READINGS IN MODERN ECONOMICS

James F. Crawford, Ph.D.

Chairman, Department of Economics
Georgia State University
33 Gilmee Street, S. E.
Atlanta, Georgia 30303

1977 W. B. SAUNDERS   PHILADELPHIA, LONDON, TORONTO

W. B. Saunders Company: West Washington Square
                           Philadelphia, PA.   19105

                           1 St. Anne's Road
                           Eastbourne, East Sussex BN21 3UN, England

                           1 Goldthorne Avenue
                           Toronto, Ontario M8Z 5T9, Canada

Cover illustration titled Planned City is an enamel on steel painting by Virgil Cantini.

READINGS IN MODERN ECONOMICS   ISBN-0-7216-2736-6

Last digit is the print number: 9 8 7 6 5 4 3 2 1

PREFACE

Economics is a fascinating, but complex, subject which is vitally important and highly relevant to all of us in our daily living. In a democratic society it is essential that citizens understand how their economic system - and other economic systems - functions. This book of readings is designed to assist in that learning process.

The readings in this volume are intended to supplement the textbook in principles of economics courses by illustrating current economic problems and issues and by showing how economic principles relate to real-life problems. Although written particularly for the Lindauer, Economics: A Modern View (Saunders, 1977), it can be used equally will with any standard principles of economics textbook. (In the correlation table on page IV the readings are keyed to most of the widely used current principles textbooks).

Several major criteria governed the choice of readings. First, articles were selected that treated important economic issues. "Fads" and issues of purely transitory interest were avoided.

Second, emphasis was placed on issues of particular significance for this era, with which students will have to cope during their lifetimes. In this connection, except in the case of a few pieces of enduring significance, the most recent articles available were sought.

Third, an effort was made to choose articles of high quality, characterized by clarity of exposition and sound economic reasoning. Most were written by leading economists.

Fourth, an effort was made to present a reasonable balance of views on controversial issues. In some areas of economics there is as yet no clear consensus as to what is "right" or "correct." Thus, in most cases the variety of opinions represented herein include the major opposing positions on unresolved or controversial issues.

Fifth, selections were chosen which could be read and understood by college students with no previous instruction in economics. (The small amount of mathematics encountered in the Readings is rudimentary.) While many of the articles are of interest and value to advanced students, emphasis was given to articles which could be understood by and would be helpful to college students taking their first courses in economics.

Finally, in choosing readings to be used in courses in economics, the discipline sometimes called "the dismal science," priority was given to articles which students would find interesting and readable.

I must express my large debt of gratitude to the many individuals who have contributed quite materially to the preparation of this volume. Owing to space limitations, I can name only a few. Most obviously, profound thanks are due to the authors and publishers who granted permission to reprint the readings herein. I would especially like to acknowledge the important contributions of Dr. Craig Marxsen, Assistant Professor of Economics at West Georgia College, who assisted in screening ariticles, read the entire manuscript and offered numerous valuable suggestions. Among my colleagues at Georgia State University, I would like to acknowledge my appreciation to Professor Andrew Hamer for writing an article especially for this book of readings, and to Professors Arthur Schreiber, Miltos Chacholiades, David Sjoquist, Paul Farnham, Ted Boyden, Jack Blicksilver, Mark Schaefer and Visiting Scholar Vera Rony for their very helpful comments and suggestions. I would like to thank Research Assistants Sharon Diamond, Jerry DeFoor and Wayne Plumly for their assistance in screening articles and Nancy Marxsen for very useful secretarial assistance. And finally, I am deeply indebted to my assistant, Bee Hutchins, for her great skill in infinite patience in enduring the burden of secretarial tasks associated with the assembling of a book of readings.

James F. Crawford

III

CORRELATION TABLE

Readings in Modern Economics	PART I			PART II		PART III		PART IV			PART V				PART VI		PART VII		PART VIII				
	A	B	C	A	B	A	B	A	B	C	D	A	B	C	A	B	A	B	A	B	C	D	E
Lindauer, Ch.	1	2	3	4, 10	6, 7 11	12, 13	14, 15 17, 27 30	22	21, 28		23	20, 21 28, 29	18, 19, 31		32, 34 36, 37	35	10	10		25			
Heilbroner, Ch.	1, 3 5, 6	2, 40, 41	4, 8, 10	16	11-14		18, 22, 27 23, 27, 28	16				17, 19, 29	30, 32	32	35, 36, 38	37	21, 34, 39	20			15		
Bach, Ch.	1, 3	4	4, 21, 22	20, 23	24, 25 27, 46	26, 30	14, 31 38, 40	30	7	33, 34		5, 32	12-14	9	41, 42	43, 44	16-18	16, 17, 19		37			45
Mansfield, Ch.	1	2, 3, 34	4, 20	7	7, 23	5, 25	5, 6, 10, 15				26	26	12-15	8	30	31, 32	16, 17	17, 33		28	18		
McConnell, Ch.	12	3, 6 46	4, 5 24, 34 36	8	23, 27-30	35	7, 9 14, 15 41	32	2, 11		39	10, 29	16, 18, 19	11	42, 44	43, 44	20-22, 45	22, 45		37, 38		41	
Miller (Macro), Ch.	1	2	3		18	10	5, 10			6		4, 6	11-13	7	14	15	16, 17	16					
Miller (Micro), Ch.	1	2, 14	3, 4	5	6, 7	8	12	10							16		17				13, 15		
Reynolds (Macro), Ch.	1	2, 3										4-6	8-11	7, 13			14, 16, 17	14, 15					
Reynolds (Micro), Ch.	1	3	2, 4 5		8, 9	10	11, 16	5			15									15, 17		12	13
Samuelson, Ch.	1	2, 42 43	3, 4 20, 21, 32	6	25, 26	8	8, 9	5, 29	41		7, 29	10	15, 18	13, 19	34, 35	33, 36	37, 38	5	40	39, 40			42, 43
Spencer, Ch.	1	2, 3 38	4	6	24, 25	30	5, 7 12, 17		9		28, 31	8, 10	13-17	13, 19	34	35, 36	18, 19 37	19, 37		32, 33	20		

CONTENTS

PART I. THE NATURE OF EONOMICS: BASIC ECONOMIC CONCEPTS

PART II. BUSINESS FIRMS AND MARKET STRUCTURE

PART III. GOVERNMENT AND THE ECONOMY

PART IV. CURRENT LABOR ISSUES

D. LABOR UNIONS AND COLLECTIVE BARGAINING

PART V. INCOME AND EMPLOYMENT ANALYSIS

A. INCOME-EXPENDITURE ANALYSIS

B. MONETARY THEORY AND POLICY

C.   INFLATION AND UNEMPLOYMENT

PART VI. THE INTERNATIONAL ECONOMY

A.   INTERNATIONAL TRADE AND MULTINATIONAL BUSINESS

B.   INTERNATIONAL MONETARY ISSUES

PART VII. ECONOMIC GROWTH AND PRODUCTIVITY

PART VIII. CURRENT ECONOMIC ISSUES AND APPLICATIONS

PART I.
THE NATURE OF
ECONOMICS:
BASIC
ECONOMIC
CONCEPTS

The study of economics is concerned with how man attempts to deal with the problem of scarcity. The articles in Part I are concerned with basic economic ideas and concepts. In sections A and B, the alternative ways of solving the economic problems which confront all societies are examined with particular emphasis on the approach of free enterprise economies. The American economy operates through a vast network of exchanges, known as markets, that set prices for goods and services. Section C examines product markets in several sectors of the economy.

Section A, Economic Ideas

In "Is There a Future for Economic Man?" David Eastburn considers the question of whether a free market system can cope with economic problems of the future. In "Why Do We Work?" Herbert Woodward argues that the Protestant work ethic has no inherent religious or moral value and is a wasteful luxury that we can ill afford in the resource-scarce world that he projects for the future.

Section B, Economic Systems

In "Homage to Adam Smith" Robert Heilbroner examines the rich intellectual heritage of Smith, "the first economist of truly philosophic temper and ability." In "The Alternative to Planning May Be Chaos" Nobel Prize-winning economist Wassily Leontief argues that more economic planning now is not only desirable but necessary for the future economic well-being of our society, while in "Planning Disaster" Henry Hazlitt presents an opposing position, pointing out what in his view is the poor record of the Federal government in its past efforts at planning. Max Lerner, in "American Capitalism: Trial Balance," attempts a cost-benefit analysis of capitalism, weighing rapid growth and economic strength, with their resultant rich variety of consumer products, against resource depletion, unplanned cities, over-size war industries, the business cycle and the evolution of private empires challenging the authority of the state itself. Nobel Prize-winning economist Kenneth

Arrow, in an interview, "Kenneth Arrow on Capitalism and Society," discusses a broad range of social, ethical and economic issues related to capitalism.

Section C, <u>Markets and Prices</u>

University of Chicago Professor D. Gale Johnson, a leading agricultural economist, forecasts that food will not get significantly more expensive in the future and explains why in "Are High Farm Prices Here to Stay?" Jeffrey Frankel, in "The Bluejeans Effect," defines four "effects whereby and individual's utility for a product is affected by the demands of his fellow consumers." One of these four, the "bluejeans effect," is Frankel's own invention. In "Seasonality of Agricultural Prices" Blaine W. Bickel notes that both the supply and demand for food fluctuate seasonally and investigates the hypothesis that seasonal price variations are identifiable from market history. Statistical and graphical methods are used to analyze six agricultural markets to determine whether this seasonality is demonstrated.

Marked changes in consumer behavior have resulted from recent economic trauma and some of these changes (confidence, reduced buying of "big ticket" items, greater avoidance of waste, shorter travel, housing, etc.) are discussed in "The Changing American Consumer." In "Criminal Behavior and the Control of Crime: An Economic Perspective" Timothy H. Hannan shows that the tools of economics can be used to analyze the criminal decision-making process.

A. Economic Ideas

Is There a Future for Economic Man?*

*By David P. Eastburn, President
Federal Reserve Bank
of Philadelphia*

Economic Man has had things pretty much his way for most of this century. But, what are his prospects for the rest of the century?

First, let's examine Economic Man for a moment. His claim to fame in economic discussion is secure. Economists long ago described him well. He is, above all, a calculating individual. He approaches problems rationally, balancing advantages and disadvantages of alternative courses of action. In the time-honored tradition of Adam Smith's "invisible hand," he considers these advantages and disadvantages in terms of his self-interest. By serving his own interests he is also serving society's interests. In the business world, Economic Man's self-interest drives him to use the resources at his disposal to generate

*An address given before a Conference on Futurism held at Eastern College, St. Davids, Pennsylvania, February 5, 1975.

the highest possible profit or income. In doing so, he is governed by the market system which harnesses the pursuit of self-interest into social good. The market registers the desires of consumers, passing them along to producers who, disciplined by the marketplace, allocate resources in the most efficient way to meet those desires. The market distributes incomes in accordance with each person's contribution to the total product. Although this may not be equality, Economic Man believes it is not only fair but necessary for progress. This is a broad-brush portrait of Economic Man as you might come upon him in a textbook.

More recently, however, Economic Man has come to convey another kind of image. This is the image of a person to whom consumption is the most important goal of life. He is typified by the affluent American with two cars, a power boat, two homes, three or four color TVs, all the

---

David P. Eastburn, "Is There a Future for Economic Man?" *Business Review*, Federal Reserve Bank of Philadelphia, April 1975, pp. 3–7. Reprinted with permission.

kitchen appliances, an electric toothbrush, and all the other "necessities" of life. His desire for more gadgets is insatiable. Therefore, his major goal for the economic system is growth. Only by a constantly and rapidly rising GNP is he able to satisfy his craving for greater material comfort. This growth is made possible by a frenetic pace of discovery and invention turned out by modern technology. If this growth uses up natural resources at a dangerous rate, this is a problem others will have to deal with in the future. If it fouls the air and water, clogs the highways, and spoils places of scenic beauty, this is a price of progress. Here is an image of Economic Man that is becoming increasingly prevalent. Although I think it is more a caricature than a portrait, it is one we must deal with in assessing Economic Man's future.

Much of what I read and hear about his future is pessimistic. Robert Heilbroner, for example, has recently explored the human prospect and arrives at a most dismal conclusion.

> Rationalize as we will, stretch the figures as favorably as honesty will permit, we cannot reconcile the requirements for a lengthy continuation of the present rate of industrialization of the globe with the capacity of existing resources or the fragile biosphere to permit or to tolerate the effects of that industrialization. Nor is it easy to foresee a willing acquiescence of humankind, individually or through its existing social organizations, in the alterations of lifeways that foresight would dictate. If then, by the question "Is there hope for man?" we ask whether it is possible to meet the challenges of the future without the payment of a fearful price, the answer must be: No, there is no such hope.[1]

If this kind of thinking is accurate, it suggests that the next quarter century would be very different from the past quarter century. Perhaps most striking, it would be a sharp shift from what has generally been a prevailing optimism of American attitude. In view of all the gloom, it seems to me that somebody should look at the other side, and examine the possibility that our society will be better able to meet the challenges ahead than many currently are forecasting.

In essence, my point is that Economic Man is most adaptable. He is not the same person now as 50 or 75 years ago. The rough edges of his philosophy and practice have been smoothed by social action—especially in the 1930s. He will not be the same person in 25 years as now. But he will still have an important role to play in our society.

How accurate this prediction turns out to be will depend heavily on how Economic Man meets three major challenges: the exhaustion of resources, the deterioration of environment, and the clamor for equality.

RESOURCES

One point of view is that Economic Man is doomed because we are certain to run out of vital natural resources. It will not be possible to continue the economic growth we have enjoyed in the past quarter century. It will not be possible to consume on the same lavish scale.

A fascinating aspect of this forecast is how rapidly it has come about. In 1958 John Kenneth Galbraith wrote *The Affluent Society*. This was hailed at the time not only as an accurate evaluation of the current state of affairs, but a perceptive appraisal of the problems ahead. Whatever they were, they were not problems of production; we had solved the production problem and now had to deal with the problems of affluence. Galbraith's analysis had a profound effect on thought at that time. It was only a few years later that *The Limits to Growth* appeared. This book, which purported to show by scientific econometric techniques that the economy could not continue growing at its recent pace, came as a shock to many who had just come to believe that Economic Man was firmly in the saddle. Some disagreed with the analysis, but it was hard to dispel the idea that, after all, we do live on a finite planet and at sometime resources will be gone. And we all have had first-hand confronta-

---

[1] Robert L. Heilbroner, *An Inquiry into the Human Prospect* (New York: W. W. Norton and Company, 1974), pp. 135–36.

tion with the problems at the gas station. Still more recently I ran across a paperback called *The End of Affluence* which, among other things, instructs Americans in how to adjust their life-styles to new realities of slower economic growth. So, within the space of relatively few years the prospects of Economic Man, in the minds of many people, have suffered a complete about-face because of new concern about resources. What are we to make of this?

Obviously, resources are finite. Economic growth uses them up—quickly if growth is rapid, less quickly if growth is slower. The difficult question is whether Economic Man is capable of dealing with the problem before it becomes catastrophic. I believe he is, by relying on two of his trusted tools—the market system and technology. The market system, if it is permitted to work, can slow down use of increasingly scarce resources and encourage development of new resources. This is the best approach to the energy problem we face right now, for example. If the price of gasoline is permitted to rise, this will cut down demand and at the same time encourage exploration of new sources of energy. A higher price for fuels will encourage technology to develop new techniques of recovery, better methods of producing nuclear energy, and even feasible processes for harnessing energy from the sun.

It is true that the market system does not work perfectly in protecting resources. For one thing, it sometimes takes the short view, overly emphasizing the present to the detriment of the future. Economic Man does look ahead, but the market does not always cause him to be sufficiently concerned with problems he may create for future generations. The market will need help, therefore, from Government. If certain resources are being used too fast and others not being developed, Government can assist by removing controls and other impediments to resource conservation as well as by legislating taxes and subsidies that nudge Economic Man in the desired direction. For example, a tax on imported oil, or on gas at the pump, or on large cars can help to conserve gasoline and stimulate development of other energy sources. The trick is for Government to work as much as possible through the market system and to capitalize on Economic Man's desires for profits and his talents in allocating resources.

ENVIRONMENT

Economic Man has neglected the environment, and his prospects are not good if he continues to do so. Economists as far back as Adam Smith recognized that the production of goods often involved costs that the producer didn't have to bear but others did. When a paper producer dumps waste into a stream and this pollutes the water supply of neighboring communities, for example, the practice entails a cost for the people in those communities, but the cost doesn't enter into the price of the paper. (In fact, the effort of cleaning up the water is actually counted as an increase in GNP rather than a subtraction from it!) These external costs of production, or externalities as economists have come to call them, while long recognized in concept, have only recently been given the attention in economics which they deserve. And it is only in the past decade or so that the environment has deteriorated so drastically that the general populace has become restive about the problem. What can Economic Man do?

The challenge is immense. It will take decades to undo past damage. But here again, the market and technology can help. The market can't do it alone, however. The fact that externalities are not included in the price of products is a defect of the price system that must be corrected. The idea is to have as much of these external costs as possible borne by those who produce them rather than by others. Economists have explored many ways of doing this, but taxation is probably the most important. The paper producer can be taxed so that he, not the community downstream, bears the cost of pollution. The result would be cleaner water.

This, of course, is easier said than done. Many external costs are hard to measure. There is political resistance to allocating costs to their sources. But the problem has been recognized and Government is increasingly aware of the role it must play. Again, the trick will be to take advantage of the market system and to harness Economic Man's sharpness in calculating profit opportunities. Technology can help by devising improved methods of production without pollution.

EQUALITY

Economic Man's prospects will not be good unless there is progress in dealing with the human inequalities which now exist. Here again, the outlook need not be one of unrelieved gloom. I think it is undoubtedly a fact that disadvantaged people throughout the world will be clamoring for a better shake. But it is also a fact that our economic system has done a great deal to upgrade living standards of lower-income groups, and I believe it can do a great deal more. As often pointed out, Marx *was* wrong in his prediction. The market-oriented countries of Europe and North America have not turned into places with a few very rich and masses of very poor. We have not had a revolution of the proletariat. The reason is that our economic system has generated a large and stable middle class. But what of the future? Two questions are vital—population growth and economic growth.

The predictions of an economist of a century and a half ago—Thomas Malthus—are now enjoying a new vogue. Malthus predicted that there was a natural tendency for population to outrun the means of subsistence. Unless population were held in check by birth control, it would be held in check by starvation. Certainly, as we look around the world, there is ample reason for pessimism. In the less-developed world of Africa, Asia, and Latin America, birth rates are enormous and population growth soars. At the same time, sources of food supply are becoming hard-pressed and unreliable. People are starving. Economic Man is limited in what he can do about this food gap. Food supplies can be enlarged through improvements in technology, changes in Government policies which limit farm output, as well as changes in social and religious customs which restrict diets. But of critical importance also is that people limit their own reproduction. As we see what has happened in developed countries in recent years, however, there is cause for hope. In many areas, births are rapidly moving toward a rate which is materially slowing population growth. With education and governmental pressure—and, I predict, eventually a changed policy of the Catholic Church—the same can happen in developing countries.

A second factor determining the future of disadvantaged people will be the rate of economic growth, and this is something Economic Man *can* do a lot about. A main reason for past improvement in living standards all around has been Economic Man's talent in producing more efficiently. He has enlarged the total size of the output pie so successfully that everyone can have more even with the same relative slices. Despite implications for our resources in the longer run, I believe it is essential to continue to press for rapid economic growth. As I explore the arguments for moving toward a stable state economy, I conclude (in addition to the feeling that life might be pretty dull) that their major defect is a lack of realism about implications for disadvantaged people. It simply does not seem in the cards to be able to redistribute the existing product in a way that would significantly help the disadvantaged. The haves would not stand for it, the have-nots would not benefit all that much. Growth strikes me as a much more realistic solution.

I recognize that there are two sides to the problem—the size of the pie and the size of the slice—absolute well-being and relative well-being. Growth, if the past is any guide, can go a long way in solving the absolute problem, but probably won't do much toward solving the relative problem. And, if so, the clamor for equality will continue. I suspect this will always be the case. It is too deeply ingrained in human nature to be otherwise.

ECONOMIC MAN IN 2000 A.D.

So it seems to me that the outlook for Economic Man is not as bleak as it is being painted these days. Nevertheless, just as his lot is not the same now as 25 years ago, it will not be the same 25 years hence. What will it be like in 2000 A.D.? As I see it, his world will be different in at least three respects: the degree of freedom which he can exercise, relationships with others, and the degree of conservatism that exists.

Freedom. I suspect there will be a trend toward less freedom in the next quarter century —at least freedom as Economic Man has known it. Much of the history of this century has been a decline of laissez-faire philosophy and practice. A continuation of the trend seems inevitable. Government has played an increasing role in the economy and will continue to do so.

Although Economic Man may not realize it, this can work to his benefit. As I have tried to show, he needs the help of Government in protecting resources, improving the environment, and bettering the lot of the disadvantaged; and unless there is substantial progress toward these goals, Economic Man does not face a happy future. However, much will depend on how Government goes about intervening in economic affairs. In the past, Government efforts in these directions have often hampered the functioning of the market system rather than improving it. Hopefully, Government will not clog it with self-defeating regulations and will see the advantage of working *with* Economic Man by utilizing the market system which is so important to them both.

All things considered, however, Economic Man will become more and more a partner of Government rather than a free agent. He will not occupy the dominating role he has grown accustomed to over most of this century.

Relationships. As the economy grows increasingly complex there will be a need for greater interdependence of the units within it. Unfortunately, there may be strong pressures for parts of it to go it alone. I don't have in mind the kind of self-sufficiency prescribed in *The End of Affluence* which I mentioned earlier. It seems unlikely that the idea of storing up food for emergencies or planting organic gardens in backyards is likely to catch on with most people. But on a larger scale it does seem likely that the desire to go it alone or to form closely knit groups will have a major impact in the world economy. Witness our own Project Independence. Witness banding together of countries to form cartels to control natural resources as the OPEC nations have done. Given this tendency, plus the clamor for equality from disadvantaged people the world over, Economic Man seems likely to be living in a world of considerable conflict. Since he thrives best in a climate of trust, specialization, and interdependence, he may find life difficult.

Conservatism. I am not thinking here in usual terms of liberal versus conservative, but in the more general sense that society is likely to become increasingly concerned with conserving what it has. It will necessarily become more conservative in the use of resources. And although I believe the economy must continue to grow to solve the problems of the disadvantaged, the idea of the stable state will gain increasing acceptance. This suggests that the dynamic economy which Economic Man is used to will become less dynamic, less growth-oriented. It is probably also true that there will be some change in life-styles. A return to the simple rural life is impossible, but there will probably be less of a drive to achieve satisfaction through consumption, less of a drive to lose oneself in work, and more interest in making productive use of leisure, more satisfaction from family and friends. It could be a less exciting but perhaps a more rewarding world.

CONCLUSION

In short, I believe the gloomy prognosis for Economic Man has been overdone. He is too adaptable not to be able to go a long way in meeting the challenges before him. But by 2000 A.D. he *is* likely to be living and working in a world that has values differing from those he has traditionally held. He is likely to need all the adaptability he can muster.

WHY DO WE WORK?

Herbert N. Woodward

WHEN THE CAVEMAN went hunting, his concern was to come back with the meat and skins to provide food and clothing for himself and his family. When the head of the modern household brings home the bacon, he or she performs the same function, but the reward is a paycheck which can be translated into food and clothing for his or her family.

We all tend to work on two levels: We work for the money to satisfy our needs and wants. We also work because we obtain personal satisfaction from doing the job. In a large, interdependent, and highly specialized society, the financial reward often becomes the sole motivation, because our economic system is so complex that tracing the effects of individual actions or inactions through the economy is a practical impossibility. Since one person's work—or failure—seldom has an identifiable effect on the large community, we focus on the employment itself instead of on what is accomplished at the job.

"Job philosophy" may be defined as the twin beliefs that (1) it is good to have more and more jobs, and (2) that everyone should work, whether there is any value in what the job produces or not. Featherbedding is an obvious example of attention on jobs for jobs' sake, instead of concern with what jobs accomplish.

We associate featherbedding with union organizations that seek to protect the jobs of their members. But the unions are not the only groups that believe in job philosophy. Any profession which restricts entry to its ranks is likely to be similarly protective. As examples, both the medical and legal professions act like trade unions in defining broadly the scope of their professions and preventing nonmembers from performing the functions they have reserved to themselves.

Job philosophy has many guises. Every community that uses legislative influence to prevent closing an obsolete governmental installation is thinking job philosophy. Every group urging a high tariff to prevent competition with American industry is asking all consumers to pay higher prices to keep certain Americans fully employed.

Once one begins to brainstorm about what

specific products or services really don't improve the quality of life, the list seems endless. Many of us work hard and get paid for contributing little or nothing to the quality of life.

What about the so-called Protestant work ethic which seems to be an essential element of our culture? The ethic came from Calvinism, a particularly strict expression of Protestantism which dates only from the 16th century. Stressing the virtue of economic labor, Calvinism was a powerful ally of the businessman who needed willing and submissive workers. Its predestinarianism tended to glorify success in business as evidence that the businessman must be one of the predestined few chosen for salvation.

The work ethic can be seen as a special device to provide a moral compulsion to work; *some* compulsion was essential to the development of the Industrial Revolution throughout the world. "Progress" and "religion" went hand in hand. For primitive and early civilized people, work as such was not a virtue. Rather than work hard, they worked as little as possible and settled for a limited standard of living. The deep-felt necessity to "acquire" virtue through hard work is a modern invention.

Where does this leave us? Where useless effort is being expended, the economy fails to benefit. In an abundant economy in an expanding world, however, the costs of job philosophy are small compared to the massive benefits from the stimulus of capitalist incentives. In the resource-scarce, conservation-minded world that seems to be ahead, we will not be able to afford job philosophy and its reckless waste of energy. If we eliminate production that does not truly contribute to the quality of life, massive unemployment will follow. But once we recognize that the so-called work ethic has no inherent religious or moral value, we will not need to resort to make-work projects just to keep the unemployed busy. Busywork will be inappropriate as a device for redistribution of income because there will be inadequate resources or energy to permit doing so many nonessentials. Instead, we may find means to replace the frenetic competition of our present society with a less pressured cooperative endeavor in which only the necessary is done. ∎

Herbert Woodward is president of International Science Industries, Inc., in Chicago.

Herbert N. Woodward, "Why Do We Work?" *Business and Society Review.* Winter 1974–75, p. 10. Reprinted from *Business and Society Review,* Winter 1974–75, Vol. 12, Copyright 1975, Warren, Gorham, and Lamont, Inc., 210 South Street, Boston, Mass. All rights reserved.

B. Economic Systems

ROBERT L. HEILBRONER

Homage to Adam Smith

Two hundred years after the publication of his magnum opus, Adam Smith remains a towering figure in the gallery of the great economists—a name for all to conjure with, the author of the most famous unread book in our profession. On the occasion of the sec- ond-hundredth birthday of *The Wealth of Nations* I should like to pay homage to Smith, recalling for all of us the reasons for his fame.

Let me begin by sketching in his life. Adam Smith was born in 1723 in Kirkaldy, Scotland, of modest

Robert L. Heilbroner, "Homage to Adam Smith." *Challenge,* March–April 1976, pp. 6–11. Copyright © 1975 and 1976 by International Arts and Sciences Press, Inc. Reprinted by permission of International Arts and Science Press, Inc.

but well-connected parents, his mother's family being substantial landowners. Kirkaldy was a small, thriving fishing village, rustic and even primitive in Smith's time, but fortunately within easy posting distance of Edinburgh. Edinburgh itself was one of the centers of the Scottish Enlightenment, that extraordinary concentration of intellectuals to whom we owe the first systematic development of sociology, anthropology, a materialist conception of history and a unique line of philosophy of which David Hume was the father. Adam Smith himself was, of course, to become responsible for the contribution of the Scottish Enlightenment to political economy.

In 1737, at the standard entering age of fourteen, Smith began his studies at the University of Glasgow, where he fell under the spell of Francis Hutcheson, a renowned moral philosopher. Graduating with a scholarship, Smith set out for Oxford, then at the nadir of its history. There he spent six years, largely untaught save by himself. Returning home, he managed to arrange a series of public lectures at Edinburgh which ranged over a wide variety of subjects, from rhetoric to history and economics. Evidently they made a considerable impression on Smith's eminent contemporaries, for in 1751 he was offered the chair in Logic at Glasgow, and soon thereafter the more remunerative and prestigious chair of Moral Philosophy, a subject that embraced theology, jurisprudence, "police and revenue" (economic administration), and the study of military power.

Smith remained at Glasgow until 1762. His fame was by that time widespread, largely as a consequence of *The Theory of Moral Sentiments,* published in 1759. The book attracted the attention of Charles Townshend, whose unhappy fate it was to become the Chancellor of the Exchequer responsible for the Stamp Tax on the American colonials. Townshend engaged Smith to be the tutor for his stepson, the young duke of Buccleuch, and Smith set off for a European sojourn that was to last almost four years. A year and a half was spent in the provinces, where Smith relieved ennui by visits to Rousseau and Voltaire; thereafter Smith and his charge moved to Paris where he found his lifelong friend Hume, then secretary to the British Embassy, and met the circle of *économistes* busy in promulgating François Quesnay's physiocratic ideas.

The stay in Paris came to an abrupt halt in 1767 when the young duke's brother was murdered in the streets. The party returned to London, where Smith was elected to the Royal Society, and where he broadened his intellectual circle to include Burke, Gibbon, Johnson, and perhaps Benjamin Franklin.

Thereafter he returned to Kirkaldy for six years, then to London for three more. Much of this time was spent in refining and polishing the treatise on political economy that had evidently been formally begun during the European tour—I say "formally" because we know from students' notes that a great deal of the *Wealth* was already conceived and even roughly composed in the early 1760s when Smith delivered the discourses known as *Lectures on Justice, Police, Revenue and Arms.*

The *Wealth* appeared in 1776 to the plaudits of his friends ("Euge! Belle!" wrote Hume), although it was not an immediate public success. Thereafter Smith went into comfortable semi-retirement. He re-edited the *Wealth* once in 1778, and made numerous revisions in his *Theory of Moral Sentiments.* Perhaps he sought to realize a promise made at the end of that book to write an account of the "general principles of law and government." We shall never know, because he insisted on his deathbed in 1790 that his extensive unpublished manuscripts be burned.

Not much by way of personal detail can be added to flesh out this chronology. We have anecdotes about Smith's absent-mindedness, his stumbling manner of speech, a nervous tremor of his head, his "vermicular" gait. A medallion by Tassie gives us a heavy-lidded profile: "I am a beau in nothing but my books," Smith once told a friend while showing off his treasured library of 3,000 volumes. No record of any romantic attachments has come down to us. Smith passed his days as a bachelor, often residing with his mother. His history is, with the exception of his intellectual life, a biography without excitement, save only for the famous incident of Adam's abduction, at age four, by a band of passing gypsies. His biographer, John Rae, has drily commented: "He would have made, I fear, a poor gypsy."

It is, of course, his ideas that command our interest; and an intellectual biography of Smith requires a far larger canvas than his private life. There is only one economist to whom it is possible to compare Smith in breadth, depth, and brilliance. This is Marx; and indeed such a comparison helps to put Smith into a proper initial perspective. As in the case of Marx, it would be a mistake to take the measure of Smith solely as an economist. Studying Marx, we are aware that *Capital* is more than a book on economics. It is the application to a given society of a larger theory of historical change, and this theory in turn—dialectical materialism—must be viewed as the application to history of a still more fundamental conception of reality itself. So too with Smith. *The Wealth of Nations* is much more than a treatise on economics. It is the application to a given society of Smith's larger views of the processes of historic evolution, and these again, like the theories of Marx, represent the working-out in history of even more fundamental premises with respect to man and the universe.

These latter views find their expression in and between the lines of *The Theory of Moral Sentiments,* the remarkable treatise on human nature that Smith published during his tenure at Glasgow. The *Theory* remains to this day a perplexing book. Rich in anecdote and ornate in style, it covers its subject in a taxonomic rather than systematic way, so that on finishing the text for the first time, one is apt to ask in bewilderment: "What is it all about?"

In the main, it is about the subject of its title— that is, it is a *theory* of "moral sentiments." Moral sentiments, in Smith's time, was the phrase used to describe the puzzling ability of man—by instinct, it was supposed, a creature of self-interest—to conceive judgments in which his self-interest was held in abeyance. Smith's analysis of the problem is original and interesting. It is based on our capacity for the feeling we call "sympathy"—that is, the capacity to imagine ourselves in another's position. This capacity does not, however, give us a mechanical means of attaining moral judgments. Rather, it requires that we form our moral opinions by bringing each case before a tribunal of judgment located within ourselves, a tribunal that Smith called the Impartial Spectator.

The idea of an Impartial Spectator smacks of a naive conception of thought, emotion, and behavior. But we must remember that Smith was writing in a period when the discipline of psychology was not yet detached from the generalized study of man to which moral philosophy addressed itself. Smith's Impartial Spectator, it soon becomes clear, is not a fanciful homunculus implanted within us, but an accretion of judgments that we have internalized by watching the appropriations and disappropriations of the world. The Spectator, in other words, is a description of man's sociality—a conception that takes on additional prescience if we see it as an imaginative prefiguring of the Freudian superego, formed in much the same way.

As economists we no longer pay much heed to Smith's concern with moral sentiments. If his *Theory* is referred to at all, it is to point to a caesura between the central role played by moral behavior in that book and its virtual disregard in the *Wealth.* There is, however, an important reason to consider *The Theory of Moral Sentiments* as an integral part of Smith's work as an economic philosopher. This is the role of the invisible hand, whose nature and functions are more clearly set forth in Smith's earlier book than in his later one.

The famous phrase is used but once in the *Wealth,* and there almost in passing (p. 423 in the Modern Library edition). But in *The Theory of Moral Sentiments* the invisible hand plays a more fundamental role. Indeed, the entire book is suffused with the idea of a Deity who entrusts the well-being of mankind to passions and propensities that work in ways veiled from the human actors themselves. "Without intending it; without knowing it," as Smith says, our pursuit of private ends promotes a larger design than our own. The invisible hand thus becomes a prime agency for human destiny, comparable in importance to the mechanism of dialectics in Marx.

When it appears in *The Wealth of Nations,* the invisible hand is used as a metaphor for the beneficent outcome of the process of competition. But in *The Theory of Moral Sentiments,* it elucidates another problem—namely, the way in which the acquisitive urge itself also redounds to a larger social purpose.

As a philosopher, Smith regards this acquisitive urge, with considerable disdain, as an indication of human shortsightedness. "The poor man's son, whom heaven in its anger has visited with ambition," he writes, "when he begins to look around him, admires the condition of the rich. He finds the cottage of his father too small for his accommodation, and fancies he should be lodged more at ease in a palace. . . . He is enchanted with the distant idea of the felicity [that money can buy]."

Accordingly, the smitten fool devotes his life to arduous labor, ruins his health and his peace of mind, and accumulates a fortune, only to discover at the end that "wealth and greatness are mere trinkets of frivolous utility . . . , enormous and operose machines contrived to produce a few trifling conveniences to the body . . . , immense fabrics which it requires the labour of a life to raise, which threaten every moment to overwhelm the person who dwells in them" (Part IV, Ch. 1).

Smith has a larger purpose in discussing the snare and delusion of riches than to reinforce the moral priggishness of the landed gentry's sons to whom he was lecturing. For quickly he goes on to say: "it is well that nature imposes upon us in this manner." The reason is that, dazzled by the imagined benefits of wealth, men undertake arduous tasks they would not otherwise perform. They "cultivate the ground, build houses, found cities and commonwealths, invent and improve all the sciences and arts . . . , turn the rude forests into agreeable and fertile plains," in short, carry out the prodigies of capitalism lauded by Marx in the *Communist Manifesto*.

Thus the dubious admiration for wealth is a passion implanted in us by a benign Deity because its operations are more to be trusted than those of rational foresight. But the passion for wealth accomplishes more than a driving purpose. It also serves a still more basic social function—the preservation of the social order that Smith, along with his Enlightenment colleagues, unabashedly elevated to prime importance.

How is social stability aided by the admiration for wealth? The answer is that we look with awe on those who have gained riches, assuming that they must be great as well as wealthy. And here is where the invisible hand again enters. "Nature has wisely judged," says Smith, "that the distinction of ranks, the peace and order of society, would rest more securely upon the plain and palpable difference of birth and fortune, than upon the invisible and often uncertain difference of wisdom and virtue" (Part VI, Sec. 2).

Thus the quest for wealth serves mankind in two "invisible" ways. It urges us to undertake private ventures, which in the end benefit society even though they prove to be empty for the protagonists. And the quest also establishes a solid basis for the sub- and superordination essential for society. Smith is certainly not sentimental or hypocritical in acknowledging this purpose. The specter of Hobbes haunted the 18th century, and tendencies to social stability were welcomed, not lamented: "The peace and order of society is of more importance," Smith writes, "than even the relief of the miserable" (ibid.). Indeed, it is again a sign of the invisible hand that men are awed by wealth, for in this way they are "taught to acquiesce with less reluctance under that government which an irresistible force imposes upon them and from which no reluctance would deliver them" (Part VI, Sec. 3).

I hope these highlights may send some readers to a perusal of Smith's second greatest work. But in this year of celebration our main attention is naturally focused on his masterpiece.

I suspect that most economists have not read *The Wealth of Nations* since dipping into a few extracts in college, and that most of them think of it as a lengthy discussion of the merits of a laissez-faire economy. Yet the *Wealth* is much more than such an encomium (a very tempered encomium, as we shall see). Written in a day when the intellectual division of labor had not progressed to the degree we are accustomed to, the *Wealth* is a work in general social science, unselfconsciously extending its analysis into universal history, European history, sociology, and political science, as well as into economic theory and policy.

When we read the book as economists, however, two major themes attract our notice. The first is the pioneering description of the mechanism by which a society of "perfect liberty" maintains internal cohesion and stability. It is difficult for us today to appreciate the originality of this conception. The two most influential economic writers of Smith's day, François Quesnay and Sir James Steuart, had no vision of the self-correcting capabilities of a society of competitive enterprises. In Quesnay's ingenious scheme for social reproduction, everything hinged on the proper division of expenditure between the surplus-yielding labor of the countryside and the "sterile" labor of the city. A division of expenditure that favored the city over the country would soon deplete the nation of its crucial fund of agricultural wealth, but no self-correcting tendency was evident to Quesnay to redress such a state of affairs. Steuart is even more concerned with the potential instability of economic society, and a primary function of his "statesman"— the phrase by which Steuart denotes the governing authority—is to detect and remedy imbalances of supply and demand. Only Hume among Smith's contemporaries had seen the possibilities of a negative feedback system as an equilibrating device, but Hume applied this brilliant insight to the mechanism of specie flow and did not generalize it with respect to the general equilibrium of the economy as a whole.

This is Smith's great accomplishment, for which one wishes he would have earned kinder words from Schumpeter or Marx. Their impatience perhaps arises because the demonstration of general equilibrium is encrusted with examples, exceptions, asides and polemics which, however much they may add to the flavor of the work, detract from its clarity. And then, of course, there is the fact that Smith was often inconsistent, not to say downright wrong.

Smith's primary achievement with respect to the problem of self-equilibration is his idea of the mobility of factors who respond to the signals of the marketplace by entering or leaving one field of application for another. This continual streaming of factors to their points of highest return not only serves to match the supplies of outputs to the demands for them, but becomes as well a means that assures the natural flow of each of the three great classes of revenue—wages, rents, and profits.

Because Smith does not have a clear or consistent theory of rents or profits—indeed, he treats rent within two pages (Modern Lib. ed., pp. 145-6) as deriving from monopoly, differential fertility, and the surplus-yielding character of the land—his effort to create a convincing theory of distribution is often seriously marred. For Marxian economists, this shortcoming is compounded by a terrible inability to differentiate between a labor-embodied and a labor-commanded theory of value, a failure for which Ricardo also gave Smith his lumps.

But it would be a great error to dwell on these deficiencies. Taking Smith even in the narrowest of categories—as a founder of microeconomics—his achievements are formidable. We owe to him the first systematic exposition of the division of labor, both among and within industries. We read Chapter Ten and discover to our astonishment that Smith knew about human capital and psychic income and the calculation of risk. We explore the neglected Digression on Silver and the chapter on Bounties and discover, as Samuel Hollender has pointed out, a stunning linkage of the role of silver in determining the money price of corn and thence of labor and other basic commodities. And of course, overarching the whole, we see two of the main premises that still undergird microeconomics: "Monopolies derange, more or less, the natural distribution of the stock [capital] of society" (p. 596), and "Consumption is the sole end and purpose of production" (p. 625).

For all his contributions as a microtheorist, the most fascinating aspect of Smith undoubtedly lies in his macroeconomic analysis, particularly in the description of the self-induced, self-maintained mechanism by which a system of "perfect liberty" will expand its volume of output.

The growth model, if we may apply so pallid a term to the historic, sociological and economic scenario of *The Wealth of Nations,* is really grounded in Book V. There we find Smith's stadial or stage-like theory of history—a conception that he had already formulated in those lectures of the early 1760s in which the framework for the *Wealth* was first articulated.

The stadial theory of history traces the progression of society through four epochs—an "early and rude" stage of hunters; a subsequent age of nomads or shepherds; a stage of settled agriculture; and a last period of manufactures and commerce. It is this last period about which, and for which, *The Wealth of Nations* is written, both to describe the tendencies and mechanisms hidden within it, and to prescribe the demolition of the archaic institutions of the preceding stage that still impair its fullest development. For Smith presages Marx in relating the changing material basis for each stage of his historic drama to an appropriate set of "superstructural" institutions. The society of hunters, having no property, says Smith, needs no or only very little government: here is Marx's primitive communism. The stage of shepherds, which witnesses the first large accumulations of wealth (primitive accumulation) also witnesses the necessity for government: "It is only under the shelter of the civil magistrate that the owner of . . . valuable property . . . can sleep a single night in security. . . . The acquisition of valuable and extensive property, therefore, requires the establishment of civil government" (p. 670).

The next stage of history—feudalism—is characterized both by the presence of manorial estates and by the emergence of commerce and early manufacture. Smith describes the interaction of these two in a manner that combines the insights of 20th century economic history with the rolling style of 18th century prose: "A revolution of the greatest importance to the public happiness was in this manner brought about by two orders of people, who had not the least intention to serve the public. To gratify the most childish vanity was the sole motive of the great proprietors. The merchants and artificers, much less ridiculous, acted merely with a view to their own interest, and in pursuit of their pedlar principle of turning a penny wherever a penny was to be got. Neither of them had either knowledge or foresight of that great revolution which the folly of one and the industry of the other was gradually bringing about" (pp. 391-2).

Thus the invisible hand conducts us to the system of perfect liberty (i.e., free contract and unimpeded competition), where the cramping institutions of feudalism and mercantilism are cast aside, and a society of contract (as Sir Henry Maine would later say) displaces one of status. It is this last stage of contractual society that displays the astonishing attributes of economic growth—attributes that have been examined in great detail by Joseph Spengler and cast into the form of a tight model by Adolph Lowe.

The model can be simply presented. A pervasive motive for self-betterment—"a desire which . . . comes with us from the womb and never leaves us until we go into the grave"—drives all manufacturers to seek wealth by expanding their enterprises. Note that the manufacturers are the only class able to expand its wealth by deliberate action: the working class has no such option and the landlord class rides passively along with the growth of population. But the manufacturer can accumulate—the classical term meaning the conjoined acts of saving and investing. His accumulations add to his capacity to employ labor and also to his stock of machinery and equipment. The enlarged stock of machinery will both allow him to employ more labor—there is no hint that machinery may be labor displacing—and will also further the all-important process of the division of labor which is the main source of increased productivity. Thus his business will expand and his profits rise, allowing still more accumulation.

In this perfectly simple, self-sustaining sequence, there is one difficulty. The process of bidding for labor will raise its wages, thereby choking off the profits from which further accumulations might be made. But now the key regulatory mechanism of the growth model comes to the rescue. As wages rise, so does the supply of labor: "The demand for men, like that for any other commodity, necessarily regulates the production of men" (p. 80). Accordingly, the rise in wages is tempered by the rightward shifting supply curve of labor. Over the long run the real recompense of labor rises, but the rise is never so abrupt that the process of accumulation is interrupted.

Does growth proceed indefinitely? Schumpeter called the model "hitchless," and there is indeed a promise of endless, smooth expansion in this perfectly geared reciprocating engine of expansion. Yet here and there in the *Wealth,* we catch disconcerting glimpses of countries that have acquired their "full complement of riches" and in which accumulation has ceased. Such countries are stagnant or worse, retrograde. Accumulation has stopped, but the multiplication of population proceeds, driving the level of real wages from its hard-won heights back to the barest of minima: "In a country fully peopled in proportion to what either its territory could maintain or its stock employ, the competition for employment would necessarily be so great as to reduce the wages of labour to what was barely sufficient to keep up the number of labourers . . ." (pp. 94-5).

Thus the growth process is not hitchless. On the contrary, its thrust becomes exhausted; a Ricardian finale is ultimately met; its terminus is decline. And this unhappy prospect is given additional significance by a second tragic theme that we discover in the *Wealth*. It is the theme of moral decay, of "alienation," that results from the impact of the division of labor on men: "In the progress of the division of labour, the employment of the far greater part of those who live by labour, that is, of the great body of the people, comes to be confined to a few very simple operations, frequently to one or two. But the understandings of the greater part of men are necessarily formed by their ordinary employments. The man whose whole life is spent in performing a few simple operations . . . generally loses the habit of such [mental] exertion, and generally becomes as stupid and ignorant as it is possible for a human creature to become" (p. 734).

This stinging indictment has disturbing implications for *The Wealth of Nations*. The degradation of labor, Smith makes clear, is not to be found in earlier stages of society. It is the product not of a society of hunters, shepherds, or agriculturists, but of a society of perfect liberty. Thus Smith's great work, often characterized as a paean to "free enterprise," is in fact a highly qualified tribute, ultimately even a condemnation. The gradient of growth, as we have seen, concludes in a reversion to bare subsistence. Therefore the decay of intelligence of the working class cannot be redeemed by a never-ending rise in living standards. And as we have just read, even during the period of material improvement, the worker must suffer the fate of moral debasement.

This prospect is further dimmed because Smith does not believe that the victims of history can rectify matters by taking them into their own hands. Unlike Marx, who looks forward to an end of the "idiocy" of country life and to a sharpening of the wits of the working class on the anvil of history, Smith sees a growth in the idiocy of city life and the reduction of the working class to a condition in which the laborer is "incapable either of comprehending [society's] interest or of understanding its connexion with his own" (p. 249). The idea of a profound revolution, a *renversement* of society, is neither within the range of Smith's imagination nor of that of any of his fellow *philosophes*. Thus beneath the surface assurance that radiates from the book, a distant tragedy of vast proportions—economic decline, moral decay—lurks within *The Wealth of Nations*. Two hundred years after its publication, one hundred after the appearance of Volume I of *Capital,* we may wonder whose measure of the future was more nearly correct—that of Marx or that of Smith.

It is pointless to conclude by trying to establish the proper place for Smith in the pantheon of economists. Reading *The Wealth of Nations* is somewhat like reading Shakespeare, because we rediscover how much of our common idiom originates in it, how many of our stock phrases were originally its brilliant *aperçus*. Adam Smith is more than the first economist of truly philosophic temper and ability. He is part of our intellectual heritage, someone to whom we owe a debt beyond any repayment.

Note: To mark the bicentennial of **The** Wealth of Nations, *Glasgow University (Clarendon Press) is issuing the first (!) complete edition of Smith's works, freshly edited. In addition there will be a biography of Smith and a collection of essays on various aspects of his work.* **R.L.H.**

A Nobel Prize-winning economist speaks out strongly
for national economic planning.

The Alternative to Not Planning
May Be Chaos: A Conversation
With Wassily Leontief

PLANNING! ABSURDITY! Today, these two words are on the lips of many economists. Professor F.A. Hayek, recipient of the 1974 Nobel Prize in economics, calls central economic planning "absurd." Yet in a time of high unemployment, galloping inflation, and exposure of widespread corruption in the corporate world, there are valid reasons to question Professor Hayek's position:

"[W]e have been able to achieve a reasonably high degree of order in our economic lives, despite modern complexities, only because our affairs have been guided not by central direction, but by the operations of the market and competition in securing the mutual adjustment of corporate efforts."

Furthermore, when Herbert Stein and Rexford Tugwell argue against planning, are they really arguing about who is to control planning? How can Walter Wriston, chairman of Citibank, whose organization issues planning reports, refer to planning as "incipient fascism"? Is it because he believes it is, or is it because he may not be one of the planners?

Finally, what is planning? Is it a plan or is it a process whereby we can consider alternative economic theories and strategies as ways to obtain national economic goals?

"The Alternative to not Planning May Be Chaos: A Conversation with Wassily Leontief," *Business and Society Review*, Spring 1976, pp. 10–17. Reprinted from *Business and Society Review*, Spring 1976, Vol. 17, Copyright 1976, Warren, Gorham and Lamont, Inc., 210 South Street, Boston, Mass. All rights reserved.

The advocates of planning take much of their theoretical sustenance from Prof. Wassily Leontief, the developer and chief proponent of a model using input/output analysis as a tool for economic planning. Professor Leontief won the Nobel Prize in economics in 1973 for his application of input/output analysis. He serves now as cochairman of the Initiative Committee for National Economic Planning.

Professor Leontief is a feisty James Cagney type, punctuating his remarks with dramatic gestures. The gestures are part of his presentation and help overcome a thick accent derived from his Russian birth. His presence is encompassing. It is almost as if he wants to surround you concretely with ideas.

He is an econometrician. His primary contribution, a unique method which models the interaction between production sectors in the economy, is different enough to fall outside the usual label of econometrics. The I/O Model is a planning tool which can be used to examine alternative strategies for general as well as specific goals.

After spending forty-five years at Harvard, Professor Leontief recently accepted an appointment as professor of economics at N.Y.U. Since his input/output model is clearly central to many of the issues raised by planning, *Business and Society Review* asked Professor Leontief to comment on the present controversy surrounding planning. This interview was conducted for the *Review* by Dr. A. Harvey Block, president of Bokonon Systems, a Washington, D.C., research firm.

Block: Professor Leontief, every so often in American history there seems to be a movement in favor of long-range economic planning. However, these efforts have always been resisted. Why do you think this is so, and would you comment on the arguments against planning?

Leontief: Americans, particularly educated Americans who have studied undergraduate economics, are taught that there is, in a free market economy, a price system guided by the invisible hand of Adam Smith. This price system is supposed to operate in an impersonal way to automatically solve economic problems.

When I explain the operation of a price system to my undergraduates I often use the analogy of an automatic computer, which automatically poses problems and then solves problems. This analogy certainly exposes this kind of thinking. First, there is always the question of what problems the computer poses and what problems it solves. In an economic sense, I have considerable skepticism about whether a competitive price system can solve the problems that Milton Friedman, or Walter Wriston of Citibank, think it can. Anybody who has had any experience with an automatic computer would be out of his mind if he would go to a computer late in the day, put in a very complicated problem, push a button, start it, go out, lock the door, and expect next morning to have the problem solved. Everyone knows that *something* will go wrong. The computer will stop, or mix up the figures, or burn out. The price system is very much like that. It does marvelous things—but it breaks down. You cannot rely on an automatic system to operate in an ideal way. You have to watch it; you have to

push it. It's like a pinball machine. You hit it, you shake it, and then, possibly, you get where you want. This is why I think the price system does not perform well. Do you consider an 8 percent unemployment rate an effective solution to the economic problems of today?

There is another aspect we must consider—and that is the Darwinian approach which says the *free* economy is a competitive system: the good man wins, the bad man goes down. This is a very expensive way of solving problems. It must have bankruptcy as an important principle. To demonstrate: You build a giant steel plant. Then, if you find no market for steel, you shut it down. It is terribly costly to solve problems by simply letting things that don't work sink.

The waste is clear. The human and social sacrifices are so great that no modern society can stand it. Look at Chile today. Mr. Friedman went there and advised them to increase unemployment to reduce inflation. And so what do they have? Twenty percent unemployment, hunger, and a society in chaos.

Block: What about John Maynard Keynes, who offered an alternative to Adam Smith and has been a stimulus for many liberal economists?

Leontief: Another solution that Americans have been educated to think can function in the absence of a plan is the Keynesian monetary solution. The Keynesian system can be best depicted as a fellow who doesn't know how a car runs. He gets in, however, and starts the ignition. The engine does not work well, so he quickly begins to play with the choke. Sometimes it works. But usually, what he does is flood the motor—and then he has to sit and wait. The choke is like the Keynesian monetary tools. It floods the economy —and we wait. But, in our economy, the wait is five years, not five minutes; and so we begin to use the choke again—and then we wait some more.

So, it is this education that has led Americans to believe in a simplistic approach of deficits and monetary policies. This is simply naïve. I think the time has arrived when we must see that simplistic solutions do not work.

Block: It's true that the economic rhetoric that prevails in this country has been one of Darwinian economics. Given that, what makes you think that people will change their attitudes toward planning now?

THE NEED FOR PLANNING

Leontief: I see, now you want me to explain why I think planning will come. I love to answer this question because it is easier for me to explain why I think planning *must* come rather than to persuade people that planning is good.

I think that the economic concerns of today are a sufficient incentive to justify the need for planning. Planning is possibly the most difficult enterprise a society can undertake and, being difficult, it may produce all kinds of troubles. However, I believe its time has come. I've found recently that a very large proportion of various groups in the population are now ready, in favor of, and pressing for planning. What groups? Labor. Not all of it—but even Mr. Dunlop (the former Secretary of Labor) really tried to plan. If you have a plan, you do not need a genius to figure out that you should *not* have 8 percent of the labor force unemployed. With a plan, it is rather simple to have reasonably full employment.

The response in the business community has been most interesting. When I talk about the business community, I always must distinguish between what the Chamber of Commerce says and what businessmen say. Chamber of Commerce spokesmen are simply twenty years behind in economic thought. Businessmen are now suffering from depression, shortages, and other troubles, and they clearly see that to have profits, along with social progress, there must be a rational approach to the economy. This calls for planning.

Block: So you think that the experience of the last twenty-five years has been sufficient to make people aware of the need for planning?

Leontief: I would go further. People are sophisticated. They now look beyond the next hill.

Wassily Leontief

Earlier, when times were good, everyone said, "Forget about planning." But now people remember the roller-coaster effects.

Block: The economic planning proposed by the Initiative Committee for National Economic Planning, which you and others formed last February, has been attacked bitterly by many leading businessmen. Walter Wriston of Citibank has called it "no less than fascism." Herbert Stein, former Chairman of the Council of Economic Advisors, has called your planning proposals "inherently undemocratic." What is your response to these criticisms? How do you account for such violent and emotional rejection?

Leontief: I do not feel that Stein's objection is emotional. As a matter of fact, it's rather calm, maybe even relaxed. What's interesting to note is that Stein says planning must involve coordination not only of the economy, but of different government departments. In other words, Stein admits that at present the Department of Agriculture does not know what the Department of Commerce does; that the Environmental Agency does not know what the Energy Agency does. Yes, it is true. However, I am not as pessimistic as Stein, who feels that just getting information from and to agencies cannot be done. To the contrary, it is within our ability to, at least, co-

17

ordinate information among different government departments. Considering that 30 percent of our economic activities are government activities, think of what a benefit this might be. Don't you think that most Americans, whatever walk of life, believe that different government departments should coordinate their efforts?

Block: What about Mr. Wriston's comments?

Leontief: Mr. Wriston's comments are a little more difficult for me. I feel his objections are philosophical—and remember, I distinguish between what businessmen think and what the Chamber of Commerce says. However, in this case, I'm afraid that Mr. Wriston was propagandized by the Chamber of Commerce, which is a kind of feedback I would not have expected. Wriston says that planning deprives us of our freedom. Let us consider this philosophically. I think that since humans were expelled from Paradise, we have functioned under all kinds and increasing amounts of restrictions. It is only the person who is ignorant of everything who thinks that everything is possible. The more you learn, the more you discover that freedom is a much narrower path. As a matter of fact, in the case of Mr. Wriston, I think his stockholders would have welcomed some planner who would have deprived him of his "freedom" to give credit to New York City when it was on the verge of bankruptcy.

Block: Are you suggesting that people like Mr. Wriston and Thomas Murphy at General Motors, by virtue of their enormous power and control, are like those who don't know about the restrictions required to be free because they are totally uncontrolled?

MORE POWERFUL THAN BANKS

Leontief: No, I don't want to say that. My position is much more charitable than yours. I think, probably face to face with Mr. Wriston, we could understand each other much better than his outburst indicates. I think he would understand that despite the strength of his bank, there are some areas which affect his bank over which he has no power. For example, he has no power to eliminate unemployment.

Block: Well, he might have the power to do

away with unemployment by reducing profits. But, if he feels profits are his responsibility. . . .

Leontief: I would think even then he couldn't. Suppose Mr. Murphy decided to eliminate unemployment by giving a job to every auto worker. Given the present economic situation, he would go bankrupt. So, if that was his goal, in order not to go bankrupt he would need planning.

Block: It seems to me that comments by business and government spokesmen suggest that the question is not whether there should be planning but who is going to do the planning.

Leontief: Yes—surprisingly, this question is usually not addressed to me by Mr. Wriston or Mr. Murphy but by radical economists who attack me and say, "What are you doing, Leontief, putting terrific power in the hands of the powerful?" My answer is that I think transferring real power from one strata to another is an incredibly difficult process. I think if planning is introduced, the power structure will remain the same and planning will be done by the same people who are now running the country. Essentially, they are doing it anyway, so to my radical friends, my answer is, "Look, since it is being done, why shouldn't it be done more efficiently?"

Block: That brings up an interesting point. If planning is to be done by the people who run this country, then we may conclude that those who are arguing against planning already control the economic fate of this country.

Leontief: Yes, but they don't plan. The trouble is that they control and influence without planning. This is extremely dangerous because we don't know what the consequences of their influence will be.

Block: What would happen if planning systems are set up and businessmen who have no interest in the social side of the economy continue to influence decisions? John Barner of Princeton makes just that point. He doesn't argue against planning; he points out that you've gone halfway. He states that if you are going to set up a planning system it must include both the social and economic aspects of society.

Leontief: Naturally, we don't limit ourselves. I mean—look, all of the municipal activities of state and local government are not pure economics. There are charges for health, education, and welfare. Certainly there is a problem of translating social benefits in terms appropriate to planning, but there have been some attempts which indicate possibilities and these must be followed up.

Block: One problem that seems to confuse the issue appears to be semantic. When one talks about planning, people assume that you have a grand design—a single master plan.

NO SINGLE SOLUTION

Leontief: No! No! False. I don't say we should have one plan. As an economist I have no more authority to know what direction the economy should go than anybody else. This is why I find all these meetings on national goals absolutely useless.

What I think we have to do is develop alternative plans and look at the consequences of each to determine what is the best tack for the country. For example, I think Mr. Reagan and Mr. Ford should put down on paper their strategies—

and the *consequences* of their strategies—so that we may examine them to decide whether they are feasible. The trouble with most politicians is that they say things will be done which nobody can do. This is levitation.

Block: Do you think that planning models have reached the level of sophistication which will permit us to examine possible alternative paths of the economy?

Leontief: Yes, I believe we now have techniques which can be used for effective planning. These techniques are very recent. They didn't even exist thirty years ago. They permit a scenario to be derived technically. Now what I suggest is that many scenarios be worked out, including one by the present administration, which talks about the economy but never gives us strategies and goals. Let these scenarios be examined by the use of a planning model and then let people see what the consequences of such actions are. Let the people be the judge.

I think that this idea holds out real hope for our society. Because if you work out the consequences of economic proposals, such as one which Mr. Reagan now offers, his position would become transparent and many people who would be inclined to support these proposals on ideological grounds may very well reject them. It is interesting that very often conservative politicians are the ones who emphasize the superficial aspects associated with cuts in spending but fail to show what the real long-term costs of these reductions are.

Block: I would like to believe that a national planning center would work. However, the history of government control of such activities—for example, Amtrak, the Post Office—is disastrous. It seems that even awareness of the problems doesn't lead to beneficial decisions.

Leontief: Let me make a distinction which is very important. I do not think that businesses should be operated by the government. The problem of efficiency still remains and much of the work required in our society needs short-term incentives to make it attractive. This is a complicated problem and should be the responsibility of business, not government.

The question, then, is whether the government has a plan, not whether the government takes over and controls business. The question is whether the government is responsible for injecting its presence in specific areas and identifying difficulties associated with particular business trends which are in conflict with the good of the society. For example, it's said that planning in Soviet Russia is a failure. However, some people find it quite remarkable that a country which is so terribly inefficient has been able to build a powerful economy second only to that of the United States. How did it happen? My explanation is this. It's a miracle that inefficient farms, inefficient offices and inefficient factories have been welded into a very powerful machine. Why? Because they do not make very *big* mistakes.

The difference between the Russian economy and ours is this. We are terribly efficient on the bottom, but we completely mess up the solutions to basic problems: energy, the cities, and so on. The Russians are terribly messy on the bottom, but they compensate by not making really big boners. My hope is that American planning, having the advantage of efficient operations on an individual-plant level, will also avoid big mistakes.

WHO WANTS PLANNING?

Block: Are there businessmen who support your proposals?

Leontief: Yes, you can get a complete list if you call *Challenge* magazine. A number of them support the planning approach, not because they favor social revolution, but because they want to keep this country's economy going. You will discover a very large number of men from industry, from trades, and from banking who now support planning. When the nature of our proposals is clear, more and more businessmen will shift and support planning.

Block: Would you care to comment about the statement by Mr. Wallich, Governor of the Federal Reserve Board, that "Planning in the United States appears to be the wrong thing in the wrong country at the wrong time"?

Leontief: I think it is the right thing at the right time because the country is in a very bad state. I do not think there is the slightest hope that conventional Keynesian methods will solve our problems. I don't think that anyone can seriously believe that after all the experimenting with monetary and fiscal policies that they can still solve the problems in this way. I think people who advocate the abolition or reduction of government efforts are not only wrong but dangerous. The best example of what happens if you abolish government activities is in Chile, which is the only country which follows Milton Friedman's Darwinian prescription of free market competition. I was surprised to hear that Mr. Friedman seems quite satisfied with the results. My feeling is that consistent application of his principles in this country would lead to absolute social disaster, if not revolution.

Block: It is interesting when one reads the critiques of the Humphrey-Javits legislation. . . .

Leontief: I am not an adherent of every letter and sentence of the Javits-Humphrey bill. The problem is that the legislative process is essentially one of compromise, so with a change here, an amendment there, it is hard to tell exactly in what form the bill will come out in the end. I do, however, support wholeheartedly their desire to establish some system for planning.

Block: Recently, Gar Alperovitz and Jeff Faux, codirectors of the Exploratory Project for Economic Alternatives, have jumped on the planning bandwagon. However, they propose that national planning be the sum total of local plans.

Leontief: Alperovitz and Faux are not technicians. They seem more interested in the politics of planning. They are selling planning like an advertiser sells a product. They don't know how difficult it is. They don't seem to understand the managerial and technical problems. You cannot do national planning by town meetings.

Block: Would you agree, then, that the climate for planning appears to be appropriate and the real battle will be over who does the planning?

Leontief: The battle will continue even when we are setting up the machinery to do the technical work of planning—information gathering and so on. My feeling is that it should happen like this.

The people engaged in the technical process of preparing the plans should not be the people who decide what plan should be accepted. The technician should be able to develop as many plans as there are different views regarding what direction the economy and our government should move.

There should be a plan which describes the operation of the economy as Mr. Wriston wants—and a plan incorporating Mr. Woodcock's ideas of economy, equity, and social justice. However, all the plans must be feasible.

A major problem is to ensure that the plans are practical. Think, for example, of pollution. One should prepare alternative ways of eliminating pollution and see what the costs in each case will be. Then and only then should the process of political maneuvering, of logrolling, take place. However, one point must be made. The choice, the maneuvering must be between practical, feasible plans. You cannot change one piece of a plan and expect it to work, and that must be made clear because everyone wants good things and very few want to pay the price. Good planning will make it impossible for the politician to spend money without seeing where it comes from and what the direct and indirect effects are.

THE ROLE OF INTUITION

Block: I have one difficulty with what you have just said. You distinguish the technicians from the decision makers. Yet we both know that in developing a planning model—for example, an input-output structure—the intuition of a technician is important. Certainly, that intuition reflects the ideological concerns of the developer.

Leontief: Yes, intuition of the technologist is very important, but if the technologist is competent, and the model he builds is an appropriate representation of the economic structure, then his philosophical bent will not influence the outcome.

Let me, as an example, illustrate with something I have recently done. I was responsible for constructing a very big model for the United Nations, projecting the world economy to the year 2000. I didn't make one projection, I made many of them. Let me describe two of the projections. One considered the following question: Imagine that the goal is to develop a plan attaining a very rapid or sharp rise in per-capita income levels of less-developed countries. You fix the taxed income level for the year 2000 and then work backwards to determine what levels of investment, what levels and direction of capital transfers, and what kind of labor input would be required.

The second projection uses the same model and the same basic data to answer a different question. Imagine the working habits, saving habits of people in the future are the same as they are now, including the habit of giving foreign aid. What would the incomes of the developing nations be as a result of this conceptualization?

The contrast between the two conceptualizations is incredible. To obtain high income levels, the transfer from developed to underdeveloped countries would have to be tremendous. The debt accumulated for loans under those circumstances would make the conditions in New York City seem simple. Technologically, it may be possible—but it is impractical. On the other hand, if everything goes as it has been, the developing countries will be in a starving position by the year 2000. What these contrasts show is that we have to have some other plan in between. Neither extreme works. But what is important to know is that before we had this computation, people argued we could have high income in developing nations without loans, without aid, while others said we can have much aid and no results will occur. Well, what we showed was what would happen under both extremes and made clear the necessity for different alternatives. My own interests in this case were not important. The technology produced the results.

Block: Well, you brought up a very important point. Given the multinational character of the world today, especially as it applies to economic resource allocation, can any form of economic planning in this country work without the co-operation of other nations?

Leontief: Let me turn the table on you. Mr. Kissinger's position at the beginning of the oil crisis was—you name it, I call it comical, some call it tragic. Mr. Kissinger came and said, "Let's plan." He invited everybody, including M. Jobert of the French foreign ministry. We should have international planning, oil allocation, what not. The trouble is, he had no planning at home. He couldn't guarantee anything. If the group made an international plan, Mr. Kissinger couldn't fulfill that the U.S. would do what he promised. Mr. Jobert, on the other hand, like many Europeans, had pretty good control of his own economy. So, Mr. Jobert looks around and he realizes that having good control of the French economy, he could make a better deal if the international economy is in chaos.

What I conclude is that to be able to deal in international bargaining, which is essentially planning, we have to have domestic planning. Otherwise, if planning stops at our shores, we will have complete chaos, which may already be true.

Let me give you one last illustration of how absurd decisions without planning information really are. Mr. Ford tried to control the oil situation by imposing a two-year import tax. A New England state sued him in court—and won. I supplied an affidavit for the state. My affidavit said that after having studied the justification by our government for this tariff, it was impossible to determine whether or not the tariff was appropriate. I argued that the government had no information. Therefore, how could they justify the tariff.

I believe that planning technology can work. In fact, it must if we are not to have chaos. But remember—I am a technician in *economics*, not theology.

HENRY HAZLITT

Planning Disaster

*A government blueprint for the economy would cost
the United States dear.*

In the past forty years, government intervention in U.S. business affairs has expanded at an accelerating rate. The result has been mounting economic disruption and inflation. But when such intrusions increasingly make things worse than they were before, their original advocates refuse either to acknowledge error or to change their ways. Instead, what they perennially urge is fresh intervention.

Hence, readers of *The New York Times* were perhaps not too surprised by the lead editorial in its issue of February 23, which proposed government "planning" of the entire economy. This editorial proved to be the opening gun in a well-orchestrated campaign. Five days later, *The Times* reported in its news columns that a group headed by Leonard Woodcock, chief of the United Auto Workers, and Wassily Leontief, the former Harvard economist, was calling for National Economic Planning. Now, we suppose, the suggestion is almost a movement.

Planning and socialism

To a seasoned observer, this movement has a curi-
ously familiar ring. More than forty years ago (in 1934), in his book *The Great Depression,* the British economist Lionel Robbins wrote: "Socialism is a term which is not universally popular. But 'planning'—ah! magic word—who would not plan? We may not all be socialists now, but we are certainly (nearly) all planners. Yet . . . what does it denote but socialism— central control of the means of production? . . . For planning involves central control. And central control excludes the right of individual disposal of one's labor, land or capital. Nothing but intellectual confusion can result from a failure to realize that Planning and Socialism are fundamentally the same. Now the leaders of opinion want planning."

The planners' first error

Three basic errors have led people to advocate the substitution of government for private planning. The first is the false assumption that there is very little private economic planning. Anticapitalist bias leads the Planners to assume that a free market economy is a chaos in which we are all either working at cross-

Henry Hazlitt, "Planning Disaster." *Challenge,* July–August 1975, pp. 44–46. Reprinted with permission of Barron's National Business and Financial Weekly, copyright © 1975.

purposes or blindly drifting along. On the contrary, in a free market most of us, and certainly the more enterprising, are constantly planning to maximize our future income, and are constantly on the alert for chances to do so.

Responding to changes in supply and demand, in relative costs, prices and profits, private entrepreneurs are constantly weighing what commodities and services to produce and in what quantities—and what will not be made at all. If there is no profit in an endeavor, it is a sign that the labor and capital devoted to it are misdirected—the value of the resources that would be consumed in the process would be greater than the worth of what was produced.

This theme, long familiar to free market economists, was brilliantly restated by Congressman Jack Kemp of New York in a speech to the House on February 24. He pointed out once more that a major function of profits is to guide and channel the elements of production so as to mesh the relative output of thousands of different commodities with demand. Profits and prices maximize production and relieve shortages quicker than any other economic system.

Another function of profits—and losses—is to put unremitting pressure on the head of every competitive enterprise to introduce further economies and efficiencies, no matter what stage these may already have reached. By rewarding the successful and eliminating the failures, the consuming public keeps channeling capital to those who have shown that they can make the most effective use of it.

Finally (and contrary to the belief of the government planners), profits are achieved less by raising prices than by introducing economies and efficiencies that cut costs of production. Biggest profits—as a percentage of sales—go to firms which have achieved the lowest costs of production. It is in this way that productivity constantly grows.

Second error

The second major error of government planners is their failure to point out that the real question being raised is not: plan or no plan? but whose plan? For when it is government that lays down a master plan, the plans of all the rest of us must be either set aside or subordinated. "Planning" means coercion.

The more sophisticated Planners (to use the capital

letter to signify advocates of state planning) disavow any such intention. They do not favor "coercive" planning, they say, but only "indicative" planning. (This phrase is also *déjà vu:* it was coined by French Planners some twenty-five years ago.) Says the new Initiative Committee for National Economic Planning: "The planning office would not set specific goals for General Motors, General Electric, General Foods or any other individual firm. But it would indicate the number of cars, the number of generators and the quantity of frozen foods we are likely to require in, say, five years, and it would try to induce the relevant industries to act accordingly."

But suppose GM or GE preferred its own estimates or guesses to those of the bureaucrats? Ah, then, we begin to get hints of coercion: "The inducements would be laws, as specific as necessary, on taxes, subsidies and environmental problems."

Third error

The third major error of the Planners is to assume that the production plans of the government bureaucrats would be more knowledgeable or objective than those of private industry. They would, in fact, be systematically worse and often disastrous.

Is there any reason to suppose that, if Planning had existed in the past, federal bureaucrats would have foreseen any earlier than private inventors and entrepreneurs the development of the railroad, the automobile, the airplane, the telephone, radio, television and a thousand other innovations? Isn't it more likely that the bureaucratic plans would have delayed or prevented these developments? Again, to take the very recent past, did our government officials foresee, even a week sooner than the heads of private oil companies, the imposition of the Arab oil embargo or the formation of the OPEC cartel?

The free market—the interplay of money prices, profits and losses—is the indispensable guide to production. Without it, no bureaucrat, no human mind, could solve the problem of what among tens of thousands of commodities and services to produce, and in what quantities, qualities, or proportions. Or by what technical methods. Nor is there any reason to suppose that the bureaucrat would even try to make objective judgments. Their production schedules would be those which appeared at the moment to have most popular appeal. If we want to know how overall Planning would work, we need only recall how specialized government planning has worked in the past.

Oil and gas

Let us confine ourselves to just two examples of past government planning—the first concerning U.S. oil and gas supply; the second, money supply. Both *The Times* and the Woodcock-Leontief group manage to imply that if government planning had already been in existence, we would have avoided our present domestic shortage of oil and natural gas. The facts notoriously point the other way. Everyone agrees that the policy of the Federal Power Commission, in keeping natural gas prices far below free-market levels for the past twenty-one years, has brought about the present alarming shortage. For price-fixing did two things: it encouraged an enormously wasteful demand for and use of natural gas, and it seriously lessened incentive to explore and drill for new supplies.

When we turn to petroleum, we are reminded that if our "environmentalists" in Congress and the bureaucracy had not for years held up authority to construct a pipeline, the United States would have access to Alaskan oil today. When the Arab embargo was imposed, government price controls on oil and allocations merely increased the disruption which that embargo caused, leading to long lines of cars at gas stations which, as in Europe, free-market prices would have made unnecessary. The U.S. government today is still keeping price controls on "old" domestic oil.

The currency

Let us turn to the currency. Here is one "commodity" whose production, in effect, we have placed entirely in the hands of a government agency, the Federal Reserve Board. The Board has used that power with sheer irresponsibility. It has turned out irredeemable paper money on the printing presses and has yielded perennial inflation over the last forty years.

Advocates of Planning persistently ignore the frightful record of past failures and catastrophes. That record, in their minds, is irrelevant. Those failures came about because the government's previous plans were wrong. But in the future they will be right, because the advocates always envisage themselves— or at least others with equally faultless foresight—in charge of the future. Harsh experience never seems to discourage the utopian statists.

American Capitalism: Trial Balance

GIVEN this culture of science and the machine, how about the system of American capitalism which organizes it? The appraisal of American capitalism as a going concern must be made largely in terms of a balance sheet. Whoever embraces its achievements should not flinch from acknowledging its costs; whoever condemns the costs should be candid enough to recognize the achievement.

The record of achievement is clear enough: a continuously rising curve of man-hour productivity; a high rate of capital formation; steadily rising profits which have made a corpse of the Marxist predictions about profits under capitalism; employment levels which in the mid-1950s were at their top peacetime pitch; a wilderness of available commodities and a strong "propensity to consume," reflecting the spread of high and increasing living standards even among middle- and low-income levels; a steadily increasing growth in real wages; a continuing secular increase in the national product; a production record which has provided the military production for two world wars and the current "readiness economy" for defense, while increasing the products available for civilian consumption; a capacity to take in its stride an ever-heavier tax structure without destroying freedom of economic movement and decision within the economy; a continuing sense of economic dynamism, and finally an economy with the capacity for changing its forms under pressure so that it could in the mid-1950s lay claim to being a "people's capitalism" even while being to a high degree a corporate and monopoly capitalism.

The debit side is also clear: a haste for profits which has used up too rapidly the land and resources of the continent and built unplanned cities; an economy which made heavy productive gains (especially in World War II) through the expansion of war industries and seems still to be buttressed by a government budget for arms which runs to 15 or 20 per cent of the Gross National Product; one which has lived like a fever-chart patient by constantly taking its pulse and has not been able to control firmly the periodic swings of prosperity and depression; one in which the Big Enterprise corporations create private empires challenging the state itself; one in which the chances for a competitive start in the race for the Big Money are less open to small businessmen and depend more upon upward movement in a corporate bureaucracy; an economy in which, despite its production levels, much remains to be done in distributing the final product more fairly.

The observer is tempted to say (with Hamlet): "Look at this picture, and here at this one."

Max Lerner, "American Capitalism: Trial Balance." In *America As A Civilization,"* Simon & Schuster, Inc., 1957, pp. 267–274. Copyright © 1957 by Max Lerner. Reprinted by permission of Simon & Schuster, Inc.

The defense of American capitalism runs largely in broad abstractions like "the American system" or "the free-enterprise economy," or in epithets like "serfdom" or "totalitarian" applied to noncapitalist systems. Underlying these catchwords are some basic arguments. One is the *argument from incentive:* that men's brains and energy work best when they have no hampering restrictions, and when they see an immediacy of relation between effort and reward. The second is the *argument from a free market:* that an economy runs best as the result of millions of individual decisions made through the operations of a free production, wage and price system; that when it goes off kilter, it can generally set itself right again by individual adjustments within a frame of government spurs and checks; and that even government regulation is best accomplished by the indirect methods of inducements and pressures on the free market, rather than the direct method of planning and control. The third is the *argument from managerial efficiency:* that the corporate managerial group is recruited from the men with the best skills, who deal with the problems of industrial production more flexibly than a governmental bureaucracy could.

The arguments, though vulnerable, are basically valid. True, the free market no longer exists in anything like its historic form, and Big Enterprise and the giant corporation, with prices largely reached by administrative decision, have in part taken its place. Yet the economy has developed its own distinctive forms of freedom, and the decisions reached in it are still freer than in a cartelized or largely government-directed economy. The system of profit and property incentives has been transformed in the giant corporation; yet new incentives have emerged that keep the corporate managers alert and drive the productive system on. The argument from corporate efficiency has much in its favor, provided we do not forget that a corporate bureaucracy has a strong inner impulse toward conformism of spirit and, like government bureaucracies, runs the danger of stagnation.

Some corollaries of these doctrines that emerge in the capitalist apologia are more open to question: the argument that the big corporations and their managers administer their power *as a trust* for the people as a whole; and the argument that there is a *harmony of interests* which ties labor and the farmers to business prosperity and therefore business decisions. While most Americans are too realistic to accept the view that Big Property is being held in trust for them, they do not resent the power of the possessing groups because they hope themselves someday to be secure enough to "take it easy." As for the harmony of interests, they may have some skepticism about it, yet they have never been caught by the European idea that class cleavages must deepen until the whole system breaks.

The real problems of capitalism, however, are not the doctrinal struggles but the operational strains—the periodic breakdowns, the sense of insecurity, the shadow of monopoly, the dependence upon war expenditures, the question of distributive justice. The American economy, because of its power and prosperity, has become the last, best hope of free economies in the world. But by the same token the issues of its capacity for survival, its social costs, and its impact on the human spirit have called in question the nature and survival value of the system of capitalism itself.

What are the elements of American capitalism as a going concern, distinguishing it from other going systems? It is customary to say that capitalism is organized as a "private-enterprise system," for private (individual or corporate) profit, with the resulting rewards protected by the state as private property. This is valid enough, except for the fact that far-reaching changes have taken place in the structure and functioning of American capitalism. The profit incentive, for example, does not operate in corporate management as it used to operate in individual enterprise, since ownership and management have split apart: it still holds, however, if it is rephrased as the drive within the manager to make the best possible profit record for the corporation. The idea of private property has also suffered a change, since industrial ownership is now widely scattered in the form of stock ownership, some of the stocks being owned by trust funds, investment trusts, other corporations, life insurance companies, and even trade-unions. The earlier picture of capitalism as a competitive system has also had to be changed. To some extent competition has been inhibited by price agreements and "oligopoly"—the control of an industry by a handful of big corporations competing only partly in price and mainly in packaging, advertising, and brand names, as in meat packing, automobiles, or cigarettes. Yet the impressive fact about the American economy is the extent to which it has effectively resisted the monopoly tendencies. The concept of bigness is not the same as the concept of monopoly, and something that can fairly be called competition is still a power regulator of the economy.

The core of capitalism then is still present. It is in essence concerned with decision-making within a profit-competitive framework. Under communism the decisions are made by a small group of political functionaries assigned to strategic industrial posts. Under democratic socialism they are made by technicians operating largely within government corporations, responsible ultimately to the people. Under American capitalism the decisions on production, pricing, advertising, and sales policies are private decisions—that is to say, they are made by individual businessmen or heads of small corporations, whether they be producers, middlemen, or retailers, and in the case of big corporations they are made by the managers to whom the power of decision is delegated by the stockholders; the decisions on wages and labor policy are generally made through collective bargaining by the managers and trade-union leaders. Obviously there are restrictions placed on these decisions by price and wage legislation, sometimes by priorities and the allocation of scarce materials in a defense economy. But within these limits the decisions are linked with ownership and management, and they are made always with a view to profit and in competition with other enterprises. At the other end of the capitalist process there are millions of decisions made by the consumer: production and investment policies are guided not by governmental decisions or by what might be considered socially necessary production but in the light of consumers' decisions about how they will spend their money and for what.

Thus at one end American capitalism is guided by decisions made by businessmen, managers, and trade-union leaders, at the other end by consumer decisions. This decision-making operates within a frame in which there are strong surviving elements of private property, private and corporate profits, and competition.

In assessing American capitalism as a going concern, one important test is the test of *productivity*. Here American capitalism shows the most impressive facet of its record. Socialists might argue that, given the resources of America and the accidents of its history, some other system of organization, ownership, and power could have attained the same productivity with a better distribution of the products. This is one of those iffy questions that will never be resolved. On the other hand it is hard to sustain the claim that the creative force in the American record of increased productivity is the capitalist entrepreneur and manager, and he alone. Science, technology, the legal and governmental framework, and the skill of the worker—all belong in the larger pattern along with the supplier of risk capital and the business organizer. Yet the American record of an increase of productivity running between 2 per cent and 3 per cent a year must be counted one of the over-all achievements of capitalism. Nor has this production record been only a matter of technology and resources. The drive toward productivity has also been due to the elements within the social structure which have invested the whole productive process with the *élan* of freedom. This is as true today as it was a century ago, as John Sawyer has shown, basing himself on the accounts of European travelers in America in the 1840s and 1850s.

All this brings us to the question of *incentive,* which is more troublesome. Those who contend that profit alone has furnished the effective incentive for industrial production must plead guilty to a lower view of human motive than applies even in an imperfect world. The fact is that the managerial function in the big corporation has been performed through incentives quite different from those of ownership profits or dividends, and more closely related to competitive performance and pride in a job well done. Through a complex mingling of profit, salary, bonus, and craftsmanship incentives, capitalism as a going concern has enlisted considerable talents in the processes of production and selling; and it has plowed back into increased production a steady portion (recently around 7 per cent) of the national product, keeping the process of capital formation an active and growing one.

It is on the test of *stability* that American capitalism is most vulnerable. American economic thought is crisscrossed by conflicts of opinion about the underlying causes of the periodic swings and breakdowns of the system, resulting in cycles of prosperity and recession, boom and depression. There are still die-hard critics of the system who believe that boom and bust are inherent in the system and will never yield to anything short of full-scale socialism. There are also True Believers of another stripe who feel, as their forerunners felt in the boom days of the 1920s, that Americans have somehow found the golden key to perpetual prosperity.

Aside from these two groups there is fairly general agreement, however, that, while the swings in the "business cycle" may not yet have been mastered, American business, labor, and government leaders have learned to detect the danger signals and put in motion some preventive measures, and have learned also—once the cycle is on its way—how to cut the length and severity of the downward swing and cushion its impact. In the mid-1950s there was an upsurge of conviction that the cycle had to a large extent been mastered and need never again operate drastically. The bitter experience after 1929 taught the nation's leaders how to use "counter-cyclical" measures in the form of tax and fiscal policies, rediscounting rates, Federal expenditures for defense and public works, state and Federal programs for building roads, schoolhouses, and hospitals. The President's Council of Economic Advisers, working with a committee of Congress, is now accepted under Republican as well as Democratic administrations. Its reports, carefully studied in business, labor, and government circles, are in effect an embryonic form of corrective and preventive planning. The government's massive role in a war-geared "readiness economy" has also given it a leverage in guiding, checking, and stimulating business activity and as such it is a form of indirect planning.

America has thus characteristically used an indirect approach to the control of the swings of business activity, aiming at stability without embracing a direct program of planning and without transferring the crucial decisions from the corporate managers and the consumers to government managers. The specter of Depression is, of course, always present. At the close of World War II there were widespread prophecies of economic catastrophe, yet the real danger proved to be not mass unemployment but inflation, not a paralysis of production but a boom induced by high demand and sustained by the armament race. This mood has lasted into the mid-1950s. Obviously there is a serious problem in the steady inflationary movement of American prices, year after year, largely due to the pressure of rising consumer demand, with its tragic effect in wiping out much of the substance and meaning of savings. Yet, while Americans are still far from solving the basic problem of boom and bust, they have at least a heightened awareness of what is involved and are willing to take decisive action. There are few economists who would accept the European notion, seemingly as widespread among scholars as among the people, that American capitalism will once again in the calculable future be as helpless as it was in the years following 1929.

On the test of *security and insecurity* American capitalism has made steady if reluctant progress. So far from interfering with prosperity, it is now accepted that effective, well-administered insurance programs make the economy more stable as well as adding to personal security. Every person must confront the tragic elements in life, but the pathetic elements can be whittled down by common action. To the degree that America has become a welfare state it is not because of effeminacy or the importation of "foreign" ideas, but of practical grappling with a deeply felt need to make the individual fate more secure.

Judged by another test—that of *income spread and distribution*—the going economy has in the past evoked strong self-criticism from American writers, if not from the economists. Especially in the decade before

World War I, and in the 1920s and 1930s, they unsparingly subjected the economy to the test of equity. The extremes of wealth and poverty, the discrepancies between the Babylonian living at the top of the pyramid and the scrimping and degradation at its base, became staples of the American self-portrait. There was a time when the prospects of the future for many Americans seemed precarious. Any European or Asian who thinks that Americans need to be prodded about this should read the almost unparalleled record in which sensitive Americans have made their own indictment of their own vaunted system. But the note of self-criticism has recently grown fainter because of the overwhelming evidence of American living standards. These have improved all through the class system as productivity has increased and the trade-unions have been able to claim a share of it for their members. The problem of poverty in America is now circumscribed within the lower fourth of the population.

One could argue, of course, that the depressed groups in backward areas in other countries are far worse off than this lower fourth in America. This would be sound if American living standards were judged by productivity in other areas of the world, but they must be judged by American productivity. In every economy, as Sumner put it, "there are dinners without appetites at one end of the table, and appetites without dinners at the other." The American economy as a production miracle has evoked life claims in America not roused in the underdeveloped economies: what would be a full meal elsewhere is a skimpy one at the table of the American business system.

The final test of a going economy is the *creativeness* it evokes and makes possible. Few systems in history have attracted so much talent and put it to use, and in no other economy have men's business abilities been so continuously tapped. The problem is not whether the economy gives scope to creativeness, but what kind of creativeness it gives scope to. The question asked is always whether a new idea or a new insight is "practical"—that is, whether it can be translated into dollar-and-cents terms. The creativeness that is not vendible is likely to be ignored and to wither. Yet within this pecuniary framework there has been broader scope for the creation of use values and life values than the critics of the money calculus have been ready to admit.

This then would be a rough trial balance of American capitalism as a going concern: that it has done brilliantly in productivity and national product; that it has done less well with the swings of the business cycle and with boom and bust, but that substantial steps have been taken to meet this; that its greatest weakness on this score lies in the dependence of the recent prosperity on the war-geared economy; that its growth in the areas of concentrated economic power has been at the expense of small business; that in its income distribution it is a good deal better than its opponents would admit but not nearly as good as its apologists claim, good enough to retain the faith of those who are fulfilled by it but not good enough to exact the loyalty of those who feel left out; that it allows for creativeness but within a limited sense of that word; that as a whole it is an economy which has wrested from the world its envy along with a grudging respect, but not its imitation.

Kenneth Arrow on Capitalism and Society

IMAGINE THE PLIGHT of the editor assigned to interview a distinguished economist about whom he knows very little. In preparation, he consults a review of the great man's work by fellow economist Paul Samuelson. There he learns that the prospective interviewee achieved fame by exploring the global stability of price formation when the Jacobian matrix $[\partial f_i/\partial p_j] = F'[P]$ is not symmetric but does have positive off-diagonal elements.

At this point one shudders at the prospect of an interview in which questions are asked on punched cards and answers are received on a printout. Happily, this was not the case. Interviewing Professor Kenneth J. Arrow proved to be a quite human experience.

Kenneth Arrow at 53 stands at the very pinnacle of his profession—a full professor of economics at Harvard, the 1972 winner of the Nobel Prize in Economic Science, and the 1973 President of the American Economic Association. He is beyond doubt one of the most formidable mathematical economists in the world today, with a reputation stemming from work done in his twenties at Stanford.

Arrow's major contributions to economic science have been in risk and decision theory, where he developed the theory of contingent securities. In addition, he first proved the "Impossibility Theorem," which demonstrates that in some circumstances consumer choices must necessarily produce irrational results.

But there is another side of Kenneth Arrow. He is a humanist as well as a mathematician, a man deeply concerned about social choices, the ethical responsibility of actors in the economy, and the future of capitalism. It was this side of Kenneth Arrow that came out in an interview with *Business and Society Review.*

JOHN McCLAUGHRY
Contributing Editor

McClaughry: You have made the point in your writings that social choice cannot be both rational and democratic. Could you tell us what you mean by that?

Arrow: The proposition has to be interpreted very carefully. What I mean basically is that an approach which is genuinely democratic could under certain circumstances run into logical inconsistencies. The problem arises because we have in the real world a large number of choices to be made in any given circumstances. There are not just two policies, but many, so we have to choose among them.

Now, if among the policies which exist we wish the process to be democratic, in the sense that everybody has an equal voice, and we also say that the choice has to be rational, then we can always find circumstances under which the choices circle.

Let me give an example that will clarify it— a very old example, developed in 1785 by the Marquis de Condorcet. Suppose there are three candidates who embody three policy choices. One-third of the people prefer Adams to Black and Black to Clark. One-third of the people prefer Black to Clark and Clark to Adams. One-third of the people prefer Clark to Adams and Adams to Black. Now what if society chooses between Adams and Black? Two-thirds of the people prefer Adams to Black. If you compare Black to Clark, you will find two-thirds of the people prefer Black to Clark; but to complete the circle, we also find two-thirds of the people prefer Clark to Adams. Now this means that a system that ranks candidates or social choices by pair-wise comparison according to majority rule *can* end up in inconsistency, depending on the particular assumptions made about how people will in fact vote. But the system presumably isn't set up in advance of knowing how people will in fact vote, so it's prepared to accommodate this situation. We discover it cannot accommodate it in a rational manner—in a manner that does not involve going around in circles.

I have essentially argued that this isn't just a matter of majority voting. It turns out that there is no kind of voting which is rational—in the sense that it makes consistent comparisons in pairs—and at the same time permits everybody an equal voice, or in fact permits every individual a voice at all! Now that means that in practice we have to accept the possibility that once in a while a system won't work, and try to design systems that will work fairly, widely, and responsibly.

McClaughry: On another matter, aside from the political process, do you believe a businessman has any responsibility to the social welfare that is inconsistent with the maximization of profit over the long run?

Arrow: Yes, I do. I certainly don't regard the maximization of long-range profits as an unimportant end from a social point of view, as well as from an individual one. I think one of the major things that a businessman can contribute to the world is to run his shop as efficiently as possible, and that does involve making profits high.

But there are other responsibilities which may interfere. The information available in the world is spread out very unevenly. The businessman typically has more information about his product —its quality, its safety—than his customers. I think that he is under a moral obligation to reveal the truth, even though this might hurt sales, and I think the economic system would run better if this obligation were understood. There may be an obligation not to produce things that would be unduly harmful because it may be very difficult to convey the fact that they'll be harmful. It may be better just not to produce them at all. I find it very difficult to justify engaging in the commercial production of narcotics, and I must say I have grave doubts about something like tobacco. Certainly, at a minimum, we would expect a full revelation of facts relating to safety. There seems to be some reason to suppose, in the case of complex machines like automobiles, that the facts about safety known to the manufacturers have not always been fully revealed. They may not *always* be known to the producer, but that simply means that he's not making tests which would be inexpensive for him but very costly to anybody else.

My argument is not just a question of morality, but also a question of overall economic efficiency. If there is uncertainty about the qualities of products and about their implications, there is going to be a suspiciousness on the part of customers. Some may refuse to purchase or consume goods which would in fact be beneficial, because the certification is inadequate. In some areas, society has long since taken precautions. One of the most striking cases is medical ethics. A physician is a rather extreme case of an entrepreneur selling a product about which he knows vastly more than his client. In this case, what the physician is basically selling *is* his superior information. This is the essence of the transaction. The manipulative skills of the surgeon are relatively secondary. Now, we do expect him to conduct his treatment in the best interests of the patient. If doctors were highly exploitative, the practice of

medicine would suffer. In the long run, doctors as a whole would lose by it because people would be too suspicious to make use of them.

McClaughry: Are you suggesting, then, that the businessman's superior knowledge about the character of his product carries with it a moral responsibility to protect the relatively ignorant consumer, even at the cost of the businessman's profits?

Arrow: That is exactly right. But I would also extend this to the question of safety in the work place. Very similar considerations apply to the relations between managers and workers as apply to the relations between managers and customers.

McClaughry: What steps could society take now, or could organizations take now, to attempt to reinstill this kind of moral responsibility for the well-being of the relatively uninformed consumer?

Arrow: I believe that what is needed is the evolution of accepted codes of ethics. This might take the form of grade labeling by a centralized agency. It may mean setting forth ethical codes calling for full revelation. The reason for the codes, and why I expect them to have some signaling value, is that any individual firm may indeed find it difficult to cut down on its long-run profits by advertising its failures. If other firms do not, that policy may put it at a competitive disadvantage. But if it is agreed upon by the industry, then the industry may benefit by the superior confidence of the consumers, and the individual firm will be protected against competitive disadvantage by the knowledge that all its competitors are doing the same.

Obviously, this may call for some kinds of sanctions, which I trust will be only in the form of publicity against noncompliers or those who fail to accept the supervision involved. But it seems to me that this idea of a coherent set of signals from some credible source, whether it be an impartial private institute of some kind or the government, can only improve the efficiency with which each part of the economy works. Essentially it has to be in a form of levying ethical requirements on individual producers. Hopefully, enforcement will come in part from the responsibility of the individual members of those organizations—from a moral sense which transcends their loyalty to the firm.

McClaughry: You favor, in effect, a highly moral and responsible conspiracy in restraint of trade?

Arrow: You have touched, of course, upon the grave danger of this sort of thing. There is the danger, and the medical profession probably illustrates it, that anything that is done for the purpose of increasing morality will wind up being to some extent a conspiracy against the public. Adam Smith remarked long ago that even when the members of a trade assembled for the purpose of social diversion, it would most likely wind up as a conspiracy against the public. I think there's a risk there. There's risk in all of these things. There's no way of setting forth mechanical rules which will prevent this from happening. I can only suggest a tension between the forces of antitrust regulation and the evolution of codes which will protect the public from, as you say, restraint of trade.

McClaughry: Classical economics focused on the all-important role of the market in determining supply, demand, and price. Businessmen have never been free from some uncertainties in appraising the future market for their products. Today, however, those uncertainties have compounded almost beyond human comprehension. Ever-changing technology, manipulation of consumer demand, a deep and often seemingly capricious government involvement in economic activity—all these and many other factors combined to create such uncertainty that the old idea of the market place seems hopelessly archaic. You won a Nobel Prize in economics for your work toward salvaging the idea of the market, by introducing the idea of the contingent market. What does that concept mean to today's business decision-maker?

Arrow: The idea of a contingent market is a theoretical construct designed to show how, in principle, the optimality notions connected with the free market can be rescued in the face of uncertainty. I never have intended this to be a realistic description of the economy, but rather an ideal against which the actual situation must be measured and the shortcomings assessed. The idea of the contingent market is that contracts for future delivery should be made contingent upon the occurrence of uncertain events. For example, there could in principle be contracts for delivery of wheat a year hence, where the contract depends upon the size of the total wheat crop. You may make one contract for delivery if the wheat crop is large, and another one if it is small.

In the real world we have a relatively small number of contingent contracts. Insurance policies are the most obvious ones. An insurance contract is specifically a payment of money if and only if some event now uncertain occurs. Of course, implicitly a lot of credit instruments which may appear on their face to be contracts for certain delivery are in fact contingent. Bankruptcy is always a possibility in any bond.

McClaughry: Would stock market puts and calls be examples of a contingent market?

Arrow: Puts and calls would be excellent examples of contingent contracts. More generally, equities are implicitly contingent contracts, although the contingencies are not spelled out very well. An equity does not offer, for example, a guarantee of dividends; it does offer a statement about dividends if and only if favorable events occur. What makes the matter more complicated is the fact that capital gains are so dominant in the value of equities.

The point is that the absence of contingent markets, the fact that a lot of things can't be insured against, that insurance covers only just a small fraction of economic risks, means to me that other kinds of institutions develop to fill the gap. And it's here where there is a great need for more analysis of the role of information channels in the business world. A lot of attempts are made to create certainty where there would otherwise be uncertainty—by advertising, by some kind of fixed commitments into the future, by laying off risks in the form of equities, by pooling risks in the form of mutual funds and conglomerates. One of the advantages of size in general, among other advantages, may simply be pooling of risks.

Uncertainty can also be reduced by acquiring information. The impact of quantity information on business decisions is something that goes beyond what can be explained in the usual neoclassical theory of the perfect market. The idea that sales are something to be anticipated, something about which there is uncertainty, really has no place in neoclassical theory. In the pure theory the price may be uncertain, but you can sell anything you want at the going price. In fact, we know that any firm, particularly one of any size, does have some consideration for its own certainty about sales. This is reflected especially in the production and investment decisions. The fact that the firm is responding to quantity signals is an indication that the market is not working as perfectly as it otherwise would. It means that the world is responding to information of a kind which would not be necessary if the market were perfect.

McClaughry: You have pointed out that increasing uncertainty in the economic field has placed ever-increasing premiums on reliable information. What do you see as the long-range future of the business information industry?

Arrow: Well, I think it's clear that the business information industry has grown enormously. New ways of acquiring information are being offered all the time—more control over the internal operations of the firm, in the form of computerization, and more knowledge being available about other firms and about the economy as a whole, offered by these forecasting services that are selling their products to business firms. There's probably some limit as to the value of this information. I'm not sure that the expansion is going to go on indefinitely for two reasons. One is that this information is a public good in many ways, particularly information about the economy as a whole. If it's available to me, it's available to everybody, and there's very little competitive advantage in getting it. Furthermore, if it's known, I can probably get the relevant part of the information cheaply. So there is the problem, as there always is with public goods, of a "free rider" situation.

The second problem is more subtle, and maybe it can be overcome. The absorption of information by the economic agent is also limited. There's no use producing a feast huge enough for twenty people for the benefit of only one, because there is only so much that one stomach can absorb. In the same way, there's a limit to the volume of information that can be absorbed by a single person. I assume there will be improvements in the psychological technology—ways of presenting information so as to be more meaningful. I dare say there will be increasing mechanization of the more routine aspects of decision making. In other words, we will have systems which will respond to a change in prices by automatically changing their product flows, their inputs, their outputs, in a mechanical way. I believe to some extent this is already done by oil companies in their refinery operations.

McClaughry: To what extent could the growing premium on information to dissipate uncertainty lead to a geographical dispersion of financial markets? Given modern communications systems, could much of Wall Street now profitably relocate away from New York City?

Arrow: In principle, yes. I must admit I am a bit puzzled as to why decentralization has not already occurred. We already have had a considerable change in the technology. Computer capabilities today, to one brought up as myself in a somewhat earlier era, are incredible. Machines that used to cost a thousand dollars and were preciously doled out to students for limited amounts of time are inferior to the sort of thing that you can now buy for $60.00 in any department store. Of course, communications when tied to these machines can make possible great decentralization. It is true, and this is connected with what I said earlier about the limits of information flow, that we have no really adequate substitute for face-to-face communication. There is a lot of empirical evidence, for example, that in accepting innovations, face-to-face contact plays a very crucial role. Things are believed and the information flow is perceived to be more reliable when it occurs on a face-to-face basis. No

doubt this is partly because when two individuals meet, they communicate in a variety of channels, many of which can not be translated into digital information. I should think, nevertheless, that the predominance of New York must to some extent be weakened. It certainly must be true in a field like securities that the physical location of the market should no longer matter at all. In fact, I really believe that the physical marketplace must become a ghost-like entity composed only of computer messages in the near future.

McClaughry: Professor Oskar Morgenstern has criticized economists for what he calls their "Walras-Pareto Fixation"—the idea that free competition leads to economic equilibrium and the greatest social good. He argues that economists have focused on purely mechanical behavior and have neglected the more complex human interactions which are deeply involved in economic decision making. It seems to me that in your analysis of the decentralization possibilities inherent in the new information industry, you are taking explicit

account of the importance of the human face-to-face interaction. Is this in a sense meeting Professor Morgenstern's challenge?

Arrow: I hope it is. No one could take any issue with Professor Morgenstern's general observations. We do know that there is such a thing as organization. It's an empirical fact. We observe it all around us. The purely competitive model really allows no room for an independent value of organization. If it occurs at all, in a competitive model, the decisions that it makes will be dictated by the necessities of the market, and there is very little scope for chance or human variation. The reason, in theory, is that those humans who make mistakes will be eliminated by competition. We know that in fact this does not occur with anything like the rapidity predicted by theory. All organizations have these human elements.

I've stressed earlier the informational element —that links in the chain of communication are in part human. They have to be human because human transducers are incredibly efficient in certain ways, though very inefficient in others. They are relatively poor in arithmetic, but they are very good at integrating disparate pieces of information. There is no likelihood that they will be replaced. So long as they exist, the qualities that make human beings differ from each other and that impede or enhance communication among them will be important.

It's also true that when there's flexibility in decision making, there's power, as well as information transfer. The ability to wield power and the efficiency with which it's harnessed for profitable aims make the difference between successful and unsuccessful firms. They may also determine whether the economy as a whole is more or less efficient. Different styles induced by social considerations, cultural education, and so forth may make the difference between the efficiencies of different economies. The real trouble is that we have very little way of getting empirical handles on these observations. This is the point where I find that the old theory still is hard to beat.

McClaughry: In recent years Soviet economists have had heated debates over state management of the economy. Professor Lieberman, for example, has argued that it is impossible to centrally manage any economic system of that size, and that a system suspiciously resembling Adam Smith's is the only answer. His opponents have conceded that this might have been so in the old pencil and paper era, but that the development of high-speed computers once again makes centralized management possible.

As I read your article, "Capitalism Has Overcome," in the *New York Times,* I got the impression that your views strongly resemble those of the more orthodox Soviet economists, in the sense that you believe that failures in the application of Keynesian techniques to our economy

can be reduced by better information and more sophisticated analytic techniques. Am I right?

Arrow: Yes and no. I think there is a big difference between the kind of Keynesian management of the economy in which you are trying to affect general overall parameters, but not make individual decisions, and the detailed centralized planning which many Soviet economists have always held to be the valid theoretical norm. There is no question that computerization in principle permits greater centralization. Centralization properly carried out can be more efficient than decentralization with weak links. On the other hand, the Soviet experience makes it abundantly clear that the amount of knowledge needed to run the economic system is so vast that the idea of centralizing it in any measurable way is simply ludicrous, even with the best computer resources in the world. I have already emphasized the role of human links. One problem is that if you centralize the economy, the information would have to be used by somebody, and no one is capable of using all of it.

But what is even more to the point is that you don't even know in advance what information to transmit. A plant manager may know from his daily experiences a great deal about the operations of his plant. He knows more than he knows he knows. Even if he were to take the time to write down everything he knows, he could not convey everything that he knows. If an emergency arose, he would react in a way that he probably would not have anticipated. The result is that there is no way of getting all the information on a central level.

The Soviet experience has in fact been, theory or no theory, Lieberman or no Lieberman, that a great many decisions are already being made all the time at the plant level. I understand a few years ago some efforts were made in the Soviet Union to introduce the quantitative methods in sociology. A research institute took as its first task to find out to what extent plant managers were fulfilling their assigned norms, particularly with regard to restrictions on the use of inputs. Well, the survey revealed that 85 percent or so of the plant managers were violating regulations in one way or another. The Soviet government responded in the most natural way to this discovery. They abolished the research institute. They knew very well that their system worked only because its regulations were being violated, and they had no intention of disturbing a good situation.

Now there's the question of how you decentralize. Lieberman's proposal certainly included many improvements. The question is not whether the decision is going to be made by the plant managers; the question is what criteria should be used so that plant operations are compatible with an efficient working of the economy. In spite of my earlier critical remarks, it remains to some extent true that profits are a fairly good measure of efficiency. Output is not a good measure of efficiency. Achieving output norms may be at the cost of very great inefficiency. They may be achievable only with very large inputs which would have much higher use elsewhere.

McClaughry: That reminds me of the story of the Soviet chandelier factory that was paid per pound of output. The result, of course, was chandeliers so heavy that they pulled ceilings out of the buildings.

Arrow: Yes, even the Soviet press is full of stories of that kind. Now their use of the profit norm is clearly just like the use of profit centers in large

corporations in the United States, which have very much the same problem. After all, General Motors is a socialist state which very considerably exceeds in scale most of the socialist states in the world.

McClaughry: Here in the United States over the next twenty years, do you see the role of the federal government over the economy increasing, or do you see, perhaps as a result of the wage and price control experience and the energy crisis, a trend back toward a freer market with less regulation?

Arrow: I think wage and price control has not turned out to be successful. I don't think it's as bad, by the way, as I would have thought beforehand. I don't think it did any good, but I don't think it did as much harm as it might have. The general experience with wage and price control, not only in the United States but elsewhere, has not been very successful and the controls have rarely been maintained. In terms of direct regulations of wages and prices, my feeling is that we will see a relaxation for a while.

What the future will bring will depend upon the future course of inflation, about which I hesitate to make any predictions. Other than wage and price controls, a lot of regulation has already gone on the books, particularly in regard to environmental matters, so that there is probably not too much room for more. There is probably still some question of the proper degree of safety regulation, both within the plant and in terms of the safety of the products. There is probably a need to internalize more of the costs, for example, of air pollution and solid waste disposal. This is a cost to the economy in producing a good, in that it ultimately has to be disposed of. My own view is to prefer taxes, which are a kind of price, to direct regulation. But it is clear that there are circumstances in which direct restrictions on noxious outputs of one kind or another will play a role. Therefore, my hope is that the detailed planning of the economy will be very limited in scope. In the overall monetary and fiscal management of the economy, I think we may have increasing sophistication and possibly more complex controls, as we learn to understand them.

McClaughry: You mentioned the problem of inflation. In your *New York Times* article, you pointed out that the leading contradictions of capitalism alleged by Marxist and other economists have proven to be more or less inconsequential. But you do observe that "the coexistence of inflation and unemployment is an intellectual riddle and an uncomfortable fact." What progress is being made to solve that riddle, other than making the fact more comfortable?

Arrow: At the moment I find myself very puzzled about inflation. On the one hand, the Western world had a long period of moderately stable prices with reasonably full employment in the postwar period. Now, we have had a radical change in the situation, beginning in the middle or late sixties. And it's not just the United States. The United States has had a very moderate rate of inflation compared to some stable countries. The United Kingdom, the very pillar of world stability, is having inflation rates that produce a very Latin American impression. It seems clear that this phenomenon has to do with worldwide demand and supply conditions and not merely with domestic policy.

It may be that the Vietnam War somehow set off a trigger, and that once inflation starts it is very hard to stop. Expectations get built in: wage negotiations are carried on with the expectation of inflation, employers are less resistant because they are expecting higher prices, and so forth. Interest rates tend to reflect expectations of inflation. So there is one view that the inflation occurred by chance, so to speak, but once it started it's hard to stop, and that's the reason for the persistence of inflation. I really must remain agnostic on this matter. I just don't have any firm feeling on what the root causes of inflation are. It may be that the world monetary system is the villain of the piece. Until we get a stable world monetary system, we are going to have expectations of inflation creating instability in the world market, which in turn reinforces inflation. I would certainly regard it as preferable to accept the inflation we have than to go back to high unemployment, which is the only obvious cure we have.

McClaughry: Professor William Shepherd, at the University of Michigan, has advanced the thesis that the major source of inflation is the existence of concentrated market power in large economic organizations. He argues that, in effect, the existence of this concentrated market power provides the fulcrum upon which the Phillips curve tilts and that the reduction of that concentration would lower the entire Phillips curve of unemployment and inflation. Do you find that argument plausible or persuasive?

Arrow: I think it may have some persuasive value in terms of superficial characteristics. In other words, it may be possible, in any moment of time, to reduce the rate of inflation by some changes in concentration, but I have grave doubts about it as a fundamental explanation for inflation. If by concentration of market power you mean unions, we face the uncomfortable fact that in the United States organized labor consti-

tutes roughly 25 percent of the labor force. It is a little hard to explain why it should have such vast power under those conditions.

Concentration of product control is even more dispersed than that. I don't quite see what the mechanism is. Furthermore, supposing there are monopolies in the economy, one would expect them to make a static gain. The monopolists, whether they be labor monopolists or capitalist monopolists, will achieve more of the total national product than they would otherwise achieve. That's what one means by a monopoly and that's what one would expect to happen. I do not see why a dynamic phenomenon would arise out of a static cause. Once the monopolists have appropriated, why should that give rise to higher and higher prices? The only way this can

be explained is that the monopolies provide a more effective transmission belt for passing on the price increases. In other words, if for some reason wages go up, for example, a monopoly will find it easier to pass through the price of the wage increase than its competitors would. But that is not very clear to me. Competitors should, according to theory, pass through wage increases quite as well as monopolies. All of them will have their costs increased, and the usual force of competition would lead to higher prices. In fact, the only real explanation for it might be that the monopolists slow down the rate of price increases and thereby make what should be a static adjustment into an endless tail-chasing, but you would ordinarily expect this process to damp down as each round should be smaller than the preceding one. I don't find it convincing that concentration of economic power is an explanation of inflation, but since I don't have an alternative theory I don't reject it out of hand.

McClaughry: Argument has long raged about whether capitalism can exist as an equilibrium system without continual growth. Is a no-growth capitalism possible, given a stable population?

Arrow: No, that I do not believe is possible. I think that the desire to make more profits by better ways of doing things is an inherent dynamic of a capitalist system. I find it very hard to believe that an economy in which technological progress is forbidden, for example, could possibly survive as a capitalistic economy. None of the dynamic sources of profits would exist; the motivation of the economy would change. The essence would be repetition and routine, and those are much better done by bureaucratic organizations than by dynamic corporations.

McClaughry: Standing here in 1974, a time when inflation, unemployment, and monetary problems dominate the headlines, and looking twenty or thirty years into the future, what is your feeling about the future state of the American economy?

Arrow: Basically, I have a very optimistic view of the economy, measured in the proper terms. I think that we can expect the rates of technological progress to be quite similar to those in the past. There will be all sorts of things now not available—maybe some not even dreamed of—that will be coming out on the market in the year 2000 to the benefit of the consumer. The pressure for improvement of social conditions—in its environmental aspects, safety aspects, and so forth—will be assuming an ever bigger role in our economic life. I think the steps already taken, if carried out, are enough. That will make quite a change by the year 2000. They are not necessarily measured in the conventional indices of economic performance, but are nevertheless improvements in human well-being. I think that in the foreseeable future we will not see the kind of unemployment that was so disastrous before World War II, nor even possibly the levels that were reached in the late fifties. Inflation, I must say, one has to be a little worried about.

I'm more nervous in many ways about the international picture than I am about the domestic. What has changed everything is the fact that the world can be annihilated by a few people's decisions. I see very little which has reduced the basic instability of the situation. It's remarkable that we have survived so long, but at any moment there's the risk that this very tenuous equilibrium will be disrupted. If we can overcome this danger, I am optimistic about our economy and its potential for increasing human well-being.

C. Markets and Prices

Are High Farm Prices Here To Stay?

The following article was written by Dr. D. Gale Johnson of the University of Chicago. An agricultural economist, Professor Johnson is Chairman of the University's Department of Economics.

A short answer to the question posed by the title of this article is: "Not for very long." This year and next should see the beginning of a significant weakening of some farm prices, though adverse weather in any major grain producing area could postpone the decline for a year or perhaps two years.

Mother Nature has been quite uncooperative in North America so far in 1974. First there was the wet weather during planting time in the Corn Belt and Northern Plains that delayed and decreased planting. Then significant areas of the Corn Belt suffered hot weather and limited rainfall for a month during a critical period of plant growth. From the first of May, when a bumper winter wheat crop and large acreages of feed grains and soybeans were expected, to mid-August the prices of wheat, corn, and soybeans increased by approximately 50%. Thus the prices of wheat and corn approached the peak levels achieved during the last eighteen months.

Even though there are good reasons to believe that prices of grains and most other farm products probably will decline significantly within the next year or two, without question a very precarious situation now exists in agriculture. Of prime importance is the fact that world stocks of grain are very low. At the beginning of the 1974-75 crop year grain stocks in the major exporting countries (the only countries with reliable stock data) were very near the minimal levels required for working stocks. A serious production shortfall in North America in 1974 could result in grain and soybean prices going above their recent peaks and could impose major burdens and hardships upon the peoples of poor countries that find it necessary to import grain.

A more permanent and pervasive problem, in the view of some observers, is a fundamental change that is said to have taken place in the basic demand and supply relationships for food products. It is claimed that a high rate of population growth and rising "real" per capita incomes have resulted in an increased demand for food that has outstripped the capacity to expand production, except at much higher real prices than we have seen in recent decades.

To me, such claims of basic changes in demand-supply relationships are not convincing. I can see no evidence that there has been a significant change in the annual rate of growth of world demand for food. The rate of world popu-

Gale Johnson, "Are High Farm Prices Here to Stay?" *Morgan Guaranty Survey*, August 1974, pp. 9–14. Reprinted with the permission of the author and the publisher.

lation growth during 1962-72 was the same as in 1952-62 and the United Nations medium projection of growth in population from 1970 to 1985 is approximately the same rate as for the past two decades—about 2% annually. Nor does there appear to have been any significant change in the growth rate of per capita income in the 1970s compared with the 1960s.

Why, then, have we seen such substantial increases in farm prices, especially for grains? The reasons are primarily to be found on the supply side, though governmental interventions in major consuming areas that prevented the rationing effects of higher prices were also important.

In the mid-1960s a series of shortfalls in grain production in China, the Soviet Union, and South Asia resulted in a substantial reduction in world grain stocks. Grain prices increased rather substantially. Grain production, especially wheat production, expanded rapidly in the major exporting countries—Australia, Canada, and the United States—from 1967 through 1969. Stocks of grain in the three countries increased rapidly and as a consequence grain prices fell. Farmers and governments reacted as one might expect. In the three countries the land devoted to wheat production declined from 45.1 million hectares in 1968 to 35.7 million hectares in 1969 and to 29.1 million hectares in 1970. The production of wheat in 1970 was 53.7 million metric tons, compared with the high level of 75.4 million metric tons in 1968. The attack of corn blight in the United States in 1970 resulted in a further reduction of grain stocks in the major exporting countries and in the world.

Major shortfalls in grain production were again a problem in South Asia, the Soviet Union, China, and Australia in the 1972-73 period. Grain production in the United States in the 1972-73 crop year was below the previous year, in part in response to low grain prices following the large 1971-72 crop. All told, world grain production in 1972-73 was approximately 5%, or 60 million metric tons, below trend production for that year. This shortfall was nearly as much as the world's grain reserves (excluding the USSR and China) in excess of working stocks. While the 1973-74 world grain crop was a relatively good one, it was not significantly in excess of trend production for that year and world grain stocks were further drawn down. As a consequence, stocks at the beginning of the current crop year (1974-75) were barely above required working stocks.

Effects of governmental policies

Demand considerations did play a role in the upsurge in grain prices in 1972-73. One important change in expected demand was the willingness of the Soviet Union to import enormous quantities of grain in 1972-73 to maintain its livestock herds. In 1963-64, following the poor 1963 crop, the Soviet Union imported enough grain to maintain direct human grain consumption. Rather unexpectedly, in 1972 the decision was made that grain was to be imported in sufficient quantities to prevent a significant drop in meat and milk production. Thus grain imports were at least twice as large as would have been called for by the policies of the 1960s.

Another demand-related factor has stemmed from the efforts in many large industrial countries to prevent the rise in world grain prices from pushing up domestic consumer or producer prices. Owing to the combined effects of the devaluation of the dollar and the variable import levies of the European Economic Community (EEC), the increase in U.S. export prices for wheat—from about $60 per ton in 1971-72 to $130 per ton in early 1973—had no effect on the consumer or producer in EEC. When wheat prices increased even further, EEC imposed export taxes and export licensing to discourage sales of domestic wheat in foreign markets. As a result, grain prices in local currencies increased by no more than 10% between 1971 and early 1974 in the Six, except for Italy. During the same period international prices of grain (in dollars) were doubling and trebling. But within EEC (except for the new members) grain became a bargain during a period of real food stringency in the world. The same nationalistic approach has been followed in Japan and the Soviet Union.

Consequently, virtually all required price adjustments have been imposed on a limited part of the world—the major grain exporters and a number of developing countries which rely heavily on food imports. There is no doubt that if there had been something approximating free trade in grains and other foods over the past few years price increases would have been significantly smaller than they have in fact been.

Except for the effect of the devaluation of the dollar, there seems to be no fundamental reason why the long-term decline in real grain prices should not reassert itself. Reflecting major gains in farm productivity, the real farm price of feed grains and hay in the United States between the years 1910-14 and 1971-72 declined by 40%. Similarly, the real price of food grains fell by 37%. In these calculations, the prices received by farmers have been adjusted to reflect the large direct government payments received in 1971-72. If these payments had not been included the declines in real prices would have been approximately 50% for all grains. The dollar devaluation effect is unlikely to increase the real prices of grains, priced in dollars, by more than 10% or 15%.

And yet, predictions are cropping up on all sides that the real costs of producing grains are likely to rise sharply. Why should that be? The reasons cited appear to be the following: first, there is relatively little uncultivated land remaining and all of the diverted acreage in the United States has been returned to production; second, increasing yields will increase costs in part because of diminishing returns from application of fertilizer; third, the prices of farm inputs—especially those based on petroleum products—will be substantially higher in the future than in the past.

On a worldwide basis, the first two reasons for rising real costs of grain can be said to be either incorrect, irrelevant, or both. There are substantial possibilities for expanding the cultivated land area in Africa, South America, South East Asia, North America, and Australia.* It is true that the potential for expanding cultivated land in parts of Asia is relatively small, but this does not mean that the real costs of producing grains must increase. It is not at all certain that cultivating additional land is generally a significantly lower-cost means of expanding output than increasing yield per acre. The answer for the past several decades in the United States appears to be that it has generally been cheaper to expand output through higher yields than by adding new land; some new land has been brought into cultivation but far more has been retired. It is clearly possible to increase yields in the developing countries, and yields have increased in the developing countries in the past three decades. But yields are still much lower in the developing countries than in the industrial countries.

The fertilizer factor

The second reason cited for higher costs—diminishing returns from fertilizer—is not a valid one. While higher yields may require more fertilizer per unit of output, it does not follow that real costs will increase due to the higher yields because fertilizer is only one of many inputs used in grain production. As yields increase per unit of land, the productivity of other inputs increases and thus contributes to lower costs if the returns to these resources remain constant. In addition, farmers do not continue to operate on a single fertilizer-yield function, but the function changes

---

* "While in some developing countries the practical ceiling on land development may have been reached, in a large part of the developing world there remains land resources which are either unutilized or are utilized in production processes with very low returns. The largest 'land-reserves' in the developing countries are in South America, Africa, and in parts of South East Asia. All of these regions suffer from specific limitations...but modern technology is increasingly able to cope with the problems and one may expect some very major development programmes for cultivated land in these regions." Preparatory Committee of the World Food Conference, *Preliminary Assessment of the World Food Situation: Present and Future*, United Nations, 1974, p. 65.

over time. As farmers use fertilizer for longer periods of time, they learn how to use fertilizer more effectively through a multitude of adjustments such as better adapted seed varieties, greater plant density, timing of application, location of fertilizer in the soil, and more effective types of fertilizer.*

There is a possibility that the prices of farm inputs having a significant energy component will be substantially higher in the future than in the past. The cost of energy is an important element in fertilizer production cost. Estimates of the Tennessee Valley Authority indicate that a five-fold increase in the price of natural gas—from $0.20 per thousand cubic feet to $1.00 per thousand cubic feet—would increase the plant-gate price of a ton of urea by $22 or approximately 24%.** But there are many other factors that affect the cost of nitrogen fertilizer, including technology, size of plants, and percentage of capacity utilized. In fact, with a natural gas price of $1.00 per thousand cubic feet, the cost of producing nitrogen fertilizer with the 1974 technology would be less than the cost with free natural gas and the 1960 technology.†

Another factor affecting the cost of fertilizers in the developing countries is the low ratio of output to capacity. In such countries most of the nitrogen plants operate at 60% to 70% of capacity. If capacity utilization were increased to the level achieved in the industrial countries of approximately 90%, fertilizer costs would decline significantly. Many developing countries protect their fertilizer industries, thus imposing unnecessarily high costs on their farmers. If a durable peace is achieved in the Middle East, enormous quantities of nitrogen fertilizer could be available at costs comparable to those of recent years.

I do not believe that a strong case for significant increases in the real costs of producing grains in the years ahead has been made. It has only been asserted. The improvements in methods of production that we have seen over the past four decades will continue into the future. There is a major potential for relatively low cost increases in output in the developing countries if the appropriate conditions are established and if we consider a dynamic rather than a static framework.

Energy intensiveness—then and now

The agriculture of the industrial countries is often accused of being highly energy intensive and increasingly so over time. In many respects the technology associated with the high yielding varieties in the developing countries has similar characteristics. Yet, surprisingly, it is not obvious that the agricultural technology associated with the major U.S. grains was more energy intensive in 1970 than it was a quarter century before. Pimentel and associates have estimated that the ratio of corn output per unit of energy declined from 3.7 in 1945 to 2.82 in 1970.* But this calculation does not tell us what the ratio of energy output to energy input would have been if 1970 technology had been used to produce the 1945 output level. The 1945 corn output was less than 60% of the 1970 output. Or put another way, the calculation does not indicate what the energy

* In a study of adjustments in the use of nitrogen fertilizer in the Corn Belt, Wallace Huffman found that there was a major change in the fertilizer-corn yield function between 1959 and 1964. The function became much flatter and even though nitrogen use per acre of corn increased 150% between 1959 and 1964 the marginal productivity of nitrogen declined very little. See Wallace Huffman, *The Contribution of Education and Extension to Differential Rates of Change*, unpublished Ph.D. dissertation, University of Chicago, 1972, pp. 27-34.

** Tennessee Valley Authority, "World Fertilizer Market Review and Outlook," in U.S. Senate Committee on Agriculture and Forestry, *U. S. and World Fertilizer Outlook*, 93d Congress, 2d Session, March 21, 1974, p. 106. Natural gas at $0.20/MCF is equivalent to petroleum at $1.54 per barrel; at $1.00/MCF for natural gas the equivalent petroleum price is $6.53 per barrel.

† *Ibid.* For a 200-ton-per-day plant using the older technology the gate price of a ton of urea if natural gas were free would be about $164. With natural gas at $1.00/MCF the gate price would be $116 for a plant producing 1000 tons of ammonia per day.

* David Pimentel, *et al.*, "Food Production and the Energy Crisis," *Science*, Vol. 172, 2 November 1973, p. 445.

output/energy input ratio would have been if the 1945 technology had been used to produce the much larger 1970 output. To have produced the 1970 corn output, with the 1945 energy inputs and methods of production, would have required 140 million acres of corn or 80 million acres more than actually was harvested in 1970.

In effect, a 32% increase in energy requirements per bushel of corn "saved" 80 million acres of cropland. If we assume that land had been available to produce the 1970 corn output with the 1945 yield, and all energy requirements are converted into gallons of gasoline, the use of 1.2 billion gallons of gasoline replaced 80 million acres of cropland. Even at today's high prices, 1.2 billion gallons of gasoline has a value at the refinery of about $325 million. Is such an exchange one that we would want to make, assuming it were possible? I think not.

Food problems in developing countries

I am confident that the world has the capacity to increase food production more rapidly than the growth of population, as it has for the past two decades. This is not solely my own view: it is the view expressed in *Preliminary Assessment of the World Food Situation: Present and Future** which was prepared for the World Food Conference to be held next November and was cited earlier in this discussion. It is also the conclusion of projections that have been made by the Economic Research Service of the U.S. Department of Agriculture.** Both of these projections are consistent with relatively low grain and food prices in international markets by the end of this decade.

But cautious optimism about the re-emergence

* Page 61.

** Economic Research Service, USDA, *World Food Situation —Trends and Prospects*, FDCD Working Paper, 1974, pp. 14-18.

of significantly lower international prices for grains should not be permitted to gloss over a number of important problems that confront the developing countries. Brief note will be made of two of these problems.

While world grain production is capable of expanding somewhat more than world demand over the next decade and at real prices not far above those of the period before the recent high prices, it is probable that grain imports by the developing countries may need to increase significantly unless recent trends are modified. As in the past two decades the growth of demand for food, especially grains, in the developing countries will be twice that of the industrial countries. Based on past trends, grain production is likely to increase at about the same rate in the two groups of countries. The growth of demand in the developing countries must be slowed and special and additional efforts to expand food production must be made. Unless this is done, the dependence on imported foods will increase to very high and perhaps not achievable levels.

For the past two decades the world has depended upon North America to hold its grain reserves. Importing countries, whether high or low income, generally held only working stocks with the expectation that the reserves in North America would be available to meet their needs. These reserves were large enough, until 1973, to provide a remarkable stability of grain prices, around a declining trend. The reserves were not the consequence of deliberate policy decisions by the American and Canadian governments to accumulate reserves but were the results of price and other agricultural policies.

Whereas the reserves accumulated prior to 1972 were inadvertently accumulated, the Agricultural Act of 1973 will require a positive policy decision for the U.S. government to accumulate stocks of grain. The minimum price support levels in the Act are low enough so that the Commodity Credit Corporation would only occasionally accumulate stocks, even if the demand-supply balance for grains eases significantly over the next few years—as it did in the 1967-69 period. And unless the United States holds reserves, Canada will not find it in its interest to do so.

It is now U.S. policy not to have governmentally held stocks of grain, except as a part of an internationally agreed program under which the costs of maintaining reserves would be shared by the importing countries. It is not clear that such an undertaking is possible, but even if it were the size of reserves is likely to be much smaller than that maintained in the past by the major grain exporters.* Consequently the developing countries are likely to be faced by much greater instability of grain prices than in the past. And, if their normal import needs increase substantially, the impact on their economies can be importantly adverse.

The potential for expanding grain and food production in the developing countries is large relative to the expected increase in demand during this century, even if population growth rates do not decline in the near future—as they must in the longer run. But this potential can only be realized if there is a substantial increase in agri-

---

* Research now under way indicates that the need to hold grain reserves in excess of working stocks is almost wholly the result of governmental interferences in grain prices and international trade. If there were free trade in grains throughout the world, there would be very little economic rationale for stockholding much in excess of working stocks.

cultural research, in the supply of modern farm inputs (fertilizer, herbicides, pesticides), and in the harnessing of irrigation water. Above all, the developing countries must provide their farmers with adequate incentives, something that many have not been willing to do.

Summing up

The world has not entered a new agricultural era in the sense that real grain and food prices will be significantly higher in the future than they have been in the past. One depressant on international prices—the overvaluation of the dollar—has been removed and because of this it may not be necessary for the United States to reintroduce subsidy programs such as we have had in the past. But other than this I can see no substantial reason for believing that demand has expanded more rapidly than anticipated or that the basic factors responsible for declining real costs of producing grain have disappeared.

Unless the basic features of the Agricultural Act of 1973 are changed, I do not see the United States once again accumulating large stocks of grain—at least not doing so unilaterally. We may find it in our interest to join with the other exporting countries and the major importers to hold stocks with an equitable sharing of costs in order to achieve a significant degree of trade liberalization. But it is not in the national interest of the United States to once again become, with Canada, the holder of the world's grain reserves.

THE BLUEJEANS EFFECT

by Jeffrey A. Frankel*

This brief note is intended to fill a small niche in consumer utility theory.

In the simplest world, a consumer's demand for a commodity is determined only by his internal utility function — subject to his budget constraint — without regard to the utility of other consumers. However there are three commonly-known "effects" whereby a consumer's utility for a commodity is affected by the demands of his fellow consumers: the "snob" effect, the "Veblen" effect, and the "bandwagon" effect. These three effects cry out for a fourth to complete the symmetry of the theoretical structure; that fourth phenomenon is the "bluejeans" effect.

Under the bluejeans effect, the lower the price of a certain commodity, the greater will be the utility held by some consumers for that commodity, for social or psychological reasons. Thus a low-priced item will face a greater demand, not just because people can afford to buy more of it, but because they receive an extra "negative prestige" from the purchase or ownership of the item. The prototypical example is bluejeans, which college students and others buy partially because of the prestige it affords them.

The four effects are defined as follows.

snob effect: The positive effect on an individual's utility function for a commodity caused by the knowledge that few others in the community consume the same commodity.

Veblen effect: The positive effect on an individual's utility function for a commodity caused by the knowledge that the price of the commodity is high. (This is the famous "conspicuous consumption" principle of Thorstein Veblen. Note that the Veblen effect and the snob effect may coincide, but only to the extent that a high price and limited consumption coincide.)

bandwagon effect: The positive effect on an individual's utility function for a commodity caused by the knowledge that many others in the community consume the same commodity. (The bandwagon effect can be viewed as a negative snob effect.)

bluejeans effect: The positive effect on an individual's utility function for a commodity caused by the knowledge that the price of the commodity is low. (In the same way as the Veblen and snob effects, the bluejeans effect and the bandwagon effect may coincide, but only to the extent that a low price and widespread consumption coincide. Also, just as the bandwagon effect is a negative snob effect, the bluejeans effect can be viewed as a negative Veblen effect.)

The symmetrical relationship among the four phenomena is shown in the table.

		VARIABLE ENTERING THE INDIVIDUAL'S UTILITY FUNCTION:	
		NUMBER OF OTHER PEOPLE CONSUMING	PRICE
SOCIAL SOURCE OF THE EFFECT:	ELITISM	Snob Effect	Veblen Effect
	POPULISM	Bandwagon Effect	Bluejeans Effect

As to the psychological causes for the bluejeans effect which would induce an individual to buy a commodity specifically because its price is low, they range from a housewife's desire to demonstrate her ability to get a good bargain, to a college student's desire to demonstrate solidarity with the working class.

REFERENCES

The best statement of the traditional three effects under which consumer utility is not interpersonally additive is made by Harvey Leibenstein, "Bandwagon, Snob, and Veblen Effects in the Theory of Consumer Demand," *Quarterly Journal of Economics,* May, 1950. His theoretical and graphical analysis can be very easily extended to the case of the bluejeans effect.

*Swarthmore College

Jeffrey A. Frankel, "The Bluejeans Effect." *The American Economist,* Spring 1975, p. 60. Reprinted with permission.

Seasonality of Agricultural Prices

By Blaine W. Bickel

History shows that prices of many agricultural products exhibit definite seasonal patterns which reflect the various marketing practices of farmers as well as the natural biological processes that govern production. For example, the movement of grain to market usually increases rather significantly during the harvest period, pushing prices down. Likewise, the bulk of the beef calf crop is produced in the spring, so that many calves reach market size at about the same time each year. This uneven flow in the supply of most farm commodities, coupled with changes in demand, produce seasonal price movements that should be considered when formulating a market strategy.

Agriculture has been, at least until recent years, an industry bound by tradition. Little effort was devoted to developing a marketing strategy, as many farmers sold their crops right out of the field. A great deal of on-farm storage capacity has been added in recent years, however, as farmers have attempted to increase their returns by waiting for a post-harvest rebound in prices. The success of this delayed-marketing strategy depends on both the magnitude of the price recovery and the degree of confidence that can be placed in the regularity of the seasonal pattern. If a price increase that exceeds storage and other holding costs is highly probable each year, the decision to postpone marketing would obviously be wise. To provide a framework for the decision-making process, the seasonal price patterns of several commodities important to Tenth Federal Reserve District[1] agriculture are examined in this article.

THE ANALYSIS

The changes in any price series over a long period of time can be attributed to secular, cyclical, seasonal, and irregular factors. Secular changes occur gradually over a long period of time. Cyclical fluctuations take place at somewhat shorter intervals and may be associated with alternating periods of expansion and contraction in the industry or with fundamental changes in market demand. Seasonal patterns tend to recur year after year, and are of prime importance to most agricultural producers. Irregular price movements cannot be predicted, and due to their random nature are quite often offset by another random movement within a relatively short period.

To analyze the seasonal pattern in a price series, it is first necessary to eliminate the secular and cyclical movements from the data. This analysis employs a statistical technique known as the ratio-to-moving average method to isolate and measure the seasonal movement.[2] Briefly, the first step is to compute a 12-month moving average from the original data to obtain the cyclical component. The original series is then divided by the 12-month moving average, which removes the long-term in-

---

1/Colorado, Kansas, Nebraska, Wyoming, 43 western Missouri counties, northern New Mexico, and most of Oklahoma.
2/Taro Yamane, *Statistics, An Introductory Analysis* (New York: Harper and Row, 1964), p. 357.

Blaine W. Bickel, "Seasonality of Agricultural Prices." *Monthly Review*, Federal Reserve Bank of Kansas City, June 1975, pp. 10–16. Reprinted with permission.

47

fluences and leaves a series that contains only seasonal and irregular components. This series is further modified by computing a 5-year moving average which minimizes the effects of the irregular factors. The result is an index that provides a quantitative measure of the amount of seasonal price fluctuation that recurs on a regular basis.[3]

Data for the analysis consist of monthly prices received by farmers for selected commodities over the 20-year period, 1955-74. The seasonal patterns of these commodities are depicted in Charts 1-6. In each of the charts, the heavy black line shows the means of the seasonal indexes for each month of the year and represents the typical seasonal price pattern for the commodity being studied. The vertical distance between this line and the index base of 100 represents the percentage that monthly prices typically vary from the average annual price, regardless of the absolute price level. The shaded area on either side of this line includes approximately two-thirds of all the monthly observations, and is referred to as the variability range.[4] When the variability range is narrow, most of the observations lie close to the average, indicating a seasonal pattern that occurs on a regular basis. As the variability range widens, a less regular seasonal pattern is indicated.

These graphic results should not be interpreted too literally. Since 20 years of data have been averaged to produce these results, the chances are relatively minor that any particular year closely follows the observed seasonal pattern. Yet, these seasonal price movements can be used as a general guide in making marketing decisions, thereby improving the chances of realizing better-than-average results over the longer run.

Wheat

Wheat is the most important cash crop in the Tenth District. In recent years, Kansas production has accounted for about half of the District's cash receipts from wheat, while much of the remainder has been contributed by Colorado and Oklahoma. The analysis deals with Kansas wheat prices only, although price patterns in the other states appear to be similar. One minor difference was observed. Because of the earlier harvest, Oklahoma prices typically reached their lowest level in June, as opposed to July in Kansas.

Chart 1 shows that the price of wheat in Kansas generally follows a predictable pattern. From a harvest low in July, prices increase steadily through December, then decline until the next harvest. A grower who sells his wheat in December can expect to receive about 4 per cent more than the annual average price, and about 11 per cent more than the July price. However, December prices exhibit considerable variation, particularly when compared to prices in November. Therefore, even though prices traditionally peak near the end of the year, one could more confidently predict above-average prices for November than for December.

The seasonal movement of Kansas wheat prices is somewhat irregular in July, August, and September as evidenced by the relatively large amount of price variability during this period. This reflects uncertainty about requirements and usage during the marketing year. Wheat is a good livestock feed, so there may be considerable substitution of wheat for corn or grain sorghum prior to the fall harvest of the latter two crops. Any change in expected production of these feed grains would therefore be reflected in wheat prices. In addition, wheat production in other parts of the world directly affects the export situation in this country, which adds to the sensitivity of Kansas wheat prices in the months immediately following harvest.

The variability range begins to narrow in October and continues this trend through November as supply and demand conditions for the marketing year become better defined. In addition, feed grain production is a known quantity by November, and the irregularity of wheat prices reaches its lowest point. As the average price moves to its December high, the variability range widens dramatically, and remains much the same

3/For a detailed description of the steps used in this analysis, see "The X-11 Variant of the Census Method II Seasonal Adjustment Program," U.S. Department of Commerce, Bureau of the Census, Technical Paper, No. 15 (Washington: U.S. Government Printing Office, 1965).
4/The vertical distance on either side of the seasonal index is ± 1 standard deviation from the mean for each month.

SEASONAL PATTERNS OF AGRICULTURAL PRICES

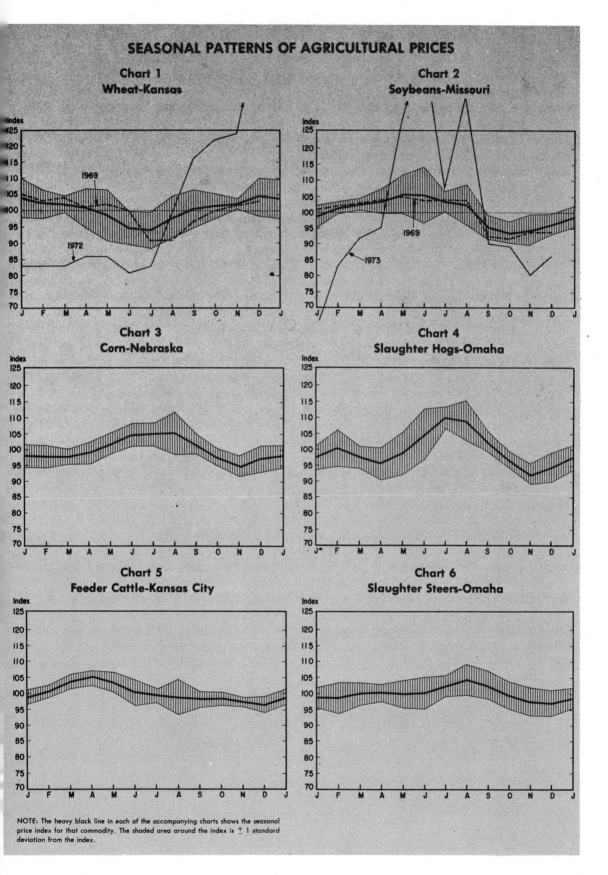

Chart 1
Wheat-Kansas

Chart 2
Soybeans-Missouri

Chart 3
Corn-Nebraska

Chart 4
Slaughter Hogs-Omaha

Chart 5
Feeder Cattle-Kansas City

Chart 6
Slaughter Steers-Omaha

NOTE: The heavy black line in each of the accompanying charts shows the seasonal price index for that commodity. The shaded area around the index is ± 1 standard deviation from the index.

through January. The decision on whether to sell stored wheat in December, or hold it until after the first of the year because of income tax considerations, is probably a major influence on the market during these 2 months. Weather extremes would also contribute to price variability at this time of year. The band continues to narrow through February and March as the relationship between supply and demand becomes well established, and weather is not usually a critical factor. But with the coming of spring, weather is of prime importance. Prices generally overreact as each new production forecast is made—whether good or bad—adding to the variability of wheat prices during this period.

If a producer elects to sell his wheat at some time other than harvest, the analysis shows that it would not normally pay to hold beyond December unless some highly unusual circumstances prevailed. Although wheat prices usually rise after harvest, this increase must be weighed against storage costs. Assuming that storage costs are 1.5 cents per bushel per month, and handling charges are 3 cents per bushel for receiving the grain and 4 cents per bushel for shipping, the breakeven price for holding wheat for the first month of the marketing year is 8.5 cents above the July price. Another 1.5 cents would be added for each additional month the grain is stored. (On-farm storage costs would differ from this example, but some costs would still be encountered.)

For a practical application of this relationship, Chart 1 shows the monthly prices received for wheat by Kansas farmers in 1969 and 1972. To facilitate comparison, these prices have been converted to an index by setting the annual average equal to 100. The year 1969 exhibited a very typical price pattern, yet storage costs would have offset the increase in wheat prices that occurred between harvest and the end of the year. Delayed marketing in 1969 would have resulted in a lower net return than marketing at harvest, for all months except November.

Chart 1 also illustrates the hazard of relying too heavily on averages. Price movements in 1972 were very unorthodox due to the unexpected and unusually large purchase of wheat by Russia. Before the extent of this transaction became known, wheat prices followed a normal seasonal pattern, but the picture changed dramatically during the second half of the year as prices exploded in response to the large export commitment.

Soybeans

Chart 2 shows the seasonal price pattern for soybeans based on Missouri prices. From a harvest low in October, soybean prices typically climb at a fairly steady pace to a May high. The total price increase over this period averages 13 per cent. The seasonal index also shows that prices remain above average through August, then drop sharply toward the October low.

Soybean prices exhibit an unusual amount of variability during the spring and summer months. Speculation about whether the supply will last until the new crop is harvested has frequently produced major price swings during this period. Weather also becomes a major factor in the summer months as changes in production estimates for the new crop can influence price behavior.

The best strategy appears to be to delay soybean marketings for at least 4 months after harvest. From February through May, and again in July, there is a good chance of receiving an above-average price. The chart shows that soybean prices have usually reached their highest level in May and June, but not with any consistency. The extremely wide confidence band shows that prices may also fall below the yearly average in June.

The wide variability of soybean prices is also illustrated in Chart 2 by superimposing two selected years on the seasonal pattern. As with wheat, the monthly prices are expressed as a percentage of the annual average. Very little deviation from the typical seasonal pattern occurred in 1969. Applying the same storage and handling costs used in the wheat example to 1969 soybean prices (October 1968 crop), the optimum selling month was May. Net returns in May were 9.5 cents per bushel more than would have been realized by selling in October.

In 1973, however, month-to-month price changes ranged from a 35 per cent increase to a 30 per cent decline in reaction to a variety of stimuli. A shortfall in Peruvian fish meal production, strong worldwide demand for high-protein feeds, and the emergence of the Soviet Union as a major soybean buyer sent prices skyrocketing early in the year. Then farmers planted the largest acreage on record and prices fell sharply in July, staged a short-lived rally, then fell again as it became apparent that supplies would exceed usage through the approaching market year. Because of this unusual price behavior, any soybean producer who held his crop beyond harvest enjoyed a tremendous increase in net returns. From an average price of $3.15 per bushel in October 1972, soybean prices peaked at $9.80 per bushel in June 1973, producing a potential net gain of $6.46 per bushel for the 8 months storage.

The evidence suggests that net returns from soybeans can usually be increased by delaying marketings for at least 4 months, but the exact timing is quite dependent on current conditions.

Corn

The seasonal pattern of Nebraska corn prices is illustrated in Chart 3. Compared with wheat and soybeans, corn prices generally display a more regular seasonal pattern as evidenced by the narrower range or variability. However, there is a longer time lag between the harvest low and the point at which corn prices move above the annual average. The lag is 6 months for corn, compared with 4 months for soybeans and only 2 months for wheat. Therefore, corn prices normally exceed the annual average only 5 months of the year, from May through September.

Nebraska corn prices usually reach their low in November and exhibit a rather quick recovery in December. Prices are very stable from January through March, then an upward movement carries corn prices to an August level that is slightly more than 5 per cent above the annual average and almost 11 per cent above the November low. Except for a bulge in August, the variability range maintains a relatively stable width. August is a critical month in the development of corn. Extremely hot or dry weather in late July or August, as in 1974, can have a devastating effect on corn production. If silk development is retarded, pollination will be hindered, and the ear will not fill properly.

In general, it appears that returns could be maximized over time by holding corn until June, July, or possibly August. Again, however, the potential increase in price must be weighed against storage costs.

Hogs

Chart 4 shows the seasonal price pattern for slaughter hogs at Omaha. The average price for all barrows and gilts sold for slaughter was used for this analysis, which undoubtedly resulted in a smoothing of the month-to-month price changes. Yet, compared with the crop prices examined, Chart 4 shows a much greater price range between the summer high and winter low.

Most hog producers strive for two pig crops each year. Hog prices are therefore unique in that they move through two corresponding up-and-down cycles each year. A major upward price movement reaches its peak in the late summer, while a secondary movement peaks in late winter. The fall pig crop is the smaller of the two, and when these pigs are marketed 6 months later, the price depressing effect is not as great as when the larger spring pig crop is marketed in the fall.

The seasonal price line reaches lows that are 4 per cent and 8 per cent below the annual average in April and November, respectively. The February peak is only slightly above the annual average, while July prices can be expected to top the yearly average by 10 per cent. The summer prices would probably be even higher except for the substantial number of sows sold for slaughter at that time of year.

If hog producers aim for July or August sales and avoid the month of November, they could expect above-average returns in most years. However, this would require shifting farrowings to January and July, when weather extremes become a critical factor unless the hog producer is equipped to furnish adequate shelter.

Feeder Cattle

The analysis of feeder cattle prices at Kansas City is depicted in Chart 5. The range through which feeder cattle prices fluctuate each year is rather limited relative to the price movements for commodities previously discussed. From the December low to the April high, the usual price increase is only 9 per cent. Considering the natural pattern of birth in the spring and marketing in the fall, it is somewhat surprising that prices vary so little. A radical departure from the usual pattern occurred in 1974, when a year-long price decline left December feeder cattle prices at approximately one-half the January level.

The apparent discrepancy in variation between prices and marketings of feeder cattle can be at least partly explained by the change in demand during the course of the year. The demand for feeder cattle to be placed in feedlots is very high in the fall of the year, so prices are only slightly below the annual average in spite of the large number of animals placed on the market at that time. Conversely, when the supply of feeder cattle falls off in the spring, prices move only 5 per cent above the annual average because a fairly sharp decline in demand also occurs at that time of year.

There is probably little the average rancher can do to alter the marketing schedule of feeder cattle. Spring calving is not a chance occurrence. It is planned to avoid weather extremes—particularly cold—which would cause undue stress on, or even loss of, new-born calves. In addition, the annual production cycle is closely associated with the grazing season. Hence, feeder cattle prices are related to the grazing season. Prices are high in the spring when cattle are needed to utilize the abundant supply of grass. As fall approaches and herds must be removed from the range as the grazing season ends, prices tend to slump below the yearly average.

The relatively narrow band around the seasonal index indicates that the price pattern is a regular one, having a high probability of recurring each year. The only exception seems to be the month of August, generally the hottest and often the driest

month. The effect of weather on range conditions, and ranchers' responses to these conditions, probably explain most of the increased price variability in August.

Slaughter Steers

The average monthly prices of all grades of steers sold for slaughter in Omaha was also analyzed. As shown in Chart 6, slaughter steer prices—like those for feeder cattle—tend to move through a rather narrow range in most years, although 1974 was an exception. Average prices change less than 8 per cent from the August high to the December low. Furthermore, the seasonal pattern is not very regular as judged by the width of the variability range.

The growth of the cattle feeding industry has undoubtedly played a major role in smoothing the line representing the seasonal index in Chart 6. Feedlots generally strive for consistency—not only in the quality of the product but also in the quantity. Some delay in marketing can occur, but once an animal reaches a certain stage of "finish," additional feeding becomes progressively more expensive and wasteful. Anything more than short-term changes in normal marketing patterns are therefore effectively eliminated.

The seasonal pattern of slaughter steer prices is especially important to the producer who markets on an irregular basis or only a few times each year. In most years, this individual should attempt to concentrate marketings in late summer and avoid the winter months when prices are usually at their low point. But this schedule may present a conflict for the feeder who purchases animals to place on feed. Assuming the typical feeding period is 140 days to 150 days, slaughter cattle that would be ready for market in late summer must be placed in the feedlot in the spring. Unfortunately, this is when feeder cattle prices are at their highest.

STATISTICAL SUMMARY

With any analysis of historical data, there is no guarantee that the observed relationships and patterns of the past will remain valid in future years.

Seasonal highs and lows may shift over time as a result of the development of new crop varieties that mature at different times of the year or as a result of new marketing practices. Although the evidence is still inconclusive, the data suggest that the low point for both wheat and soybean prices may now be occurring slightly earlier than at the beginning of the period included in the study. Earlier maturing varieties may be partly responsible for such a shift, and other technological improvements have probably contributed to this development as well. The ability to harvest and transport the crop more rapidly could result in an earlier and more concentrated marketing of the commodity.

The very fact that producers are becoming more sophisticated and market oriented in their planning can also produce changes in seasonal price patterns. If production cycles are altered to take advantage of seasonal price movements, the highs and lows may be shifted to different months. Furthermore, if marketing programs are also changed, marketings may be less concentrated and the seasonal price pattern would be smoothed as a result.

While some shifting and smoothing can be expected over a long period of time, the seasonal indexes presented in this study were found to be statistically valid. It was determined that the means of the seasonal indexes for individual months were significantly different from each other, indicating that the observed month-to-month changes were not just random movements.

As previously mentioned, price changes over time can be classified as secular, cyclical, seasonal, and irregular. The amount of price variation attributable to the seasonal component for each of the six commodities analyzed in this study is shown in Table 1. Using wheat as an example, slightly more than one-fourth of the variation from one month to the next was due to the seasonal influence. (The remainder was distributed between cyclical and irregular influences.) Expanding the

Table 1
AMOUNT OF VARIATION EXPLAINED BY SEASONAL COMPONENT

Commodity	Time Span in Months					
	1	2	3	4	5	6
	Per Cent					
Wheat	26.1	30.8	34.5	33.4	30.5	25.8
Corn	42.0	50.3	52.0	49.8	45.6	40.8
Soybeans	28.5	36.7	37.6	37.2	35.6	32.4
Slaughter Hogs	53.2	54.3	50.9	41.6	32.9	28.6
Feeder Cattle	27.6	34.9	36.1	33.1	28.9	24.5
Slaughter Cattle	34.3	36.8	37.5	34.9	32.0	29.4

time span to 3 months, more than one-third of the variation in wheat prices was due to seasonal factors. In fact, the seasonal component achieves its greatest importance during the 3-month time span in all cases except hogs. Since hog prices move through two cycles each year, it is not surprising to find the seasonal influence dominating the 1- and 2-month periods.

Beyond the sixth month, the seasonal influence declines rapidly for most commodities as the cyclical component begins to dominate the series.

CONCLUDING COMMENT

Seasonal indexes can be useful management tools for anticipating the short-run movement of commodity prices. But the average will seldom be followed exactly in any given year, so the producer needs to add his own judgment to the current situation and outlook. An understanding of seasonal price patterns can sometimes be used to schedule production to avoid low price months or to concentrate marketings in the period that offers above-average prices. This may not be the best strategy in any given year, but over time the producer should enjoy above-average results. In an industry that is frequently confronted with narrow, if not negative, profit margins, good marketing strategies are essential for the long-run survival of the firm.

The Changing American Consumer

CONSUMERS have been battered in the past year or two as seldom before—by double-digit inflation, by the worst business slump and unemployment in a generation, and by shortages (beef, sugar, gasoline).

Not surprisingly, the combination has severely bruised consumer confidence. By the first quarter of this year, the University of Michigan's index of consumer confidence had plunged to a postwar low (accompanying chart). A major consequence, meanwhile, has been a significant change in the way consumers spend their money.

Some of the shifts in buying habits probably are transitory and will fade as inflation slows, the recovery gains momentum, and incomes and employment are enlarged. But other shifts in buying patterns seem likely to prove more lasting in response to recent trends (e.g., an end to cheap energy, concern over the environment, worldwide scarcity of raw materials). Indeed, some analysts believe that the attitudes of today's consumer have changed so much compared with attitudes as recently as a few years ago that consumer markets have taken on a new shape and outlook. If such analysts are correct, implications for businessmen and investors obviously are quite far-reaching.

For many months, identification of today's new consumer has been occupying the attention of analysts in a range of industries—from chain store giants and advertising agencies to brokerage houses and research organizations. Their findings, now beginning to emerge publicly, in many cases are just what might be expected. And yet, some of the changed attitudes of consumers that have been revealed are surprising and even a bit strange.

Sorting out the causes of consumer behavior is no simple matter. Many things—economics, emotions, a combination of the two—can influence spending decisions. One determinant that looms very large, obviously, is purchasing power. As every consumer knows, rapid inflation has dealt a heavy blow to the family pocketbook. Family income in the U.S., although up 7% in 1974 to a median of $12,840, actually showed a decline of about 4% in terms of purchasing power.

Responding to "hard times"

With reduced "real" income, consumers quite understandably retrenched. Detroit felt it the hardest as auto sales plummeted. The high—and rising—price of gasoline made small foreign cars more attractive. In the buying

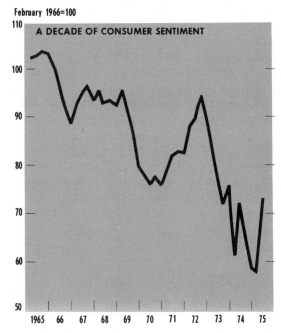

February 1966=100

A DECADE OF CONSUMER SENTIMENT

Source: Survey Research Center, University of Michigan.

"The Changing American Consumer." *Morgan Guaranty Survey,* August 1975, pp. 9–11. Reprinted with permission.

Tighter purse strings: what one survey showed

Reported activity	Percent increase in sample surveyed in 1974 over 1973:
Making fewer impulse purchases	5
Economizing on food purchases	13
Fewer expensive desserts	34
Fewer snack foods	27
Fewer prepared convenience foods	21
Economizing on services	23
Buying less new clothing	21
Postponing new car purchase	34
Postponing major appliance purchase	18
Staying at home more	13
Dining out less often	12
Planning shorter/more modest vacations	35
Planning to spend vacation at home	25
Patronizing more informal family-type eating places	71

Source: J. Walter Thompson Company, based on a sample of 2,500 consumers in autumn of last year.

equation, too, was the growing feeling among many Americans that the automobile was, after all, merely a "piece of transportation" and the simpler and more economical the better. This attitude is quite different from that of the 1950s and early 1960s, the era of tail-fin-and-chrome status seeking.

Along with reduced buying of "big ticket" items, economic uncertainty of the recent past has exerted a pervasive influence on every-day purchases. This is revealed in a study released in June by J. Walter Thompson Company.* A survey of 2,500 consumers (see table above) revealed numerous instances of "painless economies." Some examples: substituting lower-priced for higher-priced items (such as soft drink mixes rather than bottled drinks); switching to private brands rather than nationally advertised brands; buying meat substitutes (such as beans, pasta); avoiding the purchase of discretionary products (such as paper towels);

*Change in the Market Place by Joel Baumwoll, senior vice president in charge of research and planning.

and staying away from stores (to avoid impulse buying).

Significantly, JWT researchers also found an increased consumer realization that long-term future shortages are not so remote a possibility as they were once thought to be. An awareness that abundance is not boundless—something new for many Americans—has resulted in a desire to avoid waste (e.g., patching clothing, repairing rather than replacing furniture, and re-using aluminum foil).

Paradoxically, consumers also were found to be showing new interest in "top of the line" products, apparently in a search for true long-term value (especially in categories where the price differential between top and mid-line products has been decreasing). And in the auto market, cars that combine luxury equipment with economy features have proved popular with consumers. What's more, JWT researchers found a counteraction by some consumers to the need to economize—i.e., an indulgence in luxury products, perhaps to lift the gloom that had enveloped consumers. As one respondent put it: "I don't want to live my life like a corpse."

A finding that pursuit of the "good life" dies hard among consumers is not surprising. What's interesting, though, is the way consumers now are going about modifying the good life. Thus, typically, vacations are not eliminated; they are made more modest. Pleasure trips are taken closer to home. The travel industry, as a consequence, is feeling the effects, with overseas travel off and even domestic airline travel (and hotel occupancy) affected in many areas. Consumers, meanwhile, are doing more at-home entertaining. One indicator: sales of salted nuts and popcorn are way up.

Against that background of changed buying behavior, what can be expected in the years ahead from the individual consumer? The National Planning Association, also in a report released in June, ventures some forecasts on the broad pattern of consumer outlays*:

*Clambering into the Eighties, Volume Two by R. Dennis, M. Higashiyama, and T. Sivia.

• What consumers spend their money on during the next decade will depend on adjustments to energy prices and changes in demographic trends rather than on the generally increasing affluence which dominated the 1960s.

• The infant and "youth market" will begin to diminish in importance, with the number of people in the under-16 age group falling noticeably between now and 1980. This will affect purchases of scores of products from baby clothes to sports equipment.

• Transportation will replace housing in the years ahead as the No. 2 expenditure item—mostly attributable to growing outlays for gasoline and oil.

• Housing's reduced share of total consumer spending reflects, in part, an expectation by NPA analysts of somewhat less inflation in rents than in other prices over the next decade.

• Clothing purchases will account for an almost constant proportion of the consumer budget in the next ten years. On the other hand, spending on services—ranging from electric power and auto insurance to financial services—will expand significantly (see table above).

Analysts recognize, of course, that it is risky to predict consumer behavior. There is no sure-fire way to forecast what the consumer will do simply by charting how the consumer has acted in the past. New conditions could bring new responses.

Few would dispute, however, that, for consumers, times have changed. Analysis of recent behavior gives some clues at least to the motivations of consumers in today's world. And the

The shifting pattern of consumer spending

(current dollars, percent distribution)

Product group	1960	1970	1973	1979	1984
Food and tobacco	26.9	22.9	22.2	21.7	20.6
Clothing and accessories	10.2	10.2	10.1	10.0	10.2
Personal care	1.6	1.7	1.5	1.4	1.3
Housing	14.2	14.7	14.5	14.1	13.9
Household operation	14.4	14.1	14.6	13.9	13.8
Medical care expenses	5.9	7.7	7.8	8.1	8.2
Personal business	4.6	5.7	5.6	6.6	7.6
Transportation	13.3	12.6	13.6	14.3	14.6
Private education and research	1.1	1.7	1.6	2.0	2.2
Recreation	5.6	6.6	6.5	5.7	5.4
Religious and welfare activities	1.5	1.4	1.3	1.3	1.3
Foreign travel and other, net	0.7	0.8	0.7	0.8	1.0
Durable	13.9	14.8	16.2	14.0	13.6
Nondurable	46.5	42.7	42.0	41.6	39.9
Services	39.6	42.5	41.8	44.4	46.5
Total	100.0	100.0	100.0	100.0	100.0

Source: National Planning Association

sales stakes for the supermarket, the auto showroom, the appliance store, and myriad service industries are high: personal consumption expenditures now reach close to a trillion dollars a year.

Criminal Behavior And the Control Of Crime: An Economic Perspective

By Timothy H. Hannan

Crime is rational! People who engage in crimes such as burglary and robbery do so because they are the best "occupations" available to them. Sound strange? This is the view of a small but growing number of economists who have recently invaded the traditional turf of sociology and criminology to apply economic principles to the analysis of criminal behavior.

To refer to crime as rational is not to excuse those who engage in it. Crime, however, is an unfortunate fact of life, and if there is an element of rational choice involved in the decision to engage in criminal activity, then such information can prove valuable in determining which policies are likely to be effective in the control of crime.

CRIME AS A CHOICE

Economists have long viewed people as making, in their own estimations, the best choices among available alternatives. A consumer who chooses margarine over butter does so either because to him it tastes better, its price is lower, or both. Given a choice between bricklaying and farming, a worker chooses bricklaying either because he would rather lay bricks than plant corn, because bricklaying pays better, or both. People try to choose the best options available to them, and decisions to engage in many different types of criminal activity may simply be another example of this type of behavior. Crime, whether it is motivated by the desire for income or some nonmonetary gain, can be thought of as a choice, and as economists would have it, that choice in many cases may be no less rational than the everyday choices people make in determining what products to buy or what occupations to pursue.

The fact that crime is illegal and carries the

Timothy H. Hannan, "Criminal Behavior and the Control of Crime: An Economic Perspective." *Business Review,* Federal Reserve Bank of Philadelphia, November 1974, pp. 3–9.'

possibility of a fine or prison sentence need not imply that the decision to engage in it is irrational. After all, the world is filled with people who have voluntarily chosen "risky" occupations over relatively safe ones. Jet pilots, steeplejacks, and matadors all face the possibility of disaster in their chosen occupations. Yet, to conclude that their choice is irrational is to disregard the relative gains and costs that they derive from their chosen occupations. All things considered, a "dangerous" occupation may be the best available alternative, and the decision to engage in crime need not be an exception.

It is true, of course, that people are often not certain of the consequences of their behavior and may make choices which later prove to be mistakes. Because they choose a course of action without full information, some criminals may incorrectly weigh the advantages and disadvantages of engaging in crime, as opposed to pursuing the "straight and narrow." A mugger or burglar on his first job can be "collared" and sentenced to many years in prison. But such an occurrence may simply be the result of an incorrect but rational decision made on the basis of incomplete information. Like the test pilot who crashes or the businessman who goes bankrupt, the criminal can make rational choices that later prove to be mistakes.

None of this denies that some people are more emotional than others or that rational choice plays less of a role in some types of crime than it does in others. Many who engage in the so-called crimes of passion, for example, may be devoid of all reason and rationality, but it is by no means obvious that *all* such offenders act with complete disregard for the consequences of their behavior. If this is true, then viewing the criminal as rational can have at least limited applicability even to the most violent or impulsive of crimes.

CRIME: THE GAINS AND THE COSTS

If this approach has merit, what are the gains and costs associated with crime that are likely to influence the individual's decision to engage in criminal activity? Consider first the gains of crime. Criminal gains can be thought of as both monetary and nonmonetary in nature. In crimes such as burglary and robbery, monetary rewards clearly play a dominant role in determining the attractiveness of crime relative to other pursuits. All other things equal, a million-dollar "take" is better than a hundred-dollar one, just as a higher-paying occupation is more attractive than a lower-paying one if everything else about the two jobs is the same. But nonmonetary gains of crime can also be important, particularly in the case of crimes not motivated by the desire for property or income. Just as people differ in the degree of satisfaction they derived from bricklaying or farming, so too do they differ in their tastes and attitudes toward criminal activity. Some people may actually enjoy the thrill of the chase or impressing friends with the number of cars they steal or the number of purses they snatch. Others obviously do not.

There are also significant costs of crime which may weigh heavily in the decision to engage in it. One relevant cost, particularly in the case of property crimes, is the "wage rate" or monetary gain that individuals can earn in legal employment compared with the amount they can "earn" in illegal activity. If people choose to support themselves by criminal activity, they are forfeiting the wages they could have earned working on construction sites or waiting on tables. In other words, one of the costs of crime is the "opportunity cost" of foregone legal earnings. Since some people can earn very little in legal employment, criminal activity is in a very real sense "cheaper" for them than it is for those whose legal options are more rewarding, and involvement in certain types of criminal activity may vary accordingly.

Other costs may also be incurred in criminal activity. Both the probability of being arrested and convicted and the length of jail sentences meted out to convicted offenders are costs that directly influence the attractiveness of crime, and these costs too may vary significantly among individuals. The probability of an individual being convicted for an offense will clearly depend upon his skill in avoiding arrest or his ability to "beat the rap" once arrested. The cost of a prison sentence may also be greater for some people than for others. Some people may consider imprisonment and the social stigma associated with it a heavy burden, while others find it more bearable. Perhaps more important, the enforced unemployment involved in a prison sentence will result in a greater loss in income for some people than for others. Highly educated people, for whom high-paying jobs are available, will find a prison sentence much more costly than it is for low-income people, and the decision to engage in crime may reflect such influences.[1]

Thus, the decision to engage in crime can be viewed as a subjective weighing of gains and costs, like may other decisions encountered in daily life. Since the gains and costs associated with crime vary with a person's attitudes and the legal and illegal options available to him, different levels of criminal participation are to be expected for different types of people. While crime is clearly unattractive to most members of society, many categories of crime may be, to put it bluntly, the best available alternative as perceived by some individuals (see Box).

THE ECONOMIC APPROACH: WHAT DOES IT EXPLAIN?

Theories are all well and good, but is the economic approach to criminal behavior supported by any evidence from the real world? What, if anything, can it explain or predict? Although theories can never be totally proved by observing what goes on in real life, the economist's view of criminal behavior does seem to jibe well with a number of observable facts.

The Role of Legal Opportunities. Consider first the role of legal opportunities in the decision to engage in criminal activity. Crime can be thought of as "cheaper" for the low-skilled and the underemployed than it is for the more affluent members of society. Therefore, faced

with a decision to engage in a crime of a given "payoff," individuals who can earn high incomes legally should be less likely to succumb to temptation than those for whom legal opportunities are less rewarding. Put simply, they have more to lose. This prediction does seem to be borne out for many types of crimes. Presumably, bank presidents can rob liquor stores just as well as can impoverished residents of big-city ghettos. Yet, the fact that bank presidents generally refrain from such activity, while ghetto residents often do not, is at least consistent with economic prediction.[2] Other explanations are clearly possible and cannot be discounted. Yet, the widely observed fact that low-income people engage in crimes such as burglary and robbery in higher proportions than high-income people is consonant with the economic view of criminal behavior.

The Role of Punishment: Does It Deter? More support is available in reference to the deterrence effect of punishment. The role of punishment in deterring criminal behavior is an area in which economists and sociologists have often parted company. Many sociologists and criminologists have tended to view the criminal as "sick" or "abnormal" and therefore relatively unresponsive to costs. According to one advocate of this position:

> Certainty of punishment and detection may deter the normal person who thinks about his actions and the consequences, but the criminal mind does not operate like a normal mind. The criminal often acts irrespective of the consequences, learning little from experience and living for the present.[3]

Economists, of course, lean toward the opposite view, predicting that the prospect of punish-

---

[1]There are, however, some positive aspects of imprisonment. Incarceration means free room and board for those confined, and this feature of imprisonment sometimes seems to outweigh the costs when, for example, drunks prefer jail to pounding the pavements on skid row.

[2]Certainly people capable of earning high legal incomes can and do engage in embezzlement and other white-collar crimes, but this is presumably because the "payoffs" to such crimes are often very high and the probabilities of being caught are often quite low.

[3]Joel Meyer, "Reflections on Some Theories of Punishments," *Journal of Criminal Law, Criminology and Police Science* 59 (1968): 597.

DOES CRIME PAY?

The age-old question of whether crime pays has been asked anew by economists and has, in fact, stimulated a number of recent economic studies. The primary problem with a number of studies which have attempted to answer this question is that not all of the gains and costs of crime can be measured. It is not possible, for example, to measure directly the nonmonetary gains to the criminal of illegal activity or such nonmonetary costs as the loss in freedom associated with a prison sentence or the stigma suffered by criminals as a result of social disapproval. Nevertheless, a number of economists have tried to quantify the monetary gains and costs for a number of crimes and have found that, at least in strict monetary terms, criminal activity may well represent the best available alternatives for some people.

Such studies are generally limited to calculating the average net income obtained from certain economically motivated crimes and comparing the results with an estimate of the monetary loss typically suffered from punishment over time. Monetary losses from punishment are in the form of fines and foregone legal earnings resulting from a prison sentence. The table below presents one estimate of the monetary gains and costs calculated by economist William E. Cobb for those people who participated in the crimes of burglary and robbery in Norfolk, Viginia during the years 1964 and 1966.

Year	Monetary Costs of Punishment (Fines, plus Income Lost As a Result of Incarceration)	Monetary Gains From Theft
1964	$153,813	$290,339
1966	128,072	460,121

These estimates of the monetary costs of punishment are quite low because the typical thief was expected to command only a low wage in legal employment and suffer from high rates of unemployment.* Although not all of the gains and costs of crime can be measured, results such as these lend some support to the view that for some people—particularly those with few marketable skills—certain types of crime may indeed pay.

---

*See William E. Cobb, "Theft and the Two Hypotheses," Simon Rottenberg, ed., *The Economics of Crime and Punishment* (Washington: American Enterprise Institute for Public Policy Research, 1973), pp. 19–30.

ment, by raising the cost of crime, will cause fewer crimes to be committed.

In the end, this issue can be resolved only by looking at the evidence, and what evidence is available seems to substantiate the view that criminals, like other people, respond to the costs of their activities. A number of statistical investigations of the question have appeared in recent years, and nearly all have shown a strong deterrent effect of punishment, not only for property crimes, but when investigated for personal crimes as well.[4] In general, crime rates appear to be more sensitive to the probability of conviction than to the length of prison sentences, but even the length of a prison sentence is generally found to deter crime.

Such findings should hardly be surprising if one reflects on what usually occurs in the wake of a natural disaster such as a flood or hurricane. In such situations, property owners and enforcement authorities are often not around to protect property against those who would steal and loot. The probability of being caught for an offense declines dramatically. Consequently, stealing and looting often rise sharply, with even normally law-abiding citizens getting into the act. Such a response to the dramatic reduction in the cost of crime is very much in line with the economist's view of criminal behavior. In such situations people do not suddenly become "sick" or "abnormal"; they are simply making different decisions in response to a rather dramatic change in "prices."

The Problem of Repeaters. As a final example of something which may be fruitfully explained

[4]Indeed, a study by Isaac Ehrlich has found that personal crimes such as rape and murder were deterred by punishment just as effectively (or perhaps even more so) than were a number of property crimes. Many may find it hard to accept that punishment can actually deter the so-called crimes of passion, and more research using better data is clearly needed to settle the issue. For examples of studies which have attempted to measure the deterrent effect of punishment, see Isaac Ehrlich, "Participation in Illegitimate Activities: A Theoretical and Empirical Investigation," *Journal of Political Economy* 81 (1973): 521–65; Morgan O. Reynolds, "Crime for Profit: The Economics of Theft," unpublished Ph. D. thesis, University of Wisconsin (1971); and David L. Sjoquist, "Property Crime and Economic Behavior: Some Empirical Results," *American Economic Review* 63 (1973): 439–46.

by viewing the criminal as a rational decision-maker, consider the age-old problem of recidivism—the repeated relapse into criminal activity. As is well known, many people convicted and imprisoned for criminal offenses return to the life of crime almost immediately upon release from confinement. To such people, the prison gate is a "revolving door" through which they will predictably return time and time again. Many cite such records of repeated convictions as evidence that criminal behavior is irrational. Why shouldn't such people recognize the errors of their ways and realize that crime doesn't pay?

The answer to this question from an economic viewpoint is that when expected gains and expected costs are taken into account, crime may very well pay even for the person who has served several prison sentences. Suppose that prior to his first conviction, a potential offender subjectively weighs the expected gains and costs of criminal activity and rationally concludes that it is worthwhile for him to engage in an illegal act. If after conviction and imprisonment nothing has happened to reduce those expected gains or increase those expected costs, it should not be surprising to see him return to a life of crime after release from confinement. Of course, the expected gains and costs of an additional offense can change as a result of a prison sentence. On the one hand, the cost of an additional offense may increase if longer prison sentences are given to those convicted for a second time. On the other hand, if the repeat offender obtains criminal skills in prison that reduce the probability of his being arrested for a criminal act, or if his opportunities in legal employment are reduced because of the stigma of being an "ex-con," then the costs of engaging in illegal acts may actually decline as a result of a prison term. Thus, the rather high rates of recidivism in the United States may also be explainable by viewing as rational the decision to engage in crime.

THE ECONOMIC APPROACH: THE WHOLE STORY?

Although the economist's conception of crime seems to explain a good deal, clearly it cannot explain everything. For example, why do some individuals choose the life of crime, while others, faced with the same legal and illegal opportunities, refuse to engage in any illegal acts? Economists can no more answer this question than determine why some people, faced with the same set of prices and income, choose margarine instead of butter while others do not; or why, faced with the same wages, some people choose bricklaying over farming while others make the opposite choice. "There's no accounting for tastes." In the economics of crime, as in many other areas of economics, economists must accept tastes as given.

Differing tastes for criminal activity do not negate the usefulness of this approach, any more than do the differing tastes for margarine refute the economist's prediction that with a rise in its price, less of it will be purchased. It does, however, leave many tough questions for others to answer—questions that would seem to be of particular importance in fully explaining the more violent types of crimes. Why do the nonmonetary gains of some crimes differ so sharply from person to person? Why are the nonmonetary "costs" associated with the loss of freedom or social disapproval higher for some than for others? Questions such as these are important, but best left for sociologists or criminologists to ponder.

THE QUESTION OF POLICY

From the "hardliners" to those who advocate abolishing prisons, there seems to be a great diversity of opinion concerning what to do about the soaring crime rate and those who are responsible for it. Although the economist's conception of criminal behavior has its limitations, it can make policy decisions about crime a little easier by laying out alternatives a little more clearly.

What Can Be Done to Control Crime? If the criminal is not totally irrational or "sick," then illegal acts can be deterred either by decreasing the gains to such activity or increasing the costs. Efforts to reduce the gain to crime are well known in the private sector: people avoid "bad" neighborhoods at night, some take taxis instead

of subways or buses, and many carry only small amounts of cash. But reducing crime by raising costs of criminal activity is usually more relevant for governmental action, and in this area economics has something to offer both to the "get-tough hardliners" and to those who, for humanitarian reasons, wish to improve the lot of the criminal offender.

Consider the ways in which criminal activity can be made more costly to the potential offender. The first and perhaps most obvious method is simply to raise the direct costs of criminal activity—the probability of arrest and conviction and the severity of punishment. In other words, crime can be reduced by devoting more resources to police departments and by handing out stiffer sentences to individuals arrested and convicted.[5] But another means of raising the costs of crime is also available. Since one of the costs of participating in criminal acts, particularly those motivated by the desire for income, is the foregone earnings obtainable in legal pursuits, costs can also be increased by making legal activity more attractive. This implies that crime can be reduced by devoting resources to education and training or by increasing job opportunities in high-crime areas.

Thus, what may appear to be two widely differing approaches to crime control can be thought of as simply two alternate methods of raising the costs of crime, and the two approaches need not be mutually exclusive. Both sets of policies can be pursued simultaneously to reduce the number of criminal offenses.

How Much Crime Control? Closely related to the question of *what* to do to control crime is the question of *how much* should be done to control it. Certainly if enough of the economy's scarce resources were used to expand police, court, and correctional activity, or to improve the legal opportunities of criminal offenders, crime could be drastically reduced or perhaps totally eliminated. Does this mean then that governments should hire a hundred policemen for every criminal offense, impose extremely long sentences for all crimes, or spend billions to make legal pursuits more attractive to criminal offenders? The answer is clearly "no." The gain from implementing crime-control measures is the "damage" from crime that can be prevented, and if it could be prevented without cost, then wiping out all crime would pay.

But crime prevention, like so many other desirable things in life, has its price tag. To obtain less crime, resources must be shifted from other desirable uses. In addition, punishments may have to be imposed that are distasteful from a humanitarian standpoint. Hence, expanding the various areas of law enforcement or improving the legal opportunities of offenders can only be justified up to a point. As a general rule, it will pay to expand each measure designed to reduce crime only up to the point where the value of the additional crimes prevented just equals the increased cost or sacrifice associated with doing it. Beyond this point, reducing crime will simply not be worth the effort.

---

[5]Great care must be taken, however, in determining the relative punishments handed out for various types of crimes. If, for example, kidnappers are given the death penalty, then there is no increased punishment for kidnappers who also kill their victims. Clearly, the penalty structure is a very delicate creature.

CONCLUSION

The decision to engage in criminal activity may indeed be rational for many different types of crimes. If this is true, as many economists believe, then determining what policies to pursue in the fight against crime can be made a little easier. Policies that either reduce the gain or increase the costs of criminal activity can be expected to reduce the number of illegal acts committed. This means that punishment, contrary to what many may believe, is justified up to a point. So, too, are police actions designed to increase the probability of being punished for a criminal act and perhaps also policies aimed at improving the legal opportunities of criminal offenders. Understanding the determinants of criminal behavior, along with the conditions that must be met in efficiently allocating scarce resources to the control of crime, can provide useful conceptual guidelines for the tough decisions that must be made in dealing with today's soaring crime rate.

SELECTED BIBLIOGRAPHY

Reynolds, Morgan O. "The Economics of Criminal Activity." Andover, Mass.: Warner Modular Publications, Module 12, 1973.
Rottenberg, Simon, ed. *The Economics of Crime and Punishment.* Washington: American Enterprise Institute for Public Policy Research, 1973.
Tullock, Gordon. "Does Punishment Deter Crime?" *The Public Interest* 36 (1974):103–11.

PART II.
BUSINESS FIRMS
AND MARKET
STRUCTURE

If all business firms operated in a world of pure competition, then pursuit of self interest by them would, in all likelihood, serve the public interest. In fact, however, most markets are characterized by varying degrees of monopoly, or absence of competition. The selections in Part II examine some of the problems and public policy issues which arise when business firms operate in a world of imperfect competition.

Section A, The Business Firm: Ideology and Facts

In "Personal Freedoms and Economic Freedoms in the Mixed Economy" Paul Samuelson seeks to explain business ideology and the relationship between economic freedom and other kinds of freedom. With respect to the latter, he concludes that economic freedom is not a prerequisite for personal freedom in society and that the question is a matter of definition - what is freedom? In "The Function of Business" James Kuhn states that the function of business is to produce for the consumer. Businessmen often tend to forget this, he says, and think that their only function is to make a profit. In "Health Care and the United States Economic System: An Essay in Abnormal Physiology" Victor Fuchs shows that health care is a commodity similar to most other commodities in that it has value subject to a diminishing marginal ability to satisfy. Thus there exists an optimum level of utilization determined by cost and the satisfaction obtainable from other commodities.

Section B, Competition and Monopoly

In "Restrictive Labor Practices in Baseball: Time for a Change?" Janice Westerfield contends that, contrary to claims, the player reservation system does not reduce the gap between strong and weak teams. It does, however, benefit the owners by reducing player income, with consequent loss to the players. In "Forced Divestiture in Oil?" the case for breaking up petroleum companies is examined and diagnosed as weak. In "Bank Profitability and Bank Size" Edward Gallick examines recent trends in bank profitability which show that, contrary to earlier periods, since 1970 medium-size banks seem to be the most profitable, with profitability dropping off as size increases. In "'Commodity Power' is Here to Stay" C. Fred Bergsten warns of future OPEC-like cartels in such international commodities as coffee, phosphate, bauxite, bananas, tin and copper, whereas Philip Trezise reaches the opposite conclusion in "More OPECs Are Unlikely." In his view, elastic product demand and the incentive to cheat are likely to undermine the effectiveness of new international cartels. The success of OPEC, according to Trezise, was due to exceptional circumstances, including a war, which are not likely to endure.

A. The Business Firm:
Ideology and Facts

Personal Freedoms and Economic Freedoms in the Mixed Economy

Paul A. Samuelson

I

Although businessmen do not constitute a completely homogeneous group, it can be documented that generally they share a particular set of political and economic beliefs. These beliefs overlap in some degree with those of other groupings in the community; but in some degree they differ, and the differences can become quite sharp. That is, the typical view among academic economists and other social scientists on topics such as the proper role of government expenditure and regulation has become increasingly different from that of the typical view among businessmen.

How can we account for business ideology? Much of this discussion will be devoted to this question and to previous attempts to answer it. Since it takes two to make a difference, the business ideology of intellectuals will also be studied.

The second part of the essay attempts to analyze various interrelations among economic and personal freedoms. Agreeing that governments everywhere take a more active role·in the conscious direction and regulation of economic life, we may speak loosely of "a decline in business freedoms." At least some people will want to distinguish between the concept of the freedom of a seller to market his product as he wishes and the freedom of a family man to go to the church of his choice; to think and utter the thoughts of his fancy; and to read his evening paper within the four walls of his castle, with the secure feeling that the moat separating it from the outside will not be breached by bailiffs without due process of law. They will be willing to fight to the death to defend these personal freedoms but will not care to risk more than a few scratches and bruises in the cause of business or economic freedoms.

Yet it can be argued—and, hence, has been so argued—that freedom is one and indivisible: that it is as grave a sin to condemn a man's property and take it over (at court-determined cost) for an urban renewal project as it is to whisk his wife into the county jail on arbitrary charges or on no charges at all. Or (and this is by no means the same argument) that the empirical nature of the political process is such that infringement of business freedoms must lead inevitably to infringement of personal freedoms. Beliefs about the relationships between personal freedoms and economic freedoms represent one of the most important tenets in business ideology. Before beginning to analyze these specific beliefs, I will attempt to account for business ideology in general.

The Business Creed as Delusion

Although this discussion purports to be objective, by its very nature it begins with certain preconceptions. When a social scientist speaks of the puzzle of business ideology, he has already committed himself to the view that these beliefs cannot be explained in terms of their self-evident objective merits. But this is not because he has prejudged the issue from the beginning of time, having known already before his ninth-grade civics course that the pretended merits of laissez-faire are all bunk. Rather, the historian of ideas has built upon numerous earlier studies in the field of economics and politics, which suggest strongly that the conservative business ideology overstates the objective merits of its own case.

When most academic discussions of the business creed begin with this viewpoint as an explicit or implicit axiom, they unavoidably irritate the businessman that they are talking about. There is no real harm in that, any more than there is in the case where radicals become irritated when psychologists attempt to explain their behavior on the picket line in terms of jealous resentment over their mother's love for her husband. The danger is all the other way. When Western anthropologists go to live with South Sea islanders, they end up too often with an exaggerated fondness for the quaintness of the sex rituals there, in just the way that an economist working for an aid program in

Pakistan finds himself arguing with the Washington office on behalf of his constituency, using the same arguments that he had himself been previously rebutting. What one must hold against a generation of anthropologists is that they were so taken in by the phenomena they were objectively studying that they made bad empirical predictions about the hardness of the cake of custom and its resistance to material change. I need not point out the danger implied in the proverb, "To know all, is to forgive all."

But an opposite warning is also necessary. Most of the literature that I have seen on this subject starts out too blithely with the postulate that the views of the conservative businessman are palpable delusions, which must, therefore, be approached with the tools appropriate to the analysis of odd beliefs. I exaggerate a little, but copious quotation could show that I do so in a good cause.

Let me illustrate with a recent book on American intellectual history edited by Arthur M. Schlesinger, Jr., and Morton D. White.[1] This excellent work represents the joint contributions of able scholars in the diverse areas of history, literature, philosophy, sociology, and economics. Several essays touch upon the development of conservative business thought in the last century. None of them—my own included—can be fairly termed a panegyric to the views under contemplation. Indeed, the following passage by Max Lerner [2] is more typical:

One of the paradoxes of American social and intellectual history is that laissez-faire reached its height as a system of economic thought and judicial decision at the very time that its doom as a system of economic organization was already clear.

Lerner is referring here to conservative ideology at the turn of the century. Many other writers have pointed out the apparent paradox of the Jacksonian era, when the Jeffersonian idyll of the prosperous and self-sufficient farmer was being replaced by the growth of industrialism and urbanization. Yet, just as the reality was turning to interdependence and away from independence, Emerson and Tocqueville were articulating the great American belief in individualism. How explain the discrepancy between fact and word? Hallucination? Self-deception? Mendacity?

It is a widespread view among academics that conservative sermons about laissez-faire and individualism represent a simple denial of the reality of society. Maybe this is so. Maybe it is patently so, and no danger can come from prejudging the case in advance. But it is certainly a matter of some moment that what is taken for granted not be wrong. I am here stressing,

---

[1] A. M. Schlesinger, Jr., and Morton White: *Paths of American Thought*, Houghton Mifflin, Boston, 1963.

[2] *Ibid.*, p. 147. This is the opening sentence in Max Lerner's essay, The Triumph of Laissez-Faire.

without guile, *the crucial importance of a scientific assessment of the merits of an ideology as a preliminary to understanding its nonrationalistic content and function.* In handling an upset person who claims to have seen a ghost, it is of some moment to know whether he *has* seen a ghost. It is one thing to be told by an individual in a sanitarium near New York City that he is Napoleon Bonaparte and quite another to be told the same thing by a short, swarthy individual who inhabits the island of St. Helena in 1817.

The way that you calibrate the respondent's verbal behavior and the explanation appropriate to account for it is much altered in the two cases. And the way I calibrate *your* rejection of his claiming to be Napoleon is equally affected by the circumstances. What are we to think of A, who knows that B is crazy to claim he is Napoleon for the sufficient reason that all sane men should know that A is the true Napoleon?

At last I have revealed my hand; I intend to play a double game. I shall try not only to understand businessmen's beliefs about economics and business, but also intellectuals' beliefs on these matters as refracted by *their* reactions to business ideology. The mind reels at this prospect of wheels within wheels. But it is all good, clean fun. At bottom I am an intellectual myself, as ready as the next boy to throw a snowball at the top hat of a nearby tycoon (or at the mortarboard of some dear, departing colleague).

The Economist as Go-between

Actually, this is in a genuine sense no frivolous exercise. The economist is in the unique position of being able to assist the historian of thought and social movements. Just as a pathologist can help a psychiatrist appraise the meaning of a patient's assertion that he has a brain tumor, the economist can—alas, imperfectly—help certify what the reasonable facts are, the necessary benchmark against which to measure delusion and rationalization.[3]

Although the thought would spoil digestions at a downtown eating club, the economist has always played the role of interpreter to the academic community of the businessman and of material activity generally. Fifty years ago, conservative advocates would perhaps invoke the authority of the local Ph.D. in political economy; today they are more likely to regard him as an impractical enemy and send for their lawyer to find that

---

[3] An example is provided by the apparent incompatibility of individualism and a post-Jeffersonian interdependent economy. The historian needs to be told by the economist that a system of ideal pricing in perfectly competitive markets *can* coordinate the activities of quite egotistic individualist atoms through the impersonal market mechanism. (I discuss this in greater detail later.) Hence, the paradox of post-Jacksonian ideological individualism evaporates as a logical self-contradiction. The Lerner problem remains: Is it oligopolists who will be most fervent in the praise of competition and laissez-faire?

needle in the haystack of economists that a sensible man can rely on. But their view of the economist does not refute my point that we are go-betweens.

Historians and political scientists will go on taking seriously the economic doctrines of Henry George or Bernard Shaw long after any quorum of economists will deem them significant. A sociologist well-trained in what is politely called intellectual history will laugh to hear a businessman claiming that *his* investment will benefit the working man in the future. The sociologist knows that this "filter-down" theory was killed off when John Stuart Mill accepted Thornton's refutation of the classical wage-fund theory a hundred years ago. What the sociologist does not realize is that, in another form, most modern economists place some credence in that murdered notion while, perhaps, sopping their social consciences by suggesting that workers be given both the increased wages stemming from the new capital *and* the fruit of the capital itself, if it is *their* present sacrifices that are to be involved.

As the general economist is to the other social scientists and the historians, often the business economist is to the general economist. Business school economists will, I think, agree with my observation that in past decades professors in commerce departments voted more conservatively than their colleagues in economics departments. Times have changed a little. Where only two out of the hundreds of professors at the Harvard Business School chose Franklin Roosevelt over Wendell Willkie in 1940, a majority chose Kennedy over Nixon in 1960. The more things change, the less they are the same, as a Frenchman might say. Yet, it is still the case, I believe, that the majority for Kennedy was greater in the Harvard economics department (and liberal arts faculty) than in the Business School. And it is still fairly typical of colleges everywhere that business school professors are more sympathetic toward business than are members of the other faculties (with the possible exception of the engineers).

I am not saying that management school faculty members are "kept" men, apologists for business. In part, their difference in attitude may be traceable to their more detailed research into the complexities of business life; in part, to the evident attitudes of men who have chosen as their lifework the training of accountants, marketing experts, and other business practitioners. Economists who are known to be radical are less likely to be courted by business school deans and are less likely to succumb to available suitors. This may be just as well. The man who adores business is likely to lose objectivity. And the man who hates business is also handicapped in being objective. Neither Casanovas nor misogynists are apt to make cracker-jack obstetricians.

Here, I think my role as an economist can be a useful one. If you "know," as many social scientists know, that the praise of laissez-faire is beside the point, your analysis has to run along different lines than would be the case if, like Professors Frank

Knight and Milton Friedman of the University of Chicago or Professors Gottfried Haberler of Harvard and William Fellner of Yale, you "know" there is much objective merit in the viewpoint. To be sure, a rabid business spokesman like Mr. Edgar M. Queeny of the Monsanto Chemical Company [4] does not state with any meticulousness the scientific findings of economists who belong to the secret lodges of the *Mont Pelerin* Society; but, then, neither did Franklin Roosevelt catch correctly the nuances of doctrine of his brain trust in the week in question; and few of the New Frontiersmen who have returned from Washington to their ivory towers would give top grades to their intermediate students for the utterances that they admire in high officials. Samuel Johnson's dictum on walking dogs and preaching women must be invoked here.

Business Ideology on the Defensive?

Before we try to account for business ideology, it may be well to examine its importance. Certainly, one cannot take for granted that its dominance in our society can be measured by its decibel count. Happy is the nation that has no history. And most secure may be the laissez-faire economy that no one bothers to talk about. In the 1920's, when Calvin Coolidge was Chairman of the Board, the business of America was business. As a boy entrepreneur I used to sample my own wares and read in the *Saturday Evening Post* (and in the now-defunct *American Magazine*) the success stories of American businessmen. Although they appeared in the nonfiction columns, they read like fiction. (Only after 1929 did I learn that they actually were part fiction!)

Nevertheless, despite the considerable volume of such panegyrics, there seemed to be less ideological defense of private enterprise in the 1920's than appeared in the mid-1930's, when Roosevelt's New Deal was at the apex of its power and when the rearguard actions of the Liberty League served the function of self-expression more than that of persuasive social propaganda.

The felt need for articulation of business creed and *apologia* may itself be a sign of inner uncertainty on the part of the business community and conservative leaders. In the vigor of manly growth the motto is "Ask me no questions, and I'll tell you no lies." As the bachelor balds, and perhaps begins to pall, come the better rationalizations for the lively life. Eulogy and obituary are not accidentally related words.

Implicitly, I have been raising the suspicion that the business ideology may no longer have the importance for good or evil that it once had. How can this be reconciled with the common observation that radical reform has become a dead movement in American life? Communism has no following. Socialism has lost even the small appeal it once had. No utopias fire the

[4] Edgar M. Queeny, *The Spirit of Enterprise*, Scribner, New York, 1943.

imaginations of Americans and provide an alternative to the philosophy of business enterprise. In short, business is allegedly now in the saddle.

Now, this is not quite the way I hear it down at the Union League Club. There, they would be astonished to learn that they are in the saddle. The active businessman has not these many years been fearful of utopian socialists; nor of card-carrying communists, as such. He has regarded it as an over-nice distinction to worry about whether an intellectual is a fellow traveler or a lodge member. Since Karl Marx advocated a progressive income tax in the *Communist Manifesto* of 1848, why bother to distinguish between Marxians and progressives who hold such uncomfortable views? I believe it was the retired President Herbert Hoover who introduced into the vocabulary of American political life the compound word Marx-and-Keynes.

To say that people are now merely New Dealers or New Frontiersmen is not even to provide cold comfort to business ideologies. Franklin Roosevelt was the enemy, not Earl Browder or Norman Thomas. The thing to fear is not the full-fledged alternative social system, so much as the hard-to-differentiate "mixed economy." For one thing, Eugene Debs, the I.W.W., and earlier radical movements (including Populism) have, I suggest, an importance in the minds and writings of historians, social scientists, and conservative alarmists out of proportion to their actual historical importance. And although Norman Thomas can claim with some factual accuracy that many of the programs in his platform were adopted by Franklin Roosevelt, it would be politically naive to suppose that the socialist party was the spearhead and wedge for these social changes. The dawn does not pull up the sun, any more than the rear guard pushes the army in front of it.

The Mixed Economy

I question whether business has climbed back into the saddle. The story is much more complicated; history does not consist of one-way trends. History oscillates, backtracks, and spirals. Admittedly, in the twenty years after 1929 the trend seemed to be toward limitations on business, but during the last dozen years of that period, the strength of strong radical dissent was also on the ebb. One forgets how desperate the populace was in 1932. Half of the small-town editors, for example—a group usually about as conservative and reactionary as any that can be found—then favored nationalization of the banks. The success of Roosevelt's New Deal in stemming the tide of collapse acted as a lightning rod in dissipating the forces of fascism and drastic reform.

Since 1950, both in America and the West generally, there has been some comeback of private enterprise and an increasing reliance on markets rather than government controls. But even this movement has been a spotty one; thus, Germany, Japan, France, and Italy—to say nothing of The Netherlands and Great Britain—

have, by planning, interfered extensively with laissez-faire. In the United States, the Eisenhower Administration retained most of the post–1933 economic institutions. Although the Kennedy-Johnson Administration has paid less lip service to the business cause and has been regarded by businessmen as a hostile adversary, its performance has been mixed. Labor unions these days regard themselves as being in the descendancy, both in terms of public opinion and government support. It is ironical that the first major step in gutting America's egalitarian structure of taxation should have been taken by a Democratic rather than a Republican administration. And still, it is this same administration that pushes medical care for the aged, regulation of drugs and security markets, and other programs distasteful to business.

Perhaps the one discernible trend is toward less polarization of ideology; less of laissez-faire versus socialism; of freedom versus totalitarianism. This does not mean that the conflict is over, but rather that it is taking place along other battlelines. It is in this sense that I contend that the "mixed economy" is the enemy and the ever-present effective challenge of the business ideology.

The mixed economy is not a very definite concept. I have purposely left it vague, in part because that is its intrinsic nature and in part because increased precision should come at the end rather than at the beginning of extensive research.

Search for New Goals

The vagueness of the opposing ideology naturally begets a responding vagueness in the business creed itself. The old clear-cut bastions become too vulnerable. Yet, once they are left behind, the new ground to be defended becomes hard to define. This leads to a certain frustration and an urge to find a new formulation of the business creed. Professor Jesse W. Markham of Princeton University in his editor's introduction to R. Joseph Monsen, Jr., *Modern American Capitalism: Ideologies and Issues* [5] asks why capitalism, despite its demonstrated performance in producing highest real incomes, should be seriously challenged in the new uncommitted nations and at home. Markham concludes:

In this book Professor Monsen provides some meaningful and thoughtful answers to this question, the most plausible of which is the absence of a clearly articulated ideology of private capitalism.

Monsen himself puts the matter bluntly:

Americans will never be able to persuade other countries to follow an anti-communist route to development if they cannot explain and understand what they themselves are for—and why. [6]

---

[5] R. Joseph Monsen, Jr., *Modern American Capitalism: Ideologies and Issues,* Houghton Mifflin, Boston, 1963, p. vi.

[6] *Ibid.*, p. ix.

I regard the Monsen study as valuable in demonstrating the differences and the nuances in capitalist ideology. It is debatable that the best defense of a system comes from a thorough understanding of its nature and a self-conscious articulation of its merits and demerits; and, therefore, I should be less sad than Monsen if it turned out that a would-be missionary, starting out to sell the American way of life to the Hottentots, Laotians, and Yankees, were to find his eloquence paralyzed by learning from Monsen that there are at least five versions of capitalistic ideology:

1. Classical Capitalist Ideology (of the N.A.M. and the Chicago economics department).
2. Managerial Ideology of Capitalism (of the C.E.D. and *Fortune* magazine).
3. Countervailing Power Ideology (of J. Kenneth Galbraith, and of whom else?).
4. People's Capitalism (of the New York Stock Exchange's Keith Funston and the American Advertising Council).
5. Enterprise Democracy (associated with the Eisenhower Administration, and particularly with its "semi-official ideologist" Arthur Larson).

Since it is not clear that the best preparation for the soap salesman is a thorough briefing in the scientific laboratory that produces soap, one cannot be sure that Monsen's contribution towards a sixth ideology will restore the aplomb of the American missionary:

> It is suggested that the U.S.I.A.'s currently exported American Capitalist Ideology be reoriented toward these basic elements of the American system, particularly pragmatism and compromise, elements not at present included in Enterprise Democracy.[7]

A New Capitalism?

The five versions of capitalism cited from Monsen can be boiled down to two categories: old-fashioned profit maximizing markets that are perfectly or imperfectly competitive; and the newer notion of "managerial capitalism"—that the corporation (and its officials) are responsive to the interests of *all* parties it deals with—employees, customers, shareowners, the public, the federal government. I fancy that most of the big business guinea pigs dissected by Robert Heilbroner lean toward this last view. And so do the well-known writings of A. A. Berle on the separation of ownership and control of the modern corporation and on new roles of property and of corporate bureaucrats.

Many economists have been skeptical about this new capitalism. Edward S. Mason, a judicious scholar of industrial organi-

[7] *Ibid.*, p. 128.

zation, has gently debunked it. A more cavalier rejection is provided by Jack Hirshleifer:

There are several interesting things about this defense of capitalism —that capitalists are really not selfish after all. The first is that, as a defense, it is a hopeless failure. There are many reasons why this argument must fail, but perhaps the most conspicuous reason is that it is untrue. . . . What does all this prove? Simply that all the world is largely governed by self-interest, and all the world knows it. . . .[8]

Of course, every schoolboy knows that "what everybody knows" is true only about half the time. Although I agree that there is exaggeration in the new view, the matter cannot be carried far by *a priori* reasoning.

My colleague, Morris A. Adelman, in a too-little known essay, "Some Aspects of Corporate Enterprise," [9] has emphasized some of the limits of corporate political power. He has also emphasized that in these days the political power of many small businesses is more potent than that of giant corporations. Congressmen know that. Often a large firm will try to get an association of small firms linked to its cause; and an outsider is amused to see an international oil firm frightened of its domestic subsidiary, when the latter has powerful allies among the small, but numerous, local producers. General Motors would be foolish to risk the wrath of Congress by pushing its dealers around, and many a giant has been blackmailed by its numerous pygmies. Although one group may have a controlling vote in a corporation, in politics it is still one vote for one head. (The coefficients of reactionariness and of bigness are certainly *not* correlated in any simple, positive fashion.)

Adelman also has some trenchant remarks on the corporation as a profit maximizer, and I think Earl Cheit and he would form a heroic minority of dissenters against the fashionable interpretation of the Berle–Means thesis concerning dispersed ownership of corporations and its separation from management control. By and large, what is good for General Motors *is* good for Charles E. Wilson, GM president. This does not ignore the existence of some conflicts of interest between ethical and unethical inside officers. Degree of concentration of ownership among different corporations turns out on sober examination to have few predictive consequences for corporate behavior. Standard Oil of New Jersey has employee board members. Some oil companies have family control. What differences in behavior are traceable to this difference? More research would be needed to give a

[8] Jack Hirshleifer, Capitalist Ethics—Tough or Soft?, *Journal of Law and Business*, II (October 1959), p. 116. E. S. Mason, The Apologetics of "Managerialism," *The Journal of Business*, XXXI (January 1958), pp. 1–11.
[9] In R. E. Freeman, ed., *Postwar Economic Trends in the United States*, Harper, New York, 1960, pp. 291–307, particularly pp. 299–302.

significant answer to this question—a fact that you might not guess from reading the vast literature on this subject.

As Adelman has indicated, simple profit maximizing for owners and exercising trusteeship for pluralistic claimants do not lead to very significant differences in behavior. To be significantly different, a change must make a difference. When it is damnably difficult to make an operationally meaningful experiment (even in principle) in order to detect a difference, why care much? For example, some economist friends work for one of the largest companies in the world. In privacy, they have tried to get top management to admit that it "really acts so as to maximize long-run profits." They have never been able to squeeze out such an admission. Is this surprising? The men at the top are *not* completely free wills. But they have spent most of their 40 years of adulthood with the company; the crises in their lives—the "hard times"—have no more been associated with stockholder pressure than with pressure from government and labor. But suppose that such an admission had been wrung out of them? What difference would it have made? Really none at all, since this company acts much like its rivals, which are organized differently. Economists are like pedants (a redundancy!) in wanting to save the face of their principles even when naught is at stake.

If it is wrong to think that separation of ownership and control makes a great deal of difference, that does not mean that corporations can be regarded as simple conduits for funneling earnings into the hands of owners and for funneling decisions of owners into corporate acts. Large corporate oligopolies have considerable degrees of freedom in the short run (and to a degree even in the long run), which atomistic competitors lack. The folkways and mores that these authorities follow are, therefore, somewhat indeterminate and tend to be self-determining by the group.

Corporations act *as if* they were independent entities; ask any fund raiser, and he will tell you that. Corporations have behavior patterns, personalities, and styles. It is witchcraft to impute these persistent patterns of behavior back to something antecedent to the corporation called "owners," and Occam's razor can kill off these antecedent spirits. Corporations have attitudes toward Negroes and Jews, toward wage rates and work conditions, toward research and charity. To say that the vast differences in behavior between U. S. Gypsum and National Gypsum are merely reflections of the personal tastes of a man called Avery and a man called Baker is either to be saying nothing or to be saying something wrong. When Sewell Avery died, U. S. Gypsum did not change *its* spots.

Just as we call a spade a spade, we must call a corporation an actor in the scenario of economic life—no different from the rest of us puppets. This is quite distinct from the normative question whether it would be a bad thing for corporations to exercise independent choices in the pursuit of goals other than simple profit maximization. Professors Hirshleifer and other writers of the Chicago school have expressed disapproval of any such actions. There is little that is compelling in such opinions. Contrary to allegation, economic theory does not tell us that a farmer should first maximize his profits and then satisfy his personal utilities and tastes. There is no such inherent separation of functions, either in fact or in ideal theory. Similarly, in a diverse corporation there is no basis in economic theory for the assertion that decisions *should* be taken so as to maximize that single thing called "profit." Although it is possible that observing economists could more simply predict the behavior of entities that maximize a simple magnitude called "dollar profit," there is no reason why the world should accommodate itself to our desire for a lazy life.

If it comes to ethical issues of value judgment, I, for one, can as easily imagine a good society in which corporations freely act according to certain patterns as one in which private individuals are given the ostensible power to make decisions about fair employment and other practices. Indeed, one of the few positive arguments for bigness in corporations is that such entities are less able to break the law and resist the social pressures of democracy. The family farmer can and will cheat where the vast corporate farmer will not. Altruism is a scarce good, and corporations may help society economize on its use.

Explaining the Business Creed

By far the most important attempt to describe and explain the business ideology is that of Francis X. Sutton, Seymour E. Harris, Carl Kaysen, and James Tobin in the *American Business Creed*.[10] Although they are friends, I think no one will think me partial when I call them the cream of the elite of American scholarship. Here a leading sociologist, disciple of Talcott Parsons and Ford Foundation administrator, teamed up with three economists of the highest distinction. Without disrespect to my profession, one must admit that here is a case where the three economists seem pretty much won over to the view of the sociologist. (This must be qualified by the recognition that economists have never been happy about the fashionable economic interpretation of history or of events; those who knew little of technical economics have been the ardent boosters of the doctrine that economic interests are dominant in life.)

Their book has received a fair measure of attention but, except among connoisseurs, not nearly the attention it deserves. Its value is great, even though—as will become evident—I think it has essentially failed in its attempt to explain business ideology in terms of a theory of "strain" in the business role. This failure, I cannot help but think, throws some light on the weakness of

[10] Harvard University Press, Cambridge, Mass., 1956, and Schocken Paperback, New York, 1962, hereafter referred to as Sutton et al.

our present-day best sociology. In the brief space at my disposal and in view of my amateur status in these realms, I make no pretence to giving a convincing proof of the view that I have just expressed. Certainly I shall not pretend to put up a better theory than the one I criticize; but I do not think that criticism is beside the point, if it is not able to be constructive and to provide a superior alternative to what is being criticized. They also serve who merely point out that the emperor has no clothes or that the clothes he does not have fit badly.

It will be economical of space if I first quote at some length from these authors. (In every case, the emphasis is mine.)

Our aim in this study is to answer the questions: Why does the business ideology say what it does? On what theory can the themes, symbols, arguments, which form the business ideology be explained? . . . To reach the answer to our ultimate question, we first seek to define the general role of ideologies in social life. We find our answer, broadly speaking, in the strains and conflicts inherent in every institutional position in a complex society, whether the position be that of businessman, or university professor, or labor leader. These conflicts are of several kinds: conflicts between the demands of the particular position and the broader values of society; gaps between the demands of social positions and the capabilities of the human beings who hold them to fulfill these demands; inherently conflicting demands built into the social definition of certain positions. This general proposition is applied to an investigation of the particular strains inherent in the business role in the United States, and the major themes of business ideology are shown as verbal and symbolic resolutions of these conflicts. This is our central proposition . . . (page vii).

We have rejected the "interest" theory, that ideologies simply reflect the economic self-interest, narrowly conceived, of their adherents. Ideology, in this view, is merely an attempt to manipulate symbols and marshal arguments which will persuade others to take actions from which the ideologist stands to profit financially. The ideologist may or may not believe the things he says. If he does happen to believe them, it is maintained, it is only because he has succeeded by wishful thinking in convincing himself that truth and self-interest coincide.

The "interest theory" contains important elements of truth. It is easy to understand why the ideology of the domestic watch industry, both management and labor, features support of tariff protection and includes all the venerable arguments and symbols which might persuade the Tariff Commission, the Congress, and the public of the protectionist case. Were this the model for all ideology, there would indeed be little problem of explanation and little need for our book. Actually the relationship between specific ideologies and economic interest is seldom so clear. A more typical example is provided by the passionate support a businessman gives to the principle of a *balanced federal budget*. We surely cannot conclude that he has reached this position by sober calculation of his profit prospects *under balanced and unbalanced budgets*. Assessing the ultimate effects of alternative budgetary policies on the profits of a specific business firm is a formidable econometric problem. Yet businessmen speak on the subject with such confidence, emotion, and unanimity that, in the "interest theory" of ideology, we would be forced to conclude that they have no trouble knowing on which side of the issue their economic interests lie, and that varying effects on different groups of businessmen are never to be anticipated.

It is true that with sufficient ingenuity one can construct a chain which reconciles practically any ideological position to the economic interest of its holder. Or one can make the task easier by attributing to the ideologist a mistaken or unduly certain conception of his own interest. One can make the task still easier by widening the notion of self-interest to encompass psychological satisfactions other than economic returns. But these expedients are really the end of the theory they are designed to salvage. They reduce it to a tautology: "Men act in their own interests" becomes "Men act as they are motivated to act" (pages 12–13).

. . . Why do businessmen so fiercely oppose *deficit financing* on the part of the government? Such opposition cannot be the result of a rational calculation of their tangible interests. In the short run many businesses (for example, construction firms) stand to gain from this policy. It is possible that in the long run, business interests may be injured by *deficit financing*, but it is certainly not inevitable. In any particular instance it is exceedingly difficult if not impossible to assess the remote consequences of *deficit financing*. And so there is no rational basis for the simplicity and certainty of business opposition. If we stick to a theory of rational self-interest we can only dismiss examples such as this as evidence of ignorance or error. But this is obviously unsatisfactory. . . .

The clearest way to give the theory a definite character is to equate interests with objective, private economic advantage. Formulated in this way, the interest theory, *as our deficit financing example shows,* simply cannot account for a considerable part of the business ideology (pages 303–304).

A Trial Balance

Where do such explanations get us? The simple notion of strain as nervous collapse, in which the businessman says gibberish because he is in a state, is, of course, not what is intended. This is a pity, in that the vulgarization of a theory usually contains its operationally meaningful content in the sense of logical positivism and Peirce-James pragmatism.

I do not think that vulgar or sophisticated self-interest theories have been given a fair shake by the authors. The space spent on refuting what they point out is the single most popular and natural theory is, by my count, amazingly small and amazingly repetitive. You cannot get very far in proving that Americans are very tall by telling anecdotes about how many tall men you know. And this is particularly the case, if you keep repeating the one name of John Kenneth Galbraith. Yet, as my repeated italicizing of words in the quotations from the Sutton book will show, about the only case they cite in which businessmen *seem* to be acting against self-interest is the case of opposition to deficit spending (and we might add to expansionary monetary policy). Where are the hundreds of other examples? I believe I could find half a dozen, and no doubt they could triple this number. But I suspect that the end product will not be terribly impressive.

Personal views, in fact, rarely contradict personal interest. Read the papers for a month and count the score.

I agree that it is a terribly interesting question why business generally has been antiexpansionary in the area of aggregate demand. I wish the authors had addressed themselves more specifically to it. Indeed, they cite, but do not really linger on, the attempt made by Sidney S. Alexander [11] to tackle this very problem. I must report that there is more wisdom *on this specific matter* in the short essay by Alexander than in their whole book (and yet Alexander would be the first to admit that he has not said the last word on the puzzle).[12]

In my limited space I can say but little on this specific subject. Let me stress that macroeconomics is not an easy problem for a businessman or any lay person to understand. Moreover, I am not sure that businessmen are *in the concrete* opposed to expansionary policies. They have trouble in rationalizing their frequent longing for such policies, which seems to me to be natural. But when it counts, the defense producers are eager for increased expenditures. We have had much recent experience that business, if it can save face and get *its* kind of tax cut, is willing to let deficits soar in a good cause. General Motors has repeatedly criticized tight money, when it hurt sales of cars on credit. Bankers, who benefit from tight money, are its most vocal exponents.

To make the point that businessmen believe in what they say publicly, the authors quote a public opinion poll showing that the business ideology on budget balancing is that "of the population at large; a variety of polls indicates that the people as a whole are 'budget balancers,' and it seems safe to infer that the polled sentiments of businessmen would show the same pattern" (page 324). If true—and in a degree this is true—what has become of their one case where a strain theory proves to be the superior one? There is apparently no peculiar business view here that has to be explained by peculiar business-role strain!

I suspect that the Sutton group somewhat exaggerates the element of unpleasant strain involved in business, perhaps because of the natural tendency of any academic person to suppose that others experience the discomfort that *he* would experience if placed in business life. The great Cambridge physicist, J. J. Thomson (discoverer of the electron), was once asked how he felt

<hr />

[11] S. S. Alexander, Opposition to Deficit Spending for the Prevention of Unemployment, in Alvin H. Hansen et al., eds., *Income, Employment and Public Policy*, Norton, New York, 1948.

[12] Alexander classified business opposition to deficit financing under four headings: misunderstanding of the validity of the mechanism; desire to have slack labor markets to keep worker performance high relative to wages; class antagonism, which associates deficit spending with other liberal programs that are against business; fear of increasing power of the state and of groups other than the business elite. Interestingly, he omits opposition to inflation, even though he wrote during the 1947–48 postwar inflation.

about the fact that any broker in the City made three times the income he did as a professor. "But just think of the work they have to do," he replied. Like most academics, he used his preferences to project into the business role strains and unpleasantnesses that businessmen may not feel. Brokers like being brokers, hard as that is for professors of botany to believe. Business is a great game to many people. It is a relatively well-paid game, as every prospective father-in-law knows. A second-class violinist in the family is a tragedy; a third-class businessman is someone you can lean on in your old age.

In every country the party of business is the more conservative party. In every case, when it comes to marginal decisions that bear on business interests, the party of business acts friendlier to those interests. Why then deny or overlook the obvious? Admittedly, no *explanation* has been provided by this recognition. But that is no reason to reject the fact. We laugh when a Molière character speaks of the power of opium to induce sleep *because* of its "soporific" quality; however, that should never make us overlook the fact that opium does induce sleep.

Rich and (what is not necessarily the same thing) acquisitive men do labor under the strain of being natural objects of dislike and envy. The Bible tells us that and so does a theory of self-interest. It is hard for people to believe that the road to heaven is paved with selfish intentions, even when it is true. That much I grant to the business-strain theory.

In its wider sense, a strain theory that finds associated with each occupation a characteristic strain explaining its ideology comes full circle to a materialistic interpretation of ideology of the Marxian type. To see this, repeat the word "strain" over and over again. It is like repeating "ice-cream cone" over and over again; the words begin to lose meaning. But in the last case, the mind's eye can keep looking at the dripping cone. However, since strain does not mean anything so concrete as biting one's nails or experiencing facial tics and the shakes,[13] one can replace "strain" by x. A farmer believes in this or that because of the x of the farmer trade; the money lender believes what he believes because of his job's x. Why not cancel out the x and stick to the bare facts of differential ideologies, pending the time when fewer x factors than occupations can be found to provide a mnemonic pattern. On the whole, I am left with the impression that an interests-cum-prestige theory provides more of a simplifying pattern than any proposed alternative.

I could go on giving criticisms; they are not intended to be captious but are merely copied from the margin of my copy of their book. But I have said enough to demonstrate my disappointment with the strain theory of business ideology. Let me

---

[13] Apparently actuarial statistics do not show relatively more heart attacks and ulcers among business decision makers than among routine workers.

repeat that the Sutton group has been led to observe things about business strains that are interesting for their own sake, even where they fail to explain the business creed.[14]

Up to now I have largely discussed the problem of explaining business ideology without giving my evaluation of its intrinsic content. My remaining task is to appraise the specific part of it that relates to freedom and coordination.

II

As a prelude to discussing the empirical and analytical relations between business and personal freedoms (which is roughly the distinction between economic and political freedoms), I might usefully give some reflections on the nature of individualism, liberty, freedom, coercion, and the marketplace.[15]

How Divine the Natural Order?

Adam Smith, our patron saint, was critical of state interference of the prenineteenth-century type. And make no mistake about it; Smith was right. Most of the interventions into economic life by the state were then harmful both to prosperity and freedom. What Smith said needed to be said. In fact, much of what Smith said still needs to be said; good intentions by government are not enough; acts have consequences that must be taken into account, if good is to follow.

One hundred per cent individualists concentrate on the purple passage in Adam Smith, where he discerns an Invisible Hand that leads each selfish individual to contribute to the best public good. Smith had a point; but he could not have earned a passing mark in a Ph.D. oral examination by explaining just what that point was. Until this century, his followers—such as Bastiat—thought that the doctrine of the Invisible Hand meant (1) that it produced maximum feasible total satisfaction, somehow defined; or (2) that it showed that anything resulting from the voluntary agreements of uncoerced individuals must make them better (or best) off in some important sense.

[14] One can derive a superficial explanation of intellectuals' behavior from a retaliating use by a businessman of the Sutton-Parsons strain theory of academic life.

[15] Some of the following thoughts appeared in two recent lectures. Since I do not believe in elegant variations, some of the words that follow will be in the same sequence as is published elsewhere. I own to no sense of self-plagiarism since, as indicated there, many of those words were stolen from the present research investigation.

George J. Stigler and P. A. Samuelson, *A Dialogue on the Proper Economic Role of the State*, Graduate School of Business Selected Papers No. 7, 1963; P. A. Samuelson, Modern Economic Realities and Individualism, *The Texas Quarterly* (Summer 1963).

Both of these interpretations, which are still held by many modern libertarians, are wrong. They neglect the axiom concerning the ethical merits of the preexisting distribution of land, property, and genetic and acquired utilities. This is not the place for a technical discussion of economic principles, so I shall be very brief and cryptic in showing this.

First, suppose that some ethical observer, such as Jesus, Buddha, or for that matter, John Dewey or Aldous Huxley, were to examine whether the total of social utility (as that ethical observer scores the deservingness of the poor and rich, saintly and sinning individuals) was actually maximized by 1860 or 1964 laissez-faire. He might decide that a tax placed upon yachts whose proceeds go to cheapen the price of insulin to the needy increased the total of utility. Could Adam Smith prove him wrong? Could Bastiat? I think not.

Of course, they might say that there is no point in trying to compare different individuals' utilities, because they are incommensurable and can no more be added together than can apples and oranges. But if recourse is made to this argument, then the doctrine that the Invisible Hand maximizes total utility of the universe has already been discarded. If they admit that the Invisible Hand will truly maximize total social utility *provided the state intervenes so as to make the initial distribution of dollar votes ethically proper*, then they have abandoned the libertarian's position that individuals are not to be coerced, even by taxation.

In connection with the second interpretation that anything resulting from voluntary agreements is in some sense, *ipso facto*, optimal, we can reply by pointing out that when I make a purchase from a monopolistic octopus, that is a voluntary act; I can always go without Alka Seltzer or aluminum or nylon or whatever product you think is produced by a monopolist. Mere voluntarism, therefore, is not the root merit of the doctrine of the Invisible Hand; [16] what is important about it is the system of

16 Milton Friedman, *Capitalism and Freedom*, University of Chicago Press, Chicago, 1962, Chapters 1 and 2 seem grossly defective in these matters. In the first chapter, he regards market behavior as optimal merely because it is voluntary, save for the single passage: ". . . perhaps the most difficult problems arise from monopoly—which inhibits effective freedom by denying individuals alternatives to the particular exchange" and promises to discuss this matter in more detail in the next chapter. It turns out there that "Exchange is truly voluntary only when nearly equivalent alternatives exist." Why this new element of alternatives? Because, as I point out, *perfect* competition is efficient in the Pareto-optimality sense, and it is this property that modern economists have *proved* optimal (and interesting) about such competition. Libertarians, like Hayek and von Mises, would be annoyed to learn that their case stands or falls on its nearness to "perfect competition." Unlike George J. Stigler and Milton Friedman, neither of these two men has remotely the same views on perfect competition as do modern economists generally. What libertarians have in common is the hope that departures from perfect competition are not too extreme in our society; Friedman, himself, has apparently come full circle to the view that public regulation of "monopoly" and state regulation of "monopoly" are greater evils than letting well enough alone. I do not feel competent to report on the algebraic degree

checks and balances that prevails under perfect competition, and its measure of validity is at the technocratic level of efficiency, not at the ethical level of freedom and individualism. That this is so can be seen from the fact that such socialists as Oskar Lange and A. P. Lerner have advocated channeling the Invisible Hand to the task of organizing a socialistic society efficiently.

The Cash Nexus

Just as there is a sociology of family life and of politics, there is also a sociology of individualistic competition. It need not be a rich one. Ask not your neighbor's name; enquire only for his numerical schedules of supply and demand. Under perfect competition, no buyer need face a seller. Haggling in a Levantine bazaar is a sign of less-than-perfect competition.

These economic contacts between atomistic individuals may seem a little chilly or, to use the language of wine tasting, "dry." This impersonality has its good side. Negroes in the South learned long ago that their money was welcome in local department stores. Money can be liberating. It corrodes the cake of custom. It does talk. In the West Indies there is a saying, "Money whitens." Sociologists know that replacing the rule of status by the rule of contract loses something in warmth; it also gets rid of some of the bad fire of olden times.

Impersonality of market relations has another advantage, as was brought home to many "liberals" in the McCarthy era of American political life. Suppose it were efficient for the government to be the one big employer. Then if, for good or bad, a person becomes in bad odor with government, he is dropped from employment and is put on a black list. He really has no place to go then. The thought of such a dire fate must in the

---

of his agreement with Stigler and others who put considerable emphasis on antitrust action. [There appears to me to be a technical flaw in the view of Friedman and A. P. Lerner that regulated or publicly owned monopolies should always (as a matter of principle as well as pragmatic expediency) be permitted to have competition from free entrants.. The mathematics of the increasing-returns situation admits of no such theorem; it is simply false game theory and bilateral monopoly theory, which asserts that letting one more viable person in the game must lead to a "better" result in any of the conventional senses of better. To make the Scottish Airlines keep up unprofitable schedules and at the same time permit a free enterpriser to make a profit partially at the regulated lines' expense can easily result in dead-weight loss to society under the usual feasibility conditions. The crime of legally abolishing the Pony Express because it competed with the Post Office would have to be examined on all its complicated demerits.]

course of time discourage that freedom of expression of opinion that individualists most favor.[17]

Many of the people who were unjustly dropped by the federal government in that era were able to land jobs in small-scale private industry. I say small-scale industry, because large corporations are likely to be chary of hiring names that appear on anybody's black list. What about people who were justly dropped as security risks or as members of political organizations now deemed to be criminally subversive? Many of them also found jobs in the anonymity of industry.

Many conservative people, who think that such men should not remain in sensitive government work or in public employ at all, will still feel that they should not be hounded into starvation. Few want for this country the equivalent of Czarist Russia's Siberia or Stalin Russia's Siberia either. It is hard to tell on the Chicago Board of Trade the difference between the wheat produced by Republican or Democratic farmers, by teetotalers or drunkards, Theosophists or Logical Positivists. I must confess that this is a feature of a competitive system that I find attractive.

Still, I must not overstress this point. A mixed economy in a society where people are by custom *tolerant* of differences in opinion may provide greater personal freedom and security of expression than does a purer price economy where people are less tolerant. Thus, in Scandinavia and Great Britain civil servants have, in fact, not lost their jobs when parties with a new philosophy come into power. In 1953, the Eisenhower Administration "cleaned house" in many government departments for reasons unconnected with McCarthyism. In 1951, when the Tories came to power, they deliberately recruited Fabian socialists to the civil service! Business freedoms may be fewer in those countries, but an excommunist probably meets with more tolerance from employers there.

---

[17] F. A. Hayek, *The Road to Serfdom*, University of Chicago Press, Chicago, 1944, p. 119, aptly presents the following quotations from Lenin (1917) and Trotsky (1937):

> The whole of society will have become a single office and a single factory with equality of work and equality of pay.

> In a country where the sole employer is the State, opposition means death by slow starvation. The old principle: who does not work shall not eat, has been replaced by a new one: who does not obey shall not eat.

M. A. Adelman in Freeman, *op. cit.*, p. 295, says:

> . . . It has probably become clearer in the last ten years that the chief objection to socialism is not strictly economics but lies rather in its startling resemblance to the oldfashioned mining town where the one employer was also the landlord, the government, the school, etc., with the vital difference that there was a world outside the town which afforded means of escape for a few and, in time, of release for all.

See also the valuable words on this matter in Friedman, *op. cit.*, pp. 20–21.

This raises a larger question. Why should there be a perverse empirical relation between the degree to which public opinion is, in fact, tolerant and the degree to which it relies on free markets? In our history, the days of most rugged individualism —the Gilded Age and the 1920's—seem to have been the ages least tolerant of dissenting opinion.[18]

Fallacy of Freedom Algebra

I must raise some questions about the notion that absence of government means increase in "freedom." Is freedom simply a quantifiable magnitude, as much libertarian discussion seems to presume? Traffic lights coerce me and limit my freedom. Yet in the midst of a traffic jam on the unopen road, was I really "free" before there were lights? And has the algebraic total of freedom, for me or the representative motorist or the group as a whole, been increased or decreased by the introduction of well-engineered stop lights? Stop lights, you know, are also go lights.

Whatever may have been true on Turner's frontier, the modern city is crowded. Individualism and anarchy will lead to friction. We now have to coordinate and cooperate. Where cooperation is not fully forthcoming, we must introduce upon ourselves coercion. When we introduce the traffic light, we have, although the arch individualist may not like the new order, by cooperation and coercion created for ourselves greater freedom.

The principle of unbridled freedom has been abandoned; it is now just a question of haggling about the terms. On the one hand, few will deny that it is a bad thing for one man, or a few men, to impose their wills on the vast majority of mankind, particularly when that involves terrible cruelty and terrible inefficiency. Yet where does one draw the line? At a 51 per cent majority vote? Or, should there be no action taken that cannot command unanimous agreement—a position toward which such modern exponents of libertarian liberalism as Professor Milton Friedman are slowly evolving. Unanimous agreement? Well, virtually unanimous agreement, whatever that will come to mean.

The principle of unanimity is, of course, completely imprac-

[18] Years ago someone asked me, "Why is it that economists who are most libertarian in economic philosophy tend to be personally more intolerant than the average and less concerned with civil liberties and such matters?" I replied, "Is this true?" He said, "Look at the monolithic character of the three most libertarian departments of economics." I said, "The three departments most radical or anything else can hardly be expected to show average tolerance of differences." Our conversation broke off. However, in the last dozen years I have been alert to observe the attitudes and actions of economic libertarians in connection with nonmarket issues—teachers' oaths, passport squabbles, and the like. I am sorry to have to report that my friend

had a point (although there are one or two persons who are residuals from his regression).

tical. Aside from its practical inapplicability, the principle of unanimity is theoretically faulty. It leads to contradictory and intransitive decisions. By itself, it argues that just as society should not move from laissez-faire to planning because there will always be at least one objector, so society should never move from planning to freedom because there will always be at least one objector. Like standing friction, it sticks you where you are. It favors the status quo. And the status quo is certainly not to the liking of arch individualists. When you have painted yourself into a corner, what can you do? You can redefine the situation, and I predicted some years ago that there would come to be defined a privileged status quo, a set of natural rights involving individual freedoms, which alone requires unanimity before it can be departed from.[19]

At this point the logical game is up. The case for "complete freedom" has been begged, not deduced. So long as full disclosure is made, it is no crime to assume your ethical case. But will your product sell? Can you persuade others to accept your axiom, when it is in conflict with certain other desirable axioms?

Property and Human Rights

Closely related to ethical evaluation of business activity for its own sake are ethical attitudes towards the rights of property. Today, demagogues never tire of emphasizing the primacy of human over property rights; this is not an accident but rather a recognition that such sentiments evoke an increasingly resonant response from modern public opinion.

Today when we defend the rights of property, we often do so in the name of the *individual* rights of those who own property or hope one day to do so. The tides of modern politics pay little regard to the older view that property in all its prerequisites is a natural right and that whenever the democratic action of even $99\frac{44}{100}$ per cent of the electorate limits property rights in any degree, then an act of theft has taken place. Instead, the effective defense of property rights consists largely of specifying the inefficiencies that will result at the level of means and

---

[19] A friend of mine is a justly famous expert on law. He has participated in world conferences, here and behind the Iron Curtain, dealing with such weighty concepts as "the Rule of Law." Apparently, the Russians do not view the matter in quite his way. I am not sure I do. After listening to his view, an eminent judge asked him, "Was slavery in Virginia in 1859 contrary to your 'Rule of Law'?" My friend squirmed. Finally, he replied, "Yes, really. Because the law permitting slavery was essentially a *bad* law." I congratulated my friend on his good luck: how fortunate that he had happened to be born in just those few years of the globe's history when *the* Rule of Law (about equivalent to that approved by a conservative New-Deal type) happened to be in bloom. Libertarians like Hayek are on the same boat, but they want it to stop at a different port; Gladstone's age turns out to have been the nearest approach to *the* (I mean Hayek's) Rule of Law. F. A. Hayek, *op. cit.*, Chapter 6.

mechanisms from their impairment—the paralysis of risk taking, the effects upon saving, efforts and incentives; the certain or uncertain ruin that must follow wherever taxation exceeds 10 (or 90) per cent of national income.

All this may be true enough. But for some people it does not go far enough. It is a little like the saying: "Honesty is the best policy." Or, "The golden rule is good business." Beyond the level of expediency, there can be thought to be human property rights at the ethical level in the sense that the individual's property is to be taxed or affected by state action only in an orderly manner, within the framework of constitutional procedures and with "due process" being legally observed.

As a bulwark to historical property rights, this is not saying very much. To say that the electorate cannot arbitrarily do something to one millionaire without doing the same thing to another (essentially similar) millionaire provides little protection to the class of all millionaires, some of whom may even have amassed their millions at a time when it seemed reasonable *not* to anticipate policies of heavy income or capital taxation. Whether we approve or disapprove, we should face squarely the fact that neoclassical economic-welfare policies—which hold that after the ethically desirable distribution of income has been properly determined by democratic decision, a pricing system is to organize and allocate production in response to individuals' purchases—provide little protection to ancient property rights.

Personal Liberties and Rights

This makes it all the more important to study the question of the relation of property rights and market institutions to essential individual freedoms and liberties. These were enumerated by Lord Beveridge in his *Full Employment in a Free Society* as

. . . freedom of worship, speech, writing, study and teaching; freedom of assembly and association for political and other purposes, including the bringing about of a peaceful change of the governing authority; freedom of a choice of occupation; and freedom in the management of a personal income . . . including freedom to decide to spend now and save so as to have the power of spending later . . . it being recognized that none of these freedoms can be exercised irresponsibly. . . .

The list of essential liberties given above does not include liberty of a private citizen to own means of production and to employ other citizens in operating them at a wage. Whether private ownership of means of production to be operated by others is a good economic device or not, it must be judged *as a device*. (The italics are mine.) [20]

To Americans this British view is interesting, because the distinction is made clear-cut between (1) human individual civil liberties or freedoms and (2) ethical evaluations of property rights and of business activity for their own sakes. So-called diehard

[20] Norton, New York, 1945, pp. 21–23.

conservatives will not alone be shocked by the distinction. At the extreme left, violent exception will also be taken to the view that "political democracy" can exist in the absence of what is called "economic or industrial democracy." Both extremes seem to argue that the essential human freedoms are inseparable from the institutional framework under which production is carried on. But, of course, they believe this in diametrically opposite senses; the extreme conservatives at the ethical level link human freedoms with relatively unhampered free enterprise, whereas the extreme radicals proclaim that human freedoms are empty and meaningless in the absence of "industrial democracy" (in one or another of the many senses in which the last two words are used).

From the standpoint of pure logic, I believe that the two concepts are conceptually distinct at the purely ethical level of ends. Moreover, whatever its pragmatic wisdom, there appears to be nothing inherently illogical (whatever its wisdom) in the ethical belief that individual human liberties have an ethical primacy over the freedoms associated with property and commercial activity.

However, this brings us to a quite different, but possibly important, question: "Granted that human rights are to be accorded ethical primacy over property rights, is it not true that human rights can only flourish and be preserved in a society that organizes its economic activity on the basis of relatively free private enterprise?" Many economic libertarians strongly proclaim an affirmative answer to this question. Friedrich Hayek's *The Road to Serfdom* (1944) is an eloquent attempt to read this same empirical law in the tea leaves of history. Frank Knight and Milton Friedman have enunciated interesting views along the same line. It is ironical, but not incriminating, that this is a conservative's variant of the strong Marxian doctrine that economic relationships allegedly determine political relationships.

As stated, this is not at all a philosophical question. Nor is it very much a question of economics. It is primarily a political, sociological, and anthropological question. Basically, it is an empirical question of inductive extrapolation or forecasting rather than one of consistent logical deduction from universally true *a priori* premises. And unfortunately, the patterns of history have not been optimally designed to perform the controlled experiments that would enable us to make either certainty or probability inferences on the hypothesis in question.

It will be plain that I have little confidence in emphatic generalizations concerning the empirical linkage of human political rights with any one economic system. Evidence—as I understand this term—is not at hand to validate strong inferences; and such evidence as may exist has not, to my knowledge, been carefully brought together anywhere and sifted to bring out the degree of our knowledge and lack of knowledge. In a world where economists cannot even accurately predict national income one year ahead or identify the demand elasticity for a single commodity, I find it somewhat *simpliste* to think that economists can arrive at confident answers to an infinitely more complex and important question, resting primarily on noneconomic data. Certainly the degree of confidence and emphasis with which judgments on this matter are proclaimed seems to weaken rather than strengthen one's trust in their validity. I may add as a digression that I greatly resent the prevailing tendency to regard the broad questions of social development as being too important to be left to mere judicious scholarly investigation and to handle them instead by the transcendental poetic talents of a Toynbee or Spengler.

The Limited Nature of Individual Political Liberties

The above discussion has left civil liberties almost completely emasculated of intrinsic economic content. The doctrine "a man's home is his castle" is to apply to rented as well as self-owned homes. But some of the methods and tools used to analyze theoretical economic concepts do have an application in this field of political theory.

For one thing, basic civil rights of the individual are shot through with "external effects." The ideal frontier community never existed in which freedom for the individual meant that he could live on his acre of land exactly as he wished, leaving others to live as they chose on theirs. Certainly today, the right of one man to speak what he wishes conditions the rights of another man to listen to what he wishes. The right of one man to "fair" consideration for a job has implications for the right of another man to "discriminate" as to whom he shall hire. The right of one group to preach nondemocratic principles has effects on the future existence of democracy itself. In the pursuit of happiness, we all interact.

Once we have recognized these external aspects of individual rights, we must recognize that precious little is being said in the familiar qualification that people are free so long as they do not inhibit the freedom of others. Any degree of limitation on freedoms can be rationalized by this formula.

Dogmatic absolutes being thus ruled out, democratic society is left in the position of pragmatically attempting to choose among partial evils so as to preserve as much as possible of human liberties and freedoms. Nor is it only in time of war and siege that it may become necessary to sacrifice some aspects of democratic freedoms in order to prevent losing more important aspects. Those who abandon the unproved faith that democratic individualism *is by its nature viable under all conditions* must compromise with evil at every turn. And it is not at all unlikely that they will end up killing, in the name of its salvation, much of what they wish to save, perhaps in these "scorched earth" operations killing even more than realistically had to be sacrificed.

Consider the little that is known concerning the interrelations between human rights and the organization of economic activity in the U.S.A. (1870, 1920, 1964) and the U.K.; the German Empire, the Weimar Republic, and the Third Reich; Norway, Sweden, Denmark, Australia, and New Zealand; pre– and post–1917 Russia; Italy, Czechoslovakia, and the Balkans—to say nothing of China, Arabia, Fiji, and non-Western cultures. Then ask ourselves what simple truths can be confidently inferred.

For a quite different appraisal of these same matters consider, in the cited Friedman book, the first chapter, "The Relation Between Economic Freedom and Political Freedom." A few quotations cannot do him justice but can give the flavor of the divergence of his view from mine.

The citizen of Great Britain, who after World War II was not permitted to spend his vacation in the United States because of exchange control, was being deprived of an *essential* freedom no less than the citizen of the United States, who was denied the opportunity to spend his vacation in Russia because of his political views. . . .

The citizen of the United States who is compelled by law to devote something like 10 per cent of *his* income to the purchase of a particular kind of retirement contract, administered by the government, is being deprived of a corresponding part of his personal freedom (page 8). (My italics.)

So is the man who would like to exchange some of his goods with, say, a Swiss for a watch but is prevented from doing so by a quota. . . .

Historical evidence speaks with a single voice on the relation between political freedom and a free market. I know of no example in time or place of a society that has been marked by a large measure of political freedom, and that has not also used something comparable to a free market to organize the bulk of economic activity (page 9).

Economists love diagrams. Figures 1 and 2 plot economic freedom (as if it were measurable as a scalar) on the horizontal axes, and political freedom (as if that too were separately measurable as a scalar) on the vertical axes. What I regard as the grossly oversimplified views are shown in Figure 1. Social reform (moving "west") inevitably plunges society ("southward") into serfdom. Hayek does not tell us what his predicted delay period is, but since he formulated his thesis as early as 1938 (and using the simplifying assumption that we are not unknowingly now in serfdom), the mechanism must involve lags of more than a quarter of a century. Friedman also believes in strong positive correlation between Y and X but indicates that economic freedom is a necessary but not a sufficient condition for political freedom. (Sidney and Beatrice Webb, particularly in their final honeymoon stage of infatuation with Stalin's Russia, would relabel the axes as X = Economic Democracy—whatever that means—and Y = Political Democracy. The U.K. and U.S.A. they would place up in the northwest and, except *in extremis* of infatuation, would put Russia in the southeast. As Fabians, they would maneuver the U.K. eastward.)

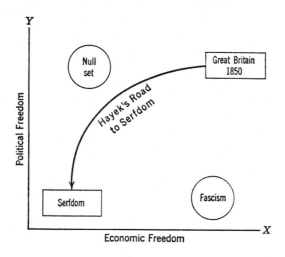

Figure 1

Figure 2 represents the more relevant question. Will a little more of the welfare state push the U.S.A. westward and necessarily southward? For years libertarians have been challenged to explain what appears to most observers to be the greater political freedoms and tolerances that prevail in Scandinavia than in America. In Norway, a professor may be a communist; a communist may sit by right on the Board of the Central Bank or as an Alternate Board member. The B.B.C. and Scandinavian airwaves seem, if anything, more catholic in their welcome to speakers of divergent views than was true in McCarthy America or is true now. In 1939, I was told that none of this would last; active government economic policy had to result in loss of civil liberties and personal freedoms. One still waits. Figure 2 does not represent my informed evaluation of the facts but merely poses the problem provocatively.

These are subjects that need serious empirical study, not strong *a priori* utterances or casual travelers' anecdotes.

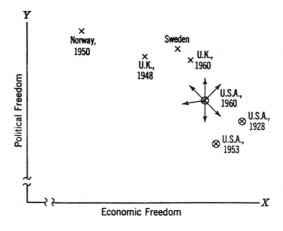

Figure 2

THE FUNCTION OF BUSINESS

James Kuhn

BUSINESSMEN FREQUENTLY COMPLAIN that Americans do not understand the profit system. Richard Gerstenberg of General Motors, for example, wrote in the New York Times that citizens need to know "what makes a profitable business tick, and most important, why it is to [their] advantage to have business profitable." Z. D. Bonner, writing in the same paper, warns that "those in business must do their level best to explain and justify the American system to their employees and the public."

Such business leaders assume something difficult to believe: that after years of working in and for a business corporation, employees do not comprehend the way they and their managers conduct business affairs, and that after lifetimes of buying and using business products, consumers do not understand the role of profits. More reasonably, one may suggest that the assumption is invalid: it is likely that business leaders do not realize how *much* Americans know about the conduct of business firms and the purposes of businessmen.

The critics of business who seek government regulation, consumer protection, conservation of resources and landscape, and equal employment opportunities are not simply naive about, or even antagonistic toward, business and its profit making. They are attempting to use government creatively—as business has long used government in gaining subsidies, contracts, special-interest legislation, favorable court rulings, and protected markets. Spokesmen for business justify such government favors as bolstering free enterprise in its striving to make profits; they loudly proclaim, and unthinkingly assert, that the basic function of business, after all, is to make a profit.

Two hundred years ago Adam Smith asserted what should be a more basic tenet of a competitive private-enterprise system: "Consumption is the sole end and purpose of production; and the interest of the producer ought to be attended to, only so far as it may be necessary for promoting that of the consumer." Acceptance of Smith's doctrine implies that the *social* function of business is not to make profits, but rather to serve consumers. Opportunities for profit making are subordinate to, and should follow from, serving consumers effectively and efficiently.

By focusing on profits, businessmen have neglected the vision and purpose of their grander and more defensible social function. That neglect has damaged their reputation and standing in the community, persuading many persons that the interests of consumers and the nation are not served by profit-making organizations.

Such a belief surely has contributed to the growing willingness of the nation to seek delivery of services on a nonprofit basis. Is it coincidental that the fastest-growing sectors of the economy over the last decade and a half have been those that produce for no profit—local government, education, and health?

Alfred North Whitehead once wrote, "A great society is one where men of business think greatly of their functions." Whitehead both challenges and judges businessmen. If they believe their only function is to make profits, they demean themselves and denigrate our society; if as a people we encourage businessmen to the high function—the necessary and essential function—of serving society to earn a profit, we call upon them to value themselves and their work for what they can do to improve the lot and ameliorate the burdens of those with whom they live.

Businessmen cannot think greatly of their social or private functions so long as they misperceive them as no more than the making of profits through any means not beyond the law. Businessmen know—as too often customers know from experience—that profits can be won by *not* serving, as well as by serving. Import quotas, special tax allowances, price fixing, built-in obsolescence, useless additives, and a multitude of other ways to increase profits by not serving consumers are too well documented to ignore.

Exhortation that profits must be protected are heard, but not heeded, by the public. Americans pay little attention to the pleas, not because they reject free enterprise, but because the pleading is too self-serving. American consumers do not decry profits for services rendered. But they must be convinced that service indeed is being, and has been, rendered. ■

James Kuhn is a professor in Columbia University's graduate school of business.

James Kuhn, "The Function of Business." *Business and Society Review*, Winter 1974–75, p. 101. Reprinted from *Business and Society Review*, Winter 1974–75, Vol. 12, Copyright 1975, Warren, Gorham and Lamont, Inc., 210 South Street, Boston, Mass. All rights reserved.

HEALTH CARE
AND THE UNITED STATES ECONOMIC SYSTEM
An Essay in Abnormal Physiology

VICTOR R. FUCHS

Health care affects and is affected by the economic system in so many ways as to preclude any attempt at complete enumeration or description. The objective of this paper is more modest. I shall assume that the reader is reasonably familiar with health care, its institutions, technology and personnel, but is less familiar with an "economic system" that is used by economists to describe and analyze economic behavior. Therefore, major emphasis will be given to indicating the place of health care in this system and showing how related economic concepts can contribute to an understanding of problems of health care in the United States. I shall also attempt to indicate some of the limitations of economics in dealing with such a complex area of human activity and concern.

INTRODUCTION
Definitions

Health care can be defined as those activities that are undertaken with the objective of restoring, preserving or enhancing the physical and mental well-being of people. These activities may be aimed at the relief of pain, the removal of disabilities, the restoration of functions, the prevention of illness and accidents or the postponement of death. Some health care is produced within the "household;" e.g., the triage, first-aid and nursing services rendered to children by parents. Some is bought and sold in the "market"; e.g., physicians' services, hospital services. Most health care is applied to identifiable individuals but some may be aimed at a population; e.g., fluoridation of a water supply.

The *economic system* consists of the network of institutions, laws and rules created by society to answer the universal economic questions: (a) What goods and services shall be produced? (b) How shall they be produced? and (c) For whom shall they be produced?[1] Every society needs an economic system because *resources* (natural, human and manmade) are scarce relative to human wants. The resources have alternative uses and there is a multiplicity of competing wants. Thus, decisions must be made regarding the use of these resources in production and the distribution of the resulting output among the members of society.

Two Fallacies

Before turning to several important issues concerning health care in relation to the economic system it will be useful to dispose of two fallacies that have frequently obstructed clear thinking in this area.

1. Resources are no longer scarce. Some people seem to be so inspired, terrified or confused by automation and other technologic advances as to proclaim the end of scarcity. A decade ago it was not unusual to find writers prophesying that in ten years no one would have to work because machines would turn out all the goods and services needed. The falsity of such predictions becomes more apparent each year. That inefficiency and waste exist in the economy cannot be denied. That some resources are underutilized is clear every time the unemployment figures are announced. That the resources devoted to war could be used to satisfy other wants is self-evident. But the fundamental fact remains that even if all these imperfections were eliminated total output would still fall far short of the amount people would like to have. Resources would still be scarce in the sense that choices would have to be made. An economic system would still be needed. Not only is this true now, but it will continue to be true in the foreseeable future. Some advances in technology make it possible to carry out current activities with fewer resources (e.g., automated laboratories), but others open up new demands (e.g., for renal dialysis or organ transplants) that put further strains on resources. Moreover, time, the ultimate scarce resource, becomes more valuable the more productive we become.[2,3]

2. Health is the most important goal. Some of those in the health field recognize that we cannot satisfy all wants, but they seem to believe that health is more important than all other goals and therefore questions of scarcity and allocation are not applicable in this area. It requires only a casual study of human behavior to reveal the fallacy of this position. Every day in manifold ways people make choices that affect health and it is clear that they frequently place a higher value on satisfying other wants; e.g., smoking, overeating, careless driving, failure to take medicine.

Criteria for an Economic System in Relation to Health Care

What is it that we want the economic system to do with respect to health care? Given the scarcity of resources and the existence of competing goals we want a system that will result in:

1. An optimum amount of resources devoted to health care;
2. These resources being combined in an optimal way;
3. An optimal distribution of health care;
4. An optimal allocation of resources between current provision of health care and investment for future health care through research, education and so forth.

The general rule for reaching such optima is "equality at the margin." For instance, the first criterion would be met if the last dollar's worth of resources devoted to health care increased human satisfaction by exactly the same amount as the last dollar's worth devoted to other goals.

The contrast between this view of a social optimum and the notion of "optimal care" as used in the health field can be appreciated with the aid of Figure 1. The relation between health and health care inputs can usually be described by a curve that may rise at an increasing rate at first, but then rises at a decreasing rate and eventually levels off or declines.[4] "Optimal care" in medicine would usually be defined as the point where no further increment in health is possible; i.e.,

FIGURE I. DETERMINATION OF OPTIMUM LEVEL OF HEALTH CARE UTILIZATION

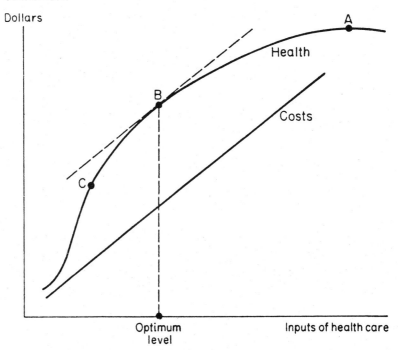

point A.[5] The social optimum, however, requires that inputs of resources not exceed the point where the value of an additional increment to health is exactly equal to the cost of the inputs required to obtain that increment (point B). It should be noted that point C, where the *ratio* of benefits to costs is at a maximum, is not the optimal point because additional inputs still add more to benefits than to costs. One of the problems with current health care policy is that it frequently fluctuates between trying to drive utilization to A, and then, in frenzied attempts to contain costs, cuts back some programs to point C or below.

Types of Economic Systems

Economists have identified three "pure types" of economic systems—traditional, centrally directed and market price. Every actual economy is a blend of types, but their relative importance can and does vary greatly. Most primitive and feudal societies rely heavily upon a traditional system; the process of decision-making is embedded in the total culture—its customs, traditions and religious rituals. In some ancient empires (Egypt, Babylonia) central direction played a major role. The basic decisions were made by one man or a small group of men who controlled the power apparatus of the society and were in a position to enforce their decisions concerning the allocation of resources and the distribution of output. This system has also been dominant in the Soviet Union since 1928 and in many other countries since World War II. The United States, Canada and most countries of Western Europe have relied heavily on a market system for the past century or two. Thus a discussion of health care and the United States economy requires a close look at the working of a market system. An additional reason for concentrating on this third type is for its normative value. Under certain specified conditions the results produced by the theoretical market system set a standard against which the performance of any real economy can be evaluated.[6]

The Elementary Model

The elementary model of a market system consists of a collection of decision-making units called *households* and another collection called *firms*. The households own all the productive resources in the society. They make these resources available to firms who transform them into goods and services, which are then distributed back to the households. The flow of resources and of goods and services is facilitated by a counterflow of money (see Figure 2).[7] This is called a market system because the exchanges of resources and of goods and services for money take place in markets where *prices* and *quantities* are determined.

These prices are the signals or controls that trigger changes in behavior as required by changes in technology or preferences. The market system is sometimes referred to as the "price" system.

In the markets for resources the households are the *suppliers* and the firms provide the *demand*. In the markets for goods and services the firms are the suppliers and the households are the source of demand. In each market the interaction between demand and supply determines the quantities and prices of the various resources and goods and services (see Figure 3).

The income of each household depends upon the quantity and quality of resources available to it (including time) and their prices; the amount of income determines its share of the total flow of goods and services. The household is assumed to spend its income (and time) in such a way as to maximize *utility* (i.e., satisfaction). It does this by following the principle of "equality at the margin;" i.e., it adjusts its purchases so that marginal utility (the satisfaction added by the last unit purchased) of each commodity is proportional to its price.

It is assumed that firms attempt to maximize *profits* (the difference between what they must pay the households for the use of resources and what they get from them for the goods and services they produce). To maximize profits they too must follow the equality at the margin rule, adjusting their use of different types of resources so that the marginal products (the addition to output obtained from one additional unit of input) are proportional to price.

If the markets are perfectly competitive and if certain other conditions are met, it can be shown that a market system produces an optimum allocation of resources, given the distribution of resources among households and given their "tastes" or preferences. The United States economy departs in many re-

FIGURE 2. ELEMENTARY MODEL OF A MARKET SYSTEM

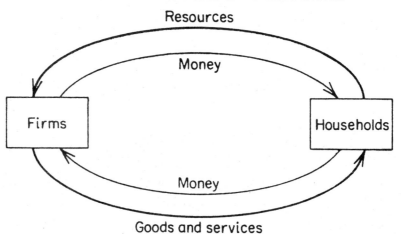

FIGURE 3. A TYPICAL MARKET

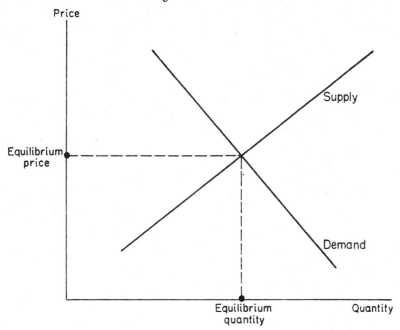

spects from the abstract perfectly competitive market system; this is particularly noticeable in the health care sector. The main body of this paper is devoted to a discussion of these departures and the problems they pose for health care policy.

IMPERFECTLY COMPETITIVE MARKETS

The essence of a competitive market is (1) that there are many well-informed buyers and sellers no one of whom is large enough to influence price; (2) that the buyers and sellers act independently (i.e., no collusion) ; and (3) that there is free entry for other buyers and sellers not currently in the market. Most health care markets depart substantially from competitive conditions, sometimes inevitably, and sometimes as the result of deliberate public or private policy. A discussion of some of the principal problems follows.

Fewness of Sellers

In most towns and even moderate size cities the market is too small to support enough hospitals or enough practitioners in each speciality to fulfill the requirements of a workably competitive market. For instance, most students of hospital costs believe there are significant economies of scale in general hospitals up to a size of 200 or 300 beds, and some believe that economies are to be realized in even larger hospitals. Assuming a ratio of four beds per 1,000 population, a city of 60,000 could support just one 240 bed hospital. Thus, it would be extremely uneconomical to require numerous competitive hospitals except in large, densely populated markets. These constraints are even more significant when specialty care is considered. It is doubtful that even a population of one million would justify enough independent maternity, open heart surgery and transplant services and the like to approximate competitive conditions.[s]

In such a condition of "natural monopoly" the traditional United States response has been to introduce public utility regulation (e.g., electricity, telephone, transportation). The results, however, have not always been satisfactory, partly because the regulators often tend to serve the regulated rather than the public and partly because it is inherently difficult to set standards of performance without competitive yardsticks. Many other countries rely on government ownership and control, but the United States experience with government hospitals has not, on balance, been favorable. Another possible solution is the development of what J. K. Galbraith has termed "countervailing power" and what the economics textbooks describe as bilateral monopoly. If, for instance, in a one-hospital town all the consumers were organized into a single body for purposes of bargaining with the hospital, at least some of the disadvantages of monopoly would be lessened.

The typical "solution" in the hospital field has been to emphasize the "nonprofit" character of the hospitals and to assume that therefore the hospital will not abuse its monopoly power. Two criticisms of this "solution" are (a) the absence of a profit incentive may lead to waste, inefficiency and unnecessary duplication, and (2) the hospitals may be run for the benefit of the physicians.[9]

Cooperation (Collusion) Among Sellers

Even when numerous sellers of the same health service are in the same market there may be significant advantages to society if they do not maintain a completely arms-length competitive posture vis-à-vis one another. The free exchange of information, cooperative efforts to meet crisis situations and reciprocal backup arrangements may help to reduce costs and increase patient satisfaction. Unfortunately, the intimacy and trust developed through such activities may spill over in less desirable directions such as price fixing, exclusion of would-be rivals and other restrictions on competition. For 200 years economists have been impressed with the wisdom of Adam Smith's observation that "people of the same trade seldom meet together, even for merriment and diversion, but the conversation ends in a conspiracy against the public, or in some contrivance to raise prices." Pathologists have been found guilty of price-fixing, and price discrimination by physicians is not uncommon.

The latter practice, which physicians view benevolently as a way of reducing inequality of access to medical care, is viewed by some economists as evidence of the use of monopoly power to maximize profits.[10]

Restrictions on Entry

Probably the most obvious and most deliberate interference with competition in the market for physicians' services is the barrier to entry imposed by compulsory licensure. The case for licensure presumably rests on the proposition that the consumer is a poor judge of the quality of medical care and therefore needs guidance concerning the qualifications of those proposing to sell such care. Assuming this to be true the need for guidance could be met by voluntary *certification*, rather than compulsory licensure. Indeed, the need could probably be better met through certification because there could be several grades or categories and periodic recertification would be more practicable (and less threatening) than periodic relicensure. Under a certification system patients would be free to choose the level of expertise that they wanted, including uncertified practitioners.

The principal objections that could be raised against such a system are that some patients might receive bad treatment at the hands of uncertified practitioners, and that it might result in an expansion of unnecessary care. The obvious advantages of such a system are greater availability of care and lower prices.

FIGURE 4. EXCESS DEMAND

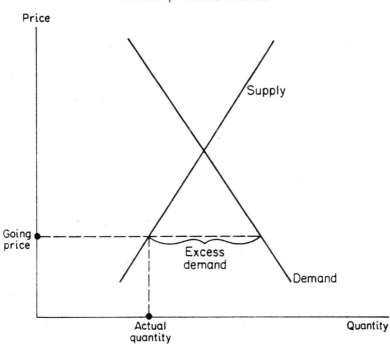

101

For certain health care needs, practitioners with lesser qualifications than present physicians have would clearly be adequate. The existing system results in some persons receiving no care, or being treated by persons without any medical training (e.g., family members, neighbors, friends).

Another example of entry restrictions is the system of limiting hospital privileges to certain physicians. This has been justified in terms of the desire to insure quality of care (in the institution) and as a way of obtaining free services from the physicians. However, it can also be viewed in an economic context as a way of limiting competition.

In general, the codes of professional ethics that physicians have evolved undoubtedly serve many useful social purposes. But it is well to recall Kenneth Arrow's observation that "codes of professional ethics, which arise out of the principal-agent relation and afford protection to the principals, can serve also as a cloak for monopoly by the agents."[11]

Disequilibrium

One disturbing characteristic of some health care markets is the failure of price to reach an equilibrium level (the level where the quantity demanded and the quantity supplied are equal). For instance, the market for house calls seems to be characterized by excess demand (see Figure 4). The "going price," about $20 per visit, is not high enough to bring supply and demand into balance. The quantity (number of house

FIGURE 5. EXCESS SUPPLY

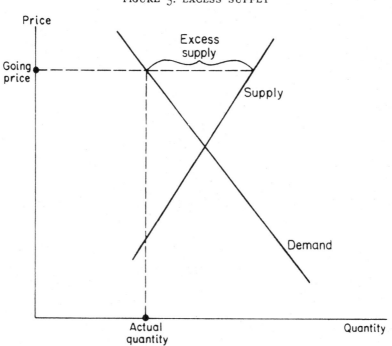

calls) that patients are willing and able to pay for at that price is much greater than the quantity physicians are willing to supply. Some observers, notably Martin Feldstein,[12] believe that the market for physicians' services in general is characterized by excess demand.

The market for general surgery, however, can best be described as an example of excess supply (see Figure 5).[13] At the going price for most general surgical procedures, $300 for a herniorrhaphy, the quantity that surgeons are willing and able to do is much greater than the quantity demanded. A condition of excess supply is also probably present for many types of specialty surgery (ophthalmology, gynecology).

The persistence of a disequilibrium price is a clear indication that the market departs substantially from the competitive norm. In the case of excess demand, physicians are apparently reluctant to let the price of house calls rise to their equilibrium level; they introduce a form of rationing instead. This may yield certain psychic satisfactions in lieu of the higher income that is clearly possible. In the excess supply example, the price fails to fall either because the individual surgeon does not think it would be to his advantage to cut price or because surgeons have collectively reached this decision. A contributing factor is the option that most surgeons have of using their nonsurgical time for general practice or other income-producing activities.

The alleged shortage of nurses indicates another potentially troublesome health care market. If what is meant by "shortage" is that it would be nice to have more nurses, no analytical problem arises and the point is trivial. In that sense there is a shortage of every type of good or service. If, however, the allegation refers to a shortage in the sense shown in Figure 4 (i.e., an excess demand for nurses), the failure of nurses' salaries to rise to their equilibrium level must be explained. Some investigators[14,15] claim that it is monopsonistic behavior on the part of hospitals that keeps nurses' salaries from rising to the point where supply and demand would be equal.

Costs of Information

The elementary competitive model assumes that all information relevant to decision-making is known by the households and firms—prices, production possibilities, utility to be derived from different commodities. In the real world, of course, such information may be difficult or even impossible to obtain. High information costs are characteristic of many health care markets; frequently the only way a person can know whether he needs to see a physician is to see a physician. The incorporation of information costs into economic analysis is relatively recent,[16] and the theory is far from complete. Many health care markets function poorly because of imperfect information but there is considerable disagreement as to how to make them function better. One point might have general validity. Where the costs of information are increased as a result of public or private policy, reversal of that policy would probably be desirable. For instance, restrictions on the right of physicians to advertise and on the right of pharmacies to advertise prices of prescription drugs ought to be reexamined in the light of the consumer's need to know more about physicians and drugs to make intelligent choices. A study of variations in restrictions on advertising by optometrists and opticians found that prices were substantially lower in states that permitted advertising.[17]

EXTERNALITIES

An externality exists when the actions taken by an individual household or firm will impose costs or confer benefits on other households or firms, and where no feasible way exists of arranging direct compensation for these costs or benefits. The presence of externalities indicates that the individual household or firm, in attempting to maximize its own utility or profit, will not make socially optimal decisions.[18] A classic example of an externality is the costs of air pollution imposed on others by the smoke emanating from a factory. Another classic example is the benefit to society that results when an individual decides to be vaccinated or treated for a communicable disease.

One way to deal with externalities is for the state to prohibit or require certain actions. Another is to attempt to modify the prices facing individual firms or households (through taxes or subsidies) so that the price properly reflects the social costs or benefits. In principle, use of the price mechanism will permit a much closer approximation to a social optimum, but practical difficulties may preclude the price approach in some situations.

Externalities are very important to health care in the broadest sense of the term. Consider, for instance, the effects of automobiles on health. The decisions of individual households involving the purchase and use of an automobile, the speed and manner of driving, the amount of maintenance and repair and even the choice of gasoline have potentially important implications for the health of others, but these implications are not reflected in the prices facing the household. Similar problems arise in connection with many other consumption or production activities that create environmental health hazards.

In seeking to reduce such hazards a few central points should be kept in mind. First, costs (resources used or wants unsatisfied) are usually associated with the reduction of hazards, and these costs frequently increase at an accelerating rate, the greater the reduction desired. It follows, therefore, that the social goal should rarely be the complete elimination of the hazard, but rather its reduction to the point where the value of a further reduction is less than the cost of achieving it. A major problem for health care policy is to identify these externalities, estimate their effects and impose appropriate taxes or subsidies so that individual households and firms, in seeking to maximize their own utility or profits, will make socially appropriate decisions.

Medical research is a good example of an activity with large external benefits, and, therefore, in the absence of specific public policy, too little will be undertaken. One solution is to permit the discoverer of new knowledge to appropriate the benefits (e.g., through patent protection), but with regard to much health research this solution will frequently not be feasible or acceptable. The alternative is for the government to subsidize research. It has done this to a considerable degree; the question is how much health research is socially desirable? The answer, in principle, is the same as for any other decision regarding the use of scarce resources—the optimum level of research is reached when the incremental value of the prospective benefits is equal to the incremental cost. The more basic the research the more likely it is to give rise to external benefits, but the more difficult it is to estimate their value or incidence.

In contrast to environmental programs and medical research, medical care today frequently does not involve significant external benefits. For instance, the benefits of most surgery accrue primarily to the patient and his family. This is equally true for treatment of most major diseases such as heart disease and cancer.[19] The best known examples of externalities arising from medical care involve the prevention of and treatment for communicable diseases. Another potentially important source of externalities is the treatment of mental illness, but lack of knowledge concerning causes or cures makes it difficult to reach firm policy conclusions in this area.

One important application of the externality idea is with respect to the problem of inequality of access to care. A frequent criticism of the market system is that it results in an unequal and "unfair" distribution of income.[20] Households that are poorly endowed with resources will earn relatively little and will command only a small share of the nation's output.

Many people would like to see a reduction of inequality, either in general or with respect to a particular commodity (medical care). To the extent that they are prepared to back their demand for less inequality through voluntary redistribution (philanthropy), no modification of the elementary model is required. We simply note that some households derive utility from giving money to others or from knowing that other households are receiving medical care. They are, therefore, willing to devote a part of their income (or part of their time) for that purpose. The purchase of a good or service for someone else is no different analytically from the purchase of a good or service for one's own household.

The externality problem arises because a philanthropic act by one household confers benefits on all other households that derive utility from observing a decrease in inequality. If each potential philanthropist considers only the psychic benefits *he* derives from reducing inequality, the total volume of philanthropy will be less than warranted by the collective desires of the group.[21]

One solution is compulsory redistribution. Society, working through government, may decide that the distribution of income resulting from the market system is inequitable or otherwise unsatisfactory and may seek to change it through taxation. This requires only a slight modification of the elementary model. The simplest way to do this is to take money away from some households and give it to others. Each household is then free to allocate its income as it pleases.

For any given amount of redistribution the utility of households is presumably maximized by a general tax on the income of some households and grants of income to others rather than by taxing particular forms of spending or by subsidizing particular types of consumption. Mathematical proofs of this proposition are available and its plausibility is obvious. If a household is offered a choice of either $100 or $100 worth of health care, it will prefer the former because it can use the additional income to buy more health care (if that is what it wants), but usually utility will be maximized by increasing consumption of many other commodities as well. Similarly, if a household is offered a choice between giving up $100 and giving up $100 worth of health care, its utility will be diminished less by the general tax on income.

Despite the obvious logic of the foregoing many nonpoor seem more inclined toward a reduction in inequality in the consumption of particular commodities (medical care is a conspicuous example) than toward a general redistribution of income.[22] Two reasons may explain this behavior. First, the nonpoor may believe that significant externalities are associated with medical care (in addition to the psychic benefits of observing a reduction in inequality) that are not associated with other commodities. The earlier discussion indicated some grounds for skepticism concerning this belief.[23] A second reason may be that the nonpoor think they know better what will maximize the utility of the poor than do the poor themselves.

A special aspect of the problem arises when the emphasis is

put on reducing inequality of access to medical care *per se* rather than raising the consumption of medical care by the poor. This goal may require rationing the amount available to the nonpoor as well as subsidizing the poor. One economist has argued that the British approach to health care through a national health service can best be understood in these terms.[24]

Compulsory Insurance

At the extreme, the demand for reductions in inequality takes the form of an assertion that "health care is a right;" that if someone needs health care society has an obligation to provide it. To the extent that society honors that obligation, the incentive for households to provide for their own health care (as through voluntary insurance) is diminished. Those without insurance and especially those individuals who prior to their illness could have afforded the normal premium, become, in effect, "freeloaders" on the rest of society.

If this behavior is widespread, the only solutions are to make insurance compulsory or to modify the ethical imperative. Thus far the United States has opted for a little of each. Insurance is virtually compulsory for many through their employment contract; on the other hand, free care is made less attractive by means tests, long waiting lines, unpleasant surroundings and similar inconveniences.

Another argument advanced in favor of compulsory insurance is that it overcomes the problem of adverse selection. If insurance is completely voluntary it may be impractical to adjust each household's premium to its expected utilization. To the extent that uniform premiums are charged, however, households with lower than average expected utilization have an incentive to drop out and this process can continue until the plan collapses.

It seems likely that the United States will move further in the direction of compulsory insurance, but this development is likely to create new problems even as it solves others. It increases the incentive to reduce health care in the home and throws more of the burden on collectively provided care. If the money price of market-provided care goes to zero, people will tend to use more than the amount they would like to use if they were free to shift resources to satisfy other wants.

SOME LIMITATIONS OF THE MODEL

The "Taste" for Health

It is becoming increasingly evident that many health problems are related to individual behavior. In the absence of dramatic breakthroughs in medical science the greatest potential for improving health is through changes in what people do and do not do to and for themselves. Household decisions concerning diet, exercise, smoking, drinking, work and recreation are of critical importance.

It is useful to distinguish between two different classes of decisions. The first consists of those that affect health, but without the decision maker's awareness of these effects. In such instances, public policies are needed to increase information. The question of how much of this activity can be justified can be answered (in principle) along the familiar lines of weighing incremental costs and benefits.

A more difficult problem is posed by those decisions that are made with full information available, and that, according to economists, reflect the household's "tastes." Tastes is a catchall term given by economists to the underlying preference patterns that determine demand at any given structure of income and prices. The overeater, the heavy smoker, the steady drinker are all presumably maximizing their utility, given their tastes. They may be knowingly shortening their lives. Should it be an object of public policy to try to change their tastes—to try to increase people's tastes for health? Economics can provide very little guidance in this area because economists have no way, even in principle, of saying what has happened to utility once tastes have changed. Economists are not, of course, alone in this dilemma. None of the other social sciences has a well-developed theory of preference formation or the capacity to make judgments about the relative merits of different social goals.

The issues involved are extremely complex. Tastes are not acquired at birth or formed in a vacuum. It seems that economists should make an effort to determine how the working of the economic system itself influences tastes. They should study the impact of advertising and other sales efforts on demand, and try to determine whether taxation or subsidies of such efforts and counter efforts are justified. Tastes are also undoubtedly influenced by the information and entertainment media, by the schools, by religious institutions and by other organizations that are either tax supported, subsidized through tax exemptions or regulated by government to some degree.

Another way of thinking about this problem has been proposed by Gary Becker and Robert Michael.[25] In their approach, all households have the same basic wants or "tastes." They try to satisfy these basic wants by producing "commodities" with the aid of purchased goods and services plus inputs of their own time. Households differ greatly in their ability to produce different "commodities" and these differences explain much of the observed differences in purchases of goods and services in the market.

This approach has been developed and applied to health by Michael Grossman.[26] In his model it is the household, not the physician or the hospital, that produces health. Health care and other goods and services (food, shelter) are used in the production of health and some goods (e.g., cigarettes) may have negative effects.

If one pursues this approach, it could be a legitimate aim of public policy to help households become more efficient producers of health.[27] The chief ways of doing this would be through health education and by providing more information about the health care that is purchased in the market. It is of some interest to note that the United States government currently assumes more responsibility for informing consumers about the quality of steaks they buy than about the quality of hospitals or physicians they use.

Behavior Within Households and Firms

A significant shortcoming of the elementary model in analyzing health care is its treatment of the firm and the household as the basic elements of analysis. In recent years some economists have directed their attention to decision-making within the firm[28-30] and within the household.[2, 31]

Attention to decision-making and allocation within the firm is particularly important if we are to try to understand one of the major institutions in health care, the nonprofit, voluntary hospital. It is relatively easy to identify several significant interest groups within the hospital—the board of directors, the management, the full-time medical staff, the attending staff—but it is more difficult to weigh their impact to formulate a predictive theory of hospital behavior. When the goals of the various interest groups are similar, the simple theory of the profit-maximizing firm may be adequate, but when they conflict, (e.g., the selection of cases for admission) such a theory is obviously incomplete.

Decision-making and allocation within the household also pose problems that have special relevance to health care. The quantity and quality of health care provided to children by parents differ greatly among households, even among households with equal incomes. The ability of parents to "produce" health for themselves and for their children seems to vary considerably. Society feels an obligation to protect the health rights of minors, but has found this difficult to do. The health care provided elderly parents by their children also varies greatly. The decline of family ties tends to shift some production of health care from households to firms, and part of the observed rising cost of health care in recent decades is undoubtedly attributable to such a shift; e.g., the growth of nursing homes.

109

This paper has discussed health care in relation to the economic system. The conference, however, is primarily concerned with technologic change, so it is appropriate to conclude with an attempt to relate the preceding discussion to technology.

Certainly the most important point to be made is that the basic economic principles concerning resource allocation and utility maximization apply in a world of technologic change as well as in a static one. Neither blanket endorsement nor condemnation of technology is rational; every change in technology involves costs and benefits and wise social policy depends upon an accurate assessment of their relative magnitudes.

There is a widespread belief that the health care sector harbors many wonderful technologic changes that have not been diffused widely and rapidly enough. An opposing view has been advanced by Richard Nelson of Yale, one of the nation's leading students of the economics of technologic change. He has written, "In both defense and health there has been a lot of R and D, and technical change has been extremely rapid; but it also has been extremely expensive and poorly screened . . . In health one has the strong impression that one of the reasons for rising health costs has been the proclivity of doctors and hospitals to adopt almost any plausible new thing—drugs, surgical methods, equipment—that increases capability in any dimension (and some for which even that isn't clear) without regard to cost."[32]

Nelson's view has considerable validity. The tendency toward rapid and indiscriminate adoption of innovations in the medical care field can be attributed in part to efforts of suppliers of the innovation, especially drug companies. Possibly the most important reason is the technologic imperative that influences medical choices.[33] This is instilled in physicians by their training, and reinforced by present systems of financing health care. It produces the attitude that if something can be done it should be done. Most medical decision-makers, be they physicians or hospital administrators, are not trained to weigh marginal benefits against marginal costs. Moreover, present methods of third party payment and provider reimbursement do not give them any inducement to acquire that ability. To be sure, patient pressure and the ethical imperative to do everything possible for the patient make this a complex problem. But a more rational approach could result in saving more lives and providing greater overall patient satisfaction.

Another popular misconception is that any change in health care technology that reduces labor requirements must be desirable. No such a priori assumption is warranted. A change in technology that is capital saving and labor intensive may be more valuable than the reverse, and a change that permits the substitution of two relatively unskilled workers for one highly skilled one may be more valuable than either.

The nature of technologic change can have profound effects on resource requirements, and some attention should be paid to this matter in granting funds for research and development. In choosing between two projects, for instance, it is not sufficient to consider only the importance of the problem and the probability of success. The granting agency should also consider what resources will be required to implement the solution if the project is successful.[34] Some technologic advances, such as the antibiotic drugs, greatly reduced the demand for physicians' services. Others, such as organ transplants, greatly increased demand.[35]

Traditional societies resist or inhibit technologic change. Society probably errs in the opposite direction. We seem to be fascinated by technology and often look to it to solve problems when less expensive solutions lie elsewhere. This may be particularly true of health care. It is to be hoped that this conference, with its emphasis on technology, will not serve to divert attention from other fundamental questions concerning the organization and financing of health care and personal responsibility for health.

Consider the problem of hospital costs. Hundreds of millions are being spent to make hospitals more efficient through new technology, but the return is likely to be small compared to the savings possible now with existing technology through reductions in utilization. Most informed observers believe that on any given day approximately 20 per cent of the patients in the average general hospital do not need to be there. Research probably will prove this to be a conservative estimate because it still assumes customary medical interventions, conventional lengths of stay and so forth.

What, for instance, is the appropriate length of stay after hernia surgery? A British team, in a carefully controlled study, showed that patients discharged one day after surgery did as well as those discharged after six days. Another British team compared surgical repair of varicose veins with injection compression sclerotherapy. The former method involves expensive hospitalization; the latter is done on an outpatient basis at minimum cost. Outcomes seem to be similar, (except that surgical patients lost four times as many days from work) and patients seem to prefer the injection/compression technique.[36]

No reasonable person would want to inhibit the development of new technologies or their application to health problems. But everyone concerned with American health care should realize that the most pressing problems are not centered around technology and their solutions will probably be found in other directions. As this paper has suggested, we need to make health care markets work better; we need to quantify and control the externalities that affect health; and we need to recognize the importance of individual behavior and personal responsibility for health. Substantial alterations in organization, financing and education are required to achieve these objectives.

These are the realities. Tomorrow's technology may help to bring about these changes, but let us not underestimate what is possible today if we have the will to do it. Let us not oversell technology. Let us not divert attention and misdirect energies that could be devoted to the complex task of creating a more equitable, more effective and more efficient health care system.

REFERENCES

[1] Samuelson, P., ECONOMICS, New York, McGraw-Hill Book Company.

[2] Becker, G. S., A Theory of the Allocation of Time, *Economic Journal,* 75, September, 1965.

[3] Linder, S. B., THE HARRIED LEISURE CLASS, New York, Columbia University Press, 1970.

[4] Health might be measured by life expectancy, absence of disabilities, speed of recovery after surgery and so forth. Health care inputs might refer to the size of a health care program, or the total amount of care given to a particular patient or a particular aspect of care such as number of tests or number of days in the hospital.

[5] This assumes that some input—e.g., the state of technology—is fixed at any given point in time.

[6] This point is well recognized in the theoretical literature on socialist planning (cf., Lange, O., On the Economic Theory of Socialism, in Lippincott, B. E. (Editor), ON THE ECONOMIC THEORY OF SOCIALISM, Minneapolis, University of Minnesota Press, 1956) and in the attempts of the Soviet government and other East European governments to make greater use of the market mechanism.

[7] The flow of resources (and the reciprocal flow of goods and services) in the United States is currently at a rate of approximately one trillion dollars per annum. About seven per cent of these resources flow to "firms" producing health care. Fifteen years ago only about 4.5 per cent of such smaller resource flow went in that direction. The resource flow, measured in dollars, depends upon the quantities of various resources and their prices. Over long periods of time prices of equivalent resources usually change at about the same rate in all sectors of the economy. Thus the increased share in dollar terms reflects a substantial increase in the share of real resources as well. This large shift of resources over a relatively short period of time is the most important element in the present "health care crisis."

[8] The fact that these services proliferate contrary to what economies of scale would indicate is the result of other problems such as the absence of appropriate incentives and constraints for physicians and hospital administrators.

[9] Pauly, M. V. and Redisch, M., The Not-for-Profit Hospital as a Physicians' Cooperative, Northwestern University, 1969, mimeographed.

[10] Kessel, R. A., Price Discrimination in Medicine, *Journal of Law and Economics,* 1, October, 1958.

[11] Arrow, K. J., The Organization of Economic Activity: Issues Pertinent to the Choice of Market vs. Non-Market Allocations, in THE ANALYSIS AND EVALUATION OF PUBLIC EXPENDITURES: THE P.P.B. SYSTEM, Subcommittee on Economy in Government of the Joint Economic Committee, 91st Congress of the United States, First Session, Volume 1, p. 62.

[12] Feldstein, M. S., The Rising Price of Physicians' Services, *The Review of Economics and Statistics,* 52, 121–133, May, 1970.

[13] Hughes, E. F. X., Fuchs, V. R., Jacoby, J. and Lewit, E., Surgical Workloads in a Community Practice, *Surgery,* 71, 315–327, March, 1972.

[14] Altman, S. H., The Structure of Nursing Education and Its Impact on Supply, in Klarman, H. E. (Editor), EMPIRICAL STUDIES IN HEALTH ECONOMICS, Baltimore, The Johns Hopkins Press, 1970.

[15] Yett, D. E., The Chronic Shortage of Nurses: A Public Policy Dilemma, in Klarman, *op. cit.*

[16] For a pioneering article see Stigler, G., The Economics of Information, *Journal of Political Economy,* 69, 213–225, June, 1961.

[17] Benham, L., The Effect of Advertising on Prices, Chicago, Graduate School of Business, 1971, mimeographed.

[18] The firm or household will presumably equate *its* marginal cost and *its* marginal benefit. The social optimum requires taking into account the costs or benefits imposed on others.

[19] When medical care keeps an employed head of family alive and well, a type of external benefit is created because society does not have to provide for his or her dependents. Much medical care, however, goes to the young or the aged or to keeping people alive but not well enough to work so it is doubtful if on balance a positive externality exists in this sense.

[20] What would constitute a "fair" distribution of income has never been satisfactorily answered by economists or anyone else. One feature of the market system that makes it attractive to some is that a household's share of goods and services will be roughly proportional to its contribution to total output as evaluated by all households collectively.

[21] Note the analogy with the individual household's decision regarding vaccination.

[22] Pauly, M. V., MEDICAL CARE AT PUBLIC EXPENSE: A STUDY IN APPLIED WELFARE ECONOMICS, New York, Praeger Publishers, Inc., 1971.

[23] However, where medical care for the poor is tied to using them for teaching and research purposes, significant externalities are probably present.

[24] Lindsay, C. M., Medical Care and the Economics of Sharing, *Economica,* 36, November, 1969.

[25] Becker, G. S. and Michael, R. T., On the Theory of Consumer Demand. 1970, mimeographed.

[26] Grossman, M., THE DEMAND FOR HEALTH: A THEORETICAL AND EMPIRICAL INVESTIGATION, New York, National Bureau of Economic Research, in press.

[27] But there would be no a priori case for favoring health over other commodities. The choice should depend upon relative costs and benefits.

[28] Cyert, R. M. and March, J. G., The Behavioral Theory of the Firm: A Behavioral Science-Economics Amalgam, in Cooper, W. W. (Editor), NEW PERSPECTIVES IN ORGANIZATION RESEARCH, New York, John Wiley & Sons, Inc., 1964.

[29] Simon, H. A. New Developments in the Theory of the Firm, *American Economic Review,* 52, 1–15, May, 1962.

[30] Williamson, O. E., CORPORATE CONTROL AND BUSINESS BEHAVIOR, Englewood-Cliffs, New Jersey, Prentice-Hall, Inc., 1970.

[31] Gronau, R., The Intrafamily Allocation of Time: The Value of the Housewives' Time, paper presented at the National Bureau of Economic Research Conference on Research in Income and Wealth, 1971.

[32] Nelson, R. R., Issues and Suggestions for the Study of Industrial Organizations in a Regime of Rapid Technical Change, in Fuchs, V. R. (Editor), POLICY ISSUES AND RESEARCH OPPORTUNITIES IN INDUSTRIAL ORGANIZATION, New York, National Bureau of Economic Research, 1972.

[33] Fuchs, V. R., The Growing Demand for Medical Care, *New England Journal of Medicine,* 279, July 25, 1968.

[34] Weisbrod, B. A., Costs and Benefits of Medical Research: A Case Study of Poliomyelitis, *Journal of Political Economy,* 79, 527–544, May–June, 1971.

113

[35] Fuchs, V. R. and Kramer, M. J., The Market for Physicians' Services in the United States, 1948–68, 1971.

[36] Ford, G. R., Innovations in Care: Treatment of Hernia and Varicose Veins, in McLachlan, G .(Editor), PORTFOLIO FOR HEALTH, London, Oxford University Press for Nuffield Provincial Hospitals Trust, 1971.

ACKNOWLEDGMENTS

I am grateful to Barry Chiswick, Michael Grossman, Edward F. X. Hughes, Ben Klein, Marcia Kramer and Robert Michael for comments on an earlier version of this paper.

This article was prepared for a conference on Technology and Health Care Systems in the 1980's, sponsored by the National Center for Health Services Research and Development and held at San Francisco, California, January 19, 1972. It will also be published in the Proceedings of that conference.

B. Competition and Monopoly

Restrictive Labor Practices in Baseball: Time for a Change?

By Janice M. Westerfield

When pitcher Jim (Catfish) Hunter was declared a free agent last December, he entertained offers from 23 of the 24 major league teams in the hottest bidding war in baseball history. He finally signed a five-year contract with the New York Yankees for a record $3.75 million. Never before had an experienced player of Hunter's caliber—he pitched the Oakland A's to three consecutive World Series Championships and is considered by many experts to be baseball's top pitcher—enjoyed free-agent status.

Competitive bidding for Hunter's services spotlighted one of professional baseball's unique labor practices—the player reservation system which can keep a player from selling his skills to the highest bidder. Sports entrepreneurs defend the noncompetitive labor practices by claiming that professional teams are unique and note that the courts

have exempted them from antitrust action. They argue that while an ordinary business is untroubled if it wipes out its competitors, a professional baseball team is in jeopardy if the financially weaker teams fail. The reason is that even the stronger teams need a league in order to operate profitably. Thus, while it's desirable to compete as hard as possible on the playing field, it's unwise for teams to compete against each other in a business manner, say the owners.

Team owners contend that baseball's restrictions on the labor market can be justified on other grounds as well. Their major contention is that the player reservation system equalizes team playing strengths and this is in the "public interest." Otherwise, the richer teams would garner the bulk of playing talent and lopsided games would result. Team owners also suggest that these noncompeti-

Janice M. Westerfield, "Restrictive Labor Practices in Baseball: Time for a Change?" *Business Review*, Federal Reserve Bank of Philadelphia, June 1975, pp. 17–26. Reprinted with permission.

tive practices help "maintain the integrity of the game" by assuring fans that players are loyal to their team. Finally, by preventing bidding wars (except in unusual circumstances), the weaker teams have greater financial security.

After Catfish Hunter declined the Philadelphia Phillies' offer of $2.6 million, Phillies President Ruly Carpenter said the rejection underscored the need for retaining the "reserve clause" in baseball. Does it? Or do the terms of the contract simply show the extent to which Hunter was previously paid less than his value to the team? An economic approach provides a much-needed dimension to the debate on the player reservation system and helps sports fans make some sense out of the industry's chaotic business conditions. In other words, who gains what under the current setup?

THE RESERVE CLAUSE

Organized baseball's exemption from an-

titrust action has encouraged collusion among the teams, allowing them to draw up explicit business rules for the conduct of the sport. (For more on baseball structure, see Box 1.) Perhaps the most important set of rules in baseball concerns the player reservation system. This system includes rules governing the acquisition of new players, the promotion of players from minor to major leagues, and movement of players from one major league team to another.

Specifically, the reserve clause in each player's contract gives a team the exclusive right to buy the player's services for the next season. In practice, it often ties a player to a team for his entire career, because under a reserve clause exclusive rights are retained by the team whether the athlete plays or not. A player may be transferred from one team to another only if the team owning his services releases him from his contract or allows another team to buy his contract and negotiate with him.

BOX 1

THE ECONOMICS OF BASEBALL STRUCTURE

Organized baseball acts like a "cartel." It restricts competition in business practices, regulates entry, and divides markets among teams in the two major leagues and several minor leagues. The antitrust exemption has encouraged teams to collude and to set up explicit business rules which are codified and open to public scrutiny. Output is limited by restricting the number of league franchises and the location of the teams. The establishment of territorial rights for each team prevents expansion teams from raiding another team's home territory. In addition to receiving income from admissions and concessions, teams benefit from the sale of radio and TV rights. Here again, rules limit competition in selling the industry's product. Leagues control the right to national broadcasts and each team holds exclusive rights to broadcast locally all home games that are not part of the league's national package. Professional baseball also has a complex set of rules dealing with interteam competition for players, the industry's most important production input. The rules governing the acquisition of new and veteran players are at the heart of the dispute on sports business practices.

In a cartel, cooperative behavior among the teams will assure greater profits than a competitive system. Yet, a particular team may increase its profits if it can convince all other teams to abide by the rules of the cartel and then itself cheat on the regulations.

BOX 1 (Continued)

For instance, a team could benefit by negotiating with players on other teams as long as the other teams do not reciprocate. To prevent secret negotiations with individual players, baseball has a "no-tampering" rule against bargaining with a player whose contract is owned by another team. Such rules, which are difficult to enforce, require serious penalties to dissuade member teams from violating them.

Organized baseball displays another cartel feature—a lack of innovation. Changes on most matters require a three-quarters majority vote in the league. Thus, on issues affecting both leagues, a mere four teams can thwart a change in major league rules. The voting rules make it difficult for organized baseball to respond to opportunities for profitable innovation. Critics claim the lack of innovation partially accounts for baseball's inability to keep its share of the total sports dollar.

Perhaps because the cartel has been slow to adjust to external changes eroding profitability, the sketchy financial data available indicates that few baseball teams are big moneymakers. The Los Angeles Dodgers and the New York Mets are probably the most profitable; they are located in large metropolitan areas and draw around two million fans apiece. In the American League the Baltimore Orioles, winner of the World Series in 1970, earned only $345,000 after taxes that year on revenues of $4.6 million—and their profit figure was believed to be the highest in the league. In 1970, a survey revealed that only half of the major league baseball teams netted an after-tax profit or broke even.* However, because of the special tax advantages of sports enterprises, such as depreciating the value of player contracts, baseball teams may actually be more profitable than the accounting figures would suggest.** Current profit figures also ignore capital gains resulting from increases in the value of the franchise.

---

*"Who Says Baseball Is Like Ballet?" Forbes, April 1, 1971, p. 30.

**Tax shelters traditionally open to sports enterprises may be threatened by a U.S. District Court ruling last February against the Atlanta Falcons. The Court reduced the allowable depreciation reductions on football player contracts and ruled that TV rights could not be depreciated. The uncertainty of tax advantages from depreciation may reduce the market value of pro sports franchises.

The player reservation system is intended to limit competition among teams for the services of players. The agreement not to compete is the key to the reserve clause's effective operation. If a particular team tries to negotiate with a player to see if he is interested in changing teams, it runs the risk of being severely penalized. By restricting the right of a player to negotiate with another team while under contract to his current team, the "no-tampering" rule deprives the player of his freedom to choose his prospective employer or place of employment. The officially stated reason for the reserve rule is that it "inhibits the moneyed clubs from acquiring all of the best talent."[1] Supporters contend that the reserve clause does tend to equalize the strengths of the poor and

---

[1] U.S., Congress, House, Committee on the Judiciary, Subcommittee on Study of Monopoly Power, Organized Baseball, 82d Cong., 2d sess., 1952, p. 105.

the rich teams. This rule is also said to ensure the honesty of the game by bolstering public confidence that players are competing to win. It is feared that a player negotiating with another team would lack the "winning spirit"—this could raise suspicions of a fix if he muffed an easy play.

DRAFTING

New Player Draft. Central to the player reservation system is the new player draft. This draft was established in 1965 when the baseball cartel realized that bonuses to amateur players were costing teams big money. Here's how it works. The names of the eligible amateur players are pooled and the teams draft the negotiation rights in reverse order of the won-lost standings. The lowest-ranking team then gets first pick of the new player draftees. The new player and the team that has drafted him have six months to negotiate a contract. During this period, the player may not negotiate or make a deal with any other team. If the player and the drafting team cannot reach an agreement, then the player returns to the pool to be drafted by a second team in the "secondary phase" of the draft. The six-month bargaining period in baseball puts the player in a slightly better negotiating position than in football where if a player cannot conclude a contract with the assigned team, he has no alternate means for reaching an agreement to play for another team. The limited time period in baseball also gives some encouragement for a team to offer a signing bonus.

The arguments advanced for the new player draft are essentially those given for the reserve clause. The primary purpose was to end the competitive bidding through bonuses which were transferring wealth from the club to the players. By drafting in the reverse order of standing, it was also argued that the weaker teams would benefit relatively more than the stronger ones.

Veteran Player Draft. Although a major league baseball team is limited to carrying about 25 players on its active roster, it may have up to 15 more players under exclusive contract. These "protected" athletes play for minor league teams affiliated with the parent club. Players *not* on the protected roster of major league teams may be reallocated by means of a veteran player draft at the end of each season. This draft attempts to equalize playing strengths by limiting direct competition for the player. First, teams draft players in reverse order of standings for a stipulated amount, currently set at $25,000. This means a team cannot bid for a player's services by promising a higher salary or offering to place him on its protected roster. Second, the drafted player must be placed under exclusive contract, thereby releasing one of the protected players and making him eligible to be drafted by other teams. Like the draft, limits on the number of protected players are alleged to equalize team strengths. Team owners argue that, otherwise, championship teams would keep too many players under exclusive contract, thereby depriving lower-ranked teams of playing talent.

"Waiver Rule." Sales of player contracts are also limited by the "waiver rule." A team wishing to sell a player's contract must "clear waivers"—that is, each team in the league must have the opportunity to buy, at a fixed price, the exclusive rights to bargain with the player. Acquisition rights for waivered players are tendered in reverse order of team standing. In baseball, even after a player is waived, he may not be free to negotiate with teams in the other league. The waiver rule is another means of restricting competition for veteran players.

THE RESERVATION SYSTEM: WHO BENEFITS, WHO DOESN'T?

Economic logic and statistical studies say a great deal about the alleged benefits of the player reservation system. First of all, economic theory suggests that artificial mechanisms designed to promote equal playing strengths among teams are unnecessary. Indeed, it runs against the economic interests of a team to become overloaded with star players. Second, even if equalizing team strengths were desirable (perhaps because team owners don't behave as economic logic would predict), the player reservation system fails to perform this task. The reason is that it doesn't prevent the most talented players from being transferred from one team to another.

The player reservation system does have some economic effects, however. It increases the financial security of team owners, for example. It does so principally by keeping player salaries lower than they would otherwise be. Financial losses to the players are considerable. Lower salaries mean that prospective players devote less time and energy to developing batting and fielding skills. The overall level of individual team quality is lower as a result.

Playing Strengths. In their support of the player reservation system, team owners view the necessity of a mechanism for equalizing playing strengths as axiomatic. Economic theory, however, suggests it's highly unlikely that the financially strong teams would buy up *all* the star players if released from the reserve clause. Any team that tries to buy up the most capable players will reach a point where it will forego the services of an additional talented player. This happens because a team has an incentive to win by a close margin rather than by clobbering its opponents. Close contests with an element of uncertainty are considered more exciting and more likely to attract fans. If lopsided sports contests discourage attendance, it will not be in the best economic interests of a strong team to buy up all the talent in the league. At some point, therefore, a strong team will be willing to pass up the services of another topflight player and see him play for another team.[2]

Supporters of the reserve system may counter that team owners may receive psychic satisfaction from hoarding expert players. Hence, the current setup is required to prevent unequal distributions of talent. Economists retort that the reserve clause and player drafts are unequal to this task. The reason is that resources tend to move toward their most highly valued uses (given well-defined property rights and small costs of exchange). The player reservation system fails to prevent player transfers from one team to another for cash or other players. If a player's services are worth most to the team having exclusive rights to his contract, then no other team will want to pay the current owners enough to bid him away. But, if the player's services are valued more highly by another team, and if the costs of transferring the player's contract are small, the team that values him most will bid the contract away from the current owners. Thus, each player will play for the team which gets the highest return from his service — the same as in most other professions operating in a free market. Player sales and trades also probably offset any equalizing effects that the new and veteran player drafts have on team strengths.

---

[2]A rich team will not purchase an unlimited number of talented players. This point is well explained by Simon Rottenberg in his classic article, "The Baseball Players' Labor Market," *Journal of Political Economy* 64 (1956): 301. "Beyond some point — say, when a team already has three .350 hitters — it will not pay to employ another .350 hitter. If a team goes on increasing the quantity of the factor, players, by hiring additional stars, it will find that the total output — that is, admission receipts — of the combined firms (and, therefore, of its own) will rise at a less rapid rate and finally will fall absolutely. At some point, therefore, a first star player is worth more to poor Team B than, say, a third star to rich Team A. At this point, B is in a position to bid players away from A in the market. A's behavior is not a function of its bank balance. It does what it calculates it is worthwhile to do; and the time comes when, in pursuing the strategy of its *own* gains, it is worthwhile, whatever the size of its cash balance, to forego the services of an expert player and see him employed by another team."

Thus, in theory, the distribution of playing talent between rich and poor teams is not affected by the reserve clause.[3]

In practice, even if a player reservation system is in effect, imbalances between weak and strong teams persist. The reserve rule has not frustrated those teams willing to outbid others for players. Franchises in areas with high drawing-potential (usually big cities) have a stronger economic base and are apt to develop stronger teams than franchises in low population areas. A look at the evidence indicates that teams in high drawing-potential areas win more than their share of championships. If team strength is measured by pennants won, from about 1900 to 1970 the four largest cities in the American League won 49 out of 68 pennants while the four largest cities in the National League won 41 out of 70.[4] These big city teams tend to bid some star players away from the low drawing-potential teams, which are usually based in smaller cities that generate lower "live gate" and TV revenues for the home team.

The limited evidence available also suggests that the distribution of playing talent is probably much the same with or without a player reservation system. A recent study was made of three four-year periods, beginning with the years 1876–79 before the reserve clause became operative in 1880 on a partial basis. During both of the successive four-year test periods, the reserve clause was extended to more and more players, yet the study uncovered no significant differences in talent distribution for the three periods.[5] The quality of the teams was measured by such factors as the number of years that teams won successive championships and the average percentage of games won (won-lost record) by a championship team. Similarly, more recent data for baseball, football, basketball, and hockey show no consistent relationship between talent distribution measures and the presence or absence of a free-agent draft.[6]

Financial Security. Although the player reservation system doesn't appear to equalize playing talent among the rich and poor teams, owners of the poorer teams do receive greater financial security. First of all, the reserve clause reduces their labor costs compared to competitive bidding. Secondly, it assures financially weaker teams exclusive rights to an asset that can be sold to richer teams. Thus, by financially aiding teams in less populous markets, the league becomes more viable.

Similarly, the new player draft is a subsidy of sorts to the weaker franchises. Since the teams draft in reverse order of standings, the weaker teams get preferential treatment. Likewise, the veteran player draft redistributes income toward the financially weaker teams. These teams purchase players from the powerhouse teams at a below open-market price; thus, the drafting teams gain wealth equal to the excess of the market price over the draft price. The rich teams apparently think it worth their while to support

---

[3]Under a reserve clause, a player will theoretically be transferred to the team for which he generates the most revenues. For example, suppose a player is worth $75,000 to the Philadelphia Phillies and $100,000 to the Atlanta Braves, and his contract is currently held by Atlanta. The Phillies will be willing to pay a maximum of $75,000 (and probably less if they hope to gain revenues by paying the player less than his value to the team). However, as long as the Braves are willing to top that figure, the player will remain on their roster.

Conversely, if the player is currently playing for the Phillies, both teams will benefit by transferring the contract to the Braves at any price between $75,000 and $100,000. At any price over $75,000, the Phillies will benefit from the sale of the contract while the Braves will be willing to pay as much as $100,000.

[4]James Quirk and Mohamed El Hodiri, "The Economic Theory of a Professional Sports League," in Roger G. Noll, ed., *Government and the Sports Business* (Washington: The Brookings Institution, 1974), p. 48.

[5]Michael E. Canes, "The Social Benefits of Restrictions on Team Quality," in Noll, op. cit., p. 85.

[6]Ibid., p. 88.

the league by bearing a larger share of the financial burden. Of course, the player reservation system is only one of many schemes which could be employed to redistribute income among league members. For example, a change in the way gate receipts are shared could also affect a redistribution of income.

Player Salaries. While the owners of the poor teams may receive some benefits relative to the rich teams, the limitations to labor mobility inherent in the player reservation system clearly reduce the financial return to the player. In fact, *the redistribution of income from the players to the owners is the primary economic effect of the player reservation system.* The player can only negotiate with the team holding exclusive rights to his contract; he cannot choose from among several bids in a free labor market where he would be paid his full value to the team. Thus, a differential can exist between the player's salary and his "worth" to the team. The cash sale of players from one team to another suggests that players receive less than they would under a competitive bidding system. The player reservation system simply gives the money acquired in exchange to the team owners instead of to the player.

The redistribution of income from players to owners leads to several secondary effects. First, lifetime player earnings are less. Not only is the player's salary lower in his first contract than it would be under competitive bidding, but he cannot expect to make up the current shortfall at anytime during his playing career. Before the free-agent draft, when big bonuses were common in the competitive bidding for new players, the bonus would at most equal the value today of the wages lost in the future as a result of the player reservation system. Thus, the player did not suffer reduced lifetime earnings. With the institution of the new player draft in 1965, direct price competition was restricted in the market for amateurs and bonuses fell considerably.

One study that estimated the extent of the wages lost under the reserve clause for three qualities of players found that baseball players suffer a financial loss of "considerable magnitude."[7] Over their playing careers, **average** players are paid about 20 percent of **the net** revenues they generate for the team. (**Net** revenues remain after training and other **costs** have been subtracted.) Star players are **paid** about 15 percent of the net revenues they generate. Ironically, only mediocre players are paid more than the revenues they generate over their shorter playing careers.

Team Quality. Since the restrictive rules in the baseball labor market reduce player salaries, skill levels and team quality are reduced over the longer haul. Amateur players can be expected to devote less effort to bettering their skills if they face lower potential earnings. Since prospective players are free to choose alternative earning possibilities, lower player salaries will also reduce the quantity of baseball talent supplied, and those amateur players who actually do become professionals will have invested less resources to sharpen their natural skills.[8] Thus, the fans as well as the players suffer under the current setup.[9]

---

[7]Gerald W. Scully, "Pay and Performance in Major League Baseball," *American Economic Review* 64 (1974): 929.

[8]Disagreement exists over whether society benefits from higher average skill levels and higher salaries for baseball players. For instance, a player paid a free market salary may feel his income has increased enough for him to substitute some leisure time for time spent in his playing career. Also, if star players receive huge salaries, amateurs are encouraged to devote more effort to sharpening their skills. For those who don't make it, some people think the effort is wasted.

[9]An argument can be made, however, that a competitive system promotes too high a level of team quality because it does not account for external factors which affect other teams in the league. For a further explanation, see Canes, op. cit., p. 94.

MODIFYING THE PLAYER RESERVATION SYSTEM

Supporters of the player reservation system claim that it equalizes team strengths. But economic logic and evidence indicate that the system hardly affects the distribution of playing talent. So, the primary benefit of restrictive labor practices in baseball may well be a fiction. At the same time, the player reservation system imposes heavy costs on the players in terms of lower wages and reduced employment choice. Thus, it may be worthwhile to consider alternative ways to achieve the secondary benefits of the reserve system—greater financial security for weaker teams—so that the reserve clause can be modified or eliminated. The player association is already moving against the player reservation system. Suits have been filed in the courts to place baseball's restrictive labor practices under Federal antitrust laws. (See Box 2.)

Some alleged benefits of the reserve clause—more equal playing strengths, greater financial gains for the weaker teams—could be met by dividing income more equally among the teams. For example, if the present 80–20 (American League) gate-sharing arrangement between home and visiting teams were altered to share revenues more equally (as in football), financial disparities among the teams would be reduced. That way a team based in a smaller population area of, say, 1.5 million would receive a larger proportion of revenues on the road and would increase its profits even if the team drew the same number of fans at home. Alternatively, it has been estimated that equal revenue sharing between home and visiting teams would reduce the number of fans needed at home to maintain the same profits, so that the minimum viable size for a franchise area would be reduced from 1.9 to 1.5 million population.[10] An even-gate split

would benefit several teams by making them more financially viable. Similarly, a team's monopoly on local broadcasting revenues in its home territory—the visiting team does not receive a share of the revenues from local broadcasts—could be modified to divide income more evenly with the same effects.

If owners as a group can realize the financial benefits of the reservation system in some other way, modification of these labor practices should be easier to accomplish. One suggestion is to combine the reserve clause with some kind of an option clause. In football, an athlete who plays out his option takes a 10 percent pay cut from his previous year's salary (which may amount to a higher percent cut of what he would have earned if he were a good player). He remains with the same team for the current season and then is a free agent who can negotiate with any other team in the league. A fairly liberal option rule in baseball could go a long way toward remedying the restrictive employment choices and the reduced lifetime earnings for the player offered by the reserve clause.

U.S. Senate hearings on the proposed basketball merger in 1972 resulted in several conditions which had to be met to obtain an antitrust exemption. Some of these could be suggested to the player association for collective bargaining in baseball. The proposed bill (which eventually died) provided that veteran player contracts were to have a negotiable duration, after which the player was free to switch teams. This proposal goes one step further than the option clause by eliminating it altogether. Another proposal would retain the amateur draft but obligate the rookie to play for the team that drafted him for at least two years, then free him to negotiate with any team. Both these measures would increase player mobility and free employment choice.

Federal legislation may well modify the player reservation system. In 1972, legislation was introduced in Congress to establish a Federal commission to regulate drafting procedures and other labor practices involving

[10]Roger G. Noll, "Attendance and Price Setting," in Noll, op. cit., p. 131.

ASSAULTS ON THE RESERVE CLAUSE
AND OTHER RESTRICTIVE LABOR PRACTICES

Baseball has been exempt from antitrust laws ever since *Federal Baseball Club* v. *National League* (1922), when the Baltimore club of the Federal League sued the American and National Leagues for attempting to buy out the members of the Federal League. The Supreme Court ruled that baseball games were exempt from antitrust because they were "purely state affairs"; interstate commerce was not the "essential thing." Thus, baseball was not subject to Federal jurisdiction over interstate commerce and the Baltimore club was not harmed "by reasons of anything forbidden in the antitrust laws." Although numerous court challenges have been made to this ruling, it has never been overturned. When professional football was placed under Federal antitrust laws (*Radovich* v. *National Football League*), the Court was pressed to make the rulings on football and baseball consistent and confessed that "were we considering the question of baseball for the first time upon a clean slate we would have no doubts" about nonexemption.*

The Court justified the continued exclusion of baseball from antitrust laws by passing the buck to Congress, which had shown little inclination to bring baseball under these laws in the preceding years, and concluded that the most appropriate way to redress the situation (if indeed, redress is called for) is "by legislation and not by court decision." Congressional reluctance to close the loophole stirred another player, outfielder Curt Flood, to turn once again to the courts. However, by 1972, the dependence of baseball structure on the legal precedents proved too difficult to overcome, and Flood lost his challenge. The majority holding reaffirmed the earlier court rulings, citing the "positive inaction" of Congress, which "allowed those decisions to stand for so long . . . and has clearly evinced a desire not to disapprove them legislatively."**

Recently hopes for a reversal were raised from another quarter. Last December a Federal judge handed down a decision concerning former quarterback Joe Kapp which could have implications for the reserve systems governing baseball, basketball, and hockey. The "Rozelle Rule" allows the football commissioner to determine compensation when an athlete plays out his option—that is, plays one more year at 90 percent of his previous salary and becomes a free agent—and accepts an offer from another team. This rule was declared an unreasonable restraint and illegal because by setting a high indemnity, the commissioner can block a player's employment choice. The decision also found that the "no-tampering rule," which operates much the same way in football as in baseball to prohibit players under contract to a team from negotiating with other teams and to provide penalties for violators, unduly restricts free employment choice. It

---

Radovich v. *National Football League*, 352 U.S. 452 (1957).

**Curtis C. Flood v. Bowie K. Kuhn et al.*, 407 U.S. at 283–84 (1972).

is this latter finding which antitrust enthusiasts hope can somehow be broadened to include baseball.

Meanwhile, assaults on the web of restrictive labor practices are coming from another Quarter—the player association. Although the Major League Players Association, the union, represents only players on the roster of the major league teams, it has the potential to affect labor relations greatly. Collective bargaining has resulted in major gains for baseball players, notably by allowing them to have a lawyer present when negotiating a contract. Baseball also has a three-man arbitration board to settle disputes such as that between Catfish Hunter and Charles O. Finley, owner of the Oakland A's. One member represents the players union, a second represents the major league owners, and the third is an impartial arbitrator. The board gives the players an advantage over the "one-man rule" policy in football that was found illegal in the Kapp case. Although the baseball players association has tried to place the player reservation system on the agenda for collective bargaining, so far the owners have refused to negotiate at all on the reserve system. However, the 1973 baseball agreement calls for a three-year study of ways to revise the player reservation system and will serve as a basis for negotiations in 1976.

restriction on competition, but the bill died in committee. The proposed bill to set conditions under which an antitrust exemption would be granted for the proposed basketball merger also hints at the possibility of government action. In any case, after the player association, Congress may be the most likely source of change in business practices in the sports labor market.

A LOOK AT THE FUTURE

Economic analysis of the baseball labor market sheds some light on the effects of the present system and possible ways of modifying it. Economic theory does not support the claim that the player reservation system reduces the disparity between the strong and the weak teams. Playing talent is probably distributed much the same with or without a reserve clause. Team owners benefit from the restrictive labor practices because income which would otherwise be paid to the players is kept by the owners. Financially weaker teams also benefit from the player

sales which transfer funds to them at the expense of the richer teams. However, the financial costs to the players are quite high under the player reservation system. Studies have shown that players are paid considerably less than the net revenues they generate for their team. Since playing skills respond positively to salary increases, lower player salaries inhibit the amount of prospective skills produced and result in lower team quality as well.

Because of the magnitude of the economic losses suffered by the players, chances are that the player reservation system will be modified in the near future, either through efforts by the player association, through court suits, or, as a last resort, by Congressional action. The crucial test will probably come in 1975–76 when the player association and the team owners negotiate a new agreement. One way out might be to combine a more equal distribution of revenues for the weaker teams with an option clause or long-term contract for the players.

124

Forced Divestiture in Oil?

DOES not the American partly live in oil? Certainly he cannot move without it. Every tenth man owns an automobile, and the rest are saving up to buy one . . .

That observation, made in 1923 by a British writer, was perceptive then—and is even more apt today. Oil use in this country has risen from 138 gallons per capita in 1923 to 1,176 gallons per capita now. (Auto ownership, meanwhile, has climbed from one in ten persons to one in two.)

That spectacular rise in demand for oil has been taken in stride by the industry, which has pushed ahead with exploration, enlarged its refining capacity, and expanded marketing facilities. The performance of the industry, on the whole, has been creditable; businessmen and consumers over the years have been able to get the fuel for their factories, for their homes, for their automobiles when they needed it—and at a relatively low cost. As a consequence, the oil industry's image during recent decades generally has been a positive one, with poll takers finding little of a negative nature when sampling public opinion.

More recently, the public mood has been changing—and for the worse for the oil companies. The change, initially, can be traced to the Arab oil embargo of 1973 and 1974 which brought gasoline shortages and lines at filling stations. And, of course, the subsequent quadrupling of OPEC oil prices—which forced a roughly 50% increase in gasoline and fuel-oil prices—added greatly to consumer dismay and anger.

A feeling has persisted among many people that the earlier shortages and the present high prices of gasoline somehow have been due to oil company "conspiracies." Frustrated by inflation at the gas pump (which aggravates the problem of generalized inflation), and upset at the inability of the U.S. government to counter OPEC, public sentiment has taken on a decidedly "anti-oil" bias.

Lashing out

The tendency to lash out at "Big Oil" is evident in the halls of Congress. In the past year, nearly forty bills which would importantly affect oil industry operations have been popped into the legislative hopper. In mid-June, the Senate Judiciary Committee approved and sent to the Senate floor the most far-reaching of those bills. Called the "Petroleum Industry Competition Act," it would force the top eighteen oil companies to divest themselves of either their exploration and production functions or their refining-marketing functions as well as, in either case, all their transportation operations (mostly pipelines). In addition, refining companies would not be permitted to extend their marketing operations through owned service stations beyond the number of such outlets they owned at the beginning of this year. Thus, integrated operations—from drilling rig to the refinery and then to the gas pump—would be banned.

The full Senate will take up the vertical divestiture measure next month—after the recess for the Democratic national convention. A companion measure in Congress would require "horizontal" divestiture, which would prohibit oil companies from operating in other types of energy such as coal, nuclear power, or geothermal steam.

The idea of divestiture is not new. Eugene V. Rostow, former head of the Yale Law School, in

---

"Forced Divestiture of Oil." *Morgan Guaranty Survey*, June 1976, pp. 3–10. Reprinted with permission.

125

1948 argued in his book, *A National Policy for the Oil Industry:* "The key to an effectively competitive reform of the petroleum industry is . . . the separation of the major companies into separate units controlling their four chief functions: production, transportation, refining, and distribution . . ."

Nothing ever came of such proposals until 1965 when, through efforts by Senator Philip Hart of Michigan, a plan to force divestiture was initially put forward in Congress. The Hart bill over the years made no headway. However, last October, in a reflection of the changed attitude toward the oil industry, a divestiture bill—offered as an amendment to a natural gas deregulation bill—narrowly lost in the Senate 55 to 45.

Little ones out of big ones

Vertical or horizontal divestiture (or the two combined) would bring about a major restructuring of a giant industry with an impact far greater than the historic 1911 breakup of Standard Oil. That action 65 years ago resulted in merely a geographic dismemberment in which individual companies confined their operations to specific regions. Many of the companies continued as integrated operations.

The world-wide assets of the companies affected by currently proposed divestiture legislation are estimated at $149 billion at the end of 1975. Those companies employed 693,000 workers. Their aggregate long-term debt amounted to nearly $23 billion and their off-balance-sheet debt exceeded $10 billion. Stock in the companies, valued at $72 billion, is held by several million investors directly—and, indirectly, by several million more through pension and mutual funds.

The bill to break up the oil companies just passed by the Senate Judiciary Committee has emerged after a decade of examination off and on by the Senate Judiciary Subcommittee on Antitrust and Monopoly. Hundreds of witnesses —oil executives, professors, federal and state officials, bankers, economists, ordinary consumers —have appeared to argue for and against the idea. Their testimony literally has filled tens of thousands of pages. Out of that massive record, proponents of divestiture have produced a bill which declares: "It is the purpose of the Congress in this act to facilitate the creation and maintenance of competition in the petroleum industry, and to require the most expeditious and equitable separation and divestment of assets and interests of vertically integrated major petroleum companies."

Companies producing 100,000 barrels of oil a day or more in the U.S. could not engage in refining, transportation, or marketing of oil. Companies refining or marketing 300,000 barrels a day or more in the U.S. could not produce or transport oil. And companies of any size that transport oil through domestic pipelines could not produce, refine, or market oil.

The bill's timetable calls for vertical disintegration of the oil companies within five years.* The table on the following page lists the eighteen companies that would be affected by divestiture.

Significantly, the oil companies are not charged with violating any laws. Instead, a breakup of the oil industry is called necessary to foster competition. Proponents of the bill argue that legislation is needed because antitrust laws have been "too slow and inadequate."

Traditionally, when looking for indications of possible anticompetitive conduct in an industry, analysts consider three criteria: concentration ratios, profitability, and ease of entry into the field.

Concentration ratios. Such ratios show the proportion of industry production or sales accounted for by a small number of firms— usually the top firm, the top four companies, and the top eight companies. The evidence is clear that oil concentration ratios are lower

---

*Horizontal divestiture, which is contained in a separate bill not acted upon as yet, would have to be completed within three years. Alarm within the industry is greatest over proposed vertical disintegration, although oil companies are very much concerned with forced divestiture horizontally. The oil industry, which has engaged in research and development for alternate energy resources for many years, feels that it has much to contribute. And quite aside from technological know-how and expertise, segmented coal or nuclear-power companies would not have the capital base needed for massive development programs.

U.S. operations only in 1974	Barrels per day		
	Crude production	Refinery throughput	Marketing
Exxon	890,000	1,123,000	1,782,000
Texaco	807,000	945,000	1,338,000
Shell	586,000	1,005,000	1,060,000
Standard Oil of Indiana	539,000	936,000	1,012,000
Gulf	476,300	813,000	860,600
Mobil	420,000	823,000	928,000
Standard Oil of California	413,080	867,000	1,006,000
Atlantic-Richfield	383,100	653,500	697,600
Getty	300,300	214,500	254,000
Union	268,400	439,100	441,200
Sun	265,588	489,988	570,546
Phillips	255,700	523,000	541,000
Continental	218,000	322,000	364,000
Cities Service	212,300	231,800	348,400
Marathon	174,039	264,415	280,106
BP-Sohio	29,646	323,336	332,996
Amerada Hess	98,816	530,000	591,000
Ashland	23,071	329,789	457,007

SOURCE: National Petroleum News Factbook, mid-May 1975.

than for U.S. businesses generally. Data from the Census of Manufactures and other sources (table on page 6) show that the four-firm concentration ratio approximates 27% for crude oil production, 34% for refining capacity, and 30% for gasoline sales. These numbers are appreciably lower than the weighted average four-firm concentration ratio for U.S. manufacturing, which works out at about 40%.*

Indeed, many other U.S. industries are decidedly more concentrated than is oil. For example, the four top companies in the copper industry account for 75% of production; the auto industry has one producer which accounts for half the market for U.S.-made cars; more than 90% of aluminum output is accounted for by four producers. In a list of 27 major industries, oil-industry concentration ranks lowest of all.

Charges of monopolistic behavior raised by proponents of divestiture seem strange in an in-

dustry where there are 50 integrated oil companies; 10,000 producers of oil and natural

U.S. Oil Industry Concentration Ratios

	Percent of U.S. industry output accounted for by:		
	Top firm	Top 4 firms	Top 8 firms
Crude oil production (1970)	8.5	27.1	49.1
Refining capacity: gasoline (1970)	9.2	34.0	59.8
Product sales: gasoline (1973)	8.0	30.0	52.4

SOURCES: Crude oil production from "Concentration Levels and Trends in the Energy Sector of the U.S. Economy" by Joseph P. Mulholland and Douglas W. Webbink, Staff Report to the Federal Trade Commission, Washington, D.C., March 1974, pp. 63-65. Gasoline refining capacity from U.S. Federal Trade Commission, "Preliminary Federal Trade Commission Staff Report on Its Investigation of the Petroleum Industry" (Washington, 1973), Table 11-3. Gasoline sales from Harold Wilson, "Exxon and Shell Score Gasoline Gains," Oil and Gas Journal, June 3, 1974. Reproduced from page 2231 of hearings of Senate Subcommittee on Antitrust and Monopoly, Part Three.

*Share of the market accounted for by top four firms in various industries, with the shares for particular industry weighted by value added.

127

gas; 100 interstate pipeline companies; 130 refining companies; 18,000 marketers of fuel oil; and 300,000 retailers of gasoline—95% of them independent businessmen—who compete for motorists' business.

Proponents of divestiture concede that concentration ratios in oil are low, but they insist such ratios should not be conventionally interpreted. The reasons they cite: the oil industry is prone to joint ventures, swap agreements, and joint services affecting pipelines, refineries, international production and distribution, domestic oil exploration and development, and bidding for federal oil leases. Such arrangements are said to create a "community of interest" which tends to bring about a "unity of attitude and action."

Unquestionably, the oil industry enters frequently into joint ventures. An obvious reason for this is the cost—and enormous risks—involved in oil exploration and development. Joint bidding on offshore oil tracts can be pro-competitive rather than anticompetitive since more companies can participate than would be the case if joint bidding were not allowed. (Actually, under a recent government ruling the seven largest oil companies can no longer bid jointly; they must bid singly or as partners with smaller companies.) Moreover, exchange and processing agreements among oil companies provide for economical use of resources. Oil is rarely found near a company's own refinery but can be exchanged with other companies for a supply which can be more efficiently used—and which is of the specific type and quality needed for each refinery. As for monopolistic control by owners of pipelines, the Interstate Commerce Commission tightly regulates pipeline transportation to be sure that nonowners get access to the lines.

Profitability. Relatively large profits for an industry over a long period of time traditionally are considered an indication that the industry possesses monopolistic power. That kind of profitability is not the case in the oil industry. In 1974, it is true, oil profits hit record highs. But that was due to inventory profits made possible by the quadrupling of the world price of oil by OPEC and by overseas sales at the higher prices. After that one-shot effect, profits dropped back to normal levels (chart on page 7). For the years 1960 through 1975, the oil industry's rate of return on shareholder's equity—what the company earns on the money the stockholders have invested—averaged just over 12%, only a bit higher than the 11.4% average return on all American manufacturing. Many other industries did better than oil companies—including soft drinks, drugs, medicines, soap, cosmetics, office equipment, and tobacco.

Entry by competitors. The third test of uncompetitive conditions is the existence of barriers to entry into the field.

The record indicates freedom of entry for individuals and groups into all phases of the oil business. For example, independent oil companies have shared in four of every five winning bids on tracts for offshore lease sales. And "independents" selling nonbrand gasoline have increased their share of the market from 23% of the total in 1967 to roughly 32% in 1975.

Vertically uncompetitive?

On the three standard "tests," it is not at all clear why anyone should think that the oil in-

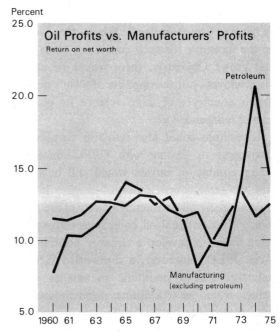

Percent

Oil Profits vs. Manufacturers' Profits
Return on net worth

Petroleum

Manufacturing (excluding petroleum)

25.0
20.0
15.0
10.0
5.0

1960 61 63 65 67 69 71 73 75

dustry needs to be dismembered. Perhaps recognizing this, those who are pushing a breakup have been emphasizing a different argument: because the oil industry is vertically integrated, its market structure lends itself to uncompetitive action. Here again, a look at the record makes the claims for divestiture appear unconvincing.

In the first place, an industry should not be presumed to be anticompetitive just because it is integrated. Economists who have written on the subject generally argue that vertical integration does not have an adverse impact on competition. Secondly, vertical integration is not peculiar to the oil industry; it is used by all sorts of businesses, large and small.

A farmer who plants vegetables, harvests them, and sells them to the public at his roadside stand is vertically integrated. Vertical integration is attractive to many different businessmen because it permits production efficiencies and spreads the risks of the business. In the case of oil, if exploration ventures prove unproductive, for example, refining or marketing activities might serve as cushioning offsets through a rough period.

Such integration is commonplace in business. Some auto companies make their own steel and glass and some operate auto dealerships. Steel companies are integrated "backward" through ownership of coal and ore mines and "forward" into production of finished products. Some newspapers own timber to assure supplies of newsprint. The industry list of integrated firms is almost endless. The key point is that there must be very strong advantages to be derived from vertical integration in order to make it so universal a method of organization.

Moreover, as a study by Professor M. A. Adelman of Massachusetts Institute of Technology has shown, the oil industry ranks far down the list in its degree of vertical integration among U.S. manufacturing industries.* As Professor Edward J. Mitchell, of the University of Michigan, put it in testimony before the Senate Antitrust and Monopoly Subcommittee in January: "The average U.S. manufacturing firm would have to divest itself of from 30% to 60% of its assets and employees just to get down to the low level of integration that exists in the petroleum industry."

Adverse consequences

Against a background of competitiveness in oil, an industry which is less integrated than most others—and which has served consumers well over the years—why the proposals for a breakup?

Would such action bring important benefits for consumers? Would a splintered oil industry be more capable of the major task of developing domestic energy resources? And would a larger group of smaller U.S. companies have more "muscle" and be better able to stand up to the OPEC cartel?

The answer to each of those questions must be "No." Dismemberment in all probability would lead to higher costs and a narrowing capital base, resulting in more expensive fuel for consumers and impeding hopes for developing an effective energy program. Such an impact on the energy program, monumentally jarring as it would be initially, would continue to be felt for years to come. The reason: divestiture standards are based on the size of production and refining-marketing operations; as today's smaller oil companies got larger and reached those artificial limits, they automatically would have to break their operations into pieces. A government sword, thus, would be hanging over their heads. Where, then, would be the incentive for such companies to expand and grow? Obviously, there would be strong disincentives—just the opposite of what's needed if this country ever is to achieve its goal of energy independence.

Divestiture could also result in reduced effectiveness in dealing with OPEC since the larger number of buyers would still be faced with the same concentration of supplier power.

*See "Concept and Statistical Measurement of Vertical Integration," in *Business Concentration and Public Policy*, National Bureau of Economic Research.

Indeed, many oil-consuming countries are combining their national oil companies—not splintering them—to develop a stronger position vis-à-vis OPEC. Moreover, a dismantled U.S. oil industry, with a multitude of smaller companies, would be at a distinct disadvantage trying to compete with the foreign giants for scarce supplies of foreign oil.

Discussion in Washington and elsewhere of the impact of dismemberment on foreign operations of U.S. oil companies has been rather muted. The reason for this, undoubtedly, is that the proposed divestiture legislation is glaringly lacking in specificity as to how it would apply abroad. Still, the broad intent of the bill is clear: U.S. companies would be required to break into segments their overseas as well as their domestic companies. For example, Exxon's production activities in the U.S. and overseas could be retained, but the company would have to divest its refining, marketing, and distribution operations in this country and abroad. Moreover, as experts in corporate law warned the Senate Antitrust Subcommittee, any long-term contracts entered into between the prohibited U.S. overseas subsidiaries and foreign companies or foreign governments would have to be terminated.

The international legal snarls that would be created by such action clearly would be immense. Foreign courts almost surely would support the contentions of foreigners that contractual obligations of U.S. overseas oil companies could not unilaterally be abrogated by the U.S. Foreign debts of U.S. overseas oil companies might be accelerated by foreign creditors concerned about the impact of dismemberment. Foreign courts might very well uphold claims for damages for breach of contract against splintered U.S. overseas companies. In short, a breakup of the U.S. oil companies would bring severe headaches abroad as well as at home.

A case of need for divestiture has not been made; appeals have been largely emotional—and proponents of a breakup have been vague about the resulting benefits. What is not at all fuzzy, however, are the tremendous risks that would be run if dismemberment is pursued.

Chief among these are the enormous procedural problems which would arise if Congress were to enact divestiture. Tearing apart a major industry is easier said than done. It would be a long, drawn-out affair dealing with immensely complicated issues. Legal experts at the hearings on the divestiture bill estimated that such a move by the government might well take ten to twenty years to complete.

Those involved in the case would include federal agencies, federal courts, oil companies, investment bankers and other financial institutions, and squadrons of lawyers. All would be caught up in a costly and arduous exercise in revising a maze of contractual arrangements on which the oil industry's financial and organizational structure now rests.

In the meantime, what would happen to this country's energy industry? How could the industry function during a period of extended litigation which would breed extreme uncertainty?

In one word, as witnesses testified, the condition of the oil industry would be chaotic. Until a divestiture plan was agreed upon, until the inevitable litigation that would follow was settled in the courts, and until dismemberment was actually carried out, no one would have any idea of what the post-divestiture oil industry would be like. Stockholders would not know what they owned—or what had been "spun off" by divestiture. How would the debts of the present companies be apportioned to each of the fragments? What kind of a capital structure would the new, smaller units have? How to judge their earnings potential? And would the smaller units be able to make it on their own in a tough, competitive industry? No one, quite literally, can know in advance the answers to those critical questions.

The financial-market implications of divestiture, quite obviously, would be sizable. Investment analysts warned the lawmakers at the hearings that a breakup of the majors—making 72 companies instead of the present 18 companies—would effectively close off a major portion of the oil industry from the capital markets for an indefinite period of time. With reduced investment, the inevitable result would be growing weakness for the oil industry in this country—and enlarged dependence on foreign suppliers of energy.

Sheer-size syndrome

Fundamentally, the dismemberment drive grows out of the deep-rooted antipathy toward bigness that keeps surfacing in American political dialogue. Fortunately, from the standpoint of the nation's economic development, the legal framework within which business operates has not heretofore reflected a preoccupation with sheer size. Size, indeed, is irrelevant in judging anticompetitive conduct; the law requires evidence of collusion or other anticompetitive behavior as the only grounds for government antitrust action.

The pervasive yearning for smaller economic units simply overlooks reality in today's world of high-cost energy. It takes unprecedented amounts of capital to find and deliver energy to consumers. The trans-Alaska pipeline, coming into operation next year, will cost something over $7 billion when completed. A single drilling platform in the North Sea, together with its associated wells and production facilities, is currently estimated to cost upwards of $750 million. An economically competitive oil refinery can cost well over $500 million these days. Such projects require companies of a size capable of raising massive amounts of capital. Smaller units in a post-divestiture market environment, if able to raise money at all, surely would have to pay much more for it, adding to operating costs. Moreover, smaller companies would either have to build smaller, less efficient units or operate on the basis of cumbersome joint ventures; one or the other alternative, however, would further add to production costs—and to the bill the consumer would have to pay. Splintering the oil companies, thus, might yield short-term political gains but, over the longer run, prove to be an economic disaster.

Radical legislative surgery, as is called for in the divestiture bill, would make sense only if it were clear that the oil industry is badly malfunctioning—and if the surgery could cure the problem without devastating "aftereffects." By reasonably objective tests, the oil industry is performing well.

Backers of the proposed divestiture law are curiously silent about its supposed benefits. They have promised nothing—not a swifter energy development effort, not cheaper gasoline and oil, not a loosening of OPEC's stranglehold on oil-consuming nations.

A recent public opinion poll indicated that a majority of Americans feel that big oil companies have "too much power." At the same time, the poll showed that Americans recognize that big oil companies are more efficient than many of the smaller ones. Such feelings, of course, are emotionally based and have nothing to do with the industry's competitive structure.

Congress, in deciding on a measure that would draw and quarter a major industry to the detriment of the nation, needs to keep sight of economic reality and eschew political convenience. Once torn apart, the pieces could not be put back again. That point was aptly made recently by Paul Frankel, chairman of Petroleum Economics Limited of London, when he warned U.S. lawmakers about "the child who, bent on finding out how the toy works, dismantles it and in the process wrecks it altogether."

Bank Profitability and Bank Size

By Edward C. Gallick

The earnings performance of commercial banks varies widely from one bank to another. Some banks earn quite high rates of return, while others turn in low rates of return. A number of factors are believed to contribute to the variability of bank profits. They include differences in bank size, location, and structure as well as differences in asset portfolios, liability composition, and quality of bank management.

This article examines the extent to which bank size is associated with bank profitability. In contrast to earlier studies on this subject, which have tended to focus on current profit disparities among selected individual banks or among well-defined bank subsamples, this study considers the profitability of all insured commercial banks in the United States during the 21-year period 1954-74.[1] Systematic differences in bank profitability by bank size, therefore, are examined from a long-run perspective. Also, to gain a better understanding of the variability of bank profits, the major components of bank profitability during the period are identified and their movements investigated. In addition, four subperiods within the 1954-74 period are considered to better evaluate the representative nature of long-run trends in profitability.

AN OVERVIEW OF PROFITABILITY: 1954-74

The overall measure of bank profitability used in this study is the rate of return on capital, defined

---

1/See William F. Ford, "Profitability: Why Do Some Banks Perform Better Than the Average? An In-Depth Analysis," *Banking*, Vol. 76, No. 16 (October 1974), pp. 29-33; Dennis A. Olson, "How High Profit Banks Get That Way," *Banking*, Vol. 67, No. 5 (May 1975), pp. 46-58; Jean L. Valerius, "Bank Profits in 1974," Federal Reserve Bank of Chicago *Business Conditions*, July 1975, pp. 13-15; Marvin M. Phaup, Jr., "Contrasts in 1974 Bank Profitability: Two Profiles," *Economic Commentary*, Federal Reserve Bank of Cleveland, August 18, 1975; and William C. Niblack, "Income and Expenses of Eighth District Member Banks," Federal Reserve Bank of St. Louis *Review*, Vol. 57, No. 8 (August 1975), pp. 20-23.

---

as the ratio of net income before taxes to total capital. Table 1 shows the rates of return on capital of all insured commercial banks in the United States by bank deposit size during the years 1954-74. As can be seen, there is considerable variability in the rates of return among deposit size groupings. Nonetheless, there is a distinct tendency for smaller banks to register lower rates of return on capital than larger banks, not only during particular years but also during the period as a whole.

Evidence of a positive association between bank size and bank profitability is depicted clearly in Chart 1. The chart shows the average rates of return on capital by banks classified according to deposit size for the entire 1954-74 period. Banks with deposits of less than $5 million, for example, had an average rate of return of 11.43 per cent—the lowest ratio of any bank size group. Then, as the chart shows, the average rates of return tend to increase as bank size increases. Banks with deposits from $5 to $10 million, $10 to $25 million, $25 to $50 million, and $50 to $100 million averaged pretax rates of return on capital of 13.97, 14.98, 15.27, and 15.20 per cent, respectively. Banks with deposits of more than $100 million, the largest banks, had an average rate of return of 15.71 per cent—the highest ratio of any group.

Components of Bank Profitability

Given the clear tendency for bank profitability to rise as bank size increases, it is useful to examine the components of bank profitability that contribute to this positive relationship. The components can be identified by reference to the definition of the rate of return on capital, which is the ratio of net income before taxes to total capital, as shown by the following equation:

Edward C. Gallick, "Bank Profitability and Bank Size." *Monthly Review*, Federal Reserve Bank of Kansas City, January 1976, pp. 11–16. Reprinted with permission.

Table 1
RATE OF RETURN ON CAPITAL, ALL INSURED COMMERCIAL BANKS, BY BANK SIZE

Year	Less than $5	$5 to $10	$10 to $25	$25 to $50	$50 to $100	More than $100
1954	13.546	15.553	17.169	18.494	18.652	17.833
1955	12.495	13.868	14.374	14.721	14.854	14.757
1956	12.168	13.238	13.943	14.471	15.001	15.055
1957	11.996	13.239	14.277	14.699	15.450	16.409
1958	12.304	14.659	16.618	18.934	18.752	20.705
1959	11.983	12.486	12.973	12.581	12.678	13.128
1960	13.027	14.583	16.191	17.488	17.568	19.280
1961	11.900	13.864	15.179	16.577	16.996	19.535
1962	11.416	13.057	13.997	14.339	15.307	16.578
1963	10.686	12.528	13.211	13.473	14.294	15.625
1964	10.984	13.051	13.576	13.849	13.622	14.639
1965	10.233	12.371	13.044	13.534	13.268	13.845
1966	11.038	12.550	13.028	13.257	13.005	13.019
1967	11.508	12.808	13.387	13.968	13.599	14.449
1968	11.826	13.751	14.414	14.703	14.075	14.463
1969	11.719	15.243	16.380	16.256	16.033	15.910
1970	12.276	15.770	16.599	16.162	15.980	15.488
1971	11.046	14.986	16.216	15.560	15.470	14.486
1972	8.766	13.966	15.797	15.719	15.267	14.439
1973	9.713	16.118	17.265	16.839	15.281	15.069
1974	9.302	15.674	16.871	14.944	14.098	15.234
1954-59	12.415	13.841	14.892	15.650	15.898	16.315
1960-64	11.603	13.417	14.431	15.145	15.557	17.131
1965-69	11.265	13.345	14.051	14.344	13.996	14.337
1970-74	10.221	15.303	16.550	15.845	15.219	* 14.943
1954-74	11.425	13.970	14.977	15.265	15.202	15.712

NOTE: Rate of return on capital defined as net income before taxes divided by total capital account. Denominators for the 1969-74 period calculated from all commercial banks. Ratios computed from aggregate dollar amounts and expressed as percentages. Post-1968 figures not strictly comparable due to changes in reporting procedures introduced in 1969. The remaining discrepancies, however, are minimal.
SOURCE: Annual Report(s) of the Federal Deposit Insurance Corporation; Assets and Liabilities: Commercial and Mutual Savings Banks, FDIC; and report(s) of income and of condition submitted to the Federal Reserve System.

(1) Rate of return on capital = $\dfrac{\text{net income}}{\text{capital}}$.

Since net income is definitionally equal to total revenues minus total expenses, the rate of return on capital can also be shown as follows:[2]

(2) Rate of return on capital = $\dfrac{\text{total revenues} - \text{total expenses}}{\text{capital}}$.

To eliminate the effects of absolute bank size on revenue, expense, and capital measures, each is deflated by total bank assets. As a result, bank profitability can be analyzed in terms of its three major components:

(3) Rate of return on capital = $\dfrac{\dfrac{\text{total revenues}}{\text{assets}} - \dfrac{\text{total expenses}}{\text{assets}}}{\dfrac{\text{capital}}{\text{assets}}}$.

This latter formulation implies that a higher rate of return on capital can result from a rise in the revenue-assets component or from a decline in either the expense-assets or the capital-assets components.

The average revenue, expense, and capital components of bank profitability during 1954-74, classified by bank size groups, are shown in Chart 1. In examining the relationship of these compo-

2/Total revenues are defined as total operating income. Total expenses equal total operating expenses plus actual net losses on loans and securities minus provision for loan losses and interest paid on capital notes and debentures. Capital includes total capital accounts.

133

nents to bank profitability, it is quite evident from the chart that the uptrend in profitability across bank size is associated with the decline in the capital-assets ratio. The smallest banks—those with deposits of less than $5 million—had an average capital to assets ratio as high as 9.80 per cent. As bank size increased, the ratio declined quite sharply, falling to 7.17 per cent for banks with deposits of $50 to $100 million. The only exception to this generally strong negative relationship between profitability and capital to assets occurred in the largest size group. These banks with deposits of more than $100 million increased their average return on capital relative to smaller sized banks despite an increase in their capital to assets.

The net income to assets component remained generally stable throughout the bank size distribution during the 1954-74 period. Banks with deposits of less than $5 million averaged a net income to assets ratio of 1.12 per cent, while banks with deposits of $50 to $100 million had a ratio of 1.09 per cent. The largest banks, however, showed a noticeable rise in their net income component to 1.17 per cent.

The general stability in the net income to assets ratios shown in Chart 1 reveals a relatively constant spread between the revenue and expense ratios. Both revenue and expense ratios tend to increase across the smaller bank sizes and decline across the larger sizes. Banks with deposits over $100 million were able to reduce expense ratios sufficiently to offset lower revenue ratios, so that their net income relative to assets posted a noticeable increase.

The rise in the net income to assets ratio of the largest banks serves to explain how they were able to increase their overall profitability despite a rise in their capital to assets ratio. As indicated by equation (3), other things equal, an increase in the capital to assets ratio would cause a decline in the rate of return on capital. In the case of the largest banks, however, the rise in the net income component more than offset the negative impact coming from the capital component. Specifically, the higher rate of return on capital shown by the largest banks, relative to banks with deposits of $50 to $100 million, was due to a larger percentage gain (7.8 per

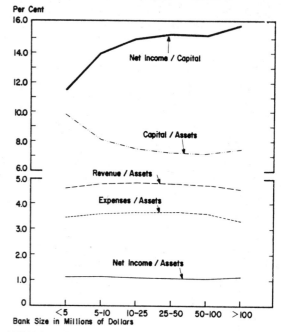

Chart 1
BANK PROFITABILITY: 1954-74

Per Cent

Net Income / Capital

Capital / Assets

Revenue / Assets

Expenses / Assets

Net Income / Assets

Bank Size in Millions of Dollars

<5   5-10   10-25   25-50   50-100   >100

SOURCE: See Table 1.

cent) in the net income component than the percentage increase (4.1 per cent) in the capital component. The net effect of these two factors enabled banks with deposits over $100 million to earn the highest average return on capital of any bank size group for the entire period.

To summarize, the average rates of return on capital of all insured banks in the United States during the 1954-74 period have displayed a marked tendency to increase as bank size increases. For all but the largest size bank category, this tendency reflects systematic movements of two factors. The capital component of bank profitability declines as bank size increases and the net income component remains relatively constant. In the case of the largest banks, the increase in the rate of return on capital is produced by an upward movement in the net income component and not by a decline in the capital component.

How representative are these long-run trends in bank profitability, and components of profitability, for individual subperiods within the 1954-74 period? The next section of this article attempts to answer this question by examining movements in bank profitability by bank size for four distinct subperiods.

PROFITABILITY WITHIN THE 1954-74 PERIOD

Representative Subperiods

The long-run systematic behavior of bank profitability across bank size is found to be representative of three subperiods: 1954-59, 1960-64, and 1965-69. To illustrate this similarity, Chart 2 contains average rates of return on capital for all insured commercial banks in the United States, grouped according to deposit size, for each of these subperiods. Also shown are the components of bank profitability for each of the subperiods.

A noticeable characteristic of each of the three representative subperiods is that the average rates of return on capital are positively associated with bank size. The smallest banks invariably record the lowest average rates of return; larger banks tend to show progressively higher rates of return; and the largest banks show the highest rates of profitability. Also clearly evident is that, for each representative subperiod, the capital to assets ratio falls across the size distribution, except in the case of the larger banks. There is, with the exception of the larger banks, a perceptible inverse relationship between bank profitability and the capital component in each of the three representative subperiods. The net income to assets ratio, and the underlying revenue and expense ratios, also behave in a similar fashion in each of the three subperiods. While little variability occurs in each of these ratios for most bank sizes, the net income to assets ratios of the largest banks rise noticeably due to a more rapid decline in the expense than in the revenue component. This rise in the net income component for the largest banks was sufficient to offset the increase in the capital component, producing a rise in the return on capital.[3]

A Nonrepresentative Subperiod

Movements in bank profitability are found to differ significantly in the 1970-74 subperiod from the long-run patterns evidenced for the entire 1954-74 period. Average rates of return for this nonrepresentative subperiod are depicted in Chart 2. As seen from the chart, rates of return on capital are only positively associated with bank size over the smaller bank groups. Thereafter, as bank size increases, profitability falls. As a consequence, the highest average rate of return of 16.55 per cent is turned in by medium sized banks with deposits of from \$10 to \$25 million. And, the profitability ratio of the largest banks of 14.94 per cent is found to be next to the lowest of any size group. In the 1970-74 subperiod, therefore, the relationship between profitability and bank size becomes negative for bank sizes larger than \$25 million in deposits.

Movements in the capital to assets ratio in the most recent subperiod are generally similar to earlier periods for small and medium bank sizes. Unlike the 1954-74 period, however, the ratio falls across the larger bank sizes. Other things equal, declines in the capital component are associated with increases in bank profitability. Hence, declines in the capital to assets ratio across bank size offer no ready explanation for the relative decline in profitability experienced by the larger sized banks during the 1970-74 period.

The dominant factor contributing to the falloff in profitability at larger sized banks is that—unlike earlier periods—the net income to assets ratio drops almost steadily as bank size increases.[4] In particular, the ratio falls for the largest banks, which is in marked contrast to earlier subperiods when the ratio at these banks increased. Underlying the downward movement of the net income ratio, as seen in Chart 2, is the fact that the revenue component remains generally flat for all but the smaller bank sizes while the expense component steadily rises as bank size increases. This pattern is particularly evident for banks with deposits over \$100 million. In brief, the decline in relative profit-

---

3/Chart 2 may appear to suggest that movements in capital are more important than movements in net income between the two largest bank sizes. Yet, in percentage terms, the increments in the net income component are larger. In the 1965-69 subperiod, for example, the capital to assets ratio increased from 7.28 per cent to 7.53 per cent, whereas the net income to assets ratio increased from 1.02 per cent to 1.08 per cent across the two largest bank sizes. In percentage terms, however, the movements in the capital and net income components are 3.43 per cent and 5.79 per cent, respectively.

4/From equation (3), other things equal, a decline in the capital component produces an increase in the rate of return on capital. Thus, the downturn in net income was sufficient to reduce the rate of return on capital, despite the reduction in the capital to assets ratio.

Chart 2
BANK PROFITABILITY IN SUBPERIODS

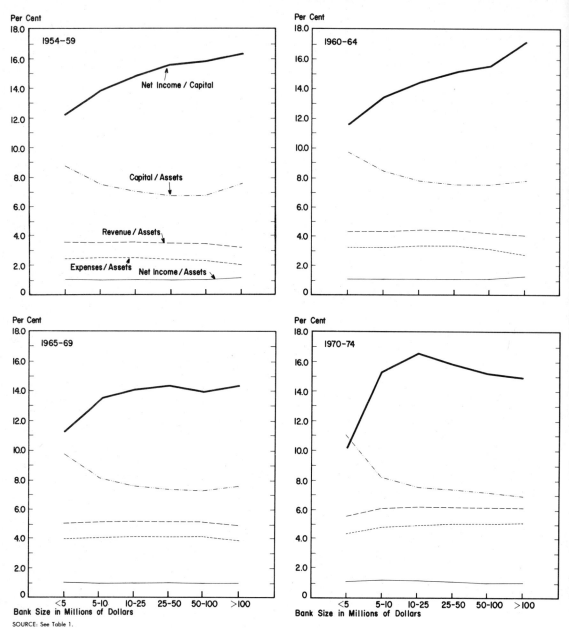

Per Cent

1954–59

Net Income / Capital

Capital / Assets

Revenue / Assets

Expenses / Assets   Net Income / Assets

Per Cent

1960–64

Per Cent

1965–69

Bank Size in Millions of Dollars

SOURCE: See Table 1.

Per Cent

1970–74

Bank Size in Millions of Dollars

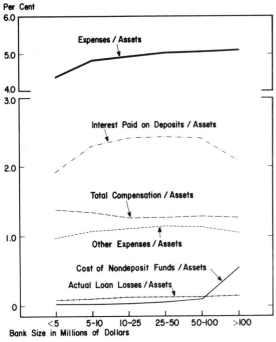

Chart 3
EXPENSE COMPONENT: 1970-74

Per Cent

- Expenses / Assets
- Interest Paid on Deposits / Assets
- Total Compensation / Assets
- Other Expenses / Assets
- Cost of Nondeposit Funds / Assets
- Actual Loan Losses / Assets

Bank Size in Millions of Dollars: <5 5-10 10-25 25-50 50-100 >100

SOURCE: See Table 1.

ability of the larger banks in the 1970-74 period is traceable to a rise in the expense component relative to the revenue component.

But what caused the expense component of bank profitability to rise at larger banks during the 1970-74 period? To examine this question, Chart 3 depicts the major items of expense relative to total assets of all commercial banks classified by deposit size during the recent period. The chart shows that all except one of the major expense items either declined or remained relatively constant over the larger bank size groups. The one expense item that increased noticeably was the cost of nondeposit sources of funds, defined as the expense of Federal funds purchased plus the interest cost on other borrowed money. In other words, the rise in the expense to assets ratio at the larger banks appears to be attributable mainly to an increase in the cost of nondeposit funds. Underlying this phenomenon is that the larger banks have relied increasingly during recent years on short-term borrowed money

to accommodate loan demand in the short run and to maintain valuable customer relationships in the long run. These bank practices, however, at times of rising interest rates and unexpectedly severe inflationary pressures—such as prevailed in the 1970-74 period—undoubtedly have served to reduce the relative profitability of the larger sized banks.[5]

SUMMARY

An examination of bank profitability according to bank deposit size reveals that during the 1954-74 period there is a clear tendency for the rate of return on capital to increase as bank size increases. Small banks show the lowest average rates of return; larger banks show progressively higher rates of return; and the largest banks post the highest rates of profitability. Except for the largest bank sizes, this tendency reflects the sharp downward movement in the capital component of bank profitability as bank size increases. The net income component of bank profitability tends on average to vary little across small and medium sized banks. Across the two largest bank sizes, however, the income component increased sufficiently to offset an upward movement in the capital component, producing a rise in the rate of return on capital.

The general pattern of bank profitability observed in the 1954-74 period was found not to hold true in the most recent subperiod of 1970-74. Rates of return on capital were positively related to bank size only over the small to medium size groups. Thereafter, as bank size increased, bank profitability decreased. Consequently, medium sized banks turned in the highest average rate of return of any size group during the recent subperiod. Contributing to this pattern of bank profitability is that the expense component—particularly for short-term borrowed money—moved up quite noticeably at larger banks. As a result, the average profitability ratio of the largest banks was found to be next to the lowest of any size group during the recent 5-year period.

5/A mild and relatively stable inflation rate averaging 1.99 per cent per annum characterized the 1954-69 period; it more than tripled to 6.14 per cent during 1970-74. It is precisely in this time interval that rates of return on capital peak over the medium sized banks and steadily decline throughout the remainder of the bank size distribution.

137

After Oil, Bananas and Bauxite?

Last year the Organization of Petroleum Exporting Countries (OPEC) successfully engineered a major increase in the world price of oil. Could producing countries band together to raise the prices of other commodities essential to the industrial world? This question is explored in the following exchange between C. Fred Bergsten and Philip H. Trezise, both senior fellows in the Brookings Foreign Policy Studies program.

Mr. Bergsten's argument is adapted from his statement of May 15, 1974, before the Subcommittee on Foreign Economic Policy of the House Committee on Foreign Affairs. Mr. Trezise's rejoinder is based on his remarks before an Open Forum meeting held at the U.S. Department of State in March.

"Commodity Power" Is Here to Stay

C. Fred Bergsten

THERE CAN NOW BE NO DOUBT that a large number of primary producing countries will make steady, determined, and often concerted efforts to raise substantially their returns from a wide range of the commodities they produce, in part through the formation of "new OPECs," and that many of them are in an excellent position to do so.

None of the individual commodities susceptible to such developments has the quantitative or qualitative importance of oil. Nor is it likely that this new commodity power will often be used, as was oil, for political reasons—though oil may well be used for that purpose again.

Nevertheless, successful "resources diplomacy" on the part of producing countries will further intensify the strong inflationary pressures now engulfing the world economy, including our own. Since many of these primary producers are developing countries, their actions will also reduce the North-South economic and political disparities that characterized the first postwar generation, and thus may put new constraints on U.S. foreign policy in the coming years.

Since I first called attention to the likelihood of these developments a year ago in "The Threat From the Third World" (*Foreign Policy*, Summer 1973), their scope and depth have expanded dramatically.

• OPEC itself effectively quadrupled the price of oil and cut production sharply. Oil is of course the most important commodity in world trade.

• The leading coffee producers have established effective control over the world coffee price. Indeed, they are so confident of success that they let expire the International Coffee Agreement, which they had previously relied on to secure the cooperation of the consuming countries in stabilizing prices. Coffee has traditionally been the second most heavily traded commodity in the world.

• The phosphate producers acted together to triple their prices. Phosphate is of course a major input to fertilizer and detergents.

• The bauxite producers have formed the International Bauxite Association. Immediately thereafter the leading producer, Jamaica, demanded a fundamental renegotiation of its present arrangements with the multinational aluminum firms now operating there, apparently including an increase in the domestic processing of the bauxite ore into alumina and six times higher taxes and royalties on all output. It is widely assumed that the other producing countries will demand terms equal to those achieved by Jamaica.

• The Latin American banana producers have organized an International Organization of Banana Exporters (known by its Spanish acronym, IPEB) and raised their prices substantially through the joint imposition of export taxes.

• The major tin producers are seeking a 42 percent increase in the guaranteed floor price maintained through the buffer stock held under the International Tin Agreement.

• The four major copper exporters, through their long-standing organization CIPEC, are now deciding how to fix a floor price for their commodity.

Several qualitative developments have accompanied this trend. More than two dozen developing countries have set up ministries of resources to pursue their new economic diplomacy. The call for new "producer associations" was a central theme at a special session of the UN General Assembly. In a recent meeting of parties to the General Agreement on Tariffs and Trade, the developing countries unanimously rejected a suggestion to consider the establishment of new international rules to guarantee access to supplies for consuming countries, analogous to the traditional GATT rules guaranteeing access to markets for producing countries.

Thus the commodity producers are aggressively seeking to improve their earnings dramatically, through whatever means they can devise to fit the opportunities available to them, and they are recording substantial successes. Two basic developments explain why they are doing so.

First, the buyers' markets of the past have largely become sellers' markets. Downturns in commodity prices usually lead declines in the business cycle by at least one quarter, which is why many observers began to predict a bursting of the commodities boom in early 1973. Yet the prices of virtually all primary products continued to rise, or declined only marginally from record levels, until very recently—at least eighteen months after they "should" have turned down—despite the sharp decline in GNP in the United States and Japan and markedly slower growth rates in nearly every other industrial country. References to unsuccessful cartelization efforts during the past decade, when buyers' markets dominated, are irrelevant to the current situation.

Economists frankly do not understand why this has happened. Double-digit inflation, itself caused partly by the rise in commodity prices, has fueled further speculation in commodities as faith in paper money folds; hence a commodity-price spiral replaces or supplements the wage-price spiral that has explained much of the inflationary bursts of the past. The advent of more flexible exchange rates, while providing a major improvement in the balance-of-payments adjustment process, may increase this effect by reducing confidence in currencies as against "real goods." The success of the new OPECs, and fears that more are coming, may add yet another loop to the spiral.

Because buyers' markets have become sellers' markets in virtually every primary product, market conditions provide an ideal setting for producers to raise their prices still further. Even the most persuasive counterargument to this thesis published so far concludes that "there is an improved climate for group pressure or price leadership, and where the trend is toward higher mineral prices . . . the new aggressive stance of producers would seem to make it irreversible." (Bension Varon and Kenji Takeuchi, "Developing Countries and Non-Fuel Minerals," *Foreign Affairs*, April 1974.) As always the rich get richer—this time, of course, with some justice in that it is the *nouveaux riches* who are benefiting.

The second fundamental change is the success of OPEC itself. There is disagreement as to whether OPEC is really a successful cartel, or whether it is simply an inner group of four or five countries that have propped up the market by restraining output, or whether the results are due solely to the activity of a single country (Saudi Arabia), or whether—in light of Middle Eastern politics—economics has anything to do with the situation.

These questions as yet have no widely accepted answers. But whatever the answer, OPEC has worked. Its success promotes "new OPECs" in several ways.

In purely economic terms, the dramatic increase in oil prices forces every oil-consuming country to maximize its own export prices so as to limit the cost to its balance of payments and internal growth. Many developing countries have no alternative; they can look only to their primary products if they are to recoup.

OPEC shows that a producer-country cartel can work. If OPEC can work for oil, similar organization may even be *easier* to form for other commodities. OPEC comprises a large number of countries reliant on a single

commodity, several of which hold very different views on important economic and political issues, including Israel. The absence of a concerted response to OPEC by the oil-consuming countries can only suggest to other primary producers that they need have little fear of even subtle retaliation against their efforts. Indeed, virtually every action taken by the industrial nations—notably the scrambles for "special deals" by the Europeans and Japanese—encouraged OPEC to take more and bigger steps.

In addition, OPEC may help its offspring directly. The Shah of Iran has spoken publicly of such possibilities, which are one way—perhaps a very profitable way —for the oil producers to mitigate the economic damage they have done to a large number of countries that are still relatively poor. Since the OPEC countries are looking for profitable ways to invest their oil earnings, simple purchases of commodities (including futures) in the open market might meet their economic and political goals simultaneously.

It is often argued that producer-country cartels for other primary products will not work even if the countries involved try to form them. That argument is not persuasive. Only three prerequisites need be satisfied for such cartels to succeed.

The economic requirement is a relatively low price elasticity of demand for the commodity in question— that is, a higher price must neither reduce final demand for the product excessively nor trigger substitution by similar commodities. Existing knowledge of these elasticities suggests that they are quite low for a wide range of primary products. Substitution—of aluminum for copper, for example—is unlikely if the prices of *all* commodities are high and rising, as they have been in recent months. Moreover, the huge investments required to develop new sources of supply or substitutes—often in "politically unstable" areas—are a major deterrent to increased production even in the medium term.

In short, it would be unwise to assume that "the market" will quickly abort the efforts of primary producers to boost their returns substantially.

The political criterion for a cartel is simply an absence of overt enmity among the participating countries. They need not be allies or even hold similar foreign policy views. Some of them would have no reason even to communicate *except* to maximize their commodity power, as in the case of Bolivia and Malaysia on tin, and Chile and Zambia on copper.

It is a common fallacy that only "shared political values" subsumed in hatred for Israel bound together the oil producers. In fact Iran, the second-biggest exporter and the leader in raising oil prices, has been consistently pro-Israeli and continued selling oil to Israel during the Yom Kippur war. Important producers such as Venezuela and Indonesia care little about Middle Eastern politics. Sharp divergences exist even within the Arab world on how best to use the oil weapon. In this case the value-sharing is far from monolithic, and hardly explains the success of OPEC.

Nor is it true that a surfeit of foreign exchange enabled the oil producers to take the risk of cartelization. Iran and several other producing countries actually held small reserves and spent everything they earned. Conversely, potential members of other cartels (Malaysia, Brazil, and Australia, among others) have sizable reserves. Poverty may encourage cartel efforts more than it will deter them. On balance, then, the foreign exchange position is not what made OPEC succeed.

Lastly, a cartel is manageable only if (a) relatively few countries are involved, or (b) a single country is willing and able to dominate the market. One or the other of these conditions is present in a wide array of markets for primary commodities.

Such generalities obviously cannot be applied without reservation to every primary product at every moment in future time. Intensive analysis of the economics and politics of individual commodities is necessary to provide a clearer fix on each.

Nevertheless, individual commodity developments—like individual acts in international trade or monetary policy—take place within a broader framework of economic and political trends. The trends outlined above, coupled with the new ability of developing countries to pursue national policies that effectively serve their interests and reflect their view that the international economic system has worked against them far too long, suggest that commodity power and resources diplomacy will be with us for a long time to come.

More OPECs Are Unlikely

Philip H. Trezise

I DO NOT BELIEVE that widespread fears about supplies of primary commodities other than oil have any substantial basis. Putting oil aside, I see small likelihood that producing countries will be able to concert effectively for very long on policies to limit supplies and raise prices. Again excepting oil, politically motivated embargoes on exports of primary commodities are improbable and in any case would be unsuccessful.

The general proposition is that the Organization of Petroleum Exporting Countries (OPEC) has provided a model for other producers of raw materials. It follows that the spectacular rise in the price of oil inevitably will lead countries producing minerals and tropical products to emulate OPEC by establishing cartels for their commodities. I think, however, that this is a misreading both of OPEC and of the possibilities for managing supplies of primary goods.

Consider first the conditions for an effective cartel—that is, for successful concerted producer action to raise prices. Broadly, they are two:

First, producers must be willing and able to withhold enough supplies to affect the market. If only some producers do the withholding, others must refrain from making up the difference. If consumers have stockpiles to draw on, the producers must hold back a greater volume of goods. And new suppliers must be kept out.

Second, consumer demand for the cartelized product must be relatively unaffected by higher prices. If consumers can do without, or economize, or find suitable substitutes, then a cartel will find the going rough even if its members are able to act together.

These are hard conditions to satisfy.

It is not a simple matter to manage the supply side. The temptation to cheat is always present among producers. Many of the countries involved have limited financial staying power. For some of the metals, which are the subject of most of the present worries, reserves are rather widely distributed. Cartels for these products must stretch over a large number of countries if they are to work. Lower grade reserves in nonmember countries will come to be exploited. And stockpiles can be put on the market.

On the demand side, price elasticities will vary among commodities. In no case, however, is it plausible that consumers will be helpless in the face of producer efforts to raise prices. The nascent banana cartel would appear to have limited market power, given the variety of fruits available to consumers. Could tin producers have significantly better prospects, considering the alternative materials that can be used for the same purposes? Copper, bauxite, rubber, coffee—whatever the product, the outlook is that higher prices will cause users in due course to reduce consumption and alter their buying habits. These frustrations always face the would-be organizers of cartels.

Oil may be said to be a special case. The price elasticities for oil are probably low everywhere. A large part of exportable output is controlled by a few producers, some of them well stocked with financial reserves. Perhaps more than any other primary product, oil is suitable for concerted measures to raise prices. The current folklore is that OPEC did indeed demonstrate in 1971 and again in 1973 the potential and the power of cartel action.

The facts about OPEC as a cartel do not quite correspond with the received wisdom.

OPEC was formed in 1959 in response to a reduction in the posted price and thus in producer country revenues from crude oil. Through the 1960s the real price of crude oil nonetheless continued downward. In 1970 Libya, which had become a major supplier of crude to Western European markets, had a revolution. The successor regime, independently of OPEC, cut output sharply in a partly political contest with the oil companies whose concessions were granted by the previous regime. Libya by itself, not OPEC, made possible the sizable price increases of 1971, which were ratified in the so-called Tripoli and Teheran agreements. The new prices would quickly have come under downward pressure from rising output in the Persian Gulf had not a surge of import demand in the United States strengthened the world oil market, fortuitously for the oil countries. U.S. imports of crude oil grew by two and one-third times between 1970 and 1973, from 1.5 million to 3.5 million barrels a day.

The round of much larger OPEC price increases in 1973 was made possible, of course, by the production cutbacks enforced in Saudi Arabia, Kuwait, and a few smaller Arab oil countries in the wake of the Yom Kippur war. Concerted action was taken by a few—not all—of the Arab countries in an atmosphere charged with high political emotion. It was certainly not an OPEC-wide master design. Most OPEC countries raised output as much as they could.

These events confirmed what was already apparent—that oil supplies from the Arab states are vulnerable in

---

time of political crisis or war in the Near East, that prices will go up when supplies are short, and that the normal producer response to higher prices is to take advantage of them. Whether they mean that OPEC could hold down production levels elsewhere if Saudi Arabia were to resume the expansion of output is much less certain. The same holds for OPEC's capability to induce or enforce producer unity as other adjustments are made in world energy markets on both the supply and demand sides.

If the oil "cartel" is a somewhat questionable proposition, cartels for other primary products are far more so. Nothing in experience indicates that a number of supplying countries can operate together in a disciplined fashion for very long. It is evident, notably in the instance of the International Coffee Agreement, that even when producers and consumers agree to cooperate to hold prices steady, serious problems arise in keeping producers in line. The truth is that most of the countries producing primary commodities have very limited capacities for managing supply. Disappointment, not success, is the likely fate of the cartels now being so easily proposed.

The policy lessons I would draw from this are not the currently conventional ones. I see little need to gear up to defend ourselves against threats from the Third World. We do have commodity problems, both in supply and trade terms, but, like all problems in foreign economic policy, they will require for their solution the acceptance of special responsibility by the industrial countries and cooperation, not confrontation, between the industrial and developing countries.

First, the major trading nations—some, particularly the United States, are great primary product exporters themselves—ought to make a strong effort to tighten the rules on export restrictions as applied by themselves. There is little prospect that the developing countries will be ready to accept any such discipline, but it should be obvious that they will scarcely feel bound to refrain from considering embargoes on exports if the United States, Japan, and the European Community are free to do as they please. In any event, it is important that the industrial countries agree to restraints on their own actions, which can be destructive of international comity whatever the developing nations may do.

Second, a case can be made for a new look at commodity agreements. As prices slip from their high levels, the developing countries are bound to come back to the question of producer-consumer cooperation to stabilize commodity prices. To be sure, the record of the past shows that stabilization agreements are hard to negotiate and perhaps harder still to operate, but the few that have been established have had their uses. Much can be said for new efforts to check commodity price fluctuations, through buffer stocks or other approaches.

The long downward trend of primary product prices from 1951 to 1968 contributed to the capacity shortages that sent prices skyrocketing in 1972–73, as well as to the frustrations of the developing world. We could, and should, try to do better as the recent boom fades and prices weaken.

PART III.
GOVERNMENT
AND THE
ECONOMY

Accompanying the rapid growth in the population and wealth of the U.S. during the 20th century has been a vast expansion in the role of government in the economy. In 1929, the public sector (Federal, state and local government) accounted for approximately 10% of GNP; by 1970 this figure had reached 34%. The most rapid growth occurred in Federal government expenditures, which benefited greatly from changing public perception of the role of government in the economy. Section A examines issues and problems of government regulation in general and in various sectors of the economy. Selections in section B review developments and issues related to government taxation and expenditures policies.

Section A, Government Regulation

In "The New Wave of Government Regulation of Business" Murray L. Weidenbaum expresses concern with the 50% increase in Federal expenditures for business regulation since 1974. Government, he says, is increasingly regulating trivia and shows no appreciation for the costs it imposes by so doing. In an interview conducted by John McClaughry, Hendrik Houthakker states the case for governmental deregulation, tax reform, and changes in antitrust laws. He evaluates Federal policies in the areas of natural gas, agriculture, transportation, and banking. In "A Dispersed or Concentrated Agriculture? -- The Role of Public Policy" Edward Harshbarger and Sheldon Stahl contend that the shift away from dispersed agriculture toward concentration has been encouraged by governmental policies. They question the desirability of this trend and call for a re-examination of agricultural policies.

Section B, Taxation and Expenditures

Genuine tax reform is very difficult, according to Joseph Pechman in "The Myths of Tax Reform," because no one wants to face up to the hard choices that it demands; beginning from scratch might be the best way. In "Egalitarianism: Mechanisms for Redistributing Income" John Cobbs says that the current trend toward income equality in the U.S. will be expensive and must be paid for by someone. In "Anatomy of a 'Fiscal Crisis'" Anthony Rufolo discusses the flight to suburbia to escape redistributive taxes and offers some solutions. Dan M. Bechter summarizes the content of Federal government spending in "Federal Government Purchases of Goods and Services," noting in particular the substantial increase in Federal transfer payments. In his view, the swings in the business cycle have been aggravated in recent years by insufficient emphasis in government spending policies on stabilization relative to other objectives. In companion piece entitled "Federal Government Spending on Interest, Transfers, and Grants" Mr. Bechter recounts the recent history of Federal transfers, grants to state and local governments, and interest on the national debt, showing the rapidly rising level of Federal spending owing to sizeable increases in domestic transfer payments and grants-in-aid to state and local governments. The article "Is the Housing Cycle Being Transformed?" reports that in the past severe cycles in housing starts ran counter to the general business cycle, thus providing a stabilizing influence in the economy. While government efforts to stabilize the housing cycle have been unsuccessful, it appears that they have pushed housing construction into a procyclical "lockstep with the overall economy." "Congress's New Grip on the Federal Purse" describes "the most significant modification of the overall federal budget in more than half a century," the Budget and Inpoundment Control Act of 1974, whereby Congress is for the first time considering the national budget as a unified whole.

Will the ACLU come to the rescue of businessmen whose civil liberties are trampled by government bureaucrats?

The New Wave of Government Regulation of Business

MURRAY L. WEIDENBAUM

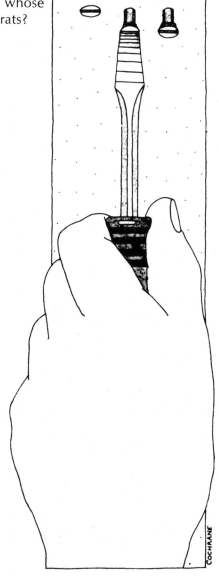

THERE IS A STRIKING but little-noticed parallel between the standard liberal concern with governmental infringement on the civil liberties of individuals and the rising conservative concern with governmental infringement on the freedom of individuals acting as business executives. The first target is often termed "Big Brother." The second could be called "Big Mother."

Many liberals are outraged by the arbitrary "no-knock" powers of federal investigative agencies,

Murray L. Weidenbaum, "The New Wave of Government Regulation of Business." *Business and Society Review,* Fall 1975, pp. 81–86. Reprinted from *Business and Society Review,* Fall 1975, Vol. 15. Copyright 1975, Warren, Gorham and Lamont, Inc., 210 South Street, Boston, Mass. All rights reserved.

yet they readily ignore the unchallenged no-knock power used by other federal agencies in their regulation of private business. Federal inspectors are an increasingly important physical presence in private industry. The Supreme Court has ruled that air pollution inspectors do not need search warrants to enter the property of suspected polluters as long as they do not enter areas closed to the public. The unannounced and warrantless inspections were held not to be in violation of constitutional protections against unreasonable search and seizure.

The inspectors of the Labor Department's Occupational Safety and Health Administration (OSHA) can go further. They have no-knock power to enter the premises of virtually any business in the United States, without a warrant or even prior announcement, to inspect for health and safety violations. Jail terms are provided in the OSHA law for anyone tipping off a "raid."

Federal regulatory agencies do not always feel obliged to follow normal standards of fairness in dealing with business firms. Consider the possibility of biased decision-making inherent in the recent agreement between the U.S. National Institute for Occupational Safety and Health (NIOSH), the agency that does the basic research underlying new OSHA regulations, and the Amalgamated Clothing Workers.

Under the agreement, the official federal study of safety and health hazards in the clothing industry is being conducted by a union employee and financed by the union. In the words of the OSHA publication which enthusiastically reported the undertaking, "The union will help obtain the cooperation of plant managers." It is painful to try to picture the reaction of a company management to the investigation of its premises by its union on behalf of the government!

THE NEW MODEL OF GOVERNMENT REGULATION

The traditional notion of government regulation of business is based on the model of the Interstate Commerce Commission: A federal commission is established to regulate a specific industry, with the related concern of promoting the well-being of that industry.

In some cases—because of the unique expertise possessed by the members of the industry, or its job enticements for regulators who leave government employment—the regulatory commission becomes a captive of the industry it is supposed to regulate, and the public or consumer interest is subordinated or even ignored. At least, this is a popular view of the federal regulatory process. In addition to the ICC, other agencies

which have been criticized on this ground include the Civil Aeronautics Board, the Federal Communications Commission, and the Federal Power Commission.

Although that type of federal regulation of business surely may continue, the new regulatory efforts established by the Congress in recent years generally follow a fundamentally different pattern. The new federal agencies are broader in scope than the ICC-CAB-FCC-FPC model. Yet in important aspects, they are far more restricted. In the cases of the Environmental Protection Agency, the Equal Employment Opportunity Commission, the Consumer Product Safety Commission, the Federal Energy Administration, and the Occupational Safety and Health Administration, the regulatory agency is not limited to a single industry. Their jurisdictions extend to the bulk of the private sector and, at times, to the public sector as well. It is this far-ranging reach that makes it impractical for any single industry to dominate these regulatory activities in the manner of the traditional model.

Yet, in comparison to the older agencies, the newer federal regulators, in many important ways, operate in a far narrower sphere. That is, they are not concerned with the totality of a company or industry, but only with the segment of operations which falls under their jurisdiction. This limitation prevents the agency from developing too close a concern with the overall well-being of any company or industry. Rather, it may result in total lack of concern about the effects of its actions on a specific company or industry.

If any special interest may come to dominate such an agency, it is the one that is preoccupied with its specific task—environmental cleanup, elimination of job discrimination, establishment of safe working conditions, reduction of product hazards, and so forth. Thus, the basic mission of the industry to provide goods and services to the public may get little attention. And matters broader than the specific charter of the regulating agency—such as productivity, economic growth, employment, effect on overall living standards, inflationary impacts—also may be ignored. At times the process may seem to be epitomized by that proverbial dentist who sees his patient as merely two rows of teeth surrounded by a mass of miscellaneous material.

The result may be a reversal of the traditional situation. Rather than being dominated by a given industry, the newer type of federal regulatory activity is far more likely to utilize the resources of various industries, or to ignore their needs, to further the specific objectives of the agency. My personal study of the activities of these new regulatory agencies reveals many negative aspects of considerable importance.

I do not quarrel with the intent of the new wave of federal regulation: safer working conditions, better products for the consumer, eliminating discrimination in employment, reducing environmental pollution, and so forth. And the programs established to deal with these problems have at times yielded significant benefits. But no realistic evaluation of government regulation comfortably fits the notion of benign and wise officials making altogether sensible decisions in the society's greater interests. Instead we find waste, bias, stupidity, concentration on trivia, conflicts among the regulators, and, worst of all, arbitrary and uncontrolled power.

The agencies carrying out federal regulation are proliferating. In the past decade alone we have seen the formation of the Consumer Product Safety Commission, the Environmental Protection Agency, the Federal Energy Administration, the Cost Accounting Standards Board, the National Bureau of Fire Prevention, the Mining Enforcement and Safety Administration, the National Highway Traffic Safety Administration, and the Occupational Safety and Health Administration, to cite the better-known ones.

The administrative cost of this army of enforcers (approximately $3 billion a year to support a regulatory work force in excess of 74,000) is quite substantial (see table on page 84). But that expense is only the tip of the iceberg. It is the costs imposed on the private sector that are really large, the added expenses—which inevitably are passed on to customers—of complying with government directives. A direct cost of government controls is the growing paperwork burden imposed on business firms: the expensive and time-consuming process of submitting reports, making applications, filling out questionnaires, replying to orders and directives, and appealing some of the regulatory rulings in the courts. There now are 5,146 different types of approved government forms. Individuals and business firms spend millions and millions of work-hours a year filling them out.

Another hidden cost of federal regulation is the reduced rate of technological innovation. The longer it takes for some change to be approved by a federal regulatory agency—a new product or a more efficient production process—the less likely it is that the change will be made. A recent case is the new asthma drug beclomethasone dipropionate (let us call it BD). Although this drug has been used by millions of asthma patients in the United Kingdom, it still has not received the approval of the U.S. Food and Drug Adminis-

tration. BD is described as a safe and effective replacement for the drugs which are now administered to chronic asthma patients, but without the adverse side effects of the drugs now in use in the United States. Unlike BD, the steroids currently used in this country, such as prednisone, can stunt growth in children, worsen diabetes, and increase weight through water retention. The delaying procedures of the FDA not only are increasing costs to drug manufacturers, but also are preventing American consumers from having access to BD.

The large private costs of government regulation sometimes arise from the attitudes of the regulators. Take the question of industrial noise. Reluctant to depend on earplugs and similar hearing protectors, EPA and OSHA are mandating extremely expensive engineering changes. The cost to industry of achieving the current ninety-decibel OSHA standard is estimated at "only" $13 billion. EPA, however, is attempting to obtain a quieter eighty-five-decibel level, at an estimated cost of $32 billion.

REGULATING TOILETS

The Council on Wage and Price Stability has urged both OSHA and EPA to study the costs and benefits of the standards. It points out that lowering allowable noise from ninety to eighty-five decibels would cost industry $19,828 a person —a sum more than adequate to provide comfortable and effective personal hearing protectors. But cost apparently is not an important factor to federal regulators.

The lack of attention to the costs of regulation gives bureaucrats the opportunity to engage in all sorts of trivia. What size to establish for toilet partitions? How big is a hole? (It depends where it is.) When is a roof a floor? What colors to paint various parts of a building? How frequently are spittoons to be cleaned? The public's taxes actually support people who are willing to establish and administer regulations dealing with these burning issues.

Consider the plight of the small businessman who tries to deal with the Occupational Safety and Health Administration (OSHA) rules without paying for expensive outside assistance. The puzzlement over OSHA regulations extends to chairman Robert Moran of the Occupational Safety and Health Review Commission, the independent agency created to hear appeals from rulings by OSHA inspectors. After citing one vague standard, he lamented:

"What do you think it tells us to do?

"I have no idea—and I don't think OSHA could tell you either, before an inspection, citation, complaint, hearing and post-hearing brief.

"I submit that there isn't a person on earth who can be certain he is in full compliance with the requirements of this standard at any particular point of time."

The operation of the Occupational Safety and Health Act provides a pertinent example of how government regulation can lose sight of the basic objective. A company which invites OSHA to the plant to tell management which practices to revise to meet the agency's standards lays itself open to citations for infractions of OSHA rules and regulations. The law makes no provision for so-called courtesy inspections. To get around the problem, one regional office of OSHA has come up with a beautifully bureaucratic solution. They suggest that companies take photographs of their premises and send them to OSHA for off-site review. After all, if the inspectors do not actually "see" the violations, they cannot issue citations for them!

CONFLICTS AMONG REGULATIONS

The proliferation of government controls has, perhaps inevitably, led to internal conflicts. In some cases, the rules of a given agency work at cross-purposes with each other. OSHA mandates back-up alarms on vehicles at construction sites. Simultaneously the agency, to protect employees against noise, requires them to wear earplugs that can make it extremely difficult to hear the alarms. More serious and more frequent are the contradictions between the rulings of two or more government agencies where the regulated have little recourse. Federal food standards require meat-packing plants to be kept clean and sanitary. Surfaces which are most easily cleaned are usually tile or stainless steel. However, these are highly reflective of noise, and may not meet OSHA noise standards.

A controversy over rest rooms furnishes another example of conflict among regulations; it also demonstrates that common sense is in short supply in the administration of government controls. The Labor Department, carrying out its weighty responsibilities under the Occupational Safety and Health Act, has provided industry with

detailed instructions concerning the size, shape, dimensions, and number of toilet seats. For well-known biological reasons, it also requires some type of lounge area to be adjacent to women's rest rooms.

However, the EEOC has entered this vital area of government-business relations and requires

FEDERAL EXPENDITURES FOR BUSINESS REGULATION
(Fiscal years, in millions of dollars)

Agency	1974	1975	1976
Agriculture	330	376	381
Health, Education and Welfare	145	173	189
Interior	59	74	79
Justice	270	345	383
Labor	231	343	397
Transportation	178	212	234
Treasury	246	306	320
Civil Aeronautics Board	89	85	85
Commodity Future Trading Commission	—	—	11
Consumer Product Safety Commission	19	43	37
Equal Employment Opportunity Commission	42	54	60
Federal Communications Commission	33	127	208
Federal Energy Administration	38	49	50
Federal Power Commission	27	37	36
Federal Trade Commission	32	41	45
International Trade Commission	7	9	10
Interstate Commerce Commission	38	47	50
National Labor Relations Board	55	63	70
National Transportation Safety Board	8	10	10
Nuclear Regulatory Commission	80	139	198
Securities and Exchange Commission	35	45	49
All Other	17	21	23
Total	1,979	2,599	2,925

that male toilet and lounge facilities must be equal to the women's. Hence, either equivalent lounges must be built adjacent to the men's toilets or the women's lounges must be dismantled, OSHA and state laws to the contrary notwithstanding. To those who may insist that nature did not create men and women with exactly identical physical characteristics and needs, we can only reply that regulation, like justice, must be blind.

UNCONTROLLED POWER OF GOVERNMENT REGULATORS

The instances of government regulators' waste and foolishness pale into insignificance when compared to the arbitrary power they can exert. To cite a member of the Consumer Product Safety Commission, "any time that consumer safety is threatened, we're going to go for the company's throat." That this statement is not merely an overblown metaphor can be seen by examining the case of Marlin Toy Products of Horicon, Wisconsin.

The firm's two main products, Flutter Ball and Birdie Ball, were plastic toys that originally held plastic pellets that rattled. This led the FDA in 1972 to place the products on its ban list because it feared that if the toys cracked, the pellets could be swallowed by a child. The company recalled the toys and redesigned its product line to eliminate the pellets, thus entitling the toys to be removed from the ban list.

The Consumer Product Safety Commission in 1973 assumed responsibility in this area. Because of an "editorial error," it put the Marlin products on its new ban list. Apparently the Commission had incorporated an out-of-date FDA list. The error was called to the Commission's attention; it replied that it was not about to recall 250,000 lists "just to take one or two toys off."

Marlin Toy Products was forced out of the toy business and had to lay off 75 percent of its employees due to the federal error. It is ironic to note that the Commission specializes in ordering companies to recall their products if any defective ones have been produced, but refuses to recall its own product when there is a defect in every single one.

A more amusing instance of the CPSC's failure to abide by its own standards involves the toy safety buttons which it intended to distribute in the fall of 1974 in an effort to make consumers more safety conscious. Only after producing 80,000 buttons did the Commission learn that its product was dangerous to children because of the lead paint and the possibility of pieces of the button breaking off and being swallowed. Unlike the procedures that it expects of the companies it regulates, the Commission presumably ran its tests after, rather than before, production. Fortunately, since it realized its error prior to public distribution of the buttons, "only" wastes of resources and tax dollars were involved.

RAMPANT BUREAUCRACY THREATENS BUSINESS

Except by anarchists, it is universally believed that the role of government is to establish the rules for the society. Government can and should act to protect consumers against rapacious sellers, individual workers against unscrupulous employers, and future generations against those who would waste the nation's resources. Yet the new wave of government regulation of business extends far beyond these sensible considerations; wittingly or not, it is changing the locus of decision making and of responsibility for a large portion of private-sector activities. Liberals and conservatives alike should be concerned about what is tantamount to a second "managerial revolution."

The first such revolution was noted by Berle and Means more than four decades ago and given the title by James Burnham a decade later. These analysts were referring to the divorce of the formal ownership of the modern corporation from the actual management. The revolution now under way is a silent bureaucratic one during which the locus of much of the decision making

149

in the American corporation is shifting once again. This time the shift is from the professional management selected by the corporation's board of directors to the vast cadre of government regulators that influences and often controls the key decisions of the typical business firm.

This revolution is neither deliberate nor violent. But a revolution it truly is, for it is forcing a fundamental change in the nature of our industrial society. Extending the analysis of Berle, Means, and Burnham to the current situation, it is not who owns the means of production but who makes the key decisions that is crucial in determining the relative distribution of public and private power.

To be sure, the process is far from complete, and it proceeds unevenly. But the results to date are clear enough. Increasingly the government is participating in and often controlling the internal decisions of business, the kinds of decisions that lie at the heart of the capitalist system: What products can be produced? Which investments can be financed? Under what conditions can products be produced? Where can they be made? How can they be marketed? What prices can be charged?

Virtually every major department of the typical industrial corporation in the United States has one or more counterparts in a federal agency that controls or strongly influences its internal decision making. When we examine the sector of industry that already is most subject to government supervision—defense production—the results are disconcerting. It is precisely the companies that are most heavily dependent on military contracts that report some of the largest cost overruns and greatest delays. The society does not get the benefit of efficiency and innovation expected from private industry. Liberals and conservatives alike should be repelled by the ultimate consequences of governmental assumption of basic entrepreneurial and management functions.

Hendrik Houthakker on the Erosion of Competition

A NYONE PROPOSING TO MAKE HAMBURGER OUT OF SACRED COWS is likely to attract attention. That is exactly what happened to Harvard professor Hendrik S. Houthakker when he advised President Ford at the 1974 "economic summit conference" that grinding up no less than forty-five sacred cows of economic regulation would work wonders for the economy. Since that time Professor Houthakker's spirited advocacy of governmental deregulation, tax reform, and antitrust changes has won him a large and still growing following among those who feel that the American system of competitive enterprise is slowly disappearing under mountains of regulations, inelasticities, and disincentives.

Hendrik Houthakker, now Henry Lee Professor of Economics at Harvard, was born in the Netherlands and took his professional training at the Universities of Amsterdam and Cambridge. Coming to the United States, he served as assistant professor at the University of Chicago, then at Stanford, and arrived at Harvard in 1960. His earlier professional work was in the field of consumption economics, and with Lester Taylor he authored the definitive *Consumer Demand in the United States* in 1966. In recent years he has specialized in regulatory policies and in international trade. In January 1969 he was appointed to a two-year term on the Council of Economic Advisers.

Like those other noted economists, Galbraith, Friedman, and Leontief, Professor Houthakker has a summer retreat in the Vermont mountains, where *Business and Society Review* interviewed him early this summer.

JOHN McCLAUGHRY
Contributing Editor

McClaughry: Professor Houthakker, you gained considerable attention last year at President Ford's economic summit conference for proposing a deregulatory program in almost every sector of our economy. Starting with the field of energy, what are some of the sacred cows of economic regulation that you're ready to consign to the slaughterhouse of regulatory reform?

Houthakker: The most important sacred cow has been wellhead control over natural gas prices;

this has been in force since the 1950s. The artificially low price caused the demand to increase far more than the supply. Thus, there have been shortages for several years now, mostly in industrial consumption of natural gas. If we let the market determine the price, there would undoubtedly be much more gas coming to market; there would be higher prices, but industry would be able to buy the gas it wants.

More recently, we have had price controls on petroleum, which, I believe, have also been very harmful. Our overall domestic petroleum production has been going down despite much higher oil prices; this is in large part due to the price control program which distinguishes between "old oil" and "new oil." The new oil is not controlled and is therefore essentially at the world price. The old oil is held down to $5.25 a barrel. Now there are all sorts of complications which we don't have to go into, but the fact is that our domestic production has so far not responded to higher prices. In fact, it is now down something like 6 percent from a year ago, and this cannot be explained entirely by the running down of our wells. There is no doubt that if the controlled price of old oil were to be increased or the controls removed altogether, there would be more secondary recovery from existing fields. We have been producing petroleum for more than a hundred years now, and most of the petroleum discovered is still in the ground. It's expensive to get out; we have to use secondary and tertiary recovery techniques which are not worthwhile at the present controlled price. Also, as long as we have price controls, people think that in the future the price will be higher and therefore they leave the stuff in the ground pending a better return.

McClaughry: Do you think it is feasible and possible for the U.S. to achieve energy independence by 1980 provided the deregulation steps are taken promptly?

Houthakker: I used to think that 1980 was a feasible target for independence. I am not too sure about it now. I would say that 1985 is perhaps a little more realistic. We can achieve independence by a number of steps, including the ones which I've just mentioned—the deregulation of gas and oil. In addition, we have to make use of the naval petroleum reserve in Alaska, which is a great source of oil; we have to have offshore drilling on the Atlantic Coast and the Pacific Coast and the Gulf of Alaska; and we have to make more use of coal.

McClaughry: One of the prime candidates for regulatory reform, according to President Ford, is the field of transportation. What might be done to free up that industry?

Houthakker: On the whole, the regulatory commissions—the Interstate Commerce Commission, the Civil Aeronautics Board, and the Federal Maritime Commission—have acted primarily as managers of cartels in their respective industries. With respect to trucking, for instance, the ICC gives out licenses subject to all sorts of restrictions. The main purpose of this is to restrain competition. Now there is plenty of evidence in this country and in other countries that competition will work in transportation and will bring about lower freight rates; therefore, we don't need this kind of cartel regulation. The ICC has also been very hard on the railroads. Originally the railroads thought they could benefit from it, but ultimately the invigorating forces of competition diminished, and most of the railroads, especially in the eastern part of the country, went further and further downhill.

I believe that at the moment the transportation industries would be hard put to deal with very vigorous competition. We have to introduce it gradually, but I believe that a lot could be done even in the short run. The costs of regulation in surface transportation are of the order of several

billion dollars a year. In the case of airlines, the problem is somewhat different, but not too much so. There again, the CAB essentially upholds a cartel, but it has done so with somewhat less consistency than the ICC. The ICC is a very old organization and there is a tremendous accumulation of legal barnacles on the Interstate Commerce Act. Under the CAB there has been no new entry into the domestic airline business. There is probably too much competition on some routes, primarily by the principle of "use it or lose it." This competition has not generally led to lower fares but has shown up in all sorts of frills. When an airline can't fill its 747, it puts a piano in the lounge and nonsense like that, so that price competition among the airlines has until very recently been almost absent. The Federal Maritime Commission from the start had the objective of controlling, which in fact means protecting, the shipping conferences.

McClaughry: How about the area of American agriculture?

Houthakker: We have made quite a bit of progress in agriculture in the last ten years or so. Starting in 1966, each farm bill brought about some liberalization, especially in the central part of agriculture, the field crops. Also, last year we abandoned the Sugar Act, which was one of the worst examples of bureaucratic overregulation. There is still a great deal to be done in the field of agricultural marketing orders—the government-supervised process for controlling price and production. The dairy industry is still controlled by measures that prevent milk from following the most economical routes. Certain parts of the country are not allowed to ship to other parts of the country. This has two effects—the milk is too expensive to the consumer in those parts that cannot be reached from everywhere else, and the farmers in the parts that are prevented from shipping to other areas of the country are correspondingly disadvantaged. It would be in the interests of both farmers and consumers if there were more freedom in the movement of dairy products. There are also marketing orders in fruits and vegetables, some of which are very harmful. One hears a lot about the poor quality and high price of tomatoes. It is almost entirely the result of marketing orders.

McClaughry: How about the banking system and such things as Regulation Q which limits the rates of interest banks can pay on savings deposits.

Houthakker: There has been a lack of competition in the banking system, especially due to protection of the savings and loan associations. Savings and loan associations were set up in an era of very low interest rates, and they generally hold a large mortgage portfolio from the past. They cannot afford to pay high interest rates, so the interest rate structure has been frozen for them at a relatively low maximum. This has in turn meant that the commercial banks do not have as much competition as they should have. I believe that the distinction between these two types of institutions should be weakened, although perhaps not eliminated entirely. Regulation Q should be removed to allow the commercial banks to compete for deposits, and savings and loan associations should engage in business other than residential financing.

McClaughry: Many economists have pointed the finger at the federal laws regarding labor unions as introducing important inelasticities and dis-

economies into the American economy. What areas in labor law would you change for a more efficient economy?

Houthakker: I am not an expert on labor law, but it is my impression that the problems in labor are relatively concentrated in two or three industries, mostly construction. The construction unions have been able to extract very large wage increases in the face, sometimes, of very considerable unemployment. This is due to a number of factors, including the apprenticeship system. There is not a sufficient inflow of new workers into the construction trades. Some time ago I saw a picture of about 5,000 young men waiting before a union office in Long Island because the electricians' union was going to admit 500 new members. Now this, I think, is completely beyond reason. The electricians' union should not be able to keep out prospective electricians. There are quite a few nonunion construction workers too, but they are generally excluded from various government projects. The Davis-Bacon Act, which effectively imposes union wages on government contracts, should be repealed. There are also a few things that should perhaps be done in the area of unemployment insurance, but I believe that the most important thing is to make sure that the unions have open membership. Unions do play a useful role on the whole, but they should not be allowed to restrict labor supply.

McClaughry: What changes in antitrust practices would you recommend to accompany these regulatory reforms?

Houthakker: To my mind, the most important change is to make the refusal to sell a per se violation of the antitrust laws in the case of large corporations. This is how large corporations enforce their market power with respect to customers. In the copper industry, for instance, the suppliers often ration their customers. They don't raise the price necessarily, but they tell their customers that "you can only get so much." The effect of this is to institutionalize the link between a firm and its customers, thereby making it more difficult for these customers to shop around. That's why I think a refusal to sell, which is a violation in some European countries, should also be made a violation here, at least in the case of large corporations. I also believe that there should be somewhat greater freedom in the area of mergers. The merger guidelines that were issued by the Justice Department in 1968 are, to my mind, too rigid. Some mergers are pro-competitive, some are not, and I don't think that simple numerical criteria can tell you which are harmful and which aren't.

McClaughry: Finally, what changes in corporate taxation policy would you recommend?

Houthakker: I think that the corporate income tax has become a real deterrent to a sound financial structure and to the capital position of private industry. I would make a number of changes. In the first place, I would make the corporate income tax progressive with respect to rates of return. I would levy a higher rate on corporations that over a period of five years have a high rate of return to capital, because in many cases this simply reflects market power rather than superior efficiency. Now, if it does reflect efficiency, then corporations could escape this higher rate by expanding, so this would be an incentive to investment by corporations that are either very efficient or have large market power.

McClaughry: That is to say, an efficient corporation which showed a higher rate of return on investment would be forced to invest its earnings in some more risky and less profitable business in order to escape the added burden of taxation?

Houthakker: Yes, or it could expand its own business. This is probably the most natural thing to do. What you have now is a corporation with lots of market power that doesn't expand as much as it otherwise could in its own industry for fear of depressing the price; but if there were graduation of the corporate income tax, then there would be an incentive to expand the capital base so that the corporate tax rate would be lower.

A second change that I would make is to allow deduction of dividends paid by corporations, just like wages and interest. I don't see any difference between interest and dividends as far as their susceptibility to tax is concerned. It's important, I think, to do this primarily to make equities more attractive to the general public. I believe that our capital markets have been distorted by insufficient issues of new equities, and that is in part caused by the double taxation of dividends, first at the corporate level, then at the individual level. Some people have proposed that this should be done by eliminating dividends from taxation at the individual level. This idea was implemented some years ago in the form of the $100 dividend exclusion. I think that is the wrong approach. From the individual's point of view it makes no difference whether his income is from dividends or from wages or from anything else; therefore I would maintain the individual taxation of dividends, but not corporate taxation of dividends.

Now, still another change I would make in the corporate income tax is to abolish all rules regarding depreciation. This hinges on the first point I mentioned, namely, the graduation with respect to rate of return. When you have graduation you no longer have to worry about corporations depreciating too much, because if they do, they reduce the capital base on which their corporate income tax is calculated. At the same time, there has been a great deal of complaint from business about the arbitrariness of the present depreciation rules, and a great deal of complaint from certain economists who feel that depreciation gives away too much tax revenue. With the system I propose, you wouldn't have to worry about that anymore.

McClaughry: How would you compare the merits of deducting paid dividends, which you just recommended, to those of imputing all earnings directly to shareholders whether or not distributed, a proposal which has been put forth by Professor Milton Friedman?

Houthakker: I don't believe that it is either equitable or practical to tax people on earnings that they have not received. If you go that way you also have to recalculate the value of various other assets and levy taxes on those. Our individual tax system is generally based on the notion that if you haven't received something then you aren't taxed upon it, and I believe that that is a sound principle. It is possible to argue that in some sense the earnings accumulated but not distributed by the corporations belong to the shareholders, but that is only a capital transaction, and to my mind it should not be subject to the income tax.

One of the effects of the second change I mentioned, namely, the exemption of dividends from the corporate income tax, would probably be that corporations will pay out more in the form of dividends, and that would eliminate to some extent the problem which Professor Friedman addresses.

McClaughry: You've proposed a number of regulatory reforms, antitrust changes, and tax changes. Suppose that the great bulk of these reforms were adopted; what kind of scenario would you paint for the American economy over the ensuing decade?

Houthakker: I would say that our economy has become inflation-prone in part because there is too much resistance to price falls. This, I think, is not what the public perceives to be the case. When people worry about inflation, they worry about price *rises*. I would say that the main problem is that prices don't fall, not that they rise so much. If the price of steel doesn't fall when there is a decline in demand for steel, it means that the output for steel has to be restricted that much more; and the natural reaction of the government, in all countries now, to falling output is to expand aggregate demand—whether its own demand or that of the taxpayers—by either fiscal or monetary policy. In either case, it validates the attempt by many industries to maintain prices in the face of falling demand. That is why every

time there is a recession we lay the groundwork for the subsequent inflation. We try to overcome the failure of private industry to lower prices by an increase in demand, which then leads to excessive price rises in the next stage. Now, I believe that the main purpose of the various reforms that I've been advocating is to increase price flexibility in the economy; this means that prices would fall to a greater extent than they do now in the face of a recession. It would make recessions shorter and make it less necessary for the government to adopt stimulative policies which result in inflation later on.

McClaughry: Recently the *Wall Street Journal* ran a rather discouraging series on various views of the future of the American economy. Almost every person interviewed seemed to feel that public support for the free enterprise system and competition was waning sharply, and that support for increased governmental intervention, price controls, and so on was growing. Indeed, an Initiative Committee for National Economic Planning—including your distinguished Harvard colleague Wassily Leontief—has gained wide publicity recently for advocating that the U.S. move toward a nationally planned economy. Do you think Americans are ready for your kind of program of deregulation and restoration of competition, or for more national economic planning?

Houthakker: At the moment we are at a crossroads as far as private enterprise is concerned. There is one school of thought, to which I belong, which holds that our private enterprise system can be saved provided it be made more competitive. The other school, which is also very widespread and to which Professor Leontief belongs, argues that private enterprise is essentially a thing of the past and thus we must now go to increased government intervention. My own observations suggest that widespread government intervention has not been a success on the whole. I'm not saying that it's always been bad. There are countries, such as Japan, where it's worked fairly well, but in Japan you don't really have government intervention—in Japan the government and business are one and the same thing. There are also countries, like France, where there has been extensive nationalization and where the economy on the whole has done very well. On the other hand, in countries like West Germany

the government has by and large abstained from detailed intervention, and German economic performance has probably been the best of any major country in the postwar period as a whole.

I happen to believe that the maintenance of private enterprise is a very important part of the maintenance and reinforcement of democracy generally. That is why I think we should try to refurbish private enterprise by making it more competitive. If it turns out that there is not enough support for that, then maybe we'll have to go the other way, but I would hope that it is only a last resort.

McClaughry: In West Germany, a capital-accumulation law has been advanced to require the industrial workers to invest in ownership shares in the German economy to give them a wealth base as well as labor income. Similar plans have been advanced in the Netherlands, France, and Italy. Is this a desirable trend?

Houthakker: I think that it is a desirable trend. I believe the prospects of private enterprise would be better if there were wider ownership of equities. This is one of the main reasons that I am in favor of exempting dividends from corporate income tax: to make equities more widely available by making corporations rely more heavily on new equity issues. I don't think we would want to do it quite the same way that it has been done in the European countries you have mentioned, but nevertheless the overall goal is a very worthwhile one.

McClaughry: Do you think this kind of policy will find increased advocacy here in the United States?

Houthakker: It's hard to say. It is not a new idea; we have had movements of this kind before, and I don't want to be too optimistic about it. The idea of "people's capitalism" has sort of a bad name because it was overemphasized. We got all these figures about thirty million shareholders, which actually doesn't mean very much. A lot finally depends on where the balance of opinion as regards private enterprise comes out. I would hope that our government will recognize the importance of preserving private enterprise and will take concrete steps, through taxation and otherwise, to provide the necessary support.

McClaughry: Would the workings of the U.S. economy be improved if owned by twice as many individuals?

Houthakker: I would certainly say so. The holding of shares now is very concentrated. As I just mentioned, figures like thirty million shareholders are very misleading because most of those hold very little in the way of shares, and the large bulk of the population holds no shares at all.

McClaughry: On a nationally televised interview program some months ago, George Meany, president of the AFL-CIO, was asked about any problems he saw in connection with Arab investment in the productive industries in the United States. Mr. Meany's reply was that he felt the Arabs should be free to invest in any enterprise whatsoever, and once they were heavily invested here, those industries should be nationalized. Would you like to comment on that prescription?

Houthakker: I hope it was a joke. It is the kind of foolishness one sometimes hears in less developed countries, too. I believe that the Arabs should indeed be free to invest in most of our industries. I would make an exception for certain defense industries and for the petroleum and other energy industries; apart from this I don't see any great harm in their investing in textiles or computers or what have you.

McClaughry: In the debate we're in at this crossroads of our economic thinking, what kind of role should our business leaders be playing? Should they be playing a basically passive role in dealing with proposals such as that of the Initiative Committee for National Economic Planning, or should they be taking a more aggressive role to champion the cause of deregulation and increased competition in the economy, even though some fairly cozy existing arrangements might thereby be jeopardized?

Houthakker: I believe that one shouldn't generalize on the role played by business leaders. Many American businessmen do not take an active part in politics and this is probably justified. I would hope that to the extent that business leaders feel it necessary to speak in public—and I certainly hope that some of them will—they will be on the side of more competitive enterprise, with everything that it entails. But I would be somewhat reluctant to see a concerted effort on the part of business because I'm afraid it would be misinterpreted by the large part of the public.

McClaughry: If the dike holding back the onrush of government regulation starts to leak, can we have confidence that there is at least one Dutchman holding his finger in it?

Houthakker: Well, I have done what little I could, and I have been quite pleased with the response there has been to this. I can say that since the forty-five sacred cows became available to the public I have had hundreds and hundreds of letters from all over the country, from people with very different outlooks, supporting this idea. That's what makes me think that private competitive enterprise should not be given up as a lost cause.

It would be very unfortunate if we went in the direction advocated by Professor Leontief and his group who have a quite unrealistic faith in government planning. The fact is that government planning would be an exercise in applied economics for which we do not as yet have adequate tools. Economics is not good enough to provide a basis for detailed planning, and it won't be good enough for quite a while. Much more research is needed. In the meantime, we would be just fooling ourselves if we were to think that the government can somehow do things better than private business can.

A Dispersed or Concentrated Agriculture?
—The Role of Public Policy

By C. Edward Harshbarger and Sheldon W. Stahl

Farmers and policymakers alike are expressing concern over the possible future direction of American agriculture. Prompting these concerns are the rapid changes that have occurred in production and marketing patterns as a result of technological improvements and certain institutional factors. In short, agriculture has evolved to the point where fewer, but larger, farms are producing most of the output and realizing the largest share of income. Moreover, many agribusiness firms are exerting pressure to more closely coordinate various production and marketing activities through contractual arrangements with producers. In fact, several commodities such as broilers, eggs, and most fruits and vegetables are presently handled in this fashion rather than through an open, competitive market.

In an earlier article, the agricultural sector of the economy was examined to determine the extent to which economic concentration has occurred in the production and marketing of farm commodities. Although the evidence in that article showed that production is clearly becoming more concentrated in the hands of large producers, the fact remains that economic power in agriculture is relatively diffused as compared with many industrial sectors of the economy. Furthermore, despite well publicized developments regarding contractual arrangements for a few commodities, more than three-fourths of total farm output continues to move through an open market of many buyers and sellers. While significant changes in marketing practices may occur for individual commodities, it is generally expected that the bulk of farm marketings will be exchanged in open markets in the foreseeable future.

Nevertheless, a crucial issue for farmers, agribusinessmen, and consumers is the organization and control of agriculture in the future. In a dispersed system consisting of many proprietary units, control would rest in the hands of many individual decisionmakers; at the opposite extreme, control would be concentrated in a relatively small number of very large firms, greatly reducing the high degree of individual freedom afforded by a dispersed system.

The family farm-open market system that is so prevalent in agriculture today is a reflection of the stance taken by public policymakers since the early days of the United States. Shortly after the nation was founded, it was decided that the public interest would best be served by encouraging wide distribution of land ownership. Thus, laws were passed that facilitated the sale and homesteading of public land into family-sized units. Similarly, the open, competitive market is a derivative of the free enterprise system that has been espoused in this nation for so many years. Reflecting the cherished concepts of freedom and equal opportunity, early policymakers established various rules

C. Edward Harshbarger and Sheldon W. Stahl, "A Dispersed or Concentrated Agriculture? The Role of Public Policy." *Monthly Review,* Federal Reserve Bank of Kansas City, March 1975, pp. 3–10. Reprinted with permission.

and regulations that heavily influenced the development of free markets in which each individual could compete to earn his just reward. Obviously, political philosophies and social goals have changed as the economy has evolved from an agrarian to a highly complex industrial structure. But the markets for agricultural products, some of which remain open while others are administered, still mirror the laws, customs, and institutions that have been supported by public policy. Hence, just as public policy has contributed to current agricultural production and marketing practices, so too will policy influence the future direction and control of American agriculture.

CONTROL AND THE PRESSURES FOR CHANGE

Unless significant changes in public policy occur, the forces affecting agricultural production and marketing trends are not likely to subside in the near future. Thus, farm numbers will continue to decline, production will become more concentrated, and further progress likely will be made in coordinating production and marketing activities through contractual arrangements. On the other hand, public policy can be a tool with which to counteract or redirect structural developments in agriculture. Before this can occur, however, a general understanding of the factors which have contributed to structural change in agriculture is required.

Market Developments and Pricing

Among those factors which have contributed to the shift from a dispersed agriculture to a more concentrated structure are the increased technical complexity of farming and the pressures to expand output to achieve lower unit costs. Technological developments have made it possible for farmers to improve production efficiency, but the sharp increase in the managerial skills required of farm decision-makers has made it more difficult to operate successfully in a competitive agricultural environment. Moreover, in recent years, the capital requirements associated with the adoption of new technology have soared, and unfortunately, many farmers could not afford the investment. While the staying power of smaller, less technologically advanced, farmers is surprisingly strong, the price-cost squeeze has forced many to seek new jobs, retire, or live on very low incomes.

The increased complexity in agricultural production and the attendant risks and financial requirements have led to greater specialization. Farmers frequently focus on one or two principal commodities in order to exploit the economies of volume production. Moreover, in those areas where they feel deficient, farmers increasingly are turning to outside specialists for the technical knowledge and financing required to operate efficiently. Sometimes it is even necessary to enter into formal contracts to secure the desired services, and when this happens, control often shifts from the farmer to the outside interests.

With few exceptions, however, most of these developments represent adjustments that would normally occur in a free, competitive market whenever new technology is introduced. As such, the role of public policy in this case should be to permit the forces in motion to operate freely unless other problems become apparent and are accorded higher priority.

The manner in which farm markets function must also be examined to explain the current structure of agriculture. The competitive market, as a socio-economic institution, has several inherent features that are desirable from a public policy standpoint. Offering an environment in which no single participant can affect price, the market brings together the disparate decisions of buyers, sellers, producers, and consumers to establish equitable market values on goods and services. In addition to guiding and directing production and consumption decisions, a competitive market affords a wide range of individual freedom in that it provides meaningful choices among alternatives and effectively limits barriers to entry or exit.

The performance of a pricing system in a competitive market can be evaluated in terms of how well it satisfies certain specified criteria. As far as agriculture is concerned, an effective pricing system is expected to facilitate the physical marketing of the commodity, yield acceptable returns to market participants, maintain reasonably stable prices, protect long-run demand by not pricing the product out of the market, assure equitable treatment of all participants, and clear the market.[2]

Most of the problems with pricing systems in agriculture revolve around the first three criteria. Probably the most important factor behind the decline of traditional open markets has been the growing inefficiency in physically moving and exchanging commodities. Direct selling, either through individual negotiation or formula pricing, as well as vertical integration have provided much greater efficiencies in assembling and handling several farm commodities. Consequently, the open market is often skirted altogether, coming into play only as a base for determining the "going price" in the negotiations. Obviously, if the central market slips in volume of sales, a question immediately arises about the validity of the reported base price as a signal of general market conditions for the industry as a whole. Where this problem has occurred, participants in the exchange must often depend upon their own abilities to acquire and translate general market news into a price.

Farmer dissatisfaction with open market results, perceived as not yielding equitable returns to market participants, represents another threat to the structural organization of agriculture. History provides several examples of farmers seeking out alternative pricing systems to gain better treatment. Owing to unstable prices, chaotic conditions, and inefficient handling, farm legislation established Federal marketing orders for fluid milk during the 1930's to instill greater stability and order in the industry. Virtually all of the selling is now done directly to the processor under a tight set of specifications. Consequently, milk prices are some of the most stable in agriculture today, thus satisfying the third criterion for successful performance of a pricing system; however, the markets do require close supervision under this arrangement.

In essence, the existence of marketing orders, formula pricing techniques, and vertical integration reflect not only the special characteristics of the commodities involved but also certain shortcomings of the market as viewed by the participants.[3] While these alternative pricing systems have produced positive benefits for certain farmers, the results in other areas have been disappointing. For example, vertical integration in the broiler industry has transformed most producers into piece-wage workers and, at the same time, has virtually eliminated the market. In fact, quotations on farm prices for broilers no longer exist. Although consumers and some producers stand to benefit from greater price stability and more efficient production, certain costs as measured by the constraints placed on farmers in making production decisions and controlling marketings must be taken into consideration before a final judgment is made on a new marketing arrangement. Public policy can play an integral role in cultivating the changes that are needed in the future while correcting for errors made in the past.

Institutional Factors

Previous research suggests that the increase in economic concentration in agriculture has also been influenced by several institutional factors. Government farm programs, for example, have probably given an unintended boost to larger farms even though various direct actions have been taken to support the smaller family units. According to one report, several important reasons for believing that price and income programs speed the trend to concentrated holdings are (1) wealthy investors, either farm or off-farm, presumably are highly responsive to protected income, (2) the stability of income promised by programs may provide improved access to big capital markets, and (3) small farmers probably have more difficulty accumulating capital for expansion even with commodity support programs.[4] Although it is difficult to specify the extent to which government programs have contributed to economic concentration in agriculture, the overall impact has been to help finance growth to larger operations that might not have occurred otherwise.

2/V. James Rhodes, "Pricing Systems—Old, New, and Options for the Future," *Bargaining in Agriculture*, North Central Regional Extension Publication 30, University of Missouri Extension Division, C 911, June 1971, p. 12.

3/The characteristics of commodities typically produced under contract or by vertically integrated industries were discussed by the authors in the article cited in footnote 1.

4/L. R. Kyle, W. B. Sundquist, and H. D. Guither, "Who Controls Agriculture Now?—The Trends Underway," *Who Will Control U.S. Agriculture?* North Central Regional Extension Publication 32, University of Illinois Cooperative Extension Service, Special Publication 27, August 1972, p. 11.

Income tax laws have also introduced an institutional bias that has accelerated the trend toward larger farms. According to Professor Levi, three features in the tax laws give preferential advantages to wealthy taxpayers who make investments in agriculture even though the system presumably is progressive in nature.[5] For example, the graduation of income tax rates, the special rates for income from capital gains, and the treatment of depreciation as a "paper loss" all work to the relative advantage of people in high tax brackets because, in essence, a larger proportion of the investment ultimately is subsidized by the Treasury. Meisner and Rhodes recently examined the changing structure of the cattle feeding industry, giving special attention to the rapid influx of outside investors who have found cattle feeding to be an attractive tax shelter.[6] For this reason and others, cattle feeding in large commercial lots expanded sharply during the 1960's. Moreover, as outside investment funds continued to roll in during the early 1970's, the industry expanded further even though the returns, without tax considerations, may not have warranted it. Certainly, part of the crisis now confronting the cattle feeding industry—not to mention its concentrated structure—is traceable to the response of outside investors to attractive concessions in the tax laws.

Aside from the obvious loss of revenue to the Treasury, tax-subsidized investments in agriculture have several other effects, not all of which are desirable. It is widely accepted that tax concessions tend to bring more risk capital into farming, especially for large scale enterprises such as cattle feeding, poultry, and orchards. They also have the effect of expanding production, thus lowering farm prices and incomes in most cases. Furthermore, because the concessions make it possible for the tax-subsidized investor to make money even though the enterprise itself shows no profit, ownership and control are frequently shifted out of the hands of farmers who may find it difficult, if not

impossible, to compete under these conditions. Clearly, the tax rules do affect structural developments in agriculture and the ability to compete for resource ownership. Preserving a dispersed agriculture will likely require, among other things, a fundamental reappraisal of the tax system by policymakers with a view toward reform in certain areas.

Maintaining Control

Assuming that managerial skills are not a limiting factor, the key to whether agriculture remains dispersed or becomes more concentrated is control. If control is to rest in the hands of the traditional farmer, certain conditions regarding access to markets and to important resources, such as land, technical knowledge, and credit, must prevail.

With respect to farmland, various policies in the past have been designed to augment a wide distribution of ownership. However, the competing demands for farmland for urbanization and recreational purposes, coupled with new laws on zoning, conservation, and pollution controls, threaten to restrict this privilege. Furthermore, the upward trend in land prices has markedly reduced the opportunities for many young farmers to purchase farm real estate despite credit policies that have generally favored farm ownership.

Access to knowledge, whether technical or market related, is another factor which can affect the structure of agriculture. Even the so-called "free" market depends on effective government regulation and information to make it workable. Each year millions of dollars are spent by public and private institutions to provide market participants with information on production estimates, expected disappearance, and the latest price developments in domestic and international markets. Competitive marketing systems cannot function effectively without good information.

Equal access to research findings from scientific experiments by public-supported institutions, such as land grant universities, has enabled many family farm units to remain technologically efficient and competitive. Any restrictions on access to this knowledge will give a special advantage to those who acquire it first. Thus, a policy to confine research mainly to private firms would likely lead to greater con-

5/Donald R. Levi, "Federal Income Tax Law—A Powerful Policy Tool," *Economic and Marketing Information for Missouri Agriculture*, Department of Agricultural Economics, University of Missouri-Columbia, Vol. 19, No. 7, (July 1971).

6/J. C. Meisner and V. James Rhodes, "The Changing Structure of U.S. Cattle Feeding," Department of Agricultural Economics, University of Missouri-Columbia, Special Report 167, November 1974.

centration in agriculture, especially if the research happened to focus on product development and promotion in vertically integrated industries.

In the last few years, one of the chief concerns in agriculture has been the sharp increase in capital requirements as land values and the amount paid out for purchased inputs have skyrocketed. Because of these developments, the risks in farming are such that, if prices received drop even modestly below costs, severe financial stress can result unless precautionary measures are taken. Sometimes these risks can be shifted to others through the use of futures markets or crop insurance. Price support programs and tax shelters also offer protection. However, some producers are finding it necessary to form contractual arrangements with processors to reduce risks, which frequently results in some loss of managerial control.

Similar problems exist with credit. Any policy that makes credit more available or less expensive to certain groups will affect the future structure and control of agriculture. The traditional sources of credit, while they have been sufficient to date, could encounter problems which may make it more difficult to finance agriculture at competitive rates. Many farmers have already boosted their borrowings to levels that seem precarious, given the high risks noted earlier. Hence, a future problem may be finding ways to increase equity capital to solidify a farmer's financial position. If increases in farm income prove inadequate, outside sources of equity capital will probably take on greater importance. There are several ways to acquire outside capital, including the sale of common or preferred stock if the farm is incorporated, but virtually all of the methods entail some loss of control. However, if these measures fall short, a higher incidence of direct ties between producers and vertically integrated organizations in order to secure funds for agriculture can probably be expected, in which case much of the control likely would shift out of the farmers' hands. Obviously, public policy may face a formidable challenge in the future in assuring that the growing credit needs of individual farmers are met within reason.

The shift in emphasis from marketing commodities to merchandising food through product development and promotion by processors and retailers suggests that several farm production units will or could be absorbed into large corporate enterprises, resulting in a more concentrated agriculture. Thus, maintaining access to markets is essential to a dispersed proprietary farming system.

Two different approaches can be used to keep marketing options open. In short, farmers may try to preserve access, as individuals, to an open market system, or they may seek to protect market access by grouping together.[7] In the group approach, certain individual prerogatives would probably be relinquished, but for some commodities, individual access may not always be attainable.

Many farmers are examining group action because they are becoming increasingly concerned about the fairness of price-making forces in deteriorating open markets and because they feel at a disadvantage in individual negotiation. While there are various ways in which group action can occur, most of the attention has focused either on vertical integration through farmer cooperatives or on horizontal bargaining associations.

A common misconception is that the primary reason for group bargaining is to raise prices above their free market level. While this objective exists, farmers may actually use bargaining just to discover a fair and stable price thought to be absent in the present pricing system.

Much of the impetus behind the cooperative movement has emanated from the Capper-Volstead Act of 1922 which explicitly allowed farmers to form cooperative associations without fear of violating the antitrust laws. But in no sense does Capper-Volstead permit farm cooperatives to do things that are otherwise illegal, such as monopolizing or restraining trade enough to unduly influence prices. Reflecting this call for surveillance, the Justice Department has recently filed civil antitrust suits against a few very large regional dairy cooperatives, charging them with illegal practices. Thus, there are limits to the power that cooperatives can exercise in behalf of their membership.

7/Rhodes, "Policies Affecting Access to Markets," *Who Will Control U.S. Agriculture?*, p. 39.

Public policy clearly encourages the cooperative concept as a means of equalizing the bargaining power of the individuals belonging to the cooperative and the large firms with which they must do business. As such, co-ops have become quite important as a means of preserving the producer's access to commodity and input markets. Furthermore, farmers are able to gain some of the benefits of industrial organization without being enveloped into a big corporate structure.

The bargaining association differs from the cooperative in that it serves as the producers' representative in contractual negotiations over prices and other terms of trade. In some cases, however, a cooperative may not only integrate forward but also serve as the bargaining agent for its members. At any rate, the greatest gains from bargaining thus far in the United States have been mainly in fluid milk and processing fruits and vegetables—both of which involve cooperative bargaining in the establishment of government marketing orders.

In essence, the overall strategy is for farmers to turn to group action as a replacement for the open market. Producers would likely forego some of their individual freedoms for the privilege of gaining greater security and less risk through their cooperatives or bargaining associations. However, some hazards are involved. For example, when a cooperative becomes large enough to compete with strong corporate interests, will it remain responsive to its membership, or has it moved beyond the farmers' ability to control it?[8] Clearly, when a cooperative becomes the only viable access to a market, the policy implications are far different than when it represents just another choice in an open market of many competing firms. Furthermore, there is evidence that some "corporate" farmers are invading the Capper-Volstead shelter in order to bargain for, or "discuss," higher prices with each other and escape antitrust prosecution. One danger is that if this practice becomes widespread, not only will these corporations lose their privileges but the whole cooperative system could be placed in jeopardy. Moreover, if agriculture becomes concentrated with limited marketing opportunities, public

policy would inevitably be forced to consider regulation of pricing practices to protect the consumer.

IMPLICATIONS FOR PUBLIC POLICY

From the foregoing discussion, it is apparent that the agricultural sector of the economy is a complex amalgam of many different organizations and ways of doing business. The relatively dispersed system that has survived in agriculture for so long has been supported by various national policies. The dissemination of information, an agricultural credit system, price support programs, and the authority for farmers to group together for bargaining purposes are but a few of the measures sanctioned by public policy. Clearly, organizational structure has historically been a public policy issue, and it will no doubt continue to be.

From the consumers' standpoint, most of the evidence suggests that under either a dispersed or a concentrated agriculture, adequate food supplies would be available. However, the implications for prices are likely to be quite different under the two systems. With a concentrated agriculture in which a few large, vertically integrated or corporate firms would dominate, monopolistic pricing could easily surface and offset the potential gains to consumers arising from closer market coordination. In this event, policymakers would find it necessary to police the performance of the pricing system very diligently—probably a cumbersome process—to protect the interests of the public.

The defense of the dispersed, competitive market system rests heavily on its socio-economic qualities of freedom and fair play as well as its ability to guide and direct resource use. As noted, obstacles arising from the complexity of many industrial processes, and problems associated with the control of markets in which merchandising techniques are emphasized, pose a serious threat to the dispersal concept. By the same token, it is becoming increasingly clear that the degree of freedom in present farm operations may have to give way to the requirements of market coordination for best meeting the demands of a sophisticated economy. Some sacrifice in individual freedom may be in order for the common good.

8/*Ibid*, p. 40.

Nevertheless, the present structure of agriculture is very competitive with control resting largely in the hands of individual producers. Furthermore, there is still considerable room to move in the direction of greater concentration for the sake of efficiency without losing these desirable features. Certainly, the competitive system—while far from perfect—possesses several admirable features that merit the continued loyalty of policymakers. Probably no other system is capable of giving so much positive direction to the economy with so little need for policing the performance.

If there is a danger, it is that control of agriculture may shift out of the hands of individual producers, not because the family farm-open market concept is an anachronism in a complex industrialized economy, but because public policy may not perceive the ultimate impact of the forces in motion until it is too late. For farmers to lose control by default would be most unfortunate, but if the trends now underway in agriculture continue unchecked, this may happen. In the final analysis, the question about the future direction and control of agriculture can be settled in a number of ways, depending on how public policy views the problem. In all probability, the final decision will hinge more on social and political viewpoints than on economic ones.

B.   Taxation and Expenditures

The Myths of Tax Reform

Every Congress begins with a determination to reform the tax system, but soon runs out of steam. The Ninety-fourth Congress is no exception. Early this year, Chairman Al Ullman bravely announced that tax reform would be high up on the agenda of the Ways and Means Committee, with only tax cuts and energy policy having higher priority. Hearings on tax reform were held during the summer, but most of the time was spent on proposals to add new tax preferences for business and investment income to the tax code rather than to cut some out. Most tax reformers believe that the best outcome for this year would be an extension of the 1975 tax cuts without any other changes in the tax law, for fear that the changes would only make matters worse.

This dismal outlook for tax reform contrasts sharply with public and professional opinion about the tax system. Demands for tax reform are heard from all sides: everybody knows that the tax system is unfair and almost hopelessly complicated. Tax rates go up to 70 percent, but very little income is subject to the top rate. Conservative and liberal experts testified this summer that Congress could substantially improve the tax system merely by repealing the preferences added to the tax law in the last five years. Even a Republican Administration acknowledges that the code contains over $90 billion of "tax expenditures"—a new term coined by tax reformers to dramatize the extent to which the tax side of the budget has been used to subsidize particular taxpayer groups. What is wrong? Why is tax reform so difficult to accomplish?

The answer is that neither the public nor the politicians want to face up to the hard choices that real tax reform requires. Before progress can be made, it will be necessary to discard some of the myths surrounding tax reform.

The first myth is that only the wealthy benefit from tax loopholes. Actually, loopholes are not confined to one part of the income scale—all income classes benefit from them. Perhaps the best way to proceed is to eliminate all the special provisions, as former Ways and Means Committee Chairman Wilbur D. Mills once suggested and even introduced a bill to that effect. If a new start could be made, it might be easier to design an individual income tax with a broad base and with tax rates that never exceeded 45 or 50 percent.

Second, the most expensive tax preferences are too often regarded as untouchable. The tax breaks for home owners, the personal deductions, income splitting, exemption for state and local bond interest, percentage depletion for independent oil producers, real estate tax shelters and capital gains have powerful lobbies behind them, yet these are the very provisions that seriously erode the income tax and violate horizontal equity. In some cases, other devices would achieve the objective of the provision at lower cost; in other cases, outright repeal is called for. But unless the major issues are tackled, there is no hope for real tax reform.

Third, it is widely accepted that the so-called middle-income classes are overtaxed and that tax reform must reduce tax burdens for this group. The fact of the matter is that, regardless of the incidence assumptions used to distribute such big taxes as the payroll tax, the corporation income tax, and the property tax, the effective tax rate paid by the middle 50 percent of income recipients is lower than the rates at the top and the bottom of the income scale. The income groups between $10,000 and $25,000 pay almost half of the total individual tax revenue, and there is no way to reduce their taxes without placing excessive burdens on incomes in other parts of the income scale.

Fourth, business and financial leaders frequently assert that there is already a capital shortage, or that a shortage is about to occur. Their solution is to reduce taxes on business and investment income through such devices as higher depreciation allowances, bigger investment credits, lower rates on capital gains, or even outright exemption for particular types of investment income. Actually, the level of private investment in the last ten years has been extremely high by any standard, and projections for the future suggest that private investment requirements will be in about the same ratio to the gross national product as, or only slightly higher than, the recent ratios have been. Furthermore, the saving needed to pay for this investment will be forthcoming, provided the federal government runs a modest surplus when the economy reaches full employment. This is well within our capability, and there is no need to distort the tax structure to achieve the same objective, particularly since the tax preferences generally cost more than the increased investment they would generate.

Fifth, there is universal agreement that the income tax must be simplified, yet the tax code and the tax return get more complicated every year. The only way to make the income tax simpler is to remove the special deductions, exclusions, and credits that are designed to help particular groups. Instead, tax reform usually winds up with compromises dictated by political considerations rather than by the logic of equitable income taxation. Congress should be aware that it will have to step on somebody's toes to simplify the tax law.

In brief, there is much to be said for wiping the slate clean and starting all over again, as Wilbur Mills suggested. Unless it is prepared to do so, Congress is deceiving itself and the public.

JOSEPH A. PECHMAN

Mr. Pechman is Director of the Economic Studies Program, the Brookings Institution and co-author of *Federal Tax Reform: The Impossible Dream?* (Brookings Institution, 1975). His views are not to be attributed to the officers, trustees or other members of the staff of the Brookings Institution.

EGALITARIANISM: MECHANISMS FOR REDISTRIBUTING INCOME

Every year, in July, the Bureau of the Census issues a modest pamphlet titled "Money Income and Poverty Status of Families and Persons in the United States." At once, the desk calculators light up all over the country—in universities and scholarly institutes, in government offices, and in the headquarters of groups such as the National Assn. for the Advancement of Colored People and the National Organization for Women. Distribution of income is the central issue in the insistent push for greater social and economic equality in the U. S. The annual report of the Census Bureau serves as a score card for the egalitarians.

This year's report, covering the calendar year 1974, shows little significant change. The U. S. economy still rewards success with incomes far greater than the average, and it still penalizes the unsuccessful with incomes below the poverty level. The bottom 20% of American families received only 5.4% of total income in 1974, while the top 20% of families got 41% of income. The bottom two-fifths got only 17.4%; the top two-fifths got 65.1%.

Income figures are among the shakiest—both in concept and in accuracy—of all the numbers that come out of the government statistics machine. They show money income before taxes, including welfare and Social Security payments at the bottom, but not including capital gains at the top. Thus, they probably understate the width of the money gap between the rich and the poor. On the other hand, they do not include benefits in kind, such as food stamps for the poor. Consequently, they may make the difference in well-being between the bottom and the top look larger than it really is.

Over the long pull the figures show a small but distinct shift toward a more equal distribution of income. In 1935-36 the bottom fifth of families got only 4.1% of income, while the top fifth got 51.7%. A substantial part of this change came during World War II, when the U. S. got its first taste of full employment. But between 1950 and 1968, the share of the bottom fifth inched up steadily—from 4.5% to 5.6%. This trend has been halted for the past six years, suggesting that the great inflation has hit the low incomes somewhat harder than the top brackets.

The number of people living in actual poverty has decreased dramatically in the past decade. In 1974 the Census Bureau estimated that 24.3 million people were below the poverty line ($2,495 for a single individual and $5,038 for a nonfarm family of four). Ten years earlier 36.1 million people were below the poverty levels of that period. Even with an increase of 1.3 million, caused by the recession, the 1974 poverty total represents only 11.6% of the U. S. population, against 11.1% in 1973 and 19% in 1964.

The biggest change in incomes since World War II has not been in the shape of the curve but in the levels. The whole income structure has been moving steadily upward. Even when the figures are adjusted for inflation they show that each quintile of the population has been pushing up to higher real incomes. The median income of all U. S. families has risen from $3,031 in 1947 to $12,840 today. Deflated for

The big target for reformers: Unequal income distribution

Top 20% of families gets 41%

Bottom 20% of families gets 5.4% of total income

2nd

3rd

4th

Percent

Families by quintiles

Data: Census Bureau

John Cobbs, "Egalitarianism: Mechanisms for Redistributing Income." *Business Week,* December 8, 1975, pp. 86, 87, 89, 90. Reprinted from *Business Week,* December 8, 1975, by special permission. Copyright 1976 by McGraw-Hill, Inc.

price changes, this change still means that real income has doubled for the family that stands at the midpoint of U.S. income, with half of all families below it and half above it.

A complex problem. On their face, these figures seem to suggest that with a little patience the U.S. could achieve a good life for everyone—though not equality—by "leveling up"—expanding the total national income so that everyone gets a larger slice. Every President since Harry Truman has tried to use economic growth to increase incomes and open up new job opportunities. The upward shift in the income structure is characteristic of an expanding economy.

But it is not as simple as that. The income figures for the bottom brackets include massive government transfer payments—including Social Security, welfare, and veterans' programs. As Joseph Pechman of the Brookings Institution points out, without these transfers the income curve would have shifted toward greater inequality in the past five years. Edgar K. Browning, in a study for the American Enterprise Institute, estimates that in 1973, transfers accounted for 69% of the income of the bottom one-fourth of all families. His definition of income, however, includes in-kind benefits, which he puts at 40% of total transfers. According to his calculations, net money transfers would account for nearly half of average income per capita in the bottom quartile.

To the real egalitarians all this is interesting but beside the point. The philosophical egalitarians like Herbert Gans of Columbia University and David Gordon of the New School of Social Research want equality for its own sake, not just as a means of reducing hardship in the bottom brackets. The minority leaders look at the figures and see that white males working full time in 1974 had a median income of $12,434, while black males got $8,705, and men of Spanish origin got $9,007. Women compare a median income of $6,957 for full-time work with the all-male median of $12,152. Municipal workers, fearful of shrinking jobs, see 41% of all income in the top quartile where it could be taxed to support bigger payrolls. Social workers simply see 24 million people living in poverty.

From one source or another, the push for equality of income as well as equality of opportunity and legal rights builds up steam.

Four main strategies are open to the government that undertakes to change the shape of the income curve and promote greater equality. It can:
- Push affirmative action programs to ensure equal job opportunities and equal pay for minorities and women.
- Increase taxes on the higher income earners and reduce taxes on the lower brackets.
- Increase transfer payments and extend them into new areas.
- Provide or subsidize public services—recreational facilities, transit, hospitals, entertainment.

In the past decade, the U.S. has tried all four approaches. As the pressure for more equality mounts, Congress and the Administration will have to decide how much further they are prepared to go. In the past, it has been possible to vote benefits for the poor without specifically facing the fact that this meant less for the rich. With federal, state, and local budgets strained to the breaking point, there is no way now to duck the issue. More spending for the bottom can be financed only by more taxes at the top. The U.S. must ask and answer the question: Just how much equality do we really want?

Jobs and pay. In the area of jobs and pay, the question has already been asked and answered. Congress and the courts have firmly committed the U.S. to equal job opportunities for everyone and equal pay for equal work. The federal government is pushing affirmative action programs in colleges—which are threatened with a shutoff in federal grants—and in private companies that want to do business with the government. As time goes on, this program undoubtedly will be strengthened and extended. The U.S. Commission on Civil Rights already has proposed a new government agency with power to enforce equal job opportunity anywhere it finds discrimination.

Affirmative action creates problems. It upsets long-established seniority rules, raises costs, and sometimes puts unqualified workers into critical jobs. Somewhere in the future there will be violent collisions between the groups backing affirmative action and the old-line unions that are still determined to restrict membership and preserve seniority rights.

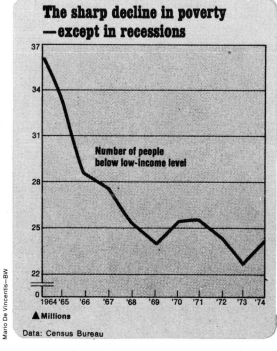

The sharp decline in poverty —except in recessions

Number of people below low-income level

Mario De Vincentis—BW

▲ Millions

Data: Census Bureau

Nevertheless, the U.S. is moving toward total equality in job opportunities and in the pay for a particular job. Over time, this will tend to establish what the economists call horizontal equality of incomes—equal rewards for equal performance throughout the economy. It will also tend to pull up the bottom of the income structure—by raising the pay of minority workers and women. If this narrows the gap between the top and the bottom, there will be a modest gain in vertical equality, but affirmative action by itself will not change the differentials between low-pay jobs and high-pay jobs.

The egalitarians, therefore, have to look elsewhere—to taxes, transfers, and public services—for mechanisms that will promote a significant move toward vertical equality in the U. S.

Tax leveling. Taxes are the obvious device, and every session of Congress yields a crop of bills designed to soak the rich and give tax exemptions to the poor. But the complex structure of U. S. taxes makes it hard to tell where the burdens would fall and what the consequences of a drastic change in tax policy would be.

The cornerstone of the federal revenue system is the individual income tax, which produced about $122 billion in fiscal 1975. On its face, this is a highly progressive tax, with rates scaling up from 14% on the first $1,000 of taxable income (for married couples) to 70% on everything over $200,000. If the tax applied to all income, without deductions or exemptions, it would be a significant leveler.

The elaborate system of exemptions and deductions confuses the picture and takes more of the progression out of the rate structure. Until Congress enacted the minimum tax in 1971, it was possible for a rich man to put his money in sheltered investments and pay no tax at all. Presumably, he had to accept a lower rate of return on his investments, but if he was rich enough, that did not matter. Tax shelters are less important to the middle-bracket earners, but the net effect of exemptions and deductions undoubtedly is to make the income tax less progressive than it looks.

The corporate income tax, which yielded some $40 billion in 1975, is progressive to the extent that shareholders bear the burden. But at least some of this tax is passed through to consumers in the form of price increases, and this bears more heavily on the low incomes than on the high. Federal excises tend to be regressive. So do tariffs.

Social Security taxes are a special case. This year employers and employees each pay 5.8% on the first $14,100 of income. This obviously takes a bigger percentage bite out of incomes below the cutoff figure than incomes above it, and in that sense the tax is regressive. But the Social Security tax is, in a way, an insurance premium. The participant is buying an annuity. The benefits are scaled so that the lower-income recipients get a better bargain than the higher incomes. Thus, the system as a whole tends to be an equalizer.

State and local taxes tend to be regressive, although as more states adopt a graduated income tax, the bite on upper incomes is increasing. Property taxes, the mainstay of the school systems, bear most heavily on the lowest incomes, where housing takes a larger proportion of the family budget. And since property taxes are deductible from taxable income on the federal returns, their impact on the middle and upper brackets is cushioned.

Joseph Pechman, whose studies of taxes are considered authoritative, adds it all up and concludes:

"The U. S. tax system is essentially proportional for the vast majority of families and therefore has little effect on the distribution of income. The very rich pay higher average effective tax rates than does the average family, but the difference is large only if the corporation income and property taxes are assumed to be borne by capital. If they are assumed to be shifted to consumers to a considerable degree, the very rich pay tax rates that are only moderately higher than the average." (*Who Bears the Tax Burden?* by Joseph A. Pechman and Benjamin A. Okner, published by the Brookings Institution.)

If Pechman is right, the present U. S. tax system is not an equalizer. It takes roughly the same proportion of income out of each bracket, leaving the differentials between top and bottom unchanged. But the potential for equalizing clearly is there: Knock out the exemptions and demolish the shelters, increase the personal deductions, raise the top bracket rates, and treat capital gains as ordinary income. You would bring the after-tax income curve a good deal closer to equal distribution.

The rebate and temporary tax cut adopted early this year as an antirecession measure were heavily loaded in favor of the low and low-middle brackets. The rebate rose from $100 at the bottom to $200 at the $10,800 level. Above the $20,000 level it scaled back down, reaching $100 at the $30,000 level. The cut amounted to 47% of the total tax for a married couple (no dependents) with an income of $5,000 but only 1% for the $25,000 couple. The bill also included a novel feature—an "earned income credit" that paid up to $400 to families with children whose earnings were in the bottom brackets.

President Ford's plan for a $28 billion permanent tax cut would abolish the earned income credit, a proposal that critics call highly regressive. But actually the tax rates that Ford proposes would make the system a good deal more progressive than it is under either the 1974 schedule or the temporary 1975 rates. At the $5,000 level, a couple with no children would get a

Ford's tax-cut proposal: More for the lower brackets

Income	1974 tax*	Ford proposal	Percent reduction
$2,000	$0	$0	0%
3,000	28	0	100
4,000	170	0	100
5,000	322	60	81
10,000	1,171	800	32
15,000	2,062	1,750	15
20,000	3,085	2,780	10
25,000	4,240	3,905	8
50,000	12,380	12,080	2

*Married couple with no dependents

cut of 81%, but a $25,000 couple would get only 8%, and a $50,000 couple 2%. Under the 1974 schedule, the $10,000 couple paid 3.6 times the tax of the $5,000 couple, though it had only twice the income. A $20,000 couple paid 2.5 times the tax of the $10,000 couple. President Ford's proposal would leave the $10,000 couple paying 13.3 times the tax of the $5,000 couple and the $20,000 couple paying 3.5 times the tax of the $10,000 couple.

The Ford Administration also is proposing to take two percentage points off the corporate income tax (now 48%). In a separate recommendation, Treasury Secretary William E. Simon has suggested allowing corporations to deduct half their dividends from taxable income and allowing stockholders a tax credit equal to half the dividends they received. Since the credit would have to be added to incomes and then subtracted from taxes, it would yield the greatest benefits to small investors with moderate incomes.

Surprisingly, the U. S. has never shown any real interest in tough estate and gift taxes, the device that the British have used to level the old class structure. By the skillful use of trusts and lifetime gift programs, it is possible to transfer enormous fortunes down through the generations more or less intact. And that is apparently the way the voters want it. Senator George McGovern lost labor votes in his Presidential campaign by suggesting a limit of $100,000 on inheritances. Robert Nisbet of Columbia University observes that the American intellectual is "more hostile to the businessman who earned his money than to the man who inherited it."

Extending transfers. Transfer payments are a double-action leveler. They shift money to the bottom brackets, and at the same time they increase the need for government revenue, which means heavier taxes on the middle and upper incomes. Unlike affirmative action programs, they are a powerful weapon for increasing the degree of vertical equality in the income structure.

In the second quarter of 1975, federal transfer payments, measured on the national income accounts basis, hit an annual rate of $150 billion. This represented 42% of total federal spending.

It also represented a breathtakingly swift expansion in transfers. As recently as fiscal 1972, the total was only $78.6 billion, or 33% of federal spending.

State and local transfers are harder to estimate, but they would add $20 billion to $30 billion to the 1975 total.

Not all of this money went to the poor, of course. The rich and poor alike draw Social Security benefits, and there is some spillover in medical care, aid to the blind, and other programs. But there is no question that without transfers, the bottom quintile of the income curve would get a much smaller share of the total.

Transfers have been the driving force in the expansion of the federal government apparatus in the past decade. The Health, Education & Welfare Dept., with 128,000 employees is now the biggest department in the government, with the exception of Defense and the Veterans Administration (195,000) which administers a huge transfer operation of its own. The "welfare industry," which reaches down through state and local governments to the kitchens of Harlem and the clothes closets of Los Angeles, has become one of the nation's biggest businesses.

Public services. The alarming growth rate and the multiplication of programs and subprograms are drawing heavy fire both from within the government and from without. Just before he left Washington, former HEW Secretary Caspar Weinberger lashed out at the "massive welfare state that has intruded into the lives and personal affairs of our citizens." He predicted: "If social programs continue growing for the next two decades at the same pace they have in the last two, we will spend more than half of our whole gross national product for domestic social programs alone by the year 2000."

Weinberger's answer to the "welfare mess" is to adopt "a completely new system that would be coordinated and administered through our tax system. . . . substitute a simple cash grant, based on need, measured by income and payable only to those who meet a strong work requirement if they are able to work."

This is a variation of the negative income tax—a guaranteed minimum income for everyone. It has strong appeal not only for conservatives but also for the egalitarians, who would simply eliminate the work requirement and increase the benefits in Weinberger's plan. Eventually, some form of minimum income probably will replace the patchwork of overlapping programs that now make up the welfare system.

But in the immediate future, these programs are due for expansion rather than simplification. A national health program is almost a sure bet within the next few years. Day nurseries for the children of working women are one of the top demands of women's groups. Federal job programs to take up the slack in chronically depressed areas will get strong backing if the economic recovery does not generate a fast increase in employment.

The federal government will also be under mounting pressure to move deeper into the area of public services. The cities and states are close to the limit of their resources. They are calling on Washington to take over.

The federal government already is spending more than $8 billion a year on education. Some of this takes the form of direct transfers—scholarships or loans to needy students—and some is earmarked for special programs such as aid to the handicapped. The rest goes to beef up school district budgets.

Housing programs, once a big item in the federal budget, have been suspended for the past three years, while the government tried to find a better way of encouraging building for low-income tenants. President Nixon proposed a system of rent subsidies for the poor, but the idea died in Congress. With the building industry still flat on its back and an acute housing shortage in prospect, a new program to provide low-income shelter is certain to be adopted sooner or later.

Mass transit is running deficits in city after city. Local governments dare not let the fare rise for fear of the voters' anger, but they find it increasingly hard to cover the loss. New York City clung to the 35¢ fare until the whole city was on the verge of collapse. Now it needs help to maintain a 50¢ fare.

And so all the mayors, governors, and local delegations to Congress converge in Washington to ask for massive expansion of federal help in providing public services. They will not get everything they want, but they are determined not to go home empty-handed.

As the egalitarians see it, people have a right to food, shelter, transportation, and entertainment. The business of government is to provide these things without regard to what they cost or where the money comes from. John Rawls, the philosopher most often quoted by the egalitarians, puts it simply: There can be no justification for differences in the conditions of individuals unless it can be shown that the difference benefits the inferior more than the superior.

171

Anatomy of a "Fiscal Crisis"

By Anthony M. Rufolo

Although the fiscal plight of New York City has been making headlines, most local governments now complain that expenditures are growing faster than taxes. Many residents demand increased services despite rising costs, but they quickly rebel at attempts to raise more tax dollars. Nearly everyone wants more goods and services for less money, so these demands don't seem unusual. It's one way for citizens to remind City Hall that every expenditure decision involves a budget tradeoff. After all, as economists never tire of pointing out, resources are limited and budgets limit their use. However, mayors in certain areas—particularly central cities—fear that if they fail to maintain the same level of services or to clamp a lid on taxes, the exodus of jobs and wealth to the suburbs may accelerate. Many of them call this a "fiscal crisis," conjuring up visions of nothing but abandoned buildings and jobless poor. Is such alarm jus-

tified, or are some city administrators simply rebelling against the constraints of their budgets?

Taxpayer Smith may forsake the paved sidewalks of the city for the manicured lawns of suburbia for any number of reasons. He may commute a greater distance for more open living space. He may want his children to attend a suburban school. If he moves from one suburb to another, generally no one would care. But a move from city to suburb makes him another statistic to furrow the city mayor's brow. The likeliest candidate for such a move is the relatively wealthy taxpayer.[1] For example, Smith's contributions to the city's coffers may be more

---

[1] One author found that "between 1959 and 1969, the median income of central city families dropped from 89 percent of that of suburban families to 83 percent." See Joseph A. Pechman, "Fiscal Federalism for the 1970's," *National Tax Journal* 24 (1971): 285.

Anthony M. Rufolo, "Anatomy of a Fiscal Crisis." *Business Review*, Federal Reserve Bank of Philadelphia, June 1975, pp. 3–12. Reprinted with permission.

than it actually costs to provide him with government services, so he pays for services for relatively poor taxpayer Jones as well. This redistribution of income provides an incentive for Smith and others like him to leave the city, thereby putting increasing pressure on city budgets. Thus, income redistribution at the local level may be a major force behind the "fiscal crisis."

So far, no major cities have folded. Perhaps the danger signals were heeded before the situation became hopeless. Recently Federal revenue-sharing funds have helped relieve the pressure on city budgets. But the underlying source of the problem may still be with us. An analysis of what makes a fiscal crisis is in order, so that the pros and cons of proposed solutions can be weighed intelligently. Perhaps there is a solution which attacks the source of the problem rather than its symptoms.

CITY VERSUS SUBURBS

Every government has budget constraints, so why must *only* major cities face crises? One reason for the difference in ability to cope is that suburban communities have been more successful in attracting the "Smiths" and banning the "Joneses."[2] This creates a problem for the city because the poor require relatively more services from government but have less ability to pay. More low-income residents force a larger tax burden on city businesses and wealthier residents or shift services away from them, or both. Some of these businesses and individuals avoid this increased burden by just moving to the suburbs. This movement in turn leads to greater tax burdens and/or decreased services for those remaining in the city. The poor don't emigrate because of inadequate low-cost housing or poor public transportation in the suburbs as well as barriers such as zoning restrictions.[3] This population shift then affects government budgets, and a quick review will show that cities' tax bases relative to expenditures are not keeping pace with the suburbs'.

The property tax is the primary source of most locally raised revenue. In the early '70s, property taxes accounted for 82 percent of all tax revenue of local governments in metropolitan areas and 40 percent of their total revenue from all sources.[4] However, this important component of the tax system has its base rising more slowly in central cities than in the suburbs. For example, real estate values in Philadelphia increased by 29 percent from 1962 to 1972 while those in the surrounding counties of Delaware, Montgomery, and Bucks posted increases of 38, 77, and 100 percent respectively (see Table 1).

At the same time population has been growing fairly fast in the suburbs while it has actually declined in Philadelphia (Table 2). The result is that tax base per person has grown at a similar rate for each county (Table 3). However, expenditure per person is rising fastest for Philadelphia (Table 4) so that even adjusting for population, total expenditures are growing faster in Philadelphia (Table 5). Thus, while expenditures are rising faster than the value of the property base in all four counties, the difference is largest for Philadelphia.

Several major cities have turned to a wage or income tax to pay for services without increasing the tax burden on real estate. In Philadelphia, for example, between 1962 and 1972 property tax revenues increased by less than 45 percent while total tax revenue almost doubled. In large part the wage tax took up the slack. Unfortunately, however, shift-

[2]There are exceptions, of course, and those suburbs which have not been successful at this face the same type of problems as the central cities.

[3]A recent New Jersey Supreme Court ruling has as its intent the removal of these barriers with respect to housing, but its impact cannot yet be determined. See "Zoning and the Citizen" in the *New York Times*, April 1, 1975.

[4]U.S. Department of Commerce, Bureau of the Census, *1972 Census of Governments, Local Government in Metropolitan Areas*, p. 8.

TABLE 1
THE TAX BASE* (MARKET VALUE OF REAL ESTATE) IS RISING FASTER IN THE SUBURBS**

	Philadelphia County	Bucks County	Delaware County	Montgomery County
1962	$5889.8	$1237.9	$2142.8	$2664.5
1972	7617.0	2474.8	2961.2	4708.5
Change (1962–72)	$1727.2	$1236.9	$ 818.4	$2044.0
Percent Change (1962–72)	29.3%	99.9%	38.2%	76.7%

*Dollar figures are in millions.

**Chester County is not included because it is not contiguous to Philadelphia County.

SOURCE: Pennsylvania Department of Commerce, *Pennsylvania Statistical Abstract*.

TABLE 2
BUT SO IS THE POPULATION

	Philadelphia County	Bucks County	Delaware County	Montgomery County
1962	2,002,512	308,567	553,154	516,682
1972	1,950,098	415,056	601,425	623,921
Percent Change	−2.6%	34.5%	8.7%	20.8%

SOURCE: U.S. Department of Commerce, *Census of Governments —Compendium of Government Finance*, Table 53.

TABLE 3
LEAVING TAX BASE PER PERSON GROWING AT SIMILAR RATES

	Philadelphia County	Bucks County	Delaware County	Montgomery County
1962	$2941.2	$4011.8	$3873.8	$5156.9
1972	3906.0	5962.6	4923.6	7546.6
Percent Change (1962–72)	32.8%	48.6%	27.1%	46.3%

SOURCE: Tables 1 and 2.

174

TABLE 4
EXPENDITURE PER PERSON IS RISING SIGNIFICANTLY FASTER IN PHILADELPHIA THAN IN SURROUNDING COUNTIES*

	Philadelphia County			Montgomery County			Delaware County			Bucks County		
	1962	1972	Percent Change	1962	1972	Percent Change	1962	1972	Percent Change	1962	1972	Percent Change
Expenditure per Person	$209	$635	203.8%	$183	$436	138.2%	$155	$326	110.3%	$213	$463	117.4%
Revenue per Person	$209	$590	182.3%	$169	$432	155.6%	$145	$338	133.1%	$185	$455	145.9%
Intergovernmental	34	216	535.3	29	92	217.2	26	96	269.2	44	150	240.9
Own Sources	175	374	113.7	140	340	142.9	119	242	103.4	154	305	98.1
Intergovernmental as Percent of Total	16%	37%	131%**	17%	21%	24%**	18%	28%	56%**	24%	33%	37%**

*Dollar figures are in millions.

**Represents rate of growth of intergovernmental as percentage of total revenue.

SOURCE: Same as Table 2.

TABLE 5
WHILE TOTAL EXPENDITURES ARE RISING ONLY SLIGHTLY FASTER

	Philadelphia County			Montgomery County			Delaware County			Bucks County		
	1962	1972	Percent Change	1962	1972	Percent Change	1962	1972	Percent Change	1962	1972	Percent Change
General Revenue	$418.6	$1151.6	175.1%	$87.4	$269.5	288.4%	$80.0	$203.8	154.8%	$57.0	$188.5	230.7%
Intergovernmental	67.8	421.9	522.3	14.8	57.2	286.5	14.2	58.0	308.5	13.6	62.2	360.3
Own Sources	350.9	729.7	108.1	72.5	212.3	192.8	65.8	145.8	121.6	47.4	126.4	166.7
Taxes	279.4	557.0	99.4	58.5	168.1	185.9	53.2	118.7	123.1	32.1	96.2	199.6
Property	162.9	231.3	42.0	53.2	152.6	186.8	49.4	111.4	125.5	27.6	84.8	207.2
Other	116.5	325.7	179.6	5.5	15.5	181.8	3.8	7.4	94.7	4.5	11.4	153.3
Direct General Expenditures	$417.6	$1237.9	196.4%	$94.7	$272.2	186.4%	$85.7	$196.1	128.8%	$65.6	$192.2	193.0%

*Dollar figures are in millions.

SOURCE: Same as Table 2.

ing to a different tax is not likely to alleviate the problem (see Box 1). City residents paying more in total local taxes than it costs to serve them are still likely to have an incentive to move to the suburbs. It is this incentive that is at least partially behind the fiscal plight of many major cities.

LOCAL INCOME REDISTRIBUTION: AN INCENTIVE TO MOVE?

Most people consider political factors as the primary determinants of the tax rates and services provided by a local community. Residents as voters register their desires through elections, and the elected representatives try to coordinate the often conflicting goals of various groups. Some economists, however, emphasize a rather different aspect of this process. They point out that communities can be considered as sellers of a package of goods and services who charge a certain tax-price for the package. So while a resident/voter can try to influence what local government does, he can also decide to move to a community more tailored to his

BOX 1

HIGHER RESOURCE COSTS VERSUS INCOME REDISTRIBUTION

There are, of course, many reasons why a central city might have faster growing expenditures per capita than do the suburbs. However, most of these phenomena do not create distortions in the economy. When the higher expenditures and, hence, higher taxes represent the cost of serving residents, then the movement of residents to find more services for fewer tax dollars is beneficial to the economy. For example, if wages and land costs are rising fast in the city and this raises the cost of running local government, then someone who moves out frees the resources which were used to provide him with services. This person is made better off and no one is worse off. However, if taxes are high in order to pay for the services which someone else receives, then moving out lowers the city's income by more than it lowers expenses. In this situation, even people who would be willing to pay the cost of service to them may be driven away. This then raises the tax burden and/or lowers service levels for those remaining and may lead to the cumulative process discussed in the text.

The same situation arises no matter who is being subsidized. For example, some people argue that suburbanites directly exploit the central city. They commute in and impose costs on the local government and then leave without paying any taxes. Partially in response to this argument, some central cities levy wage or income taxes; however, there is very little evidence to support this allegation.* To the extent that this does happen, a wage tax can offset the income redistribution to suburbanites; but if it does not happen, the wage tax will distort location decisions in favor of suburban jobs. The discussion in the text is equally applicable to all types of local income redistribution.

---

*For a detailed discussion, see "Suburban Exploitation of Central Cities," by David F. Bradford and Wallace E. Oates, presented at the Urban Institute conference on "Economic Policy and the Distribution of Benefits," held in Washington, D. C., March 23–24, 1972.

preferences. Consumers in a sense "shop" among communities much as they shop among stores for goods.

Unfortunately, though, this analogy has its limitations. There are easily recognizable differences between the way stores sell and the way local governments "sell." Stores charge directly for the items bought while governments charge indirectly by taxing sources such as property or income. This difference affects people when they are "community shopping."

The major effect is that people do not necessarily contribute equally to the cost of public goods and services, even if they receive the same benefits. For example, with a property tax, a person with a small house might pay much less in taxes than a neighbor with a big house although both may send the same number of children to the same school. This local redistribution of income may be desirable on equity grounds (if we accept "ability to pay" as our equity criterion), since presumably the resident of the larger house is wealthier. (See Box 2.) However, such a situation motivates the person paying higher

BOX 2

EQUITY, PRODUCTION EFFICIENCY, AND SOCIAL EFFICIENCY

There are two criteria which appear to be used most in judging governmental actions—equity and efficiency. Equity relates to "equal treatment." Unfortunately, this is about all that can be said in this area without provoking some controversy. Does it relate to equal treatment of equals or equal treatment of everyone? Should the poor get the same as the rich, or more, or less?* Government is often in the position to provide different levels of services to different groups or to charge them different taxes. When government actions in this regard favor the poor, there is essentially a transfer of income. This transfer of income is carried out for equity purposes. Thus, one goal of government could be to promote equity through income redistribution.

Efficiency can be broken down into production versus social efficiency. We can look at production efficiency as being the least costly production of a given good or service and social efficiency as being the production of goods and services most desired by consumers. For example, a firm may be a very efficient producer of buggy whips in terms of keeping the cost per whip down, but it may be wasting resources because no one wants buggy whips. This would be a case of production efficiency which is not social efficiency. In a competitive economy, such a firm would go out of business; however, government subsidies might allow it to remain in operation. Similarly, other firms in some noncompetitive positions may be producing desirable goods but in a very costly manner. As long as the goods are worth more than the resources used in producing them and they would not otherwise be produced, then it may be socially efficient to provide them although we don't have productive efficiency. Thus, productive efficiency and social efficiency are two other possible goals of government.

---

*For a treatment of some of the issues, see Anita A. Summers, "Equity in School Financing: The Courts Move In," *Business Review* of the Federal Reserve Bank of Philadelphia, March 1973, pp. 3–13.

taxes to try isolating himself from the person paying lower taxes, since the wealthier resident is, in a sense, paying part of the poorer person's bill. Each person has an incentive to live in a community in which he has less property (and hence lower tax payments) than anyone else in the community. Of course, everyone cannot have less than the average amount. The only stable solution to this type of system would seem to be one in which each resident of a community has approximately the same amount of property and makes similar tax payments.[5] All persons who want smaller houses or apartments would be kept out by zoning laws or similar arrangements.

---

[5]Renters are assumed to pay property taxes through their rent payments.

Redistribution and Efficiency. Economics tells us that if the price of something corresponds to the costs of providing it, then our scarce resources will be channeled to their most highly valued uses. When local governments charge tax "prices" unrelated to the costs of the services they provide, these resources may end up in inefficient uses. For example, consider our friend Smith's decision to move from the city to the suburbs. Suppose he was entirely happy with the services he received but discovered the same services could be received in suburbia for lower taxes. If the cost were the same in the two places, but taxes were higher because of local income redistribution, then Smith's move would waste both the resources involved in the actual move and those used in his daily commuting. However, if taxes were different because the suburban government had lower costs, then Smith's move would result in the saving of resources employed in providing the services. This saving would be balanced against the cost of Smith's moving and commuting. In this case moving would mean not only a cost saving to him, but more efficient use of society's resources would result (Box 2).

If suburban communities succeed in keeping out low-income residents, they reduce the incentive for *current suburbanites* to move around. This can cut the loss of resources resulting from a game of "musical chairs" among communities. However, this cannot reduce the loss of resources because of excess movements out of the city, and it reinforces the result of little or no income redistribution at the local level.

This description of how people choose a community may seem an extreme case, and it certainly omits other important factors which shape a location decision. However, tax-benefit considerations may have significantly influenced the movement to suburbia and may have helped create communities where all the residents have very similar characteristics. To the extent that this process really operates, it can thwart the attempt

of cities to pay for the services they provide by redistributing income through taxes. In fact, attempts to redistribute income locally through taxes can not only influence the movement of people and jobs out of the city, but can also backfire and deepen the plight of the poor.

Redistribution and Low-Income Residents. If attempts to redistribute income lead to separation of families by income class, then the poor could be worse off than if no income redistribution were attempted. This is because current financing only allows communities with a large tax base per person to provide large amounts of goods and services per person. Thus, it is usually necessary for each resident of such a community to buy a large house or rent an expensive apartment. A poor family desiring high levels of some public services (education, for example) would then have to pay for large amounts of housing as well as for the services they desire. While low-income families might be able to afford payments for the services, they obviously cannot also afford large payments for housing. Efforts to encourage low-income housing in the suburbs have encountered stiff opposition, with income redistribution probably a major objection. The likely outcome is that the poor with their demand for services are "locked" into the central city. And, there's the heart of a "fiscal crisis."

So, cities face the problem of providing goods and services which are increasingly more costly to a population which has a growing percentage of those with the least ability to pay. This leads to high-tax and low-service levels for those who can pay. To avoid income redistribution payments at the local level, some people who would otherwise have stayed in the city may incur the costs of moving and commuting. They might also move to a community which provides a different amount of public services than they would choose if they were bearing the direct cost.

The net result is likely to be some waste of society's resources, very little actual income redistribution at the local level, and forces continuing to militate against locating in the central city. While there are many factors creating fiscal pressure on the city, this one may truly be called a "fiscal crisis," for the situation cannot be controlled from within the city. However, this does not imply that all cries of "crisis" should be treated the same. If the city is driving away jobs and residents because it has high production costs or is inefficient, the situation should be labeled an internal management problem, not a crisis.

PROPOSED SOLUTIONS

Two often-proposed methods of aiding the central city are the formation of a metropolitan or regional government and the sharing of revenue by the state or Federal Government. Either method can achieve the goal of relieving the fiscal pressure on central cities, but each also has shortcomings.

Metropolitan Government: A Loss of Competition. A metropolitan government consists of a central city and all of its suburbs replacing many local governments. Proponents of this approach argue that it would eliminate competition for the tax base at the local level.[6] Individuals or businesses would have to move outside the metropolitan area to escape paying their share of taxes. The problem with this solution is that local government competition can be desirable.

Local government, locally financed, is beneficial in two important respects. The first is that to some extent it forces people to reveal what they are willing to pay for government services. Suppose property taxes were used only to finance goods and services whose costs are approximately proportional to the amount of property people own. It is then likely that the "shopping" element of community choice would direct people with similar preferences for government services to the same communities. They would not have any incentive to move to communities that provided more of these services than they wanted because they would have to pay the cost. Similarly, people would not have an incentive to move to communities providing too little of these services because the resultant tax savings would not compensate them for having less of these services.

The second benefit (and perhaps that which advocates of local government stress most) is the wider range of choice which results from many "suppliers" (governmental units). For example, suppose that Jones would like more police protection than would Smith. If they live in the same community, both cannot be satisfied. Voting may lead to some compromise, perhaps less than Jones would like to "purchase," but more than Smith wants to pay for. However, if Jones and Smith each move to other communities populated with residents of similar tastes, each may be able to achieve his desired level of police protection. A more inclusive metropolitan government is not likely to offer as much variety.

This is not meant to imply that local government would not have fiscal pressures in the absence of local income redistribution. Most economists now agree that suburbanization would have occurred even if central cities had had no fiscal or social problems.[7] Also, people in every community will want to

---

[6]There are a number of arguments related to coordinating the actions of local governments which are also expounded by proponents but which will not be covered here. For a discussion of these arguments and alternative forms of metropolitan government, see L. Christine Grad, "Blueprint for Metropolitan Reform," *Business Review* of the Federal Reserve Bank of Philadelphia, October 1971, pp. 12–17.

[7]For example, see Edwin S. Mills and James MacKinnon, "Notes on the New Urban Economics," *Bell Journal of Economics and Management Science* 4 (1973): 593–601, 596.

minimize their costs for particular services. But this type of incentive serves to inform government of what the residents want. In this case, a community may lose residents by not providing the desired level of services or by being inefficient, but it will not lose residents because another community is a "tax haven."

Sharing Revenue Distorts "Prices." The sharing revenues approach leaves government units unchanged but provides funds from state or Federal sources to relieve the fiscal pressure on local government. Tax collections are made from all over the state or even the country, making tax avoidance very difficult.

Sharing revenue has been with us for some time, although large-scale transfers of unconditional funds are relatively recent occurrences. Table 5 shows that funds from the state and Federal governments have been growing faster for Philadelphia than for any of its neighboring Pennsylvania counties. In fact, while Philadelphia had the largest percentage increase in expenditures, the growth of transfer funds has been sufficient to give it the smallest percentage increase in taxes and in total revenue from local sources. Thus, sharing revenue has, indeed, relieved some of the fiscal pressure on central cities and other local governments. However, this solution also has a drawback.

Revenue sharing does not force people to relate their tax payments to the cost of providing services. If one community should consistently get more in transfer funds than another, it will become more attractive relative to the second community. In addition, each community will still have incentives to attract businesses and individuals who pay more in taxes than it costs to serve them and to keep others out. Because the "prices" of services in one community versus another still do not reflect the cost of resources used in providing these services, people will expend time and money in relocating. Moreover, they will not move to the community which can best satisfy their preferences with the least use of resources.

LOCAL FINANCING WITHOUT INCENTIVES TO MOVE

It may sound like local tax financing will always create incentives for people to separate into similar income groups, but this is not true. This result arises from attempts to redistribute income locally through the tax process. If Smith's taxes represent the cost of serving him, then it doesn't matter much to the community whether or not he lives there. Neither a new rich neighbor nor a new poor one would alter the taxes or benefits for current residents of the community. For example, if the property tax were restricted to financing services whose cost is approximately proportional to the amounts of property in the community just as the property tax is, then people with large houses would have no *tax* incentive to bar construction of small houses. Such services as fire protection are likely to fit into this category. Thus, owners of large houses on large lots (which are likely to require more fire equipment and create a bigger area to cover than do small houses on small lots) would pay higher taxes to offset the higher costs imposed on the community. No doubt there are other reasons why people might want similar houses in the same community (such as aesthetic appeal and a desire to socialize with people of similar income), but such considerations often relate more to an immediate neighborhood than to an entire town.

When a government service has costs which are not related to property, then the property tax should not be used for financing. Similarly, if the cost of serving someone is not related to his income, then a local income tax should not be used to finance that service. Certainly, we would seldom expect to find an exact correspondence between a certain tax and the cost of providing a particular service. But now taxes and services are usually completely unrelated. Take welfare as an example. Most people agree that society has some obligation to care for the indigent, but why should the burden fall on property owners in a particular community? This is definitely an area where direct payments from the Federal Government would lead to more equal treatment for the poor in different communities and would relieve an unfair burden on city property owners. This proposal would, in turn, reduce the incentive to move strictly to avoid local tax payments aimed at redistributing income.

Another benefit of such a system is that the range of choices available to many people would increase. Education is a good example. "Charging" on the basis of the number of schoolchildren avoids income redistribution at the local level. Given that government has assumed the financing of the service, the funds should come from state or Federal sources. One way would be for the state to issue a voucher which would be used to "pay" for schooling.[8] Each student would receive a voucher and present it to the school he attends. The school would then redeem the voucher with the state or Federal government for its operating funds. Local communities might continue to *provide* school services, but there would no longer be any reason to restrict entrance to local residents. Thus, a family would not have to relocate to obtain the educational services it desires.

In short, let local government continue to finance those services which do not result in significant income redistribution. And, whenever possible do this with taxes that closely reflect the costs of providing services.

[8]The voucher plan allows parents to determine what school to send their children to while having the state continue to finance the education. See David W. Lyon, "Capitalism in the Classroom: Education Vouchers," *Business Review* of the Federal Reserve Bank of Philadelphia, December 1971, pp. 3–10.

Let the state and Federal governments finance services which entail significant income redistribution. Income redistribution can be more effectively administered at these higher levels of government. The difficulty in avoiding broader-based taxes will reduce the amount of resources spent in trying to avoid them. At the same time, the benefits of local choice can be maintained or increased.

SUMMING UP

Now, what about that "fiscal crisis"? To the extent that such a crisis exists, it is at least partly caused by communities using local taxes to finance public goods and services in such a way that some redistribution of income results. When this effect is large, communities are forced both to compete for citizens who make a net contribution to the local treasury and to keep out those who are a net drain. This can lead to segregation by income, and it's possible for this to make everyone, including the poor, worse off than if no such attempt were made.

The benefits of many communities offering a range of services are very real. Financing the wrong services—ones where taxes are not linked to costs—by means of local taxes is likely to cause inefficient use of resources and excessive decentralization of people and businesses. It is time for a rational approach to financing government expenditures, and this includes a recognition that efficiency and equity may require one level of government to raise taxes while another provides goods or services. However, it also requires the recognition that competition at the local level can be beneficial. There is no reason for city governments to be spared from having to accept the tradeoff of taxes and services faced by other governments. But there is also no reason for them to shoulder most of the burden of financing services for the poor.

Federal Government Purchases of Goods and Services

By Dan M. Bechter

Federal government spending has grown enormously over the years. Total expenditures for the current fiscal year will likely exceed $370 billion, more than twice the amount spent during the peak Vietnam war year of 1968, and more than 10 times the average annual amount spent a generation ago during the peacetime years, 1947-49. The rapid growth and huge size of these outlays have attracted much attention, and with good reason: Federal government spending profoundly affects the economy.

The economic effects of spending by the Federal government are not fully understood. It is clear, however, that while it might be all right for certain purposes to treat one dollar of Federal expenditure like any other, the kind of economic impact depends importantly on the type of expenditure. In particular, the economic effects of increases in Federal government transfer payments, such as social security benefits, will differ in some ways from the effects of increases in Federal government purchases of goods and services. Thus, a preoccupation with total spending by the Federal government can lead to conclusions which may differ from those reached when it is noted that the composition of that total has shifted dramatically toward transfers and away from purchases.

This article reviews trends in total Federal government spending, takes up the question of how economic effects differ according to the type of expenditure, and then focuses on Federal government purchases of goods and services. A subsequent article will deal in some detail with Federal government transfer payments.

FEDERAL GOVERNMENT SPENDING SINCE 1929

Total spending by the Federal government is commonly used as a measure of the "size of the Federal government." This is unfortunate. None of the usually implied concepts of the Federal government's magnitude—employment, influence on the lives of Americans (and others), or resources required—is measured by its total expenditures. This is not to deny that the total on the outlays side of the Federal budget is an important figure, for it is the amount that must be financed by taxation or borrowing. And this amount has increased dramatically since World War II, significantly faster than the rate of inflation (Chart 1).

As already noted, the first step toward a better understanding of Federal government spending is to distinguish between the two principal types of expenditures, transfer payments and purchases of goods and services. The second step is to make allowance in the historical series for the declining value of the dollar. Chart 2 shows the two major expenditure components adjusted for inflation. In the past, most Federal expenditures were for national defense. Now, the Department of Health, Education, and Welfare (HEW) distributes more in transfer payments than the Department of Defense

---

Dan M. Bechter, "Federal Government Purchases of Goods and Services." *Monthly Review,* Federal Reserve Bank of Kansas City, November 1975, pp. 3–10. Reprinted with permission.

Chart 1
FEDERAL GOVERNMENT EXPENDITURES AND INFLATION

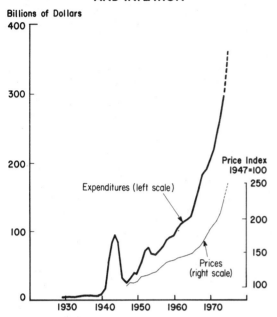

Billions of Dollars

Expenditures (left scale)

Price Index 1947=100

Prices (right scale)

Chart 2
FEDERAL PURCHASES AND TRANSFERS IN REAL TERMS

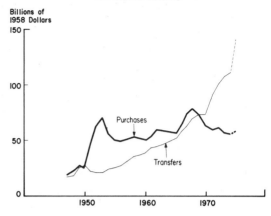

Billions of 1958 Dollars

Purchases

Transfers

spends for goods and services.

An individual taxpayer concerned about the size of his own tax liability may not particularly care how his tax dollar is split between the financing of Federal government purchases and transfer payments. However, the distinction is important in terms of effects on the economy. Federal government expenditures on goods and services deny other sectors some of the country's total output, or, more meaningfully, the use of part of the country's resources. Not so with Federal transfer payments, which leave resource claims within non-Federal sectors. For example, resources used to build a jet fighter for the Air Force are not available for the production of goods and services for the rest of the economy. In contrast, an increase in social security benefits and taxes redistributes purchasing power among non-Federal sectors and does not translate into an increase in the Federal government's claim on resources.[1]

The declining absolute amount of real Federal government purchases of goods and services since 1968 (Chart 2) together with the rising productive capacity of this nation has meant a declining share of the central government's claim to resources in recent years (Chart 3). The relative size of the public sector (all government), however, is still about the same as it was in 1952. As Table 1 shows, the declining Federal share of output since 1952 has been offset by a rising share of goods and services purchased by state and local governments, a trend helped along by revenue sharing and other Federal grants in aid to state and local governments. Consumer and business shares have remained relatively stable. By this one measure, then, since the Korean war period, "big" government has declined in size relative to other sectors, and especially relative to "small" government. Chart 4 tells a similar story with employment data.

DEFENSE PURCHASES

Most Federal government purchases of goods and services are for national defense. This proportion has trended downward, however, as has the ratio of defense expenditures to gross national product (Chart 5). Purchases of goods and services

---

1/Another important implication of the compositional shift in Federal spending is a declining fiscal stimulus for a deficit of a given size. This is because a dollar's worth of transfers has less of a stimulating effect on the economy than a dollar's worth of purchases. See "Federal Fiscal Policy, 1965-72," *Federal Reserve Bulletin*, Vol. 59, No. 6 (June 1973).

Chart 3
REAL FEDERAL PURCHASES AS A SHARE OF REAL GNP

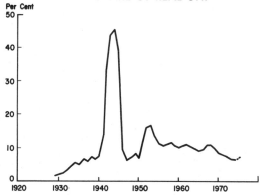

Per Cent

1920	1930	1940	1950	1960	1970

Table 1
SHARES OF GROSS NATIONAL PRODUCT BY FINAL DEMAND CATEGORY
Selected Years, 1929-75

| | Share of Actual Gross National Product | | | | Fed. Gov't. |
| | Private | | Government | | Share of |
Year	Consumption	Investment	State and Local	Federal	Potential GNP*
1929	.75	.16	.07	.01	.01
1940	.71	.13	.08	.06	.05
1943	.52	.03	.04	.42	.42
1947	.69	.15	.05	.05	.04
1952	.63	.15	.07	.15	.16
1955	.64	.17	.08	.11	.11
1958	.65	.14	.09	.12	.12
1964	.63	.15	.10	.10	.10
1967	.62	.15	.11	.11	.11
1974	.63	.15	.14	.08	.08
1975 est.	.65	.11	.15	.09	.08

*This ratio better measures the Federal government's share of the nation's capacity. Shares of actual GNP are affected by the business cycle.
SOURCE: U. S. Department of Commerce.

for national defense amounted to $83.1 billion during the fiscal year that ended June 30, 1975.

The Federal payroll for national defense accounts for a big chunk of defense expenditures. During fiscal year 1975, the Department of Defense bought 95 per cent of defense goods and services, spending an estimated $21.2 billion on salaries and benefits for 2.1 million active military personnel. An additional $1.6 billion went for pay and benefits to reserve forces. The Department of Defense also employs, in military functions, close to 1 million civilians, or about one-half of all Federal civilian employees excluding postal workers. Their salaries and benefits came to an estimated $14.5 billion in fiscal year 1975.[2] Thus, the Federal payroll for national defense totaled $38 billion in fiscal year 1975, or 46 per cent of national defense purchases, and two-thirds of total compensation in Federal employment exclusive of postal workers.

National defense purchases of goods and services are directly responsible for many jobs in the private sector, too. In full-time equivalents, perhaps 3 million non-Federal employees are involved at some stage with the production of goods and services for national defense although only an estimate

[2]/Military personnel in the Coast Guard (Department of Transportation), numbering 36,000, received $380 million in compensation. Another 6,250 Federal civilian employees earned $94 million working for the Coast Guard, and 8,200 more earned an estimated $180 million working defense-related jobs for the Energy Research and Development Administration or the Nuclear Regulatory Commission.

is possible. Over 1 million workers are currently employed by "defense product industries," but some industries in this classification also produce nondefense goods. Thus, their total employment tends to overstate the number of workers at the final stage of defense production. On the other hand, data on defense product industries exclude significant amounts of defense work carried on by companies and establishments in industries classified otherwise.[3] And, of course, the initial and intermediate levels in the production of defense goods are not included in these tabulations. Nonetheless, employment in defense product industries does serve as a useful index of defense activity.

NONDEFENSE PURCHASES

Nondefense purchases of goods and services by Federal civilian agencies totaled $41.1 billion, or half the amount of defense purchases, during fiscal year 1975. Nondefense expenditures include such programs as operating national forest, park, and recreation areas; space exploration; promotion of commerce; acquisition and disposal of agricultural

[3]/Defense Indicators, U. S. Department of Commerce, July 1975, p.2.

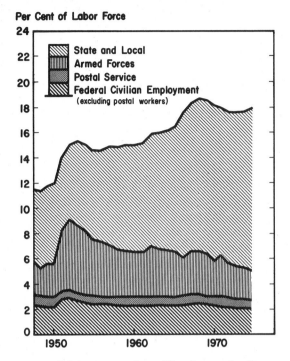

Chart 4
GOVERNMENT EMPLOYMENT

Per Cent of Labor Force

State and Local
Armed Forces
Postal Service
Federal Civilian Employment
(excluding postal workers)

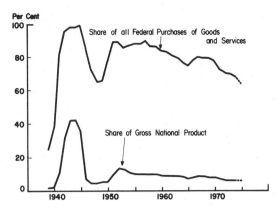

Chart 5
NATIONAL DEFENSE PURCHASES

Per Cent

Share of all Federal Purchases of Goods
and Services

Share of Gross National Product

commodities; construction of flood control and navigation projects; operation of the Federal airway system; a wide variety of medical and other scientific research; the capital outlay of Government-sponsored enterprises; Federal law enforcement; and operation of veterans hospitals.[4] Excluded are operating expenditures of government enterprises. Roughly one-half of nondefense spending on goods and services compensates about 1 million Federal government employees, most of whom work in the executive branch. Not included in the 1 million are 557,000 permanent and 140,000 part-time Postal Service employees whose $11 billion in pay and benefits in 1975 required more than all of the $10.3 billion in nonsubsidy revenues of this government enterprise. Fewer than 50,000 people work for the legislative and judicial branches of the Federal government.

As noted earlier, transfer payments are not part of purchases of goods and services by the Federal government. But the cost of administering these transfers is. Thus, 5 per cent of the $112 billion spent during fiscal 1975 by HEW went for goods and services; the rest was transfer payments. In contrast, 92.5 per cent of the Department of Defense expenditures went for goods and services, the other 7.5 per cent going for military retirement pay, a transfer.

INDUSTRY EFFECTS

To what extent do various industries benefit from Federal government purchases of goods and services? This question has been answered for 1963 with input-output analysis, which shows the interdependencies of industries in the economy.[5] The input-output technique permits the determination of indirect, as well as direct, effects of Federal purchases on industries. An example of a direct effect is the impact on the aircraft industry of the purchase of a jet fighter. Indirect effects on other industries arising from this final sale would occur in the preproduction phase as the aircraft company bought controls, fabricated aluminum, and other intermediate goods and services necessary to build the

4/*Special Analysis Budget of the United States Government, Fiscal Year 1976* (Washington: U. S. Government Printing Office, 1975), p.13.

5/Irvin Stern, "Industry Effects of Government Expenditures: An Input-Output Analysis," U. S. Department of Commerce, *Survey of Current Business,* May 1975, pp. 9-23. More recent data are not available.

Table 2

INDUSTRIAL DEPENDENCE ON FEDERAL GOVERNMENT PURCHASES OF GOODS AND SERVICES, SELECTED INDUSTRIES, 1963

	Where Each Dollar of Fed. Purchases Went	Per Cent of Output Attributable to Fed. Gov. Purchases	
		Total	Direct
The 7 industries most dependent on Federal purchases:			
Ordnance and accessories	.0827	90.1	84.1
Aircraft and parts	.1175	77.9	52.6
Radio, television, & communication equipment	.0731	48.7	37.7
Electronic components & accessories	.0062	38.8	8.8
Nonferrous metal ores mining	.0038	31.7	15.8
Machine shop products	.0008	31.3	2.2
Transportation equipment other than for motor vehicles & aircraft	.0175	26.8	23.0
The top 10 industries in dollar sales to the Federal government:			
Aircraft, ordnance, radio & television (see above)			
New construction	.0625	6.1	6.1
Gross imports	.0413	14.7	9.8
Business services	.0309	10.9	5.5
Medical educational services & nonprofit organizations	.0221	4.6	4.3
Construction maintenance & repair	.0221	10.4	7.1
Transportation & warehousing services	.0206	9.5	5.0
Chemicals & selected products	.0162	12.8	6.1
Total of above 14 industry categories	.5173		
Federal government industry*	.3813	100.0	100.0
All other industry	.1014		
All industry total	1.0000		5.5†

*Compensation of Federal government employees.
†Federal purchases/GNP.

jet. The producers of these intermediate inputs require inputs of their own from other industries, which means more indirect effects, and so on down the production chain to the primary materials industries.

Table 2 shows the effects of Federal purchases on certain industries in 1963. The defense industries exhibit the strongest ties to these purchases. In 1963, 8.27 per cent of Federal purchases (or 8.27 cents of a representative purchase dollar) went directly for the output of the ordnance industry, accounting for 84.1 per cent of its sales. Another 6 per cent of ordnance revenues were due to indirect effects from Federal purchases from other industries. It is readily seen from the table that some industries selling very little directly to the Federal government are heavily dependent on the indirect effects of Federal purchases (e.g., machine shop products). The sales of most industries, of course, depend in at least a small way on the Federal government's final demand.

REGIONAL EFFECTS

The ladder of production that supplies the Federal government with goods and services gives rise to income at every rung. From a regional point of view, this income is an outside source of dollars that supports the area economy.

The most easily identifiable source of income from Federal government purchases is the Federal payroll. Most Federal employees, like the rest of the population, live in or near cities. In 1972, 84 per cent of the total Federal civilian payroll went to U.S. government workers living in Standard Metropolitan Statistical Areas. Of total military pay, 75 per cent was for officers and enlisted men stationed in these urban locations. The military and civilian payrolls of the Federal government are by no means evenly distributed over cities. Thus, metropolitan areas of roughly the same size exhibit wide variations in the degree to which they depend on Federal pay as a source of income from the outside. For example, compare Lawton, Okla., with St. Joseph, Mo., in Table 3.

A community's total income depends indirectly as well as directly on its sales to outsiders. Income earned from such "exports" is spent partly on local goods and services, giving rise to other income, which itself is respent, and so on. Not all of an area's income attributable to Federal purchases of goods and services can be considered export income, since some of these expenditures go for local needs. For example, the salaries of regional Social Security personnel are not for exported services to the extent that the work done by these Federal employees is for residents of that region. In

Table 3					
FEDERAL PAYROLL AS A SOURCE OF PERSONAL INCOME IN SELECTED STANDARD METROPOLITAN STATISTICAL AREAS (SMSA's), 1972					
Millions of Dollars					
Area	Federal Payroll			Total Personal Income	Federal Payroll as Per Cent of Area Income
	Total	Civilian	Military		
United States	51,475	32,930	18,545	935,350	5.5
All SMSA's	41,777	27,787	13,990	734,865	5.7
Four SMSA's with big Federal payrolls:					
Washington, D.C.	5,526	4,690	836	17,578	31.4
New York	1,398	1,234	164	60,674	2.3
Philadelphia	1,369	950	419	24,103	5.7
San Diego	1,340	379	961	6,822	19.6
Tenth District SMSA's*	2,668	1,625	1,043	28,657	12.5
Colorado:					
Colorado Springs	391	92	299	1,110	35.2
Denver-Boulder	496	359	137	6,797	7.3
Pueblo	43	40	3	486	8.8
Kansas:					
Topeka	80	40	40	837	9.5
Wichita	102	44	58	1,705	5.9
Missouri:					
Kansas City†	346	282	64	6,396	5.4
St. Joseph	9	7	2	426	2.1
Nebraska:					
Lincoln	36	31	5	796	4.5
Omaha*	227	98	129	2,548	8.9
New Mexico:					
Albuquerque	184	131	53	1,458	12.6
Oklahoma:					
Lawton	201	50	151	371	54.1
Oklahoma City	440	386	54	3,105	14.2
Tulsa	52	41	11	2,339	2.2
Wyoming:					
Cheyenne	61	24	37	283	21.5

*Includes Pottawattamie county in Iowa, part of the Omaha SMSA, but the Tenth District total excludes Nebraska's Dakota county, which is in the Sioux City, Iowa SMSA.
†Includes Johnson and Wyandotte counties in Kansas.
SOURCE: U. S. Department of Commerce, Survey of Current Business, May 1974, Part II.

Table 4		
NET VALUE OF MILITARY PROCUREMENT ACTIONS, SELECTED STATES, FISCAL YEAR 1975		
	Amounts in Thousands	Per Cent
Total U. S. Prime Defense Procurement Awarded	43,355,471	
Distributed by State	37,319,429	100.0
The 4 biggest recipients	16,024,232	42.9
California	7,907,977	21.2
Connecticut	2,348,567	6.3
New York	3,743,942	10.0
Texas	2,023,746	5.4
Tenth District States	2,547,747	6.8
Colorado	293,803	0.8
Kansas	504,566	1.4
Missouri (state total)	1,361,409	3.7
Nebraska	49,860	0.1
New Mexico (state total)	93,812	0.3
Oklahoma (state total)	215,329	0.6
Wyoming	28,968	0.1

SOURCE: Prime Contract Awards, Department of Defense, Fiscal Year 1975.

areas where the ratio of Federal purchases to total purchases is significantly higher than average, there is a strong presumption that Federal demand is a major determinant of that area's economic activity.[6] Needless to say, that is the case in the Washington, D.C. metropolitan area, where 31 per cent of all personal income is Federal payroll, and where

6/Federal transfer payments can also be a major source of outside income. This will be covered in a subsequent article.

other Federal purchases of goods and services and spending by Federal employees is responsible for most of the remainder. (Empirical studies have shown that one to two dollars of additional local income is associated with each dollar of export income. The larger and more self-sufficient the region, the higher is this multiplier.)

The regional impacts of Federal purchases other than payroll are more difficult to determine. To the extent that certain industries are regionally concentrated, input-output analysis gives some idea of this impact. For example, a regional impact is indicated by those sales of the motor vehicle industry due to Federal government purchases. For one category of nonpayroll purchases, defense procurement, regional data are available. Expenditures on procurement by defense agencies account for one-fourth of all Federal purchases other than payroll. Final sales do not equal income, of course, nor do they show indirect industry effects. But it is probably true that those states which sell most of the defense goods to the Federal government are also those that would show the highest income benefits from defense procurement activity (Table 4).

INFLATIONARY EFFECTS?

Does an increase in Federal government purchases of goods and services cause more inflation? The answer is not an unequivocal yes; it depends on factors such as how the increase is financed, how close the economy is to its capacity level of output, and to what extent the pricing system is permitted to guide and direct.

If resources are fully employed and the Federal government creates new money to finance its additional spending, the result is more inflation. If, however, the increased demand of the Federal government is financed in a way that decreases demand in other sectors by the same amount, inflation can be kept at bay. Taxation reduces demand in the private sector. So does Federal borrowing from the available flow of saving. Deficit spending at full employment need not be inflationary, so long as it is not accompanied by an increase in the money supply or its velocity (rate of circulation) that is greater than the increase in output.

If the economy is operating substantially below capacity, an increase in Federal government purchases of goods and services stimulates production and puts unemployed resources to work (if markets are not immobilized by controls or monopoly elements). In such a circumstance, a case can be made for financing additional government purchases with new money, since the result of more money can be more output rather than higher prices (growth considerations aside, this cannot be true at capacity, where output is, by definition, a maximum). With underemployment, the Federal government will not need to reduce the demand of other sectors in order to provide for its increased purchases. To some degree, therefore, taxation and borrowing of old money can be avoided at least temporarily without disastrous inflationary consequences.

So much for theory; what is the record? A comparison of annual rates of change of the price level with same-year (or previous-year) percentage changes in real Federal purchases shows no consistent relationship between the two. In the past quarter century, the rate of inflation has just as often

as not gone in a direction opposite to that of real Federal spending on goods and services.[7] Clearly, the behavior of this one category of aggregate demand cannot provide much of a foundation for explaining the rate of change of the price level. One must look further to such factors as changes in the money supply and its velocity, and how Federal expenditures were financed.

STABILIZING ROLE

Federal government purchases of goods and services could be increased or decreased to help iron out business cycles. But Federal purchases usually are justified by criteria other than their stabilizing effect. According to one principle, the government should use resources (buy goods and services) only to provide desired quantities of public needs, such as national defense, that would not be provided by an aggregation of individual market decisions. This rule does not leave room for using Federal purchases as a means to stimulate or cool off the economy. Also, because of production lead-time, start-up costs, and penalty costs associated with project termination, it is technically very difficult to use purchases of goods and services as a flexible policy tool. Fiscal policy, therefore, frequently has been limited to the tax and transfer functions in the Federal budget. In the past 25 years, the two largest increases in real Federal expenditures for goods and services accompanied war, in the two 3-year periods 1951-53 and 1966-68. During these two periods, the economy reached capacity-straining levels of production not experienced since 1948, a peacetime year of economic boom supported by all major sectors of final demand, including Federal purchases, which rose 24 per cent from their postwar low.[8] After the Korean war and the peak of the Vietnam conflict, in 1954-55 and 1969-70, Fed-

7/In the national income accounts, defense goods are recorded as purchases when they are delivered rather than when ordered or produced. Before delivery, these goods are included in the inventory component of GNP and are not counted as government expenditures. Thus, the inflationary impact of defense spending could be realized well before purchases are recorded in the accounts. It turns out, however, that the correlation between defense purchases and prior-year rates of inflation is also poor.

8/The increases in Federal purchases in 1948 were primarily in the nondefense category, including added emphases on natural resource development and on transportation and communication.

eral expenditures on goods and services declined dramatically. Federal purchases also declined in successive years in 1959-60 and 1973-74. Each of these four 2-year periods included, by no coincidence, a recession. If changes in Federal demand did not cause these booms and busts, it certainly did not smooth the swings.

Federal purchases more often than not have changed in ways that aggravate the business cycle. In the past 28 years, 1948-75, the unemployment rate has averaged above 5 per cent half of the time. Real Federal purchases decreased in 7 of those years, and increased by more than 3 per cent in only 4, the two pairs of years 1957-58 and 1961-62, two truly contra-cyclical episodes for Federal demand. Of the 14 years in which the unemployment rate averaged less than 5 per cent, Federal expenditures on goods and services fell, in contra-cyclical fashion, in only 5, perhaps by too much, as recessions usually followed.

To summarize, Federal purchases have often changed in the wrong direction in terms of stabilization. When the direction has been right, the magnitude of change sometimes has not fit the situation. As noted above, however, Federal purchases of goods and services are only a small part of the fiscal stabilization package. And, conversely, stabilization is not the major goal of Federal purchases. Changes in taxes and transfers can be used to offset adverse effects on the economy that might result from changes in demand for output by the Federal government or, for that matter, any other sector in the economy. The fact that Federal purchases appear to have added amplitude to the business cycle suggests that fiscal stabilization policy has been an inadequate tool. Specifically, if more Federal purchases are required when the economy's capacity is already strained, the stabilization goal argues for bigger tax increases (or transfer decreases) than have been observed under these circumstances in the past. By the same token, if Federal purchases are being cut back at the same time that the economy is slumping, bigger-than-observed tax cuts or transfer increases are indicated.

SUMMARY

Total spending by the Federal government has risen rapidly in recent years. Huge increases in Federal transfer payments are the reason, because Federal purchases of goods and services have declined substantially in real terms. Transfers to persons have displaced expenditures for national defense as the largest expenditure category in the Federal budget. Only purchases use up resources; transfers do not increase the Federal government's resource requirements. Consequently, the share of the nation's productive capacity that is required to directly supply Federal demand is the lowest it has been in 25 years. Meanwhile, the share of output purchased by state and local governments has increased.

Two-thirds of Federal expenditures on goods and services go for national defense. In both defense and nondefense categories, the Federal payroll accounts for about half of all purchases. A big proportion of nonpayroll purchases are for defense and aerospace activities. Several industries depend heavily on such expenditures. Regional economies, too, show varying degrees of dependence on Federal purchases.

Inflation cannot be explained solely by changes in Federal purchases of goods and services. But changes in these expenditures apparently have aggravated the business cycle over the years, contributing to recessions, and to overstimulation in boom periods. Apparently, considerations other than stabilization have made the Federal government unwilling to choose adequate revenue and expenditure policies to offset the sometimes destabilizing effect of changes in Federal purchases.

189

Federal Government Spending on Interest, Transfers, and Grants

By Dan M. Bechter

The changing composition of Federal Government spending tells a story of trends and swings in national priorities during our country's two-century history. From the earliest years through the 1920's, the expenditure side of the Federal budget primarily reflected the nation's involvement in wars. Expenditures would increase to pay the cost of a conflict. Then, after the war, total spending would decline, and the budgetary emphasis would shift from paying for arms to paying interest on a war-inflated public debt.

Those who worry about today's national debt may derive some comfort from knowing that in most years before 1803, interest on the public debt claimed more than half of the outlays of the Federal Government. With the exception of veterans' compensation and pensions, Federal spending for social welfare was virtually unknown during the Republic's first 150 years. During fiscal year 1976, expenditures for income security, health, education, and veterans' benefits will account for 53 per cent of Federal budgetary outlays. In contrast, net interest on the public debt now claims about 8 per cent of the budget.

Federal spending for social welfare has roots in the Great Depression. By 1939, such expenditures had risen to 44 per cent of Federal outlays, or to over 50 per cent, if veterans' services and benefits are included. But World War II reversed this trend by ending the Depression and by requiring enormous defense expenditures. Veterans' benefits increased sharply after the war, but Federal spending on other welfare programs fell to nearly one-fourth the prewar dollar amount. Not until the late 1950's did the Federal Government again spend as much on social welfare as it did in 1939.

Clearly, major shifts in the composition of Federal Government expenditures are nothing new. But the trend of the past 20 years is not a repeat performance of historical cycles in Federal spending. It is a compositional shift that underlines a national commitment to use Federal spending as an instrument for redistributing income in relatively good times as well as in depressed economic periods. Thus the percentage of Federal outlays going for purchases of goods and services (two-thirds of which is currently for national defense) has declined from 64 per cent in 1956 to 55 per cent

---

Dan M. Bechter, "Federal Government Spending on Interest, Transfers, and Grants." *Monthly Review,* Federal Reserve Bank of Kansas City, May 1976, pp. 14–19. Reprinted with permission.

in 1966 and, with accelerating momentum, to 35 per cent in 1976. A previous article has dealt with the implications of changes in Federal spending for goods and services.[1] This article is about the other principal subdivisions of Federal outlays—interest on the public debt, domestic transfer payments, and grants-in-aid to state and local governments.

INTEREST ON THE NATIONAL DEBT

All but 1.3 per cent of the gross debt of the U.S. Government is in the form of marketable bonds, notes, and bills and certain nonmarketable series issued by the U.S. Treasury. Issues of several Federal Government agencies, such as the Export-Import Bank, the Tennessee Valley Authority, and the Federal Housing Administration, account for the remainder. A large proportion of gross Federal debt—43 per cent at the end of 1975—is held by Federal Government agencies, primarily in trust funds, and the Federal Reserve Banks. Thus, much of the interest paid on the gross Federal debt amounts to internal bookkeeping transactions that do not affect the public.

Net Federal indebtedness is that amount that the Federal Government owes to domestic and foreign investors. To the extent that the net Federal debt is held by U.S. investors, interest payments do not constitute a net burden on this nation's economy. No external burden is involved on domestically held debt because tax receipts from Americans are used to pay interest to Americans. However, even though "we pay interest to ourselves" on a national debt that "we owe to ourselves," a burden to current and future generations from past wars has been said to exist. This burden, the argument goes, is in the form of what might have been, had wars not interrupted the development of resources and the advancement of technology. According to this point of view, private investment has been crowded out by

[1] Dan M. Bechter, "Federal Government Purchases of Goods and Services," Federal Reserve Bank of Kansas City *Monthly Review*, November 1975.

Government borrowing over the years, and the amount of interest on the Federal debt can be considered a rough estimate of the additional national income that would have been generated by that foregone investment. This argument has merit, but it is by no means clear that Government borrowing always crowds out private investment, or that Government spending slows technological change. In particular, when resources are underutilized, deficit spending by the Federal Government can stimulate economic activity, including private investment.

Americans do not hold as much of the net Federal debt as they did formerly; a growing share is owed to investors outside the United States. Foreign holdings of U.S. debt have increased dramatically in relative importance since 1969. Increases in the early 1970's were due to an overvalued dollar, but more recently oil exporting nations have accumulated dollar claims in several forms, including U.S. Government securities. At the end of 1975, investments of foreign and international accounts included an estimated 20 per cent of the net Federal debt.

The real burden of externally held Federal debt is borne by Americans when foreigners convert this debt to dollars, or use the interest on it to buy U.S. goods and services. To the extent that U.S. debt is held by foreigners, Americans are borrowing from future domestic output to satisfy current demands. On the one hand, it is fortunate that other countries have been willing to accumulate dollar balances because if economic activity is constrained by an inflation-fighting policy, an increase in exports would require an offsetting decrease in domestic purchases of goods and services. On the other hand, were inflation not such a problem, this period of underutilized resources would be an ideal time for the stimulus that a major increase in exports would provide.

Various categories of domestic investors hold net Federal debt. Individuals hold the largest

share, about one-fourth of the total. Commercial banks hold almost as much. The remaining 30 per cent that is not part of foreign accounts investment is divided up among state and local governments, thrift institutions, insurance companies, other corporations, nonprofit institutions, corporate pension trust funds, dealers and brokers, and other miscellaneous investors.

Interest payments from the Federal Government to the private sector have risen sharply in recent years, for four reasons. First, the rate of growth of the net Federal debt has accelerated. From 1964 to 1969, it grew 1.2 per cent; from 1969 to 1974, 17.7 per cent. Then, in fiscal 1975 alone, privately held Federal debt grew 17.5 per cent, a postwar record. Second, interest rates have trended upward. Between 1964 and 1974, the average annual yield on 3-month Treasury bills increased 122 per cent; on 3 to 5 year issues, it increased 92 per cent. Bond interest—the yield on securities with many years to maturity—increased 60 per cent or more, with the greater increases associated with the shorter maturities. Third, the maturity distribution of the Federal debt has shifted toward shorter issues, where rates have been rising the fastest.[2] In 1964, the average time to maturity of marketable public debt was 5 years; in 1974, it averaged 3 years. In 1964, 39 per cent of the marketable public debt came due within the year; in 1974, that percentage had risen to 52. Over most of this period, the upward push on interest payments that came from the shift to the shorter maturities with rapidly rising rates was offset by the fact that the shorter debt instruments carried lower yields. But this normal relationship between yield and maturity underwent a twist in mid-1973, so that for more than a year there was a fourth reason why interest payments on the Federal debt were rising—Treasury bill rates were higher than those on notes at a time when (and largely because) a growing proportion of the Federal debt was being shifted into bills.

Although the size of the net Federal debt jumped almost 30 per cent during calendar 1975, interest payments grew less than half as fast, thanks primarily to falling interest rates on Treasury bills. A further decrease, to 2 years 9 months, in the marketable debt's length of time to maturity helped the Treasury draw even greater benefit, for the short term, from declining interest rates.

The Federal Government's interest payments to the public have increased dramatically in the past 10 years, but so have most other economic variables measured in dollars, because of inflation. Relative magnitudes, therefore, are more meaningful. As a share of the nation's potential output, Federal interest payments to the public have stayed about the same for many years.

DOMESTIC TRANSFER PAYMENTS

While all nonpurchase expenditures by the Federal Government must be transfer payments of some sort, the category known as domestic transfer payments includes only certain types. In particular, it excludes interest payments on Federal debt and subsidy payments to business and government enterprises. Domestic transfer payments are payments directly to (or in behalf of) individuals because of their personal (nonbusiness) special circumstances. Included in this category are social insurance and veterans' benefits; food stamp expenditures; retirement benefits for railroad workers, civil servants, and military personnel; benefits to individuals who are learning, training, or employed under manpower programs; and supplemental security income benefits for the aged, blind, and disabled. This is not an exhaustive list of Federal spending for social welfare. Other "human resources" programs are financed by the Federal Government through grants-in-aid to state and local governments. But these expenditures, considered in the following section, are not Federal transfers directly to persons.

---

[2] A major reason for this shift is the law that limits the rate of interest that the Federal Government can pay on long-term issues. Since the ceiling rate is below the market rate, bonds of longer maturities cannot be sold. Thus the U.S. Treasury has been forced to concentrate on short issues in its debt expansion and refunding operations. By doing so, of course, it has pushed up short rates faster than if a wider range of maturities could have been offered.

During the fiscal year ending June 30, 1976, domestic transfer payments are expected to total $155 billion, almost 5 times more than 10 years earlier, and more than double the amount in fiscal year 1972. Inflation explains some, but not all, of this growth—consumer prices have not doubled in the past decade. Most of the rapid increase in transfer payments is attributable to escalating benefits under old welfare programs and the adoption of new programs since the early 1960's. These new programs did not come about by chance. For better or worse, the economic and political climates of the 1960's favored the increased use of Federal expenditures as a mechanism to reduce the hardships of those living on low incomes, as well as a means to compensate those unduly harmed by recession and inflation.

In the absence of compensatory measures, inflation and economic growth redistribute income and wealth in favor of the productive members of society and against those who are not employed. One of the ways that Congress has offset prosperity's redistributive effects and simultaneously acted to support persons with low incomes is by legislating substantial increases in old age, survivors, and disability benefits. Between 1965 and 1973, partly because of such legislation and partly as a result of the increases in average benefits and in number of beneficiaries, total payments under these Social Security programs rose at an average annual rate of 14 per cent. Even faster rates of growth were recorded by Federal civil service retirement benefits, military retirement pay, and manpower training programs. Excluding unemployment benefits, which will be discussed separately, the slowest growing domestic transfer programs between 1965 and 1973 were railroad retirement and veterans' benefits which grew at about 10 per cent annual rates. The medicare, food stamp, and coal miner programs were begun and grew rapidly in those years. All told, the average annual rate of growth of domestic transfer payments, excluding unemployment benefits, came to 15 per cent from 1965 to 1973.

National income grew at an 8 per cent rate during that period, substantially less than the 15 per cent increase in transfer payments. Clearly, income was distributed from those who worked to those who did not. About half of the 8 per cent rate of gain in money income of the employed represented an increase in purchasing power, and this was much more than enough to finance the increase in domestic transfer payments. Even though transfers grew faster, their absolute increase of $60 billion from 1965 to 1973 was dwarfed by the $500 billion increase in national income, four-fifths of which was employee compensation. Only relative after-tax shares of national income shifted toward the nonproductive and those of low productivity.

The story was quite different between 1973 and 1975. The two fiscal years from mid-1973 to mid-1975, or fiscal years 1974 and 1975, included five quarters of recession. Because of continued inflation, national income did grow in money terms over that period, by about a 6 per cent annual rate. But domestic transfer payments jumped at a 23 per cent annual rate. A shift in relative shares occurred, and this time some of the gain by transfer recipients did come at the absolute expense of the employed. This is because real output declined, so that the redistributed purchasing power had to be spent on fewer goods and services.

Payments in most categories of domestic transfers continued to rise from mid-1973 to mid-1975. Coal miner benefits were the exception: they were flat. Consumer prices rose at a 10 per cent average annual rate in those 2 years, which partly explains the accelerated rates of growth of civil service retirement benefits (25 per cent), military retired pay (20 per cent), veterans' benefits (15 per cent), medicare (25 per cent), and other Social Security benefits (15 per cent). To some extent, growth of benefits in these categories reflects the recession. Relatively poor economic conditions tend to encourage retirement, for example.

The most pronounced impact of recession on domestic transfer payments is shown in unemployment benefits, which increased more than 2½ times between 1973 and 1975, and by food stamp payments, which increased 67 per cent. These increased transfers are similar to the others in that they do represent a redistribution of income from the working to the idle population. They differ, however, in that the unemployed are cyclically idle, drawing benefits that will eventually decline as the economy recovers.

During the current fiscal year which ends June 30, 1976, domestic transfers are estimated to total 18 per cent more than in fiscal 1975. At least half of this increase is attributable to the still depressed economy—the high unemployment benefits and other payments that are larger under such conditions. On the brighter side, however, the economy is recovering from the recession of 1974-75, and the increase in real national income will again be far more than enough to "pay" for the increase in real transfer payments.

GRANTS-IN-AID TO MUNICIPAL GOVERNMENTS

Federal grants-in-aid to state and local governments have grown almost as fast as domestic transfer payments in the past decade. The growth rates of the two would have been even closer, had the Federal Supplementary Security Income program, a domestic transfer category new in 1974, not replaced some state income assistance programs that had been funded by Federal grants. For fiscal year 1976, grants-in-aid are estimated to total $60 billion, compared to $155 billion in domestic transfer payments.

More than half of Federal grants-in-aid to state and local governments finance social welfare activities. The programs receiving the most money include aid to families with dependent children, school lunch and other child nutrition, medicaid, and several programs in education, training, and social services. The shorter end of Federal grants-in-aid (about 45 per cent of the total) goes for various purposes. Highways and general purpose fiscal assistance (primarily revenue sharing) split half of nonwelfare grants. Other programs supported include environmental improvement, urban mass transit, airport construction, scientific research, community and regional develop-

ment, natural resource and energy, and law enforcement and justice.

The amounts of aid granted to states by the Federal Government differ. On a per capita basis, states with relatively more poverty tend to receive the most Federal social welfare assistance. The big, thinly populated western states also rank high in per capita grants because, on a per person basis, they receive more Federal money for highway construction, and because they share, with the Federal Government, revenues from extensive Federal lands within their boundaries. Ranking lowest in per capita aid are the midwestern states, where Federal land is scarce, where relatively few people live on low incomes, and where highway construction is closer to average on a per person basis.

CONCLUDING NOTE ON INCOME REDISTRIBUTION

In the past several years, Federal spending has grown rapidly because of the very large increases in domestic transfer payments and grants-in-aid to state and local governments. Both of these expenditure categories are weighted heavily toward human resources, or social welfare, programs. Their intent, as indicated earlier in this article, has been to better spread the costs of the battles against inflation and recession, and to reduce income inequality. Because of the failures and abuses of some programs, and the high cost of the total package, many people, both liberal and conservative, are disillusioned with Federal welfare activity. But there can be little doubt that despite the waste, fraud, and economic inefficiency of Federal redistributive spending, the overall effect of these programs has been to alleviate those severe hardship cases that are directly due to inadequate income. Money measures of income still show more than 10 per cent of U.S residents living below the arbitrarily defined poverty level. But, as Edgar Browning establishes, money income data miss the fact that many welfare programs provide income in kind. In other words, he argues, few Americans today live below a poverty level of consumption.[3]

[3] *Redistribution and the Welfare System.* American Enterprise Institute for Public Policy Research, Washington, D.C., 1975.

Is The Housing Cycle Being Transformed?

IN the dim past, the housing market—whether for a picture window in the suburbs or for a city walk-up—usually involved three parties: a builder, a banker, and a buyer. For more than 40 years, however, there's been a fourth party in the act: the federal government. Indeed, government's role in helping to provide shelter has become so pervasive that most Americans now take it for granted.

There are federal programs to guarantee and insure mortgages, to subsidize interest rates, to entice home buyers with tax credits, and to spur construction of housing units for a gamut of special groups from the aged and the poor to farmers, college students, and war veterans.

In this Everyman's approach, the government's goal has been to help people acquire a home or rental unit when they could not meet the market test. In 1949 that goal took the form of a statutory commitment to a "decent home . . . for every American family."

Until about ten years ago, government's role in housing had been largely supportive; little effort had been made to manage the timing of the housing cycle. Of late, however, the nature of government involvement has changed in a way that raises some disquieting questions about housing's impact on the future stability of the economy.

Housing construction in postwar America has ridden a rollercoaster—surging to the heights

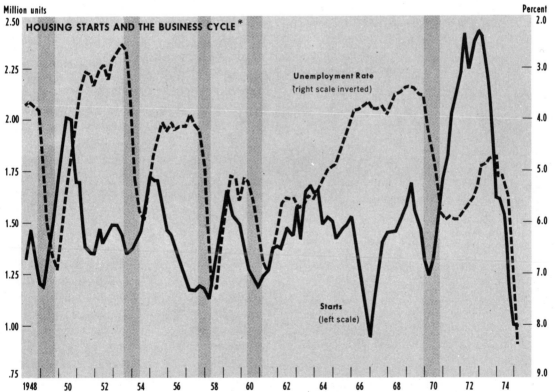

HOUSING STARTS AND THE BUSINESS CYCLE *

Million units — 2.50

Percent — 2.0

Unemployment Rate
(right scale inverted)

Starts
(left scale)

1948 50 52 54 56 58 60 62 64 66 68 70 72 74

*Quarterly plottings; starts are seasonally adjusted annual rates. Shaded areas represent recession periods as designated by the National Bureau of Economic Research.

"Is the Housing Cycle Being Transformed?" *Morgan Guaranty Survey*, July 1975, pp. 3–8. Reprinted with permission.

and then plunging. In all, housing starts have gone through seven major cycles since the end of World War II (chart above).

Over the years, the housing rollercoaster has generally run on a contra-cyclical track:* housing activity has tended to rise when the over-all economy was slackening; conversely, housing has headed downward—taking pressure off real resources—in the late stages of business expansions. Thus, housing has acted (to change the image) as a balance wheel for the economy.

From the standpoint of over-all economic stability, there is an advantage to having an important component of investment demand serve as a balance wheel for the rest of the economy. As for the nation's housing needs, how well American families are housed depends little on any year's new building activity, but on the size and condition of the housing stock. Loss of housing output in any one year, by and large, has relatively little effect on the stock. And yet there is one obvious drawback. In instances of particularly severe impact, the toll is extremely heavy in terms of unemployment for building workers and disruption of the activities of builder organizations. It is principally for that reason that government has sought to stabilize housing construction.

The goal has proved elusive—despite a massive enlargement of government efforts in the housing field. Meanwhile, an unwelcome by-product of such efforts appears to be the upsetting of the earlier balance-wheel effect. Suddenly, housing—at least in the current cycle—seems to have become "pro-cyclical." As a consequence, housing accentuated the 1974 business slump (instead of cushioning it). And it is distinctly possible that government's current efforts to stimulate housing may bear fruit, not in the recovery period but later and thus exaggerate the next cyclical upswing in general business activity. Government may, indeed, be in the process of unwittingly transforming the housing cycle in a most fundamental sense.

New conditions, new policies

To see how the transformation has come about, it is necessary to look back, briefly, on the government's earlier pattern of involvement.

For a long time, government housing policies, curiously enough, had actually tended to intensify the contra-cyclical role of housing: in the 1950s and for much of the 1960s, FHA and VA rates often were pegged—in part because of their political sensitivity—unrealistically low. Discounts or "points" limited the extent to which statutory rate ceilings interrupted the flow of mortgage credit in this important sector of the market. But at times large discounts were limited by regulation and some major lenders shied away from them as a matter of policy. Even when "points" were legal and acceptable to the lender they generated understandable buyer resistance.

Moreover, FHA/VA backing was extensively used by nationwide lenders—especially life insurance companies and savings banks—which by law and by custom enjoyed considerable flexibility to shift among various investments according to the returns offered. Thus, the below-market ceiling rates on FHA/VA loans, which made government-backed mortgages unattractive, served to reinforce the contra-cyclical nature of home building.

Beginning in 1966—and as a consequence of the credit crunch in that year—government involvement in the housing market changed in character. The credit crunch brought with it much greater volatility in interest rates and credit availability than had characterized previous booms. Thrift institutions, as a result, suffered heavy deposit drains as investors sought higher yields in open-market paper. To offset dwindling mortgage loans by the thrifts, government-sponsored agencies made heavy purchases of mortgages (with funds raised by the issuance of securities), and the federal home loan banks made large advances.

The same pattern of aggressive government

---

*In the postwar recessions prior to the current one, housing expenditures have either actually risen or accounted for relatively little of the over-all drop in GNP. In the ensuing expansions, measured four quarters following the trough, contra-cyclical support from housing was even more evident. In an industry that has accounted for 4½% of GNP on average in the postwar period, the rise in housing expenditures accounted for anywhere from 6% to 29% of the gain in over-all GNP in the first year of cyclical expansion following recession troughs. On average, housing's contribution to the initial four quarters of recovery periods approached one-fifth of the gain in GNP.

intervention was followed in late 1969 and early 1970. By mid-1970, general economic forces had once again moved in housing's favor: heavy flows of funds into thrift institutions, declines in mortgage rates, a backlog of postponed demand were marshaled. But what was most conspicuous about government's massive support to housing in the post-1970-recession period is that it did not diminish significantly *after* housing picked up real momentum of its own. Purchases of mortgages by the federal government and its sponsored agencies in 1971 and 1972 averaged $5.5 billion per year—even greater than 1969 and 1970 support levels. Thus, the agencies added to the flood of funds available through private channels and in the process pushed the housing boom to higher and higher levels (starts soared to a record annual rate of 2.4 million units in late 1972 and early 1973).

Continued federal participation in the mortgage market in 1971 and 1972—making housing pronouncedly pro-cyclical for the first time in the postwar period—reflected to a large extent purchases of subsidized mortgages on properties owned or rented by low- and moderate-income families. A significant expansion of the subsidy concept evolved out of the Housing and Urban Development Act of 1968, an act which established a production goal of six million units of new housing for low- and moderate-income families within a decade. Starts subsidized by the Department of Housing & Urban Development (HUD) in 1971 and 1972 averaged almost 300,000 units a year, the majority built under Sections 235 and 236 of the 1968 act.

Under Section 235, low-income families were eligible to buy a house with an effective interest cost as low as 1%. Section 236 provided similar subsidies for rental units. In early 1973, Section 235 and 236 programs were "temporarily suspended"—partly as a result of reports of fraud and maladministration in many cities. More importantly, the suspension two years ago of these and other housing programs was motivated by Administration fears of the huge long-run costs involved in efforts to provide subsidies, for example, as deep as those available under the 1968 act. Such costs have been officially estimated at between $65 billion and $85 billion over a forty-year

"GOVERNMENT" SUPPORT FOR THE MORTGAGE MARKET

Billions of dollars

	Increase in residential mortgage holdings of all lenders	Increase in holdings of federal gov. and its sponsored credit agencies*	Change in advances extended by federal home loan banks	Combined "government" support	"Government" as a percent of total increase in holdings
1952-65 (annual average)	13.4	0.4	0.4	0.8	6
1966	13.8	2.8	0.9	3.7	27
1967	16.0	2.1	−2.5	−0.4	—
1968	18.6	2.8	0.9	3.7	20
1969	20.4	4.6	4.0	8.6	42
1970	19.2	5.7	1.3	7.0	36
1971	36.8	5.7	−2.7	3.0	8
1972	51.2	5.2	**	5.2	10
1973	50.3	7.6	7.2	14.8	29
1974	37.9	13.8	6.7	20.5	54

Source: Flow of funds accounts.
*Includes mortgage pools backing securities guaranteed by the Government National Mortgage Association.
**Less than $50 million.

period, even if no added subsidized units were built.

In addition to a major increase in starts subsidized by HUD, the early 1970s also witnessed a significant increase in rural housing starts built under subsidies provided by the Farmers Home Administration. All told, the production of subsidized units under all programs averaged more than 400,000 units in 1971 and 1972. (This federally inspired spurt in housing came about at a time when privately sponsored condominium and apartment projects—financed through the burgeoning real estate investment trusts, themselves creatures of special federal tax laws—were creating problems of over-building in many parts of the country.)

In retrospect, it is clear that the extraordinary diversion of more resources into housing than would otherwise have been the case was particularly ill-timed. By late 1972 and early 1973 —when, as indicated, housing starts were running at a record high—the economy was beginning to show signs of capacity strains which gave rise to pressures on raw-materials prices (including important housing inputs like lumber and copper) and later to a generalized inflationary outburst. While the housing boom certainly reflected influences other than public policy actions, it seems apparent that government stimulation of housing—which continued long after the financial forces favorable to home building were put in place and housing was indeed showing strong momentum—contributed to those inflationary pressures.

Housing in lockstep

Whatever the inflationary role played by government stimulation of housing, the experience of 1973 and 1974 once again demonstrated that home building cannot stand up to the forces of inflation and the monetary re-

straint applied in an effort to check that inflation. Despite massive efforts by government to cushion housing against the jolts of credit restraint, starts by late 1974 had fallen to a million units at an annual rate, an eight-year low. And yet in 1974 mortgage support by the federal government and its sponsored agencies approached $14 billion (box page 6); additionally, advances extended to savings and loan associations grew almost $7 billion. All told, more than half of the increase in residential mortgage credit was supplied by government intermediation in 1974. If the pools of mortgages backing securities guaranteed by HUD are included, "federalization" of the mortgage market reached 80% in the third quarter of last year.

Intensified federal efforts in the housing field, thus, have not brought the sought-after stability. At the same time, however, housing now seems to have been pushed into lockstep with the over-all economy. Its movements have tended to accentuate the business cycle instead of, as in the past, muting it.

More of the same seems to lie ahead. Most analysts are convinced that a revival in housing activity is all but assured before long. Record deposit flows into thrift institutions in the first half of the year presage an ample supply of mortgage credit. And the advent earlier this year of significantly lower inflation rates, together with a pickup in the tempo of business activity in coming months, will go far—in time —to arrest the imbalance between home prices and rents and family income that has played such a negative role in the housing picture in the last year or so.

Housing's recovery, though now in lockstep, normally could be expected to break ranks and move into its own cycle. Such a pattern would be the natural result when, as the over-all recovery gains momentum late this year and next, credit demands rise and interest rates firm. The housing expansion, being so sensitive to credit-market developments, would normally begin to slow. In that case, housing's performance in the recent past would be no more than an aberration: housing would return to its former contra-cyclical path.

It's possible, however, that the normal course of events for housing may not recur, particularly if the recovery later this year proves to be draggy. Pressures in that event could mount in Congress to stimulate the recovery by administering a hypo for housing more potent than the expansion of HUD's mortgage-purchase programs signed into law earlier this month. Indeed, Congress in this session wanted to pump much more federal money into housing than the Administration thought appropriate. While the President's veto in June of an elaboratively stimulative housing bill was sustained by Congress, against the background of a possibly sluggish recovery it would not be surprising to see efforts among the lawmakers to resurrect a broad range of programs to boost housing.

Clearly, there is a need—recognized in a long history of legislation—for a government role in housing. But it also needs to be recognized that such programs, when pushed too hard for too long, can be detrimental. The danger now is that housing, already on a pro-cyclical course, may be artificially forced along that track. What that would lead to, in all probability, would be an artificial and unsustainable level of home-building activity in a year or two which ultimately would do serious damage both to housing and to the general economy.

Congress's New Grip on the Federal Purse

AT mid-month, Congress made legislative history of prime fiscal importance: House and Senate lawmakers—implementing provisions of the Budget and Impoundment Control Act of 1974—jointly agreed on targets for spending, revenues, and the deficit for the fiscal year beginning July 1. The action formalized a radically new approach to the budget process, and it marked one of the most significant modifications of the over-all federal budget system in more than half a century.*

Estimating that revenues will total $298.2 billion, the lawmakers specified that expenditures should not exceed $367 billion. That combination of income and outgo—were it to be realized—would produce a deficit $8.8 billion larger than the $60 billion President Ford said at the end of March he would accept. The bigger deficit is mainly attributable to a feeling in Congress that more spending than the President has proposed is needed as an economic stimulus.

Quite aside from the differences over how much stimulus is needed, the House-Senate action is significant for an added reason: the lawmakers have selected a goal for spending that is very much *lower* than would result from adding up, function by function, the spending plans of the individual committees of Congress. The combined spending figure of all House committees was $30 billion higher than

spending proposed by the House Budget Committee. Incredibly, the combined spending figure of all Senate committees was $54 billion larger than the outlays adopted by the Senate Budget Committee. If all the Senate spending intentions were translated into fact, the resulting deficit for fiscal 1976 (assuming $298 billion of revenues) would be $121 billion.

To be sure, the recommended budget levels are only a trial run; the new budget process does not take effect officially until next year. Still, the action is significant because, for the first time, congressional committees will now be under pressure to think in terms of an over-all financial plan. Actions taken this month will be hard to ignore later.

The budget overview concept is intended to remedy the most glaring defect in budget procedures: the fact that Congress has not considered the national budget (both spending and revenues) as a unified whole. Instead, Congress has broken the budget up into unrelated fragments.

In neither House nor Senate deliberations has there been any effective link between revenues and expenditures. In the House, tax bills go to the Ways and Means Committee; in the Senate, to the Finance Committee. In both cases they are considered apart from questions of spending. Moreover, the appropriation proposals put forward in the President's budget, instead of being considered by Congress in a single bill, are divided up into a dozen or more different measures. These are considered separately by the twelve appropriations subcommittees—agriculture, defense, public works, and so on—in each branch of Congress.

The various subcommittees finish their work at different times so that the appropriation total comes before the parent committees and the

---

* The last successful basic reform of the federal budget process occurred in 1921. The Budget and Accounting Act of that year, which President Harding signed, had its origins in a study commissioned by President Taft in 1909. Later the House of Representatives appointed a Select Committee on the Budget, and its work led finally to a 1921 law which, dealing chiefly with the Executive branch, for the first time prescribed formal annual budgetary procedures. The major innovation was a centrally prepared budget under a newly created Budget Bureau. A major effort at streamlining the congressional budget was undertaken shortly after World War II. As subsequent discussion in this article explores, it failed.

"Congress's New Grip on the Federal Purse." *Morgan Guaranty Survey,* May 1975, pp. 5–11. Reprinted with permission.

SHAPING THE 1976 BUDGET— A VARIETY OF PRESCRIPTIONS
(Billions of dollars)

	Spending	Revenues	Deficit
Administration (February 3) ..	349.4	297.5	51.9
Administration (early May) ...	355.0	295.0	60.0
House Budget Committee	368.2	295.0	73.2
Full House......	368.2	298.2	70.0
Senate Budget Committee	365.0	295.4	69.6
Full Senate......	365.0	297.8	67.2
House-Senate Conferees	367.0	298.2	68.8

full Congress in individual pieces. The most critical inadequacy is that there can be no opportunity to weigh the merits of one proposed expenditure against those of others and to establish a scale of priorities. That piecemeal approach—which has given the annual budget exercise a haphazard flavor—now stands a good chance of yielding to a much sounder and more coherent procedure.

Under the Constitution, primary responsibility for the budget is lodged in Congress. The sweeping transformation now under way clearly enhances congressional control of the budget process. Under the 1974 budget law, the new system becomes mandatory in fiscal year 1977, which begins October 1, 1976.*

The current dry run in Congress reveals a

---

* The 1976 budget covers the fiscal year beginning July 1, 1975 and ending June 30, 1976. However, subsequent fiscal years will start on October 1 and end September 30. As a result, there will be a three-month transition quarter between fiscal years 1976 and 1977. By starting the budget year in October, Congress will have three months longer than it has had for budget deliberations before a new fiscal year begins.

whole new procedure for shaping the federal budget. Both the House and the Senate have new budget committees with many top-quality staff members. In addition there's a new set of initials that budget watchers will have to learn: CBO (for Congressional Budget Office). CBO will provide the two budget committees and Congress with fiscal and economic expertise. CBO's staff of economists, lawyers, financial analysts, and computer specialists is expected to reach 120 by year-end and could be double that number a year later. The CBO and the House and Senate Budget Committees give Congress the equivalent of the Administration's Office of Management and Budget.

A fiscal timetable

A significant feature of the new budget machinery is its tight timetable, shown in the box on page 7. Here, briefly, is how the new system will work.

The process begins in the autumn of each year. The President must submit by November 10 a "current services" budget. This will indicate how much it would cost to maintain existing federal programs for the following fiscal year. Next will come the actual budget message of the President, submitted, as is now the case, within fifteen days after the convening of Congress in January.

By mid-March, all of the appropriations, tax, and legislative committees will have to estimate the expected costs of programs under their jurisdictions for the coming year and submit those numbers to the budget committees. In mid-April the budget committees will propose over-all spending targets, revenue estimates, and the resulting budget deficit or surplus for the new budget year. Congress will vote on those targets in a concurrent resolution (which lacks the force of law and is not signed by the

CONGRESSIONAL BUDGET SCHEDULE

On or before:	Action to be completed:
November 10	President submits current services budget.*
Fifteen days after Congress meets	President submits regular budget.
March 15	Committees and joint committees submit reports to Budget Committees.
April 1	Congressional Budget Office submits report to Budget Committees.
April 15	Budget Committees report first concurrent resolution on the budget to their Houses.
May 15	Committees report bills and resolutions authorizing new budget authority.
May 15	Congress completes action on first concurrent resolution on the budget.
Seven days after Labor Day	Congress completes action on bills and resolutions providing new budget authority and new spending authority.
September 15	Congress completes action on second required concurrent resolution on the budget.
September 25	Congress completes action on reconciliation bill or resolution, or both, implementing second required concurrent resolution.
October 1	Fiscal year begins.

*Covers costs of extending existing programs and activities through the upcoming fiscal year.

President). The resolution, besides setting overall targets, will also divide spending among sixteen broad functions such as defense, agriculture, health, veterans, and so on. Passage of the resolution must be completed by May 15.

Once the targets are approved, Congress will proceed as before, shaping the government's programs, holding hearings, passing money bills. Within a week after Labor Day, Congress is supposed to have passed all spending bills. By mid-September Congress will add up all the money bills that have been approved and compare the result with the targets voted earlier in the year—that is, in the concurrent resolution. If the total of the various programs exceeds the spending targets adopted in the spring, the Appropriations Committees might be asked to report legislation rescinding spending authority in appropriations bills already enacted. Or the House Ways and Means Committee and the Senate Finance Committee might be asked to report new tax legislation. In short, by late September, Congress will have taken an overall look at income and outgo, decided on priorities, and have passed a second resolution either reaffirming or revising the target figures adopted in May.

A crunch could come, obviously, in September of each year. Given the historic penchant for individual congressional committees to enlarge existing federal programs and to embrace new ones, Congress each September could be faced with a fiscal dilemma: to trim some cloth to fit the pattern voted in spring or else to enlarge the pattern to accommodate the old piecemeal spending approach.

In this year's "dry run," Congress will approve only aggregate targets for spending and will not have to decree in the resolutions how the money is to be spent. Next year, however, Congress must decide not only what the nation can afford over all, but also where the money will go according to individual functional categories.

Where the money goes

As part of this year's trial, the House and Senate Budget Committees have provided breakdowns, by sixteen functional categories, of where the money might go in the coming fiscal year. Generally, the budget committees would spend much less than the Administration would on defense and international affairs while spending considerably more on job programs, public works, and income maintenance. When compared with proposed spending by individual committees of Congress, the budget com-

mittees' recommendations are sharply lower all along the line. The table on page 9 shows, by function, the dramatic differences in spending as proposed by the budget committees, the Administration, and the individual committees in Congress.

Support for less spending than individual committees would like has, of course, come early in the legislative session. The question is whether such backing would fade in late September (on what henceforth would be the eve of the new fiscal year) when a need to retrench would require lawmakers to make hard choices —to sustain individual pet projects or give them the axe.

Looking back: reform manqué

Judging from past efforts at budget reform, one needs to be somewhat cautious about making confident predictions. The most ambitious earlier attempt at budget reform occurred with passage of the Legislative Reorganization Act of 1946. Section 138 of that law provided for joint meetings, early in each session of Congress, of four committees: House Ways and Means, House Appropriations, Senate Finance, and Senate Appropriations.

The combined group was designated the Joint Committee on the Legislative Budget and was directed to examine the budget proposals made by the President. By February 15 of each year it was to submit to the full Congress in the form of a concurrent resolution (1) its own estimates of anticipated receipts and expenditures for the ensuing fiscal year and (2) its recommendations as to the maximum amount to be appropriated for expenditures. If accepted by both House and Senate, the concurrent resolution presumably was to be "binding" on Congress during the remainder of the session.

HOW BUDGETS COMPARE BY FUNCTION

(Billions of dollars)

	House Budget Committee spending as compared with—		Senate Budget Committee spending as compared with—	
	Administration	House Committees	Administration	Senate Committees
National defense	−4.3	−6.3	−2.8	−6.2
International affairs	−1.4	−1.4	−1.4	−1.3
General science, space, technology	*	*	*	− .1
Natural resources, environment, energy	−1.5	−2.0	1.7	−5.6
Agriculture	*	− .9	.2	− .4
Commerce, transportation	6.1	−2.4	2.9	−4.4
Community, regional development	3.6	−2.0	.7	−3.4
Education, manpower, social services	5.8	−1.6	4.8	−11.9
Health	2.7	−1.8	2.9	−3.3
Income security	5.2	−5.7	7.4	−10.8
Veterans' benefits, services	1.9	− .3	1.3	− .7
Law enforcement, justice	*	*	.1	− .1
General government	.2	− .8	*	− .7
Revenue sharing, general fiscal assistance	*	*	*	−5.0
Interest	.6	.6	.9	*
Allowances	−7.0	−7.4	−7.0	− .4
Undistributed offsetting receipts	4.0	*	4.0	*
Total	18.9	−30.2	15.7	−54.3

*Difference less than $100 million.

The experiment fizzled out quickly. In only two Congressional sessions—those of 1947 and 1948—were the provisions of Section 138 followed. In 1947 the Joint Committee's recommendation for an appropriations ceiling was accepted in a resolution adopted by the House but was amended in the Senate. When the conference committee that was appointed to reconcile the differences could not agree, the "legislative budget" of that session simply died. In 1948 both chambers reached agreement on an appropriations ceiling, but the concurrent resolution was couched in extremely general terms which provided no real guidance to the apppropriations committees. Congress responded by simply ignoring its own self-imposed ceiling, voting total appropriations $6 billion higher than the specified ceiling and thus making the whole procedure pointless.

In 1950, after the failure of the legislative budget approach, Congress tried a new method to achieve budget control: it combined appropriations bills in each house into one omnibus measure. This was an idea long advocated by the late Senator Harry F. Byrd, of Virginia, who waged an unceasing struggle for better control of federal spending. The omnibus bill was to provide an opportunity, prior to final action on any particular appropriations request, to re-examine each spending program in the light of all the others. However, outbreak of the Korean War at mid-year brought huge supplemental appropriations, so that there was not a definitive test of the omnibus method.

A major stumbling block for the 1950 experiment was the attitude of many of the chairmen of the appropriations subcommittees who felt that the omnibus procedure gave undue influence to the chairmen of the parent committees. Their pique was a major obstacle to sound budget reform. The Senate proposed a return to the omnibus spending bill in 1953 but the House showed no interest and that approach was abandoned.

Through the rest of the 1950s and into the 1960s the idea of reviving the joint budget committee concept had a durable if quite ineffective existence. Between 1952 and 1965, for example, the Senate no fewer than seven times approved bills providing somewhat different procedures from those of the Legislative Reorganization Act of 1946 for achieving improved congressional handling of the budget submitted by the President. The House, however, did not act on any of the bills.

Over the years Congress has tried various other approaches to budget control—notably ceilings on the federal debt and expenditure ceilings (in the late 1960s and early 1970s). Both approaches proved futile; putting a lid on the federal debt was doomed to failure as long as Congress voted more spending than it raised in taxes, and spending ceilings didn't work simply because the lawmakers poked holes through the ceiling with "exceptions" for "uncontrollable items" such as veterans' benefits, interest on the debt, and Social Security outlays.

More recently, Presidential efforts to control the budget—particularly under President Nixon—relied on impoundment: a refusal to spend funds voted by Congress (a practice that goes back to the days of Jefferson). But that approach, at best, was a temporary, stop-gap effort to prevent a budget crisis. And besides, Congress has increasingly regarded impoundment as unacceptable Presidential interference with its constitutional prerogatives to decide where money will be spent and in what amounts. Indeed, in last year's law providing for new budget procedures, Congress tightened up on Presidential impoundment. For example, impoundments are now considered illegal if they make program implementation impossible. Some other impoundments are legal only if Congress specifically approves them. Brief deferrals of spending authority, however, are legal, unless reversed by either the House or Senate.

Turning on the machinery

Against that background, it's plain that there is a new determination in Congress to play a more dominant role in shaping the federal budget. The machinery is in place; what's needed is to implement budget control legislation adopted last year.

Whether the new process succeeds or fails is of much more than passing significance. As

Dr. Arthur F. Burns, chairman of the Federal Reserve Board, noted in a speech in Washington on May 6 before the Society of American Business Writers:

> No major democracy that I know of has had a more deficient legislative budget process than the United States—with revenue decisions separated from spending decisions and the latter handled in piecemeal fashion. Budgets in this country have just happened. They certainly haven't been planned.
>
> We are now attempting to change that by adopting integrated congressional decisions on revenues and expenditures. . . . The potential gain for the nation from budget reform is enormous even in this first year of "dry run." If, in fact, the work of the new budget committees produces in the Congress a deeper understanding of the impossibility of safely undertaking all the ventures being urged by individual legislators, a constructive beginning toward a healthier economic environment will have been made.

This is not to say, of course, that budget targets set in the spring need to be cast in concrete. The set of anticipations (economic, foreign policy, etc.) on which a budget plan is based obviously may not be fulfilled. Major surprises, should they come along, clearly might justify considerable revisions of the budget plan. If, for example, economic recovery fails to materialize as expected, or if it is exceptionally weak and fitful, additional stimulus would be appropriate. Alternatively, if recovery is strongly vigorous it may well be prudent to withdraw or scale back some of the stimulants now being provided. (Dr. Burns, calling for such "contingency planning," has suggested that the President send to Congress a "massive deferral and recision bill which might or might not be used.") Financial plans for government, no less than for corporations, must change if conditions change. No one could meaningfully label the new budget process a failure without regard to that kind of consideration.

Distressing in the extreme, however, would be actions by individual committees which would make the new budget process no more than an elaborate charade. That would be the case if lawmakers return to helter-skelter spending without regard for priority needs or availability of revenues to pay the bill.

All eyes will be on the lawmakers in coming weeks and months as the budget drama unfolds. Will cherished committee prerogatives yield? Can Congress swallow a sizable dose of self-discipline? Hopefully, affirmative answers will emerge. But for now at least, few would deny that there has been an important and promising beginning.

PART IV.
CURRENT LABOR ISSUES

A century ago the U.S. was a predominantly agricultural society. The coming of industrialization, which made possible unprecedented improvements in living standards, also produced serious new labor problems and accentuated old ones. As workers were subjected to industrial discipline, the conditions were ripe for the development of large-scale unionism. (Labor unions appear in most free industrial societies as one of the institutions through which the divergent interests of workers and management may be resolved.) Other labor issues of the late 1970's include: unemployment from various causes; industrial accidents and disease; providing for income in old age; financing health care; technological job displacement; worker skill obsolescence; job discrimination; and training and retraining workers with usable skills, to name a few. The selections in Part IV are addressed to some of these problems.

Section A, Labor Markets

In "College and the Changing Job Market" William Haber replies to charges that too many Americans go to college by pointing out that our age is characterized by "a tremendous explosion of knowledge accompanied simultaneously by a rapid obsolescence of old knowledge." He feels we need more education, not less, to deal with tomorrow's surprises. The article "Woman's Labor Market Experience" by the U.S. Department of Labor's Bureau of Labor Statistics provides a statistical profile of working women who now comprise almost half of our femal population. Carl Rosenfeld's article, "Jobseeking Methods Used by American Workers," provides a statistical analysis of the various ways in which people look for jobs. Elinor Abramson in her article, "Projected Demand for and Supply of Ph.D. Manpower, 1972-1985," predicts that by 1985 there will be twice as many new Ph.D's as job openings for them if current trends continue.

Section B, Unemployment Insurance

In Martin Feldstein's article, "Unemployment Compensation: Its Effect on Unemployment," he considers the work disincentive effect of unemployment compensation when taxes are taken into account. In "Do Benefits Cause Unemployed to Hold Out for Better Jobs?" Professors Ehrenberg and Oaxaca report on the effects of unemployment insurance on the duration of unemployment and on the level of compensation on reemployment. In "Unemployment Insurance: A Critique" Steven Zell examines some major criticisms of our unemployment insurance system. He reports that empirical evidence "seems to indicate that U.I. benefits are responsible for a sizable increase in the duration of unemployment of the insured unemployed."

Section C, Economic Security

In "The Challenge to Mandatory Retirement" Norman Wood discusses the Murgia vs. Commonwealth of Massachusetts case in which a state police lieutenant charges that mandatory retirement at 50 violates his civil rights and represents age discrimination. In "Future Dimensions in Pension Legislation" U.S. Senator Jacob Javits offers some suggestions on how to make the Employee Retirement Income Security Act (ERISA), the new pension reform law, work. Wilber Cohen, in "Social

Security 40 Years Later," tells us that, though the social security system has and will have problems, it "is a sound structure on which we can build and adapt to changing needs." In an article entitled "Propping up Social Security," Business Week magazine reports that a substantial gap is developing between benefits and receipts under the present Social Security law. In the past 20 years, benefits have risen sharply, payroll taxes have gone up dramatically, and Social Security represents a growing proportion of the tax dollar. Tadashi Hanami in "The Life-time Employment System in Japan: Its Reality and Future" describes how Japanese paternalism provides labor with a unique system characterized by a high degree of job security, a seniority wage system, a solid bond of loyalty between worker and employer, and a broad spectrum of anti-alienation fringes. Hanami describes the system and examines its prospects for the future.

Section D, Labor Unions and Collective Bargaining

In "Unions, Critics, and Collective Bargaining" Profess Tim Bornstein weighs the shortcomings and accomplishments of contemporary American unions. In "Wage Determination Processes" George Taylor, from the rich perspective of his long ex-perience as practitioner and scholar, contrasts collective bargaining to other procedures for wage determination. In "Reflections on Public Sector Collective Bargaining" Benjamin Aaron notes that during the sixties, union membership among public employees more than doubled, but more recently this trend has slowed in the face of a depressed economy. In "The Incidence of Collective Bargaining Once More" Professor M. Bronfenbrenner inquires, Who ultimately bears the cost of wages estab-lished by collective bargaining?

A. Labor Markets

College and the Changing Job Market

by William Haber

Public discussion about higher education in recent years has been concerned with several key issues. One of these is the question as to whether we have "over-

WILLIAM HABER, former dean of the college of literature, is now professor emeritus of economics and adviser to the executive officers of the University of Michigan. This article is from a presentation Dr. Haber made to an honors convocation at the university in March 1976.

sold" a college or university education. Are there too many young men and women who continue their education beyond high school? The numbers in the United States are, of course, astounding: more than 10.1 million students are enrolled in more than 2,600 colleges and universities. This number represents more than 45 percent of the college age group, a proportion whose magnitude is not duplicated in any other coun-

William Haber, "College and the Changing Job Market." *The American Federationist*, June 1976, pp. 23–25. Reprinted with permission.

try. Only the Soviet Union, where the comparable figure is 27 percent, comes close. In West Germany it is only about 14 percent; in Japan only about 16 percent; in France and England 10 percent. The comparable percentage is not known for the People's Republic of China, but it is clearly below any of these cited. The problem in gauging other nations is complicated by how one defines a post-secondary education.

In any event, the widely prevailing opinion is that Americans are being overeducated and that much of our college and university enrollment is unnecessary. It is even said that it is economically unjustified. Recent data suggested, for example, that perhaps for the first time in American history, the earning power of real wages of college graduates has actually declined. Quite apart from the problem of finding jobs, many have begun to question the economic value of a college education. It is suggested that from a purely economic point of view, it is not now irrational to skip college. For more and more people it is not unreasonable to forget about a college education and go to work after high school.

It is somewhat too early to tell whether the stabilization or decline in college enrollment is influenced to any extent by the belief college is unnecessary or is solely the result of other factors. It is clear however that the real income of a non-college wage earner or salaried person has gone up and, relatively speaking, the real income of the college graduate has gone down. When this is coupled with a substantial increase in the cost of a college education, the economic benefits of college are being subjected to serious question.

The labor market has been "glutted" with college graduates, even before the present recession, the most serious in 25 years. The glut is the result of pushing college education for the past quarter century. It is also observed that the problem exists not only in this country but in other nations with a substantial proportion of their post-high school age group enrolled in colleges and universities. Legislators and other state officials now talk about training students for whom there are no jobs and are beginning to look at manpower requirements when appropriating funds for institutions of higher learning.

I do not believe too many young men and women are going to college. First, concerning the recession, this is not an apocalyptic period. Public policy concerning education and professional development should not be unduly influenced by the transitional employment levels which characterize an unstable economy. I do not see all doom and gloom ahead of us. Perhaps five or more years from now we shall be concerned about labor shortages rather than mass unemployment.

Quite apart from the question as to whether economic advancement is the only purpose of a college or university education, I maintain that our educational policies and individual decisions on going to college should not depend on employment fluctuations which create occasional labor surpluses. The proportion of college graduates who are unemployed is probably relatively small—but such data are unfortunately not readily available. In my judgment, except for new job seekers, the overwhelming proportion of college graduates who have been working before the recession are still working.

How are we to explain the high proportion of the post-secondary school group who continue their education in some college or university, public or private? All of us are aware that we are living through a period of great social and economic change. Some have called this the age of transformation. It is neither an overstatement nor an exaggeration to say that these have, in fact, been revolutionary times. The certainty of rapid, headlong change has faced every institution and every individual. The idea of change is perennial. It is not new. What is significant about these times is its pervasive character. It faces us on every front, at a pace and at a tempo which is unprecedented. All of us are vulnerable and must learn to accept it, to accommodate to it and perhaps even to manage it. The late atomic scientist Robert Oppenheimer observed that the one thing that is new is the prevalence of newness. The "futurists" are speculating about the world in the year 2000. Some of the vast changes of the past 30 years will continue and the year 2000 is very likely to be as different from 1975 as 1975 was from the year 1800. It is difficult for most of us to conceptualize this. Yet it is wise to remember that except for science fiction writers, hardly any of us in 1950 expected the exciting developments which have influenced our life in the past quarter century.

The United States is a different country than it was when I was a college student. Whether it is better or worse is a value judgment and each of us has our own opinion. It is only clear that it is not the same and little would be gained by search for the good old days. I like the title of Otto Bettmann's recent book. "The Good Old Days—They Were Terrible." Among the forces which have changed America, perhaps the most important is the research and development revolution. Our national outlays for research and development approach nearly $30 billion per year. This is a vast sum, even taking into account the decline in the purchasing power of the dollar. Its object is to make a new tomorrow; to make obsolete our present methods, processes, materials and technologies. Today, for instance, the University of Michigan has a research budget approaching $70 million—none of it from the state legislature. Professors today are involved not only in transmitting the knowledge of the ages but in creating new knowledge. We show our expectation of new knowledge when we shock our professors with the "publish or perish" challenge.

The research revolution has created a new industry—the industry of "discovery." It has led to a tremendous explosion of knowledge accompanied simultaneously by a rapid obsolescence of old knowledge. It may startle us to learn that a Ph.D. in mathematics is said to have about six years of "intellectual capital." Unless one keep up, the intellectual obsolescence begins to set in. A Ph.D. in physics is said to possess only eight years of such capital and a Ph.D. in engineering about 10 years. It is hard to determine how much intellectual capital an MD has, for after many years he is still "practicing."

A rather subversive idea once occurred to me—that the Ph.D. degree should expire in 10 years unless renewed by another and more up-to-date examination. I desisted from doing so for fear that someone would suggest that the BA degree should be printed on paper which deteriorates and thus ceases to exist in five years.

It is no simple task to determine how many tens of thousands of engineers are already obsolete. And the question may well be asked about every other discipline. Former HEW Secretary John W. Gardner calls attention to this problem in his book, "The Ever Renewing Society." The research revolution has changed America as no other single development. It has created a new technology. Automation and the computer have been joined into what has come to be known as continuous automation. Hundreds of thousands of workers have been eliminated from the basic production industry, whose output has not declined.

One of the results has been a revolution in skills and this has gone farther in our own country than anywhere else. Of the more than 90 million persons in the American workforce, only one out of three is engaged in production. He or she is "making" something—a chair, a suit, a table, a brick. Two out of three are not producers. This is not the same as saying that they are unproductive. And the process is continuing. Many millions of Americans now hold dead-end jobs—jobs which have no future and are rapidly disappearing. Those who hold them must adapt themselves to new skill requirements; they must be trained and retrained. Many of these tasks were once respectable bookkeepers, accountants, meter readers or elevator operators.

As a result, I have serious doubts as to whether we ought to teach anything as specific as an occupation. We need to find something that resembles a family of occupations, a cluster of jobs. We need to teach adaptive skills. It has been observed that 50 percent of the 1985 workforce will be engaged on skills and jobs which have not yet been invented or developed. Everyone, whether in production or non-production, needs to be retrained perhaps two or three times in an occupational lifetime. This is no less true for a craftsman in factories and shops than for doctors, lawyers and professors. The obsolescence of knowledge plays havoc with everyone.

How does this subject relate to whether there are too many college students? Simply this: our society is being transformed more rapidly than we realize into one which is professional, managerial and technical; into one where the overwhelming proportion of jobs will be not in industry or agriculture but in government, the universities, in public health, in the professions, in teaching, in preaching, in treating people, in the arts and in the sciences—all white-collar jobs requiring a degree of education and mental agility, different from the production job. And an increasing proportion of these jobs will be in research. It has been suggested that one third of our gross national product is generated by the "knowledge sector" of our society. "Bread and butter work" is of declining im-

portance in this country and especially for the younger generation.

To prepare ourselves for a society we must be innovative and inventive. A university or college education becomes indispensable. Those who analyze the forces which explain economic growth in the United States give credit to inputs of labor and capital, but far greater credit to the increased education and advances in knowledge of our workforce and managers. Moreover, more years of schooling prepare us to accommodate to the forces of change. Tomorrow's America will require more and not fewer men and women prepared to deal with tomorrow's problems and fill tomorrow's jobs.

It has been suggested that this appraisal may be far less applicable to graduate work for those masters' and doctorate candidates who aspire to teach. The number of teachers we need and can employ is, of course, influenced by the number of students and by financial resources of government units. Currently there are probably more teachers than there are jobs. Population trends and economic conditions cannot be disregarded in counseling those who prepare for a teaching career. On the other hand, it would be completely foreign to our traditions to have a quota system, to allocate the number of students in each discipline. We need to provide information of trends and developments—but not compulsion. Freedom to choose is what distinguishes our system of education from that in China and the Soviet Union.

The Ph.D. area is somewhat more complicated. Long-term projections of manpower requirements suggest that we may have been overproducing Ph.Ds in some disciplines. Much depends upon what we think about the future growth of the American economy. If one were to assume that the era of growth has come to an end and that we are now—and for the long future—living in an economy of scarcity, it follows that not only our educational system but much else in our society requires rethinking. I am not prepared to accept the idea that "small is beautiful," that we are about to have zero population and zero growth, or that the United States in this bicentennial year will begin to stand still economically and in population.

Consequently, I conclude that while more careful, long-term manpower planning is essential for the Ph.D. and professional education in general, the economic problems of the moment are transitory and do not represent a long-term trend.

Never in our nation's history has our country been in greater need of an informed and educated citizenry. Only those so prepared can comprehend and grapple with the complex problems which face us at home and abroad. The political leaders, the best and the most nobly motivated, cannot do so without an informed citizenry. The general level of education of the public governs the pace at which knowledge is absorbed. Public disenchantment with college and university education comes at a bad time in our nation's history. The electorate will be faced with overwhelming decisions, more complex and costly than at any time in our history.

Women's Labor Market Experience

LABOR FORCE PARTICIPATION

The proportion of women of working age in the labor market, which was 33.9 percent in 1950, rose by one-third to 44.7 percent in 1973.[2] This rapid rise in women's labor force participation rates during the past quarter century has had a marked effect on the size and composition of the work force, on the growth in national product, and on the lifestyles of both men and women. Among the many factors promoting or discouraging labor force entry, several—including marital status, presence and age of children, educational level, husband's income, race, general economic conditions, and potential earnings—can play a determining role in the decision of a woman to seek paid work.

The Age Factor

Although the effects of age on women's labor force activity resemble those prevailing 25 years ago, important changes have occurred in participation rates at all ages (see chart 6). During the 1950's and early 1960's, the proportion of older women in the work force rose dramatically (partly

[2] *Handbook of Labor Statistics* (Washington : U.S. Department of Labor, Bureau of Labor Statistics, 1974), table 2, p. 31.

because many women who had worked during World War II were eager to seek employment

CHART 6

WOMEN'S WORKLIFE PATTERNS ARE CHANGING RAPIDLY.

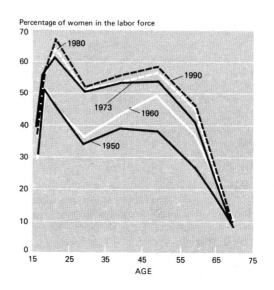

Percentage of women in the labor force

Source: U.S. Department of Labor.

TABLE 1. LABOR FORCE PARTICIPATION RATES OF WOMEN, BY AGE GROUP, SELECTED YEARS 1950 TO 1973 AND PROJECTED 1980 AND 1990

Age	1950	1960	1970	1973	1980	1990
Total	33. 9	37. 8	43. 4	44. 7	45. 6	46. 5
16 and 17 years	30. 1	29. 1	34. 9	39. 1	36. 1	37. 4
18 and 19 years	51. 3	51. 1	53. 7	56. 9	55. 0	56. 3
20 to 24 years	46. 1	46. 2	57. 8	61. 1	63. 6	36. 4
25 to 34 years	34. 0	36. 0	45. 0	50. 1	50. 4	51. 6
35 to 44 years	39. 1	43. 5	51. 1	53. 3	53. 5	55. 4
45 to 54 years	38. 0	49. 8	54. 4	53. 7	56. 6	58. 3
55 to 64 years	27. 0	37. 2	43. 0	41. 1	45. 1	46. 1
65 years and over	9. 7	10. 8	9. 7	8. 9	9. 1	8. 8

SOURCE: *Handbook of Labor Statistics* (Washington: U.S. Department of Labor, Bureau of Labor Statistics, 1974), table 2, p. 31.

"Women's Labor Market Experience." From *Manpower Report of the President,* U. S. Government Printing Office, 1975, pp. 56–63.

again, once their children had entered or completed school). From 38 percent in 1950, the participation rate for women 45 to 54 years of age rose to 51 percent in 1964, while the rate for women 55 to 64 rose from 27 percent to 40 percent (see table 1). The mid-1960's then saw an upsurge in participation by younger women, as the 20- to 24-year-old group increased its participation rate from 50 percent in 1964 to 61 percent in 1973, and the 25- to 34-year age group from 37 percent to 50 percent during the same period. Both the earlier rise in participation by older women and the later rise by younger women were accompanied by a steady growth in participation by the intermediate 35- to 44-year age group during the two and a half decades.

Increases in labor force participation rates are expected to continue for all but the youngest and oldest groups, but a remarkable shift has already occurred.[3] While age still has the same relative effect on participation rates as it did in 1950, the growth in participation rates for all women has been so rapid that the proportion of women aged 25 to 34 who are in the work force today has reached the rate of the most active age groups of 1950. And mothers with school-age children are just as likely to work today as were unmarried young women of the 1950's.

Marital Status and Children

Women who have never married have much higher rates of labor force activity than do women who have (see table 2). Still, the participation rates of married women have risen sharply since 1950, when they were 14 percentage points below the rate for widowed, divorced, or separated women and nearly 27 percentage points below that for single women. While just over half of the single women were in the work force, the same was true of less than 1 out of every 4 married women with husbands present. By 1974, however, 43 per-

TABLE 2. LABOR FORCE PARTICIPATION RATES[1] OF WOMEN, BY MARITAL STATUS, SELECTED YEARS, 1950 TO 1974

Year	Never married	Married, husband present	Widowed, divorced, or separated
1950	50. 5	23. 8	37. 8
1955	46. 4	27. 7	39. 6
1960	44. 1	30. 5	40. 0
1965	40. 5	34. 7	38. 9
1970	53. 0	40. 8	39. 1
1973	55. 8	42. 2	39. 6
1974	57. 2	43. 0	40. 9

[1] Percent of noninstitutional population in the labor force.

cent of married women with husbands present were in the labor force, compared with 57 percent of single and 41 percent of widowed, separated, or divorced women.[4] Thus, while marriage still reduces the labor market activity of women, its impact has been greatly lessened. Participation rates for married women are expected to continue to rise, as marital status becomes a less significant factor in determining work force activity.

Married women, however, still have significantly different participation rates when they have preschool-age children (chart 7). In March 1974, married women without children under 18 years of age had a participation rate of 43.0 percent, and married women with only school-age children had a participation rate of about 51 percent. By contrast, the rate for married women with preschool-age children was 36 percent, while that for women with both preschool- and school-age children was 33 percent.

Although the presence of preschool-age children therefore remains a significant factor in reducing the participation rates of married women, it is important to note a considerable growth in work force participation of this group. In fact, married women with preschool-age children are now in the work force as often as were married women who either had no children under 18 or who had only school-age children in 1950. This development is certain to have important consequences in terms of the cumulative labor force experience and employment continuity of working wives.

The presence of greater numbers of children in the same age group tends to reduce the participation rate of married women, but the age of the children statistically swamps the effect of greater numbers. For example, 59 percent of the married

[3] Bureau of Labor Statistics projections of participation rates in 1980 and 1990 may be understated, given the sharp drop in birth rates during the early 1970's and the continued improvement in women's educational levels. Recent research, such as that by M. G. Sobol, "A Dynamic Analysis of Labor Force Participation of Married Women of Childbearing Age," *Journal of Human Resources,* Fall 1973, indicates that expected family size and wife's education are "of utmost significance" in predicting participation rates. On the basis of these trends, a sizable increase in the labor force participation of married women may be expected. Lower levels of economic activity could lower female work rates, but the composition of any long-term rise in unemployment is uncertain and more women, instead of fewer, may seek jobs if men are displaced. Already, some of the projected participation rates for 1980 and 1990 have been surpassed by several age groups in 1973. Even if there is a short-term setback in the growth of female work force activity, it appears that female participation rates could grow somewhat faster than has been projected.

[4] For more information on the current labor force participation of women, see Howard Hayghe, "Marital and Family Characteristics of Workers, March 1974," *Monthly Labor Review,* January 1975, pp. 60–64.

213

CHART 7

THE PRESENCE OF PRESCHOOL CHILDREN REMAINS IMPORTANT IN REDUCING LABOR FORCE PARTICIPATION AMONG MARRIED WOMEN.

Labor force participation
(March 1974)

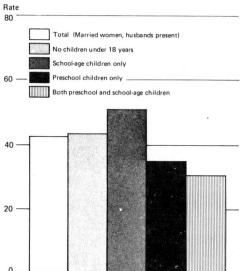

MARRIED WOMEN

Source: U.S. Department of Labor.

women aged 30 to 34 with three or more children aged 12 to 17 worked in 1970. But when only one child under 3 years of age was present, the participation rate was 32 percent.

However, just as the impact of household duties on women's market work has lessened, so too the constraints imposed by having young children seem to be less severe than in earlier years (or, conversely, the financial and psychological constraints of not working may have become more crucial). Whereas 1950 participation rates for 25- to 34-year-old women were about one-fourth lower than the rates for women aged 20 to 24, by 1974 the participation rate of the 25-to-34 group was less than a fifth below that of the younger women. If this trend continues, traditional female worklife patterns will gradually be replaced by something closer to the patterns of their male coworkers.

Educational Attainment and Husbands' Earnings

Another important factor in female participation rates is the level of education attained. Work

force activity rises with educational attainment in a consistent pattern, except for the slightly lower rates for women with 1 to 3 years of college, whose earnings differ only moderately from those of high school graduates. The association of earnings with educational attainment provides a partial explanation of this positive correlation; earnings rise with increased educational attainment, the higher wages providing an added incentive to many women to undertake paid work, even when it is combined with household obligations. In 1952, the average level of educational attainment for working women in the United States was 12.0 years, rising to 12.2 years in 1962 and 12.4 years in 1972—a steady growth that has attracted some women into a widening range of jobs.

It should be noted, however, that higher earnings provide only a portion of the explanation for higher labor force participation rates among college-educated women. Other causal elements may include, for example, the fact that commitment to a particular vocation is likely to be more intense among women who have been willing to pursue supplementary years of education. Exposure in college to an emphasis on lifetime careers may well be another factor of considerable importance in influencing decisions to work.

Although improved educational levels and earnings have been accompanied by higher work force rates for women, higher earnings by husbands have been associated with lower participation rates by their wives. While this still appears to be true to some extent, two important changes have occurred in the last 20 years. First, there has been a continuing upward shift in participation rates by wives with husbands at all income levels, reflecting women's improved earnings and employment opportunities as well as the continuing pressure of family budgetary needs. The positive effect of increases in women's own earnings has more than offset the negative impact of higher earnings of husbands, resulting in increases in both family income and the participation rate of wives over time.

Second, the inverse relationship between husbands' earnings and wives' participation rates has become less consistent. While 1951 participation rates of wives were highest for those whose husbands earned less than $3,000 (in 1973 dollars), wives whose husbands' earnings were in the $5,000-to-$6,999 bracket (in 1973 dollars) were the most likely to be in the labor market by 1960; by 1973, the highest participation rates had shifted to wives with husbands earning between $7,000 and $9,999 (in 1973 dollars). The increased earnings and employment opportunities available to wives with higher levels of educational attainment thus may be changing the earlier inverse relationship be-

214

tween husbands' earnings and wives' participation rates.

Racial Factors

It is important to consider the effect of race, along with age, education, and husbands' earnings, on female labor force participation rates. Except among those who are single or aged 16 to 24 years, the proportion of black women of working age who are in the labor market is significantly higher than that of white women, irrespective of the other factors considered. At each age level, except in the 16- to 24-year-old groups, black women had higher participation rates in 1973, as shown below:

Labor force participation rates of women, 1973

Age	Black	White
16 to 17 years	24. 3	41. 7
18 to 19 years	45. 1	58. 9
20 to 24 years	57. 5	61. 6
25 to 34 years	61. 0	48. 5
35 to 44 years	60. 7	52. 2
45 to 54 years	56. 4	53. 4
55 to 64 years	44. 7	40. 8

SOURCE: *Handbook of Labor Statistics*, 1974, table 4, pp. 38–39.

The lower participation rates for younger black women appear to be slightly more related to such factors as school attendance and job-search difficulties than to home maintenance responsibilities. In a 1973 survey of young women aged 16 to 24 who were not in the labor force, 44.1 percent of the whites, but only 36.7 percent of the blacks, gave home responsibilities as the reason for nonparticipation. In contrast, 46.0 percent of the black women in the sample listed school responsibilities, while only 42.8 percent of the white ones gave this reason.[5]

Except for single women, who are primarily in the 16- to 24-year age group and have lower participation rates, and women who head families, black women have higher rates of labor market activity than white ones of comparable marital status. For example, among married women, blacks display higher participation rates than whites, regardless of husbands' earnings. Indeed, 54 percent of black married women with husbands present were in the labor force in 1973, in contrast to 41 percent of white women of similar marital status; and 44 percent of black women who were widowed, divorced, or separated were working or seeking work, in contrast to 39 percent of their white counterparts. The presence of children, especially young children, is also less of a constraint to black

married women than it is to white ones. While 54 percent of black women with children under 6 years of age were labor force members in 1973, this was true of only 31 percent of white women with pre-school-age children.

Education, particularly college education, raises participation rates more for black than for white women. However, while black women (including those whose husbands earn $10,000 or more per year) have traditionally shown a much greater attachment to the labor force than white women, the recent rise in white women's participation rates has been much faster, as the following tabulation shows:

Labor force participation rates of women

Selected years	Black	White
1950	46. 9	32. 6
1955	46. 1	34. 5
1960	48. 2	36. 5
1965	48. 6	38. 1
1970	49. 5	42. 6
1973	49. 1	44. 1
1974	49. 1	45. 2

SOURCE: U.S. Department of Labor, Bureau of Labor Statistics.

Consequently, the longstanding difference between participation rates of black and white women is narrowing, as the general rise in these rates continues.

OCCUPATIONS AND PAY

Differences in the occupational distribution of men and women workers remain substantial, both among industry groups and between white- and blue-collar categories. For example, women account for 49 percent of white-collar workers, but only 17 percent of those in blue-collar jobs; similarly, in the service sector, 63 percent of jobholders are women. These differences require further breakdown, however, since significant variations occur within occupational groups. For example, approximately equal proportions of women and men are professional or technical workers, but women are heavily concentrated in the lower paying teaching and nursing fields, while more men are found in such higher paying professions as law, medicine, and engineering.

The service sector remains the most important employer of women, as shown in chart 8. Nearly one-fourth of all women workers are employed in the industry, where they make up over one-half of all employees.

Within the service industry category, nearly two-thirds of the workers in education, and three-fourths of those in medical-health and personal

---

[5] *Handbook of Labor Statistics*, 1974, table 9, pp. 49–50.

CHART 8

WOMEN CONTINUE TO FIND JOBS MORE EASILY IN SOME INDUSTRIES THAN IN OTHERS.

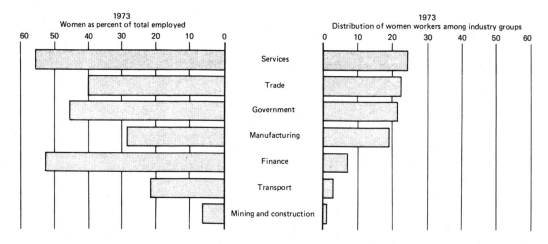

1973
Women as percent of total employed

1973
Distribution of women workers among industry groups

Services
Trade
Government
Manufacturing
Finance
Transport
Mining and construction

Source: U.S. Department of Labor.

services (including work performed in hotels and private homes), are female.[6] The predominance of women in these areas has been attributed to the similarity of the work to the activities traditionally carried out by women in the home. Teaching children and young adults, nursing the sick, and preparing food are seen as extensions of what women do as homemakers. In addition, the availability of part-time or shift work in this sector [7] is attractive to women who have young children.

The growing number of services available in recent years has provided more and more jobs in the types of work that were familiar to women. Conversely, the rapid growth in the American economy during that period was made possible because the fastest growing sector had access to a large supply of women workers who were able to perform a wide range of services.[8] Tradition notwithstanding, women are also heavily represented in government, retail trade, and manufacturing. Indeed, in 1973, these three groups, along with the service category, accounted for nearly 90 percent of female employment.

Women workers have also entered other indus-

trial sectors in significant numbers, however. Women's share of employment in finance, for example, now exceeds half of all jobs; and in transportation, women have more than one-fifth of the total employment.

These apparent gains are tempered, however, by the continued poor representation of women in senior positions within each industry category. There has been a significant decline within the service sector in the proportion of women in professional and technical positions over the last quarter century, offsetting the increase in the numbers of professional and technical women in the trade and manufacturing groups.

Still, some penetration of the industrial sectors traditionally closed to women is occurring. Associated with this is an increase in the proportion of women seeking the necessary training required to undertake new career opportunities. However, much greater progress is needed in this regard if an oversupply of women in the traditional areas of employment is to be avoided in the future,[9] and if women are to attain the level of

[6] E. Waldman and B. J. McEaddy, "Where Women Work—An Analysis by Industry and Occupation," *Monthly Labor Review*, May 1974, pp. 3–13.

[7] Nearly half of all voluntary part-time workers are in the finance and service industry groups. *Handbook of Labor Statistics*, 1974, table 22, p. 78.

[8] For an analysis of this trend, see V. K. Oppenheimer, *The Female Labor Force in the United States* (Berkeley: University of California Press, 1970).

[9] Neal H. Rosenthal, in *College Educated Workers, 1968–80* (Washington: U.S. Department of Labor, Bureau of Labor Statistics, 1970), BLS Bulletin 1676, p. 4, states: "Over the 1968–80 period, the number of women graduates is expected to increase two-thirds, or twice the rate [of increase] for men. Traditional 'women's' fields will not be able to absorb this increase because about 2 out of every 5 women in professional and related jobs are elementary or secondary school teachers. . . . Some may enter social work, chemistry, engineering, or other shortage areas to help achieve a supply-demand balance and improve their own employment prospects. Unless women enlarge the range of occupations, strong competition for jobs may develop."

responsibility within the labor force that their proportional representation in the labor market warrants.

Certain issues—the scheduling of work, the level of unemployment suffered, and wages earned—are of particular importance in this context:

—*Full-Time and Part-Time Work*: About 7 out of 10 women workers have full-time jobs at some time during the year, but only about 4 out of 10 maintain full-time jobs throughout the year. Students, women with family responsibilities, and women over 65 years of age often prefer part-time employment, which is most frequently available in the service and trade industry categories.

—*Unemployment*: Teenage black women suffer the highest unemployment rates of any group classified by age, race, or sex. About 1 out of every 3 young minority women was unemployed in 1974. White women of all ages and minority women aged 20 and over suffered less joblessness than black female teenagers—but, for all classifications, the unemployment rates for women are significantly higher than those for men (often because of the difficulties experienced by many women in finding re-entry jobs after a period of absence from the labor force). Recent job market trends show a worsening of female unemployment as the labor market continues to slacken, particularly as layoffs first affect those with the least seniority. Recently hired workers, including many women and minority group members, have become the early casualties of the economic downturn. In some cases, such layoffs have highlighted the potential legal conflict between affirmative action plans and seniority rules within individual firms, but litigation on this issue is still in process.

—*Earnings*: Nearly two-thirds of all full-time, year-round female workers earned less than $7,000 in 1972. In the same year, over three-fourths of full-time, year-round male workers earned over $7,000.[10] Moreover, the large earnings differential between male and female workers has persisted over the past two decades, even when adjusted for hours of work and level of education (see chart 9).

Furthermore, a classification of occupations by earnings reveals a marked similarity to a classification of jobs by sex. In fact, overall

[10] Revised tables for the "Fact Sheet on the Earnings Gap" (Washington: U.S. Department of Labor, Women's Bureau, March 1974).

CHART 9

THE LARGE EARNINGS DIFFERENTIAL BETWEEN MALE AND FEMALE WORKERS STILL EXISTS.

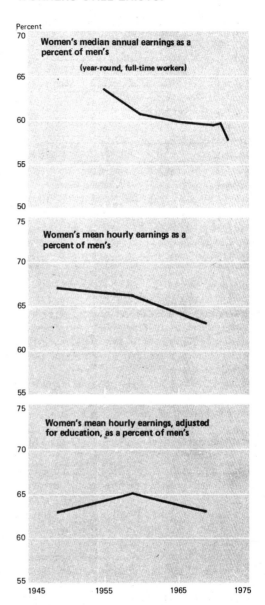

Note: The annual earnings data for 1970-72 are not strictly comparable with those for prior years, which are for wage and salary income only and do not include earnings of self-employed persons.

Source: U.S. Department of Labor and Council of Economic Advisers.

average earnings in private industry were $4.06 per hour in March 1974, but average rates in occupations with high proportions of women were often nearer to $3 than to $4. By contrast, the areas of extensive unioniza-

217

tion and the lowest female participation, construction (where only 6 percent of the workers were women) and mining (with 8 percent women), had average earnings of $6.75 and $4.99, respectively.

Women are not only concentrated in the lower paying industries but they are also found in relatively large numbers in non-unionized business enterprises and in the lower paying occupational groups, including clerical workers and service workers. In addition, even when both sexes are well represented in an occupational group, women's earnings are substantially lower than those of men (see table 3).

Various studies have found the overall discrepancy between male and female earnings to be around 40 percent.[11] Some researchers have argued that they could explain nearly all of this sex differential by controlling for such factors as part-time employment and differences in job responsibilities, education, and length of service.[12] Most of these studies, however, find that large differentials remain; in addition, case studies have found earnings differences even for the same job assignment and with great similarity in performance.[13] One case study indicated that variations in such factors as education and experience ex-

TABLE 3. MEDIAN INCOMES OF FULL-TIME WOMEN WORKERS BY OCCUPATION, 1972

Major occupation group	Median income	Percent of men's income
Professional and technical workers__	$8,796	68
Nonfarm managers and administrators_____	7,306	53
Clerical workers_____	6,039	63
Sales workers_____	4,575	40
Operatives, including transportation_	5,021	58
Service workers (except private household)_____	4,606	59
Private household_____	2,365	(1)
Nonfarm laborers_____	4,755	63

[1] Percent not shown where median income of men is based on fewer than 75,000 individuals.

SOURCE: Revised tables for the "Fact Sheet on the Earnings Gap" (Washington: U. S. Department of Labor, Women's Bureau, March 1974).

plained only half of the difference between men and women in job level assignments.[14]

Although recent action to strengthen equal pay laws may eventually overcome discrimination in earnings for the same job assignments, it will be much more difficult to remove discrimination in the making of job assignments. However, recent evidence suggests that pressures for change may be building. While the average annual discrepancy between the mean incomes of men and women working full time, year round remained substantially unchanged over the 1969–73 period, reports of occupational discrimination doubled.[15]

To a considerable degree, female occupational distribution results from a culmination of influences that start in childhood. Role differentiation in early life later affects educational and occupational choices, hours and location of work, and other factors which relegate women to lower level positions in the lower paying industries. Altering this occupational distribution requires not only the legal prohibition of discrimination but also some fundamental changes in attitudes within the home, the school, and the workplace.

[11] Some examples of unadjusted differentials found are 58 percent in L. E. Suter and H. P. Miller, "Income Differences Between Men and Career Women," *American Journal of Sociology*, January 1973, p. 962; 45 percent in M. S. Cohen, "Sex Differences in Compensation," *The Journal of Human Resources*, Fall 1971, p. 435; 40 percent in V. R. Fuchs, "Differences in Hourly Earnings Between Men and Women," *Monthly Labor Review*, May 1971, p. 10; and 35 percent in R. Oaxaca, "Sex Discrimination in Wages" in Ashenfelter and Rees (eds.), *Discrimination in Labor Markets* (Princeton, N.J.: Princeton University Press, 1973), p. 148.

[12] Cohen, op. cit., found that these factors explained 38 percent of the differential; Fuchs, op. cit., 34 percent; and Oaxaca, op. cit., 29 percent. See also the *Economic Report of the President* (Washington: U.S. Council of Economic Advisers, February 1974), pp. 154–161, for a discussion of the impact of labor force intermittency on women's earnings.

[13] C. R. Martin, Jr., "Support for Women's Lib: Management Performance," *Southern Journal of Business*, February 1972, p. 25.

[14] B. G. Malkiel and J. A. Malkiel, "Male-Female Pay Differentials in Professional Employment," *American Economic Review*, September 1973, p. 703.

[15] G. L. Staines and R. P. Quinn, "Trends in Objective and Subjective Sex Discrimination in Occupations: 1969–73" (Ann Arbor: University of Michigan, Survey Research Center, 1974).

JOBSEEKING METHODS USED BY AMERICAN WORKERS

CARL ROSENFELD

To IMPROVE programs designed to help workers seeking jobs, the Manpower Administration of the U.S. Department of Labor financed a nationwide sample survey conducted in January 1973 of successful jobseekers to determine which search methods they used and the effectiveness of the various methods. Following are highlights from the preliminary analysis of results:

1. The method most commonly used by all jobseekers, by 2 out of 3, was direct application to employers without suggestions or referrals by anyone.

2. Direct application was also named by the largest proportion of workers as the method by which they found their present jobs. Next in rank were: Asking friends about jobs where they work, and answering local newspaper ads.

3. About half of all persons who applied directly to employers for work found their current jobs that way, about double the percentage for the methods with the next two highest rates.

4. The four methods most commonly used and the method most frequently named as the one by which they obtained their jobs were the same for men and women, and, with minor exceptions, for most classifications of workers by other characteristics.

5. Greater proportions of blacks than whites asked friends and relatives about jobs where they work, took Civil Service tests, checked with the State employment service, and contacted local assistance organizations.

6. Nearly half of the jobseekers who were employed just before beginning their job search started to look for a new job while still at work on their old one. Among those who did not look for a job while still working, 2 out of 5 began their job search within 1 or 2 days after leaving their old job.

7. One out of three jobseekers turned down a job offer. Blacks were less likely than whites to refuse jobs. Of those who turned down job offers, 3 out of 10 declined them because of low pay.

The survey, conducted by the Bureau of the Census for the Bureau of Labor Statistics, covered nearly 16 million wage and salary workers 16 years old and over who were not in school and who had started their current jobs during 1972. About 5.5 million of these workers had not found it necessary to look for work because they returned to jobs held formerly, were offered jobs, had entered a family business, or other reasons. Of the 10.4 million who actively sought work, about half began their search either as new entrants or reentrants to the labor force. The remainder had lost or quit their jobs or wanted to change jobs.

The men and women who had looked for work were asked to complete a questionnaire relating to their job search and to their employment situation just before starting the search. Questions included all methods used to find work; the method by which they obtained their present job; and the number of weeks, average number of hours spent per week, and the distance traveled looking for work.

Methods used

Those who had actively looked for work were asked to check from a list of 20 those methods they had used in the search for their present job. On average, workers used four methods; about 1 out of 5 used only one method and over one-third used five methods or more. Men used an average of 4.2 methods in their search compared with 3.7 for women. The average was 3.9 for whites and 4.5 for blacks and other races.

By far, the most often cited method was direct application to employers without suggestions or referrals by anyone. (See table 1.) Two-thirds of

Carl Rosenfeld is an economist in the Division of Labor Force Studies, Bureau of Labor Statistics.

Carl Rosenfeld, "Jobseeking Methods Used by American Workers," *Monthly Labor Reveiw,* August 1975, pp. 39–42. Reprinted with permission.

all jobseekers used this method. Methods used by between one-half and one-third of the jobseekers were asking friends about openings where they worked and about jobs elsewhere, answering ads in local newspapers, and using the State employment service.

Generally, there was little difference between men and women in the degree to which they used the several methods. However, much larger proportions of men reported asking friends and relatives, and using the State employment service and union hiring halls. Blacks were less likely than whites to have applied directly to employers or to have answered local newspaper ads, but were more likely to have asked friends and relatives, taken Civil Service tests, or used the State employment service. A larger proportion of blacks than of whites contacted local organizations, such as the Urban League and welfare or social organizations, for job leads.

Method of obtaining jobs

After the respondents listed all the methods they used to find work, they were asked to select from the list the method by which they obtained their present job. The three top-ranking methods were direct application to employers, asking friends about jobs, and answering advertisements in newspapers. (See table 2.) About the same proportion of workers found jobs through the State employment service as through private employment agencies. Direct application ranked first for all groups of workers, but there were a number of differences among worker groups in the succeeding rankings of most useful methods. Among blacks, the second- and third-ranking methods were asking friends about jobs where they work and using the State employment service.

For some occupational groups, there were wide

Table 1. Methods used to look for work, by sex and race, January 1973

Job search method	Percent who used each method					Method used to get job					Effectiveness rate [1]				
	Sex			Race		Sex			Race		Sex			Race	
	Both sexes	Men	Women	White	Negro and other races	Both sexes	Men	Women	White	Negro and other races	Both sexes	Men	Women	White	Negro and other races
Total: Number (thousands)	10,437	5,749	4,688	9,302	1,135	10,437	5,749	4,688	9,302	1,135					
Percent						100.0	100.0	100.0	100.0	100.0					
Applied directly to employer without suggestions or referrals by anyone	66.0	67.3	64.4	66.6	60.7	34.9	35.1	34.6	35.7	27.7	47.7	47.0	48.5	48.8	38.1
Asked friends:															
About jobs where they work	50.8	53.8	47.2	49.9	58.4	12.4	13.8	10.7	12.0	16.4	22.1	23.2	20.5	21.9	23.4
About jobs elsewhere	41.8	45.9	36.6	41.6	43.5	5.5	6.2	4.8	5.7	4.0	11.9	12.1	11.7	12.5	7.7
Asked relatives:															
About jobs where they work	28.4	31.0	25.1	27.4	36.5	6.1	6.9	5.1	5.7	9.3	19.3	20.1	18.2	19.0	21.3
About jobs elsewhere	27.3	30.1	23.9	26.8	30.9	2.2	2.7	1.7	2.3	1.9	7.4	8.0	6.4	7.7	5.1
Answered newspaper ads:															
Local	45.9	44.6	47.5	46.7	39.6	12.2	10.3	14.5	12.8	6.4	23.9	20.9	27.5	25.0	13.6
Nonlocal	11.7	14.2	8.6	11.7	11.9	1.3	1.4	1.1	1.3	.8	10.0	9.1	11.9	10.5	5.9
Checked with private employment agency	21.0	19.9	22.4	21.0	20.9	5.6	3.8	7.9	5.8	3.8	24.2	17.1	31.9	25.3	15.2
Checked with State employment service	33.5	37.1	29.2	32.1	44.9	5.1	5.0	5.2	4.4	10.8	13.7	12.1	16.2	12.6	20.1
Contacted school placement office	12.5	12.0	13.0	12.2	14.4	3.0	3.1	2.8	3.0	2.3	21.4	23.0	19.6	22.5	13.5
Took Civil Service test	15.3	15.4	15.2	14.6	21.1	2.1	1.6	2.8	2.0	3.3	12.5	9.2	16.6	12.4	13.0
Asked teacher or professor for job leads	10.4	9.2	11.8	10.3	10.7	1.4	1.2	1.6	1.4	1.6	12.1	11.9	12.5	12.1	12.4
Checked with union hiring hall	6.0	9.9	1.1	5.7	8.4	1.5	2.6	.1	1.4	1.9	22.2	23.7	(²)	22.6	18.9
Contacted local organization	5.6	5.5	5.7	4.0	18.6	.8	.7	.9	.4	3.9	12.7	11.0	14.7	9.9	17.6
Answered ads in professional or trade journals or periodicals	4.9	6.7	2.6	4.7	6.4	.4	.5	.3	.4	.2	7.3	6.5	9.9	8.1	(²)
Placed ads in newspapers:															
Local	1.6	1.7	1.4	1.3	3.4	.2	.1	.4	.2	.1	12.9	5.1	(²)	16.0	(²)
Nonlocal	.5	.7	.2	.5	1.0	(³)	(³)	-----	(³)	-----	(²)	(²)	-----	(²)	-----
Went to place where employers come to pick up people	1.4	2.0	.7	1.1	3.9	.1	.1	.2	.1	.4	8.2	4.3	(²)	7.9	(²)
Placed ads in professional or trade journals or periodicals	.6	.8	.4	.5	1.1	(³)	-----	(³)	(³)	-----	(²)	-----	(²)	(²)	-----
Other	11.8	11.9	11.5	11.8	11.7	5.2	5.1	5.3	5.2	5.1	39.7	38.5	41.5	40.1	36.4

[1] Number of persons reporting method used to get job divided by total number of persons who used the method to find a job.

[2] Base less than 75,000.

[3] Less than 0.05 percent.

NOTE: The approximately 3.5 million persons in this survey who checked for jobs with the State employment services do not represent all persons who filed new or renewed job applications during 1972.

Table 2. Method by which current job was obtained, by selected characteristics, January 1973

[Percent distribution]

Characteristics	Total	Applied directly to employer	Ask friends about jobs		Ask relatives about jobs		Answer ads in local paper	Private employment agency	State employment service	School placement office	Civil Service test	All other methods
			Where they worked	Elsewhere	Where they worked	Elsewhere						
Total, all persons	100.0	34.9	12.4	5.5	6.1	2.2	12.2	5.6	5.1	3.0	2.1	10.9
OCCUPATION												
Professional and managerial	100.0	29.0	8.3	8.7	2.9	1.8	11.0	7.0	1.8	8.0	3.7	17.8
Professional	100.0	30.7	8.6	7.8	2.5	1.4	9.0	5.6	1.6	10.2	4.0	18.5
Managerial	100.0	24.3	7.6	11.1	3.9	2.7	16.5	10.9	2.5	1.9	3.1	15.5
Clerical and sales	100.0	29.7	11.9	4.3	4.8	2.1	15.1	12.4	5.6	2.5	3.3	8.4
Sales	100.0	42.8	12.3	5.8	3.8	1.9	16.8	4.3	2.2	1.9		8.4
Clerical	100.0	25.4	11.8	3.9	5.1	2.1	14.5	15.1	6.7	2.7	4.3	8.4
Craft workers, total	100.0	41.1	14.4	4.8	7.1	1.9	9.5	1.5	4.2	.6	.4	14.6
Union members	100.0	30.9	10.3	5.6	5.3	2.3	7.6	.7	3.3	.7	....	33.2
Nonunion members	100.0	45.4	16.1	4.5	7.8	1.7	10.3	1.8	4.6	.6	.6	6.7
Operatives, total	100.0	41.5	13.6	4.6	8.8	2.2	10.8	1.2	7.0	1.1	.4	8.6
Union members	100.0	41.0	11.4	5.4	5.2	1.4	11.1	1.4	8.2	....	.5	14.4
Nonunion members	100.0	41.6	14.1	4.4	9.7	2.4	10.7	1.2	6.7	1.4	.4	7.3
Nonfarm laborers	100.0	40.1	15.1	4.3	9.6	7.1	6.4	.5	5.9	1.1	.7	9.4
Service workers, except private household	100.0	38.7	15.4	5.6	6.9	1.2	14.8	1.3	5.7	2.2	2.0	6.2
AGE												
16 to 24 years	100.0	33.8	13.2	4.9	8.2	3.3	9.8	5.9	5.0	4.6	1.8	9.5
25 to 44 years	100.0	35.5	11.9	5.8	4.7	1.3	13.6	5.7	5.4	1.8	2.7	11.6
25 to 34 years	100.0	34.0	11.5	6.2	5.2	1.8	13.4	6.2	5.4	2.3	3.0	11.2
35 to 44 years	100.0	38.6	12.9	5.1	3.6	.4	14.2	4.6	5.5	.7	2.2	12.4
45 years and over	100.0	36.9	11.0	6.9	2.4	1.1	16.7	4.3	4.2	.4	1.4	14.6
45 to 54 years	100.0	35.5	11.5	8.6	2.4	1.5	16.8	4.8	3.6	.3	1.8	13.3
55 to 64 years	100.0	38.1	11.3	4.2	2.7	.6	17.0	3.9	4.8	.6	.6	16.4
65 years and over	(1)	....										
EDUCATION												
Elementary school: 8 years or less	100.0	49.9	6.7	4.1	6.1	.1	10.4	.5	9.6	....	.5	12.0
High school: 4 years or more	100.0	35.8	10.0	4.3	4.3	1.8	20.4	5.3	6.6	1.2	1.5	8.8
College: 4 years or more	100.0	33.1	7.5	5.2	1.1	.7	13.2	7.8	2.4	10.2	1.8	16.9
REASON FOR STARTING TO LOOK FOR WORK												
Quit job	100.0	38.2	10.2	4.9	6.1	2.8	13.5	7.9	5.1	.8	.8	9.7
Lost job	100.0	34.5	11.7	5.9	5.5	2.0	13.0	4.3	7.8	.8	1.5	12.9
Wanted different job before quitting	100.0	32.6	14.0	6.9	6.9	1.6	12.9	7.6	2.7	1.5	5.1	8.1
Left or finished school	100.0	31.6	12.4	5.8	6.8	3.8	6.0	5.2	4.4	8.8	3.0	12.3
Wanted to work while in school	100.0	31.1	19.6	4.6	4.8	2.2	7.9	1.4	3.0	14.3	....	11.3
Was keeping house and wanted a job	100.0	40.2	11.3	3.8	6.2	1.2	18.8	5.5	4.6	.2	2.3	5.8

[1] Percent not shown where base is less than 75,000.

differences between men and women in the proportions of jobseekers who obtained jobs through a specific method. Among professional and technical workers, a smaller proportion of men than women obtained their jobs by applying directly to employers but larger proportions by answering newspaper ads, and checking with private employment agencies. Among clerical workers, more men than women got jobs through friends, relatives, and school placement offices and fewer through newspaper ads, private agencies, and Civil Service procedures. Among service workers, a higher proportion of men than women got their jobs through friends, relatives, the State employment service, and Civil Service and smaller proportions by applying directly to employers and by answering newspaper ads.

In each occupational group for which comparisons could be made, there were some methods by which relatively more blacks than whites obtained jobs. For example, among professional and technical workers, more blacks than whites obtained jobs through friends and Civil Service procedures and fewer by applying directly to employers or through private employment agencies. Fewer blacks than whites got jobs by answering newspaper ads and more got jobs from the State employment service if they were clerical or service workers, or operatives (except transport). For blacks in the latter two groups, local organizations were an important source of leads.

Effectiveness of job search methods

The effectiveness of each job search method may be expressed as the proportion of persons using it who obtained their current jobs by that method. The method with the highest effectiveness rate, by far, was application directly to an employer—48 percent of all persons who used this method reported that they had obtained their job that way (table 1). As indicated earlier, this method was also used by the greatest proportion of jobseekers.

This method was followed by six others which had effectiveness rates about half that of direct application—private employment agencies, local newspaper ads, asking friends about jobs where they work, union hiring halls, school placement offices, and asking relatives about jobs where they work. Although the effectiveness rates were high for persons who used hiring halls and school placement offices, comparatively few persons used these methods.

There was little difference between men and women in the effectiveness rate of a given method, with two exceptions. The rates for women were about double those for men for private agencies and Civil Service.

The effectiveness rates for several job methods differed sharply for blacks and whites. Black jobseekers found direct application somewhat less effective than did white jobseekers. Other methods that were much less effective for blacks included use of private employment agencies, newspaper ads, and school placement offices. However, blacks had greater success with local organizations such as community action groups and the Urban League, and they were more likely to use this service. Similarly, the State employment service, which was used by more of the blacks, had a higher effectiveness rate for blacks than whites.

The most effective job search method, next to applying directly to an employer, also varied sharply by occupation. The hiring hall was second most effective for craft workers, operatives, and nonfarm laborers. Local newspaper ads had the second highest rate for managers and administrators, transport equipment operatives, sales workers, and service workers. School placement offices were the second most effective for professional and technical workers and the private employment agency was second for clerical workers.

Intensity of job search

The jobseekers generally spent relatively few hours a week looking for a job. About 66 percent reported they usually looked for 5 hours a week or less, and about 20 percent for 11 hours or more. (See table 3.) Women devoted fewer hours to their job search than men. The distributions by amount of time were about the same for white and black workers.

The jobseekers generally restricted their job search to a relatively short distance from their homes. About 4 out of 10 looked no farther than 10 miles and another 3 out of 10 went up to 25 miles; only 1 out of 10 went over 100 miles. Men tended to go farther than women and whites farther than blacks.

Additional information on the jobfinding process will appear in a forthcoming BLS bulletin. □

Table 3. Selected data on jobfinding activity, by sex and race, January 1973

[Percent distribution]

Item	Both sexes	Men	Women	White	Negro and other races
Total who looked for work	100.0	100.0	100.0	100.0	100.0
HOURS USUALLY LOOKED FOR WORK A WEEK					
5 hours or less	64.9	59.9	71.1	65.3	61.5
6 to 10 hours	16.1	16.9	15.2	15.7	19.9
11 to 20 hours	10.6	12.4	8.3	10.7	10.1
21 hours or more	8.4	10.8	5.4	8.3	8.5
FARTHEST DISTANCE TRAVELED TO LOOK FOR WORK					
Under 5 miles	20.7	15.0	27.9	20.3	24.3
5 to 10 miles	22.4	18.3	27.6	22.0	26.2
11 to 25 miles	29.6	29.7	29.6	29.6	29.8
26 to 50 miles	14.4	18.6	9.0	14.7	11.0
51 to 100 miles	4.3	6.4	1.7	4.3	4.2
101 miles or more	8.5	12.0	4.2	9.0	4.7
NUMBER OF WEEKS LOOKED FOR WORK					
Under 5 weeks	59.9	57.7	62.6	60.1	57.9
5 to 10 weeks	18.4	19.5	16.9	18.4	17.9
11 to 14 weeks	6.6	6.9	6.1	6.5	6.7
15 to 26 weeks	8.6	9.2	8.0	8.5	9.6
27 weeks or more	6.6	6.6	6.5	6.4	7.9
NUMBER OF METHODS USED TO FIND A JOB					
1 method	19.8	17.9	22.1	20.2	16.6
2 methods	18.3	17.3	19.5	18.7	15.4
3 or 4 methods	25.8	24.8	27.0	25.9	25.1
5 methods or more	36.1	39.9	31.4	35.3	42.9
JOB OFFER					
Turned down a job offer	32.3	32.6	31.9	33.5	22.2
Did not turn down a job offer	67.7	67.4	67.1	66.5	77.8
JOB SEARCH WHILE EMPLOYED					
Started to look while still working—percent of those employed just prior to job search	48.4	49.2	46.9	49.0	43.4

PROJECTED DEMAND FOR AND SUPPLY OF PH. D. MANPOWER, 1972–85

ELINOR W. ABRAMSON

BY 1985, JOBS requiring doctorates will increase to about 475,000, if trends continue in the use of Ph. D.'s relative to other workers in the same occupation (table 1). Demand for Ph. D.'s between 1972 and 1985 will grow nearly twice as fast as for all workers, but more slowly than for college graduates as a whole, according to a Bureau of Labor Statistics study.

About 335,000 holders of doctorates were employed in 1972. Nearly one-half had doctorates in engineering or natural science. Approximately 70 percent worked in educational institutions; smaller proportions were employed in private industry, government, and nonprofit organizations. Almost one-half of all Ph. D.'s were employed in teaching, while one-third were working in research and development. Smaller proportions were employed in administration, provided professional services to individuals, and were also engaged in other activities.

Projected growth rates will vary among different employers as well as among occupational fields. Demand for Ph. D.'s in educational institutions is expected to increase by only 32 percent; in government, almost 55 percent; in nonprofit organizations, 79 percent; and in industry and business, 100 percent.

Job openings for doctorate holders will number about 187,000 between 1972 and 1985 (table 2). One-fourth will replace Ph. D. workers who retire, die, or leave the labor force for other reasons, and about three-fourths will be needed for occupational growth. Most of the openings resulting from growth will stem from increased numbers of workers in each field (employment expansion). The remainder will result from the educational upgrading of jobs and will reflect the projected increase in the proportion of workers in each field holding a doctorate.

Table 1. Ph. D. employment, 1972, and demand, 1985

Field	Employment, 1972	Demand, 1985	Percent change, 1972–85
All fields	334,600	474,900	41.9
Engineering and natural science	161,700	243,700	50.7
Engineering	31,000	59,100	90.5
Physical science	63,800	91,700	43.8
Chemistry	35,900	50,500	40.7
Physics	22,600	29,400	30.0
Life science	54,500	73,100	34.2
Mathematics	12,400	19,800	59.3
Social science and psychology	63,800	87,100	36.5
Psychology	22,700	34,400	51.7
Arts and humanities	38,800	49,400	27.3
Education	58,300	79,200	35.9
Business and commerce	5,400	6,300	18.2
Other fields	6,700	9,100	37.2

NOTE: Because of rounding, sums of individual items may not equal totals.

Table 2. Source of demand for Ph. D.'s, 1972–85

Field	Total demand	Growth			Replacement needs
		Total	Educational upgrading	Employment expansion	
All fields	187,400	140,300	30,800	109,500	47,100
Engineering and natural science	105,600	82,000	19,900	62,100	23,600
Engineering	33,300	28,100	5,500	22,600	5,200
Physical science	37,100	28,000	8,900	19,100	9,100
Chemistry	19,600	14,600	7,100	7,500	5,000
Physics	9,700	6,700	1,100	5,600	3,000
Life science	26,000	18,600	3,400	15,200	7,400
Mathematics	9,300	7,400	2,100	5,300	1,900
Social science and psychology	32,100	23,300	4,900	18,400	8,800
Psychology	15,000	11,700	4,100	7,600	3,300
Arts and humanities	15,700	10,600	200	10,400	5,100
Education	28,900	20,900	4,000	16,900	8,000
Business and commerce	1,700	1,000	300	900	700
Other fields	3,400	2,500	1,700	800	900

NOTE: Because of rounding, sums of individual items may not equal totals.

Elinor W. Abramson is an economist in the Division of Manpower and Occupational Outlook, Bureau of Labor Statistics.

Elinor W. Abramson, "Projected Demand and Supply of Ph.D. Manpower." *Monthly Labor Review,* December 1975, pp. 52–53. Reprinted with permission.

Table 3.   Supply of and demand for Ph. D.'s, 1985

[In thousands]

Field	New supply, 1972–85	Openings, 1972–85	Difference
All fields	583.4	187.4	396.0
Engineering and natural science	224.4	105.6	118.8
Engineering	50.3	33.3	17.0
Physical science	60.3	37.1	23.2
Chemistry	25.8	19.6.	6.2
Physics	19.9	9.7	10.2
Life science	92.2	26.0	66.2
Mathematics	21.6	9.3	12.3
Social science and psychology	101.6	32.1	69.5
Psychology	37.7	15.0	22.7
Arts and humanities	79.6	15.7	63.9
Education	148.8	28.9	119.9
Business and commerce	19.2	1.7	17.5
Other fields	9.7	3.4	6.3

NOTE: Because of rounding, sums of individual items may not equal totals.

Based on the U.S. Office of Education's projections of earned degrees, the supply of new Ph. D.'s between 1972 and 1985 is estimated at about 580,000 persons (table 3). Therefore, if present trends continue in patterns of use of Ph. D.'s relative to other workers and in the proportion of persons obtaining doctorates, by 1985 the number of Ph. D.'s would be more than double the number of jobs traditionally available to Ph. D.'s.

The implications of this projected imbalance between supply and demand are of concern to individuals, universities, employers, and society. Underemployment is likely to increase and salary differentials paid to Ph. D.'s may narrow in relation to other workers. Universities may not have adequate funds to train and employ Ph. D.'s. Employers may have to consider ways to restructure jobs to make use of Ph. D.'s. Society will have to determine the course of future support of graduate education in terms of its anticipated needs and resources.

B. Unemployment Insurance

Unemployment compensation: its effect on unemployment

MARTIN FELDSTEIN

Under the economic conditions that have prevailed in the postwar period, our current system of unemployment compensation is likely to have increased the average rate of unemployment. The common presumption, that unemployment compensation reduces unemployment because it automatically increases government spending when unemployment rises, is really irrelevant. The same fiscal stimulus would now be provided through other expenditure increases or tax cuts by a government committed to maintaining aggregate demand. The primary effect on aggregate unemployment of our current system of unemployment compensation is not its contribution to aggregate demand but its adverse impact on the incentives of employers and employees. As a result, unemployment compensation is likely to increase nearly all sources of unemployment: seasonal and cyclical variations in the demand for labor, weak labor force attachment, and unnecessarily long durations of unemployment.

Our current system of unemployment compensation has two distinct but related bad incentives. First, for those who are already unemployed, it greatly reduces and often almost eliminates the cost of increasing the period of unemployment. Second,

and more generally, for all types of unsteady work—seasonal, cyclical, and casual—it raises the net wage to the employee relative to the cost to the employer. The first of these effects provides an incentive to inappropriately long durations of unemployment. The second provides both employers and employees with the incentive to organize production in a way that increases the level of unemployment by making the seasonal and cyclical variation in unemployment too large and by making casual and temporary jobs too common.

The high rate of wage replacement

The reform of unemployment insurance is fundamentally impeded by the false notion that unemployment benefits replace only a small fraction of lost wages. The most common assertion is that benefits provide only about *one-third* of the unemployed individual's usual pay. A more accurate description is that unemployment insurance currently replaces *two-thirds* or more of lost net income. In some extreme cases, the individual may receive more net income by being unemployed than by returning to work at the previous wage.

To understand the high replacement rate, it is useful to examine a detailed example. Consider a worker in Massachusetts in 1975 with a wife and two children. His gross earnings are $120 per week or $6,240 per year if he experiences no unemployment. She earns $80 per week or $4,160 per year if she experiences no unemployment. If he is unemployed for 10 weeks, he loses $1,200 in gross earnings but only $227 in net income. How does this happen? A reduction of $1,200 in annual earnings reduces his Federal income tax by $194, his social security payroll tax by $71, and his Massa-

Martin Feldstein is professor of economics, Harvard University. The title of his full paper presented at the IRRA meeting is "The Unemployment Caused by Unemployment Insurance."

Martin Feldstein, "Unemployment Compensation—Its Effect on Unemployment." *Monthly Labor Review,* March 1976, pp. 39–41. Reprinted with permission of the author. Based on a paper entitled "The Unemployment Caused by Unemployment Insurance", which appeared in the *Proceedings of the 28th Annual Meeting, Industrial Relations Research Association* (Madison, WI.: The Association, 1976).

chusetts income tax by $60. The total reduction in taxes is $325. Thus net after-tax wages fall by only $875.

Unemployment compensation consists of 50 percent of his wage plus dependents' allowances of $6 per week for each child. Total unemployment compensation is therefore $648. These benefits, which are not taxable, therefore replace 74 percent of the net wage loss of $875. Viewed slightly differently, *the combination of taxes and unemployment compensation imposes an effective marginal tax rate of 81 percent*—that is, the man's net earnings fall by only 19 percent of his gross pay (by $227 out of $1,200) when he is unemployed for 10 weeks. Moreover, part of this difference in income would be offset by the cost of transportation to work and other expenses associated with employment.

Because of the original 1-week waiting period, even these remarkable figures understate the effect of unemployment compensation on the cost to the individual of remaining unemployed longer.[1] If he stays unemployed for 11 weeks instead of 10, he loses an additional $120 in gross earnings but only $15.50 in net income. The reward for working is less than $0.50 per hour. The implied tax rate is 87 percent.

These astounding figures are not very sensitive to the specific details of the family in the example or to the use of Massachusetts rules. For a wide variety of representative unemployed men in the Nation, the compensation benefits replace more than 60 percent of lost net income; for women who are unemployed, the typical replacement rates are close to 80 percent. In the more generous States, the rate on net earnings is generally over 80 percent.[2]

The common statistic that average benefits are only about one-third of average covered wages is a misleading observation for two reasons. One reason is that the average benefit refers to those who become unemployed, while the average wage refers to all covered workers. Since the lower paid workers are more likely to become unemployed, the average wage overstates even the *gross* earnings of these unemployed. The other reason is that the figure of one-third is a ratio of *nontaxable* benefits to gross wages. The incorrect perception of the relative level of unemployment compensation reflects a failure to recognize the high *marginal* tax rates currently paid by individuals in the middle- and low-income ranges. The combination of Federal and State income tax and the social security payroll tax generally makes the marginal tax rate of such individuals 30 percent or higher. The majority of unemployment compensation recipients collect benefits that are at least 50 percent of their previous gross wage. These benefits are not taxed, so a 30-percent marginal tax rate on earnings (or a 70-percent net income)

implies that the ratio of benefits to net earnings is five–sevenths, or that benefits replace more than 70 percent of the net wage.

These very high replacement rates are quite unintentional. They reflect the fact that the system of taxation has changed dramatically since the origin of the unemployment insurance program. The Federal income tax was then very small and restricted to high-income families and State income taxes were virtually nonexistent. By 1974, the percentage of the population covered by taxable returns had increased to over 80 percent, and the Federal income tax rate at the median taxable income was over 19 percent. In addition, there are sizable State income tax rates and a 5.85-percent social security payroll tax.

Effect on temporary layoffs

Although most discussions of the adverse impact of unemployment insurance focus on the prolonged duration of job search, I believe that the effect on the frequency and duration of temporary layoffs is at least as important. The high level of untaxed benefits and the inadequate system of experience rating used in the financing of unemployment insurance provide very strong incentives for an excessive volume of temporary unemployment.[3]

Employees on layoff receive a substantial subsidy from the unemployment insurance system because of the ineffective method of experience rating. Employers now contribute to their State's unemployment insurance fund on the basis of the unemployment experience of their own previous employees.[4] But the current system of experience rating is a very imperfect check on the substantial subsidy entailed by unemployment compensation. A crucial feature of the unemployment insurance tax is that there is a relatively low maximum rate and a positive minimum rate. As a result, many firms with high layoff rates have "negative balances" in their accounts, that is, they have paid less in taxes than their employees have received in benefits. These firms with high unemployment rates face the maximum tax rate; an increase in layoffs causes no increase in tax payments. Similarly, the large number of firms with substantial positive balances face the minimum rate and would continue to do so even if their rate of layoffs increased, as long as that increase was not too great.[5]

With effective experience rating, the frequency and duration of temporary layoffs would reflect the employers' attempts to produce at minimum cost and the employees' balancing of higher wages and periods of temporary layoff. In contrast, the current inadequate experience rating and the tax-free status of unemployment compensation induce employers and employees to organize production and work rules in ways that create excessive unemployment.

It is not surprising that temporary layoffs are such an important part of unemployment in an economy in which a spell of temporary unemployment is almost costless to both the worker and the firm. ☐

————FOOTNOTES————

[1] There is typically a 1-week waiting period *per benefit year*. An individual with more than 1 spell in 12 months only has to "forgo a week's benefits" during the first spell.

[2] For a detailed analysis, see Martin Feldstein, "Unemployment Compensation: Adverse Incentives and Distribution Anomalies," *National Tax Journal*, June 1974, p. 231.

These replacement rates are based on typical earnings for men and women in each State.

[3] See Martin Feldstein, "The Importance of Temporary Layoffs: An Empirical Analysis," *Brookings Papers on Economic Activity*, 1975, No. 3.

[4] A full analytic model of temporary layoffs and experience rating is presented in Martin Feldstein "Temporary Layoffs in the Theory of Unemployment," *Journal of Political Economy*, June 1976 (forthcoming).

[5] For a detailed study of experience rating, see Joseph Becker, *Experience Rating in Unemployment Insurance* (Baltimore, Johns Hopkins University Press, 1972).

Do benefits cause unemployed to hold out for better jobs?

RONALD G. EHRENBERG AND
RONALD L. OAXACA

The recent economic recession has occasioned alarming increases in the program costs of various public assistance and social insurance systems. Budgetary pressures brought on by recession-cum-inflation have rekindled criticism of the scope and variety of existing social programs. Such programs are undergoing intense scrutiny. Part of this process of re-evaluation involves an examination of the actual effects of a public program in comparison with its intended effects. Among those programs experiencing a revival of interest in their actual functioning is the Unemployment Insurance (UI) system.

Intuitively, one would expect that the UI system leads to more unemployment and longer durations of unemployment than would occur in the absence of a UI system. This is, of course, an implication of standard job-search models. Empirical studies support the hypothesis that UI benefits lead to more unemployment and longer durations of unemployment.[1] However, job-search models also imply that increases in UI benefits will raise an individual's expected post-unemployment wage. It is reasoned that the income maintenance afforded by unemployment insurance benefits encourages the unemployed to engage in productive job search. In short, unemployment insurance benefits enable unemployed workers to hold out for jobs that are more commensurate with their skills. This aspect of the unemployment insurance benefits-job search process has until recently been subordinate to the unemployment duration side of the picture. The potential impact of unemployment insurance benefits on the post-unemployment wage has not enjoyed atten-

tion equal to that generated by previous studies of the effects of unemployment insurance benefits on the unemployment rate and the duration of unemployment.

A knowledge of the wage gain aspects of an unemployment insurance system is essential to public policy regarding the choice of optimal unemployment insurance benefit levels. The social costs and social benefits of replacing a portion of an individual's pre-unemployment wage while he or she is unemployed need to be compared. The social costs can be measured by the present discounted value of the output foregone during the additional job-search period engendered by the availability of unemployment insurance benefits. Social benefits can be measured by the present discounted value of the additional future earnings made possible by longer search.[2]

Our study of the unemployment insurance system is directed toward estimation of the effects of unemployment insurance benefits on the expected duration of unemployment and on the expected post-unemployment wage. These effects are estimated separately for various demographic groups. Our model entails simultaneous estimation of the effects of unemployment compensation on post-unemployment wage rates and the duration of unemployment, and is described in detail in a longer version of this paper.[3]

Data source

Our data are taken from the National Longitudinal Survey. Four cohorts of approximately 5,000 individuals each were surveyed annually over the period 1966–71. These cohorts are as follows: Males 45–59 years of age in 1966; females 30–44 years of age in 1967; males 14–24 years of age in 1966; and females 14–24 years of age in 1968. The general restrictions we placed on the subsamples for this study required that (1) the respondent be employed at two consecutive survey dates with reported spells and weeks of unemployment between the survey dates, and (2) the respondent's hourly wage be reported at each of the two consecutive survey dates. Additional restrictions were imposed separately on each of the four demographic groups depending on circumstances specific to the group.[4]

Empirical results

Our findings, based on the results of regressions for each of the four age-sex groups, show that un-

Ronald G. Ehrenberg is professor of economics and labor economics, Cornell University, and Ronald L. Oaxaca is professor of economics, University of Massachusetts. The title of their full paper is "Impacts of Unemployment Insurance on the Duration of Unemployment and the Post-Unemployment Wage." Their research was supported by a grant from the U.S. Office of the Assistant Secretary for Policy, Evaluation, and Research, Department of Labor.

Ronald G. Ehrenberg and Ronald L. Oaxaca, "Do Benefits Cause Unemployed to Hold Out for Better Jobs?" *Monthly Labor Review*, March 1976, pp. 37–39. Reprinted with permission of the authors. Based on a paper entitled "Impacts of Unemployment Insurance on the Duration of Unemployment and the Post-Unemployment Wage", which appeared in the *Proceedings of the 28th Annual Meeting, Industrial Relations Research Association* (Madison, WI.: The Association, 1976).

employment insurance benefits lead to longer durations of unemployment for all of the groups in our study.[5] These effects are statistically significant. Benefits also lead to larger wage increases for all groups, but these effects are statistically significant only among females age 30–44 and older males.

One measure of the impact of benefits is the amount by which they raise the average duration of unemployment and average percentage wage gain above what they would be in the absence of benefits. Since our samples include many individuals who did not receive benefits, the sample average wage replacement ratios are far below the actual average among unemployment insurance recipients. We find that the presence of benefits raised the average duration of unemployment among males age 45–59 by 1 week and less than a week for the other groups. The presence of benefits raised the percentage wage gains above what they would be in the absence of benefits by 9 percentage points and 3 percentage points for older males and females 30–44, respectively. The effects of raising benefits as a fraction of the pre-unemployment wage from 0.5 to 0.6 are to raise the duration of unemployment by almost 2 weeks for older males and less than a week for the other groups. This increment in the wage replacement ratio would lead to an increase in the percentage wage gain of 7 percentage points among older males and about 1.5 percentage points for females age 30–44. Raising the wage replacement ratio can be interpreted as an increase in actual benefits or, in the present context, as an increase in the coverage of the unemployment insurance system.

The ratio of the percentage wage change effects of unemployment insurance benefits to the change in duration of unemployment caused by unemployment insurance benefits yields the percentage wage change per week of unemployment. Thus, for example, an increase in the wage replacement ratio from 0.5 to 0.6 implies that each week of unemployment (job search) leads to an increase in the percentage wage change by 3.7 percentage points for older males, 3.5 percentage points for females age 30–44, 2.7 percentage points for males age 14–24, and 0.7 percentage points for females age 14–24. We emphasize, however, that the estimates for the younger cohorts are *not* statistically significantly different from zero.

Summary and conclusions

Our study confirms that unemployment insurance benefits lead to longer spells of unemployment. While unemployment insurance benefits also raise post-unemployment wages, these wage effects are statistically significant only in the cases of older males and females age 30–44. Thus the predictions of the search models are satisfied for these older groups of workers, but not for the 14–24 year-old cohorts. At the margin, the percentage wage gain for each additional week of unemployment is larger among older workers and among males.

At this time, we can only speculate as to why unemployment insurance benefits have no statistically significant effect on the post-unemployment wages of younger workers. It is possible that these benefits are used by younger workers to subsidize nonmarket activities rather than job search. A second explanation is that younger workers are not very productive searchers. A third explanation may be that many of the younger workers who receive such benefits choose to search for more pleasant jobs which also pay lower wages because of compensating differentials. A fourth possibility is that many of the younger recipients of unemployment insurance benefits may search for jobs offering better opportunities for on-the-job training. If this is true, we would expect their post-unemployment wages to be relatively low because of worker investment in on-the-job training. Consequently, concentration on the post-unemployment wage may be myopic, and the returns to job search would be appropriately measured by examining changes in lifetime earnings streams. Additional research is needed to explain this apparent failure of unemployment insurance benefits to raise post-unemployment wages among younger workers. It is important for policy purposes to know why there is no short-run impact of unemployment insurance benefits on the wages of younger workers. The case for providing unemployment insurance benefits would undoubtedly be strengthened if the fourth (and possibly, the third) explanation given above turned out to be true. □

FOOTNOTES

[1] See Gene Chapin, "Unemployment Insurance, Job Search and the Demand for Leisure," *Western Economic Journal,* March 1971, pp. 102–07, and Raymond Munts, "Partial Benefit Schedules in Unemployment Insurance: Their Effect on Work Incentives," *Journal of Human Resources,* Spring 1970, pp. 160–76.

[2] Assuming of course that the wage truly reflects productivity.

[3] The representative type of model from which ours is drawn is found in Dale Mortensen, "Job Search, the Duration of Unemployment, and the Phillips Curve," *American Economic Review,* December 1970, pp. 847–62.

[4] The details of the selection criteria used in defining the various subsamples in the study will be found in Ronald G. Ehrenberg and Ronald L. Oaxaca, *The Economic Effects of Unemployment Insurance Benefits on Unemployed Workers Job Search,* final report to be submitted to the U.S. Department of Labor under contract L74-49.

[5] The complete regression results are available from the authors upon request.

UNEMPLOYMENT INSURANCE

Part III: A Critique

By Steven P. Zell

F our decades after its creation, the
Federal-state system of unemployment
insurance (UI) remains one of our nation's
principal tools for economic stabilization. As
has been seen in Parts I and II of this series,
the UI system has evolved into an enormously
complex and varied organization.[1] Almost every
facet of the system has expanded tremendously.
For example, since the mid-1950's, the number
of covered workers has grown far more rapidly
than the total work force, the level of average
weekly benefits adjusted for inflation has
increased almost twice as fast as real average
spendable weekly earnings, and the potential
duration of benefits has been expanded from 26
weeks to 65 weeks.[2]

In recent years, economists have become
extremely interested in the potential impact of
these changes on the level of unemployment.
Since the earnings a worker foregoes while
unemployed can be thought of as the cost of

that unemployment, economic theory predicts
that as this cost is reduced via liberalized
unemployment benefits, the level of unemployment in the economy might increase.
Considerable research has been conducted on
the nature and magnitude of these unintended
effects of the UI program, often with
conflicting results. This concluding article on
unemployment insurance will examine some of
the major criticisms of the UI system in the
light of this research.

WHAT ARE WORK DISINCENTIVE EFFECTS?

Ever since the program's inception, UI
benefits have been designed with two basic
objectives directly related to the unemployed
worker. First, on the assumption that the
worker was involuntarily unemployed for a
short period, benefits were established to
replace a portion of his lost wages. Second,
benefits were to go only to "regular" workers,
and could not be set at so high a level as to
make the receipt of benefits more attractive
than working.

The difficulty with the second objective lies
in that the desirability of working, or the

---

[1] Parts I and II appeared, respectively, in the February
1976 and June 1976 issues of this *Review*.

[2] For one estimate of these changes from 1955 to 1973, see
George M. von Furstenberg, "Stabilization Characteristics
of Unemployment Insurance," unpublished paper, Council
of Economic Advisors, p. 5.

Steven P. Zell, "Unemployment Insurance, A Critique." *Monthly Review,* Federal Reserve Bank of
Kansas City, July–August 1976, pp. 14–22. Reprinted with permission.

acceptability of a particular job, is affected by a large number of economic and noneconomic factors. On the noneconomic side, "some workers are choosier than others about jobs. Some place a higher value on spending time at home with their families than do others. And the psychic costs of being unemployed are higher for some workers than for others."[3] Economically, the important question is how costly is unemployment and what alternative assets and income sources are available? If other things are equal, the better a worker can afford to be unemployed, "the less effort he is likely to devote to searching for a job and the more selective he is likely to be about the kind of job he will accept."[4]

The UI system can be said to have work disincentive effects to the extent that it results in a voluntary reduction in the supply of labor in the economy. For example, an unemployed worker might turn down as unsuitable a job which, in the absence of UI, he would have accepted. Similarly, a worker, knowing that his plant will be closing, might delay searching for a job in the knowledge that he can depend on UI benefits when he decides to search. Unlike collecting benefits under the pretense of seeking work, however, neither of these acts is illegal nor constitutes fraud. Furthermore, to the extent that additional job search results in higher paying, more stable employment, the work disincentive effects might prove to have net positive results.[5] Whether or not these work disincentive effects should be discouraged depends, then, on their relative mix of negative and positive effects. Determining the net effect,

however, is not simple. For example, though UI benefits lower the cost of search, they simultaneously lower the cost of increased leisure which might well be substituted for both work and job search. Secondly, even if additional job search does result in more pleasant or higher paying jobs, the subsidization of individual searchers can be justified only if it can be shown that an improved job match constitutes some benefit to society which does not simultaneously accrue to the individual searcher. Otherwise, the worker would be likely to search the optimum amount in the absence of subsidies.[6]

THE CENTER OF THE CONTROVERSY

While some research had been done previously on the unintended effects of the UI system, by far the greatest impact has resulted from the findings of Professor Martin S. Feldstein of Harvard University. In a study prepared for the Joint Economic Committee of Congress in September 1973, and reiterated in numerous professional and popular articles since that time, Feldstein concluded that the unemployment insurance system was responsible for a significant part of the observed unemployment in the United States.[7] Much of the research that has been conducted since that

---

[3] Raymond Munts and Irwin Garfinkel, *The Work Disincentive Effects of Unemployment Insurance* (Kalamazoo: The W. E. Upjohn Institute, September 1974), p. 56.

[4] *Ibid.*, p. 56.

[5] See Steven P. Zell, "Recent Developments in The Theory of Unemployment," Federal Reserve Bank of Kansas City *Monthly Review*, September-October 1975, pp. 5-6, for a discussion of the job-search, labor-turnover theory of unemployment.

[6] Kathleen Classen, *The Effect of Unemployment Insurance on the Duration of Unemployment and Subsequent Earnings*, The Public Research Institute of the Center for Naval Analyses, September 1975, p. 1.

[7] Martin S. Feldstein, *Lowering The Permanent Rate of Unemployment*, U.S. Congress, Joint Economic Committee, 92nd Congress, 2nd Session, September 1973 (Washington, D.C.: Government Printing Office, 1973).

Feldstein originally presented these views in hearings before the Joint Economic Committee, 92nd Congress, 2nd Session in 1972, published as "Policies to Lower the Permanent Rate of Unemployment." See also "The Economics of the New Unemployment," *The Public Interest*, No. 33, Fall 1973, pp. 28-42, "Unemployment Compensation: Adverse Incentives and Distributional Anomalies," *National Tax Journal*, Vol. 27, No. 2, June 1974, pp. 231-44, and "Unemployment Insurance: Time for Reform," *Harvard Business Review*, March-April 1974, pp. 51-61.

date on the UI system has been an attempt to either support or contradict Feldstein's findings and methodology.

Feldstein's Research

Feldstein begins his analysis with a discussion of the major characteristics of unemployment in the United States during nonrecessionary times. First, the *duration* of unemployment is quite short. For example, in 1973, when the unemployment rate was a relatively high 4.9 per cent, more than half of the unemployed were without jobs for less than 5 weeks and less than 8 per cent were unemployed for more than 30 weeks. Second, *job losers* account for less than half of all the unemployed, the remainder consisting of job quitters, new entrants, and reentrants to the labor force. Third, *turnover* is extremely high, especially in manufacturing, where "total hirings and separations have each exceeded 4% of the labor force per month for more than a decade."[8] Lastly, most layoffs are brief and *temporary*. The average manufacturing company rehires about 85 per cent of those it lays off.

All of these factors are very important for understanding the effects of the UI system on unemployment. Consider, for example, the duration of unemployment. The total amount of unemployment in the economy is the sum over all individuals of the number of times they are unemployed multiplied by the average duration of their spells of unemployment. Therefore, unemployment can be increased by either increasing the number of spells of unemployment or lengthening the duration of the spells. Feldstein stresses that, in a variety of ways, unemployment insurance has both of these effects.

The Effects of UI on the Structure of Employment

According to Feldstein, the negative aspects of UI affect not only the unemployed worker but the structure of employment as well. UI benefits are financed by a payroll tax which tends to vary with the amount of labor turnover of the particular firm. However, because this "experience rating" system is imperfect, former employees of firms with high turnover can receive UI benefits well in excess of the tax cost to the firm.[9] This creates an incentive for both employers and employees to structure employment with too much seasonal and cyclical variation and too many casual jobs. It has this effect because the net wage to employees (wages plus unemployment benefits) exceeds the cost to employers. "Because the price of unstable labor has been artificially subsidized, employers organize production in a way that makes too much use of unstable employment. Similarly, the economy as a whole consumes relatively too much of the goods that are produced in this way," because the prices of these goods are artifically low.[10]

Likewise, workers may be induced to accept seasonal, cyclical, or temporary jobs, even knowing they are likely to be laid off, because they know that unemployment benefits will be available to supplement their lost income. The net effect is the preservation and expansion of the *secondary sector* of the dual labor market, with its low wages, poor working conditions, layoffs, little chance for advancement, and high turnover.[11]

In the absence of unemployment compensation, most workers could be induced to accept unstable work only if the wages were sufficiently higher than those in available stable employment so as to compensate for the greater probability of becoming unemployed. Similarly, if employers had to pay the full cost of UI benefits, they would tend to incur the expense

---

8 Feldstein, *Harvard Business Review,* p. 53.

9 Zell, "Unemployment Insurance Part I," pp. 13, 16-17, footnote 18, and discussion later in the present article.

10 Feldstein, *The Public Interest,* p. 34.

11 See Zell, "Recent Developments in The Theory of Unemployment," pp. 7-10.

Table 1
REPLACEMENT OF LOST AFTER-TAX WAGES BY UI BENEFITS
(Kansas City, Mo., 1975)*

	Hourly Wage			
	$3/Hour	$4/Hour	$5/Hour	$6/Hour
1. Gross Wage Income - 52 weeks of work	$6,240	$8,320	$10,400	$12,480
2. Gross Wage Income - 39 weeks (without UI)	4,680†	6,240	7,800	9,360
3. Gross Wage Lost	1,560	2,080	2,600	3,120
4. After-Tax Income - 52 weeks	5,902	7,292	8,789	10,292
5. After-Tax Income - 39 weeks	4,691†	5,902	6,922	8,049
6. Net Wage Lost	1,211	1,390	1,867	2,243
7. UI Benefit	1,014	1,105	1,105	1,105
8. Net Total Income Lost	197	285	762	1,138
9. Replacement Rate (#7 ÷ #6) %	84	79	59	49
10. Implicit Tax Rate [100−(#8 ÷ #3) 100] %	87	86	71	64

*Calculations assume 13 weeks of unemployment. After-tax income is net of all Federal, State, and local income taxes and the Social Security tax.
†After-tax income exceeds gross wage income due to low-income allowance.

of improved scheduling, greater inventory variability, more off-season work, and new technology so as to reduce the instability of employment. Finally, consumer demand for the output of these firms would fall as their prices rose, further reducing the amount of unstable employment.

The Effects of UI on the Duration of Unemployment

The second side of Feldstein's argument pertains to the work disincentive effects of unemployment compensation. Feldstein dismisses as a myth the often cited figure that UI benefits replace, on the average, about one-third of lost weekly wages. The flaw in these data, he notes, is that they ignore the fact that wages are taxed while UI benefits are not. Taking into consideration Federal and state income taxes and the Social Security tax, Feldstein found in his initial research that UI benefits in the state of Massachusetts for a family of four would replace more than 80 per

cent of the wages lost from an additional week of unemployment. Under some special circumstances, the wage replacement figure might even exceed 100 per cent.

Criticized on the grounds that Massachusetts was an atypical state, Feldstein calculated wage replacement ratios for all states and for 13 different family types. His findings confirmed his initial results. Men and women with median earnings for their state were entitled to unemployment benefits which replaced, respectively, over 60 per cent and over 70 per cent of lost weekly after-tax wages. Furthermore, the income replacement effect is greater for those persons with lower-than-average earnings; e.g., men and women whose income was only 70 per cent of the median for their state had replacement rates of 69 per cent and 78 per cent, respectively.

Similar calculations for Kansas City, Mo., in 1975 also confirm Feldstein's findings (Table 1). In each of four cases, a married worker, earning either $3, $4, $5, or $6 per hour, was assumed to have two dependent children and a nonworking spouse. Consider the worker who earned $3 per hour. If he worked 52 weeks during the year, his gross wage income would have been $6,240. Had he been unemployed for 13 weeks, this would have dropped to $4,680, yielding a loss of $1,560. This, however, represents his lost *gross* wages. Taking into consideration his reduced liability for Federal, state, and local income taxes and the Social Security tax, the amount of lost *net* wages would total only $1,211. His UI benefit entitlement of $1,014 for 13 weeks of unemployment would therefore replace 84 per cent of this net *wage* loss yielding a net *income* loss of only $197. Looked at another way, since working an extra 13 weeks yields the worker $1,560 of additional *gross* income, but only $197 of additional *net* income, the implicit tax rate on this extra work is 87 per cent. By staying unemployed 13 weeks rather than 12 weeks, the worker would actually lose only $15.20, or $0.38 per hour.

Distributional and Unemployment Effects

Feldstein uses his results to examine two important questions: (1) What groups in the population benefit most from the present structure of UI benefits? and (2) What are the total effects on unemployment of the distortions introduced by UI?

On this second question, Feldstein provides some rough estimates of the magnitudes that might be involved.

For example, a reduction of three weeks in the average ten-week spell of insured unemployment would lower the overall unemployment rate by 0.75 [percentage points]. If one-third of the purely seasonal unemployment were avoided, the overall unemployment rate would fall by an additional 0.25 [percentage points]. Reducing the cyclical variation in labor demand by 20% would reduce average unemployment by another 0.25 [percentage points].[12]

Given a labor force of almost 94 million persons, these changes could represent a decrease in unemployment of almost 1.2 million persons.[13]

Regarding the first question, if it were true that the poor are the greatest beneficiaries of UI benefits, some of the distortions introduced by the system might be justified. Unfortunately, this is not the case. In a study using 1970 data, Feldstein discovered that, "Half of the benefits go to the families in the top half of the income distribution. Fifteen per cent of the benefits . . . went to the 18 per cent of families with incomes over $20,000. Only 17 per cent of the benefits went to families with incomes under $5,000."[14] Some of the reasons given for these surprising facts pertain to the different employment characteristics of poor workers relative to those with higher incomes, as well as to the basic structure of the UI system. When unemployed, poor workers are more likely to have quit their last job, to have worked too little to earn sufficient wage credits, or to have worked in employment not covered by the UI system. Even when qualifying for benefits, poor workers will frequently qualify for less than the maximum duration and will more often exhaust their benefits. Middle and higher income workers, on the other hand, will be entitled to higher benefits, will more often have two wage earners in a family, thus increasing the risk of unemployment, and be more likely to be laid off only temporarily and recalled by the same firm.

In addition to the fact that middle and higher income workers receive a dispro-

---

[12] Feldstein, *Harvard Business Review*, p. 58.

[13] The research of Stephen Marston and of Kathleen Classen, discussed below, presents alternative interpretations and estimates of these changes.

[14] Feldstein, *National Tax Journal*, p. 237.

portionate share of UI benefits, a further distortion is added by the tax system. Because higher income families are in higher income-tax brackets, the tax savings resulting from the fact that UI benefits are not taxed go far more than proportionately to these higher income families. Thus, while 29 per cent of all families earned over $15,000 in 1970, they received 34 per cent of the UI tax savings. On the other hand, the 28 per cent of all families with incomes below $5,000 received only 15 per cent of the tax savings.[15]

If unemployment benefits were taxed as income, the Government would receive about $1 billion in additional revenue (in nonrecessionary periods) and part of the regressivity of UI benefits would be reversed. Furthermore, the work disincentive effect of UI payments would be somewhat reduced. For example, in Kansas City, Mo., the effective tax rate on the income earned by accepting a job after 12 weeks of unemployment rather than 13 weeks would drop from 87 per cent to 76 per cent for the worker earning $3 per hour, if UI benefits were taxable.

RESOLVING THE CONTROVERSY

While many of Feldstein's findings pertaining to disincentive effects on individuals and firms are intuitively persuasive, his claims for their magnitude, especially in the aggregate, have been extensively debated. Much of the early criticism of his research, however, was based more on differing views of the structure and operation of the labor market than on contradictory empirical results.[16]

The two most important criticisms were, first, that there was little evidence confirming the significant effect of the UI system on either the duration of unemployment or the amount

of seasonal, cyclical, or unstable employment in the economy. Second, it was argued, whatever effects there were on unemployment duration, they would be unlikely to be of such magnitude as to significantly affect the overall unemployment rate. While data problems continue, especially regarding the effects of UI on the structure of employment, recent research has greatly clarified the duration issue and other important questions about the impact of the UI system.

Recent Research on Duration

In a 1975 study for the Brookings Institution, Stephen T. Marston developed a sophisticated model for estimating the effects of UI benefits on the duration of unemployment.[17] Like Feldstein, Marston compared the duration of unemployment of insured and uninsured workers, hoping to estimate the disincentive effects of UI benefits. Correctly criticizing Feldstein for misinterpreting published duration data, Marston adjusted these data through a complex procedure which he hypothesized would yield more accurate results. In this manner, Marston calculated that unemployment insurance lengthens the expected duration of completed spells of unemployment for the insured by between 15.7 per cent and 31.4 per cent. The net effect of this, according to Marston, would be to raise the overall unemployment rate by about 0.2 to 0.3 percentage points. This contrasts with Feldstein's rough estimate that the unemployment rate might be lowered by 0.75 percentage points by reducing the effect of UI benefits on unemployment duration.

Numerous problems exist, however, in interpreting Marston's results. The most important of these problems is inherent in any comparison of insured and uninsured workers. Basically, most insured unemployed workers

[15] *Ibid.*
[16] See *Comments* by R. A. Gordon, Bennett Harrison, Charles C. Holt, Hyman Kaitz, and Frank C. Pierson, and Feldstein's reply in Feldstein, *Lowering the Permanent Rate of Unemployment.* pp. 56-101.

[17] Stephen T. Marston, "The Impact of Unemployment Insurance on Job Search," *Brookings Papers on Economic Activity.* 1975: 1.

are job losers. On the other hand, the uninsured unemployed have either quit, been fired for misconduct, are new entrants or reentrants to the labor force, have not earned sufficient wage credits, or worked in uncovered employment. Furthermore, even the job loser group studied is a special group of such workers, since many job losers never become unemployed at all. Thus, besides the adjustments made by Marston to compensate for the differing demographic characteristics of the two groups, it is extremely difficult, if not impossible, to disentangle behavioral differences due to being an insured worker from those due to being a job loser.[18]

Other difficulties also exist with Marston's study. Because of problems with the restrictive nature of available data, Marston was required to use extremely "complex and often arbitrary techniques [to] circumvent these problems."[19] As a consequence, it is difficult to assess the accuracy of his results or to interpret their meaning. For example, by adjusting for factors allegedly omitted by Marston, Feldstein deduces from Marston's figures that UI, operating solely through extended duration, causes an increase of 0.69 percentage points in the overall unemployment rate.[20] Similarly, Hall notes that other findings of Marston's show that right after exhausting benefits, the rate of leaving unemployment rises rapidly. "Part of that increase clearly consists of people who leave the labor force, but part clearly consists of those who take jobs. If every insured worker were delaying his exit from unemployment to the same degree as,

apparently, do those who have exhausted their benefits, unemployment insurance would be lengthening unemployment substantially."[21] Marston does make the excellent point that in an economy with limited employment opportunities, shortening the unemployment duration of some workers by eliminating UI might well result in the displacement of other workers, thus reducing the aggregate effect on unemployment. Nevertheless, it appears that there are more fruitful approaches that can be taken to examine the duration issue.

One such approach is found in a study conducted by Kathleen Classen of the Public Research Institute of the Center for Naval Analyses. For her study, Classen had the advantage of a body of data which permits the examination within a single state of similar individuals who receive different benefit amounts. In Pennsylvania, benefits were significantly increased in 1968 only for those workers earning above a specified level. By examining a sample of claimants who filed the year before and the year after the change in the benefit schedule, Classen was able to estimate the effects of an increase in weekly benefit amount (WBA) on the duration of unemployment while avoiding many of the pitfalls inherent in other data sources.[22]

Looking first at aggregate data, Classen found a significant rise in the duration of unemployment for that group of individuals entitled to a WBA increase (of $15 from $45 to $65). On the other hand, those claimants entitled to only a very small benefit increase experienced an actual decline in unemployment duration. Studying the data through regression analysis confirmed these initial findings. Specifically, a $10 increase in WBA resulted in a 1.1 week increase in the average

---

[18] See *Comments* by Robert C. Hall, pp. 51-52 and by Feldstein, pp. 52-58 in Marston, "The Impact . . . ". Both give several reasons why job losers would be likely to suffer shorter periods of joblessness than other unemployed workers, irrespective of UI benefits. If this is true, then Marston's study underestimates the true insured-uninsured duration differential.

[19] Kathleen Classen, p. 11, and Feldstein, *Comments*, pp. 54-56.

[20] Feldstein, *Comments*, pp. 54-55.

---

[21] Hall, *Comments*, p. 50.

[22] In an appendix to her Pennsylvania work, Classen examined similar data for Arizona and obtained strikingly similar results despite major differences between the UI systems of the two states.

unemployment duration of all claimants. Furthermore, when persons who were recalled by their former employers were excluded from the sample (on the grounds that their unemployment duration was largely determined by their employer and thus not a function of their WBA), the length of time by which duration was extended by a $10 rise in WBA climbed to 1.6 weeks. If these relationships are applicable to the nation as a whole they would imply that a $10 increase in WBA for all covered workers would have increased the unemployment rate for these workers by about 0.6 percentage points, a very large increase.[23]

Other Research

Several researchers, including Classen, have examined the related question of whether increased UI benefits result in longer and more productive job search, and, thereby, in better worker-job matches. If this is the case, it might be argued that the benefits deriving to society from improved job matches would more than compensate for the increased duration of unemployment.[24] Four papers dealing with this issue were presented at the Symposium on the Economics of Unemployment Insurance, held at the University of Pittsburgh on April 8-9, 1976.[25] The basic question examined by these papers was whether there was a positive relationship between UI benefits and, presumably as a result of increased job search, post-unemployment wages. The results ranged from no (Classen), to strongly yes for older men (Ehrenberg - Oaxaca).

In an incisive commentary on these papers, however, Professor Finis Welch of UCLA showed that none of the studies really proved its case.[26] During the examination of data provided by the "real" world, econometric difficulties combine with institutional factors to enormously complicate the estimation procedure. For example, state benefit formulas determine a claimant's WBA as a direct function of his pre-unemployment wages. Thus, by trying to find a relationship between WBA and post-unemployment wages, one is actually estimating the relationship between pre- and post-unemployment wages. Not surprisingly, this relationship is strong and positive. This finding, however, reveals little about the relationship between UI benefits and job-search productivity. Furthermore, Welch noted, the fact that employers must initially pay (through higher taxes) for increased UI benefits could very well lower, over time, the entire schedule of wages employers are willing to offer. Since both pre- **and** post-unemployment wages could be lowered by increasing UI benefits (though not necessarily to the same degree), a theoretical case can be made for either a positive or a negative relationship between UI benefits and post-unemployment wages. Whatever the results, however, they would yield no clear information on the productivity of job search. It appears, therefore, that much more work must be done before a definite relationship between UI benefits and productive job search can be determined.

In addition to the above questions, many other important UI issues have yet to be examined in depth. Frank Brechling has

---

[23] Including the SUA program (see Part II), over 90 per cent of the labor force is employed in or unemployed from covered industries. While there are some econometric problems with Classen's methodology, it appears that her findings are of the right order of magnitude.

[24] As noted on page 15, however, subsidization of job search can be justified only if the benefits to society from this increased search do not simultaneously accrue to the searcher who would otherwise be likely to search the optimum amount in the absence of subsidies.

[25] Kathleen Classen, "Effects . . . "; Jerry L. Kingston and Paul L. Burgess, "Unemployment Insurance and Earnings Changes From the Preunemployment to the Postunemployment Year"; Arlene Holen, "Effects of Unemployment Insurance Entitlement on Duration and Job Search Outcome"; and Ronald G. Ehrenberg and Ronald L. Oaxaca, "Unemployment Insurance, Duration of Unemployment, and Subsequent Wage Gain."

[26] Finis Welch, "What Have We Learned From Empirical Studies of Unemployment Insurance?", unpublished paper presented at the Symposium.

conducted an extensive theoretical study designed to discover the incentive effects on individual firms of the unemployment insurance tax as it currently operates in most states.[27] Brechling theorizes, for example, that the structure of the current experience rating system of UI taxation affects the hiring and layoff policies of firms in a complicated manner with potentially strong policy implications. The actual magnitude of these effects, however, remains to be estimated.

A related issue is that of determining who ultimately pays the tax cost of financing unemployment insurance. While employers initially pay the UI payroll tax, it is unlikely that they absorb all of the cost. Some of it is certainly passed on to consumers in the form of higher prices. In addition, much of it may be indirectly paid by labor in the form of lower wage offers made by employers, substitution of capital for labor in some processes, and the reluctance of employers to hire from groups with a history of high turnover.[28] Furthermore, because some industries have very high turnover while others have very stable employment, there is an implicit cross-subsidization among industries and a potential distortion in the use of the nation's resources. The issues involved in these and other questions are very complicated, however, and much more theoretical and empirical work must be done before the magnitude of the effects can be estimated and the related policy implications assessed.

SUMMARY AND CONCLUSIONS

In this final article of a three-part series on unemployment insurance, some of the

[27] Frank Brechling, "The Incentive Effects of the U.S. Unemployment Insurance Tax," PRI 173-75, June 1975, and "Unemployment Insurance Taxes and Labor Turnover: Summary of Theoretical Findings," PRI 75-5, December 1975, Public Research Institute.

[28] For a preliminary theoretical study of this issue, see Charles E. McLure, Jr., "The Incidence of the Financing of Unemployment Insurance," unpublished paper, Department of Economics, Rice University.

important issues regarding the unintended effects of the UI system have been examined. Ever since the inception of the system, economists have been concerned that the payment of UI benefits might result in a reduction of work effort or in an increase in unemployment duration. This possibility was recently highlighted by Martin Feldstein of Harvard University.

In his controversial 1972 congressional testimony, Feldstein illustrated how UI benefits replace most of the after-tax income that is lost from being unemployed. Feldstein also noted that because the system permits workers to receive benefits in excess of the cost to their former employers, an excessive amount of seasonal, cyclical, and temporary employment is encouraged. Much of the research done since then has attempted to either support or contradict Feldstein's findings and methodology.

Of the issues involved in the UI controversy, the one receiving the closest scrutiny has been the effect of UI on the duration of unemployment. While Feldstein suggested the potential for such an effect, he never accurately estimated its magnitude. Recent research, especially that studying the marginal effect on duration of increasing benefits, seems to indicate that UI benefits are responsible for a sizable increase in the duration of unemployment of the insured unemployed.

On the question of whether this extended unemployment duration is spent in productive job search (yielding higher post-unemployment wages), the results are unclear. A theoretical case can be made for expecting either a positive or a negative relationship between unemployment benefits and post-unemployment wages. Furthermore, the very formulas by which UI benefit levels are determined (i.e., based on pre-unemployment wages) may make the empirical estimation of this relationship impossible using available data. Clearly, new experiments will have to be developed to deal with this issue.

C. Economic Security

The Challenge to Mandatory Retirement

By NORMAN J. WOOD

Professor of Economics, University of Georgia.

A NEW CIVIL RIGHTS effort is slowly developing in the courts,
the Congress and state legislatures. The goal of this movement
is to abolish the accepted practice of forcing workers to retire at a
certain age without regard to their physical or mental condition or
their desire to continue work.

Recently, a three-judge federal panel in Massachusetts held that
a state statute which requires members of the state police force to
retire at age 50 discriminates on the basis of age and therefore is
unconstitutional.[1] The District Court ruled that the forced retirement
of Robert D. Murgia, a state police lieutenant colonel, violated the
guarantees of due process and equal protection provided by the Four-
teenth Amendment of the Constitution. The U. S. Supreme Court
has agreed to consider the state's appeal.

The campaign against mandatory retirement raises extremely
difficult social issues. On the one hand, it can be argued that mandatory retirement condemns able older workers to a life of enforced
idleness and deprives society of their talent and experience.

On the other hand, defenders of mandatory retirement argue that
it is necessary in order to create job openings and promotion opportunities for younger people. Employers also contend that it would
be more difficult to carry out federal directives to increase the hiring

---

[1] *Murgia v. Commonwealth of Massachusetts*, 8 EPD ¶9519 (DC Mass. 1974).

Norman J. Wood, "The Challenge to Mandatory Retirement." *Labor Law Journal,* July 1976, pp.
437–440. Reprinted with permisison of the author and the publisher. Reproduced from the July 1976
issue of the *Labor Law Journal,* published and copyrighted 1976 by the Commerce Clearing House,
Inc., 4025 W. Peterson Avenue, Chicago, Illinois 60646.

of women and minorities without mandatory retirements. They further argue that their inability to set retirement rules would wreak havoc with pension plans in which contributions are calculated on the basis of a predictable number of workers retiring at a fixed age. Hence both businesses and unions, while often expressing sympathy for older people who want to work, usually oppose efforts to ban mandatory retirement.

The courts, Congress, and state legislatures have generally supported mandatory retirement. The *Murgia* case is believed to be the first in which a court has endorsed a constitutional argument against mandatory retirement. In two earlier cases, the Supreme Court ruled against older workers appealing adverse judgments by lower courts.[2]

[2] *McIlvaine v. Pennsylvania State Police*, 6 EPD ¶ 8860 (Pa. Sup. Court, 1973) and *Weisbrod v. Lynn,* 9 EPD ¶ 10,001 (Dist. of Columbia, 1974).

Counsel for defendants in mandatory retirement cases have argued that retirement rules, whether resulting from laws or company policies, imply that a person is unable to continue working because of age. They further contend that age is only a crude measure of a person's physical and mental abilities, qualities which can be measured only by individual examinations—that a person is constitutionally entitled to work, and the test of whether he is able to do so should not be his age. They argue further that there is no statutory age associated with the ability to work—a worker may be in good health at age 70 or in poor health at age 35. Defenders of the present system insist there is at least a general correlation between age and the ability to work, and contend that employers have little choice except to use age as a neutral guideline in establishing retirement rules.

In the *Murgia* case, the District Court found undisputed testimony that at the time of his discharge, Robert Murgia was in excellent physical health and was capable of performing the duties of a state police officer, whether involving physical or psychological stress associated with his work. The court therefore held that the only question requiring serious considera-

tion was whether mandatory retirement at age 50 was rationally related to maintaining vigorous and healthy personnel.

The District Court said that since officers were given comprehensive physical examinations annually, the arbitrary standard of mandatory retirement at age 50 was not a reasonable one. The court drew a parallel with the *LaFleur*[3] case, by stating that where individualized medical screening was not only available but required, mandatory retirement at age 50 was no more related to a protectable state interest than the mandatory discharge of school teachers in their fourth month of pregnancy. Furthermore, the court found that Massachusetts state police records showed the rate of discharge of officers for non-injury disability was no greater at ages 48 or 49 than at ages 40 or 41; in fact, it was lower for the 48 and 49 year old officers during the five years prior to Robert Murgia's mandatory retirement. From these statistics, the court concluded that there was no reason to believe that age 50 is within, or even significantly approaching, a range where changes of conditions warrant a change of

[3] *Cleveland Board of Education v. LaFleur*, 7 EPD ¶ 9072 (U. S. Supreme Court, 1974).

treatment—rather, the statistics contradict that supposition.

How is the Supreme Court likely to rule in the *Murgia* case? In two recent cases the court has upheld mandatory retirement. Early in 1975 it rejected the appeal of a 70-year-old former federal employee who sought to overturn the government's mandatory retirement rules as an unconstitutional "irrebuttable presumption" that an older person wasn't fit to work.[4] A federal District Court had dismissed the employee's claim, stating that, although the employee was fully qualified both physically and mentally, the Supreme Court's decision in a case with substantially similar questions was that mandatory retirement age provisions were not "suspect" nor were they an "irrebutable presumption" of incompetency. Thus far, the Supreme Court has declined to consider the legal theory that mandatory retirement discriminates against older workers in violation of the Constitution's equal protection clause. In March, 1974, the court dismissed the appeal of a 60-year-old Pennsylvania state trooper who was fighting his forced retirement partially on the grounds of equal protection.[5]

Lower courts have been just as zealous in upholding mandatory retirement. In January, 1975, an Arizona court upheld the compulsory retirement, at age 65, of a highly regarded junior high school teacher.[6] In the same month, a Nevada court also upheld the forced retirement of a teacher,[7] and a California court, in December, 1974, upheld the forced retirement at age 55 of a National League baseball umpire.[8] Further,

the courts have firmly upheld the involuntary retirement provisions of the Age Discrimination in Employment Act. This Act contains an exception for any "bona-fide" employment benefit plan such as retirement, pension, or insurance plan, which is not a subterfuge to evade the purposes of the Act.[9] In a case involving the Taft Broadcasting Company, a federal court ruled that the company could require employee retirement at age 60 because that provision was part of a "bona-fide" pension plan.[10]

Legislation

Opponents of mandatory retirement hope to persuade federal and state legislators to change laws that sanction the present system. In Congress, Senators Church (D. Idaho) and Fong (R. Hawaii) are sponsoring a bill that would extend to persons over 65 the current federal protections against age discrimination in hiring, firing, and promotions. In the House, Representative Findley (R. Illinois) is sponsoring a bill banning mandatory retirement. A bill to ban forced retirement was introduced in the Illinois State Legislature in 1975, and passed the state house, but died in the senate.

In finding for Robert Murgia, the Massachusetts District Court stated that "the only question requiring serious consideration is whether mandatory retirement at age 50 is rationally related to maintaining a vigorous, healthy personnel." Even the plaintiff's expert witnesses conceded that there was a general relationship between advancing age and decreasing physical ability to respond to the demands of the job. On the other hand, the state did not dispute the expert's testimony that the relationship between chronological age and functional age varies greatly from one individual to another. The state's position was that in matters of this

---

[4] *Weisbrod v. Lynn,* cited at note 2.
[5] *McIlvaine v. Pennsylvania State Police,* cited at note 2.
[6] *Lewis v. Tucson School District No. 1,* 9 EPD ¶ 9944 (Ariz. Ct. of Appeals, 1975).
[7] *Clark Co. School District v. Beebe,* 9 EPD ¶ 1030 (Nev. Sup. Ct., 1975).
[8] *Steiner v. National League of Professional Baseball Clubs,* 8 EPD ¶ 9800 (DC Calif., 1974).

[9] *Age Discrimination in Employment Act of 1967,* 29 U.S.C. 623.
[10] *Brennan v. Taft Broadcasting,* 7 EPD ¶ 9232 (DC Ala. 1973).

nature it is administratively reasonable to select an arbitrary cut-off, and that irrationality is not established by the fact that certain individuals are thereby disadvantaged. In upholding Robert Murgia's claim the District Court further stated that "individual testing is not impracticable, but rather is the order of the day. There is no suggestion that it is more burdensome to examine an officer at age 50 than it was at age 49."

There are literally thousands of state statutes which create classifications permanent in duration, which are less than perfect, and which might be improved upon by individualized determinations. Countless state and federal statutes draw lines similar to those drawn by mandatory retirement regulations, which under the District Court's line of analysis in *Murgia* might well be considered arbitrary in individual cases.

State codes, for example, draw lines with respect to age for several purposes: voting, marriage, the purchase of alcoholic beverages, permission to operate a motor vehicle, etc. Nothing in the District Court's opinion clearly demonstrates why its logic would not equally well sustain a challenge to these laws from a 17-year-old who insist that he is just as well informed for voting purposes as an 18-year-old, or from numerous other persons who fall on the outside of lines drawn by these and similar statutes.

All legislation involves the drawing of lines. This necessarily results in particular individuals who are disadvantaged by the lines drawn being, for many purposes, virtually indistinguishable from those individuals who benefit from the legislative classification. The *Murgia* case raises the difficult question of whether individualized determination would represent a triumph for civil rights or whether it would represent nothing less than an attack upon the lawmaking process itself.   **[The End]**

Future Dimensions
in Pension Legislation

By JACOB K. JAVITS

U. S. Senator, R. - New York

THE NEW PENSION REFORM LAW is a major achievement towards advancing greater participation of workers in our nation's economy by guaranteeing them greater retirement security under private pension programs. But, it is not enough to celebrate the enactment of landmark pension law or to recount the series of hard-fought legislative triumphs that made it possible.

What is needed is some plain talk about what has to be done to make the law work effectively. What does the private sector need to do to strengthen the value of the private plan in the midst of those whose demands led to reform in the first place? What are the elements that will make the law work? What will assist in the sound expansion of pension plans for workers? What will increase the social usefulness of pension plans?

First, I suggest it would be useful if there existed a detente between those who administer the plans and the agencies charged with administering the law. It seems to me wide of the mark to rekindle the flames of controversy over each provision of the new law which some elements of the private sector find distasteful. Instead, every effort should be made to exhaust the available administrative procedures before concluding that specific provisions are unworkable or that the rationale behind them is faulty. These judgments cannot and should not be made on a fragmentary experience of administering the law or on the basis of self-serving "scare" tactics.

Second, and here I refer specifically to the controversy brewing over the fiduciary standards, it should not be lightly assumed that dilution of these standards, either in terms of prohibited conflicts of interest or in terms of personal liability for imprudent investments, is a matter that will be fully understood or appreciated by those who are beneficiaries of the plans and who have entrusted *their* hard-earned pension funds to the supervision of supposedly loyal and competent managers.

Trustee Liability

Those who are advising pension fund trustees to resign in order to avoid potential liability for their decisions not only completely misin-

Jacob K. Javits, "Future Dimensions in Pension Legislation." *Labor Law Journal*, July 1975, pp. 391–395. Reprinted with permission of the author and the publisher. Reproduced from the July 1975 issue of the *Labor Law Journal*, published and copyrighted 1975 by the Commerce Clearing House, Inc., 4025 W. Peterson Avenue, Chicago, Illinois 60646.

terpret the scope of the "prudent man" rule, but also do a great disservice to the pension industry as a whole. They misinterpret the prudent man rule because they erroneously assume that a mistake in judgment by a trustee is grounds for a lawsuit against him.

I can assure you that was not the intent of the Congress, and every lawyer who has made a careful study of the law and its history knows this to be true. Certainly, personal liability attaches when a trustee is guilty of negligence, mismanagement, or worse—as for any fiduciary. But, liability does not attach because a trustee failed to be clairvoyant.

Further, those who are advising trustees to resign cannot help but create the public impression that the reason trustees cannot function under the new law is not because its requirements are onerous or unusual. Rather, the impression is left that the majority of such trustees are incompetent. Since nothing could be further from the truth, I suggest this approach is no way to build confidence in the private enterprise system.

If this attitude persists, it may well be that the only appropriate way to amend the law would be by constructing a federal legal list of proper investments for pension trustees—similar to the rule in New York with respect to the administration of widow's estates.

Handling Technical Flaws

In bringing to light the technical flaws in the new law, attention must be given not only to those provisions which unduly burden plan administrators but also to those which present problems to workers. Clearly, there are some provisions which through inadvertence have created technical difficulties. Most of these, I believe, can be handled by administrative procedures. In those cases where this cannot be feasibly accomplished, we will, of course, have to consider appropriate technical amendments to the law.

But, let no one be misled by the use of the word "technical." That is not going to be a subterfuge to whittle down the protections granted to workers. The vast majority of responsible elements in the private sector fully support these protections, and they received overwhelming bipartisan support in Congress. In this regard, I should point out that we often tend to emphasize the complaints of those who are well-financed and articulate. Yet, a review of my correspondence indicates that complaints from workers concerning their problems under the new pension reform law outrun the complaints from plan administrators by a margin of at least 4 to 1.

The pension reform law is a bright spot in what otherwise appears to many to have been a dismal failure of traditional political attitudes. People generally recognize that Congress did its best to be fair to workers and also be practical about how much regulation could be attempted. It is not a perfect law, but there is an enormous reservoir of respect for the determination and dedication by which Congress achieved this conspicuous first step. Accordingly, everything positive the private sector does to strengthen the administration of the new law and improve it in the eyes of workers will have a tremendous effect in strengthening the role of private pension programs and encouraging their expansion.

We should not let the day-to-day problems that spring from the complexities of the law cause us to feel that we can or should turn back the clock to pre-reform days. That would be a tragic error even if it were practically possible; and it is not practically possible. Nor should we let our concerns with administrative problems and agency delays in issuing interpretations and regulations obscure the primary objectives the law seeks to secure. The law will work only if it succeeds in fulfilling these objectives in the minds of 35 million workers covered by private pension plans.

New Challenges

I can fully appreciate the practical problems that lawyers, actuaries, consultants, administrators, etc. are struggling with. But, private pension plans must now prepare to confront new and more profound challenges. These may include proposals for accelerated vesting, portability, greater integration with Social Security, flexible individual retirement schedules, new and redesigned employee profit-sharing and stock ownership programs, expansion of the IRA concept, broader survivor benefits, and employee participation in plan administration.

The pension reform law mandates Congressional studies into a wide range of problems with the view toward developing further legislation. These problems are to be dealt with by a joint Congressional Task Force. They include, among those already mentioned, the question of extending the law's coverage to state and local government plans and the impact of federal preemption of state law, particularly in the welfare plan area. All these areas of inquiry are significant, and on the basis of careful Congressional study could result in further amendments to the pension reform law.

Mandatory Retirement

First, I think that it is becoming increasingly apparent that relatively large numbers of workers are dissatisfied over the concept of a mandatory retirement age, i.e. age 65. It appears that many wish to have the option of retiring on some reasonable income prior to that point, and judging from my mail, just as many would like to

have the option of working beyond age 65.

So far, the mandatory retirement age of 65 has withstood assault in the Supreme Court and under the age discrimination law. This may sound like heresy, but I believe that mandatory retirement at age 65 can no longer be regarded as a sacred cow.

Accordingly, we should begin to grapple with the concept of a flexible retirement age, with all that that implies in terms of pension plan design and the manpower situation. This is not a matter which should be dismissed lightly. The fact of the matter is that many working, as well as older, Americans feel quite strongly on this issue and I have no doubt they will become more vocal as time goes on.

Integration with Social Security

For the last several months, a controversy has raged over the future financing of the Social Security system and about clamping a lid on present benefit levels and cost-of-living additions. Without reviewing here all the various options that have been presented by the various contending parties, I think it is plain to see that lower and middle income workers are feeling the pinch of the higher payroll taxes that have gone into effect. For the first time, serious and legitimate concern has been expressed over the long-term prospects for adequately financing Social Security.

What I find most interesting about this discussion is its virtual indifference to the role that private pension plans have in meeting the retirement security needs of our nation's work force. The notion that Social Security can be substantially revised without impacting heavily on the private pension sector is appalling. I am at a loss to understand why no serious effort has really been undertaken to determine whether a greater role could be played by private pension plans in meeting our nation's retirement income objectives.

For example, a fresh and more useful approach might be to establish a national policy of guaranteeing for every American worker on retirement 75% of his pre-retirement income, with appropriate cost-of-living adjustments. Then, having established that national objective, attention should be paid to rearranging the Social Security system and private pension plans in such a way as to produce the result I have described. In those instances where private plans finance the major portion of this national retirement objective, appropriate offsets to employer and employee payroll taxes should be considered.

Investment Policy

Aside from the fiduciary standards established under the pension reform law, there are no specific guidelines created for the investment of pension funds and none have been proposed. In general, this is in keeping with the essentially private and voluntary nature of the plans and the dynamic characteristics of the funds as a source of capital.

Yet, for some time I have been disturbed over the failure of these huge pension reserves, now in excess of $160 billion, to be invested in the most socially effective manner. There is, of course, a justification on the part of those who argue that market forces are the most rational mechanisms for channeling pension resources and that government intervention with respect to investment guidelines would be tantamount to gross interference with private decisions.

Nevertheless, I am persuaded that some mechanism must be devised to create a more harmonious relationship between the economic power of pension funds and our nation's social needs. In this connection, I have had on the drawing boards for a couple of months, and intend to introduce shortly, a bill which will establish a number of selective tax incentives for pension funds that invest at least 10% of their assets in qualified "housing" investments. This approach may well constitute the only practical solution to the type of problem I have described; and there can be no doubt that the housing market would benefit greatly from an infusion of pension fund money.

Profit-Sharing and Stock Ownership

Finally, we have been hearing a great deal lately about employee stock ownership as a means of solving some of our economic ills. Indeed, a species of a stock ownership proposal appears in connection with the recently enacted tax cut bill. The subject is one which is clouded by confusion and by overinflated promotional claims. But, it is one which, nonetheless, has immense potential significance for both management and labor. It is an area which the labor bar, and indeed the entire trade union movement, has neglected for too long.

It is incumbent on those who play a role in the collective bargaining process to now consider seriously the advantages of spreading corporate ownerism among workers. This would reduce job dissatisfaction, encourage quality production, and strengthen our nation's economy.

The main problem, of course, is to secure greater advantages of profit-sharing and stock ownership for workers without sacrificing or eroding their legitimate claims for adequate wages or salaries and other necessary fringe benefits. This should be done in a manner which maintains a due regard for the special interests of both management and labor and the collective bargaining process. It is that problem which I will attempt to address in future legislation, and which I hope will stimulate wide interest among the labor law bar and the public generally.

Conclusion

I have no doubt that the pension reform law of 1974 will generate substantial legislative additions in the future. The numbers of retired Americans are growing larger every year and have a strong interest in achieving broader pension protection. The law itself will need to be revised and improved. That, of course, was contemplated by the legislation and is inherent in some of the problems that have come to light since its passage.

Of even greater significance, however, are the implications of the older American population explosion. The Congress may need to find, sooner than it thinks, more comprehensive and fundamental solutions to the problems of allocating national resources to the retired while pursuing policies geared to restoring full employment, price stability, and adequate economic growth.

[The End]

Social Security 40 Years Later

by Wilbur J. Cohen

The Social Security program has been improved and extended by the Congress in major respects some 15 times since the law was first enacted in 1935. Very substantial progress has been made. Some setbacks have occurred from time to time.

But the story of the evolution and growth of the Social Security system is one of the most significant and successful illustrations of incremental and pragmatic development in social legislation in the 200-year history of the nation.

The original act provided for only two social insurance programs: old age insurance and unemployment insurance. Over the years, additional insurance protection has been added and the program has come to protect the entire family.

In 1939, survivors insurance was added which provided monthly life insurance payments to the widow and dependent children of a deceased worker. Today, the face value of this life insurance under Social Security is approximately a trillion dollars and is nearly equivalent to the total of all private life insurance in the United States. In addition, some 800,000 young people at any one time are able to finish high school and go to college, even though the breadwinner has died or is disabled or retired since monthly payments are made to the dependents up to age 22 if attending school. Social Security is one of the largest student aid programs in the nation.

In 1956, disability insurance was added to the program. Today, over 1.3 million disabled workers are getting disability benefits. An additional one million persons receive payments as the dependents of such employees. The law now provides medical insurance protection to some 22 million aged persons and several million disabled persons. Both hospital and physicians' services are covered.

Nine out of 10 workers are covered under Social Security, including members of the armed forces, the self-employed, the farmers, and farm workers, domestic help, and just about everyone except certain government employees who are protected by separate systems. Over 90 percent of all people 65 and over

WILBUR J. COHEN is a former secretary of the Department of Health, Education and Welfare and was a member of the original Social Security Board set up under the act. He presently is dean of the College of Education, University of Michigan.

are eligible under the program; 95 out of 100 mothers and children in the country would be entitled to monthly benefits in the event of the death of the main breadwinner in the family; and 85 out of every 100

Wilbur J. Cohen, "Social Security 40 Years Later." *The American Federationist,* December 1975, pp. 9–13. Reprinted with permission.

248

workers would be entitled to disability insurance benefits in the event of total permanent disability.

The Social Security Act was one of the most far-reaching pieces of social legislation ever enacted by Congress. Its passage marked both the end of a long struggle for protecting and enhancing the human rights of the aged, unemployed and dependent children and the beginning of a new era of social reform.

As a former Secretary of Health, Education, and Welfare, I can testify from my personal experience what conscientious and dedicated support the officers and rank and file of the AFL-CIO have given to the basic philosophy and improvement of the Social Security program. While some economists from the Brookings Institution, the University of Chicago, and Harvard University complain about the so-called "regressivity" of the payroll tax, or the possible adverse impact of these taxes on future capital formation, the organized labor movement defends the "earned right" and "contributory social insurance" philosophy which assures workers and their families of the payment of benefits irrespective of the political ups-and-downs in Congress. The strong support of the AFL-CIO for Social Security, health insurance, unemployment insurance, and related social welfare programs has benefitted millions of persons both in and out of the organized labor movement.

In the United States the term "social security" has been used to identify the broad range of programs covered under the Social Security Act. But in popular parlance through the years it has come to be particularly identified with the Old Age Insurance Program (now Old Age, Survivors, Disability, and Health Insurance). When the man on the street today says social security, he is usually referring to the specific program of OASDHI.

It is no exaggeration to say that, in one way or another, the lives of every one of the 215 million people in the United States presently is affected by the overall Social Security program. Today, over 100 million people have worked long enough in employment covered by the Social Security Act to be insured for benefits, and over 32 million individuals regularly receive such benefits each month (OASDHI). In addition, several million individuals currently receive weekly unemployment insurance benefits, some 11 million persons receive welfare checks each month (AFDC), another 4 million aged, blind and disabled persons receive supplemental security income (SSI), some 25 million persons received aid from Medicaid last year, and millions of others receive social services and child welfare services and have their medical bills paid for through the maternal and child health and crippled children's provisions of Social Security.

Social Security has become an accepted part of the American way of life. Over $100 billion was paid out under the Social Security Act last year. Along with other federal, state and private pension and social welfare programs, the total amount being currently disbursed exceeds $15 billion a month—a significant volume of purchasing power which has set a floor under consumer income and moderated the adverse economic impact of the recession on families and the economy.

The widespread acceptance of Social Security is due in large part to the contributory earnings-related social insurance philosophy. This aspect, strongly supported by the AFL-CIO, emphasizes the work ethic and both individual and social responsibility. This philosophy appeals to liberals and conservatives, Democrats and Republicans and most individuals in all socio-economic groups. The federal statutory right to earned benefits without recourse to welfare or resource restrictions appeals to minorities as well as the majority. The low cost of administering the program (only 2 percent of benefits) has made the Social Security program a distinctive and acceptable feature of a free society.

But despite the remarkable achievements, there are many proposals for changes and reforms in the program. Looking ahead, the number of persons age 65 and over will grow from the present 22 million to 30 million by the year 2000 and 50 million by the year 2030. We must begin to consider how to prepare our society for a much greater proportion of older people—perhaps 15 percent of the total population. The long-run implications need imaginative consideration.

The next Advisory Council on Social Security should consider this situation and to present recommendations for the considerations of the President and the Congress.

There are, however, important short-run changes needing prompt attention. The most immediate is congressional action is to increase the maximum earnings base, which is now $15,300 a year, for contributions and benefits. Under the existing law which provides for the automatic increase in wages, this figure is estimated to be about $17,000 in 1977. An increase to about $24,000 in 1977 and succeeding years would result in enough additional income to cover expected expenditures in the near future and rebuild the reserve fund. It is essential that Congress enact such legislation to foreclose anxieties about the future financing of the system.

The most far-reaching legislation needed is the enactment of a national health insurance plan as part of the Social Security system. Those persons like myself who are proponents of public-sector responsibility in a national health insurance plan believe that only through the public sector can equity to all participating individuals be assured. Equity in this context means assurance of similar treatment of individuals in similar circumstances with respect to financing costs, access to the delivery system, adjudication of grievances, and similar matters. Private plans cannot meet all these requirements.

A great deal of opposition to the payroll tax has been engendered recently by staff members of the Brookings Institution, the newer brand of elitist economists, including both right-wingers like Professor Milton Friedman and newspaper columnists and magazine writers. The argument is made that the payroll tax is a "regressive" tax and the system is a "rip-off" on lower-paid workers.

It is said that Social Security contributions are regressive because the wealthy pay smaller percentages of their earned income than do the poor, in contrast to the general income tax, under which the wealthy pay higher percentages. If Social Security collections were taxes for general support of the government, this

charge would be unanswerable; one can hardly imagine that Congress would ever have imposed these levies, or would now allow them to remain on the law books, except as a part of a social insurance system. This charge illustrates, indeed, the fallacy of looking at the two parts of Social Security in isolation from each other, an approach which inevitably distorts the issues and loads the argument.

The issue here is not whether Social Security taxes are regressive but whether the Social Security system taking into account both benefits and contributions, is subject to this charge. The answer is "no."

The benefit formula in OASDHI is so designed as to give a larger return for each dollar of contributions to the low-wage earner than to the high. While there are other factors to be considered, some favoring the poor and some working against them, the net effect of the system is to transfer some income from the more affluent as a group to the less affluent. It is legitimate to argue that the system ought to be made more progressive than it is, as for instance by the introduction of. a government contribution derived from general revenues, but it is not legitimate to argue, by disregarding the benefit payments, that the total system as now structured is regressive.

Another contention which has gained in prominence with the increasing amount of contributions is that, regardless of the liberality of future returns, the present burden is simply more than people in low- and moderate-income brackets ought to bear out of current earnings. It is often pointed out that many of these people pay more in Social Security than in income taxes. Many persons pay more for any number of things than they pay in income taxes, and there is nothing inherently inequitable in charging them

more for the important protections afforded by Social Security than they are charged for the general support of government.

The resolution of these various financing issues is the enactment of a comprehensive national social insurance program, including cash benefits and medical coverage, which will be financed on a tripartite basis with contributions from employers, employees, and general revenues of the federal government.

One of the provisions in the OASDHI program most frequently under attack primarily from conservatives is the test of retirement. This test, indeed, has been a bone of contention for many years with support for its abandonment and for the automatic payment of benefits upon attainment of age 65. The retirement test is the mechanism to determine if a loss of income has occurred due to retirement, its effect being reduction or suspension of benefits for periods in which earnings are above stated amounts. The amounts will be increased to keep up to date with rising earnings by the automatic adjustment provisions in present law and, of course, as in the past they may be further increased by amendments to the law, but the present structure of the test is probably as fair a method as can be devised if retirement is not to be abandoned altogether as a condition of eligibility.

Some people believe, however, that this condition of eligibility is basically unfair in depriving people of benefits for continuing to work after reaching 65, and that it is undesirable because it stands in the way of people on the benefit roll who wish to supplement their Social Security income as much as they can. Those who support the retirement test, as does the AFL-CIO, point out that its abolition would cost the equivalent of a .34 percent increase in the combined employer-employee contribution rate and would benefit less than one-tenth of the people over age 65 who are otherwise eligible for benefits.

They ask whether funds in this amount are better used to supplement the incomes of those who still have substantial earning power or by spreading the funds among the nine-tenths who do not, or cannot, earn enough to bring them within the ambit of the retirement test. Arguments such as these have persisted over the years, but they have no bearing on the soundness or durability of the Social Security system; abolition of the retirement test would aggravate somewhat the problem of financing, but it would no more spell the doom of the program than does retention of the test. Congress has repeatedly considered this issue and concluded that adaptation of the test to fit rising levels of earnings is preferable to its repeal.

A different attack on the retirement test, however, does have destructive implications. This is the contention that if benefits are withheld on account of earnings, they should also be withheld on account of the receipt of private pension payments, dividends, interest, or other unearned income—in other words, that the payment of benefits should be conditioned on a means test. This change would deprive the program of one of its major strengths, its encouragement of people in their working years to supplement their Social Security protection through savings and private pension plans. The change, indeed, would in all likelihood mean the end of contributory social insurance, since the masses of self-supporting people would hardly put up with paying Social Security contributions if they knew they would get nothing in return unless they should ultimately fall into the ranks of the indigent.

The provisions incorporated in the 1939 amendments to provide benefits to wives, widows and dependent parents have been of inestimable value in promoting family security. Since that time the proportion women in the paid labor market has increased. The basic law needs to be reexamined in the light of these changed conditions. The existing discrimination against some women should be eliminated, especially that against divorced women and married women who work for substantial periods of time.

Two benefit improvements need to be made to take account especially of problems arising from the recession: individuals age 55 and over who are totally disabled for their regular and customary work should be entitled to benefits, and those persons between age 60 and 62 should be entitled to draw their Social Security benefits on actuarially reduced amounts.

To assure that the Social Security program is administered without regard to partisan political influence, the program should be placed under a board with terms of office rotated to assure the political independence of the board members.

A major restructuring of our federal-state unemployment insurance system is long overdue. There is an urgent need for a comprehensive national health security program as part of the Social Security system. We need a restructuring of the medical delivery system, a comprehensive system of social services and a national supplemental income system which will underpin all other programs. The need for further reduction in the number of persons in poverty should be a high priority of national policy. A program of full employment is essential to make it possible for all other social programs to operate effectively and efficiently.

In the interim we must improve the present welfare system by providing some kind of national floor in the program for aid to families with dependent children (AFDC), and by authorizing the same kind of automatic device to relate these payments to the increase in the cost of living as exists for OASDHI and SSI.

The $2.5 billion annual limitation established in 1972 on federal financing of social services in Title XX of the Act is clearly inadequate. The goal should be at least $5 billion annually for 1980.

The Social Security program is a sound structure on which we can build and adapt to changing needs. It is one of the institutions we have built with care and intelligence. We have both the economic resources and the administrative capacity to continue to improve it incrementally in relation to our national priorities and productivity.

Despite the remarkable progress made since the original act was passed, President Roosevelt's words are still pertinent—the structure of Social Security is still being built and is by no means complete. The next decade should produce still further improvements in the program.

PROPPING UP SOCIAL SECURITY

The system doesn't have to go broke if Congress would stop playing politics

Attacks on the Social Security system are hardly new. Ever since the program was born in the shadow of the Depression, critics have decried its compulsory nature, charged that it undermined thrift, and insisted that it was just a plain bad buy for the man in the street. But none of these or other criticisms ever succeeded in weakening the great love affair between the American people and the Social Security system, as those politicians who have tried to make curbing the system a political issue have found out to their electoral grief.

Now, however, a new specter haunts Social Security, charges that the system is doomed to bankruptcy in the long run unless there is either a massive increase in already hefty payroll taxes or a major cut in benefits. And because the system is already running somewhat in the red and facing large deficits in the future (chart, page 35), concerns about its financial stability are suddenly credible to a public already shaken by the fiscal crises that have rocked some of the nation's banks, industrial corporations, and municipalities. To make matters worse, complaints about unfair treatment of such groups as working wives and poor wage earners are also on the upswing.

Although there may be more reason to worry about Social Security now than at any time in its 41-year-history, a careful analysis of the system suggests that its outlook is far from catastrophic. As Social Security Commissioner James B. Cardwell puts it: "The public's benefits are not in jeopardy."

But, as Cardwell himself concedes,

there is also little doubt that the program must be modified to remedy potentially damaging defects and restore public confidence. For without such modifications, the imposing edifice carefully built up over many years to underpin the security of the nation's aged could begin to crack at the seams with incalculable damage to the quality and comity of American life.

The urgent issues

Business, which coughed up some $36.3 billion last year as its share of payroll taxes, has a special stake in remedying the situation. Says Victor Zink, director of employee benefits at General Motors Corp.: "Costs and benefits under both the private pension system and Social Security have been rising so rapidly that we've got to start

thinking about integrating them. But we can't make any progress until Social Security's problems are resolved."

Such appeals have not fallen on deaf ears. Congress is already grappling with a number of issues that have taken on urgency in recent years:

- Current projections indicate that the Old Age, Survivors & Disability Insurance (OASDI) trust funds will be exhausted by the early 1980s. (Social Security is backed up by three trust funds—for old age and survivors' insurance, disability insurance, and hospital insurance—which are respectively financed by payroll tax rates of 4.375%, 0.575%, and 0.9% to make up the total 5.85% rate levied on both employees and employers.) The hospital insurance fund is currently in healthy surplus, but during the next 75 years, experts predict a widening deficit for the other two insurance programs that could eventually require a tripling of the current tax rate unless changes in financing and benefits are made.
- A number of economists believe that pay-as-you-go Social Security financing depresses private savings and thus impedes the capital accumulation and investment necessary to insure adequate economic growth. This effect may have been negligible in the past but appears to be intensifying with expansion of the system.
- With the steady rise in the payroll tax rate, the painful impact of Social Security taxes on the working poor has been increasing. As it stands now, these regressive taxes claim a far greater percentage of the earnings of poor and middle-income workers than they do of the well-to-do.
- Complaints about inequities in the Social Security benefit structure are growing louder. Critics claim that it discriminates against working wives, single people, and retirees who must work to make ends meet.

Insiders defend the system

Don Carl Steffen

Cardwell: Benefits are not in jeopardy.

Ball: The system protects against loss of earnings.

Myers: Means testing is demeaning to the elderly.

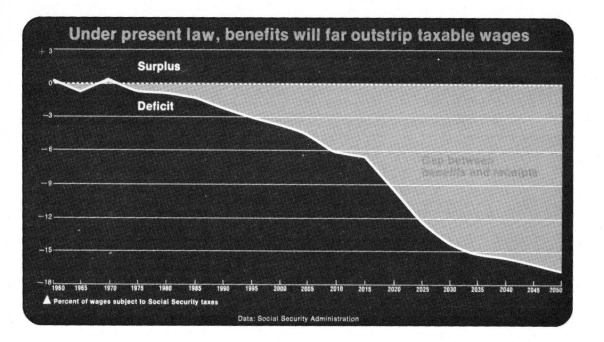

Under present law, benefits will far outstrip taxable wages

Surplus

Deficit

Gap between benefits and receipts

▲ Percent of wages subject to Social Security taxes

Data: Social Security Administration

■ Some observers believe the tension between Social Security's two not entirely consistent goals of providing benefits related to retirees' previous earnings (its insurance function) and lifting all beneficiaries out of poverty (its welfare function) is beginning to undermine the system. Recent reform in public assistance programs, particularly the creation of the supplemental security income program (SSI) may make it feasible to start shifting some of the welfare burden to other programs that are more efficient because they are geared specifically to need.

A floor of protection

To fully understand the system's problems, one must hark back to Social Security's origins in the Depression. Even in those parlous times, many Americans regarded the notion of a government old-age insurance program with suspicion and feared that it would undermine the Puritan virtues of work and thrift. Thus the system that President Roosevelt's braintrusters came up with in the mid-1930s was necessarily something less than a comprehensive program. As Roosevelt himself remarked in signing the Social Security Act of 1935, it was "a cornerstone which is being built, but which is by no means complete."

In its original design, Social Security was a modest insurance scheme financed by compulsory employer and employee contributions to a trust fund that would provide wage-related benefits to workers as a matter of right. Its goal was not to provide the bulk of

retirement income, but only a "floor of protection" to be supplemented by private savings and pensions.

Even before the first Social Security benefits were paid in 1940, however, two critical changes were made that have characterized the system ever since. The first was to put funding on a pay-as-you-go basis with the trust fund acting mainly as a safety buffer in case of economic adversity. One reason for the change was the realization that meaningful pensions could not be paid out for many years if they were to be based mainly on retirees' own contributions.

Relying on current tax receipts to pay for current benefits is not unique to the U. S., but is in fact an earmark of almost every Social Security system. In economic terms, says economist John A. Brittain of the Brookings Institution, Social Security is basically an "intergenerational transfer system" in which today's workers finance the pensions of yesterday's workers in the confidence—confirmed by government legislation—that tomorrow's workers will do likewise. And the financial soundness of such a system is maintained by setting present and future benefit and tax levels in a way that receipts promise to balance expenditures.

The second major change in the original scheme was to emphasize the principle of social adequacy or need. The benefit schedule was weighted in favor of low-income workers by providing them with greater benefits relative to their earnings and contributions than higher-income workers. And retirees with dependent wives got more than

single retirees, regardless of their contributions. Over the years, the tilt favoring low-income earners has been increased by raising the minimum pension considerably.

Social Security experts like to explain the system by terming it social insurance. "Unlike private insurance, social insurance tries to meet the goals of both individual equity and social adequacy, but with emphasis on the latter," notes Robert Myers, former chief actuary of the Social Security Administration. Myers concedes, however, that most Americans tend to believe their taxes pay for their own future benefits.

The benefit bandwagon

This belief, reinforced by Congress' tendency to match each tax boost with a boost in scheduled benefits, is obviously the big reason for Social Security's staunch political support in the past. Though the system has successfully alleviated serious poverty among the elderly, it has also benefited the middle class. In the past 20 years the maximum pension for a newly retiring worker and spouse has jumped from $156 a month to $581. Over the years survivors, disability, and hospital insurance have been added to the original pension package. No less than one out of every seven Americans now receive benefits.

Despite the benefit largesse, however, enthusiasm for Social Security has begun to wane recently in the wake of escalating taxes and charges that the system is on the verge of bankruptcy. "In actuality," says Brittain, "Social Security is backed by the most solid source of funds known, the federal taxing power. The bankruptcy charge is a senseless generator of fear."

The buildup of revenues

Ironically, none of the system's current financial problems were apparent in mid-1972 when Congress passed a hefty 20% boost in benefits. The move came in the wake of a startling finding by the 1971 Social Security Advisory Council that the program was greatly overfinanced and would produce cumulative reserves approaching a trillion dollars by the year 2025, an accumulation the council deemed both "unnecessary and undesirable."

The council's assessment of payroll taxes as a veritable money machine stemmed from an accounting practice that had consistently tended to underestimate tax revenues. In projecting the long-range costs of the program, the Social Security actuary had assumed "for fiscal prudence" that average taxable wage levels would remain stable. Since wage levels inevitably rose, the result was a periodic buildup in revenues that Congress ladled out in higher benefits every few years, usually before elections.

By 1972, however, criticism of the "unrealistic" level-wage assumption had meshed with a desire to protect retirees against the ravages of inflation and concern by economists that the periodic buildup and dispersal of Social Security funds could play havoc with macroeconomic policy. Always ready to sweeten the benefit pot on the eve of an election, Congress responded by passing a bill that mandated "realistic" wage assumptions, doled out the resulting projected actuarial surplus via the 20% benefit boost, and indexed benefits to inflation and maximum taxable wages to future wage movements. "This legislation is financed on a conservative basis," then-Chairman Wilbur Mills of the Ways & Means Committee told the House. "I can assure the membership that we will take in each year more than we will be paying out."

What Mills and his colleagues failed to appreciate was how fragile actuarial assumptions can be. (Ignored in the rush to passage were warnings from former chief actuary Myers that the level-wage assumption provided a desirable margin for error, since it permitted benefit improvements only after—not before—surplus revenues began to materialize.) Almost before it started rolling, the new actuarial ap-

plecart was upset by the surge of double-digit inflation combined with the deepest economic slump since the Depression. Benefits geared to inflation have jumped substantially, while unemployment has cut heavily into revenues. At the same time, disability benefit claims have increased far beyond original projections. As a result of these unanticipated developments, the $44.4 billion OASDI trust funds are expected to pay out some $4.3 billion more than they take in this year and to be virtually exhausted by the early 1980s.

This short-run deficit is not the only financial problem threatening Social Security. Revised actuarial projections in recent years have uncovered a slowly widening long-run deficit that—unless corrected—could put an untenable burden on future generations and result in a doubling or tripling of the Social Security tax rate within 75 years.

The irony is that this deficit is not set in concrete, but results mainly from a mistake in the benefit formula which can be easily corrected if legislators can summon the political will to act. In setting up the automatic benefit escalator in 1972, Congress stipulated that benefits for current and future retirees would both be adjusted periodically to keep pace with inflation and that the maximum taxable wage base would be raised in line with average wages.

An offset to inflation

No one objects to raising benefits for people already retired to keep pace with living costs. The problem is that the 1972 formula also raises scheduled benefits for people not yet retired, whose wages tend to be pushed up by inflation anyhow. And this, in effect, gives current workers a double offset to inflation. To take a simplified example, if living costs rise by 10%, a worker is likely to get a 10% raise, and this automatically boosts his scheduled benefits, which are tied to his earnings. But under the new law, all scheduled benefits would also be raised by 10%. So workers tend to get two inflation adjustments. And if rapid inflation lasts long enough, some could wind up with higher pensions than their former wages.

The problem is exacerbated by long-run demographic trends. As a result of the postwar baby boom, the nation's aged population will climb by some 66%, or 21 million people, between the years 2005 and 2030. At the same time, if present low fertility rates continue, the working population will stabilize or even decline. Under pay-as-you-go fi-

nancing, this means that there may be only a little more than two workers to support each pensioner, compared with 3.2 today. And each worker would necessarily have to shoulder a larger burden in taxes.

Happily there is no shortage of suggestions to cure Social Security's financial woes, though there is considerable ideological debate over which one to adopt. To eliminate the short-term deficit, for example, the Administration has proposed raising the basic payroll tax of 5.85% for employees and employers to 6.15% starting next year—a step that has the support of such business groups as the U. S. Chamber of Commerce and the National Assn. of Manufacturers as the most fiscally responsible solution. But organized labor and liberal Democrats oppose a higher tax rate because of its impact on low- and middle-income workers.

Another proposal is to increase revenues by raising the wage base—the amount of earnings subject to payroll taxes. Such groups as the AFL-CIO and the National Council of Senior Citizens have long favored this idea as a way to reduce the regressiveness of the payroll tax. "Some 97% of covered workers had all of their wages taxed when the program was originally set up," notes Lawrence Smedley, associate director of the AFL-CIO's Social Security Dept. "Now only 85% have all of their wages taxed."

Republicans and the business community are adamant in their opposition, however. For one thing, the wage base has already been rising precipitously from $7,800 in 1971 to $15,300 this year, and it will continue up in line with average wage gains. Then, too, a boost in the wage base would trigger higher future benefits for those whose taxes would go up, and as Commissioner Cardwell comments, "This is hardly prudent when we are concerned with holding down the program's long-term expenditures." Finally, many businessmen worry about the impact on private savings and investment. "The higher the wage base goes, the less funds are available for individual savings and private pensions," warns J. Henry Smith, retired board chairman of Equitable Life Assurance Society of the U. S.

A third option would be to supplement the payroll tax with some form of general revenue financing. Liberal economists have long favored this idea because it partly substitutes progressive income and corporate taxes for the payroll tax. But many critics—including the Ford Administration—feel it would erode the "earned right" nature of the program and result in the loss of

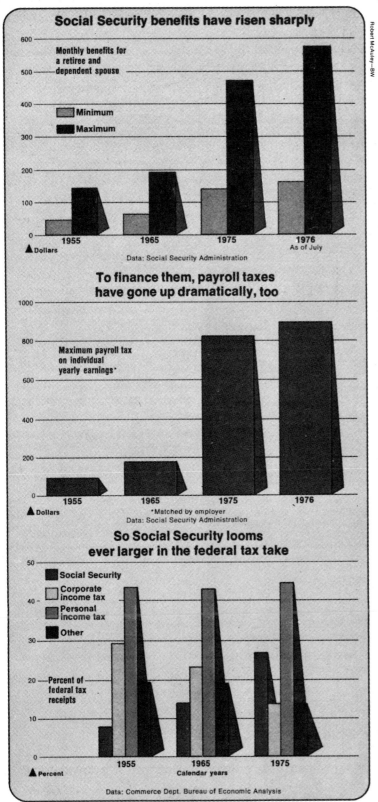

Social Security benefits have risen sharply

Monthly benefits for a retiree and dependent spouse

■ Minimum
■ Maximum

1955   1965   1975   1976 As of July

▲ Dollars

Data: Social Security Administration

To finance them, payroll taxes have gone up dramatically, too

Maximum payroll tax on individual yearly earnings*

1955   1965   1975   1976

▲ Dollars

*Matched by employer
Data: Social Security Administration

So Social Security looms ever larger in the federal tax take

■ Social Security
□ Corporate income tax
▨ Personal income tax
■ Other

Percent of federal tax receipts

1955   1965   1975

▲ Percent

Calendar years

Data: Commerce Dept. Bureau of Economic Analysis

the fiscal discipline that the need to rely on earmarked taxes imposes on Congress's generosity.

Reducing the deficit

Whatever way Congress finds to cover the short-term deficit (a compromise solution is the most likely), it is also likely to act within the next year to reduce the projected long-term deficit. One simple way would be to adopt a 1975 Social Security Advisory Council proposal to change the benefit formula so that it would provide stable replacement ratios. Under this approach, future retirees would receive pensions that are equal to the same percentage of their recent taxable wages as today's new retirees receive. (Current replacement ratios for single workers retiring at 65 range between 62% for someone who earned $3,400 a year to 31% for someone earning $14,100.) Since real wages will inevitably rise in the future as a result of productivity gains, this approach would provide higher average pensions in line with higher living standards.

One difficulty with the council approach is that it does not eliminate that part of the projected deficit occurring in the next century when the retired population grows dramatically. Recently, a Congressional advisory panel headed by Harvard University economist William C. Hsiao suggested an alternative formula that would do just that. The formula would keep the real value of pensions from eroding in the sense that someone earning $10,000 in 1976 dollars 50 years from now would get the same real pension as today's retiree. But it would result in lower average replacement ratios because most wages would have risen considerably in 50 years putting retirees in a lower benefit bracket. "This approach," says Hsiao, "would not only eliminate the threat of a deficit, but with a few other adjustments could result in stable tax rates for the foreseeable future—reducing the chance that future generations would refuse to pay the tax bill for today's workers."

Although the advisory council approach has garnered the widest support so far (the Administration, the AFL-CIO, and the National Assn. of Manufacturers all favor it) a growing number of economists advocate the Hsiao formula. Henry J. Aaron of the Brookings Institution, for example, argues that it "would leave more options open for spending the productivity dividend of economic growth. Congress could still raise pensions in the future, but it could also decide that other programs such as housing, health insurance, or defense have greater claims on available funds." And Harvard economist Martin S. Feldstein likes the Hsiao formula because it would leave more room for private pension plans and individual savings in retirement planning.

Feldstein regards this effect as crucial in light of fears about a pending capital shortage. He believes that the mushrooming growth of Social Security is largely responsible for the fact that the savings rate—that is, the ratio of savings to disposable income—has failed to rise in the postwar period despite the steady climb in incomes. In essence, current workers have decided to save less because they anticipate receiving Social Security pensions and regard their payroll taxes as a form of forced savings. By Feldstein's calculations, Social Security has cut personal savings by 40% to 50%.

Feldstein argues that Congress

has been relatively small, at least until the past few years. "The negative impact has been largely offset by the desire to save for the earlier retirement that Social Security has made possible," she says. Munnell concedes that continued benefit increases could seriously depress savings in the future, but argues that "there are more equitable and efficient ways to stimulate savings and investment than raising payroll taxes."

The impact on the poor

Despite its controversial nature, the notion of building up a larger trust fund to augment savings is likely to receive more attention in the years ahead. Several countries, notably Swe-

den either by raising prices or trimming wage boosts.

Defenders of the system argue that the regressive tax is balanced by the progressive benefit schedule, which gives low-income workers a bigger return on their contributions than higher-income workers. However, a recent study by Brookings' Aaron concludes that the poor actually fare worse than higher-income groups because they tend to start working earlier and thus pay taxes longer, and they die earlier and thus receive benefits for a shorter period.

Economists like Aaron and John Brittain have long argued that the same "ability to pay" criterion that governs the progressive income tax should be applied to Social Security taxes through the use of deductions and low-income allowances—with the tax loss made up out of general revenues. But many Social Security advocates, though sympathetic, have resisted the idea. "It is important for even low-income workers to feel that they have paid something for their benefits," insists Robert Ball, former Social Security commissioner.

Outside economists look at Social Security

Steve Hansen

Hsiao: A formula that ends the threat of a deficit.

Munnell: Phase down the welfare function.

Feldstein: Benefit boosts have dampened saving.

should consider accumulating a larger trust fund to enhance economic growth and to lower the cost burden for future generations. "A 2% rise in the tax rate, he says, "would produce a surplus of $15 billion a year to buy government debt that would otherwise be held by private investors." And the capital formation resulting from such increased savings would result in higher productivity and lower unemployment—all of which would eventually reduce the system's need for tax revenues.

Not everyone agrees with Feldstein's analysis. Back in 1965, for example, two separate studies found that persons covered by private pension plans tend to save more than those not covered. These results suggest that participating in a pension plan (and presumably Social Security) focuses attention on retirement and makes saving for retirement more feasible.

Moreover, recent research by economist Alicia H. Munnell of the Federal Reserve Bank of Boston indicates that Social Security's net effect on savings

den whose trust fund reserves are invested in housing mortages and local government securities, have already taken this tack.

Meanwhile, the call for higher taxes has highlighted another issue that has long rankled economists and social critics: the painful impact of Social Security taxes on poor and middle-income wage-earners. Roughly half of all working Americans shell out more for payroll taxes than they do for income taxes, and last year some 15 million of this group were deemed too poor to pay any federal income taxes at all.

Conservative economist Milton Friedman calls the Social Security tax "the most regressive tax in our tax system." A person earning just $5,000, for example, will have 5.85% of his wages deducted from his paycheck, while a $50,000-a-year man (or woman) will pay less than 2% of his salary. To make matters worse, most economists believe that employees wind up bearing the employer's share of payroll taxes, since employers eventually pass on the bur-

Perhaps predictably, politicians have already found a way to resolve this dilemma. In 1973, Senator Russell B. Long (D-La.) proposed an amendment to the Social Security Act that would provide a fully refundable tax credit to low-income workers with dependent children. The credit was 10% of household earnings up to $4,000 and was phased out at higher income levels. Last year it was finally passed as part of the Tax Reduction Act of 1975, allowing Social Security officials and the public to accept it as more of a step toward a negative income tax than a weakening of the Social Security contributory principle. And now the push is on to extend it to childless individuals who make up the bulk of low wage earners, a move that would subtantially offset the regressive impact of payroll taxes on the working poor.

Congress is also looking more critically at the benefit side of Social Security. Changes in work and retirement patterns in recent decades combined with the hefty growth in benefits have resulted in a rising tide of complaints from groups who feel they are discriminated against by the benefit structure.

One of the hottest issues is the retirement test, which penalizes current pensioners up to 72 years old by reducing their Social Security checks by 50¢ for every dollar they earn over $2,760 (the limit on nonpenalized earnings is raised each year in line with average wages). The elderly bemoan the loss of benefits which their taxes presumably paid for, and claim that it is unfair to penalize those who must work to supplement their Social Security pensions.

The system's defenders insist that such complaints misconstrue the nature of the program. "Social Security was never meant to provide annuities, but to protect people specifically against the loss of earned income," says Robert Ball. The Social Security Administration estimates that eliminating the retirement test would cost more than $6 billion a year and would help only 10% of pensioners.

Dartmouth economist Colin D. Campbell, however, argues that "the earnings test has significantly reduced labor force participation by the elderly. This made sense during the Thirties when jobs were very scarce, but it makes less sense now when enforced retirement can be detrimental to both the elderly and society." Over the long run, Campbell believes that prolonged working careers would actually alleviate financial problems because the working aged would continue to pay Social Security taxes.

A question of equity

Meanwhile, still another benefits issue has taken on urgency in recent years: the question of sexual and "marital" discrimination. For example, the present law insists that husbands must prove dependency in order to qualify for the same dependent's and survivor's benefits that wives can apply for automatically. And the benefit schedule provides far lower pensions to single people and working couples in return for their taxes than it does to couples with a nonworking wife. Because a married man receives an additional 50% of his primary pension to support a dependent wife, a working couple may actually wind up with a smaller combined pension than a couple in which only the husband worked and paid less in taxes than the working couple did.

The 50% wife's benefit, of course, seemed a necessity in the Thirties when incomes were severely depressed and women's participation in the labor force was low. But in an era in which most women work, it has begun to look more and more like a windfall benefit.

Can such equity issues be resolved? The answer is obviously yes—but not overnight. Because most of the proposed solutions involve higher costs not lower ones and because the system is currently in financial distress, progress will necessarily be slow.

The clauses involving sexual discrimination will be the first to go, since recent court decisions suggest that they are illegal anyhow. The retirement test is also likely to be eased soon, though not entirely eliminated. The inequities caused by the dependent wife's benefit are more difficult to resolve. Perhaps the most sensible solution in the light of women's working trends would be to slowly reduce the dependent wife's benefit over a period of several decades, but voters are not likely to applaud this idea.

To many economists, the most attractive long-run solution to Social Security's problems would involve a radical restructuring of the system. In a critique published in 1968 by the Brookings Institution, economists Aaron, Joseph A. Pechman, and Michael K. Taussig put the matter succinctly. Social Security's basic dilemma, they wrote, is that it "has attempted to solve two problems with one instrument: How to prevent destitution among the aged poor, and how to assure people [who had] adequate incomes before retirement, benefits that are related to their previous standard of living. The earnings replacement function calls for benefit payments without an income test. Basic income support, on the other hand, can be carried out most efficiently if payments are confined to households with low income."

The ultimate solution that the authors prescribed for this dilemma was to assign Social Security's two functions to two linked but separate systems. A restructured Social Security system itself would provide pensions equal to a fixed percentage of retirees' previous earnings. And a reformed welfare or negative income tax system financed out of general revenues would take on the task of supplementing the incomes of those aged workers whose Social Security checks left them below the poverty line.

Eight years ago, the Brookings economists doubted that such a transformation was feasible in the foreseeable future. But a forthcoming book on the future of Social Security by Alicia Munnell to be published by the Brookings Institution suggests that this may no longer be true. According to Munnell, the creation of the new nationwide supplemental security income (SSI) program has provided a striking opportunity to shift the focus of Social Security back toward its original insurance function.

SSI, of course, is the federally sponsored welfare program administered by the Social Security Administration, which in 1974 replaced the fragmented network of state-run public assistance programs for the aged, blind, and disabled. Since it already provides an income floor for the elderly (currently $168 a month for individuals and $252 for married couples), Munnell argues that it should be expanded to relieve Social Security of most of its welfare function. She also recommends that Social Security should be gradually converted into a proportional system that provides each beneficary with the same flat percentage of past earnings up to the taxable wage base.

Such a streamlined Social Security system would have numerous advantages, reasons Munnell. Rid of its welfare function, it would be far less expensive than the present system, which by providing high minimum pensions often winds up giving windfall benefits to the non-needy in its attempt to alleviate poverty. With each beneficiary receiving a pension strictly related to his past earnings and contributions, complaints about inequities in the benefit structure would vanish. Perhaps most important, such reform would permit a more rational allocation of roles to both Social Security and the private pension system in meeting the problem of retirement income support.

However appealing this prescription appears in the abstract, it disturbs many Social Security advocates who feel the system's great strength and justification lie precisely in its blending of the goals of individual equity and social adequacy. "Means tested programs have never worked well," says Robert Myers, "and they are particularly demeaning to the elderly. Moving away from the concept of social insurance would violate the nature of the system."

Though Myers may well be right, the Social Security pendulum does seem to be swinging back toward the goal of individual equity. Currently some 2.3 million Social Security beneficiaries also receive SSI supplementary checks, and the fact that both programs are administered by the Social Security Administration has probably blunted the stigma of welfare for many recipients. Moreover, the 1975 advisory council specifically recommended that Social Security's minimum-payment floor should be frozen so that its real value would decline in future years.

The fact is, of course, that Social Security is not an immutable institution but a dynamic system that must inevitably respond to changing conditions in a dynamic society. And in this sense its current financial problems may prove a blessing in disguise. As one Capitol Hill observer remarks: "A few years ago, Social Security had so much political momentum that no one wanted to criticize it. Now Congress cannot avoid taking a searching look at the entire system." ∎

The Lifetime Employment System in Japan:
Its Reality and Future

Tadashi A. Hanami

The Japanese employer-employee relationship is unique among the world's industrial relations systems. What are its prospects for international use?

IN THE LAST few decades several Western industrial societies have been suffering from a malfunctioning of their industrial relations systems. From time to time world interest has shifted from one country to another in search of an "ideal" pattern of industrial relations. After the decline of the British system, which once had been the model of modern industrial relations, the American system gained reputation. In turn, German, Dutch, and Scandinavian systems have been paid much tribute. Now, it appears to be the turn of the Japanese.

Recent developments of Japanese business activities in the advanced Western countries raise some stimulating questions. One question, for example, is whether Japanese business is likely to

---

Dr. Hanami *this past year was a Visiting Professor at the Center for Japanese and Korean Studies, University of California, Berkeley. He is Professor of Law, Sophia University, Tokyo, Japan.*

keep its traditional pattern in another society—a society with its own established system. Another question is whether Japanese business can maintain its well-known efficiency in a different environment and with a labor force of a different nature.

In this short article, the author will not assess the pros and cons of the Japanese system. The purpose is to present a brief description of the Japanese employer-employee relationship and the prospect of its future development and use in the era of multinationals. There have been a number of works on the Japanese system. The most accurate analysis in English of the employer-employee relationship for blue-collar workers in Japan can be found in Cole's *Japanese Blue Collar*;[1] for white-collar workers, in Rohlen's *For Harmony and Strength*.[2] Dore's *British Factory—Japanese Factory*[3] provides an excellent comparative study of British and Japanese employer-employee relationships.

The labor force in Japanese enterprises is divided into two categories:

Tadashi A. Hanami, "The Lifetime Employment System in Japan: Its Reality and Future." *Atlanta Economic Review*, May–June 1976, pp. 35–39. Reprinted with permission.

regular employees and temporary employees. In most enterprises, except perhaps very small ones, the regular employees are dominant in terms of number as well as in significance. Statistical accounts of the percentage of temporary employees among the total persons employed are not available. The percentage of the various types of temporary employees, including daily workers, among total newly employed in each year has been slightly less than 20% in these several years: in 1970, 19.4%; in 1971, 17.0%; and in 1973, 19.5%.[4]

Each enterprise recruits most of its regular employees fresh from school, in April right after graduation. There is no legal obligation for them to stay in a particular enterprise longer than one year. Article 14 of the Labor Standards Law of 1947 provides: "Labor contract, excluding those without any set period, shall not be concluded for a period longer than one year except those requiring a definite period for the completion of a project." Nor do employers have a legal obligation to keep them; employees may be dismissed with or without notice, depending on the reason for the dismissal. According to Article 20 of the Labor Standards Law, the employer must give at least 30 days advance notice before dismissal or pay 30 days average wage "except when the continuance of the enterprise is made impossible by reason of some natural calamity or other inevitable cause, or when the dismissal is caused by reason of the employee's responsibility."

However, after a certain period of probation (ranging usually from 14 days to 6 months, depending on the enterprise and the several other factors), once employees become regular employees. they usually are expected to stay at the particular enterprise until they reach a certain retirement age prescribed in the work rules of the enterprise. The retirement age normally is between 55 and 60 years old, depending on the specific enterprise and other factors. Employers are not expected to dismiss the regular employees. Dismissals are largely the result of grave misconduct of the employees or an unusual decline of business. Japanese enterprises employ temporary employees (the second category) in order to cope with normal business fluctuations. These temporary workers are employed for a certain period, mostly one or two weeks, but sometimes one or two months. As long as business is booming, their contracts are renewed. However, when the enterprise considers it necessary to cut the number of the employees, it simply refuses to renew the contracts for the temporary employees. In other words, the temporary employees are the shock absorbers of business fluctuations in a lifetime employment system.

The Seniority Wage System

Under the lifetime employment system, regular employees enjoy annual wage increments which are given automatically with growing length of service. Thus the total income of each employee increases in accordance with length of service. In addition to monthly wages, most Japanese enterprises pay bonuses, which range from three to six times the average monthly wages, depending on the business situation of the company in each year.

Retirement allowances, paid in a lump sum, also are calculated on length of service. The allowances paid to employees retiring at the prescribed retirement age are particularly generous, thus encouraging the regular employees to stay with the company.

As a result of the seniority wage system, wages of employees of the same age and with the same educational background basically tend to be similar. Some important exceptions will be discussed subsequently. Moreover, as already indicated, dismissal is rather exceptional under the lifetime employment system. What, then, makes the individual employees work hard in a system under which they possibly may be idle but still can expect to keep their jobs and enjoy wage increases every year? How do most Japanese workers become so diligent as to surprise Westerners? It is true that even in Japan payment based on results does exist and certain segments of wages are linked with efficiency. But these are not important factors motivating Japanese employees to work as hard as they do.

One of the key points of the "mystery" of Japanese efficiency is the promotion system and the hard competition among the employees recruited in the same year. Although the wages are decided basically by the educational background and length of service, after a few years of employment, when promotion to responsible positions begins, differences do come about. Only some of the employees recruited in a given year are promoted to higher positions. Some are delayed in promotion; some are never promoted beyond a given level. After many years, the difference becomes more and more important. Since everybody is expected to stay at the particular enterprise for life, those recruited in the same year compete with each other very hard. The anxiety and frustration taking place among the employees at the time of the yearly personnel changes is well described by Rohlen.[5] The substantial retirement provisions for those high in the company also are incentives. Even a blue-collar worker may become head of a plant. Others may end up as *kachō* (chief of section). A university graduate may even become president of the company, while most of his colleagues might still be *buchō* (chief of department) when they retire. This difference in ranking and status causes substantial differences in total wages among the same age group with the same educational background. (See Exhibit 1.)

Loyalty

Another crucial factor of Japanese employees' diligence is their strong loyalty to and identification with the enterprise. Since they stay at one enterprise for life, their fate and well-being depend almost entirely on the prosperity of the enterprise. Furthermore, most of the Japanese enterprises still maintain their nature as traditional social groups in which members possess a strong sense of homogeneity and exclusiveness. Thus the relationship between employer and employees is not to be explained in simple contractual terms. Both parties to the relationship "are bound as one by fate in conditions which produce a tie between man and man often as firm and close as that between husband and wife."[6]

It is common knowledge among Westerners that the Japanese company often refers to itself as an "enterprise-family," employer and employees being "family members." This enterprise-family consciousness produces a total commitment of the employees toward the enterprise. However, their personal sentimentally or emotionally oriented commitment is nurtured and reinforced by the welfare policy of the enterprise. Japanese enterprises take care of the total personal lives of the employees, including their family members.

Functional Diffuseness

The employer-employee relationship in Japan is something more than a mere exchange of labor and wages. First, Japanese enterprises train their newly employed labor force, either by their own training facilities or on the job. As mentioned, most of the employees are recruited directly from school, and the Japanese educational system as a whole is more or less oriented toward general education rather than toward occupational training. Therefore, the enterprises must train their labor force by themselves. In addition, most employees are not hired for a particular job. During their long careers at the same enterprise they are expected to transfer from one job to another. They are trained and retrained, especially after each transfer. The frequent transfer is one of the characteristics of the Japanese employer-employee relationship. This gives the Japanese enterprises greater flexibility to cope with technological change, expansion of business scope, and the opening of new plants ("scrap-and-build") because of innovation and to respond to changing business conditions. Dore points out the high degree of job interchangeability in the Japanese

Exhibit 1: Wage Differences Among Employees of Same Age and Educational Background

Salaries*

Age	Middle School Graduate		High School Graduate		University Graduate	
	Minimum	Maximum	Minimum	Maximum	Minimum	Maximum
18	100	121	117	117		
22					157	157
23	133	160	134	176		
30	155	209	195	257	198	324
45	267	317/356	359	476		

*Basic element only, of male lifetime employees at Hitachi Co. (minimum for 18-year-old middle school graduate = 100).
Source: Dore, British Factory—Japanese Factory, p. 101.

factory: "Workers can be 'posted' within the firm from one factory to another for months or years at a time, much as soldiers are posted to a new station."[7]

The educational function of Japanese enterprises is not limited to job training. A variety of courses are provided for the employees, including traditional subjects as tea ceremony, flower-arrangement, or Zen, in addition to general education courses. Some companies run their own adult education programs at a level equivalent to senior high school or college. Graduates of such programs are treated as high school or university graduates in terms of working conditions.

The enterprises also take care of the education of the employees' children. In contemporary Japan, the competition to enter better schools is very keen. The enterprise tries to utilize personal connections with school teachers in order to facilitate the admission of employees' children. In case of a transfer to another locality which makes a change of school necessary, one of the most important functions of the personnel division of the company is to secure admission of the employee's children to a good school.

The enterprises also provide recreation facilities such as sports fields, equipment, vacation facilities, and recreational lessons. In every enterprise, the company trip, once or twice a year, is a big event. The companies make arrangements for transportation and hotel reservations and provide substantial financial help, supplementing the amount contributed by the individual employee. Employers and employees eat together during such trips. In the evening they usually hold dinner parties with heavy drinking. Everybody, including the president of the company, is supposed to get completely drunk and utterly frank so as to release tensions and develop mutual trust between all of the enterprise-family members.

Athletic matches held by companies also are big events. Unions join management in organizing several kinds of such matches and other hobbies. Exhibitions of paintings, calligraphy, flower arrangements, and so on also are very popular. The company journals or newspapers often publish employees' essays and poems and sometimes novels.

The companies also take care of more personal matters, such as weddings and funerals of employees and their family members. In Japan, even now, most marriages are arranged marriages. Arrangements usually are made by relatives or friends but often also by the employees' superiors at the working place. At the wedding parties, in both "arranged" and "love" marriages, the superiors, and sometimes the executives or even the president, depending on the status of the groom or bride, are always invited and often play the role of go-betweens. Rohlen describes most vividly the reality of such arrangements in a Japanese bank.[8]

To the funeral of an employee or his

family members, companies always send flowers and their employees to help the bereaved. In the case of funerals of employees with distinguished contribution to the company, a company official usually presides over the ceremony and the company pays all the expenses.

The most important function of Japanese companies is one which in most industrialized societies usually is presumed to be cared for by social security or social welfare. Japanese companies usually provide family allowances based on the number of dependents, housing allowances, commutation allowances, and so on, in addition to basic wages. Often they provide company housing facilities and dormitories. Larger plants and offices have their own clinics to provide medical care for the employees.

The lump-sum retirement allowances are intended to make it possible for the retired employees to buy a small house or start a small business on which they can depend for the rest of their lives without much worry. After the end of World War II, because of inflation and the increase in the price of real estate, these retirement sums are no longer sufficient. In recent years, therefore, some of the public companies have begun to pay pensions in addition to the public pensions provided by the national social security systems.

Japanese enterprises also are playing an important role in coping with the unemployment problem by refraining as far as possible from dismissing regular employees. The inefficient or idle, rather than being dismissed, are assigned to unimportant jobs and not promoted. Dismissal of regular employees by redundancy also is exceptional. Companies try to avoid this as far as possible. First, surplus labor in a certain division, plant, or job category does not cause redundancy. Employees are not attached to a certain job. When there is a labor surplus in a certain part of the enterprise, employees are likely to be transferred to another unit. Second, the enterprises try to find or sometimes create work especially for surplus labor. The most remarkable case of this sort is that of a large steel company which started to plant trees on the spacious grounds surrounding its steel mill. It thus produced some work for those who became redundant by production cuts during the recession after the oil crisis. Another company began planting orange groves for the same reason.

Using one of Talcott Parsons' pattern variables for the distinction between the attributes of "traditional" and "industrial" societies,[9] Japanese enterprises, being a clear case of functional diffuseness, can be designated as "traditional." However, the fact is that the "traditional" features of Japanese enterprises have been advantageous in contributing to the astonishing efficiency of Japanese business in technological development and expansion of operations.

Labor Market Changes

The main features of the lifetime employment system were institutionalized early in the postwar period. Following James Abbeglen's 1958 book, *The Japanese Factory*,[10] it has been commonly held that the lifetime employment system is a practice which grew out of traditional social relations. In fact, however, it was established by some of the big enterprises during and after World War I[11] and was institutionalized in today's form after World War II.[12] Its features have been modified as a result of the changing industrial structure and labor market. After 1955, the Japanese economy continued to expand, with an annual GNP growth rate of around 17% or 18%. At the same time, the redistribution of output by industries has been quite significant: primary industries declined, whereas manufacturing and construction expanded markedly. Between 1955 and 1967, the number of firms in manufacturing industries increased by 138%, the number of employees by 175%, and value-added by 677%.[13] Chemical and heavy industries developed greatly between 1955 and 1968. In manufacturing, the portion accounted for by the machinery industry increased from 18.5% to 31.4%.[14]

Changes in the labor market after

1955 directly reflected the rapid expansion of the Japanese economy and its structural change. The number of employees in manufacturing industries increased 30% from 1955 to 1959, became 1.5 times the 1955 level by 1961 and nearly 1.7 times by 1963. In particular, by 1966 the number of employees in enterprises with more than 30 employees had increased 66% over 1955; by 1963 the number had more than doubled the 1955 count.[15]

The constant labor surplus, a major feature of the Japanese economy throughout the period of modernization, has now finally disappeared. This labor surplus was characterized by a high unemployment rate, disguised unemployment, and very poor living conditions for most of the agricultural families. For the first time in Japanese history, a labor shortage has emerged. It is particularly noteworthy in this context that this labor shortage applies most strongly to young workers, especially new graduates from junior and senior high schools. In April 1970, seven job vacancies were reported for each junior high school graduate. The demand for new school graduates has been especially strong in the manufacturing industries. After 1962, about 80% of the junior high school graduates and 45% of the senior high school graduates entered the manufacturing industries. Another remarkable trend in the labor market after 1955 has been the increasing amount of labor mobility. The total number of employees changing jobs increased from 425,000 in 1959 to 802,000 in 1962, nearly doubling.[16]

Other conspicuous phenomena caused by the labor shortage are the rising labor force participation of females and the growing tendency of women to stay longer in their jobs. In Japan, as in many other industrial societies, women workers traditionally have been regarded as temporary workers. The labor shortage and other factors such as the changing character of labor caused by technological change, changes in living styles and housing conditions, and availability of household appliances have contributed to the breakthrough from the traditional pattern. The number of female employees nearly doubled between 1955 and 1969. Female employees now constitute one third of the total employed labor force. The portion of married women among the total number of women employees exceeded 50% in 1969. Part-time female employees account for a significant portion of these increases, especially of the married female employee sector. They have become a last resort for much-needed additional labor.

Impact of the Change: The labor shortage has caused some changes in the established pattern of the lifetime employment system. First, the shortage of young people in the labor force, especially new graduates, contributed to a decrease in wage differences by age and by size of the enterprise. Starting wages have increased more rapidly in the smaller enterprises than in larger enterprises (Exhibit 2). The narrowing wage difference by age has been caused not only by the difficulty of obtaining

---

Exhibit 2: Wage Indexes by Enterprise Size

Enterprise Size (Employees)	1958	1968
500 and more	100.0	100.0
100-499	69.7	74.5
30-99	54.7	61.7
5-29	43.6	49.3

Source: Ministry of Labor, *Monthly Labor Survey.*

---

young labor but also by the stronger demand for younger workers who are more adjustable to rapid technological change.

Second, the labor shortage has led to a growing labor mobility. The trend to move, to seek better working conditions and brighter career prospects, certainly is new. Under the lifetime employment system, the better employees stay at the particular enterprise and get promoted and enjoy the privileges of seniority. But, due to the strong labor shortage, especially for competent and adjustable workers with technical knowledge and skill, a number of enterprises have started to recruit employees from other companies. They offer conditions equivalent to or sometimes better than those of their own regular employees. This trend is a sharp contrast to the traditional pattern, under which most of the employees recruited from other enterprises are regarded as temporary employees or at least are given disadvantageous working conditions compared with conditions given those recruited immediately after graduation.

However, in spite of the impact of this new practice of "pulling-out" workers from other companies, its effect on the employment system should not be magnified. Labor mobility is growing, but this trend still does not reflect a general practice. "Pulling-out" has become popular in the case of salesmen, technical engineers, and other highly skilled workers, but ordinary workers continue to be recruited from among new graduates. And the enterprises naturally are reluctant to let their own capable employees be recruited by competing companies. Similarly, after enticing employees from other companies, they very much want to keep them. In this sense, this practice, while seemingly weakening the lifetime employment system, tends to strengthen it in a modified form. In fact, protection from employee-raiding by other companies was the major motivation for the evolution of the lifetime employment system in the prewar period.[17]

In this connection, we should also consider Galbraith's contention that the impact of technological innovation and high industrialization may serve to strengthen the identification of employees with their own respective enterprises.[18] On the one hand, this may be true even in Japan. On the other hand, it also is possible that technocrats, with their universal knowledge and techniques which are applicable in other companies, generally may be more mobile than are the traditional regular Japanese employees. This observation may be particularly applicable to technocrats at the lower levels of the organization who are still out of the inner circle and are impatient to be admitted into that circle.

Another factor likely to sustain the lifetime employment system is the fact that because of the labor shortage, temporary employees are staying longer in one enterprise. Female employees, especially, are encouraged to remain with the organization. The longer they stay, the more they want to be promoted and receive treatment equal to that received by regular employees. Some of the enterprises have started to regularize the status of temporary employees, even part-time employees. This development is not a decline of the system but only a modification. That this represents a new trend in the Japanese employer-employee relations system is supported by the fact that it has occurred in spite of the economic recession following the oil crisis. These changes, plus the growing scope of the international phase of the Japanese employment system, will have an impact as yet unknown.

Impact of Foreign Enterprises

The business activities of foreign enterprises in Japan are still rather limited in terms of number of employees and sales volume. Employees working in foreign enterprises in Japan account for only 0.7% of all Japanese employees. The total sales volume of those firms accounted for only 1.5% of the Japanese total in 1972.[19] Thus the impact on the Japanese industrial relations system is not significant at the present time. Moreover, most foreign enterprises are attempting to adjust themselves to Japanese employment practices rather than asserting their own patterns, although sometimes they do cause friction in industrial relations.[20]

Foreign activities of Japanese enterprises are still in the early stage of development of multinational enterprises. In 1971 Japanese foreign investment in total was only 2% of GNP or 18.6% of the annual value of exports.[21] Furthermore, until quite recently most Japanese foreign investment has been directed to the developing countries. The enterprises, especially those operating in Southeast Asia, are trying to retain skilled labor, in short supply in such areas, and increase productivity by providing health care, housing, and education for workers. This suggests that they will develop a model similar to, if not quite the same as, the model of the Japanese employment system.

Japanese enterprises operating in the industrialized countries have no necessity to develop a labor force by themselves. Yet a recent study by Johnson and Ouchi[22] suggests that some of the Japanese enterprises in the United States are taking the typical Japanese approach to personnel management. Such companies have been more successful in reducing absenteeism and turnover than have some other Japanese companies which have handled their labor force in American fashion. (Somewhat different observations have been made by Harari and Zeira.)[23] The findings of Johnson and Ouchi are quite similar to my own personal observation of Japanese enterprises operating in Southeast Asia.

Thus, on the one hand, because of the limited scope of both foreign business in Japan and Japanese activities abroad, the international impact on Japanese industrial relations is not yet serious. On the other hand, there is a possibility, not only in the developing areas but also in the developed countries, that the Japanese employment oped in a modified form by Japanese business.

If we broaden the scope of our observation from the limited field of the employment system to the whole system of industrial relations, the Japanese pattern (in particular, enterprise unionism and enterprise bargaining) is likely to be adopted—again in a modified form. One notable case is the growing importance of plant-level bargaining, caused by technological change and changes in the nature of work in modern industries. Another is the growing development of enterprise bargaining on an international level, necessitated by the expanding worldwide activities of multinationals. A more detailed analysis of the future development of the Japanese industrial relations system and multinationals can be found in the author's work, "The Multinational Corporation and Japanese Industrial Relations."[24]
system will be maintained and will have a positive impact on the management style prevalent in the host countries.

There is no vital and distinct factor likely to cause a drastic change in the Japanese employment system in the near future. The system will be modified in response to future developments in technology and the industrial structure. In foreign countries, some of its features could be maintained and devel-

---

1. Robert E. Cole, *Japanese Blue Collar* (Berkeley, University of California Press, 1973).

2. Thomas P. Rohlen, *For Harmony and Strength* (Berkeley, University of California Press, 1974).

3. Ronald Dore, *British Factory—Japanese Factory* (Berkeley, University of California Press, 1973).

4. Ministry of Labor, *Rodō Tōkei Yōran*, Summary of Labor Statistics (Tokyo, Ministry of Labor, 1974), p. 67.

5. Rohlen, *For Harmony and Strength*, p. 136.

6. Chie Nakane, *Japanese Society* (Harmondsworth, Penguin Books Ltd., 1973), p. 15.

7. Dore, *British Factory—Japanese Factory*, p. 40.

8. Rohlen, *For Harmony and Strength*, p. 235.

9. Talcott Parsons, *The Social System* (London, Tavistock Publication Ltd., 1952), pp. 51-67 and 182-191.

10. James Abbeglen, *The Japanese Factory* (Glencoe, Free Press, 1958).

11. Cole, *Japanese Blue Collar*, p. 131.

12. Tadashi A. Hanami, "Future Industrial Relations—Japan," *Bulletin of the International Institute for Labor Studies*, no. 10, 1972, Geneva, p. 85.

13. Ibid., p. 100.

14. Ibid., pp. 100-101.

15. Ibid., p. 101.

16. Ibid., p. 103.

17. Koji Taira, *Economic Development and the Labor Market in Japan* (New York, Columbia University Press, 1970), p. 151; and Robert Evans Jr., *The Labor Economics of Japan and the United States* (New York, Praeger Publishers, 1971), p. 40.

18. John Kenneth Galbraith, *The New Industrial State* (Boston, Houghton Mifflin Co., 1967), pp. 149-158.

19. Ministry of International Trade and Industry, *The Trend of Foreign Enterprises* (Tokyo, MITI, 1973), p. 14.

20. Tadashi A. Hanami, "The Multinational Corporation and Japanese Industrial Relations," in *International Labor and Multinational Enterprise*, edited by Duane Kujawa (New York, Praeger Publishers, Inc., 1975).

21. Ministry of International Trade and Industry, *White Paper on International Trade* (Tokyo, MITI, 1973), p. 197.

22. Richard Tanner Johnson and William G. Ouchi, "Made in America (under Japanese management)," *Harvard Business Review*, September-October 1974, pp. 61-69.

23. Ehud Harari and Yoran Zeira, "Morale Problem in Non-American Multinational Corporations in the U.S.," *Management International Review*, November 1974, pp. 43-53.

24. Hanami, "The Multinational Corporation and Japanese Industrial Relations."

D. Labor Unions and Collective Bargaining

Unions, Critics, and Collective Bargaining

By TIM BORNSTEIN

Professor of Law and Industrial Relations, University of Massachusetts/Amherst.

THERE ARE MORE THAN 165,000 collective bargaining agreements in the United States today. Their provisions govern the wages and working conditions of more than twenty million persons, from steelworkers and sailors to police and professors. Each agreement is negotiated individually at two or three year intervals—item by item, word by word—to meet the needs of a single employer or group of employers and a defined group of employees. Each set of negotiations is a potential source of industrial conflict if collective bargaining fails. Moreover, each grievance that arises during the life of a collective agreement—probably millions annually—is also a potential source of industrial conflict.

Despite this vast potential for conflict, there is no labor-management crisis in America. The leading explanation is that the system of collective bargaining that has emerged over the last century works extremely well in resolving some of the most difficult problems of employment relations in the modern world. The vast majority of labor agreements, more than 99 percent, have been negotiated without strikes, lockouts or other forms of labor conflict. Violence, once a common feature of American industrial relations, has virtually disappeared. While not generally appreciated by the public or by policymakers, it is, nonetheless, a fact that since the strike-laden years immediately following World War II collective bargaining in America has been a success story.

Tim Bornstein, "Unions, Critics, and Collective Bargaining." *Labor Law Journal*, October 1976, pp. 614-622.

Collective bargaining, like political democracy or universal public education, is a social invention. It was created in response to the special needs of industrial society. Like other social inventions, its success depends upon its responsiveness to changing social conditions. Whether one looks at the evidence of international comparisons, or historical standards, or at the more conventional standards of industrial peace and economic progress, collective bargaining in America is one of the most successful institutions of the 20th Century.

There are many calls for reform of America's social, political, and economic institutions, but few calls for reform of the structure of collective bargaining. Candidates for public office rarely discuss labor relations problems. Political party platforms, which are as comprehensive as a five year old's Christmas list to Santa Claus, usually ignore

collective bargaining. Newspaper editors, who are professionally expert in identifying our national ills, rarely call for changes in the fundamental structure of American labor-management relations. And, among scholars and researchers, labor issues lag far behind such other troubled and fashionable fields of inquiry as unemployment, poverty, race relations, urban affairs, public health, education, the political system, the environment, defense, and foreign affairs.

Even strikes, which historically have been an irritant to the public, have receded into the background of national anxieties as effective collective bargaining has diminished their number and impact. Since the late 1960's, there has been a surge of strikes among newly organized and militant government employees; these strikes, both because of their novelty and their disruptiveness, have frequently received headline treatment. Yet few responsible observers contend that strikes by public employees constitute a grave national problem. In fact, American unions have themselves come to look on strikes with increasing distaste. There has not been a strike in the basic steel industry, for example, since 1959, virtually erasing that industry's once notorious record for workdays lost to labor disputes. Even the protracted strike in the rubber industry in 1976 turned out to be more the cause of irritation than of widespread industrial dislocation.

Fashionable Despair

Success of the collective bargaining system has not been universally admired, however. Success may be dull, while struggle is romantic. Reformers who found the cause of collective bargaining vital and absorbing in the 1930's, when it was vigorously opposed by management, find it tedious and dull today in its maturity. Indeed, it has long been fashionable for social critics to despair of unions and collective bargaining as irremediably conservative and uninteresting fixtures of American society. Articulate critics from *The New York Times* to *Ramparts* accuse unions and collective bargaining of promoting a host of vices: racism, sexism, insensitivity to aspirations of the young and poor, hostility to technological innovation, a leaning towards violence, jingoistic support of imperialistic foreign policies, and political partnership with venal power brokers in the Democratic party. While extreme and unbalanced, these charges are not without substance, for an informed observer can point to many examples involving individual unions and individual collective bargaining relationships that would abundantly document them. But it is a monstrous untruth to assert, as some critics do, that these vices accurately characterize American unions and the institution of collective bargaining.

In some instances, these charges are so excessive that one can only conclude that they are a polemical camouflage for critics' unspoken complaint that American unions have rejected left-wing ideologies in favor of serving their members through the moderate and pragmatic, but effective, institution of collective bargaining. They may also conceal a disappointment that American employers have been unfaithful to their sinister role in the 19th Century Marxist script as uncompromising enemies of the working class.

To the dismay of radicals here and abroad, American workers are not infused with a sense of class consciousness or class militancy. Most workers, their unions, and the institution of collective bargaining are in the mainstream of the nation's social values: progressive, but not radical; tolerant of differences, but not of extremism; respectful of tangible achievement, but skeptical of rhetoric; willing to innovate and experiment, but cautious about radical change; generous and open by nature, but far from saintly. Union leaders, whose role in the collective bargaining system is crucial, are realists whose dominant vision is that their members aspire to fair treatment, fair compensation, and job security in the workplace—not to radical social reform. With this vision, is it surprising that union leaders are suspicious of those who would draw them away from their preoccupation with collective bargaining into such high-risk games as political revolution, radical reform of the political party system, or warfare against private enterprise?

A Folk Hero

Because unions have increasingly shunned radical politics and have, instead, devoted their energies and resources to collective bargaining, their leaders are often bracketed— by their critics—with the most reactionary forces in American life. George Meany is no folk hero on the campus; on the contrary, he is viewed by the New Left and Old Left alike as an enemy.[1] Liberals and academics have had no folk hero in high office in the labor movement since Walter Reuther's death in an air crash in 1970.[2] Symbolically, his death marked the end of a generation of disenchantment in the liberal and academic communities with unions and collective bargaining, disenchantment that began in earnest in 1949 when the old CIO expelled its communist-dominated affiliates and that reached its zenith

[1] Former North Carolina Senator Sam Ervin—elderly, long-time spokesman for the most right wing economic forces of the "Old South," foremost opponent of civil rights laws, and consistent opponent of legislation to improve the welfare of workers—was knighted as a campus folk hero virtually overnight because of his admirable work as chairman of the Senate Watergate investigating committee in 1973. His folksy humor was repeated in every campus gathering. His face was memorialized on sweat shirts along with such other folk heroes as Fidel Castro, Chairman Mao and Beethoven. But George Meany is held in contempt. While one might regard his remarkable intellectual and physical vigor in his 80's as exemplary of contributions that elderly citizens can make to society, his critics see him only as a stubborn old man. While one might appreciate Meany's toughness and pragmatism as an accurate reflection of the essential character of American unions, his critics regard these qualities as proof of his lack of idealism. His critics even fasten on his Bronx accent and his weakness for cigars and golf as evidence of the decadence of the man and the institution that he heads.

[2] Cesár Chavez of the United Farm Workers has become a minor folk hero on the campus and among liberals. He has both personal charm and charisma of the type that made Reuther so attractive. Chavez brought a social movement to life by his rhetoric and his sacrifice. But his admirers too willingly overlook his faults as the executive of an organization that is entrusted with serious administrative tasks. In his fight with the Teamsters, his supporters have been too partisan to appreciate that the Teamsters are very good contract negotiators and administrators, whereas the Teamsters have been too smug and cynical to appreciate that Chavez is not just another union leader and the UFW is not just another union.

in 1972 when the AFL-CIO refused to endorse George McGovern's candidacy.

Reuther's impassioned rhetoric of social reform, his newsworthy alliances with leaders of civil rights and civil liberties causes, his outspoken criticism of business leaders and especially of his colleagues in the labor movement, and his ascetic personal habits set him apart from most other union leaders—indeed, from leaders in other fields as well. Walter Reuther was an exceptional man, but he did not lack for pragmatism. He was not a labor saint; he was not a Eugene V. Debs.

His leadership of the United Automobile Workers was sustained for 25 years by his dynamism and effectiveness at the negotiating table, not by his role as social reformer which was frequently a liability among UAW members and the UAW bureaucracy. Ostensibly, Reuther led the UAW out of the AFL-CIO in 1968 because of dissatisfaction with its lack of commitment to social reform and its lack of energy in organizing the unorganized, but some observers friendly to Reuther were convinced that he was motivated, at least in part, by personal disappointment in failing to become president of the AFL-CIO.[3]

If American unions have been unresponsive, even hostile, to critics from the campus and elsewhere, the explanation is not that the critics' voices have been unheard or that their views have been misunderstood. The explanation is more basic. The critics ask the unions to exchange their commitment to what they view

as their finest and most enduring achievement in American history— establishment of the system of collective bargaining in law and in daily practice—for an ill-defined role in an ill-defined program of social reform. It is their tenacious adherence to collective bargaining and their rejection of ideology, which is so common to foreign labor movements, that explains better than other factors the gap between unions and liberal critics.

Not Political Parties

Why should American unions turn from the well-understood and tangible goals of collective bargaining for a place in the never-never land of radical social reform? In substance, they made that choice in the 1890's when the pragmatic AF of L under Sam Gompers' leadership shaped the modern labor movement, leaving the quixotic, reformist Knights of Labor as only a memory in the museum of social history. Unions in America have chosen to define a role for themselves that is intimately tied to the collective bargaining system which, in turn, is concerned with the welfare of employees and the success of management at the workplace.

American unions have decided, in effect, that they do not *also* wish to be political parties, or the alter ego of political parties, or the organizational edge of revolution. Unions have been concerned with better housing, education, race relations, and a thousand and one other worthy social causes, but they have rejected a role as the institutional conscience for social reform in America.

---

[3] Several months after leaving the AFL-CIO, Reuther's UAW formed a curious coalition with the Teamsters with grand ambitions to organize the unorganized *and* to engage in social reform. The Teamsters Union has the most checkered history of all major unions. Its erstwhile leaders, Dave Beck and Jimmy Hoffa, are household names commonly associated with the worst excesses in organizational venality. But the Teamsters' treasury was large, which fitted Reuther's collective bargaining and reformist aspirations nicely. Shortly after Reuther's death this alliance disintegrated.

To left wing critics of British unions, the late Allan Flanders of Nuffield College, Oxford, replied:

"What I find so objectionable as well as invalid in the Marxist view is its implicit contempt for 'pure and simple' trade unionism. Trade unions, by doggedly sticking to their immediate ends and refusing to be captured and exploited by any political party, have gradually transformed society. Only not according to the sacred texts or the dialectical laws! That they may be right in preferring reform to revolution, and unity to discord, never crosses the mind of those whose theory tells them all the answers."[4]

American unions and their leaders have a vivid, sometimes excessively vivid, recollection of the historical opposition of government and business to collective bargaining throughout the 19th Century and well into the 20th Century. Long after enactment of the Wagner Act of 1935, which guaranteed the right of private sector employees to join unions and engage in collective bargaining, large sections of management ignored the law and resisted any form of bilateral decision-making with workers' representatives. Indeed, several of the most violent labor-management confrontations in American history took place in the late 1930's—notably in steel, automobile, textile and coal mining industries—*after* Congress had established collective bargaining as the bedrock feature of our national labor policy and after the Supreme Court (voting five to four) declared the Wagner Act constitutional.

American management has become reconciled to collective bargaining and, in rare instances, endorses its contribution to productivity and stability, although even now not without reservations. Remembering the birth pangs of collective bargaining, it is natural that unionists view its achievements with great pride and its critics with distaste.

Goals Achieved

The pragmatic unionist argues that through collective bargaining American unions have already achieved for their members many of the goals that European unions are still striving to gain through legislation. Fair wages, maximum hours, overtime pay, health and life insurance, pensions, seniority protection, vacations, sick leave, protection from arbitrary discipline—these are typical features of the *typical* collective bargaining contract in America.

Some of the more significant collective bargaining agreements go much further in providing added benefits and other forms of job security, such as dental and psychiatric benefits, supplemental unemployment benefits, sabbatical leaves, guaranteed annual income, educational tuition, and the like. These benefits have contributed to what some social critics uncharitably call *enbourgeoisiement* of the American working class. To many unionists, the process of *enbourgeoisiement* is precisely what they have always hoped to gain for their members.

Some of them are over-zealous in their own defense and no less so in attacking their critics. Michael LaVelle, a tough talking steelworker and shop steward turned newspaper columnist, asserts with foolish extravagance: "I have read most of George Meany's speeches and much of the literature by intellectuals who hate him. I find this difference: George Meany has done more to advance the meek and to heed the calls of workers than all of the intellectuals from Karl Marx to Herbert Marcuse."[5]

[4] Allan Flanders, *Management and Unions: The Theory and Reform of Industrial Relations.* Faber and Faber, London: 1970, p. 39.

[5] Michael LaVelle, *Red, White & Blue-Collar Views.* Saturday Review Press/E. P. Dutton & Co., Inc., New York: 1975, p. 181.

While collective bargaining directly benefits only those who are part of the system, it is not a closed system. Under American law, the right to join unions for purposes of collective bargaining is guaranteed to most workers in most industries, private and public sector alike. Farm workers are an unfortunate exception, as are government employees in many states.

Moreover, as every freshman economics student knows, negotiated wage and benefit patterns often have a far-reaching impact on employment standards of unorganized employees within a single firm and on wholly unorganized industries. During the 1970 strike against General Motors, there were widely publicized interviews with white collar workers, including middle managers, who were secretly hoping that the UAW, which did not represent them, would succeed in its bargaining objectives. They anticipated correctly that GM would be obliged to extend to white collar workers and managers the benefits negotiated by the UAW for its members.

Paul Jacobs has earned the title of dean of the critics of American unions by his authorship of an insightful and widely quoted tract in 1963 entitled *Old Before Its Time: Collective Bargaining at 28*.[6] He urged the unions to abandon their emphasis on "the obsolescent tool of collective bargaining" and to turn, instead, to politics as the primary means of achieving "industrial justice." Jacobs, along with such other critics as Paul Sultan, Irving Kristol, Jeremy Brecher, Stanley Aranowitz and Solomon Barkin, claim special credibility for their arguments by virtue of their one-time association or sympathy with unions.

"Fugitives"

Not surprisingly, unions are especially sensitive to criticism from former friends and colleagues. The late Joseph Beirne, long-time president of the Communications Workers, lashed out at these "fugitives" from the world of unionism who, "while professing total dedication to the ideals and objectives of the labor movement, shed well-paid public tears over its supposed failure to live up to those ideals and objectives."[7] Despite union tenderness when criticized by former associates, are not they at least as well qualified to evaluate union goals and strategies as anyone else? It is, one suspects, not just substantive criticism that provokes union anger towards critics; it may also be the pious and superior tone of the criticism.

Paul Jacobs, a thoughtful observer of American social life, was as entitled and qualified to evaluate union goals and strategies as anyone in the labor movement itself. Indeed, one of the traditional problems of American unions is that they fail to articulate their objectives persuasively to outsiders, a small evidence of which is the paucity of books and articles by unionists on labor relations or any other subject. But Jacobs unwisely went much further than to argue for a change of goals and strategies. He warned unions that they faced elimination as a major institutional force in society if they ignored his advice:

"The place of unions in the struc-

***

[6] Paul Jacobs, *Old Before Its Time: Collective Bargaining at 28*. Center for the Study of Democratic Institutions, Santa Barbara: 1963.

[7] Joseph A. Beirne, *Challenge to Labor: New Roles for American Trade Unions*. Prentice-Hall, Englewood Cliffs, N. J.: 1969, p. 131.

ture of industrial justice will continue to grow smaller unless unions return to the political function that once was primary with them. They will need to design new political tools and new forms of political participation, for it is clear that future union-management relations will depend less and less on sheer economics and more and more on political instruments and political techniques. . . .

"Now unions must move on from the simple economic level. In Israel, in the Scandinavian countries, in England, and in many other foreign lands unions are an integral part of the political system, not onlookers as they are in America where the simplistic AFL tradition of rewarding friends and punishing enemies in the political arena is still dominant. The tragedy of American unions is that they who did so much to create the old collective bargaining system are taking so minor and unimportant a role in developing a new one. It may mean their death."

He was wrong. And to be wrong —plainly and demonstrably—is a fatal flaw in one who would be a prophet. American unions ignored his advice to shift emphasis from "obsolete" collective bargaining to politics. They have not been tempted to start a labor party or to join hands with radical political movements, yet their institutional authority has not diminished by any objective measure. On the contrary, they have grown in membership and in influence during the last decade and a half. Indeed, at the time that Jacobs, in 1963, was predicting their demise, union membership began to rise at a rate more rapid than in any period since 1935-

1945, the greatest spurt of unionism in American history.

Moreover, much of this growth has been in fields that are new to collective bargaining, especially in public employment, education and health care.[8] Collective bargaining has not only reached entirely new fields of employment but also it has moved up the socio-economic ladder, attracting for the first time large numbers of professors, physicians, social workers, professional engineers and scientists, lawyers and other members of the professional-managerial strata of the economy.

Influence

Membership data do not measure social influence, of course, but there is little evidence that labor's overall influence has been diminishing in Washington, in state capitols, or in town halls in the last decade or so. *U. S. News & World Report's* annual survey of national leadership in April, 1976, a poll conducted among 1400 leading public figures, ranked organized labor as the fourth most powerful institution in the nation, following the White House, the Supreme Court, and television. Labor was *perceived*, according to this poll, as more influential than the Senate, the bureaucracy, industry, the House of Representatives, and the press. Of course, perceptions of power may be inaccurate, for measurement is difficult. Still, there is little doubt that during the Kennedy-Johnson years, 1961-1968, union influence was enormous as measured by political appointments, legislation, and access to executive power.

What is surprising, however, is that the AFL-CIO and many individual

---

[8] According to the most recent study of the Bureau of Labor Statistics in the *1975 Directory of National Unions and Employee Associations,* union membership in the United States rose from 17 million in 1960 to over 20 million in 1974. Unions, however, represented 23.6% of the total national labor force in 1960, falling to 21.6% in 1974, probably because of the decline in the number of manufacturing and unskilled jobs.

unions exercised substantial influence during the first Nixon administration, whose election the unions bitterly opposed. In Congress, while labor experienced many failures during the Nixon years, it can count a number of significant victories: It played a leading role in defeating Nixon's 1969 nominations of Haynsworth and Carswell to the Supreme Court; it lead support for enactment of the Occupational Safety and Health Act of 1970; it persuaded Nixon to expand and vastly improve the system of collective bargaining in the Federal service through his promulgation of Executive Order 11491; and it secured improvements in minimum wage legislation. On the state level, unions were extremely successful during the 1960's and early 1970's in promoting enactment of collective bargaining legislation for public employees in over half the states.

Collective bargaining as a mechanism for resolving disputes between groups has moved beyond its traditional context of labor-management relations into a number of new and important settings. Three major tenets of labor-management collective bargaining—recognition of a collective bargaining agent, negotiation in good faith over relevant issues, and incorporation of understandings into a written contract—have been used increasingly in disputes between landlords and tenants, students and universities, prisoners and prison administrations, civil rights organizations and municipal governments, and physicians and health insurers.

If American unions have continued to concentrate their energies on collective bargaining, ignoring their critics' advice to concentrate on radical politics on the European model, have European unions fared so much better? There is slight evidence that they have, much that they have not.

The English labor movement's close linkage with the Labor Party has traditionally been admired by left wing critics of American unions and collective bargaining, perhaps because the English labor movement and the Labor Party have adopted socialism as their unquestioned (and unquestioning) ideological objective. That admiration has recently become muted, however.

Britain's unemployment has risen to the highest levels since the Depression; productivity in basic industries has declined to among the lowest in the industrialized world; the quality of public services has seriously deteriorated; inflation has been more severe than in any other country in the West, except for sick Italy; lack of opportunity has inspired thousands of talented young professionals to emigrate; tensions between working-class whites and the Black and Asian communities have produced nasty racial problems for British cities; Britain's involvement in the religious strife in Northern Ireland has become a costly burden on human and other resources; assorted Marxists and moderates are engaged in bitter power struggles within several of Britain's largest unions; education and housing policies are widely regarded as disastrously chaotic; the standard of living for all Britons has continued to fall since the early 1970's; and, reflecting this widespread social disorganization, the pound sterling has fallen so low as to imperil its viability as an international currency. The conduct of collective bargaining itself in Britain, which was the home of modern collective bargaining, has been a matter of sadness and ridicule for two decades.

One British writer not incorrectly notes that there is a "common belief that the British system of industrial relations is akin to an anarchist's football match where the referee has no whistle."[9] No objective observer attributes these pervasive troubles *solely* to the labor movement's close connections with the Labor Party or *solely* to the socialist policies of the Labor Party. Obviously the problems of modern Britain are inordinately complex. At the same time, however, those critics of the American system of collective bargaining who call for a radical, Marxist alternative no longer point to Britain as a model.

Flaws and Accomplishments

Collective bargaining in America is not without a number of well-known flaws. For example, it favors stronger parties over the weaker, regardless of the substantive merits of their claims. It assumes the validity of economic conflict, strikes and lockouts, as an essential lubricant to the system. It serves primarily the interests of immediate parties to bargaining and is often insensitive to the impact of their decisions on the community. At the same time, collective bargaining at its best is no more than an effective system for reconciling conflicts between labor and management. It is not designed or suited to deal with other social problems: there is no *collective bargaining approach* to housing, education, environment, foreign affairs, or civil rights policy outside the employment relationship.

But the case for collective bargaining is not that it is a model of social engineering or that it purports to have long-term solutions to all social ills. Its claim, more narrowly, is that since World War II it has compiled a tangible record of success and flexibility in the face of continuing social and economic challenges in the workplace, that it has contributed to creating and sustaining a high level of economic productivity and prosperity, that it has largely replaced strikes and violence with negotiations, and that it has brought principles of participation, due process, and fair treatment to millions of wage earners.

[The End]

GEORGE W. TAYLOR

Wage Determination Processes

*T*he widespread use of collective bargaining in recent years, particularly its government-enforced adoption in the mass-production industries, has brought about important changes in the forces that have to be reconciled in the process of wage determination. One of the necessary steps in developing a wage theory for this day and age, therefore, is the formulation of a theory of collective bargaining. Such a theory will be concerned with the fashioning of wage decisions within the range of policy-making and administrative latitude that negotiators possess.

In this chapter the characteristics of collective bargaining as a wage-determining institution are contrasted with alternative processes which have been and still are utilized. Each process has particular characteristics. Each process constitutes a unique decision-making mechanism and has a marked influence upon the substantive terms of employment. Contrasts between the several processes are particularly cogent as respects the factor of consent, the nature of the agreement, and the consequences of nonagreement.

CONSENT AND THE AGREEMENT

In our kind of a democracy the primary criterion for wage determination is the mutual acceptance of employment terms by the parties of direct interest.[1] The essentiality of this criterion derives from a conviction that employment terms should not be imposed upon either employees or employers.

This basic concept of wage determination has shortcomings that sometimes give rise to doubts about the efficacy of the concept. Employees and employers are sometimes disposed, it is said, to ignore the "needs of the consumer." Negotiators may even fail on occasion to conserve what

---

[1] A lack of public interest is not implied. Indeed, legislation affecting the processes of determination has been enacted because of public concern about maintaining an "equality of bargaining power." During national emergencies, even the substantive terms of employment have been fixed by government rule. With these exceptions, important though they be, wage determination is conceived essentially as private agreement making between employees and the employer.

George W. Taylor, "Wage Determination Processes." In *New Concepts in Wage Determination*, George W. Taylor and Frank C. Pierson, eds. McGraw-Hill Book Company, Inc., 1957, pp. 83–113. From *New Concepts in Wage Determination*, by George W. Taylor and Frank C. Pierson. Copyright © 1957 by McGraw-Hill Book Company. Used with permission of McGraw-Hill Book Company.

appears to be their own economic interests—especially their long-run interests—when they determine wages. The risk that faulty decisions will sometimes be made is inherent in a decentralized system of wage determination grounded upon private negotiation and agreement. Within broad limits, however, such shortcomings are tolerated because the advantages of private agreement making are highly prized.

Employees and employers thus have a responsibility to reconcile their conflicting wage objectives. They are under strong inducement to do so. The rule of "no contract, no work," which applies in the absence of mutual understanding, is a powerful motivating force. Wage determination may be defined, therefore, as the process of discovering those wage rates, and related terms of employment, which the employer will make available and at which employees will work in the immediate future.

Equality of Bargaining Power

The idea that wages are to be determined only by a mutual understanding between employees and the employer is, in essence, a simple proposition. Effectuation of the idea, however, has given rise to complex and controversial problems. The quality of the employee consent, and of the employer consent as well, has become a matter of general interest and of political concern. A coerced consent is not sufficient. The search has been for a process, or processes, of wage determination that will ensure, as far as possible, a validation of the terms of employment by a negotiated agreement between employees and employers who possess what is termed an "equality of bargaining power." This aspect of wage determination largely dominated the history of employer-employee relations in the United States for more than a hundred years.[2]

One way of giving substance to the elusive notion of equality of bargaining power is to evaluate the consequences to employees and to employers of a failure to agree under alternate processes of wage determination. If a negotiating impasse results in overwhelmingly serious consequences to one party but is of little consequence to the other, a so-called inequality of bargaining power may be said to obtain. If either party possesses what is deemed to be a coercive power, then the process of wage determination from which that power derives is likely to become the subject of governmental regulation. However, when the consequences of nonagreement are serious to both parties, standards of wage determination are sometimes evolved which are mutually regarded as fair and equitable. Changes in the costs of living, the so-called annual improvement factor, comparative wage rates, and other points of reference are being more and more extensively used in the formulation of wage policies.

[2] Early in the nineteenth century attempts of employees to organize unions in order to strengthen their bargaining position were forestalled by court decisions in the famous "conspiracy cases." This policy was subsequently modified. Through the Wagner Act, enacted in 1935, the government facilitated the organization of employees for collective bargaining. In 1947, through the Taft-Hartley Act, the government limited the economic power of unions and regulated certain aspects of collective bargaining. The processes of wage determination have thus been of continuing interest to governmental agencies.

The factor of consent involves much more than an economic power relationship.

Public opinion about what constitutes coercive power in wage determination changes from time to time, especially with fluctuations in business and employment opportunities. Serious questions in this area do not ordinarily arise, however, if the employees and the employer see eye to eye about the procedures and the standards by which they will reconcile their wage differences. Securing such an understanding is the crux of the problem of effectuating a private process for determining wages. There is, to be sure, a risk that arrangements quite acceptable to employees and employers may be contrary to consumer interests. The extent to which the private wage-determination system will be subjected to governmental regulation depends, in part at least, upon the public appraisal of the seriousness of this risk.

A widespread loss of employee confidence in so-called individual bargaining[3]—finally shared by the general public—culminated in the Wagner Act, with its governmental support of collective bargaining. Lack of employer confidence in unregulated collective bargaining—finally shared by the general public—resulted in the Taft-Hartley Act. However, employees and employers in many plants and industries have achieved—and are increasingly achieving—a considerable meeting of minds about the process and the standards they will use to determine wages. Nor can it be said that collusion in disregard of consumer interests typifies these understandings.

The procedures for establishing wages, as distinct from the substance of the determination, have long been a separate problem. The consent factor has been mainly responsible. It is not at all implied that the process of determination and the substantive terms of employment are unrelated. But the mutual acceptance of wages, effected under a determination system appraised as "fair" by employees and employer, gives those wages a rightness and a usefulness not otherwise attainable.

Concessions made by the employer and by the employees to achieve an agreement may create economic problems. They may necessitate subsequent economic adjustments. There is, nevertheless, a considerable tolerance about such results[4] because of an overriding desire to ensure against the imposition of the conditions of employment by one party upon the other or by some "outside" agency upon both the employee and the employer. The factor of consent is a vital consideration in wage determination.

[3] As will be noted presently, it is more precise to say that the employees' loss of confidence in management-administered wage determination gave rise to a demand for collective bargaining.

[4] There are limits to the public acceptability of the results of private agreement making. Minimum-wage legislation, for example, reflects a conclusion that employees, organized or unorganized, should receive at least a specified wage as a legal right. The national wage-stabilization programs of World War II and the Korean conflict were designed to forestall wage increases that employees could achieve and which employers were often willing to concede.

Nature of the Wage Agreement

It is necessary then that wages, and related employment terms as well, be validated by an understanding between employees and employers. Several kinds of agreement-making processes are utilized to arrive at various kinds of agreements. What roles are assigned to the employees and to the employer in formulating, modifying, and rejecting proposed terms? Do employees individually accept or reject terms which the employer formulates and institutes? Or should employees more directly participate in the development and in the administration of wage policy? In other words, how are wage decisions made? These questions reflect the wide differences of opinion which have been voiced over the years about the desirability of the collective-bargaining kind of agreement making.

An important characteristic of collective bargaining is that certain policy-making and administrative functions are shared by the management and the designated union representatives of the employees. Employment terms have to be agreed upon by the union and the management before they are put into effect, i.e., before they are offered to individual workers who still retain the right to accept or reject employment at available terms. But the basic wage decisions are made jointly by union and management representatives.

It is significant to note the increase in subjects dealt with by collective bargaining over the years. Organized employees have successfully asserted an interest in bringing more and more employment terms under the joint-determination process. Fewer terms are formulated by management alone. The wage agreement has become a comprehensive and a detailed document covering wages and many related conditions of employment.

In examining the behavior of wages, it is consequently becoming increasingly difficult to isolate wages from the total conditions of employment. "Rule-of-thumb" comparisons of basic wage rates do not take into account critical variations in overtime opportunities, promotion rules, old-age retirement benefits, provisions for health insurance, grievance procedures, production standards, work loads, and a host of other conditions which are integral parts of the wage agreement. A few examples will illustrate. The likelihood of rapid promotions may be more important to employees than the hiring rate. Relatively low wage rates have been acceptable to employees in some cases when explicit assurance of considerable overtime work at premium rates was given.

Many of the clauses governing "conditions" are not so directly or specifically related to the level of wage rates. In their application, however, virtually every one of these clauses has an indirect bearing upon labor costs and employee earnings. The limitation of the employer's right to discipline "for cause" as determined by an arbitrator is one example. In ways that will be subsequently outlined, the effect of such clauses upon costs and earnings and upon the relative competitive position of a company depends upon the manner of their administration in day-by-day operations.

Another distinguishing characteristic of collective bargaining should be particularly noted. A union-management agreement covering all the matters subject to negotiation is ordinarily a prerequisite to the production of goods. "No contract, no work" is the slogan which epitomizes this idea. The employer's right unilaterally to install conditions of employment—to which employees then individually react—is further restricted by law. It will be recalled that in the Inland Steel Case, decided in 1948, the National Labor Relations Board ruled that old-age retirement pensions were a form of wages and subject, therefore, to compulsory collective bargaining under the Taft-Hartley Act.[5] The immediate effect of the ruling was not only to extend the scope of negotiations but to limit the right of management unilaterally to institute an old-age retirement program or unilaterally to make changes in an existing one. Such questions were assigned to the joint-determination process. To the extent that the employees support their union representatives on these or other issues, a union-management agreement is a prerequisite to the performance of productive operations.

The particular kind of employee-employer understandings which are required to validate the conditions of work through collective bargaining is a matter of no little significance in explaining the behavior of wages. The nature of the agreement is a critical aspect of wage determination.

Consequences of Nonagreement

The latitude of employees and employer to reject employment terms is particularly significant as long as mutual acceptance remains a basic criterion. What happens if there is no agreement? What are the consequences of nonagreement? These questions must be answered when a final decision is made about accepting or rejecting the terms offered by "the other side."

The upper and the lower limits of the negotiating area are those points at which employer and employees consider the costs of settlement prohibitive. These limits are not precise. They are variously conceived at the start of particular negotiations. They change as a breakdown of negotiations becomes imminent. Modifications occur in order to terminate a strike. The real limits are seldom disclosed in negotiations. Bargaining tactics and negotiating skills must be included, therefore, among the various factors which fashion the wage agreement. The limits within which a wage settlement is achievable, however, are singularly dependent upon the particular process of determination which is utilized, for the consequences of nonagreement vary significantly between the several processes.

The need for an agreement is felt both by employees and by employers, but usually with differing degrees of urgency. This affects their readiness to modify positions in order to consummate the essential understanding. The individual employee who fails to get the raise which his wife urged him to go after, and to which he feels entitled, placates the family by reporting: "The boss said I was entirely free to get a job somewhere else." The union leader explains to a critical membership that "after all, we got as much as could be secured without a strike. You don't want a strike, do you?" The industrial relations director tells his colleagues that a far-reaching concession would never have been made to a union except

[5] This decision was later upheld by the Supreme Court. *Inland Steel Company v. NLRB*, 336 U.S. 960 (1949).

for the undesirability of an imminent work stoppage. A satisfactory understanding of wage behavior is not possible without recognizing the vital role played in the determination processes by the factor which is here designated as the consequences of nonagreement.

Virtually all wage agreements, and particularly those arrived at by collective bargaining, represent compromises between conflicting objectives. Being differently oriented, the wage objectives of employees and of the employer are bound to be different. An employee whose wife has been urging the need for more money to meet current and accumulating bills is not likely to have an all-absorbing interest in a company's understandable concern about a possible worsening of its competitive position or the need to provide for future expansion of facilities. Strong claims for attention to both short-term and long-term economic well-being arise during wage negotiations. They have somehow to be balanced and reconciled. Not without reason have wage negotiations been designated as "a give-and-take proposition."

Nor can subjective attitudes be lightly dismissed. It has often been observed that the desires and opinions of men are fundamental facts. At any event the conflicting positions which they engender have to be reconciled. In some cases employees simply cannot see why they should receive lower wages or lesser increases than neighbors who do "the same kind of work" for another company. A management does not want to "upset wage levels in an area" and thereby incur the disapproval of those who manage other companies. Institutional considerations are sometimes paramount. Wage changes, or the lack of them, are related to the so-called union-security issue. The examples could be multiplied of similar determinants of the range of acceptability within which a wage agreement has to be consummated.

Every wage negotiation, under each process of determination, has its own peculiar characteristics. The differences which must be reconciled are variously oriented. Thus, as stated previously, wage negotiation may be conceived as a system of communication between employees and employers, regarding their respective needs, directed toward the discovery of those terms at which employers will provide jobs and at which employees will work in the near future. Under each process of determination, penalties accrue from a failure to discover—or for undue delay in discovering—such terms. The need to avoid the consequences of nonagreement constitutes the ultimate motivation for the concessions which are given and taken whenever wage decisions are made.

The Wage-determination Processes

The processes by which the essential employee-employer agreement is developed constitute a significant aspect of wage determination. The consent factor is variously evaluated under the alternative processes; this factor has influenced specifically the development and growth of collective bargaining with a marked effect upon the nature of the agreement and the consequences of nonagreement. These considerations are pertinent because, within the range of latitude in which wage decisions are made, substantive terms depend upon the process of wage determination that is utilized.

Four principal processes of wage determination are examined in the balance of this chapter: (1) individual bargaining, (2) management-administered wage determination, (3) collective bargaining, and (4) union-administered wage determination.[6] For clarity of analysis, each of these four processes is discussed as though it were a clearly identifiable type. The agreement-making procedures followed in particular cases, however, do not always fall neatly and exclusively into one of these categories. There are overlapping characteristics.[7] The present analysis is designed to provide guides, or bench marks, for discovering the dominant characteristics of a particular wage-setting arrangement and their effects upon wages.

INDIVIDUAL BARGAINING

Considerable public and governmental support for collective bargaining derives from the conviction that the worker who negotiates individually suffers from "inequality of bargaining power." The consequences of non-agreement are, in fact, often far more serious for the individual employee whose job is at stake than for the employer who is negotiating for the service of but one of many employees. This characteristic of so-called individual bargaining is not emphasized by those who contend that so-called voluntarism in labor-management relations is best preserved by a process requiring the explicit consent of each individual employee to the employment terms at which he will work.

However, the fact is that individual bargaining simply cannot be practiced in many sectors of our complex industrial economy. The individual necessities and desires of each employee have to be subordinated to general rules and regulations which cannot be avoided when large numbers of employees are brought together to work as a coordinated production unit. How are wages and related conditions of work to be specified when the individual employee cannot participate directly in their formulation? This has long been the fundamental question about the manner of wage determination.

It is only in relatively small concerns that individual bargaining is at all feasible. Some service businesses and small manufacturing establishments assign only one or two employees to a certain operation. Each employee may even perform a variety of tasks which change from day to day. Job assignments are not clearly defined, therefore, and the employee does not work at a specialized task. Virtually every employee can be a "key employee" in the sense that the loss of his services could seriously affect the employer's ability to operate successfully. The consequences of nonagreement are significant enough, both to employee and to employer,

---

[6] There has been experience in the United States with a fifth process, i.e., governmental determination. It is assumed, however, that resort to this process will continue to be limited to periods of national emergency.

[7] If the coercive power is great enough on either side, collective bargaining may take on some of the characteristics of either management-administered wage determination or union-administered wage determination. Individual bargaining may be practiced under any type.

to induce "give-and-take" negotiations between them. A considerable individual variation in employment terms must also be compatible with operational needs. Wages are then determined for the man, rather than for a job. Scheduled hours of work are also sometimes negotiated separately for different employees where their work is not interdependent. Some cannot get to work as early as others; so it is agreed that one employee will work from 7 A.M. to 3 P.M., while another will work from 8:30 A.M. to 4:30 P.M.

There are circumstances, then, under which the determination of wages can be worked out as a series of individual arrangements between each employee and the employer. A high degree of voluntarism then obtains. Nor need the individual employee be burdened by an inequality of bargaining power if he fills a key job. Indeed, when business is good and when manpower is in short supply, small employers frequently complain about having "too little left" for themselves after making the concessions necessary to hold the "experienced" workers upon whom they are dependent. Such employers have been known to establish a market-wide association committed to the "stabilization" of wages. They look to joint employer action to attain what they consider an equality of bargaining power.

Individual bargaining on a give-and-take basis becomes less and less practical when a small company expands. More workers are hired. Groups of workers are assigned to perform a specialized task in repetitive fashion. Differences in rates of pay within a job classification give rise to so many claims of discriminatory treatment that a standard job rate has to be specified. Wage differentials between the various occupational groups also have to be decided upon. Since the jobs are interdependent, shop rules must be promulgated for general application to all employees in order to facilitate the flow of production and to provide supervisors with guides for dealing with employees. As the plant becomes larger, wage administration becomes necessary; that is, decisions have to be made as respects wage structure and conditions of work.

Individual bargaining is effectively utilized to the satisfaction of employees and employer in many small enterprises. However, it may be noted that multiemployer bargaining, or so-called industry-wide collective bargaining, has been widely adopted in the small-scale industries. In those situations, the jobs usually have common craftlike characteristics and the employees look essentially to the labor market rather than to a particular employer for their job opportunities. Waiters and cooks are an example. They seek uniform market rates of pay, particularly to avoid a deterioration of work standards in times of poor business. The employers then frequently associate and negotiate for a master agreement, not solely to achieve a stronger bargaining position, but to avoid an upward spiraling of wages in times of good business. Individual bargaining has but a limited applicability in a complex industrial society.

MANAGEMENT-ADMINISTERED WAGE DETERMINATION

Wage determination in a mass-production economy has come to involve administrative decision making, i.e., the formulation and effectuation of wage programs. The wage-administration function is particularly crucial in manufacturing, where the large majority of jobs are specialized and repetitive. They are the so-called semiskilled jobs. Most employees can perform any of them effectively with but limited training. Scores—or even hundreds—of employees perform the same job and are responsible for about the same rate of production. Their work is interdependent with similar groups of employees. Standard occupational wage rates, uniform hours of work schedules, and generally applicable conditions of employment are an unavoidable concomitant of manufacturing operations in which the specialized work of many individual employees must be closely scheduled and coordinated.

With a few possible exceptions, there are no "key" employees among the semiskilled employees in manufacturing.[8] The loss of any one man's services is frequently of little or no concern to the employer. Retention of his job, however, is frequently a matter of considerable urgency to the employee. A change of employment is likely to result in the loss of important rights derived from seniority standing. The right of an individual employee to quit his job, therefore, is of limited significance, at least as far as longer-service employees are concerned, in fashioning the conditions of employment.

Craft versus Factory Labor

Another notable change in the employer-employee relationship occurred with industrialization. A new answer was given to the query: For what are wages paid? Wages are paid to skilled craftsmen and to so-called semiskilled factory employees on the basis of quite different assumptions. Skilled craftsmen—those who serve an apprenticeship or have equivalent all-round skills—receive an hourly wage to compensate for the performance of all kinds of work, simple or complex, encompassed by a craft jurisdiction. Possessing a reservoir of general-purpose skills, readily transferable from one employment to another, the craftsman is paid the same wage whenever any of those skills are drawn upon. This concept of wage determination is epitomized by the phrase: "A man is worthy of his hire."

Certain standard conditions of employment for craftsmen can be and are rather generally established by multiemployer bargaining conducted separately for each labor market. This seems to derive, at least in part, from a market orientation rather than an employer orientation of the employees. Because their skills are readily transferable from one employer

---

[8] Those who are "key" employees may engage in a limited form of individual bargaining. Their ability to do so effectively, however, is inhibited by management's concern lest "concessions" to an individual employee generate a demand for their general application.

to another, craftsmen look to an entire labor market for their job opportunities and for their economic security. The factory employee, however, is more company-oriented.[9] He looks to a certain employer for job opportunities and economic security. The effort of skilled craftsmen to maintain or extend their craft jurisdiction is, in a sense, the counterpart of the insistence of factory employees upon seniority rights.[10]

The wage rates for most manufacturing operations (the unskilled and semiskilled jobs) are not related to a man's mastery of related skills. They are, rather, dependent upon an evaluation of the skill and effort required to perform each particular job assignment.[11] Work assignments in a manufacturing plant vary from time to time, and so does the employee's wage. A man is paid for what he does rather than for what he *can* do. The wage depends in part upon administrative measurements of so-called job content. It is notable, however, that the craftsmen in the mass-manufacturing industries (including those on maintenance work) are usually paid as craftsmen; that is, their wages are dependent upon all-around capacity rather than upon particular work assignments. This contrast serves to highlight differences in wage concepts.

Wage determination in factories has a further distinguishing characteristic. Since wage relationships are based primarily upon an administrative evaluation of the elements which constitute each job, the job description is important. When the job description changes because of the addition or elimination of duties, a new wage rate may have to be decided upon. The negotiation of wage rates for new or changed jobs is an administrative aspect of wage determination which is among the most controversial and exacting aspects of labor-management relations in manufacturing. The standard output for which a particular wage is payable, i.e., the specification of a "fair day's work for a fair day's pay," is a further task which wage administrators have found to be elusive and controversial.

Various administrative aspects of wage determination, such as those already mentioned, have been conceived by many a company as an es-

[9] The difference in orientation is illustrated by collectively bargained programs for old-age retirement benefits. Craftsmen tend to establish labor-market funds to which the employers contribute a fixed percentage of each payroll as their sole obligation and from which benefits are paid on the basis of the employees' length of service in the industry. In manufacturing industries, however, a company accepts responsibility for making specified benefits available based upon the employees' length of service with the company.

[10] Not many years ago, a job counselor would advise young men to "learn a trade; then you will be able to earn a good living anywhere." With the growth of large-scale manufacturing operations, it is as appropriate to suggest: "Get a job with a large company and accumulate seniority."

[11] Although unions in manufacturing industries have accepted this view in general, they have sought certain modifications—for example, increasing wages as productivity increases regardless of the effort and skill factors.

sential part of the managerial function which should not be shared either with individual employees or with a union. Under collective bargaining these administrative functions are commonly shared between management and union representatives.

It is also important to note the continuous nature of the bargaining over wages and employment conditions which more or less typifies collective bargaining in manufacturing industries. This application of general policies, whether enunciated in a formal labor agreement or not, to the day-by-day operations of a plant give rise to so-called employee grievances. An employee challenges the equity of the rates set by the industrial engineering department on a new job or he questions the selection of another employee for promotion. He objects to overtime rules and sometimes grows restive, for real or imaginary reasons, about the way he is treated by a foreman. These examples could be multiplied many times. Decisions made to settle grievances are among the administrative determinants of labor costs and employee earnings.

An individual employee negotiating a grievance on his own behalf, is likely to feel that he does not bargain on equal terms with the employer. Use of his ultimate economic power, i.e., quitting the job, may carry little or no weight in support of the employee's position. It is not implied, however, that individual employee grievances are invariably mishandled by management. Many an unorganized company "leans over backward" in disposing of grievances in order to avoid the charge of unfair or discriminatory treatment. Some personnel departments are expected to "represent" the employee whose grievance is under consideration. Even so, the bargaining is largely restricted to the application of a company policy and does not embrace the substance of the policies. Under collective bargaining, the union is a joint administrator with management, not only in formulating wage policy, but in applying it in the day-by-day operation of a plant.

As industrial expansion occurred, a distinctive process of wage determination came into being. In the absence of collective bargaining, the basic wage-rate schedule and related conditions of employment, including grievance-handling policies, are enunciated by the management without the direct participation of employees. The terms of employment are then proffered to employees for their individual acceptance or rejection. This process is here designated as management-administered wage determination.

Employee Consent to Management-administered Wage Rates

The several ways by which the individual employee can, in effect, reject the proffered terms constitute a restraint upon the unorganized employer in the formulation and application of wage policies. A voluntary severance of employment by an employee constitutes a summary rejection. Employee-turnover data are an important measure of the acceptability of available employment terms. The individual employee can also ostensibly accept the proffered terms and, while remaining on the job as a matter of necessity, give less than a full productive effort. The morale factor has become important in the wage-determination process. Devices such as attitude surveys have been developed to measure this kind of rejection. The employee can reject proffered terms in another way. He can decide that an altogether different process of wage determination —collective bargaining—is essential for his economic well-being. In years past, individual employees were often inhibited in exercising their right to join a union. It was the strengthening of the right of employees in mass-production industries to form unions and, by their vote, to require the employer to substitute collective bargaining for management-administered wage determination that made the Wagner Act so controversial; for this placed an additional restraint upon management in the making of wage decisions.

Under management-administered wage determination, the reaction of individual employees to the management wage decisions can induce their modification. The costs of a high labor-turnover or of impaired employee morale can become prohibitive. The disposition of employees to organize into a union can also result in an improvement of the terms of employment. However, these forms of employee influence upon the formulation and administration of wage policies are indirect and may have costly consequences to employees. Quitting a job may be a serious proposition since seniority rights are involved. Loafing on the job can result in disciplinary action by management. Improvements in employment terms resulting from high labor turnover, moreover, benefit only those who did not quit their jobs. The employee drive for collective bargaining in many plants was doubtless grounded in a desire for less costly and less risky means of rejecting employment terms.

Only a relatively few large manufacturing companies in the mass-production industries have successfully developed management-administered wage determination. A large majority of their employees are convinced of the fairness and equity of the conditions of employment made available by management even in the absence of direct participation in their formulation. Employees do not reject the management-administered terms by quitting their jobs, by unduly restricting their effort on the job, or by voting for union representation. These companies have apparently recognized that the genuine consent of a substantial majority of the employees is essential to a satisfactory and continuing status for management-administered wage determination. Some management representatives have expressed the view that continued adherence to management-administered wage determination might require even higher wages and better working conditions than would be granted under collective bargaining.[12]

The great labor relations issue of the past twenty years has been over the use of management-administered wage determination or of collective bargaining in the manufacturing industries. Collective bargaining is a process which stands in marked contrast to management-administered wage determination.

[12] It is reasoned, in effect, that the weight of a recommendation of union representatives to the employees is considerable when wage increases are less than expected or when wage decreases are unavoidable.

COLLECTIVE BARGAINING

The Wagner Act established, as a matter of law, the right of employees in an appropriate bargaining unit to decide, by majority vote, whether or not collective bargaining should be utilized as the wage-determining process. This right was reaffirmed by the Taft-Hartley Act. The consequent widespread introduction of collective bargaining in the manufacturing industries was a momentous event in the development of wage-determination processes.

Under collective bargaining the terms of employment have to be approved, prior to being placed in effect, by the union as well as by the employer. Employees also participate through their shop committeemen and union stewards in applying the terms of the union-company agreement to day-by-day operational problems. Certain administrative functions of wage determination are thus shared by company and union representatives.

Individual employees can react to the terms made available by the union-management agreement in much the same manner as when management-administered wage determination obtains. They can individually quit their jobs, give less than adequate productive performance, or even take steps to eliminate collective bargaining.[13] If virtually all the employees are union members, especially if they participate in union affairs, the collectively bargained terms are likely to be acceptable to at least a majority of the employees. However, this is not inevitable. The union membership may be a bare majority of all employees and a wage settlement may be approved by a close vote among the relatively few members who attend a ratification meeting. Individual employees and particular groups of employees may be quite dissatisfied with the results of collective bargaining. Many employees, on the other hand, are disposed to approve of the collective-bargaining process, even when they do not avail themselves of their participation rights, on the assumption that the proffered terms are likely to be more favorable to them if the union has participated in their formulation.

There are logical reasons, therefore, for viewing collective bargaining as essentially a process of union-management wage administration, i.e., joint formulation and application of labor policy. Once an agreement is worked out by company and union negotiators, they have a joint interest in convincing the employees that a "good settlement" has been reached. Their roles tend to change from opposing advocates to cooperators. Occasionally company and union representatives stand shoulder to shoulder in defending a wage settlement against the onslaught of a dissatisfied employee constituency.

One of the most important characteristics of collective bargaining is the essentiality of a union-management agreement as a condition precedent to work performance. As already noted, this is in marked contrast to management-administered wage determination. The strike threat unquestionably has to be reckoned with when wages are determined by collective bargaining.

[13] The Taft-Hartley Act provides for decertification elections through which the employees can change unions or eliminate collective bargaining.

The theory of collective bargaining, certainly as conceived by the labor unions, encompasses the idea that individual employees have no right to work at employment terms rejected by the union. Otherwise the union would not be a coadministrator nor would it be the exclusive bargaining representative for all employees. Whether or not the union function should be so conceived is perhaps the most controversial concept in the field of wage determination. Experience indicates, however, that difficulties are encountered if the union is presumed to act as the bargaining representative for its members only. Indeed, it is ordinarily not at all feasible to formulate one set of working conditions for union members and other terms for nonunion members.

A strong tendency exists for a company to accept the union as the bargaining representative for all employees, i.e., to concede exclusive bargaining rights, when it decides that "collective bargaining is here to stay." In acceding to so-called union-security demands, many a company has concluded that, under collective bargaining, the opportunity of the individual employee to participate in wage determination accrues primarily from union membership. This would seem to be essentially the case if the exclusive bargaining right of the union is recognized.

Wage Negotiations under Collective Bargaining

Under collective bargaining, therefore, basic decisions respecting wages and conditions of employment are a matter of joint management-union determination. In this process, wages are frequently balanced with "conditions" and a choice is often made between alternative changes in employment terms. For example, the union may withdraw a claim for a union shop in return for a significant increase in wages. A choice may be made between a general wage increase for all employees and old-age retirement benefits or health insurance which will actually be received by but a part of the work force.

As a result of their growing importance, these alternate choices constitute a new dimension in wage determination. The cost of the so-called fringes, or collateral wage provisions, cannot always be readily translated into a precise "wage-per-hour equivalent." Especially when company commitments are long-term ones—as in the case of many old-age retirement programs—their ultimate cost can at best only be approximated when they are instituted. Labor turnover, changes in the composition of the work force, the rate of interest earned on reserve funds, the rate of plant operation, and other variable factors will fashion the ultimate cost.

It has become increasingly difficult accurately to anticipate the economic consequences of a collectively bargained labor agreement. This is not only because of the so-called fringes. How will a seniority rule negotiated to regulate the promotion, layoff, and recall of employees affect the labor cost? Is it better for a multiplant company, whose employees are deeply concerned about the possible loss of jobs because of impending technological changes, to agree to interplant seniority or to severance pay? Will higher or lower costs result from a no-strike clause accompanied by a provision for the arbitration of all grievances? Easy answers are not available to these and many similar questions. The results will be determined by practice in the day-by-day operations of the future.

Appraising the economic consequences of a labor agreement becomes an even more elusive undertaking when tactical considerations are dominant. In the late 1930's, for example, relatively large wage increases were volunteered by many a management to their nonunionized employees in order to "show the workers they don't need a union." If the plant became organized anyway, as was often the case, a further wage increase was insisted upon by the union in order to complete its organizational program, i.e., to give tangible proof of the advantages of the union to the employees. In this type of situation wages were increased first in an effort to forestall unionization and then to assist in assuring continued employee support for the union.

Institutional necessities, as appraised by the union leaders, have also sometimes affected the character of wage adjustments. Because a wage settlement is subject to at least the simple majority-vote approval of those attending a ratification meeting and actually needs an even greater degree of employee acceptance to be really workable, a union leader may have to make certain that a settlement will be particularly acceptable to employees in those occupational groups which make up the bulk of the work force. The general across-the-board increases, so typical of wage settlements in recent years, were not unrelated to the need to gain the approval of the relatively large number of semiskilled and relatively unskilled employees. There have been times, however, when this kind of wage administration has resulted in the strenuous opposition of skilled employees.

Because of the interjection of conditioning factors like those mentioned, the terms of employment specified by joint agreement between a union and the employer are likely to be different than they would be under management-administered wage determination. The extent of the difference, however, depends upon the manner in which the management and the union undertake their joint administrative functions. In some situations the union is relatively passive and the administrative responsibilities devolve primarily upon management. In others the union asserts positive policies. There are few, if any, collective-bargaining arrangements without their own peculiar characteristics in these respects.

Agreement Making and Agreement Administration

If the economic consequences of the total agreement arrived at by collective bargaining are significantly indeterminable, how do employer and union representatives decide upon the relative acceptability or the relative unacceptability of particular conditions of employment? How is a balanced "package" of employment conditions evolved in collective bargaining?

In ways presently to be discussed, the immediate consequences of nonagreement are a persuasive force. No one can participate extensively in collective-bargaining negotiations, however, and remain unaware of the concern of those on each side of the bargaining table with the company's competitive position. An employer is reluctant to acquiesce in any important "improvement" of employment conditions which will not apply to his competitors. Nor will a union lightly assume the risk of unemployment which is accentuated when a company "is pushed too far out in front."

Interplant and intercompany comparisons of the various conditions of employment, and of changes in them, are well-nigh universal in collective bargaining. Clauses are carried over verbatim from one labor agreement to another, sometimes even when the transfer seems to be patently inappropriate. The formulation of wage agreements has strong intercompany characteristics. This is most notable in the consummation of master agreements in multiemployer bargaining, but it is also quite pronounced even in company-by-company bargaining.

There has been a marked tendency, then, for the terms of collectively bargained settlements to be similar among competing concerns. A high degree of uniformity respecting the scope of collective bargaining, i.e., the subjects dealt with by joint negotiation, is the result. The application of a labor agreement, however, is generally the joint responsibility of local union representatives and local management representatives. Even though identical clauses may be in the labor agreements of two or more companies, wide variations in their application are the rule. The local understandings that are devised to give "meaning" to the clauses are an important aspect of collective bargaining.

Local understandings and practices have been known to negate entirely the terms of a formal labor agreement. A critical impasse developed during a negotiation some few years ago. Company representatives refused to agree to any seniority clause unless it provided for taking the ability as well as the seniority of employees into account in the making of promotions. The union finally acceded. A recent investigation showed that the principle gained by the employer was actually never effectuated. As a matter of plant practice, promotions were made on a "straight seniority" basis by foremen who either did not know how to combine ability and seniority factors in deciding upon promotions or were reluctant to create grievances and trouble with union representatives by deviating from a straight seniority approach.

The clauses of a labor agreement are not self-effectuating. An adequate comprehension of the wages and conditions of employment at various companies cannot be achieved, therefore, by a simple comparison of formal labor-agreement terms. How a particular term of a labor agreement works out depends upon the policies and practices followed in its effectuation. As an additional telling example, consider a standard clause providing simply for an equal division of overtime work among the employees in each department. The management of one company agreed with the contention of local union representatives that the clause should be "strictly" interpreted. Employees who were lowest in the amount of overtime worked were assigned to jobs for which overtime was scheduled without regard to previous experience. Another company, subject to the identical clause, convinced its employees and their local union representatives that men should be assigned to overtime work on the basis of management's appraisal of their ability to perform the jobs but that every effort would be made to ensure all men in the department an equal number of overtime hours during each six-month period. In one case the assignment of inexperienced men to overtime work increased unit labor costs by an estimated 25 per cent in addition to the premium pay. Production dropped precipitately and quality standards were adversely affected. In the other case, the regular rate of production and quality standards were fully maintained during the overtime hours, and the requirement that overtime be shared entailed virtually no increase in labor costs. The respective competitive positions of the two companies were obviously affected to a marked extent by the effectuating policies which were agreed upon locally. In other words, the administrative decisions were a vital part of wage determination.

The cost and earnings effects of labor-agreement clauses are significantly dependent upon the way those clauses are applied. The acceptability or unacceptability of many proposals made in contract negotiations consequently depends—sometimes to a marked extent—upon the kind of union-management relationship which obtains. What operating policies and procedures can minimize the cost impact or maximize the wage possibilities of a proposed clause? What will be the incidence of a particular clause in view of the state of the labor relationship in a company or in a plant? These questions can be far more important than the way a clause is worded. It is often said unofficially that "the words of the labor agreement don't mean nearly so much as the way the parties work and live together."

The quality of the relations which have been developed between the company and its employees and between the company and the union representatives largely determines the way in which a collective-bargaining agreement operates in practice. The day-by-day administration of a labor agreement can be either orderly and reasonable or chaotic and vindictive. Sometimes the agreement is operated as a "living document." During times of good business every clause of a collective agreement is rigorously "lived up to" and even extended in its scope through the manner of settling day-by-day problems. When business is bad, however, the agreement terms will be narrowly applied or even ignored. But such give-and-take flexibility is not an inherent characteristic of collective bargaining. The labor agreement is viewed in some cases as a rigid statement of the rights conceded to the union and as a very inflexible document. If a union is weak or its leadership ineffective, the employer may successfully assert extensive decision-making rights. On the other hand, the union may be able to take over a large share of the decision-making function. The labor agreement greatly influences but does not inexorably determine the conditions of employment.

Nature of Effectuation

Under collective bargaining, then, union representatives share with management, in various ways, the function of formulating and applying the employment terms. An employee can individually reject these terms —most summarily by quitting his job—but he cannot bargain directly for terms at variance from those covered by the labor agreement.[14] Employees occasionally combine their individual protests and engage in a wildcat strike, but both the union and management, i.e., the joint administrators of the conditions of employment, are responsible for taking action

[14] Individual bargaining may be conducted regarding other terms of employment and, to a limited extent, may even be provided for in the agreement if, for example, minimum rates or conditions are specified.

against such activities. It is significant, indeed, that the union is often held "responsible" for such "illegal" stoppages. Such a responsibility, it would seem, cannot be assigned unless the union is recognized as the exclusive bargaining representative of all employees.

The labor agreement is effectuated jointly by negotiations between local management and union representatives. The factor of consent thus assumes far-reaching implications. Local negotiations are vital.[15] Precedent-making applications of the agreement terms are made and substance is given to rather bare clauses. Supplemental agreements are also negotiated locally to dispose of problems not "covered" by the terms of the formal labor agreement. A considerable decision-making latitude is thus possessed by those who are responsible for applying the wage agreement to the day-by-day operation of a business.

Because of the characteristics here noted, it is logical to view collective bargaining, particularly as developed in manufacturing industries, as a process of union-management administration of the conditions of employment. The quality of the decisions, for which union and management representatives are jointly responsible, is determined in large measure by the characteristics of the labor relationship which obtains. This is another way of saying that collective bargaining is a continuing process. So is the determination of wages and related conditions of employment.

Motivations for Union-Management Agreement

In the absence of collective bargaining, the specification and application of employment terms are essentially administrative functions of management. When collective bargaining is practiced, those terms and their application must be validated by an agreement between the employer and the union. What induces such an agreement?

In performing their joint administrative function, representatives of the union and of the management have to anticipate the reactions of the employees. Serious membership dissatisfaction with the terms of a settlement can lead either to loss of support for the union or in demands for greater militancy in the future. Nor can there be certainty about the willingness of the employees or of the employer to "take a strike" in support of particular demands.

Negotiating tactics and rituals have come into being to mask union weaknesses deriving from the employees' unwillingness to strike and management weaknesses resulting from the employer's inability to forego production. The discovery of those terms which will be really accepted in order to avoid a work stoppage, or to terminate one, is the fundamental task of negotiators.

In a real sense, the right to strike provides the employees with a more effective way of rejecting an employer offer than obtains in the absence of collective bargaining. Rejection does not entail a severance of employ-

[15] Some grievance problems can be disposed of by the employee and his immediate supervisor. Questions arise, however, about the extent to which grievances can be so disposed of without "interpreting" the labor agreement in ways which are unacceptable to a majority of the employees or to the union leaders. Settlements of this kind may also establish precedents adverse to the employer's interest and result in so-called "whipsawing."

ment. When a collective-bargaining impasse occurs, all employees in the bargaining unit temporarily lose their employment opportunities. They do not usually lose their jobs. Management may replace "economic strikers" or seek to operate during a strike with employees who choose to exercise an individual "right to work." Such courses of action, however, are no longer standard practices. Companies which have decided, as a matter of policy, to "make collective bargaining work" do not attempt to operate during a strike. The strike is conceived as an institutional incident concomitant to a particular process of wage determination. In some cases, the management and the union even consummate a "strike agreement." The company agrees not to undertake production activities until a labor agreement is reached. The union agrees that maintenance work and office activities can be conducted by the company without union interference.

It is usually worth some concessions on the part of both employer and employees to avoid the costs of a strike. However, the extent to which a union can influence the specification of employment terms—in acting jointly with management to perform the decision-making function—depends, in the last analysis, upon the willingness of the employees to "hit the bricks" if necessary to achieve a certain goal. This may or may not exert sufficient economic pressure upon the employer to bring about the desired recognition of union demands. Additional uncertainties about employee reactions are thus introduced by collective bargaining and make judgments about wages more difficult.

It is often said that a union cannot win a long strike. A short strike, on the other hand, may hold an altogether different prospect. When it seems virtually certain that any walkout will be brief, employees are strongly disposed to approve strike action. This propensity is particularly strong among employees who have long been working a full schedule with plenty of overtime. A brief spell of unemployment, even without pay, is sometimes attractive—say at the start of a hunting season—and pressure can thereby be painlessly applied to induce concessions from the employer.

By and large, however, employees are averse to a strike. They are willing to "accept less" if that is necessary to get an agreement and "much less" if a protracted strike is the alternative. Depending largely upon this week's wages for this week's living, employees have inadequate reserves to carry them through a long period of no earning.[16] There is always the risk, too, that a lengthy shutdown will result in an impairment of job opportunities if the company loses market outlets or discontinues operations.

Under some circumstances, strike action will be strongly supported by the union membership despite the prospect of a lengthy stoppage. This has happened most commonly when the employer position was widely interpreted as part of a move to "break the union." A protracted strike may then be knowingly undertaken by the employees to defend their

[16] On occasion, strike benefits have approximated regular earnings. Employees have then been disposed to continue a strike indefinitely—often to the financial and negotiating embarrassment of the union.

right to collective bargaining as a "matter of principle." Such a strike may also be called, of course, to reject an employer proposal which is deemed to be entirely unreasonable and inequitable in terms of employee needs.

This brief attention to the consequences of a collective-bargaining impasse upon employees illustrates some of the potent restraints upon union negotiators. The consequences of a failure to agree can also be adverse to the employer. The seriousness with which an employer contemplates a possible interruption to production, however, depends upon the circumstances of each case. If inventories are high, or if production needs can be readily met by purchases from other companies, a company may face a shutdown with considerable equanimity. Moreover, profit margins may be so narrow that a company prefers a work stoppage, whatever the duration, to any increase in labor cost. The threat of a work stoppage, therefore, does not inevitably induce concessions. There are limits to the terms which the union can achieve.

It is, however, frequently "worth something" to an employer to avoid a strike. Even a brief stoppage of operations entails the added expense of closing down and starting up again. Nor can it be assumed that the terms of employment agreed upon to terminate a strike will be more favorable than a settlement negotiated without a work stoppage. Lack of an agreement can be quite serious to the employer if the flow of goods to customers is interrupted. Many an employer concession has been made solely to avoid the risk that outlets for goods, carefully nurtured over many years, might dry up because of a loss of customer confidence in the dependability of its customary source of supply. These and similar factors induce employer concessions in collective bargaining.

The weight of customer needs in wage negotiations is closely related to the employee unit for which a particular negotiation is conducted. Many multiplant companies seek to bargain separately and at different times, either with the same union or with different unions, for each plant at which similar products are manufactured. A threatened work stoppage at but one of these plants is less likely to impel employer concessions than a collective-bargaining impasse in negotiations covering all the plants. Unions have understandably sought company-wide bargaining under these circumstances to maximize their bargaining power. The situation is quite different if the operations of a multiplant company are integrated. Successive threats of localized stoppages at each plant would then constitute a series of negotiating crises because the entire operation would be affected.

Important variations in the substance of the labor agreement can arise, therefore, from differences in the employee unit represented in negotiations. There are other pointed illustrations of this circumstance. For example, when competition between several producers is spirited, a strike limited to one company means that competitors will continue to produce goods and thereby gain a temporary advantage from the selective work stoppage. Vast employer wage concessions have sometimes been made by a company anxious to avoid a selective stoppage. Such concessions then typically become a pattern for application to other companies. While the company selected for "breakthrough" negotiations is under strong pressure to make concessions, the union faces but a limited unemployment problem among its total membership if an impasse occurs. Working employees may even be assessed to support the strikers. Out of such situations has come a strong impulse among employers for multi-employer bargaining or for a uniform expiration date for the various agreements.

An employer who is unable to stand even a brief interruption of production without large losses has an urgent need for a labor agreement and is likely to make substantial concessions to get one. The union bargaining position is then strong because the employees are not likely to be seriously disadvantaged by a short strike. There are some cogent illustrations of this. Construction companies working against an imminent deadline for completing a building have made significant concessions to ensure the uninterrupted services of their employees and thereby avoid penalties for delays in performance. Concessions have also been exacted from an employer who is under strong compulsion to keep men on the job in order to get a ship unloaded before substantial demurrage charges accrue. Despite worry over a poor financial position, some companies have nevertheless agreed to wage increases, adamantly insisted upon by a union, simply because a strike would have resulted in "sudden death," whereas uninterrupted production has given a chance—even an outside chance—for business survival. The coercive cases are fortunately not typical.[17] They do illustrate how employment terms can be dependent upon the employer's urgent need to avoid the consequences of nonagreement. Many wage rates and conditions can only be explained in terms of this factor.

Consequences of Nonagreement

Balancing the consequences of nonagreement to employer and to employees is usually far less one-sided than in the cases just mentioned. The union will make concessions to avoid a work stoppage which would lack membership support. Management will make concessions that are, in its judgment, less expensive than the increased overhead costs of idle facilities, the loss of profitable sales, and the possible loss of customers. Within an area bounded by the points at which the costs of settlement are deemed to be excessive, union and company negotiators jointly formulate the terms of employment.

However, the limits are variable. If profits and employment opportunities are low, the negotiating area is narrow. On the other hand, if the customer demand for goods is so avid that increased wage costs can be "passed along" in product price, a stoppage of production tends to appear justifiable to a management only if necessary to forestall the most extreme union demands. Consumer interest in the substance of wage agreements run high when negotiations are conducted under such influences.[18]

---

[17] They resemble union-administered wage determination more than collective bargaining.

[18] This consumer interest has been most pronounced during wartime emergencies, when the customary restraints upon negotiators are virtually nonexistent. Under these conditions, intensive efforts to achieve so-called wage stabilization and price stabilization were made by the government on two occasions in the past fifteen years.

Wage increases then connote price increases. The employee risk of losing employment opportunities and the employer's risk of losing sales and profits are both minimized.

In preparing for a wage negotiation, steps are sometimes taken by one or both sides to minimize their bargaining weaknesses. Prior to negotiations, the employer may accumulate inventories or lay plans to secure goods from "outside sources" if necessary. Wildcat strikes sometimes "spontaneously" occur, or the union authorizes grievance strikes, if they are not outlawed by a labor agreement, to prevent inventory accumulation. The union may create a "strike fund" to encourage employees to stand ready, if necessary, to endure a work stoppage. Such tactics are designed to limit the adverse consequences of nonagreement and thereby support negotiating claims.

Since collective bargaining is essentially a form of joint management-union administration, the labor leader has a key function to perform in wage determination. He shares with management the responsibility for formulating conditions of employment which will prove acceptable to the great majority of the employees. Some labor leaders have been able to initiate new demands and develop an employee willingness to strike for them in prosperous industries where employers have been most anxious to avoid work stoppages. Under less favorable economic circumstances, the union leader has to take defensive positions. He may have to convince a skeptical membership of the wisdom and necessity for taking far less than they have demanded as an "irreducible minimum." He may even have to gain membership acceptance of wage cuts proposed by the employer and agreed to by a union negotiating committee. While they are anxious to avoid a strike, the "rank and file" still tend to insist upon more favorable terms than can possibly be secured even as a strike settlement. It is a sobering experience to be with a union president at a membership meeting when he recommends employee approval of a wage agreement just consummated. His lot is not a happy one when the settlement provides few or no gains at a time when workers in other industries are securing significant improvements in working conditions.

Forces not encountered in any other process of wage determination thus have to be reconciled in collective bargaining. Tactical positioning and negotiating skills can account for sizable differences in wage settlements. Economic strength can be exaggerated and economic weakness can be masked.[19] Tactical moves and persuasiveness in argument are important. Small wonder that most employers did not welcome collective bargaining with open arms. The extent to which many employers have successfully geared their labor relations policies to collective-bargaining requirements, however, is one of the outstanding achievements of American industry.

[19] In the "now-it-can-be-told" sessions subsequent to a wage conference, a union negotiator will admit that, despite any impression to the contrary, he would have had to recede somewhat further from his "final" position rather than to strike for it. And the management negotiator will surmise that maybe "a penny or two" might have been forthcoming if that had been necessary to "settle the deal."

UNION-ADMINISTERED WAGE DETERMINATION

In the preceding discussion of collective bargaining, it was generally assumed that a kind of "equality of bargaining power" exists. In other words, each party is assumed to be interested in give-and-take negotiations if for no other reason than to avoid the adverse consequences of nonagreement. As long as the negotiator on each side of the table possesses a significant economic power, it is likely that the fundamental needs of each party will be conserved in a settlement.

Whether or not collective bargaining works out in practice, as is assumed by its theory, and also whether or not consumer interests are adequately protected, have been subjects of controversy in recent years. Attention has been directed to those large and pervasive unions which have been able at times to bypass give-and-take negotiations. In some small-scale industries, for example, the "big" union may unilaterally specify standard conditions of employment which are then presented separately to each "little" employer for acceptance or rejection in their entirety. The employer does not participate in the formulation of employment terms and may have little influence in their application. This process is here termed union-administered wage determination.[20]

Neither the union nor the employees have a great stake in any one of the negotiations conducted separately with one of a score or more of small employers in an industry. Only a small fraction of the industry's total job opportunities is involved. If negotiations break down, the relatively few strikers can ordinarily be placed by the union in other establishments or the strikers can be supported by the nonstriking union members. While the union is under no great pressure to complete an agreement, the small employer urgently needs one. He is unable to endure being singled out for a protracted stoppage.

The ability of the union to assume an administrative initiative in formulating employment terms does not necessarily mean that the resultant process of wage determination is unacceptable to the employers.[21] By recognizing its responsibility to gain overwhelming approval of the employers to its programs, a union can achieve accepted leadership status in wage determination. Such a position among employers has been achieved, it is sometimes said, by the Amalgamated Clothing Workers and the International Ladies' Garment Workers' Union.

A comment made some years ago by a union representative about union-administered wage determination is pertinent. He said, in substance: "We price our labor just as a retailer prices his wares. Sales are made only at the price tag figure. Anyone may buy or refrain from buying as he chooses." The analogy is not exact. Under union-administered wage determination, a fixed price may be effectively established for a total labor supply. The reasoning is similar, however, to the argument

---

[20] It can be compared to management-administered wage determination which involves the unilateral specification of terms by the employer and their proffer for acceptance or rejection in their entirety by each individual employee.

[21] Neither must the possession of a superior bargaining power by the employer under management-administered wage determination result inevitably in the nonacceptability of this process to employees.

often used in support of management-administered wage determination. It is frequently said by a company representative: "We offer wages and conditions as good as are compatible with the needs of the company and with the provision of steady jobs to employees. If any employee can do better elsewhere, he is free to quit his job at any time."

Other recently cited illustrations of union-administered wage determination include the practices of some locals of the International Brotherhood of Teamsters and Helpers. Small operators of trucks frequently complain about the loss of their collective bargaining rights, i.e., their right to participate directly with the union in formulating the terms of employment applicable to their operations. The story told by these small operators goes something like this: "A union representative comes to see me. He deposits on the desk a so-called labor agreement, drawn up by the union, and says, 'Sign here or we'll strike you tomorrow morning.' I can't stand a strike, so I sign." Sometimes the employer complains that his employees were not even members of the union. He may also explain that, subsequent to signing, he had no alternative but to seek devious ways and means of securing relief from the particularly onerous terms of an agreement.

Multiemployer Bargaining

Certain sections of the Taft-Hartley Act were devised in an attempt to redress the employer's inequality of bargaining power in small-scale industries.[22] Quite a different remedy has been sought by employers on their own initiative. In order to ensure direct participation with the union in formulating and applying the terms of employment, many associations for multiemployer collective bargaining have been created in small-scale industries. Representatives of the union and of the employers' association are responsible for the negotiations undertaken to consummate a master agreement applicable to all the companies. If negotiations fail, each employer is unable to operate, but so are his competitors. The consequence of nonagreement is minimized for the individual employer. At the same time the union is under greater pressure to meet employer terms, for only by an agreement can extensive unemployment among the union membership be avoided. To a large extent multiemployer bargaining has been developed by small employers in their search for an "equality of bargaining power" in dealing with a relatively powerful union. Since a strike can cut completely the consumer supply of goods or services, multiemployer bargaining peculiarly involves the public interest and has been the subject of considerable governmental scrutiny.

It would be a mistake, however, to conclude that multiemployer bargaining has been developed only in small-scale industries. Some of the conditions of employment of such diverse occupational group as coal miners, railroad workers, clothing workers, building-trade employees, printing employees, and glassworkers are also fixed by multiemployer

[22] A purpose of the Wagner Act, on the other hand, was to give employees a legal right to collective bargaining when they objected to their lack of participation in the establishment of employment conditions under management-administered wage determination

collective bargaining. An essentially similar process is also in effect in the steel industry. Separate agreements are consummated by the United Steelworkers of America and each of the major basic steel producers. These agreements expire, however, on the same dates. The basic terms of a key labor agreement consummated with one company are usually extended to all the steel companies. It is logical, therefore, to classify the wage-determination process in the steel industry as a form of multiemployer bargaining.

Employers frequently pool their economic power in order to participate more effectively with the union in formulating employment terms, rather than to forestall union-administered wage determination. They are doubtless concerned about the intolerable position each would be in if singled out by the union to negotiate under the threat of being shut down while competitors operate. Furthermore, a pattern-following company may lose much of its right to participate in the establishment of its own conditions of employment.

Disadvantages may also accrue to a union in bargaining with one concern at a time. Especially when concessions are not easily obtainable, the employees of one company are likely to be unenthusiastic about striking while fellow union members remain at work and subsequently receive any benefits gained by the localized strike. Augmented employer resistance may also arise about acceding to union proposals in the absence of definite assurance that they would also apply to competitors.[23] This factor has been of overriding importance to the unions in small-scale industries which have encouraged, or even assisted, the formation of employer associations to engage in industry-wide bargaining. Nor will a union see advantages in company-by-company bargaining if that entails, especially in times of poor business, the risk of establishing a pattern-making standard with the company least able and willing to be generous in its offers.

Union-administered wage determination is not commonly encountered, for multiemployer bargaining has usually been developed whenever a union possesses a predominant economic power in negotiations conducted on a company-by-company basis. Although employers have thereby improved their position, they are not always satisfied with the results attained. There are drawbacks, moreover, in being subject to the standard terms of a master agreement, particularly if it is broad in scope and inflexibly applied. It is notable, however, that an estimated one-third of the 15 million employees under labor agreements are covered by multiemployer arrangements.

THE DECISION-MAKING ASPECTS OF WAGE DETERMINATION

Wage determination is private agreement making in which variously conceived and differently oriented objectives of employees and employers have to be accommodated and reconciled. Long-run economic considerations are among the factors which are taken into account. But many

[23] The so-called "most-favored-nation" clause is occasionally incorporated in a labor agreement. This provides that the labor agreement will be modified to conform to any more favorable terms subsequently negotiated by the union with a competitor.

kinds of shorter-run necessities are also among the forces which condition a settlement. Subjective attitudes, adherence to particular principles, and institutional needs create some of the forces which have to be reconciled. Each wage negotiation thus has some unique characteristics. Each case involves a balancing of many forces. How to gain mutual consent is the crux of the matter.

Unless the wage-determination process permits a significant latitude for decision making, accommodation of differences by agreement between employees and employers can scarcely be expected. The adoption of a wage-determination system grounded upon private agreement making reflects a conviction that employers and employees do possess decision-making latitude. Because of the importance attributed to mutual consent, wage negotiation may be defined as the discovery of those terms at which, despite the differences between them, employers will make jobs available and employees will work in the immediate future.

Wage theory has been useful in emphasizing the role of market forces in directing wage decisions. The reality of this element is attested in the conduct of every wage negotiation. There are points at which the costs of a settlement are deemed so prohibitive that employees and employers prefer the consequences of nonagreement. The location of these critical points by employees and by employers, or by their representatives, is perhaps the most important phase of wage determination. In the making of these decisions, market forces are evaluated. Because future plans and future prospects are involved, the evaluations will differ in various cases. Moreover, many other considerations have to be taken into account in deciding the points at which the consequences of nonagreement will be assumed and in defining the negotiating area within which the essential agreement is achievable.

Within the negotiating area, the precise decision regarding wages is fashioned not only by the relative urgencies of the need for an agreement but also by the negotiating tactics and bargaining skills which are exercised. Administrative decisions have to be made; that is, a wage policy is formulated and a program for its effectuation and application is devised. For example, what basis of job evaluation should be utilized and should a wage increase be in the form of a general increase in cents per hour or in a uniform percentage increase? Decisions are made between alternative courses—for example, a general wage increase may be weighed against seniority rules or so-called fringes. These, too, are decisions of considerable import. The complex administrative aspects of wage determination have not been adequately analyzed in their relation to the broad wage-determination problem.

It is concluded that the processes of wage determination, i.e., the various kinds of agreement-making mechanisms which are utilized, have a major influence upon wages and related conditions of employment. Whether collective bargaining or management-administered wage determination is practiced, for instance, has an important bearing upon the location of the points at which the costs of an agreement are appraised as prohibitive. In other words, the agreement-making process influences the way in which the area of negotiation is defined. In their effects upon the consequences of nonagreement, the processes also influence the wage decision made within the negotiating area.

It is a notable fact that, while recognizing the limitations imposed upon them by market forces, employers and employees widely appraise the processes of wage determination as significant to labor costs and to employee earnings. This aspect of wage determination has constituted the most controversial of the employee-employer relations problems. While insisting that employers and employees have an obligation to work out their own employment terms, the government has become particularly interested in the agreement-making processes by which they do so. Not without cause have the Wagner Act and the Taft-Hartley Act been among the most controversial laws of this generation.

The search has been for a process, or for processes, of wage determination in which employees and employers, possessing an equality of bargaining power, will jointly participate in formulating and applying the terms of employment. In supporting collective bargaining, as well as its regulation, the government has sought to minimize unilateral or coercive wage decisions. It is believed in the United States that employment terms have a particular rightness and an incomparable usefulness when they are developed by an agreement-making process recognized as fair and equitable by both employees and employers. Problems concerning the processes for formulating and applying wage policies have been distinguished from the substantive terms of employment and their economic consequences, although they are not unrelated.

Collective bargaining, which is essentially a system of wage determination in which the employer shares administrative decision-making responsibilities with the union, has emerged as the process by which critical wage decisions are made.

In the absence of collective bargaining, particularly in the manufacturing industries, the employer promulgates and applies policies respecting the conditions of employment as part of the managerial function. The employees influence the terms of employment through their right individually to react to the conditions which the employer makes available. They do so in an indirect manner, however, and sometimes at considerable personal cost. An outright rejection means quitting the job. But there are some cases in which the employees find this process of wage determination acceptable. Many employees in many industries, however, were convinced that such a process was disadvantageous to them; that is, they believed they lacked an equality of bargaining power.

Since the passage of the Wagner Act, employees have had a legal right to select union representatives with whom the employer is required to share the administrative function of promulgating and applying agreement terms. A far-reaching change occurred in the determination of wages with the widespread adoption of collective bargaining. Under collective bargaining, unless and until a management-union agreement is consummated, the employer must reckon with the risks and the costs of a total work stoppage. So must the employees, who can, however, reject the employment terms offered by the employer without a permanent loss of their jobs.

The functions assigned to union and company negotiators are administrative. The employees retain the right individually to reject the terms available through the labor agreement just as they can reject the terms of employment when proffered by the employer alone. With collective bargaining, however, a potent force is added to wage determination—the consequences of nonagreement between the company and the union.

To ignore the far-reaching effect of collective bargaining upon the substance of wage determination is to ignore problems which are among the most complex in the labor-management relationship. One of the tasks of wage theory is to explain how the pressing long-run and short-run needs of employers and employees, economic and noneconomic, are reconciled through the collectively bargained agreement. The purpose of this chapter has been to initiate such a discussion.

Reflections on Public Sector Collective Bargaining

By BENJAMIN AARON

Professor of Law, University of California, Los Angeles.

The Changing Environment

AT THE BEGINNING of the present decade, the outlook for collective bargaining in the public sector was roseate. During the preceding 10 years, government employment had increased 44.1 percent, from 8.8 million in October 1960 to 12.6 million in October 1969, while state and local government had increased from 6.3 to 9.7 million.[1] In early 1970, 24 states had 34 different mandatory statutes requiring either meet-and-confer or collective bargaining relationships; 11 states had 14 permissive statutes, making meet-and-confer or collective bargaining relationships permissible; and 14 states had statutes granting to selected groups of employees only such minimal rights as the right to join a union or to present proposals to the employer.[2]

Organization of public employees had continued to gain momentum. In the period between 1962 and 1968, union and association membership among government employees had almost doubled, from 1.2 to 2.2 million; unions of public employees made membership gains of 135.5 percent, compared to a gain of about 5 percent among private-sector unions.[3]

In a few years, the picture has changed. The current status of collective bargaining in the public sector is uncertain; the immediate future appears bleak. What has happened to the surging, triumphant organizational movement among government employees which swept across the country during the 1960's and which appeared to be surmounting every barrier placed in its path? The answer, my friends, is blowing in the wind—the chill wind of a depressed economy. Although there are a few signs of recovery in the private sector, the situation in the public sector seems, if anything, to be getting worse.

---

[1] U. S. Department of Commerce, Bureau of the Census, *Public Employment in 1969* (April 1970), cited in National Governors' Conference, *1970 Supplement to Report of Task Force on State and Local Government Labor Relations* (Chicago: Public Personnel Ass'n, 1971), p. 1.

[2] American Bar Ass'n, Section of Labor Relations Law, *Report of the Committee on State Labor Law* (1970), pp. 94-95.

[3] Harry P. Cohany and Lucretia M. Dewey, "Union Membership Among Government Employees," *Monthly Labor Review,* vol. 93 (July 1970), pp. 15-16.

Benjamin Aaron, "Reflections on Public Sector Collective Bargaining." *Labor Law Journal,* August 1976, pp. 453–460. Reproduced from the August 1976 issue of the *Labor Law Journal,* published and copyrighted 1976 by the Commerce Clearing House, Inc., 4025 H. Peterson Avenue, Chicago, Illinois 60646.

It is unnecessary to dwell on the highly publicized plight of New York City by way of illustration; indeed, to do so would be misleading. Almost every major city in the country is in financial trouble. Last February, for example, Mayor Coleman Young of Detroit told the Congressional Joint Economic Committee that his city, which has already dismissed 18 percent of its municipal workers, faces financial disaster within a year. Detroit now has a budget deficit of $50 million in the current fiscal year, which could grow to $700 million by 1980 unless federal aid is forthcoming. Young also predicted that Philadelphia, San Francisco, and other major cities could follow Detroit into financial collapse.[4]

Effects of the Crunch

The main theme of a national conference last January in Washington, D. C., on "Public Sector Labor Relations in a Troubled Economy," concerned possible or likely effects of the anticipated financial crunch on various areas of the public sector. Thus, Dean Alan K. Campbell, of the Maxwell School, Syracuse University, stated in part: "The necessary 'holding the line' for public expenditures is also bound to reduce the level and quality of public service. Not only is this likely to weaken the already deteriorating economic base of some jurisdictions, but additionally it will particularly hurt those dependent on public services."[5]

Another speaker, Dr. Donald R. Magruder, executive director of the Florida School Boards Association, declared: "This same economic pinch will affect some collective bargaining laws presently in force, and also . . . any new state legislation to be considered for adoption. Legislators will be more cautious about abdicating final decision-making authority, particularly in the budget area, and serious consideration will be given to the retention of the final budgetary decision to be made by the legislative body . . . ."[6]

Much of the current commentary on economic problems in the public sector assumes, whether implicitly or explicitly, that collective bargaining in general, and the allegedly rapacious demands of some unions in particular, are largely responsible for the present financial plight of state and local governmental jurisdictions. How much truth is there in that assumption?

It is, of course, true that public service is a labor-intensive product, and that the major expense of government is employee compensation, accounting for 75 to 85 percent of governmental budgets. In the years 1970-74 tax collections by local governments increased 40 percent, while city and county payrolls rose 46 percent and 57.7 percent, respectively.[7] Those figures however, are misleading. Payroll increases reflect not only rates of pay, but also increased employment. To illustrate, during this same 1970-74 period the number of employees rose 11 percent in the cities and 20.8 percent in the counties. If one looks at the average earnings of full-time city and county employees between 1970 and 1974, the picture is different; earnings of city employees (excluding teachers) rose by only 34 percent, and those of county employees by only 32 percent.[8]

[4] *Los Angeles Times*, Feb. 26, 1976, § 1, p. 1.

[5] LMRS *Newsletter*, vol. 7 (Feb. 1976), p. 1.

[6] *Ibid.*

[7] Marion Ross, "The Local Government Budget Crisis: Is Bargaining to Blame?," *California Public Employee Relations*, No. 27 (Dec. 1975), pp. 2-12.

[8] U. S. Department of Commerce, Bureau of the Census, *City Employment in 1974* (June 1975), and *County Employment in 1974* (June 1975), cited in Ross, p. 5.

An additional perspective on pay increases for public-sector employees can be gained by comparing those of several key occupational groups—urban public classroom teachers, police, and firefighters—with earnings of production and nonsupervisory workers in the private nonfarm sector. For the five-year period ending 1973-74, the differences were not significant.[9]

These comparisons, and other factors, have led Professor Marion Ross to conclude: "When looked at in conjunction with the eroding tax base and rising interest cost, these bare figures cast doubt on the allegations that collective bargaining in the public sector accounts in large measure for the financial difficulties of cities. Particular wage increases have received so much attention that other reasons for payroll increases have been largely overlooked."[10]

"Square Atop a Tinderbox"

Regardless of the reasons, however, labor costs in the public sector continue to rise at a time of shrinking government revenues and increasing resistance to tax increases. Strikes by public employees are also on the rise. Secretary of Labor Usery, surveying the outlook for 1976 when he was still Director of the Federal Mediation and Conciliation Service, commented pungently: "We are sitting square atop a tinderbox" in the public sector.[11]

The picture in this regard is grim, not only for the general public, but also for the strikers and for the various labor organizations which represent them. In California, for example, most informed observers believe that recent strikes in several cities, especially the current strike of city employees in San Francisco, have aroused such hostile reactions among large numbers of the public throughout the state that even the faint hope for enactment of a comprehensive collective bargaining law for state, county, and municipal employees in the immediate future has been extinguished.

Dismal as the overall situation may be, however, it should not be exaggerated or misread. There is no indication of a reversal in the trend toward increasing resort to collective bargaining in the public sector, although it may be slowing down in specific areas. According to a recent Census Bureau report, 51 percent, or 4.7 million, of the nation's full-time, nonfederal public employees belonged to employee labor organizations in October 1974. This represented a gain of about 10 percent in the previous two-year period. During the same period the number of nonfederal public-sector labor-management agreements rose 21.9 percent, to 23,820, of which 6,659 were memoranda of understanding (MOUs). At local levels, where most of the membership gains occurred, collective agreements increased by 30 percent in the two-year period, compared with an increase of only 9 percent in MOUs.[12]

What we are witnessing, therefore, is not so much a decline in collective bargaining in the public sector, as a period of hard bargaining in an environment of severe economic restraint and increasing public hostility. I propose now to comment briefly on several of the current suggestions for

---

[9] See U. S. Department of Labor, *Current Wage Developments*, Feb. 1975, p. 42, and *Monthly Labor Review*, vol. 98 (Oct. 1975), p. 93, cited in Ross, p. 5.

[10] Ross, cited at note 7, p. 5.

[11] LMRS *Newsletter*, vol. 7 (Feb. 1976), p. 5.

[12] U. S. Department of Commerce, Bureau of the Census, *Labor-Management Relations in State and Local Governments: 1974*, quoted in BNA *Daily Labor Report*, No. 49 (Mar. 11, 1976), pp. A-1—A-2.

dealing with some collective bargaining issues, as well as on the reactions to those suggestions by the parties directly involved.

Some Current Proposals

Reduction of Services and of Employment. The most obvious, as well as the most logical, response to public complaints against the rising costs of government is to reduce such costs. One way to accomplish this is to reduce the number of services provided, which, in turn, will reduce the number of employees required. Some cities and states have done just that, but the method has its limitations. First, the average citizen's insistence upon eating his cake and having it, too, is well known. Demands for reduction in public services almost invariably emphasize that the services to be reduced are those provided primarily for some other group. Second, the employees who would be affected by reduction of services are quite understandably opposed to that particular method of cutting costs, not only because it hurts them personally, but also because they frequently identify with the needs and aspirations of those special publics that they serve.

Even that modern Savonarola, Governor Brown of California, whose popularity has remained surprisingly high despite his constant emphasis upon the need to "lower our expectations" and to abandon our wasteful and self-indulgent ways, has encountered fierce opposition in his efforts to cut back on the number of employees in some departments of the state government. Then, too, a planned reduction of services is likely to raise issues that have the highest potential for polarizing various elements in a given community. In Southern California, for example, residents of elegant but fire-prone housing areas strongly resist proposals to reduce the number of firefighters on duty during the hours when fewer fires occur, while at the same time demanding that welfare expenditures be cut.

Purely for political reasons, therefore, and without regard to more fundamental issues involving competing equities, reduction of services and of the number of full-time public employees as a means of curbing the rising costs of government has only a limited utility.

Productivity Bargaining. The latest glamour term in the public collective bargaining lexicon is productivity bargaining. It is a phrase that comes trippingly off the tongue; it has a pleasant ring to it; no one denies that it is a Good Thing. It appears to have replaced, at least for the time being, "communications" and "human relations" in the minds of public managers as the primary desideratum in collective bargaining. Let me say, at once, that I have nothing against the concept of productivity bargaining; the problem is that the term, like the others I mentioned, is one of fathomless ambiguity and means different things to the various participating or affected parties.

This observation is clearly illustrated by the way the term has been bandied about in the press and in numerous conferences on employee relations in the public sector. The same point was noted by Robert McKersie and Laurence Hunter in their book, *Pay, Productivity and Collective Bargaining,* in which they offered alternative definitions of productivity bargaining: one focusing on the payment system, i.e., more pay for greater worker output; the other focusing on distribution of cost savings resulting from changes in organization and working methods according to some previously agreed upon formula.[13] In addition, many persons think of productivity bargaining as a way of getting more work for the same amount of money or the same amount of work with fewer employees. Others conceive of it as a way to improve the quality of the employees' working life, principally through increased worker participation in managerial decisions.

In his recent evaluation of productivity bargaining in the public sector, McKersie notes an increasing interest in that concept in the past few years, but expresses the opinion that "at the county and municipal levels, the idea will never become a fad."[14] His reasons are instructive:

"Most productivity improvement programs initiated in the future [he concludes] will run the 'gauntlet' of collective bargaining. Management will be forced by the realities of increasing union strength and interest as well as the advantages of collaboration to bring their productivity plans to the bargaining table, i.e., to engage in productivity bargaining."[15]

The key word here is "bargaining," as Rudolph Oswald stresses in his essay in the same IRRA volume. Asserting that productivity improvements in the public sector "are peculiarly labor-oriented, rather than technology induced," he continues:

"However, before one can move to productivity bargaining, there must be a strong underpinning of true collective bargaining. Without that base, there is no foundation to build on for future mutual trust. Job and income maintenance guarantees are also prerequisites for achieving employee cooperation to change work methods. Only then can the worker approach the changes secure in the knowledge that the productivity program will not threaten his livelihood."[16]

Here, then, according to Oswald, is part of the problem: In times of financial stress and pressures to cut costs, the resulting actions by management tend to undermine the basic premises of collective bragaining. Nor is that all. As strikes increase and public resentment against government employees continues to rise, public managers become less willing to take responsibility for decisions reached in collective bargaining. This accounts for, among other things, the relatively high incidence in recent weeks of what seem to me idiotic and unworkable proposals to require instant public referenda on all new wage bargains in the public sector before they can be put into effect.

A Prescription for Crisis

In a recent address,[17] Donald H. Wollett, the Director of Employee Relations in New York State, offered his "prescription for crisis," which seems to me to make a lot of sense. In essence, he recommends that public management accept its responsibilities to take the initiative in eliminating waste and mismanagement in its own ranks,

[13] Robert B. McKersie and Laurence C. Hunter, *Pay, Productivity and Collective Bargaining* (London: Macmillan, 1973), pp. 4-5, quoted in Robert B. McKersie, "An Evaluation of Productivity Bargaining in the Public Sector," in *Collective Bargaining and Productivity,* eds. Gerald Somers, Arvid Anderson, Malcolm Denise, and Leonard Sayles (Madison: IRRA, 1975), p. 52.

[14] *Ibid.,* p. 62.

[15] *Ibid.* (Emphasis supplied).

[16] Rudolph A. Oswald, "Bargaining and Productivity in the Public Sector: A Union View," in Somers, Anderson, Denise, and Sayles, pp. 100-01.

[17] Donald H. Wollett, "Public Employee Bargaining in Crisis," an address to the International Personnel Management Association, Albany, New York, Jan. 28, 1976.

and then to persuade labor organizations that certain hard choices must be made if the collective enterprise is to survive.

As he says, responsible unions can and will take "no" for an answer to unacceptable economic demands if, but only if, all other options have been carefully explored and the reasons for their rejection convincingly made. To put the matter in another way, what is needed now is not less collective bargaining, but more. And both sides must be prepared to carry out their responsibilities, not only to protect their own institutional interests, but also to safeguard those of the general public, of which they also are a part.

Naivete or Reality?

I realize that there is a strong temptation to dismiss what I have just said as naive rhetoric, the triumph of hope over experience. But let me put this question: Does anyone in this audience really believe that the problems of maintaining adequate public services at a cost the consumers are willing and able to pay in times of economic restraint or, for that matter, at any time, can be solved by the unilateral action of management or of employees, or by legislative fiat?

The plain fact is that collective bargaining in the public sector is a reality; it is here to stay; it is, I believe, an irreversible process. Our job is not to prevent it, abolish it, or contain it. Rather, our job is to try to make it work better. I shall conclude, therefore, with some observations about the conditions I think necessary in order to make collective bargaining perform more efficiently.

Essential Conditions

Nothing I have to say on this subject is new, but it all bears repetition. First, collective bargaining in the public sector requires a proper statutory framework. Executive orders or administrative regulations are not an acceptable substitute. An adequate statute or ordinance must provide, at a minimum, for the following rights:[18] (1) the absolute right of all government employees at state and local levels to organize and to engage in collective bargaining (as distinguished from meet-and-confer procedures) over wages, hours, and other terms and conditions of employment; (2) the right to an orderly procedure for dealing with all questions of representation, including determination of appropriate bargaining units, conduct of elections, and related matters; (3) the right to negotiate for a provision in collective agreements for the final and binding arbitration of grievances by a neutral third party; (4) the right, in the absence of a legal right to strike, to an impasse procedure leading to settlement of disputes over interests; (5) the right of access to an independent agency with the power and the means adequately to administer all provisions of the statute; and (6) the right to judicial review of any final orders of that agency.

Second, these rights of government employees must be matched by statutory guarantees of public management's right to manage. By this I do not mean that legislative bodies should require that broad management rights clauses be written into all collective agreements, or that the scope of bargaining should be sharply restricted by statute. Such tactics merely serve to frustrate collective bargaining. I am thinking, rather, of provisions that

[18] These rights were first enumerated in Benjamin Aaron, "Federal Bills Analyzed and Appraised," LMSR *Newsletter,* vol. 5 (Nov. 1974), p. 4.

make it possible for government managers to organize strong management teams consisting of persons unhampered by conflicts of interest in the performance of their duties.

Third, because collective bargaining is a relatively new phenomenon in the public sector, both sides, but especially management, need to develop and to maintain training programs in the philosophy and techniques of collective bargaining.

Fourth, we need credible alternatives to the strike and, yes, to the lockout. One of the safest predictions one can make is that, before long, governmental bodies in this country will discover, as their counterparts in Sweden have learned, that the lockout is a feasible and effective weapon in some types of interests disputes. I have never favored strikes by public employees, but our experience over the last 15 years has convinced me that neither statutes nor judicial decisions can prevent their occurrence. I am also convinced, however, that public employees will avail themselves in most instances of any feasible alternatives to the strike.

Providing such alternatives is a very difficult, but not impossible, task. I say "alternatives" because I do not think any one procedure will be adequate for all groups and situations. That is one reason why I oppose a single, preemptive federal law governing collective bargaining in the public sector, and why I favor continuing experimentation within the borders of the separate states.

In respect of impasse procedures, it seems to me unfortunate that some labor and management groups uncriti-

cally lump all the various procedures designed to settle unresolved interests disputes into the category of compulsory arbitration, and then damn them indiscriminately because they bear that label. Granted that arbitration works best when it is voluntary rather than mandatory, we ought not to allow the best to become the enemy of the better. There may be instances in which compulsory arbitration is clearly a better way to settle a dispute than is a resort to a strike or a lockout. More important still, some of the procedures which, if allowed to run their course, would culminate in some form of imposed settlement, will themselves engender a willingness in both parties to reach a voluntary agreement at an earlier stage in the process. The Michigan final-offer statute, which covers police, firefighters, and deputy sheriffs, and which applies only to economic issues, is one example of such a procedure.[19]

Commitment

Fifth, we need a stronger commitment by public management and by public organizations to making collective bargaining work. This is the same point made by Wollett to which I referred earlier. Although it may seem parodoxical, public management has lagged most in its willingness and ability to manage within a system in which decision-making is shared in varying degrees with employee organizations. Too many public managers confuse management with dictation; too few of them are willing to accept the responsibility to initiate ideas about reducing costs, increasing productivity, and improving the quality of working life, to defend those ideas in frank discussions with employee

[19] See Charles M. Rehmus, "Is a 'Final Offer' Ever Final?" in *Arbitration—1974, Proceedings of the Twenty-Seventh Annual* *Meeting, National Academy of Arbitrators,* eds. Barbara D. Dennis and Gerald Somers (Washington: BNA, 1975), pp. 77-81.

representatives, and to compromise when necessary.

Employee organizations have a responsibility to accept the limits imposed by external conditions, to give up certain guarantees in respect of wages and working conditions that have carried over from the time when there was no collective bargaining, and to refrain from "end runs" to legislative bodies in order to secure through lobbying what they failed to achieve through collective bargaining.

In conclusion, let me remind you that the course of collective bargaining anywhere, like that of true love, never did run smooth. In times of economic stress or of great social unrest, collective bargaining in both the public and the private sectors is apt to encounter difficulties. Although the outlook for collective bargaining in the public sector in the immediate future is fraught with troubles, I am confident that it will survive and continue to spread.

[The End]

THE INCIDENCE OF COLLECTIVE BARGAINING ONCE MORE[*]

M. BRONFENBRENNER

Michigan State University

I

A few years ago I tried to work out some ideas on "The Incidence of Collective Bargaining" before the American Economic Association.[1] The results satisfied neither my critics nor myself, and I confess inconsistencies between my earlier paper and my present opinion.

Some of the peculiar difficulties of the subject may be clarified by reference to the theory of tax incidence, which is our model here. There is a perennial dispute in tax incidence theory as to whether one should or should not take account of the way the tax receipts are spent. There is another perennial dispute as to whether one should compare the post-tax situation with the situation which would have existed without any tax at all, or with the situation which would have existed had some other tax, such as a proportional income tax, been used to raise the same revenue.

Analogous methodological problems give us pause in discussing the incidence of collective bargaining. Should we confine ourselves to the incidence of collective bargaining narrowly construed? Or should we take into account the incidence of the political and other activities,[2] including pressure on the monetary authorities, which unions may undertake in aid of their bargaining positions? I take the first and more restrictive position, which seems to be necessary for

[*] Delivered at the Memphis meeting of the Southern Economic Association, November 8, 1957.

[1] M. Bronfenbrenner, "The Incidence of Collective Bargaining," American Economic Association, *Proceedings* (1954), pp. 293–307.

[2] As an apt example of these "other" activities we may cite the recent role of the United Mine Workers in assisting in the organization of the American Coal Shipping Company to increase the world demand for American coal. (For this illustration I am indebted to my colleague, Charles P. Larrowe.)

Martin Bronfenbrenner, "The Incidence of Collective Bargaining Once More." *Southern Economic Journal*, April 1958, pp. 398–406.

analytical precision. But on the other hand, the political activities of unions are interwoven so inextricably with their collective bargaining that to ignore the political side makes our results unverifiable.[3]

Let me digress to illustrate what is worrying me. It may be that one important effect of collective bargaining by some unions is to price labor out of certain occupations, and to lower wage rates indirectly wherever the displaced workers go. In such a case its incidence would be on workers down-graded or disemployed. But at the same time, suppose that the political activities of the same unions have been directed at increasing employment opportunities for their members, so that the net result of all union activities taken together has been to down-grade and disemploy nobody—rather the reverse. For analytical purposes I separate the two effects, and talk of the incidence of collective bargaining on down-graded and disemployed workers—who may be invisible! This unhappy situation becomes less happy when we realize that the collective bargaining policies of unions might be quite different were their political pressures less effective.

II

So much by way of overture or prelude; There seem to be six main theories of incidence in the economic literature, which can be sub-divided into two groups of three theories each. The first group of theories maintains that incidence exists. These theories maintain, that is to say, that union members make gains at some other group's expense as a result of collective bargaining. The second group of theories maintains that incidence does not exist. These theories maintain, that is to say, either that union members make no gains as a result of collective bargaining that they could not have made in the free market, or else that their gains come out of increased rates of economic activity and growth rather than out of the incomes of anyone else.

1. The "redistribution" theory. Collective bargaining redistributes income in favor of "laborers" and against "capitalists"—meaning receivers of rent and interest as well as receivers of profits in the strict sense. The incidence of collective bargaining is then on the capitalist class.

2. The "reallocation" theory, which is perhaps more entitled than any other to be called "orthodox." The labor share of privately produced national income stays more or less constant—a kind of statistical wages fund—while collective bargaining distributes further this more or less constant share. Members of the most aggressively organized trades and industries get more. Their increases spread "sympathetically" to a number of related trades, industries, and localities, by raising their supply schedules. At the same time, these increases reduce employment opportunities, displace workers into other labor markets, and hold wage rates down in these other markets. Sometimes the displacement is into unemployment or involuntary entrepreneurship of the peanut-stand variety, if organization is sufficiently broad. More frequently it is into some less aggres-

---

[3] Many writers accordingly discuss all trade union activities simultaneously, a practice defended most explicitly by Clark Kerr ("Labor's Income Share and the Labor Movement," in George W. Taylor and Frank C. Pierson [ed.], *New Concepts in Wage Determination*, "The term 'trade unionism,' instead of 'collective bargaining,' is used deliberately. Unions can and do affect actions of both employers and governments, and some of both kinds of action have potential or actual consequences for distributive shares. To explore the impact of unionism in only the economic sphere and not also in the political sphere is to tell but half the tale." [New York: McGraw-Hill, 1957], p. 266).

sively organized type of labor. Part of the incidence of collective bargaining is on these displaced workers regardless of what finally happens to them.

The remainder of the incidence, by this same theory, is on that particular sub-class of consumers who consume most heavily those goods and services whose production costs and selling prices have been raised by wage increases, and who consume least heavily those goods and services whose production costs and selling prices have been pushed down by the displacement. These are however not "consumers" as a whole. Another sub-class of consumers may very well be net gainers in consequence of collective bargaining, and we shall ignore in the discussion which follows any effects of relative price changes on "consumers" as such.

3. The "inflationary" theory. The main effect of collective bargaining is to force up money wages and prices. Its incidence is on fixed income receivers whose incomes lag behind the inflationary movement.

Passing to the theories which deny any incidence of collective bargaining, we have:

4. The "illusion" theory. Collective bargaining gives the members of established unions[4] no more on the average than they could have expected through the competitive labor market as it operates on the wages of comparable unorganized workers.

5. The "productivity" theory. Collective bargaining increases the rate of economic growth, in the first place, by "shocking" employers into increasing their efficiency and introducing innovations of many kinds. At the same time it insures workers against wage cuts and unemployment when their productivity rises, and increases worker cooperation with technical progress. A differentially higher rate of growth results over-all. Out of the differential it has been possible to increase the pay of organized workers without injury to any other group.

6. The "consumption" theory. This is an extension of the redistribution theory which stresses longer-run effects. Collective bargaining redistributes income from the rich to the poor, which raises purchasing power, which in turn permits full consumption and full production, and leaves even capitalists no worse off in the long run than they would have been without it.

Speaking ideologically for a moment, the redistribution, productivity, and consumption theories are usually presented as pro-union in their implications. The reallocation, inflation, and illusion theories, differing widely among themselves, share a certain anti-union flavor, although many illusion theorists maintain pro-union policy positions on sociological or political grounds.

The six theories are overlapping rather than mutually exclusive, and it is common to find writers holding more than one. Pro-union writers often combine redistribution and consumption theories, and often add productivity theories as well. Anti-union writers often combine reallocation and inflation theories, and speak of "unemployment and inflation" as consequences of union power.

III

The literature on the incidence of collective bargaining is not one of which we can be proud as professional economists. Some writers present their views

---

[4] An upward fillip to wage rates as the immediate consequence of organization is recognized quite generally, and may be attributed to the overcoming of labor monopsony. By "established" unions we mean unions for whose members this short-run fillip has already come and gone.

as matters of common notoriety, without rebutting or even mentioning the views of others. There is a certain amount of question-begging, and otherwise playing fast and loose with the evidence. (For example, when union wages rise faster than non-union ones within some industry, this is taken to show that collective bargaining has raised them. But when the opposite is the case, this allegedly proves that collective bargaining raises non-union wages as well.) I have also seen the fact of economic growth—the fact that all major groups have enjoyed rising real incomes since 1900—used as evidence that collective bargaining has had no incidence.

Advocates of redistribution theories, and of the consumption theories often built upon them, assume that the share of manual or production workers in private national income has risen as a consequence of collective bargaining, or if they can isolate no rise, they assume that it would have fallen without collective bargaining because the over-all capital-labor ratio has risen. Neither of these propositions is tenable without supporting evidence, and the little evidence I have seen points in opposite directions.[5] Nor have proponents of productivity theories, to the best of my knowledge, investigated by crafts or industries the empirical relations between union strength and the growth of productivity. We still do not know the comparative importance of union encouragement to efficiency in the use of machines and raw-material and union encouragement to "feather-bedding" in the use of direct man-power.[6]

A final criticism of the literature is a certain tendency to generalize, to erect universal theories of incidence, based on one or a few specific episodes in recent economic history. The reallocation theorists of the 1920's and the 1930's in the United States and Great Britain seem to have been thinking about 1920–22 or 1929–33, when union wage rates were maintained while other wage rates fell, and when employment shifted (for whatever reason) largely away from sectors of union strength to sectors of union weakness. The American under-employment inflation of 1936–37, followed by the downturn of 1937–38, may have been uniquely important in providing supporting evidence for writers combining misallocation with inflation theories.[7] The even more unusual circumstances of 1945–48 in the United States, when an inflation burst forth into the daylight after four years of wartime suppression, saw the emergence and development of the illusion theory. Currently (1955–57) it is the inflation theory which is fashionable, mainly because of the effects of wage increases on industrial costs— despite the occasional use of collective bargaining as a screen for increased profit margins and the matching of union wage increases in many weakly organized trades (such as teaching) where shortages have been recognized.

---

[5] For a useful summary, see Kerr, *op. cit.*, pp. 279–294. For the United States in particular, we quote from p. 281: "Over the past century [including both periods of union strength and weakness] labor's share has risen primarily as employed persons have become a more important component in our population. In other words, employees are not comparatively better off as individuals; there are, however, many more of them."

[6] Here again, the relevant literature has been reviewed by Kerr, "Productivity and Labour Relations," *Reprint 96* of the University of California Institute of Industrial Relations (1957). The results are most inconclusive.

[7] The standard presentations of this viewpoint are probably H. C. Simons, *Economic Policy for a Free Society* (Chicago: University of Chicago Press, 1948), ch. 6, (originally published 1944); C. E. Lindblom, *Unions and Capitalism* (New Haven: Yale University Press, 1949), ch. 11; and Fritz Machlup, *Political Economy of Monopoly* (Baltimore: Johns Hopkins University Press, 1952), ch. 9–10.

IV

I take an electic position, trying harder to escape logical than temporal inconsistency. My view is that different theories (or combinations of theories) apply in good times than in bad, and different theories under easy money than under tight. We must, moreover, deal with continua, not dichotomies, especially since some crafts, industries, and areas are generally enjoying prosperity at the same time that others are suffering depression and still others are in an intermediate state.

When a craft, industry, or locality is enjoying prosperity, with money easy but prices temporarily stable, the major effect of collective bargaining is to get inflation under way from the cost side. Wage increases over and above productivity increases, and above wage increases obtainable under competition, can be secured and passed on (or magnified) in price increases. The money supply expands, or its velocity of circulation is allowed to increase without offset, so that the increased wages and prices cause no credit stringency. (The increased wages and prices are not only *financed*, but *underwritten* or *validated*, by easy money.) [8] When times are good but money is tight, any appreciable rise in prices in a strongly organized sector of the economy is accompanied or followed by a stringency of credit, with unfavorable effects on wages, prices, output, and employment generally. This is a reallocation effect, from whose consequences the original price- and wage-raising sectors are often insulated by their particular situations of prosperity. Thus a wage and price rise in autos or steel may lead through tight money to wage cuts or unemployment in textiles or construction—but *not* in autos and steel, the original "culprits."

When a craft, industry, or locality is suffering hard times, the major incidence of collective bargaining seems to be the reallocation one, which might alternatively be called anti-deflationary. Money wages are held at the levels of the last prosperity; or rather, they are nearly as likely to rise as to fall. Employment falls off in terms of hours, and usually also in terms of men. The unemployed go elsewhere; new entrants enter elsewhere; wages are often forced down elsewhere. The resulting displacement may be upward, as when coal miners from Kentucky become auto workers in Detroit. More commonly, if

---

[8] A clear distinction should be, but usually is not, made between that degree of monetary ease which finances a wage increase in the first instance, and that further degree of monetary ease which underwrites or validates it by providing higher money purchasing power at higher money prices. In an earlier essay, "A Contribution to the Aggregative Theory of Wages," *Journal of Political Economy* (1956), pp. 459–469, assuming the first and lesser degree of monetary ease, I arrived at essentially classical inverse relations between wage rates and employment. In the present passage, assuming the second and greater degree of monetary ease, I suppose the Keynesian independence between wage rates and aggregate employment, my concern being concentrated on inflationary consequences. It would be easy to go to super-Keynesian direct relations between wage rates and employment under this degree of monetary ease, if the initial position were one of less than full employment.

hard times are general, displacement will be downward, involving more unemployment of old skills than development of new ones. Accompanying the displacement and reallocation are assorted reactions favorable and unfavorable to particular classes of consumers, as relative prices follow the relative wage movements.

Monetary policy makes little difference here; easy money in depressions has been compared often and aptly to "pushing on a string." Fiscal policy, especially government spending, is more significant. The special phenomenon of unemployment (or under-employment) inflation often results when, as under the New Deal in 1936–37, collective bargaining diverts expansionary fiscal policy to wage rates rather than employment.

With an important limitation, in conclusion, one may concur with Sumner Slichter[9] as to the inflationary bias in our collective bargaining arrangements, if not in his recommendation to accept the resulting inflation gracefully. The limitation is to good times with temporary price stability. If times are bad or money is tight, collective bargaining reallocates labor and changes relative prices rather than inflating the general price level—except insofar as it generates unemployment inflation from expansionary fiscal policy during depressions. And at other extreme, when inflation gets under way for other reasons than collective bargaining, as it did in the American 1945–48 and 1950–51, bargained labor markets often escalate and inflate no faster than competitive ones, if the excess demand for labor at prevailing wage rates is at all general.[10]

In both good and bad times, but primarily the latter, collective bargaining probably also induces a slight redistribution of income in favor of wages and against profits. The evidence which has convinced me of this underlying movement was developed by H. M. Levinson,[11] but I shall not reproduce his statistical tabulations here. For those unfamiliar with his work, let me say only that he has broken down the private sector of the American economy into one group of industries where unionism or the threat of unionism are important and another group where neither unionism nor its threat is of much immediate significance. (The first or union group includes manufacturing, mining, construction, transportation, and public utilities. The second or non-union group includes agriculture, trade, finance, and services.) Levinson's figures indicate that in the union group the generation since 1929 has seen a shift from property income (rent and

[9] Sumner H. Slichter, "Do the Wage-Fixing Arrangements in the American Labor Market Have an Inflationary Bias?," American Economic Association, *Proceedings* (1954), pp. 342–346.

[10] Compare particularly Albert Rees, "The Economic Impact of Collective Bargaining in the Steel and Coal Industries During the Postwar Period," Industrial Relations Research Association, *Proceedings* (1950), pp. 203–210.

[11] For the period 1929–1947, see H. M. Levinson, *Unionism, Wage Trends, and Income Distribution, 1914–1947* (Ann Arbor: University of Michigan Press, 1951), esp. Table 25, p. 106. The results are extended through 1952 in Levinson, "Collective Bargaining and Income Distribution," American Economic Association, *Proceedings* (1954), pp. 308–316, esp. Table 1, p. 309. For further extension (through 1954) of some of Levinson's results see Kerr, "Labor's Income Share," *op. cit.*, esp. Table 2, p. 285.

interest) to *wages*, whereas in the non-union group the shift has been from property income to *profits*, including both dividends and entrepreneurial income. I am impressed in each case by the *intra-industry* shifts only, computed after changes in the relative importance of different industries have been eliminated statistically.[12] The differences between the union and non-union groups are slight, and may not be statistically significant; they may also be sensitive to the particular choices of initial and terminal dates. But with these hesitancies and reservations, Levinson's hesitant and reserved conclusion seems acceptable, that a small amount of redistribution results from the collective bargaining process. (There is also supporting evidence from Great Britain and Western Europe.[13]) It is, however, probably unwise to go further and suggest any kind of consumption theory of incidence, or rather of non-incidence, on the basis of differences so small as those Levinson has isolated.

In summary, then, my eclectic theory of the incidence of collective bargaining is an inflationary theory for an easy-money prosperity, or for a depression with a carelessly expansionist fiscal policy, an illusion theory once inflation is under way, and a reallocation theory for most other circumstances. A redistributionist strain underlies the entire process, but on a scale too small to produce significant consumption effects or otherwise to influence the course of prosperity or depression. The illusion theory also warns us usefully at all times against exaggerating the quantitative significance of the other patterns of incidence.[14] The evidence for and against the productivity theory still awaits detailed examination.

V

Thus far nothing has been said of Lloyd Reynolds' *Evolution of Wage Structure*,[15] perhaps the decade's most significant contribution to the literature of the incidence of collective bargaining. This omission has been neither accidental nor disrespectful. Reynolds' conclusions do not fit neatly into our clas-

[12] Kerr, in criticizing Levinson's study (and other studies with similar results) does not distinguish between *intra-industry* and *total* share shifts (*ibid.*, p. 284 f.). The force of his criticism, and of other criticisms along the same line, is thereby reduced substantially.

[13] E. H. Phelps Brown and P. E. Hart, "The Share of Wages in National Income," *Economic Journal*, June 1952, esp. p. 276 f. and Phelps Brown, "The Long-Term Movement of Real Wages" in John T. Dunlop (ed.), *Theory of Wage Determination* (London: Macmillan, 1957), pp. 48–65. Phelps Brown stresses the conventional element in profit margins, which can be squeezed by the coincidence of a "hard" labor market (aggressive collective bargaining) and a "soft" product market (generally depressed conditions and/or aggressive price competition). For additional consideration of the American results, see William Fellner, *Competition Among the Few* (New York: Knopf, 1949), pp. 317–321; Sumner H. Slichter, *Economics of Collective Bargaining* (Berkeley: University of California Press, 1950); pp. 36–38; George J. Stigler, *Theory of Price* (Revised edition; New York: Macmillan, 1952), p. 259.

[14] Thus for example Milton Friedman suggests 15–20 percent as the probable limit of upward wage distortion and 4 percent as the probable limit of downward wage distortion in connection with what we call the reallocation theory. Friedman, "Significance of Labor Unions for Economic Policy," in D. McC. Wright (ed.), *The Impact of the Union* (New York: Harcourt Brace, 1951), p. 216.

[15] Lloyd G. Reynolds and Cynthia Taft, *The Evolution of Wage Structure* (New Haven:

sification of incidence theories. He and his collaborators have asked different questions, and turned the whole discussion in a different direction.

Given the imperfections of actual non-union labor markets, Reynolds inquires whether collective bargaining has shifted wage structures closer to or further from the "competitive norm" than they would otherwise have been. This competitive norm is thought of as devoid not only of collective bargaining but also of employer monopsony, worker ignorance and immobility, and also "non-competing groups" of privileged workers. Reynolds concludes in general, and with reservations, that the countervailing power of unions, exercised through collective bargaining, has brought actual wage structures closer to the competitive pattern than they previously were.

It does not seem impossible to translate Reynolds' conclusions into my own terms, although my translation lacks Reynolds' approval. We may say, for example, that the redistributive effect of collective bargaining represents mainly the countervailing of monopsonistic exploitation and a movement toward the competitive norm. We may also suggest that many who suffer from reallocation or inflation effects are white-collar folk who have traditionally formed a closed group with respect to recruitment from the ranks of manual workers, so that these effects, too, may be presented as competitive rather than the reverse.

Translation in the opposite direction is more difficult, but it serves to point up both my agreements and my disagreements with Reynolds' position. We may for translation purposes employ the hackneyed expression "labor aristocracy", subdividing it further into an old aristocracy and a new one, corresponding respectively to the elites of craft and of industrial unionism, and then proceed.

The old labor aristocracy consisted of members of the skilled trades, which old-style collective bargaining established as non-competing groups, often with monopoly power as against their small employers. On balance this kind of collective bargaining, with the incidence patterns we have ascribed to it, was probably an anti-competitive force despite its anti-monopsony aspects.

Reynolds bases his argument, however, mainly on the new labor aristocracy. This includes workers of all degrees of skill, but fortunate enough to work for large firms with substantial monopoly power and profits on the selling sides of their several markets, and therefore substantial ability to pay wage increases. Here collective bargaining as carried on mainly by industrial unions has had complex consequences. It has counteracted the monopsony power of

Yale University Press, 1955), esp. ch. 7, 13. (See also Reynolds, "The Impact of Collective Bargaining on the Wage Structure in the United States" in Dunlop, *op. cit.*, pp. 194–221 for a more condensed and less positive presentation of the same point of view.) Reynolds has also contributed to the discussion along less unconventional lines in his "General Level of Wages," in Taylor and Pierson (*op. cit.*). Here he traces in some detail the routes by which money wage increases may increase the labor share, in accordance with what we have called the redistribution theory of incidence (p. 253 f.). He also sets himself against the inflationary theory in a manner justified when monetary authorities do not allow tight money policy to be influenced by the results of collective bargaining (pp. 243 f., 249 f.).

these employers in hiring labor—clearly a competitive effect, which Reynolds stresses, and probably a redistributive one as regards incidence in the sense of the present discussion. But at the same time collective bargaining has raised these employers' costs, justified if not forced increases in their selling prices, and given their workers some share in what would otherwise have been their monopoly profits.

Should we call this a movement towards competition in general? From the viewpoint of the functional income distribution, it might appear so. Collective bargaining raises the labor share, and retards the shift to profits which Mrs. Robinson and others foresee as the ultimate end of a "world of monopolies".[16] But I have my doubts, which spring from the inflation and reallocation theories of incidence. There seem to be elements of collusion or conspiracy against consumers of particular products and fixed-income groups in general, elements of labor support for monopolistic restrictions, elements of cultivation of monopoly profits as pools for wage increases to strategic groups of organized workers—"palace slaves," Lenin would have called them.[17] These are reflected in the inflation and reallocation patterns of incidence of collective bargaining as has been said, and it is by no means certain that the injured parties are confined to the monopsonists or the non-competing groups of yesteryear. Do they not include family farmers and agricultural workers, unskilled employees in domestic and service trades, widows and orphans, pensioners and annuitants, racial and religious minorities? Inflation and reallocation, like the biblical rain, fall alike on the just and the unjust. Reynolds' theory has conjured up for the just an umbrella that the good Lord may thus far have neglected to provide.

[16] Although stated most explicitly by Mrs. Robinson in *Economics of Imperfect Competition* (London: Macmillan, 1933), Book X, the notion of a trend toward monopoly correlated with a reduction of the distributive share of labor dates back to Marx and beyond. Among the spate of turn-of-the-century "Distribution" books it is found most clearly in John R. Commons, *Distribution of Wealth* (New York: Macmillan, 1893), pp. 101–107, 198–200, 229–237, 246–248, ch. 6. It underlies the aggregative wage theory of Michal Kalecki, "The Distribution of the National Income," reprinted in William Fellner and B. F. Haley, (ed.), *Readings in the Theory of Income Distribution* (Philadelphia and Toronto: Blakiston, 1946), selection 11. For a critical survey of this literature, beginning with Mrs. Robinson, see Dean A. Worcester, Jr., "Monopoly and Income Distribution," Western Economic Association, *Proceedings* (1956), pp. 36–41.

[17] The writer has expressed these doubts previously at somewhat greater length. See M. Bronfenbrenner, "Wages in Excess of Marginal Review Productivity," *Southern Economic Journal*, January 1950, pp. 307–309. Similar doubts were likewise not unknown to the founding fathers of labor economics. Compare *e.g.,* the discussion of "Capital and labor hunting together, their prey being the people who needed cheap housing" in John R. Commons, *Economics of Collective Action* (New York: Macmillan, 1950), p. 31 ff. But as Kerr reminds us, collusive agreements between monopolistic employers and their favored employees antedated powerful trade unions, his wry comment ("Labor's Income Share," *op. cit.,* p. 272) being: "It is very difficult to keep the employers indefinitely from giving away their profits in part to their employees, in one way or another."

PART V.
INCOME AND
EMPLOYMENT
ANALYSIS

The famous British economist John Maynard Keynes showed that, sometimes unfortunately, the level of income (and output) depends upon how much people choose
to spend, and this choice may be inconsistent with the level of output that would
employ all of a nation's available labor and property resources. Selections in
this part focus on some of the issues surrounding this basic problem.

Section A, Income-Expenditure Analysis

In "The Coming of J.M. Keynes" John Kenneth Galbraith provides a brief summary
of Keynes' General Theory, describes its initial reception in the United States,
its subsequent widespread acceptance and its profound influence in the post World
War II era. Oskar Morgenstern in "Does GNP Measure Growth and Welfare?" points out
that we really don't know what GNP is measuring - he uses the example of traffic
jam which increases GNP by causing everyone to burn more gas. And he says that
there exists no "generally accepted scientific concept which would give us the
basis for a reliable numerical measurement of the rate of growth." Kenneth Stewart
in "National Income Accounting and Economic Welfare: The Concepts of GNP and MEW"
discusses the Nordhaus-Tobin Measure of Economic Welfare (MEW). MEW is GNP modified by subtracting certain "bads" (like pollution), excluding some services (like
increased police services to fight crime) and adding some household activities.
Stewart concludes that MEW seems to measure consumption, not welfare, and that it
isn't an adequate measure because it is full of guesswork. In "The Consumer Price
Index: How Will the 1977 Revision Affect It?" Julius Shiskin describes the many
ways the CPI will be changed in the 1977 revision. By the end of 1975, John
Kendrick states in "Measuring America's Wealth," the net national wealth of the
U.S. totaled about $26,530 per capita. Kendrick discusses how this figure has
changed and what it measures.

Section B, Monetary Theory and Policy

In "Persepctive on Inflation" 1976 Nobel Prize winner Milton Friedman relates
how wage and price controls "ended in utter failure and the emergence into the
open of suppressed inflation." The expanding money supply, he contends, caused
the rise in prices. "Money Growth Feeds World Inflation" discusses the crucial
role of the growth in the world money stock in triggering the current general inflation. In "MV = PT" Tilford Gaines discusses recent U.S. monetary and fiscal
policy in terms of the equation of exchange. In "The Making of Monetary Policy:
Description and Analysis" Willian Poole describes how the Federal Reserve Bank
selects a money growth target and criticizes its attempts to manipulate the Federal
funds rate in order to reach that target. In Professor Poole's view, one widely

321

shared by monetary economists, the Federal Reserve pays too much attention to interest rates and too little to the quantity of money.

Section C, <u>Inflation and Unemployment</u>

W. Philip Gramm in "Inflation: Its Cause and Cure" argues that the basic cause of our inflations is the government's printing of money, which is, in turn, forced upon the government because it creates large deficits. "Does Inflation Ride Escalators? Not Yet, Pay Council Study Finds" is a review of H.M. Douty's study which found a low correlation between inflation and escalator clauses. In "Indexing Inflation: Remedy or Malady?" Vencent Gennaro discusses the ways in which indexes (e.g., escalators) are currently used, their advantages and disadvantages, and ways in which their use could be extended. In "Is Continuing Inflation Inevitable?" Thomes Maloy advocates jointly determined wage-price guideposts, coupled with some kind of sanctions such as tax penalties. In "Full Employment: The Inflation Myth" current Secretary of Labor Ray Marshall endorses the Humphrey-Hawkins Bill, emphasizing that public employment is non-inflationary approach to the reduction of unemployment. In the <u>Business Week</u> ariticle, "Why Recovering Economies Don't Create Enough New Jobs," unemployment in the U.S. today is assessed mainly as a structural unemployment problem (the loss of jobs due to changes in the economic environment such as population shifts and changes in consumer tastes) which could not be expected to respond siginficantly to monetary and fiscal policy. The liberal and conservative approaches to the problem of unemployment are discussed and the experiences of European countries are compared with those of the U.S. "Recent Developements in the Theory of Unemployment" by Steven Zell examines four recent theoretical explanations for the problem of unemployment with emphasis on labor market stucture and behavior: the theory of structural unemployment; the job-search, labor-turnover theory; the theory of human capital; and the dual labor market hypothesis. In "Unemployment: Exposing the Inflation Alibi" Charles Killinsworth offers the view, as do other writers in this series, that unemployment today is largely structural in nature. He favors a Public Service Employment program and rejects the notion that we can't reduce unemployment without causing more inflation.

The way we look at our economic system today was prefigured by J. M. Keynes and his disciples in the 1930s.

The Coming of J. M. Keynes

JOHN KENNETH GALBRAITH

IN 1935, AT THE AGE OF fifty-two, John Maynard Keynes might well have been considered at the peak of a reasonably remarkable career. His views of the Versailles Treaty had been vindicated, although they had also encouraged the Germans in resisting the reparations which had helped the vindication. He had assuredly been right on Churchill and the return to gold. In 1930, he had published what he had intended as his master work, the two-volume *A Treatise on*

John Kenneth Galbraith is now developing a television series with the British Broadcasting Corporation. His article is based on his book *Money: Whence it Came, Where it Went,* currently being published by Houghton Mifflin Company, copyright © 1975, John Kenneth Galbraith.

Money. Tall, angular, arrogant, very English, he was very much a figure in the London intellectual world.

In fact, most of his reputation was still to be made, a circumstance of which he was wholly aware. Writing to George Bernard Shaw on New Year's Day, 1935, he said: "To understand my state of mind, you have to know that I believe myself to be writing a book on economic theory which will largely revolutionise—not, I suppose, at once but in the course of the next ten years—the way the world thinks about economic problems." So it developed.

What made the book, and Keynes's further reputation, was his instinct that there were forces in the modern economy that were frustrating the most important assumption made by men of orthodox mind—the assumption that, left to itself and given time, the economic system would find its equilibrium with all or nearly all its willing workers employed. More than the orthodox views were involved. Were Keynes's instinct right, the hopes of the monetary radicals would also be destroyed. A change in the gold content of the dollar or an increase in banks' reserves would not mean more borrowers, more deposits, more money and a surge of the economy back to full employment. The level of trade might be indifferent to the supply of money. The loans might be available in the banks; the returns from borrowing, given the natural tendency of the economy to low performance and unemployment, might be such that no one would want to borrow. It followed, as the failures of the gold-buying policy and open-market operations were beginning in the mid-1930s to suggest, that monetary policy would not work. It was essentially passive or permissive. What was needed was a policy that increased the supply of money available for use and then ensured its use. Then the state of trade would have to improve.

The conclusion as to the proper policy was one to which Keynes came well before he got around to its theoretical justification. In the late 1920s he helped persuade Lloyd George, in the latter's last effort at a comeback, to support a major program of borrowing for public works to cure unemployment. The borrowing created the money; its use for public works ensured its expenditure and the effect on production. And at the end of 1933, as the American gold-buying program was negating both the hopes of its supporters and the fears of its opponents, he urged the same course on Roosevelt. "I lay overwhelming emphasis on the increase of national purchasing power resulting from government expenditure which is financed by loans," he wrote in a letter to the New York Times. The New Dealers should not content themselves with making funds available to be borrowed and spent; they must borrow and spend. Nothing could be left to hope or chance.

The theoretical justification came in the book Keynes mentioned to Shaw, The General Theory of Employment Interest and Money, published in Britain in February 1936, and in the United States a few months later. Keynes had long been suspect among his colleagues for the clarity of his writing and thought, the two often going together. In The General Theory he redeemed his academic reputation. It is a work of profound obscurity, badly written and prematurely published. All economists claim to have read it. Only a few have. The rest feel a secret guilt that they never will.

THE REIGN OF SAY'S LAW

The belief that the economy would find its equilibrium at full employment depended partly on what had long been called Say's Law—for J.B. Say, the French counterpart and interpreter of Adam Smith—and partly on the corrective movement of wages, prices and interest rates when there was unemployment. Say's Law, not a thing of startling complexity, held that, from the proceeds of every sale of goods, there was paid out to someone somewhere in wages, salaries, interest, rent or profit (or there was taken from the man who absorbed a loss) the wherewithal to buy that item. As with one item, so with all. This being so, there could not be a shortage of purchasing power in the economy. Movements in prices, wages and interest rates then validated J.B. Say and also ensured that the fundamental tendency of the economy would be to operation at full employment. People and firms saved from their income, and this saving had, obviously, to be spent. This happened when it was invested in housing, plant, capital equipment. If people saved more than was invested, the surplus of savings would bring down interest rates. Investment would thus be stimulated and saving (at least in theory) discouraged. So the excess of savings would be eliminated and Say sustained. Prices of goods would also fall in consequence of any shortfall in purchasing power that resulted from an excess of savings. This would encourage buying and, by reducing the income from which savings were made, also reduce savings. Again Say was sustained.

Until Keynes, Say's law had ruled in economics for more than a century. And the rule was no casual thing: to a remarkable degree acceptance of Say was the test by which reputable economists were distinguished from the crackpots.

Supplementing Say, as noted, were the forces

that kept the economy at full employment. These too were relatively straightforward. Were there unemployment, the competition for jobs would bring a fall in wage rates. Prices would be less immediately affected by the unemployment. The relationship of prices to costs would thus be made more attractive—real wages would fall—and workers whose employment was previously unprofitable to employers would now be hired. The fall in wages would not affect purchasing power; because of Say, that was always sufficient. Employment would continue to expand until the approach to full employment raised wage costs and arrested the hiring. Thus did the economy find its equilibrium at or very near full employ-

ment. From this also came the one decisive recommendation of the orthodox economists for ending unemployment. Do nothing to interfere with the reduction of wages in a depression. Resist all siren voices, including that of Herbert Hoover who, it will be recalled, urged against wage cuts. On no matter was compassion so soft-headed, for to keep up wages merely perpetuated the sorrow of unemployment and the sorrows of the unemployed.

This was the doctrine, perhaps more accurately the theology, that Keynes brought to an end. There are numerous points of entry on his argument; perhaps the easiest is by way of the rate of interest. Interest, he held, was not the price people were paid to save. Rather it was what they got for keeping their assets in plant, machinery or similarly unliquid forms of investment —in his language, what was paid to overcome their liquidity preference. Accordingly, a fall in interest rates might not discourage savings, encourage investment, ensure that all savings would be used. It might cause investors to retreat into cash or its equivalent. So interest rates no longer came to the support of Say's Law to ensure that savings would be spent. And if Say's Law was no longer a reliable axiom of life, the notion of a shortage of purchasing power could no longer be excluded from calculation. It might, among other things, be the consequence of a reduction in wages.

What people sought to save, in Keynes's view, had still to be brought to equal what they wanted to invest. But the adjustment mechanism, he argued, was not the rate of interest but the total output of the economy. If efforts to save exceeded the desire to invest, the resulting shortage of purchasing power or demand caused output to fall. And it kept falling until employment and income had been so reduced that savings were also reduced or made negative. In this fashion savings were brought into line with investment—which also, meanwhile, would have fallen but by not so much. The economic equilibrium so established, it will be evident, was now one in which there was not full employment but unemployment. Thus unemployment for Keynes was a natural condition of the economy.

There was much else. And not all of Keynes's argument survived. The liquidity-preference theory of interest, for example, though it served Keynes's argument, did not gain permanent acceptance as a description of reality. But on two things Keynes was immediately influential. Say's Law sank without trace. There could, it was henceforth agreed, be oversaving. And there could, as its counterpart, be a shortage of effective demand for what was being produced. And the notion that the economy could find its equilibrium with unemployment—a thought admirably reinforced by the everyday evidence of the 1930s—was also almost immediately influential.

COMPETITION AND CONCENTRATION

If Keynes seemed radical to some in his time, he was, in one important respect, completely orthodox. The economic structure which he assumed was that which economists had anciently avowed—that of competition, freely moving prices and the ultimate, uninhibited control of economic behavior by the market. There were unions but they made relatively little difference to Keynes. Corporations and corporate power made no real difference at all. In fact, both unions and corporations, as Keynes wrote, were acting to affirm his thesis. He had support for his ideas that he did not use.

Thus, during the fifty years before Keynes, in all of the industrial countries, corporations had gained greatly in influence and market power. It was the textbook time of what was coming to be called corporate concentration. With the United States in some measure the exception, there had been also the rise of the modern trade union. And in the latter 1930s, under the aegis of the New Deal and in response to the organization drive of the CIO, the United States had come abreast of other countries in union organization. The effect of both corporate concentration and union strength was to make radically more unreliable the adjustments which were assumed to sustain Say's Law and the full-employment equilibrium.

In 1920, it has been noticed, farm prices fell more rapidly and much more severely than did prices of industrial products. The reason, not subject seriously to debate, was that the industrial corporations had the power in their markets—the power normally associated with monopoly or oligopoly—to temper or arrest the decline. Farmers and other small entrepreneurs lacked such power. Again, from 1929 to 1932, farm prices at wholesale fell by more than half. Nonfarm prices fell by less than a quarter. This disparate movement was influentially studied by Gardiner C. Means, at the time employed in the United States Department of Agriculture. To the

better-controlled industrial prices he gave the enduring term administered prices.

The Keynesian adjustment to an excess of savings is through a reduction in aggregate demand. When demand falls, something must give, and what gives must be either prices or production. If prices can be held up by the market power of the corporation, it is production that must fall. When production falls, so will employment. With corporate market power, unemployment will thus become a highly distinctive feature of the Keynesian adjustment. And the reduced spending of those who lose their jobs or who fear that they will lose their jobs can be expected to have a further depressing effect on output and employment. Plausibly this effect on output and employment will be far greater than that which might come, in a competitive economy, from the reduction in prices and wages that Keynes, in the main, envisaged.

The rise of the trade union also made hash of the orthodox hope that wage reductions would serve as a stabilizing influence, act to correct unemployment. Whatever the merits of wage reductions to increase employment, they would not so serve if they did not occur. And one of the first purposes of a union was to resist such reductions. The adjustment in money wages that Keynes thought of dubious corrective value was something that was increasingly less likely to occur. But the unemployment which was now the alternative to wage reductions could have an even greater effect in reducing aggregate demand than the adjustment Keynes did discuss.

HITLER LICKED UNEMPLOYMENT

The rise of the corporations and the unions had another importance for the Keynesian system. They were to be the prime instrument of its failure when inflation, as well as depression, became the problem.

By the mid-1930s there was also in existence an advanced demonstration of the Keynesian system. This was the economic policy of Adolf Hitler and the Third Reich. It involved large-scale borrowing for public expenditures, and at first this was principally for civilian works—railroads, canals, and the *Autobahnen*. The result was a far more effective attack on unemployment than in any other industrial country. By 1935, German unemployment was minimal. According to economist Joan Robinson, "Hitler had already found how to cure unemployment before Keynes had finished explaining why it occurred." In 1936, as prices and wages came under upward pressure, Hitler took the further step of combining an expansive employment policy with comprehensive price controls.

The Nazi economic policy, it should be noted, was an *ad hoc* response to what seemed overriding circumstance. The unemployment position was desperate. So money was borrowed and people put to work. When rising wages and prices threatened stability, a price ceiling was imposed. Although there had been much discussion of such policy in pre-Hitler Germany, it seems doubtful if it was highly influential. Hitler and his cohorts were not a bookish lot. Nevertheless the elimination of unemployment in Germany during the Great Depression without inflation—and with initial reliance on essentially civilian activities—was a signal accomplishment. It has rarely been praised and not much remarked. The notion that Hitler could do no good extends to his economics as it does, more plausibly, to all else.

THE DEBATE GROWS STRONG

Thus the effect of *The General Theory* was to legitimatize ideas that were in circulation. What had been the aberrations of cranks and crackpots became now respectable scholarly discussion. To suggest that there might be oversaving now no longer cost a man his degree or, necessarily, his promotion. That the proper remedy for oversaving was public spending financed by borrowing was henceforth a fit topic for discussion—although it continued to provoke bitter rebuke. The way was now open for public action.

The Keynesian ideas passed into the domain of public policy by way of the universities. If this was a revolution, it was not of the streets or of the shops but of the seminar rooms. Keynes was taken up, in the main, by younger scholars. Economists are economical, among other things, of ideas; most make those of their graduate days do for a lifetime. So change comes not from men and women changing their minds but from the change from one generation to the next. Keynes's great contemporaries, almost without exception, reviewed his book and found it wrong. This conviction they then, with a few exceptions, carried into retirement and perhaps beyond.

The principal British center of Keynesian discussion was, as might be expected, the University of Cambridge; here the ideas were brilliantly examined and explained by two younger colleagues of Keynes, R. F. Kahn and Joan Robinson. It was through Harvard that the Keynesian ideas reached the United States. In the months following the appearance of *The General Theory* the discussion was nearly continuous—an interested student could attend a seminar, formal or more often highly informal, on *The General Theory* almost any evening. Students who had been at Cambridge, England, and had known Keynes became minor oracles in Cambridge, Massachusetts—valued courts of appeal on what Keynes really meant.

In time, Harvard alumni became aware of the Keynesian ferment and were distressed. (In later years a small organization, the Veritas Foundation, was formed to combat the menace.) The older faculty members, though tolerant, were not approving. In the autumn of 1936, the University celebrated its three hundredth anniversary. It was known that honorary degrees would be given to the greatest men in the various fields of science, social science, arts and public life, and that Franklin D. Roosevelt, to the distress of many distinguished graduates, was to give one of the principal speeches. The younger members of the Departments of Government and Economics offered suggestions to their elders as to proper recipients of the degrees; the thought was to propose names that, by their plausibility, would cause the maximum of embarrassment. The name so chosen by the political scientists was Leon Trotsky; by the younger economists, it was

Keynes. Neither man was honored. Those who were are mostly forgotten.

From 1938 on, however, a senior member of the Harvard faculty, just arrived from the University of Minnesota, was vital for winning acceptance for Keynes. This was Avlin H. Hansen. Hansen's initial reaction to *The General Theory* as a reviewer was cool; however, he had a notable, even exceptional, capacity to change his mind. Soon his seminar on fiscal policy was a major focus of both theoretical and practical discussion. In the late 1930s it was joined by a steady flow of Washington officials. Thus it became, in appreciable measure, the avenue by which the Keynesian ideas went on to Washington. Hansen also wrote lucidly and indefatigably on Keynesian policy. Less lucid but even more indefatigable was another, somewhat younger Harvard professor, Seymour E. Harris. Hansen, Harris and, with his pioneering textbook, Paul A. Samuelson were the men who brought the Keynesian ideas to Americans.

THE THEORY HITS WASHINGTON

However, Washington in the second half of the 1930s was also fertile ground. The failure of monetary policy, along with the folding up of the NRA, had left the Administration with no clear design for ending unemployment and promoting recovery. One possibility was an attack on monopoly. Monopolies were wicked; something good would surely come from harassing them. More logically, the market power of monopoly, as just noted, meant that prices remained high in face of falling demand. It was output and employment that suffered. To restore competition would presumably reduce the influence of administered prices, diminish the importance of this cause of unemployment. In the latter 1930s there was a marked revival of interest in antitrust enforcement in Washington. It proceeded from this view of matters.

The difficulty was that market power and price administration were not a problem of a few firms; they were pervasive in the American economy. So the remedy required a complete restructuring of that economy. To spend money, as the experience of the early 1930s with public works was by now showing, took time. But it was a marvel of immediacy as compared with the time that would be needed to bring the antitrust laws to bear on all American corporations that had power over their prices. And not many in the New Deal were willing to propose the logical companion step, which was to disintegrate the trade unions. So there remained only Keynes.

From the time of the publication of *The General Theory* forward, the center of Keynesian evangelism in Washington was the Board of Governors of the Federal Reserve System. History seemed to be proceeding in an exceptionally logical way. Monetary policy resulted only in an increase in excess reserves. Those responsible

were turning, accordingly, to the less passive, more certain fiscal policy that ensured that the money would be spent. In fact, the role of the Federal Reserve was mostly an accident. Lauchlin Currie, having anticipated Keynes, was notably open to his ideas. He was now Director of Research for the Board. And the Chairman was Marriner Eccles, whose description of a bank run we have read. Eccles, reflecting on his own perilous experience as a banker and the deprivations and perils of Utah farmers and businessmen during the Depression, had been led quite independently to the view that the government should intervene in the economy along Keynesian lines. Thus the emergence of the Federal Reserve, after the publication of *The General Theory*, as the entering Washington wedge of Keynes.

Currie proceeded in a more practical way. In 1939, he moved from the Federal Reserve to the White House as, in fact though not in title, economic adviser to FDR, the first such in a long line. At the White House he constituted himself an employment agency and general dispatcher for government economists. As openings of importance developed anywhere in the government, he endeavored to see that they were filled by people of assured Keynesian convictions. By the end of the 1930s he had established an informal network of such converts extending into all of the fiscally significant agencies. All remained in close communication on ideas and policies. Neither Currie nor any of those involved regarded this as a conspiracy. It merely seemed the necessary and sensible thing to do.

THE LIMITS OF THE 1930s

Keynesian policy in these years was circumscribed by the small role available for taxation. Partly this was circumstance. Before World War II, the government of the United States was a small thing; in 1930, total expenditures were $1.4 billion; in 1940, still less than $10 billion. Purchases by the Federal government of goods and services were 2 percent of Gross National Product in 1930 and 6 percent in 1940. In the latter 1950s and 1960s, in comparison, they ranged from 10 to 12 percent.

Federal expenditures being small, so were the taxes to cover them. In later years Keynesian policy would come to depend heavily on two types of tax changes. One is the tendency of both the corporate and the personal income taxes to adjust themselves in a fortuitous way. When output and employment fall, so do profits and incomes, including those incomes subject to surtax. And as incomes fall, so, and more than proportionately, do the taxes paid. The reverse holds when output, employment, profits and incomes increase. In the 1930s, taxes being small, this effect was negligible.

In later years also, the idea of tax reduction to increase the deficit and thus expand borrowing and spending from borrowed funds would gain acceptance. In the 1930s, with the budget out of balance, a tax cut in order to increase the deficit seemed a far too radical step even to the most persuaded Keynesians. Currie, and perhaps a few others, saw the failure to urge taxes as a flaw in the policy. In general, however, Keynesian policy was considered identical with increasing public spending.

This, too, had an adverse political effect. Spending was not then for such socially reputable purposes as national defense. Rather it had the spendthrift aspect invariably associated with outlays for the average citizen or the poor. And Keynesian policy shared this reputation. In later times, when Keynesian policy to expand output came to lay greater emphasis on the use of taxes, attitudes would greatly change. Among the beneficiaries of tax reduction would be the affluent and the rich. Economic stimulation that works through the increased outlays of the affluent has, inevitably, an aspect of soundness and sanity that is lacking in expenditures on behalf of the undeserving poor. The shift from use of spending to use of tax reduction would have much to do with making Keynesian stimulation of the economy respectable.

So, as far as the 1930s went, the practical effect of Keynes was not very great. In 1932, 1933 and 1934, the revenues of the Federal government had been less than half of expenditures—a greater relative imbalance than in any peacetime year since. In the fiscal year ending June 30, 1932, revenues were $1.9 billion, expenditures $4.7 billion. But in relation to the economy these magnitudes were, as noted, far from impressive. Then, after 1934, revenues gained relatively on expenditures. By the fiscal year ending in June 1938, the deficit was only $1.2 billion on expenditures of $6.8 billion. It rose again in consequence of the recession of 1937-1938, and part of the increase was deliberate. It was then, for the first time, that the deficit was justified, at least by policy-makers to themselves, by Keynesian policy. But the magnitudes were still small. In the 1939 fiscal year the deficit, for example, was only $3.9 billion, the same amount as in the year following. This was only marginally greater than the $3.6 billion deficit in 1934. Clearly the triumph of Keynesian policy was not overwhelming.

The Great Depression did not, in fact, end. It was swept away by World War II. This was, in a grim sense, the triumph of the Keynesian policy. But the problem it posed was not employment and output; it was inflation. And for this, as was to be learned again a quarter century on, the Keynesian system did not answer.

The father of "game theory" challenges our assumptions on growth, utility, and welfare.

Does GNP Measure Growth and Welfare?

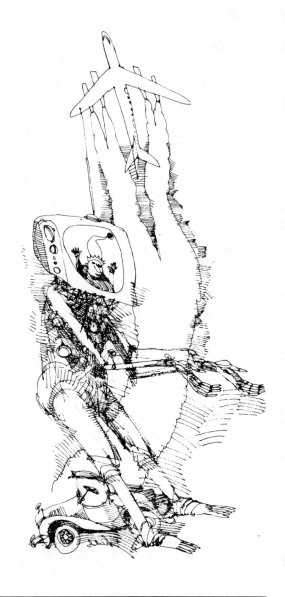

OSKAR MORGENSTERN

T HE QUESTION POSED by the above title raises a number of deep problems of economic science. The question seems simple, yet in those few words—measurement, growth, and welfare—culminate the problems of large

Oskar Morgenstern, who with John von Neumann wrote the now-classic *Theory of Games and Economic Behavior* in 1944, is professor of economics at New York University. His article is adapted from his recent remarks at the university's Key Issues Lecture Series.

Oskar Morgenstern, "Does GNP Measure Growth and Welfare?" *Business and Society Review*, Fall 1975, pp. 23–31. Reprinted from *Business and Society Review*, Fall 1975, Vol. 15. Copyright 1975. Warren, Gorham, and Lamont, Inc., 210 South Street, Boston, Mass. All rights reserved.

areas with which economists have been concerned for centuries. How nice it would be, then, if one could report that now we have one single concept and, indeed, one single number which could summarize variations of growth and welfare. As we shall see, this unfortunately is not the case.

To begin with measurement: All sciences have to come to grips with that problem. It is an extremely difficult one and each science has its own troubles. When a measurement in any field has become possible this is rightly hailed as a great achievement, as a step toward new discoveries and innumerable applications. Even to have a precise measure of time is difficult: Clocks are a late development in human history, and to this day we try to make them more and more accurate, because so much depends on them. So it is not surprising that when it was recently reported that the rotation of the earth—our finest measure of time—may have slowed down during the last year by one second, this caused great interest in physics and astronomy. From this reaction we also get an idea of the high standards in those sciences. In other fields we measure blood pressure, barometric pressure, the composition of blood, temperature, the speed of light, etc., etc., sometimes crudely, sometimes with extraordinary precision.

THINK FIRST, COUNT LATER

Although in the physical and even in the biological sciences a great and firm tradition has been built up over the centuries, the matter of observation and measurement is never closed. Science is never finished; rather, for all time, science is only an approximation of the underlying reality. It may surprise you that in spite of this great tradition Einstein more than once remarked to me, "Most scientists naively think they know what they should observe and how they should measure it." And he had the natural sciences in mind!

How, then, is the situation in the social sciences, in particular in economics? In some manner we seem to be more fortunate than the natural sciences. Nature shows itself to our senses essentially in a qualitative way, and to get to numbers of high precision requires great effort and is a formidable achievement. But in economics we can count the number of inhabitants of a town or a country, the number of motor cars, of checks cashed, of tons of steel produced, of . . . well of almost anything—or so it seems. Since it looks to be so simple to observe and count, there is in economics—as well as in other social sciences —no tradition which would enforce high standards. Counting seems natural, and what is counted is readily accepted. But that is true only up to the point where broader notions are encountered, notions such as "growth" and "welfare." Or even more basic, the question of what is "value" and "utility" promptly causes great difficulty.

Suddenly we see that we have to have sharp *concepts*, that we must ask questions to which we normally get only qualitative, not—at least not right away—quantitative answers. There is little doubt what an individual is, or a motor car, or a check. But to observe "growth," or "utility," or "welfare" for a whole nation is an entirely different matter. Surely people are involved, or cars that can be counted, or monies changing hands, and so on; but to state how the economy grows, and whether welfare changes and by how much, are entirely different matters. Such words mean very different things to different people. For many, they are abstractions that mean nothing concrete or tangible. It is a long way from that to truly scientific, objective knowledge. What we need are concepts. There is no escape from that, no matter how primitive our approach may be.

Let us first look at "growth." That is clearly a notion that applies to an organism. The human body grows, stops growing, and eventually dies. The body has many parts and many functions. It grows not only all together, as a whole, but parts of it grow at different rates (and not forever, as Galileo knew); and the whole is of unimaginable complexity, which modern biology reveals to us in a rapid though still partial manner. In the whole process of organic growth there is control, genetic planning, and unified function. Can the economy be compared with this so that we can transfer the notion of organic growth from this area to our field? One thing the economy certainly has in common with the human body: The economy is also of the highest complexity. Consequently one must expect that even an adequate qualitative description is correspondingly difficult.

I find, however, that very few people, even few economists—or should I say regretfully, especially economists—have a real appreciation and understanding of the immense complexity of an economic system. Now, I have used the word *system,* but it is not even clear whether that word is appropriate, because we do not understand fully the organizing principles that make possible the economic life of a nation. One need only observe what happens in an ordinary person's day and what is considered to be absolutely obvious and normal. We take a bus or train in the morning, we go to stores, we buy, the money is accepted with which we pay, or we pay by a check which will be transmitted—by mails about which we have no control whatsoever—to an anonymous institution, possibly far away; the stores order and have things in stock; they set prices on the basis of the expectation of what competitors might be doing; we buy on the basis of expectation as to what our needs might be in the future and how they will be met; we spend our money today because we expect that our salaries, or incomes from other sources, actually will be paid at certain dates in the near or more distant future, etc., etc.

In all this, there is no central genetic regulation, nobody who plans for all, no one to whom everybody is responsible. We carry a great deal of information in our heads, and that which we do not carry we can find in newspapers which gather information and are printed, again motivated only by their own self-interest, namely, to be published and sold with profit. At present—at this very moment—raw materials are being produced, and there is no conceivable way of telling how they will be finally molded, into which kind of finished products they will be turned. A steel producer has no idea whether his steel will be used for the making of tanks, or ships, or paper clips.

And yet all this works, and works miraculously well, although of course it is easily subject to great disturbances. The astonishing fact is not that the thing works so well, but that it works at all. It is only when we realize the complexity of the economy that we begin to see, and possibly understand, how dangerous it is to interfere in these matters. The economic system is subject to great changes caused by technology, by political events, by changes in the desires and wishes of consumers.

Any living organism is in many ways a very much simpler matter. However, if one knows anything at all about physiology, one finds that statement horrendous, because one can hardly imagine anything more finely tuned and more complicated than, let us say, the human body, not to mention the brain, which, without any doubt, is the most complicated thing of whose existence we are aware in the whole universe, and whose functioning we clearly do not understand, although we have a tremendous amount of knowledge of it. The fact is that the human body has one specific purpose: to stay functioning, to stay alive. We cannot say that the economic system has any such clear purpose.

INTRODUCING A LITTLE CHAOS

In the light of such observations, one should be extremely modest in making proposals for policy. In general, I would say that unless we are reasonably sure that we know what the consequences of new policy measures will be—for example, of new taxes introduced, prices regulated, etc., etc.—we should leave things alone. One ought interfere only if one believes that one understands the consequences of the interference. The same is true of medicine: It took a long time to come from the witch doctor to the modern brain surgeon. While presumably the human physiology—or that of any other biological entity—stays practically the same throughout centuries or millenia (although subject to evolution over hundreds of thousands of years), the economic system—to make things still more difficult—is constantly being changed, especially by technology. Technology is an interference from the outside; it is absorbed in a manner which those who bring it into economic existence think to be profitable for them, but whose global effects they neither understand nor care about. Clearly, this compounds the difficulties of policy, because what might have been a suitable measure to achieve desired results at one time may no longer have any validity under present or future circumstances. It takes a long time to develop a scientifically acceptable new idea of policy; and while it is being born, if that happens at all, new features appear in the economic life. For example, Keynesian policy ideas of the 1930s are being adopted by the U. S. government now—a time when they have virtually no applicability whatsoever.

Thus, the "growth" of an economy is a very different matter from the growth of an organism. The economy has neither a beginning nor an end.

In addition, as was already said, the economy is constantly in flux. So it is perhaps not surprising that, apart from some highly technical and abstract models of economic expansion—which is not the same thing as growth—there simply does not exist a generally accepted scientific concept which would give us the basis for a reliable numerical measurement of the *rate* of growth.

WHAT ABOUT GNP?

But, you say, there is GNP, gross national product, i.e., the turnover in an economy in a unit period—a hallowed notion in contemporary economics. It is used with abandon. I shall say more about it later. For now I want to point out only *one* of its quantitative features: It is expressed by a *single number*, a so-called scalar. We discussed organic growth of a human body. Would anybody in his senses imagine that there could be a single scalar number which would adequately describe the development of a human from babyhood to maturity to old age: the growth of the body, of the mind, of capabilities? The idea is so grotesque and ludicrous that we can dismiss it from the outset. We have just seen that the economy, too, is of high complexity; therefore, to think that its description, or rather its changes, could be given and measured—accurately, without the slightest error of measurement—by one scalar number is equally absurd.

Just to show the absurdity and limitation of this popular alleged "concept," consider this: *Anything* that leads to a transaction in monetary form, where goods or services change hands against money, is recorded as *positive*. No matter what is being sold, it is added to GNP. It may have been sales of goods already stocked, it may have been a car just coming out of a factory: it does not matter. Neither does it matter what *kind* of product it is: atomic bombs, drugs, cars, food, aesthetic pollution by new billboards . . . you name it. Clearly, that goes against common sense. Why should all products and services be treated alike? Why should I accept more nuclear weapons as part of the "growth" of the economy? Of course, one could argue that one is interested only in *transactions*. But then one would have a great deal of explaining to do about how a larger number of transactions can possibly be related to "welfare." Does the uncontrolled increase of cancer cells in a child mean "growth"?

There are other and equally well-known difficulties. Many services are rendered and many goods are produced that never enter a market. Thus they escape GNP. As has been often noted, if housewives were being paid by their husbands GNP would rise, although there would not be one iota of difference in production or services. There are many similar situations.

Another trouble with the GNP concept is that it measures, or rather expresses, as positive (i.e., as adding to GNP) the *malfunctions* of the economic system or society. To wit: if we are stuck in one of the thousands of traffic jams, if airplanes are stacked and cannot land on schedule, if fires

break out, or other disasters occur that require repair—*up goes the GNP*. More gasoline is used, fares go up, overtime has to be paid, and so on. It would be difficult to find in any other science a "measure" which simultaneously tells opposite stories of the functioning of a complex system with *one* single scalar number! If we merely improve the scheduling of airplanes and stagger the times of automobile traffic, and nothing else is changed—*down goes GNP!* It goes *up*, on the other hand, if industry pollutes the air and we create other industries to remove the polluting substances.

So we see that there is real trouble with the basic underlying notion of GNP. It is not an acceptable scientific concept for the purposes for which it is used. The fact that it violates common sense might not be considered critical. There are, after all, many concepts in physics which common sense could never create or might reject, such as "curved space." But these concepts are the product of powerful theories and are needed when a scientific field is already well developed. The GNP action, however, is nothing of this kind. It expresses a trivial idea which is clearly accessible to scrutiny by common sense. Therefore its current, indiscriminate uses are suspect, and it is certainly questionable that it should be used to tell us about growth and welfare.

At this point it is proper to recall Einstein's remark that it seems, to many, obvious what one should observe. Surely transactions occur all the time in the economy, but that does not mean that they offer the proper way to describe the functioning of the economy. Perhaps only *some* transactions—a selection made on the basis of a powerful theory—can give us the desired information. But what we see is that the corrections —or better, the changes—of GNP figures made by elimination of the effect of seasonal variations, price changes, etc.—thereby obtaining a stable base, free of inflation's distortion—in no way touch the fundamental issues and objections.

SMALLER IS BETTER

GNP is a global notion. It is undifferentiated. It falls into the pattern of modern *macroeconomics*, which attempts to relate, say, the *total* quantity of money in circulation to *total* employment, *total* output of industry, etc. It is tempting to do so, and it would simplify economic reasoning enormously if one could discover strict interdependencies. Yet there is great danger in these efforts: For example, the same increase in the quantity of money will have very different consequences if it goes to consumers rather than to producers. This difference is obliterated when one restricts oneself to the macro entities. (It is interesting to note that modern science goes in exactly the opposite direction: More and more,

finer distinctions are made. First, one has a molecule; then an atom; then the electron; then more and more elementary particles; then subparticles; and only by these steps does one arrive at a better understanding of matter.) But GNP, as an alleged global measure, runs precisely counter to the spirit of modern science. (I am tempted here to quote St. Augustine: "For so it is, oh my Lord God, I measure it, but what it is that I measure I do not know."

When we talk about "economic welfare" we are entering upon a field where other great difficulties arise. Economists have struggled with the problem of welfare for centuries. Countless volumes have been written about it, but there still is no consensus. It is therefore likely that using a primitive notion such as GNP to measure that much-disputed thing will come to naught. But first let us examine briefly where the difficulties lie with respect to economic welfare. Most of us will think at first of our own, personal situation: possessions, income, stability of income, needs (as perceived), health, obligations to others, prices of the goods and services to be bought over some more or less specified period of time, etc. In short, our personal welfare is composed of many variables. Over time, some variables may go up while others go down. In some cases these movements cancel out: income may rise in the same proportion as the prices of the goods I want and so all stays the same. But when some prices of relevance to us go up and others go down, then it is not so obvious whether and how our individual welfare has been affected.

WHAT DO WE MEAN BY VALUE?

The principal attribute of individual welfare is, in the last analysis, what value or utility people attach to their possessions and income. What determines value has puzzled economists for ages. Is there an objective value applicable for everyone, in any circumstance, at any time? How is value produced? What affects value? The answers have ranged from the assertion that there are absolute values to the statement that the economic value of an object is only what you can sell it for—"Res tantum valet quantum vendi potest"—which is certainly true in the stock market, although there is also the assertion of an "intrinsic" value which often differs in both directions from the sales value. Though all this may seem to be a confusing situation, there is today no doubt that—apart from the few remaining adherents of the superseded labor-value theory—utility attributed by individuals to goods and services is all that matters. Utility is based on individual preferences, and these are related to the objective, technical characteristics of the desired goods and services. An individual can compare the utilities he expects to derive from goods even though they are all different.

But here we come to an end: Utility is strictly an individual matter. Exactly the same bundle of goods will have a very different utility for different persons.

Of course, it is likely that persons in a given income class have similar needs and are concerned about the prices of similar bunches of goods. But if I take a good from A, for whom it has some utility, and give it to B, for whom also it has some utility, it does not follow that I have diminished A as much as I have improved B's position. The point is, different individuals' utilities are not comparable. There is no known way to find out objectively whether I transfer the same utility (for example, by taxation) from one to the other.

Economists have thought of one way which seems to give us information about general welfare, which is what we are really interested in (and what GNP is somehow expected to measure). It is the Pareto optimum, which says the following:

If we look at a community and add a good to one party without at the same time diminishing any other party of that community, then we can say that the welfare of the whole group has increased. This seems plausible and harmless, and we find the Pareto optimum extolled and used in almost every textbook in economics. Yet how can we find out when a person feels diminished? Only by questioning, for there is no objective way of observing the phenomenon. A person might even feel diminished when something is given to him that he does not want or cannot use. And might not A feel diminished when he gets nothing and someone else gets an addition? This can certainly happen—even when nothing is actually taken from him.

If the only way to find out whether someone benefits or is diminished is to ask them, then we face other problems. Do they tell us the truth? Necessarily? Always? May they not be playing a game in order to extract some greater benefit? So we see that this seemingly innocent and seemingly workable concept is applicable at best under severely restrictive conditions which may never exist in reality. In reality, of course, we determine social preferences and act accordingly. We tax people and we transfer income. We build public works, establish museums, run a military force, and so on. But all this is the product of political decision-making processes, based on voting or on dictates, with only vague ideas of what might be good for the society and increase its "welfare." But there is no strictly scientific basis. There is power—or at best persuasion.

The upshot of all this is that welfare is an elusive concept that has great intuitive appeal—but means different things to different people and groups of people. It is a concept that slips through our net the moment we want to make it objective. I say this with all due respect to the many economists, past and present, who have given so much thought to this matter. Many valuable attempts have been made, but, as so often in science, much has to be discarded that was once acceptable. There is a great challenge here to economic science. To find some day a satisfactory description of "welfare" and then also to tell us how to measure it.

A POSSIBLE APPROACH

A promising development is the study of the "social indicators." This movement recognizes

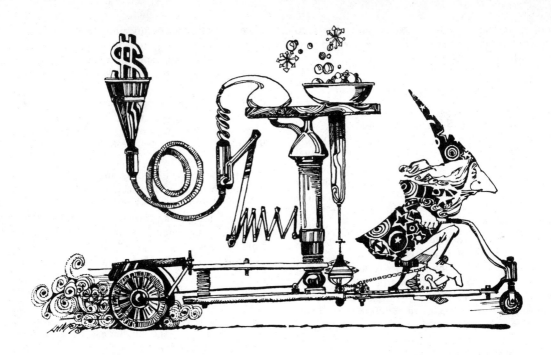

that a positively valued social development depends on the simultaneous weighing of several variables. For example, an increase in production is not good if it is accompanied by more pollution; a rise in income is not beneficial if there is deterioration of its present distribution. Incidentally, note that when I speak of "deterioration of income distribution" I appear to be able to tell in a scientifically objective way when a particular income distribution is "better" than another. This would again involve interpersonal comparisons of utility, which we know have to be ruled out. Yet, to take an extreme case, common sense tells us that if 90 percent of the national income goes to 5 percent of the population, that country is no better off than if even a slightly smaller income is distributed more equally among the inhabitants. This clash of insight with our inability to make scientifically acceptable statements is most disturbing.

There are many interrelated factors on which welfare, whether personal or communal, depends. Even to describe them, to enumerate them and put them into a coherent picture, is a difficult task. Any differentiation which forces us to make more and more distinctions and leads us away from simple global expression is in the right scientific spirit.

A poorly defined, hard-to-capture, yet exceedingly important phenomenon such as welfare is supposed to be measured with extraordinary precision by another phenomenon, GNP, that records nothing better than the total hodgepodge of transactions in the economy. The idea has no chance of finding any scientifically valid justification whatsoever. It is another instance, as was the case in growth, of demanding that a single, scalar number produce wonders of measurement.

Attempts have been made to improve upon the GNP concept, for example, by considering gross *domestic* product, or attempting to arrive at some measure of *net* output so that the "productivity of an economy" can be determined. Such efforts, to make finer and finer distinctions clearly go in the right direction; however, conceptual difficulties arise then, too. For example, the notion of "productivity" applies easily to processes where we observe physical tangible inputs and outputs. (These can also be expressed in monetary terms, though this is not a simple matter.) However, perhaps only 40 percent of the U.S. economy today involves physical output; the rest is "services." And no one has come forth with good ideas on how to measure productivity of lawyers, doctors, teachers, policemen, hospitals, scientists, musicians, or actors. Yet they all have some kind of "output"—conceivably even a "net" output. But what is it, and how do we compare these heterogeneous services with each other? What is hoped for is, again, a primitive, single, scalar number!

MEASURING: HARDER THAN IT LOOKS

Now let me turn to the way in which one deals with the numbers purporting to measure GNP. Let us forget for the time being all that was said in criticism of GNP. Let us merely look at the measurement itself.

Measurement is demanding, and accurate measurement exceedingly so. It may interest you that even today we do not know the relatively simple matter of the moon's *precise* distance from earth —though man has visited the moon! What is more, we cannot prove the stability in the large of the moon's orbit around the earth. (We can only prove it "in the small." For the whole proof we would need to know the moon's behavior from the beginning to the end.) Exactly the same is true regarding the entire planetary system. Should not these two considerations make us economists exceedingly modest and cautious when discussing measurement of complex economic-social situations, or the stability of the economic universe?

But what happens in reality?

Mountains of economic statistics pour forth continuously from government and business— millions of numbers, immense detail, comprehensive aggregates, and sophisticated index numbers. Many numbers have been, so to speak, laundered; for example, seasonal variations are eliminated in order to show the alleged "true" movement of some activities. In other cases, numbers are obtained by carefully studied sampling processes; powerful statistical theory is used, and sampling errors are carefully spelled out.

But one characteristic pervades all: *We virtually never encounter the words* "perhaps," "approximately," "about," "maybe," and so on, or see a sign saying: "± x percent." That is vastly different from the natural sciences, where it is standard to ask immediately what the error of observation might be. (A notable exception is S.N. Kuznets who, in his valuable work on national income, has shown that some of the figures may err by more than 20 percent.) Some things *seem* easy to measure, e.g., the number of inhabitants in a country. But in the U.S. Census of 1950, about 5 million people— equivalent to a good-sized city, say Chicago—were not counted! In some Asiatic countries the population count is said to have errors of ±20 percent. Who knows the population of China, or of some African countries? For very gross comparisons this may not matter too much, but the frequently and freely used international per capita income data are often meaningless.

Errors there must be. The extent of *admissible* error depends on the use for which the measurement is needed. (Cross-section data for nuclear reactors may have an error of ±50 percent. But the reactors work!) Of course, the smaller the error, the better. Reduction of error is usually expensive, and how much one wants to spend on error reduction depends, again, on the use to be made of the measurement or observation. Also, if a good number has to be combined with a poor one, there is not much point in making the good number even better.

Since errors range from very small to very large, is there a generally accepted standard? The answer is that one should always state honestly what error is involved, in whatever field. This is common in physics and, I regret to say, almost totally lacking in economics and the other social sciences. I am referring to the basic errors in variables, i.e., errors in the basic observations, not to sampling errors and the like. There will have to be a change in attitudes, in demands, in standards. No compromise is possible.

THE USES OF GNP FIGURES

Now we come to the point of looking at the *calculations* made with the GNP figures. It is well to start by quoting one of the greatest mathematicians of all time, C.F.W. Gauss: "The lack of mathematical insight shows up in nothing as surprisingly as in unbounded precision in numerical computations." There are countless illustrations for such activity, not only in economics, but in all social sciences. This is another sign of their lack of maturity compared to the physical sciences. There seems to be a love for a string of decimal places so long as to be meaningless. Yet Norbert Wiener, also an eminent mathematician, observed to me: "Economics is a one-digit science." (I would be inclined to agree in general, but there are a few areas where our power of interpretation is great enough to handle two, perhaps even three, digits.)

GNP figures are principally used to calculate rates of change—presumably rates of growth, because that is what the world has been made aware of. Governments everywhere look hypnotized at these calculations. Systems are judged by the numbers generated even for the short intervals of a quarter year—so brief a period that one must be astonished that all the hundreds of thousands of underlying figures could even be collected, much less collected without any error whatsoever! Or if there are errors, perhaps they very kindly distribute themselves in such manner that they all cancel out? As to both propositions the facts are, of course, quite the contrary. There *must* be errors: We live in a "stochastic universe," which means that the world is to a large measure indeterminable. And that errors in economic observations would cancel out precisely—well, I shall give an illustration of a "one percent error" in calculation. Suppose you have two consecutive GNP numbers—whatever their absolute values be —such that the second one is 3 percent larger than the first. Now assume that the first is overstated (i.e., errs) by 1 percent, and that the second is understated by the same amount. Then the rate of growth, instead of being $+3$ percent, is in fact $+5.03$ percent—a difference of two-thirds! And if the errors are the other way around, so that the first figure is faulty by -1 percent and the second by $+1$ percent, then the rate of growth is only 0.97 percent. And that is with merely a *one* percent error, tiny by almost any standard. (In physics, observations with only a 3 percent error are frequently very good and useful measurements.)

Simple as these considerations are, they are basic. They illustrate precisely the importance of the statement quoted from Gauss. In gathering the thousands of underlying figures, there are delays and corrections. The respective statistical offices naturally want to do a good job, so they correct the initial figures as faults are discovered.

(The yearly GNP often requires up to *ten years* before a final figure is presented.) In the course of these successive revisions, there are plus and minus changes of the order of 2, 3, or sometimes more percent. (Quarterly figures are subject to more and even bigger corrections.) All this plays havoc with the initially calculated rate of change, which is what government and private economists base forecasts and remedial measures on.

Is it not peculiar that governments submit to being judged by numbers as primitive as those here discussed? Not that one would want to deny that some parts of this phenomenon can be expressed numerically. But to proceed as though all can be put into one single number that is free of all possible faults—that is unacceptable. What is more, these numbers are supposed to be comparable internationally. Whether it be India or Sweden or China or the U.S., the "precise" rates of growth are compared with each other—despite the fact that for some countries even the number of inhabitants is only vaguely known. Why would statesmen expose themselves to this kind of evaluation?

Economists have to share in the blame. They have introduced the notion of "fine tuning" the economy, the idea that one can control the whole so precisely as to judge its performance by, and adjust its functionings to, the *second* digits of growth rates, when in truth even the *first* digit is in doubt. (One hears a little less, however, about the fine tuning recently in view of the fact that rather gross events—such as high unemployment, high interest rates, and steep oil price increases—are with us.)

We would of course like to know whether, and how much, and in what direction the economy has grown, and how economic welfare has been changed. We would like to have good, trustworthy, numerical expressions for these. Alas, the GNP concept is primitive in the extreme, and "social welfare" is still so difficult and controversial that given its inherent great conceptual difficulties, we have no measure at present which does not involve political, moral, or other prejudices.

National Income Accounting and Economic Welfare: The Concepts of GNP and MEW

by KENNETH STEWART

T HE MOST comprehensive indicator of economic performance in the nation in a given year is gross national product (GNP). Changes in GNP reflect both changes in prices and changes in the physical volume of output. GNP adjusted for price level changes is generally accepted as a reliable indicator of growth in the nation's total production and is used by economic analysts to indicate whether the economy is expanding or contracting. Policymakers use GNP data, along with other measures of economic activity, in the formulation and subsequent evaluation of stabilization policy.

A growing GNP is generally associated with expanding opportunities for employment and an increasing amount of material welfare. Economic policy facilitating GNP growth is formulated, in part, as a means of reducing both unemployment and poverty. But a growing GNP has also been accompanied by urban decay and pollution, which are not accounted for in national income data. Critics of economic growth, as measured by national income data, argue that such data tend to emphasize the growth of material welfare while ignoring what is happening to the "quality of life" or "social welfare." GNP has been growing, but what has been happening to total welfare?

William Nordhaus and James Tobin recently proposed an indicator to obtain a measure of "economic welfare" or "standard of living" to complement GNP.[1] This indicator, referred to as "Measure of Economic

Welfare" (MEW), would modify the present GNP measure primarily in three ways: 1) by subtracting estimates of certain costs or "bads", such as pollution, from the national income total; 2) by excluding some services, such as police services, since it is possible that increased police budgets to combat rising crime do not indicate an increase in welfare; and 3) by adding to GNP some activities, such as household activities (housework, home repairs, etc.) and leisure, which are not included in the GNP total.

This article discusses the Nordhaus-Tobin measure of economic welfare. Since they use GNP as a point of departure, the concept of GNP is reviewed in the first part of this paper and then compared with the proposed MEW concept.

DEFINITION AND CONCEPT OF GNP

Gross national product can be defined as the market value of domestic current final output.[2] It provides a measure of the nation's aggregate economic activity — income or output — measured in terms of current market prices over a given period of time, usually a year.

Two methods can be used in measuring the nation's income or output — the income approach and the expenditure approach. The income approach determines gross national income by totaling the various income shares of the factors of production, such as compensation of employees, rental income, proprietors' income,

---

[1]William Nordhaus and James Tobin, "Is Growth Obsolete?", *Economic Growth,* Fiftieth Anniversary Colloquium, Vol. 5 (New York: National Bureau of Economic Research, 1972).

[2]For further discussion of the GNP concept, see Armen A. Alchian and William R. Allen, *University Economics,* 3rd ed. (Belmont, California: Wadsworth Publishing Company, Inc., 1972), especially pp. 529-533.

Kenneth Stewart, "National Income Accounting and Economic Welfare: The Concepts of GNP and MEW." *Review,* Federal Reserve Bank of St. Louis, April 1974, pp. 18–23, Reprinted with permission.

net interest, and corporate profits (and adding in an allowance for depreciation, indirect business taxes, and other smaller items). The expenditure approach determines the current value of production basically by totaling all expenditures for final goods and services based on type of purchase and expenditure (plus the net change in business inventory). Expenditures in the national income accounts are classified as personal consumption expenditures, gross private domestic investment, government purchases of goods and services, and net exports. The two approaches provide approximately the same total, for expenditures on final goods and services provide income to the factors of production which produced these items.

In general, nonmarketed goods, such as goods and services produced and consumed by the household (which would include meals prepared in the home and home repairs) are not included as part of the nation's measured income. The exclusion of such productive work performed by household members limits the validity of the GNP concept as a measure of the nation's *total* product.[3]

It also should be stressed that not all market transactions are included in determining GNP, for this

would involve double-counting. Final products are not normally resold; intermediate products are resold in some form. For example, flour sold by a miller to a baker is resold in the form of bread. To count the flour sold by the miller and the bread sold by the baker as part of GNP would involve double-counting the value of the flour.[4]

Market transactions involving the exchange of wealth or claims to wealth are also excluded in the determination of GNP. Exchange of stocks on the stock market and exchange of bonds in the securities markets only shift ownership of claims to existing assets from one person to another. For the most part, the sale of a used car has a similar effect. In both cases, no increase in production or productive capacity is directly related to the exchange of these assets. Included in GNP, however, are some of the dealer costs associated with these transactions. These costs include, among other things, the salaries and the commissions of the stock and security brokers and used car salesmen, since they provide a current service in the exchange of existing assets. In determining what is included in GNP, the emphasis is on current economic activities which are "productive" in the sense of creating income. A sale of a new car would be included in GNP for this is an end item of current productive activity.

The concept of GNP then necessarily implies selection of what one considers "productive activity". In determining GNP, one must use some criteria of production which are based on an implicit or explicit value judgment. To quote Simon Kuznets, a pioneer in developing national income accounting concepts:

> . . . if no criteria of social productivity are used, national income becomes a mechanical total of all net receipts of individuals and business agencies, regardless for what activity or even whether there is any activity. It would include the compensation of robbers, murderers, drug peddlers, and smugglers, differential gains from the transfer of claims, and pure transfers such as gifts and contributions, which, in the absence of a productivity criterion, cannot be distinguished from payments for services. Such a judgmentless estimate would be of little use, since, to measure all market transactions, some gross rather

---

[3]A leading authority on national income determination, Simon Kuznets, considered this problem when discussing issues involved in defining national income. He argued against the inclusion of nonmarket activities in general, but cautioned in the interpretation of data which exclude such activities: "The national income estimator must choose between comprehensive definition — with the consequence that large sectors of the economy either cannot be measured on a continuous basis or cannot be included with more precisely measurable sectors because the errors are so enormous — and a narrower definition that confines economic activities to those market-bound — for which tolerably reliable estimates can be made. In current national income measurement in this country, the decision is usually in favor of the second alternative. And it finds support in the argument that the activities so segregated for measurement are the ones subject primarily to economic criteria and rationale; whereas those that are not directed at the market are much more a part of life in general. One may and does discharge a housekeeper for inefficiency in managing a household, but by itself this is rarely a ground for divorce . . . .

"The national income estimator cannot do much about such omissions, since scarcity or lack of data is inherent in the nature of the omitted areas. But in interpreting national income movements in terms of satisfying consumers' wants, the limitation of national income largely to noncasual market-bound activities must be stressed. In this country as in many others where the market is always being extended, the relative importance of the household as a source of consumer goods is declining. Many activities formerly performed by the housewife or other members of the family and not measured (baking, sewing, canning, etc.) have progressively been taken over by business enterprises and gone into market-bound activities; other household functions have vanished without leaving a direct substitute in business activity. Hence, national income totals tend to exaggerate the upward movement in the supply of goods to consumers, if such supply is comprehensively defined as coming from both market-bound and family activities." [Simon Kuznets, *National Income: A Summary of Findings* (New York: National Bureau of Economic Research, Inc., 1946), pp. 124-125.]

[4]At the end of an accounting period, any increase in the inventory of raw materials (or intermediate products) is included as part of the total product of that period. Double-counting can be avoided by totaling only the market value of "final" products, such as bread (plus an allowance for changes in inventories), or by totaling the sum of the "value added" by *all* firms. Value added by a firm equals the market revenues received by the firm minus the cost of the raw materials. In the above example the value added by the baker would be the revenues received through the sale of the bread minus the cost of the flour and other ingredients.

340

than net total is requisite. It would measure neither the positive contribution of the country's economic system to the needs of its members for purposes of consumption or capital formation nor the sum total of what the inhabitants of the country *think* their income is.[5]

Kuznets favored a policy of making any underlying "scheme of values or social philosophy" explicit and allow it to guide the selection of the data.

HISTORICAL DEVELOPMENT OF GNP

The concept of "production" or "productive activity" in the measurement of national income has been given different meanings by various writers and governments. In *The Wealth of Nations*, which was first published in 1776, Adam Smith distinguished productive activities as the making of material goods only; all services, such as those provided by churchmen, lawyers, doctors, musicians, etc., were considered unproductive since "the work of all of them perishes in the very instant of its production."[6]

Smith's concept of productivity was perpetuated in the writings of David Ricardo and John Stuart Mill and formed the basis of the primary national income estimates in England and France for nearly a century. It was not until Alfred Marshall identified the production of goods and services with the creation of utility in the latter part of the nineteenth century that estimators in these two countries returned to a broader concept of production.[7] This broader concept included services as well as material commodities in the measurement of output. Karl Marx accepted Smith's distinction, and consequently, the Soviet Union and other communist countries of Eastern Europe adopted a concept of national product that basically excludes all those services which do not contribute to material production.[8]

---

[5]Simon Kuznets, *National Income and Its Composition, 1919-1938*, Vol. 1 (New York: National Bureau of Economic Research, 1941), p. 4. In 1971, Kuznets received the Nobel Prize in Economics, which was awarded, in part, for his work on developing measurements of national income.

[6]Adam Smith, *The Wealth of Nations* (New York: The Modern Library, 1937), p. 315.

[7]Earlier estimators of national income had used a more comprehensive production concept. See International Encyclopedia of the Social Sciences, s.v. "National Income and Product Accounts: Developments up to World War I."

[8]See Moshe Yanovsky, *Social Accounting Systems* (Chicago: Aldine Publishing Company, 1965), pp. 112-115. Other aspects of national income accounting in the Soviet Union are also influenced by the writings of Marx. For example, following Marx's theory of value, income is related to only one factor of production — social labor.

In the United States, studies on the measurement of national income appeared in the mid-nineteenth century, and the National Bureau of Economic Research published several studies in the 1920s. Spurred by the economic depression and increasing government involvement in economic affairs, the Department of Commerce established a National Income Division in the late 1930s which prepared estimates of national income data on an official basis. Official figures of U.S. national income and product first appeared in the *Survey of Current Business* in 1942 and were published in accounting form for the first time in 1947. Various revisions and refinements have been made since, but the basic structure of national income accounting has not been altered greatly.[9]

PROPOSED MEASURE OF ECONOMIC WELFARE

National income or GNP in the United States today is basically a measure of the market value of goods and services produced during a given period of time.[10] As two proponents of an indicator to measure economic welfare, William Nordhaus and James Tobin do not question the usefulness of the GNP data as a measure of production. They consider GNP data indispensable for short-run stabilization policy and for assessing the economy's long-run growth in productive capacity. They do question, however, the usefulness of GNP data in evaluating the growth of economic welfare.

Nordhaus and Tobin would like to see the development of a new concept to measure the growth of economic welfare, and their argument for the development of such a concept is as follows:

> An obvious shortcoming of GNP is that it is an index of production, not consumption. The goal of economic activity, after all, is consumption. Although this is the central premise of economics, the profession has been slow to develop, either conceptually or statistically, a measure of economic performance oriented to consumption, broadly defined and carefully calculated. We have constructed a primitive and experimental 'measure of economic welfare' (MEW), in which we attempt to allow for the more

---

[9]The present U.S. national income accounting system consists of five interlocking accounts: National Income and Product Account, Personal Income and Outlay Account, Government Receipts and Expenditures Account, Foreign Transactions Account, and Gross Savings and Investment Account.

[10]The major exceptions concerning production of goods and services which are not marketed but included in the measurement of GNP are estimates of food produced and consumed on farms, financial services of commercial banks and other financial intermediaries, and the rental value of owner-occupied houses.

obvious discrepancies between GNP and economic welfare.[11]

To construct their measure of welfare or consumption, Nordhaus and Tobin make several modifications to the existing national income accounts. These modifications fall into three general categories: 1) reclassification of GNP expenditures as consumption, investment, and intermediate; 2) imputation for the services of consumer capital, leisure, and household activities; and 3) correction for some of the disamenities of urbanization and industrialization.[12]

Sustainable MEW

These modifications are shown in Table I. In essence, this table provides various additions and subtractions to gross national product, or net national product, to arrive at what is labeled sustainable MEW.[13]

Capital Consumption — Sustainable MEW as a measure of consumption is somewhat similar to the concept of net national product (NNP) as a measure of production. Part of the output included in GNP will be used to repair and replace the existing stock of capital goods. This portion of output is classified as the capital consumption allowance. The subtraction of the capital consumption allowance from GNP gives NNP. NNP tells us how much current income or production can be consumed consistent with the maintenance of productive capacity or income potential.

In a similar manner, the Nordhaus-Tobin concept of sustainable MEW provides a measure of "the amount of consumption in any year that is consistent with sustained steady growth in per capita consumption at the trend rate of technological progress." The sustainable MEW concept then considers not only the amount of capital which must be replaced in a period to maintain consumption at the existing level, but also how much additional investment or abstention from consumption in the current period must be made in order to keep consumption per capita growing at some

Table I

GROSS NATIONAL PRODUCT AND MEASURE OF ECONOMIC WELFARE (MEW): 1929 AND 1965
(Billions of Dollars, 1958 Prices)

	1929	1965
Gross National Product	$203.6	$ 617.8
Less: capital consumption, NIPA[1]	— 20.0	— 54.7
Net National Product, NIPA	183.6	563.1
Less: NIPA final output reclassified as regrettables and intermediates		
a) Government	— 6.7	— 63.2
b) Private	— 10.3	— 30.9
Imputations for items not included in NIPA		
Plus: a) Leisure	339.5	626.9
b) Nonmarket activity	87.5	295.4
c) Services of public and private capital	29.7	78.9
Less: d) Disamenities	— 12.5	— 34.6
Less: Additional capital consumption	— 19.3	— 92.7
Less: Growth requirement	— 46.1	— 101.8
Sustainable MEW[2]	543.6	1241.1

[1]NIPA refers to National Income and Product Accounts.
[2]MEW figures are based on using variant B as a deflator.

Source: William Nordhaus and James Tobin, "Is Growth Obsolete?", *Economic Growth*, Fiftieth Anniversary Colloquium, Vol. 5 (New York: National Bureau of Economic Research, 1972), p. 55.

rate which is based on technological progress.[14] After estimates for both the capital consumption allowance and the growth requirement are made, these estimates are subtracted from GNP.

Intermediates and Regrettables — Some output, classified as final output for GNP purposes, is reclassified as regrettables and intermediates by Nordhaus and Tobin and is excluded from MEW.

By intermediate product, Nordhaus and Tobin mean "goods and services whose contributions to present or future consumer welfare are completely counted in the values of other goods and services";[15] they are "not directly sources of utility themselves but are regrettably necessary inputs to activities that may yield utility."[16] Regrettables represent expenditures for national security, prestige, or diplomacy, which in the judgement of Nordhaus and Tobin, do not directly increase the economic welfare of households. No sharp dividing line exists between what is classified as intermediates or regrettables.

Some private expenditures and some Government expenditures are reclassified as intermediate products

---

[11]Nordhaus and Tobin, "Is Growth Obsolete?", p. 4.

[12]Ibid., p. 5.

[13]Another concept, labeled actual MEW, consists only of total consumption for a given period and does not take into account any investment expenditures.

[14]Sustainable MEW omits capital expenditures required to maintain the capital-output ratio. According to the authors, "It allows for capital depreciation, for equipping new members of the labor force, and for increasing capital per worker at the trend rate of productivity change." See Nordhaus and Tobin, "Is Growth Obsolete?", pp. 24-25.

[15]Ibid., p. 5.

[16]Ibid., p. 7.

or regrettables. Private expenditures, such as personal business expenses and a part of transportation expenditures in the GNP accounts, would be reclassified as intermediate products. A major portion of Government purchases, such as national defense, space research and technology, international affairs and finance, veterans benefits, general government, and civilian safety (police, fire, and correction) are reclassified as regrettables or intermediate products and subtracted from GNP.[17]

Imputations – The authors impute an estimate for many activities which they feel have a positive or negative effect on social welfare but are not considered in the determination of GNP. Specifically, imputations are made for leisure, nonmarket activity, disamenities, and services of public and private capital.

The most substantial modifications to GNP in obtaining a measure for sustainable MEW are the result of the imputations for leisure and nonmarket activity. Leisure is important to a welfare index, for welfare could rise (consumption of leisure) while GNP falls if employees voluntarily decide to work less. An estimate for nonmarket activity or household production and consumption, such as meals, cleaning, and home repairs, is also added to GNP to obtain MEW.

An estimate for the disamenities of urbanization is subtracted from the GNP data in determining MEW. This estimate considers social costs which are not included in the costs of producing consumption goods and services.[18] These costs would include pollution, litter, congestion, noise, and insecurity. The estimate

of these costs is based on the income differentials between large cities and smaller towns and rural areas. Assuming that people can choose residential locations, a portion of the observed income differential can be considered a "disamenity premium" which compensates individuals for unpleasantness associated with living in urban areas.[19]

Services of public and private capital is the last category of imputations for items not included in GNP. The only imputation made for the services of capital in determining GNP is the addition of an estimate for the services received from owner-occupied housing. The MEW concept would extend imputations from capital to include services from Government structures (excluding military) and services from consumer durable goods (under the MEW concept, consumer durables are reclassified as investment goods rather than consumption).

Assessment of MEW

Nordhaus and Tobin state that they are after a measure of consumption, "broadly defined and carefully calculated," but then label this measure a "measure of economic welfare." However, consumption and welfare are two different (although related) concepts. Welfare would depend on the amount of total satisfaction one receives from total consumption, and, among other things, would depend also on the distribution of income. Nordhaus and Tobin realize the problems involved in trying to measure welfare and state that they "cannot . . . estimate how well individual and collective happiness are correlated with consumption."[20] In a comment on the Nordhaus-Tobin MEW concept, Robin C. O. Matthews points out that debates in the 1940s recognized such distinctions between consumption and welfare, and argues that the MEW concept is a measure of consumption not a measure of welfare.[21]

Obtaining reliable estimates of various economic activities which are not included in the national income accounts poses a serious problem in computing MEW. The problems involved in obtaining an accu-

[17]Ibid., p. 7. Kuznets supported the notion that many government services should be treated as intermediate goods rather than final product. He argued that services to businesses such as economic legislation and the maintenance of internal and external security is not a direct service to consumers but a cost of maintaining society at large: "a *condition* of economic production rather than an activity directly yielding final economic goods." He supports the exclusion of these government activities from a country's output by emphasizing that the total which is sought is "that of product, of end-result of activity – not of the volume of activity itself." See Simon Kuznets, "Discussion of the New Department of Commerce Income Series: National Income: A New Version," *The Review of Economics and Statistics* (August 1948), pp. 156-157. Also see Martin J. Bailey, "Appendix: The Concept of Income," *National Income and the Price Level*, 2nd ed. (New York: McGraw-Hill Book Company, 1971), pp. 272-274. For an argument against such exclusion see Milton Gilbert, George Jaszi, Edward F. Denison, and Charles F. Schwartz, "Objectives of National Income Measurement: A Reply to Professor Kuznets." *The Review of Economics and Statistics* (August 1948), pp. 183-189.

[18]For an economic analysis concerning problems of social costs, see R. H. Coase, "The Problem of Social Cost," *The Journal of Law and Economics* (October 1960), pp. 1-44.

[19]According to the authors, the disamenity premium was about 8 percent of average family disposable income in 1965. Since income differentials have tended to induce migration to urban areas, only a portion of the estimated income differential is subtracted from the GNP accounts as a disamenity premium.

[20]Nordhaus and Tobin, "Is Growth Obsolete?", p. 25.

[21]Robin C. O. Matthews, "Discussion," *Economic Growth*, Fiftieth Anniversary Colloquium, Vol. 5 (New York: National Bureau of Economic Research, 1972), p. 91.

rate measure of household activities is one of the reasons why such activities are not included in measured GNP. The authors of MEW recognize this problem and attempt to estimate the reliability of various components of MEW.

Nordhaus and Tobin rank the reliability of the components of MEW as having a low error, medium error, high error, or very high error. Data in the national income accounts, such as GNP, are used as a benchmark in determining reliability and are put in the low error category. Components in the very high error category are judged to have about ten times the percentage error of GNP. The imputations for leisure, nonmarket activities, and disamenity fall into this very high error category. The imputations for these activities, however, account for much of the difference between GNP and MEW.

The imputations for leisure and household activities, in terms of constant prices, vary greatly depending on how current price estimates are deflated. The authors obtained constant price estimates of both activities by deflating current prices by a consumption deflator and by deflating by wage rates. The accompanying chart presents three different growth paths of sustainable MEW which depend on how leisure and nonmarket activities are deflated. The authors indicate a preference for variant B which deflates leisure by a wage index and which deflates nonmarket activity by a consumption deflator.[22]

All three variants of MEW show a positive rate of growth over time, which indicates that real consumption per capita has been increasing. According to variant C, per capita sustainable MEW grew at a 3.6 percent average compound annual rate from 1929 to 1965, which is slightly faster than the 3.1 percent rate for NNP. In the same time period, variant B grew at a 2.3 percent rate and variant A at a 1.8 percent rate.

Nordhaus and Tobin have provided an estimate of sustainable consumption over time. After allowing for some of the disamenities of modern production techniques and urban congestion, their estimates show that net consumption has been growing, but probably at a slower rate than total measured output. They recognize that many unsolved problems are posed by their MEW concept, but view the measure as an attempt to obtain an indicator of the growth in economic welfare. Perhaps the intent and conclusions of

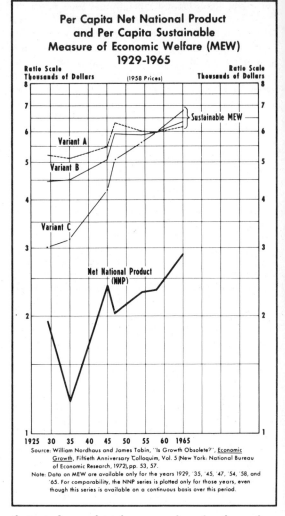

Per Capita Net National Product and Per Capita Sustainable Measure of Economic Welfare (MEW) 1929-1965

Source: William Nordhaus and James Tobin, "Is Growth Obsolete?", Economic Growth, Fiftieth Anniversary Colloquium, Vol. 5 (New York: National Bureau of Economic Research, 1972), pp. 53, 57.
Note: Data on MEW are available only for the years 1929, '35, '45, '47, '54, '58, and '65. For comparability, the NNP series is plotted only for those years, even though this series is available on a continuous basis over this period.

their study can best be summed up by the authors themselves:

We recognize that our proposal is controversial on conceptual and theoretical grounds and that many of the numerical expedients in its execution are dubious. Nevertheless, the challenge to economists to produce relevant welfare-oriented measures seems compelling enough to justify some risk-taking. We hope that others will be challenged, or provoked, to tackle the problem with different assumptions, more refined procedures, and better data. We hope also that further investigations will be concerned with the distribution, as well as the mean value, of a measure of economic welfare, an aspect we have not been able to consider.[23]

---

[22]Variant A deflates both leisure and nonmarket activity by a wage index, and variant C deflates both activities by a consumption deflator.

---

[23]Nordhaus and Tobin, "Is Growth Obsolete?", p. 26.

The Consumer Price Index:
How Will the 1977 Revision Affect It?

Julius Shiskin
Commissioner of Labor Statistics

The Consumer Price Index is being updated and revised after more than a decade of service without major improvements. Weights will be based on current data, the monthly sample will be improved, the stores selected will be representative, and the conceptual basis of the new index will be modernized. Those changes will result in two indexes instead of one — the familiar index for urban wage earners and clerical workers, and a new index for all urban households. In addition, more cities will be included, the rent survey will be taken monthly, and many other improvements will be incorporated. A by-product, the information from the consumer expenditure survey, may prove useful in market analysis and in other research.

INTRODUCTION

THE CONSUMER PRICE Index is currently being updated and revised for the first time since 1963. The results of these efforts will be introduced in the indexes to be published in the spring of 1977. Some of the results will be clearly visible. For example, there will be two indexes — the present index for wage earners and clerical workers and a new index for all urban households — instead of one. There will also be many less visible innovations in methods and procedures which will yield more accurate indexes, for example, the method of selecting individual items to be priced in each retail outlet.

The experience in conducting this revision has made clear the need for a more modern method of updating the CPI. Instead of a periodic effort undertaken once every 10 years or so, a series of continuous surveys should be initiated, so that when the revisions are made, they will be based on current data.

As background for considering the revision program, the uses of the CPI and the concepts upon which it is based will be examined. After that review, the 1977 CPI revision will be described and evaluated.

USES OF THE CPI

The CPI measures the change in price of a constant market basket of goods and services. One use, therefore, is as an index of price change; during periods of price rise, it is an index of inflation. In this use, the CPI serves as an economic indicator. It is watched closely as a measure of the success or failure of government economic policy.

A second use of the CPI is as a deflator of other economic series — that is, to adjust other series for changes of prices. These include retail sales, hourly and weekly earnings, and some of the personal consumption expenditures of the GNP — all important series in themselves as measures of economic performance.

A third major use of the CPI is as an escalator of income payments. When dependents are taken into account, somewhere in the neighborhood of one-half of the population are directly affected by changes in the Consumer Price Index. However, most of the income payments involved are to persons at the lower end of the income distribution representing approximately 10 to 15 percent of

Julius Shiskin, "The Consumer Price Index: How Will the 1977 Revision Affect It?" *Business Economics*, March 1976, pp. 1–9. Reprinted with permission of the author and the publisher.

total income payments. Nevertheless, a 1-percent increase in the index can trigger about a $1 billion increase in income payments. So, an error of only 0.1 percent can potentially lead to the misdirection of over $100 million.

The accuracy of the CPI is also very important when the index is used to deflate other economic series. If the CPI measures an out-dated market basket, for instance, the significance of any inaccuracy is heightened since the index is used to deflate economic indicators such as wages and retail sales. Errors in the deflation of these indicators can result in misleading economic signals at crucial junctures in the business cycle.

Finally, while it is difficult to estimate the effects of an error in the Consumer Price Index on economic policy decisions, it is clear that — with inflation a major economic problem of the day — the stakes involved in an accurate Consumer Price Index are very great relative to the costs.

CPI CONCEPTS

These three uses of the CPI — as an indicator of inflation, a deflator of other indexes, and an escalator — require some variations in the basic concept of the CPI. Certain uses require a price index while others require a cost-of-living index.

The Consumer Price Index compares what the "market basket" of goods and services cost this month against what it cost a month ago, or a year ago, or 10 years ago, or in 1967 (the base year for the current index). Say that in 1967 the prescribed market basket could have been purchased for $100. In August, 1975 the CPI was 162.8. That means that the same combination of goods and services that could have been obtained for $100 in 1967 cost $162.80 in August, 1975.

This does not, however, imply that consumers will actually purchase the same set of goods and services year after year. Consumers tend to adjust their shopping practices to the relative prices they encounter in the marketplace and to substitute items whose purchase price has increased little for items whose price has increased greatly, in order to obtain the greatest satisfaction from their expenditures. For example, if the prices of certain cuts of beef rise rapidly while prices of chicken do not, consumers may shift to consuming more poultry and less beef. If the price of repairing an item increases greatly relative to the price of replacing that item, householders may opt to buy a new one rather than get the old one repaired.

The CPI does not take this sort of substitution into account, as a cost-of-living index would, but rather is predicated on the purchase of the same market basket, in the same proportions (or weight), month after month. This is one reason why it is called a price index and not a cost-of-living index — although the public often refers to it as a cost-of-living index, and it is frequently used in that way. There are other major differences between the two types of indexes. For instance, the CPI does not include income and social security taxes since, unlike sales taxes, these costs are not directly associated with retail prices of specific goods and services, whereas a true cost-of-living index would explicitly account for them.

New Products

The CPI does not immediately reflect changes in expenditure patterns, nor can it immediately adjust to the introduction into the economy of new products or services. For example, the increased use of convenience foods and the rise in "fast-food" eating places were well-established phenomena before they could be adequately reflected in the index. Similarly, a product which has fallen from public favor — either because its place is taken by a better product, or simply because of a change in fashion or consumer preference — may continue for a time to carry a disproportionate weight in the index until it can be appropriately phased out.

The Consumer Price Index does not attempt to report these changes in the style of living. It simply measures the changes in prices for a scientifically selected sample of goods and services which is based on the average experience of certain population groups. Items in the market basket for which the CPI measures price changes run the gamut from bread and butter to television and bowling fees, from prenatal and obstetrics services to charges for funeral services, from popular paperbacks to college textbooks. The CPI never has been limited to price changes of so-called necessities.

Expenditures by a cross section of consumers living in a representative selection of urban places, as disclosed by the Consumer Expenditure Surveys, provide the basis both for the selection of items to be priced and the importance of each of these items in the index structure. The weights reflect the experience of renters and of homeowners; of car owners and of carless families and individuals; of families with many children, childless families, and single consumers.

Since the CPI is based on expenditures, it does not reflect noncash consumption, such as fringe benefits received as part of a job, services supplied by government agencies without payment of a special tax fee, and so on. When the relative importance of such an item changes over time — as with medical care, for which employers and the government have in recent years assumed an increased proportion of the expense — these changes must be taken into account in interpretation of the index.

The Cost of Living Index

Given the different uses to which the CPI is put, it is interesting to examine how a cost-of-living measure might perform in practice vis-à-vis a price index. A full treatment of this question is beyond the scope of this paper, but a brief discussion may help to illustrate what, in the final analysis, is a very complex comparison.

Very few studies have been undertaken to analyze the actual numerical differences that would result if a true cost-of-living index were developed and compared with the CPI. BLS recently completed studies that compared fixed-weight indexes for various CPI components with indexes that adjusted the market basket for substitution. The difference between the two kinds of indexes averaged about one-tenth of an index point per year.

We can speculate, given several assumptions, that the differences between a price index and a cost-of-living index would be small in stable economic periods. When changes in relative prices and government activity are minor, changes in taxes and substitutions in the market basket would be at a minimum. However, in turbulent economic periods such as we have recently experienced, these differentiating elements may change in magnitude. If they change in the same direction, the net effect may again be little difference between the CPI and a cost-of-living index; for example, taxes increase, so that the CPI understates the cost of living, while the rate of substitution also is high, so that the CPI overstates the cost of living. However, if taxes decreased while substitution was high, the CPI could differ significantly from a cost-of-living index since both of these elements would reduce the cost of living relative to changes shown by the CPI.

Later in this paper our plan for frequent monitoring of consumers' spending will be described. When implemented this monitoring will make it possible for us to know when the typical market basket has changed substantially, thereby providing the means for assuring that the CPI will be a reasonable approximation of the cost of living, while retaining its basic character as a price index. The market basket would still change infrequently, not more than once every five years or so, and only when consumer spending patterns changed significantly in terms of standards which would be specified in advance.

Quality Changes

Let us now turn from the conceptual differences between a price index and a cost-of-living index and discuss one of the most difficult conceptual problems faced in compiling a price index — quality change. Both products and consumption patterns are constantly changing. An example familiar to many consumers is that of passenger automobiles, where — with each model change — the BLS faces the problem of separating out the actual price rise from the changes in quality.

The value of the quality change in the new model should not be reflected as a price change, since the goal of the index is to measure the cost to consumers of purchasing a constant market basket of goods and services of constant quality through time. Ideally, estimates would be obtained for the value of each change in quality that occurred as a result of a change in the model or item priced; and this estimate would be based on the consumers' valuation of a change in quality.

However, this direct measurement of quality is extremely difficult since the direct valuation of a change in quality to consumers is rarely possible. Therefore, an indirect method is used that measures the quality change by the change in unit cost of production associated with particular changes in quality. For new features, this estimate is based on all direct and indirect costs incurred for manufacture or purchase of components, assembly and installation of the feature, plus the established company mark-up to selling price applicable to passenger cars. This applies to all items which represent entirely new features installed as standard equipment, that is, do not replace or modify any previously existing feature on cars in the same or comparable series. For all items that replace or modify some previously existing feature, the estimate is based on the difference in cost between the old and the new feature. In other words, the estimate of cost as described for new items is computed for both the new and the old feature. The difference between these values is used as the estimate of quality change.

The new car series selected for pricing at the beginning of each model year are those most nearly equivalent to the series priced in the preceding year. Four criteria govern the selection of a specific series. First, it must be produced by the same manufacturer. Second, it must have the same body type. Third, it must be in the same size class. Fourth, principal features must be comparable.

The third condition, which treats the different size classes as essentially different items for indexing purposes, occasionally presents a problem of identity when a modification in size shifts the automobile into another size class.

There have been reports that many of the 1977 model cars will be scaled down to smaller wheelbases. This would present a problem in making quality adjustments. Most of the move to longer wheelbases on full-size cars took place in the late fifties, before the current quality adjustment procedure was instituted. Therefore, no quality adjustment was made to reflect the fact that the sample cars were made longer. We have only had to deal with the problem of shifting sizes a few times since the establishment of the present adjustment methodology. Each case was handled on an *ad hoc* basis according to the data available regarding the many features involved, such as seating capacity and trunk space. Thus, there is no clear precedent for dealing with radical changes in the size of automobiles. We will have to weigh all of the factors that will affect quality as well as examine the history of adjustments made due to size changes over the years.

The kinds of changes for which quality adjustments are made in the CPI new car index include structural and engineering changes which affect safety, the healthfulness of the outside environment, reliability, performance, durability, economy, carrying capacity, maneuverability, comfort and convenience. While it was first felt that antipollution equipment on automobiles did not represent an increase in quality because the utility to the purchaser was difficult to determine, it was later concluded that the devices did represent an improvement in quality for consumers in general, and therefore an increase in physical quanitiy. Consequently, quality adjustments are made for additions of pollution controls to automobiles.

The kinds of changes for which quality adjustments are not made include changes in style or appearance designed solely to make the product seem new or different, such as trim and configuration, unless these features were previously offered as options and were purchased by a large proportion of customers. Occasionally, new technology makes it possible to achieve recognizably better quality at no increase in cost, or possibly at a reduction in cost. Since no satisfactory technique has been developed for placing a value on such a change, it is ignored and prices are directly compared. The BLS is continually researching better methods to measure quality change, but has not as yet developed a viable alternative to the present methods.

THE 1977 CPI REVISION

Against this background of what the CPI is and how it is used, let us now turn to the 1977 CPI revision. This revision is the first since the early 1960's and constitutes a large-scale effort to (1) update the weights assigned to the various spending categories, such as food, clothing, shelter, medical care, and so on; (2) update the sample of items priced each month in the ongoing CPI; (3) update the sample of retail stores; and (4) modernize the conceptual basis and statistical methods employed in the CPI.

Many improvements and innovations will be introduced as a result of the revision, but only a few will be visible in the final indexes to be published. Index users will see that (1) a new index will be issued that represents 80 percent of the population in addition to the current index which represents roughly 35 to 40 percent; (2) monthly or quarterly indexes will be published for 28 cities compared with 24 at present; (3) regional indexes will be available for urban areas of different population-size classes; and (4) some index components reported will be of a more general character, covering a type of good or service instead of a very specific item.

In addition to these visible changes in the CPI, there will be some less obvious improvements: (1) the fixed market basket will be a more accurate reflection of purchases; (2) the outlets surveyed will be more representative of those actually frequented; (3) there will be some increase in monthly pricing, and quarterly pricing will, by and large, be replaced by bimonthly pricing; and (4) the measurement errors will be substantially lower than those of the current CPI. These improvements will be accomplished through a series of innovations introduced in the revision process.

Consumer Price Index for All Urban Households

The most obvious innovation is the addition of a new Consumer Price Index for All Urban Households. One of the major problems related to the revision program has been to determine just who should make up the index population. The present index represents the experience of wage earners and clerical workers, and therefore is, strictly speaking, appropriate for only this group. However, a more comprehensive consumer price index is needed to escalate the income payments for other population groups and to measure inflation and guide monetary and fiscal policy. Therefore, the Bureau of Labor Statistics will issue two indexes starting in April, 1977 — the traditional index and a new index that covers all urban households. Both indexes will incorporate improvements being developed as part of the revision program.

The expansion of population coverage in the all urban households index will increase coverage to about 80 percent of the total noninstitutional population, contrasted with the current coverage of between 35 and 40 percent for the wage earner and clerical worker index. We expect the average annual income of the two index populations to be roughly the same, since the addition of the retired and the unemployed will tend to offset the income increase resulting from the addition of professional workers.

In the 1960's, food price increases averaged 2.7 percent a year; fuels and utilities, 1.0 percent; and services, 3.5 percent. From 1972 to 1973, foods rose 20.1 percent; fuels and utilities, 11.5 percent; and services, 6.2 percent. Today no one can tell which components of the index — food, fuels, services — are likely to be rising most rapidly in 1977 and later years. Nor can anyone say whether the all urban households index will rise more or less rapidly than an index for wage earners and clerical workers alone. Some students of the index speculate that movement of the comprehensive index will closely parallel that of the urban wage earner index. But one cannot speak authoritatively on this matter until empirical evidence is available.

The question is complex and involves more than just the expenditure weights assigned to various items. The items surveyed and the kinds of outlets sampled are also important factors. Some people have argued that the prices of some luxury items have risen much more rapidly than have the prices of more prosaic commodities; others have noted that prices of some very low cost items, not now included, have also risen more than the average. This implies that prices of goods purchased by groups not covered by the urban wage earner and clerical worker index (professional workers, the self-employed, the unemployed and retired persons) have risen more than average. But in fact we know very little about differences in the movements of price indexes which might be constructed for different population groups.

Expanded City Coverage

Monthly or quarterly indexes will be published for 28 cities compared with 24 at present. The present sample of 56 Standard Metropolitan Statistical Areas (designated by the names of their central cities) was selected on the basis of the 1960 Census of Population using probability methods. It was designed to represent the entire urban portion of the country.

For the revised index, prices will be collected in 85 areas, with the area selection based on the 1970 Census of Population. The 85-area design lends itself to further expansion to at least 156 areas, if needed. Of the 85 areas, 28 are self-representing and 57 are representative of the balance of the SMSA's and the remainder of the urban population. It is to be noted that this increase in the number of areas covered makes it possible substantially to reduce the number of price quotations collected.

The increase in the number of areas to be sampled will make it possible not only to publish indexes for an additional 4 cities, but also to improve the reliability of the national Consumer Price Index, the indexes recently introduced for different regions of the country and for urban areas classified by size of population. In addition, for the first time, regional indexes for cities of different population-size classes can be published. Therefore, cities that are not specifically reported in the CPI will be able better to approximate an index for themselves by using the appropriate population-size class for their region.

Improved Item Selection

The components of the CPI will look different as a result of the method of selecting the particular, detailed items to be priced each month. At the present time, a fixed basket of about 400 specific items are priced each month. While most outlets in the survey carry the items as described, occasionally an outlet does not stock the item and another item is chosen that most closely fits the description. This current approach confines the items which can be priced and reported in the CPI to a relatively narrow segment of the quality range available for each CPI component.

An improved process, called "store specific pricing," has been designed to choose the detailed items to be priced. The first difference between this and the present method is in the way the con-

tents of the fixed market basket are classified. Instead of detailed descriptions of items, the sample basket will contain item descriptions of a more general nature — perhaps whole fresh milk instead of Vitamin D, Grade A Homogenized milk in half-gallon containers. The second difference is in the method of selecting the specific items to be priced from these general item categories. In order that the items priced will truly represent the purchases of the index population, the specific items to be priced are chosen separately in each outlet surveyed. For example, the fixed market basket specifies that fresh whole milk is to be priced.

However, the specific kind of whole fresh milk to be priced is determined separately in each outlet through a "disaggregation" probability process. Each kind of whole milk is assigned a probability, based on sales receipts. (If Vitamin D, Homogenized milk in half-gallon containers makes up 70 percent of the receipts for fresh whole milk, and the same milk in quart containers accounts for 10 percent of all whole milk sales, then the half-gallon container will have 7 times more chance of being chosen than the quart container.) After probabilities are assigned, one of the kinds of milk is chosen using an objective selection process. The particular container of milk that is selected will be priced each month in that outlet. Therefore, in the aggregate, high-volume items will be chosen most often, but the low-volume items will also be represented, in proportion to their share of total expenditures. The character of the published CPI components, then, will be more representative of the range of typical items purchased.

The published CPI components will be for the general item categories, such as fresh whole milk, eggs, and butter. There will be a minimum of 250 such categories. In addition, we expect that some specific detailed items will be selected often enough in the disaggregation process that an index for each of these high-volume items can be published in the monthly CPI.

Some other important but not obvious innovations are associated with the three basic elements in any CPI revision: (1) determining what people buy; (2) determining where they buy it; and (3) improving statistical techniques.

Consumer Expenditure Survey

The first element, determining what people buy, requires data collection from a series of sample surveys. The most important of these is the Consumer Expenditure Survey. The latest such survey differs from previous surveys in several aspects of design and collection methods. It was accomplished by the combined resources of the Nation's two major economic statistical agencies, the Bureau of the Census and the Bureau of Labor Statistics. BLS developed the questionnaire content and specified the output. Census selected the household sample and conducted the interviews. This household sample was spread throughout 216 areas of the country, representing rural as well as urban sectors, compared with 66 areas in the previous Consumer Expenditure Survey. Most of the information was obtained in a series of quarterly interviews involving about 20,000 families. The data collected in this survey covered the calendar years 1972 and 1973.

The remaining information was obtained from another sample of about 20,000 families, who were asked to complete a 2-week diary, in order to obtain data on small, frequent purchases, such as food and personal care items, which are typically difficult to recall over a longer period. The diary collection program started and ended six months later than the quarterly survey and covered the period July 1972—June 1974.

The Consumer Expenditure Survey is expected to provide a sound basis for the selection and weighting of items in the market basket. As with the previous revision, data from the Consumer Expenditure Survey will be used to select a stratified probability sample of items (the market basket) within the universe of items classified into expenditure classes.

Data from the 1972—73 Consumer Expenditure Survey are now being used in the revision process and are also being compiled and cross-tabulated for analysis. Later in this talk I will cite some of the findings from the preliminary data on expenditures for automobiles.

Rent Survey

A new sample design has been developed to improve the timeliness of the rent index, as well as its accuracy. The current method collects data quarterly for half of the sample, while the new method provides for monthly data collection. Also, data will be collected on rent for the previous month as well as the current month on each visit. As a result of these innovations, comparisons of rent for the current month can be made with rent for the immediately preceding month, rather than only with rent for six months ago. The measurement of short-term changes is a critical requirement for the Consumer Price Index. The current rent system does not provide an adequate measure of monthly change. The revised system will yield accurate short-term changes while allowing for close to a 50-percent reduction in sample size.

Home Ownership

In addition to the rent survey, alternative methods for reporting the home ownership component of the index are being tested. The treatment of owner-occupied housing presents a two-tiered problem. At the first level, a decision must be made as to the concept under which housing is to be priced. After that decision is made, a second is required on the most accurate and most efficient way of measuring prices and price changes under that concept.

The problem with housing — and with all durable goods — is that the purchase of a house is not the same as consumption. In effect, the current index treatment of housing implies that those individuals who purchase a house this year consume the total value of the house — purchase price, as well as total financing costs — this year. And those individuals living in previously purchased houses spend nothing on housing in this year. In other words, the entire "consumption" of the purchase price plus financing costs is attributed to the year of purchase.

Another way of looking at it is that what is really being "consumed" by the owner living in a house is housing services — that is, shelter, and accommodation for food preparation and consumption, recreation, entertaining, laundry, and so forth. Obviously, the owner does not consume all these services in the year of purchase, but continues to consume them over the years of living in that house. (In the same way, a renter consumes housing services during the time of residence in a rented house or apartment.)

If a decision is made to price the flow of housing services, the problem will be to develop a technique for estimating the price of owner-occupied housing. There are two methods which can be used. The first is to use a *rental equivalence* technique — in effect, measure what you would charge if you rented the house to yourself in an assumed arms-length transaction. The second is to establish a *user-cost function* for the provision of housing services — that is, to measure the major cost components that an owner incurs in providing himself housing. These would include mortgage and equity financing costs, maintenance costs, taxes, and the variety of other expenses that go into providing housing services.

Both approaches present considerable data problems and are still being studied. We have not as yet made a final decision on our treatment of owner-occupied housing — one of the most important components in the CPI.

Point-of-Purchase Survey

All of the less visible innovations discussed to this point have related to the first element in the revision process — determining what people buy. The second step in a CPI revision, determining where people buy, marks a major innovation in this revision. A "Point-of-Purchase" survey has been conducted to provide data on the retail stores, mail order houses, bowling alleys, doctors' offices, and other places where goods and services are bought. Approximately 20,000 families were asked in 1974 where they purchased various types of goods and services. From the survey results, a full probability sample of retail stores and other outlets to be used in collecting data for the monthly index will be developed for the first time. Here again the Bureau of the Census served as collection agent, under contract with BLS.

Improved Statistical Techniques

Innovations to improve statistical methods include the development of four regional market baskets, a more complex error measurement procedure which will yield better estimates of the sampling error, and a program to measure data quality that will be followed by corrective action where necessary. One of the most important improvements in statistical techniques is the increase in frequency with which prices will be collected for the revised indexes.

At present, about 48 percent of the items (in terms of their weight in the index) included in the CPI market basket are priced every month. In the revised index, about 53 percent are scheduled to be priced every month. Furthermore, about 41 percent of the index weight, now priced once a quarter, will be priced every other month. While it would not make much sense to price certain items monthly, for example, college tuition and taxes, the percentage priced monthly could effectively be increased to about 85 percent. The additional annual cost of the CPI (with this level of monthly pricing) would, however, be substantial — about $2 million a year over estimated annual costs of about $7 million for the revised indexes.

The use of quarterly or bimonthly instead of monthly pricing introduces a lag in the index. For this reason, the CPI today lags the reference month by .72 months. The revised index will lag by .37 months. Expansion of monthly pricing to 85 percent would reduce the lag to .20 months. The lag must be taken into account not only in interpreting current changes in the CPI, but also in interpreting current changes in other indicators, such as wages and retail sales, which are deflated by the CPI.

What difference will all of these improvements and innovations have on the CPI for wage and clerical workers? We will not know that until the first monthly index is computed using the revised methods in 1977. However, the last revision resulted in a difference between the old and revised indexes of 0.2 percent over a course of six months. It is to be noted, however, that this difference could today involve substantial amounts in income payments, because of escalation.

The 1972–73 Consumer Expenditure Survey

So much for the improvements and innovations in the CPI revision. Let us turn now to data from the 1972–73 Consumer Expenditure Survey.

I have referred to the 1972–73 Consumer Expenditure Survey as a source of weights and item samples for the revised CPI. The survey is also an extremely valuable source of data for economic analysis because it is the only source that relates expenditures to the socio-economic characteristics of the population. When processing is completed, we will have expenditure data for food, housing, apparel, durables, medical care, etc. by income group, family size, age of head, region of the country and other characteristics. Some selected data have been published and more will follow as processing is completed.

Some examples of the findings that have already emerged from first-year data of the 1972–73 Consumer Expenditure Survey follow. More than 50 percent of the total number of families consist of only one or two persons. Some of the signs of economic well-being appear to rise with family size until a five-person family is reached. Then family income declines, homeownership declines, education declines, car ownership declines, and food away from home declines. There is apparently a segment of lower income families in this group which is pulling the average down.

A look at expenditures by the age of the head of the family reveals that the under-25 group, which contains many single individuals, eats away from home a good deal, having the highest ratio of food away from home to total food. It also spends a relatively high proportion of income on gasoline and on personal care products. The over-65 group eats away from home very little, drives very little, but maintains expenditures for gas and electricity and other fuels that go with maintaining a home. Personal care products have a lesser claim on income for this group than for families with younger heads.

Now let us turn to the findings on automobile expenditures. For motor vehicles we have collected information on purchases of new and used cars by make and model and imports by country of origin; other vehicles such as trucks, trailers and campers; and methods of financing. While processing and review of the data are not yet completed, we have analyzed some preliminary tabulations. The results are about what was expected, but they do provide quantitative confirmation of what otherwise was only assumed. They aslo provide some information that may be useful in analyzing the market.

For instance, families with age of head between 25 and 35 purchased about 30 percent of the new imports reported although constituting about 20 percent of total families. The data also indicate that they bought a higher percent of the less expensive imports than the other age groups. I emphasize this young age group because in 1980 such households are projected to constitute almost one-quarter of all households, by far the largest age group. On the other hand, the households headed by age group 45–54 is expected to decline in absolute numbers and even more as a proportion of the growing total. Families in this declining group have higher incomes and expenditures and spent 50 percent more on domestic new cars in 1972 than did the younger group, and also spent more on larger, more expensive cars than any other age group. Another interesting statistic relates to purchases of trucks. About 2.5 percent of the families reported non-business purchase of new and used trucks, largely in the $6–20,000 income groups. The value of truck purchases was largest in the

South and West, as might be expected and these are the areas of growing population.

These examples illustrate the uses of the survey data not only for current market analysis, but also for planning purposes when tied to projections of demographic characteristics.

LONG-RUN REVISION PLANS

Now that the current CPI revision is well on its way to completion, we are already in the midst of plans for a long-run improvement of the revision process. The automobile data summarized for 1972 dramatically demonstrates the basic problem with the CPI revision process. When the revised CPI is first issued in the spring of 1977, the data used to revise the market basket will be three to four years old. Since the data were collected, we have experienced the oil embargo and the subsequent consumer responses to the high cost of gasoline, including dramatic changes in automobile expenditures. We need to improve the CPI revision process so that it can respond more promptly to changes in consumer buying habits. For example, the weights in the revised CPI in 1977 will be nonrepresentative to the extent that consumers may have changed the percent of their total expenditures spent for gasoline, heating oil, car payments, and other items significantly affected by the higher cost of oil. Rapid rises in food prices since the 1972—73 Consumer Expenditure Survey may have similarly produced a shift in consumer buying patterns.

Costs provide another reason to change the current approach to CPI revision. The 1950—52 revision of the consumer price index took three years and cost $4 million; the 1960—64 revision took five years and cost $6.5 million; present estimates are that the current revision will take eight years and cost about $42 million. Most of these expenditures were made prior to 1975. The cost in 1975 dollars would be almost $47 million.

Endless delays and ever-rising costs — including those for gearing up for a decennial effort — suggest that a better method must be used to collect consumer expenditure data and update the Consumer Price Index. Over the past decade, statistical agencies over the world have shifted to smaller decennial or quinquennial programs supplemented by annual, quarterly, and monthly sample surveys. The BLS has proposed, and limited funds have been provided, to plan a continuing quarterly expenditure survey. Such a survey would provide more timeliness and greater flexibility than the present method. Data from an ongoing quarterly consumer expenditure survey could also be used for numerous analytical studies on a current basis. Thus, it should give us prompt information for assessing the effect of a rise in food and fuel prices on spending patterns, or of a tax rebate on spending and saving. Furthermore, a continuing survey could, after the initial period, be tabulated rapidly so that shifts in spending patterns and market baskets could be analyzed and information provided for more frequent updating of the Consumer Price Index, if that turned out to be necessary. While the continuous consumer expenditure survey would cost more than the present decennial effort, it would also provide more — for example, data for following changes in consumption patterns of different income groups.

The long-term improvements to the CPI revision process include a second aspect — a continuous program of outlet sample updating. The objective is to insure that the new indexes properly reflect the market place on a continuing basis by revising approximately one-quarter of the CPI outlet sample each year. To achieve this objective, a "Point-of-Purchase" survey would be conducted by the Bureau of the Census in one-fourth of the 85 pricing areas each year. The results of these surveys would be used to select a new sample of outlets for each pricing area covered. Thus, each year one-fourth of the sample would be updated, resulting in an entire CPI outlet sample revision every four years. This is the estimated maximum time period during which the outlet sample would remain sufficiently representative of the market place. This ongoing "Point-of-Purchase" survey would (1) replace the large-scale, expensive, periodic efforts previously conducted on a 10- to 12-year cycle and (2) provide, for the first time, an objective, statistically based means of maintaining the outlet sample as firms disappear from the market place, as new outlets come into existence, or as consumers change the type and locations of outlets in which they shop.

In view of the high stakes — both in terms of economic policy decision making and the escalation of income payments, there is a compelling need to modify the decennial method of updating the expenditure weights and the outlet sample for the CPI.

Decisions on the future of a continuing quarterly consumer expenditure survey and an ongoing Point-of-Purchase Survey will, of course, depend in the end upon Congressional and Administration priorities for these programs relative to other program objectives. We are hopeful the means will soon be found to allow BLS to move ahead to an Ongoing Point-of-Purchase Survey and to a continuing quarterly expenditure survey.

Measuring America's Wealth

The following article was written by Dr. John W. Kendrick, Professor of Economics at The George Washington University. Dr. Kendrick is a consultant to The Conference Board, where his latest project is a forthcoming report entitled Partial and Total Productivity.

WEALTH is productive power. It represents capacity to produce output and income. By a broad definition, wealth includes human resources in addition to man-made structures, equipment and inventories, and natural resources. This article, however, is confined to a review of trends in real tangible nonhuman wealth, by sector and type.

Estimates of wealth are important for analyzing movements in production and in measuring and analyzing productivity trends—particularly productivity trends in the business sector for which independent output estimates are available. When combined with financial asset and liability data, tangible wealth estimates make possible the development of balance sheets for the nation as a whole and for its major sectors. Balance sheets are, of course, requisite to studies of the changing financial structure of the various sectors (households, business, government) and for estimation of rates of return on assets and net worth.

Despite the importance of national wealth estimates for macro-economic and industry analyses, they are not yet prepared as a regular part of official national accounts. Nevertheless, significant progress toward that goal has been made since I wrote an article on wealth a decade ago for *The Morgan Guaranty Survey*. The Bureau of Economic Analysis (BEA) in the U.S. Department of Commerce has published estimates of fixed stocks of capital in the private business economy, business-sector inventories, residential structures, and net foreign assets. Estimates of stocks of consumer durable goods have been completed, and work is under way on governmental capital stocks. Eventually, if all goes well, annual estimates of national wealth, by major sector and type, will be published as a regular complement to the official national income and product accounts. To fill the gap meanwhile—and to supplement the planned Commerce Department series—I have recently completed estimates of national wealth in current and constant prices as part of a Conference Board research report.* The box on pages 8 and 9 sets forth the conceptual framework underlying such estimates and presents a national balance sheet for the U.S.

National wealth, total and per capita

At the end of 1975, net national wealth—or net worth—is estimated at close to $5,700 billion (table on page 6). This tremendous sum is easier to grasp when it is averaged out to $26,530 for each of the men, women, and children residing in the United States, or about $106,000 for the typical family of four. The per-capita numbers relate not only to the direct holdings of individuals in the personal sector,

*See John W. Kendrick, with Kyu Sik Lee and Jean Lomask: *The Gross National Wealth of the United States, by Sector and Industry*. That study, to be published soon by the Conference Board, is the basis for this article. The Conference Board study generally provides more sectoral detail than does the Commerce Department analysis and also provides quarterly estimates of wealth for the business sector (by the three broad groupings used by BEA—farming, manufacturing, and nonfarm nonmanufacturing—for the period since 1948 and by 30 industry groups since 1968). The quarterly estimates make possible analysis of cycles as well as of trends.

John W. Kendrick, "Measuring America's Wealth." *Morgan Guaranty Survey*, May 1976, pp. 5–13. Reprinted with the permission of the author and the publisher.

National Wealth of the United States

Yearend values

	1925	1929	1948	1957	1966	1973	1975
Net national wealth (billions of dollars)	357.2	403.3	897.0	1,582.0	2,552.0	4,719.1	5,684.0
Price deflator (1958 = 100)	44.1	42.8	77.6	99.0	118.7	174.3	200.7
Real net national wealth (billions of 1958 dollars)	810.0	942.3	1,157.0	1,597.0	2,149.0	2,707.0	2,833.0
Population (millions)	116.6	122.5	146.0	173.5	195.4	211.2	214.4
Real net national wealth per capita (1958 dollars)	6,947	7,692	7,921	9,206	11,000	12,817	13,212

which comprise about 40% of the net national wealth (NNW), but also to their share of business and public domestic wealth plus net foreign assets.

Since this is America's bicentennial, it may be of interest to compare the current national wealth with an estimate for 1775, based on data assembled by economic historians from probate inventories and accounts of estate executors or administrators in sample counties of the thirteen colonies.* Estimated wealth at that time amounted to a bit under $4 billion, or $1,550 per capita (in 1975 prices). Thus, while population grew by about ninety-fold, from under 2½ million in 1775, over the two centuries, real wealth per capita grew seventeen-fold, which works out to a 1.4% average annual rate of increase. In other words, real NNW per capita more than doubled every 50 years, on average.

During the most recent half-century, 1925-1975, real wealth grew at an average annual rate of 2½%, or 1.3% per capita (table on page 7). But the growth of wealth was severely

retarded by the Great Depression of the 1930s, and the postwar record was decidedly better. Between 1948 and 1973, total real NNW grew fairly steadily at a pace of about 3½% a year, almost 2% per annum faster than population. The relatively strong growth of wealth in the postwar period reflects the generally strong advance of output and income since World War II and the relative mildness of the economic contractions that have been experienced.

Reflecting a deceleration in population growth, the growth of real per-capita NNW actually accelerated from a 1.7% annual rate between 1948 and 1957 to 2.2% in the 1966-73 period. The rate dropped to 1.5% between 1973 and 1975 due to the recession of that period.

In making comparisons of output and wealth, gross estimates of both—that is, gross national product (GNP) and gross national wealth (GNW)—are appropriate. At the end of 1975, GNW exceeded $9 trillion, approximately six times the official GNP estimate for the year. When GNP is adjusted to include the rental values of nonbusiness wealth for consistency with GNW, the capital coefficient (ratio of GNW to GNP) is approximately 5.

---

*See Alice Hanson Jones, *Wealth of the Colonies on the Eve of the American Revolution*, New York: Columbia University Press, 1976.

Change in National Wealth

Average annual percentage rate

	1925-75	1925-29	1929-48	1948-57	1957-66	1966-73	1973-75
Net national wealth	5.7	3.1	4.3	6.5	5.5	9.2	9.7
Price deflator	3.1	−0.7	3.2	2.7	2.0	5.6	7.3
Real net national wealth	2.5	3.9	1.1	3.7	3.4	3.4	2.3
Population	1.2	1.3	0.9	1.9	1.3	1.1	0.8
Real net national wealth per capita	1.3	2.6	0.2	1.7	2.0	2.2	1.5

Between 1925 and 1975 real GNW increased at an average annual rate of 2.7% compared with 3.2% for real GNP. The decline in the real GNW/GNP ratio of 0.5% a year, on average, reflected primarily an increase in capital productivity of the business sector. In current dollars, the ratio fell less because the price deflator for GNW rose more than that for GNP. In the final sub-period 1966-1973, the real GNW/GNP ratio was constant, reflecting a marked slowdown in business-sector productivity gains. A rise in the ratio between 1973 and 1975 reflected the contraction of real GNP at a time of continued increase in real wealth.

Composition by sector and type

There were pronounced shifts in the sectoral composition of real GNW, as indicated by the accompanying table:

	Percentages of Real GNW		
	1925	1948	1975
Personal sector	29.5	28.6	40.3
Business sector	56.4	39.6	37.3
Government sector	12.0	29.8	21.3
Net foreign assets	2.1	2.0	1.2

The strong relative growth of personal-sector wealth since 1948 is particularly noteworthy. By 1975 real wealth in the personal sector exceeded that of the business sector. Most of the decline in the business proportion of total wealth had occurred by the end of World War II, when the strong relative expansion of government assets reached its peak. Since then the public share has receded, but by 1975 it was still much higher than in the 1920s. The growth of net foreign assets since 1948 has been less than the growth of domestic wealth, and by 1975 net foreign assets comprised only 1.2% of the national total.

In all domestic sectors real wealth rose considerably faster than employment. In the business sector this was a significant cause of rising labor productivity. With respect to the other sectors, it suggests that the official real GNP estimates understate growth as well as absolute magnitudes. That is possible because the Commerce Department makes no direct estimate of the output of either households or governments. Rather, it estimates gross product originating in those sectors from information on labor compensation. If labor productivity rose in those sectors (as it did in the business sector), labor compensation data alone would understate the sectoral output increases. Adding in the rental values of nonbusiness stocks of capital results in a stronger growth of real nonbusiness product, and of total real GNP, than shown by the official *(continued on page 10)*

CONSTRUCTING A BALANCE SHEET FOR THE U.S.

A national balance sheet for the United States combining the tangible wealth estimates with financial asset and liability data prepared by the Federal Reserve Board has been constructed for 1973 and is presented in the accompanying table (balance sheets for other years have not yet been completed). Holdings of domestic U.S. financial assets are shown by major categories, along with a single figure representing U.S. ownership of foreign financial assets, including U.S. equity interest in direct investments abroad. To these are added monetary gold and domestic tangible assets comprising inventories, structures, equipment, and land, in order to obtain total assets. From these are subtracted liabilities and corporate equities (since stock values were included with assets) in order to calculate net worth.

The domestic financial assets and liabilities to U.S. residents cancel one another so that national net worth equals tangible assets, plus monetary gold, plus net foreign assets (financial claims on foreigners less foreign claims on U.S. residents). This is what economists understand as national wealth. On the one hand, it is the net worth of the nation. On the other hand, it is the productive tangible resources of the country plus our net claims on the productive resources of other countries. The equality between net worth and productive resources at the national level is, of course, not matched by equality in individual sectors. The personal sector's net worth is generally larger than its tangible assets, since its financial claims exceed liabilities. The opposite is true of business which is a debtor, on balance.

To be consistent with gross national product (GNP), which is valued in market prices or approximations thereto, national and sector balance sheets and the tangible wealth components must be valued likewise rather than at acquisition or original costs as is customary in corporate balance sheets. In the case of tangible assets, land is valued at market prices. Inventories have been revalued from book to current market replacement costs. Newly purchased equipment and structures are valued at market. But since most aging fixed assets are not traded in organized markets, their values are estimated in terms of depreciated replacement costs as a proxy for market values. Theoretically, market values represent the present (discounted) value of the expected net income from the capital goods over their lifetimes. Obviously, depreciated replacement costs are only a rough approximation of true values. Also, for purposes of relating capital to production, we estimate capital on a gross basis (that is, with no subtraction of depreciation), since the current productive capacity of fixed assets generally does not decline in step with depreciated value.

Real wealth (i.e., wealth in constant prices) grows as a result of saving and investment. In the case of depreciable capital goods, the change in net wealth between successive dates equals gross investment less depreciation charges during the period; the change in gross wealth equals gross investment less retirements (all in constant prices). In fact, depreciable wealth is generally estimated by the "perpetual inventory" method, whereby real net investment by type is cumulated over time, and then revalued to current prices. In current prices, changes in wealth reflect not only net investment but also price changes.

The Commerce Department defines investment narrowly to include only business capital formation, residential construction, and net foreign investment. This analysis defines tangible investment and the resulting wealth more broadly to include purchases of structures and equipment and inventory accumulation of all sectors—households and governments as well as business.

Combined Balance Sheet of the United States
on December 31, 1973
(Billions of dollars)

Assets

Demand deposits and currency (a)	296.0
Time and savings accounts	703.1
Insurance and pension reserves	458.1
Corporate equities	896.7
Government obligations	612.1
Corporate bonds	247.4
Mortgages	429.8
Other credit instruments	788.8
Security and trade credit	261.6
Other (b)	346.0
U. S. foreign assets	213.7
Monetary gold	11.7
Inventories	564.6
Structures	1,042.1
Equipment	2,202.1
Land	848.4
Total	9,922.2

Liabilities and net worth

Liabilities	
To U. S. residents (c)	4,142.9
To foreigners	163.5
Corporate equities	896.7
Net worth (or net national wealth)	4,719.1
Total	9,922.2

(a) Includes Treasury currency and IMF position.
(b) Includes interbank claims, taxes payable, and miscellaneous.
(c) The breakdown of this aggregate is the same as shown for domestic financial assets owned by U. S. residents, except for corporate equity shares, which are shown separately.

SOURCES: Tangible assets (net of depreciation reserves) are estimates of The Conference Board. The foreign assets, liabilities, and monetary gold estimates are from the U. S. Department of Commerce, *Survey of Current Business*, October 1975. The other estimates are derived from the Federal Reserve Board, *Introduction to Flow of Funds*, February 1975.

estimates. It also is of interest that U.S. income and product originating in the rest of the world rose more than net foreign assets, suggesting a higher rate of return on foreign investments in recent years than in the 1920s.

There also were marked shifts in the composition of real gross domestic wealth (GDW) by type, as indicated by the following table:

| | Percentages of Real GDW | | |
	1925	1948	1975
Equipment	19.9	31.3	36.5
Structures	55.8	48.3	44.9
Land	15.9	12.7	10.1
Inventories	8.4	7.7	8.5

The proportion of equipment, including consumer durables, rose markedly, while the relative declines in both structures and land reduced the real estate component of real GDW from more than 71% in 1925 to 55% a half century later. In current prices, however, the real estate proportion remained constant due to a relative increase in prices of land and structures. The share of equipment rose to a lesser extent based on current value measures, while the inventory proportion fell somewhat since the prices of goods entering inventories rose less than capital-goods prices. Although the proportions of wealth by type differ somewhat among the several sectors, the compositional changes for each were generally in the same directions as for the aggregate.

Real gross wealth of the business sector has grown less rapidly in the postwar period than has real gross business product. Thus, the real capital coefficient fell from 2.81 in 1948 to 2.22 in 1973. This implies a rise in capital productivity (measured by the relationship between real product and real capital) at an average annual rate of almost 1%.

The growth of business-capital productivity was achieved at a time of substantial increase in real gross capital stocks per person engaged in production (employees plus proprietors). The climb during the 1948-73 period in real capital per person averaged about 2% a year—from $16,730 to almost $27,000 in 1973 (at 1958 prices). This was a major contributor to the 2.9% a year average rate of increase in "labor productivity," as measured by real output per person engaged in production.

The rate of growth of real gross business capital accelerated somewhat over the several postwar sub-periods bounded by cycle peaks; but the rate of increase in labor force and employment accelerated even more. Consequently, the rate of increase in real capital per person engaged in production decelerated from a 2.2% annual rate in the 1948-57 period to 1.6% in the 1966-73 period. This was undoubtedly a factor in the deceleration of labor productivity increase down to 1.9% a year in the 1966-73 period. The rate of increase of capital productivity decelerated even more to 0.3% a year between 1966 and 1973. Thus, the growth of total factor productivity also decelerated markedly after 1966.

The productivity slowdown after 1966 was a factor in accelerating inflation, retardation of advances in living standards, decreased international competitiveness of American products, and the eventual devaluations of the dollar. Factors adduced to explain the slowdown of productivity include the general instability of the economic environment; a shift in labor force mix toward lower-productivity workers, especially youths; a decline in the ratio of research-and-development outlays to GNP; distortions of cost-price relations during the 1971-74 period of price-and-wage control—generating misallocations of investments and capacity bottlenecks; and—finally—the general societal tensions that grew out of the Vietnam war and Watergate. The creation in 1970 of what is now called the National Center for Productivity and Quality of Working Life was one response to the problems. And in the last several years some of the forces depressing productivity appear to be reversing themselves—quite apart from the normal cyclical recovery of productivity which has been going on since early 1975.

Examination of the composition of real gross business capital in terms of the three industry segments for which the Commerce Department provides estimates shows (table on this page) that the farm proportion declined between 1948 and 1973 (from 18% to less than 12%), that manufacturing held fairly steady (at about a fifth of the total), and that nonfarm nonmanufacturing rose (from about 62% to 67%). These proportions differ from shares in real product owing to differences in capital coefficients which, in 1973, were 7.0 for farming, 2.5 for nonfarm nonmanufacturing, and 1.3 for manufacturing.

The inverse of these capital coefficients—providing a measure of capital productivity—rose in all segments over the quarter-century, but least in farming. But in the final sub-period, 1966-73, capital productivity growth accelerated in farming while it decelerated in manufacturing and declined absolutely in the residual segment.

Real gross capital stocks per person engaged in production rose at average annual rates of 4.6% in farming, 2.2% in manufacturing, and 1.6% in the residual segment. These rates generally paralleled rates of gain in real product per person. The positive correlation also tended to prevail in the sub-periods.

The capital productivity series fluctuated over the business cycle in both nonfarm segments, particularly in manufacturing. It tended

Real Gross Capital Stocks of U. S. Private Domestic Business Sector

	1948	*1957*	*1966*	*1973*
Total, billions of 1958 dollars	800	1,024	1,320	1,660
Percent distribution				
Farming	17.6	16.3	13.6	11.7
Manufacturing	19.9	22.0	21.5	21.2
Nonfarm non-manufacturing	62.5	61.8	64.9	67.1

to lead turns in general business activity at cyclical peaks, as output rose less than real capital, but to move coincidentally with general business activity cyclical troughs.

The only industry group which showed no increase in real gross capital was railroad transportation, whose share of total nonmanufacturing capital fell from near 30% in 1948 to under 14% in 1973. Real estate and mining also showed less than average increases in real gross capital and therefore declining proportions of the nonmanufacturing total. The other seven groups increased relatively. Seven of the 20 manufacturing industry groups also showed relative increases.

In 1973 capital coefficients in nonmanufacturing ranged from about 1.0 for contract construction to 10.7 for railroads. In manufacturing, the ratios ranged from 0.6 in the miscellaneous group to 5.1 for petroleum and coal products. Consequently, industry proportions of gross capital usually differed considerably from proportions of gross product.

Between 1948 and 1973 capital productivity rose in more than two thirds of the industry groups. Among industry groups showing large increases were the utilities, real estate,

Capital and Labor Productivity Ratios

Average annual percentage rates of change, 1948-1973

	Real product per unit of real capital	Real product per person engaged in production	Real capital per person engaged in production
Private domestic business sector:	0.9	2.9	1.9
Farming	0.3	4.8	4.6
Manufacturing	1.0	3.2	2.2
Nonfarm non-manufacturing	0.7	2.2	1.6
Manufacturing industry groups:			
Food	2.1	3.5	1.4
Tobacco	1.1	2.7	1.6
Textiles	2.2	4.1	1.9
Apparel	0.1	1.9	1.8
Lumber and products	1.5	4.2	2.2
Furniture and fixtures	2.6	2.5	−0.2
Paper	2.2	3.3	1.1
Printing and publishing	0.9	2.1	1.3
Chemicals	3.6	6.4	2.7
Petroleum and coal	2.1	4.8	2.7
Rubber and plastics	3.4	4.5	1.0
Leather and products	−0.7	1.0	1.8
Stone, clay, and glass	0.5	2.8	2.3
Primary metals	1.1	2.4	1.4
Fabricated metals	1.1	2.2	1.1
Machinery, except electrical	1.0	3.2	2.1
Electrical machinery	−0.5	3.7	3.2
Transportation equipment	−0.1	3.0	3.0
Instruments	0	4.1	4.1
Miscellaneous manufactures	2.7	3.0	0.3
Nonmanufacturing industry groups:			
Mining	1.2	3.6	2.5
Construction	−3.8	0.8	4.7
Trade	0.4	2.3	1.9
Railroads	0.5	4.6	3.9
Nonrail transport	−0.2	2.9	3.1
Communications	1.1	5.2	4.1
Public utilities	1.8	5.0	3.0
Finance and insurance	−2.1	−0.6	2.0
Real estate	2.3	3.0	0.4
Services	−0.3	1.0	1.4

chemicals, and rubber and plastic products. But in the final sub-period 1966-73, half or more of the industries in both manufacturing and nonmanufacturing registered declines in capital productivity, contributing to the deceleration in both segments.

There were large differences among the industries in gross capital per person engaged in production. In manufacturing the range in 1973 was from little more than $4,000 to over $100,000 (in 1958 prices). In nonmanufacturing, requirements per person ranged from about $5,000 in contract construction (which leases much of its equipment) up to about $230,000 in public utilities and railroads. Between 1948 and 1973, real capital requirements per person rose in all industry groups but one (furniture). But rates of increase decelerated in most nonmanufacturing industries during the several sub-periods, particularly in the 1966-73 period. As in the segments, there was a significant positive correlation between industry rates of increase in real capital per person and in real product per person.

Capital requirements: 1980 and beyond

A major use of estimates of real stocks of capital is for projections of investment requirements in future years. For the business sector this involves projecting real gross product, preferably by industry groupings, and capital coefficients in order to obtain estimates of real capital stocks in a given target year, gross and/or net of depreciation allowances. The difference between current real stocks and those projected for the target year, plus estimated real retirements and/or depreciation, yield estimates of the required new gross fixed investment. These estimates can be converted to an average annual requirements basis.

In view of ongoing discussions concerning large capital requirements and the possible inadequacy of investment and capacity by the end of this decade, Commerce Department analysts recently went through the kind of exercise described above.* By breaking down a real GNP projection for 1980 by detailed types of final goods and services, they were able to translate aggregate output into industry outputs by use of an input-output table. Then by applying capital coefficients projected to 1980

—taking account, as best they could, of recent trends—they arrived at their capital requirement estimates. In addition, the Commerce Department analysts took account of the investments required by the various industries to meet existing regulations relating to pollution control.

The projections indicate that the cumulative gross investment requirements for the five-year period 1976-1980 would somewhat exceed 12% of projected GNP, compared with 10.4% in the prior decade. Even if corporate profits and cash flow continue to recover smartly from the recent recession, it is doubtful if fixed investment demand will grow as much relative to GNP as the Commerce Department projections indicate is needed, unless special investment incentives are provided.

This is not the place to discuss the various tax and other incentives that have been proposed to stimulate private investment. Suffice it to note that if after-tax profit rates are not adequate, the growth of capital per person engaged in production will be less than in the past, which will tend to reduce the growth of labor productivity and real income per capita. Even worse, capacity bottlenecks may again appear in the latter 1970s, as in 1973 and 1974, making more unlikely the achievement of high-level employment.

In any case, the type of exercise undertaken by Commerce Department analysts demonstrates the importance for projections and policy formulation of estimates of real national wealth, by sector and industry. Commerce had to rely for industry detail on private estimates which are not wholly consistent with their sector aggregates. It is to be hoped that the Commerce Department will develop consistent industry estimates of good quality in order to permit improvements in empirical analyses and projections of capital and output.

*See BEA, U.S. Department of Commerce, "A Study of Fixed Capital Requirements of the U.S. Business Economy, 1971-1980," Springfield, Va., National Technical Information Service PB 248690, December 1975. A summary is contained in the annual report of the Council of Economic Advisers for 1975.

B. Monetary Theory and Policy

BY MILTON FRIEDMAN

PERSPECTIVE ON INFLATION

Double-digit inflation is the new scare word. We are warned that it is here to stay. Predictions that inflation will be "only" 6 or 7 per cent by the end of the year are greeted as wildly optimistic.

As one who believes that inflation is a serious danger to our society, I deplore this widespread lack of perspective. I fear that exaggerating and misrepresenting the current situation will weaken our will to meet the real problem.

MISLEADING INDEX NUMBERS

True, computed price-index numbers record double-digit inflation in early 1974. But these computed price-index numbers overstate the "real" inflation. To see why they do, it is necessary to consider the whole period since Aug. 15, 1971, when President Nixon froze prices and wages. Shortly thereafter, I wrote in this space: "Officially computed index numbers . . . will . . . show a dramatic improvement . . . and depart increasingly from reality . . . How will it end? Sooner or later . . . as all previous attempts to freeze prices and wages have ended . . . in utter failure and the emergence into the open of suppressed inflation" (NEWSWEEK, Aug. 30, 1971).

Precisely that has occurred. The recent explosion in the index reflects largely the unveiling of previously suppressed price increases. The recorded rate of inflation was below the true rate in late 1971 and 1972. It has been above the true rate since mid-1973. This is primarily a catch-up.

The catch-up will no doubt carry too far, but we should shortly be back to the basic underlying inflation of about 6 per cent per year. That should be an occasion for concern, not for congratulation. Inflation was running at only 4½ per cent in 1971 when political pressures "forced" President Nixon to freeze prices and wages.

But you will reproach me: what of oil and food to which every government official has pointed? Are they not the obvious immediate cause of the price explosion? Not at all. It is essential to distinguish changes in *relative* prices from changes in *absolute* prices. The special conditions that drove up the prices of oil and food re-

quired purchasers to spend more on them, leaving less to spend on other items. Did that not force other prices to go down or to rise less rapidly than otherwise? Why should the *average* level of all prices be affected significantly by changes in the prices of

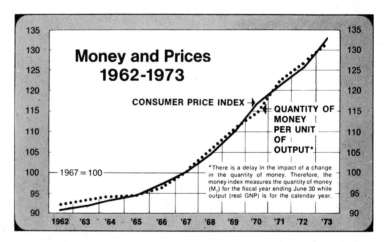

some things relative to others? Thanks to delays in adjustment, the rapid rises in oil and food prices may have temporarily raised the rate of inflation somewhat. In the main, however, they have been convenient excuses for besieged government officials and harried journalists rather than reasons for the price explosion.

The basic source of inflation is the faster growth in the quantity of mon-

---

ey than in output. From the fourth quarter of 1970 (the final quarter of the 1970 recession) to the fourth quarter of 1973 (the final quarter of the subsequent expansion) the quantity of money (M_2=currency plus all commercial bank deposits other than large CD's) grew at the average rate of 10.4 per cent per year; output (GNP at constant prices) at 5.5 per cent. The growth rate of money exceeded that of output by 4.9 percentage points which, by no coincidence, is almost precisely equal to the rate of inflation in consumer prices (5.1 per cent). However, the 5.1 per cent is an average of 3.4 per cent for the first two years, when inflation was being suppressed by controls, and 8.4 per cent for the final year.

CHERCHEZ LA MONNAIE

The same story is told by the chart that plots for the past twelve years consumer prices and the ratio of the quantity of money to output, both expressed as index numbers with 1970=100. Prices have clearly danced to the tune of money. But in 1972, the price index fell below the monetary ratio; in 1973, it overshot the monetary ratio.

For the long pull, averaging booms with recessions, we cannot expect output to grow by more than about 4 per cent per year. If the relation that has prevailed between money and prices for the past dozen years continues,* and if the Federal Reserve continues to permit the quantity of money to grow by 10 per cent a year,

*It has prevailed for as far back as the data go, which is more than 100 years for the U.S. and Japan, 90 years for Britain, and shorter periods for other countries. However, the relation in the U.S. for the past dozen years is closer than the average relation.

inflation will proceed at a rate of about 6 per cent. Judged not by pronouncements, not by intentions, but by performance, that is the rate that monetary policy for the past four years has been directed at producing.

Like you, and like the Fed, I regard 6 per cent inflation as much too high. I therefore welcome the Federal Reserve's announced intention to reduce the rate of monetary growth. Unfortunately, there is as yet little sign of any change in performance. The widespread impression that the Fed has tightened is based on the mistake of judging monetary policy by interest rates, which the Fed cannot control, rather than by the quantity of money, which it can. The quantity of money is still growing as rapidly as it has for the past four years.

The future well-being of this country depends critically on whether, this time, intentions are translated promptly into performance.

Money Growth Feeds World Inflation

The world has been through an extraordinary surge of inflation in the past five years. A market basket of goods and services which would have cost an American consumer $100 in 1970 would today cost $143 — or 43% more. Comparable increases in other industrial countries include 37% in Germany, 76% in Japan, and 100% in the United Kingdom. While prices have generally been rising since World War II, previous increases did not approach these rates.

There 'has been no shortage of explanations for the recent inflation. The oil embargo, poor crops, changes in the Humboldt current, growing union power, and the end of U.S. wage and price controls are only a few of the factors advanced to account for it. But the fact that the inflation has been so pervasive and persistent suggests that more general forces may be operating.

Monetary aggregates and inflation

A prime candidate for examination is monetary expansion. A very important trend in the industrial countries over recent years has been rapid growth of their monetary aggregates — money stocks, bank reserves, and similar measures. The table shows growth rates of the money stock as most commonly defined (currency plus checking account deposits, or M1) in major countries over the past 10 years. In most countries, money growth accelerated in recent years. The table also shows rates of price increase, indicating a similar pattern of acceleration.

In the simplest terms, inflation occurs when spending increases faster than an economy's ability to increase production. Theory and evidence show that spending — and inflation — are closely associated with the stocks of monetary aggregates in an economy, and with changes in these stocks. There is a clear theoretical presumption that the money stock is the driving monetary variable in the inflation process. Money is what people spend and react to.

Inflation is by nature a national phenomenon: prices are costs that are paid by individuals living in individual countries, although some of the goods they buy may be imported. On an individual country basis, however, the bursts of money growth and of inflation do not necessarily coincide. Interdependence of economies causes some inflationary pressures to show up in countries other than where the money growth occurred.

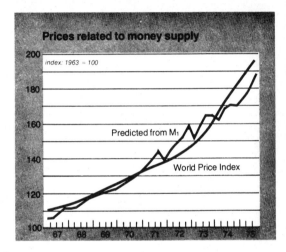

Prices related to money supply

If the acceleration of inflation in recent years were due entirely to episodic factors such as poor harvests, it would not be possible to analyze the world inflation rate simply on the basis of world monetary growth. On the other hand, if the inflation is due more to accelerated monetary growth, with specifics such as harvests governing the timing and location of price increases, a monetary analysis of inflation would be effective.

The first chart suggests that a monetary analysis is indeed effective. The chart shows the world price index since 1966 and the index predicted statistically on the basis of world money stock (M1) behavior. (In this analysis, "world" refers to the 11-country totals as shown in the table.) Money growth can't account for every wiggle in the price line, most notably in 1974 when disturbances in the markets for food and fuel had genuinely large impacts on prices. Still, the evidence does show that the world inflation surge of recent years owes much to a pickup in the pace at which the world

Average annual increase of money stock and price level in major countries

(percent per year)

	Money stock		Price level	
	1965-70	1970-75	1965-70	1970-75
United States	5.2	6.3	4.3	6.7
Canada	8.2	4.1	3.9	7.3
Belgium	5.7	10.9	3.5	8.4
France	5.1	11.3	4.4	8.8
Germany	6.5	9.8	2.4	6.1
Italy	16.2	16.1	3.0	11.4
Japan	16.2	18.5	5.4	11.4
Netherlands	8.6	12.3	4.8	8.6
United Kingdom	3.6	10.9	4.6	13.0
11-country total*	3.0	9.1	4.2	8.5

*Totals include Spain and Mexico. The 11-country money stock was calculated by converting each country's money stock into SDRs and adding. The conversion used prevailing exchange rates in each past time period and the reformed SDR (see October 1975 *Business in Brief* for an article on the SDR). The 11-country price index is an average, weighted by nations' GNPs, calculated by Chase Econometric Associates.

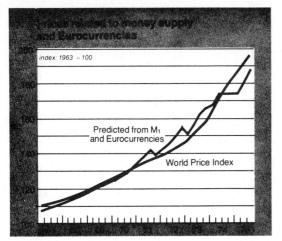

Trade related to money supply
and Eurocurrencies

index: 1963 = 100

Predicted from M₁
and Eurocurrencies

World Price Index

money stock has grown, rather than being exclusively due to special factors beyond the reach of economic policy.

When the statistical analysis is done for the major industrial countries one by one — relating each one's price behavior to the behavior of its money stock — predicted price behavior is less close to the actual. An important reason for this is interdependence. Trade and investment are now sufficiently harmonized that bulges in money growth make themselves felt in prices well beyond the home country's borders. Because of this, it is appropriate to think of inflation as a truly global problem. While a country can make progress at slowing its inflation by controlling its money growth, it needs the cooperation of its trading partners if it is to reap the full potential from an inflation-control program.

The Eurocurrency market

This line of reasoning makes it relevant to examine the role of Eurocurrency deposits in the generation of global inflation. These are deposits booked in one country but denominated in the currency of another country. They are in many ways similar to domestic money, but are not counted in the money stock of any individual country. If Eurocurrency deposits serve to fuel world inflation by stimulating spending, the analysis here would be improved by taking their growth into account.

There are two related arguments against including Eurocurrency deposits in the world money stock. First, they are predominantly time deposits, whereas the narrowly defined money stock (M1) includes only currency and demand deposits — the most directly spendable assets. Second, a major portion of Eurocurrency deposits are investments by nature rather than working balances. Nevertheless, a case can be made for including Eurocurrencies in the world money

stock, even when money is defined as only currency and demand deposits. These deposits certainly have considerable "moneyness," and while they are largely time deposits, they are typically of rather short maturity. If holders of Eurocurrency deposits think of them as to some extent substitutes for demand deposits, then the existence of Eurocurrency deposits raises the amount of spending which takes place with any given actual money stock.

To assess the practical impact that Eurocurrency deposits have on world prices, it is not appropriate simply to relate prices to the Eurocurrency stock; if there is an effect, it should occur because these deposits function as money and thus should be analyzed along with the money stock. That is, world prices should be related to the world money stock plus Eurocurrency deposits. The results of doing this are in the second chart. The fit between the actual price path and the statistically predicted path is indeed closer than in the money-only analysis in the first chart.

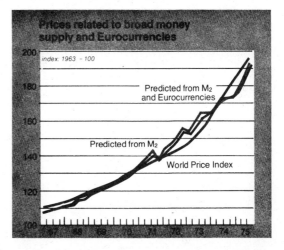

Prices related to broad money
supply and Eurocurrencies

index: 1963 = 100

Predicted from M₂
and Eurocurrencies

Predicted from M₂

World Price Index

It can be plausibly argued that Eurocurrency deposits are more similar to broadly defined national money stocks — which include some domestic time deposits — than to narrowly defined money (currency and demand deposits). The third chart shows the relationship of world prices to the broadly defined world money supply (M2) and to M2 plus Eurocurrency deposits. Here again, the relationship of the statistically predicted price level to the actual level is closer when Eurocurrency deposits are included in the monetary variable.

It thus appears that Eurocurrency deposits have indeed served as money to an identifiable extent, with their growth contributing to the world price rise over the past eight years. While it is far from the whole story, the volume of Eurocurrency holdings warrants explicit attention in future analysis of world inflation.

MV=PT

March 1976

TILFORD GAINES
Senior Vice President and Economist
Manufacturers Hanover Trust

MANUFACTURERS HANOVER TRUST

One of the many tautologies in economics is the proposition that the supply of money (M) multiplied by its velocity (V) (the number of times the supply of money turns over) must equal the volume of transactions (T) adjusted by the level of prices (P). It would be difficult to imagine a more obvious identity.

Just recently the role of velocity in the equation has attracted new interest. In explaining why the money supply has failed to grow at target rates in recent months, despite expanding economic activity and falling interest rates, Federal Reserve spokesmen have pointed to a rapid growth in money velocity. In other words, MV has been on target even though M, and particularly M_1, has not been. To the extent that this has been the case, the slow growth of the money supply has not imposed a drag on real economic growth as it might otherwise have.

This issue is more than academic to monetary policy officials and to economists generally. From the point of view of the monetary economists the issue is important because many of them have argued that velocity tends to be fairly constant, and that short-term jiggles in the rate of velocity represent nothing more than the result of monetary policies that alternatively accelerate or slow monetary growth, which lead to alternate periods of lower or higher interest rates and, as a result, to either tighter or looser cash management in the private economy. The difficulty this time around, however, is the fact that short-term interest rates have been falling while velocity has been rising—so that economizing on cash balances has not been the motivating force. From the point of view of monetary officials the concern is the obvious one of wishing to be sure they are doing their jobs as they intend.

Influences on Velocity of Money

The fact that money velocity has been rising rapidly is pointed up by the table:

Date	Change in M_1 (per cent)	Change in Velocity (per cent)	90 Day Treasury Bills (per cent)
1968	7.1	1.9	5.4
1969	6.0	1.7	6.7
1970	3.9	1.2	6.4
1971	6.7	1.5	4.4
1972	7.1	2.9	4.1
1973	7.5	3.9	7.1
1974	5.5	2.2	7.9
1975	4.3	2.2	5.8
1975: 1	1.0	−2.7	5.8
1975: 2	7.4	0.2	5.4
1975: 3	7.0	11.4	6.4
1975: 4	2.5	9.0	5.7

What are the influences upon velocity? There are a great many, most of which point toward a secular up-trend in the turnover rate of money. For example, as the society becomes more affluent and moves to higher *real* levels of income and spending, it is not necessary for the typical household or company to hold as large cash balances relative to income. As industry has tended to become more concentrated in ownership, cash management expertise has been extended from parent companies to new acquisitions, reducing their needs for cash. Given the uncertainty in business and households this past year, the tendency to save more out of income has been balanced by a desire to earn a maximum rate of return on savings.

Many reasons might be given for expecting a long-term, secular rise in velocity, but they would not explain the apparent upward shift in the velocity function during 1975. At least two reasons might be advanced for this shift. First, the strong upturn in real Gross National Product in the last half of the year was paralleled by a strong improvement in real disposable income. The latter led to a surge in personal expenditures that involved an accelerated use of credit cards. While credit cards have been on the scene for a long while, their popularity and usage has grown particularly rapidly in recent years. The strong growth in personal income and expenditures against the trend growth in credit card usage accounted for the surge in credit card usage—and to the extent that a family buys on credit it does not require the money balances it would if it were buying for cash.

Another influence, but one that it is not possible to document, was the result of a change in Federal Reserve regulation promulgated late in 1975. Under this change, commercial banks were permitted to accept passbook savings accounts from business concerns on the same basis as such accounts from individuals, in amounts up to $150,000. Federal Reserve officials have indicated their feeling that this regulatory change may have led to a fairly substantial shift of smaller corporate balances from demand deposits to time deposits. And since demand deposits along with cash constitute money supply (M_1), even the shift of a few billion dollars could lead to a major downward effect for the basic money supply without affecting the M_2 results, which include time deposits.

What Is The "Money Supply"?

An evaluation of a given "MV" performance most obviously rests upon an appraisal of money supply (M_1 or M_2) as well as an attempt to explain why velocity behaved as it did. This leads to one of the most abstruse debates among economists. At one time in our history, money supply was defined as gold and/or other "coin of the realm." (Quite a number of people would prefer that it still be so defined.) The growing use of demand deposit checking accounts in commercial banks for the settlement of claims necessitated a broader definition that included such demand deposits in the money supply, because owners considered them the equivalent of cash in the wallet.

Where do we go now? With the growing use of "negotiable orders of withdrawal" upon thrift institutions, a wholly new "demand deposit" is developing. Were all the deposits at savings and loan associations and mutual savings banks to be counted as demand deposits, the M_1 money supply would be pushed up by $54.3 billion or 18.8 per cent. And would it stop there, or are there other forms of financial claims that might be placed on a demand-transferable basis?

The questions raised by the NOW accounts are only illustrative of the terminological and philosophical questions raised by any definition of money. If the simplistic but relevant equation $MV = PT$ is to have meaning, it is necessary first that we understand its terms. In particular, the value of M is a determinant of the value of V, so we can not understand the value of the left term if we do not know what M really means. It would seem reasonable to suggest that M should include *any financial claim or guaranteed right to credit* the holders of which consider to be the equivalent of cash. Substitution for M, by M_2, M_3, etc. simply obfuscates the issue. A case can be made for the proposition that a relevant definition of "money" should include all liquid claims held in the private sector, not only demand deposits and regular savings accounts but also such negotiable short-term assets as treasury bills and other money market paper.

To a degree, even longer-term assets such as common stock and bonds that are traded in broad markets could be considered part of the money stock. It is a well-established fact that a run up in stock prices of the sort we have enjoyed in recent weeks causes investors and business corporations to feel wealthier and spend more, just as an accelerated growth in the money supply does.

Viewed in this perspective, the job of the Federal Reserve in managing the monetary aggregates becomes far more complex than those who tell the Fed simply to manage the money supply can ever comprehend. Recently there has been a development that underscores the Fed's dilemma. In 1975 the Treasury issued a net total of some $85 billion of new debt, the large bulk of it in short-term, highly liquid obligations. Borrowing by the Treasury and the government agencies threatens to be nearly as large this year. The debt was easily absorbed because of the weakness of demand for business credit, but this year could be a different story as economic recovery continues and business credit needs grow. Of the $85.8 billion total for last year, commercial banks bought $29.1 billion and nonfinancial corporations $14.8 billion. To some analysts this was a happy outcome since it strengthened the tightly strained liquidity of banks and industry. From the point of view of the Federal Reserve, however, it was a disturbing development. The availability of a vastly increased total of easily marketable short-term investments probably will mean that the Fed will have to press even harder than otherwise to prevent excessive inflationary economic growth. The ability at will and at minimum risk of loss to convert these short-term assets into cash for lending or investment could be a major roadblock in the way of noninflationary monetary policy.

So, what is "money"? Because of the definitional difficulties in arriving at a firm answer, it might be best to retreat to the present definition with an understanding that this "money" is only part of a spectrum of monetary and credit variables that the Federal Reserve should attempt to regulate. It might be possible to construct an index of "liquidity" that would assign weights to all these various financial assets, to which could be added factors for business and consumer credit lines. Federal Reserve targets could then be devised in terms of this index. But this concept appears to be far too elaborate and probably would lead to the same rigidities and misinterpretations that the recent emphasis upon the money supply statistic has engendered. On the other hand, it would be much more comprehensive than M_1 alone and would provide a means for the Congress and the public to judge monetary policy performance.

Interest Rates

In the eyes of many people, including political critics, the most important role for the Federal Reserve is the regulation of interest rates—and most critics would want rates to be low. There should be no question that the Fed can control interest rates. It did so during the Second World War, with great precision, by standing ready to buy all Government securities offered to it at pegged rates that ranged from ⅜ per cent on ninety day bills to 2.5 per cent on long-term bonds. Interest rates were controlled, but at the cost of no control over the money and credit aggregates—between 1941 and 1946 the money supply grew by 126.3 per cent and total liquidity by even more. As a result, consumer prices in this five year interval rose by 32.7 per cent.

Recently the Federal Reserve has once again been criticized for paying too much attention to interest rates in its execution of policy. At each meeting of the Federal Open Market Committee, the Manager of the Open Market Account is instructed to achieve (1) a certain rate of growth in the money supply and (2) a Federal funds rate that holds within a prescribed range. The principle underlying the dual target is that at any given Federal Funds rate a chain reaction will be triggered through other short-term interest rates that will encourage or discourage bank credit growth and, thereby, move the money supply in the desired direction. Open market operations have been successful in managing the Federal funds rate and other short market rates, but the transition from interest rates to money supply has been highly erratic. Money supply (M_1) by quarters last year grew at annual rates of .06 per cent, 7.4 per cent, 7.0 per cent, and 2.5 per cent. These quarterly growth rates compare with a desired growth rate of 5 to 7.5 per cent.

If the Federal funds rate performs so poorly as the mechanism for transforming policy intentions into money supply results, why does the Fed persist in using it? The answer, very simply, is that there is no other operating method that might promise to do better. For years, the Fed pursued objectives in terms of "net borrowed" or "net free" bank reserves, but two problems arose. One was the difficulties encountered in achieving a net reserve target. The other was the fact that, even when achieved, net reserve

totals did not translate at all well into money supply results. The same has generally been true of such other targets as the "monetary base."

The problem is that all those people who for years told the Fed to manage the money supply toward a constant target rate of growth neglected to tell them how to do it. American financial interrelationships have long been far more intricate than simplistic monetary theory could possibly comprehend. The growing importance of international financial flows in recent years has added immensely to the complexity of the entire system. Part of the inherent complexity was summed up in the preceding discussion of velocity and of the conceptual difficulty of defining what the money supply is or should be. But analysis of such broad aggregates and understanding of what they mean must rest upon a thorough knowledge of the structure of financial markets and of how these markets affect the real economy. It is quite one thing to analyze historical time series and conclude that such and such a statistical variable will, over time, have such and such a likely effect upon another variable. But the Federal Reserve authorities do not have the luxury of such a long view. They have to operate from day to day and hope that the cumulative results of their hourly decisions will add up, over time, to monetary policy actions most conducive to a strong economy and to the well-being of the entire country.

In the months just ahead the Federal Reserve may have some particularly difficult challenges in terms of interest rates, money supply, and money velocity. As noted earlier, the U.S. Treasury and agencies were able to borrow $85 billion net without strain in 1975 because business was repaying debt, but this year the $80 billion plus that they will have to borrow will be in competition with private borrowing demands. Almost all forecasts of the economy for 1976 call for real growth of five to seven per cent and inflation that would bring nominal GNP growth up to eleven or twelve per cent. Even the impressive rebuilding of liquidity achieved by corporations last year plus sharply higher profits will not permit them to avoid fairly heavy recourse to external financing, particularly in the short-term market. And there's the rub. Will the credit markets be able to handle the volume of public and private borrowing to be expected in 1976 without a moderately large increase in interest rates or without an excessively expansive monetary policy?

The cynics have a ready answer. Since this is an election year, they are saying the Fed *obviously* will inflate money and credit supplies by whatever amount is necessary to avoid anything like a credit "crunch" or sharply higher interest rates. The cynics are badly informed. It is true that Federal Reserve policy was far too easy in the fall of 1972, but that was due to an underestimate of the strength of the boom then emerging rather than to the fact that 1972 was an election year. Federal Reserve officials have made it clear that they will not be swayed by political concerns in shaping monetary policy this year, and there is every reason to believe they mean what they say.

The prospect is that monetary policy in 1976 will remain on a steady course in terms of the money and credit targets it seeks to achieve. Such a policy course would provide enough money and credit to support the rate of real growth projected for the economy, but would stop short of underwriting a new round of inflation.

In Conclusion

A wide-ranging debate is now underway as to whether or not a more liberal fiscal policy, involving even larger deficits in the short run than are now projected, might prove to be a wise policy course. The theory is that by enlarging personal income and profits more quickly, the resultant revenues would ultimately bring the budget into better balance.

There is, indeed, a deceptive attractiveness to this proposition. Certainly everyone would wish to see the unemployment rate brought down more rapidly than can be anticipated with the actual set of fiscal and monetary policies that would appear to be in store. It even appears that this is a way to have one's cake and eat it too.

One of the many difficulties with the proposition is that it ignores the monetary, liquidity and interest rate implications in the short run during which deficits would be enlarged. The point made earlier that the liquid assets generated by budget deficits bear a close relationship to money cannot be overemphasized. To the extent that reliquidating the economy through a flood of short-term Treasury paper makes it necessary for the Federal Reserve to pursue an even more restrictive policy leading to even higher interest rates might more than offset any stimulus to the economy from the larger deficits.

It might then be argued that this would be only a short-term problem, but another economic rule of thumb is that "we are all dead in the long run." One might hope and expect that the Administration and the Congress would give careful attention to the liquidity and monetary policy implications of excessively large budget deficits.

THE MAKING OF MONETARY POLICY:
DESCRIPTION AND ANALYSIS*

WILLIAM POOLE
Brown University

At the present time Federal Reserve policy-making may be viewed as having a two-part structure. First, based on a four to eight quarter economic forecast, the Fed selects a target rate of money growth. Second, based on a short-term money market forecast, the Fed selects a Federal funds rate range thought to be consistent with the money growth target. The procedure followed in selecting the money growth target is "state-of-the-art" but the policy implementation based on controlling the Federal funds rate has permitted an undesirable pro-cyclical behavior of the money stock.

From talking with economists and reading the financial press it has become apparent to me that the basic procedures followed by the Federal Reserve in making and implementing monetary policy over the past few years are not well understood. This lack of understanding is unfortunate since it has reduced the effectiveness of communication between Fed and non-Fed economists. One purpose of this paper is to present a simple description of current policy procedures in the hope of improving the on-going debate over monetary policy. A second purpose is to analyze the effectiveness of current procedures in order to identify the major problem areas.[1]

No attempt will be made to examine the complex economic and political considerations underlying monetary policy decisions. Instead, my purpose is to describe the framework within which the basic policy decisions are made. This policy framework has a clear and simple logical structure revolving around the distinctions of basic policy vs. implementation, and goals vs. instruments.

The logical structure of current policy formulation applied at each FOMC meeting may be described as follows: a) the Federal Reserve board staff presents an economic forecast four to eight quarters into the future, with the forecast being dependent on alternative paths for the money stock (primarily M_1); b) the FOMC selects a near-term target money path, after considering the forecasting uncertainties, the risks

*Reprinted from *New England Economic Review*, March/April 1975, p. 21-30, with a few minor changes in the text and the addition of footnotes 4, 8, and 14. An earlier draft of this paper was read at the Western Economic Association Meetings, Las Vegas, June, 1974.

1. For another description of current Fed procedures, see "Numerical Specifications of Financial Variables and Their Role in Monetary Policy," *Federal Reserve Bulletin*, May, 1974.

William Poole, "The Making of Monetary Policy: Description and Analysis." *Economic Inquiry*, Journal of the Western Economic Association, June 1975, pp. 253–265. Reprinted with permission of the author and the publisher.

of various types of errors, the trade-offs between unemployment and inflation, etc.; c) The Board staff presents short-run (two to six months) money market forecasts indicating alternative short-run paths of monetary and reserve aggregates under alternative paths for the Federal funds rate; d) The FOMC selects a target range for the Federal funds rate, and a guideline as to how the manager of the open market account should adjust the funds rate within the target range in response to new information.

The instructions to the open market account manager apply until the next FOMC meeting. Thus, the money stock is treated as the policy instrument with respect to the basic long-run goals of policy — inflation and unemployment — while the Federal funds rate is treated as the policy instrument with respect to the short-run target — the rate of growth of the money stock. This logical structure will now be described in more detail.

I. THE FORMULATION OF BASIC POLICY

Several times a year the staff of the Federal Reserve Board prepares a comprehensive economic forecast extending four to eight quarters into the future. Between the major forecasting efforts, the previous forecast is updated for each month's FOMC meeting. Since the economic forecast is a major input to the basic policy decision, an understanding of the determination of the basic policy stance requires an understanding of how the forecast is prepared.

The Board staff has two somewhat independent forecasting efforts. The first is the judgmental forecast. Based on an assumed "standard" monetary policy — a rate of growth of money typically approximating the target rate accepted at the previous FOMC meeting — staff experts on various sectors of the economy prepare detailed projections of the various GNP components. These projections are then modified as necessary to produce an internally consistent forecast for the entire economy.

The second forecasting effort is based on a modified version of the MIT-University of Pennsylvania-Social Science Research Council (MPS) econometric model of the United States. Following usual model forecasting procedures, forecasts of exogenous variables, including the "standard" monetary policy assumption, are fed into the model and equations are adjusted judgmentally to obtain the standard model forecast.

The judgmental and model forecasts are compared, and the differences between them studied. Adjustments are then made in both forecasts so that they agree in basic respects. Once this process is complete, it is fairly straightforward to simulate the model under alternative monetary policy assumptions in order to forecast the effects of various hypothetical monetary policies.

At the same time the Board staff is preparing its economic forecast, less extensive forecasting efforts are being pursued at the 12 Federal Reserve Banks. These forecasts are not ordinarily written up in any detail, but serve to brief the bank presidents before they go to the FOMC meetings.

The individual members of the FOMC may or may not accept the details of any particular forecast. Nevertheless, each FOMC member may be viewed as having some forecast in mind along with a notion of the range of uncertainty around his own projections. Given his projections as to how the economy is likely to respond to alternative monetary policies — projections which play the role of the estimated structure of the economy in control theory — each FOMC member attempts to optimize his views of the objective function containing the inflation rate, the unemployment rate, and other less important variables such as conditions in particular sectors of the economy.

After debating the issues surrounding the economic forecast, the FOMC decides on its basic monetary stance. Judging from the FOMC *Policy Record*, which is published in the *Federal Reserve Bulletin* approximately three months after each FOMC meeting, the basic policy stance has changed relatively little since 1970, the year in which monetary aggregates targets were first specified. Over this period the *Policy Record* has typically described the policy target as being "moderate" or "modest" growth in the monetary aggregates. That there have been some, but relatively small changes in the monetary growth targets may be inferred by such language as, "The Committee agreed that the economic situation and outlook called for moderate growth in monetary aggregates over the longer run, including a slightly higher rate of growth in M_1 than contemplated earlier."[2]

The procedures outlined above follow quite closely the generally accepted theoretical policy-making model that has been developed in the literature over the postwar period. The constraint on policy imposed by the structure of the economy is clearly specified in the detailed economic forecast. The uncertainties over the outlook and over the effects of policy are understood. There is an awareness that policy actions affect the economy with a lag, and accordingly the money growth target is set in a forward-looking way rather than simply in response to the current business situation. It should be noted, however, that the fact that the money growth target has been adjusted relatively little over the past few years does not reflect acceptance of a stable money growth norm as proposed by Friedman; rather, it reflects the FOMC's judgment over this period that large changes in monetary policy have not been required and, in addition, the FOMC's implicit acceptance of the Brainard (1967)

2. "Record of Policy Actions of the Federal Open Market Committee, Meeting Held January 1-22, 1974," *Federal Reserve Bulletin*, April, 1974, p. 279.

argument that "multiplier uncertainty" calls for less aggressive use of policy instruments than would be the case without the uncertainty.

These procedures may be fairly characterized as "state-of-the-art." The forecasting effort is at least as good as can be found in any government agency, university, or private firm. It seems doubtful that any group of academic economists, including those who make up the "Shadow Open Market Committee"[3] led by Karl Brunner and Allan Meltzer would, if they sat on the FOMC, do the job much differently. As I see it, the only important questions about these procedures involve the willingness of the Federal Reserve to use the minor instruments of monetary policy — changes in reserve requirements on various categories of deposits and non-deposit liabilities, interest rate ceilings, and moral suasion.

II. THE SHORT-RUN IMPLEMENTATION OF POLICY

The short-run policy implementation procedure involves the use of the Federal funds rate as the policy instrument to keep the level of the money stock in a neighborhood around the long-run growth path selected in the manner described in the previous section. This decision process makes use of a money market forecast projecting short-run growth in monetary and reserve aggregates under alternative Federal funds rate assumptions. The FOMC selects the target Federal funds rate based on how much interest rate pressure seems appropriate under the prevailing conditions.

The money market projections are based on a combination of model and judgmental forecasts. The model used is a monthly financial model developed at the Board. These projections may be interpreted as the estimated constraints within which the Federal funds rate policy is to be optimized.

Starting with the Policy Record for the January 21-22, 1974 FOMC meeting, the numerical target ranges for the short-run operating targets are now reported regularly. The relevant paragraph from the January 21-22, 1974 *Policy Record* reads as follows:

> The Committee agreed that the economic situation and outlook called for moderate growth in monetary aggregates over the longer run, including a slightly higher rate of growth in M_1 than contemplated earlier. Taking account of the staff analysis, the Committee concluded that growth in M_1 and M_2 over the January-February period at annual rates within ranges of tolerance of 3 to 6 percent and 6 to 9 percent, respectively, would be consistent with its longer-

3. The "Shadow Open Market Committee" consists of a group of private economists who have generally been critical of Federal Reserve policy. The group holds mock FOMC meetings several times a year and then publicizes its monetary policy "decisions."

run objectives for the monetary aggregates. The members agreed that such growth rates would be likely to involve RPD growth during the January-February period at an annual rate within a 4¾ to 7¾ percent range of tolerance, and they decided that in the period until the next meeting the weekly average Federal funds rate might be permitted to vary in an orderly fashion from as low as 8¾ percent to as high as 10 percent, if necessary, in the course of operations. It was understood that a slight easing in reserve and money market conditions would be sought promptly, provided that the data becoming available later in the week of the meeting did not suggest that the monetary aggregates were growing rapidly.

The interpretation of this paragraph is that considering the near-term money market projections, M_1 and M_2 growth in the ranges indicated would be consistent with maintaining these variables in the neighborhood of their longer-run target paths. Member bank reserves required against private deposits (RPD) would be expected to grow at a 4¾ to 7¾ percent rate. The Open Market Desk was expected to hold the Federal funds rate within the 8¾ to 10 percent range, with the rate being shaded toward the lower end of that range if M_1 and M_2 were growing within their tolerance ranges. If the M_1 and M_2 growth rates were above (below) the upper (lower) ends of their tolerance ranges, it was understood that the Open Market Desk should push the funds rate toward the upper (lower) end of its tolerance range.[4]

The Federal Reserve does not, of course, control the Federal funds rate exactly, which it could do, if desired, by offering to borrow or lend unlimited amounts of Federal funds at a posted rate. Instead, the Open Market Desk talks with Federal funds brokers by phone several times each day, and supplies (absorbs) reserves if the funds rate is higher (lower) than desired. The reserves are supplied or absorbed either through standard open market operations or by regular, or reserve, repurchase agreements with government securities dealers. Desk control of the Federal funds rate through these procedures is not exact, but generally the Desk is able to hold the funds rate within a range that is narrower than the tolerance range specified by the FOMC.

The FOMC instructions to the Open Market Desk apply over the month between FOMC meetings. However, the FOMC holds interim

4. As noted in the previous section, the MPS model simulations are performed using M_1 as the policy variable. The use of both M_1 and M_2 in the FOMC's instructions to the Desk of significance only in the relatively infrequent instances when the two measures have different implications for the movement of the funds rate. The Desk is more likely to move the funds rate if both M_1 and M_2 are outside their tolerance ranges on the same side. Although the RPD measure was introduced in an effort to gain greater control over the monetary aggregates, in fact RPD's have had essentially no operating significance. Under lagged reserve requirements RPD's largely reflect changes in the money stock two weeks earlier and cannot be independently adjusted without causing either reserve deficiencies or excesses.

meetings (usually by telephone or by wire) from time to time to adjust the instructions if events so require. In particular, the Federal funds rate tolerance range and the monetary aggregates tolerance ranges sometimes turn out to be seriously inconsistent. In this situation the Desk ordinarily holds the funds rate within its tolerance range permitting money growth to fall outside its range, unless the FOMC holds an interim meeting to consider revising the range on the funds rate. On rare occasions it also happens that market pressures become so great that the Desk decides not to supply or absorb the inordinately large amounts of reserves that would be necessary to hold the funds rate within its tolerance range; in such a case the funds rate, for all practical purposes, is set free for a few days and the FOMC instructions changed to reflect the market realities.[5]

The procedures used to set the target rate of growth of money were described in the previous section as "state-of-the-art." The short-run policy implementation procedures, however, cannot be so described, or at least not without adding that there are sharp differences of opinion over the merits of current operating techniques. While both defenders critics of the current techniques agree that they do not produce accurate control of the money aggregates, there is considerable disagreement over both the need for close short-run control of money growth and the technical possibilities of obtaining tighter control.

The most important consequence of the current operating procedures is that they have permitted procyclical fluctuations in the rate of growth of money. The rate of growth of the money stock (M_1) was higher in each of the expansionary years, 1971, 1972, and 1973, than in the recession year of 1970. An especially unfortunate period was mid-1972 to mid-1973. Using quarterly average data to smooth monthly aberrations, the money stock rose at a 7.7 percent rate (continuously compounded) between the second quarter of 1972 and the second quarter of 1973.

To some extent, the high rate of growth of money from mid-1972 to mid-1973 was not understood at the time because the contemporary data understated money growth. Nevertheless, even before the data revisions published in the February, 1974 *Federal Reserve Bulletin*, the M_1 series showed a 6.7 percent increase from the second quarter of 1972 to the second quarter of 1973. Moreover, the *Policy Record* indicates that the rate of growth of money was deemed too high at the time; for practically every FOMC meeting during this period the *Policy Record* reported that the target rate of money growth was lower than the actual rate of growth over the preceding months.

It might be argued that the problem in this period was not in the control procedure per se but in the willingness of the FOMC to move the

---

5. A recent example of such an occasion occurred in early July, 1974. See the *Policy Record* for the FOMC meeting of June 18, 1974 and the subsequent interim meetings of July 5 and June 10 (*Federal Reserve Bulletin*, September 1974, pp. 656-63).

funds rate enough. Two answers may be given to this argument. First, using monthly average data, the Federal funds rate in fact rose in every single month from June 1972 to June 1973, increasing from 4.46 percent to 8.49 percent. Ex post. it is obvious that the funds rate did not rise enough to hold money growth to its target rate, but the problem is that ex ante no one knows how much is "enough." This observation raises my second point. While it is true that, other things equal, an increase in the Federal funds rate reduces the rate of money growth, in fact it appears that continuous and unpredictable shifts in supply and demand functions destroy the forecasting value of the theoretical relationship. The R^2's of equations linking the funds rate and money growth are near zero beyond the sample periods used to estimate the equations.[6]

Given the absence of a tight relationship between money growth and the funds rate it is not surprising that the FOMC does not move the funds rate "enough." In fact, the Brainard argument on the importance of multiplier uncertainty would seem to suggest that modest moves in policy instruments are optimal under such circumstances. Moreover, given the fluctuations in the Federal funds rate in recent years, there can hardly be said to be a prima facie case that the rate doesn't move "enough."

The basic problem is that the Federal funds rate is not the appropriate instrument for the implementation of monetary policy; a bank reserve target, or non-borrowed monetary base target, would work much better. If the Open Market Desk controlled the monetary base errors would, of course, still be made in hitting the M_1 target since the relationship between the base and M_1 is not constant. However, the errors would be self-limiting because the ratio of the base to M_1 does not wander off continuously and rapidly in one direction or the other as does the relationship between the funds rate and the money stock.

The primary objection to using a reserves target has been that short-term interest rates would fluctuate widely, even wildly, under such a policy. Since reserves themselves cannot be controlled precisely and since the banking system cannot effortlessly bring deposits into line with a given quantity of reserves, banks would not infrequently find themselves with substantial reserve deficiencies or excesses that would lead them to bid interest rates sharply up or down.

This argument certainly has some validity, but it can easily be met. Relatively simple reforms in the reserve requirement regulations could

---

6. See, for example, Davis and Shadrack (1974). The authors argue that the post-sample performance of an equation linking the growth in the money stock to the Federal funds rate and other variables is reasonably good in spite of the fact that the post-sample root mean square error (RMSE) is 50 percent larger than the within-sample standard error. Moreover, from Table VII of this paper it is possible to calculate that the RMSE of the naive forecast that the money stock will rise by $1 billion per month is 0.874, only slightly above the post-sample RMSE of 0.781 for the equation reported by Davis and Shadrack employing the Federal funds rate (Equation (2) in Tables V and VI).

essentially eliminate the problem of undue short-run volatility in interest rates under a reserves target.[7]

Most of the needed changes could be instituted by the Federal Reserve within its current legal authority. Indeed, there is one simple reform that alone would solve the very short-run interest rate volatility problem. That reform would be to alter the reserve carry-over regulations to permit a bank to carry over a reserve deficiency, or reserve excess, of unlimited size and for as many weeks as desired, but with the provision that in each statement week required reserves would be increased by 110 percent of any reserve deficiency, or decreased by 90 percent of any reserve excess, in the previous statement week. With this carry-over regulation, a bank that, for example, expected the Federal funds rate to be 10 percent next week would this week have no incentive to lend Federal funds at a rate below 9 percent or to borrow at a rate above 11 percent. The Federal funds rate could be made even more stable week by week, if desired, by requiring a carry-over of 105 percent, rather than 110 percent, of any deficiency and 95 percent of any excess.

This carry-over regulation would retain a substantial incentive for banks to meet their reserve requirements exactly. At a Federal funds rate equal to the rate expected to prevail in the following week, under the 90/110 percent deficiency/excess carry-over proposal the penalty (at an annual rate) for not meeting reserve requirements exactly would be 10 percent of the Federal funds rate provided that the excess reserves carry-over were fully utilized, or the deficient reserves carry-over fully met, the following week. It would not generally be profitable for a bank to carry excesses (or deficiencies) over several weeks since the reserves available after n weeks would amount to 100 times 0.9^n percent of the original amount available. For a deliberate plan to carry excess (deficient) reserves over for n weeks to be profitable, a bank would have to anticipate that the funds rate would rise (fall) at a compound rate of 10 percent per week for n weeks.[8]

While this carry-over proposal reduces the incentive for banks to adjust as compared to a system with no carry-over and unlimited Federal funds rates fluctuations, it increases the adjustment pressures as compared to the current system. Instead of accumulating deficiencies, banks with insufficient reserves to cover requirements are currently supplied with additional reserves by the Fed open market operations needed to keep the funds rate from rising. Moreover, Fed open market purchases of government securities, whether outright or through repurchase agree-

---

7. Possible reforms in reserve requirement regulations were examined in some detail in Poole and Lieberman, (1972).

8. My original treatment of this carry-over proposal as published in the *New England Economic Review* seriously overstated the penalties implied by excess or deficient reserves. I am indebted to Mr. David H. Kopf of the Federal Reserve Bank of New York for finding my error and bringing it to my attention.

ments, directly increase the money stock to the extent that the securities are purchased from members of the non-bank public. This direct impact on the money stock is avoided when banks are forced to borrow from the Fed or to use a deficiency carry-over privilege.

There is a substantial advantage to building in a market mechanism to smooth the Federal funds rate rather than relying on the Open Market Desk to do the smoothing. The Desk and market mechanisms both work equally well in smoothing purely banking disturbances — changes in float, shifts in deposits between banks with different marginal reserves requirements, etc., — but the market mechanism is much less likely to smooth interest rates when they ought not to be smoothed. It is generally accepted that interest rates ought not to be held unchanged when aggregate demand disturbances occur since interest rate changes tend to reduce the impact of such disturbances on economic activity. If there are, for example, heavy credit demands associated with an investment boom, interest rates will rise unless cushioned by reserve injections by the Open Market Desk.

Current operating procedures not only fail to distinguish between disturbances that should and should not be cushioned, but also generate market expectations that increase the volatility of the government secur-

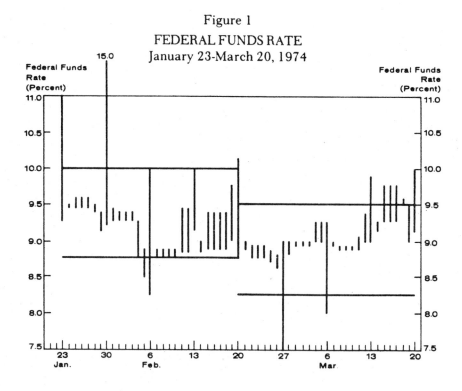

Figure 1

FEDERAL FUNDS RATE

January 23-March 20, 1974

ities market thereby generating perverse changes in the short-run rate of growth of money.[9] The reason for this result is that the procedures followed by the FOMC and the Open Market Desk set up clear speculative opportunities for holders, and potential holders, of Treasury bills and other money market instruments.[10]

As an aid to understanding this argument, consider Figure 1. The daily high and low Federal funds rates are indicated by the ends of the vertical bars over the January 23-March 19, 1974 period. At the January 21-22 FOMC meeting the tolerance range was set at 8.75 percent to 10 percent; this range is indicated by the horizontal lines for the January 23-February 20 period. At the February 20 FOMC meeting the tolerance range was moved to 8¼ percent to 9½ percent, as indicated by the horizontal lines for the February 21-March 19 period.

The FOMC gave two interim instructions to the Open Market Desk in March, neither of which is indicated in the figure. On March 1 it was decided,

> "that in light of the recent marked rise in market interest rates and the highly sensitive state of financial markets, the System [should] conduct reserve operations in a manner expected to be consistent with maintenance of the funds rate at the prevailing level of about 9 percent for the time being."[11]

Then on March 11, it was decided,

> "that the System [should] return to conducting reserve operations in a manner consistent with the full range of tolerance for the Federal funds rate agreed upon at the February meeting. However, in light of recent increases in market interest rates and the sensitive state of financial markets, the Account Manager would be expected to proceed very cautiously in operations thought likely to be consistent with a rise in the weekly average funds rate above 9 percent."[12]

One other aspect of the figure needs to be explained. The dates indicated on the horizontal axis are Wednesdays. Wednesday is the last day of the reserve settlement period, and reserve pressures are frequently so substantial on Wednesdays that the Open Market Desk is unable to keep the Federal funds rate within its tolerance range. It should be noted that practically all the cases in which the funds rate falls outside its tolerance range are on Wednesdays.

9. This argument is presented in more detail in Poole (forthcoming).

10. The argument in the paragraphs below should be considered tentative since I have not as yet gathered evidence to support it.

11. *Policy Record* for FOMC meeting of February 20, 1974, *Federal Reserve Bulletin*, May, 1974, p. 357.

12. *Ibid.*, p. 357.

Although the *Policy Record* has only recently reported the numerical tolerance range for the Federal funds rate, the Fed's operating procedures as described above have for some time been well understood by sophisticated bankers and government securities dealers. The basic procedures could be inferred by closely watching Fed behavior, and, of course, knowledgeable Federal Reserve employees have from time to time resigned their posts in order to accept positions at banks and other financial institutions.

The financial community knows, therefore, that the Desk supplies and absorbs reserves to hold the funds rate within an intervention range typically narrower than the tolerance range, and moves its intervention range within the tolerance range depending on how the monetary aggregates are behaving. Furthermore, the financial community expects that the FOMC will move the tolerance range in light of the behavior of the monetary aggregates. Finally, it is clear that the Desk intervention points tend to move smoothly rather than jumping sharply and discretely.

Knowing all this, it is not difficult for the financial community to guess which way the funds rate will move over the near term. If money growth has been high, it is expected that the funds rate will rise; such a conjecture is readily confirmed when the Desk is observed to supply reserves at a higher funds rate than it had in the recent past. As these expectations develop, rates on other money market instruments jump sharply upward. Given that bank lending rates apparently lag a bit behind money market rates, it becomes cheaper for business firms to meet temporary cash needs by borrowing from banks on their credit lines than for them to sell holdings of bills, CDs, etc.[13] The result, of course, is an expansion of bank credit and deposits; the additional required reserves generate additional upward pressure on the Federal funds rate which the Open Market Desk cushions by injecting more reserves.

Still another mechanism may be operating to expand money growth when bill and CD rates rise relative to the funds rate. Smaller banks tend to be consistent net sellers (lenders) of Federal funds, selling more or less depending on their reserve needs. These banks also adjust their reserve positions to some extent through purchases and sales of liquid money market assets such as Treasury bills, CDs issued by other banks, etc. Large banks, on the other hand, tend to be net buyers of Federal funds, and they also rely heavily on liability management — the sale of large negotiable CDs in the open market. In adjusting reserve positions, then, smaller banks are asset managers and larger banks are liability managers.

13. Using weekly average data over the sample period 7/7/65 through 5/29/74, the highest simple correlation between the prime rate and the Federal gunds rate is between the prime rate for week *t* and the funds for week *t*−6. This evidence for a lag in the bank lending rate is suggestive but hardly conclusive since non-rate lending terms might adjust more quickly.

When bill rates rise relative to the funds rate, the smaller banks may invest in bills, CDs, and commercial paper with short maturities and sell smaller amounts of Federal funds day by day. To some extent these purchases of money market instruments will be made from the non-bank public, adding to the money stock. There is some initial upward pressure on the Federal funds rate, but the upward pressure is probably small because with lagged reserve requirements the increase in deposits does not affect required reserves for two weeks. When required reserves do rise, however, the upward pressure on the funds rate is cushioned by Federal Reserve intervention in the market.

To complete the argument it is necessary to consider the behavior of the large banks which, generally, are consistent net buyers of Federal funds. Since the large banks rely on liability management, their behavior is not symmetrical with that of the small banks. If the large banks sold exactly the quantity of large CDs that the small banks purchased, then demand deposits would not be affected. However, the small banks not only buy CDs but also other money market instruments which they must buy from the non-bank public because the large banks have very limited holdings of such paper.

In summary, my empirical conjectures — none of which have been tested carefully to my knowledge — on the effects of current Federal Reserve operating procedures on money creation are: a) bank lending rates tend to lag behind rates on negotiable money market instruments; b) business firms raising additional short-term funds tend to borrow from banks while retaining holdings of negotiable money market instruments when money market rates are higher than normal relative to bank lending rates; c) commercial banks relying primarily on asset management reduce their sales of Federal funds and increase their holdings of negotiable money market instruments when money market rates are high relative to the Federal funds rate; d) as a result of liability management by large banks, the ratio of the growth in large negotiable CDs to total demand deposits rises when demand deposits are growing rapidly. All of these propositions are meant to apply in the other direction when rates on negotiable money market instruments fall relative to the Federal funds rate because of developing expectations that the Fed will lower the funds rate.

III. CONCLUDING COMMENTS

The introduction in 1970 of monetary aggregates targets marks a major change in Federal Reserve policy-making. This change is of great

---

14. This statement was probably rash at the time it was written (June, 1974); the behavior of the money stock in the second half of 1974 has certainly proven it to be so. Nevertheless, I am optimistic that the Federal Reserve will come to interpret the events since 1970 as providing confirmation of the wisdom of the 1970 decision adopting monetary aggregates targets and will in time reform its procedures so that the targets are realized.

significance because a long period of substantially accelerated or deceler-ated money growth is much less likely to occur than it was before 1970.[14]

The Federal Reserve's short-run procedures, however, are still basically the same as they were before 1970, and these procedures permit abnormally high or low money growth to occur for many months at a time. In fact, the increased emphasis on monetary aggregates in the longer-run context probably generates market expectations that make the operating procedures less satisfactory than before in terms of short-run stability of both money growth and money market rates.

The Federal Reserve should, therefore, move promptly to complete the transition to an aggregates approach to monetary policy. Reserve regulations should be reformed to increase the stability of the relationship between bank reserves and the money stock and to make it possible for the market to smooth out transitory disturbances to short-term interest rates. When these regulatory reforms are adopted, the FOMC should give instructions to the Open Market Desk in terms of a bank reserve aggregate and the Federal funds rate should be permitted to fluctuate freely.

Nothing in these proposed reforms implies that the Federal Reserve should withdraw from the business of operating a discretionary monetary policy. Whether or not the Fed should follow a constant money growth rate rule is a separate issue. The argument of this paper is simply that changes in the money stock, whether they be smooth or variable, ought to occur because the policy-makers want them to occur, rather than as an unwanted result of the operating procedures used to implement policy decisions.

REFERENCES

1. Brainard, William, "Uncertainty and the Effectiveness of Policy," *American Economic Review* 57, (May, 1967), 411-25.

2. Davis, Richard G., and Shadrack, Frederick C., "Forecasting Monetary Aggregates with Reduced Form Equations," in *Monetary Aggregates and Monetary Policy* (Federal Reserve Bank of New York, 1974).

3. Poole, William, "Benefits and Costs of Stable Monetary Growth," (forthcoming).

4. Poole, William, and Lieberman, Charles, "Improving Monetary Control," in Okun, Arthur M., and Perry, George L. (eds.), *Brookings Papers on Economic Activity*, 2:1972, 293-335.

C. Inflation and Unemployment

Inflation: Its Cause and Cure

W. PHILIP GRAMM

W. Philip Gramm is a professor of economics at Texas A&M University in College Station, Texas. Professor Gramm has published articles in various economic journals on topics ranging from environment to monetary and banking theory. He is a consultant to the U.S. and Canadian Governments on matters of energy and economics. Professor Gramm presented this paper at the Federal Reserve Bank of St. Louis on February 7, 1975.

We ARE today experiencing the most prolonged period of rapid inflation in the history of the United States. While we have had short periods where inflation rates have been more intense, a decade of high inflation rates is without precedent in the history of the Republic. As an index of how severe price increases have been for the last decade, the consumer price index, which measures the price of a market basket of goods and services purchased by the American consumer, is up 66 percent; the wholesale price index, which measures the price of raw materials used in the production process, is up 75 percent from a decade ago. Not only have we experienced a decade of high inflation rates, but in the last year the rate of price increase has quickened. The consumer price index is up 12 percent from a year ago and the wholesale price index is up 20 percent. These harsh economic facts suggest two questions: (1) how did we get in such a mess, and (2) how do we get out?

The first question is easy to answer. There are data on inflation which go back to the 15th century, when

gold was discovered in America, transported to Spain, and permeated the European market. Since that time there has *never* been a prolonged general price inflation that was not preceded by and directly related to a growth in the money supply. In our economy, growth in the money supply occurs principally when the Government spends more than it taxes and prints money to make up part of the deficit.

The History of U.S. Inflation

We have incurred five major inflations in the history of the United States: the Revolutionary War inflation, the War of 1812 inflation, the Civil War inflation, the World War II inflation, and the Vietnam War inflation. All five of these inflations have had the same cause — a rapid increase in the money supply. Under the Articles of Confederation, the Continental Congress did not have the power to tax. It was therefore forced to issue paper currency to fight the Revolutionary War. The paper currency units were called Continental Dollars. You have all heard the saying "not worth a Continental," a statement derived from the fact that when Continental Dollars were redeemed at the end of the Revolutionary War, they were redeemed at 2 cents on the dollar in gold and silver. The paper currency depreciated very rapidly because

Note: An earlier version of this paper was presented at Hillsdale College, Hillsdale, Michigan, in connection with a seminar sponsored by the Center for Constructive Alternatives entitled "Energy or Exhaustion: The Planet as Provider." See *imprimis* (November 1974), pp. 1-6.

W. Philip Gramm, "Inflation: Its Causes and Cure." *Review*, Federal Reserve Bank of St. Louis, February 1975, pp. 2–7. Reprinted with permission.

of the tremendous quantity which was issued. In essence, the Continental Congress was entering the American market and competing against private citizens for goods and services with newly issued Continental currency, buying goods at a more rapid rate than the economy was producing them. Prices, therefore, were driven up.

In reviewing our first inflationary experience as a nation, it is important to note that at the end of the Revolutionary War the Congress established the First Bank of the United States, which systematically withdrew Continental Notes from circulation. Prices then leveled off and fell back toward their original level.

The next major inflation in American history followed the War of 1812, which was basically a carbon copy of the Revolutionary War inflation. The principal method of deriving Federal revenue was imposing import taxes or tariffs. But we were at war with our major trading partner, England, and tariffs had fallen off drastically. In order to fight the war we therefore issued large quantities of paper currency which produced a rise in the general price level. Again, however, to the credit of our forebearers, when the war was over the Congress established a Second Bank of the United States that redeemed paper currency at par. Prices leveled off and declined back toward their original level as the paper currency was withdrawn from circulation.

The next major inflation in American history occurred during the American Civil War. The Federal Government ran a $1 billion deficit, which was without precedence in history. It financed a large part of this deficit by issuing Greenback Notes. These Greenback Notes expanded the money supply by over 150 percent, and prices roughly doubled from 1860 to 1865. At the end of the war taxes were left at their war-time level and Government spending was cut back drastically. The Government surplus drew Greenbacks out of circulation and the Treasurer of the United States burned them. As the money supply declined prices fell off, and by 1879 we went back on the gold standard at exactly the same par value that existed in 1860 because prices had been driven back down to their previous level.

The next major inflation in American history occurred in World War II. The Federal Government ran a large deficit and the money stock more than doubled as the Federal Reserve monetized a part of the debt. As the Government entered the market armed with newly printed money, it drove up prices, increasing overall prices by over 60 percent during the Second World War. By the end of 1946, we were approaching a balanced budget, and by 1947 price increases had ceased. We established a period from 1947 to 1962 (except 1950) which proved to be one of the most prolonged periods of stable prices and stable economic growth in the Twentieth Century.

The Current Inflation

The next major inflation in American history occurred with the initiation of massive Government expenditures on the Vietnam War. *We are today in the fifth major inflation in American history — and its source is identical to the four inflations that preceded it. The current inflation differs only by the fact that it has been carried over into a peacetime period; this is the only peace-time inflation of any real significance in the entire history of our country. Our present inflation has been caused by the fact that since 1965 the Federal Government has run a $100 billion deficit and has financed 40 percent of that deficit by printing money.*

It is fundamentally important to note the difference in the impact on the economy caused by Federal financing through taxation and borrowing, as opposed to printing money. When the Government taxes and spends the receipts of those taxes, the ability of the private consumer to purchase goods and services is diminished by the amount of the tax. Therefore, the increase in total spending as a result of the increase in Government spending is quite small. If the Government goes onto the bond market and sells bonds, competing with private firms and private individuals for loanable funds, the competition simply drives up interest rates as Government diverts funds away from private investment projects. In this case, private spending falls by the amount that public spending increases. In the case of selling Government bonds to the Federal Reserve, which in turn gives the Treasury the capacity to write checks drawn on the Federal Reserve, there is no corresponding decrease in private spending. So the increase in Government spending represents a net increase in total demand for goods and services.

There is a simple rule of thumb to follow in gauging the relation between the growth in the money stock, the growth in the economy, and changes in prices. Remember what money is used for — it is used to buy and sell goods and services and consummate exchange. We have found in economics that as the level of economic activity grows with the growth in income and commerce, the demand for money grows by a corresponding amount. So if the economy grows at about 3 percent a year, which has been the average growth rate throughout the entire history of the United States, then the economy will absorb a 3 percent growth in the money supply with no change in prices. For example, from 1947 to 1962 the Federal Government ran small deficits and the money stock grew at about 3 percent per year as the Federal Reserve purchased Government securities in the open market to keep interest rates low. The economy grew at about 3 percent a year so that the increase in money supply was simply absorbed in the consummation of exchange, and prices remained virtually stable for the entire period. One exception was the year 1950, when the economic impact of the Korean conflict was felt; the money supply grew by 10 percent and prices increased 10 percent.

Beginning in 1964 we had large increases in Federal spending to finance unprecedented domestic expenditures on the War on Poverty and on Great Society programs. With the escalation of the war in Vietnam we saw the Government deficit rise from a fairly low level in 1964 to $25 billion a year in 1968. The so-called anti-inflationary surcharge imposed in 1968 had no real impact on inflation rates because Government expenditures grew more rapidly than tax receipts. As a result, in 1968 we ran a record peacetime deficit and the money supply grew by almost 8 percent.

In 1969, when President Nixon took office, we made the only real attempt in the whole inflationary period to stop the inflation. Beginning in January, President Nixon brought the budget into balance, and the rate of growth in the money stock from January to June was zero percent. This policy worked because the rate of price increase, which was almost 6 percent on an annual basis in December and January, had fallen to a 2.7 percent rate by June. But in April, May, and June the unemployment rate jumped significantly.

Unemployment rose principally because in the wage negotiations which occurred in the fall of 1968, wage contracts were based on the assumption of a continuation of 5-7 percent inflation rates. This expectation was realistic, given our previous five-year experience. So an employer who expected the productivity of his workers to rise by 2 percent was willing to negotiate a 7-9 percent wage increase if he expected the price of his product to rise by 5-7 percent. Workers, being aware of the same set of circumstances, were unwilling to accept any smaller pay increase. If the Federal Government had continued its expansionary monetary and fiscal policy, such wage negotiations would have caused no changes in the unemployment rate. But when the Federal Government reversed its monetary policy in an attempt to stabilize prices, and the rate of price increase fell below 3 percent by June, the wages that had been negotiated in the fall of 1968 were too high for full employment and workers were laid off.

The Federal Government at this point faced a crucial decision between two options. (1) It could reverse its monetary policy, reinflate, and therefore seek to drive up prices, which would produce a fall in real wages to the point necessary to produce full employment; or (2) it could maintain its monetary policy, and allow the new contracts written in the fall of 1969 to be based on a 2.7 percent inflation rate and a higher unemployment rate.

In 1969 and 1970 the Government reversed its pol-

icy and began to inflate at an increasing rate in the last six months of 1969 and 1970. By January of 1971 the inflation rate was back up to a 6 percent annual rate and the unemployment rate was beginning to slide. Since June of 1969, when we abandoned our only real attempt to stop the inflation, we have made no significant attempt to bring inflation under control in this country. We have sought to find easier solutions to our economic dilemma. At first, in the second half of 1969, we tried a voluntary approach. Then in 1971 we went to the mandatory approach when we imposed wage and price controls and attempted to freeze prices and wages in the United States by Government edict.

While we in economics have a lot of data on inflation, we have even more data on wage and price controls. In fact, our first history of wage and price controls occurred 5,000 years ago when price controls were imposed in the fifth dynasty of ancient Egypt. Pericles imposed price controls in ancient Athens, and Diocletian imposed wage and price controls in ancient Rome. *And from the fifth dynasty of ancient Egypt to President Nixon's Phase IV price controls, all of these experiences have one thing in common — not one has ever worked. And they do not work for a very simple reason: they freeze prices at a level where the quantity demanded exceeds the quantity supplied. They simply turn price increases into shortages and stifle the incentive to produce, therefore causing output to fall.*

We have in fact produced a minor miracle in the United States in the 1970s, in that at various times we have produced a grain and a meat shortage through Government policy — in a country that has the most fertile land, the highest level of capital equipment and technology in agriculture, and the best educated farmer in the world. We have produced shortages of critical inputs to the production process, sending the country into a recession.

If one looks at what the Government says it is doing in its "anti-inflation" policy, and then looks at the growth in the monetary base to see what it is actually doing, there is only one conclusion that can be drawn. That conclusion is that Federal anti-inflation policy since June of 1969 has been a "fraud." *Over the last 12 months the monetary base has grown at almost an 8 percent annual rate. Never in history has such a rate of monetary expansion failed to produce rapid inflation.*

Pointing the Finger of Guilt

When the Federal Government, in June 1969, stopped trying to do anything about inflation it turned its activities toward developing scapegoats in order to get Americans to blame their neighbor for their problems. Had the scapegoat strategy not been so effective, it would be humorous. How does this strategy work? Well, you have all heard it. It works basically as follows. A bureaucrat goes to a businessman and says, "Why are you increasing your prices?" And the businessman says, "Because our costs are rising." And then the bureaucrat says, "What is your major cost?" And the businessman says, "labor." And then the bureaucrat concludes, "Well, labor unions cause inflation." And then the same bureaucrat goes to union leaders and says, "Why are you demanding such high wage increases?" And union leaders note that the consumer price index is up 12 percent in the past year, and that wages of hourly workers are 4 percent lower than they were a year ago in terms of real purchasing power dollars. And the bureaucrat says, "Well, who sets prices anyway?" And the labor leaders say, "businessmen." And the bureaucrat concludes, "Well, through price collusion and administered prices, businessmen create inflation."

Then, of course, another popular version of scapegoatism was employed by former Treasury Secretary John Connally. He said, "We are all causing inflation through our greed. We are all so greedy in competing against each other for goods and services that we are, through this competition, driving up prices. We have all just got to stand back and quit being so greedy." I guess the low point in scapegoatism was reached when Herbert Stein pronounced, just before his retirement from the Council of Economic Advisers, that the American people were responsible for inflation.

Picking up the scapegoat theme, Jack Anderson wrote an article in which he said high interest rates are the result of banker collusion in an attempt to drive up the interest rate to make fat profits at the public's expense. This statement, I think, showed that Jack Anderson knows nothing about banking and finance and nothing about economic history, because never in the history of the United States have we had high inflation rates which have failed to produce high interest rates, except during periods of capital rationing.

Our high interest rates over the last year, which have disrupted the long-term capital market, have been caused by irresponsible Government policy. I think it is important that we not allow bankers and businessmen to be used as scapegoats for Government failure. In fact, if one looks at nominal interest rates and the current inflation rates and attempts to draw any parallel between current interest rates, in terms of real resources borrowed, relative to real resources paid back, interest rates last year were not at historic highs, as we were told in the newspaper and on the news. They were at historic lows. We hear from Washington that Government economists marvel at record demand in the short-term credit market in the face of record

high interest rates, but if one can borrow at 12.5 percent on prime commercial paper and the inflation rate is 12 percent, he is paying back in real terms only 0.5 percent interest. *It is indeed no marvel that the demand for capital in the short-term credit market has been at a record high, because real interest rates have been at a record low.* Indeed, if the Federal Reserve had not been following an easy money policy through open market purchases of Government securities, interest rates on short-term credit would probably have reached 15 percent last year.

The Costs of Inflation

While high nominal interest rates have not disrupted the short-term credit market, they have had a disastrous effect on the long-term credit market, and the reason is very simple to understand. Historically, we in the United States have been blessed with fiscally responsible Government. Indeed, if you throw out all the war years in American history, prices on the average have remained constant or fallen slightly throughout the entire history of the United States. As a result, we have had historically low nominal interest rates. Therefore, borrowers are loathe to commit themselves over 25 - 30 years to a nominal interest rate that, although it may be 2 percent or negative (in real terms) at current inflation rates, might later turn out to be an extremely disadvantageous rate if the current inflation should end. Secondly, at high inflation rates, funds have been diverted from their traditional channels, whereby savings flowed into commercial banks and savings and loans institutions, and were in turn loaned out to businesses to build new factories, to generate jobs, and to build new homes. As a result of high inflation rates and interest ceilings on banks and savings and loan associations, funds have been diverted into land and commodity speculation and large Government bond issues.

We are all aware of the impact of inflation on income redistribution, particularly on those with fixed salaries, the old, and the poor. There is no question that this is a major cost of inflation. But an additional, more important cost is the impact caused by diverting funds from traditional channels and disrupting the link between the saver and the investor. In this way, we are today planting seeds which will yield lower economic growth rates for a decade.

Today we have a 7.1 percent unemployment rate which is highly concentrated in two industries — the construction industry and the automobile industry. As the effects of the recession in these industries spread, the unemployment rate will rise further. High interest rates, uncertainty about future prices, and the availability of gasoline go a long way in explaining the plight of these industries. While the $52 billion deficit in fiscal 1975 will stimulate these industries, most of the stimulation will occur in nondepressed industries. A deficit of such magnitude will assure that interest rates will be bid up as Government competes with private industry for loanable funds. If the Federal Reserve monetizes 40 percent of this deficit, as it has done over the last decade, the money supply will expand by over 20 percent and double-digit inflation will occur in 1976, even if we experience the most rapid economic recovery in American history.

Government: The Cause of Inflation

How do we stop the inflation? Inflation has one cause and it has but one cure. And that one cure is to slow the rate of growth in the money supply. This can be accomplished only by closing the Government deficit. Our inflation has resulted from the prevalence of a bankrupt (and bankrupting) idea within Government that money solves problems. If one looks at the historic growth pattern of Government spending over the history of the United States, it is very easy to discern that within the last 15 years there has been a fundamental change within our Government. From the birth of the United States it took over 180 years for the Federal budget to grow from roughly zero to $100 billion. It took only ten years to grow from $100 billion to $200 billion, and it has taken only four years for it to grow from $200 billion to $300 billion. Despite the fact that Federal tax collections have grown by 110 percent over a decade, over three times the rate of economic growth, the Federal Government has failed to live within its budget. According to Treasury Secretary William Simon, *the Federal Government is deficit financing at such a rate that today it is absorbing 60 percent of all the funds raised in U.S. capital markets.*

In January I had the pleasure of working in Washington for my Congressman, Olin Teague, on the Energy Emergency Act. While I was there, Congressman Teague asked me if I would read some of the bills that he had to vote on during the period I was working for him. I noticed that despite the fact that I make my living reading and writing, I was unable to read the bills as fast as they came in, so the stack on my desk kept getting higher and higher. Finally, I realized that it was physically impossible for any Congressman to read the bills he had to vote on. I assert here today that no member of the United States Congress read the $25 billion education act that has just become law. The sheer bulk of paperwork is so great that no effective research is being done in the Congress by those who are actually engaged in the process of making decisions in the public interest. We are experiencing an attempt by the Congress to substitute money for ideas.

Probably the best statement of the money-solves-problems philosophy that I have ever heard was John Lindsay's statement shortly after he became mayor of New York. The gist of John Lindsay's message was as follows: people think New York City has a lot of problems, but New York City has only one problem — private affluence and public poverty. If my budget were simply twice what it is today I could solve every problem in New York City. The day John Lindsay left office his budget was over 2 times what it was the day he took office, and by every index from garbage collection to crime in the streets, New York City was a worse place to live the day he left than the day he came. And the reason is that money does not solve problems, ideas solve problems. And Government has had few viable ideas in 40 years.

The best personal example that I have witnessed of the bankruptcy of Government with regard to new and viable ideas was a call I received back in January. I was working in my office at Texas A & M and my secretary, who gets excited with very little provocation, came into my office and said, "Dr. Gramm, you're not going to believe this, but the President of the United States is on the telephone." And I said, "You're right, I don't believe it." Nevertheless, I picked up the phone and a very stern sounding lady said, "Is this Dr. W. Philip Gramm of Texas A & M University?" I said, "Yes, Ma'm." She said, "Dr. Gramm, this is the White House calling."

So I sat on the edge of my chair awaiting some message — some mission from my President — and a member of the White House staff came on the phone. He said, "Dr. Gramm, your name has been given to us by some very, very important people. We think you might be the kind of person that can help us develop a new and viable energy program, a system of Government controls and subsidies, a system of Government and industry mutual research and project participation. And as an index of our commitment to this project we are willing to commit $20 billion."

He went on and used every 25-cent word in the English language. When he got through, being an Aggie, I said simply, "It is a happy coincidence that out of 211 million Americans you have called the right man, because I know exactly what to do." I told him that I envisioned a system which was not going to cost a penny, but in fact would make money. It would be so productive that we could tax its output and finance Government programs on the basis of its productivity. I told him that I envisioned a system whereby we would allow people to own property, and we would allow them to combine this property with their God-given talents to produce output. We would allow them to sell output in a free market so that each individual, in attempting to maximize his own welfare, would operate at maximum efficiency. And each consumer, in attempting to maximize his own individual welfare, would economize on the things that were scarce and therefore expensive, and substitute for them things that were abundant and therefore cheap. In such a system, by rewarding production and innovation, we could assure a maximum level of economic growth. I told him that I was basically a modest person and that I wanted him to know this was not totally my idea; that in fact if he would like a written reference, he might look at Adam Smith's *Wealth of Nations*, written in 1776. And I hung up.

Well, I assumed that I would never hear from the White House again, but indeed they went to a great deal of trouble to get in touch with me. And that's how, as I expressed it, for about a two-month period, while I didn't invent free enterprise, I had the sole Washington distributorship on it.

Conclusion

If we are to ever put an end to spiralling prices, shortages, high interest rates and, economic stagnation, we must stop the growth of Government and put our monetary and fiscal house in order. To reverse the trend of fiscal irresponsibility we need strong leadership, which is a scarce commodity in Washington today. We must resist the siren song of more and more Government spending and more and more Government controls, and stand up for the free enterprise system which has made us prosperous and free.

The hour is late. It has become quite fashionable to proclaim the inevitability of the demise of our system. Such a philosophy is a convenient escape. For if there is not hope, we are not obligated to do anything. In fact, there is no real reason for pessimism. We have human talents on our side. We have money and economic power on our side, and most important, we have history on our side. We have, in the American free enterprise system, the most successful economic system in the world. It has elevated us from a powerless nation, 90 percent of whose citizens were in poverty — by any measure — at the time of the Revolution, into the greatest agricultural and industrial power on earth. So successful is our system and so high are the aspirations of the American people that we define poverty at an income level that is higher than the average income level of the world's second most powerful nation. Yet, paradoxically, this great system is under attack at all levels of Government, and is being replaced by a system which has never worked in history and which is working effectively no where in the world today. The greatest product in history is not selling for the simple reason that it has no salesman. Those within our Government who supposedly represent our views are defending our system with an ineptitude unparalled in the history of the Republic. To reverse this trend we need but a unit of will.

I wish to tell you today that I am optimistic about the future of America, and I am optimistic about the future of the American free enterprise system. If we have learned anything in the 1970s, it is that big Government cannot solve problems, and that spending more of the taxpayers' money cannot turn a bad idea into a good one. Everywhere I go in Texas and in our nation I find the American people feel a sense of helplessness. They know big Government is not working, they know something is out of kilter, but they don't know what to do about it. What we need today, more than at any time in the history of the United States, is a new wave of leadership to turn this country around. We need this leadership to fulfill the ideals and aspirations of a revolution which occurred almost two hundred years ago. In the coming struggle for the survival and the success of the American experiment, I call upon you as our business and civic leaders not to be merely passive observers, but to be active participants. While I cannot speak for the actions of others, in my own case I mean not only to participate, I mean in that participation to lead.

DOES INFLATION RIDE ESCALATORS?
NOT YET, PAY COUNCIL STUDY FINDS

COST-OF-LIVING escalator clauses in major union contracts have not been a major contributing factor to recent inflation rates, but future ramifications of the widespread use of these clauses are uncertain. These are the findings of a study conducted for the Council on Wage and Price Stability by H. M. Douty, an economic consultant and former Bureau of Labor Statistics economist. The conclusion that the correlation between inflation and escalator clauses "does not appear to have been great" is based on data showing relatively limited use of escalators through 1974, that average wage compensation, to those with escalator provisions, equaled not more than half the increase in the Consumer Price Index between 1968 and 1974, that consumer price increases are equally reflected in contracts without escalator clauses as well as in wage decisions in the nonunion sector, and that the direct contribution of escalator increases to total wage adjustments is small, even in the union sector. Douty says escalators could be inflationary in the future if they become more "widespread and geared to frequent reviews and small changes in the Consumer Price Index."

When the Vietnam-induced wage-price spiral began in 1966, only about 20 percent of workers under major collective bargaining agreements were covered by escalator clauses. During the 1970–71 recession, the rate of price increases moderated but wages rose about as rapidly as during the previous economic expansion, placing pressure on costs and prices and transforming "demand-induced" inflation into a "cost" inflation. On the wage side, escalator coverage had increased only moderately by 1971 to 28 percent of workers under major agreements. Thus, the relatively high rate of wage increases primarily reflected nonescalated gains in the union sector and sizable adjustments in the pay of nonunion workers.

Douty attributes the growth in escalator coverage to the "length and severity" of the 1966–74 inflation but notes that adjustments in 1968–74 were below the level of consumer price increases. Further, for the same period of time, cost-related wage adjustments were reflected to a much greater percentage in first-year and deferred increases and only to a much lesser extent in escalator increments. Thus, pressure to keep wages in line with price increases was reflected more in the general wage settlement than in the addition of an escalator clause.

Although noting that the effect of escalation on the level of wages generally cannot be definitively answered, Douty points to two sets of indexes whose similarity of movement is striking. The first relates to the adjusted average hourly earnings in the private nonfarm sector. This series serves as a "rough measure of change in the level of rates of pay" for production and nonsupervisory union and nonunion workers, who numbered 53 million in 1974. The second set of indexes relates to average effective general wage changes under major collective bargaining agreements in 1974 and covers about 10.2 million workers. For both, annual rates of increase over the 1965–74 period were 6.2 percent in terms of money wages and 1.1 percent in real terms. Further, the year-to-year changes show that since 1969, the union sector has been better able to protect its real wage position. The corresponding "spread of escalator agreements probably has contributed to this result," Douty observes.

According to the consultant, "if inflation persists, escalator clause coverage will continue to expand and there will be a tendency for the adaption of escalator provisions that compensate more rapidly and completely than many now do for living cost changes;" the future effect of these clauses will depend on several factors. The first relates to the use of the Consumer Price Index as the basis of the escalation formula. A spurt in the Consumer Price Index could be due to a price change in one major component, yet would still lead to employee wage escalation and a resultant rise in general price levels and inflation. Secondly, Douty finds escalator clauses inherently capricious. Firms cannot anticipate escalator-triggered wage increases and thus may be forced to increase employee compensation at times when they cannot raise prices. Finally, a widespread use of escalator clauses tied to frequent and small changes in the price index may contribute to the inflationary process by removing wage-to-price lags. In Douty's view, these lags tend to slow down inflation because nonunion wage increases and collective bargaining occur rarely more often than once a year.

H. M. Douty's study may be obtained from the Council on Wage and Price Stability, Executive Office of the President. □

"Does Inflation Ride Escalators?" *Monthly Labor Review*, November 1975, pp. 65–66. Reprinted with permission.

Indexing Inflation: Remedy or Malady?

By Vincent A. Gennaro

When people could still talk about price increases lightly, inflation was sometimes referred to as "crab grass on the lawn of prosperity." Since most people will tolerate a little crab grass and a little inflation, the analogy appeared apt. Unlike crab grass, however, inflation is not disdained because it is ugly or rapacious. The arbitrary and unpredictable redistributions of income and wealth that stem from unexpected inflation underlie its unpopularity. Some economists believe, however, that many of inflation's ill effects can be softened or eliminated through a program known as "indexing" or "monetary correction." They argue that an indexing program has the additional benefit of making it easier to wipe out the crab grass of inflation while preserving the lawn of prosperity.

Indexing is a method of linking various payments made under contract (wages, rent, and interest) to selected price indices by periodically "adjusting" for price level changes. When prices go up, indexed payments go up, while price level declines mean lower payments. The idea is by no means new. Its origins date back as far as the 1700s. Under the name of "tabular standard" it was proposed in detail in the late nineteenth century by the English economist Alfred Marshall. Recently the idea has been employed extensively in Brazil, Chile, and Israel. The intention of indexing is to alleviate some of the ill effects of inflation or deflation.

Indexing exists in the United States as well to some extent (see Table 1). Nearly 5.1 million workers have cost-of-living escalator clauses in their contracts while another 13 million receive indexed food stamps. In all, nearly one out of every four persons has some income tied to the cost of living. Many would like to see still more comprehensive application of escalator clauses. A program of indexing, however, has its "costs."

Vincent A. Gennaro, "Indexing Inflation—Remedy or Malady?" *Business Review*, Federal Reserve Bank of Philadelphia, March 1975, pp. 3–13. Reprinted with permission.

TABLE 1
ESCALATION AND THE CONSUMER PRICE INDEX

The number of people known to be receiving automatically escalated payments based on the Bureau of Labor Statistics' Consumer Price Index includes:

	Millions
Wage earners covered by union contracts	5.1
Social Security beneficiaries	28.9
Retired military and Federal Civil Service employees and survivors	1.9
Postal workers	0.6
Food stamp recipients	13.0
Total	49.5

Many other people receive automatically escalated payments although the exact number is not known. Among them:

(1) State and local employees and retirees

(2) Alimony and child care recipients

(3) Lessors with CPI adjustments in leases

(4) Royalty recipients covered by escalator clauses

(5) Beneficiaries of certain insurance and annuity policies

SOURCE: *Morgan Guaranty Survey*, May 1974.

Whether or not indexing is acceptable to society depends on how its benefits stack up against its costs.

INFLATION'S ILL EFFECTS

Inflation has many "costs" which impinge on individual members of society. Perhaps the most distressing of these ill effects is the "surprise" decline in purchasing power which results from an unexpected rise in prices. The same market basket of goods and services purchased in the past takes more and more dollars from our wallets. For those individuals with few assets, standards of living must decline when their incomes fail to keep pace with inflation. Likewise, those households that depend solely on fixed incomes in the form of pensions, insurance benefits, or interest on assets will be among the losers in terms of declining living standards. There will also be gainers—those whose incomes rise faster than prices and output in general—but the income redistributions which result may generate social as well as economic distress.[1]

For example, even if wages increase to keep pace with prices, workers will find larger por-

---

[1]For a more complete discussion of the effects of inflation, see W. Lee Hoskins, "Inflation: Gainers and Losers," *Business Review* of the Federal Reserve Bank of Philadelphia, February 1970, pp 23–30.

tions of their income being redistributed to the Government during inflationary periods. Because of the graduated tax system, the Internal Revenue Service claims a larger chunk of inflation-boosted earnings. A worker whose earned income is presently $15,000 will be rapidly pushed into a higher tax bracket despite the fact that his annual pay raises of, say, 10 percent only about maintains his pretax purchasing power. At that rate, 20 years hence his annual salary will be $100,912, putting him in a 50-percent bracket under the current Federal tax structure. In inflation-adjusted terms, he is considerably worse off *after taxes* even though his wages have kept pace with inflation. In this example, the Federal Government is a gainer and the wage earner is a loser as a result of inflation.

Redistribution in wealth, the value of accumulated savings, can also result when inflation is not accurately anticipated. If actual inflation is greater than expected, net borrowers (those who have borrowed more than they have loaned out) will gain as they repay "cheaper" dollars, and lenders will suffer. If actual inflation is less than expected, net lenders will gain as the dollars they are repaid are worth more in purchasing-power terms than lenders had expected. For example, suppose you lend a friend $100 at 8 percent interest, *expecting* that prices will rise 5 percent before the loan is repaid. If prices actually rise only 2 percent, you are better off since your inflation-adjusted or real return is 6 percent, rather than the 3 percent you were anticipating. But if prices rise 7 percent, your real return is only 1 percent, and the borrower has gained at your expense. All of these unforeseen changes in wealth and income resulting from unexpected inflation could be greatly reduced if wage contracts or loans took account of unexpected as well as expected future price changes.

In sum, unexpected inflation exacts social costs in the form of arbitrary redistributions of income and wealth. Economic decision-makers, such as households and firms, will try to avoid these costs by devoting resources, including their own time and effort, to the task of protecting themselves from the redistributional impact of inflation. In fact, the value of these resources in alternative uses should also be considered a cost of unanticipated inflation.

INDEXING'S BENEFITS

One method of removing the ill effects of inflation is to eliminate inflation itself. However, this solution is difficult to carry out and may take considerable time. In the interim, a policy of "indexing" can ease the burden inflation exacts on unwary economic decision-makers. Indexing would act as an "insurance policy," guarding against losses from *unexpected* price changes. If wages were indexed (by way of an escalator clause), they would increase when prices rise. Constant purchasing power would thus be maintained despite price increases.[2] Currently, inflation expectations are taken into consideration in wage contracts that are not indexed. If expectations prove to differ greatly from the actual rate, however, then workers or employers may suffer. If inflation is underestimated in the contract settlement, workers' real wages will fall during the contract period—that is, money wages will rise less than prices. If inflation is overestimated, workers will get real wage gains. Indexing in wage contracts eliminates such "surprises" about real wages. A contract with an escalator clause means that labor and management bargain over "real" wages rather than so-called money wages.

Interest payments can also be indexed, eliminating the need for borrowers and lenders to guess at the rate of inflation.[3] For example, suppose the annual rate is 10 percent, the in-

---

[2] Wages could also be adjusted to account for productivity changes, so that purchasing power can actually rise or fall accordingly.

[3] Presently, these inflation expectations are built into many interest rates. If a lender, for example, desires a *real* (inflation-adjusted) rate of return of 3 percent and anticipates an annual rate of inflation of 5 percent over the contract period, he will require an 8-percent market interest rate. The 3 percent covers the risk and the opportunity cost of tying up his money, while the 5 percent will be to maintain his purchasing power (to stay even in real terms). If the actual rate of inflation turned out to be 9 percent, the lender would be

TABLE 2
ADJUSTING PRINCIPAL FOR 10 PERCENT INFLATION
ASSURES LENDER OF HIGHER GAINS TO OFFSET INFLATION

	Without Indexing	With Indexing
Principal	$1,000	$1,000
"Adjustment" Made to Principal for 10 Percent Inflation	0	+ 100
"Adjusted Principal"	1,000	1,100
Interest (5 Percent)	50	55
Balance (Principal and Interest)	1,050	1,155

terest rate paid annually on passbook savings accounts by a bank is 5 percent, and the balance (principal) in the account for the last year is $1,000 (see Table 2). Without indexing, the holder of the passbook would have $1,050 after one year. This amounts to a loss in real dollars or purchasing power of $50, since one would need $1,100 now to buy what he could with $1,000 a year ago. If savings deposits were indexed, first the principal would be "corrected" for inflation, then the interest rate would be applied to the corrected principal. With indexing the new balance is $1,155, compared to $1,050 without indexing, and the 5-percent stated rate of interest represents the *real* rate of interest—the rate of return in terms of increased purchasing power. The asset side of a bank's balance sheet would likewise be indexed, of course.

Unlike wages and interest which require adjustments, aggregate profits (business revenues minus costs) will automatically keep pace with

price level changes. For the economy as a whole, the average percentage change in the price of business inputs—that is, labor, land, and capital—will equal the average percentage change in the price of business output—the goods produced and sold (see Table 3). In such a case, profits increase by the same percentage. This occurs with no forced adjustment on profits directly—rather, the input prices are escalated when output prices rise in general.

How would indexing originate in various business contracts? In a market-oriented economy, escalation of wages and interest payments in private contracts would be decided by the parties involved, not by a program imposed by the Federal Government. (In Brazil the program was imposed by government decree. See Box 1 for discussion.) The Government's role in indexing private payments would be to remove any barriers (such as interest rate ceilings) to an indexed agreement and provide the kind of price indices required to allow indexing to work equitably and efficiently.

Indexing of the Federal Government's own revenues and expenditures is a different matter, however, because these changes would require explicit legislation. Currently, social security payments and government pensions are tied to

losing money in real terms. Under indexing the interest rate could be stated at 3 percent. The interest payment would be tied to the price level and fluctuate accordingly, eliminating the need to bear the risk of price changes. It would also alleviate the unforeseen transfer of wealth during unexpected inflation. Neither the borrower nor lender would lose or gain because of unanticipated inflation or deflation.

TABLE 3
PROFITS INCREASE "AUTOMATICALLY" UNDER INDEXING PROGRAM BY SAME PERCENTAGE AS PRICES IN GENERAL

Total Profits, No Inflation		Total Profits, Indexed for 10 Percent Inflation	
Revenues	$300	Revenues	$330
− Costs	200	− Costs	220
Profits	$100	Profits	$110

Percentage Change in Profits: $\dfrac{10}{100} = 10$ Percent

BOX 1

THE BRAZILIAN EXPERIENCE

The final verdict is not yet in on indexing in Brazil. Many believe, however, that it has contributed to improved performance of the Brazilian economy over the last decade.

From 1959 to 1965 inflation in Brazil raged at an average annual rate of over 53 percent, while the economy grew, in real terms, at a rate of 5 to 6 percent annually. Even as far back as 1950 inflation proved to be very disruptive to the financial system. Since usury laws limited interest rates to 12 percent, banks began charging commission fees on top of the maximum rate. But lending rates still lagged far behind the inflation rate. Compounding the problem, banks could not offer high enough interest rates to depositors to attract or even maintain savings deposits. This resulted in banks limiting loans to terms of 120 days or less.

Consequently, housing markets suffered. However, consumers did not halt their borrowing. Anticipation of future price rises spurred consumers to buy now even if they had to borrow at "high" interest rates, which were considered a bargain in their inflationary economy. The nation was indeed troubled. In 1964 the Brazilians implemented their comprehensive system of indexing after the military overthrow of the Goulart government. The inflation rate has gone from 91.6 percent in 1963 to less than 20 percent in 1973, while the average annual real growth rate for the last five years has been roughly 10 percent.

This is not to say that indexing alone was responsible for this performance. It was accompanied by slashed budgetary deficits, a watchful regulatory eye on money supply growth, and various wage-price controls.

Not everyone benefited equally in the post-1964 Brazilian economy. Real wages of unskilled workers declined more than 30 percent while the real minimum wage declined 20 percent from 1964 to 1967. (However, since 1967 there has been a steady rise in the average real wage.) Indexing was responsible in part for this decline. It was used not as a device to help labor keep pace with inflation, but as an instrument of anti-inflationary policy.* Wages were tied to a formula which had a built-in bias toward lower wage adjustments. The formula included an unrealistically low expected inflation rate and did not allow for retroactive correction of its inaccuracies.** The result was a decline in labor's relative share of national income.

It is possible, however, that this redistribution of wealth and income can be partly attributed to factors other than indexing. Brazil's fiscal policy is conducive to these inequities. There are liberal tax incentives to those who invest in the securities markets, favoring those with capital to invest and hardly beneficial to the "poor."

There have also been structural changes in the educational distribution of the Brazilian work force. Aside from the increase in the average level of education of the labor force from 1960 to 1970, the variation of the level of education increased greatly. Education did not grow uniformly throughout the labor force, leading to a decline in the income share of unskilled laborers.***

There are limitations in appraising indexing on the basis of the Brazilian experience. First, the effects of indexing cannot easily be isolated from the effects of any other economic policy of the same time, making the results difficult to evaluate. Also the degree of comparability between the United States and Brazil is dubious. Brazil has neither a strong union movement nor the sophisticated financial markets of the United States—not to mention the disparity of the rates of inflation between the two nations. In addition, the type of government in the two countries is different.

---

*Walter W. Heller and Albert Fishlow, "Painless Inflation through Indexing? Should We follow Brazil's Example?" *Bank Letter of National City Bank of Minneapolis*, June 20, 1974.
**Indexing in Brazil was not merely offered to workers as an alternative; it was imposed by government decree.
***Albert Fishlow, "Brazilian Size Distribution of Income," *American Economic Review* 62 (May 1972): 401.

the Consumer Price Index. However, items such as Federal income tax brackets, personal exemptions, and corporate and capital gains taxes can also be adjusted for inflation. Consequently, the taxes paid by individuals and businesses would be affected.

For example, indexing could alter the manner in which firms report their earnings, so that profits resulting purely from inflation would not be taxed. Companies would be permitted to revalue or index such balance sheet items as working capital and fixed assets (building and equipment) in accordance with the rate of inflation. As prices rise, the value of fixed assets on a firm's financial statements would be revalued upward to reflect the higher price the firm would have to pay to replace its equipment. This would au-

tomatically increase the depreciation expense—the amount the firm is allowed to charge as an expense against current income to cover the cost of worn-out buildings and machinery. Reported earnings would be lower than they would be in an nonindexed world, and firms would consequently pay lower taxes. The working capital adjustment has a similar effect, lowering both reported earnings and taxes. Aside from making the tax system more equitable by taxing real purchasing power instead of dollars, shareholders would benefit from more accurate information on a firm's performance. The distorting impact of inflation on reported profits would be sharply curtailed.

Aside from the effects on business taxation, indexing would also alter the personal income tax considerably. The Federal Government would no longer receive higher real revenues as a by-product of inflation (see Box 2). During inflation, the ceilings on tax brackets could be escalated. If, for example, an income tax range were $0–$1,000 and a 10-percent inflation occurred, this bracket would be revised to $0–$1,100. Thus, a person who increased his dollar income from $950 to $1,045, leaving his real purchasing power unchanged, would not be pushed into a higher tax bracket as he would be in a nonindexed world. The personal exemption could be similarly adjusted, and the inflation component could be removed from capital gains before the tax rate is applied. All these tax adjustments would deprive the Federal Government of its "extra" tax gains accruing from inflation and prevent Uncle Sam from being one of inflation's big winners.[4]

Indexing does not remove all the ill effects of inflation, however. In actual practice it is quite

---

[4]The Federal Government also gains if inflation is unanticipated because it is the largest net debtor in our economy.

difficult to link *all* payments to a price index. For example, it's highly unlikely that the cash in people's pockets would be protected against inflation. Thus, holders of money balances would continue to lose purchasing power during inflation. In addition, the fact that there may be time lags between periods of adjustments means some inequities will remain under indexing. Ideally, to eliminate lags between price changes and the compensation for such changes, the adjustments would be daily or even continuous. This, too, is impractical. These imperfections must be weighed in considering the merits of comprehensive indexing.

It remains true, however, that an indexing program will eliminate a good deal of the redistribution of income and wealth that results from unanticipated inflation. Most observers agree that such redistributions are "costly" both economically and politically and should be avoided. However, many feel that the bad "side effects" associated with an indexing "cure" rule it out as a viable means of reducing the social ills associated with inflation.

BOX 2

WITH NO INDEXING, INFLATION INCREASES INDIVIDUAL TAX BURDENS . . .

Table A—Tax Brackets Are <u>Not</u> Adjusted for Inflation

	(1)	(2)	(3)	(4)	(5)	(6)
Year	Inflation Rate	Real Value of Taxable Income	Taxable Income in Current Dollars	Effective Tax Rate	Taxes Paid*	Real Value of After-Tax Income
1	0%	$10,000	$10,000	20.9%	$2,090	$7,910
2	10	10,000	11,000	21.3	2,340	7,873
3	10	10,000	12,000	22.0	2,659	7,802
4	10	10,000	13,310	22.6	3,010	7,739
5	10	10,000	14,641	23.3	3,409	7,672
10	10	10,000	23,579	28.1	6,622	7,192

*Calculation of taxes paid was based on 1972 Federal Income Tax, Schedule X, Single Taxpayers.

BOX 2 (Continued)
BUT INDIVIDUALS STAY EVEN WHEN TAX BRACKETS ARE INDEXED.

Table B—Tax Brackets Are Adjusted for Inflation

	(1)	(2)	(3)	(4)	(5)	(6)
Year	Inflation Rate	Real Value of Taxable Income	Taxable Income in Current Dollars	Effective Tax Rate	Taxes Paid*	Real Value of After-Tax Income
1	0%	$10,000	$10,000	20.9%	$2,090	$7,910
2	10	10,000	11,000	20.9	2,299	7,910
3	10	10,000	12,100	20.9	2,529	7,910
4	10	10,000	13,310	20.9	2,782	7,910
5	10	10,000	14,641	20.9	3,060	7,910
10	10	10,000	23,579	20.9	4,928	7,910

*For this calculation it was assumed that the income breakpoints in Schedule X were adjusted upward by the inflation rate (1).

Tables A and B show a hypothetical example of an individual's income tax payments. In both cases it is assumed that the inflation rate is 10 percent per year and that the person's real taxable income (2) is protected from inflation by indexing. His current dollar income (3) increases each year by a percentage equal to the inflation rate (1). The effective tax rate (4) represents the proportion of current dollar income going to taxes (5). Real after-tax income (6) (representing what the person could spend in terms of goods and services) shows the inflation-adjusted purchasing power remaining after taxes have been paid.

In Table A, although income is escalated, the tax brackets are not adjusted for inflation. Even though real taxable income (2) remains constant, after-tax income (6) falls. Since the tax rate is based on current dollar income (3), as income increases to keep pace with prices, the individual is forced into a higher tax bracket (4). Not only does the tax payment rise in dollars, but also as a percent of his earnings.

In Table B, not only is income escalated, but the tax brackets are also adjusted for inflation. The tax rate (4) is now based on real taxable income (2). As current dollar income increases with prices, the worker is not forced into a higher tax bracket and his real spendable income remains unchanged.

OBJECTIONS AND BARRIERS TO INDEXING

Perhaps the most popular objection to comprehensive indexing is the claim that such a program represents a "policy of despair"—throwing in the towel in the fight against inflation. Opponents argue that by making inflation more tolerable, indexing reduces the will to combat inflation. However, advocates of indexing make a strong argument that instead of weakening the fight against inflation, indexing actually makes it easier to combat inflation. Indexing, they say, reduces the burden—typically reflected in increasing unemployment—of an anti-inflation effort.

Policymakers are faced with a cruel dilemma. Reducing a demand-related inflation typically requires slowing the rate of increase in total spending. Slower growth in demand, however, usually results in higher unemployment. Consequently, decision-makers follow "gradualist" policies which attempt to reduce *slowly* the inflation so as to minimize the adverse employment effects. In an indexed economy, however, policymakers can act more vigorously in the anti-inflation effort because the increase in unemployment will be smaller than that which occurs in an nonindexed economy, say the proponents of indexing.

Firms' decisions about how many workers to hire depend mainly on real wages—money wages adjusted for inflation.[5] As real wages rise, other things equal, firms will hire fewer workers or begin furloughing some of their existing labor force. According to this argument, firms that include escalator clauses in their contracts bargain in terms of *real wages* and, consequently, know what real wages will be over the life of the contract. Other businesses which do not include indexing clauses in their wage agreements can only forecast what real wages will be over the contract horizon. If prices increase more slowly than these firms had expected, real wages will increase. In a competitive economy, such a "surprise" increase in real wages will mean that firms will cut back on production and hire fewer workers. These unexpected increases in real wages are quite likely to occur during the initial phases of a restricitve anti-inflation policy since workers will be attempting to "compensate" for past inflation and hedge against future inflation by demanding higher wages. Thus, restrictive policies are generally accompanied by rising unemployment. If all wage bargains are indexed, however, there is no need to "compensate" for past inflation or build in hedges against unexpected future inflation in wage agreements. Thus, real wages will not increase as rapidly in a fully indexed economy during a restrictive monetary policy, and the rise in unemployment consequently will be smaller.[6] With fewer unemployed laborers, it becomes politically easier to adhere to a dedicated anti-inflation program.

Indexing, then, according to this view, operates so as to change the terms of the cost-benefit calculation which underlies society's decision about how much effort to devote to fighting inflation. Only if society decides that as a result of indexing the costs of fighting inflation have increased significantly relative to the benefits, will the "will to combat inflation" be weakened. It is by no means clear that this *must* be the result if comprehensive indexing is implemented, however. In fact, indexing's supporters would argue that the cost of fighting inflation has been reduced and therefore the will to fight inflation may be increased.

Another objection to indexing is the contention that such a mechanism would "institutionalize" a wage-price inflationary spiral. According to this view, widespread indexing would alter the structure of the economy—that is, cause it to respond in a more inflationary way to irregularities such as a crop shortage or an increase in the price of crude oil. These unpredictable inflationary shocks would be expected to feed through the economy at a faster pace. The inflationary rise in the price of oil, for example, will quickly result in increased wages for workers in *all* industries. Those firms whose product prices had increased less than the average will find their profit margins squeezed since their wage costs increased by a greater percentage than their prices. Such firms are victims of "cost-push" pressure to raise their prices further to restore previous profit margins. Thus, indexing perpetuates inflation, or so the argument goes.

---

[5]For empirical evidence, see Robert E. Lucas, Jr. and Leonard A. Rapping, "Real Wages, Employment, and Inflation," Edmund S. Phelps *et al.*, eds., *Microeconomic Foundations of Employment and Inflation Theory* (New York: W. W. Norton and Company, 1970), pp. 257–305.

[6]Indexing is a two-sided coin, however. If the Government is pursuing expansionary policies, fewer jobs would be created for each dollar of stimulus provided by fiscal or monetary policies, since wage gains would proceed *more* rapidly than in a nonindexed economy.

The argument doesn't go far enough, however, contend proponents of indexing. First, it ignores what happens to those firms whose prices had initially increased more than the average as a result of oil price rises. Even after the wages of their workers have been escalated, their profit margins will be fatter. If these firms are in competitive industries, swollen profit margins will attract new firms, thus stimulating additional production. This pressure of profits pulling new firms into an industry should reduce the rate at which an industry's profits are rising.[7] Only if "cost-push" pressures for increases in the rate of price changes are greater than "profit-pull" pressures for reductions in the rate of price increases can inflation accelerate as a result of indexing.

The "cost-push" spiral argument also ignores development on the demand side of the economy. When the price level rises as a result of some external shock, more money is required to conduct the same amount of real economic activity. If the money supply is not increased enough to accommodate the price rise, the rate of increase in aggregate demand will eventually be slowed. A restrictive monetary policy will thus reduce pressures on prices, but at a cost in terms of higher unemployment. These unemployment costs in turn are higher *without indexing* than with it.

Another argument against indexing relates to the problem of measuring inflation. Suppose, after hearing the arguments about its relative merits, society should conclude that there is only a small risk that indexing will perpetuate inflation by institutionalizing a wage-price spiral or by reducing the public will to combat general price increases. Should contract forms be altered immediately to include escalator clauses? Not necessarily, for there still may be substantial costs to implementing a comprehensive program. In particular, the inherent inability of price indices to capture changes fully in the cost of living presents an obstacle.[8] Because of their failure to adjust adequately for both quality changes and for behavior changes by the public when prices rise (for example, buying artificial sweeteners when sugar prices rise), all price indices currently available give biased measures of true changes in the cost of living, say opponents of indexing. The reply from supporters of indexing, however, is that the method of constructing price indices can be modified to attempt to measure changes in the cost of living more accurately. Such changes would be costly in terms of both money and time but could be done.

Another possible snag associated with implementing indexing would be the problem of escalating everyone's income with a single index that is based on one subgroup of the population. Suppose this price index rises more rapidly than the living costs of other subgroups of the population. If so, these other subgroups would receive escalated incomes in excess of what they would have received if their wages were escalated by their own "index." This would give them an unwarranted increase in income. Conversely, certain subgroups could receive a smaller escalator than warranted by increases in their cost of living. Thus, income shares could continue to shift under a program based on a single price index. However, proponents of indexing say that this problem can be circumscribed by using a number of price indices that would be more satisfactory from both an economic and a political view.

NOT A CURE-ALL

Indexing cannot by itself reduce the rate of inflation. Nor for that matter is that its intention. What *does* it offer, then?

- It can reduce inflation's arbitrary redistributional effects, especially as they affect the Federal Government.
- It could provide a less uncomfortable environment for anti-inflationary policies and cushion the otherwise harsh effects of bringing a sky-high inflation rate down to earth.
- Or, negatively, it might possibly institutionalize inflation more into the fabric of society. However, this is not a necessary consequence of indexing as some have suggested.

Whatever its other merits or shortcomings, however, indexing will not reduce the importance of monetary and fiscal policies in combating inflation. Ultimately it will be these policies that will reduce the rate of inflation while indexing could play a supplementary role. That role could be quite useful, however, if indexing, like the best "pain killer," not only alleviates the "pain," but also facilitates the "cure" by assuring the cooperation of the "patient."

[7]In many cases, however, there are barriers to entry into an industry. Effective barriers may prevent "profit-pull" pressures from slowing the rate at which current prices are rising.

[8]For a more complete discussion on the reliability of price indices, see David B. Thomas, "How Reliable Are Those Price and Employment Measures?" *Business Review* of the Federal Reserve Bank of Philadelphia, April 1973, pp. 17–22.

Thomas M. Maloy

Is Continuing Inflation Inevitable?

Reasonable price stability can be attained by implementing flexible wage-price guideposts which interfere as little as possible in the free market and by securing the active participation of both business and labor in setting the standards.

INFLATION has been our most severe economic problem for almost a decade. The tendency for prices to rise even in periods of relatively high unemployment is now well established. This is troubling to economists, who are accustomed to thinking about economic policy in terms of either unemployment or inflation. When both are occurring simultaneously, the task of economic policy is complicated further.

Mr. Maloy *is Assistant Professor of Economics at the University of Wisconsin-Eau Claire. He taught previously at Cleveland State University, Cleveland, Ohio. Labor economics is one of his specialized fields.*

In the last few years particularly, it has become apparent that the supposed tradeoff between unemployment and inflation depicted by the Phillips curve is misleading. If one plots rates of inflation and unemployment on a chart, the result in recent years resembles a scatter diagram. If the Phillips curve did approximate reality at one time, this no longer appears to be true, and the term stagflation has crept into the economic vocabulary.

There are those such as Edmund Phelps and Milton Friedman, of course, who have long argued that no such tradeoff exists, except perhaps for a short period of time while individuals are adjusting their expectations to the higher rate of inflation. After this adjustment period, the "natural" rate of unemployment will continue at the higher inflationary level.

If the relationship depicted by the Phillips curve proved accurate, the job of economic policy, although difficult, would be rather well defined. Monetary and fiscal policy could aim in the direction of keeping unemployment down to the minimum level consistent with what is considered tolerable inflation. That view of the economy appears in fact to have been the dominant one of Administration economists in the mid-1960s. Recent experience, however, in which inflation has accelerated to double digit rates while unemployment hovers several percentage points over the traditional high full employment level (4%), makes it apparent that this view is an inaccurate picture of present reality.

Thomas M. Maloy, "Is Continuing Inflation Inevitable?" *Atlanta Economic Review,* May–June 1975, pp. 52–54. Reprinted with permission.

If it is true that higher rates of inflation have not appeared to purchase a permanently reduced unemployment rate, it is also a fact that inducing a higher rate of unemployment has failed to make much headway against inflation. Most recent inflation has been from the supply side, caused primarily by the pressure of organized labor groups or monopolistically controlled industries. This is obvious from the fact that real GNP was declining throughout 1974 while prices during that time were increasing at an annual rate of over 10%. Such inflation could hardly be attributable to demand pressures. It is also true that such inflation appears to resist the usual monetary and fiscal tools. Although it is no doubt true that even this cost-push inflation eventually would yield to monetary and fiscal restraint, the prolonged recession that would be necessary is neither politically nor economically expedient.

It therefore becomes necessary to devise alternative policies to deal with those inflationary pressures that exist in the absence of excess demand. This is especially true in view of the strong inflationary forces that permeate the U.S. economy from the supply side. There is a substantial degree of concentrated economic power residing in firms, unions, and other political pressure groups. Each is out for a larger share of the economic pie, and the ultimate effect is to drive up costs and prices. As inflation proceeds, each feels it must pursue its economic goals aggressively in order to keep one step ahead of the accelerating inflation.

In spite of the fact that these inflationary pressures are built into the U.S. economic system, it nevertheless should be possible to keep the inflation within reasonable bounds. This can be accomplished, however, only if it becomes painful for firms and unions which have substantial market power to exercise that power with little regard for the public interest.

It is the position of this article that flexible wage-price guideposts can aid substantially in attaining reasonable price stability, if certain actions are taken in both the formulation and administration of these standards. Guideposts are vastly preferable to direct controls, for which increasing support seems to be developing.

The problem with controls, as opposed to guideposts, was vividly demonstrated by the experience of the Nixon Administration. Controls were reluctantly introduced in the summer of 1971, when unemployment was drawing substantial criticism at the same time that inflation was also a problem. The freeze that was adopted at that time and the successively more liberal phases introduced after the three-month freeze were an attempt to keep prices in check while policy was directed at reducing unemployment.

The dismal record of the economy under those controls was not unexpected by many economists. By the end of Phase II, prices were rising at an annual rate of 4%. Some inflation, nevertheless, had been repressed, and it has been accelerating ever since. Recent experience suggests that the aftermath of controls will see greater inflation and a more difficult task of restraining it than had the inflation been permitted to occur without any resort to controls. The controls were too rigid, and they were not perceived as equitable by labor and management. Controls may give the illusion of progress for a short while, but they create shortages and eventually make inflation worse, since basically they are an attempt to dictate decisions normally made in a free market.

Making Guideposts Work

If controls performed as poorly as indicated, is there any reason to be optimistic about achieving better results with guideposts? There is reason to think that this approach can be successful if properly implemented and if government macroeconomic policies are not overly stimulative. Guideposts can be framed in such a way as to interfere as little as possible in the free market, thereby substantially avoiding the basic problem brought on by controls.

Many critics question how a system of voluntary standards and government appeals could cause any wage or price below that which would maximize net income. Gardner Ackley, chairman of the Council of Economic Advisers during our first experience with these standards in the early 1960s, responds as follows:

"Is it not the answer that, in collective bargaining and most industrial pricing, wage rates and prices are set not by impersonal market forces but rather by human (usually collective) decisions. The decision makers have room for judgment or there would be no decision.

"I believe that the guideposts did have some impact on wage decisions, primarily through influencing employers' bargaining positions, rather than by directly affecting union attitudes or aggressiveness, although I do not rule that out."[1]

There is evidence that the guideposts during the period mentioned did attain a measure of success in preventing prices from rising as fast as they would have risen in the absence of such guideposts.[2] This is true even though the guideposts during that period met neither of the conditions which will maximize their effectiveness.

There appear to be two major ways in which the success of guideposts as a means of reducing inflation can be enhanced. The first step is to secure the active participation of both business and labor in recognition of the problem and in assisting government in formulating the basic standard. Such a policy would ensure greater acceptance of the standards and more adherence to them. This was not done in the 1960s, when they were unilaterally determined by government.[3]

The lack of labor participation in helping to determine the guideposts during our previous experience with these standards was a factor in the hostility which labor displayed to them. The AFL-CIO became a vigorous foe of guideposts and pointed to a number of specific defects that it perceived in the standards as they were then devised.[4] Business leaders also showed little sympathy for guideposts. Although some reaction against the guideposts by business and labor is probably inevitable, this could be held to a minimum by having both parties in at the planning stage.

The second method for ensuring that guideposts will have their desired effect of aiding in the fight against inflation is to provide firms with an economic incentive to resist costly wage settlements. This would be necessary, it should be pointed out, only in industries where significant market power exists, since the forces of competition should ensure relative price stability elsewhere.

In concentrated industries, however, there is considerable merit in the suggestion that has recently been advanced that the corporate income tax be used as a vehicle for ensuring that firms keep labor contracts within productivity guidelines. Wage settlements in excess of national productivity would subject the firm to additional taxes.[5] This appears to be a promising method of providing the guideposts with some teeth. Administration of the plan by the Internal Revenue Service need not be cumbersome, and such a plan also should be politically palatable. In any event, some such method of penalizing wage settlements in excess of productivity are worth careful consideration as a means of inhibiting cost-push inflation.

If such a policy is to be implemented, it is important that the standards be realistic and flexible. Inflation would have to be brought under control over a period of years, and the allowable rise in prices could be set rather high at first and reduced in each succeeding year. Each year the tripartite board would announce the allowable standards for the following year. This initially would mean substantial inflation, but still less than would occur in the absence of such a policy. Slow but steady progress would be the objective. Such a policy, if announced in advance, would have the effect of gradually reducing wage demands by unions. This is so because the primary wage goal of unions is to increase real wages, and the prospect of diminishing rates of inflation therefore would put less of a premium on high money wage settlements.

Flexibility for this plan is important in another respect. It is essential that exceptions to the guideposts that are in effect be made in certain circumstances without the suggested penalty. Where bona fide shortages exist, for example, and higher prices are considered essential to a greater long-run supply, deviations from the suggested guideposts would be reasonable. Such exceptions would apply only after careful study by appropriate government officials.

Longer Term Measures

There also exist a number of steps, long urged by economists, which would aid in the attainment of more stable prices over the long run. Although it is doubtful that such measures will be adopted in the future irrespective of their value, it nevertheless is worthwhile to mention a few of the most important. These would include:

1. More vigorous use of antitrust laws to reduce monopoly power.

2. Reduction of tariffs and other barriers to international trade.

3. Efforts to raise output. Greater investment in scientific and technological research would help, as would efforts to raise savings, stimulate investment, and increase the rate of economic growth.

4. Continuing efforts to educate the public on the need for moderation in wage and price decisions.

Conclusion

There currently is a pressing need for a policy which will keep inflation within reasonable bounds (2% to 3% per annum) without resorting to rigid controls. The wage-price guideposts, jointly determined and coupled with some device to give the guideposts some force, qualify well for this task. At the same time, fiscal and monetary restraint and an ambitious effort to make some progress toward some of the longer term objectives mentioned here would aid significantly in achieving price stability.

There is no question that a movement back to reasonably stable prices will take time. It appears doubtful that completely stable prices can be achieved in the foreseeable future. Progress is possible, however, by flexible guideposts which could allow for successively lower annual rates of price increases and penalties for exceeding these standards. Our recent experience with direct controls suggests that they have been largely ineffective in reducing inflation, but they have encouraged shortages. The proposal suggested here is one that could be implemented with a minimum of interference in the free market.

1. Gardner Ackley, "An Incomes Policy for the 1970's," *Review of Economics and Statistics*, August 1972, p. 220.

2. See, for example, George S. Perry, "Wages and the Guideposts," *American Economic Review*, September 1967.

3. Ackley, "An Incomes Policy for the 1970's," p. 221.

4. Report of the Economic Policy Committee to the AFL-CIO Executive Council on *The Wage Guidelines* (February 26, 1966, Bal Harbour, Florida).

5. Henry C. Wallich and Sidney Weintraub, "A Tax-Based Incomes Policy," *Journal of Economic Issues*, June 1972.

Full Employment: The Inflation Myth

by Ray Marshall

It is clear from the experiences since Congress first passed the employment act of 1946 that traditional monetary-fiscal policies and market forces alone cannot produce the full employment and balanced growth envisioned in the Humphrey-Hawkins bill.

Traditional monetary-fiscal policies are important but they alone clearly will not produce full employment without intolerable levels of inflation because labor market segmentation is such that some markets will be very tight while there is substantial unemployment in others. For example, increasing the money supply in order to reduce unemployment might generate inflation in tight medical or professional labor markets while having very little effect on unemployment in rural areas and central cities or among teenagers. Such problem areas require concentrated selective efforts to combat unemployment directly.

Selective programs have to complement general economic policies in order to achieve reasonable price stability and full employment. Critics of Humphrey-Hawkins tend to minimize the importance of these

RAY MARSHALL is a professor of economics at the University of Texas at Austin and president of the National Rural Center. This article is excerpted from his testimony to the Joint Economic Committee of Congress.

selective policies for two reasons: (1) They think tight labor markets alone will dissolve most structural problems and, (2) The manpower or specific labor market programs of the 1960s are presumed to have been ineffective.

Tight labor markets during World War II and in the South during the 1950s did not by themselves erode discrimination against women and minorities—selective programs, including antidiscrimination laws, also were required.

Similarly, public employment is the cheapest—and therefore the least inflationary—way to reduce unemployment. For example, the Congressional Budget Office estimates the annual net cost of creating a job through a public employment to be much less than the cost per job of a tax cut. The CBO concludes: ". . . a 3 percent adult unemployment target does not seem unrealistic if employment programs are effective in dealing with the special factors contributing to high employment for certain groups and are not limited to across-the-board measures or programs that simply create jobs without increasing employment stability or job attachment."

Although it is fashionable to criticize the manpower programs of the 1960s, the overwhelming weight of evidence supports the conclusion that these programs

Ray Marshall, "Full Employment—The Inflation Myth." *The American Federationist,* August 1976, pp. 6–10. Reprinted with permission.

made significant improvements in labor markets and were, on balance, cost effective for the government and the participants.

The manpower programs of the 1960s were not as effective as they might have been because they were experimental, many of them were really income maintenance programs, and the budgetary support for these programs was small relative to the need and relative to the size of monetary-fiscal policies.

The experiences of the 1960s, while generally favorable, therefore provide little guidance to what could happen if an effective array of selective public and private programs could be developed. Clearly, however, these specific policies, including public employment, must be a necessary part of any program to achieve full employment without high levels of inflation.

There is a mistaken belief that full employment would necessarily lead to intolerable levels of inflation. Most such estimates are based on the relations of gross national product, prices and employment of the 1960s and 1970s, which would not necessarily be the relationship if the Humphrey-Hawkins bill were passed and if the bill assumed a necessary inverse relationship between inflation and unemployment. In particular:

• There seems to be general agreement that public employment (which includes public service employment, public works by private profit and non-profit contractors and supported work) is by far the cheapest way to reduce unemployment. Therefore the GNP would not have to grow as much as would be required to produce full employment by market forces or monetary-fiscal policies alone.

• Full employment would reduce many transfer payments in programs like unemployment compensation, which are inflationary because they constitute income payments with no corresponding output of goods and services. Full employment also would reduce the inflationary impact of federal deficits created because of unemployment.

• A full employment economy could erode many of the causes of inefficiency the present system yields. Many industries have adapted to very inefficient and wasteful employment systems because they are able to shift the costs of inefficiency to workers in the form of low wages and unemployment. These inefficient systems will persist so long as there is mass unemployment in low-wage labor markets.

Critics of Humphrey-Hawkins often display a strange theory of inflation. They believe that all expenditures of public money necessarily cause inflation. Inflation reflects the relationship between money and goods. It may be moderated in a negative way by restricting the supply of money and goods in the hope that growth in the output of goods and services will fall by less than the growth in the money supply, causing the rate of inflation to decline.

This is a negative approach and it is very costly in terms of lost output to the nation, rising unemployment and higher welfare costs, and human misery for those who are unemployed.

A more positive approach is to attack unemployment and inflation simultaneously. The best attack on inflation is to increase output and improve productivity and efficiency through fully utilizing the nation's productive potential. If we increase the output of goods and services as fast as we increase the money supply, the result will not be inflationary.

Critics of this positive approach think spending money is always inflationary, and that high levels of unemployment are necessary in order to check inflation. They forget that the effect on prices depends on what you get for your money, and all of the evidence suggests that the cost of achieving full employment by the combination of the general and selective procedures outlined in the Humphrey-Hawkins bill would be a very good deal.

Because of unemployment in casual occupations, many employers have been able to perpetuate labor surpluses and wage payment systems which provide little incentive for managerial efficiency. There is no need to introduce efficient technology or to otherwise develop efficient labor utilization systems where there is a surplus of low-wage labor augmented by a steady flow of legal and illegal immigrants and millions of people displaced by technological changes in agriculture. Humphrey-Hawkins could provide alternatives for these workers and offer incentives for private employers to rationalize their labor markets in order to provide more regular and better jobs without increasing labor costs.

If workers had some assurance of continued full employment, many impediments to improved efficiency and productivity would be overcome. Full employment would facilitate the continued reduction in the waste caused by discrimination. Experience shows tight labor markets to be effective forces in overcoming resistance to the employment of women and minorities as well as in providing employers with incentives to hire them.

Full employment also would reduce some of the resistance to increased productivity and efficiency caused by a prevailing "depression mentality." If workers had greater assurance of job security, they could do a great deal to increase efficiency and productivity. Moreover, greater continuity of employment in many casual occupations, like agriculture and construction, is a substitute for higher wage rates. In other words, inflationary wage pressures would be moderated by greater income from more work at existing wage rates.

Surprisingly, much of the criticism of the Humphrey-Hawkins bill has been the argument that the payment of prevailing wages on public employment programs would be inflationary because public programs would bid unskilled and semi-skilled workers away from private employers, causing the wages of the private sector employees to be raised. This outcome is neither predetermined nor very likely for the following reasons:

• Raising the wages of marginal workers is not a necessary outcome of the Humphrey-Hawkins bill, but even if it were, there is no assurance that the results would be either undesirable or inflationary. In addition to the effect noted earlier of encouraging employers to do more to rationalize secondary labor markets, improve jobs, increase efficiency, and generate productivity gains without increasing labor costs, the Humphrey-Hawkins bill would provide the stimulus to create better as well as more jobs. There can be no more effective way of overcoming some of the nation's most important social and economic problems than improving the quality and quantity of jobs available to the poor and near poor.

• The assumption that low-income workers would necessarily be paid more than they were "worth" if they worked on public jobs is invalid. If prevailing wages are paid, wages and productivity would increase at the same time, causing no increase in inflationary pressure.

Undoubtedly, the achievement of full employment would not be easy and no one knows how hard it would be to achieve the target established in Humphrey-Hawkins.

Curiously, however, some critics emphasize the "fuzzy" definitions in the bill, but then calculate precise number of jobs needed to achieve that fuzzy goal. As pointed out earlier, we cannot use past parameters to estimate the costs of this bill or its impact because that bill would create many new relationships and much would depend on the mix of policies used to promote full employment.

This mix could include:

• Stimulating the private sector, which could be done by monetary or fiscal policies, which must remain the basic tools of economic policy. However, monetary-fiscal policies alone are not likely to produce full employment without intolerable levels of inflation.

• Measures to promote the development of lagging regions and areas. The bill should give more specific attention to rural development, but a balanced growth policy including a rural-urban balance policy is compatible with the provisions of Humphrey-Hawkins. Since many productive jobs could be created in rural areas with relatively low cost by private profit and non-profit organizations, a rural development strategy could do much to solve the employment problems of rural and urban places. One of the most important requirements for development in depressed areas is a system to make credit available to people who are unable to obtain credit from existing sources.

• Public employment could take a variety of forms, making it difficult to calculate costs unless the specific forms were explicitly mentioned.

Costs in a public service employment program (to put workers on government payrolls at prevailing government rates) would cost more than some programs, less than others. For instance, a public service employment program would cost more than Operation Mainstream, where older workers, mainly in rural areas, were employed on useful projects for public and non-profit organizations. That program, in turn, has a different cost than a supported work program for youths. The public employment provisions of Humphrey-Hawkins are sufficiently flexible to permit a wide range of alternatives.

The critics of the legislation often seize upon a particular alternative which may or may not be the one adopted. It is often assumed, for example, that public employment means only public service or government employment. Experience shows this kind of program to have the advantage of supporting local governments, but it does very little to put the disadvantaged to work or to guarantee that governments hire people who could not have been hired in the absence of the programs. Privately operated public works or supported work programs can do more to put the disadvantaged or the unemployed to work faster.

As was noted, attention should be given to manpower and other specific policies to improve the operation of labor markets. These specific policies will make it possible for more general economic policies to reduce unemployment with less inflationary impact.

Careful attention should be given to wage and price policies. It is unrealistic to assume that wage and price controls can be effective for very long in an economy characterized by relatively free market forces and collective bargaining. It is easy to specify general criteria for wage and price controls but impossible to either implement them or to devise a formula to set wages and prices that will not cause serious labor or product market maladjustments.

General wage and price controls are difficult to apply because they must operate against powerful market forces. There are, however, conditions under which wage and price controls might be successful for short periods of time. A wage-price freeze can temporarily halt price increases and perhaps break inflationary psychologies. But, because of inherent inequities and the dynamic nature of the economy, the longer a freeze stays in force the more untenable it becomes.

If there were an effective controls mechanism on the price side—which there was not in the nation's recent experience with controls—then an effort on wages might succeed if geared to the realities of each industry and set up as an adjunct of collective bargaining. Because they are designed to provide jobs, overcome bottlenecks and improve the operation of labor markets, manpower and other specific labor market policies have the advantage of working with basic labor market forces rather than against them as is the case with wage and price controls.

The wage policies for the jobs guaranteed by Humphrey-Hawkins also are very important and will be difficult to administer.

But some of the critics, in addition to revealing misunderstanding of labor market procedures and presuming a knowledge of the program mix that they don't have, also ignore the safeguards built into the Humphrey-Hawkins bill.

There is no evidence that workers would leave many good private sector jobs where they have seniority and other benefits in order to acquire public employment jobs. A worker cannot ordinarily voluntarily quit a private job and draw unemployment insurance—he must lose his job for reasons beyond his control. That same condition could be imposed for public jobs under Humphrey-Hawkins.

The prevailing rates mentioned in the full employ-

nothing wrong with allowing the best qualified unemployed workers to fill those jobs—there's nothing in the bill that requires jobs to be provided regardless of qualifications.

The assumption that workers would leave private sector jobs to get public jobs, and that the size of the government's jobs program would thus grow rapidly, is a strange theory of labor market behavior. Besides the bill contains safeguards to prevent this from happening.

Moreover, the argument assumes that employers of low-wage workers would not adjust their wages and employment conditions in order to retain their workers. But research and demonstration work in agricultural and other low-wage labor markets indicates that if they are forced to do so, employers can do much to rationalize labor markets. In the absence of an outside stimulus (like upward pressure on wages by governments or unions) where there are surplus labor supplies, these employers have little incentive to use labor efficiently. Humphrey-Hawkins, by giving workers options, could force employers to improve employment systems without significantly increasing labor costs. It is in the national interest to provide better jobs for low-income people who are willing and able to work. We also must not use public programs to force people into menial low-wage jobs much below their qualifications.

In short, the critics have devised an unlikely scenario for the impact of Humphrey-Hawkins. Others can be developed which are more compatible with the intent of the bill and which would not be as inflationary. Again, however, we cannot use past parameters to estimate the impact of the Humphrey-Hawkins bill.

Finally, we must consider the alternatives to paying decent wages for useful work. Would it be better to have these workers continue to be unemployed and drawing extended unemployment insurance, or on welfare, or continuing to work in lousy, dead-end, low-wage jobs?

It would seem much better public policy and much less inflationary to put these workers to work doing useful things in keeping with their abilities and motivations. In calculating the costs of a full employment program we must take a systems approach which looks at the net impacts and not just at the wage costs.

Some critics argue that the Humphrey-Hawkins target of 3 percent unemployment for adults within four years is unrealistic because it would require sustained growth rates greater than we have ever been able to achieve. This criticism also seems to me to be unwarranted for the following reasons:

—We do not know what growth rate in the GNP would be required to achieve this target because estimates based on the GNP assume most of the job creation to be in the private sector, as was the case in the past. These GNP estimates would not apply to a public employment strategy. Moreover, the cost of creating the necessary jobs would depend on the program mix.

—It would undoubtedly be very difficult to achieve

ment bill need not be union wage rates, but might be jobs at or near the minimum wage. They also need not be regular government jobs, because, as noted earlier, the bill allows for several other possibilities. Moreover, there is no convincing evidence that public jobs have higher wage rates than similar private jobs—as mentioned, the contrary is more likely to be the case. And regardless, making wage comparisons between public and private jobs is a hazardous undertaking, because job content is so rarely the same.

Nor is there any reason, given the flexibility provided in the Humphrey-Hawkins bill, why the total benefit package on the public jobs should not be sufficiently lower than comparable private jobs to encourage workers to leave public for private jobs when jobs in the private sector became available. One way to encourage this would be the trigger mechanism contemplated in the bill. Another way would be to discourage public service employment in favor of various forms of more temporary public works projects—ranging all the way from regular construction to maintenance, light construction and environmental controls. These programs are easily phased out as unemployment declines.

Humphrey-Hawkins also contains major safeguards against the kinds of abuses contemplated by some critics. The Secretary of Labor is required to establish a program to ascertain qualifications of workers and would therefore be able to match workers and jobs. In public works programs, private employers—profit or non-profit—would do this automatically. This procedure could prevent workers from upgrading themselves very much unless they had the qualifications for the public employment jobs.

An example sometimes cited, that janitors, porters and cleaners could work as construction laborers, is not valid because construction laborers are fairly skilled and their jobs cannot be filled by people without training or experience. However, if the workers can do the work and the jobs are available, there's

the 3 percent target, but this does not mean we should not try. It is true, as some argue, that public policy currently suffers from the exaggerated promises of past rhetoric. The solution is not to avoid promise, but to mobilize to make those promises a reality.

Achieving the goal will, in addition to monetary-fiscal and specific labor market policies, require many other policies, including the following, all of which seem practical objectives:

• Stopping the flow of illegal aliens into the country and relating the flow of legal aliens more to labor market needs. Although there is no way to knowing for sure, illegal aliens probably accounted for at least 10 percent of the growth in the labor market during the 1960s. The labor certification process should be coordinated with realistic efforts to attract native workers.

• Strengthened approaches to the reduction of discrimination.

• Rationalize labor markets to reduce waste and inefficiency.

• A development strategy for rural areas and central cities.

• The perfection of a public employment program including public service employment, public works and supported work.

The goal of reducing unemployment to what is now called "frictional" unemployment is likely to be difficult to achieve, but desirable. Any calculation of the costs of achieving this objective must deduct the material and human costs of not doing anything.

In the final analysis, it will be better public policy to pay people to do constructive work than to support them through income maintenance programs to do nothing. We must not only strive for more jobs, but better ones as well.

WHY RECOVERING ECONOMIES DON'T CREATE ENOUGH NEW JOBS

A radical change in political economics:
Conventional fiscal stimulation doesn't work

Despite encouraging news about the strength of the U. S. economic recovery, one critical problem stubbornly persists. Even with recovery, unemployment will stick at a very high level: at least 5% through 1980. In Europe, too, economists and politicians anticipate that unemployment rates will not drop back to the rates of the early 1970s again in this decade. In the Western world, something has changed radically in political economics. Economists and politicians now agree that by themselves the traditional modes of stimulating economies by government spending or increasing the money supply will not end high unemployment. These conventional policies, used to excess, will only create additional inflation in economies that have suffered far too much inflation for years.

The fear is that the high unemployment rates in so many countries will trigger severe political upheavals. Communists are already close to participating in the governments of Italy and Portugal. France's government has been weakened in the past 12 months because of its inability to improve the economic picture in the face of 4.8% unemployment. In Great Britain, the Labor Party has had to aban-

don some of its cherished goals to try to get the economy back on track, and unemployment has hit levels unheard of since the Depression.

In the U. S., even if economic conditions continue to improve in line with the more optimistic forecasts, the unemployment rate will still be above 7% on election day in November. Even more worrisome is that trimming two more percentage points off that level by 1980 will require the creation of 12 million new jobs, more than have ever been generated so quickly in peacetime.

Doing less, many experts in political economy as well as politicians fear, would be not only economically costly but also politically and socially dangerous. "I'm concerned about the young people, especially the blacks," says manpower expert Lloyd Ulman of the University of California. "The less they squawk now, the more of a problem we are storing up for the future." Adds William A. Niskanen Jr., chief economist for Ford Motor Co.: "Unemployment insurance and welfare are two reasons why there isn't blood in the streets with today's unemployment rates."

What makes unemployment more in-

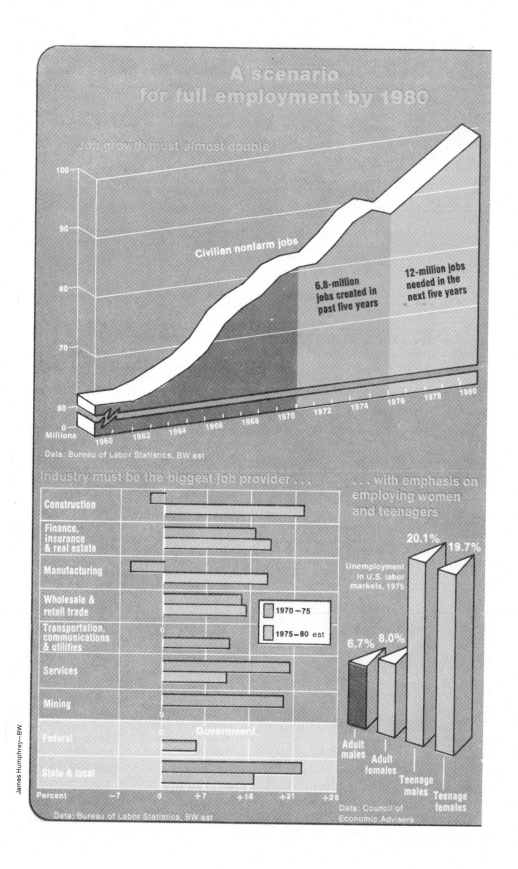

A scenario
for full employment by 1980

Job growth must almost double

Civilian nonfarm jobs

6.8-million jobs created in past five years

12-million jobs needed in the next five years

Millions
1960 1962 1964 1966 1968 1970 1972 1974 1976 1978 1980

Data: Bureau of Labor Statistics, BW est

Industry must be the biggest job provider . . .

Construction
Finance, insurance & real estate
Manufacturing
Wholesale & retail trade
Transportation, communications & utilities
Services
Mining

1970—75
1975—80 est

Government
Federal
State & local

Percent   −7   0   +7   +14   +21   +28

Data: Bureau of Labor Statistics, BW est

. . . with emphasis on employing women and teenagers

Unemployment in U.S. labor markets, 1975

20.1%   19.7%

6.7%   8.0%

Adult males   Adult females   Teenage males   Teenage females

Data: Council of Economic Advisers

James Humphrey—BW

409

tractable than ever is its structure, with the heaviest concentration of joblessness among teen-agers, minorities such as blacks and Hispanics, and older workers who have been displaced by technology or foreign competition. Among teen-agers, the unemployment rate is 19.2%; among blacks, 13.7%; among black teen-agers, a staggering 35.2%. But the outlook for a 57-year-old man laid off by W. T. Grant, a shoe manufacturer, or a specialty steel maker, is equally bleak.

Two views of government

Sometimes the mere identification of a problem points the way to its solution. But this is distinctly not the case with employment, for there are many difficulties standing in the way of a policy that could come to grips with the problem, at least in the U. S.

The greatest obstacle is deep public ambivalence toward the role of government in the labor markets. Polls consistently show that the public says that it wants less government involvement in the economy. But the polls also indicate that an overwhelming majority of the population believes that the government should guarantee jobs for all who want to work.

This confusion has fostered a deepening political split that prevents the formation of a consensus on how to deal with unemployment. The Republican approach has been to play on the public's dislike of big government. The Democrats talk of the need for an active manpower policy to raise employment, implying more government. The current election campaign has polarized these differences, as campaigns always do.

This divided opinion has created an economic situation that is eerily reminiscent of some of Karl Marx's predictions. A fundamental tenet of Marxist thinking is that advanced capitalism could not work without the existence of "an industrial reserve army of the unemployed." The U. S. response to unemployment has created such an army; Washington has dealt with joblessness mainly by extending unemployment compensation at levels that keep people from starving and rioting. But almost no one would disagree that the dole is an unsatisfactory way of handling unemployment.

Taken at their word, neither President Ford nor the Democrats believe in making the dole permanent. Unemployment insurance alone cost the nation $18 billion in fiscal 1976, and that expenditure neither creates jobs nor improves the quality of the work force. But politicians will have to take further action by this fall, since an estimated 2 million unemployed are expected to exhaust their benefits this year.

Ford contends that the way to generate enough jobs is to rely on the private sector and to continue to pursue a policy of gradual economic growth. The cornerstone of that policy, which has widespread support among businessmen and conservative economists, is to free funds for capital investment by significantly reducing the size of government. Ford proposes to further encourage investment by cutting government regulations and providing tax incentives to business.

The liberal approach

Although they agree that the private sector must provide the bulk of the jobs, the Democrats and liberal economists argue that Ford's policies work too slowly, if they work at all. By the Administration's own calculations, the economy must grow at 6% a year for the next five years in order to produce enough jobs—more than 2 million a year—to absorb new entrants to the labor force and reemploy those still jobless as a result of the recession. The economy has never grown that fast for so long, and liberal economists think such expansion is virtually impossible to achieve with the Administration's minimalist fiscal policy.

Most liberals and Democratic Presidential candidates maintain that more stimulus is needed now. But their dilemma is that high rates of growth are very risky when inflation is still running at 6% and is expected to hover around 5% for the rest of the decade. Perhaps the most significant change in economic thinking over the past 10 years is the liberals' recognition that conventional monetary and fiscal policies are insufficient to achieve full employment (unofficially defined as 4% unemployment) without serious inflationary consequences.

"The Administration is cautious about stimulating the economy, but the liberals are plenty cautious too," says the University of California's Ulman. "More important, the liberals now know that the speed of the recovery affects inflation."

The liberals are groping for solutions. They are examining ways to expand and improve the the manpower programs of the 1960s. And they are exploring new approaches, such as the comprehensive training and placement policies used in many European nations, an enlarged role for government planning, and an expanded national computer job bank to facilitate the relocation of workers.

A blueprint of the new policy direction for the Democrats may be the just-introduced revision of the controversial Humphrey-Hawkins full-employment bill, which would replace the Employment Act of 1946. The new bill, worked out in conjunction with liberal economists and labor leaders, sets a full-employment target of 3% unemployment and commits the Administration, Congress, and the Federal Reserve Board to design policies to hit annual interim unemployment goals. Where macroeconomic policies fall short, they would be augmented with countercyclical aid to state and local governments and manpower programs for hard-hit industries and regions, with special attention to young people.

"This bill would formally add manpower programs to the mix of conventional economic policies," says Jerry Jazinowski, a staff economist on the Joint Economic Committee who helped draft the bill. In this respect, the U. S. is only now beginning to think about job-creating measures that have long been staples of economic policy in other industrialized countries. Generally, Europe has been far more innovative at this than has the U. S.

But the crucial difference is that the Europeans and Japanese rely far more heavily on central government planning than has ever been considered in the U. S. The Humphrey-Hawkins bill would take a large step in that direction. Even if it does not become the touchstone for the Democrats—it is unlikely to pass this year—the liberals are clearly pushing for far more direct government intervention in the labor markets, a policy shift resisted by Republicans and conservative economists.

The issue will not be resolved fully in this year's election, but the future direction of economic policy is emerging. Neither the Democratic Congress nor the Administration is likely to allow 2 million people to exhaust their benefits. But the Democrats will continue to push for additional manpower policies, and even if President Ford wins, they will keep control of Congress, and some new programs will be passed or old ones expanded.

In the final analysis, a much larger government role in the labor markets seems inevitable. In particular, the old approaches cannot deal with the growing problem of meeting young people's and women's desire to work.

The roots of the problem

Today's high unemployment rates and tomorrow's employment problems are rooted in a generation of demographic and social changes that have swelled the number of teen-agers and women in the labor force and have greatly heightened the economic expectations of disadvantaged minorities. These changes have caused "structural problems," which means that workers do not fit into the labor market because of a lack of skills or discrimination. As economist Robert J. Gordon of Northwestern University puts it: "Our economy suffers from a serious mismatch between available jobs and available workers."

The structural problems of the labor market, which go far beyond the unemployment caused by the recession, are best illustrated by the relatively high rates of unemployment for women and teen-agers (chart, page 116) as well as for blacks. In the past 15 years, because of the postwar baby boom, the number of teen-agers in the labor force has increased from 4.8 million to 8.8 million. Even were this number smaller, it would still be difficult to absorb these teen-agers into the work force; they lack skills, and employers are unwilling to incur the cost of training them since they change jobs frequently.

Responding to changing views of their role in society and inflationary pressures on family budgets, women have entered the labor force in even greater numbers than have teen-agers. Since 1960 the percentage of women seeking work has increased from 37.8% to 46.4%, while that of men has declined from 84% to 78.5%. The greatest uncertainty clouding the employment picture is the extent to which this trend will continue. "There have been consistent underestimates of women's desire to work, and our estimates of job needs may be too low," says Eli

Ginzberg, chairman of the National Commission on Manpower Policy.

Growing numbers are the biggest problem presented by teen-agers and women. But disadvantaged minorities, especially the blacks and the Spanish speaking, have chronically been a "bad fit" in the labor market because of discrimination, inadequate education, and lack of skills.

The persistence of high unemployment for blacks, women, and teen-agers even in the best of times is the main reason that liberals now accept the inadequacy of traditional policies. As the over-all jobless rate declines, monetary and fiscal policies have less and less impact on structural unemployment. But inflationary bottlenecks develop as a result of shortages of key labor skills. In the 1960s liberal economists believed that the point at which such bottlenecks emerged, causing inflation to accelerate, was 4%. By 1970 many thought it was 5%, and now some think it may even be 6%.

The solutions

"If we use only aggregate demand measures, we may be forced to take 5.5% to 6% unemployment, says economist Charles Holt of the Urban Institute. Most liberals are less pessimistic, but most are paying more attention to using manpower programs—which can be targeted at specific unemployment problems—as the means of getting unemployment close to the old full-employment goal of 4%.

Liberals regard the present programs, most of which come under the Comprehensive Employment & Training Act of 1973 (CETA), as inadequate. They maintain that funding is too low and, more important, that decentralized control of the program prohibits efficient use of the money. "The philosophy of the Office of Management & Budget is to put the money on a stump and run," says Orley C. Ashenfelter, Princeton economist and former director of the Labor Dept.'s Office of Manpower Policy Evaluation & Research. "There is a very large question whether the state and local governments direct all the funds into the designated programs."

The main thrust of U.S. manpower policy since the 1960s has been to upgrade the employability of youths by teaching them jobs skills through class-room and on-the-job training and, to a limited extent, through public or subsidized private employment. Supporters of manpower policy argue that this is the best way to make a dent in the teen-age unemployment problem as well as to insure the future quality of the work force.

"Teen-agers are growing up into the 20 to 24 age group and beyond without adequate work experience," says Robert A. Gordon, University of California professor and former president of the American Economic Assn. Gordon maintains that the jobless rate of workers aged 25 to 34 began to rise in the late 1960s and early 1970s while unemployment among older workers remained very low. "This reflects the inability of younger workers to get jobs that provide the opportunity to move up the skill ladder, and it could have a significant impact on the long-term inflation outlook," he warns.

Gordon argues that much more has to be done to get business involved in training younger workers. "The business community and high schools should cooperate and provide course credits for on-the-job experience," he says. He also believes that programs such as those of the National Alliance of Businessmen are "the kind of effort that business should be making."

The NAB, set up in late 1960s as a response to the riots, sent top executives into the ghettos to recruit. But the organization has become much less active in recent years. "Business should be subsidizing this program now, but it is costly, and it is difficult to hire minority workers when you are laying off your regular employees," says Gordon. "A more serious problem is that business in general doesn't seem to perceive a problem, and too many simply don't give a damn."

Gordon has strong words for the unions, too. "Unions could do a lot more," he says. "They should loosen up on the seniority system and push employers to restructure jobs to open the lower rungs on the job ladder."

The unions are of two minds. They agree that youth unemployment is the most serious long-term labor market problem, but they see their primary responsibility as protecting the jobs of their members. But they do favor providing work experience for youths without disrupting the labor markets.

"We have to provide the opportunity

for kids to learn how to work," says I. W. Abel, United Steelworkers president and a one-time mill hand. "First you have to teach people how to get up in the morning. You have to get them used to the idea you're going to come home sore after a hard day's work."

Abel and other union leaders favor a revival of the Depression-era Civilian Conservation Corps, which would provide this basic training while employing youth in constructive work. "There were minuses to programs like the CCC, but there is the need," says Nathaniel Goldfinger, director of research for the AFL-CIO. "The CCC got the kids off the urban streets, and Senator Humphrey says we are 15 years behind on reforestation of the country."

The first step

Manpower policy enthusiasts believe that training is only the first step. "What we need is an across-the-board strategy that integrates manpower training and subsidized jobs in the private and public sectors with income-maintenance programs for the poor," says Holt of the Urban Institute. Currently the federal government is supporting 330,000 state and local government employees through CETA at a cost of $2.7 billion. This program aims at putting unemployed people to work while helping local jurisdictions during periods of financial distress.

At present, public service employment exists at the whim of Congress and the Administration. Most liberals would like to make it permanent and automatic: Funds would be released when unemployment rates reach a trigger level and cut back when the jobless rate falls. "We need a two-tier program," says Gordon of the University of California. "One program should be permanent to deal with structural unemployment, and the other should be countercyclical."

Holt also advocates greatly expanding the U. S. Employment Service (table, p. 120) into a national computerized job-matching system and providing financial aid to help relocate the unemployed. In 1971 he and several colleagues proposed a comprehensive set of such programs that at the time would have cost $14 billion. The price tag is now $18 billion, but Holt emphasizes that this is relatively inexpensive when "the country is spending that much on unemployment compensation."

Another idea that has attracted support on Capitol Hill is employment subsidies to business in the form of either tax credits or direct cash grants. Representative James C. Wright Jr. (D-Tex.) has introduced a bill that would give "incentive grants" of up to $3,500 a year to employers that hire people unemployed for four months or more. The idea is to encourage business to take less productive workers. "It is better to put people to work whose productivity is only 50% than to pay for 100% welfare," says Holt.

Lessons from abroad

What troubles many of those seeking new policy directions is that the government not only does too little, it does it in a piecemeal, uncoordinated fashion. They are looking to Europe—and to Sweden in particular—where integrated manpower programs have been a way of life for decades. Sweden has the world's most comprehensive policy. It provides employment and investment subsidies to business, manpower training and placement subsidies, and regional development assistance as well as public works and public service employment.

What distinguishes Sweden's program is that it is highly centralized and functions as an integral part of national economic planning. "The Swedes have a central authority armed with power, and they have a selection of policy alternatives which enable them to deal with specific problems," says Ulman. He points out that the Swedes will subsidize business to keep people on the job, but they will not provide open-ended support for weak industries, as Britain does. "The Swedes are rather ruthless with weak companies, and they have the retraining and relocation policies to allow them to fail," he says.

The Swedish philosophy is to identify potential problems and to prevent them. "You have to tackle the problem of unemployment before you have unemployment," says Prime Minister Olof Palme. "It's a matter of priorities—you have to decide whether you want to spend money on more gadgets or on improving the quality of life."

Palme says that the first priority is full employment; inflation comes second. The Swedes work to hit an employment target and then adjust policies to deal with inflation if it becomes a problem. They then handle any unemployment resulting from the anti-inflationary measures by attacking trouble spots. In effect, Sweden's economic policy is a bundle of tools that they have used to hold their unemployment rate at a mere 1.6%.

Most other European countries are not faring as well. Although their unemployment rates are well below that of the U.S., the industrialized countries are suffering their first real bout of serious unemployment since the postwar recovery. Roland Tavitian, director of employment policy at the European Community in Brussels, says that until six months ago the governments believed that high unemployment was temporary but that now there is concern that the problem will last until well into the 1980s. "The question is whether these countries can tolerate a long period of high unemployment," he says. "I'm worried. This situation is likely to generate serious social tensions and is threatening the existing social and political balances."

The most widespread tactic for dealing with unemployment is subsidizing industry to maintain payrolls. In France the government is forcing business to carry excess employees. French companies are also receiving subsidies to retrain workers, and the government will give straight grants of up to 20% of plant, equipment, and startup costs to companies that relocate in depressed areas.

In Italy companies are reducing the workweek, and the loss of income is partly made up by government subsidies. The government is also bailing out companies in danger of going under. And, because the political situation is so precarious, unions are often taking matters into their own hands and occupying plants that threaten to close.

In addition to bailing out companies such as Chrysler UK, the British have been gearing up public service programs. The government has increased grants to municipalities or community groups for projects of "local value." And the government extends "temporary employment subsidies" to employers who postpone laying off workers, recruitment subsidies to those who hire school dropouts, and grants to industries for "countercyclical stockbuilding."

Germany's response

Even though the number of unemployed rose to 1.3 million recently, the highest since the early 1950s, Germany has been the slowest to react to the problem. One reason is that German workers get benefits that amount to nearly full pay for one year after being laid off. Because of a growing recognition that the problem may not go away by itself, however, German Economics Minister Hans Friderichs has developed a plan to get the country back to full employment by the early 1980s.

The plan calls for German labor, whose share of national income has increased from 55% to 60% during the late 60s and early 70s, to restrain its wage demands in order to leave more profit to encourage investment and thus more jobs. And it calls for German industry to concentrate more investment on high-technology products in which the country has an edge.

Such proposals are very similar to those of the Ford Administration. It is no coincidence that at a meeting of the Organization for Economic Cooperation & Development (OECD) labor ministers to discuss what could be done about unemployment, Germany and the U.S. agreed that the best course of action was to move slowly. As U.S. Labor Secretary W.J. Usery Jr. put it: "We recognize that stimulation could cause increased instability and endanger chances for a return to sustainable growth, which we believe offers the safest road to full employment."

The Ford Administration opposes not only further monetary and fiscal stimulation but also the specific manpower programs adopted by most European nations. It argues that the programs the U.S. already has are adequate and that any additional efforts would, in the President's words, "do little to create jobs" and would result in "excessive federal spending."

Ford has backed up this view by vetoing every major jobs bill passed by Congress, the latest a $6.2 billion public works bill. And the Administration would like to see existing programs cut back. It has proposed that the public service employment provisions of CETA be phased out next year.

Conservative economists, in and out of the Administration, maintain that such programs are ineffective because they do not create new jobs but merely substitute government jobs for those

414

in the private sector. They also argue that state and local governments use public service employment funds to hire back workers they have just laid off or to hire the best-qualified people rather than the hard-core unemployed. Administration economists claim that each new job added through public service employment costs $90,000. Defenders of the program argue that the so-called substitution effect is small when the economy is weak because state and local governments are under severe budget constraints and, without the aid, would have to cut payrolls.

Public works programs are just as deficient, claim the conservatives, mainly because their impact is felt long after the money is committed. They point out that the accelerated public works program of the early 1960s did not begin to create jobs until the mid-60s, when the aid was no longer needed. In his veto of the public works bill, Ford said that it would create "almost no new jobs in the immediate future" and that its "peak impact" would be in "late 1977 or early 1978."

Supporters of the measure claim that it would avoid the long time lag associated with public works because only projects that could use on-site labor within 90 days would qualify. Furthermore, they say that, given the Administration's own projections of high unemployment for the rest of the decade, the program would still be helpful, even if there were long lags.

One area in which the Administration encounters less opposition is manpower training. It maintains that there is no evidence that the extensive programs of the 1960s actually improved job opportunities for participants. Supporters concede that those programs were so poorly designed that they often trained people for jobs that did not exist. "We haven't looked far enough ahead to see where jobs will be coming from," says the University of California's Gordon, who believes that the answer is to design and administer the programs better.

Although the Administration has many specific objections to each of these programs, it dislikes them primarily because they would mean an expanded federal government role in the private economy. Most businessmen wholeheartedly agree. "The private sector can alleviate unemployment if the government would stop gobbling up the money," says William P. Drake, chairman and president of Pennwalt Corp. "The government should cut back on some programs. If the $6.2 billion from the vetoed make-jobs program were made available to industry, it could create more permanent jobs, and it could do it faster."

The key to expanded employment, businessmen say, is more capital investment. They believe that the government has a role here: to provide tax incentives and reduce or eliminate costly regulation. "If you are not going to have money invested in tools of production, you're not going to provide new jobs," says Bracy D. Smith, vice-president and controller of U. S. Steel Corp. "Training people is not going to provide the jobs."

How businessmen see it

Most businessmen also complain that government regulations of all sorts are as much an obstacle to investment as taxes. William J. De Lancey, president of Republic Steel Corp., notes that his company recently canceled a $350 million capital investment project in Gadsden, Ala., that would have meant more than 1,000 jobs during construction and a 40% increase in the plant's work force, in part because of the cost of government-required environmental controls.

Government employment regulations such as the minimum wage and unemployment insurance also discourage hiring say businessmen. William A. Kistler Jr., executive vice-president of Hughes Tool Co., says, "The minimum wage law was the most damaging piece of legislation ever passed. It has eliminated thousands of jobs at service stations and dry cleaners."

The minimum wage has long been highly controversial. Even many liberals now believe that a two-tier minimum is needed, with a lower rate for teen-agers. Such a provision exists for "student-learners," but stringent requirements and extensive red tape have prevented its broad application. The unions vigorously oppose "subminimum" rates because they fear that cheap teen-age labor would increase the employment of youth at the expense of adult workers.

Some businessmen argue that lowering unemployment benefits and cutting back their duration would boost employment by forcing laid-off workers to seek jobs at available wages. "Unemployed workers are buffered by jobless benefits and welfare," says Ford's Niskanen. "With high benefits, workers tend to stay off the job longer and wait for openings at rates of pay close to their previous wages."

Union-negotiated fringe benefits, together with government-imposed payroll taxes for worker's compensation and social security, are further disincentives to hiring, businessmen say. These factors add to the cost of hiring additional workers and, because overtime does not add to fringe benefit costs, it often is cheaper to work the existing labor force extra hours, even at time-and-half, than to increase employment. Businessmen also complain

The federal government's $7 billion grab bag of employment programs

PROGRAM	WHO BENEFITS	1976 COST
Public service employment	About 330,000 people who would otherwise be unemployed are now working under this program of temporary jobs in state and local government.	$2.7 billion
Manpower training	Young people about to enter the adult labor force can qualify for a set of programs designed to upgrade skills. Approaches include on-the-job training, classroom work, apprenticeship, and rehabilitation. Some programs are earmarked for veterans, former prisoners, migrant workers, and other groups with special problems.	$2.5 billion
Vocational education	About 15 million students this year are expected to participate in programs to train them for specific job skills through regular secondary education and community colleges.	$673 million
U.S. Employment Service	Any job seeker can use federal and state unemployment services to match skills with available jobs. Counseling, testing, and placement are being supplemented with a computerized job bank. The USES expects 13 million placement applications this year.	$492 million
Economic development	Out-of-work people in depressed areas can find work in federally funded public works that provide community facilities as well as jobs.	$448.4 million
Summer youth employment	About 740,000 young people who otherwise could not find summer work will be given nine-week jobs.	$440 million
Relocation and training assistance	Workers who have lost jobs to increased import competition can be retrained and relocated under the Trade Act of 1974. Of 2,300 people the Labor Dept. hoped to relocate this year, only eight were actually relocated.	$3.2 million

Data: Labor Dept., OMB, Congressional Budget Office, Office of Education, Commerce Dept.

that seniority rules often force them to retain unproductive workers.

Even if labor market impediments were removed, many executives are concerned about finding enough qualified people and would like to see more business involvement in manpower training. "We have the jobs and we have the people, but we just can't make a marriage," says Peter B. McKallagat, manager of employment for Gillette Co. He would like to see better communication between business and schools on both the high school and the college level. "Too few students know much about business," he says. "We need stronger working relations with guidance counselors and professors."

And not all businessmen believe that direct government job creation is bad. As John R. Selby, president of Standard Pressed Steel Co., puts it: "Right now, I doubt there is a soul who would say the interstate highway construction jobs weren't worthwhile, and they stimulated more than just the construction industry. I would like to see more programs like that."

Generating jobs

One way or another, however, business believes it can generate the jobs. But how and where is by no means certain. It is indisputable that the service industries, which are highly labor intensive, along with state and local government, have provided by far the largest proportion of new jobs over the past 25 years (table). "The growth of these sectors reflects the fact that the country has become much wealthier," says Ashenfelter of Princeton. "Education, health, and other services are luxury items, but the public wants them and can afford them. I don't buy the argument that the government should do anything special for the private sector. The public should determine whether it wants private goods or public services."

The public demand for these services is reflected in the diminishing role of manufacturing in the economy. Over the past 25 years, employment in manufacturing has grown very slowly, partly because fewer and fewer workers have been needed to produce more and more goods. In the steel industry, for example, employment dropped 15% between 1960 and 1974, while output increased 47%. Although few economists dispute the fact that more investment in manufacturing is essential to the fundamental health of the economy, it is questionable how many jobs will be created.

In support of their proposals to increase capital investment, such as Ford's suggested tax credit for business investment in areas of high unemployment, Administration economists argue that although the initial job creation may be low, expanding and modernizing the productive base will provide the foundation for job growth in the long run. The question raised by the liberals is whether the country can afford to wait. ∎

Recent Developments in
The Theory of Unemployment

By Steven P. Zell

O ver the 40 years since the Great Depression, economists have developed a variety of theories to explain the phenomenon of unemployment. Many of these explanations are products of their time, emerging as the result of major social and economic developments. Yet, all such models have at least one thing in common. They represent attempts by their proponents to provide a theoretical framework within which policy prescriptions can be developed.

This article examines four recent theoretical explanations for the problem of unemployment: the theory of structural unemployment, the job-search, labor-turnover theory, the theory of human capital, and the dual labor market hypothesis. These alternative approaches are examined with particular emphasis on their respective views of the structure and behavior of the labor market, and especially, on the policy prescriptions which follow from these different views.

INADEQUATE DEMAND OR STRUCTURAL UNEMPLOYMENT?

Given the experience of the Great Depression, there has understandably been much interest in diagnosing the causes of unemployment. From a policy standpoint, however, the more important question is why workers who lose their jobs are not quickly reemployed, and why many new entrants or reentrants to the labor force remain without jobs. As noted by Gilpatrick, if reemployment is assured, the reasons for the original unemployment are of little interest. Thus, "the causes blocking reemployment are the proper targets for policy."[1]

One long-standing controversy over the persistence of unemployment developed in the late 1950's and early 1960's between the advocates of inadequate aggregate demand theory and the proponents of the school of structural unemployment. This controversy arose at a time when the national unemployment rate seemed to lose its resiliency. From 1951 through 1957, the unemployment rate exceeded 5 per cent of the labor force only in one year, 1954. Then, after reaching its recession high of 6.8 per cent in 1958, the unemployment rate did not fall below 5 per cent for 7 years.

In 1961, the Joint Economic Committee conducted a series of hearings[2] to try to determine whether structural factors or inadequate demand were responsible for the high unemployment the country had been experiencing since the closing months of 1957. The distinction between these two explanations for the persistence of unemployment appeared crucial

---

1/Eleanor G. Gilpatrick, *Structural Unemployment and Aggregate Demand* (Baltimore: Johns Hopkins Press, 1966), p. 2.
2/U. S. Congress, Joint Economic Committee, Subcommittee on Economic Statistics, *Higher Unemployment Rates, 1957-60: Structural Transformation or Inadequate Demand,* 87th Congress, 1st Session (Washington: U. S. Government Printing Office, 1961).

Steven P. Zell, "Recent Developments in the Theory of Unemployment." *Monthly Review,* Federal Reserve Bank of Kansas City, September–October,1975, pp. 3–10. Reprinted with permission.

from the viewpoint of policy. The advocates of the inadequate demand theory, most notably Walter Heller, then chairman of the Council of Economic Advisors, tended to dismiss the significance of structural unemployment. They argued instead that the persistently high unemployment was due to the incomplete recovery from the 1957-58 recession. The solution therefore lay in more expansionary fiscal policies such as lower taxes and greater government spending.

The structuralists, on the other hand, viewed the unemployment as arising from a change in the composition of labor skill requirements relative to labor skill availability. They argued that this structural mismatch could arise in several ways, regardless of the level of aggregate demand. For example, technology may change, the demand for certain products may disappear, raw materials may be used up in a given geographic area, a factory or industry may change its location, or the proportion of different skill groups in the population may change over time.

As long as the labor force is able to adapt to these changes, said the structuralists, no problem exists. But if people are unwilling or unable to move to a different geographic area where workers with their qualifications are in demand, if their skills have become obsolete, or if their skills are of limited transferability and their numbers in the labor force increase without a concommitant increase in the demand for their services, structural unemployment is the result.[3]

Arguing that a combination of these developments was at the root of the persistently high unemployment, the structuralists claimed that a policy of adapting the unemployed to available job openings would substantially reduce the unemployment rate at the *current* level of national income. Because they believed the problem to be structural in nature, they further claimed that an attempt to reduce the unemployment through increasing aggregate demand would succeed only at the cost of substantial inflation as bottlenecks appeared.[4]

Following extensive debate, the inadequate demand view prevailed in Washington, and the 1964 income tax cut was passed in an attempt to stimulate demand. This provided a test of these two alternative theories which seemed to substantiate the inadequate demand position. In 1965, the unemployment rate fell below 5 per cent and then remained below 4 per cent from 1966 to 1969.[5] Nevertheless, a great deal of interesting work has been done on the concept of structural unemployment, and it remains a potentially useful tool for explaining certain occurrences of unemployment, especially when the economy is functioning much closer to full employment than was the case in the late 1950's and early 1960's.[6]

SOME NEW THEORIES OF UNEMPLOYMENT

Since the structuralist-inadequate demand controversy of the early 1960's, economists have generally agreed about the cause of the increase in unemployment and its persistence during and following a recession. The recessionary falloff in the demand for goods and services leads to a rise in the unemployment rate, while the uncertainty of a recovery, the increased productivity of those already employed, and the knowledge of the availability of a pool of unemployed workers delays rehiring once the economy begins to turn around. Yet even when the economy was functioning near the limits of its capacity, as in the late 1960's, the overall unemployment rate still hovered just below 4 per cent of the labor force, while for some population groups, it was considerably higher.

Observing this phenomenon, several economists attempted to answer what has become a central question in current unemployment

3/Gilpatrick, pp. 4-5. Also Barbara R. Bergmann and David E. Kaun, *Structural Unemployment in the United States,* U. S. Department of Commerce (Washington: U. S. Government Printing Office, 1966), pp. 4-5.

The classic example of workers' unwillingness to move to another geographic area is the case of unemployed coal miners in Appalachia in the 1950's and 1960's. Similarly, railroad firemen represent persons whose skills have become obsolete, while minority teenagers, with skills of limited transferability, have increased their labor supply in excess of the increase in the demand for their services.

4/Richard Perlman, *Labor Theory* (New York: John Wiley and Sons, 1969), p. 167.
5/Besides the tax cut, spending for the Vietnam war greatly stimulated the economy during these years. While the resulting fall in unemployment supports the view that demand had been inadequate, the accompanying climb in the rate of inflation, to a level consistently above 3 per cent since 1966, points to the existence of inflationary bottlenecks which arise when the economy is subjected to too rapid a rate of expansion.
6/Gilpatrick, *Structural Unemployment and Aggregate Demand,* and especially Perlman, *Labor Theory,* ch. 7, present strong evidence of the existence of structural unemployment and argue convincingly that "much of the confusion in evaluating the impact of structural aspects has resulted from illogical or loose definitions of the term . . .".

theory: "Why is the unemployment rate so high at full employment?"[7] Three important theories which deal directly with this question are, respectively, the job-search, labor-turnover theory; the theory of human capital; and the dual labor market hypothesis.

The notion of the level of "full employment unemployment" is not unambiguous. One approach suggests that the level of "full employment unemployment" in the United States is a rate of unemployment (say, 4 to 5 per cent) which, if maintained permanently, is compatible with some steady rate of inflation (say, 3 to 4 per cent per year).[8] When the economy is operating at full employment (as defined in this way), an increase in aggregate demand can lower the unemployment rate further, but only at the expense of higher and higher rates of inflation. The question that the various theories of unemployment must deal with is why the full employment level of unemployment (resulting in a steady and relatively low rate of inflation) is reached at so high a rate of unemployment.

The Job-Search, Labor-Turnover Theory

Of the three theories of unemployment noted, the formal search-turnover model most directly draws a functional relationship between unemployment and inflation.[9] Characterized as "a rigorous theoretical development of the traditional notions of frictional unemployment,"[10] the search-turnover theory views unemployment as the result of a search process, where both employers and workers have limited information about the opportunities in the labor market. According to this explanation, when a worker begins looking for a job, either from a state of nonparticipation or previous employment, it is generally not in his economic interest to take the first available

position. Lacking basic information on the opportunities in the labor market, the worker instead searches for information on the types of jobs, level of wages, and working conditions available to a person of his qualifications. He therefore spends time unemployed while learning about jobs and waiting for better job offers.

Thus, according to the search-turnover theory, unemployment represents a type of investment by workers in obtaining information about the labor market. Unemployment persists because the labor market is inefficient in providing this information and thus fails to quickly match workers and job vacancies. Taking the existing patterns of labor supply and demand as given, the proponents of this theory suggest that unemployment can be substantially reduced through a comprehensive program of manpower policies. In particular, this would include a several-fold expansion in the Federal-State Employment Service to improve the quality and speed of worker-job matches and to reduce turnover; improved vocational counseling and expanded job opportunities for youth to reduce their high turnover and to increase their future productivity; training and job restructuring to reduce skill shortages in certain occupations; support of geographic mobility to reduce pockets of high unemployment while good jobs remain unfilled elsewhere; and elimination of institutional barriers, such as union restrictions on entry and occupational licensing, which increase unemployment by reducing the efficiency of search. All of these policies are based on the belief that an improvement in the inflation-unemployment trade-off can only be achieved by reducing the "frictions" within the labor market and thereby improving its efficiency.[11]

There is much to be said for this view of the labor market with its emphasis on turnover as the principal element in unemployment. Data on the duration of unemployment in the United States indicate clearly that the Keynes-

---

7/This is the title of a study by Robert E. Hall, "Why Is The Unemployment Rate So High At Full Employment?" *Brookings Papers on Economic Activity (No. 3: 1970)*, pp. 369-402.

8/Hall, "Why . . .", p. 370. It has been suggested that because of a changing age-sex composition of the labor force, the trade-off between the rates of unemployment and inflation may actually be worsening over time. See George L. Perry, "Changing Labor Markets and Inflation," *Brookings Papers on Economic Activity (No. 3: 1970)*, pp. 411-41.

9/See, for example, Charles Holt and Associates, "Manpower Proposals for Phase III," *Brookings Papers on Economic Activity (No. 3: 1971)*, pp. 703-22.

10/Robert E. Hall, "Prospects for Shifting the Phillips Curve Through Manpower Policies," *Brookings Papers on Economic Activity (No. 3: 1971)*, p. 660. Frictional unemployment is temporary unemployment which arises due to the time required for finding or changing jobs.

11/Holt, "Manpower Proposals . . .", pp. 712-16. Along the lines of the first of these proposals, the U. S. Manpower Administration has recently initiated a 15-state, Federally funded pilot program designed to encourage both employers and employees to register their manpower needs and skills with their state office of employment security. Missouri is one of the participants in this project. Dale Leibach, "Program To Match Jobs To People," *Kansas City Times*, July 11, 1975.

ian view—that high unemployment is caused by the long-term inability of some fraction of the labor force to find jobs—is invalid in the modern U.S. economy when it is functioning near "full-employment." Instead, the high unemployment rates are the result of frequent, generally short spells of unemployment.[12]

Nevertheless, Hall and other economists find fault with the implicit premise of the search theorists that "every person who finds himself out of work is spending a few weeks between jobs in the normal advancement of his career."[13] This, they feel, incorrectly represents the labor market situation of teenagers, of women, and, in particular, of the unskilled and uneducated segments of the labor force.

> The central problem seems to be that some groups in the labor force have rates of unemployment that are far in excess of the rates that would accord with the hypothesis that the unemployed are making a normal transition from one job to another. Some groups exhibit what seems to be a pathological instability in holding jobs.[14]

Both the theory of human capital and the dual labor market hypothesis represent attempts to explain this seemingly pathological job instability. Yet, because they represent very different viewpoints as to the nature of the problem, their respective analyses and policy prescriptions differ greatly.

The Theory of Human Capital

In many respects, the theory of human capital is simply a logical extension of the underlying assumptions about human behavior on which most of modern economic theory is based. According to these assumptions, economic man is rational man, and all of his decisions are based on deliberate economic calculations.

The theory of human capital extends this concept to the determination of the distribution of income and unemployment. Emphasiz-ing individual choice, this theory concludes that the existing distribution of income and unemployment reflects differences in the levels of education and training, which, in turn, are the direct result of decisions by individuals whether or not to invest in themselves.[15] From this premise it follows that the unemployment problem of disadvantaged workers is a problem on the supply side rather than on the demand side of the labor market. That is, because these workers lack the basic skills necessary to make it worthwhile for employers to hire them at the prevailing level of wages, the amount of labor they are willing to supply at this wage level exceeds the demand for their services by employers, and unemployment results. Thus, the inability of these workers to find and hold stable employment is due to insufficient investment in their own human capital. This theory suggests, then, that the appropriate policy to reduce the unemployment of disadvantaged workers consists of extensive manpower training and skill upgrading.

In many respects, this policy prescription is very similar to that of the structuralists, and both of these schools strongly influenced the format of the great majority of modern Federal manpower programs. These programs began in 1961 with an emphasis on training unemployed workers in regions with high unemployment, but gradually shifted their focus from regional unemployment to unemployment of specific groups of disadvantaged workers.

The theoretical foundation for the earliest of these programs was provided by the theory of structural unemployment. Holding that structural factors and wage rigidities prevented employers from hiring poorly or inappropriately trained workers, this theory suggested that training would raise the productivity of these workers to a level where they could obtain employment. Thus, though the structuralists viewed the unemployment as arising from a structural disequilibrium in the labor market, while the human capital school saw the problem as one of inadequate personal investment by individuals, both agreed the solu-

12/Hall, "Prospects . . .", p. 660. Also see Hall, "Turnover in the Labor Force," *Brookings Papers on Economic Activity* (No. 3: 1972), pp. 709-56 and Steven P. Zell, *A Comparative Study of the Labor Market Characteristics of Return Migrants and Non-Migrants in Puerto Rico* (Commonwealth of Puerto Rico, Puerto Rico Planning Board, Bureau of Social Analysis, 1974), chs. 6 and 8.

13/Hall, "Why . . .", p. 389.
14/*Ibid.*

15/Peter B. Doeringer and Michael J. Piore, "Unemployment and the 'Dual Labor Market'," *The Public Interest*, No. 38, Winter 1975, pp. 69-70.

tion lay in expanded training for unemployed disadvantaged workers.[16]

In the late 1960's, however, it was observed that despite substantial labor market tightening and numerous low-paying job vacancies, disadvantaged workers continued to experience high rates of unemployment. As correctly noted by the search theorists, the problem was clearly not one of a chronic job shortage for disadvantaged workers, but rather a situation of excessively high labor turnover. Nevertheless, the human capital approach still appeared to be relevant if its emphasis was changed from merely qualifying these workers for any job, to qualifying them for good high-paying jobs at which they might stay.[17]

The Dual Labor Market Hypothesis

To another group of economists, however, both the human capital and search-turnover approaches seemed seriously flawed. While these two theories differ in many respects, they share the belief that labor markets are shaped by economic motivation within an essentially competitive framework. "Relative wages are assumed to be flexible, employers are believed willing and able to adjust their employment in response to changes in wages and productivity, and workers are assumed to make training and information investments easily in response to changes in relative wages."[18]

Claiming that these premises were unrealistic and misleading, these economists developed an alternative view of labor market behavior which has come to be known as the dual labor market hypothesis. An outgrowth of both the civil rights and anti-poverty experience of the 1960's, this school views unemployment as "rooted less in individual behav-

ior than in the character of institutions and the social patterns that derive from them."[19] Much more of a "sociological" and "institutional" approach rather than a purely economic approach to the labor market, it deals specifically with trying to explain the seemingly excessive job turnover in what its proponents call "the secondary sector."

As advanced by Peter B. Doeringer, Michael J. Piore, and others,[20] the hypothesis views the economy as being conceptually divisible into a primary and a secondary sector. The *primary sector* is characterized by good jobs, high wages, satisfactory working conditions, employment stability, and prospects for promotion. The *secondary sector,* its antithesis, is characterized by bad jobs, low wages, poor working conditions, layoffs, little chance for advancement, and high turnover. When a primary-sector worker becomes unemployed, he is unemployed in the involuntary, Keynesian sense. He is out of his accustomed place in life, and though he may temporarily accept other, less attractive work, he is essentially waiting to regain his lost position. Unemployment in the secondary sector, however, is not at all like this. Rather than consisting of people waiting to regain a lost position, it is more a process of shuttling from one low-paying position to another.[21]

According to this theory, while white adult males are usually employed in the primary sector, women, teenagers and, in particular, minority groups are generally confined to the secondary sector. But because secondary firms provide little specific on-the-job training, because there is only a limited chance for advancement, and because a worker's current wage is unlikely to differ widely from that available in a great number of other similar jobs, a worker finds little incentive to either stay on the job or to perform particularly well at it. Hence, once a worker is in the secondary sector, the unstable work environment encourages the adoption of certain poor work habits: "casual devotion to job, reporting for work late

---

16/While one policy prescription of the search-turnover approach also stresses job training, this is done as part of a multifaceted program operating on both the demand and supply sides. Thus, in addition to providing job training for workers, it is also proposed that employers be aided in restructuring their jobs to better fit available manpower. The emphasis is not one of upgrading the skills of the disadvantaged, *per se,* but rather one that concentrates on eliminating skill mismatches in sectors of the economy which contribute excessively to inflation. "The unskilled and disadvantaged . . . will benefit disproportionately from the vacuum effects of general upgrading and the overall reduction of unemployment that can occur." Holt, pp. 720-21.
17/Hall, "Prospects . . .", pp. 661, 674-81.
18/Doeringer and Piore, "Unemployment . . .", p. 71.

19/*Ibid*, p. 72.
20/Peter B. Doeringer and Michael J. Piore, *Internal Labor Markets and Manpower Analysis* (New York: Heath, 1971) and Michael J. Piore, "Jobs and Training," in Samuel H. Beer and Richard Barringers (eds.), *The State and the Poor* (Winthrop, 1970).
21/Doeringer and Piore, "Unemployment . . .", pp. 70-71.

422

or not at all on some days, and quitting without good reason often within months of taking the job."[22] It is these habits which most clearly distinguish the primary and secondary sectors and which make movement into the primary sector so much more difficult. In addition, this vicious circle is reinforced as secondary-sector employers are unwilling to invest heavily in the training of a work force which is prone to high turnover, and simultaneously, are less reluctant to fire a worker in whom they have little invested.[23] These factors thus tend to result in entrapment in the secondary sector.

Above and beyond this entrapment, which helps to perpetuate the low productivity of secondary workers, the dualists identify two principal explanations for the continued duality in the face of market forces which would tend to eliminate the wage disparity between the two sectors.

The first of these explanations, restrictive practices, generally represents legalized barriers to the occupational mobility of workers. The prime example of this is occupational licensing by the state, where access to the skilled trades is often controlled by license boards composed of licensed members of the supervised occupations. These persons have strong economic incentive to keep the number of workers permitted to practice their trade at an artificially low level in order to raise the wages of those already licensed. A similar restrictive practice is followed by unions who can maintain an artificial scarcity of good jobs either through a close control of the number of apprentices (as in the craft unions) or through negotiating so high a wage that employers decide to hire fewer workers than are willing to work at that high a wage level.[24]

The second explanation for the continued duality, discrimination, is viewed as operating in two ways, through statistical discrimination, and discrimination pure and simple. Statistical discrimination represents an attempt to simplify the hiring procedure by assuming that certain poor work habits are closely related to personal characteristics such as race, age, or sex. Under this procedure, a number of job candidates may be wrongly rejected even though they are actually qualified. This kind of discrimination, in conjunction with outright discrimination, enlarges the secondary work force while reducing the supply of labor to the primary sector. It thereby gains the economic support both of secondary employers, who now pay a lower wage, and of primary employees, who now receive a higher wage. Furthermore, although primary employers receive no economic gain from outright discrimination, the higher wages they must pay are compensated by the reduced costs of screening job candidates through the use of statistical discrimination.[25]

If this dual labor market schema is correct, then the potential effectiveness of the skill training programs proposed by the human capital school is open to serious question. The dualists have noted that a great part of the training necessary for workers to satisfactorily perform in the primary sector cannot be purchased in schools or elsewhere. Rather, it is only available on the job, and, in order to acquire this training, the worker first must be hired, and then must be accepted by the established group of workers who must teach him what they are doing. In other words, "social acceptability," which is directly related to such characteristics as race, sex, and shared social beliefs, is a key factor in obtaining "primary-sector" skills and a job in the primary sector, and this "social acceptability" cannot be purchased in the usual sense.[26]

Within this framework, the proponents of the dual labor market hypothesis develop a number of policy options which focus on the *institutional* forces they feel underlie the structure and behavior of the labor market. In particular, they propose policies to eliminate discrimination and restrictive practices which have kept people out of the primary sector, and policies to shift the demand for labor, and thus jobs, out of the secondary and into the primary sector.

While their anti-discrimination policy calls for an intensive, but straightforward, use of instruments like civil rights legislation and Fed-

22/Hall, "Prospects...", p. 683.
23/Doeringer and Piore, *Internal Labor Markets*, pp. 165-72. Also, Michael L. Wachter, "Primary and Secondary Labor Markets: A Critique of the Dual Approach," *Brookings Papers on Economic Activity (No. 3: 1974)*, p. 651.
24/Hall, "Prospects...", p. 684.

25/Piore, "Jobs and Training," p. 56.
26/Doeringer and Piore, "Unemployment...", p. 72.

eral contract compliance programs, the dual-ists' proposals for shifting jobs from the secondary to the primary sector are more complicated. Basically, the dualists suggest a two-pronged attack: (1) having the government impose the characteristics of the primary sector on the secondary sector through expanded coverage of (and higher) minimum wages, encouraging unionization, and expanded coverage of social legislation; and (2) adopting a long-run, stable, full-employment policy.

The first set of programs is designed primarily to convert secondary sector jobs into jobs with primary-type characteristics. Some examples of occupations which, to some extent, have already undergone this type of conversion are longshoring, unskilled construction labor, and office cleaning. It is assumed that these policies, which, in effect, are designed to legislate higher wages, would also tend to stabilize employment and develop promotional ladders as the alternative, secondary job structure becomes more costly for employers. Hospital and hotel jobs, for example, might be particularly susceptible to this kind of conversion.[27]

The second type of program, adopting a long-run, stable, full-employment policy, is directed at significantly expanding the primary sector. While acknowledging that the full-employment policy which has been followed in this country has not accomplished this goal, the dualists claim that this has been due to its stop-and-go nature. Employers who believe an expansion to be temporary, say the dualists, are reluctant to admit workers to the primary labor market. Rather than incur the costs of training and providing career benefits, and the problems which might arise from the structural changes involved in this expansion, employers would rather rely on subcontracting and temporary employment from the secondary sector. If, however, employers can be con-struments like civil rights legislation and Fed-full-employment, corresponding to an unemployment rate of between 3 and 4 per cent, they would then be much more likely, claim the dualists, to significantly expand the number of jobs in the primary sector.[28]

CONCLUSION

The dual labor market approach, with its emphasis on the interrelationship between economic, sociological, and institutional variables, has attracted considerable attention in recent years both within and outside the economic profession.[29] Nevertheless, neither it alone nor the alternative theories of human capital and search-turnover, present a complete picture of the problem of unemployment. Due to the complexity of the labor market, all three theories fail to consider important aspects of the problem, and all three necessarily incorporate simplifying assumptions about the structure and behavior of the labor market.

Thus, for example, the dualists, in their policy prescriptions, implicitly assume that secondary workers have all of the necessary human capital needed to succeed in primary-type employment. To the extent that this assumption is incorrect, their proposals to legislate higher wages in the secondary sector and to expand the primary sector could lead to both higher unemployment and inflation unless also coupled with programs to encourage formation of physical and human capital, improve job matches, and discourage turnover. Therefore, rather than choosing between the alternative theories, it is more instructive to view them as an important set of complementary perspectives on the nature of unemployment, which, when taken together, correctly portray the problem of unemployment as a complex interrelationship of supply, demand, informational, and institutional factors.

27/Doeringer and Piore, "Internal . . .", pp. 181-82, and Wachter, pp. 672-73.

28/Doeringer and Piore, "Unemployment . . .", pp. 78-79.
29/See Wachter, p. 638, and Hall, "Prospects . . .", p. 682.

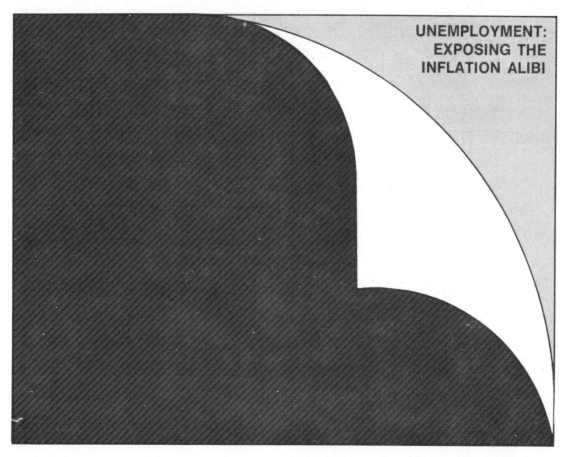

UNEMPLOYMENT: EXPOSING THE INFLATION ALIBI

by Charles C. Killingsworth

In his presidential campaign in 1960, when the average number of unemployed U.S. workers was 3.9 million, John F. Kennedy made unemployment one cf the major issues and he promised to "get this country moving again." After Kennedy won the election, there was a national debate about how best to reduce unemployment; but scarcely anyone questioned the basic proposition that an unemployed total of around 4 million workers was intolerable.

During calendar year 1975, the total number of unemployed averaged 7.7 million workers, or 8.5 percent of the labor force, and Administration spokesmen "projected" unemployment rates well above most postwar recession highs for most of the rest of the 1970s. Yet the public discussion of the unemployment problem was strangely muted, except for complaints by union leaders. The national Administration was reported to believe that no measures to reduce unemployment beyond those already in place were necessary or desirable, and its actions confirmed that report. With a few notable exceptions, most nation-

CHARLES C. KILLINGSWORTH is a professor of economics at Michigan State University.

ally known political figures had little to say and less to propose about unemployment. The general public was reported to believe that the most important national economic problem was not unemployment, but inflation. True to the old American advice to make a virtue of necessity, some people are now arguing that we need high levels of unemployment, at least for a few years, in order to end inflation.

In the euphoria of the mid-1960s, it was fashionable to say that never again could a democratic government permit high levels of unemployment for extended periods. Today, almost any proposal to reduce unemployment invites the accusation that the proposer is "in favor of inflation." Many economists and most political figures avoid that accusation like the plague. The present checkmate is largely a product of the view, which has become widely prevalent in the past decade, that there is a "trade-off" between unemployment and price increases—if you want less of one, you must accept more of the other.

To take a critical look at this proposition as applied to the current situation in the nation and to evaluate our present efforts to deal with unemployment, it is necessary to deal with how much unem-

Charles C. Killingsworth, "Unemployment: Exposing the Inflation Alibi." *The American Federationist,* February 1976, pp. 9–18. Reprinted with permission.

UNEMPLOYMENT IN PERCENT

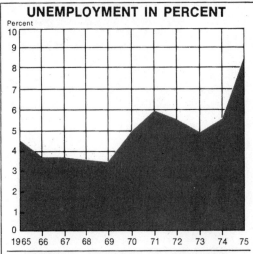

UNEMPLOYMENT IN MILLIONS

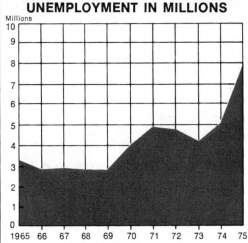

PUBLIC SERVICE JOBS
(1974-75)

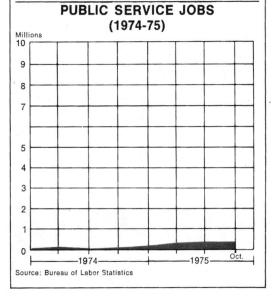

Source: Bureau of Labor Statistics

ployment we have now; the outlook for unemployment; a "trade-off" between unemployment and inflation; what we are doing now about unemployment; and what additional steps are needed to deal with unemployment.

How much unemployment Do we have now?

Employment, as officially reported, peaked in July 1974 at 86.4 million persons, and dropped to 83.9 million in March 1975, a decrease of 2.5 million. From March to December 1975, total employment increased by 1.7 million—apparently justifying the conclusion that the revival of the market economy had restored about 65 percent of the recession-caused job loss. This interpretation of the figures is misleading because it ignores the effect on employment figures of the expansion of two federally financed job creation programs. One of these is Public Service Employment under the Comprehensive Employment and Training Act, and the other is the College Work-Study program. Enrollees in both programs are counted as "employed" in the labor market statistics. But the jobs involved are not "market-generated" in any generally accepted sense of that term. The PSE enrollees are those who have had a substantial period of unemployment and have been unable to find jobs in the normal labor market. The College Work-Study enrollees are students who need to work for pay a few hours per week in order to stay in school (and without the program they would presumably be unemployed or not in the labor force). If the total employment figures are adjusted to exclude these manpower program jobs, the decrease in employment between July 1974 and March 1975 was 2.7 million jobs, and the increase from March to December becomes 1.3 million jobs. Economic recovery has offset only 50 percent of the recession job loss, rather than 65 percent as the unadjusted figures suggest.

The unemployment figures are also misleading. The expansion of PSE program jobs and the increase in the "discouraged worker" total both contributed to a substantial understatement of the number of people who wanted jobs in the regular labor market but could not find them. Adjusting the May 1975 official unemployment rate for both of these factors gives a recalculated rate of 10 percent rather than the official 9.2 percent rate reported for that month. The official unemployment rate for December 1975 was 8.3 percent. When this figure is adjusted as above for the recent increases in discouraged workers and manpower program job slots, it becomes 9.2 percent.

The distribution of unemployment among various sub-groups of the labor force must also be considered. In December 1975, when the national unemployment rate was reported as 8.3 percent, married men with spouse present had a reported rate of 4.7 percent, while black teenagers had a rate of 35.9 percent. Professional and technical workers had a reported rate of 3.1 percent and nonfarm laborers had a 14.6 percent rate. The rate for government workers was 4.3 percent, and that for construction workers was 16.2 percent. Other striking differentials could be cited, but these examples perhaps suffice to make the point that the national unemployment rate averages together very large differences in unemployment among various groups in the labor force. And the greatest difference of all is hardly ever mentioned—whatever the national unemployment rate is said to be, the individual without a job has a personal unemployment rate of 100 percent.

One final aspect of the reported unemployment figures needs no comment. In November 1975, the BLS reported, the number of workers without a job for six months or longer rose to a total of 1.7 million, which was the highest total in the post-World War II period; the figure for December showed no significant change.

What is the outlook For unemployment?

Unemployment is one of the "lagging indicators" in a recovery period. The unemployment rate has a historical tendency to recover more slowly than other measures of economic activity after a recession has bottomed out. By mid-January 1976 it was perhaps still too early to say that a clear pattern has emerged. Nevertheless, for what it is worth, scarcely any forecaster now predicts a return to pre-recession unemployment levels within the next 12 to 18 months. The consensus appears to cluster around an unemployment rate of about 7.5 percent by the end of 1976.

Many, perhaps most, economic forecasts nowadays are based upon computer simulations of the whole economy. There are other, less mechanistic ways to analyze the outlook for unemployment. One is to consider the behavior of the unemployment rate after the trough (lowest point) month of each of the five post-war recessions. There is a pronounced tendency over time for the unemployment rate to recede less and less from the recession high after the economy as a whole has begun to recover. This tendency is particularly apparent in the last two recovery periods. During the recovery period following the 1969-70 recession, the unemployment rate remained close to the recession high throughout the economic expansion. In the present recovery period, the same pattern seems to be emerging. In 1975, the unemployment rate fluctuated in a narrow range of 8.3 percent to 8.6 percent from July to December, with no trend evident.

When a rise in unemployment began in early 1970, Chairman Herbert Stein of the President's Council of Economic Advisers asserted that this was a "transitional" problem. In the light of hindsight, it seems unmistakably clear that it was the low unemployment rates of the late 1960s that were "transitional," and that the chronically high unemployment rates of the 1970s reflect the reappearance of some basic imbalances in the economy that were temporarily masked by the effects of the Vietnam War and the new programs of the Great Society. Furthermore, there is evidence which suggests that the lingering effects of some employment problems of the 1950s and 1960s may be augmented by some new problems in the late 1970s.

The disturbing fact is that some of the industries that contributed substantially to the growth of employment throughout the years since World War II now show signs of stagnation or decline. These include automobiles, education, health care, construction and national defense.

Automobiles: A striking aspect of the growth of the U.S. automobile industry in the 20th century is that the automobile population was growing much more rapidly than the human population throughout most of the century. In the most recent years, the growth rate of the auto industry has slowed primarily because of an approach to what appears to be an upper limit. The latest figures indicate we now have one car for every two men, women, children and infants in the United States. Recent developments have accentuated the long-run trend to slower growth in this industry. Huge price increases, even if largely caused by forces beyond the control of the industry, have adversely affected sales prospects. Past and anticipated increases in the price of gasoline, insurance, financing, repairs, and so on have contributed to slower sales. News headlines made much of large percentage increases in automobile sales in December 1975 compared to the previous year. Rarely mentioned was the fact that December 1974 was an extremely depressed sales period and that December 1975 sales were still far below pre-recession projections.

In the early 1970s, the automobile industry was getting about 4 percent of total disposable personal income for its products. In most of 1975 it has been getting only about 2.5 percent of a smaller total. In 1973, the industry employed about 950,000 workers; in 1975, the average for the year will probably be about 200,000 less than that. Wassily Leontief, an economics professor at Harvard, has estimated that for each 10 workers in the automobile and parts industry, about 15 workers in other industries supply raw materials—glass, rubber, steel, textiles, copper and so on. This estimate implies a loss of another 300,000 jobs in the raw materials industries because of the continuing slump in autos, or a total of 500,000 in 1975. Some of this job loss is temporary, as is demonstrated by the recent increase in sales. But it seems highly doubtful under present circumstances that the automobile and related industries will ever again provide regular jobs for as large a proportion of the labor force as in the 1970-73 period. Unit sales may recover and conceivably even equal past highs; but the smaller cars that will surely be emphasized require less materials and fewer man-hours to produce.

Education: From 1950 to the 1970s, this nation increased its spending on education at all levels almost

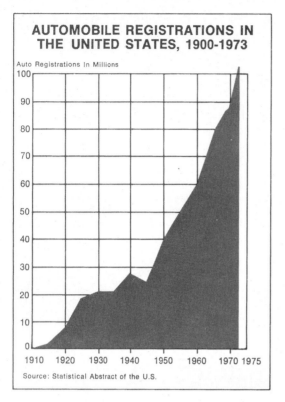

AUTOMOBILE REGISTRATIONS IN THE UNITED STATES, 1900-1973

Auto Registrations In Millions

Source: Statistical Abstract of the U.S.

ten-fold—from $8.8 billion in 1950 to $83 billion in 1972. The percentage of Gross National Product going to education increased from 3.4 percent in 1950 to 7.9 percent in 1972. Since 1972, the dollars have further increased, but the share of education in GNP has been going down rather than up. Enrollments are down also, but by much less than the decrease in the share of GNP. No single factor can completely explain this rather sudden reversal. However, there has undoubtedly been some public disillusionment with education as the purported best road to the good life, and education has fared rather badly in the increasingly tough competition for tax dollars.

The reduction in demand for teachers has had an adverse effect on the labor market for all new college graduates. In recent years, the largest single source of employment for them has been education. The sudden change in this sector of the labor market has to some extent contributed to the devaluation of the college degree as a ticket for a job; and thus we have a self-reinforcing process. The decline in the prospects for this industry contributes to a further decline in its prospects. In the years ahead, the likelihood is that education will be taking less than its former share of a growing labor force, rather than a growing share as in the past two decades.

Health care has been another of the great growth industries since World War II. The nation spent $12 billion (4.6 percent of GNP) on health care in 1950;

the expenditure in fiscal year 1975 was $118 billion (8.3 percent of GNP). In the three preceding years, however, health care costs as a percentage of GNP had leveled off at about 7.8 percent and the increased percentage in 1975 was partly the result of a sharp decline in total GNP and partly the result of continued large price increases for health care. Between 1960 and 1970, employment in health care fields had increased by about 50 percent—from 2 million in 1960 to 3 million in 1970; but the next decennial census is likely to show little if any further increase in employment, unless comprehensive health care legislation is passed, which is far from certain.

The labor market implications of the leveling-off of employment in health care may not be entirely obvious. The greatest expansion in employment in this industry from 1960 to 1970, both in percentage terms and in absolute numbers, was at the lower skill levels. Thus, the increase in physicians, dentists and related practitioners was only 17 percent; the increase in health service workers (assistants, aides, and the like) was 67 percent. If the labor requirements of the health care industry diminish to the replacement level, this will have a significant effect on the supply of new jobs in the economy with a relatively short training period.

The construction industry has the highest unemployment rate reported for any of the standard industry classifications—16.2 percent in December 1975. This is a cyclically sensitive industry, of course, but its present difficulties have deeper roots than the recent recession. In the consumer market, construction and site costs have far outstripped the growth in disposable personal income in the past decade. In the government market, the great boom in education construction has ended; the great national network of freeways is virtually completed; and proposals for other kinds of public structures must compete with other rising claims on tax dollars. From 1950 to 1974, the percentage of the labor force employed in construction decreased somewhat, but in absolute numbers the industry provided 1.2 million more jobs in 1974 than in 1950. With 700,000 of its present work force now unemployed, construction is not likely to offer large numbers of new jobs in the next few years—unless, of course, the federal government steps in with a big new public works program.

War: Over the past 40 years, wars and preparation for wars have had larger effects on the labor market figures than most analysts have recognized. Large increases in the size of the armed forces during a war reduce the number of young men in the civilian labor force. Large orders for conventional weapons and other equipment such as wheeled vehicles, ammunition, helmets, and so on, create large numbers of assembly-line jobs for semi-skilled workers. During the period of heavy production for the Vietnam War from 1965 to 1968, defense industries provided 48 percent of the new blue-collar jobs in the economy.

Now war appears to be a likely candidate for listing among the declining industries. The number of persons now serving in the Armed Forces is the lowest since 1950. In the past five years, national defense expenditures as a percentage of GNP have marched steadily downward—from 9 percent in 1969 to 6 percent in 1974. Some of this reduction may be attributed to the U.S. withdrawal from Vietnam; but the GNP percentage for 1974 is the lowest since 1950.

Other industries perhaps belong on this list of "endangered species," but this listing is intended to be illustrative rather than exhaustive. The basic point is not that the country is headed for another depression like the one in the 1930s. The market presumably will again generate a growing total of jobs. There will be new growth industries. Most people will live lives of comfortable affluence. But we will face a massive problem of redeployment of our labor force—a problem that is likely to equal or exceed the comparable problem of the 1950s and early 1960s.

We never really solved that problem, although the effects of the Vietnam War led some people to believe for a time that we did. The Vietnam War removed about a million young men from the civilian population (most of whom would have been in the labor force except for the war); and war production provided a large number of temporary jobs for blue-collar workers. The growth of manpower programs during the late 1960s, and the classification of many of the enrollees as "employed" in labor market statistics, also contributed to the appearance of full employment.

The war ended; war production was sharply cut back; hundreds of thousands of former draftees were returned to civilian life; manpower programs leveled off or were, in some instances, reduced in size; and the labor force resumed its normal rate of growth. The forces of change in the American economy left large numbers of workers stranded in the wrong cities. Monetary policy was directed toward the control of inflation, and fiscal policy did not avert the deepest recession since the 1930s. The recession aggravated the displacement effects of structural change while leading many analysts to believe that all of the unemployment was caused by the business cycle and the fight against inflation.

The question now is whether we must accept, for the rest of the decade, unemployment rates that have generally been regarded as intolerable since the end of World War II, or whether some combination of manpower and fiscal policies can prevent the blighting of millions of lives to which some of our national leaders appear to have resigned themselves.

Is there a "trade-off" Between unemployment and inflation?

In 1958, Professor A. W. Phillips, of Australian National University, published an article titled, "The Relation Between Unemployment and the Rate of Change of Money Wage Rates in the United King-

dom, 1861-1957." His findings were not entirely free from ambiguity and, at least by contemporary standards, his methodology was not impeccable. But almost immediately the so-called "Phillips curve" became a major factor in employment policy.

And many economists, with varying degrees of success, tried to determine whether the Phillips curve relationship was applicable to American experience. Some analysts found little need for data. The relationship was so logical and so consistent with economic theory that, if the data did not plainly show it, there must be something wrong with the data. With the passage of time, the relationship tended to become one between the level of unemployment and rate of inflation—rather than the rate of change of money wage rates—although some analysts still recognize that a change in money wage rates is far from synonymous with a change in the general level of prices. The most common statement of the doctrine is that if you want less unemployment, you must accept more price increase; and if you want less price increase, you must accept more unemployment.

The data invoked to provide empirical support for this concept have turned out to be fractious. At least for the United States, the alleged relationship cannot be convincingly demonstrated in any straightforward manner. On the simplest level, for example, the data show that the United States had quite low unemployment rates—at times less than 3 percent—through most of the years 1951, 1952 and 1953. Yet coincident with their low unemployment rates, we also had very low rates of price increase. There were wage and price controls during part of this period, but their abrupt removal early in 1953 made no difference. On the other hand, in the three years since 1972, we have had unemployment rates that were extremely high by post-war standards—and we have had very rapid price inflation as well.

Various strategies have been followed to overcome such fractiousness of the data. Leads and lags of varying duration have been tried. Additional variables have been thrown into the equations, often with little effort to justify their use except for the fact that more satisfactory results were thereby produced. Some analysts say that the Phillips curve describes a short-run relationship; others say that it describes a long-run relationship. If all else fails, or seems inadequate, there is the useful notion of a "shifting" Phillips curve —that is, a relationship that changes over time.

Despite these difficulties, the Phillips curve has gained increasing influence in policy-making. When men in high office tell us that we must accept high unemployment rates for years into the future in order to bring inflation under control, they are echoing the Phillips curve doctrine. But, as often happens, as the acceptance of the Phillips curve among economic policy makers has spread, skeptics have arisen among the prominent members of the economics profession. For example, Chairman Arthur F. Burns of the Federal Reserve in a recent speech remarked as follows: "Whatever may have been true in the past, there is no longer a meaningful trade-off between unemployment and inflation." Burns proposed a program of direct attack on what he presented as the real causes of inflation, and he prefaced a program for the reduction of unemployment with the following observations:

"I believe that the ultimate objective of labor market policies should be to eliminate all involuntary unemployment. This is not a radical or impractical goal," Burns said. Others, like Burns, have pointed out that to a large degree, recent increases in the price level have obviously been caused by factors that are wholly unrelated to the state of the labor market—the outstanding examples being world-wide crop failures, the unilateral decisions of the Arab oil cartel, and the tightness, in the recent past, in world markets for raw materials.

Forty-five years ago, there was general agreement among the world's leading economists that the only way to reduce unemployment was to reduce wages. One of the great achievements of J. M. Keynes was to demonstrate the fallacy of this doctrine. Cutting wages might induce some employers to hire more workers, he said, but he pointed out that that was certainly not the only way or the most effective way to reduce unemployment. Like the insistence on wage-cutting, the Phillips curve concept surely has a kernel of truth in it. Some approaches to the reduction of unemployment would be quite likely to generate upward pressure on the price level. But there is really no convincing proof of the widely accepted belief that any reduction in unemployment, no matter how much and no matter what means are employed, will cause more inflation. It is true that few, if any, professional economists would state the doctrine quite so crudely. But many, perhaps a majority, would still accept the generalization that there is some kind of "trade-off" between inflation and unemployment. Belief in such a trade-off has become an important barrier in the way of a substantial reduction in unemployment. Yet this widely held belief in a "trade-off" lacks a substantial basis in either experience or analysis.

What are we doing now About unemployment?

In terms of numbers of workers involved, by far the largest present program for dealing with unemployment is unemployment compensation. It has developed into a kind of ad hoc set of programs with some variation in financing arrangements and duration of benefits. In general, the maximum duration for any recipient is 65 weeks, or approximately 15 months. By the best estimates available, the U.S. spent a total of $12.1 billion on all of the main unemployment compensation programs in fiscal year 1974-75, and it is estimated another $20.6 billion will be spent in fiscal year 1975-76. During most of calendar 1975,

between 6 and 7 million workers were receiving benefits. In the closing months of the year, the number of claimants showed a downward trend, partly as a result of exhaustion of eligibility.

In terms of numbers of dollars, the biggest effort to date against unemployment is tax-cutting. The total value of tax cuts, personal and business, and rebates in 1975 is estimated at approximately $22 billion. Although the tax cuts were not motivated solely by benevolence toward the unemployed, the reduction of unemployment was said to be one of the intended benefits of the tax cuts. It is difficult to estimate how many jobs were or will be created by the tax cuts. However, the Congressional Budget Office has recently published impact estimates which imply that the 1975 tax cuts will produce from 660,000 to 880,000 jobs after 24 months.

The Public Service Employment program is currently financed at a level of about $3 billion per year, and Department of Labor estimates place the current number of enrollments at about 325,000.

Other programs aid the unemployed, such as food stamps, Aid to Families with Dependent Children (AFDC), general relief, and so on, but the amounts going to the unemployed cannot be determined with precision. There are also many private programs, such as supplementary unemployment benefits (SUB) in automobiles, rubber, steel and some other industries. In some companies, the reserve funds have been depleted and payments have been reduced or terminated. Finally, training programs for the unemployed are provided by many state and local units with funds provided by the federal government.

What should we be doing About unemployment?

It is far easier to point out what is wrong with what we are doing now about unemployment than it is to say what would be better. But both matters must be considered.

For the last 40 years, unemployment compensation has been considered "the first line of defense" against the financial losses imposed by unemployment. Therefore, the salient features of the system have always included limited duration of benefits, a relationship between wages previously earned and the size of the benefit amount, and employer experience rating. The current use of this system to cope with very long-term unemployment threatens to change the system itself in rather fundamental ways. Such use is creating future problems for the states that now have the highest levels of unemployment.

As of October 1975, 11 states had had to borrow funds from the federal government to continue to pay unemployment benefits. By the middle of calendar year 1976, it is likely that more than half of all the states will be borrowing money to pay benefits. Those states that exhaust their reserve funds and borrow will have to tax the employers in their boundaries more heavily in the future to repay the loans than will the states that have been more fortunate. Therefore, the states with the largest present unemployment problems will have a competitive disadvantage as compared with the states that have been less affected.

The greatest shortcoming in such heavy reliance on unemployment compensation is that this program pays huge sums of money to millions of people for doing nothing and going nowhere. When we are dealing with relatively short-term unemployment, the unemployment compensation system functions well. It is a most useful social invention which has contributed significantly to the moderation of past business cycles and has alleviated much hardship. But unemployment compensation is much less defensible as a program to deal with a high level of long-term unemployment, particularly when structural changes in the economy are contributing to the unemployment. This approach contributes nothing to the solution of such structural problems—aside from income maintenance. If we want to meet some part of the very longterm unemployment problem with a minimum income guarantee, we can devise a more rational and more equitably financed system than the present patchwork of add-ons to the existing unemployment compensation system. Under the present system, many people who are not in need are eligible for benefits; others who are in need are not eligible.

Unemployment compensation payments do not encourage preparation for a change in occupation or place of residence, which will be required of many people if they are to adjust to the effects of structural change. A minor exception is that under one of the special programs, if training opportunities are available and if the recipient would benefit from such training, he or she may be required to enroll. The Administration's opposition to further extensions of unemployment benefits deserves support, provided other programs are developed to meet the needs of the long-term unemployed.

Tax-cutting is perhaps irresistibly seductive for politicians and addictive for economists, who have joined opponents of "big government" in proclaiming the virtues of tax-cutting. Yet only rarely has the effectiveness of tax-cutting as a remedy for unemployment been dispassionately examined. In discussions during recent years, the main evidence on this point has often been said to be what happened in the late 1960s. We had a $14 billion tax cut in 1964, when the unemployment rate was around 5.4 percent; by 1968, the unemployment rate was down to 3.6 percent (annual average) and in 1969 it was 3.5 percent. Many economists have attributed all of this reduction in unemployment to fiscal policy (a few would give some of the credit to monetary policy as well). This interpretation rests upon a fallacy that is easily revealed: the definition of unemployment was changed twice during the period of 1965-1967 and in combination the definition changes reduced the reported unemployment rate by about 0.7 percent. The Viet-

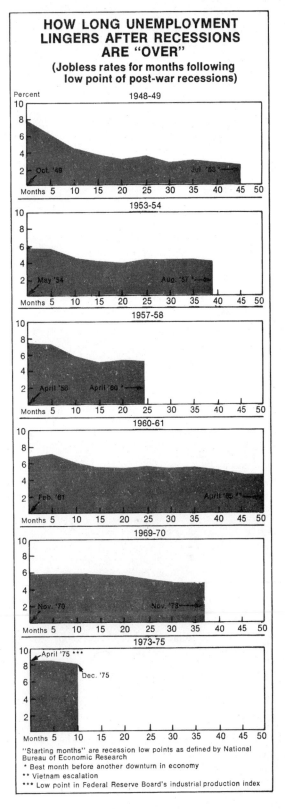

HOW LONG UNEMPLOYMENT LINGERS AFTER RECESSIONS ARE "OVER"
(Jobless rates for months following low point of post-war recessions)

"Starting months" are recession low points as defined by National Bureau of Economic Research
* Best month before another downturn in economy
** Vietnam escalation
*** Low point in Federal Reserve Board's industrial production index

431

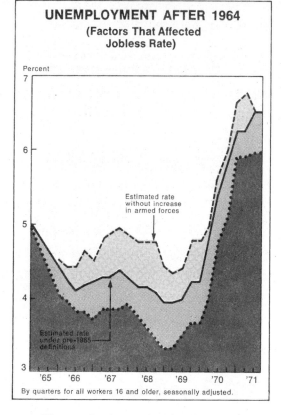

UNEMPLOYMENT AFTER 1964
(Factors That Affected Jobless Rate)

Percent

Estimated rate
without increase
in armed forces

Estimated rate
under pre-1965
definitions

'65 '66 '67 '68 '69 '70 '71

By quarters for all workers 16 and older, seasonally adjusted.

660,000 to 880,000 after 24 months—for an initial cost of about $22 billion. By contrast, the estimated net cost per public service employment job after 24 months is $2,600 to $3,500, according to the Congressional Budget Office study. The heavy emphasis on tax-cutting in the employment policy recommendations of many economists in recent years is not justified by considerations of cost-effectiveness.

Two other weaknesses of tax-cutting as a remedy for unemployment should be noted. First, the experience of the 1960s shows that this remedy apparently does the least for the most disadvantaged members of the labor force. Despite the tax cut in 1964, and also despite manpower programs which emphasized enrollment of the disadvantaged, black teenage unemployment, for example, did not decline at all during the great boom of the 1960s. Second, and related, there is general agreement that tax-cutting, and fiscal and monetary policy generally, are not the most effective tools for dealing with structural unemployment. Indeed, Keynes himself, in the late 1930s, took the position that expansion of aggregate demand by itself would do little to remedy structural imbalances.

While tax cuts are limited as an instrument of job creation, it must be noted that the unusual aspects of the situation made the extension of the 1975 tax cuts imperative. The expiration of the 1975 tax cuts on schedule on Dec. 31, 1975, obviously would have constituted a large tax increase. The modest economic recovery thus far achieved could have been endangered. And the impact, in the form of sharply increased withholding rates, would have been immediate. In a less exigent situation, an argument could have been made for more cost-effective uses of the public revenues; but given the realities, there was no reasonable alternative to the extension of the 1975 tax cuts. It must be recognized, at the same time, that this extension will make only a nominal contribution to the reduction of unemployment, if the impact estimates of the Congressional Budget Office are accepted as accurate.

For a time a few months ago, it seemed that Public Service Employment was almost everyone's favorite remedy for unemployment. More recently, there has been a reaction—or overreaction—against the earlier enthusiasm. The criticisms are numerous and varied: PSE jobs are not going to the right people; there are "leakages" that reduce the anticipated impact of the nominal job slots by 50 to 90 percent; it doesn't make sense to have cities hiring new people with federal money while they are laying off their regular employees. And so on.

Few informed people would argue that the existing PSE program is the best of its kind that could be devised by the mind of man. The present program was the product of legislative compromise and urgency, plus an effort to fit the program into the untried framework of state and local administration that is provided under the Comprehensive Employment and

nam War, as already noted, reduced the size of the civilian labor force significantly; a conservative estimate of the effect on the reported unemployment rate is a reduction of 0.5 percent. Other factors—equally unrelated to fiscal and monetary policy—also contributed to lower unemployment during the late 1960s. But considering only the definition changes and the Vietnam War effects, in combination they contributed about two-thirds of the reduction in the reported unemployment rate in the second half of the 1960s. To attribute the entire reduction to monetary and fiscal policy imputes to such policy about three times as large an effect as is justified by the facts. The point is not that tax-cutting has no effect on unemployment; rather, the point is that the magnitude of the effect has usually been substantially exaggerated in recent years.

The impact estimates of the Congressional Budget Office support this conclusion. These estimates cover four types of programs for the relief of unemployment: public works, anti-recession grants to state and local governments, public service employment and federal tax cuts. According to the estimates, tax cuts have the smallest impact on employment of any of the four types of programs, assuming equal numbers of dollars are involved. The Congressional Budget Office estimates imply that the net cost per job created by tax cuts after 24 months is in the range of $17,000 to $21,000. As previously noted, the estimated number of jobs created by the 1975 tax cuts will be from

UNEMPLOYMENT INSURANCE PROGRAMS

Program	How Financed	Maximum Duration of Benefits	Expected Expenditures Fiscal Years (Billions of dollars) 1975	1976
1. Regular Unemployment Insurance	State unemployment tax on employer payrolls finances benefits; federal unemployment tax monies used to cover state administration costs and to maintain a loan fund.	26 weeks	$10.0*	$13.5*
2. Federal-State Extended Benefits	50 percent from state unemployment taxes and 50 percent from federal unemployment tax.	13 weeks	$1.2	$3.3
3. Federal Supplemental Benefits (FSB)	Federal unemployment tax— now financed by repayable advances from general revenues.	26 weeks	$0.8	$2.5
4. Supplemental Unemployment Assistance (SUA) for workers not covered by above.	General federal revenues	39 weeks	$0.2	$1.3
		TOTAL	**$12.2**	**$20.6**

* ($544.6 million was borrowed from the loan fund in 1975; between $3 and $5 billion in loans is expected for 1976.)

Source: Unemployment Insurance Service, U.S. Department of Labor.

Training Act. Improvements can and should be made in the program. Tighter eligibility requirements should be enacted and enforced. Target groups should be limited. Prime sponsors in addition to governmental units should be encouraged. The "leakage" argument rests far more on speculation than on hard evidence; and such leakage, at its worst, would not render the program less effective than tax-cutting. But if convincing evidence of a serious leakage problem does emerge, the obvious solution for it is federal administration.

The most valid criticism of the PSE program is that it is far too small to make a real dent in unemployment. Currently, the number of job slots funded equals about 4 percent of the total number counted as unemployed. In the years of the Great Depression, we provided jobs, under roughly equivalent programs, for 30 to 35 percent of the unemployed. Today, a program of comparable size would provide 2.3 to 2.7 million job slots, or eight to nine times as many as are now funded.

Now that the PSE program is increasingly subject to criticism, including some that is not justified, it is essential to emphasize two advantages of basic importance:
● It is better for society in general and better for the individuals involved to pay them for working

than it is to pay them for not working. Society gets the benefit of the goods and services thus produced, and the individual has a better chance of hanging on to his or her self-respect and ability to work.

● A PSE program is much more cost-effective than tax-cutting as a way of providing jobs for the unemployed. As already noted, the Congressional Budget Office impact estimates imply the lowest net cost per job created for this program; the estimate is a net cost of $2,600 to $3,500 per job created after 24 months. In a broader kind of cost accounting, that net dollar cost must be set off against the value of the goods and services produced by the PSE worker. A careful analysis of experience under the 1971 Public Employment Program concluded that the great majority of the enrollees performed work that was as useful as that of regular employees of state and local governments.

There are indications that one consequence of the recent popularity of PSE programs at the local level has been a sharp cutback in expenditures for manpower training programs. Such a cutback is surely shortsighted. Obviously, it does does not make sense to train people for jobs that are not available, and manpower training has had a bad press on this point. It has also become faddish to assert that manpower training has been shown to be a "failure." This assertion is reiterated reflexively by some persons who

433

appear never to have examined the available facts. Some programs in some locations have "failed;" for example, training for welfare clients, especially enrollees in the AFDC program. It is nonsensical to generalize from such incidents to a sweeping conclusion. The fact is that the great majority of careful studies of manpower training programs show positive rates of return for the investment in training. Some critics have raised questions about the methodology of such studies, and some of the methodological criticisms are justified. But the reality is that in the social sciences, methodologically impeccable experiments are more of a Utopian vision than a practical possibility. At the present writing, the weight of the evidence decidedly supports a finding that manpower training has been successful. Hard evidence of "failure" is virtually non-existent. Given this state of affairs, policy should ignore the mythmakers and revive manpower training, while continuing careful evaluation studies.

Finally, we need some new approaches to the old problem of depressed areas and sick industries. Perhaps it is not excessively pessimistic to say that our previous efforts in this area have accomplished little more than to show us what does not work. Of course, there are exceptions. For example, during the 1960s, there was experimentation with programs to increase worker mobility, and some of the programs reportedly were relatively successful. Yet we have no federal programs of this kind in operation today. This body of experience should be reviewed and consideration given to substantial efforts in this area. Renewed attention should be given to other direct approaches to the reduction of excessive local or regional unemployment.

For a decade or so, many analysts believed that employment policy was virtually synonymous with fiscal and monetary policy—or, to simplify even further, that if you want to reduce unemployment, you need only to reduce federal taxes. The ultimate illusion was that government had mastered the unemployment problem and all that remained was to master the technique of "fine-tuning." The development of persistent and excessive unemployment after U.S. withdrawal from Vietnam, and the catastrophic rise of unemployment in the current recession, may have corrected the complacency of the 1960s and the early 1970s. But excessive optimism has been replaced by a virtual paralysis of employment policy. The source of the paralysis is a new simplism: that the country needs to have 7 or 8 million unemployed workers at least for the next few years in order to bring inflation under control.

This "need" is but another illusion. It is certainly possible to find ways of reducing unemployment that would make the inflation problem worse. But the rate of unemployment does not uniquely determine the rate of inflation. And unemployment can be reduced far below 7 or 8 million without aggravating inflation. We have some weapons at hand that can be effectively

utilized, and we need to invent some new ones. But the one weapon that will not help is "benign neglect."

In summary, the following recommendations emerge:

● The extension of the 1975 tax cut is necessary in order to avoid a seriously adverse effect on the present recovery.

● In the longer run, employment policy should recognize that tax cuts are less cost-effective than many other programs for the relief of unemployment. Tax cuts may be justified as a general stimulus to the economy, but other ways of assisting the unemployed produce more jobs at less cost.

● The present reliance on unemployment compensation as the primary means to relieve long-term unemployment is excessive and deplorable. More efficient programs of income support for the long-term unemployed can be designed. Such programs should not be financed by the unemployment insurance system, which was designed to handle basically short-term unemployment. No further extension of duration of benefits, or any additional temporary programs for special groups of the unemployed should be adopted, provided that alternative sources of support as just suggested are provided.

● The Public Service Employment program, including youth employment efforts and public works, should be enlarged to provide approximately 1 million jobs, and eligibility should be more strictly limited to long-term unemployed. If substantial proof of substitution of PSE workers for regular public employees is developed, consideration should be given to federal administration of at least part of the program, and greater involvement of non-profit, non-governmental organizations should be encouraged.

● Despite glib assertions to the contrary, manpower training programs generally cannot accurately be called a "failure." On the contrary, the weight of the evidence supports the conclusion that the monetary returns to manpower training usually exceed the costs of such programs. Manpower training is currently being under-utilized, and greater reliance on manpower training should be stimulated.

● A significant portion of the current unemployment problem is structural in nature, and many idled workers will be unable to return to their former lines of employment. Many of these workers will need extensive retraining, relocation and other services. A substantial start should be made on the development of such services.

● The claim that we cannot reduce our present grossly excessive unemployment without seriously increasing inflationary pressures should be rejected. That claim is not supported by experience or analysis. If the vigor and health of our society are to be preserved, we must prevent the loss of hundreds of billions of dollars in production and the blighting of millions of human lives which are promised by the projected unemployment rates in the range of 6 to 8 percent for the remainder of this decade.

PART VI.
THE
INTERNATIONAL
ECONOMY

Sovereign nations do not live in isolation. They exchange goods and services with one another because such international exchange facilitates an international division of labor and specialization, producing a rising standard of living. Flows of labor, capital, technology and enterpreneurship also cross national frontiers. As the economic interdependence of nations has increased with modern developments in transportation and communication, it has given rise to may interesting and challenging international economic problems and these, in turn, to international political problems. In recent years, international economic issues have been dramatized by several events such as the 1973 oil crisis, the creation of Special Drawing Rights (also known as paper gold), the suspension of the 1944 Bretton Woods System and the adoption of flexible exchange rates, to name only a few. Part VI presents a collection of articles which examine significant economic issues of the world economy.

Section A, International Trade and Multinational Business

Export controls on grain shipments to Russia will not control price increases according to Clifton Luttrell in "Grain Exports and Inflation," an article that reviews the classical view of free trade and reminds us of its continuing applicability. "Foreign Raw Materials: How Critical Are They?" from the Morgan Guaranty Survey lists a dozen metals largely or entirely imported from other countries, gives the location of the world's major reserves, and suggests that recycling, new technology, stock piling, and more expensive alternatives all offer substantial protection for the U.S. against overseas raw material cartels and supply interruptions. In "Trends in U.S. Export Prices and OPEC Oil Prices," Edward E. Murphy and Jorge F. Perez-Lopez report that "OPEC has experienced large gains in the purchasing power of its barrel revenue" and, therefore, American export inflation does not justify OPEC price increases as some have argued. Sheldon Stahl, in "The Multinational Corporation; A Controversial Force," finds that the U.S. has become increasingly concerned with multinationals because within the past 20 years we have experienced a large capital outflow to Western Europe and a deterioration in the overall U.S. balance of payments position (until very recently). Stahl examines the motives of multinationals and their impact on the U.S. economy.

Section B, International Monetary Issues

"Worldwide Stagflation" is a thoughtful piece by Paul Samuelson on the cause of simultaneous worldwide inflation and high unemployment. He emphasizes the role of international monetary forces as transmitters of unemployment and inflation from

one nation to another and argues that overvaluation of the dollar was a major
cause of inflation abroad. In "Interdependence, Exchange Rate Flexibility, and
National Economies" Donald Kohn contrasts fixed and flexible exchange rates and
"explores some of the more important conceptual implications of the growth in
interdependence." James Burtle in "Some Problems in Living with a System of Floating Exchange Rates" discusses some of the reasons behind the slow adjustment of exchange rates to equilibrium following an exchange rate change. In "The U.S. Dollar
in International Markets: Mid-1970 to Mid-1976" Donald Kemp reviews the recent
experience with generally floating exchange rates between the U.S. dollar and the
currencies of the United States' major trading partners. "Balance-of-Payments
Concepts--What Do They Really Mean?" by the same author provides a comprehensive
review of several balances in the balance of payments account as currently reported:
Current Account, Basic Balance, Net Liquidity Balance and Official Settlements Balance. He concludes that "Under freely floating exchange rates there are no meaningful balance-of-payments concepts, because in this case, international transactions
have no impact on the money supply." He proposes that these balance be no longer
calculated and reported.

A. International Trade and Multinational Business

Grain Exports and Inflation

CLIFTON B. LUTTRELL

PRIVATE grain exporters have notified the United States Department of Agriculture (USDA) of their intentions to sell more than 10 million tons of grain to the Russians in the current marketing year. The sales include 177 million bushels of corn, 154 million bushels of wheat, and 50.5 million bushels of barley.[1] They constitute about 3, 7, and 13 percent, respectively, of the prospective corn, wheat, and barley crops and are equivalent to 13, 18, and 84 percent, respectively, of our average annual exports of these crops to all foreign purchasers for the past five years.

The grain sales to Russia this year are for cash. They carry neither a Government price subsidy nor a Government credit arrangement. Payments for the shipments will be made with funds which can be used immediately to purchase goods and services from abroad.

This is in contrast to the 1972 sales which involved substantial Government subsidies. The U.S. Government at that time maintained a subsidy on all wheat sold in foreign markets. The subsidy kept the international price for U.S. wheat at a lower level than the domestic price. These subsidies were a holdover from the old farm programs which were designed to reduce the domestic grain supply and increase domestic grain prices. In addition to the price subsidies, the Russians received a subsidized credit of $750 million that was

made available over a three-year period for purchasing the grain.

This year, however, no export subsidies on wheat are available and no subsidized credit is granted to the purchaser. Consequently, most of the basic economic arguments against the 1972 transactions are missing.

Nevertheless, the recent sales to Russia, like the earlier sales, have received considerable criticism. Some analysts have argued that the exports will contribute to higher food prices and to inflation.[2] The rising prices of grain and soybeans during recent weeks are pointed to as evidence of the inflationary effects of the sales. Higher grain and soybean prices contribute to higher meat and poultry prices which, in turn, are believed to spill over into higher prices for industrial raw materials. Hence, restrictions on grain exports have been proposed in order to halt this asserted inflationary impact.

Basic Issue is Free International Trade

In the controversy over the entry of Russia into the domestic grain market, one major point has been largely overlooked. Restrictions on grain exports to the Russians will not prevent domestic grain prices from

[2]For examples of such views, see "Russia Feeds U.S. Inflation," *Business Week*, August 11, 1975, pp. 14-15; "Prices: A Rude Surprise," *Time* Magazine, August 4, 1975, p. 59; and Robert E. Grant, "Mr. Butz and the Grain Sales to Russia," *The Wall Street Journal*, July 28, 1975.

[1]*The Wall Street Journal*, July 24, 1975.

Clifton B. Luttrell, "Grain Exports and Inflation." *Review*, Federal Reserve Bank of St. Louis, September 1975, pp. 2-4. Reprinted with permission.

rising unless restrictions are placed on *all* grain exports. If, for example, the Russians purchased grain exclusively from Canada, prices there and in other world trading centers would rise and U.S. grain dealers would have the incentive to sell in those markets. Grain markets are international and prices in these markets reflect international supply and demand conditions. Grain will flow to those locations where the price is highest so long as the price differential exceeds transportation costs. Thus, as long as the United States ships grain freely to any other nation, sales to Russia by U.S. dealers will have no more of an impact on domestic grain prices than the same amount of sales by the Canadian Grain Commission or by Australian dealers. Consequently, preventing a rise in domestic grain prices involves the imposition of comprehensive controls on grain exports to all nations.

Total Export Controls Have Short-Run Appeal

Comprehensive export controls could be used *in the short run* to limit the quantity of grain exports, reduce domestic grain prices, and raise world grain prices. The Organization of Petroleum Exporting Countries (OPEC) is an example of an action where a minimum price has been set on petroleum exports. This has led to the accumulation of a surplus of oil in member countries since the rest of the world has not been willing to purchase all the oil produced by the cartel at the prevailing fixed prices. The effect on the quantity and price of goods exported is the same whether the action is initiated by export controls or by artificial price supports.

Some nations, by imposing such controls, are able to increase their wealth since in the short run the gains from higher prices more than offset the decline in the quantity of their exports. The OPEC members have received more foreign exchange for a smaller amount of exported oil than formerly.

It does not appear that American wheat farmers are in the same position as OPEC. While it may be true that total world grain consumption does not fall sharply in response to higher prices, the United States faces strong competition from other grain producing nations. If we were to limit, through export controls, the amount of grain we make available in the world market, the effect would certainly be a somewhat higher world price than otherwise would be the case, since the United States supplies a major portion of the world's grain exports. But our restrictions would cause other grain producing countries to increase *their* exports. Our competitors, instead of American grain farmers, would surely gain. Small wonder, then, that grain farmers are objecting vociferously to proposals to restrict grain exports — domestic grain prices will almost certainly be lower than world grain prices.

Historically, popular and political demands for international trade restrictions generally have been for limitations on imports, through the imposition of either tariffs or quotas. These restrictions have penalized consumers who have been forced to pay higher prices for protected goods in order to benefit producers who could not compete effectively in a free market. In contrast, export restrictions initially hurt producers by depriving them of access to free world markets, and help consumers by increasing the domestic supply. However, over the longer run it is not simply a case of helping one group at the expense of another. Accepted economic theory implies that, in general, trade restrictions make this country as well as the entire world less well off.

Classical View of Free Trade Still Persuasive

Despite some occasional short-run gains from international trade restrictions, the classical view of international exchange remains persuasive. In 1776 Adam Smith outlined a system of free trade among nations with arguments which are still held as valid by most economic analysts.[3] He pointed to the gains from the specialization of labor and trade in a small community. Through such specialization and exchange of goods and services the total volume of real product is increased and the costs of goods and services are lower than if each person attempted to be self-sufficient.

Smith postulated that the gains accruing from the specialization of labor and other resources in a local economy are not basically different from those accruing from the specialization of resource use and exchange among nations.[4] He contended that the benefits stem directly from imports rather than from exports. Gains accrue because the imported commodities can be acquired through trade at a lower cost than similar or substitutable commodities can be produced domestically.

The mutual gains from trade can be demonstrated with a simple example using only two countries and two goods. Suppose we consider some hypothetical cost of production figures for the United States and West Germany, as in Table I.

Table I		
COST OF PRODUCTION		
Product	In the United States	In West Germany
Wheat, per bushel	$2.50	DM 5
Wine, per barrel	$5.00	DM 5

In the United States, we must devote to the production of every barrel of wine resources which could otherwise produce two bushels of wheat, while West Germany gives up only one bushel per barrel of wine. Alternatively, we can say that the United States gets two bushels of wheat for every barrel of wine we give up in production, while West Germany gets only one. Clearly, the U.S. is a more efficient (that is, lower cost) producer of wheat, and West Germany is a more efficient producer of wine.

Suppose with an exchange rate of 1.5 Deutschmarks

---

[3]Adam Smith, *The Wealth of Nations* (New York: The Modern Library, 1937), pp. 3-4.

[4]Ibid, p. 424.

per dollar, we decide to export 100 bushels of wheat for which we give up potential production of 50 barrels of wine. In order to get the $250 to pay for the wheat, West Germany gives us DM 375 (1.5 x $250) which we in turn can use to buy 75 barrels of wine, surely an improvement over the 50 we gave up. Notice also that Germany's DM 375, which purchased 100 bushels of wheat in the United States, would have yielded only 75 bushels of domestically produced wheat.

This example shows that countries engaging in trade are able to get more goods and services from their endowments of resources than they could by using those resources to produce solely for their own consumption. Each is encouraged to expand the production of those goods which it produces more efficiently and to trade them for goods which others can produce at lower cost. Conversely, any restriction which turns a country back toward greater self-sufficiency attains it at the cost of getting less from its resources — that is, a lower standard of living.

The Case at Hand

Considering the nation as a whole, what might we expect to result from the imposition of restrictions on the amount of grain exported? Given an inelastic demand for grain, a small decline in U.S. grain exports could cause a relatively large increase in the world price of grain in the short run. Total receipts derived from grain exports would then be greater than in the absence of export restrictions. Depending on the extent to which U.S. farmers participate in the higher returns from the world grain market, both farmers and consumers could gain relative to the free market solution. On the other hand, if the world price of grain did not rise sufficiently to offset the reduced volume of grain exports (that is, if demand for grain is elastic), total receipts derived from these sales would be less than without the grain export limitations. The dollar price of foreign currency would then be higher, resulting in higher prices paid for the foreign goods and services we import. In this case the farmer is obviously worse off and the consumer is either better or worse off, depending on one's purchases of domestic food relative to imported goods and services. So even immediately, the restrictions which lead to lower domestic grain prices might not provide an unmixed blessing for American consumers.

In the longer run, however, the effects of export restrictions are more drastic (and we have learned how difficult it is to escape from "temporary" government policies, once they are established). Grain farmers, finding that they are not allowed to garner the profits which they would receive from free trade as a result of their superior efficiency as compared to their foreign competitors, will reduce grain production and turn to alternative forms of employment. In short, resources which were previously used to produce goods which we could sell to other countries in exchange for commodities which they produce more cheaply are now used to produce those commodities for ourselves — at a higher cost.

Will Unrestricted Grain Exports Cause Inflation?

The belief that inflationary pressures arise from the unrestricted export of grain stems from a basic confusion between the forces which cause changes in *relative* prices and those which affect the general price *level*. It is quite true that an increase in foreign demand, if it is allowed to be effective, would raise the price of grain and grain-related products. It is *not* true, however, that this effect would spill over to higher prices for other goods. The increased demand for dollars to buy the grain would make imported goods and services less costly to Americans — if not now, then at some time in the future. This, in turn, would exert a downward pressure on the prices of domestic goods which compete with imports. Further, the higher price of dollars to foreigners would induce them to buy fewer American goods, leaving more available for domestic consumption and making them cheaper to us.

On the other hand, a rise in the price level (that is, a rise in the average of prices of all goods) occurs when we have more money to spend on an unchanged stock of goods and services or if we were to have the same amount of money to spend on a smaller quantity. This would certainly occur if we were to give our grain away, receiving nothing in return. Since this is not the question in the recent grain sales, there is no reason to expect that allowing farmers to sell their output as profitably as they can will contribute to inflation.

It is far more likely that a higher price level will follow from a long-run policy of export restriction on farm products. The resultant shift of resources out of agriculture into other uses implies that we will have fewer of all goods and services than we could otherwise have. Without reduced money supply growth and with a smaller commodity bundle available for domestic purchase, aggravated inflation is to be expected.

Summary

Export controls on grain shipments to Russia have been proposed. It is contended that such exports lead to higher food prices and further inflation. Restrictions on exports to Russia, however, will not prevent domestic grain prices from rising unless comprehensive controls are placed on all grain exports.

Comprehensive export controls have appeal in the short run since they tend to restrict current domestic food prices. In the longer run the effects of export controls are always harmful. They result in a decline in the world value of the dollar, an increase in the price of imported goods, less output from our productive resources, a higher average price level, and a lower standard of living.

Foreign Raw Materials: How Critical Are They?

OVER the past twenty years a gradual erosion has taken place in this country's self-sufficiency in raw materials. Domestic output of a broad range of basic metals and minerals—quite aside from oil—has lagged behind the rise in consumption. The U.S., as a consequence, has entered a new era—one marked by mounting dependency on foreign resources.

The U.S., for example, for a long time has been completely dependent on imports for its cobalt, chromium, manganese, and tin. Foreign sources last year supplied 84% of the bauxite consumed in the U.S., 92% of the nickel, and 82% of the mercury (box on page 10). In the last decade alone, reliance on foreign-source tungsten has doubled, and imports as a percentage of consumption of many other commodities from asbestos to zinc have shown sizable increases.

In some cases—such as lead and mercury—increasing concern with industrial pollution control has resulted in curtailed domestic smelter production. In others, foreign sources have been tapped simply because it is easier and cheaper. Iron ore is one example of many. High-grade iron ore can be brought in from Venezuela, for instance, for several dollars a ton less than low-grade ore can be produced in Michigan's Mesabi Range.

The mounting dependence of the U.S. and other developed nations on imported raw materials is bringing a significant change in relations between consumers and suppliers. Particularly in the environment of the recent past—featured by a world-wide boom among industrialized nations—producer countries have found that their rich mineral endowment can be used to score gains, both economic and political.

Oil, of course, is today's most publicized example. But many other commodities have been affected in one way or another. Prices have been raised. Producer nations have insisted that raw products be processed to a greater degree at home. And in many places local ownership of production facilities has been increased—in some cases to 100%—through nationalization and other governmental actions.

Is there a possibility of new cartels similar to the one formed by foreign oil producers?

The question is not merely academic, judging by the statements of officials of some producer nations. They have heralded the dawning of a new era of "product diplomacy." Not unnoticed, too, was the meeting earlier this month in Guinea of seven major bauxite producers. Press reports told of the formation of a "bauxite club," but indicated that—for now, anyway—the governments had decided against embargo or price control moves similar to those of the Organization of Petroleum Exporting Countries.

A key consideration in all this, of course, is the degree of concentration of world mineral reserves. Providence, in sprinkling minerals around the earth's crust, has favored some areas in a lavish way while scrimping in others. A relatively few countries, thus, hold the bulk of a number of major minerals. (In the case of the U.S., even though abundantly blessed, its rapid—some would say profligate—chew-up of minerals has depleted many of its reserves.)

The pattern of concentration for a dozen key minerals is shown in the box on page 11. It lists U.S. reserves along with those of other nations which individually account for at least 8% of total world reserves.

Examples of concentration: Australia and Guinea together are found to have more than half of the world's bauxite reserves. South Africa

---

"Foreign Raw Materials: How Critical Are They?" *Morgan Guaranty Survey*, March 1974, pp. 9–13. Reprinted with permission.

alone has 63% of chromium reserves and, with Southern Rhodesia added, the concentration rises to 96%. Spain has just under half of world mercury reserves. Three countries—Thailand, Malaysia, Indonesia—have 60% of tin reserves. And nearly half of world reserves of nickel is held by two countries: New Caledonia and Canada.

Note, however, that the pattern of concentration shown by official reserve estimates is necessarily a qualified and limited one. Reserves are defined as known, identified deposits of mineral-bearing rock from which minerals can be extracted profitably with existing technology and under present economic conditions. New discoveries could swiftly change the picture. So, too, could new breakthroughs in extractive technology. (For example, not long ago a new chemical "flotation" method was developed to produce pellets of iron from low-grade ore. Minable crude ore reserves of the U.S., as a consequence, were increased by 750 million tons or

U.S. IMPORT DEPENDENCE

	Imports as a percent of consumption in 1973
Bauxite	84
Chromium	100
Cobalt	100
Copper	8
Iron Ore	29
Lead	19
Manganese	100
Mercury	82
Nickel	92
Tin	100
Tungsten	56
Zinc	50

about 8%.) And under changed economic conditions, and with upward adjustments in prices, the size of many nations' mineral reserves would be significantly altered.

Still, for the present, concentration of reserves would appear to indicate that raw-material producing nations are in a position to determine market conditions. In actuality, however, the real story may be quite different for a variety of reasons. Among them:

• Substitutes can be found and synthetics developed for many commodities if they should get too costly or scarce.

• Producing countries have different cultural and historical backgrounds and diverse political and economic philosophies which would work against cohesion.

• Most producers, unlike the Arab nations, lack financial reserves to squeeze back production without impairing their economic growth.

• Loss of sales and reduced output in producer countries, where mining payrolls account for a large share of the work force, would quickly bring political repercussions at home.

• Finally, demand for many metals and minerals can be expected to rise unevenly and in times of economic recession actually to decline. The coincidence of business-cycle exuberance among industrialized nations in the recent past, in short, may well have been a transitory phenomenon. A direct consequence could be a weakening of producers' bargaining position.

This country has buffers, too, against possible foreign moves to control prices and supplies of exportable commodities. One such buffer is the nation's stockpile of 91 assorted commodities. As one example, the U.S. has about a year's supply of bauxite squirreled away, an amount adequate to absorb any shock from market disruption in the short term.

In April of last year the national stockpile

441

WHO'S GOT THE MAJOR MINERAL RESERVES

	Percentage of world reserves		Percentage of world reserves
Bauxite		**Manganese**	
Australia	30.3	Gabon	15.0
Guinea	22.6	Republic of South Africa	8.5
United States	.3	United States	—
Other Free World	43.0	Other Free World	35.0
Communist Countries	3.9	Communist Countries	41.5
Chromium		**Mercury**	
Republic of South Africa	62.9	Spain	49.1
Southern Rhodesia	32.9	Yugoslavia	8.7
United States	—	United States	7.2
Other Free World	2.8	Other Free World	21.9
Communist Countries	1.3	Communist Countries	13.2
Cobalt		**Nickel**	
Zaire	27.5	New Caledonia	33.3
New Caledonia & Australia	27.1	Canada	13.6
Zambia	14.0	Cuba	9.1
United States	1.0	United States	.4
Other Free World	8.5	Other Free World	21.9
Communist Countries	21.9	Communist Countries	21.6
Copper		**Tin**	
United States	22.4	Thailand	33.5
Chile	15.7	Malaysia	14.4
Canada	8.9	Indonesia	13.2
Other Free World	41.6	United States	.1
Communist Countries	11.4	Other Free World	21.8
Iron Ore		Communist Countries	17.1
Canada	14.5	**Tungsten**	
Brazil	10.8	United States	6.4
United States	3.6	Other Free World	16.1
Other Free World	24.5	Communist Countries	77.5
Communist Countries	46.6	**Zinc**	
Lead		Canada	26.0
United States	38.9	United States	22.9
Canada	13.2	Other Free World	35.9
Australia	8.3	Communist Countries	15.3
Other Free World	22.2		
Communist Countries	17.4		

NOTE: Reserves are defined as known, identified deposits of mineral-bearing rock from which minerals can be extracted profitably with existing technology and under present economic conditions. Aside from the U.S., nations shown are those which individually account for at least 8% of total world reserves. "Communist Countries" category excludes Yugoslavia.

target level was lowered to $702 million by the Nixon Administration—a reduction of approximately 90% (box on page 13). Against a background of the energy squeeze, shortages, and rising commodity prices, the correctness of the decision to slash stockpiles seems less clear cut now than it did a year ago. Indeed, some lawmakers in Congress are beginning openly to attack the decision. An issue in the debate is whether the basic concept of a stockpile should be changed from that of a strategic store of key minerals useful in times of conflict to one of a "commodity bank" in which minerals could be released to the market in times of shortages and built up in times of reduced world-wide demand.

Riding a recycle

Yet another buffer is the ability to reduce needs for imported commodities by recycling—"mining" trash dumps, industrial scrap piles, even farm refuse. Last year, for example, no less than 15% of domestic copper demand was met from recovered scrap. Almost half of domestic consumption of lead also came from the recycling of scrap. As commodity prices have moved up, more recycling has been taking place.

In the longer run, of course, higher prices for foreign commodities would lead to increased exploitation of domestic resources. Aluminum, for instance, is the third most abundant element in the earth's crust. Potential domestic resources of aluminum derived from ores other than bauxite are virtually inexhaustible. At present, however, the catch is cost; it is generally unprofitable at current prices to tap such sources. Tungsten is another example. The U.S. has potential independence in tungsten—but only at a price (by some estimates, $65 a ton) considerably above that at which it is now available in world markets

(about $50 a ton). Manganese, available in vast quantities on the ocean floors, is another mineral in which the U.S. could be self-sufficient—but at a price considerably above the present.

More attention is now being paid to the development of domestic self-sufficiency in energy as stressed in President Nixon's "Project Independence." Such concern is bound to rub off on mineral industries besides oil. The aluminum industry, for example, uses about 4% of the nation's electricity each year, making it one of the most power-consuming sectors in the economy. Promising new processes are being developed which not only will produce aluminum with 30% less power than before, but also will produce it without bauxite—using, instead, clays and shales which exist almost everywhere.

Substitutions—for instance, plastics for copper and zinc—can help to lessen somewhat the need for scarce commodities. (Ironically, the substitutes themselves can run short; plastics, for instance, have a petroleum base.) That's been happening, of course, in many products and industries, including the U.S. Treasury's money-making business. Silver coins have long since been replaced by copper-clad coins—and now the copper penny itself is an endangered specie. Rising copper prices have made it all but uneconomical to coin the penny in copper.* The Bureau of the Mint has asked Congress for permission to make the penny out of aluminum—at a saving to taxpayers of $40 million a year, owing to aluminum's lower price.

Despite all this, however, it seems clear that for many years to come the U.S. will need to depend to an important degree on imported minerals and metals. Foreign suppliers of such com-

* If the price of copper should rise above $1.20 a pound (copper futures contracts in New York recently were quoted around $1.15 a pound) it would cost the Treasury more than one cent to make a penny, according to metals experts. Pennies would disappear on a mass scale, the experts predict, if the copper price should rise to $1.50 a pound.

SLIMMING THE STOCKPILE

THE nation's stockpile of key minerals and metals has been shrinking slowly but steadily for more than a decade.

The government had $8.7 billion of commodities stored in the stockpile in 1962. That proved to be the peak; midway in the Kennedy Administration the decision was made to scale back the mountain of commodities. Reductions continued in the Johnson Administration, partly as a way to enhance government revenues and improve the budget picture, and in President Nixon's first term.

Last April, the Nixon Administration proposed a more drastic slimming down of the stockpile. It suggested to Congress a new target level of only $702 million—about a tenth of the $6.9 billion worth of commodities in the stockpile at that time. One objective was to combat inflation by increasing the supply of industrial commodities, some of whose prices had increased by more than 30% in the previous twelve months. Another consideration was the decision by military analysts that it was no longer necessary to store three years' supplies to tide the nation over a war emergency.

Congress, in recent months, has questioned the advisability of a drastic shrinking of the stockpile. Lawmakers on the Joint Committee on Defense Production feel that sales from the stockpile would not be of major significance in cooling inflation, and when weighted against the future possibility of foreign embargo and price control of commodities, a large stockpile would be a form of low-cost insurance against shortages.

Eight metals account for the bulk of the stockpile's value. Here are the eight, showing the quantity at the peak level reached in 1962, the current size of the stockpile, and the proposed target level put forth by the Nixon Administration in April 1973.

STOCKPILE PROFILE

	At stockpile peak (12/31/62)		Latest (12/31/73)		New objective	
	Thousand tons	Months' supply	Thousand tons	Months' supply	Thousand tons	Months' supply
Tin	347	77	231	50	41	8
Chromium	5,343	57	1,953	17	445	4
Aluminum	1,970	9	457	1	0	0
Tungsten	81	141	40	61	2	3
Manganese	10,028	65	3,705	23	751	5
Lead	1,386	15	829	6	65	1
Zinc	1,581	14	639	4	203	1
Copper	1,133	8	259	1	0	0

NOTE: Months' supply under the new objective is based on average consumption per month in 1973.

modities, in turn, will be needing the huge U.S. market and U.S. technological know-how to make possible their own economic development and rising levels of living.

Thus, it should be abundantly evident that producers and consumers are interdependent. It is to be hoped that it will also be recognized that commodity confrontations are wasteful, highly disruptive of efficient allocation of resources, and fraught with peril for both sides.

Trends in
U.S. export prices
and
OPEC oil prices

Indexes covering principal categories
of U.S.–OPEC trade between January
1974 and June 1975 indicate U.S.
export prices have not risen relative
to OPEC revenue per barrel of crude oil

EDWARD E. MURPHY AND JORGE F. PEREZ-LOPEZ

MUCH ATTENTION in recent months has centered on the question of inflation in the industrial countries and its impact on the purchasing power of oil revenues received by members of the Organization of Petroleum Exporting Countries (OPEC).[1] It had been argued by some that because of inflation in the industrial countries since January 1974, it would be necessary for OPEC to increase the price of oil to compensate for a decline in purchasing power of the revenues of its members.[2] [OPEC increased the posted price of crude oil an additional 10 percent as of October 1, 1975.] Others had argued that in view of the price increases in 1973 and 1974, the purchasing power of OPEC revenues had been greatly increased.[3]

The purpose of this analysis is to estimate from the available data on U.S. export prices and OPEC pricing policy the trend of purchasing power of OPEC revenue per barrel of oil vis-a-vis exports from the United States. To do this, it was necessary to construct both an index of OPEC revenue per barrel of crude oil and an index of U.S. export prices for the types and classes of nonmilitary products imported by the OPEC countries from the United States.[4] The main findings of the study are:

1. During 1974 and the first half of 1975, OPEC revenue per barrel of oil did not suffer losses in purchasing power vis-a-vis the United States. The available evidence suggests, in fact, that OPEC revenue per barrel may have gained with respect to the export prices of U.S. goods. Specifically, during these 18 months, export prices of the principal categories of U.S. nonmilitary goods of the types and amounts purchased by OPEC countries increased by between 7.2 percent and 9.7 percent, depending on which of two different calculations is used.[5] During the same period, however, OPEC increased its rev-

enue per barrel of crude oil by 9.6 percent by raising the royalty rates and tax rates levied on oil exports.

2. If the period examined is extended 6 months to cover the 24 months from June 1973 to June 1975, then it is clear there has been a dramatic increase in the purchasing power of OPEC revenue per barrel of oil.[6] Specifically, between June 1973 and June 1975, OPEC revenue per barrel increased by 499 percent, while U.S. export prices increased by 31.1 percent.[7]

U.S. trade with OPEC countries

U.S. nonmilitary exports to OPEC countries for 1973, the last year for which complete and disaggregated data are available, amounted to slightly over $3.3 billion, which is about 22 percent of total value of Organization for Economic Cooperation and Development (OECD) exports to OPEC for that year.[8] The members of the OECD referred to here are the principal industrial countries of Western Europe plus the United States, Canada, and Japan.

The bulk of U.S. nonmilitary exports to OPEC for 1973 were concentrated in manufactured goods and food. Table 1 shows the distribution of the value of U.S. nonmilitary exports to OPEC by broad categories of the Standard International Trade Classification scheme (SITC) of the United Nations.[9]

An examination of table 1 shows that machinery and transport equipment (SITC 7) and food (SITC 0) accounted for nearly 70 percent of the value of U.S. exports of nonmilitary goods to OPEC for 1973. Manufactured goods classified chiefly by material (SITC 6) and chemicals (SITC 5) accounted for about 18 percent of total value. Of less significance were crude materials (SITC 2), miscellaneous manufactured articles, not elsewhere classified (SITC 8), and beverages and tobacco (SITC 1). Mineral fuels, lubricants, and related materials (SITC 3) were almost negligible. Commodities and transactions not

---

Edward E. Murphy is chief of the Division of International Prices, Bureau of Labor Statistics, and Jorge F. Perez-Lopez is an economist in the Division.

Edward E. Murphy and Jorge F. Perez-Lopez, "Trends in U. S. Export Prices and OPEC Oil Prices." *Monthly Labor Review*, November 1975, pp. 36–42. Reprinted with permission.

Table 1. U.S. exports of nonmilitary products to OPEC countries during 1973 by SITC section

SITC section	Description	U.S. exports to OPEC, all categories		Value of U.S. exports to OPEC covered by U.S. export prices to the world	
		Value (in dollars)	Percent	Value (in dollars)	Percent [1]
	Total	3,334,973,423	100.00	2,011,620,616	60.32
0	Food and live animals	589,766,770	17.68	448,238,106	[2] 13.44
1	Beverages and tobacco	49,329,433	1.48	0	0
2	Crude materials, inedible, except fuels	122,532,361	3.67	446,282	0.01
3	Mineral fuels, lubricants, and related materials	19,137,834	.57	1,443,106	0.04
4	Oils and fats, animal and vegetable	53,065,094	1.59	0	0
5	Chemicals	243,446,386	7.30	22,978,260	0.69
6	Manufactured goods classified chiefly by material	370,463,370	11.11	84,552,230	2.54
7	Machinery and transport equipment	1,698,676,502	50.94	1,406,772,627	42.18
8	Miscellaneous manufactured articles, not elsewhere classified	138,287,874	4.15	47,190,005	1.42
9	Commodities and transactions not classified according to kind	50,267,799	1.51	0	0

[1] Each element of the third column as percent of total U.S. exports to OPEC ($3,334,973,423).

[2] Includes domestic wholesale prices for milled rice and dried leguminous vegetables.

SOURCE: U.S. Exports—Schedule B Commodity by Country, Report FT-410, December 1973 (Bureau of the Census, 1974).

classified according to kind (SITC 9), a general category that groups shipments valued under $250 regardless of commodity, zoo animals, value of repairs on imported items to be exported, and so on, accounted for about 1.5 percent of the total value of U.S. exports to OPEC.

Prices of U.S. export commodities

The price data used in this investigation have been brought together from three different sources. Price data for manufactured products were obtained from the U.S. export price index program of the Bureau of Labor Statistics. The BLS prices are export prices to the world collected from U.S. exporting firms, whether or not U.S.-owned, for specific and important U.S. exports. Complete specifications are obtained for each product priced. In addition to physical descriptions, the specifications include class of buyer, size of transaction, applicable discounts, currency, mode of transport, port, and packing.

The products selected are classified by Schedule B, the principal scheme for classifying and recording the type, value, number, and destination of U.S.

exports.[10] Adjustments are made in reported prices for quality change. The prices are collected directly from the firms in each reference month. For the period 1964–73, the reference month is June of each year. Beginning with 1974, the reference month is the last month of each quarter.

This procedure for obtaining specification prices means that within an index or a category within an index, the specification priced for one firm most likely will be different from the specification priced for another firm. The advantage of this procedure is that specification prices are used in the indexes and, at the same time, the products most representative of each firm's export sales are included in the indexes. The potential problem thus avoided is that a single national or regional specification for the United States may not accommodate product differences among firms, and indeed may be unrepresentative of the bulk of transactions in a product for all firms.[11]

The composite price behavior of the items selected and priced for each Schedule B category has been considered as representative of the other nonpriced items in the same seven-digit class.[12] The sample of products and price trends reported may thus be taken to represent U.S. exports to the world, and will be applicable to any country or group of countries *except to the extent their experience diverges from the average for all countries.* The price trends will correspond more closely to the trend of prices paid for U.S. products by any buying country or group of countries as the number and variety of products covered is increased in categories which correspond

Table 2. Export price index for all covered U.S. nonmilitary commodities bought by OPEC countries, 1964–75

[June 1967 = 100]

Date	Commodities
June 1964	97.1
June 1965	96.2
June 1966	96.9
June 1967	100.0
June 1968	102.1
June 1969	105.0
June 1970	106.8
June 1971	114.0
June 1972	116.0
June 1973	132.0
January 1974	[1] 161.5
March 1974	161.8
June 1974	159.1
September 1974	169.7
December 1974	179.0
March 1975	174.8
June 1975	173.1

[1] Manufactures interpolated using wholesale price index rate of change for all manufactures for the period January 1974 to March 1974.

Table 3. Changes in variables determining Saudi Arabian oil revenues, 1974–75

Date	Posted price (dollars per barrel)	Royalty rate (percent)	Tax rate (percent)	Production cost (cents per barrel)	Buy-back percentage of posted price
1974:					
January	11.651	12.50	55	10	93.00
March	11.651	12.50	55	10	93.00
June	11.651	12.50	55	10	93.00
September	11.651	14.50	55	10	94.86
December	11.251	20.00	85	12	94.80
1975:					
March	11.251	20.00	85	12	93.00
June	11.251	20.00	85	12	93.00

to those purchased by the group of countries. More than 530 Schedule B categories were included in this analysis. They account for 60.3 percent of the value of U.S. exports to OPEC. Because of space limitations, the Schedule B numbers are not reproduced here. However, table 1 shows the distribution of total value of U.S. exports to OPEC according to SITC sections and the total value of exports that correspond to categories for which U.S. export prices to the world are available.

The products for which export prices are collected by BLS are concentrated in manufactured goods— SITC 6, manufactured articles classified chiefly by material; SITC 7, machinery and transport equipment; and SITC 8, miscellaneous manufactured articles.[13] As may be seen from table 1, these three categories accounted for nearly two-thirds of U.S. exports to OPEC in 1973.[14] Export price series corresponding to categories covering about 70 percent of the value of the manufactures in SITC 6, 7, and 8 were used in the investigation.

An adjustment was necessary because U.S. export prices for manufactured goods are not available for January 1974, the beginning of the principal period being examined. Quarterly collection of U.S. export prices began in March 1974. Prior to that date, export prices were collected in June of each year beginning with 1964. Thus, actual U.S. export price data for manufactured goods are available for June 1973 and March 1974, but they are not available for January 1974. However, it is possible to estimate the level of U.S. export prices to OPEC countries for manufactures in January 1974 by interpolating the export price index time series using the change in U.S. domestic manufactures prices between January 1974 and March 1974. The U.S. wholesale price index rate of change between January and March

1974 was calculated for the all manufactured commodities category and applied to U.S. export prices for manufactures for March 1974 to estimate the level of the export prices for manufactured commodities for January 1974.

At the present time, BLS does not collect export prices for agricultural commodities. Therefore, in order to cover this important category, which accounts for 17 percent of U.S. exports to OPEC, it was necessary to obtain price data from two sources. Export prices for wheat and corn were obtained from the U.S. Department of Agriculture.[15] For milled rice and dried leguminous vegetables, domestic U.S. wholesale prices from the Wholesale Price Index were used as a proxy for export price indexes.[16] These four agricultural products account for about 76 percent of the value of agricultural commodities exported from the United States to OPEC and 13.4 percent of the value of all U.S. nonmilitary exports to OPEC.

The price index of U.S. exports to OPEC countries calculated here is a weighted average of changes of individual prices of U.S. export products. The weights used are the value of U.S. exports to OPEC countries calculated at the most detailed product level for 1973.

The export price index (XPI) is of the Laspeyres form, so that at time t

$$XPI_t = \sum_j \sum_{i=1}^{n_j} \frac{1}{n_j} \cdot \frac{P_{i\varepsilon j,t}}{P_{i\varepsilon j,t-1}} \cdot w_j$$

where
- j = seven digit Schedule B commodity
- n_j = number of price relatives within each j
- w_j = share of value of U.S. exports to OPEC for each j in 1973
- $\frac{P_{i\varepsilon j,t}}{P_{i\varepsilon j,t-1}}$ = price relative of iεj (the ith item within j)

and where

$$w_j = \frac{V_j}{\sum_j V_j}$$

and V_j = value of U.S. exports to OPEC in 1973 for each j.[17]

In cases where BLS has already published an export price index for an SITC subgroup, that index was entered in the above formula and assigned a weight equal to the share of that subgroup in the value of U.S. exports to OPEC.[18]

The index as calculated thus assigns an importance to each product which is proportionate to its importance in U.S. sales to OPEC in the base period.

Price trends for U.S. goods bought by OPEC

Using the price data described above, an index was prepared for the kinds of U.S. goods exported to OPEC. The prices have been weighted by the relative value of U.S. exports to OPEC of each of the detailed commodities for which U.S. export prices to the world were available. The export categories covered contain slightly over 60 percent of the total value of U.S. exports to OPEC.[19] The index shows an increase of 73.1 percent between June 1967 and June 1975. (See table 2.)

The change of U.S. prices over the period January 1974 to June 1975, measured in table 2, for all the types of commodities exported to OPEC countries which we have covered is estimated to be 7.2 percent. Calculations which include certain domestic U.S. prices for the commodities for which directly collected export prices are not available raise this estimate to 9.7 percent.[20]

OPEC revenue per barrel of oil

The discussion of the purchasing power of OPEC oil exports has been couched in terms of the purchasing power per unit of oil exports. In the case of oil, the published prices (called posted prices) are not the actual transaction prices; that is, the posted prices are not the prices paid by the buyers and they are not the prices received by the sellers. To examine the trend of selling prices of oil, it is necessary to

Table 4. Changes in posted prices and government revenue on equity oil for Arabian light crude, 1964–75

[Dollars per barrel]

Date	Posted price	Government revenues from royalties and taxes
June 1964	1.800	0.990
June 1965	1.800	.990
June 1966	1.800	.990
June 1967	1.800	.990
June 1968	1.800	.990
June 1969	1.800	.990
June 1970	1.800	.990
June 1971	2.285	1.325
June 1972	2.479	1.448
June 1973	2.898	1.702
January 1974	11.651	7.008
March 1974	11.651	7.008
June 1974	11.651	7.008
September 1974	11.651	7.113
December 1974	11.251	9.799
March 1975	11.251	9.799
June 1975	11.251	9.799

Table 5. Buy-back prices for Saudi Arabian light crude, 1974–75

[Dollars per barrel]

Date	Posted price	Buy-back (percent)	Buy-back price
1974:			
January	11.651	93.00	10.835
March	11.651	93.00	10.835
June	11.651	93.00	10.835
September	11.651	94.86	11.052
December	11.251	94.80	10.666
1975:			
March	11.251	93.00	10.463
June	11.251	93.00	10.463

make a special calculation of the revenues received by the OPEC sellers of oil on a unit basis.

As sellers of crude oil, the OPEC countries derive their revenues from a combination of two principal sources: (1) taxes and royalties per barrel paid by oil companies that have an equity investment in the country for the extraction of oil, and/or (2) sale of state-owned crude by the OPEC country to the oil companies.[21] The first source of revenue is generally referred to as taxes and revenues on "equity" oil, while the second corresponds to receipts for "buy-back" oil (that is, state-owned oil).

The posted price is an artificial price set by OPEC, which is used as a base to calculate the amount of royalties and taxes and to determine the level of the buy-back price. Therefore, given any posted price, other variables such as the royalty rates, the tax rates, and the buy-back rates determine the revenue received per barrel by the OPEC governments.[22]

The series for OPEC revenues per barrel of crude oil presented here is based on revenues from sale of light crude oil received by Saudi Arabia, the world's largest crude oil exporter. Arabian light crude, 34° API, f.o.b. Ras Tanura, is used as the pricing standard for crude oil by OPEC countries. Adjustments of price for other crude oils are made for deviations in density, sulphur content, and differentials in transportation costs. Since most pricing decisions by OPEC are based on Arabian light crude, and OPEC has generally followed the leadership of Saudi Arabia in determining the level of government revenues per barrel, Saudi Arabian revenue per barrel of light crude oil can validly be used to indicate trends in OPEC revenue per barrel.

The revenue per barrel is the weighted average of the revenue per barrel from equity oil and the revenue per barrel from buy-back oil. It is calculated by a formula which incorporates the various tax and royalty rates, buy-back rates, production costs, and the posted price.

Revenue per barrel =
  (royalty per barrel + tax per barrel) (share of equity oil in production) + (buy-back price per barrel) (share of buy-back oil in production)

where:

Royalty per barrel = (posted price per barrel) (royalty rate)
Tax per barrel = [posted price per barrel−(royalty per barrel + production cost per barrel)] (tax rate)
Buy-back price per barrel = (posted price per barrel) (buy-back rate)

The revenue per barrel of Saudi Arabia for Arabian light crude was calculated by substituting in the formula the relevant Saudi Arabian values for royalty rates, tax rates, production shares, and so forth. (See tables 3, 4, and 5 for values used.) The results of these calculations are shown in table 6, where it may be seen that revenue per barrel remained at $0.99 until after June 1970, when it began to increase. It reached a level of $10.32 in December 1974 and decreased to $10.198 in March 1975. There was no change between March 1975 and June 1975. This series, showing Saudi Arabian revenue per barrel, has been used here as the proxy for all OPEC revenue per

Table 6. Saudi Arabian revenue per barrel of crude oil, 1964–75

[Dollars per barrel]

Date	Revenue per barrel from—		Revenue per barrel [1]
	Equity oil	Buy-back oil	
June 1964	0.990	(2)	0.990
June 1965	.990	(2)	.990
June 1966	.990	(2)	.990
June 1967	.990	(2)	.990
June 1968	.990	(2)	.990
June 1969	.990	(2)	.990
June 1970	.990	(2)	.990
June 1971	1.325	(2)	1.325
June 1972	1.448	(2)	1.448
June 1973	1.702	(2)	1.702
January 1974	7.008	10.835	9.304
March 1974	7.008	10.835	9.304
June 1974	7.008	10.835	9.304
September 1974	7.113	11.052	9.476
December 1974	9.799	10.666	10.320
March 1975	9.799	10.463	10.198
June 1975	9.799	10.463	10.198

[1] Weighted average of government revenues from equity oil and buy-back oil. Calculated based on total sales of 95 percent of all crude—40 percent equity oil and 60 percent buy-back oil.

[2] From June 1964 to June 1973, the buy-back price is not available since during this period almost all oil was equity oil. Changes in participation agreements that gave rise to the differential price treatment of the two oils occurred in late 1973.

Table 7. Comparison of export price index for U.S. goods bought by OPEC countries and index of OPEC revenue per barrel of crude oil, 1964–75

[June 1967 = 100]

Date	U.S. export price index to OPEC	Index of OPEC revenue per barrel
June 1964	97.1	100.0
June 1965	96.2	100.0
June 1966	96.9	100.0
June 1967	100.0	100.0
June 1968	102.1	100.0
June 1969	105.0	100.0
June 1970	106.8	100.0
June 1971	114.0	133.8
June 1972	116.0	146.3
June 1973	132.0	171.9
January 1974	161.5	939.8
March 1974	161.8	939.8
June 1974	159.1	939.8
September 1974	169.7	957.2
December 1974	179.0	1,042.4
March 1975	174.8	1,030.1
June 1975	173.1	1,030.1

barrel. The series was converted to index number form and is shown in table 7.

Comparison of trends

It is interesting to compare the U.S. export price index for the types of goods exported to OPEC and an index which shows the growth of OPEC government revenue per barrel of crude oil.

June 1967–June 1975. A comparison of these two series for the period June 1967 to June 1975 shows that gains in OPEC revenue per barrel far outweighed increases in U.S. export prices, resulting in large increases in the purchasing power of OPEC revenue per barrel. Indeed, while U.S. export prices to OPEC countries as measured here increased by about 73 percent between June 1967 and June 1975, OPEC revenue per barrel of crude oil rose by 930 percent. (See table 7 and chart 1.)

January 1974–June 1975. An examination of trends in the period following the dramatic oil price increases late in 1973 reveals there has been no decline in purchasing power of OPEC revenue per barrel vis-a-vis U.S. export prices. During 1974, the U.S. export price index developed here increased by approximately 11 percent. OPEC revenue per barrel of crude oil also increased by approximately 11 percent during 1974.[23] During the first half of 1975, U.S. export prices to OPEC countries declined by about 3.3

449

percent from their level at the end of the fourth quarter 1974. Over the same period, OPEC revenue

per barrel decreased by 1.2 percent. Thus, for the six consecutive quarters from January 1974 through June 1975, U.S. export prices to OPEC rose by about 7.2 percent, while OPEC revenue per barrel increased by approximately 9.6 percent.

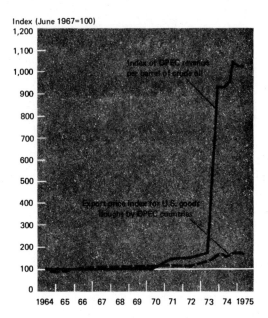

Chart 1.

Export price index for U. S. goods bought by OPEC countries and index of OPEC revenue per barrel of crude oil, 1964-75

Index (June 1967=100)

Summary

This investigation has provided measures of the trend of U.S. export prices for the types of goods exported to the OPEC countries. The measures use U.S. prices to the world weighted by U.S. trade with OPEC. The U.S. export price index calculated here, when compared with OPEC revenue per barrel, shows that OPEC has experienced large gains in the purchasing power of its per barrel revenue.

During 1974, U.S. export price increases were matched by increases in OPEC revenue per barrel. During 1975, U.S. export prices to OPEC decreased while OPEC revenue per barrel of oil remained unchanged. From January 1974 to June 1975, the 7.2-percent price increase which has occurred for U.S. exports has been exceeded by the 9.6-percent increase in the revenue per barrel of oil charged by OPEC. (For an alternative calculation, see the appendix.) It appears, therefore, that OPEC's purchasing power per barrel of oil has not decreased between January 1974 and June 1975 with respect to U.S. products of the nonmilitary types purchased by OPEC. □

<hr>

————FOOTNOTES————

ACKNOWLEDGMENT: The authors are grateful to Jose Alonso and William Alterman of the Division of International Prices for preparation of the computer programs and to Glenn Stadsklev of the Office of Survey Management for the system redesign and data processing required for the large amount of price data used in the preparation of this report. Helpful comments were received from W. John Layng of the Office of Prices and Living Conditions.

[1] Current members of OPEC, which was created in 1960, are Algeria, Ecuador, Gabon, Indonesia, Iran, Iraq, Kuwait, Libya, Nigeria, Qatar, Saudi Arabia, United Arab Emirates, and Venezuela. Ecuador was admitted as a full member in November 1973 and Gabon was admitted as a full member in June 1975.

[2] For example, a communique issued at the conclusion of the June 1975 Ministerial Meeting of OPEC in Gabon, published in The New York Times, June 12, 1975, p. 57, reported, among other things, that:

. . . in view of increasing inflation, the depreciation of the value of the dollar and the consequent erosion of the real value of the oil revenue of member countries, the conference decided to readjust crude oil prices as from October 1, 1975.

Specific reference to the period Jan. 1, 1974, to September 1975, was made by an official of one OPEC member government in an advertisement in The New York Times, June 5, 1975, p. 23 and The Washington Post of the same date in which he states:

An early upward revision of petroleum price by OPEC members has become an economic necessity in view of the persistent rise in import prices of oil exporting nations from the industrial nations. . . . It has been reported that according to OECD estimates the export prices of OECD countries to OPEC members had increased by 25 percent during 1974 and a further increase of 10 to 15 percent is anticipated until the end of September 1975—i.e., the expiration date of OPEC oil price freeze. Thus the oil exporting nations will be losing after allowing for some adjustments during 1974 between 30 and 35 percent of the purchasing power of their dollar earnings from oil exports between January 1974 and September 1975.

[3] For example, see *World Oil Price Increases and the Inflation in OPEC's Import Costs* (New York, Petroleum Industry Research Foundation, Inc., 1975), p. 2. Mimeographed.

[4] The price data are not specifically for any one buying country, but rather refer to the world market for U.S. products. The weights used are the value of U.S. export shipments to OPEC in 1973. See the discussion of these points in the section on prices of U.S. export commodities.

[5] The former figure refers to product categories for which direct pricing of exports is available and accounts for 60.3 percent of the value of U.S. exports to OPEC. U.S. domestic wholesale price trends for the remaining products, but excluding direct energy products, combined with the price trends of the directly priced exports, yields the latter figure. See the appendix for discussion of the 9.7 percent figure. The lower figure is discussed in the text.

[6] This was due to the large increases in oil prices in October 1973 and January 1974. In fact, oil prices began rising faster than U.S. export prices between 1970 and 1971 and continued to do so, with only minor interruptions, as can be seen from table 7.

[7] The remarkable effect of a slight alteration in the base period dramatizes the significance of the choice of a base period. Much of the analysis of this paper refers to 1974 and the first half of 1975, because the recent OPEC statements on the purchasing power of its revenue refer to price changes in 1974 and 1975. The reader can calculate the trend of the purchasing power of OPEC revenue per barrel vis-a-vis the United States from any of several possible base periods by using the data in table 7.

[8] Data on military exports are not available. After the analysis here was completed, the trade data for 1974 became available, and showed that the value of U.S. exports to OPEC were approximately twice the level of 1973. However, for purposes of price index construction, the distribution of value by product (that is, the weights) is important; the absolute value of trade is not important in this context. We calculated the correlation coefficient between the detailed weight structures for 1973 and 1974; it is .955. Thus the structure of U.S. trade with OPEC in 1974 was almost the same as that of 1973 even though the dollar value of trade had doubled. The use of 1974 weights thus cannot be expected to change significantly the indexes calculated here.

[9] For a full explanation of the SITC, see *Standard International Trade Classification, Revised* (New York, United Nations, 1961), Statistical Papers Series M, No. 34.

[10] *Schedule B, Statistical Classification of Domestic and Foreign Commodities Exported from the United States*, Jan. 1, 1971, and annual revisions (Bureau of the Census).

[11] The use of actual prices instead of unit values results in indexes that measure pure price change. That is, they do not also incorporate movements due to shifts in the composition of products within categories, and adjustments can be made for changes in quality or other specifications. For a description of the problems of unit-value indexes, see Irving Kravis and Robert E. Lipsey, "International Prices and Price Proxies," in Nancy E. Ruggles and others, *The Role of the Computer in Economic and Social Research in Latin America* (New York, National Bureau of Economic Research, 1974).

[12] Schedule B is the most detailed classification scheme available for classifying U.S. export products.

[13] Coverage is being extended to include all U.S. exports in the next few years.

[14] The same coverage holds for 1974, though the dollar amounts are larger.

[15] *Grain Market News* (U.S. Department of Agriculture), various issues.

[16] *Wholesale Prices and Price Indexes* (Bureau of Labor Statistics), various issues. In general, domestic wholesale prices have proved to be good proxies for export prices only in a limited number of cases. In the case of these two products, it has not been possible to examine quantitatively how well the proxy relation holds. However, both products are important export items and, since the lifting of export subsidies in 1972, domestic U.S. wholesale prices are probably a good mirror of the world price. For a discussion of the proxy relation of wholesale prices to export prices, see Kravis and Lipsey, "International Prices."

[17] Calculated from *U.S. Exports—Schedule B Commodity by Country*, Report FT-410, annual 1973, and errata (Bureau of the Census, 1974).

[18] For export price index series published by the Bureau of Labor Statistics, see *U.S. Export Price Indexes, First Quarter 1975* (USDL–75–270).

[19] See table 1. The weights used in the index were calculated at varying levels of disaggregation: the 4- and 7-digit product categories of Schedule B. Schedule B is the principal scheme for recording the value, description, and destination of U.S. exports. See, for example, *Schedule B, Statistical Classification of Domestic and Foreign Commodities Exported from the United States*.

[20] The latter calculation excludes fuels, lubricants, petroleum-related chemicals and fertilizers which together account for 4.5 percent of the value of U.S. exports to OPEC. This and other aspects of the noncovered commodities are discussed in the appendix.

[21] State-owned oil sold at auction accounts for less than 5 percent of production. It has not been included in the calculations made here.

[22] Since October 1973, the OPEC countries have unilaterally determined the level of all these variables.

[23] OPEC revenue per barrel rose over this period, although posted prices for crude oil remained stable and even decreased from November 1974 through the first quarter 1975. The revenue increase was accomplished by raising the royalty and tax rates. (See table 3.)

The Multinational Corporation: A Controversial Force

By Sheldon W. Stahl

There appears to be a growing awareness on the part of many observers of the importance of the multinational corporation (MNC) as a force in world trade and commerce. In 1973, when the gross world product was estimated to be about $3 trillion, approximately 15 per cent, or $450 billion, was accounted for by MNC's. Of this amount, U. S. firms generated nearly one-half. An even more graphic means of illustrating the dimensions of the large multinational firms is to compare their gross annual sales with the gross national products of various countries. These data are presented in Table 1, and they serve to point out not only the heterogeneity of the multinational companies, but their massive size as well.[1] In addition, the table clearly demonstrates that while U. S. firms loomed large, the multinational phenomenon is not uniquely American—a factor which should be borne in mind in light of the many criticisms which have been directed at the multinationals.

In a recent, and generally critical book dealing with MNC's, the authors observed:

> The global corporation is the most powerful human organization yet devised for colonizing the future. By scanning the entire planet for opportunities, by shifting its resources from industry to industry and country to country, and by keeping its overriding goal simple—worldwide profit maximization—it has become an institution of

unique power. . . . They (the managers) exploit the advantages of mobility while workers and governments are still tied to particular territories. . . . In making decisions today they are creating a politics for the next generation.[2]

At the same time, there are many who view the growing internationalization of production engendered by the MNC not only as a highly positive development, but perhaps on a par with the Industrial Revolution of the 18th century insofar as its ultimate impact is concerned. Thus, the investment and operations decisions of corporations come to be viewed in global dimensions with regard to resource allocation and maximization of welfare. And, in this scheme of things, the multinational company becomes the key vehicle for bringing about a world economic system in which the allocation of resources is rationalized to a far greater degree than had ever been the case in the past. Additionally, it is held that if the developing countries seize the opportunities for enhancing their economic growth that result from the activities of the multinational companies, there may be a significant rise in living standards for a vast, impoverished area of the world.

Yet, if this somewhat idealized view of the positive potential of the multinationals has considerable appeal to many, there also remains for many a far less flattering or beneficent view. For example, representatives of organized labor have charged that through the transfer of U.S. technol-

---

1/Since gross national product figures are calculated on a value-added basis—which counts only the value added at each successive stage of production—while gross annual sales of business are not so calculated, comparisons such as those offered in Table 1 should be interpreted with this qualification in mind. Nonetheless, even if one were to divide gross sales figures by two to compensate for double-counting, MNC's would still be massive compared with many nations.

2/Richard J. Barnet and Ronald E. Muller, "Global Reach: The Power of the Multinational Corporations" (New York: Simon and Schuster, 1974), p. 373.

Sheldon W. Stahl, "The Multinational Corporation: A Controversial Force." *Monthly Review*, Federal Reserve Bank of Kansas City, January 1976, pp. 3–10. Reprinted with permission.

Table 1
NATIONS AND CORPORATIONS
Gross National Product or Gross Annual Sales
in Billions of U.S. Dollars

1.	United States	$974.10	51. Egypt	$ 6.58
2.	Soviet Union	504.70	52. Thailand	6.51
3.	Japan	197.18	53. ITT	6.36
4.	West Germany	186.35	54. TEXACO	6.35
5.	France	147.53	55. Portugal	6.22
6.	Britain	121.02	56. New Zealand	6.08
7.	Italy	93.19	57. Peru	5.92
8.	China	82.50	58. WESTERN ELECTRIC	5.86
9.	Canada	80.38	59. Nigeria	5.80
10.	India	52.92	60. Taiwan	5.46
11.	Poland	42.32	61. GULF OIL	5.40
12.	East Germany	37.61	62. U. S. STEEL	4.81
13.	Australia	36.10	63. Cuba	4.80
14.	Brazil	34.60	64. Israel	4.39
15.	Mexico	33.18	65. VOLKSWAGENWERK	4.31
16.	Sweden	32.58	66. WESTINGHOUSE ELEC.	4.31
17.	Spain	32.26	67. STANDARD OIL (Calif.)	4.19
18.	Netherlands	31.25	68. Algeria	4.18
19.	Czechoslovakia	28.84	69. PHILIPS ELECTRIC	4.16
20.	Romania	28.01	70. Ireland	4.10
21.	Belgium	25.70	71. BRITISH PETROLEUM	4.06
22.	Argentina	25.42	72. Malaysia	3.84
23.	GENERAL MOTORS	24.30	73. LING-TEMCO-VOUGHT	3.77
24.	Switzerland	20.48	74. STANDARD OIL (Ind.)	3.73
25.	Pakistan	17.50	75. BOEING	3.68
26.	South Africa	16.69	76. DUPONT	3.62
27.	STANDARD OIL (N.J.)	16.55	77. Hong Kong	3.62
28.	Denmark	15.57	78. SHELL OIL	3.59
29.	FORD MOTOR	14.98	79. IMPERIAL CHEMICAL	3.51
30.	Austria	14.31	80. BRITISH STEEL	3.50
31.	Yugoslavia	14.02	81. North Korea	3.50
32.	Indonesia	12.60	82. GENERAL TELEPHONE	3.44
33.	Bulgaria	11.82	83. NIPPON STEEL	3.40
34.	Norway	11.39	84. Morocco	3.34
35.	Hungary	11.33	85. HITACHI	3.33
36.	ROYAL DUTCH/SHELL	10.80	86. RCA	3.30
37.	Philippines	10.23	87. GOODYEAR TIRE	3.20
38.	Finland	10.20	88. SIEMENS	3.20
39.	Iran	10.18	89. South Vietnam	3.20
40.	Venezuela	9.58	90. Libya	3.14
41.	Greece	9.54	91. Saudi Arabia	3.14
42.	Turkey	9.04	92. SWIFT	3.08
43.	GENERAL ELECTRIC	8.73	93. FARBWERKE HOECHST	3.03
44.	South Korea	8.21	94. UNION CARBIDE	3.03
45.	IBM	7.50	95. DAIMLER-BENZ	3.02
46.	Chile	7.39	96. PROCTOR & GAMBLE	2.98
47.	MOBIL OIL	7.26	97. AUGUST THYSSENHUTTE	2.96
48.	CHRYSLER	7.00	98. BETHLEHEM STEEL	2.94
49.	UNILEVER	6.88	99. BASF	2.87
50.	Colombia	6.61		

NOTE: This table uses 1970 figures for all except the centrally planned economies (excluding China) and General Motors Corp., for which 1969 figures are used.
SOURCE: Lester Brown, "The Interdependence of Nations" (New York: Foreign Policy Association, 1972), pp. 14-15.

ogy and productive facilities to foreign countries, the MNC's have not only exported American jobs, but have, at the same time, eroded our tax base and worsened our balance of payments problems. If it appears that many observers here in the United States are increasingly concerned about the economic impact of multinationals, it would appear equally true that there is rising uneasiness abroad with regard to the activities of U. S. MNC's. Many foreign countries have come to view these corporations as simply an extension of American influence and dominance in the economic sphere, with interests that may not necessarily coincide with what they perceive to be their own national interests. In their shrillest form, allegations have been made that multinational firms simply constitute a subtle form of economic imperialism. Reduced to a less emotional theme, the question of national control over the means of production is becoming a major issue of political debate in country after country. One need look no further than our neighbor to the north, Canada, to be made aware of the increasingly strict controls that have been imposed on the inflow of equity capital from abroad.

The rising tide of U. S. concern over the activities of the multinationals appears to coincide with two developments which have taken place within roughly the last 2 decades. One is the massive flow of U. S. capital into Western Europe—increasingly in the form of direct investment in manufacturing industries. The second factor is the deterioration—until quite recently—in the overall U. S. balance-of-payments position. Without question, the influx of U. S. capital into Western Europe contributed to the rebirth of Europe's economic infrastructure and brought with it a dramatic upsurge in production, employment, and incomes. But along with this rise in living standards, these countries have emerged in a relatively few years as very formidable competitors of the United States both here at home and in our foreign markets. In this regard, the MNC's through their successful foreign operations are alleged to have created the very export competition which, critics say, has undermined our export position, and which allegedly threatens U.S. living standards and job security.

In the analysis which follows, this charge, as well as a number of major problems which have emerged with the growth of MNC's, will be examined. Before looking at some of the economic areas of impact of the MNC's, however, it is helpful to try to clearly define the MNC, as well as to shed some light on the motives for investing abroad.

DEFINITIONS AND MOTIVES

The term "corporation" can be defined precisely. However, there is no universal agreement on exactly what constitutes an MNC. In discussing firms which have international operations, the terms "multinational" and "international" are often used interchangeably. Initially, firms with a high percentage of foreign sales which represented principally exports from the home country were so designated. With the postwar growth in importance of foreign sales traceable to direct foreign investment rather than simply to home country exports, the terms became somewhat less precise. However, a look at some of the representative MNC's shown in Table 1 suggests that those firms have a number of readily identifiable characteristics. They operate in many countries; within those countries, in addition to production, they are quite likely to be engaged in research and development; their management is multinational in character; and stock ownership is typically multinational. The MNC's activities transcend national boundaries and their strategies are directed from a corporate center which may be far removed from where a particular activity takes place. Such corporations have large financial resources, and given their management capabilities, they are able to exploit profitable opportunities throughout the world. Although no precise quantitative frame of reference has been placed on MNC's, knowledgeable authorities suggest that the typical multinational company would have annual net sales of $100 million to several billion dollars, with their foreign sales representing a significant share—some have suggested 25 per cent—of their total sales. Similarly, direct foreign investment in productive facilities in one or more foreign countries may approximate at least 15-20 per cent of the company's total investment outlays.

In addition to defining and attaching some quantitative dimensions to the MNC, it is helpful to distinguish between two principal types, since their economic impact and their rationale for investment abroad are likely to vary according to type. MNC's may be either vertically or horizontally integrated. Vertical integration occurs when the various components used in some final product or products are produced by subsidiaries located in different countries. This might be the case where component part production requires a significant amount of either unskilled or semiskilled labor. Depending upon the number of stages in the fabrication process, the MNC might be highly vulnerable to interruptions in production at one or several steps along the way. Thus, the likelihood of uninterrupted production will be a primary factor in the choice of investment locations, as well as the relative costs of production.

The second type of MNC, the horizontally integrated company, typically is made up of a parent company and one or more foreign-based subsidiaries. These subsidiaries are independent units in their productive capacity, and are set up to produce and sell the company's products in the surrounding overseas region. Although the parent company may set up a branch firm abroad to produce for the American market, in the case of sales to foreign customers, the MNC will usually go the overseas subsidiary route in order to take advantage of the competitive edge afforded by a tariff structure which penalizes foreign imports. In addition, differences in national tastes and traditions frequently necessitate special designs for particular markets. In these instances, even in the absence of tariff or other cost considerations, MNC's will locate close to their potential customers and will therefore disperse their productive facilities.

Despite the allegations by some labor spokesmen that MNC's represent "runaway" firms which produce abroad in order to take advantage of lower foreign wage rates, more often than not, this simply is not true. For the process by which a firm becomes an MNC is an evolutionary one in response to a variety of motives and seldom involves an abrupt or dramatic reversal of previous corporate policies or objectives. The development of an MNC will ordinarily proceed through a number of steps. Initially, the firm will export abroad, selling its products through overseas distributors. A second stage involves the establishment of overseas sales subsidiaries. This is followed by the building of plants abroad, and constitutes direct investment. These plants may be used either for local assembly or full production. Finally, the regional subsidiaries are given full operating authority, and at this point the role of the parent company becomes one of planning and coordination.

Except in the obvious case of the extractive industries which must, of necessity, place their direct investments in those countries where the raw materials are located, the reasons for the movement of direct investment capital abroad are more varied than those alleged by many critics of the MNC. The desire to get around tariff barriers has already been alluded to as a motive, and indeed this was a major consideration for U. S. companies wishing to do business in the European Economic Community. Similarly, where local taste and design differences exist, both production and transportation costs may be minimized by locating close to the markets to be served. Related to this, in part, is the desire to diversify product lines in order to guard against fluctuations in earnings either from cyclical movements in economic activity, labor strife, or interruptions to supply.

While all of the above, in varying degrees, serve to motivate direct foreign investment, perhaps the most important and the most fundamental motivation is simply to tap foreign markets. More than 90 per cent of the output of U.S.-owned firms abroad is absorbed by local rather than U. S. markets. Thus, corporate strategies are directed primarily at either preserving or preempting market shares from actual or potential competitors—U. S. and foreign based. Although a good deal of this direct investment activity may be basically defensive in nature, it can also take on a more aggressive tone when large firms seek to develop new markets outside their home base in order to sustain continued overall rapid growth rates. Where these markets have requirements which make it difficult to service them efficiently via exports from domestic operations, investment capital will move abroad.

The above discussion stresses market motivation as a primary factor in explaining the flow of direct investment overseas. This is not to deny that cost considerations may be important as well. However, cost comparisons are seldom the predominant factor in reaching a basic decision as to whether to invest abroad or in the United States. There have been a number of highly controversial and well-documented cases in which U. S. firms have shifted their production abroad. Unlike most of our direct overseas investment, which is in relatively high-cost industrial countries, these went to the less-developed countries principally because of the large pool of low-wage labor, and involved mainly the consumer electronics, footwear, toy, and apparel industries. Not only do these examples constitute a relatively minor part of our total direct foreign investment, but even in these instances where cost factors are assumed to be of primary importance, there still remains a very strong element of market focus. But in contrast with the examples cited earlier, the market focus in these cases relates to the domestic rather than the foreign market. For all, or nearly all, of the output of the U.S.-owned plants abroad is returned for sale in the U. S. market. It should be noted that in these examples of "runaway" firms, the industries of which they are a part are generally labor-intensive with labor costs representing a high proportion both of the total cost and the value of the output. Within those industries affected, the negative impact on the U. S. work force has been significant and, as noted earlier, has generated heated discussion over the broader impact of multinational business on a number of facets of the American economy.

THE ECONOMIC IMPACT

Perhaps one of the most comprehensive investigations of some of the more important implications of multinational firms was undertaken by the U. S. Tariff Commission at the behest of the Senate Finance Committee. The report is entitled "Implications of Multinational Firms for World Trade and Investment and for U. S. Trade and Labor," and was released in February 1973. Much of the data was obtained from the Bureau of Economic Analysis of the U. S. Department of Commerce and was the result of a special census which encompassed all known U.S.-based MNC's, covering 3,400 U. S. parent companies and approximately 23,000 foreign affiliates. That survey was supplemented by a sample survey of MNC operations for the calendar year 1970. Comparison data were based on the benchmark years 1966 and 1970. Although those responsible for the report candidly acknowledge a number of technical shortfalls and urge further substantive research into the area, the report does provide a wealth of data as well as a number of important insights into both the operations and some of the implications of the MNC's. The observations which follow are drawn largely from the Tariff Commission report.

The Impact of U.S.-Based MNC's on World Trade

During the period covered in the study, the U.S.-based MNC's bulked large in overall world trade, but they did not dominate it. A basic reason was that the major share of their foreign output, particularly in the manufacturing sector which was the most dynamic in terms of MNC expansion, was sold in the countries where it was produced. The MNC's, including parents and affiliates, generated about 25 per cent of world exports of all commodities, but accounted for about one-fifth of world exports of manufactured goods. At the same time, it was observed that MNC worldwide exports, and in particular exports of manufactured goods, were growing faster than those of the world as a whole in the 1966-70 period.

The Impact of Multinational Firms on U. S. Trade

One of the more frequent allegations regarding MNC's is that they displace domestic production—hence jobs—by increased imports from their affiliates. At the same time, some charge that by using affiliate output to serve foreign markets, they tend to reduce our exports to those markets. Regarding these allegations, the Tariff Commission found a close association between U. S. foreign investment and U. S. exports, but a weak association between the level of foreign investment and the degree of import penetration. Those industries which were the larger direct investors abroad were also the industries generating the largest amount of U. S. industrial exports. With regard to trade levels, then, the evidence suggested that the MNC's played a larger role as exporters than as importers. However, a partial indication of the extent to which the U. S. trade balance may have suffered adversely from MNC activities may be discerned by examining changes in the U. S. trade position.

Changes in U. S. exports and imports may be affected by MNC's in two ways. By their shipments from and to the United States—their exports and imports—they exert a direct effect. Additionally, they may exert an indirect effect by substituting the production of their foreign affiliates for U. S. exports in foreign markets. From 1966-70, the Tariff Commission study showed that overall, U. S. MNC's generated $3.4 billion more in new exports than in new imports, while at the same time non-MNC's in manufacturing generated an import surplus of $3.6 billion, suggesting that the direct trade effects of MNC's were highly favorable to the United States. An estimation of the indirect effects also proved favorable, with U. S. exports showing a net gain of $400 million over the same period.

Yet, it would not be wholly correct to infer from the existence of export balances for some firms or industries versus import balances for others, that the former were automatically more beneficial to the U. S. economy than the latter. The amount of imports used by a firm is quite obviously related to the kind of product it produces, and it would be clearly wrong to conclude that a firm which may be a heavy importer is, because of that fact, somehow damaging the U. S. economy. For many U. S. firms—among them a number of vertically integrated MNC's, as noted earlier—import large amounts of raw materials or other intermediate inputs and export little, if any, of their final product. To the extent that these imports contribute to the firm's overall productive efficiency, its sales of final products in the U. S. market might well substitute for those of would-be foreign exporters. Such a benefit to the overall U. S. trade balance, though perhaps less visible than increased exports, is nonetheless equally real.

The result overall, for manufacturing, shows that the impact of MNC's on changes in U. S. trade from 1966 through 1970 appeared to be highly favorable. As might be expected, however, on an industry-by-industry basis, there was a good deal of variance. Of the 24 industries in which comparisons could be made, 16 industries showed a net increase in U. S. exports of $7.3 billion for the period, while 8 industries showed net new imports of $3.4 billion. Despite the apparent favorable outcome overall, the wide variations in industry performance do lend some credence to the notion that for some groups of workers, the MNC development may have been costly.

The Impact of MNC's on U. S. Labor

If some groups of workers have been clearly harmed as a result of the growth of MNC's, is it true, as has been alleged by many within organized labor, that the spread of multinational business has reduced overall employment in the United States? In order to measure the impact of U. S. direct investment abroad on domestic employment, for the period 1966-70, the Tariff Commission study attempted to estimate what would have happened if the multinationals had not invested abroad. It did this by making estimates based on three different sets of assumptions. The first, and most pessimistic estimate, assumes that in the absence of U. S. plants overseas, the foreign countries would not resort to local production to replace that lost output, but would import the entire output from plants within the United States. Given this assumption, the presence of U. S. plants abroad represents a net loss of 1.3 million U. S. jobs. The second estimate was arrived at by assuming that foreign countries would replace half of the output of the U. S. overseas plants with local production and import the remainder from the United States. Using this assumption, there is a net loss of 400,000 U. S. jobs. Finally, in order to incorporate more realism, the Commission assumed the following: in the absence of U. S. MNC's, foreigners would not have substituted their own plants, and U. S. exports to those countries could reasonably have been expected to have maintained only the share of world exports of manufactures that they held in 1960-61, rather than to have taken completely the markets abroad served by the MNC's affiliate plants. With these more realistic assumptions, there is a net gain in U. S. manufacturing employment of roughly 500,000 jobs.

Ultimately, the kind of job loss or gain that may result depends upon the time scale involved. In the short run, a domestic job loss is a near certainty where production is shifted abroad. Over the longer run, however, if one expects our international accounts to tend toward equilibrium, some positive offset is likely to occur in some other industry. Perhaps the principal difficulty the MNC's pose is that, because they are typically in the technological forefront, they serve as a much quicker transmission belt for technological change than otherwise. The more rapid the change or the dispersion of production to new locations, the more rapidly adjustment problems arise for the work force in the short run, even though this same process might, in the longer run, benefit the general welfare.

An important point brought out by the analysis was that there was significant variation on an industry-by-industry basis. For example, even under the most pessimistic assumption, there are still some industries which show gains in employment. In the case of industries that are experiencing difficulties from foreign competition, the appropriate public policy response should be couched in terms of the broad U. S. national interest. For labor is not only a producer, but a consumer as well. From the perspective of the consumer, it seems reasonably clear that there have been sizable benefits in terms of a wider range of high quality, lower-priced goods as a result of the overseas production opportunities made possible by U. S. foreign investment and by our liberal trade policies. At the same time, this may be of little solace to those U. S. workers whose incomes have been terminated as a consequence of job loss to foreign competition. Yet, basically, high levels of production, employment, and income in the United States depend upon a vigorous economy which is competitive and profitable in the world economy. Thus, advocacy by labor of restrictions on U. S. trade and investment appear to be not only ill-founded, but short-sighted as well. For such a course would generate retaliation by other nations and would lead ultimately to reduced levels of trade and investment with consequent reductions in income and employment both here and abroad. Rather, in those instances where U. S. industries have been adversely affected by foreign competition, a more forward-looking approach would involve adjustment assistance to domestic firms and adequate compensation and retraining opportunities for labor, plus a vigorous pursuit of more equitable trade and investment rules from our trading partners.

Technology and the MNC's

The U. S. based multinationals play a key role in the development of new domestic technology. At the same time, they are the principal vehicles for both exporting and importing technology. The study found that exports of technology exceeded imports by a factor of more than 10 to 1, for the 1966-70 period. In addition, the high technology industries tended to place more direct investment abroad—as compared to investment at home —than did either the medium or low technology industries. Thus, it might seem a foregone conclusion that, inasmuch as the high technology MNC's are both the major developers and exporters of U. S. technology as well as major investors abroad, they contributed significantly to the relative decline in our trade of high technology products. However, the study found that this was not the case. Over the 1966-70 period, the MNC's in the high technology industries generated about $6.1 billion in net new exports, while the non-MNC's in the same industries generated about $2.1 billion in net new imports. On balance, then, it would appear that the MNC's have aided rather than impeded the growth of U. S. export trade in high technology goods. It should be pointed out, though, that this observation would likely be just as true for those high technology firms which were not MNC's. Thus, our favorable export experience in high technology goods may not solely be a function of the unique character of MNC's, but rather may reflect the experience of high technology firms, some of which happen to be MNC's.

The U. S. Balance-of-Payments Impact

In the second half of the 1960's, aggregate U. S. balance-of-payments performance was marked by considerable deterioration, traceable chiefly to transactions with Canada and Japan. The alleged negative payments role of the MNC's was alluded to earlier. In examining these allegations, the Commission found that in the period 1966-70, the position of the MNC's in terms of the "basic balance" (current account and long-term capital account combined) improved by $2.8 billion, while non-MNC's in the private sector showed a decline of $3.3 billion. The MNC's appeared to be a major factor in the adverse shift in the payments balance with Canada—primarily because of trade in automobiles. But this came about as a result of a treaty with Canada, rather than decisions by the MNC's involved. With respect to our payments balance with Japan, the MNC's were a positive force.

Despite the generally favorable payments impact of MNC's reported by the Tariff Commission, several qualifications should be borne in mind. Just as an examination of import versus export balances was not adequate to assess the impact of MNC's on U. S. trade, similarly, comparisons of MNC versus non-MNC basic balance positions provide only a very cursory and incomplete indication of the impact of MNC's on the overall U. S. payments balance. Moreover, to the extent that there is at work a long-run adjustment process toward equilibrium in our international accounts, generalizations based on fragmentary evidence for a short time period must be viewed with extreme caution as a guide to the future.

SOME FINAL OBSERVATIONS

The subject of MNC's is charged with a good deal of emotion. At home, they are the object of a wide range of allegations, most of which do not appear to be borne out under investigation. Yet, the evidence is not absolutely conclusive. For public policy then, until long-run benefit/cost ratios for MNC's can be more clearly determined, the appropriate policy stance would seem to be one of neutrality in either promoting or discouraging MNC development. Certainly, to the extent that public policies focus on ways of maintaining a vigorous and healthy American economy, any adjustments necessitated by MNC activities in particular industries can proceed more smoothly.

In a larger sense, the promise of the MNC in a world characterized by increasing economic interdependencies and a growing awareness of the need to maximize the efficiency with which resources are utilized should be apparent. As a force for breaking down national barriers and integrating economic relationships throughout the world, the MNC may be uniquely able to help create a true world economy. Yet, this promise of the MNC coincides with a growing wave of economic nationalism, particularly in many of the smaller and less affluent nations. Fears and resentment of the MNC run deep in the impoverished countries of the Third World, where paradoxically MNC's account for most of the employment in the advanced sectors of the economy. For frequently, the immediate interests of the MNC and the host government may not coincide and in such instances the issue of who is the boss becomes of paramount importance.

The MNC may represent one part of the practical answer to the question of how a truly viable world economic system can be created. But the conflicts which have arisen between the MNC with its supranational point of view, and the host of newly emerging and already existing nations with their narrower national economic concerns, will have to be resolved before the MNC can play its positive role. Whether the MNC will, in the future, be a positive force contributing to the uplifting and economic betterment of much of the world, or whether it will become a divisive force leading to distrust and hostility, depends to a large degree upon how those conflicts are resolved.

B. International Monetary Issues

Worldwide Stagflation

The following article was written by Professor Paul A. Samuelson of the Massachusetts Institute of Technology. The article is adapted from a memorandum prepared last autumn by Dr. Samuelson for the West German Council of Economic Advisers. Copyright © 1974 by Paul A. Samuelson.

THE international economy has seen in recent years a reacceleration of inflation in virtually every region. Creeping inflation that had earlier displayed a 3% or 4% or 5% average yearly trend has generally more than doubled that rate. Although the sharpest upswing has been in the prices of those staples that move heavily in international trade—food, fiber, fuels, and metals—there also has generally been a decided quickening in the pace of wage inflation and of price increases for domestic services and goods.

The current inflation, to be sure, has not represented hyperinflation or galloping inflation of the 1920-23 German experience or the Hungarian and Chinese experiences after World War II; nor is it akin to the 300% rate of inflation reached in Chile at the end of the Allende regime, or (as yet) akin to the chronic Latin American inflation that has averaged out to more than 20% per year for decades and even generations. However, the magnitude of the inflation makes it a matter of acute concern and public debate, particularly because of widespread uneasiness that it may well accelerate further. Inflation is indeed a prime election issue in many countries.

Compounding the economic problem of inflation is the fact that, often and in many countries, there persists a simultaneous problem of unemployment and stagnant growth. "Stagflation" is a new name for a new disease: stagflation involves inflationary rises in prices and wages at the same time that people are unable to find jobs and firms are unable to find customers for what their plants can produce.

Fallacious single-cause explanations

A variety of monistic explanations have been offered for the current inflation. The monetarists, of course, identify excessive growth of the money supply as the sole or prime cause. Other economists trace the global speedup of inflation principally to the long string of balance-of-payments deficits experienced by the U.S. in the 1960s. And for still others, wage-push is the villain, with the wage explosion that has occurred so widely in recent years attributed to various structural changes in the labor market that are said to have worsened the so-called Phillips-Curve trade-off between movements in unemployment and wages.* Other monistic explanations of current inflation relate to forces disturbing individual commodity or labor markets: to droughts, floods, strikes, cartel behavior, and so on. And a great number of people are convinced, of course, that our inflationary troubles trace to the rise in both the official and unofficial prices of gold—that is, to the general devaluation of currencies vis-à-vis gold that has occurred in the last several years. A related explanation runs in terms of the additional depreciation of particular currencies—such as the dollar—against other major currencies, a phenomenon that links domestic cost and price increases to exogenous forces abroad.

One could expand the list of monistic explanations. They make for dramatic reading. But, alas, the claims of one cause to be the sole cause invalidate such claims for the rest. As we apply the best tools of modern economic analysis to the pattern of available evidence, I believe that no monistic theory can be validly maintained. One is forced by the facts of experience into an eclectic position. It is not a case where intellectual indecision or uncertainty leads to a hedged position of eclecticism. It is rather that explanation of the varied pattern of ongoing experience calls for bold combination of causations.

I certainly have no doubt that the Asian and African droughts and Soviet crop shortfalls have been one critical element in the international run-up of food prices. Sudden supply shifts combined with sudden demand shifts obviously tend to produce dramatic price fluctuations, particularly in an area such as agriculture where changes in prices do not quickly induce either enlarged supply or reduced demand. Microeconomic commodity inflation—whether in food, in fuels, or indeed in any important sector of the domestic or international economy—refuses to remain microeconomic. It is true that a family which spends more on beef or electricity than it has been spending previously may spend less for other things, tending thereby to depress their prices. And one could conceive of money wage rates falling when bad harvests or dear Near-East oil induces a lower real wage rate. But this sort of offsetting occurrence seems to happen only in history books. In the world in which we actually live, strong upside price pressures originating in a particular sector tend to disturb the whole price structure and raise its average level. This is partly because fiscal and monetary policies—for reasons I explore in the paragraphs that follow—generally work in a way that prevents compensatory price declines from occurring. It is also because existing institutional arrangements (such as escalator clauses in collective-bargaining contracts) tend to set in motion a phase of price-wage leapfrogging whenever a major instance of microeconomic inflation erupts. If one focuses narrowly on some especially visible part of the complicated transmission process—on explosive wage behavior or rapid monetary growth—it may well seem that the critical causal element has been identified. But that is illusory. Monetary expansion, for instance, is typically more the result than the cause of sustained general inflation, simply because in the end central bankers—like governments—must be responsive to public opinion of populist electorates. They must be accommodative and avoid policies that would acutely worsen short-run unemployment and stagnation problems. The whole explanation of the inflation we are experiencing is something more than the sum of its separate parts. But it is not something other than the combination of those analytically distinguishable separate strands of causation.

Overview of global inflation

I believe that the present inflation is rooted deep in the nature of the mixed economy. And it

---

* The Phillips Curve takes its name from A. W. Phillips, a New Zealand economist who concluded from study of data covering almost a century of British experience that percentage changes in money wage rates can be explained largely by the level of unemployment and the rate of change of unemployment. Oversimplified, Phillips' thesis is: The softer the job market, the weaker are wage pressures.

is the mixed economy—which is not laissez-faire capitalism any more than it is centrally-controlled state socialism—that characterizes most of the world today: North America, Western Europe and Australasia, Japan, and much of the developing world outside of Eastern Europe and mainland Asia.

For one thing, we live in the Age After Keynes. Electorates all over the world have eaten of the fruit of the tree of modern economic knowledge and there is no going back to an earlier age. High employment or full employment is everywhere a goal insisted upon by the electorate of all political persuasions. A half century ago there was no comparable political sentiment effective against incurring prolonged depression or even stagnation; rather there was often a preoccupation with the perils of inflation, of budget and foreign-trade deficits. This shift in populist attitudes of governments necessarily shifts the odds against stable prices (and of course against falling prices). No longer can one expect half the peace-time years to experience falling prices. If general price levels rarely stand still and often rise, then the secular trend of prices must be upward on the average.

What needs emphasis is the universal character of this common *Zeitgeist*. It used to be said, of course, that Germany was an exception. Because of traumatic memories of the inflation of the early 1920s, the German voter, it used to be claimed, would put effective political pressures on the side of price stability—even at the cost of considerable transitional unemployment. Whatever plausibility that hypothesis once had, its credibility surely has gradually weakened as the years have passed? Only a fraction of the population now alive could actually have experienced the hyperinflation. The vividness of any memory must be attenuated through time. This is not to deny that the German Phillips Curve of earlier years represented, in some respects, the envy of most other industrialized nations. However, although I cannot profess to be anything of

an expert on local German conditions, the available statistical evidence strongly suggests to me that *since 1969 there also has been a deterioration in the trade-off relation between German labor market conditions and wage inflation.* Thus, even in Germany, we seem to have a new bias toward chronic inflation.

The present diagnosis is in some ways *not* a pessimistic one. The microeconomic laws of supply and demand that have pulled the prices of major staples to high levels can be expected at least in some instances to pull those same prices downward. Indeed, the prices of many key farm products are now well below earlier peaks, and outside the U.S. a number of metal prices have recently come down appreciably. Microeconomic commodity inflation—except perhaps for OPEC oil—does not have the irreversible character that we properly associate with cost-push inflation in the mixed economy. Moreover, the pre-World War II pattern of a common synchronous business cycle has to a considerable extent reappeared. The coincidence of business cycle exuberance widely throughout the world in 1972-73 was a prime reason for the intensity of inflationary pressure. Now, we seem to be witnessing a widespread relaxation of demand in many countries at the same time. The old-fashioned business cycle has been tamed in the Age After Keynes, but it is by no means yet dead.

A pessimistic diagnosis?

But in a deeper sense, for anyone who is nostalgic for an era in which prices are reasonably stable and in which the purchasing power of money might even rise under the impact of cost-reducing technical change and innovation, the present general diagnosis may be profoundly pessimistic. The modern mixed economy simply will not tolerate that large numbers of people starve or suffer. The old dictum, "He who will not take any kind of work that is offered him, however disagreeable and low-paid it may be, must be starved into doing so," just does not hold any more. And its degree of relevance fades with each passing decade. So be it. Few of us, in the affluent West at least, would want to turn back the clock to an earlier epoch. But it is a corollary of this deep-seated structural change in both attitudes and institutions that prices and wages are increasingly rigid against downward movement. In 1921 general wage rates in urban Britain or America might drop by 10% or even 20%. Today, even relatively large numbers of unemployed put little effective downward pressure on general wage and cost levels. Thus, during the U.S. recession of 1969-70, the rate of unemployment went from 3⅓% of the labor force up to 6% without doing very much even to slow down the positive rate of increase of money wage rates; and it never did slow the rate of wage increase down to the level of average labor-productivity improvement in the American economy. Looking beyond 1974, one must expect that union wage settlements will lose their "moderate" character and move from the 5%-to-7% annual range up toward the 10%-to-12% range.

Specific factors in recent inflation

Besides the broad deep-rooted structural changes here and abroad that have created a new bias toward inflation, the acceleration of price increases in recent years traces to a number of special disturbances — most of which I have enumerated. The food and fuel problems are uppermost in the minds of people at the moment perhaps, but a great deal of attention—deservedly so—also has been paid to balance-of-payments disequilibrium, particularly to the U.S. payments deficits of the 1960s. From 1959 to 1971, the U.S. dollar was overvalued in my view. Even if this opinion is not accepted for the first five years of this period, after the Viet Nam War few could doubt that the overvaluation of the dollar was worsening. This must, in some degree, have contributed to inflation in Western Europe and Japan.

The mechanisms through which the overvaluation of the dollar contributed to global inflation are multivarious but are not in doubt. The swelling of U.S. imports of goods and services provided strong export markets for the surplus countries such as Germany and Japan Export orders, microeconomically, raised the prices German firms could charge; they also reduced the excess capacity in the export sectors, raising real marginal costs there and hence the mark prices charged to either Germans or non-Germans. The enhanced incomes enjoyed in the export sectors were, in turn, respent on local goods and services, putting upward price and wage pressures in those sectors. Thus, whether we use the language of microeconomics or the Keynesian multiplier language of macroeconomics, one understands how the international U.S. payments deficit contributed to inflation in other countries. (In the U.S., the ability to get goods from abroad did—but in an inadequate degree—do something to lessen upward pressure on the U.S. wage and price level.)

The tendency for the rest of the world to import some inflation from the United States was reinforced, moreover, by the workings of the Bretton Woods system. Prior to 1971, the surplus countries generally supported the official parity of the U.S. dollar. This meant that firms and persons in Western Europe were, in the end, given local currencies by their own central banks. This added to their local supplies of money. And one does not have to be an over-simple monetarist to recognize that the effect of such an increase in money is to strengthen the direct stimulative multiplier effect that flows from an export surplus. Inevitably, of course, the policy of "benign neglect" in the U.S. with regard to the payments deficit was bound to create apprehension and to induce a speculative flight out of the dollar and into the undervalued currencies of the surplus countries. When that happened, a further bulge occurred in local money supplies outside the U.S., thereby intensifying the multiplier process.

Could not the nations with undervalued currencies have insulated themselves from importing some inflation from the American deficit? Of course they could have. But it would not have been technically all that easy. And it would have involved many politically unpopular measures.

A surplus country, for instance, could have refused to support the dollar at its official parity. Instead it could have let its currency appreciate against the dollar without limit. This would have stopped the stimulative multiplier process. No dollars would have come into the surplus country, and hence there would have been no enlargement of the local money supply via central banking absorption of dollars. In time, the appreciation of the surplus country's currency could have been expected to have stimulated imports and weakened exports. And with the risks from speculation becoming two-sided under a regime of freely fluctuating exchange rates, there presumably would have ceased to be one-way speculative movements. These possibilities are not, of course, entirely academic. The German government on several occasions most particularly did follow a deliberate policy of currency appreciation beginning in the early 1960s. The results, it is true, were not wholly in keeping with textbook doctrine, especially as regards Germany's trade surplus. *But appreciation of the mark undoubtedly did keep the price level in Germany from being as high as it would have been otherwise.* The German man in the street understandably complains about the inflation he has experienced: he would have more to complain about under a Bretton Woods regime of pegged exchange rates at the 1960 dollar-mark parity.

Alternatively, while still supporting an overvalued dollar's official parity, the monetary and fiscal authorities of any country in payments surplus, could, in principle, have *offset* the inflationary pressures imported from abroad. Higher taxes and lower government expenditures could have been employed to produce a negative fiscal-policy multiplier effect just large enough to offset the stimulative export multiplicand. And as the central bank of the surplus country absorbed dollars (or SDRs or, before 1967, official gold), it could have arranged *offsetting sterilization operations* to keep its domestic supply of money from expanding. The central bank, that is, could have engaged in whatever open-market sale of government securities was needed to keep the supply of currency plus demand deposits at a target set by some perfectionist monetarist. None of this would have been easy; and it would have run into great political resistances. But, in principle, it would not have been unfeasible.

Trade and payments considerations

For the future, there is reason to think that the American dollar is no longer overvalued from a long-run point of view. This has to be a tentative judgment, especially because of the difficulties involved in assessing the outlook for food exports and oil imports over a several year span. But with the dollar now showing a cumulative trade-weighted average depreciation of about 18% from June 1970 parities vis-à-vis 14 other major currencies, it is not unreasonable to think that the period of chronic balance-of-payments disequilibrium for the U.S. is over, at least in relation to other oil-consuming industrialized countries. (Germany may still be an exception to this: she still runs a surprisingly strong payments surplus in mid-1974.) If this is so, the stimulative multiplier process described above that prodded global inflation rates higher may have run its course. Countries no longer with chronic surpluses thus could get some relief from "imported" inflationary pressures. This would be decidedly the case if the overhang of dollars accumulated prior to the Spring of 1973 was gradually to be reduced by U.S. payments strength. However, it's a bit premature as yet to count on such a relative surplus trend.

There is another facet of international economic relations that must be analyzed if we are to understand the recent worldwide speeding up of the rate of inflation. Ten years ago the need to compete for world export business served effectively to hold down many prices in the European and Japanese economies. Professor Erik Lindahl of Sweden and others have described the dual-price system that emerged: a domestic price index of commodities sheltered from international competition rose steadily in the early 1960s at 4% per annum or more; at the same time a price index of standardized goods moving in international trade was held down to virtual stability by the need to compete with exporters abroad. What was true for Sweden was also true for other countries: Italy and Japan provide good examples of the dual-price system at work; a striking contrast exists between them and the United States, which because of its continental size and tradition of domestic orientation lacked such a dual-price system.

What needs emphasis is the fact that for many years this element of international competition did serve to restrain price increases for industrial goods and to moderate the over-all rate of inflation. It is a nice analytical question as to how equilibrium could be maintained for long in a common labor market between two such disparate sectors—one with selling prices rising several percent more per year than the other. Undoubtedly, a squeezing of profit margins in the competitive international sector provides part of the explanation. The influence of keen competition in that sector also may have done much to induce more rapid technical productivity advances and rationalizations than occurred in the domestic sector. Gradually, however, it clearly became more and more difficult to insulate the two sectors from one another. *And some part of the explanation for the recent worldwide quickening of inflation of industrial prices must be found in the fact that, at long last, stability in the price levels of internationally traded goods did come to an end.*

On the brighter side

Precise forecasting of global price trends during the next several years is beyond my ability. For the relatively near-term, I am encouraged chiefly by two considerations: first, by the incipient evidence that high prices recently for food and fibers may well be inducing a significantly enlarged flow of goods onto markets; second, by the indications that simultaneity in business-cycle situations in different countries—characteristic of the century before World War II—is reconstituting itself. In 1974, this second consideration carries disinflationary implications because we seem to be witnessing a rather general easing of demand pressures. Indeed, some concern is being voiced (e.g., an article in *The Economist* of June 1 titled, "The Approaching Depression") that we have entered into an oil-affected period of sluggishness internationally that will cumulate into very serious unemployment. While the extreme view strikes me as unjustifiably alarmist, I do believe that the fact that the present circumstance of economies tending to be in step together heightens prospects that price increases will moderate for a while. Parenthetically, I would note that I see no compelling reason why in the Age After Keynes this coming of business cycles into goose step should have to prevail in the future. As in the 1950s and 1960s, America can still have its minirecessions when other countries are having their booms — and vice versa.

The longer-run outlook

Apart from the relatively near-term, however, I do not think anyone ought to count strongly on persistent improvement in price performance. Certainly, it seems only realistic to perceive the outlook for the mixed economies not as an outlook for stable prices but rather for a series of compromises which will make for creeping or trotting inflation. The problem is how to keep the creep or trot from accelerating. This includes the challenge of finding new macroeconomic policies beyond conventional fiscal and monetary policies that will enable a happier compromise between the evils of unemployment and of price inflation. The rhetoric of John Kenneth Galbraith notwithstanding, direct wage and price controls are not an incomes policy that, in my assessment of experience, modern mixed economies know how to use effectively in other than the short run. Periodically, for short periods, price-wage freezes and phases of price-wage regulation for large-scale economic units can be used to advantage. Presidential or Ministerial wage-price guidelines and guideposts also have a limited function; but experience does not make one optimistic that these can be relied on much in the longer run.

Manpower and labor market programs to reduce the structural elements of unemployment certainly need to be explored further; but it is not clear from experience in the United States or in Europe that they have anywhere been able to solve the problem of giving a much-improved Phillips Curve to any economy.

Since I have been stressing that, even with creeping inflation, we are left with stagflation imperfections and trade-offs as people increasingly come to anticipate any maintained rate of inflation and to become habituated to that unchanging rate—then why do I not recommend a Draconian policy of insisting upon absolutely stable prices at whatever cost to current unemployment and short-run growth, always in the hope that after this original costly investment in fighting inflation has been made the economy can live happily ever afterwards with stable prices and nothing worse than moderate amounts of unemployment? I think making any such recommendation is academic, since in any modern mixed economy — featured politically by very limited tolerance of policies of constraint — it will assuredly never be followed. But more than that: I am not persuaded by the force of theoretical argument, or by the statistical and historical data so far available for different mixed economies, that even in the longest run the benefits to be derived from militant anti-inflationary policies don't carry excessive costs as far as average levels of unemployment and growth are concerned. And even if the benefits did decisively outweigh the costs in the longest run, history is a onetime thing and mankind at this stage of the game can ill afford to make irreversible academic experiments whose outcomes are necessarily doubtful and whose execution could put strains on the already-strained political consensus of modern nations.

What is not academic is the more relevant debate going on behind the scenes of official life: Would it not be desirable, in the interests of keeping inflation from accelerating, to countenance and even contrive slow U.S. growth for two or three years, so that unemployment will remain above the 5½ % level? Even if desirable, is such austerity feasible in the present American political environment?

Interdependence, Exchange Rate Flexibility, And National Economies

By Donald L. Kohn

Over the past 20 years, economic relations among countries have been marked by an increasing degree of interdependence. A rapid expansion has occurred in the quantity of goods and financial assets traded across international borders and these trade and capital flows have become quite sensitive to differences in price and interest rate levels. As a result of the growth of international transactions, countries have benefited greatly in the form of larger output through more efficient use of productive inputs.

The rise in interdependence, however, has made it increasingly difficult for a national economy to follow a path that is not consistent with worldwide economic conditions. That is, the costs of greater international trade and interdependence have been increased vulnerability to disturbances arising in other countries and a possible reduction of national autonomy in deciding on levels of domestic prices and economic activity. As a reaction, governments have increasingly accepted greater flexibility in their exchange rates in the hope that they might obtain better control of internal economic targets.

The growth of interdependence and exchange rate flexibility has important implications for the performance of a national economy. For one, the effectiveness of traditional monetary and fiscal tools in an open economy is greatly influenced by the type of exchange rate system in operation. Even the channels through which these policies affect aggregate demand may be different when foreign trade and capital flows are important. Greater interdependence and exchange rate flexibility also affect how an economy will react to an economic event in another country.

This article explores some of the more important conceptual implications of the growth in interdependence and the move to flexible exchange rates. Monetary and fiscal policy actions are examined both for their effects in the country initiating such actions and for their impact on other countries of the world. Also examined is the impact that an abrupt shrinkage in the supply of an important commodity will have on countries importing that commodity. The consequences of these events will be compared under systems of fixed and flexible exchange rates. Throughout, it will be assumed that the markets for goods and services and credit are highly integrated. In such an environment, small deviations from the world levels of prices or interest rates will elicit very large flows of goods or capital moving from an area of low yield or price to one in which high yield or price prevails.[1]

1/This does not imply that price and interest rate levels cannot be changed by the actions of a large country which purchases a significant portion of world output, only that eventually the same prices or interest rates—at whatever level—will prevail throughout the world. No explicit distinction is made between stock and flow adjustments to price or yield changes. It is assumed that the stock adjustment is so large and persists for so long that in the intermediate term considered by this article it can be treated as a flow adjustment.

Donald Kohn, "Interdependence, Exchange Rates, Flexibility and National Economies." *Monthly Review,* Federal Reserve Bank of Kansas City, April 1975, pp. 3–10. Reprinted with permission.

MONETARY DISTURBANCE

Fixed Exchange Rates

When exchange rates are fixed, a monetary policy disturbance involving a change in the money stock at home or abroad tends to have little effect on income in its country of origin.[2] This is especially true of small countries with limited foreign exchange reserves. If the monetary authorities in such a country were to attempt to increase its money stock, they would first purchase securities so as to provide more bank reserves. The security purchase and money stock increase would put downward pressure on interest rates and cause capital to leave the country.[3] To prevent the exchange rate from falling below its fixed rate, the government of the expanding country must then meet the resulting new demand for foreign exchange with sales of its international reserves. This action, however, would reduce the reserves of the banking system and cause the money stock to contract. Hence, the initial increase in the money stock would tend to be offset by its subsequent decline. The monetary authorities might try to maintain a higher money stock level by continuously injecting new reserves into the banking system. They would find, though, that their ability to sterilize the external deficit in this manner would be limited by their holdings of international reserves—for these reserves would continue to fall as long as the money stock and interest rates deviated from their initial levels.

If it took some time for capital flows to respond to lower interest rate levels, then the country might temporarily increase its demands for goods and services. In an open economy, at least part of that new demand would find an outlet in purchases from overseas. This would put additional downward pressure on the exchange rate, result in a further drop in international reserves, and speed the return of the money stock to its initial level. Monetary policy, therefore, changes the level of international reserves but has no more than a temporary impact on domestic money supply, prices, and incomes.[4]

If a large country increased its money supply, the results might be somewhat different. An increase in the money supply by a large country, i.e., one which purchases a significant amount of the world's output, would lead to an increase in demand for foreign goods and services and may raise the level of prices throughout the world. Similarly, an increase in that country's money stock would lower interest rates worldwide.[5] Consequently, the country would not be subject to the capital and product flows of the magnitude necessary to bring its income and interest rates back to their pre-expansion levels. Nonetheless, even a large country is likely to experience reserve outflows in response to a monetary expansion. The impact of the reserve outflow may be temporarily delayed if the country's foreign reserves are very large or if other countries hold the large country's currency as international reserves. In either event, the central bank could temporarily sterilize the reserve outflow and allow the money stock to remain higher for a considerable time period. In this interim period, the large country would then experi-

---

2/The same type of analysis would hold for other monetary disturbances such as a change in people's desire to hold money.

Parts of this section follow the general outlines of the monetary theory of the balance of payments. See Harry G. Johnson, "The Monetary Approach to Balance of Payments Theory," *Journal of Financial and Quantitative Analysis*, March 1972, pp. 1555-72.

A summary of much of the research done on monetary and fiscal policy under fixed and flexible exchange rates can be found in Robert M. Stern, *The Balance of Payments* (Aldine: Chicago, 1973), especially Chapter 10.

3/This ignores the possibility that the forward rate on the country's currency may adjust so as to allow it to maintain a different interest rate. The more exchange rates are really considered to be fixed and immutable, the more remote is this possibility.

4/For a country attempting to contract its money supply, the process would be a mirror image. A trade and capital account surplus would give rise to reserve inflows which would reexpand money. The central bank's ability to offset or sterilize this inflow would be limited by its holdings of domestic assets.

5/If the money stock increase were continuous and inflationary, interest rates would eventually have to rise to incorporate revised inflationary expectations.

ence increased income and, if it is near full employment, increased prices. Eventually, the country would begin to run out of reserves and would be forced to reduce its money stock. But because of higher world prices and lower interest rates, reserve outflows would tend to cease when the money stock, income, and prices were above their previous levels. For the large reserve currency country, therefore, monetary policy can have a considerable short-run impact on income and some smaller long-run effects, too.

When a large country acts to increase its money supply, smaller countries may be subject to some irresistible consequences of that action when exchange rates are fixed. The increase in demand by a large country would be felt by the rest of the world as a rising demand for exports, which would cause rising pressures on prices and incomes worldwide. In addition, the reserve outflows of the large country would swell the reserves and money supplies in the rest of the world. Businesses and consumers would find that the initiating country's external deficits would provide them with the cash balances necessary to finance rising levels of expenditures. If a small country tried to resist these inflationary pressures by sterilizing the reserve inflows and keeping interest rates high, it would simply attract even more reserves. In brief, control over the money stock or inflation rate in the rest of the world could be greatly impaired. The inflation rate would be identical everywhere, tied to the monetary expansion of the large country.

These relationships were quite evident in the events of the mid-1960's through 1971. During that time, the United States was the dominant reserve currency country and, consequently, was in a position to incur large external deficits. In the late 1960's, many European countries complained that excessive monetary expansion and inflation in the United States were causing, through capital outflows and trade deficits, monetary expansion and

demand pressures in the rest of the world. Foreign countries also found that their attempts to dampen internal demand to resist inflationary pressures only elicited larger reserve inflows. One response to this problem was the proliferation of controls on capital movements into European countries. These attempts to gain policy maneuverability by decreasing interdependence proved only temporarily successful, however, because the means of avoiding controls grew as quickly as the controls themselves.

The problem became more acute in 1970 and 1971, as the Europeans attempted to tighten their monetary policy while U.S. monetary policy was loosened in response to the U.S. recession. The Eurodollar market became a turntable on which dollar outflows from the United States were borrowed by European companies and converted into their own currencies for domestic use. Thus, integrated capital markets and fixed exchange rates meant that the European countries had largely lost control of internal monetary conditions and the ability to use monetary policy to achieve domestic income and inflation targets.

The United States, despite its large size and the special status of the dollar, found that it too was vulnerable to foreign capital flows that weakened monetary policy. In 1969, the Federal Reserve was trying to dampen inflation in the United States by reducing credit granted to American borrowers. The high interest rates and slow monetary growth in the United States, however, attracted capital from abroad, especially through the mechanism of U.S. bank borrowing in the Eurodollar market. For a time, therefore, U.S. banks were able to lessen the effects of the restrictive Federal Reserve policy by borrowing abroad and re-lending in the United States.

Flexible Rates

With flexible exchange rates, just as under fixed rates, a small country that increased its money stock would have a tendency toward lower interest rates and would incur capital outflows. Also, an increase in its money stock would cause its residents to demand more of all goods, including imports. Under fixed exchange rates, as described earlier, the deficit in trade and capital accounts would give rise to a reserve outflow that would tend to reverse the money supply increase. With flexible rates, however, the monetary authorities would not purchase or sell international reserves to keep the exchange rate within a prescribed fixed range. Consequently, the deficit would not lead to an offsetting reduction in bank reserves and the money stock. Rather, the country's increased demand for foreign currency would cause its own currency to depreciate, or decline, in price. As its currency depreciates, the country's exports become less expensive to foreigners and imports cost its own residents more. As a result, both residents and foreigners demand more of the economy's output and nominal income rises. This is what the monetary authorities intended when they increased the money stock. Therefore, even though the traditional channels of monetary influence through interest rates would be eliminated by integrated capital markets, monetary policy can be quite effective by affecting import and export demand through changes in the exchange rate.

When exchange rates are flexible, monetary policy works in large countries in the same way it does in small countries. An increase in the money stock of the large country will result through trade and capital flows in the depreciation of its currency. This depreciation will stimulate production through its effects on internal demand. In the case of the large country, however, the capital outflow may be large enough to lower interest rates worldwide.

By allowing its exchange rate to fluctuate, a small country need not accept the effects of a monetary expansion transmitted from the larger country. The depreciation of the large country's currency and coincident appreciation of the small country's currency will prevent additional domestic demand in the large country from being translated into new demands for the small country's exports. Domestic producers in the large country will feel the entire impact of the monetary expansion. As a result, the large country may find that money stock increases produce greater inflation under flexible than fixed rates. For the small country, the exchange rate might appreciate so much that its income was reduced.[6] Under flexible exchange rates, however, the small country can increase its money stock to offset the effects of the excessive appreciation and retain control over its income level.

EXPENDITURE DISTURBANCE

Fixed Rates

An expenditure disturbance is a change in spending plans which is independent of a change in the money stock. One example of an expenditure disturbance would be a change in fiscal policy—the taxing and spending decisions of government. Under fixed exchange rates, an increase in expenditures in a small country can be a very effective means of increasing income. As with an increase in the money supply, part of the increase in spending will be deflected to foreign commodities and result in higher imports. This will create a balance of payments deficit that will drain reserves, reduce the money stock, and counteract the expansive fiscal policy. But the increased spending will also put pressure on domestic credit markets and tend to raise interest rates above the worldwide level. This

---

6/Appreciation beyond the level necessary to protect small country income from large country expansion may be made necessary by the new lower world interest rate which increases the demand for money at every income level. Sales of financial assets by small country residents to obtain higher money balances put upward pressure on interest rates which attracts capital and drives up the exchange rate thus reducing income.

will promote an inward flow of foreign capital and a gain in international reserves. The latter reserve inflow will more than offset any tendency for reserves to decline due to the trade account deficit. That is because, if imports are a reasonably stable proportion of income, the trade deficit would be limited by the size of the rise in income. On the other hand, when capital markets are fully integrated, the tendency toward higher interest rates will call forth a flood of incoming capital. The net increase in international reserves—unless neutralized by the central bank through sales of domestic assets—will enable the money stock to increase, thereby validating and reinforcing the expansive thrust of fiscal policy. In brief, while monetary policy by itself is ineffective under fixed rates, an increase in the money stock which accompanies an expenditure shift can be quite powerful since it will not be subsequently offset by a reserve outflow.[7]

If a large country adopted an expansionary fiscal policy under fixed exchange rates, the same processes would work in the same directions as they do for a small country but the end result may differ. That is because the increased demand and subsequent net reserve inflow may have important effects on the rest of the world which, in turn, would feed back into the large country. As demand by large country residents for the products of other countries grows, total demand in other countries would also tend to expand. This would raise price and interest rate levels everywhere, but the impact would be greatest in the initiating country. Capital

would flow into the large countries until its interest rates were reduced to the world level—now somewhat higher than they were initially. Because of the raised world interest rate level, the money stock and income increase in the large country would not be as great as it would have been had the country left the rest of the world unaffected.

The country facing an expenditure shift in a large country, especially an important trading partner, may experience important effects on its own economy. As pointed out earlier, interest rates in the smaller country would definitely be higher. Also, income in the smaller country would have two opposing forces working on it: the expansionary impact of demand from the country initiating the expenditure increase, and the contractionary effects of a lower money supply due to a reserve outflow to the larger country. Whether income in the smaller country will be higher or lower after the first expenditure change depends on the relative strength of these two forces.

Flexible Rates

Far different results would be obtained if a small country tried an expansionary fiscal policy under flexible exchange rates. The tendency toward balance of payments surplus under fixed rates would be translated into an appreciating exchange rate. This would dampen internal demand by reducing exports and increasing imports. Since no reserves can be gained or lost when governments do not intervene in the exchange market, the increased expenditures cannot be validated by increases in the money stock. The currency would continue to appreciate as long as expenditure demands were in excess of their old level. The process would stop when the currency appreciation had decreased demand by exactly the amount it had increased originally. When there are fluctuating exchange rates and integrated capital markets, fiscal policy tends to have no effect.

7/This scenario and much of the ensuing discussion of expenditure disturbances assume that the government demands domestic, rather than foreign, output and that the existence of unemployed resources means that increases in domestic output can take place at a constant price level. See Robert Mundell, "Capital Mobility and Stabilization Policy under Fixed and Flexible Exchange Rates," reprinted as Chapter 18 of Robert Mundell, *International Economics* (New York: The Macmillan Company, 1968), p. 251. If there were any tendency for government purchases to raise prices, perhaps because the economy was near full employment, then imports would increase and the effect on income of the increase in government spending would be nullified by a larger trade deficit.

A large country would find its fiscal policy effectiveness reduced under flexible rates, but not eliminated. The initial increase in income in the large country increases demand in the rest of the world. Under flexible rates, however, the capital inflow would tend to appreciate the large country's currency. While the appreciation reduces demand on the large country's resources, it adds to the upward pressures on demand in the rest of the world by increasing their exports and decreasing their imports. Some of this foreign demand will return again to the large country as demand for its exports. If the countries are close to full employment, worldwide inflation will result. If unused capacity exists, real incomes will rise.

From the viewpoint of the small country facing a fiscal expansion in a large country, flexible rates would greatly increase its vulnerability to an unwanted rise in nominal income. Under fixed rates, the increase in demand in the small country was offset by a declining money supply. No such cushion exists with flexible rates. The large country's disturbance would have a considerable impact on the rest of the world.

This kind of business cycle transmission may have been operating at the end of 1974 and into 1975. The U.S. economy was declining more rapidly than that of most of the rest of the world. The decline was marked in part by slow monetary growth but even more importantly by downward expenditure adjustments in housing and durable goods purchases. The fall in demand resulted in lower interest rates and an outflow of capital from the United States. With exchange rates under a system of managed floating, the dollar began to depreciate against the currencies of most other industrialized countries. This development was beneficial to the United States as it tended to deflect foreign and domestic demand to U.S. products and so cushioned the fall in U.S. income. In other countries, the in-creased imports and decreased exports resulting from dollar depreciation tended to reduce income and output at a time when their economies were already weak. Consequently, they moved to support the dollar and control the appreciation of their own currencies.

SUPPLY DISTURBANCE

A supply disturbance is a sizable and unanticipated reduction in the supply, or an increase in the price, of an important international commodity. With the growth of interdependence, the potential for serious disturbances of this type has increased sharply. Important examples of supply disturbances have occurred recently in both food and petroleum products. Since food demand declines very little as its price rises, very large price increases were necessary to ration the shortfalls in supply. In the case of petroleum, the supply reductions occurred from a deliberate decision by many petroleum producing countries to band together to increase their profits. As with food, petroleum demand is not very responsive to price changes over the short run, so the producers found they could temporarily raise the price of oil substantially with only minor cutbacks in production.

From the viewpoint of the importing country, the effects of a supply disturbance in a commodity facing inelastic demands are many faceted and mostly bad. Given the short-run unresponsiveness of demand, the importing country will spend relatively more of its income on imports and domestic demand for internally produced goods will fall. As domestic demand falls, so will domestic incomes, unless the fall in demand is cushioned by the exporter spending its new export receipts in the importing country. This effect on income is analogous to a decline in planned expenditures or a tighter fiscal policy. There is also a monetary effect analogous to a reduction in the money supply. The monetary effect arises because the higher import prices cause an increase in the country's average price level.[8] At higher prices, there will be an increase in the demand for money balances to purchase the same level of real output. People desiring to increase their money balances will, in turn, tend to sell other financial assets and drive up interest rates. This increase in the demand for money caused by higher prices will have the same impact on the economy as a reduction in the supply of money.

For the importing countries, the supply disturbance can be viewed as a reduction in expenditure occurring simultaneously with a fall in the money stock. Under fixed rates, if the recessionary tendencies of the expenditure shift dominate—perhaps because the country spends a high proportion of its income on the particular product—the fall in domestic income will cause interest rates to fall, capital to flow out, and an ensuing decline in the money stock that will further reduce income. If the monetary effects dominate, lower domestic income will be accompanied by higher interest rates, capital inflows, and an expanding money stock. In this case, the capital inflows and expanding money stock with fixed rates will ameliorate the fall in internal demand.

When exchange rates are flexible, countries that would have been made worse off under fixed rates are helped by exchange rate movements. If the expenditure shift dominates, the fall in income will cause interest rates to fall, capital to flow out, and the exchange rate to decline. The ensuing increased demand for exports and import substitutes will then cushion the fall in internal demand. In this case, the country is better off under floating rates. When the monetary effect dominates, however, the fall in income will be accompanied by higher interest rates, capital inflows, and an appreciating exchange rate that will

serve to further reduce income. In this case, the country is worse off under floating rates.

Whatever the exchange rate regime, a country facing a supply reduction is likely to experience a reduced level of real income and output for some time, especially when domestic prices and wages adjust slowly to changing demand conditions. To a lesser extent, it is also true over a longer term. Eventually, the pressure of falling domestic demand will tend to reduce domestic prices relative to import prices. Also, the investment of any capital inflows will reduce interest rates and stimulate interest sensitive spending. As a result, internal demand will rise. Even after full employment is attained, however, the importing country will be worse off than it was before foreign prices increased in that it would take a higher proportion of its production to purchase the same level of imports.

The behavior of income and trade balances in the wake of the petroleum price increases of 1973 and 1974 combine elements of adjustment under both fixed and flexible exchange rates. Petroleum producers accept payment in dollars, which are rarely converted into their own currencies. Consequently, the petroleum deficit cannot be offset by changing exchange rates. The petroleum exporters have little choice but to save much of their new income by investing their surpluses in the importing countries. The industrialized world as a whole has a petroleum deficit matched by a capital reflow of "petrodollars." This deficit is fixed in terms of dollars and is based on the price and quantity of oil purchased.

Exchange rates among oil consuming nations do fluctuate and will rise or fall in part depending on a country's ability to attract capital to offset its trade account deficits. Countries with small capital inflows will find their currencies depreciating. Their oil imports will be offset by a rise in exports to other countries, and their short-run income adjustment may be relatively mild. Countries which

---

8/It is assumed that the fall in domestic demand is unlikely to cause much, if any, decline in domestic prices in the short run.

attract a large inflow of petrodollars will have appreciating currencies. As a result, their trade deficits will tend to swell beyond that which can be attributed to oil imports. Floating rates in this hybrid system therefore serve to allocate the given petroleum deficit among consuming nations.

CONCLUSION

The integration of world markets for goods and credit has led to a heightened degree of economic interdependence among nations. Sensitive trade and capital flows govern the impact of economic events in their country of origin and facilitate their transmission to other countries of the world. The exact way in which countries interact in response to economic events depends, in part, on the exchange rate system under which they operate. A corollary notion is that countries might wish to choose their policy of exchange market intervention with an eye to the type of economic disturbances they expect to be most important at home and abroad.

If a country intended to rely on monetary policy to achieve its income, employment, and price targets, or felt it was subject to unwanted monetary influences from the actions of large and important trading partners, then it should choose to allow its exchange rate to fluctuate. Under flexible exchange rates, its own monetary policy gains effectiveness by inducing changes in exchange rates that push foreign and domestic demands on its resources in the desired direction. The country avoids importing monetary inflation or deflation by not letting its international reserves be changed and by allowing the exchange rate to neutralize potential changes in demand coming from abroad.

On the other hand, a country which felt it wanted to run an effective fiscal policy or felt most threatened by shifts in expenditure flows abroad might opt for a fixed exchange rate system. Fiscal policy in an integrated world is most effective under fixed rates because it will be accompanied by capital flows which validate and reinforce the initial fiscal policy impulse. When there are expenditure shifts in other countries, fixed rates will tend to minimize their effects at home because the capital and trade accounts will move in opposite directions.

No exchange rate system will protect a country against the effects of a sudden cutback in the supply of an important import. Countries that would tend to attract a lot of capital under these circumstances would find that fixed exchange rates will minimize the effect on income. Countries in which the trade deficit would dominate a capital inflow should choose fluctuating exchange rates.

In the 1970's, there has been a pronounced movement toward increased flexibility in exchange rates. This is implicitly a concession that, at least over the long run, monetary disturbances and monetary policy dominate the determination of income. Within a shorter period, however, there may be some justification for exchange market intervention, if it is believed that expenditure shifts are pulling exchange rates away from levels consistent with long-run monetary equilibrium. Of course, no country can unilaterally decide its own exchange rate regime. The nature of the transactions in which one currency is traded for another requires at least implicit agreement by those on the other side of the trades. Countries must agree among themselves on the importance of various types of policies and disturbances and formulate an exchange rate system to maximize national decisionmaking power, while retaining the fruits of an interdependent world economy.

Some Problems in Living with a System of Floating Exchange Rates

James L. Burtle

Vice President of the Business Economics Group
W. R. Grace & Co.

The adjustment of exchange rates to equilibrium levels has turned out to be quite slow. The author examines several factors tending to initially push the foreign exchange market into greater disequilibrium thus making the J curve more pronounced than otherwise would be expected. Included are the impact of multinational companies, the discouragement of forward foreign exchange speculation and the lack of an international store of value.

WORLD trade and investment have continued to rise since early 1971 when foreign exchange rates became more flexible. There has been no decline in world trade because of competitive devaluations; forecasts of widespread beggar-thy-neighbor policies destroying world commercial relations simply have not materialized.[1] Foreign exchange risks under the system of more flexible rates have not been a significant restraint on international investment.

In spite of these basically favorable reactions to flexible rates, there is disappointment with the slow speed and roundabout path of adjustment of exchange rates to equilibrium levels. More recently developed econometric models of exchange rate adjustment[2] seem to indicate that there is a long

This article is based on a paper given at a NABE seminar in October, 1973.

See end of text for footnotes.

lag of perhaps as much as twenty quarters in reactions to an exchange rate change. This means that for several periods following a devaluation, demand elasticities for exports and imports of the country that devalues are not large enough to result in trade balance improvement. Instead there is trade balance deterioration. Later on, however, as buyers adjust to changed prices in the devaluing country, overall demand elasticities become elastic and the balance of trade improves for the devaluing country. This is the analytical machinery behind the widely noted J curve in the adjustment of international trade balances and was very likely a factor in the decline, up to July 1973, in the value of the dollar followed by marked recovery later on in the same year.

Thus the ancient argument between the elasticity optimists—who believe that demand elasticities in international trade are big enough to restore balance of payments equilibrium—and the elasticity pessimists on the other side has ended with a victory for the optimists from a long-run comparative statics point of view. But this is a somewhat pyrrhic victory because, in the short-run following most devaluations, market reactions tell the story envisaged by the elasticity pessimists.

As the J curve becomes more widely recognized, however, it might be thought that this roundabout path in the adjustment of the foreign exchange market would correct itself automatically. Speculators would see the dip in the J curve and buy (or sell) enough of the relevant currency to push it up (or down) in the direction of long-run equilibrium. But thus far there have been ten-

James L. Burtle, "Some Problems in Living With a System of Floating Exchange Rates." *Business Economics,* May 1974, pp. 52–55. Reprinted with permission of the author and the publisher.

475

dencies to push the foreign exchange market into greater disequilibrium rather than providing for its quick and easy equilibration. Without attempting to be exhaustive of all disequilibrating factors, the next three sections discuss the following elements that seem to be of major importance in making the J curve more pronounced than we should otherwise expect:

• Although multinational companies have clearly defined policies against speculation in foreign exchange, their accounting and administrative practices tend to encourage excessive hedging of balance sheet items that should not be hedged.

• Equilibrating speculation on the forward foreign exchange market is discouraged by governments and central banks and also by the large commercial banks through which the foreign exchange market is organized.

• Because the world monetary system provides no store of international value for asset holders who want to be protected against all currency losses, there is a tendency for funds to shift endlessly in search of the unattainable goal of a permanently stable currency.

Multinational Businesses in the Foreign Exchange Market

Multinational corporations are sometimes accused of disrupting foreign exchange markets by large scale speculative movements of funds from one currency to another. But for most corporate officers, at least at high levels, the possibility of gains from foreign currency speculation is strongly outweighed by the danger of severe criticism if there are losses from such gambling. Insofar as multinational corporations are disruptive of foreign exchange markets this comes not mainly from speculation but from playing it too conservatively—from over-hedging rather than from excessive speculation.

Much over-hedging arises from accounting practices that tend to overstate what a company would lose from a devaluation or revaluation. In the United States the usual practice is to adjust *exposed* items in the company balance sheet to show gains and losses from devaluations and revaluations. Exposed items are those parts of the balance sheet that change in value whenever there is a devaluation or revaluation. There are two types of exposed positions: *short positions* and *long positions*. Short positions in a balance sheet represent a company obligation or liability. Long positions represent a company asset, including accounts receivable. In general a company loses from a short position if there is a revaluation—it has to pay off its debts at a revalued exchange rate. Likewise it loses from a long position if there is a devaluation—holdings of the company are reduced in value and its receivables are taken in devalued currency.

But not all items in a company balance sheet are considered to be exposed. In almost all accounting systems it is assumed that cash and accounts receivable are exposed but that fixed assets are not exposed. However, long-term debt and inventories are taken as exposed in some accounting systems, a practice that can lead to serious overcovering and result in moving excessive amounts of funds between countries and in excessive hedging activity on foreign exchange forward markets.

This is not the place for a full discussion of the complexities of various systems of foreign exchange accounting. But some examples may be given of cases where coverage of balance sheet positions seems illogical and excessive. The first case arises from the classification of a long-term debt as a *short* exposure subject to loss if there is a revaluation. This may be reasonable if the borrowed funds are taken out of the lending country, but not if the loan is used to buy a fixed asset in the lending country. In the latter case, the ultimate purchase is the fixed asset which is traditionally not exposed. Put it another way: the dollar value of the servicing costs of the debt and the dollar value of the stream of future incomes from the asset would be roughly offsetting.

There are also cases where inventories are wrongly considered to be exposed. An extreme case would be inventories of goods to be exported for dollars. In other cases inventories are treated as exposed even though price rises in the local currency offset losses from devaluations. Exceptions, where inventories are clearly exposed, might arise for utilities, food, drugs, and inventories of other consumer goods vulnerable to price controls.

The tendency of multinational corporations to over-hedge balance sheet positions is sometimes exacerbated under decentralized management systems. It might be argued that if one subsidiary in a company has a long position and another a short position and if a devaluation was expected, no action should be required because the long and short positions would offset each other. It may not work out that way, however, because the subsidiary with the long position would not want a loss from devaluation on its books even though this loss was offset elsewhere in the company. Thus the total amount of hedging activity by company subsidiaries may be greater than what is required for the consolidated position of the whole company.

The Forward Market
For Foreign Exchange

One now largely discredited argument against exchange rate flexibility was that there would be no forward markets for major currencies. Forward contracts are now readily available for sterling, Canadian dollars, marks, French francs, Belgian francs, Swiss francs, and guilders. With somewhat less reliability, forward contracts can usually be obtained for lire and yen. But the availability of forward contracts does not mean that the market works perfectly.

The main difficulty with the foreign exchange market is that it lacks a strong enough speculative side. As already discussed, there is a tendency of multinationals to over-hedge in the foreign exchange market. This would not matter if cases of over-hedging were offset, as seems to happen in commodity markets, by a large number of speculators willing to take the risks that hedgers do not want.

In other words, the effect of the J curve on exchange rates—perhaps made more oscillatory by company over-hedging—could be smoothed by a strong speculative side of the market. But, unlike in most commodity markets, this does not happen because some governments and private banks, through which foreign exchange trading is carried out, attempt to restrict speculative trading in forward contracts.

Some governments which allow spot rates to fluctuate are, nevertheless, fearful of a free forward market at least for their own citizens. Sometimes it is believed that speculators will be destabilizing for the market although the argument just cited points in the opposite direction. In other cases, governments and central bankers that intervene in foreign exchange markets (but without total stabilization of spot rates) find that their intervention policies become too complicated to implement when they are faced with the whole structure of spot rates, forward rates and also the relevant interest rates involved in interest arbitrage. They tend to restrict the forward foreign exchange market rather than give up the intervention game.

It is well known that at least in the United States, the big banks, who are the major foreign exchange dealers, do not want speculators. This author once thought that the banks discourage speculation in the foreign exchange forward market because of a puritanic bias against gambling. But this view appears to be wrong. The development of an active spot and forward market for currencies has in any case been a strain (though sometimes a profitable strain) on the facilities that banks have available for foreign exchange trading even though most of their customers are now big companies for whom individual transactions usually exceed $100,000. Speculation would, on the other hand, tend to be in the form of a large number of relatively small bets on the foreign exchange forward markets. The banks understandably fear being swamped looking after the needs of a myriad of *little guys* often with no sizeable deposit balances or strong credit ratings. In security or commodity markets potential obligations are guaranteed by margin requirements. But the banks today apparently regard the enforcement of margin requirements as a nuisance that they—already under severe pressure for foreign exchange personnel and other facilities—would not consider profitable to handle.

It is an interesting hypothesis—though one perhaps impossible of verification—that before the Smithsonian Agreement the banks assumed the speculative side of the foreign exchange market. They had confidence in their ability to judge when fears of devaluations were unwarranted and thus made money by offsetting short positions. After the Smithsonian Agreement, however, banks became more fearful of losses from trading on their own account and made more rigid rules that their foreign exchange books for each day should be balanced. As a result there was less of an equilibrating speculative offset for the July, 1973 dive of the dollar.

It might be argued that, because of the complexity of the market, there will always be only a relatively small number of speculative traders in foreign exchange. Even a small number of speculators can, however, be stabilizing of forward rates if the demand for hedge contracts, sometimes because of rigid company rules, is highly inelastic. A relatively small number of speculative contracts supplied under these conditions, could substantially lower forward discounts or premiums.

The Lack of a Store of Value
in the World Monetary System

We have already considered how the amplitude of the J curve is widened by over-hedging by multinational companies and by the near-absence of a speculative side to the foreign exchange market. Moreover the J curve type of adjustment is made more oscillatory and slow to converge to equilibrium because of the lack of any store of value in the system for individuals who want to be independent of currency changes. Without a store of value there will tend to be large shifts from currency to currency in an effort to find the will-o'-the-wisp of a money of steady value.

Gold was once the store of value in the monetary system and it cannot be excluded that it might regain this role. But, unless there is a gold-buying policy of central banks to maintain the price of gold, it seems likely to become more like a commodity with its value affected too much for store of value purposes by the vagaries of its demand for jewelry, industrial uses and traditional hoarding. Gold at a fixed price supported by central bank purchases has the well-known objections that (a) its supply is erratic and, therefore, no one knows how much money supply will be generated by official gold purchases and (b) its use as a store of value is a waste of resources—why dig it when you can print it?

In the IMF Committee of Twenty there have been discussions of the possibility that SDR's might take the place of gold and dollars in central bank reserves. But most of these discussions have envisaged SDR's as held only by central banks. This will enable central banks to have a store of value, but nothing is being considered to provide a store of value for individuals. This writer agrees with a recommendation of the late Paul Einzig that SDR's should be privately held.

Aside from providing for a store of value for individuals, a privately held SDR has two advantages:

• Central banks could use it as an intervention currency when they enter foreign exchange markets. Otherwise countries will be obliged to hold each other's currencies for intervention purposes and there will be a strong danger of drifting back to the use of reserve currencies which most monetary reformers want to avoid.

• The private market would give an indication of when too many SDR's are being issued. Overissue of SDR's is a danger because of pressures from developing countries to link SDR issue to economic aid. But without a free private market for SDR's there will be no clear indicators of excessive SDR issue.

There is, however, the problem raised by Fred Hirsch[3] that, if a publicly held SDR is not rejected, it could easily become over-accepted thus supplanting national currencies, becoming a world money, and leading us back to a type of gold standard with paper gold. Under these conditions countries lose control over their own money supplies. The problem is to find a way out of the dilemma between a worthless SDR from overissue and a financially imperialistic SDR that might arise if its issue were restrained by a market mechanism. One possible solution is to give SDR's the desirable properties of gold that do not apply to currencies. Holders of gold have one advantage over holders of currencies in that the stocks of gold will rise in value if there is severe inflation while money would lose its value. SDR's could be given this property by indexing them as proposed by Modigliani and Askari[4] (though these writers do not propose private holding of SDR's). Indexed SDR's would be tied to a weighted average of world prices and, unlike currencies, would not substantially lose value from inflation. In order to further distinguish SDR's from money they would not be permitted to earn interest. Under these conditions, though many details remain to be worked out, the SDR would provide a store of value for those who want it, but its non-interest earning property would discourage its widespread holding to such an extent that there would be a rejection of national currencies.

[1] There is a serious question as to whether these policies were ever important with respect to currency devaluation, cf. Sidney Rolfe and James Burtle: *The Great Wheel: The International Monetary System* (Quandrangle, New York, 1974).

[2] H. B. Junz and R. R. Rhomberg, "Price Competitiveness in Export Trade Among Industrial Countries," *American Economic Review*, May, 1973.

Michael Beenstock and Patrick Minford, *A Quarterly Model of World Trade and Prices, 1955-1972*, June, 1973 (Unpublished).

[3] Fred Hirsch: "An SDR Standard; Impetus, Elements, and Impediments" in *Princeton Essays in International Finance*, June, 1973.

[4] Franco Modigliani and Hossein Askari: "The Reform of the International Payments System" in *Princeton Essays in International Finance*, September, 1971.

The U.S. Dollar in International Markets: Mid-1970 to Mid-1976

DONALD S. KEMP

ONE of the most controversial issues in the area of international trade and finance has been that of the relative desirability of fixed versus floating exchange rates. Disagreement on this issue is widespread and has been, in the recent past, the major stumbling block to a general agreement within the International Monetary Fund (IMF) regarding the future form of the international payments mechanism.

This article addresses four issues related to the recent experience with generally floating exchange rates between the U.S. dollar and the currencies of nine of the United States' major trading partners.[1] The intervention activities of the Federal Reserve System in recent years are analyzed in order to get some idea of the extent to which exchange rates have been managed. Next, the question of measuring how much exchange rates have actually fluctuated in recent years is addressed. Some criteria are developed for and employed in evaluating whether the observed changes should be regarded as excessive. Finally, the issue of the likely causes of the observed exchange rate changes is explored.

Fixed Versus Floating Exchange Rates: The Issues

The theoretical arguments which surround the issue of fixed versus floating exchange rates are all well-known and will be discussed only briefly here.[2] On one side of this issue there are the fixed rate advocates who contend that exchange rate changes un-

der a system of floating rates will be largely the result of speculation rather than the result of changes in fundamental economic factors.[3] This speculation, in turn, is presumed to be destabilizing. In other words, instead of dampening fluctuations in exchange rates, speculation will make the rates unnecessarily erratic. Furthermore, it is feared that these speculatively generated exchange rate changes will be so large and unpredictable as to disrupt international trade and investment.

On the other side of this issue are the floating rate advocates, who say that while exchange rates will change under a floating rate system, they will do so primarily in response to changes in fundamental economic factors. These individuals maintain that while speculation will undoubtedly occur in foreign exchange markets under a system of floating rates, such speculation will, on balance, not be destabilizing. In other words, speculation will have the effect of dampening fluctuations in exchange rates as they respond to changes in these fundamental factors.[4]

If the empirical evidence of the past few years shows that a significant portion of the fluctuation in exchange rates has been independent of changes in fundamental factors, then such fluctuations should be viewed with concern. On the other hand, if exchange rates have fluctuated in a pattern consistent with changes in fundamental factors, there is much less cause for concern. In such a case, the candidates for government stabilization actions are not the exchange rates themselves, but rather the underlying factors

---

[1]It is crucial from the outset that the reader recognize that the recent experience with floating exchange rates differs significantly from an experiment with the pure "freely floating" exchange rates dealt with in most of the theoretical literature. For one thing, some of the currencies analyzed in this article were officially pegged to others during all or part of the period covered by the study. For another, the rates have been "managed" through official market interventions rather than left alone to float completely free in response to nongovernmental market influences.

[2]For a discussion of the arguments for and against floating exchange rates, see M. O. Clement, Richard L. Pfister, and Kenneth J. Rothwell, *Theoretical Issues in International Economics*, ed. Jesse W. Markham (Boston: Houghton Mifflin Company, 1967), pp. 249-83; and Gottfried Haberler, Henry C. Wallich, Peter B. Kenen, Milton Friedman, and Fritz Machlup, "Round Table on Exchange Rate Policy," *The American Economic Review* (May 1969), pp. 357-69.

[3]The fundamental factors affecting exchange rates in the long run are relative rates of inflation and monetary expansion. These factors are considered fundamental in the sense that their impact on exchange rates can be justified on the basis of economic theory alone.

[4]For a theoretical discussion of the question of the stability of foreign exchange markets, see Kurt F. Hausafus, "Trade Finance, Capital Movements and the Stability of the Foreign Exchange Market," *International Economic Review* (June 1975), pp. 404-14. For an empirical evaluation of the stability issue, see Jerome L. Stein and Edward Tower, "The Short-Run Stability of the Foreign Exchange Market," *The Review of Economics and Statistics* (May 1967), pp. 173-85; and Michael P. Dooley and Jeffrey R. Shafer, "Analysis of Short-Run Exchange Rate Behavior, March 1973 to September 1975," *International Finance Discussion Papers*, International Finance Division, Board of Governors of the Federal Reserve System, No. 76 (February 1976).

Donald S. Kemp, "The U. S. Dollar in International Markets: Mid-1970 to Mid-1976." *Review*, Federal Reserve Bank of St. Louis, August 1976, pp. 7–14. Reprinted with permission.

479

Table I

TREASURY AND FEDERAL RESERVE FOREIGN EXCHANGE OPERATIONS[1]
March 1971 — April 1976
(Millions of U.S. Dollars)

Time Period	Total Purchases	Total Sales	Net Purchases	Total Intervention
February 1976 — April 1976	$301.4	$ 270.4	$ 31.0	$ 571.8
August 1975 — January 1976	227.2	106.5	102.7	333.7
February 1975 — July 1975		1,045.0	−1,045.0	1,045.0
August 1974 — January 1975		742.3	− 742.3	742.3
February 1974 — July 1974	3.7	527.0	− 523.3	530.7
August 1973 — January 1974	584.2	247.5	336.7	831.7
March 1973 — July 1973		273.5	− 273.5	273.5
October 1972 — February 1973	215.0	339.0	− 144.4	554.0
April 1972 — September 1972	299.5	41.7	257.8	341.2
October 1971 — March 1972	55.0		55.0	55.0
March 1971 — September 1971		75.7	− 75.7	75.7

Time Period	Belgian Franc P	Belgian Franc S	French Franc P	French Franc S	German Mark P	German Mark S	Japanese Yen P	Japanese Yen S	Netherlands Guilder P	Netherlands Guilder S	Swiss Franc P	Swiss Franc S	U.K. Pound P	U.K. Pound S
Feb. 1976 — April 1976	$74.9	$	$	$	$173.7	$250.8	$	$	$19.6	$19.6	$ 33.2	$	$	$
Aug. 1975 — Jan. 1976	74.4				149.7	106.5						3.1		
Feb. 1975 — July 1975		29.8		45.6		740.6				96.3		132.8		
Aug. 1974 — Jan. 1975		16.2				619.2				43.3		63.6		
Feb. 1974 — July 1974		21.2		33.7	3.7	469.8				2.3				
Aug. 1973 — Jan. 1974	36.2		33.1		510.6	244.6	4.3			2.9				
March 1973 — July 1973		6.0		47.0		220.5								
Oct. 1972 — Feb. 1973	80.0					318.6					20.4	135.0		
April 1972 — Sept. 1972		10.2				21.4								299.5
Oct. 1971 — March 1972	20.0													35.0
March 1971 — Sept. 1971						75.7								

P — Purchases
S — Sales
[1]Canada and Italy are not listed separately in this table because no data relating specifically to these countries were available.

that contribute to the fluctuations. Indeed, if exchange rate changes reflect movements in macroeconomic conditions within countries, such changes in exchange rates have been beneficial in terms of dampening the international transmission of economic disturbances.[5]

Intervention Activities

During the period covered in this article, exchange rates were neither absolutely fixed at an officially specified level nor were they allowed to float completely free of official foreign exchange market intervention. Such an arrangement has come to be known as "managed floating". In fact, many advocates of a freely floating exchange rate system argue that the present exchange rate system has been so highly "managed" that its performance is not a fair measure of how a "freely floating" exchange rate system would work if fully adopted.

Because of the sparseness of information relating to the intervention activities of the United States and its major trading partners, it is difficult to assess the validity of the above argument. The only official source of information regarding foreign exchange market intervention activities is a quarterly report issued by the Federal Reserve Board of Governors.[6]

[5]This is a fundamental assertion of the advocates of flexible exchange rates. The supporting arguments can be found in Milton Friedman, "The Case for Flexible Exchange Rates," *Essays in Positive Economics* (Chicago: The University of Chicago Press, 1953), pp. 157-203; and Harry G. Johnson, "The Case for Flexible Exchange Rates, 1969," this *Review* (June 1969), pp. 12-24.

[6]This information can be found in a series of reports titled "Treasury and Federal Reserve Foreign Exchange Operations." These reports are usually published in the March, June, September, and December issues of the Federal Reserve *Bulletin*.

In addition to being highly aggregated with respect to U.S. activities, the figures given in these reports almost completely exclude the activities of other central banks. Since other central banks have, in total, intervened in foreign exchange markets with much greater frequency and in much larger dollar amounts than the United States, the numbers provided in these reports underestimate the total amount of intervention that has taken place. However, since it is reasonable to suppose that the United States and other countries take cooperative action and thus intervene on the same side of the markets, these numbers should at least give an indication of the general thrust of worldwide intervention activities during a given period. The data reported in Table I have been gleaned from the Federal Reserve reports.

Recognizing these caveats, there are still some interesting patterns which show up in Table I. First, the currencies in which the System has undertaken the greatest amount of intervention are those that have fluctuated the most (see Table II).[7] Secondly, the total amount of intervention undertaken by the Federal Reserve in the generalized float period (after March 1973) is actually greater than the amount undertaken prior to the generalized float. However, since this observation is based on data having significant shortcomings, firm conclusions should be drawn with care.

How Much Have Exchange Rates Actually Fluctuated?

In investigating the extent to which exchange rates have actually fluctuated in recent years, the concern is not with the net change in exchange rates over long intervals of time, but rather with how much they have fluctuated over short intervals. The reason for concentrating on short intervals (a day, a month, or a quarter) is that it is the short-term fluctuations that are most often attributed to destabilizing speculative forces and are of greatest concern to those engaged in international commerce.

The daily exchange rates between the U.S. dollar and the currencies of the United States' largest trading partners are used to measure the amount of exchange rate fluctuation that has actually been experienced during the past few years. Monthly

averages of these daily exchange rate levels were computed for the time period covering June 1970 through June 1976, and quarterly averages of these monthly levels were computed from the second quarter of 1970 through the second quarter of 1976. The statistical distributions of the percentage changes in these daily, monthly, and quarterly series were then analyzed.[8] The results are presented in Table II.[9]

The first set of results covers the period beginning approximately with the floating of the Canadian dollar in June 1970 and ending in June 1976. The second set of results covers the period June 1970 through February 1973, just prior to the beginning of the current generalized float. The last set of results covers the period of the generalized float (March 1973 - June 1976).

Evaluation of Measured Variability

Unfortunately, there exists no consensus regarding what constitutes excessive exchange rate fluctuations. Hence, there is no standard against which the fluctuations of the past few years can be compared. The approach adopted here is to assume that the fixed bands agreed upon in the Smithsonian accord represent at least a loose consensus on acceptable short-run ranges for exchange rate fluctuations. The performance of exchange rates over the past few years is then compared with these bands.

At the Smithsonian meetings of December 1971, the members of the Group of Ten agreed to permit their currencies to fluctuate within a 2.25 percent range on each side of mutually acceptable central values. In other words, it was agreed that the value of each of the currencies of the United States' major trading partners would be allowed to fluctuate within

---

[7]The interpretation of this observation is a matter of dispute. Many floating rate advocates maintain the possibility that the intervention itself was a source of confusion in foreign exchange markets and, therefore, exacerbated exchange rate movements. On the other hand, many analysts contend that the rates would have fluctuated much more had the intervention not taken place.

[8]The distributions of the *absolute values* of percentage changes were also analyzed. However, there was no significant difference between these results and those of the *actual* exchange rate changes analyzed in this article.

[9]It is usually assumed that data on daily exchange rate changes are normally distributed. Furthermore, upon invoking the Central Limit Theorem, the same assumption is usually made about the distribution of the changes in the monthly and quarterly averages of daily exchange rates. However, the assumption of normality of daily exchange rate changes has been questioned recently by Janice M. Westerfield, "Empirical Properties Of Foreign Exchange Rates Under Fixed and Floating Rate Regimes," *Philadelphia Fed Research Papers* (December 1975).

An analysis of the third and fourth moments about the mean of the data employed in this study leads to no firm conclusions regarding the validity of the normality assumption. However, as expected, the assumption seems to have greater justification in the case of monthly and quarterly averages than in the case of daily levels. Thus, the normal model may not be the most accurate description of the distribution of exchange rate changes. If it is not, then the usefulness of the means and variances reported in Table II is diminished.

Table II

Distribution of Percentage Changes in Exchange Rates Between the U.S. Dollar and the Currencies of Its Major Trading Partners

Time Period and Time Interval	Statistic	Belgium	Canada	France	Germany	Italy	Japan	Netherlands	Switzerland	U.K.
Daily Changes from June 1, 1970 to June 30, 1976 (1494 Observations)	Mean	0.016%	0.007%	0.012%	0.025%	−0.018%	0.013%	0.020%	0.039%	−0.019%
	Std. Dev.	0.526	0.177	0.540	0.552	0.465	0.446	0.476	0.588	0.389
Monthly Changes from June 1970 to June 1976 (73 Observations)	Mean	0.335	0.136	0.239	0.507	−0.387	0.268	0.415	0.798	−0.408
	Std. Dev.	2.336	0.715	2.397	2.720	2.120	1.961	2.403	2.576	1.751
Quarterly Changes from II/70 to II/76 (25 Observations)	Mean	1.034	0.376	0.760	1.588	−1.164	0.773	1.259	2.299	−1.068
	Std. Dev.	4.316	1.369	4.481	5.090	4.090	3.409	4.174	4.418	3.742
Daily Changes from June 1, 1970 to February 28, 1973 (669 Observations)	Mean	0.035	0.012	0.030	0.038	0.016	0.046	0.037	0.049	0.006
	Std. Dev.	0.301	0.208	0.342	0.373	0.195	0.488	0.295	0.301	0.245
Monthly Changes from June 1970 to February 1973 (33 Observations)	Mean	0.538	0.230	0.458	0.584	0.279	0.799	0.566	0.728	0.038
	Std. Dev.	1.255	0.766	1.447	1.286	0.601	1.844	1.335	1.798	1.296
Quarterly Changes from II/70 to I/73 (12 Observations)	Mean	1.506	0.620	1.284	1.756	0.747	2.123	1.557	1.931	0.083
	Std. Dev.	2.475	1.256	2.577	2.309	1.096	3.109	2.415	2.889	2.592
Daily Changes from March 2, 1973 to June 30, 1976 (824 Observations)	Mean	0.001	0.003	−0.004	0.013	−0.048	−0.013	0.007	0.032	−0.040
	Std. Dev.	0.654	0.148	0.658	0.662	0.597	0.408	0.583	0.744	0.474
Monthly Changes from March 1973 to June 1976 (40 Observations)	Mean	0.168	0.058	0.058	0.444	−0.937	−0.170	0.290	0.856	−0.775
	Std. Dev.	2.952	0.670	2.969	3.506	2.705	1.968	3.027	3.096	1.994
Quarterly Changes from II/73 to II/76 (13 Observations)	Mean	0.598	0.151	0.276	1.433	−2.928	−0.473	0.984	2.639	−2.131
	Std. Dev.	5.587	1.479	5.792	6.846	5.033	3.298	5.415	5.580	4.393

a 4.5 percent band vis-a-vis the U.S. dollar.[10] Therefore the 4.5 percent band is used here as a standard for evaluating the degree of the exchange rate fluctuation during the past few years.[11]

A review of Table II indicates that in no instance did the mean of the percentage change in the exchange rate of the U.S. dollar vis-a-vis each of the other nine currencies exceed 4.5 percent over either daily, monthly, or quarterly intervals. In addition, in no instance did the standard deviation of the percentage exchange rate changes exceed 4.5 percent for either the daily or monthly data.

In the case of quarterly data for Belgium, France, Germany, Italy, Switzerland, and the Netherlands, however, the standard deviation did exceed 4.5

[10]While each currency was restricted to a 4.5 percent band vis-a-vis the U.S. dollar, each could fluctuate by up to 9 percent vis-a-vis a third currency. For example, suppose currency A was at the top of its 4.5 percent band and currency B was at the bottom of its 4.5 percent band vis-a-vis the dollar. If these two currencies were to switch positions within their respective bands, the value of each would change by 9 percent relative to one another while changing by only 4.5 percent relative to the U.S. dollar. For these same reasons, any two currencies of the European Snake can fluctuate by up to 4.5 percent vis-a-vis one another under current Snake rules. This point is discussed at greater length in "The European System of Narrower Exchange Rate Margins," *Monthly Report of the Deutsche Bundesbank* (January 1976), pp. 22-29.

[11]The Smithsonian agreement did not specify the appropriate time interval over which the 4.5 percent constraint was to apply. It merely stated that the constraint would be binding until a "fundamental disequilibrium" arose. Therefore, in comparing recent exchange rate movements over *specific* time intervals (days, months, and quarters) with the 4.5 percent Smithsonian band, the 4.5 percent figure must be taken merely as a *guideline* to what may have been considered acceptable variation over these intervals. One should also keep in mind that the considerations which led to the Smithsonian agreement were formed against a backdrop of inflation that was relatively mild in terms of both levels and inter-country differences compared to the experience which has followed this agreement. Hence, considerably greater fluctuations might have been considered acceptable in these latter years. Thus, given the economic environment of the past few years, the 4.5 percent constraint may represent an unduly restrictive standard of comparison.

percent during the period of the generalized float. In evaluating this last finding, one should keep in mind that the currencies of these countries (with the exception of Italy) were joined together in a currency block for much of the generalized float period. As such, if the major block currency (the German mark) were to fluctuate relative to the dollar by a given percent over a given interval for any reason, all of the other block currencies would automatically fluctuate in a similar pattern.[12]

Causes of the Observed Fluctuations in Exchange Rates

Much of the discussion about the relative desirability of fixed versus floating exchange rates relates to questions about the stability of the foreign exchange markets. This issue is tied to the question of whether or not speculation in these markets is destabilizing. With destabilizing speculation, exchange rate expectations based on fundamental factors are said to be weakly held and, hence, traders are unwilling to take large positions on the basis of these expectations. The resulting exchange rate path is then dominated by price runs and bandwagon effects and is, therefore, unnecessarily erratic.

A set of tests were performed to determine how prevalent such runs and bandwagon effects have been in foreign exchange markets since June 1970. These tests examine whether the number of runs observed in foreign exchange markets can be distinguished from the number that would be generated by a completely random process. Such so-called "runs tests" are useful in determining whether the behavior of exchange rates has been consistent with the hypothesis that speculation in these markets is destabilizing — a prevalence of sustained runs (that is, bandwagons) up or down.[13]

Runs tests for randomness were performed for each of the exchange rate series discussed in the pre-

[12]While this observation says nothing about the cause of the comparatively large fluctuations experienced by the block currencies as a group, it does call attention to the possibility that the source of fluctuations of any one of these currencies may lie more in the fact that the currency was a member of the block, rather than in any other factor.

[13]In this test a run is defined as a sequence of changes of the same sign that is preceded and followed by a sequence of changes of the other sign. If speculation is stabilizing, the runs that do appear are due to *changes* in fundamental factors. Since one would expect that *changes* in these fundamental factors occur on a random basis, expectations are that they would cause neither more nor less runs than would any random process. For a discussion of the runs test utilized in this article, see Dick A. Leabo, *Basic Statistics*, 4th ed. (Homewood, Illinois: Richard D. Irwin, Inc., 1972), pp. 545-47.

Table III

Runs Test for Randomness of Exchange Rate Fluctuations

	TIME PERIODS		
	I	II	III
Belgium			
Daily	−0.010	0.029	−0.035
Monthly	−0.058	−0.070	−0.042
Quarterly	−0.114	0.392	−0.212
Canada			
Daily	−0.085	−0.060	−0.103
Monthly	−0.282	−0.191	−0.362
Quarterly	−0.381	−0.163	−0.603
France			
Daily	−0.004	0.012	−0.018
Monthly	−0.210	−0.151	−0.258
Quarterly	−0.233	0.392	−0.603
Germany			
Daily	−0.027	−0.001	−0.044
Monthly	−0.197	−0.121	−0.242
Quarterly	−0.141	−0.131	−0.080
Italy			
Daily	−0.019	0.071	−0.060
Monthly	−0.128	0.164	−0.304
Quarterly	−0.218	0.174	0.095
Japan			
Daily	0.0	0.088	−0.031
Monthly	−0.339	−0.129	−0.336
Quarterly	−0.353	−0.696	−0.080
Netherlands			
Daily	−0.047	−0.052	−0.039
Monthly	−0.010	0.050	−0.042
Quarterly	−0.459	−0.654	−0.212
Switzerland			
Daily	−0.031	−0.049	−0.020
Monthly	−0.307	−0.222	−0.374
Quarterly	0.012	0.131	−0.028
U.K.			
Daily	−0.029	0.057	−0.098
Monthly	−0.395	−0.302	−0.430
Quarterly	−0.355	−0.554	0.097

Daily	I = June 1, 1970 — June 30, 1976
	II = June 1, 1970 — February 28, 1973
	III = March 2, 1973 — June 30, 1976
Monthly	I = June 1970 — June 1976
	II = June 1970 — February 1973
	III = March 1973 — June 1976
Quarterly	I = II/1970 - II/1976
	II = II/1970 - I/1973
	III = II/1973 - II/1976

ceding sections of this article. The results of these tests are presented in Table III. A positive value for the test statistic indicates that the number of runs in the sample exceeds the expected number for a random ordering. A negative value for the test statistic indicates fewer than the expected number of runs. The hypothesis of nonrandom ordering is rejected with 95 percent confidence only if the value of the test statistic lies within a range of ± 1.96. The data presented in Table III indicate that the hypothesis that exchange rate changes were generated by a nonrandom process should be rejected on the basis of this test and these data. As such, these results permit conditional rejection of the view that observed exchange rate fluctuations have been the result of destabilizing speculation.

What are the Relevant Fundamental Factors?

The data presented in the preceding section cast doubt on the view that exchange rate changes have been the result of destabilizing speculation. However, the alternative hypothesis, that exchange rates change primarily in response to changes in fundamental factors, has not been explicitly developed or considered.

Exchange rate theory indicates that the predominant factor determining exchange rate changes in the long run is the degree of inflationary pressure in one country relative to inflationary pressure in another country.[14] This theory can be well illustrated by a simple two-country example. Suppose there are only two countries in the world, country A and country B. A high degree of inflationary pressure in country A relative to that existing in country B implies an increase in country A's demand for all products, including those produced in country B. This increased demand for country B's products results in an increase in the demand for country B's currency in country A and causes the price of currency B to rise (in terms of the currency of country A). In other words, currency A will depreciate and currency B will appreciate.[15] In addition, if the rate of growth of a country's money stock plays a dominant role in the determination of inflationary pressures, a strong relationship will be expected to exist between exchange rate changes and relative rates of monetary growth.[16]

The longer the time horizon, the more pronounced these relationships will be. Inflationary pressures become established only in the long run and the full impact of differing inflationary pressures on exchange rates could be resisted by governments in the short and intermediate runs. Under a system of freely floating or loosely managed exchange rates, necessary adjustments to changes in such fundamental factors are permitted to occur gradually. However, when exchange rates are narrowly fixed or tightly managed (as within the European Snake, for example) exchange market pressures are not relieved in a slow and orderly fashion. However, once market participants sense the presence of pent-up market forces which favor realignment, taking into account changes in fundamental factors, exchange market pressures surge and result in "currency crises" and sudden large jolts in exchange rates. Thus, while the relationship between exchange rates and relative inflationary pressures (as measured by changes in price indices) may not be strong in the short run, the longer the time frame, the stronger this relationship becomes.

In order to perform a test of the relative inflationary pressure hypothesis of exchange rate determination, the following series were constructed. The simple percentage change in the value of the U.S. dollar vis-a-vis each of the other nine currencies reviewed was calculated over the same three time periods analyzed in the preceding tests. The same computations were then performed for the simple percentage changes in two proxies for inflationary pressure (the consumer price index, CPI, and the wholesale price index, WPI), and for the money stock in each of the respective countries relative to the simple percentage

---

[14]The future can be divided into three different time frames — the long run, the intermediate run, and the short run — during which different factors are the dominant influence on exchange rate movements. Just where one of these time frames begins and ends cannot be precisely specified. This analysis concentrates on the long run only, which is defined here as any period extending for more than a quarter.

[15]Inflationary pressures are empirically approximated by observed changes in some very broad and imperfect index of *all* prices. These indices attempt to capture increases in the prices of foreign as well as domestically supplied products. However, the majority of the items included in these indices are domestically supplied.

Any increase in inflationary pressures will be reflected in an increase in the demand for foreign as well as domestically supplied products. The increased demand for domestically supplied products will result in an increase in the price of those products. An increase in the demand for products produced in foreign countries will result in a rise in the price of the foreign exchange needed to purchase those products (depreciation of the domestic currency). It is reasonable to expect that the increase in the price of foreign exchange (which immediately increases the domestic price of foreign produced products) will occur faster than the increase in the prices of *all* of the other products covered by some overall price index. As such, it is entirely possible that inflationary pressures will be reflected in exchange rates before they are reflected in changes in overall price indices. For this reason, exchange rate changes may precede the relative movement in price indices in the short run, but this does not indicate that exchange rate changes have *caused* the movement in price indices.

[16]See Donald S. Kemp, "A Monetary View of the Balance of Payments," this *Review* (April 1975), pp. 20-21.

changes in their U.S. counterparts. In other words, for each time period the simple percentage change in the CPI, WPI, and money stock for the United States was substracted from the simple percentage change in the foreign counterparts of these measures.

A correlation test was then performed to determine the degree of relationship between the simple percentage change in exchange rate series and each of the other series described above.[17] If it is true that exchange rate movements reflect relative inflationary pressures and relative rates of money growth among countries, then the exchange rate series would be negatively correlated with each of the other three series. That is, those countries whose currencies appreciated the most relative to the U.S. dollar should be those countries whose inflation and money growth rates were smallest relative to the inflation and money growth rates in the United States.

The results, reported in Table IV, indicate that for all time periods there exists a statistically significant negative correlation between the WPI series and the exchange rate series. In addition, with the exception of the June 1970 through February 1973 period, the correlation between both the CPI and the money stock series and the exchange rate series is also negative and statistically significant. These results are noteworthy in two respects. First, the results which cover the entire time period since June 1970 indicate that there does in fact exist a statistically significant negative correlation between the exchange rate series and each of the other series. Second, there is a striking dissimilarity between the results for the pregeneralized float period and those for the generalized float period. This indicates that when the exchange rates had the greatest amount of freedom to respond to changes in fundamental factors, their observed movements paralleled relative inflation and money growth rates most closely. The results reported in Table IV thus lend support to the hypothesis that movements in exchange rates, particularly in the long run, are determined by relative inflationary pressures and relative rates of money growth.[18] In addition

---

[17]The particular measure of correlation utilized here is the Pearsonian Correlation Coefficient.

[18]The same test which led to the results presented in Table IV was conducted using data for all OECD member countries for which data are currently available. This same test was also performed using data for all of the 46 IMF member countries which account for about 90 percent of total U.S. trade and for which data are currently available. The results of both tests were virtually identical in their implications, if not in their exact numerical value, with those presented in Table IV. Thus, the conclusions drawn from Table IV do not appear to be sensitive to the sample of countries chosen for analysis.

Table IV

CORRELATION TEST

Percent Changes in Exchange Rates Correlated with:	Time Period	Correlation Coefficient	Number of Observations[1]
Relative Percent Changes in CPI[2]	June 1970- March 1976	−0.789[3]	9
	June 1970- Feb. 1973	0.002	9
	March 1973- March 1976	−0.922[3]	9
Relative Percent Changes in WPI[2]	June 1970- March 1976	−0.945[3]	8[4]
	June 1970- Feb. 1973	−0.858[3]	9
	March 1973- March 1976	−0.946[3]	8
Relative Percent Changes in Money Supply[2]	June 1970- Jan. 1976	−0.667[5]	7[6]
	June 1970- Feb. 1973	0.199	8
	March 1973- Jan. 1976	−0.829[3]	8

[1]The countries covered in this test are Belgium, Canada, France, Germany, Italy, the Netherlands, Japan, Switzerland, and the United Kingdom.
[2]The derivation of these series is explained in detail in the text.
[3]Significantly different from zero at the 99 percent level.
[4]The Netherlands was excluded from this test, as well as from the test covering March 1973-March 1976, because monthly WPI data are not currently available beyond December 1975.
[5]Significantly different from zero at the 90 percent level.
[6]The United Kingdom was excluded from this test, as well as from the test covering June 1970-February 1973, because monthly money supply figures are not available for the United Kingdom until October 1971. Italy was also excluded from this test, as well as from the test covering March 1973-January 1976, because monthly money supply figures for Italy are not available beyond September 1975.

to these results, graphic illustrations of the relationships between exchange rate changes and the relative inflation and money growth series during the generalized float are presented in Chart I.

The observed negative correlation between relative rates of inflation and exchange rate changes says nothing about the direction of causality which underlies this relationship. Some analysts claim, for example, that changes in exchange rates "cause" changes in relative rates of inflation. However, evidence in favor of the alternative argument, that exchange rate changes were "caused" by the differences in inflation rates, is given by the last set of results in Table IV. One body of economic thought holds that relative rates of monetary expansion are the predominant factor in explaining relative rates of inflation in the long run. Applied to the argument advanced in this article, this view implies a strong negative correlation between exchange rate movements and relative rates of money growth, as shown in Table IV. On the other hand, the argument that changes in ex-

–Chart I
**Relationship Between Exchange Rate Changes,
Relative Rates of Inflation,
and Relative Rates of Money Growth**

Relative Change in Money Stock — March 1973 - January 1976 — Relative Change in Money Stock

%ΔER=17.299− .956(%ΔMS$_{foreign}$ − %ΔMS$_{u.s.}$)
(3.257) (3.626)
R^2 .62

JAPAN, U.K., FRANCE, CANADA, BELGIUM, NETHERLANDS, GERMANY, SWITZERLAND

Relative Change in CPI — March 1973 - March 1976 — Relative Change in CPI

%ΔER= .6765 .936(%ΔCPI$_{foreign}$ − %ΔCPI$_{u.s.}$)
(2.417) (6.280)
R^2 .85

U.K., ITALY, JAPAN, FRANCE, BELGIUM, CANADA, NETHERLANDS, SWITZERLAND, GERMANY

Relative Change in WPI — March 1973 - March 1976 — Relative Change in WPI

%ΔER= .347 .693(%ΔWPI$_{foreign}$ − %ΔWPI$_{u.s.}$)
(.152) (7.163)
R^2 .90

ITALY, U.K., JAPAN, CANADA, FRANCE, BELGIUM, GERMANY, SWITZERLAND

Simple Percentage Change in Exchange Rates
Note: Numbers in parentheses below coefficients are t ratios.

change rates "cause" inflation offers no explanation of these results.[19]

Conclusion

The thrust of this article has been an empirical review of the recent experience with generally floating exchange rates between the U.S. dollar and the currencies of the United States' major trading partners. The evidence presented herein casts doubt on the view that exchange rate changes are the result of destabilizing speculation, even in the short run. It is also demonstrated that in the long run exchange rates have changed in a pattern consistent with changes in fundamental economic factors.

An implication of these findings is that the prospects for a return to a viable fixed exchange rate regime are remote as long as there remains as wide a spectrum of economic policies among countries as has been the case for the past few years. The unacceptability of such a regime has been amply demonstrated recently by the futile efforts to hold together the European Currency Snake and the virtual abandonment by the Common Market of any plans for a closer Economic and Monetary Union. It is no coincidence that all but one *large* country departed from the Snake and that the dream of an economically united Europe vanished simultaneously. The reason is that the Common Market countries have recognized that no country that believes it has an option will be willing to subjugate its own economic policies to the monetary discipline practiced in another country (in the current situation the other country is West Germany). These experiences amply demonstrate that the time has not yet arrived for the kind of economic policy coordination that a fixed exchange rate system requires. While such coordination may or may not be a laudable goal to strive for, the world should accept the facts as they currently are and admit that, as of now, such an arrangement is nowhere in sight.

---

[19]For some samples of other recent studies which arrive at the same conclusion regarding the relative inflation and money growth rate hypothesis of exchange rate determination, see David Kern, "Inflation Implications in Foreign Exchange Rate Forecasting," *Euromoney* (April 1976), pp. 62-69; and D. King, "The Performance of Exchange Rates in the Recent Period of Floating: Exchange Rates and Relative Rates of Inflation," unpublished memorandum (New York: Foreign Research Division, Federal Reserve Bank of New York, March 15, 1976). King's work also provides some evidence favoring the inflation to depreciation direction of causality. For an analysis of an earlier period of floating rates, see John S. Hodgson, "An Analysis of Floating Exchange Rates: The Dollar — Sterling Rate, 1919-1925," *The Southern Economic Journal* (October 1972), pp. 249-57.

Balance-of-Payments Concepts – What Do They Really Mean?

DONALD S. KEMP

T HE Advisory Committee on Balance-of-Payments Statistics Presentation of the Office of Management and Budget is currently holding meetings on the usefulness of current balance-of-payments concepts. The Committee is interested in hearing suggestions regarding ways in which international data may be presented in a more useful format. These hearings reflect a growing concern in government, academia, and the business community over the meaning of balance-of-payments data as currently reported.

While the subject of balance-of-payments reporting techniques has been debated since the inception of the practice, the debates have intensified lately as a result of a number of factors. On the one hand, there has been a surge of interest in what has been called the monetary approach to the balance of payments.[1] This approach to payments theory views international transactions within a framework that differs significantly from the current conventional wisdom.[2] If one views international transactions within this monetary framework, the currently employed balance-of-payments concepts have little meaning. On the other hand, the problems of interpreting current balance-

of-payments concepts have further intensified as a result of the evolution of a system of floating exchange rates among the world's major trading countries and the rapid accumulation of international reserves by the members of the Organization of Petroleum Exporting Countries (OPEC).

This article discusses the general concept of the balance of payments as well as the appropriateness of various measures of this concept. Its aim is to foster a better understanding of the balance of payments and the meaning of the various measures of this concept that are currently used. In light of the issues raised in this discussion, some proposals for the reform of the method of presenting data relating to international transactions will be made. The discussion will allude to the following propositions:

1) There is a widespread misunderstanding of the forces that give rise to, and the impact of, balance-of-payments deficits and surpluses and exchange rate movements.

2) This misunderstanding has led to undue concern on the part of policymakers, inducing costly recommendations for trade restrictions, controls on capital movements, and export promotion in order to solve balance-of-payments and exchange rate "problems" which simply do not exist.

3) The way balance-of-payments statistics are currently reported serves to exacerbate these misunderstandings.

4) The above propositions apply under both fixed and floating exchange rates. However, the problems alluded to are particularly acute now that we have switched from one exchange rate regime to another.

NOTE: The author acknowledges the helpful comments on earlier drafts from Allan H. Meltzer and Wilson E. Schmidt. They are, of course, blameless for any remaining errors.

[1]For a discussion of this approach, see Donald S. Kemp, "A Monetary View of the Balance of Payments," this *Review* (April 1975), pp. 14-22.

[2]The monetary approach is concerned with the impact of the *balance of payments* on the domestic economy via its impact on the money supply. In contrast, the current conventional wisdom in payments theory (the elasticities and absorption approaches) is concerned primarily with the *balance of trade* alone and assumes that either there are no monetary consequences associated with international transactions or, to the extent the potential for such consequences exists, they can be and are neutralized by domestic monetary authorities.

This is because the implications of the switch are confusing in themselves and because many of the ways in which balance-of-payments statistics are reported have been made completely obsolete as a result of the switch.

FUNDAMENTAL MISUNDERSTANDING

The fundamental misunderstanding alluded to in the first proposition stems from the fact that most balance-of-payments analyses focus on either the current or the capital account separately. In order to place the balance of payments in its proper perspective, it is necessary that all accounts be considered simultaneously. In addition, one must recognize that the transactions recorded in balance-of-payments statistics bear the same relationship to foreign and domestic monetary policies as do purely domestic transactions to domestic monetary policy.

Viewed within a monetary framework, balance-of-payments surpluses and deficits and movements in exchange rates are the result of a disparity between the demand for and supply of money. The exact process by which the disparity is corrected is a technical issue and subject to alternative interpretations.[3] Basically, however, when such a disparity exists, spending units attempt to draw down (build up) their money balances through the purchase (sale) of real and/or financial assets. In so doing they increase (decrease) the demand for all assets. Under alternative situations the exact pattern by which spending units adjust their money balances in this fashion will be different. The pattern will depend on, at a minimum, the cause of the change in the quantity of money supplied relative to the quantity demanded, the initial conditions under which the change occurred, and the impact of other exogenous events on spending units. However, the point is that an excess supply of or demand for money will be cleared through the markets for goods, services, and securities. Furthermore, and what is crucial for an understanding of the balance of payments, in an open economy (one in which there are international trade and capital transactions) the markets through which money balances are adjusted extend beyond national boundaries.[4]

Suppose, for example, that the domestic monetary authorities increase the money supply in country j, which leads to an increase in the demand for goods, services, and securities in that country. Any such increase in domestic demand will result in a tendency for prices of domestic real and financial assets in country j to rise, in the short run, relative to those in foreign markets. As a result, spending units in country j will simultaneously reduce their purchases of domestic real and financial assets in favor of foreign assets while domestic suppliers of these assets will seek to sell more at home and less abroad. At the same time, foreign spending units will decrease their purchases of the assets of country j and foreign suppliers will attempt to sell more of their own assets in country j. All of these factors work in favor of an increase in the demand for imports and a decrease in the demand for exports in country j.[5]

Adjustment Under a System of Fixed Exchange Rates

Under a system of fixed exchange rates, the adjustments described above will result in an accumulation of money balances by foreigners in return for the real and financial assets they sell to spending units in country j. This exchange of money balances for real and financial assets will be captured in the balance-of-payments statistics as an overall deficit in the trade and capital accounts.[6] The foreign recipients of these money balances have the option of converting them into their own currencies at their respective central banks. These foreign central banks will then present the balances they accumulate through such conversions to the central bank in country j in return for primary reserve assets. Since these primary reserve assets are one of the components of a country's monetary base (and thus a determinant of its money supply), the effect of this transaction will be a decrease in the money supply of country j back towards its initial level and an increase in the money supplies of its surplus trading partners.

[3]For a thorough discussion of the process by which such a disparity is corrected, see Roger W. Spencer, "Channels of Monetary Influence: A Survey," this *Review* (November 1974), pp. 8-26.

[4]The existence of free international markets for goods, services, and securities is a fundamental assertion of the monetary approach to the balance of payments. See Kemp, "A Monetary View of the Balance of Payments," p. 16.

[5]The terms "imports" and "exports" refer to more than just imports and exports of goods and services. It includes all transactions which involve the purchase or sale of domestic assets (real and financial) in foreign markets. For example, the purchase of a foreign security by a U.S. citizen would be considered an import.

[6]A deficit in the trade account reflects an exchange of money balances for real assets (goods and services). A deficit in the capital account reflects the exchange of money balances for financial assets. In order to determine the total accumulation of money balances by foreigners, it is necessary to combine all of the trade and capital accounts.

Under a system of fixed exchange rates, the primary channel by which international trade · and capital transactions can have an impact on aggregate economic activity is via the international reserve flows described above and their subsequent impact on the money supply (both foreign and domestic).[7] However, one is unable to gauge the magnitude of this impact by looking at either the trade or the capital accounts separately. For example, the effects on aggregate economic activity of a deficit in the merchandise trade account *alone* could be partially or fully neutralized by a surplus in one of the capital accounts. If such a situation arose, the negative aggregate demand effects resulting from an increase in imports of goods would be partially or fully offset by an inflow of capital and a resulting increase in investment demand. If the two effects fully offset each other, there would be no gain or loss of international reserves and the money supply would not be affected by the international trade and capital transactions.

In light of the above considerations, the crucial balance-of-payments concept is that which captures all transactions reflecting the adjustment of the supply of money to the level demanded. That is, the balance-of-payments concept which is most useful as a measure of the impact of international transactions on the domestic economy is one in which the only transactions considered "below the line" are those which have an influence on domestic and foreign money supplies.[8]

Henceforth, we will refer to this balance as the *money account*. For the United States this account would be composed of a composite of changes in U.S. primary reserve assets (gold and holdings of foreign currency balances) and changes in foreign deposits at Federal Reserve Banks.[9]

Adjustment Under a System of Freely Floating Exchange Rates

Under a system of freely floating exchange rates the balance of payments (on a money account basis) is always in equilibrium (total imports equal total exports) and there are no money supply changes associated with foreign transactions. In this case the adjustment to the disparity between the supply of and demand for money is accomplished by changes in domestic prices and exchange rates (which change concomitantly with, and accommodate, the required movement in domestic price levels).

In order to analyze the process by which the required adjustment takes place under freely floating exchange rates, it is necessary to begin with an analysis of the market for foreign exchange. The demand for imports determines the demand for foreign exchange and the demand for exports determines the supply of foreign exchange. The exchange rate will always seek the level at which the quantities of foreign exchange supplied and demanded are equal, and thus also the level at which the value of import demand equals the value of export demand. Thus, in value terms, imports will always equal exports and there is never either a surplus or a deficit in the balance of payments (on a money account basis).

[7]Within the monetary approach framework there are other channels through which international transactions can have an impact on aggregate economic activity. For example, some changes in the terms of trade and in the volume of trade and capital flows can affect the productive capacity of a given economy. However, it should be noted that both of these channels relate to the concept of the gains from trade, which is distinctly different from the concept of the balance of payments. The only other channel through which international transactions can have an impact on aggregate economic activity is through their impact on the ownership of the total money stock. For example, the size of the total U.S. money stock (as currently measured) is not affected by changes in foreign-owned deposits at U.S. commercial banks. However, the distribution of the total U.S. money stock between U.S. and foreign ownership is affected by such changes. This source of international influence· on the U.S. economy would be significant only if the volume of foreign-owned deposits was large and if the behavior pattern of foreign dollar owners differed significantly from that of domestic dollar owners. The evidence relating to this issue is, as yet, highly tentative. However, the consensus seems to be that the influence of foreign-owned deposits on the U.S. economy is minimal. For a discussion of the concept of a domestically owned money stock, see Albert E. Burger and Anatol Balbach, "Measurement of the Domestic Money Stock," this *Review* (May 1972), pp. 10-23.

[8]Balance-of-payments accounting is based on the principle of double entry bookkeeping. Total debits must equal total credits, and therefore it is impossible for the entire balance of payments to show either a deficit or a surplus. The only way we can observe a difference between credits and debits is to

select certain items out of the balance of payments and compare credits and debits for the given subset of items. A particular subset is usually chosen because the net of the transactions included therein is significant, for some reason, in sign and amount. According to current usage, an imaginary line is drawn through the balance of payments so that the items selected for a subset appear "above the line" and the remaining items are said to be "below the line." For a more thorough discussion of standard balance-of-payments statistics presentation, see John Pippenger, "Balance-of-Payments Deficits: Measurement and Interpretation," this *Review* (November 1973), pp. 6-14.

[9]The *money account* captures the net impact of all international transactions on the U.S. money supply. Of all international transactions, the only ones that affect the money supply are those that affect some component of the monetary base. Since U.S. holdings of gold and foreign currency balances (primary reserve assets) and foreign deposits at Federal Reserve Banks are the only components of the monetary base that are affected by international transactions, the entire impact of these transactions on the money supply can be captured by observing the changes in these items. As such, the *money account* includes changes in only these items below the line.

Let us now return to the previous example in which there is an increase in the quantity of money supplied relative to the quantity demanded. As in our previous example, there will be an increase in the demand for imports (the demand for foreign exchange) and a decrease in the demand for exports (the supply of foreign exchange). Under freely floating exchange rates, the inevitable consequence will be a rise in the exchange rate (the price of foreign currencies in terms of the domestic currency).[10] As such, a rise in the exchange rate is the natural consequence of the existing money stock exceeding the quantity of money demanded.

The upshot of the foregoing analysis is that under fixed exchange rates the crucial balance-of-payments concept for gauging the impact of international trade and capital transactions on the domestic economy is the balance in the money account. Furthermore, exchange rate movements and money account deficits and surpluses are merely part of the adjustment mechanism by which a disparity between the existing supply of and demand for money is being corrected. They are symptoms of a problem, but they themselves are not the problem. The fact is that equality between the supply of and demand for money must and will be restored, and the money account deficits and surpluses and exchange rate movements are merely a mechanism by which the required adjustment is accommodated.

Most furor over balance-of-payments statistics and exchange rate movements stems from the failure to recognize the above proposition. For example, the belief is widespread that deficits in the trade account are "bad" because they represent a net drain on demand for the output produced in the deficit country. In reality, however, one is unable to gauge the impact of international transactions on domestic demand by focusing on the trade account alone. Even if a trade account deficit is not offset by a surplus in the capital account, the resultant deficit in the money account merely reflects the fact that the stock of money exceeds the quantity of money demanded. Somehow this disparity must be and is corrected. In a regime of fixed exchange rates, the money stock will be decreased automatically through the outflow of international reserves which is associated with the money account deficit.

In a similar fashion, most concern over the depreciation of a currency in a regime of floating exchange rates is also misdirected. It is curious that the belief is widely held that the depreciation of a nation's currency is a cause of domestic inflation. To the contrary, depreciations are not the source, but are the result of inflationary pressures. The depreciation occurs for the same reason that money account deficits occur with fixed exchange rates — that is, because there exists a disparity between the supply of and demand for money which must be corrected.

When such a disparity exists under floating exchange rates, the excess supply of money itself will result in an increase in the demand for domestically supplied real and financial assets as well as for foreign exchange (the demand for foreign supplies of real and financial assets). Consequently, all prices (the price of foreign exchange included) will rise. As with all increases in the price level, the result will be an increase in the demand for money as spending units attempt to maintain the real value of that proportion of their wealth that they elect to hold in the form of money balances. In short, the original disparity between the demand for and supply of money will be corrected via a rise in domestic prices and a depreciation in the foreign value of the domestic currency (a rise in the price of foreign exchange).

In view of the foregoing analysis, balance-of-payments deficits and surpluses and exchange rate movements should *not* be viewed as evils that are to be avoided at all costs. They are not problems in themselves, but are one of the means by which other problems are corrected. In fact, in light of the nature of the forces which give rise to them, they are, in a sense, desirable.

BALANCE-OF-PAYMENTS CONCEPTS

Since they are summaries, balance-of-payments data are presented in categories composed of similar types of international transactions (for example, merchandise trade, long-term capital, etc.). The transactions grouped together in any particular category are similar in that, given the existing institutional framework within which they occur, the forces giving rise to, and the impact of, them is supposed to be similar.[11] To the extent that any set of groupings ever was appropriate or informationally useful, this usefulness can be greatly diminished if there are changes in the forces which give rise to, or the impact of, that

---

[10]That is, the domestic currency will depreciate in value relative to other currencies. Other currencies will now be worth more units of domestic currency than before.

[11]See Exhibit I and Table I for an outline of the groupings currently employed in balance-of-payments data presentation. These illustrations will be useful references for the remainder of this article.

Exhibit I

SUMMARY EXPLANATION OF U.S. BALANCE OF PAYMENTS

(To be used in conjunction with Table I)

The U.S. balance of payments is a summary record of all international transactions by the Government, business, and private U.S. residents occurring during a specified period of time.

As a series of accounts and as a measure of economic behavior, balance of payments transactions are grouped into seven categories: merchandise trade, services, transfer payments, long-term capital, short-term private capital, miscellaneous, and liquid private capital. We successively add the net balances of the above categories in order to obtain:

- Merchandise Trade Balance
- Goods and Services Balance
- Current Account Balance
- Basic Balance
- Net Liquidity Balance
- Official Settlements Balance

Below the dashed line there are two additional categories, U.S. liabilities to foreign official holders and U.S. reserve assets. These serve to finance the transactions recorded above the dashed line.

There are interrelationships between these accounts. For example, the credit entry associated with an export of goods could result from the debit entry of a private bank loan, a Government grant, a private grant, or an increase in U.S. holdings of foreign currency or gold.

Merchandise Trade: Exports and imports are a measure of physical goods which cross U.S. boundaries. The receipt of dollars for exports is recorded as a plus and the payments for imports are recorded as a minus in this account.

Services: Included in this account are the receipt of earnings on U.S. investments abroad and the payments of earnings on foreign investments in the U.S. Sales of military equipment to foreigners and purchases from foreigners for both military equipment and for U.S. military stations abroad are also included in this category.

Transfer Payments: Private transfers represent gifts and similar payments by Americans to foreign residents. Government transfers represent payments associated with foreign assistance programs and may be utilized by foreign governments to finance trade with the United States.

Long-term Capital: Long-term private capital records all changes in U.S. private assets and liabilities to foreigners, both real and financial. Private U.S. purchases of foreign assets are recorded as payments of dollars to foreigners, and private foreign purchases of U.S. assets are recorded as receipts of dollars from foreigners. Government capital transactions represent long-term loans of the U.S. Government to foreign governments.

Short-term Private Capital: Nonliquid liabilities refers to capital inflows, such as loans by foreign banks to U.S. corporations, and nonliquid claims refers to capital outflows, such as U.S. bank loans to foreigners. These items represent trade financing and cash items in the process of collection which have maturities of less than three months. The distinction between short-term private capital and liquid private capital is that the transactions recorded in the former account are considered not readily transferable.

Miscellaneous: Allocations of special drawing rights (SDRs) represent the receipt of the U.S. share of supplemental reserve assets issued by the International Monetary Fund. SDRs are recorded here when they are initially received by the United States. The category errors and omissions is the statistical discrepancy between all specifically identifiable receipts and payments. It is believed to be largely unrecorded short-term private capital movements.

Liquid Private Capital: This account records changes in U.S. short-term liabilities to foreigners, and changes in U.S. short-term claims reported by U.S. banks on foreigners.

NOTE: For analytical purposes the dashed line below the official settlements balance could be moved. For example, if this line were placed under one of the balances above, then all transactions below that line would serve as financing, or offsetting, items for the balance above.

Table I

U. S. BALANCE OF PAYMENTS, 1974p
(Billions of Dollars)

		Net Balance	Cumulative Net Balance
Merchandise Trade:			
Exports	+ 97.1		
Imports	−103.0		
Merchandise Trade Balance		− 5.9	− 5.9
Services:			
Military Receipts	+ 3.0		
Military Payments	− 5.1		
Income on U. S. Investments Abroad	+ 29.9		
Payments for Foreign Investments in U. S.	− 16.7		
Receipts from Travel & Transportation	+ 10.2		
Payments for Travel & Transportation	− 12.7		
Other Services (net)	+ 0.3		
Balance on Services		+ 9.1	
Goods and Services Balance			+ 3.2
Transfer Payments:			
Private	− 1.1		
Government	− 6.1		
Balance on Transfer Payments		− 7.2	
Current Account Balance			− 4.0
Long-term Capital:			
Direct Investment Receipts	+ 2.3		
Direct Investment Payments	− 6.8		
Portfolio Investment Receipts	+ 1.2		
Portfolio Investment Payments	− 2.0		
Government Loans (net)	+ 1.0		
Other Long-term (net)	− 2.4		
Balance on Long-term Capital		− 6.7	
Basic Balance			−10.6
Short-term Private Capital:			
Nonliquid Liabilities	+ 1.7		
Nonliquid Claims	− 14.7		
Balance on Short-term Private Capital		−13.0	
Miscellaneous:			
Allocation of Special Drawing Rights (SDR)	*		
Errors and Omissions	+ 5.2		
Balance on Miscellaneous Items		+ 5.2	
Net Liquidity Balance			−18.3
Liquid Private Capital:			
Liabilities to Foreigners	+ 15.7		
Claims on Foreigners	− 5.5		
Balance on Liquid Private Capital		+10.3	
Official Settlements Balance			− 8.1
The Official Settlements Balance is Financed by Changes in:			
U. S. Liabilities to Foreign Official Holders:			
Liquid Liabilities	+ 8.3		
Readily Marketable Liabilities	+ 0.6		
Special Liabilities	+ 0.7		
Balance on Liabilities to Foreign Official Holders		+ 9.5	
U. S. Reserve Assets:			
Gold	0.0		
Special Drawing Rights	− 0.2		
Convertible Currencies	0.0		
IMF Gold Tranche	− 1.3		
Balance on Reserve Assets		− 1.4	
Total Financing of Official Settlements Balance			+ 8.1

*There was no SDR allocation for 1974.
P — Preliminary
NOTE: Figures may not add because of rounding.

particular set of transactions, or if there are changes in the institutional framework within which these transactions occur. Thus, given the changes which have occurred in the field of international trade and finance in the last few years, it would not be at all surprising to find that some previously meaningful balance-of-payments groupings had become almost meaningless.

Foremost among these changes has been the movement of the world's major trading nations from a fixed to a floating exchange rate regime and the surge in the accumulation of official reserves by OPEC members. In this section the current methods of presenting balance-of-payments statistics will be analyzed in light of these changes. Each individual account will be discussed in terms of its relevance prior to these changes and, where appropriate, in light of the movement to floating exchange rates and the rapid growth of OPEC reserves.

Current Account

The current account measures the extent to which the United States is a net borrower from, or net lender to, foreign countries as a group. With the exception of unilateral transfers (gifts and similar payments by American governmental units and private citizens to foreign residents), all of the transactions recorded above the line in this account represent the transfer of real assets (goods and services) between the United States and its trading partners.[12] The transactions recorded below the line in this account represent the means by which the United States is able to finance the purchase of net imports from other countries or, in the case of a surplus, how net exports have been financed by our trading partners. For example, the United States had a $4 billion deficit on current account in 1974. This means that, on balance, the United States received $4 billion more in goods and services (imports) than it gave up (exports) in return. The United States was able to do this by borrowing $4 billion from foreigners. The borrowing was financed through a net of all of the transactions which appear below the line in the current account. Thus, for the purpose of balance-of-payments analysis, the value of

the current account balance lies in its usefulness as a measure of the net transfer of real resources between the United States and the rest of the world. Another way of viewing this balance is that it measures the change in our net foreign investment. In other words, in 1974 foreigners invested (made loans amounting to) $4 billion in the United States.

This balance carries additional significance in that it is a component of the nation's GNP accounts. It is included in the GNP accounts because it is *supposed* to capture the contribution of foreigners to domestic aggregate demand. However, it alone tells us very little about the impact of international transactions on domestic economic activity. It only measures the magnitude of foreign demand for current output (goods and services) and completely ignores the impact of foreign investment decisions on U.S. economic activity. As mentioned previously, transactions in the capital account could offset completely the impact of current account transactions on the U.S. money supply. As such, implications drawn from the current account regarding the domestic impact of foreign transactions can be highly misleading.

These same objections are equally appropriate, if not more so, to the two more narrowly defined balance-of-payments concepts — the merchandise trade balance and the goods and services balance. While these balances are among those which receive the greatest amount of attention, their implications for the domestic economy are greatly overstated.

Basic Balance

The basic balance isolates long-term capital transactions above the line along with all of the transactions included in the current account. All capital flows involving assets whose original maturity exceeds one year are defined as long term, and therefore "basic" transactions. The original theoretical justification for the basic balance seems to be that it catches the *persistent* forces at work in the balance of payments and thus could be a leading indicator of long-run trends.

However, this is clearly not the case. Both portfolio investments and long-term private loans are included in long-term capital, and both are now highly sensitive to short-run changes in interest rates and changes in expectations about relative inflation rates, monetary policies, and growth. The meaningfulness of the long-term capital concept might have some appeal on a theoretical basis, but data problems make its em-

---

[12]The current account excludes earnings on direct investments which are both earned and reinvested abroad. However, these reinvested earnings are no different than other sources of U.S. income from abroad in the sense that they represent a transfer of command over real resources. In recent years these reinvested earnings have been quite large. For example, in 1971 they amounted to $3.2 billion, while in 1972 and 1973 they amounted to $4.7 billion and $8.1 billion, respectively.

pirical counterpart extremely difficult to construct and, therefore, it is not very useful.

Net Liquidity Balance

The net liquidity balance may be thought of as a measure of the total of U.S. dollars which accrue to foreigners, during an accounting period, as a result of all of the transactions recorded above the line — that is, imports and exports of goods and services, unilateral transfers, inflows and outflows of long-term capital, and nonliquid short-term capital. Below the line it combines the changes in our reserve assets and the changes in our liquid liabilities to both private and official foreigners. The original intent of this balance was to measure the change in *potential* pressure on our reserve assets. The thinking was that official institutions could use their dollar assets to buy our reserve assets; private holdings of dollars were a potential threat if private foreigners sold their dollars to central banks, who could in turn use them to buy our reserve assets.

There are a number of problems with this measure which make its relevance and usefulness highly questionable. These problems are both theoretical and empirical and are greatly magnified by the recent institutional changes which have occurred in international finance.

The main empirical problem with this measure is that it attempts to distinguish between liquid and nonliquid liabilities. Every U.S. liability to foreigners has a combination of attributes, some of which qualify them for classification as liquid and some of which qualify them for classification as nonliquid. As a result, the classification of many assets as liquid or nonliquid must be somewhat arbitrary. For example, foreign portfolio investments in the United States are classified as nonliquid liabilities. However, these liabilities of the United States are readily convertible into liquid form — that is, they may be sold at any moment in time for cash or a demand deposit. Thus, the exchange market implications of the growth of foreign portfolio investments in the United States are not much different from those of a growth in foreign-held bank deposits (which are classified as liquid).

Suppose, however, that all liabilities to foreigners could be meaningfully subdivided into liquid and nonliquid categories. It would still be inaccurate to declare that all liquid liabilities to foreigners represent potential pressure on our reserve assets. There are many reasons why foreigners wish to hold liquid claims against the United States, not the least of which is for transactions purposes. The U.S. dollar is indeed an international currency which may be used in transactions throughout the world. Only those foreign-held claims which are in excess of those desired for transactions purposes can be rightfully considered as a potential source of pressure on our reserve assets.

While it is surely impossible, for empirical as well as theoretical reasons, to determine what proportion of total U.S. liabilities are being held for transactions purposes, the proportion is probably large. In order to determine accurately potential pressures on our reserve assets, it would be necessary to further subdivide U.S. liquid liabilities to foreigners into those held for transactions purposes and those held for speculative (or other) purposes. Indeed, it is only this latter category of liquid claims that represent potential pressures on our reserve assets.

The above problems have become decidedly more acute in the wake of the quadrupling of petroleum prices and the surge in the dollar holdings of OPEC members. Since the transacting currency of OPEC members is the U.S. dollar, the role of the dollar as an international medium of exchange, and thus its transactions demand, has been greatly enhanced. At the same time, many OPEC members have been accumulating extensive dollar denominated liquid claims. While this may be only a short-run phenomenon, the fact is that these liquid U.S. liabilities do not represent a potential threat to our reserve assets. Rather, these liabilities represent only a short-term depository for OPEC receipts while they decide how they wish to extend the maturity distribution of their claims into long-term (and therefore nonliquid in balance-of-payments parlance) investments.

To the extent that there ever did exist a conceptual basis for trying to measure the net liquidity balance, that basis no longer exists as a result of the shift from a system of fixed to one of floating exchange rates. With floating exchange rates there is no potential pressure on our primary reserve assets because the dollar is no longer convertible into them.[13]

---

[13]Under fixed exchange rates the United States stood ready to buy and sell foreign currencies in order to support the value of the dollar at a specific price in terms of other currencies. Primary reserve assets (international reserves) are stocks of gold and foreign currencies held by the U.S. Government in the event that such market intervention became necessary. For example, a decrease in the demand for dollars vis-a-vis gold or foreign currencies was accommodated by the purchase of dollars in return for foreign currencies or gold from the stocks of reserve assets. Thus, the dollar was said to be readily convertible into our reserve assets. How-

Official Settlements Balance

The official settlements balance is intended to measure the change in dollar balances which accrue to foreign official institutions only. In this balance-of-payments concept all private transactions are counted above the line, whereas in the net liquidity balance some private transactions (liquid private capital flows) are counted below the line. The original intent of this balance was to measure *directly* the net exchange pressure on the dollar and on U.S. reserve assets.[14] Since only those dollar denominated U.S. liabilities which are held by foreign official institutions could be exchanged for reserve assets, this balance focuses on only those transactions which give rise to changes in these liabilities.

The usefulness of this balance has always rested on the questionable distinction between private and official transactions. The idea is that all transactions listed above the line are the result of market-determined private (autonomous) actions and all transactions below the line are the result of official (accommodating) actions undertaken in support of fixed exchange rates. The thinking was that all official transactions could be considered as accommodating and all private transactions as autonomous. This probably never was the case and certainly is not the case now, given recent institutional changes in international finance.

The rapid accumulation of reserves by official agencies of OPEC members are included below the line in this balance, but they are clearly not the result of official action aimed at stabilizing exchange rates. These OPEC reserves largely represent investment decisions by OPEC members which are based on considerations of income, liquidity, and risk. In other words, many official transactions are clearly autonomous and not accommodating, and should therefore

---

ever, with floating exchange rates the U.S. Government is no longer *obligated* to intervene in the market for foreign currencies and changes in the demand for the dollar are accommodated by movements in the dollar exchange rate. In other words, with floating exchange rates the U.S. Government no longer *guarantees* the convertibility of the dollar into its reserve assets.

[14] The official settlements balance was originally supposed to reflect the effects of past measures taken in support of the fixed dollar exchange rate, while the net liquidity balance was supposed to reflect the potential need for such measures in the future. This is because the net liquidity balance includes liquid *private* capital, a potential source of future pressure on fixed exchange rates, below the line. On the other hand, in the official settlements balance the only transactions carried below the line are those which reflect past *official* measures.

be included with other autonomous transactions above the line.

While the above discussion relates to the blurred distinction between autonomous and accommodating transactions, there are other problems which blur the distinction between private and official transactions. For example, many foreign official institutions invest their dollar balances in the Eurodollar market. The result of such transactions on the balance-of-payments accounts is to increase private (Eurodollar bank) claims on the United States and reduce official claims. However, in reality, since the foreign official institution still maintains ownership and control of a claim against the United States, there has been no reduction in official claims against it.

To the extent that the official settlements balance ever did measure what it was supposed to measure, the relevance of this concept has disappeared as a result of the shift to floating exchange rates. As a result of this shift, exchange rate authorities are no longer *obligated* to prevent movements in exchange rates through official intervention in the foreign exchange market. The net exchange pressure on the dollar is no longer captured by changes in reserve asset holdings.

PROPOSALS FOR REFORM

In view of the considerations aired in the foregoing discussion, it is often the case that the present method of presenting balance-of-payments data is more misleading than useful. In some instances the balances currently reported have absolutely no economic meaning and often do not give an accurate measure of the impact of international trade and capital transactions on aggregate economic activity. This is because none of the currently reported balances capture the effects of international transactions on the money supply, and it is primarily through their effects on the money supply that these transactions have any appreciable impact on aggregate economic activity.

Under fixed exchange rates there is only one really meaningful balance — the balance in the money account. This account is the only one that captures the effect of international transactions on the money supply. However, at present this balance is not reported. Under freely floating exchange rates there are no meaningful balance-of-payments concepts, because in this case international transactions have no impact on the money supply. In this case the money account is always in balance, and therefore of no significance.

Thus, there is little, if any, reason why the publication of balance-of-payments data in the currently employed format should be continued. Not only is this format virtually without economic meaning, but it is often quite misleading. While there are many theoretical and empirical problems associated with any kind of aggregation of data pertaining to international transactions, the problems are unnecessarily exacerbated by the present practice of drawing balances on the various subaccounts (that is, the merchandise trade balance, the goods and services balance, the current account balance, etc.). These problems could be significantly reduced if the data were just presented and no balances were drawn.

In a world of freely floating exchange rates, changing pressures on the dollar are captured by movements in the exchange rate and not by some theoretically and empirically meaningless balances. For this reason, it would be helpful if international trade data were to include changes in the effective exchange rate.[15] However, we recognize that the current exchange rate arrangement cannot be realistically considered as an experiment with freely floating exchange rates. It is rather an experiment with a "managed float."[16] Whether recent official intervention activities have had any effect on the exchange rate or not, the fact is that they, as will any official exchange rate intervention activities, have had an impact on the U.S. monetary base. Thus, as it turns out, given the current "managed float," both the money account balance and changes in the effective exchange rate each convey some useful information.

Thus, any proposals for reform of the methods of presenting balance-of-payments data should include, at a minimum, a recommendation that the currently employed balances not be drawn and that the words "deficit" and "surplus" be dropped from any reference to international data. This would not prevent individuals from computing balances if they wished; it would only remove the implied government sanction of these concepts as economically meaningful.

In addition, any proposed reforms should address themselves to the obviously arbitrary classification of certain transactions as relating to liquid, illiquid, short-

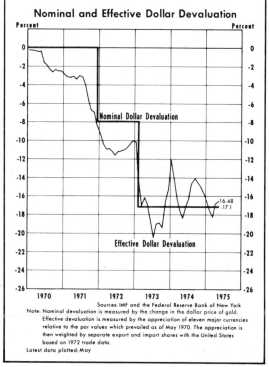

Exhibit II

INTERNATIONAL TRANSACTIONS, 1974p

	Millions of Dollars
Merchandise Exports	$100,047
Merchandise Imports	108,027
Service Exports	42,600
Service Imports	31,431
Unilateral Transfers (Net)	9,005
Direct Investment Abroad	6,801
Direct Investment in U.S.	2,308
Portfolio Investment Abroad	1,951
Portfolio Investment in U.S.	1,199
Deposits Abroad (Demand, Time, at Central Bank)	1,129
Deposits in U.S. (Demand, Time, at Central Bank)	20,746
Money Account Balance	46

Sources: *Survey of Current Business*, Board of Governors of the Federal Reserve System *Bulletin*, *Treasury Bulletin*.

Nominal and Effective Dollar Devaluation

Note: Nominal devaluation is measured by the change in the dollar price of gold. Effective devaluation is measured by the appreciation of eleven major currencies relative to the par values which prevailed as of May 1970. The appreciation is then weighted by separate export and import shares with the United States based on 1972 trade data.
Latest data plotted: May

Sources: IMF and the Federal Reserve Bank of New York

term, or long-term capital flows. They should also recognize that under a managed float changing pressures on the dollar are captured by movements in the exchange rate and the money account balance. With these goals in mind, a classification scheme similar to that presented in Exhibit II is suggested.

[15] The change in the effective exchange rate is a trade weighted average of changes in the exchange rate between the dollar and the currencies of the United States' trading partners.

[16] In other words, exchange rates are currently neither fixed at an officially specified level nor are they allowed to move completely free of official foreign exchange market intervention.

The advantages of this type of approach to the classification of international data are as follows:

1) No balances are computed or reported.

2) It allows individuals to make their own judgments regarding whether or not a particular transaction is related to liquid, illiquid, short-term, or long-term capital flows and to draw their own conclusions regarding the significance of changes in these flows.

3) It recognizes that pressures on the dollar are reflected in changes in exchange rates and in the money account balance and not by changes in the volume of a particular subset of transactions.

CONCLUSION

The current method of presenting data relating to international commerce attempts to group transactions so that the net of the transactions included in any category (the balance in that account) is significant for some reason in sign and amount. The transactions grouped together in any particular category are *supposed* to be similar in that, given the existing institutional framework within which they occur, the forces giving rise to, and the impact of, them is *supposed* to be similar. The idea is that the balance in that account should serve as a guide to policymakers as they attempt to gauge the impact of international transactions on domestic economic activity.

A particular balance is an appropriate guide to policy or is informationally useful only to the extent that it is based upon a correct perception of the forces which give rise to, and the impact of, the transactions included therein. The thrust of this article is that the balances highlighted in current balance-of-payments statistics are based on an incorrect perception of such

forces and impacts. As such, these balances have very little economic meaning and are, therefore, often a misleading guide to policymakers. As an alternative, it is suggested that international trade and capital transactions be viewed within the framework presented in the first sections of this article.

Therefore, the conclusion of this article is that the present methods of presenting data concerning international transactions should be reformed so that it more closely reflects the underlying economic realities of international commerce. At a minimum, any such reform should include a discontinuation of the practice of calculating the balances which are currently presented. While this would not prevent individuals who wish to do so from calculating such balances, it would remove the implied governmental sanction of these balances as having some special economic or policy implications.

In addition, the above reform would also result in a discontinuation of the constant references to "deficits" and "surpluses" in the balance of payments. The words "deficits" and "surpluses" in this regard convey meanings that are not at all appropriate to the realities of the impact of international commerce on domestic economic activity. For example, every month we hear that the merchandise trade account was either in "deficit" or "surplus." A deficit in this account merely means that the United States imported more merchandise than it exported during that month. In other words, the United States received more goods during that month than it was forced to give up, and it was able to do so by borrowing from foreigners. Despite the stigma associated with the word "deficit", this information tells us virtually nothing about the overall impact of international commerce on domestic economic activity.

PART VII.
ECONOMIC
GROWTH
AND
PRODUCTIVITY

The poet E. E. Cummings wrote that "progress in a comfortable disease." Indeed, those who see growth largely in terms of pollution and accelerated depletion of natural resources would regard progress as a terminal disease. But doomsday theories notwithstanding, most economists feel that the benefits of growth outweigh the costs. Thus, the selection in Part VII tend to view growth as desirable and necessary.

Section A, Economic Growth

In the piece "Is the End of the World at Hand" by Robert M. Solow, the author, asserts that Jay Forrester and other doomsday modelers find their conclusions very close to the surface. "It is, in fact, more nearly an assumption that a conclusion, in the sense that the chain of logic from the assumptions to the conclusion is very short and rather obvious." He is convinced that the economy will deal with the problem associated with growth much more effectively than Forrester would have us believe. Solow regards the desirability of growth as a separate issue but points out that it is the direction of growth that must command our attention if we fear that growth threatens the quality of life. In a speech entitled "Recovery and Growth Without Inflation" Irving Friedman argues that inflation is a serious global problem that must be halted before it becomes hyperinflation. He believes that out efforts should be aimed at increasing output and presents a list of proposals intended to achieve this goal. In "The Outlook for Long-Run Economic Growth" Leonall Anderson predicts future growth for the next 25 years based on data from 1948 to 1973. A marked slowing of growth is predicted, and some of the implications of this finding are discussed.

Section B, Productivity

In "The Agriculture of the U.S." Earl Heady poses a number of questions fundamental to the future of U.S. agriculture -- and the U.S. economy: "How did American agriculture attain such world supremacy in productivity?" "Has the Agricultural sector in the U.S. reached the limits of its productive capacity, or can that capacity be further increased?" "Can the keys to such productivity be transmitted to other countries?". In "Why Productivity Is Important" Geoffrey Moore reminds us that real income rises with productivity, that rising labor pro-

497

ductivity stimulates employment rather than displacing labor, as some suspect, and that rising productivity prevents rising prices by holding down unti costs. Leon Greenberg, in "The Need for Productivity Growth," surveys the aims and achievments of the National Commission on Productivity. He examines the slowdown in the productivity in the U.S. in recent years and considers the implications for the future, especially the decade ahead.

A. Economic Growth

Is the End of the World at Hand?

ROBERT M. SOLOW

*To grow or not to grow: that never was the question until recently.
But a computer model developed by MIT's Jay Forrester projects
imminent collapse for the world economy unless we call a halt
to growth now. Professor Solow has some doubts which he expressed
at a Symposium on the Limits to Growth held at Lehigh University.*

I was having a hard time figuring out how to begin when I came across an excerpt from an interview with my MIT colleague Professor Jay Forrester, who is either the Christopher Columbus or the Dr. Strangelove of this business, depending on how you look at it. Forrester said he would like to see about 100 individuals, the most gifted and best qualified in the world, brought together in a team to make a psychosocial analysis of the problem of world equilibrium. He thought it would take about ten years. When he was asked to define the composition of his problem-solving group, Forrester said: "Above all it shouldn't be mostly made up of professors. One would include people who had been successful in their personal careers, whether in politics, business, or anywhere else. We should also need radical philosophers, but we should take care to keep out representatives of the social sciences. Such people always want to go to the bottom of a particular problem. What we want to look at are the problems caused by interactions."

ROBERT M. SOLOW is Professor of Economics at MIT. His paper, along with
others presented at Lehigh University, will appear in *The Economic Growth
Controversy,* to be published this spring by International Arts & Sciences Press, Inc.

I don't know what you call people who believe they can be wrong about everything in particular, but expect to be lucky enough somehow to get it right on the interactions. They may be descendants of the famous merchant Lapidus, who said he lost money on every item he sold, but made it up on the volume. Well, I suppose that as an economist I am a representative of the social sciences; and I'm prepared to play out the role by talking about first principles and trying to say what the Growth vs. No-Growth business is really all about. This is going to involve me in the old academic ploy of saying over and over again what I'm not talking about before I ever actually say what I think I am talking about. But I'm afraid that some of those boring distinctions are part of the price you have to pay for getting it right.

First of all, there are (at least) two separate questions you can ask about the prospects for economic growth. You can ask: Is growth desirable? Or you can ask: Is growth possible? I suppose that if continued economic growth is not possible, it hardly matters whether or not it's desirable. But if it is possible, it's presumably not inevitable, so we can discuss whether we should want it. But they are separate questions, and an answer to one of them is not necessarily an answer to the other. My main business is with the question about the possibility of continued growth; I want to discuss the validity of the negative answer given by the "Doomsday Models" associated with the names of Forrester and Meadows (and MIT!) and, to a lesser extent, with the group of English scientists who published a manifesto called "Blueprint for Survival." The main concern of Dr. E. J. Mishan [whose article will appear in a later issue], on the other hand, was with the desirability of continued economic growth (and, at least by implication, with the desirability of past economic growth). If I spend a few minutes poaching on his territory, it is mainly because that seems like a good way to get some concepts straight, but also just to keep a discussion going.

Sorting out the issues

Arguments about the desirability of economic growth often turn quickly into arguments about the "quality" of modern life. One gets the notion that you favor growth if you are the sort of person whose idea of heaven is to drive at 90 miles an hour down a six-lane highway reading billboards, in order to pollute the air over some crowded lake with the exhaust from twin 100-horsepower outboards, and whose idea of food is Cocoa Krispies. On the other hand, to be against economic growth is to be a granola-eating, backpacking, transcendental-meditating canoe freak. That may even be a true statistical association, but I will argue that there is no necessary or logical connection between your answer to the growth question and your answer to the quality-of-life question. Suppose there were no issue about economic growth; suppose it were impossible; suppose each man or each woman were equipped to have only two children (one bomb under each wing); suppose we were stuck with the technology we have now and had no concept of invention, or even of increased mechanization through capital investment. We could still argue about the relative merits of cutting timber for building houses or leaving it stand to be enjoyed as forest. Some people would still be willing to breathe carbon monoxide in big cities in return for the excitement of urban life, while others would prefer cleaner air and fewer TV channels. Macy's would still not tell Gimbel's. Admen would still try to tell you that all those beautiful women are actually just looking for somebody who smokes Winchesters, thus managing to insult both men and women at once. Some people would still bring transistor radios to the beach. All or nearly all of the arguments about the quality of life would be just as valid if the question of growth never arose.

I won't go so far as to say there is no connection. In particular, one can argue that if population density were low enough, people would interfere much less with each other, and everyone could find a part of the world and style of civilization that suited him. Then differences of opinion about the quality of life wouldn't matter so much. Even if I grant the truth of that observation, it is still the case that, from here on out, questions about the quality of life are separable from questions about the desirability of growth. If growth stopped, there would be just about as much to complain about; and, as I shall argue later on, one can imagine continued growth that is directed against pollution, against congestion, against sliced white bread.

I suppose it is only fair to admit that if you get very enthusiastic about economic growth you are likely to be attracted to easily quantifiable and measurable things as objects of study, to point at with pride or to view with alarm. You are likely to pay less attention to important, intangible aspects of the standard of living. Although you can't know whether people are happier than they used to be, you can at least determine that they drink more orange juice or take more aspirin. But that's mere weakness of imagination and has nothing to do in principle with the desirability of economic growth, let alone with its possibility.

There is another practical argument that is often

made; and although it is important, it sometimes serves as a way of avoiding coming to grips with the real issues. This argument says that economic growth, increasing output per person, is the only way we are likely to achieve a more equitable distribution of income in society. There is a lot of home truth in that. It is inevitably less likely that a middle-class electorate will vote to redistribute part of its own income to the poor than that it will be willing to allocate a slightly larger

share of a growing total. Even more pessimistically, I might suggest that even a given relative distribution of income, supposing it cannot be made more nearly equal, for political or other reasons, is less unattractive if the absolute standard of living at the bottom is fairly high than it is if the absolute standard at the bottom is very low. From this point of view, even if economic growth doesn't lead to more equity in distribution, it makes the inequity we've got more tolerable. I think it is one of the lessons of history as recent as the McGovern campaign that this is a realistic statement of the prospects.

It is even clearer if one looks, not at the distribution of income within a rich country like the U.S., but at the distribution of income between the developed countries of the world and the undeveloped ones. The rich Western nations have never been able to agree on the principle of allocating as much as one percent of their GNP to aid undeveloped countries. They are unlikely to be willing to share their wealth on any substantial scale with the poor countries. Even if they were, there are so many more poor people in the world that an equally shared income would be quite low. The *only* prospect of a decent life for Asia, Africa, and Latin America is in more total output.

But I point this out only to warn you that it is not the heart of the question. I think that those who oppose continued growth should in honesty face up to the implications of their position for distributional equity and the prospects of the world's poor. I think those who favor continued growth on the grounds that only thus can we achieve some real equality ought to be serious about that. If economic growth with equality is a good thing, it doesn't follow that economic growth with a lot of pious talk about equality is a good thing. In principle, we can have growth with or without equity; and we can have stagnation with or without equity. An argument about first principles should keep those things separate.

What has posterity done for us?

Well, then, what *is* the problem of economic growth all about? (I'm giving a definition now, not stating a fact, so all I can say is that I think this way of looking at it contributes to clarity of thought.) Whenever there is a question about what to *do*, the desirability of economic growth turns on the claims of the future against the claims of the present. The pro-growth-man is someone who is prepared to sacrifice something useful and desirable right now so that people should be better off in the future; the anti-growth-man is someone who thinks that is unnecessary or undesirable. The nature of the sacrifice of present enjoyment for future enjoyment can be almost anything. The classic example is investment: We can use our labor and our resources to build very durable things like roads or subways or factories or blast furnaces or dams that will be used for a long time by people who were not even born when those things were created, and so will certainly have contributed nothing to their construction. That labor and those resources can just as well be used to produce shorter-run pleasures for us now.

Such a sacrifice of current consumption on behalf of the future may not strike you as much of a sacrifice. But that's because you live in a country that is already rich; if you had lived in Stalin's Russia, that need to sacrifice would be one of the reasons you would have been given to explain why you had to live without comfort and pleasures while the Ministry of Heavy Industry got all the play. If you lived in an underdeveloped country now you would face the same problem: What shall you do with the foreign currency earned by sales of cocoa or copper or crude oil—spend it on imports of consumer goods for those alive and working now, or spend it on imports of machinery to start building an industry that may help to raise the standard of living in 30 years' time?

There are other ways in which the same choice can be made, including, for instance, the direction of intellectual resources to the invention of things (like the generation of electricity from nuclear fusion) that will benefit future generations. Paradoxically, one of the ways in which the present can do something for the future is to conserve natural resources. If we get along with less lumber now so that there will be more forests standing for our grandchildren, or if we limit the present consumption of oil or zinc so that there will be some left for the twenty-first century, or if we worry about siltation behind dams that would otherwise be fun for fishermen and water-skiers, in all those cases we are promoting economic growth. I call that paradoxical because I think most people identify the conservation freak with the anti-growth party whereas, in this view of the matter, the conservationist is trading present satisfaction for future satisfaction, that is, he is promoting economic growth. I think the confusion comes from mixing up the quality-of-life problem with the growth problem. But it is nonetheless a confusion.

Why should we be concerned with the welfare of posterity, given the indubitable fact that posterity has never done a thing for us? I am not anthropologist enough to know how rare or common it is that our culture should teach us to care not only about our children but about their children, and their children. I suppose there are good Darwinian reasons why cultures without any future-orientation should fail to survive very long in the course of history. (But remember that they had a merry time of it while they lasted!) Moreover, we now enjoy the investments made by our ancestors, so there is a kind of equity in passing it on. Also, unless something terrible happens, there will be a lot more future than there has been past; and, for better or worse—probably worse—there will be more people at each future instant than there are now or have been. So all in all, the future will involve many more man-years of life than the present or the past, and a kind of intergenerational democracy suggests that all those man-years-to-be deserve some consideration out of sheer numbers.

On the other hand, *if* continued economic growth is possible—which is the question I'm coming to—then it is very likely that posterity will be richer than we are even if we make no special efforts on its behalf. If history offers any guide, then, in the developed part of the world at least, the accumulation of technological knowledge will probably make our great-grandchildren better off than we are, even if we make no great effort in that direction. Leaving aside the possibility of greater equality—I have already discussed that—there is hardly a crying need for posterity to be on average very much richer than we are. Why should we poor folk make any sacrifices for those who will in any

case live in luxury in the future? Of course, if the end of the world is at hand, if continued economic growth is *not* possible, then we ought to care more about posterity, because they won't be so well off. Paradoxically, if continued growth is not possible, or less possible, then we probably ought to do more to promote it. Actually, there's no paradox in that, as every student of economics will realize, because it is a way of saying that the marginal return on investment is high.

Overshoot, collapse, doom

There is, as you know, a school of thought that claims that continued economic growth is in fact not possible anymore, or at least not for very long. This judgment has been expressed more or less casually by several observers in recent years. What distinguishes the "Doomsday Models" from their predecessors is that they claim to much more than a casual judgment: they deduce their beliefs about future prospects from mathematical models or systems analysis. They don't merely say that the end of the world is at hand—they can show you computer output that says the same thing.

Characteristically, the Doomsday Models do more than just say that continued economic growth is impossible. They tell us why: in brief, because (*a*) the earth's natural resources will soon be used up; (*b*) increased industrial production will soon strangle us in pollution; and (*c*) increasing population will eventually outrun the world's capacity to grow food, so that famine must eventually result. And, finally, the models tell us one more thing: the world will end with a bang, not a whimper. The natural evolution of the world economy is not at all toward some kind of smooth approach to its natural limits, wherever they are. Instead, it is inevitable—unless we make drastic changes in the way we live and organize ourselves—that the world will overshoot any level of population and production it can possibly sustain and will then collapse, probably by the middle of the next century.

I would like to say why I think that the Doomsday Models are bad science and therefore bad guides to public policy. I hope nobody will conclude that I believe the problems of population control, environmental degradation, and resource exhaustion to be unimportant, or that I am one of those people who believe that an adequate response to such problems is a vague confidence that some technological solution will turn up. On the contrary, it is precisely because these are important problems that public policy had better be based on sound and careful analysis. I want to explain some of my reasons for believing that the global models don't provide even the beginnings of a foundation of that kind.

The first thing to realize is that the characteristic conclusion of the Doomsday Models is very near the surface. It is, in fact, more nearly an assumption than a conclusion, in the sense that the chain of logic from the assumptions to the conclusion is very short and rather obvious.

The basic assumption is that stocks of things like the world's natural resources and the waste-disposal capacity of the environment are finite, that the world economy tends to consume the stock at an increasing rate (through the mining of minerals and the production of goods), and that there are no built-in mechanisms by which approaching exhaustion tends to turn off consumption gradually and in advance. You hardly need a giant computer to tell you that a system with those behavior rules is going to bounce off its ceiling and collapse to a low level. Then, in case anyone is inclined to relax into the optimistic belief that maybe things aren't that bad, we are told: Imagine that the stock of natural resources were actually twice as big as the best current evidence suggests, or imagine that the annual amount of pollution could be halved all at once and then set to growing again. All that would happen is that the date of collapse would be postponed by T years, where T is not a large number. But once you grasp the quite simple essence of the models, this should come as no surprise. It is important to realize where these powerful conclusions come from, because, if you ask yourself "Why didn't I realize earlier that the end of the world was at hand?" the answer is not that you weren't clever enough to figure it out for yourself. The answer is that the imminent end of the world is an immediate deduction from certain assumptions, and one must really ask if the assumptions are any good.

It is a commonplace that if you calculate the annual output of any production process, large or small, and divide it by the annual employment of labor, you get a ratio that is called the productivity of labor. At the most aggregative level, for example, we can say that the GNP in 1971 was $1,050 billion and that about 82 million people were employed in producing it, so that GNP per worker or the productivity of a year of labor was about $12,800. Symmetrically, though the usage is less common, one could just as well calculate the GNP per unit of some particular natural resource and call that the productivity of coal, or GNP per pound of vanadium. We usually think of the productivity of labor as rising more or less exponentially, say at 2 or 3 percent a year, because that is the way it has in fact behaved over the past century or so

since the statistics began to be collected. The rate of increase in the productivity of labor is not a constant of nature. Sometimes it is faster, sometimes slower. For example, we know that labor productivity must have increased more slowly a long time ago, because if we extrapolate backward at 2 percent a year, we come to a much lower labor productivity in 1492 than can possibly have been the case. And the productivity of labor has risen faster in the past 25 years than in the 50 years before that. It also varies from place to place, being faster in Japan and Germany and slower in Great Britain, for reasons that are not at all certain. But it rises, and we expect it to keep rising.

Now, how about the productivity of natural resources? All the Doomsday Models will allow is a one-time hypothetical increase in the world supply of natural resources, which is the equivalent of a one-time increase in the productivity of natural resources. Why shouldn't the productivity of most natural resources rise more or less steadily through time, like the productivity of labor?

Of course it does for some resources, but not for others. Real GNP roughly doubled between 1950 and 1970. But the consumption of primary and scrap iron increased by about 20 percent, so the productivity of iron, GNP per ton of iron, increased by about 2.5 percent a year on the average during those 20 years. The U.S. consumption of manganese rose by 30 percent in the same period, so the productivity of manganese went up by some 70 percent in 20 years, a bit under 2.25 percent a year. Aggregate consumption of nickel just about doubled, like GNP, so the productivity of nickel didn't change. U.S. consumption of copper, both primary and secondary, went up by a third between 1951 and 1970, so GNP per pound of copper rose at 2 percent a year on the average. The story on lead and zinc is very similar, so their productivity increased at some 2 percent a year. The productivity of bituminous coal rose at 3 percent a year.

Naturally, there are important exceptions, and unimportant exceptions. GNP per barrel of oil was about the same in 1970 as in 1951: no productivity increase there. The consumption of natural gas tripled in the same period, so GNP per cubic foot of natural gas fell at about 2.5 percent a year. Our industrial demand for aluminum quadrupled in two decades, so the productivity of aluminum fell at a good 3.5 percent a year. And industrial demand for columbium was multiplied by a factor of 25: in 1951 we managed $2.25 million of GNP (in 1967 prices) per pound of columbium, whereas in 1970 we were down to $170 thousand of GNP per pound of columbium. On the other hand, it is a little hard to imagine civilization toppling because of a shortage of columbium.

Obviously many factors combine to govern the course of the productivity of any given mineral over time. When a rare natural resource is first available, it acquires new uses with a rush; and consumption goes up much faster than GNP. That's the columbium story, no doubt, and, to a lesser extent, the vanadium story. But once the novelty has worn off, the productivity of a resource tends to rise as better or worse substitutes for it appear, as new commodities replace old ones, and as manufacturing processes improve. One of the reasons the productivity of copper rises is because that of aluminum falls, as aluminum replaces copper in many uses. The same is true of coal and oil. A resource, like petroleum, which is versatile because of its role as a source of energy, is an interesting special case. It is hardly any wonder that the productivity of petroleum has stagnated, because the consumption of energy—both as electricity for domestic and industrial use and in the automobile—has recently increased even faster than GNP. But no one can doubt that we will run out of oil, that coal and nuclear fission will replace oil as the major sources of energy. It is already becoming probable that the high-value use of oil will soon be as feed stock for the petrochemical industries, rather than as a source of energy. Sooner or later, the productivity of oil will rise out of sight, because the production and consumption of oil will eventually dwindle toward zero, but real GNP will not.

So there really is no reason why we should not think of the productivity of natural resources as increasing more or less exponentially over time. But then overshoot and collapse are no longer the inevitable trajectory of the world system, and the typical assumption-conclusion of the Doomsday Models falls by the wayside. We are in a different sort of ball game. The system might still burn itself out and collapse in finite time, but one cannot say with any honesty that it *must*. It all depends on the particular, detailed facts of modern economic life as well as on the economic policies we and the rest of the world pursue. I don't want to argue for any particular counterstory; all I want to say now is that the overshoot-collapse pattern is built into the models very near the surface, by assumption, and by implausible assumption at that.

Scarcity—and high prices

There is at least one reason for believing that the Doomsday story is almost certainly wrong. The most glaring defect of the Forrester-Meadows models is the absence of any sort of functioning price system. I am no believer that the market is always right, and I am certainly no advocate of laissez-faire where the environment is concerned. But the price system is, after all, the main social institution evolved by capitalist economies (and, to an increasing extent, socialist economies too) for registering and reacting to relative scarcity. There are several ways that the working of the price system will push our society into faster and more systematic increases in the productivity of natural resources.

First of all, let me go back to the analogy between natural resources and labor. We are not surprised to learn that industry quite consciously tries to make inventions that save labor, i.e., permit the same product to be made with fewer man-hours of work. After all, on the average, labor costs amount to almost three-fourths of all costs in our economy. An invention that reduces labor requirements per unit of GNP by 1 percent reduces all costs by about 0.75 percent. Natural resource costs are a much smaller proportion of total GNP, something nearer 5 percent. So industry and engineering have a much stronger motive to reduce labor requirements by 1 percent than to reduce resource requirements by 1 percent, assuming—which may or not be true—that it is about as hard to do one as to do the other. But then, as the earth's supply of particular natural resources nears exhaustion, and as natural resources become more and more valuable, the motive to economize those natural resources should become as strong as the motive to economize labor. The productivity of resources should rise faster than now—it is hard to imagine otherwise.

There are other ways in which the market mechanism can be expected to push us all to economize on natural resources as they become scarcer. Higher and rising prices of exhaustible resources lead competing producers to substitute other materials that are more plentiful and therefore cheaper. To the extent that it is impossible to design around or find substitutes for expensive natural resources, the prices of commodities that contain a lot of them will rise relative to the prices of other goods and services that don't use up a lot of resources. Consumers will be driven to buy fewer resource-intensive goods and more of other things. All these effects work automatically to increase the productivity of natural resources, i.e., to reduce resource requirements per unit of GNP.

As I mentioned a moment ago, this is not an argument for laissez-faire. We may feel that the private decisions of buyers and sellers give inadequate representation to future generations. Or we may feel that private interests are in conflict with a distinct public interest—strip-mining of coal is an obvious case in point, and there are many others as soon as we begin to think about environmental effects. Private market responses may be too uncoordinated, too slow, based on insufficient and faulty information. In every case there will be actions that public agencies can take and should take; and it will be a major political struggle to see that they are taken. But I don't see how one can have the slightest confidence in the predictions of models that seem to make no room for the operation of everyday market forces. If the forecasts are wrong, then so are the policy implications, to the extent that there are any realistic policy implications.

Every analysis of resource scarcity has to come to terms with the fact that the prices of natural resources and resource products have not shown any tendency to rise over the past half-century, relative to the prices of other things. This must mean that there have so far been adequate offsets to any progressive impoverishment of deposits—like improvements in the technology of extraction, savings in end uses, or the availability of cheaper substitutes. The situation could, of course, change; and very likely some day it will. If the experienced and expert participants in the market now believed that resource prices would be sharply higher at some foreseeable time, prices would *already* be rising, as I will try to explain in a moment. The historical steadiness of resource prices suggests that buyers and sellers in the market have not been acting as if they foresaw exhaustion in the absence

of substitutes, and therefore sharply higher future prices. They may turn out to be wrong; but the Doomsday Models give us absolutely no reason to expect that—in fact, they claim to get whatever meager empirical basis they have from such experts.

Why is it true that if the market saw higher prices in the future, prices would already be rising? It is a rather technical point, but I want to explain it because, in a way, it summarizes the important thing about natural resources: conserving a mineral deposit is just as much of an investment as building a factory, and it has to be analyzed that way. Any owner of a mineral deposit owns a valuable asset, whether the owner is a private capitalist or the government of an underdeveloped country. The asset is worth keeping only if at the margin it earns a return equal to that earned on other kinds of assets. A factory produces things each year of its life, but a mineral deposit just lies there: its owner can realize a return only if he either mines the deposit or if it *increases in value*. So if you are sitting on your little pile of X and confidently expect to be able to sell it for a very high price in the year 2000 because it will be very scarce by then, you must be earning your 5 percent a year, or 10 percent a year, or whatever the going rate of return is, each year between now and 2000. The only way this can happen is for the value of X to go up by 5 percent a year or 10 percent a year. And that means that anyone who wants to use any X any time between now and 2000 will have to pay a price for it that is rising at that same 5 percent or 10 percent a year. Well, it's not happening. Of course, we are exploiting our hoard of exhaustible resources; we have no choice about that. We are certainly exploiting it wastefully, in the sense that we allow each other to dump waste products into the environment without full accounting for costs. But there is very little evidence that we are exploiting it too fast.

Crowding on planet earth

I have less to say about the question of population growth, because it doesn't seem to involve any difficult conceptual problems. At any time, in any place, there is presumably an optimal size of population—with the property that the average person would be somewhat worse off if the population were a bit larger, and also worse off if the population were a bit smaller. In any real case it must be very difficult to know what the optimum population is, especially because it will change over time as technology changes, and also because it is probably more like a band or zone than a sharply defined number. I mean that if you could somehow plot a graph of economic welfare per person against population size, there would be a very gentle dome or plateau at the top, rather than a sharp peak.

I don't intend to guess what the optimal population for the United States may be. But I am prepared to hazard the guess that there is no point in opting for a perceptibly larger population than we now have, and we might well be content with a slightly smaller one. (I want to emphasize the likelihood that a 15 percent larger or 15 percent smaller population would make very little difference in our standard of well-being. I also want to emphasize that I am talking only about our own country. The underdeveloped world offers very special problems.) My general reason for believing that we should not want a substantially larger population is this. We all know the bad consequences of too large a population: crowding, congestion, excessive pollution, the disappearance of open space—that is why the curve of average well-being eventually turns down at large population sizes. Why does the curve ever climb to a peak in the first place? The generic reason is because of what economists call economies of scale, because it takes a population of a certain size and density to support an efficient chemical industry, or publishing industry, or symphony orchestra, or engineering university, or airline, or computer hardware and software industry, especially if you would like several firms in each, so that they can be partially regulated by their own competition. But after all, it only takes a population of a *certain* size or density to get the benefit of these economies of scale. And I'm prepared to guess that the U.S. economy is already big enough to do so; I find it hard to believe that sheer efficiency would be much served in the United States by having a larger market.

As it happens, recent figures seem to show that the United States is heading for a stationary population: that is to say, the current generation of parents seems to be establishing fertility patterns that will, if continued, cause the population to stabilize some time during the next century. Even so, the absolute size of the population will increase for a while, and level off higher than it is now, because decades of population growth have left us with a bulge of population in the childbearing ages. But I have already argued that a few million more or less hardly make a difference; and a population that has once stabilized might actually decrease, if that came to seem desirable.

At the present moment, at least for the United States, the danger of rapid population growth seems to be the wrong thing to worry about. The main object of public policy in this field ought to be to ensure that the choice of family size is truly a voluntary choice, that access to the best birth-control methods be made universal. That seems to be all that is needed. Of course, we know very little about what governs voluntary fertility, about why the typical notion of a good family size changes from generation to generation. So it is certainly possible that these recent developments will reverse themselves and that population control will again appear on the agenda of public policy. This remains to be seen.

In all this I have said nothing about the Doomsday Models because there is practically nothing that needs to be said. So far as we can tell, they make one very bad mistake: in the face of reason, common sense, and systematic evidence, they seem to assume that at high standards of living, people want more children as they become more affluent (though over most of the observed range, a higher standard of living goes along with smaller families). That error is certainly a serious one in terms of the recent American data—but perhaps it explains why some friends of mine were able to report that they had run a version of the Forrester World Dynamics Model starting with a population of two people and discovered that it blew up in 500 years. Apart from placing the date of the Garden of Eden in the fifteenth century, what else is new?

There is another analytical error in the models, as Fred Singer has pointed out. Suppose resource exhaustion or increased pollution conspires to bring a reduction in industrial production. The model then says that birth rates will rise because, in the past, low industrial output has been associated with high birth rates. But there is nothing in historical evidence to suggest that a once-rich country will go *back* to high birth rates if (as I doubt will happen) its standard of living falls from an accustomed high level. Common sense suggests that a society in such a position would fight to preserve its standard of living by reducing the desired family size. In any case, this is another example of a poorly founded—or unfounded—assumption introduced to support the likelihood of overshoot-and-collapse.

Paying for pollution

Resource exhaustion and overpopulation: that leaves pollution as the last of the Doomsday Devils. The subject is worth a whole lecture in itself, because it is one of those problems about which economists actually have something important to say to the world, not just to each other. But I must be brief. Fine print aside, I think that what one gets from the Doomsday literature is the notion that air and water and noise pollution are an inescapable accompaniment of economic growth, especially industrial growth. If that is true, then to be against pollution is to be against growth. I realize that in putting the matter so crudely I have been unjust; nevertheless, that is the message that comes across. I think that way of looking at the pollution problem is wrong.

A correct analysis goes something like this. Excessive pollution and degradation of the environment certainly accompany industrial growth and the increasing population density that goes with it. But they are by no means an inescapable by-product. Excessive pollution happens because of an important flaw in the price system. Factories, power plants, municipal sewers, drivers of cars, strip-miners of coal and deep-miners of coal, and all sorts of generators of waste are allowed to dump that waste into the environment, into the atmosphere and into running water and the oceans, without paying the full cost of what they do. No wonder they do too much. So would you, and so would I. In fact, we actually do—directly as drivers of cars, indirectly as we buy some products at a price which is lower than it ought to be because the producer is not required to pay for using the environment to carry away his wastes, and even more indirectly as we buy things that are made with things that pollute the environment.

This flaw in the price system exists because a scarce resource (the waste-disposal capacity of the environment) goes unpriced; and that happens because it is owned by all of us, as it should be. The flaw can be corrected, either by the simple expedient of regulating the discharge of wastes to the environment by direct control or by the slightly more complicated device of charging special prices—user taxes—to those who dispose of wastes in air or water. These effluent charges do three things: they make pollution-intensive goods expensive, and so reduce the consumption of them; they make pollution-intensive methods of production costly, and so promote abatement of pollution by producers; they generate revenue that can, if desired, be used for the further purification of air or water or for other environmental improvements. Most economists prefer this device of effluent charges to regulation by direct order. This is more than an occupational peculiarity. Use of the price system has certain advantages in efficiency and decentralization. Imposing a physical limit on, say, sulfur dioxide emission is, after all, a little peculiar. It says that you may do so much of a bad thing and pay nothing for the privilege, but after that,

the price is infinite. Not surprisingly, one can find a more efficient schedule of pollution abatement through a more sensitive tax schedule.

But this difference of opinion is minor compared with the larger point that needs to be made. The annual cost that would be necessary to meet decent pollution-abatement standards by the end of the century is large, but not staggering. One estimate says that in 1970 we spent about $8.5 billion (in 1967 prices), or 1 percent of GNP, for pollution abatement. An active pollution abatement policy would cost perhaps $50 billion a year by 2000, which would be about 2 percent of GNP by then. That is a small investment of resources: you can see how small it is when you consider that GNP grows by 4 percent or so every year, on the average. Cleaning up air and water would entail a cost that would be a bit like losing one-half of one year's growth, between now and the year 2000. What stands between us and a decent environment is not the curse of industrialization, not an unbearable burden of cost, but just the need to organize ourselves consciously to do some simple and knowable things. Compared with the possibility of an active abatement policy, the policy of stopping economic growth in order to stop pollution would be incredibly inefficient. It would not actually accomplish much, because one really wants to reduce the amount of, say, hydrocarbon emission to a third or a half of *what it is now*. And what no-growth would accomplish, it would do by cutting off your face to spite your nose.

The end of the world— a matter of timing

In the end, that is really my complaint about the Doomsday school. It diverts attention from the really important things that can actually be done, step by step, to make things better. The end of the world *is* at hand—the earth, if you take the long view, will fall into the sun in a few billion years anyway, unless some other disaster happens first. In the meantime, I think we'd be better off passing a strong sulfur-emissions tax, or getting some Highway Trust Fund money allocated to mass transit, or building a humane and decent floor under family incomes, or overriding President Nixon's veto of a strong Water Quality Act, or reforming the tax system or fending off starvation in Bengal—instead of worrying about the generalized "predicament of mankind."

Recovery and Growth Without Inflation

An address delivered by
Irving S. Friedman
Senior Vice President
and
Senior Adviser
for International Operations
Citibank, N.A.
June 17, 1976
before the
International Monetary Conference
San Francisco, California

I am convinced that a solution to modern inflation is inextricably linked to a series of grave socioeconomic problems. Notable among these are mass unemployment, widespread poverty, inequalities in income distribution, inequities in consumption, and chronic social and political instability.

I will not review in detail what can be read elsewhere.(1) Instead, I will concentrate on what is new and on how we might approach a still murky future. I must stress at the outset, however, that this can only be done by maintaining a *global* perspective, including the developing countries, and by keeping our eyes fixed on *longer-term* objectives.

The achievement of our society's goals is gravely threatened by a relatively new phe-

nomenon—"persistent inflation." It is necessary to take the longer view to detect its characteristics and devise its remedy. Whereas past inflations were either temporary, local or mild enough not to disrupt world economies, modern inflation is continuous, worldwide and accelerating in magnitude over the longer run.(2)

Inflation has traditionally been viewed as a monetary phenomenon with attention focused on prices, costs, money supply, interest and exchange rates, monetary and fiscal policies. I do not disagree with this approach. Indeed, studies that relate recent acceleration of worldwide inflation to large increases in monetary reserves are quite useful.(3) Clearly, increases in money supply since World War II have tended to expand more

Irving S. Friedman, "Recovery and Growth Without Inflation." From an address before the International Monetary Conference, San Francisco, California, June 17, 1976. Reprinted with permission of the author and Citibank.

rapidly than increases in real output, and inflation can be described and analyzed in those terms.

My intention, however, is to search behind the monetary veil for lasting solutions. Even in its monetary aspects, modern inflation differs from past inflations in various ways:

- Increases in prices and costs have been sustained over a long period at very high rates.
- These increases have persisted through all phases of the business cycle.
- Money supply has increased more rapidly than real output and income.
- Interest rates have been high.

Beyond these monetary distinctions, however, lie different basic or societal causes, and the most important of these today is secular worldwide scarcity confronted by rapidly increasing secular demand everywhere.

What is meant by "scarcity" and how is it brought about? One decisive factor has been the steady rise in aspirations for a better life by all classes in the industrial nations, and all peoples in the developing countries.

Rapid improvement in worldwide communications technology has acquainted people in many countries with living standards, including consumer goods and comforts, so far available to only a few nations. "Scarcity," however, is not absolute and unchanging even within one country. It tends to be whatever the society defines it to be. Thus, the causes and effects of inflation are seen in the behavior of people. This is why I regard mine as a *societal* approach to inflation. It is not in opposition to a monetary approach. In fact, the principal objective of a societal approach is to help find ways of achieving enduring monetary stability.

Before we can deal effectively with persistent inflation, I believe it is necessary to accept four underlying assumptions:

- There has been a fundamental change in recent decades in the nature and impact of inflation.
- Complacency that finds moderate inflation rates "acceptable" is wrong. It fails to perceive the true economic impact. To end inflation is to end inflation. Period. It is not

to achieve lower rates than in some prior period, or to avoid that accident of the decimal system called "double-digit inflation."

- Major changes both nationally and internationally are required, not simply improvement of past remedies applicable to temporary and local inflations.
- Modern inflation can be ended within the framework of existing socioeconomic systems. Major changes are needed, however, in policies and institutions in such areas as taxation, subsidization and other government expenditures, savings, patterns of consumption, investment and international trade. Such changes can be made within the structure of the market-price mechanism and varying levels of government controls, intervention and ownership, as each nation chooses.

I learned a great deal from my fellow economists—academic and nonacademic—and from economic history. But I learned mostly from that harsh, but wise, teacher—experience. My own views on inflation are mostly derived from my career experience, mainly in the International Monetary Fund and the World Bank. We should not overlook the rich historical experience of both industrial and developing countries in seeking a better understanding of inflation and ways and means of bringing it to an end.

Whatever the school of thought, however, prior literature on the causes of inflation has failed to account for its stubborn persistence since the 1930s. Insufficient attention has been directed to great national differences in inflationary behavior and to the simultaneous existence of this phenomenon in virtually all countries.(4)

So far, there are no comprehensive mathematical approaches to inflation analysis, modeling and forecasting, in which causes and effects of inflation are considered to be social and political, as well as economic.(5)

The failure to see that the very continuation of low rates of inflation would lead to a new phenomenon, namely, "persistent inflation," was the great error of the 1950s and 1960s. The failure to see that persistent inflation cannot be cured on a national basis alone was another great error. There is evidence in our intellectual and political circles that these errors are now beginning to be perceived; for example, the increasing attention being given to the importance of inflationary expectations in explaining monetary and real economic behavior.

Persistent Inflation and Its Effects

Persistent inflation took hold gradually in different countries at different times and at very different rates.(6) Its deeply rooted social and political causes are also quite different from those that produce temporary inflation. Consequently, modern inflation can be eliminated only if its societal causes are well understood. More importantly, its damaging societal effects must be sufficiently exposed to produce a general consensus that persistent inflation, like persistent high levels of unemployment and persistent economic stagnation, is intolerable in modern societies. Its continuation is likely to lead to further scarcities and bottlenecks in production and distribution. The oil embargo and price increases by the OPEC countries, though surprising and politically motivated, showed how global frictions are intensified by persistent inflation.

This analysis led to the expectation that the subsequent recession would prove more intractable and difficult to manage than the previous postwar recessions and that inflation would continue to be strong by historical standards despite a cyclical downturn. Foreign exchange stability, as I predicted in 1972, could not be maintained.

My earlier analyses convinced me that various attempts to *dampen* inflation could succeed only *temporarily*. One attempt was to keep a firm rein on monetary policy, while accepting higher and more prolonged unemployment. Another was to accept the distortions caused by government controls to get a temporary respite. Still another way was to induce some major sector of society—labor, profit earners, the young, the old—to adjust its living standards downward. Everybody offered someone else as the sacrificial lamb— another example of the pernicious effect of persistent inflation on the values of society! But no group would accept the dampening

of inflation at its own expense for long. The expectation that inflation would continue indefinitely assured that conditions of confrontation and hostility would remain.

The problems of inequity caused by inflation worsened, as various corrective measures proved ineffective. Cost-of-living adjustments, other indexation, periodic increases in government salaries, food stamps, rent controls, artificially low public utility rates, price controls, embargoes on food exports, rising welfare payments—none of these could equalize the impact of inflation on everyone. For example, with the costs of food, housing and education rising faster than the general price level, many who were ostensibly protected by cost-of-living adjustments found themselves consuming a very different basket of goods and services. Many governments and corporations had to retract their income-adjustment promises.

Persistent inflation was already eroding the productive capacity and efficiency of national economies, before the oil price rise, by distorting the flow of savings into unproductive channels, such as government subsidies or inflation-hedge investments like real estate. Although economic uncertainties caused people to save more, those savings were being attracted into consumer-goods industries. An overemphasis on "consumerism" fostered nonessential and often wasteful consumption.

Because of the way persistent inflation influences decision-making, my fear then as now is that recovery strategies will be based on consumption rather than investment. Such strategies accelerate inflation before economies can be strengthened by needed investments.

Persistent inflation widened the gap between the needs of the world and the productive capacity required to satisfy them. The problem was contained while industrial countries grew fast enough to increase output and living standards. It went unnoticed that full employment was being reached at real growth rates that were, in my judgment, lower than would have been achieved in a noninflationary environment under appropriate policies. The world at large greatly needed, and still needs, this increased capacity in industrial, as well as nonindustrial, regions and countries.

I expressed doubt in the early 1970s that even a worldwide recession would end inflation. And, it has not. Indeed, many economists—myself included—expect prices to accelerate again during the current upswing and in the years ahead.

My predictions on the future course of modern inflation are influenced by the public's response to past government initiatives. Although today's relatively high inflation rates in industrial countries are considerably lower in almost every case than the peaks reached during the last upswing, neither inflation nor inflationary expectation has been eliminated. Conversely, current rates are generally higher than the low points reached during previous downswings, thus indicating a long-term accelerating trend. Moreover, the recent easing of inflation rates was achieved only after a large majority of industrial nations *simultaneously* gave top priority to fighting inflation. Their determination is attested by levels of unemployment once considered politically unacceptable and publicly intolerable. (See table on page 8.)

I believe these general observations are borne out by particular national experiences in the last few years. In the *United States,* prices (as measured by the consumer price index) rose more than 12% from the fourth quarter 1973 to the fourth quarter 1974, and only about 7% from then to the fourth quarter 1975. The cost of this reduction in the inflation rate, however, was a two-year rise in unemployment from under 5% to almost 9%, and a 7.5% decline in industrial production. Consumer prices in the first quarter 1976 were 6.4% higher than in the comparable period 1975, but only 3.9% (annual rate) higher than in the fourth quarter. The underlying inflation rate is considered by Federal Reserve Board Chairman Arthur Burns to be in the range of 6%–7%.

Canada's experiment with an incomes policy, since fourth quarter 1975, is expected to slow inflation from prior annual rates of 12% and 10%. Nationwide unemployment, seasonally adjusted, increased from a 5.5% rate to a 7% rate over the two years; however, regional and seasonal unemployment are particularly high. Inflationary price trends may be dampened temporarily by the incomes policy, but inflationary pressures remain strong.

Japan experienced her highest annual increase when consumer prices jumped 23.9% from fourth quarter 1973 to fourth quarter 1974. It slowed to less than 10% the following year. Over the same two years, however, unemployment increased from 1.2% to 2.1%, and would have climbed higher but for the tradition of job tenure. The inflation rate should decline further to about 7%, closer to the United States and Germany than to Italy or the United Kingdom, but inflationary pressures are still strong.

In *France,* the annual inflation rate is expected to remain close to 10% during the coming year. Productivity remains low, even in the recovery phase of a business cycle. The government is creating more jobs—especially for young people—through deficit spending and is urging the private sector to keep people employed despite lower productivity and higher wages and material costs. But higher costs will be passed on in higher prices.

In *Germany,* a reduction in the inflation rate from 7.3% during 1973 to 5.6% during 1975 cost a tripling of the unemployment rate to almost 5%. Though the money supply was drastically curtailed in 1973, expansion in 1974 and 1975 will assure upward pressure on prices in the coming year. Inflationary pressures are comparatively weak, but strong by modern German standards.

In the *United Kingdom,* prices increased 10% during 1973, 18% during 1974, and 25% during 1975, while unemployment was doubling from 2.2% to 4.8%. It is hoped that a more restrictive monetary policy combined with a decline in real wages will reduce the inflation rate by half in the coming year.

In *Italy,* wages have consistently outpaced consumer prices. A drop in the annual inflation rate, from 25% during 1974 to around 11% during 1975, reflected the government's tighter fiscal policies, supplemented by the Bank of Italy's more stringent monetary stance. Meanwhile, the unemployment rate hovers in the 3%–3.5% range. Inflationary

TABLE. Annual Percentage Changes in Money Supply (M1), Industrial Production, Wage Rates, and Consumer Prices Compared with Unemployment Rate of Fourth Quarter

Fourth Quarters

Country	1973/1972					1974/1973					1975/1974				
	M	P	W	Pr	U	M	P	W	Pr	U	M	P	W	Pr	U
U.S.	7.1	5.6	7.4	8.4	4.8	2.8	−4.5	10.0	12.1	6.7	4.9	−3.1	6.9	7.3	8.5
Canada	5.9	6.0	9.6	9.0	5.5	1.0	−1.1	16.7	12.0	5.6	19.7	−2.6	13.3	10.1	7.0
Japan	16.9	13.6	19.5	15.0	1.2	11.6	−13.0	26.1	23.9	1.6	11.1	−1.7	13.6	9.0	2.1
France	9.7	3.4	14.7	8.3	2.0*	15.1	−2.5	19.4	15.0	2.9*	12.8	−4.2	19.6	9.9	4.3*
Germany	0.7	4.1	11.0	7.3	1.6	12.1	−5.5	10.6	6.4	3.6	13.9	−0.1	6.5	5.6	4.9
U.K.	6.5	3.8	12.8	10.3	2.2	11.0	−4.7	25.3	18.2	2.9	18.9	−4.8	21.8	25.3	4.8
Italy	17.5	10.4	23.3	11.6	3.0	9.4	−6.9	27.1	24.7	3.1	12.5	−0.6	22.3	11.6	3.5

*Citibank estimate.

Key:
M = Money Supply (M1)
P = Industrial Production
W = Wage Rates
Pr = Consumer Price Index
U = Unemployment Rate

Sources:
International Monetary Fund (*International Financial Statistics*)
U.S. Department of Commerce (*Survey of Current Business*)
International Labour Organization (*International Labour Statistics*)
Organization for Economic Cooperation and Development (*Main Economic Indicators*)

pressures remain strong, compared with other industrial countries, and the outlook remains clouded with political uncertainties.

This brief seven-nation survey illustrates the difficulties that each country faced in fighting inflation and recession concurrently.

But it is inconclusive as to what might have happened had strong anti-inflationary fiscal and monetary policies been pursued simultaneously by these and most other industrial countries. Evidently, widespread concern that recession might deepen into a global depression, like that of the 1930s, prevented the people and their governments from accepting prolonged and severe unemployment as the cost of controlling inflation.

There is a deep conviction within modern society that business recessions will simply not be allowed to endure. So long as basic subsistence is guaranteed by transfer payments, personal expectations will be based on long-term experience and not short-term business cycles. Nevertheless, business cycles do superimpose various economic effects on the secular trend. Downswings tend to delay consumption, increase savings, and postpone improvements in material well-being—but *not* the expectation of future material well-being. In my opinion, recent cyclical changes, including a severe recession, have thus far had no decisive influence on long-run expectations of persistent inflation. Consequently, we must find other ways of dealing with the problem.

My own judgment is that more efforts will be devoted to fighting inflation without prolonged recessions or economic stagnation. But all efforts will fail that do not recognize the novel character of modern inflation. Current suggestions for various controls and incomes policies once again reflect the mistaken view that modern inflation is essentially temporary. Until policymakers understand that inflation is persistent, and is so perceived by most people, their policies will have little chance of success.

Where Are We Now?

It may be useful to review where we stand right now, before considering what steps to take:

- The expectation of persistent inflation is part of all decision-making by consumers, investors and savers, private and governmental.
- Unemployment, both cyclical and structural, is relatively high by historical standards.

- Neither the private sector nor the government has been able to devise effective protection against persistent inflation.
- Uncertainties caused by inflation continue to disrupt business and public planning and budgeting.
- The private sector has come under increased government controls, with the prospect of more.
- Inflation has so deteriorated many public services that they represent a major handicap to both economic growth and the quality of life.
- Inflation has made impractical the achievement of stable exchange rate relations.

What Should We Do?

In my judgment, inflation cannot persist indefinitely. If not curtailed, it will end in either hyperinflation or social and political disorders severe enough to compel drastic solutions. This process is already evident in some countries. We must, therefore, seek other ways of coping with persistent inflation.

Since there are no practical short-term remedies for inflation, we will have to look beyond the next one or two business cycles and design a simultaneous, cooperative, longer-term approach to be applied by the governments of the leading industrial nations. I believe such an approach would end inflation within one decade. There would be major benefits, moreover, along the way. First, countries would be tackling their major social and economic problems, which require solutions in any case. Second, inflationary expectations would subside as people saw their basic problems being addressed. Third, the shift from secular accelerating price rises to secular decelerating price rises would allow more economic decisions to be made without the built-in hedge against long-run inflation.

Over the past 25 years we have had an accelerating price trend. Each successive U.S. business cycle has started from a price level higher than the last. We must now achieve a secular deceleration in the price trend, keeping inflation rates stable during the upswings of the business cycle and reducing them during the recession phase until we finally get to zero inflation.

The principal thrust of my recommended policy is to increase global output while reformulating expectations of improved material well-being to realizable levels. Therefore, my approach emphasizes supply management; in contrast, other approaches have emphasized demand and incomes management. Though definitions of need, want, poverty and subsistence vary, minimal standards have risen everywhere. We can modify extravagant expectations, but the prospect remains that the world will live for some decades in an era of scarcity. Though the affluent society will be enjoyed by a relative few, living standards for the majority of mankind will probably continue to rise.

Since my subject is *global* inflation, I will suggest approaches applicable to most countries. I will, however, distinguish *global* actions, requiring international cooperation, from *national* actions. My suggestions are not intended to be exhaustive or absolute, but they should indicate how a societal approach can help to achieve higher levels of employment and sustained satisfactory growth rates without persistent inflation.

Global Actions

1. The world food problem is being tackled from many sides in an effort to eliminate shocks to national and world economies from recurring food scarcities. This cannot be done quickly, but it can and must be done because food prices are a key element in inflation in both industrial and developing countries.

2. The crucial role of energy sources and distribution is a perfect example of a problem that can only be solved on a global basis. Clearly, the United States cannot solve its energy problems independent of supply and demand conditions in other countries. What is less often recognized is how an effective attack on world energy needs could help to eliminate inflation.

3. Another area for global action against inflation is nonpetroleum minerals and industrial primary products. Although the urgency is not as apparent, postponing invest-

ments here could produce bottlenecks and scarcities with resulting strong inflationary effects on the world economy. Assuring adequate availability of these products—in terms of *future* needs—would achieve a less inflation-prone world economy.

4. Today there are vast pools of unemployed or inefficiently employed labor in the developing world. As the general population grows, the underemployed labor pools—both young and old—enlarge. (7) Our ability to mobilize the unemployed and increase the productivity of the employed is paramount in relieving world scarcity and thereby reducing persistent inflation.

5. Because asymmetry is common between a country's investment needs and its savings —sometimes deficit, sometimes surplus—the international capital flows that produce equilibrium represent a further area for global cooperation. The strength of private and public financial intermediaries in handling capital flows has been well demonstrated in the past two years. These essential mechanisms must remain strong, if national and international efforts to increase world output on an efficient basis are to succeed.

6. Any concerted attack on global inflation must include effective functioning of the international monetary system. Persistent inflation, as noted earlier, creates great uncertainty—directly in prices and costs, indirectly in social and political consequences. But the particular uncertainty of fluctuating exchange rates cannot be eliminated while industrial countries are experiencing inflation of significantly different orders of magnitude.

I will not dwell on the question of floating against stable exchange rates. There are two points, however, that I should like to make, which are often slighted in more general discussions:

First, we can reduce uncertainties by increasing the resources of the International Monetary Fund. This will enlarge the safety net under the international monetary system and enable countries and entities within countries to pursue better developmental, as well as anti-cyclical, policies.

Second, a key role for the international monetary system is helping countries harmonize their anti-inflation efforts by evaluating the external aspects of national programs. The IMF, the Organization for Economic Cooperation and Development, and the Bank for International Settlements are making major contributions in this area.

National Programs

As to national initiatives, I want to reemphasize that I am not designing a "package" of policies for any particular country. I do believe, however, that an effective attack on persistent inflation can be mounted if the following general policies are applied in a long-term, non-partisan manner.

In addition to the obvious suggestion that countries with high population growth rates do everything possible to implement effective family planning programs, the specific proposals are

1. Countries should aim at combined public and private voluntary savings in the range of 25%–30% of gross domestic product—perhaps higher in industrial countries. Where necessary, institutional mechanisms, including tax and interest-rate policies, should be changed to achieve these savings. Voluntary savings should be encouraged with recognition given to the general social benefits from such savings. This would achieve desired changes in consumption while encouraging productive activities. For example, earned income that is saved in financial forms could be exempted from taxation or taxed at lower rates, then treated as taxable current income later when spent. Similar tax treatment could be applied to business earnings invested in productive facilities, as is now done in Brazil. Greater flexibility could be given to financial institutions to attract household savings.

2. Measures should be taken to attract savings into high-productivity investments instead of consumption. We should emphasize the importance of the investment-consumption trade-off in contrast to the unemployment-inflation trade-off. (8)

Public investments are not "costless" when they are financed by printing money. Until the true economic and social costs are better understood, the concept of priorities is meaningless. Owing to strong worldwide demand

514

for investment capital, interest rates are likely to remain high. In this manner, the market mechanism allocates savings most efficiently.

3. A combined savings and investment program designed to deal with the basic causes of inflation would sustain higher growth rates and raise living standards for all. Among lower income groups, a higher proportion of income would go to consumption. The highest income groups would devote a larger proportion of income to savings, but would still increase consumption.

4. The selection of priorities for spending the national product lies at the heart of any country's effort to end persistent inflation. What is often lacking, however, is recognition of the tight interdependence of economic units within a country. These interactions must be well understood by policymakers and in political systems based on public consensus, by everyone.

Making and implementing priorities are specific and difficult tasks, whose details can be filled in only at appropriate levels—national, regional or municipal. It remains for political, business, and academic leaders to provide the overview of anticipated interactions.

5. In setting priorities, value systems are of prime importance. What seems urgent to one community—encouraging entry into the labor force, providing tax incentives for specified investments, increasing or decreasing transfer payments to the sick and the aged—may be unacceptable to another community. Some may prefer to tax luxury consumption —others, to reduce taxes on business profits.

6. If national priorities reflect value judgments, they also reflect the world's diverse economies and societies. Germany, France and the United States, for example, are all market-oriented economies, yet they differ widely on the role that government should play in such areas as public ownership of industry, regulation and centralized planning.

Other special efforts that I personally would advocate are improving living standards for the poorest half of the population, creating jobs for the *chronically* unemployed, and channeling savings to areas of production with the largest unutilized manpower. I

would also promote greater awareness of the true costs of public services—and encourage public utility rates that truly reflect those costs. Indeed, all subsidies granted to enterprises—public and private—should be open and come through the budgetary process. How else can people choose intelligently what they wish to subsidize? In general, I would do everything possible to reduce the relative importance of transfer payments and increase the relative importance of earned income. Finally, I would promote more intensive analyses of such problem areas as education, transportation and health as they relate to the urbanization of industrial nations and both urban and rural growth in the developing countries. Until these key problems are resolved, we have little hope of coping with persistent inflation.

Modern inflation is the product of modern relationships among people. In turn, it strains those relationships, diverts us from our social, political and economic goals and creates inequities we cannot in good conscience tolerate. Because it is a fairly new phenomenon, different in *kind* from earlier inflations, unprecedented and innovative actions are required over many years to end it. We should begin now to build the necessary public consensus by defining the destructive impact of persistent inflation.

Fortunately, there is much to learn from the experiences of other countries, in both analyses and remedies. Examples include

- Brazil—success in directing investments into top priority areas while maintaining a vigorous private sector
- France — a tradition of strong central government and administrative credit controls
- Mexico—intensive efforts to reconcile high growth rates with cautious monetary policy
- Argentina—a shift from almost hyperinflation to an orderly economic program
- Japan — maintenance of high growth rates while diversifying export capacity and strengthening competitiveness
- India — monetary policies that keep down the rate of inflation while the govern-

ment overcontrols the economy and limits the use of monetary instruments

Examples could be multiplied indefinitely, but these will serve to illustrate the national experiences that we can draw upon in achieving effective programs and policies to end persistent inflation.

We must try to get back to conditions of monetary stability. I believe experience shows we cannot achieve this stability by monetary policy alone, or by price and wage controls. We are left with the need for anti-inflationary fiscal and monetary policies, but redefined in each country to reflect the realities of modern societies and the integrated global economy.

NOTES

1. See Irving S. Friedman. *Inflation, a World-Wide Disaster*. Boston: Houghton Mifflin, 1973. Available in various translations.

2. Charting the U.S. consumer price index from 1800 to 1975 shows that "persistent" inflation was not known before World War II. After every wartime peak, prices declined and remained fairly stable between wars. But since the end of World War II—partly because of more localized military conflicts in Korea and Southeast Asia—prices have climbed steadily. Countries such as the United Kingdom and Germany had similar experiences. Between the world wars and before World War I, prices were either fairly stable or rose only moderately.

3. H. Robert Heller. *International Reserves and World-Wide Inflation*. IMF Staff Papers. XXIII: 1, March 1976. Postulates a causal link between changes in international reserves and changes in world prices. Changes in global international reserves have a direct and an indirect impact on the world money supply, and these changes in the world money supply in turn influence the worldwide rate of inflation.
David I. Fand. "World Reserves and World Inflation." Banca Nazionale del Lavoro. *Quarterly Review*. Dec. 1975. Theorizes that redundant reserves may have relaxed the pressure on individual countries to pursue internal anti-inflationary policies, thereby magnifying and intensifying the expansionary influences from trading partners.
Tom de Vries. "Jamaica or the Non-Reform of the International Monetary System." *Foreign Affairs*. 54:3, April 1976. Maintains that excess international liquidity was largely responsible for the outbreak of severe worldwide inflation in the early 1970s.

global econometric approach to inflation, which conceivably should be present in multinational econometric models (such as LINK Project and SIMLINK World Bank model), is still in its early stages of sophistication and does not yet satisfy the needs of theory and practice.

6. In general, the countries of the developing world have experienced much higher inflation rates than most of the industrial nations, even though price performance in the industrial nations varied widely. Significantly, inflation has accelerated in all the leading industrial nations in the past five years to rates as high as those experienced previously only by developing nations.

7. The International Labour Office (ILO) estimates that in the 30 years 1970–2000 more than one billion people will be added to the world's labor force, if current trends continue.

8. To achieve the desired allocation of savings, different practices and policies can be used. Some countries might seek a desired pattern of consumption through selective fiscal measures combined with general credit policies. This approach is common in Europe. Other countries, like Mexico, may use selective credit and fiscal policies. Still other countries will focus on the need for growth, natural resource endowment and productive potential as starting points for allocating savings. Finally, some countries will be influenced by the relative efficiency of existing institutions, such as multi-purpose banking systems.

4. The IMF recently began calculating world and regional measures of inflation based on consumer price indexes published by individual countries. According to these calculations, published in the IMF's *International Financial Statistics*, world consumer prices are now almost four times as high as they were at the end of World War II. Between 1950 and 1970, world inflation continued at an average annual rate of less than 4%. In the past five years, this jumped to almost 10%.
The world and regional measures of inflation based on consumer prices are calculated from the geometric means of the monthly values of the country data in index form. The weights are the 1970 dollar values of GDP. Geometric means are used to assure that if all of the countries of an area have constant—but different—rates of increase, the regional averages will have a constant rate of increase.

5. Since A. W. Phillips published his influential paper in 1958, inflation has been the subject of more detailed econometric investigations, first in the United States and then in other industrial countries. Econometric models for national economies, generally incorporating Phillips-type approaches, were rather successful in forecasting inflation up to the late 1960s. Lack of a relevant background theory, explaining the behavior of world prices in the last six to eight years, has impeded the development of new econometric models. The St. Louis model (L. C. Andersen, and K. M. Carlson. "St. Louis Model Revisited." *International Economic Review*. June 1974. pp. 305–7) produced fairly accurate forecasts of the GNP price deflator for the United States in the late 60s, but yielded very imprecise predictions in 1972 and 1973. This prompted a search for new approaches to modeling inflation. Data Resources Inc., for example, introduced the "inflation severity factor."
Sophisticated and scientifically valid econometric methods for explaining recent inflation have yet to be developed. The

The Outlook for Long-Run Economic Growth

Leonall C. Andersen

Economic Adviser
*Federal Reserve Bank of St. Louis**

The growth of potential output of goods and services from 1948 to 1973 is reviewed, and future growth trends predicted for the next quarter century. Careful analysis and reasoning lead the author to present two cases based on different assumptions about underlying trends. Both result in marked slowing in the rate of growth of potential output, with the most likely case resulting in future real growth between two and three percent. Some implications are a slower rise in the U.S. standard of living, opposition to government redistribution of incomes, questioning of government use of resources, and difficulties in effectively using monetary and fiscal policies.

AT THIS TIME of year, a popular exercise is to present one's views regarding the short-term economic outlook. My views on this subject differ very little from what appears to be the general consensus among forecasters. The most likely course of our economy during 1976 is one of rather moderate growth of output, inflation in the five to six percent range by the year's end, and a slowly falling unemployment rate. So instead of elaborating on my views of the short-run outlook, I will focus attention on the outlook for our economy's ability to produce goods and services over the next quarter century.

Such an exercise is important from several aspects. Growth of real output has a direct bearing on improvements in our standard of living. Knowledge regarding the most likely future growth of potential output is important in conducting appropriate economic stabilization actions. Such knowledge is also important because growth of potential output should be given consideration in making decisions regarding government actions which expand its use of resources relative to that of the private sector or attempt to increase the real incomes of certain economic groups relative to other groups. And, of course, projections of long-run potential output growth are essential in business planning.

In this paper I will first analyze the growth of potential output of goods and services during the period 1948 to 1973. Next, I will discuss the outlook in this regard over the next quarter century. Last, I will draw some implications of this outlook for the future.

MEASURING POTENTIAL OUTPUT

Before proceeding further, it is necessary to identify the appropriate measure of potential output. A common practice has been to accept the estimates of potential output developed by the President's Council of Economic Advisors. Their estimates are shown in Chart I. You will note that these estimates generally go from peak-to-peak levels of real GNP. This measure is based on an

*The views expressed are the author's and do not necessarily represent those held by the Federal Reserve Board or its officers.

Leonall C. Andersen, "The Outlook for Long Run Economic Growth." *Business Economics*, September 1976, pp. 32–39. Reprinted with permission of the author and the publisher.

unemployment rate presumed to represent full-employment and projections of the trend growth of the labor force and productivity. I view this measure as primarily one of technical, or engineering, potential.

I believe, however, that a more appropriate measure of potential output would be one based on the amount of output which could be expected to evolve over the long-run as a result of the interaction of market forces. A calculated trend of real GNP, as shown in Chart I, is my method of approximating such a measure of potential output. Attention is given in this discussion, however, to private sector output as a proxy for real GNP because of limitations on the availability of detailed data required for my analysis.

Let us now turn to my first topic — an analysis of the trend growth of potential output of goods and services from 1948 to 1973. This period was selected so as to have the beginning and terminal points at comparable positions in business fluctuations. Also, our economy was subjected to some rather severe shocks over the past two years, which actually reduced potential output at that time and probably retarded its growth for some time in the future.

Since my remarks will be based on trend growth rates, let me digress for a moment to explain my estimation procedures. Log-linear trends are estimated by regressions in which t (time) and t^2 are the independent variables. The t^2 term is included to allow for the possibility of an acceleration or a deceleration in a trend. In such a case, the trend growth rate changed over the estimation period.

According to my calculations, potential output grew at an accelerating rate during the period 1948 to 1973. The annual trend rate of increase was a 3.2 percent rate for the first quarter of 1948 and a 4.3 percent rate for the fourth quarter of 1973.

The factors which constrain, or limit, the growth of potential output can be summarized in economic magnitudes called "proximate determinants." Of course, underlying the movements in each proximate determinant are the influences of many different factors. The following analysis identifies five proximate determinants; they are listed in the left-hand column of Table I.

PROXIMATE DETERMINANTS OF OUTPUT

The foremost proximate determinant, population of labor force age (16 to 64), represents the potential number of persons available for employment in the over-all production of goods and services. The second one is the ratio of total employment to population of labor force age. The third one is the ratio of private sector employment to total employment. The fourth one is the ratio of man hours worked to the number employed in the private sector. The last proximate determinant is the overall productivity in the use of the services of labor and capital in the production of goods and services. It is measured by private sector output per man hour worked.

Before proceeding further, there is one term — employment — whose definition requires elaboration. Total employment is defined as the number of jobs and is measured by payroll data submitted

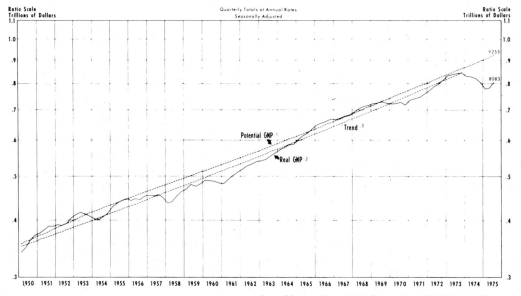

Chart 1
Real Output

by employers in both the government and private sectors. Also, members of the armed forces are included in government employment; they represent as much a use of labor resources as does employment in other branches of government or in the private sector.

Table 1 presents calculations of the trend growth rates of each proximate determinant for the first quarter of 1948 and the fourth quarter of 1973. The sum of these five growth rates for a given quarter equals the trend rate of growth of potential output. This table indicates that movements in factors influencing two of the proximate determinants accounted for most of the observed movement in the trend rate of growth of potential output. There was a marked acceleration in the growth of population of labor force age from a .5 percent rate to a 2 percent rate, which more than offset the influence of factors leading to a deceleration in growth of productivity from a 3.4 percent rate to a 2.6 percent rate.

LOOKING AHEAD

I now turn to my second topic — the outlook for growth of potential output over the next quarter century. In developing the outlook, the long-run growth rates of the five proximate determinants must be projected. One projection is that for growth of population of labor force age, for which the Bureau of the Census has projected a marked slowdown in growth from about a 2 percent rate at the present time. Using their projected levels of population of labor force age and calculating the rate of change over successive five year periods indicates a slowdown to about a 1.4 percent rate

by 1980, a further slowdown to about a .7 percent rate by 1990, and then a slight increase to around a 1 percent rate at the turn of the century.

Given this projected slower growth of population of labor force age, growth of potential output will be reduced substantially over the next quarter century unless offset by changes in growth of the other four proximate determinants. For example, if the other proximate determinants were to continue to change at their trend rates of late 1973, the trend growth of potential output would decelerate from a 4.3 percent rate to a 3.6 percent rate in 1980, to a 2.9 percent rate in 1990, and then increase to a 3.3 percent rate at the turn of the century.

An obvious question to be raised is, "What would most likely be the trends in the other four proximate determinants over the next twenty-five years?" To answer it, one must examine possible changes over time in the factors influencing each proximate determinant. Each of these will be analyzed separately, although there are interactions among them. I will attempt to weave some of these interactions into my analysis, but the following analysis should be taken as a statement of the influence of some possible developments and not as a definitive statement of all the interactions.

The Percent Population Employed

From 1948 to 1973, the ratio of employment to population of labor force age increased at a .2 percent annual rate. Labor market studies show that during that period the labor force participation rate for women increased, more than offsetting a decrease in the labor force participation rate for

Table 1

Projections of Growth of Potential
Private Sector Output and of Output Per Capita
(Annual Rates of Change)

	Estimated		Case I Projections			Case II Projections		
	1948–I	1973–IV	1980–IV	1990–IV	2000–IV	1980–IV	1990–IV	2000–IV
Population of Labor Force Age*	.5%	2.0%	1.4%	.7%	1.1%	1.4%	.7%	1.1%
Ratio of Total Employment to Population of Labor Force Age	.2	.2	.0	.0	.0	.0	.0	.0
Ratio of Private Sector Employment to Total Employment	− .4	− .2	− .2	− .2	− .2	− .2	− .2	− .2
Ratio of Man Hours Worked to Private Sector Employment	− .4	− .4	− .4	− .4	− .4	− .4	− .4	− .4
Productivity	3.4	2.6	3.0	3.0	3.0	2.0	2.0	2.0
Potential Private Sector Output	3.2	4.3	3.8	3.1	3.5	2.8	2.1	2.5
Total Population*	1.7	.7	.9	.9	.6	.9	.9	.6
Potential Output Per Capita	1.5	3.6	2.9	2.2	2.9	1.9	1.2	1.9

* U. S. Bureau of the Census, "Population Estimates and Projections," Series P–25, No. 601 (October 1975), Series II, Table 8.

men. Factors contributing to the rise in the participation rate for women were a change in the attitudes of society toward women holding jobs, the desire of mothers of the Post-World War II baby boom to take a job when their children entered school or left home, and the decisions in recent years of young married couples to postpone having a family. A movement towards an earlier age of retirement contributed to a declining participation rate for men.

Also, there is evidence, which will be discussed shortly, that firms tended to substitute labor for capital at a prevailing real wage rate. As a result, a rising real wage, partly in response to this substitution and partly in response to rising productivity, tended to increase the incentive of some individuals to choose work over leisure.

In recent years, however, three major developments have occurred which will tend to retard the trend rate of increase in the ratio of employment to population of labor force age. One development has been the recent evidence that young married couples, who have deferred starting a family, plan to start one in their late 20's and early 30's. Also, much of the rise in the participation rate of women resulting from their entering the labor market as their children got older will subside as the baby boom moves through the age distribution. As a result of these two developments, the participation rate for women will not increase as fast as previously. A third development has been the recent national policy of greatly expanding welfare programs. Such a development tends to make it increasingly less attractive for some individuals to enter the job market at a prevailing real wage rate than in the past. Also, future developments, to be discussed shortly, most likely will reduce the rate of increase in the real wage, thereby tending to decrease the incentive of some individuals to choose work over leisure.

Assuming that the movement towards an earlier retirement age continues as in the past, these developments will tend to reduce the trend growth in the ratio of employment to population of labor force age. I assume there will be no trend growth in this ratio during the balance of this century.

Private Sector Employment

The next proximate determinant is the ratio of private sector employment to total employment. Chart 2 indicates that from 1948 to 1973 this ratio decreased, reflecting a faster growth of government employment relative to private sector employment. The percent of the total number employed accounted for by government employment rose from 11 to 17 percent. Increases in the population of labor force age and in the ratio of total employment to population of labor force age were matched by growth of government employment. As a result, Chart 2 shows that the ratio of private sector employment to population of labor force age had virtually no trend from 1948 to 1973.

The outlook for growth of potential output over the next quarter century will thus be influenced by growth of government employment relative to private sector employment. Given what appears to be the present momentum in increasing government involvement in the economy, I assume that the trend in this ratio will be the same rate of decrease as in late 1973.

Average Hours Worked and Productivity

The next proximate determinant is the average number of hours worked per employee. This average decreased at a .4 percent trend rate from 1948 to 1973. Given the continuing movement towards a shorter work week, more holidays, and longer vacations, I assume that this rate of decrease will continue in the future.

The last proximate determinant of growth of potential output to be projected is growth of productivity. From 1948 to 1973, the trend growth of productivity decreased from a 3.4 percent rate to a 2.6 percent rate. Factors underlying growth of productivity (measured by output per man-hour) are changes in the quality of labor, in the efficiency in the use of resources, and in the amount of physical capital relative to labor input. In addition, there are changes in the mix of output among sectors having different rates of productivity growth.

Let us examine the movements in the factors influencing productivity growth from 1948 to 1973. Over this period the quality of labor, as measured by average years of education, increased considerably. Developments leading to more education were the G.I. Bill, expansion of in-house training programs, and rising real incomes associated with increased education and skills. The period was also one of a great number of technological advancements and improvements in managerial methods which increased efficiency.

The amount of physical capital relative to labor input in private sector production of goods and services is measured by the ratio of the capital stock (plant and equipment) to man-hours worked. From 1948 to 1973, both the capital stock and the number of man-hours worked in the private sector grew at an increasing rate. Although growth in the capital stock on average was greater than growth in man-hours worked, the acceleration in man-hours worked was greater. As a result, the trend growth in the amount of capital per man-hour worked decreased from a 3.1 percent rate in 1948 to a 2 percent rate in 1973. This deceleration in the trend growth is consistent with the proposition that the improvement in the quality of labor was such that firms tended to substitute labor for capital at a prevailing real wage rate. There also was a shift in the composition of output from agriculture and manufacturing, in which productivity gains have been relatively high, to service industries, in which productivity gains have been relatively low.

The relatively high rate of productivity growth and its subsequent slowdown was the net result of

Chart 2

Employment Ratios

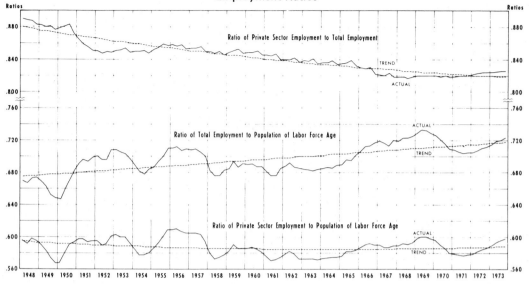

Prepared by Federal Reserve Bank of St. Louis

the influence of these four factors. An increasing quality of labor, the growing efficiency in the use of resources, and an increasing ratio of capital to man-hours worked gave a strong upward thrust to productivity. The induced slowdown in the rate of increase in the ratio of capital to man-hours worked and the shift of output to industries with relatively low productivity gains tended to retard the trend growth rate of productivity over time.

Projecting Productivity Growth

But what productivity growth may be expected to occur over the next quarter century? To answer this question it is helpful to compare the recent movement in productivity with historical movements. Studies by Solomon Fabricant have found that productivity has grown in a wave like fashion over fairly long periods of time. So it is not uncommon to find a period of decelerating growth like the one experienced since 1948. These studies also indicate that the long-run growth of productivity increased from a 2 percent annual rate over the period 1889 to 1919 to a 2.6 percent annual rate over the period 1919 to 1957. It is therefore possible that the recent movement in productivity represents a new trend growth rate.

One possibility is that growth of productivity since 1948 represents a further increase in its trend rate of growth. An approximation of a possible new trend rate of increase would be 3 percent, the average rate over the 1948 to 1973 period. Another possibility is that productivity over the next twenty-five years will grow at a trend rate significantly different than 3 percent. So let us examine some possible developments which will tend to

have an influence on future growth of productivity.

Given my assumptions regarding the likely trend growth rates of the four proximate determinants other than productivity, the trend growth rate of man-hours worked is projected to decrease by about one-third its 1.6 percent rate in late 1973. A projection of changes in the ratio of capital to man-hours worked, therefore, will depend primarily on projected growth of capital. The trend in the ratio of net real investment to net real private sector output is a summary measure of the influence of changes in the factors determining the desire of individuals to save relative to real income (that is, the desire to allocate current resources to capital accumulation) and the desire of business firms to invest relative to real income (that is, the desire to use current resources for capital accumulation).

Chart III shows that the trend in the ratio of net real investment to net real private sector output fell in the late 1940s and early 1950s, was about constant to late 1961, and then grew at an accelerating rate to the end of 1973. An explanation of its behavior prior to late 1961 involves, first, the diversion of resources to the Korean War effort. Then, there followed three recessions in rapid order, which created much uncertainty and, therefore, reduced the desire of firms to invest. After 1961 the major technological developments which occurred following World War II began to have their main impact on the productivity of capital. Also, uncertainty was reduced by a long period of continuous economic expansion from 1962 to 1969. Both of these developments tended to increase the desire of firms to invest. A partial off-

521

Chart 3
Ratio of Net Investment to Net Private Sector Output*

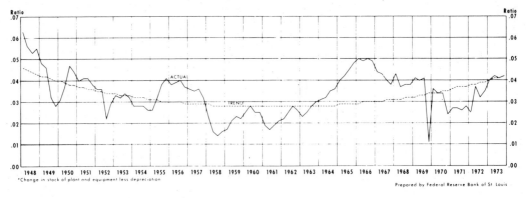

setting influence was an apparent substitution of labor for capital at the prevailing real wage rate. Assuming no change in the desire to save, the ratio of net investment to net private sector output thus began to rise after 1961.

Declining Capital Productivity

As we look to the future, there have occurred several developments recently which will tend to reduce the ratio of net real investment to net real private sector output. Growth in the productivity of capital can be expected to slow as the influence of the earlier wave of technological advances is assimilated in production processes. There has been an acceleration in government efforts to redistribute incomes from those who save a relatively large proportion of their income to those who primarily consume. Also, with increasing government involvement in economic activity, a growing share of our resources will, by government direction, be allocated to production of goods and services other than capital. Government actions with regard to economic stabilization efforts and with regard to regulations imposed on industry and their administration of such regulations have resulted in increased uncertainty. All of these developments will tend to reduce the ratio of net real investment to net private sector output.

With the projected slower growth of labor resources, there will be a tendency to substitute capital for labor, but such a development will gradually evolve over time. Consequently, it will only partially offset the depressing influence of the other developments mentioned on investment. As a result, the ratio of real net investment to real net private sector output will tend to decrease significantly during much of the next quarter century, unless another wave of technological innovation occurs. If the decrease in this ratio is sufficiently large, growth of capital can be reduced to such an extent that the ratio of capital to man-hours worked will grow slower than in 1973. As a result there

will be a tendency for growth of productivity to slow.

Other developments will also tend to retard growth of productivity. A significant shift in the composition of output toward service industries will most likely continue. Also, there is considerable doubt on the part of many educators that further increases in the average years of education will continue. Gains in efficiency are also likely to slow as the influence of previous innovations become fully implemented.

POTENTIAL OUTPUT

If the preceeding analysis is reasonably correct, the trend growth of productivity will be less than 3 percent. With the prevailing attitudes regarding the "desirability" of expanding further the role of government, I foresee a major decrease in the proportion of output allocated to capital accumulation. Because of this and the other developments tending to decrease growth in productivity, I assume that the trend growth of productivity falls to a 2 percent annual rate of increase over the next quarter century. Such a trend rate of increase, however, is only moderately lower than that of late 1973.

Table I presents projections of growth of potential private sector output, under these two assumptions regarding the trend growth rate of productivity. Case I assumes that productivity increases at a 3 percent trend rate. Case II assumes productivity increases at a 2 percent trend rate. Assumptions regarding trend growth rates of the other four proximate determinants are the same in each case. In both cases, there is a marked slowing in the growth of potential output from its 4.3 percent trend rate in 1973. Case II, the one I believe to be more likely to happen, projects trend growth rates of potential output over the next twenty-five years ranging between approximately two and three percent.

FUTURE IMPLICATIONS

So I now come to my final topic — some of the implications of such a deceleration in the growth of potential output. A foremost implication is that the trend growth rate in our standard of living, measured by potential output per capita, will slow considerably. This will be a marked departure from the experience of the past (see Table I). From 1948 to 1973, the standard of living grew at an accelerating pace, increasing from a 1.5 percent rate in 1948 to a 3.6 percent rate in 1973. Case II suggests that growth of our standard of living could dip to about a 1 percent rate of increase in 1990, followed by an acceleration at the end of the century to a rate slightly higher than the 1.5 percent rate which prevailed in 1948.

Another implication is that a great controversy could arise regarding government efforts to carry out a further redistribution of real incomes. With potential output growth in the past outstripping population growth by a considerable margin, programs to redistribute incomes could be implemented with little controversy arising. The reason for this is that the margin was so large that real incomes of all groups could rise at an increasing rate, even with the redistribution that occurred. In the future, however, the margin between growth of potential output and of population is projected to narrow considerably. As a result, continuation of efforts to redistribute income could mean that the standard of living of some groups would have to actually decrease rather than just increase at a slower rate than otherwise.

Another implication is that continuation of government programs which increase its use of resources will come into sharper conflict with the private sector's use. In the past, such a conflict was relatively moderate because accelerating growth of potential output permitted increasing growth in both uses of resources. At the slower projected growth rate of potential output, however, a continued increase in growth of the government's use of resources at its past rate would entail a decrease in the amount of resources available to private sector production.

The projection of slower growth of potential output has important implications for future economic stabilization actions. Monetary and fiscal actions designed to stimulate growth of aggregate demand so as to achieve a growth rate of actual output equal to the 4.3 percent growth rate of potential output that occurred in the early 1970's will be highly inflationary. Evaluation of our economy's short-run economic performance will have to be made relative to a much lower rate of growth in potential output. In other words, a whole new environment will exist with regard to the achievements one can expect from economic stabilization actions.

A final implication concerns business planning for the future. Growth of resources will be significantly less than business has been accustomed to in the past. This will be particularly true for labor resources, mainly because of the marked decrease projected for growth in population of labor force age. Business in recent years has designed plant and equipment and adopted production processes within the context of accelerating growth in the number of persons potentially available for employment. In the future, however, business plans for expansion and production processes will have to take into consideration the marked slow-down in growth of labor resources. Also, the composition of output can be expected to shift towards those products which use less labor inputs relative to capital.

In conclusion, let me summarize my views regarding the long-run economic outlook. It is my opinion that over the next twenty-five years the growth rate of potential output will decrease by a significant amount from its relatively high rate in the early 1970's. The two major causes of this slowdown are a marked decrease in the growth of population of labor force age and a decrease in the growth of productivity.

The next quarter century will also be a time of great controversy because the economic reality of slower growth in potential output will impinge on the fulfillment of the desires of many. In the 1960's and early 1970's this nation was able to achieve many political, social and personal objectives without much controversy, mainly because growth of potential output accelerated. Consequently, aspirations of the American people advanced to a high level. Given the projected slower growth of potential output, unless these aspirations are lowered, we can expect many acrimonious confrontations among groups in our society in the future. The resolution of these confrontations that finally evolves will have an important bearing on growth of potential output; but I will make no predictions in this regard.

B. Productivity

The Agriculture of the U.S.

*Its high productivity is a result of two centuries of development
policy: low prices for land and other things needed for farming,
stable prices for farm products and the promotion of innovation*

by Earl O. Heady

The agriculture of the U.S. currently plays a vital and unique role in
the economy of both the nation
and the world. In the nation the agricultural sector has enjoyed high profits during the past three years when most other
sectors of the economy were experiencing a recession and a decline in income.
Employment in agriculture remained
quite stable, even though elsewhere in
the economy the rate of unemployment
greatly increased. Moreover, the secular
trend of workers migrating out of agricultural jobs as a result of technological
change in agriculture has recently slackened. Over the past several years capital
assets, particularly land, have sharply
increased in value to record levels. In
contrast, the value of corporate bonds
and common stocks were strongly depressed during much of the same period.
Even during the worldwide recession
from 1973 through 1975 the dollar value of farm exports rose to an annual
average level of $18.5 billion, an annual

increase of 167 percent over the period
between 1968 and 1972. Agricultural
exports have accounted for a growing
portion of the nation's foreign exchange
and have played an important role in
creating for the U.S. a positive balance
of trade.

In the economy of the world American agriculture dominated food exports.
Between 1973 and 1975 grain exports
from the U.S. accounted for 65 percent
of the world's total grain exports. The
importance of American agriculture in
solving world food problems is obvious.
Currently the product of nearly one in
every five crop acres in the U.S. is exported, and the output of a full 14 percent of our farm work force moves into
world markets. Yet agriculture employs
only 5 percent of the labor force in the
U.S., and only 4.4 percent of the nation's
population. No other important food-
producing country of large population
approaches the U.S. in the degree to
which it has reduced its farm labor

Earl O. Heady, "The Agriculture of the U. S." *Scientific American,* September 1976, pp. 107, 108, 110,
115, 118, 121, 122, 123, 126, 127. Reprinted with permission. Copyright © 1976 by Scientific American, Inc. All rights reserved.

force. It is the great productivity of American agriculture that enables the nation to acquire its food with minimal labor.

How did American agriculture attain such world supremacy in productivity? Has the agricultural sector in the U.S. reached the limits of its productive capacity, or can that capacity be further increased? Can the keys to such productivity be transported to other countries? What future economic and social problems, if any, are in store for the agricultural sector in the U.S.? How would such problems affect rural communities and other segments of the society?

Agricultural economists and other agricultural specialists in the U.S. have been probing the world of the developing countries over the past two decades to find the key to successful agricultural development. They need not have traveled so far; the secrets of successful agricultural development are best found in the past history of the U.S.

Over the past 200 years the U.S. has had the best, the most logical and the most successful program of agricultural development anywhere in the world. Other countries would do well to copy it. Although the program was put together piecemeal over many decades, by and large instruments of policy were consciously devised to encourage the agricultural sector to expand its resources and increase its output. As a result of such conscious policy the consumer in the U.S., and to a lesser extent in the rest of the world, has realized a favorable price for food. By 1971 only 15.7 percent of the disposable income of the average American consumer was spent for food. (In 1975 that figure rose to 16.8 percent because of inflation.) By way of comparison, in developing countries in 1971 the average consumer spent 65 percent of his disposable income for food, in the U.S.S.R. he spent 30 percent and in the countries of the European Economic Community he spent 26 percent.

What are the specific elements of a successful and conscious agricultural development policy? First, the policy must enlarge the farmer's supply of major resources and keep their prices low. Second, it must keep the prices of the commodities produced on the farm relatively high and stable. Third, it must create a tenure system that structures the operating costs of the farms in a way that is favorable to innovation. Fourth, it must encourage research and technology, and it must maintain an adequate and continuous flow of information to the farmer on the availability of new techniques and technology. The U.S. has implemented all these elements in its agricultural development policy, some-

times separately, usually in combination with one another. Over the decades the specific methods by which the Government has implemented its agricultural policy have changed, but the general principle of encouraging agricultural development has remained the same.

At the beginning of the nation's agricultural development land was abundant and labor was cheap. Capital inputs such as farm machinery, fertilizer and food for the farmer's family were relatively modest, and most of them were produced on the farm. Farmers created their own power in the form of the physical work of family members and of animals raised on the farm. They also harnessed energy from the sun for that work in the form of crops grown on the farm and eaten by the people or the animals. The farmers generated their own fertilizer by rotating crops and by utilizing the wastes from the animals. The rotation of crops also controlled insects to some extent.

Because of the availability of land farms expanded rapidly across the nation. The growth in their output could be readily absorbed by the market. The demand for food was quite elastic because of the steady increase in population, in per capita income and in food exports. Food-marketing facilities also expanded through public policies that provided land grants to railroad builders. With the markets growing and the demand for food increasing, the agricultural policy was predominantly a developmental one emphasizing large supplies of major farm resources and low prices for them. In general, the nation's development policy for agriculture benefited farmers through low property values (and therefore low land costs) and high income, and it simultaneously benefited consumers with favorable real prices for food.

American agricultural policy in the 19th century was certainly the most successful policy for development the world had yet seen. After the U.S. had expanded to the Pacific and the public domain for land grants was exhausted, the Government did not terminate the agricultural development policy. It simply shifted its emphasis. Instead of concentrating on expansion it began to emphasize productivity. It turned to scientific knowledge and new technology as capital resources to be supplied either at low cost or free. The Morrill Act of 1862 created the land-grant college system to encourage research and to extend new technical knowledge to farmers. The new resources were an effective substitute for land: between 1910 and 1970 the output of American agriculture approximately doubled; furthermore, by 1970 the nation was producing

PRINCIPAL GRAINS GROWN IN THE U.S. are shown on this outline map of the nation. The dots in white represent acreage devoted to wheat raised for human consumption. The dots in black represent acreage devoted to the major feed grains (corn, grain sorghum, barley and oats) raised for livestock. The author suggests that if American consumers reduced their meat intake by 25 percent, and if silage were substituted for 25 percent of the grain fed to livestock, American grain exports to poor countries could more than double.

its food on considerably fewer acres than it had been in 1910, and production-control programs were in effect. The results of public investment in technical improvement in agriculture were particularly apparent after 1940 as research became more refined and systematic. Moreover, the technologies incorporated into the new farming practices were low in cost compared with the quantity of agricultural products to which they gave rise. Hence the new capital technologies were adopted rapidly, and by the 1950's they became an effective substitute not only for land but also for labor. The result was that between 1950 and 1955 more than a million workers migrated out of the agricultural sector into other sectors of the economy.

Other Government development policies also helped to increase the supply of resources for agriculture and thereby reduce their cost. The Federal Farm Loan Act of 1916 and subsequent legislation provided publicly supported means whereby farmers could obtain capital assets such as farm machinery at lower interest rates than those prevailing in the open market. Similarly, the National Reclamation Act of 1902 provided means by which semiarid land in the West was supplied to farmers at subsidized prices to encourage them to develop it through irrigation.

The nation's development policy for agriculture has been implemented vigorously over most of the past 200 years. It is still in force. It is reflected in publicly supported research, education, farm credits and other programs that develop new capital technologies and encourage their exploitation by farmers. The development policy for agriculture in the U.S. is a landmark example to which the governments of developing nations might pay heed as they struggle to raise their food production above the level of subsistence.

A nation can rely on a development policy to simultaneously benefit farmers and consumers only when the demand for food is both elastic and growing. Although that was the case in the U.S. until early in the 20th century, by the 1920's the per capita income had risen high enough for the domestic demand for food to have become highly inelastic. That is, incomes had risen to the level where consumers were able to buy all the food they needed and further increases in income could have little effect on food consumption. The result of such inelasticity is that an increase in food output of 1 percent leads to a decrease in food prices of more than 1 percent. If other factors, such as exports, remain at constant levels, an increase in farm production greater than the rate of population growth causes the market price of food to decline at a rate greater than the growth of demand. The total real market revenue from agricultural products thus declines.

Such a decline began in the 1920's and was intensified by the Great Depression of the 1930's. It was relieved during World War II and the period of postwar reconstruction, when the U.S. exported food to countries whose agricultural production had been disrupted by the war. By 1950, however, world agricultural production had recovered. Again the market situation for U.S. farm commodities was one of highly inelastic demand both at home and abroad. The conditions of the 1920's had returned. Agricultural development and greater farm output alone could no longer guarantee gains simultaneously to both farmers and consumers because the benefits and the costs of continued development were inequitably distributed. As farm output continued to grow, the consumers were benefited by lower real prices for food but the farmers suffered from a decline in income.

To counteract the effects of inelastic demand agricultural policy in the U.S. took yet another course. It began providing a series of compensatory programs to maintain farm income at acceptable levels. Farmers were paid to reduce their planted acreage and output. Their reduced output supported higher prices of food on the market. Farmers were also lent money and storage facilities in ways such that the rate at which their products were put on the market was controlled. Furthermore, international food-aid programs were devised to subsidize exports—sometimes in effect giving produce away—both to help increase the demand for food and to encourage developing countries to accept it. Such programs, financed by the public through taxes during the 1930's and again from the 1950's through 1972, were compensatory in two senses. First, the programs directly paid farmers to compensate them for reductions in their income from the market as the supply of food increased more rapidly than the demand. Second, by controlling farm production the programs offset or compensated for the greater productivity of farms that had been promoted through agricultural research, soil conservation, irrigation and other development efforts.

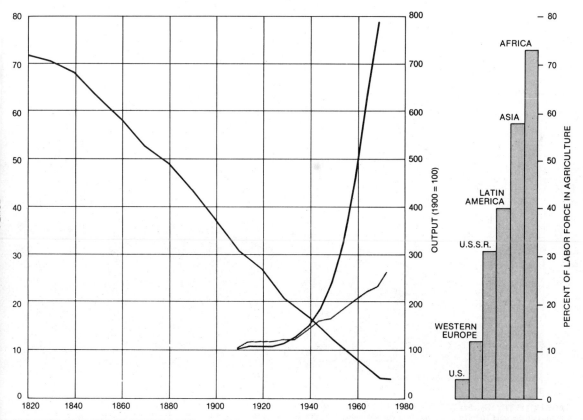

PERCENT OF LABOR FORCE ON THE LAND in the U.S. (*black*) has declined steadily over the past 150 years (*left*). Yet between 1910 and 1970 the absolute output of farms has approximately doubled (*light color*). Moreover, the productivity of American farms per farm worker has increased enormously (*dark color*). For the purposes of comparison the percent of the labor force on the land in other parts of the world is shown by the bar graph at the right. The percentages are averages for very large areas and conceal such information as the fact that 7 percent of the labor force of Israel is engaged in agriculture, whereas 91 percent of the labor force of Chad is so engaged.

527

After the 1930's, then, the U.S. had in operation both development programs and compensatory programs. The compensatory programs did not totally offset or eliminate the effects of the development programs. As agriculture continued to improve its technology the programs controlling the supply of food to the market served only to slow the growth of farm output, not to stop it. Between 1950 and 1972 the price of new capital technologies remained favorable with respect to the moderate market prices of produce, and agricultural productivity continued to advance. Farms became larger and more specialized, handling either crops or livestock instead of both. Farms growing crops greatly increased their utilization of fertilizers, pesticides, farm machinery and other capital items. For example, the use of fertilizer increased by 276 percent between 1950 and 1972. The use of powered machines increased by only 30 percent, but in 1972 there were substantially fewer farms than there were in 1950, and the average farm was more highly mechanized than its counterpart in 1950. The result was that farm labor declined by 54 percent over that period as labor productivity quadrupled and total farm output increased by 55 percent.

The compensatory programs called for large outlays of funds, and by the 1960's the public was spending heavily. By 1968 the total cost of the programs was $5.7 billion per year, and by 1972 it had reached $7 billion. More than a third of all the wheat grown in the U.S. was exported in 1965, and more than a fourth of it was exported in 1970. Other exports subsidized under foreign food-aid programs were feed grains, rice, tobacco and milk. The decade beginning with 1970 hence appeared at the outset to be a continuation of the 1950's and 1960's.

No one, however, could have foreseen the failure of the Russian wheat crop in 1972. As a result between 1971 and 1972 American wheat exports almost doubled. Feed-grain exports also grew. With the failure of the Peruvian anchovy catch in 1973 and 1974, and the consequent protein shortage in areas that relied on the anchovies as a feed supplement, in 1973 American exports of protein-rich soybeans more than doubled over those in 1971.

With such high export levels the prices of farm commodities rose sharply. Furthermore, American crops showed record yields in both 1974 and 1975. Thus farm income also attained

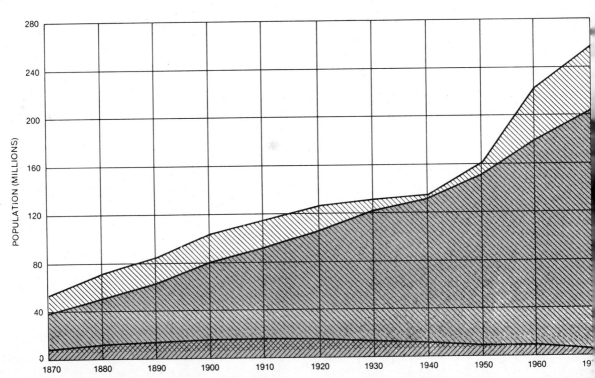

PRODUCTIVITY OF AMERICAN AGRICULTURE has been high for most of the past 100 years as a result of the agricultural policy in the U.S. The gray area represents the total population of the U.S. at 10-year intervals from 1870 through 1970. The black hatched area shows the number of workers in agriculture for the same period. The colored hatched area shows the number of people those American farm workers could feed. Although the absolute number of people on the land in 1970 was approximately half the number of people on the land in 1870, the productivity per worker was 10 times greater in 1970. Currently American agriculture can feed about 50 million more people than live in the country, and some 20 percent of all farm produce is exported. The limits of productivity have not been reached

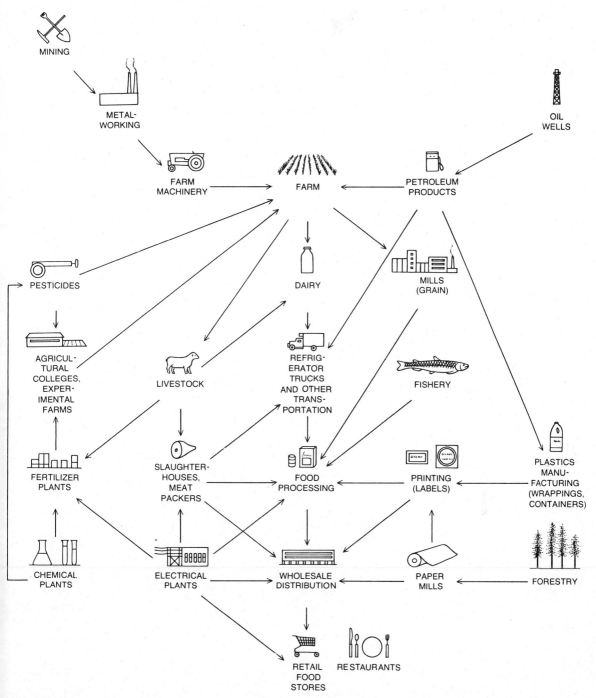

MINING

METAL-
WORKING

OIL
WELLS

FARM
MACHINERY

FARM

PETROLEUM
PRODUCTS

PESTICIDES

DAIRY

MILLS
(GRAIN)

AGRICUL-
TURAL
COLLEGES,
EXPER-
IMENTAL
FARMS

LIVESTOCK

REFRIG-
ERATOR
TRUCKS
AND OTHER
TRANS-
PORTATION

FISHERY

PLASTICS
MANU-
FACTURING
(WRAPPINGS,
CONTAINERS)

FERTILIZER
PLANTS

SLAUGHTER-
HOUSES,
MEAT
PACKERS

FOOD
PROCESSING

PRINTING
(LABELS)

CHEMICAL
PLANTS

ELECTRICAL
PLANTS

WHOLESALE
DISTRIBUTION

PAPER
MILLS

FORESTRY

RETAIL
FOOD
STORES

RESTAURANTS

THE "AGRIBUSINESS," or entire food industry of the U.S., is intricately interwoven with many sectors of the economy and encompasses far more than farming. The flow chart gives a visual impression of the interaction of farming and other activities. On the input side of the farm are industries that supply such items as farm machinery and fertilizer; on the output side of the farm is the food-processing industry. Input-output chart on page 122 shows the interaction of farming and industry in greater detail in terms of sums of money.

record levels. The rapid upward movement in income has put farmers in a highly favorable position with regard to capital assets. Although some farmers took advantage of the opportunity to repay their mortgage before it came due, the majority put their higher earnings into acquiring new farm equipment, upgrading their living facilities and enlarging their farms by buying more land. As a result farm real estate values more than doubled between 1970 and 1975.

The supply-control programs were eliminated early in 1974. Hence for the past three years U.S. agriculture has been operating in a free market.

Although the compensatory programs have held farm incomes at acceptable levels, they have had an adverse effect on some groups and conditions off the farm, an effect that has not been lessened even though the programs have been discontinued. The change in the very nature of farming, with its higher productivity and greater degree of mechanization, has severely affected rural communities in agricultural areas. With the decline in the farm population the demand for the goods and services of businesses in country towns has been eroded. Employment and income opportunities in typical rural communities have therefore declined markedly. As people migrated out of the rural communities, there were fewer people left to participate in the services of schools,

medical facilities and other institutions. With the lessened demand such services retreated in quantity and quality and advanced in cost.

Nonfarm groups in the rural communities took large capital losses as country businesses closed down and their operators moved elsewhere, in many cases leaving their dwellings to decay. Although the compensatory programs helped to prevent farms from losing their income, there were no similar programs for other enterprises in rural areas.

Rapid agricultural development in the U.S. in recent decades has also had a heavy impact on the environment. Farms have become larger and more specialized in crops such as wheat, corn and soybeans, depleting the soil of certain specific nutrients and thus requiring larger amounts of fertilizer. As Government supply-control programs curtailed the areas planted to crops in the 1950's and 1960's, farmers cultivated their remaining land more intensively and applied even larger quantities of fertilizers and pesticides. The burden placed on streams and lakes by the runoff of silt and farm chemicals therefore increased.

On the other hand, the development of American agriculture has fostered the growth of an entire agricultural industry—"agribusiness"—of which farming is only a small part. The modern agricultural industry has three ma-

Why Productivity is Important

Geoffrey H. Moore

Vice President—Research
National Bureau of Economic Research
and
Senior Research Fellow
The Hoover Institution, Stanford University

Productivity growth has played a key role in insuring higher real wages and in combating inflation over the last quarter of a century. These facts and others relating to productivity are documented as the relation of hourly compensation, productivity and unit labor costs is sketched, and the relation of the latter to total costs, prices and profits is outlined. Future real economic growth without inflation will depend on high rates of productivity growth.

I N RECENT MONTHS productivity has almost become a household word in view of the wider understanding that (1) long-term growth in productivity is a key to greater real income, and (2) productivity gains enhance the prospect for containing inflation. What are the facts underlying these propositions?

Productivity Trends and Real Income

Over the long run, the growth in real wages in the private sector — that is, hourly compensation adjusted for changes in purchasing power — has been nearly the same as the growth in output per manhour. Both rose at an average rate of nearly three percent per year during the past two decades. As a result, by the fourth quarter of 1972, production per hour in the private sector was nearly double its 1950 level, and real wages per hour also had nearly doubled.

In the latter half of the 1960's, when inflation accelerated and productivity growth slackened, growth in real wages also slowed. Productivity growth fell from three percent a year during 1950–65 to about two percent during 1065–69; meanwhile, increases in real hourly wages fell from a three percent rate to about two-and-one-half percent. Recently, however, there has been a turnaround. Productivity rose sharply in 1971 and 1972 and so did real earnings.

These recent changes reflect one of the most important results of the effort to control inflation and to spur economic expansion — the rise in workers' real earnings. The spiraling inflation of 1965–69 increased the average wage, but most of the increase was eaten up by increases in prices. During 1970 and early 1971 anti-inflation policies began to pay off — the rate of increase in the Consumer Price Index fell below four percent, and productivity and real earnings began to rise. Finally, during the past year the rate of price inflation has fallen still farther, while productivity and real earnings have had their best growth in years.

Clearly, productivity increases become translated into real earnings gains.

Productivity Change and Employment

It is often thought that one of the dangers of productivity increases is that they automatically lead to layoffs. The increase in real earnings per worker would not help much if fewer people were employed. This view is based in part on the belief that with a given increase in output, the larger the increase in productivity the smaller the increase in employment. There is nothing wrong with this

---

An earlier version of this article appeared in the Washington Post, November 19, 1972; reproduced by permission.

---

arithmetic, but happily the economy does not generally work that way.

Studies of various industries, by the Bureau of Labor Statistics and the National Bureau of Economic Research, indicate that there is no general tendency for rapid productivity improvement to reduce employment growth. Many industries, such as air transportation and radio and TV, have experienced high productivity growth, large output increases and expanded employment. One reason is that a rise in productivity can reduce costs and prices, stimulate demand and output, and thereby create more jobs, not fewer. In farming, on the other hand, where productivity growth has been outstanding, employment has declined. The process can work either way, and there seems to be no simple rule.

Productivity, Costs and Prices

Productivity — or output per manhour — affects the price level through its influence on unit labor costs. When wage increases exceed productivity increases, labor costs per unit of output rise.

Over the last quarter-century, that is what has happened. Hourly compensation in the corporate sector increased at an average rate of five percent per year (see Chart 1).[1] Productivity gains averaged three percent. Hence, unit labor costs increased two percent per year. However, there was substantial variation about these averages. In many years the gains in productivity greatly exceeded three percent; in others there was virtually no increase. On the other hand, the rate of increase in compensation was much steadier, year in and year out. As a result, unit labor cost changes have been extremely sensitive to productivity changes. The years in which productivity increased the most are those in which unit labor costs rose the least, or actually fell, and vice versa (compare the two top lines in the chart). During the present expansion, the upsurge in productivity growth has been a major

---

*The corporate sector data are used in Chart 1 and Table 1 instead of the more comprehensive data for the total private or private nonfarm sectors because corporate profits can be distinguished from other nonlabor payments (depreciation, interest, rental income and indirect taxes). As the chart shows, the cyclical behavior of unit profits is altogether different from that of other nonlabor payments. The corporate data, by the same token, also permit one to compute total costs per unit of output and hence to compare the movements of costs and prices.

Table 1

Rates of Change in Productivity, Costs, and Profits During Periods
of Rapid and Slow Inflation, Nonfinancial Corporations

Periods When Implicit Price Deflator Rose Less than 2% Per Year	Average Rate of Change Per Year[1]							
	Implicit Price Deflator	Output Per Manhour	Compensation Per Manhour	Unit Labor Costs	Unit Nonlabor Costs	Total Unit Costs	Unit Profits	Real Compensation Per Manhour[2]
IV 1950 – I 1953	3.7	2.7	7.7	5.0	4.0	4.7	0.5	3.0
IV 1955 – IV 1958	3.1	1.7	5.7	4.1	7.3	4.8	− 4.9	3.3
III 1966 – I 1972	3.1	2.6	6.7	4.1	5.8	4.5	− 5.3	2.3
Average, 3 Periods	3.3	2.3	6.7	4.4	5.7	4.7	− 3.2	2.8
Periods When Implicit Price Deflator Rose Less than 2% Per Year								
III 1949 – III 1950	0.3	4.6	3.6	−0.9	6.3	0.5	0.2	4.7
II 1953 – III 1955	1.0	4.2	4.5	0.5	4.3	1.3	1.5	4.4
I 1959 – II 1966	0.8	3.7	3.8	0.1	1.0	0.3	4.0	2.5
Average, 3 Periods	0.7	4.2	4.0	−0.1	3.9	0.7	1.9	3.9
II 1972 – IV 1972	1.5	5.1	6.2	1.1	0.4	0.9	7.2	2.8

[1] Based on percentage changes over four-quarter spans, dated in the terminal quarter of the span

[2] Compensation per manhour deflated by the consumer price index. The rates of change in the consumer price index, for the periods given above, are: 4.6, 2.4, 4.4, 3.8 (av.); −1.0, 0.2, 1.4, 0.2 (av.); 3.3.

SOURCE: Bureau of Labor Statistics

Chart 1

PRODUCTIVITY AND RELATED MEASURES
NONFINANCIAL CORPORATIONS
PERCENT CHANGE FROM SAME QUARTER A YEAR AGO

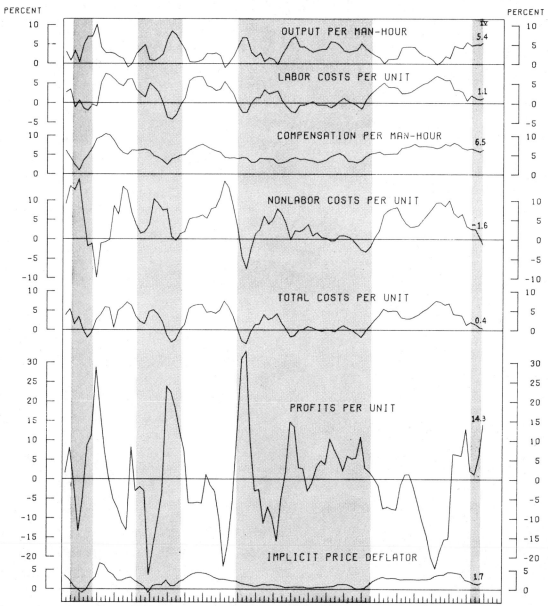

Shaded areas represent periods when the implicit price deflator for the corporate sector rose less than two percent per year.

Source: Bureau of Labor Statistics

force retarding labor cost increases despite the continued rise in wages.

Since labor costs are a major proportion of total costs of production in the corporate sector as a whole, labor cost movements have dominated those of total costs. Price movements have not been as volatile as those of labor and total costs, but the largest increases in prices have usually occurred when costs rose the most, which is also when productivity rose the least.

The greater stability of prices than of costs, and the important influence of productivity change upon cost changes implies that productivity and corporate profits are closely related. For example, the most rapid increases in profits per unit of output occurred in 1950–51, 1955, 1959, the early 1960's, and during 1971–72. These are just the points when productivity gains were the greatest. Virtually every movement in the top line of the chart (output per manhour) is reflected in the profits line.

While the factors that explain these relationships are complicated, productivity has obviously played a critical role in the movements of prices, costs and profits. In the past twenty-five years, there have been only three periods when the price level, as measured for the corporate sector of the economy, rose less than two percent per year (Table 1). In each of these periods (1949–50, 1953–55, 1959–66), productivity rose about four percent. The rest of the time, when prices rose faster, the productivity growth rate was around two-and-one-half percent or less. Wage increases in each of the periods of relative price stability were about equal to productivity growth, i.e., four percent per year, and this virtually stabilized costs of production. Although wages rose faster — six to seven percent per year — in the periods of rapid inflation, this did not help *real* wages, because prices also rose faster. In short, wage and productivity increases of around four percent per year were associated with little inflation in prices and substantial gains in real wages.

The lesson is clear that productivity growth has helped to insure less inflation and higher real wages without adversely affecting overall employment. The record justifies the view that if we are to look forward to an era of real economic growth without inflation, we would be well advised to seek high rates of productivity growth.

The Need for Productivity Growth

Leon Greenberg
Staff Director
National Commission on Productivity

The work and agenda for the National Commission on Productivity are explored. The slowdown in recent years in productivity is examined and implications for the future are drawn therefrom. The potential impact of small changes in productivity for the coming decade is detailed. The great significance of productivity is emphasized, particularly for an era when social and economic requirements are rising.

A DESCRIPTION OF the role and function of a National Commission on Productivity is more meaningful when placed in the proper setting of the reasons underlying its creation. This paper therefore begins with the economic background of the Commission.

The big push for the Commission came from the deep concern over inflation and the deteriorating position of the U.S. in world trade. In the summer of 1970, when President Nixon appointed the Commission members, prices and costs had been rising at high rates. Productivity, which could play an important role in reducing costs and ameliorating the price rise, appeared to be undergoing a serious deceleration in its rate of growth.

A year later the productivity rate had deteriorated some more. In the four year period ending in 1970 output per man hour rose at an annual rate of 1.7 percent compared with a rate of 3.1 percent for the previous 16 years. Of course, we know that the productivity growth rate is closely related to the business cycle and to the rate of increase in output. Part of the reason for the small increase in output per man hour in the last four years is unquestionably tied to the slow rise of Gross National Product. However, that does not appear to be a sufficient explanation. We computed a simple regression of productivity and output changes —using 4 year moving averages—for the period 1950-66. That regression shows that the increase in output per man hour in the past four years was at least 0.5 percentage points lower than what the output rate indicates it should have been.

Was the slowdown pervasive? Indeed it was. The figures show that in every major industry division there was a fall-off in the productivity growth rate in the last four years. Again we must take account of the influence of output changes. When this is done we find that the worst deterioration in the rate of productivity growth occurred in mining, communications, utilities, transportation, and finance, insurance, and real estate. Trade and service also slowed down but to a lesser degree. There were sizable decreases in the rates for construction and manufacturing but they seem highly correlated with cyclical changes and productivity is likely to recover when output in these sectors picks up.

Other statistical aspects of recent cost-price developments are familiar to you. While the deterioration in productivity growth was taking place, hourly compensation went up at a higher than average rate and unit labor costs and prices rose. Meanwhile, Western Europe and Japan were closing the cost gap and our competitive position in international trade worsened.

Cost and Price Stability

So one reason for a National Commission effort to restore the rate of productivity growth to at least its postwar average, is the need for greater stability of unit costs and prices. There are other reasons, however, for seeking that goal. In fact, social and economic requirements indicate that we ought to set our sights on a goal which is higher than 3.1 percent.

Among the economic and social demands are those which might be grouped· under the heading of the physical quality of life—to maintain a clean environment, to restructure our cities, to provide mass transit facilities. It is likely that the costs of these activities will have to be borne by the community at large. These could be paid for out of increased taxes but the tax burden can be avoided by higher productivity—assuming, of course, that higher productivity is accompanied by higher output.

You're probably familiar with how that might work— but let me refresh your memory. A 0.1 percent increase in the rate of growth of output per man-hour translates to about $1 billion of GNP in 1971. By 1980, adding 0.1 percent to a "normal" economic growth rate of 4 percent would produce about $15.0 billion additional GNP—in real terms. For the decade as a whole, a 0.1

Leon Greenberg, "The Need for Productivity Growth." *Business Economics,* January 1972, pp. 24–26.
Reprinted with permission of the author and the publisher.

percent difference in the annual growth rate could provide about $60.0 billion of GNP.

Income aspirations also provide an enormous potential for growth. Median family income in 1970 was about $9,500. If productivity were to rise at a 3 percent rate and previous trend relationships were to continue, we could expect real median family income to reach about $15,000 in 20 years. A family income of $15,000 is certainly beyond the bounds of poverty, but it does not convey a picture of glut or gloss.

The Shift Effect

There is another economic factor whose potential negative effect on productivity needs to be counteracted—that's the shift effect. The increasing importance of the low productivity industries will lower the productivity growth rate by 0.2 of a percent during the decade of the seventies. That's not much, but in the past 20 years inter-industry shifts raised the rate by 0.2 percent. That's a 0.4 percent swing—which translates into a lot of GNP dollars.

It is in the framework of these economic trends and social objectives that the National Commission on Productivity is operating. Perhaps the initial spark for its creation came from the fires of inflation, but the other demands on productivity were recognized in its infancy.

Let me turn now to what the National Commission on Productivity is, what it's been doing and what it might do—as well as what it won't do.

The Commission is composed of top-level representatives of industry, labor, government and the public.

Such a group has no operating authority. It can make recommendations to the President for public and private actions to improve productivity. But it is not likely to produce inventions or new technological breakthroughs which will have an immediate impact. It

cannot open a faucet and get a sudden gush of productivity. It cannot produce an action which will have the quick and dramatic impact of a wage-price freeze.

The Commission can, however, do a great deal to provide momentum for an improved productivity performance in the relatively near future. We cannot overlook the long-run implications of accelerated growth —the current state of ecology warns us about that—but our goals will be concentrated on achievement in the decade of the seventies, not in the year 2000.

The Commission's Agenda

The major efforts of the Productivity Commission are likely to include the following:

1. Improving the conditions under which technology and other productivity advancements can take place. This covers such topics as manpower development, labor-management cooperation, incentives to workers, and incentives for investment.

2. Setting the stage for continued long-term improvements in the growth of productivity. Under this heading the leading factors are education and research and development.

3. Examining the special problem of special industries and making recommendations for improving their performance.

4. Examining the impact of changing attitudes toward work—not only of factory and service workers but also of the white collar worker and, in particular, the recent college graduate.

5. Promoting a wider public understanding and appreciation of the importance of productivity.

During the past year the Commission has considered and deliberated over several topics on which we have prepared issue papers for further discussion. The topics are:

1. Productivity bargaining and manpower adjustments. Productivity bargaining refers to agreements between

PERCENT CHARGE IN OUTPUT AND OUTPUT PER MAN-HOUR

Sector	Output			Productivity		
	50-66	66-70	70-71 [I]	50-66	66-70	70-71 [I]
Total Private	3.5	2.7	2.1	3.1	1.7	4.0
Nonfarm	3.7	2.8	2.0	2.6	1.4	3.6
	50-66	66-70	Difference	50-66	66-70	Difference
Goods						
Farm	1.3	0.6	− .7	5.7	5.4	− .3
Mining	1.8	2.6	.8	3.8	2.6	−1.2
Manufacturing	3.4	2.3	−1.1	2.8	2.3	− .5
Construction	2.0	−1.0	−3.0	1.5	−1.6	−3.1
Services						
Communication	6.8	7.8	1.0	5.7	3.3	−2.4
Utilities	6.4	5.9	− .5	5.8	3.9	−1.9
FIRE	4.7	2.8	−1.9	2.0	−0.8	−2.8
Trade	3.8	3.5	− .3	2.8	1.8	−1.0
Transportation	2.1	3.0	.9	3.1	2.5	− .6
Services	3.9	3.3	− .6	1.5	0.6	− .9

[I] First half to first half.

SOURCE: Based on data from Bureau of Labor Statistics, some of which have not been published. Figures for some sectors, especially Construction, FIRE and Services, are considered to be weak statistically. They are shown primarily to compare recent with past changes.

workers and management where workers agree to relinquish certain work rules or practices which they have considered to be within their rights, and management agrees to certain job or income guarantees in exchange. The manpower adjustment issue deals not just with the cold efficiency of labor market operations but also with job or income adjustments for those relatively few individuals who may be seriously hurt in the process of technological or other productivity changes.

2. Capital requirements for the seventies. This includes analysis of availability of investment funds from internal corporate resources or from external sources.

3. Impact of education and research and development on productivity.

4. Improving productivity in government—Federal, State and local.

In preparing background materials for these issues, we have had excellent cooperation from government agencies—in particular the BLS, Office of Assistant Secretary for Economic Affairs at the Department of Commerce, OMB, and the National Science Foundation. We have also had some work done by researchers at the University of Chicago and the Urban Institute.

Immediate Topics

The program for the rest of this fiscal year has not been made final—and may be affected by the developments in the economic stabilization program. Among the topics being considered are:

1. Impact of government activities on the public sector, including such items as procurement and contracting practices, local building codes, licensing and other regulations.

2. Special industry studies. For this purpose it seems useful to put the industries into 3 groups:

   a. Productivity laggards—Industries with chronically low rates of productivity growth, especially the growing service sector, and additional attention to government at all levels.

   b. Industries with deteriorating productivity performance.

   c. Industries subject to high degree of international competition.

   For all three groups we ought to try to identify the productivity problems and recommend solutions. For the last group it would be interesting to find out what assistance these industries get from their governments in other countries.

3. Incentives and sharing plans.

4. Special problems affecting all industries, such as absenteeism and turnover, and changing attitudes toward work.

This last item for possible study brings me back to the early part of my paper and my reference to the slowdown in productivity. We cannot test whether the reduced rate is due to worker attitudes but we can assume that improved attitudes can lead to improved productivity. There are two aspects to this issue.

First, I think there is a misconception among the public about productivity. The word conjures up pictures of efficiency experts, cracking the whip and, as President Nixon noted in his Labor Day speech, a speed up. We know, as economists, that productivity can be achieved without these evils and that the entire population, including the worker, ultimately derive their economic well-being from higher productivity.

For these reasons we ought to mount an additional campaign to explain what productivity is and what its benefits can be. We must also take care not to deceive anyone. Workers also fear technological unemployment and sometimes that fear is realized—so appropriate programs to alleviate real technological unemployment are an important correlative of the educational campaign.

The second aspect of the attitude issue relates to the growing suspicion that work has become more and more of an anathema to workers. I don't think that is an accurate description of the change that has taken place.

The desires for achievement, recognition, creativity, companionship—all potentially available in a work environment—are still present in most humans. What has changed significantly is the relative affluence of the worker. This affluence allows him the luxury of being more discriminatory about his employment. The youth of the affluent society is often in a position to reject types of employment which displease him. But that same youngster will work very hard at the task he finally chooses for himself.

Despite the general affluence of our society there are still many persons who do not have a wide option of job selectivity. The worker often takes a job which he eventually finds boring or otherwise distasteful. In this case his earnings, while not munificent, are high enough to permit him to be somewhat more selective about the number of days he works.

This phenomenon needs further study. We ought to learn more about the causes of absenteeism and job satisfaction. Meanwhile, there is a strong hint that we ought to give more attention to enriching, humanizing, and otherwise making the place of employment a better place to live as well as work.

PART VIII.
CURRENT
ECONOMIC
ISSUES AND
APPLICATIONS

Energy; urban problems such as housing, crime and transportation; minority problems such as racial, sex and age discrimination; population; the environment; and health care are just a few of the pressing and exceptionally difficult issues confronting society today. And most of these problems can be expected to continue well into the future. In each of these areas the reader should learn to ask: What are the identifiable problems? How did they arise or develop? What economic principles and concepts are useful in developing answers or solutions?

Section A, Energy

In "Overview of the Energy Shortage Situation: How Real Is It and What Are the Options for the 1970's and the Necessary Policy Decisions to Make Them Viable" David White finds that the recent upward trend in energy costs is a reversal of the historical downward trend. In his view, cost factors will prevent synthetic fuels derived from coal and oil shale from becoming major energy sources before the 1990's. The author concludes that the domestic "supply-demand balance by the end of the decade will require both higher energy prices and major policy changes." In "The Invisible Crisis," James Cook presents data showing that the present high vulnerability of the U.S. to an oil embargo is likely to increase over time. In "The Battle for Energy Independence: How Much of a Good Thing?" Timothy Hannan reviews various "weapons" in "Uncle Sam's arsenal" which can be used to combat the energy problem: research and development, voluntary conservation, rationing, the tariff, the quota and oil storage. He then reminds us that all of these are costly and that gains must be weighed against costs.

Section B, Urban Issues

In "The Changing Face of Our Cities," Andrew Hamer traces the development of the typical city during the 19th and 20th centuries, showing how it changed in response to changes in transportation and energy-use technology. Changes in technology also encouraged dispersion, leaving the cities of the Industrial Heartland stagnant, ill-structured and ripe for the urban crises. The author examines the current state of the inner cities of the Industrial Heartland and the forces which, on balance, might leave them looking like "European cities after World War II." "Money Bait" by John Fischer, although dated in some respects, retains much of its freshness after a decade and half and contains an important message regarding industrial development. The prize industries for any community to capture today are those which produce small-size, high-value products. Those areas which seem to capture such industries offer two powerful attractions: "(1) A pleasant environment to live in; (2) Great Universities." The trick is to attract brainpower -- first-rate scientists, technicians and executives -- which is the one indispensable resource for these industries.

Section C, Population and Environment

In "Population and the Environmental Crisis" Carl Madden provides a summary and discussion of some of the general findings of the "doomsday modelers," Forrester and Meadows at MIT (note: these findings were the central subject of an earlier article, Solow's "Is the End of the World at Hand?"). In an article entitled "An Economic Approach to Family Size: A New Perspective on Population Growth" Donald Mullineaux discusses some of the variables which need be considered in predicting future population trends. In "Value Systems in Conflict: Economics Versus Ecology" Hazel Henderson calls for a searching re-examining of existing goals and values, some of which we are deeply committed to, as a necessary condition for the reconciliation of conflicting value systems, e.g., growth vs. ecology. In "Environmental Law and Occupational Health" Norman Wood provides a detailed analysis of laws dealing with occupational safety and health and offers several proposals for improvements.

Section D, Economics of Health Insurance

The article entitled "The Debate Over National Health Insurance" in the Morgan Guaranty Survey describes the Ford Administration's approach to health care in some detail and discusses the Kennedy proposal as well as the high costs which it may involve. In "Health Care Cost: A Distorted Issue" Rashi Fein presents a favorable view of national health insurance and concludes that "national health insurance is within our means." In "Medical Care-- Resource Allocation and Costs" from the Economic Report of the President 1976 the rapid rate of inflation in the medical component of the CPI (much faster than CPI) is attributed to a system which is increasingly paid for by third parties.

Section E, The Future

In "Recovery and Beyond: An SR-Harvard Business School Colloquium" Professors Lodge, Lintner, Markham, Stobaugh, and Goldberg discuss a broad range of economic topics of the present and future.

A. Energy

Overview of the Energy Shortage Situation: How Real is it and What are the Options for the 1970's and the Necessary Policy Decisions to Make them Viable

David C. White
Director, Energy Laboratory
Massachusetts Institute of Technology

The author traces the historical trend of energy consumption and then notes that domestic energy costs have shifted from an historic pattern of decreasing to increasing, in real terms. The domestic energy supply potential and demand responsiveness at various prices is examined and the conclusion drawn that a supply-demand balance by the end of the decade will require both higher energy prices and major policy changes. These policy changes are outlined.

This is an edited version of a paper presented at a NABE Seminar in Pittsburgh on May 7, 1974. See end of text for footnotes.

THE FIRST challenge of the energy shortages of late 1973 and early 1974 was to make short range adjustments in both production and consumption to bring supply and demand into balance with minimum disruption. In large measure the nation did this. There were some lines at gasoline stations, increased prices, voluntary cutbacks in the use of scarce fuels, and some improvements in energy use practices in all sectors. The mixture of shortages and changing prices has in the short term established energy as a central news item as well as a recognized vital commodity to industry and the average citizen. Everyone now knows what the energy professional has known for many years: that energy fuels are a fundamental element of an industrialized economy. Energy today is taking its place along with food as one of the major underpinnings of modern society.

The suddenness and intensiveness of the worldwide disruption that resulted from a modest reduction in energy supply availability has surprised most citizens, their government representatives, and many industrial leaders. From many there are cries of "How could this have happened?", followed by an intensive effort to assign the blame. However, the blame is not going to be easy to assign nor are the causes or corrective measures fully known.

All of us can point our fingers at obvious defects in the U.S. energy system. A few are: natural gas wellhead price regulations, state prorationing of petroleum supplies, tax incentives that are domestic energy supply disincentives, environmental standards poorly understood and administered, lack of definitive federal lands leasing policy, lack of effective energy siting and licensing policy, and economically ineffective regulatory pricing policies. Overall our energy system is a confused mix of free market practices, cost subsidies, price regulations, and finally, price controls. It is little wonder that distress signals in the industry are poorly interpreted; in fact, it is a wonder they can be detected at all.

The mix of separate agencies, regulatory bodies, laws and industry practices are a natural result of an industry that has evolved in stages from the beginning of the industrial revolution. The past 150 years have seen new fuels introduced along with new devices to consume those fuels at an ever-increasing rate. Energy is supplied by many different fuels, with a degree of inter-substitutability between fuels that is high in the long-term although often effectively zero for a given capital stock of energy producing or consuming equipment. An important feature of all fuels is that they are depletable natural resources and their composition and concentration in the natural state varies radically. Our industrialized society has found that the fuels most convenient to use are the products derived from liquid and gaseous petroleum. These products, formed and concentrated in discrete reservoirs over billions of years, have been preprocessed by nature into a form almost ideally suited to an industrialized society. It is important to observe that it is the petroleum fuels which are easiest to transport, process, and consume effectively and they are also easiest to recover from their natural state. These preferred fuels are the least costly to obtain and deliver to the ultimate consumer.

The abundance and low cost of these petroleum fuels has played a major role in establishing the U.S. energy ethic: *low price energy is a fundamental right of U.S. citizens.* It is this belief which has led to regulatory policies in which price is determined by average production costs instead of the marginal costs of the next marketably available unit of substitutable fuel. This one basic confusion of the role of pricing is at the heart of much of the heated and often confused dialogue about excess profits, price gouging, etc., that is taking place today.

In the U.S. economy, a company that makes large profits, and incidentally, therefore, pays large taxes, is a model company to be admired and whose stocks are sought at a premium. In the case of energy companies there are problems of monopoly by virtue of inflexible distribution systems (electricity and natural gas), and possibly monopoly or oligopoly by virtue of industry structure including certain specialized subsidies that may be outmoded or ineffective. However, none of these are inherently different from other industries, and laws are available or can be passed to deal with these issues. Yet in the case of the energy industries the U.S. ethic that energy must be cheap and that no unit of energy should be priced above production and distribution cost plus a *fair return* has the industry locked into a path that is bound to be self-defeating. This philosophy and its senseless application pervades both the production and consumption of energy and is one root cause of our present dilemma. Herein lies a fundamental challenge to economists to develop ways to deal equitably with energy suppliers and consumers for an industry which is in some sectors inherently monopolistic, in others inherently low cost, and in others inherently high cost, yet the combined output of all segments of the industry are increasingly needed and most of the energy products are potentially substitutable at the point of consumption, at least if one allows time for equipment modification. The challenge of how best to develop market practices, regulatory practices and government policies that maximize the productivity of this large, complicated and vital industry needs careful reconsideration by economists and industrialists. There are cost changes and pricing changes which must be evaluated and integrated into new government and industrial practices.

Historical Trends

The consumption of energy in all forms has grown steadily in the U.S. along with the GNP and the population since the beginning of the industrial revolution. In fact, in the last 100 years energy consumption has grown by a factor of 20 (see Fig. 1) of which a factor of 5 has been due to population growth and a factor of 4 due to energy use per capita (see Fig. 2). The increased use of energy per capita has accompanied increased industrialization, and has been further accelerated by the general economic level (affluence) of society as a whole. The average growth rate of energy utilization for a century has been 3%, yet in 1973, even with shortages in the last quarter and major efforts to reduce energy use, the annual growth rate for all energy was 4.8%, while petroleum, our domestic fuel in shortest supply, grew at a rate of 5.2%. This trend is not new, in fact, 1972 was similar with petroleum consumption growing at 8% (see Fig. 3). The decade of the sixties also showed a steadily growing demand for energy fuels, particularly petroleum products in all forms.

One important characteristic of energy con-

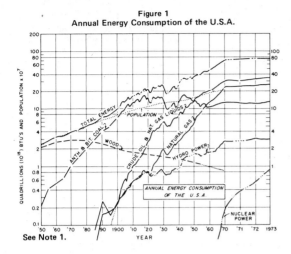

Figure 1
Annual Energy Consumption of the U.S.A.

See Note 1.

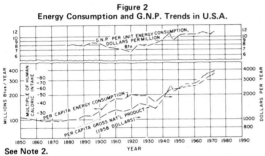

Figure 2
Energy Consumption and G.N.P. Trends in U.S.A.

See Note 2.

introduced into the energy consumption picture that, while currently disrupting, may be a long overdue correction in the economics of energy supply and demand. The U.S. established early in its history a policy of cheap energy for all consuming sectors. The vast domestic resources of energy fuels — solid, liquid and gaseous fossil fuels plus more recently, nuclear fuel — made it possible to supply almost any demand and to do so in decreasing constant dollars. The U.S. national policy of cheap energy started initially because energy was in fact relatively inexpensive to find, process, and deliver to markets until the 1950's. The next unit of available fuel in the marketplace came at a decreasing marginal cost and there was every economic incentive to stimulate energy demand. During the period of decreasing marginal costs regulatory legislation of electricity and natural gas developed since they were monopolistic by virtue of an inflexible distribution system to the consumers. There developed, therefore, a pricing system based on average production costs that was effective for suppliers and acceptable to consumers in a market of de-

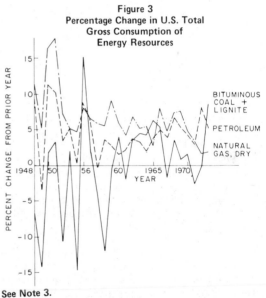

Figure 3
Percentage Change in U.S. Total Gross Consumption of Energy Resources

See Note 3.

sumption is clearly evident in Figure 4 which plots percentage growth in GNP and energy versus time. Increases and decreases in GNP growth are closely followed by energy growth changes. The last six months, where energy has been short and sharply increasing in price, has shown conversely that energy availability is a major factor in GNP growth. Figure 3, which plots percentage change in annual fuel consumption for the three major fossil fuels, shows that major percentage shifts between fuels occur that are separate and distinct from total fuel use. Such factors as environmental constraints, price and availability all influence the intersubstitutibility between fuels. The sharp increase in coal offsetting the drop in petroleum and low growth of natural gas in 1973 is an example of this interfuel shift.

The U.S. energy consumption picture is being copied by all nations and a plot of GNP/capita vs. energy consumption/capita world-wide shows that, regardless of the state of industrialization or economic development, there is a relationship between economic development and energy use that is amazingly consistent (see Fig. 5). One is forced to conclude that if historical trends on energy availability and relative prices (pre-1973) continue, the world-wide demand for energy with growing industrialization will follow the exponential growth trends set by the western industrialized nations.

There is, however, a new element that has been

Figure 4
U.S. Total Gross Consumption of Energy Resources and U.S. Gross National Product: Percentage Change

See Note 4.

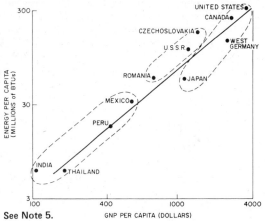

Figure 5
1965 Per Capita GNP and Energy Consumption Worldwide

See Note 5.

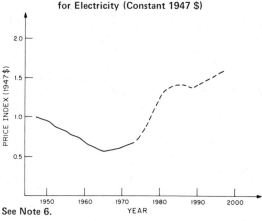

Figure 6
National Aggregated Average Price Index
for Electricity (Constant 1947 $)

See Note 6.

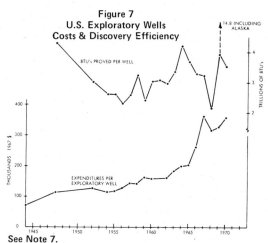

Figure 7
U.S. Exploratory Wells
Costs & Discovery Efficiency

See Note 7.

creasing marginal costs. This practice of average cost pricing in these regulated energy industries exists today, even though the cost picture has changed drastically.

Marginal costs of electric power as reflected in the price index in 1947 dollars in Figure 6 show a shift from decreasing costs to increasing costs since 1965. One major factor in this shift is the capital cost of new plants which shows a factor of 4 increase for both fossil and nuclear plants from plants coming on line in 1972 to those on order for operation in 1982. Rapidly escalating fuel costs and decreased availability of many of the large-scale plants are also important factors in this trend.

Marginal costs of exploration for domestic petroleum have reversed trends and are increasing (see Fig. 7). Almost two decades of this trend has shifted resource development to meet demand to cheaper sources, namely world petroleum resources. The result is that the U.S. shifted from a net exporter of energy fuel to an importer at an ever-increasing rate as the imbalance between domestic marginal costs and prices grew larger. Thus, the stage was set for difficulties when some unusual event should occur. In October 1973 that event took place and now the market readjustment process is occurring. The adjustments are confusing, disruptive, and for many, inequitable since not only has the historical pricing distorted supply practices but consumption practices as well. There is, therefore, a large stock of consuming equipment designed for energy utilization at the wrong price and the time it will take to adjust or replace this equipment is years or decades. The rapid adjustment in pricing that is taking place and which over the long-term must occur when one realistically evaluates new supply costs is creating a short-term economic disruption of major proportions that can only grow worse if it is not dealt with realistically.

Domestic Energy Supply Potential

The domestic resource base of fossil and nuclear fuels is still large compared with even present consumption levels. Resources are always difficult to estimate for at least two reasons. First, until they are actually discovered they must be estimated from geological data alone, and second, once discovered, the amount recoverable depends upon both price and technology. Any discussion of resources tends to be a mixture of true resource uncertainty and confusion as to the underlying assumptions on recovery methods and prices. The recently released A.P.I. reserve data on petroleum has this problem, because it assumes a price substantially below the current market and thus underestimates current reserves. Even though the resource base is large, there are many technological and economic problems to be overcome to deliver these energy resources to the marketplace in a form that is usable by current equipment, and environmentally acceptable to society.

One problem with which the U.S. is faced today is central to policy formulation for the rest of the 1970's is: *What portion of the U.S. energy demand can be met with domestic supply at what prices, utilizing which fuels, requiring what technology, and requiring what lead times to bring into effective utilization?* A supply curve of domestic fuels dealing with these factors is not available nor fully able to be estimated. Neither is the demand curve known nor can it be effectively estimated since the U.S. history of energy utilization has been developed in a framework of decreasing real costs for energy supplies, except for the last six months. Mixed into both the supply and demand picture is the further complication of the last decade of growing environmental impact of energy production and utilization with which government and society generally are struggling to deal effectively. Thus the basic information to make joint predictions of future supply-demand responsiveness is not available and decisions must be reached under conditions of high uncertainty where costs and risk are extremely large for both producers and consumers of energy fuels.

In the face of such obstacles what is the best course of action? As a technologist and systems analyst and not a businessman or economist, there seems to me to be some essential information needed to determine effective action:

- Form the best estimates of supply availability versus price and time for all fuels.
- Form the best estimates of demand responsiveness to price and technology adjustments.
- Identify major uncertainties and critical bottlenecks influencing the supply-demand responses.
- Identify the most effective changes to remove bottlenecks in either production or consumption practices.
- Identify the system configuration most effective to deal with the uncertainty level of the relevant components.
- Identify major detrimental effects that can occur from existing system operation and plan compensating mechanisms.

In the case of the U.S. energy picture, to what do these guidelines lead? The three dominant energy fuels in 1973 are petroleum, 46%; natural gas, 31%; and coal, 18%. The remaining 5% is composed of hydro and nuclear production of electricity. The fossil fuels dominate energy for the 1970's

Conventional Fossil Fuels

The MIT Energy Laboratory[8] has used current econometric models to estimate supply responsiveness of the three major fuels by the end of this decade at prices from $1.25 to $2.00 per million Btu's*. These studies indicate that the above prices for domestic petroleum generate supply responses of from −10% to +30% over 1973 production. For this same price range the domestic natural gas supply increases from 35% to 55% under a pricing policy of phased deregulation of new gas. The coal responsiveness is 15% to 25% over current consumption depending upon sulfur requirements, strip mining practices and transportation rate structures. Thus, the total supply for the price range of $1.25 to $2.00 per million Btu is, by the end of the 1970's, increased 10% to 30% over 1973 production. These substantially higher prices over pre-1973 prices thus do have a supply response but a relatively limited one during the decade of the 1970's.

The demand response to this same range of prices has also been estimated. At the $1.25 per million Btu price the aggregated demand is up 25% while at $2.00 per million Btu the demand is up only 15% over 1973 demand. Thus the demand-supply clearing price for domestic fuels, assuming maximum responsiveness of both supply and demand, seems to be approximately $2.00 per million Btu in 1973 dollars by the end of the decade. This figure is probably low considering both the physical and political constraints to be overcome.

The precision of these estimates are subject to substantial error and can only be considered as general guidelines. They indicate, however, that domestic supply-demand balance by the end of the 1970's can only be obtained at a high price, if at all. In addition to price, it also requires major changes in government policy such as phased decontrol of natural gas, liberal coal mining policies with minimum environmental constraints, and expanded leasing policies on federal lands for all energy fuels. The combination of high prices and policy changes raises the question of what other options are available.

Synthetic Fuels

Natural alternates to the conventional fossil fuels are synthetic fuels — low and high Btu gas from coal and syncrude from coal or oil shale.

Synthetic fuels, particularly gasification and lique-faction of coal, is an old technology developed primarily by Germany in the 1940's but allowed to effectively languish in the last three decades because of the price advantage of natural petroleum products. Currently, major efforts are underway to update and improve this technology so as to make the large quantities of domestic coal and oil shale an effective domestic supply source.

Most of the new technologies are in the pilot or prepilot plant stage. Thus, processes are in a state of flux and capital costs as well as total costs subject to substantial uncertainty. To establish some measure of the state of the synthetic technology the MIT Energy Laboratory evaluated current literature on those processes and developed a set of comparative costs to the extent it was possible to do so. Using a standard plant size of 250×10^9 Btu per day equivalent, the data summarized in Tables 1 and 2 were prepared.

Several interesting items arise from these data. The capital cost of all synthetic fuel plants supplying methane or a syncrude seem to be remarkably similar and range from 350 to 400 million dollars per daily 250×10^9 Btu. The cost of the products also cluster in the range of $1.25 to $1.75 per million Btu. These costs include a 15% charge for capital. The capital requirements for those plants is high since it takes approximately four dollars of investment to generate an annual million Btu's of product whose cost at the plant is estimated to range between $1.25 and $1.75. These costs contain neither profits nor allowance for risk. If for this high risk, capital intensive industry a pre tax return on capital at 25% is required to generate the necessary capital, the price must contain an additional $1.00 to cover the

Table 1

Capital Cost of Synthetic Fuels Plants, 1973 Dollars
(250×10^9 Btu/day of product)

Process	$ millions	Product
SNG Present Lurgi Technology	$400	250×10^6 cf/day
SNG New Technology	$300 to 350	250×10^6 cf/day
SNG Oil Shale	$350	250×10^6 cf/day
Syncrude from coal	$350	40,000 bbl/day
Syncrude from oil shale	$450*	40,000 bbl/day
Methanol	$350	12,500 tons/day

* Includes mine and waste disposal. The plant alone costs perhaps
  $300 million.
  See Note 9.

Table 2

Annual Charges, $ millions, 1973 dollars
(250×10^9 Btu/day of Product)

| | SNG | | Syncrude | | |
	Lurgi	New	Coal	Shale	Methanol
Capital @ 15%/yr	$ 58.5	$ 44	$ 51	$37	$ 51
Operating Costs	22.2	16	22	22	44
Fuel Costs					
Shale				37*	
Coal @ 32¢/MMBtu	48	44	37	37	48
TOTAL	$129	$104	$110	$96	$143
Per 10^6 Btu in product	$1.56	$1.26	$1.33	$1.17	$1.73
$ Per Barrel (oil equivalent)	$9.05	$7.30	$7.70	$6.80	$10.00

* This represents costs of mining, crushing, handling and spent shale disposal; includes write off of mine and solids handling equipment. See Note 10.

capital investment of $4.00. This translates into a price of $2.25 to $2.75 per million Btu at the plant. Thus a reasonable price estimate of a synthetic fuel seems to be between $12.50 and $16.50 per barrel with the higher price being more probable.

Recognizing that there are large uncertainties in these estimated prices, the data strongly indicates that the synthetic fuel industry needs major technological improvements and costs reductions to be an economically acceptable energy supply alternative.

In addition to price there is a further critical problem. A gasification plant for coal that produces 250 million cu. ft. per day (250×10^9 Btu/day) requires an input of 15,000 tons of coal per day or 5 million tons annually. It takes 12 such plants to generate one trillion cu. ft. of methane annually. It takes 72 similar size liquefaction plants (40,000 bbl./day and 10,000 tons coal/day) to yield one billion barrels of syncrude annually. A 1% contribution to the estimated energy demand by the end of the decade is approximately 0.5 billion annual barrels of oil equivalent. Even this modest contribution would require 36 syncrude plants consuming 120 million tons of coal annually. The time required to design and construct a typical syncrude plant once protype experience is obtained is approximately 5 years and requires 1.5 million man hours of technical labor and 10 million man hours of craftsman and manual labor. The major architect-engineering firms of the U.S. face an approximate tripling in size in this decade to meet projects already under contract for electric power plants and conventional fossil fuel facilities.[11] This raises a serious question of the potential expansion capability of this sector to take on the radically new technology of a synthetic fuel industry.

Considering the current state of technology, the long proving time for new technology, the large technical and craftsman manpower inputs to the complex plants for synthetic fuels, and the large numbers of plants required to significantly contribute to domestic demand for energy fuels, one is forced to conclude the synthetic fuels industry as a major energy source is many years into the future − probably well into the 1990's.

The simplest summary of the synthetic fuel technology is that it is truly difficult to produce in man-made plants liquid and gaseous fuels from solid fossil fuels that are equivalent to those that nature produced and concentrated in natural reservoirs over billions of years. The synthetic fuel industry is going to be truly hard pressed to compete with natural petroleum products and cannot do so in the 1970's.

Other Technology

Other energy sources not requiring fossil fuels as the primary energy input are nuclear, solar and geothermal sources. Solar energy can be used for space conditioning in residential and commercial building utilizing current laboratory technology. Because past low prices for energy have made solar heating uneconomical, there has been no industry developed to supply solar heating components. As prices rise these conditions will change. The time, however, to establish a new industry supplying essentially a consumer-dominated market is long and fraught with difficulties. Consumer-dominated products incur large distribution costs and carry a high introduction cost entailing substantial risk. Merely calculating materials of construction and labor costs under ideal conditions vastly underestimates the economic break-even point of a new consumer product. This has often been done in predicting the economic point at which solar power can compete with other fuels. Add to this the variability of solar power, hence the need for energy storage and usually supplementation by other sources and one has a complicated picture for a solar industry development. The time will be years and probably decades.

Solar energy for electricity generation is even more complicated and is always fighting the capital and land costs inherent in a low intensity-diffuse and variable power source. Economic solar power for electricity generation is still in the exploratory research phase.

Geothermal energy from dry and wet steam reservoirs is exploitable with known technology. Geological explorations to locate sources, the handling of corrosive vapors, and the disposal of waste heat because of the low temperatures involved are all problems. Geothermal steam has a utility whenever it exists and is being developed today. Geothermal steam, however, cannot supply more than a very small fraction of energy demand. Deep hot rock geothermal sources are an interesting energy source but no technology exists to utilize them effectively. It is still a research area.

Nuclear fission power is the only non-fossil fuel source currently available that is backed by a fully developed industry structure to manufacture, install, operate and deliver power to consumers. The past twenty years of development and operating experience has brought this industry to a point of maturity where it can be a major energy supply source. There are problems of siting, licensing, safety, construction costs, and social acceptance which must be overcome for this industry to fully develop its potential. To the present heated and often irrational dialogues on both sides, there is little that can be added in a short paragraph other than to draw a parallel between this developed industry now facing many problems including social acceptance and the as yet infant synthetic fuel industry. I find no inherent advantage of synthetic fuel plants over nuclear plants in terms of costs, environmental impacts, desirability to have in densely populated urban areas, etc. To believe the synthetic fuel industry can develop faster, with fewer problems, and be more acceptable is mixing fact with fantasy. Such fantasy is always expensive as past experience has proven many times over.

Energy Productivity

The discussion in previous sections has stressed supply potential and realistic pricing to stimulate supply and also establish demand at a cost effective and sustainable level. Because of the many decades of low prices in energy markets there are many industrial, commercial and consumer practices that are far from optimal for today's and future energy prices. The transition to a period of rising prices is going to be extremely difficult and major social inequities may well develop in the process. One difficulty of price driven changes for the energy system is that it is a system where the time delays for well managed change are long or are extremely expensive where change is forced rapidly. The current disruption in automobile sales is a graphic example of this phenomenon and the responsiveness in this instance of both suppliers and purchasers is still not known.

The list of potential changes in industrial processes, commercial and residential construction, automobile design, goods transport, urban transportation, consumer product design, resource utilization, etc. is almost without end. It is not reasonable to believe that an instantaneous change can occur in all wasteful practices stimulated by a history of very low price energy. Yet it should be a national goal to stimulate such changes as rapidly as possible. The U.S. energy consumption per capita of twice the rest of the industrialized world (see Fig. 8) is probably sustainable only at a major cost to other sectors of the economy. The development of methods to stimulate investment in improved energy productivity is of equal or greater importance to investment in new depletable energy supplies. A Btu saved through increased use efficiency is a recurring saving for the total life of consuming equipment. The internationalization into design procedures of life cycle energy costs and the communication to purchasers of the value of such changes is a major task for forward-looking industry and government. Sensible energy pricing and sound equipment design to save valuable resources is the challenge of the decade.

Reduction in demand to bring supply into balance at acceptable prices is of critical importance. Increased energy productivity, which industry has the knowledge to make happen, is preferred to shortages and rationing. Consumer markets are disaggregated and, in many instances, ineffective in understanding and responding to energy consumption practices even with major price changes. Industry can affect an unresponsive or uninformed consuming public by taking the lead for introducing improved energy-consuming equipment. Government regulations and incentives may well be needed but leadership by progressive industries is critical to any effective program of improved energy productivity.

Conclusion

The previous discussion of alternate supply-

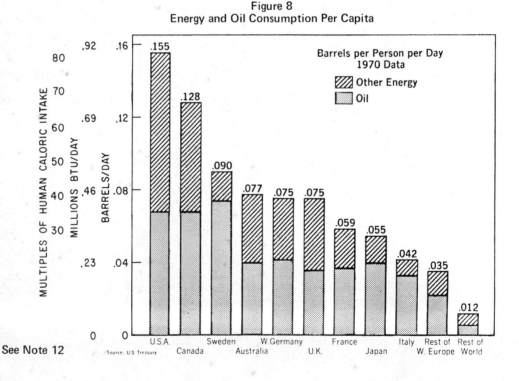

Figure 8
Energy and Oil Consumption Per Capita

See Note 12

demand strategies for the 1970's and beyond shows major uncertainties in all sections, but for domestic supplies the evidence is overwhelming that future prices in real terms must increase. The evidence indicates that the period of low energy costs and decreasing real prices which has prevailed throughout most of our period of industrial growth is past history. The evidence also indicates that the communication of this fact to energy consumers has been delayed by artificial distortion of costs and pricing through regulation and subsidies. It is still the central thrust of most government policy to maintain the historic U.S. pattern of cheap energy. The future strength of the U.S. economy rests squarely on this being the correct policy. Two questions must be answered: can cheap energy be sustained and is cheap energy the proper policy?

In my opinion the answer to both questions is no. Real costs of domestic energy fuels are increasing and at some point these costs must be reflected in price or be supported by ever growing government subsidies. Industrial, commercial and residential energy use practices are determined by price and a distortion of price distorts consumption. Artificially delaying pricing information builds internal stresses which can only result in major disturbances when those stresses are relieved by discontinuous price changes.

The single most important future energy policy is to establish a pricing system that reflects real costs and expected future costs so as to give true signals to all consuming sectors. Energy planning and change takes decades and pricing policies must be sensitive to this inherent delayed response characteristic of all energy sectors. Communicating the shift from decreasing cost to increasing costs to all energy consuming sectors and developing new policies to accomodate this major shift is the single most important task for government and all industry supplying and using energy fuels.

To accomplish this goal, a first question must be — What is the industry structure which can be most responsive to changing price trends coupled with uncertainties? A tightly regulated and centrally controlled economic system is inherently slow to respond to a reversal in the slope of cost changes since it includes both averaging and consensus for adjustments and decisions. High uncertainty coupled with radical changes in cost trends, requires a high degree of local flexibility. In economic systems this can be obtained best in a free market not dominated by single sources — either government or private. A maximum use of free market pricing is a preferred response to radical changes in cost trends complicated by uncertainty.

If a free market is to work, a dominant question for the 1970's is the availability of domestic supply and flexibility of demand under alternative energy policies. The projection by the M.I.T. Energy Laboratory[13] of supply increases and demand decreases with rising prices yield a market clearing price by the end of the 1970's somewhere around or even above $2.00 per million Btu in 1973 dollars. This clearing price, which is above current foreign petroleum landed in the U.S., requires major bottlenecks to be cleared to allow rapid expansion of domestic production of all fuels. Even with the bottlenecks removed both the supply and demand responses require that the high clearing prices be established in a climate where they are considered secure to stimulate maximum investment in new supplies and maximum investment in increased energy productivity to reduce demand. The probabilities that all bottlenecks are removed is low and thus this clearing price is also probably low.

A major question for planning is the potential for exploitation of the large resources of domestic solid fuels — coal and oil shale. The M.I.T. Energy Laboratory study[14] indicates that high prices for synthetic fuels are highly probable although no firm cost or price can be determined. A price of $2.25 to $2.75 per million Btu with the upper range most probable is suggested as likely. This high price does not seem to make synthetic fuels a realistic marginal price setter for fuel in the next decade. Rapid stimulation of production capacity by rushing unproven technology into full operation does not, therefore, seem to be a cost effective policy option. Considering the long lead times for developing new technology, the need for testing technology in full scale plants for approximately a decade to develop valid operational data, and the probable future need for a synthetic fuel technology suggests a synthetic fuels policy of maximum acceleration of technology development without immediate production commitment.

There is some indication that oil shale may be lower in cost and come into production ahead of coal-derived fuels. Even so, major production in the next decade seems doubtful.

The use of coal in direct combustion processes is proven technology that requires basic improvements to reduce environmental impacts. The central research and development issue on coal is modified combustion to minimize SO_2 and NO_x and stack gas clean up to remove SO_2 and particulates. Every incentive to accelerate this technology development is vital.

Coal availability for industrial use depends upon

leasing policy, environmental impacts and transportation costs. All are predominately government dominated issues. The environmental impact can best be handled by internalizing costs and M.I.T. Energy Laboratory data[15] shows such costs to be well below other costs, particularly transportation. The central price setter for coal in industrialized markets is thus transportation where rate regulation plays a dominant role. Rate structures that subsidize other sectors of transportation will be an unfortunate deterrent to a competitive coal industry.

The central question for the supply of domestic petroleum products, which are the major fuels of the next decade or more, is what, if any, bottlenecks must be removed for any improvement to occur. Two major distortions in pricing are natural gas regulation at the well head, and price controls on crude petroleum and its products. Constraints build a multi-tier pricing system and lead to industry practices to maximize profits that inevitably increase shortages, unbalance regional fuel availability, and generate large economic inequities. For example, the eastern seaboard is penalized by low interstate pricing of natural gas because it transfers gas to intra-state markets, decreases supply and creates shortages in interstate markets. This generates the absurd situation of a market for imported LNG at $1.25 and higher per million Btu at eastern ports being used to supplement $0.50 to $0.75 per million Btu gas delivered by pipeline.

Other bottlenecks that must be dealt with relate to the large fraction of future energy resources on federal lands. The availability of these resources for development is vital. Present practice is to use lease sales and this does generate substantial financial returns to the government. The very large funds required for leases coupled with the risk involved in exploration stimulates oligopolic arrangements that are potentially detrimental. Careful consideration of alternatives backed by quantitive data of methods which broaden participation in exploration and allow equivalent or greater return to the government are needed. Royalty participation is one alternative worthy of considerable study, particularly when marginal prices in depleted fields or synthetic fuels will probably become the price setters. Coupled with the leasing of federal lands are the environmental impacts associated with resource development. Environmental protection costs money, but so does environmetal degradation. If industry protects the environment the cost is inherently internalized in the fuel cost. If not, society absorbs the cost as a hidden tax. Internalization of environmental costs in price will aid the market system to help establish sensible consumption practices.

The shift to free market pricing from a period in which the two dominant fuels, petroleum and natural gas, have been held below probable future market clearing prices by either regulation or imported fuels raises major questions about consumer inequties by price changes they could not antici-

pate nor be protected against. The very large cost differences in the spectrum of fuels supplied having the same chemical composition means extremely high rents to some segments of the industry. This raises the question of how to return these rents to produce more supply or capture them through taxation. Any response to the issue is complicated by a set of subsidies — depletion allowance, and domestic and foreign tax credits which are cost reducing subsidies that are equally as disturbing to market prices as government price regulations and controls. The most equitable way to deal with any industry costs and profits seems to be equal treatment under normal corporate tax laws. The removal of subsidies and also price controls coupled with the use of normal corporate taxes to reduce income transfer from the consuming sector to the supplying sector is one way to help maintain social equity.

The large price increases that have occurred and which will probably be sustained raise the issue of major disposable income loss to all of society but disproportionately so to the lower income groups. A program of tax relief or subsidy of energy expenses may be necessary for some income groups during periods of rapid price changes. Given time, the equipment and the practices of the consuming sector can respond to new prices and the need for such subsidies should disappear.

The critical issue to a satisfactory domestic fuels policy is the management of international resources introduced into the U.S. supply system. The last six months has shown that the political domination of economic markets is not only possible, but highly probable. Availability and price of world petroleum resources is a subject of intense debate among experts in the energy area and no consensus exists. The capital and operating costs to deliver a unit of petroleum at the well head is lower in large fields that are not heavily depleted; i.e. most fields outside the continental U.S. International oil before royalties (or taxes) has a substantial cost advantage over domestic oil. Some international oil has a high degree of security and supply from a multitude of independent sources also carries a reasonable level of security. The only rational decision on international oil seems to be an amount that will moderate the high marginal cost of some domestic fuels, but not destroy domestic supply capability. This seems to require a highly flexible import system that is moderated by domestic supply response as well as international factors. The past five years, during which increasing imports were maintained in the face of a rapidly decreasing reserve production ratio, do not portray a well managed import policy. However, a policy of isolationism in energy markets is equally undesirable. Many U.S. goods are needed in world markets and world resource inputs are a vital part of the U.S. economy. Efficient development of all domestic fuel resources is desirable, but these alone cannot meet demand during the 1970's. Imports must play a role in the short term and for this century all evidence points to imports as a significant part of any long term fuels policy. The issue of security then seems to entail protection against short term interruption of six months to several years. One possible policy is stockpiling, of which one form is to maintain excess reserve production capacity. This entails a cost, but so does any policy of security.

The importance of U.S. energy policy to the economy and the all-pervading nature of energy in industrial and social structure of the nation require the full involvement of the political process in establishing an energy policy that effectively represents the many constituencies involved.

In reviewing the factors most important in developing an energy policy for the 1970's and beyond, one major item stands out:

> Domestic energy costs have shifted from a historic pattern of decreasing to increasing in real terms. These changes need to be reflected in future energy supply and consumption practices.

The major policies which have been suggested here to meet this changed condition are:

1. Maximum use of free market pricing and minimization of market domination by government or single industries.

2. Minimizing government controls of fuel prices, in particular natural gas phased deregulation at the well head and removal of petroleum crude oil plus product price controls.

3. Government stimulation of and subsidies for synthetic fuel technology from research through to one of a kind full scale operating plants without artificially subsidizing tull scale industry to force development of unproven and non-economic technology.

4. A broadened program of federal lands availability for resource development that includes other methods of participation in addition to lease sales. Royalty sharing is an interesting alternative for a future market of rising prices.

5. Stimulate development of processes for clean combustion of coal, including incentives and subsidies to develop proven technology for emission control of SO_2, NO_x and particulates.

6. Maximum environmental protection as standard industrial practice with the costs internalized in prices.

7. A flexible policy of fuel imports that looks for multiple sources, and stockpiling to deal with security issues. Careful maintenance of domestic reserve production ratios must be one part of such a policy to assure a healthy domestic industry.

8. Elimination of special subsidies and price controls coupled with the use of normal corporate taxes to deal with large rents that will accrue in a free market for some low cost fuel sources.

9. Tax relief or subsidies for some segments of society who face major inequities during periods of rapidly changing fuel prices.

10. Maximum stimulation of energy productivity in all consuming sectors through use of selective incentives to deal with markets such as the disaggregated housing industry, where the price mechanism may not be effective.

FOOTNOTES

[1] H.C. Hottel and J.B. Howard, *New Energy Technology — Some Facts and Assessments*. Cambridge, Mass.: MIT Press. 1971. p. 5.

[2] *Ibid*. p. 7.

[3] Walter G. Dupree Jr. and James A. West, *U.S. Energy through the Year 2000*, U.S. Dept. of Interior, Washington, D.C.: U.S. Government Printing Office, Dec. 1972. More recent data from DOI News Releases.

[4] *Ibid*. GNP data from U.S. Bureau of Economic Analysis.

[5] Joel Darmstadter, with Perry D. Teitelbaum and Jaroslav G. Polach, *Energy in the World Economy: A Statistical Review of Trends in Output, Trade, and Consumption since 1925*. For Resources for the Future, Inc., Baltimore, Md.: John Hopkins Press. 1971.

[6] Gregory C. Daley, "Nuclear Power Development — An Interfuel Competition Analysis." MIT Masters Thesis, May 1974.

[7] Martin L. Baughman, "Energy: A Unified View," Notes on "Energy System Modeling — Interfuel Competition." Aug. 2, 1973.

[8] MIT Energy Laboratory Policy Study Group, "Energy Self-Sufficiency: An Economic Evaluation." *Technology Review*, May 1974.

[9] *Ibid*.

[10] *Ibid*.

[11] *Ibid*.

[12] Bureau of National Affairs, Inc., "Energy Users Report," 1973, p. 81:4103.

[13] MIT Energy Laboratory Policy Study Group, *op. cit.*

[14] *Ibid*.

[15] *Ibid*.

The Invisible Crisis

That's what they are calling the energy situation, but the fact is that the crisis is visible enough for those who care to face the facts.

By JAMES COOK

IF YOU THINK the energy crisis is past, consider this: In 1976 the U.S. may spend as much as $35 billion on imported oil; by 1980, even if oil prices do not go up, we will probably be spending $45 billion. If oil sells for, say, $15 a barrel in 1980, the import figure will be closer to $60 billion.

As recently as 1971, the U.S. spent only $3.7 billion on foreign oil.

Let's put these figures in perspective: Our total imports this year will be about $112 billion, our total exports $110 billion.

Thanks largely to the boom in agricultural exports, the U.S. has gotten through so far in remarkably good shape. But can we continue to count on food exports to keep us from running a deep balance-of-payments deficit? Most of the experts think not.

And that's just our *financial* vulnerability to the energy situation. Consider the political vulnerability. When our oil imports were under $4 billion, most of the oil came from Canada, Venezuela and other nearby, generally friendly countries. But Canada will soon cease exporting oil, and Venezuela has cut back. By the end of this decade—only 3½ years from now—the U.S. will be buying 25% of all its oil, well over 10% of all its energy, from Arab countries.

What would happen if we could not get this Arab oil in the quantities we need and at a price we can afford? Listen to John H. Lichtblau, head of New York's Petroleum Industry Research Foundation: "You could cut 2.5 million barrels a day from the 7 million barrels a day of gasoline demand by eliminating nonessential driving. You could cut 10% to 15% from our heating oil consumption, another 15% from electric utilities. You could curtail airplane travel. But you'd have massive unemployment, gasoline stations shutting down by the thousands, motels and resorts and everything that goes with it—a recession in the auto and tire industries. You can do these things during a war because there's so much use for labor in the military industries, but you do it in peacetime, and you have nothing to make up for it. You create a disastrous recession."

The 1973-74 embargo, according to Federal Energy Administration estimates, cost the U.S. $10 billion to $20 billion in gross national product and perhaps 500,000 jobs. If a six-month embargo were imposed next year, according to the Congressional Research Service's energy expert, Herman T. Franssen, it could cost the U.S. as much as $56 billion in gross

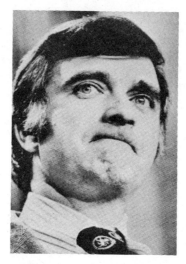

Realist? "We've had three embargo situations in the last 15 or 20 years," says FEA Administrator Frank Zarb, "and there's not much to suggest that there won't be another."

national product and 1.5 million jobs.

The one certainty is that the U.S.' vulnerability to supply interruptions will get worse, not better, for some years to come, and there's not much anybody can do about it: We are paying now for past neglect. U.S. oil and gas reserves are running out, and in the short run there is nothing to replace them but imported oil. U.S. oil production has already declined more than 13% from its 1970 peak and will probably go on dropping until Alaskan production temporarily interrupts the decline. U.S. natural gas production is declining even more rapidly—off 11% since production peaked out two years ago and likely to go on declining for the foreseeable future. With Canada and Venezuela running out of oil themselves, there are only the Eastern Hemisphere producers

and the Arabs to fill the gap. "For the next year or two," says Lichtblau, "our vulnerability to an embargo increases every day."

"It's very easy to figure out where you're going over the next five years," says Eric Zausner, the Merlin of FEA's computer forecasting program, "because there's not too much that can happen that isn't already going on. The next two or three years are easy." Easy, meaning bad.

In looking for additional oil supplies, the U.S. doesn't have much to choose from. Of the 10 million barrels a day of unused production capacity around the world, more than 70% is concentrated in Arab countries, 46% in Kuwait and Saudi Arabia alone. And it's not simply a question of existing capacity. The Arabian peninsula offers the principal source of future capacity as well. Though it accounts for less than a fourth of the world's production, the Arabian peninsula possesses more than a third of the world's petroleum reserves. As one Exxon economist says: "Not many OPEC nations outside the Persian Gulf have much expansion capability. We see the Arabian peninsula as the big flywheel for future demand."

To a large extent, the degree of the U.S.' import dependency is contingent on whether the growth in U.S. energy demand settles back—as most experts expect it to—to under 3% annually, as against the preembargo level of roughly 4%. If energy demand grows *less* than that, the problem recedes; but nobody thinks that likely. And if it grows more rapidly, the problem increases. At the height of the oil embargo, bureaucrats, politicians and citizens alike talked about the need for small cars, for holding highway speeds to 55 miles an hour, for turning thermostats down to 68, and though the emergency faded, energy consumption declined two years in a row, the first such decline since the end of World War II.

Some of the drop in demand was due to a fluke: Five straight years of unexpectedly warm winters averted predicted shortages of natural gas and heating oil. But many energy experts nonetheless began to suggest conservation could go a long way toward keeping the growth in de-

---

James Cook, "The Invisible Crisis." *Forbes*, July 15, 1976, pp. 26–29. Reprinted by permission of *Forbes Magazine* from the July 15, 1976 issue.

mand under control. Industry made impressive savings—one former FEA official predicts it could cut its energy costs another 15% to 25% without any further investment, and Congress gave private conservation a significant long-term boost by decreeing that new cars must average 20 miles to the gallon by 1980, 27.5 mpg by 1985, vs. 17.6 mpg today.

As the U.S. comes out of the recession, however, oil demand is in fact up something like 4.2%—about in line with the 4% most were expecting. What worries a lot of observers is that gasoline demand—which amounts to about 45% of total petroleum demand—has been rising alarmingly. After having lagged for two years, it's gaining by 6%, 7% and even 8%. That's substantially more than anyone had foreseen, and suggests that the American people have returned to their wasteful ways. "The increase in gasoline demand is not related to the economic recovery," observes Clement Malin, assistant administrator for International Energy Affairs at FEA. "So that seems to put us back on the track we were on before 1973." The difference is far from inconsequential. Over a five-year period, a percentage point difference in the rate of growth comes to 1 million barrels a day.

The Wrong Way

How, in a democracy, do you get people to use less oil? The best way, the time-tested way, is the way of the marketplace. You simply let prices rise—or push them up through higher taxes. But the U.S. is not doing this. Instead, it forces its oil producers to sell their domestic oil for much less than the world price. "Old" oil—that is, oil that was brought into production before price controls went into effect in 1973—is price-controlled at $5.20 a barrel; "new" oil at $11.63. This compares with a delivered price for imported oil of $13.27 a barrel.

Since 59% of the U.S.' oil needs still

Doomsday. This sign in FEA's Washington office signals the number of days' supply of oil the U.S. has left to it—3,865 when this picture was taken, and that's just over ten years' supply.

come from domestic wells, this gives U.S. consumers and U.S. industry a short-lived and illusory advantage in the form of cheaper energy. The advantage is *short-lived* because it will diminish as the proportion of imported oil goes up. It is *illusory* because it encourages Americans to continue to use more oil than they should.

The situation is even worse in natural gas, which provides 28% of the U.S.' energy needs (oil provides 46%, coal 19%, nuclear 2%). Regulated gas sold in the interstate market—and that's 60% of U.S. consumption—goes for a maximum of 52 cents per thousand cubic feet, and an average of 30 cents, less than a sixth the price of equivalent oil. Why? Because that's the federal law.

Unavailable Alternatives

In theory, the U.S. could still put itself in a position to meet most of its energy needs from its own resources. For this it would not have to depend on new energy sources like oil shale or tar sands, or even from technological advances like synthetic oil and gas; all of these may be too high-cost ever to be economic. The U.S. could be self-sufficient on its recoverable coal reserves—284 billion tons, enough to last 450 years at current rates of consumption. On top of this, the U.S. has a large uranium reserve for nuclear power production.

So far, however, the U.S. has been unable to channel these coal and uranium resources into reducing its dependence on imported oil. Other energy-related concerns have continued to seem more important—the health and safety of mine workers and citizens, the integrity of the earth, air and water. As a result, it has been impossible for the U.S. to make any

appreciable increase in its coal production. Mining coal poses such a threat to our earth and water resources that the Department of the Interior has temporarily banned the leasing of federal coal lands, and burning it threatens to poison the very air we breathe. All these hazards may be considerably exaggerated, but they help explain why, between 1970 and 1975, coal production rose only 5.5%, to 646 million tons.

In the end, the environmental and safety objections can be met—at a price—but as things now stand, coal labors at a further disadvantage: It cannot compete easily with *underpriced*—by law—fuels like domestic oil and gas. In the first four months of this year, when oil demand was up 3.6%, coal production was up only 2%. At least one coal producer complains that his production has been squeezed out of the utility market by dump sales of natural gas. The FEA hopes coal production will increase to over 1 billion tons by 1985, but the prospects are dim. "We will be lucky," says Ford, Bacon & Davis' energy expert, Gerard C. Gambs, "to be producing 800 million tons by 1985." Every 100-million-ton shortfall means 1 million barrels a day of additional imported oil.

The U.S.' nuclear future seems a bit brighter now that California voters have defeated the dishonest and well-financed effort by the so-called antinukes to put nuclear energy out of business in their state. But horrendous hurdles still exist. Environmentalists have so succeeded in delaying construction of nuclear plants that they now can take as much as twice as long to build in the U.S. as anywhere else in the world. More seriously, uncertainties about the pattern of future demand and the availability of capital to finance new construction have caused the utilities to cancel 70% of the plant capacity originally scheduled for operation in 1985. Even so, if the 175 plants licensed or under construction are built on schedule, the U.S. should be getting 10% of its energy from nuclear power by 1985, *vs.* 2.5% today, an increase of roughly 100 million kilowatts. But for every 10 million kw of capacity that doesn't get built, the U.S. will probably import 280,000 barrels a day of oil.

Federal Energy Administrator Frank Zarb and the FEA continue to have high hopes for the future of domestic oil and gas. Under the proper circumstances, the FEA forecasts 12.9 million barrels a day of production in 1985, *vs.* 8.3 million today, and gas production of 22.3 trillion cubic feet, *vs.* 20.1 trillion today. But this projected gas production depends on the timely deregulation of the price (something Congress has refused to do for two decades), while the projected oil production hinges on the development of various new areas—the Gulf of Alaska, the outer continental shelf—and so far such development has fallen well behind schedule.

There may be as many as 127 billion barrels or as few as 50 billion on the outer continental shelf, as the U.S. Geological Survey suggests, but the range suggests the risk. Last December the Interior Department put 1.3 million acres of offshore oil leases up for auction, and found takers for only a third. Eight outer continental shelf sales are scheduled for this year, but only half are likely to take place. The risks are enormous, and with no certainty that Congress will deregulate oil when the present price-control program expires in 1979, the rewards are not all that spectacular. FEA is equally optimistic over the prospects for secondary and tertiary recovery, but with old oil held at $5.20 a barrel, the incentive is noticeably lacking. Nothing is more illustrative of the stupidity of U.S. energy policy than its effect on secondary recovery. At $5.20 a barrel, it rarely pays.

The only new major domestic source of oil on the horizon at the moment is the Alaskan North Slope —1.2 million barrels a day initially; 2.4 million by 1985, enough to meet a year or two of additional growth in U.S. demand. The law requires Alaskan oil be committed to the U.S. market, though just how much of Alaska's output the U.S. will be able to use itself is very much an open question. Since the pipeline got under way, demand has slackened, and Congress has decided to bring the Naval Petroleum Reserves at Elk Hills, Calif. into production. West Coast refineries do not yet have the ability to refine more than a portion of Alaska's crude production, and if they did—something an enormous cap-

In Jeopardy? Some 3,955 imperfect welds threaten to delay the opening of the Alaskan pipeline by seven to 18 months, depriving the U.S. of 1.2 million barrels of oil a day at a time when supplies are expected to begin tightening.

ital investment could cure—the West Coast market is not large enough to absorb much more than 800,000 barrels a day of its output. There are as yet no pipeline facilities for moving Alaskan oil inland to the Midwest, though there are schemes aplenty, and once the pipeline hits full production, not enough ships to move the excess to East Coast refineries.

Thus the oil companies face the prospect of having to ask the President and Congress for permission to ship at least a portion of the pipeline's output abroad—to Japan most likely. Either that or shut in part of a $7-billion investment. Given the way oil is normally exchanged around the world, the resulting increase in U.S. imports would be balanced by a corresponding increase in U.S. exports —but politicians are obtuse in such matters. And a request to sell Alaskan oil to Japan is likely to create a political brouhaha that could make the furor over breaking up the oil companies seem like a storm in a teacup.

Contrived Complacency

So far, however, Congress has refused to take seriously our growing dependence upon imported fuel or the hazard this dependence could pose to the U.S. economy and the independence of U.S. foreign policy. "The energy crisis ended," coos Secretary of the Treasury William Simon, "and we weathered the storm." As a former head of the FEA, Simon

ought to know better. In emphasizing the *possibility* of energy independence, the FEA has inevitably deemphasized its *improbability* and encouraged Congress and many others in and out of government in their complacency.

"From our standpoint," the FEA's Zarb says, "we can't conceive the nation will allow imports to go to 12 million and 13 million barrels a day by 1985. We don't believe our policymakers will allow that to happen." But given how long things have been permitted to slide, is there anything the policymakers can do?

Zarb knows better than most that the policymakers in Washington do not even want to hear how serious the energy supply situation is, much less do anything about it. They prefer to worry about more politically sexy issues like the dismemberment of the oil companies, the removal of the depletion allowance and the imposition of price controls on new oil.

One of the few constructive moves to date is the Strategic Petroleum Reserve that Congress mandated last December. Under the legislation, the FEA is required to put a 90-day supply of oil in storage—up to a maximum of 1 billion barrels—for use in an emergency. The oil will be stored in salt domes and abandoned mines close to tanker terminals, refineries or pipelines, so that the U.S. will have time to cope with any embargo or other interruption in supply without having to resort to paratroops and without undergoing severe dislocations in the economy.

The program will be costly. A billion barrels could cost upwards of $10 billion, depending upon what price the oil is bought at, but that's still less than the 1973-75 embargo cost the gross national product. At the moment, assuming a 6-million-barrel-a-day import level, the FEA has set 540 million barrels as its initial target. Assuming that no embargo would be more than 50% effective, as most experts think likely, that would give the U.S. six months' protection—more if the U.S. imposed conservation measures, as surely it would do. Moreover, the very existence of such a reserve should discourage the imposition of an embargo. "If they know any embargo would take over half a year to take effect," says John Lichtblau, "they will know that for the first six or eight months they would hurt only themselves."

Once the strategic reserve is in place, the U.S. and the industrial West in general will have an oil weapon of their own for the first time since the Organization of Petroleum Exporting Countries seized control of the oil price five years ago. Just as an embargo against the U.S. forces the U.S.' partners in the international energy-sharing agreement to put pressure on the U.S. to moderate the actions that provoked the embargo, so the strategic reserve could enable the U.S. to take selective action against individual producing countries.

Once the strategic reserve is in place, many of the producing countries—those with large populations, relatively little oil and high absorptive capacity—would be damaged more by the loss of six months' oil revenues than the U.S. would be by the loss of six months' supply of oil. "We could use our oil reserves," one observer comments, "literally to bring another country to its knees."

Unfortunately, such measures, defensive or offensive, are impossible until the strategic reserve is in place, and that's unlikely to happen any time soon. FEA has drawn up an initial budget (yet to be approved by Congress) of $314 million for facilities and site acquisition and another $550 million for the acquisition of the first 50 million barrels of oil. By 1978 the U.S. is required to have 150 million barrels in storage—seven to eight weeks' supply—but not until 1982 is the reserve required to be in place. So much for the urgency with which Congress views the problem.

"If we had a billion barrels in storage, today," Frank Zarb concedes, "it would change a lot of things, including our bargaining position in respect to the producing nations. It would shift the balance in international oil."

Nature's Dirty Trick

But even the strategic reserve would be effective only as a short-term weapon. The long-range problem is one that defies rational solution, because it is a problem posed by nature, by geology, rather than by economics or politics. The problem is that the producing countries with the largest reserves are Saudi Arabia, Iran, Kuwait, Libya and the United Arab Emirates. By a dangerous twist of nature, with the exception of Iran, these happen to be the countries with the smallest populations, and, as a result, the least need for the revenues their oil production generates. Producing at little more than 65% of its present capacity, Saudi Arabia last year raked in something like $26 billion in oil revenues. With a population of under 9 million and a society still at a relatively low level of development, the Saudis succeeded in investing less than $6 billion in their domestic economy. That left them with the difficult task of investing the

remaining $20 billion elsewhere in the world—often in countries where it did not always seem welcome.

Confronted with similar surpluses, Kuwait has already set a 2-million-barrel-a-day limit on its oil production (57% of capacity) and Saudi Arabia itself—in the aftermath of the 1973-74 embargo—set a 8.5-million-barrel-a-day limit on its production, vs. output of 7.1 million barrels a day last year. What this means is that, if Saudi Arabia decided to hold its production at present limits as Kuwait has already announced it will do, the world will have relatively little excess oil-producing capacity to take care of the inevitable growth in demand in the late Seventies. And why *should* the Saudis expand their output? Hard put to invest $20 billion a year in excess oil revenues, it faces the prospect of having to invest $30 billion, even $45 billion if its production expands to its present limits.

It's no secret that a debate has been going on for some time within the Saudi Arabian royal family about the wisdom of maintaining even today's production levels. So far, the conservationists have not prevailed, but the potential remains. "We are in a position to reduce our production to 3 million, 3.5 million barrels a day," Saudi Arabia's oil minister,

Embargo isn't the only threat to the world's oil supply. All of Saudi Arabia's crude converges on Ras Tanura through 1,000 miles of pipeline, affording terrorists ample opportunity for sabotage.

Sheik Ahmed Zaki Yamani, told FORBES a few months ago. But he added, "This is a theoretical question. We are against doing it." Says Abdul Hadi Taher, head of Petromin, Saudi Arabia's government oil company, "We are planning on increasing capacity now, in a kind of goodwill gesture, to assure the world the oil is available when it is needed." Thus is the entire industrial world at the mercy of a mere handful of men—the few thousand descendants of the desert warrior Abdul Aziz ibn Saud—who virtually own Saudi Arabia.

"If we really want them to export that much oil," says Herman T. Franssen, "we've got to find some way for them to invest their money, some outlet to bridge the time until they can utilize that capital. They look to the U.S. for an answer, and it had better be a good one."

"The energy problem," says New York oil consultant Walter J. Levy, "is an invisible crisis. Our balance-of-payments drain is invisible. And if five or ten years from now the flow of oil declines, that again is invisible. But it is there."

"Sometimes," says Frank Zarb, "you get the feeling you're living in that society that used to behead the bearers of bad news. People don't want to hear it anymore. But that doesn't make it any less true or urgent." Zarb has kept his head longer than any of the four administrators who preceded him, but he played an equivocal role—on the one hand encouraging Congress in its delusions of independence and on the other periodically puncturing its complacency with a forthright warning of disaster. "An embargo is certainly possible," he repeats in the tone of one who has said it all too often before, "and entirely likely." But then everyone knows that.

"There has been a failure," says Interior Secretary Thomas Kleppe, "by government, by industry, by the academic community, by the press—by everyone who knows the facts—to communicate to the American people the severity of the energy crisis.... We are threatened with political and economic bondage not unlike that which touched off the American Revolution some two centuries ago."

If the next administration—Democratic or Republican—wishes to lead the American people and not simply drift with the political breezes, the energy situation is a golden opportunity for such leadership. An ordinary politician would shun the problem—too many risks. Clearly, the need is for extraordinary policies—policies aimed at the history books rather than vagaries of political poles. ∎

The Battle for Energy Independence: How Much of a Good Thing?*

By Timothy H. Hannan

Abundant low-cost energy has been fundamental to the American way of life for a long time. It's hard indeed to imagine Americans without their climate-controlled houses, aluminum cans, and large gasoline-burning automobiles. Yet, as anyone who cooled his heels in a gasoline line last year can testify, a stable source of abundant low-cost energy can no longer be taken for granted. Domestic demand for energy has increased rapidly in recent years; domestic supply has not. To help fill this widening gap, Uncle Sam has relied increasingly on imports from the Middle East, where a volatile mixture of oil and politics has already resulted in one serious embargo and poses an ever-present threat of future embargoes.

As the recent gasoline lines and closed factories so dramatically demonstrated, a sudden curtailment of foreign oil can cause considerable economic disruption in a nation grown accustomed to relative energy abundance. To reduce the threat of similar economic disruptions in the future, the nation has embarked on a policy of energy self-sufficiency. Government funds are being allocated to stimulate research and development of alternative sources of energy, voluntary conservation efforts are being promoted, and—just to help voluntary conservation along—tariffs are being imposed on imported oil.

All of this brings up the question of the desirability of these efforts and the degree to which they should be pursued to bring about energy self-sufficiency. As economists never tire of proclaiming, resources are not limitless. The economy cannot at the same time satisfy all desires for more goods and services, higher quality environment, and greater reliance on domestic production of energy. In the area of energy policy, this means that hard choices must be made not only among the various methods of reducing

---

*This article deals primarily with the economic issues involved in seeking energy independence. Political or diplomatic considerations also may be important in determining the degree of energy self-sufficiency appropriate for the United States.

Timothy Hannan, "The Battle for Energy Independence: How Much of a Good Thing?" *Business Review*, Federal Reserve Bank of Philadelphia, July–August 1975, pp. 3–10. Reprinted with permission.

energy dependence but also among the various levels to which energy dependence should ideally be reduced. Because resources are scarce, complete energy self-sufficiency in the near future may come at a very high price indeed.

ENERGY DEPENDENCE: HOW CAN IT BE REDUCED?

Uncle Sam's arsenal contains many weapons to combat the energy problem. Most are designed to cut U. S. consumption of energy, boost domestic production of energy, or perhaps achieve some combination of the two. But as the current debate over energy policy serves to emphasize, the various methods of reducing energy dependence are not identical, and much controversy remains concerning the appropriate path to follow. Consider a few of the more important alternatives available.

Research and Development. Government-funded research designed to accelerate development of alternative sources of energy can play an important role in enhancing the nation's domestic production of energy, particularly in the long run.[1] The future availability of low-cost energy from nuclear, solar, and geothermal sources, or from synthetic fuels and oil shale deposits, may require substantial investments in research and development. Although the return to such investments may prove quite significant, so too may be the time required for these investments to pay off in the form of abundant low-cost energy. Thus, research and development of new technologies is generally viewed as having only long-run significance.

Voluntary Conservation. In addition to efforts designed to increase domestic energy production, a reduction in dependence on foreign sources of energy can also be achieved by policies designed to reduce domestic demand. Voluntary conservation is a currently practiced example of such a policy, and it has met with at least limited success. However, often self-interest and the goals of voluntary conservation don't jibe. An individual who believes his neighbors will adequately conserve energy may find it in his self-interest not to do so. Because of this "free-rider problem," as economists often call it, conservation on a voluntary basis is generally recognized as having significant limitations. For this reason, policymakers have increasingly called for mandatory, and perhaps less palatable, means of reducing energy dependence.

Rationing. Mandatory conservation through rationing is one such policy and has in fact been proposed by a number of national leaders. The problems involved in developing an equitable rationing system, however, are simply enormous. Decisions would have to be made on how to allocate gasoline, fuel oils, jet fuel, diesel fuel, and many other refinery products to the thousands of categories of consumers—a function which, according to Treasury Secretary William E. Simon, would require 15,000 to 20,000 full-time employees, incur $2 billion in Federal costs, and require 3000 state and local boards to handle the exceptions.[2] Perhaps more important, rationing does not provide the needed incentives for suppliers

---

[1] Although the private sector must be counted on to undertake most of the energy research and development, Government-funded research may prove to be quite important. Development of new energy technologies often involves expanding basic knowledge of fundamental processes. In such cases, research and development may provide a large gain to the economy as a whole, but there may be little opportunity for any one firm to derive a large enough part of this gain to warrant undertaking the research. Hence, Government participation in such efforts is needed.

[2] Statement of the Hon. William E. Simon, Secretary of the Treasury, before the Ways and Means Committee of the U.S. House of Representatives, January 22, 1974, *Department of Treasury News*, pp. 9–10.

of domestic energy to increase domestic production. Without new energy production, rationing would continue to be needed many years into the future.

The Tariff. Imposing a tariff on imported oil is another tool available to policymakers. A tariff is simply a tax placed on each unit or the value of each unit of an imported good, and its imposition on oil is designed to increase the price paid for imported oil. Of major significance is the tariff's effect on the price of domestic oil. With the imposition of a tariff, domestic oil becomes relatively more attractive to consumers of energy. As long as the price of foreign oil exceeds that of domestic oil, users will try to buy from domestic producers. When this happens (and as long as at least some domestic oil is not subject to Government price controls), the average price of domestic oil will be bid up to a higher level.[3]

Because of the dual role of prices in discouraging consumption and promoting production, this whole process results in less dependence on foreign energy sources. First, the rise in the price of oil, both foreign and domestic, will cause domestic purchasers of energy to review their expenditures and cut down on the more easily avoided uses of energy. In the industrial sector, for example, firms that did not consider energy conservation measures worthwhile when energy prices were low will now find it profitable to eliminate heat leaks, switch to less energy-intensive technologies, or improve waste-heat recovery systems. Consumers who once drove large automobiles 30 miles to work and failed to insulate their homes will now find public transportation, small cars,

and six-inch insulation remarkably "good buys."

Second, unlike a policy of voluntary conservation or mandatory conservation through rationing, the impact of the tariff in reducing energy dependence is not limited to that of simply discouraging consumption. This is because a price rise brought on by the tariff will also increase the incentives of domestic producers to bring more energy to the market. Economic rewards are important. Faced with a rise in the price of energy, producers of coal, oil, and other sources of energy can be expected to search for and develop additional sources. Energy deposits identified by geologists but previously too costly to work—such as the vast oil shale deposits in Colorado and Wyoming—may now be tapped simply because higher prices make doing so profitable. And efforts to develop new technologies in the production of energy may be stimulated for the same reason.

Thus, by raising the prices we must pay for energy, a tariff on imported oil both reduces domestic consumption of energy and increases domestic production—making the nation less dependent on foreign sources of energy.

The Quota. Unlike the tariff, the quota restricts imports in terms of quantities, rather than in terms of a tax on each unit or on the value of each unit. Its impact, however, is quite similar. Like the tariff, the quota (by directly reducing the supply of imported oil, rather than by directly increasing its price) causes an increase in demand for domestic energy. Since a significant portion of domestic energy production is not subject to price controls, this means that the average price of domestic energy will rise, performing the dual function of discouraging domestic consumption and encouraging long-run domestic production. Thus, the quota, like the tariff, provides policymakers with a double-barreled weapon that can be used to make the nation more self-sufficient in energy.

---

[3]Government price controls are currently in effect on only a portion of domestically produced crude oil. In applying price controls, a distinction has been made between "old oil" and "new oil." New oil is defined as all oil produced on a property in excess of output in the same month of 1972. New oil and oil from wells producing less than ten barrels per day are not subject to price controls. Domestic "old oil," however, is currently held at a price of $5.25 per barrel.

The tariff and the quota can differ in terms of the revenue that they generate for the Government or in terms of the predictability of their economic impact (see Box 1). In general, however, the similarities are more strik-

tariff arrangements are designed to reduce imports by either reducing domestic consumption of energy, increasing domestic production, or achieving some combination of the two. But as some economists have

BOX 1

TARIFFS AND QUOTAS: THE SIMILARITIES AND THE DIFFERENCES

The economic impact of tariffs and quotas can be quite similar. In fact, for any given tariff, there is a theoretically equivalent quota. If supply and demand responses to price changes are known with certainty, it is possible to predict the level of imports that will result under a certain tariff and simply impose that quota to achieve the same result.

There are, however, some potential differences between the two means of restricting imports. One potential difference is the revenue that they generate for Uncle Sam's coffers. Since a tariff is a tax, it provides revenue for the Treasury as long as it doesn't discourage all imports. But a quota is not a tax. It simply sets the level of imports allowed into the country and therefore does not generally provide revenue to the Government. Both means of restricting oil imports cause the domestic price to rise above the world price, but the difference goes to the Government in the case of the tariff and usually to the oil importers in the case of the quota. However, even this distinction can be eliminated if, under a quota, the Government chooses to auction off import licenses. By pursuing such a scheme, the Government could obtain roughly the same funds from selling import licenses under a quota as could be collected under a tariff. With the right conditions, both approaches can generate the same revenue.

A potentially more important difference between a tariff and a quota stems from the fact that it is often not possible to predict future changes in supply and demand conditions. Under these circumstances, tariffs and quotas thought to be the same can have divergent results. For example, if world oil prices decline unexpectedly, a tariff will result in an unexpected increase in the percentage of the domestic market supplied by foreign oil, while a quota will not. Also, the failure of domestic supply to expand as expected will lead under a tariff to an increase in imports, but under a quota it will cause an unanticipated increase in the price of domestic oil. Because of uncertainty, the tariff and quota can lead to unexpected and different results.

ing than the differences. Both provide an incentive for domestic production, both discourage domestic consumption, and, to bring about these results, both require that we pay higher prices for energy.

Oil Storage. Policies such as Government-funded research and development, voluntary conservation, rationing, and quota or

been pointing out, there are also ways to soften those periodic blows from the Middle East without significantly reducing overall imports of oil, and a policy of oil storage is perhaps the most frequently mentioned example.

Storage performs the function of being an alternate source of supply when the going gets rough. By stockpiling oil bought from foreign sources or by storing domestic oil in the ground in the form of reserve capacity, sudden shortages of imported oil can be partially or totally filled by dipping into a stockpile accumulated for just such a rainy day. Oil storage, then, is another of the many potentially useful steps that can be taken to ensure a steady supply of energy.

REDUCING ENERGY DEPENDENCE: THE GAINS AND THE COSTS

Clearly, there is a potential gain to all such efforts designed to reduce the nation's vulnerability to oil embargoes.[4] When the spigots are turned off temporarily in the Middle East the resulting economic disruptions can cause considerable hardships. This is because domestic supply patterns and domestic consumption patterns cannot be changed readily at a moment's notice. It takes time to expand domestic energy production and introduce expensive production technologies which are not required when Middle East oil is flowing freely. And on the consumption side, it takes time to change over to more energy-efficient applicances, smaller automobiles, better-insulated buildings, and less energy-intensive technologies in commerce and industry. Because of this short-run inability to adjust to less energy, sudden embargoes can mean production bottlenecks, factory layoffs, cold homes, and other hardships. Therefore, the advantage of policies designed to avoid or reduce their impact can be large. This can be true even of policies such as a tariff or a quota, which are designed to replace temporary curtailments in imported oil with a permanent one. Because periodic sharp reductions in imported

oil can be so severe in the short run, there may be a positive gain from policies designed to discourage imports gradually in the long run. These long-run policies can cause the economy to make adjustments without the major disruptions associated with sudden embargoes.

By cutting consumption, increasing production, or stockpiling reserves, the country can help protect itself from future embargoes. Of particular importance, the nation's foreign and domestic policies do not have to be unduly influenced by foreign producers of oil.

But while there's something to be gained from such policies, there are also significant costs. Because resources are indeed scarce, reducing the nation's vulnerability to foreign oil embargoes requires sacrifice. If it is to be achieved through increased domestic production, large expenditures may be required for further exploration and for research and development of alternate sources of energy. If it is to be achieved by reducing domestic consumption, money will have to be spent on better insulation, more efficient engines, and improved heat-recovery systems. Moreover, we will have to get along on less energy consumption even when embargoes are not underway. Tariffs and quotas also impose these kinds of costs since they are simply tools designed to increase production and decrease consumption. And because they do so by raising the price of energy, they also bring about higher gas prices, higher heating fuel costs, and higher prices of goods whose production requires large amounts of energy. Even an oil storage policy, which is not designed specifically to reduce consumption or increase production, may require considerable sacrifice in the form of large expenditures on oil storage facilities.

THE QUESTION OF POLICY

As is the case with so many economic problems, hard choices must be made among competing ends. To protect the nation from

---

[4]In addifion to avoiding or reducing the impact of embargoes, policies designed to make the nation more self-sufficient in energy can also help the balance of payments problem. However, since fluctuating exchange rates tend to correct imbalances in the balance of payments, this advantage may not be a very significant one.

future oil embargoes, substantial sums may have to be expended and hardships may have to be endured. This means that the benefits of reducing the country's vulnerability to foreign oil embargoes must be weighed against the costs of bringing about such a result.

In such circumstances, economists often apply a simple rule: increase the activity so long as the additional gain that results exceeds the additional cost. In the present case, this means that it is worthwhile to increase activities such as research and development efforts, oil storage programs, tariffs or quotas, and conservation programs only to the point where the additional gain associated with insulation from embargoes equals the increased costs of such efforts. Beyond such a point, devoting more resources to the effort simply will not pay.

Where this point lies is always difficult to determine without further information.[5] This framework, however, does establish the probability that a number of policies designed to reduce our vulnerability to foreign embargoes—tariffs, research and development, and oil storage, for example—may indeed be justified *up to a point*. But perhaps more important, it can prove useful in analyzing the desirability of a much publicized goal—that of achieving complete energy self-sufficiency.

COMPLETE ENERGY SELF-SUFFICIENCY?

To reduce the nation's dependence on unstable sources of foreign energy is one thing; to eliminate it is another. This difference in degree can be extremely important. It is no doubt possible to achieve total energy self-

---

[5]On the one hand, if the probability of a recurrence of last year's embargo is low, as many believe, then the fruits of even the smallest efforts to reduce the nation's vulnerability to foreign oil embargoes may not be worth the cost. On the other hand, if the probability of recurring embargoes is high, then substantial efforts may be justified.

sufficiency even in the near future if we are willing to pay the price for it. Imports of foreign energy can be prohibited by quota, extreme conservation measures can be imposed, or tariffs can be set high enough to discourage all imports of oil, causing the price of energy to rise until the domestic supply of energy satisfies domestic demand. (See Box 2.) All of this can be done, but is a policy of energy self-sufficiency, carried *to this extreme*, worth the costs? There are a number of reasons to suggest that striving for total self-sufficiency, at least in the near future, may not be worth the sacrifice.

Those Last Steps toward Self-Sufficiency. One reason is that as the U. S. approaches energy self-sufficiency, the cost of taking such additional steps may increase, while the advantage of making an already relatively self-sufficient nation still more sufficient may not be great. The additional costs are particularly important. The nation moves toward energy self-sufficiency by expanding domestic production and reducing domestic demand, but the further that either of these activities are pursued, the greater will be the sacrifice required. Expanding domestic supply in the near future will require that we turn to increasingly costly methods of energy production, and reducing domestic consumption will require that increasingly high-valued uses of energy be abandoned. The sacrifice required to change the thermostat from 75 to 65 degrees may not be great, but that required by an additional 10-degree twist of the dial may be substantial. It is for these reasons that total energy self-sufficiency, at least in the near future, may be too much of a good thing. Put simply, the gain from making those last steps toward energy self-sufficiency may not be worth the higher costs required to complete the trip. It may be better to settle for something less.

Risk-Free Sources of Foreign Energy. Not all of the oil currently being imported into this country comes from the politically volatile

BOX 2

THE "PRICE" OF ENERGY SELF-SUFFICIENCY

A rough idea of the energy prices required to achieve energy self-sufficiency by 1980 can be obtained from a number of supply and demand estimates presented below.

ENERGY EQUILIBRIUM IN 1980

Fuel	Millions of Barrels of Oil per Day Equivalent, at Prices Per Barrel*		
	$7	$9	$11
Domestic Supply			
Crude oil and natural gas liquids	10.6	10.7	10.9
(including Alaskan)	(2.0)	(2.0)	(2.0)
Natural gas	14.7	14.5	14.4
Coal	6.1	8.0	8.0
Uranium and hydroelectric	5.2	5.2	5.2
New technology	0.0	0.0	0.1
Total Supply	36.6	38.4	38.6
Domestic Demand	44.2	42.4	40.6
Net imports	7.6	4.0	2.0

SOURCE: *Energy Self-Sufficiency, An Economic Evaluation* (Washington: American Enterprise Institute for Public Policy Research, 1974), p. 8.

*A fuel is made "oil equivalent" by finding the number of barrels of oil which has the same heating value as a given quantity of that fuel.

These estimates, which were derived from a number of statistical studies, indicate the supply of different fuels and the total domestic demand for energy that can be expected at the prices of $7, $9, and $11 per barrel (in constant 1973 dollars). As economic theory would suggest, higher prices mean more energy will be produced domestically and less of it will be consumed.

But here is where part of the problem of energy self-sufficiency emerges. As should be noted from the Table, the expected supply of various types of energy in 1980 is relatively unresponsive to price increases. In addition, the reduction in domestic demand for energy that can be expected to result from a price increase is estimated to be quite small. This means that in order to reach the point at which domestic supply equals domestic demand, which is required if no energy is to be imported, we may have to pay prices significantly higher than $11 per barrel (in constant 1973 dollars). As can be seen, this is significantly higher than the price of energy that would be required if we relied on some imports.

Middle East. Much comes from countries that are less likely to institute embargoes. A sufficiently restrictive policy can eliminate imports from relatively secure sources just as well as it can eliminate those from insecure sources. But why bear the cost if little is to come out of it? The primary gain from reducing imports is the reduction in periodic disruptions resulting from embargoes, but if a source of supply is relatively secure, there is little reason to incur the higher costs required to eliminate such imports. This means that policies should be less restrictive toward secure sources of foreign energy than those required by insecure sources—yet another reason to question the advisability of total energy self-sufficiency.

Oil Storage. If the goal of complete energy self-sufficiency means eliminating all oil imports, then the advantage of oil storage policies is another reason why the goal may not be desirable. If the cost of storing oil and using it during embargoes is not excessive, it may well pay to store at least some oil to smooth out the disruptions when they occur.[6]

But if a policy of oil storage is undertaken, what does this mean for the goal of self-sufficiency? Simply stated, it reduces the need to eliminate all imports. A substantial part of the gain from reducing imports is the resulting reduction in the economic impact of embargoes. But if a storage policy is instituted, embargoes become less serious, thus reducing the gain to be obtained by eliminating all oil imports. This does not necessarily mean that all efforts to increase energy self-sufficiency should be abandoned in the presence of a storage policy. Some movement toward self-sufficiency may still be justified. However, it does provide yet another reason to question the goal of independence from all sources of foreign energy.

CONCLUSION

Uncle Sam's arsenal contains many weapons that can be used to reduce the nation's vulnerability to periodic oil embargoes. Some, such as voluntary conservation programs and mandatory conservation through rationing, are designed to reduce domestic consumption. Others, such as efforts to develop alternative sources of energy, are designed to increase domestic production. Still others, such as oil storage policies, are designed to soften the blow of periodic embargoes without significantly reducing overall imports. Because all are costly, however, a proper balance must be struck between the gains and costs resulting from their use. Reducing the nation's vulnerability to a sudden oil embargo is important, but so too are the substantial sacrifices required to do it. Since periodic oil embargoes can cause serious economic disruptions, it may well pay to reduce our dependence on foreign sources of energy, at least to a degree. But running the full distance to achieve total self-sufficiency in the next few years may simply not be worth the cost required. 🖝

---

[6]Storage can take the form of either increasing domestic reserve capacity or stockpiling oil purchased abroad. The question of whether reserve capacity or storage from foreign sources is better is a simple cost calculation. If the landed price of foreign oil plus storage is less than the incremental cost of developing domestic capacity, then storage of foreign oil is preferable, and vice versa.

B. Urban and Minority Issues

Andrew M. Hamer*
Georgia State University

The Changing Face of Our Cities

The threat of bankruptcy plagues the mayors of some of our most important cities. Urban centers that exude vigor in their glass-and-steel skylines are also known for blocks of abandoned industrial and residential buildings. Crime and the fear of crime leave city streets empty from dusk to dawn. Outside our urban cores, the surrounding suburbs stand as symbols of the unequal distribution of wealth, income and education achievement that comes from hemming in the disadvantaged within the boundaries of the central cities. And, everywhere, there is the pervasive sight of congested streets and roads given over to automobility gone wild. Somehow the promise of our cities one hundred years ago has been tarnished, leading some analysts to conclude that those centers will soon die because they have become obsolete.

The present crisis, and its ultimate outcome, can only be understood in historical perspective. We must explore why cities developed in the first place, why they became tightly clustered, what forces led to the dispersed urban areas of today, and why the problem seems particularly acute only in some parts of the country. To preview, the answer lies less in some awful conspiracy and more in an understanding of modern economic growth. Rising incomes and technological changes have eroded the economic importance of particular regions of the United States and of the historic centers of our individual urban areas. In a sense, individuals and businesses have managed to expand the number of locations where consumer satisfaction and economic profitability can be maximized. The original advantage of the early sites of American economic development has been dissipated to a large degree. Public policy has merely compounded the problems, often through inaction or a failure to fully understand the consequences of otherwise meritorious actions.

Andrew Hamer, "The Changing Face of Our Cities." Prepared for this volume by Andrew Hamer, Associate Professor of Economics, Georgia State University.

The Nineteenth Century City

Prior to the last one hundred years cities of substantial size arose at strategic breaks in the national transportation network, where goods were collected from various points and distributed to various other points. These transshipment centers included river and sea ports and railroad terminals. Those centers which were situated in such a way as to service a large market area could increase their competitive advantage by providing a series of freight-related services such as insurance, credit, and intelligence. The cost of these services depended on the number of competing, specialist firms in any one line of activity that could be sustained by the volume of traffic. Cities were, therefore, places where the general level of economic activity spawned special cost-cutting services that benefited all those who shipped products to and from points within a region. These so-called economies of agglomeration were the foundation of concentrated or urban living.

In time, all forms of economic activity came to depend on these agglomeration economies. Prior to the Civil War most production was dependent on the location of randomly scattered natural resources, such as good farm land, mines, and the power provided by water falls and rapids. The typical products of the era were, therefore, resource oriented. Changing consumer tastes, backed by rising purchasing power, combined with new technology to create new products which were more dependent upon the assemblage of component parts from various industries by a labor force of varying skills working in factories powered by steam. The necessity of being close to a natural resource declined, on the average, as these new products began to dominate the output of the nation. Now it was important for the typical producer to rely on easy access to other producers, to solicit the services of specialized rental and repair firms, and to expand the reliance on the financial, legal and marketing institutions required to sell to a growing national mass market. Once again, the lowest costs were to be obtained by firms that gravitated toward centers whose activity level was high enough to generate large numbers of competing specialized firms in banking, advertising, etc. Economies of agglomeration became important for an even larger number of American businesses. These same agglomeration effects were at work in generating the supply of labor of varying skills needed to do business. Large urban centers attracted migrants in search of employment opportunities and of a greater variety of consumer-oriented services (which were themselves created by urban agglomerations). These migrants lowered the costs of all urban firms by creating a pool of competing labor of varying skills that could not be assembled easily in rural settings.

If the logic of nineteenth century economic development dictated that growth take place increasingly in these urban centers, then why did urban areas all follow a similar spatial configuration? In particular, why were urban areas so compact? The Compact City grew out of the primitive level of the technology of moving people and goods within urban settings. The Compact City was dependent on horse-drawn wagons to move freight to and from businesses and the terminals or ports. The steam-powered railroad was not suited for the stop-go pattern of urban pick-up and delivery; the enormous economic advantages of the railroad, evident on regional and transcontinental runs, were therefore neutralized. Businesses relying on freight were forced to cluster around ports or terminals. Paper-passing activities required messenger boys working on foot until the period (after 1900) when the telephone became into widespread use. Even then, confidential discussions or complex issues required face-to-face meetings among executives of firms producing goods and supplying services such as banking, insurance, advertising, and legal advice.

Until the latter part of the 1890s the labor force was forced to cluster near the sources of employment in what were, in fact, walking cities. It was in the residential sector, however, that the first breaks in the Compact City began to appear. The introduction of the electric streetcar gave those families in the upper half of the income distribution an opportunity to satisfy a taste for more housing space in lower density settings. Those rural areas surrounding the Compact City which were supplied with electric street car lines yielded low-cost land, easy access to downtown work locations, and a relatively high level of environmental amenities. Increasing numbers of households evaluated the trade-off between commuting costs and spacious living and chose to move outward. In other words, as the tyranny of narrow locational constraints was broken, the Compact City began to suffer.

The Twentieth.Century Unshackled Metropolis

The electric streetcar was, in some respects, a conservative force. For, though it encouraged suburbanization, it tended to restrict it to the narrow corridors along which the costly street car lines were built. Lateral movement, between one line and another, was difficult outside of the downtown; the areas between the street car lines remained largely untouched. What emerged, then, was a star-shaped pattern of development focused on the central employment center. Many writers on urban problems today view this pattern of development with nostalgia, because it has become identified as the embodiment of good planning and civic virtue. In fact, of course, it was but a very temporary way-station to the patterns we know today.

By 1920 several forces indicated clearly that employment suburbanization was inevitable. The pick-up truck emerged as a substitute for the horse-drawn wagon, able to carry small loads at faster speeds and lower costs. The opportunity this innovation provided for a move away from the congested, high-cost industrial center was matched by new pressures to alter the prevailing production format in the factories. Earlier, the reliance on water power had kept industries relatively scattered and without any discernible urban focus. The introduction of the steam-powered equipment had permitted concentrated urban development. Yet the source of steam power, because of its inefficiency, had to be kept close to the machinery, forcing factories into cluttered, narrow spaces in multi-storied structures. Electric power changed all that. Now machines could be powered by individual electric motors and arranged in ways that could speed up immeasurably the pace of production. For firms with fairly standardized products, mass production could now be organized most efficiently in spacious, single-story buildings where continuously flowing materials were brought to the stationary worker. The implications of these technological advances were obvious: the prototype factory would rely on more land per worker and cheap land was available, as before, in the suburbs. Any concern about being able to assemble a labor force at increasing distances from the business core was dissipated by the rapid spread of yet another set of

innovations: the automobile and the bus. Low-cost roads, initially unimproved, could fan out across the urban area, opening of those rural zones between the street car lines that were previously underdeveloped. This new form of transportation was much more flexible than anything introduced before and the residential sector began to react to this phenomenon, aided again, by the all-pervasive improvement in living standards that accompanied modern economic growth.

Factories were not the only business organizations affected. Retailers, aware of the consumers' impatience with long trips for shopping purposes, followed the suburbanites and provided that rising source of purchasing power with an ever-growing array of goods and services at locations distant from the downtown. With the outflow of manufacturers and retailers, the wholesalers servicing the urban markets were also free to use trucks and follow their customers. Distributors adapted their locations to the demands of scattered customers for frequent deliveries of small lots of products by setting up truck-oriented, land-extensive structures on the periphery of the old Compact City.

Eventually, in the last decade, even the office industry has become unshackled. These paper-passing factories have become increasingly oriented to routine operations that require little of that face-to-face communication that initially attached offices to the old core. Reliable labor power became available in outlying residential areas, eager to work in the more relaxed, pastoral surroundings of the office park. The exodus from the boundaries of the old Compact City was slower than in certain other industries, if only because some executives involved in face-to-face communication often wished to supervise the routine operations which could be spun-off to suburban sites. But the logic of decentralization has become evident in this sector as in the others already cited.

In any short discussion of this subject the misleading impression may arise that the forces at work are somehow instantaneous in their impact. In fact, there is a considerable lag between the emergence of new pressures to decentralize and the fact of widespread decentralization. Decentralization depends not only on new businesses and households that ignore the Compact City in making their first location decision, it also relies on relocations. By their very nature, moves are disruptive and therefore costly ventures that are taken only after considerable deliberation. Established businesses must modify the profitability of different locations as seen by new firms, by considering the costs of relocation. The disposal or movement of fixed assets as well as the disruption of established supplier or customer contacts may delay relocation for long periods of time. Similarly, households' perceptions of the location of the preferred residential areas is translated into moves only where the discrepancy between existing and desired area becomes so great that the costs of housing search and moving become acceptable. To these forces, operating at all times, must be added to conservative barriers in existence until 1945: the Great Depression and World War II.

Over a fifteen year period, uncertainty over economic conditions and governmental restrictions or new construction created a false sense of security for advocates of the Compact City. Once these factors were removed, what appeared to be a flood of relocations began to take place by those who had long postponed their decision to decentralize.

In the context of these rather overwhelming forces pushing for decentralization, the policies of the Federal and local governments can best be viewed as permissive. The widespread demand for public support of homeownership led to the introduction of public subsidies that benefited the construction of low-density homes on suburban land. The rising rates of automobile ownership and the increasing importance attached to truck freight led to public sponsorship of vast road building projects. These reduced the "friction of space," cutting the time required to move from one part of an urban area to another. In the absence of a national urban policy, only limited subsidies were provided to encourage attempts to rebuild the Compact City through costly land assembly, demolition, and new construction. The suburban areas, with their vast supplies of vacant, low-cost land were blessed in other ways as well. The very viability of privately-financed housing and industrial projects is affected by the way land is used in the area surrounding such investments. Financial institutions are extremely reluctant to help revitalize any area which is or might soon be physically deteriorated. This is so not only because the suburbs provided an attractive alternative but because the realized profits from any venture are believed to be dependent on the health of the entire neighborhood where such a venture is located. Luxury apartment housing in a slum neighborhood is not likely to attract high-rent paying customers. Much the same can be said about a business complex whose success depends on attracting skilled workers who wish to work in safe, attractive, surroundings when given a choice. The use of Federal and local funds to counter this problem by subsidizing large-scale demolition and rebuilding projects through Urban Renewal has been limited to a few showcase projects. Overall, the old core cities have had to fend for themselves.

The Regional Factor in the Urban Crisis

Inevitably, the cost of building in the core city and the degree to which negative neighborhood effects discouraged private financing, was to be felt first in those areas which developed before urban low density living became possible.

In general, those urban areas tend to be located in New England, the Middle Atlantic and the Middle West. The urban areas of the so-called Sunbelt States (Southeast, Southwest, and West) are newer, have more vacant land within their borders and are easier to adapt to low-density because they emerged during the period (after 1910-1920) when the prevailing technology and the level of incomes pointed toward decentralization.

Economic development during the nineteenth and early twentieth century was focused on that portion of the United States known as the Industrial Heartland. The coincidence of the large market created by the early population of the Northeast and Middle West and a large natural resource base (iron ore, coal, etc.) made that part of the nation a core area of American economic growth. Elsewhere either because of sparse original population or because of public policy (the Southeast's devastation and slow rebuilding after the Civil War), the regions were colonial hinterlands whose urban focii grew rapidly only in the last fifty to sixty years. The increasing ability to choose among alternative locations, which characterized urban decentralization, can also be found in regional development. The natural resources of the Sunbelt (including, as the name implies, the relatively mild winter weather) provided a basis for farming and mining industries. These, in turn, spawned a large inflow of workers and later of private and public investments. Rising incomes and growing populations provided a basis for rapid diversification of the Sunbelt economy into those economic activities which are urban in their orientation. Ironically, it is possible to see a close parallel between the growth and relative decline of the Industrial Heartland in the face of Sunbelt competition, and the historical changes affecting the Compact City. In both cases, the freeing up of locational decisions by households and businesses worked against the interest of the original center of economic development.

The consequences of the trends reviewed so far can be illustrated in a number of ways. Table I provides urban population and employment trends since World War II for major cities in the Industrial Heartland (Boston, Philadelphia, St. Louis and Chicago) and in the Sunbelt (Houston, Dallas, Denver, and Los Angeles). Generally, the older cities show moderate to sharp declines in population, manufacturing, wholesale, and retail employment, even while their respective suburbs register healthy gains in the same categories. In private service employment (including the office industry), the central cities have done remarkably well, though the suburbs have grown faster. Public employment statistics at the local, state and Federal level are not readily assembled for the entire period under study. Nevertheless the evidence suggests that growth has taken place at rates not unlike those of the private service sector. Once again, the central cities of the Industrial Heartland have managed to share amply in such growth. The Sunbelt cities have not only shared in the older cities' public and private service employment gains, they have managed to record rapid increases in population and employment generally. Their suburbs have also been very successful.

It can be argued on the basis of the evidence in Table I and elsewhere that the core cities of the Industrial Heartland were saved from possible extinction due to irrelevance by the upsurge of the service sector in the twentieth century U.S. economy. Rising average incomes and the increasing complexity of dealing with large regional and national markets have spawned a vast array of activities aimed at finding new outlets for purchasing power (ex. recreational activities), enhancing the speed at which businesses can make decisions (ex. computers) regulating the side-effects of growth, (ex. pollution control) and dealing with the consequences of unequal income distribution (ex. welfare). Because the office industry in general, and government in particular, have historically been less sensitive to locational costs and because political pressure or political necessity concentrates public employment in core areas, the central cities everywhere have benefited handsomely from the growth of the service sector. The selective nature of employment decentralization may not last indefinitely, as already noted in the discussion of the office industry. Public employment growth has also begun to react negatively to public reluctance to pay for the cost of rapid growth in the size and the pay scales of government workers. It is possible that stability or decline in public employment combined with the dispersal of private offices to the suburbs may eventually bring about the extinction of the Industrial Heartland core cities as predicted by the more pessimistic analysts.

Of far more immediate importance is the selective nature of population decentralization, which is not reflected in Table I. The decline or stability of the Industrial Heartland core city populations fails to underscore the fact that minority groups, in general, and poor people, in particular, make up an increasing percentage of the remaining inhabitants. The reasons for this trend are varied. Partly they reflect a careless national policy and partly they represent the outcome of deliberate, exclusionary plans by suburban jurisdictions. At the national level, little attempt was made to control the surge to the major cities that occurred among rural and small town inhabitants during and after World War II. In particular, Federal policies encouraged the rapid displacement of low-skilled farm laborers from Southern farms. In the search for alternate opportunities, these laborers left the South in search of what they viewed as high-growth areas relatively free of blatant racial obstructionism. What they found in the major cities of the Industrial Heartland were limited opportunities for upward economic mobility combined with successful exclusion from all but close-in, older suburbs. The suburbs restricted the construction of low-cost housing or mobile home parks, and were abetted in their efforts by the relative newness of the housing stock, which did not share the rent or price-depressing obsolescence of older, core city apartments and homes. This selective suburbanization has been a fundamental key to the fate of slow-growing or stagnating core cities. Though there are anecdoctal accounts in the news media of a return of middle- and upper-income families to the core cities, the net effect is clear: prosperous households have fled the older core cities in such large numbers as to make a "back to the city" movement insignificant. Such outside factors as an "Energy Crisis" are more likely to encourage core city jobs to flow to preferred residential locations in the suburbs than to bring suburban households back to the crowded central city.

A Look at the Consequences of Selective Suburbanization

While metropolitan areas, as a whole, are quite healthy in all parts of the United States, the central cities, especially in the Industrial Heartland, are suffering the effects of selective suburbanization. The disproportionate core city concentration of the poor and of minority groups to which whites feel an aversion has created a major national problem. Poverty restricts family access to purchasing power, impairs the ability of low-income individuals to absorb vocational and traditional education, and creates the preconditions for a turn to criminal activity that threatens property and life. Thus core cities, even after discounting the aid from Federal and state governments, are saddled with a disproportinate burden in trying to provide poverty-linked public services whose standards are inflated over time by rising expectations of what is appropriate. At the same time, the size of the public employee sector in our largest cities has encouraged militant unionism, with resulting increased costs in pay and fringe benefits. Because local government is very labor-intensive, it is difficult to automate such activity, and the higher labor costs are not offset by improved work performance per worker. Rising costs have burdened the core cities at a time when some important sources of revenue (property taxes on middle- and upper-income residences, sales taxes on retail activity) are being lost to the suburbs. Even in cases where economic activity has not declined absolutely, such as the office industry, the cities must set aside an important fraction of office building property taxes and office worker sales taxes on downtown purchases to pay the costs associated with congestion. For, the success in retaining a healthy office industry has been associated, inevitably, with a trend whereby a large fraction of core city workers commute from the suburbs every working day. The central cities must cope with this vast array of problems with full awareness of the fact that it is in an economic battle with the surrounding suburbs, a battle which all sides perceive as hinging, in part, on the higher tax rates of the core city. Thus there is a limit beyond which the central cities simply refuse to raise taxes even if the problems faced cannot be resolved without greater local fiscal effort. Finally our perception of the urban crisis is affected by visual observation. The newer suburbs may suffer from monotonous residential areas and garrish commercial "strips." Nevertheless, the central cities, especially those in the Industrial Heartland, are faced with a large stock of public and private structures which are technologically obsolescent. In many cases vacant residential and industrial buildings, rundown schools and public service structures create neighborhoods that are increasingly unattractive and threatened with wholesale abandonment by all but the most desperate individuals. The visual impact of abandonment is not unlike that of European cities after World War II and no national or local policy exists to reverse this type of blight.

Money alone will not necessarily cure the ills of the core cities. Appropriate analyses that weight the impact of alternate strategies are sorely needed. But the absence of a commitment to restructure the older cities in the nation, where so many of our less fortunate citizens live in great numbers, inevitably leads to the fear and pessimism that are the hallmarks of the urban crisis.

Table I

Population and Employment Trends in Selected Major Cities and
Metropolitan Areas Since World War II

City / Rest of Metropolis	Population		Manufacturing		Wholesale		Retail		Service	
	1950	1970	1947	1972	1948	1972	1948	1972	1948	1972
Houston	596,163	1,232,407	40,563	105,000	20,754	55,499	39,389	90,372	10,567	70,014
	339,376	752,578	25,410	54,700	873	7,260	10,131	34,570	1,529	16,008
Dallas	434,462	844,401	34,245	106,900	25,197	50,128	37,000	66,415	9,554	48,893
	309,039	711,923	8,429	61,200	1,207	10,696	9,475	38,864	1,811	13,126
Denver	415,786	514,678	30,876	41,500	18,224	27,625	30,737	38,663	7,127	30,450
	196,342	715,120	3,371	53,900	424	8,938	3,705	47,823	428	17,819
Los Angeles	1,970,358	2,816,111	167,156	281,000	66,063	78,795	23,746	165,375	33,848	156,310
	2,181,329	4,220,352	185,516	751,900	25,843	98,943	218,467	236,049	28,557	140,932
Boston	801,444	641,071	101,722	59,400	46,337	26,134	74,310	53,217	14,641	51,254
	1,609,128	2,112,629	169,643	213,600	14,204	51,571	66,874	144,070	13,088	58,561
Philadelphia	2,071,605	1,948,609	328,630	203,000	62,728	49,388	124,258	95,653	28,872	66,623
	1,599,443	2,869,305	203,862	295,100	8,241	49,904	60,616	160,905	9,422	60,428
St. Louis	856,796	622,236	172,946	97,600	43,169	26,679	66,561	36,461	14,799	32,653
	898,538	1,740,781	80,046	158,300	4,874	29,397	31,819	95,797	4,671	34,950
Chicago	3,620,962	3,362,825	667,407	430,100	136,193	101,195	259,396	193,096	69,430	157,315
	1,925,058	3,612,081	189,679	479,200	9,574	92,998	65,419	236,749	12,915	87,837

Data Sources: For each of the years and categories cited, a census of the particular activity was undertaken by the Bureau of the Census, U.S. Department of Commerce. The results are published separately and then assembled in summary form in publications like the annual County and City Data Book. The data are listed for the core city on the numerator and for the remainder of the officially defined metropolitan area on the denominator. All metropolitan areas are defined to include the cities and surrounding counties appropriate for the 1970 definition, even when that definition was not in use in earlier years. In any such cases the data were reassembled to reflect 1970 definitions. In some cases, most clearly in Houston, the growth of core city population and employment reflects the ability of younger cities to annex surrounding suburban territory over time.

Money Bait

ALMOST by accident, a new method has been discovered for attracting wealth. It has never been publicly reported, so far as I can find—although one group of financiers is now quietly using it in an operation which promises to be highly profitable. Apparently they are the first to fully understand the formula, and to put it to deliberate use.

Earlier it had been tested successfully in two states—Massachusetts and California—but these demonstrations were inadvertent. Most of the people concerned did not quite grasp what was happening, or why. This isn't surprising, because the demonstrations occurred piecemeal, over a period of about fifteen years, without any conscious plan.

Once the formula is widely known, however, it should be possible to apply it more quickly in at least a dozen other places. The South, Puerto Rico, and the Pacific Northwest look like the best bets. All of them have one of the two vital ingredients, and probably can create the other if they really try. The result might well be a surprisingly rapid rise in new factories, skilled employment, and per capita income. In certain other states, however, it is never likely to work, for reasons to be noted in a moment.

Our poorer communities have, of course, been looking for just such a recipe for generations. They have tried many kinds of lures to attract new industries. The favorite has been tax concessions—sometimes, as in the case of Puerto Rico, complete tax exemption for as long as twenty years. Often they have put up new buildings and offered them at low rent (or none) to any factory that would move in. In addition they usually have promised cheap labor, and some Southern states have hinted loudly that newcomers wouldn't have to worry about trouble with labor unions.

All too frequently the catch has proved disappointing. For the kind of industry that will snap at such bait is hardly worth having. The South, for example, succeeded in enticing a good many textile mills away from New England—but the industry already was in decline, and its low wages certainly have bestowed no crescendo of prosperity on the Carolinas or Georgia.

On the other hand, the exciting growth industries—electronics, for instance—aren't interested in cheap labor. They need highly skilled men and are willing to pay almost any price to get them—as anyone can see by glancing at the help-wanted ads in *Scientific American* or the Sunday *New York Times*. Neither are they much interested in low taxes, because low taxes mean poor schools. Such schools can't turn out the kind of brains these industries need; moreover, the men they seek aren't willing to settle in communities where their children will be doomed to a second-rate education.

In fact, the major growth industries of the postwar era—the prizes any ambitious community would love to get—differ in six important characteristics from the old-fashioned industries such as steel, textiles, and automobiles:

1. They mostly produce items of small size but great value: transistors, magnetic tape, automation-control instruments, micro-bearings, computers, missile-fuel pumps, pharmaceuticals, inertial-guidance systems, to mention a few.

2. They do not use huge tonnages of raw material and fuel.

3. Consequently they don't have to locate near ore bodies or coal mines. Nor are they dependent on river transport or rail lines. Indeed so far as physical requirements are concerned, they can locate practically anywhere they please.

4. Their plants usually operate without noise, smoke, or smell. Therefore they don't blight the surrounding neighborhoods as a steel mill or paper factory does. On the contrary, these new-type factories are often an enhancement to the community. The cluster of Johnson & Johnson plants near New Brunswick, New Jersey—each a handsome specimen of architecture in a campus-like setting—is a noteworthy example.

5. They aren't greatly concerned about unions. For one thing, their scientific and other white-collar workers are almost impossible to organize. For another, wage costs aren't decisive. What is decisive is the quality of the product—plus constant innovation of improved or entirely new

items. If a production team can come up with a better silicon diode or a more efficient process for making antibiotics, management isn't inclined to haggle about salaries.

6. Their one critical requirement, therefore, is brain power. If they hope to stay ahead of the competition, they must at all costs attract (and hold) really first-rate scientists, technicians, and executives.

I T is interesting to note the places where such industries have, in fact, chosen to locate. Although some are scattered in many parts of the country, they have tended to gravitate toward two great concentrations: one in Southern California, the other in the Boston area. In the latter, they have sprouted thickest along Route 128—the semicircular expressway built a few years ago through what was then open countryside to by-pass the traffic-choked metropolitan area of Boston. According to Dr. F. Leroy Foster, director of the Division of Sponsored Research for Massachusetts Institute of Technology, more than four hundred plants are now turning out electronic components or associated products within a twenty-mile radius of the Charles River Basin, the center of the area. Virtually all of them have been established since the war, and most within the last ten years.

The comparable concentration in Southern California covers a wider area, and has been even more spectacular in its rate of growth. San Diego, for instance, increased its factory employment by 54 per cent between 1954 and 1959, while Los Angeles reported a 21 per cent gain.

Why have such plants sprung up in these two places—rather than in, say, Arkansas, Mississippi, or upstate New York, which need new industry much more desperately? Certainly not because California and Massachusetts did a better promotion job or offered bigger tax and wage incentives; their promotion has been negligible and their tax incentives nil.

By happenstance, however, both areas did offer two powerful attractions:

1. A pleasant environment to live in.
2. Great universities.

These often turned out to be the decisive considerations for a management which was worrying about the recruitment of key personnel.

To begin with, many of the people they wanted already had their roots down in these communities. They were faculty members or graduate students at MIT, Harvard, Boston University, Brandeis, or at Caltech, Stanford, or one of the many campuses of the University of California. (Indeed such people frequently start a factory themselves. MIT alumni have organized seventy-five new companies in the Boston area since the war. And the firm which eventually grew into the Raytheon Company was originally founded by Dr. Vannevar Bush—wartime director

of the Office of Scientific Research and Development—and two friends, who wanted to make a special kind of thermostat. Raytheon now employs 40,000 people—the great majority in twenty-five plants near Boston.)

Moreover, other scientists can easily be persuaded to move to an area which has a complex of good universities. There they can keep in touch with the research under way in the best laboratories. They can consult whenever necessary with the leading minds in their fields.*

Above all, they have company. In the evenings they can visit with friends who share their interests and talk their language. And not merely with other scientists. These people frequently are true intellectuals, with a wide range of interests. They like to live in a community of scholars —historians, writers, sociologists, even an occasional artist—and they enjoy being near good libraries, good orchestras, good art galleries. If you plunked them down in Spearfish, South Dakota, they would go out of their minds with boredom; no amount of money could persuade them to stay there.

Robert S. McNamara is a case in point. A Phi Beta Kappa and once an assistant professor at Harvard, he is typical of the new breed of corporate executive. And it is significant that even after he became president of the Ford Motor Company he continued to live in Ann Arbor— thirty-eight miles from his office—because, as *Time* reported, "it is a university town" and he had "a liking for the academic life." (Or, to put it less tactfully, no intellectual is likely to live in Detroit if he can avoid it.) Dr. Bush provides another object lesson. After his retirement as president of the Carnegie Institution, he returned to MIT because he enjoyed "the excitement of its intellectual ferment."

By coincidence, both Southern California and the Boston area offered not only intellectual ferment but also pleasant places to live. The charms of Southern California (for some people, anyhow) are well known. And the construction of Route 128 made it possible for a man to live in the Boston suburbs, or in the rolling, wooded hills beyond, and still drive to his plant in a few minutes.

It is no coincidence, of course, that these localities also had good schools. Any area that abounds in first-rate universities is almost sure to have better-than-average primary and secondary schools, both public and private. For almost

* Dr. Wernher von Braun, the rocket scientist, recently made the same point in asking the Alabama legislature for money to expand a small research center near the state university. "It's not water, or real estate, or labor, or power, or cheap taxes which brings industry," he said. "It's brainpower. . . . What do you think attracted the aircraft industry to the Los Angeles area? The desert and smog? No, it was UCLA [and the other great universities there]."

by definition, intellectuals are passionate about education, and insist on getting the best they can for their children.

Finally, such people are apt to be sensitive to their physical surroundings. Because they detest ugliness, they can sometimes muster enough public opinion to fight back the tide of billboards, juke joints, used-car lots, and Tastee-Freez stands which has overwhelmed so much of the American landscape. (Witness the civic uproar which saved Walden Pond.) Both Los Angeles and downtown Boston are hideous enough, God knows, but their outlying academic communities generally have managed to preserve little islands of green and ordered serenity.

Since the key men in a space-age factory also are likely to value these things, it is only sensible to locate the plant where they are already available. Provided, of course, that the universities are there too.

T H E business firm which first spotted this pattern of behavior, and tried to make a profit out of it, apparently was the City Investing Company of New York City.

It discovered one-half of the formula about eight years ago. Its original idea was to buy up a twenty-thousand-acre tract of woodland on the west side of the Hudson River, thirty miles from Manhattan, and to develop there a cluster of modern research establishments. Each plant could be set in its own tree-shaded campus, a comfortable distance away from any other. Each employee could have his own country estate—within walking distance of his work.

On paper, this idyllic planned community sounded irresistible to the new type of science-based industries and their egghead personnel. Moreover, the company spared nothing to make its Sterling Forest development into a sylvan paradise. It found a choice site—close to Tuxedo Park and West Point, within easy reach of the New York Thruway, endowed with a brook and three lakes—and it spent hundreds of thousands of dollars on landscaping, flowers, and shrubs.

But, alas, the scientists didn't swarm in with the expected alacrity.

In 1957 the Union Carbide Nuclear Company did begin to do some research there, and has since opened a new center, while the Sterling Forest management put up an International Research Building of its own. But there was no stampede like the one Boston and California had enjoyed.

The trouble, it seems, was that the scientists were afraid they would be lonesome. Who could they talk to out there in those woods? Chipmunks? Gardeners? Their wives?

So in 1960 the City Investing people hit upon the missing half of the formula. What they needed, obviously, was a university.

Last December they got it. The company gave a thousand acres of land to New York University, on condition that it would establish there a major campus for its science departments. The school's president promptly announced plans for setting up an atomic-reactor laboratory, classrooms and quarters for graduate students, adult education programs, and housing for faculty and research personnel. The development may take twenty years to complete, he explained, but eventually the new campus will be fit company for the six campuses which NYU already operates.

That evidently turned the trick. Four corporations made plans to install research units in the Sterling Forest area, before the university got around to laying its first brick.

Few private financiers are likely to command the resources (or the foresight) to carry through similar schemes. But the technique seems made to order for states that are eager to attract modern industry. Some already have a good start, even though they don't realize it.

In North Carolina, for example, the area between Chapel Hill and Durham looks like a natural for such an enterprise. Both are pleasant towns. They are surrounded by unspoiled (well, all right, not *hopelessly* spoiled) countryside; it could be handsomely developed—at a profit —by public purchase and zoning. The Blue Ridge Mountains are an easy drive to the west, the Cape Hatteras beach about the same distance east. In sum, a potential for The

Good Life as promising as anything Massachusetts or California can offer.

And here are two of the best educational institutions in the South: the University of North Carolina and Duke. Around this nucleus the state could—if it made a determined effort—build up a truly great intellectual center. It might become not just the best in its region, but one of the best in America. Inevitably it would give North Carolina the educational leadership of the South —and as a consequence, leadership in modern industry as well.

It would cost money of course. A doubling of teachers' salaries, new buildings, urban renewal, parks and landscaping, a long-range, well-thought-out regional plan: all of these would have to be financed somehow. (The big national foundations and the tobacco industry might both be eager to help.) But in the end the investment ought to pay off bountifully. In New England the factory sales of electronic equipment alone amounted to $749 million in 1959, and are expected to pass $2 billion by 1970. Already these factories have created jobs for nearly a hundred thousand people—almost as many as the payroll of the region's entire textile industry.

COMPARABLE opportunities would seem to be open to Puerto Rico, with its climatic advantages and a university already growing rapidly in stature; to the Puget Sound region; to Wisconsin, Michigan, and a few other areas which already have some of the basic ingredients.

For certain states, however, this sort of development seems out of the question. How could anybody create either a great university or an enticing environment in Kansas or North Dakota? The Deep South will continue to lose, rather than attract, educated people so long as it threatens to destroy its public-school system over the integration issue. (The North Carolinians, notoriously more commonsensical than most Southerners, seem likely to solve this problem without much uproar.) Texas, Arizona, Colorado, and Nevada—plus some others—have not yet demonstrated that respect for intellect and education which is necessary to the growth of great universities. Maine and Idaho probably couldn't raise the money.

Clearly the new recipe for industrialization will not work everywhere —but it does look too good to remain indefinitely the secret weapon of Massachusetts, California, and the City Investing Company. It will be entertaining to see what community first shows enough enterprise to try to break their monopoly.

———

C. Population and the Environment

Population and the
Environmental Crisis

Carl H. Madden
Chief Economist
Chamber of Commerce of the United States

For the world as a whole, overpopulation represents a serious survival problem. The clash between population growth and technology and ecology represents a crisis of culture. Policy in this area should view "human bodies and individuals" as they were "part of the capital stock." Economic and population policy, therefore, should explore the measurable benefits which people in comprehensive understanding and rational action would contribute to the growth of income and wealth, the enhancement of the environment, the survival of the species, and the realization of mankind's possibilities.

IN EXAMINING THE QUESTION of environment and population policy, too many people are demanding answers to questions that they have not bothered to ask. An answer without a question is no answer at all. The environmental crisis pressing hard on mankind today calls less for answers to questions we have never bothered to ask than it calls for a search for what questions we ought to be asking.

It is hardly news any longer that mankind is moving towards a mounting crisis, as the world's rapidly growing population and industrialization deplete the earth's resources and pollute the environment. But it can be argued that those whose answer is "Stop economic growth" may not have asked the significant questions before they gave the answer. Yet, it should be added: the voices of the dissidents have great value because even if they give no answer, they demand of the conventional wisdom that it begin asking more significant questions.

Population and Culture

Population policy illustrates the need facing mankind to invent new culture within which action perceived as rational promotes his survival as a species. The unprecedented power given mankind by science and technology places him in a race between utopia and oblivion, a race threatened by reliance on traditional or ancestral wisdom. "Out-breeding, out-gunning, or out-producing other groups," Brock Chisholm told the twenty-third American Assembly, "can no longer be counted on to provide security, prosperity, or peace, or even survival." In the three great world problems of security, population, and food, today's threat is to the

Carl H. Madden, "Population and the Environmental Crisis." *Business Economics,* January 1972, pp. 12–17. Reprinted with permission of the author and the publisher.

whole human race, requiring for resolution independent thought rather more than methods learned from parents or tradition.

The ancient survival system depended on defense against attack by family, clan, tribe, city, state, principality, kingdom, empire, or nation. It required the largest possible number of fighting men, exclusive loyalty, the best weapons, unquestioning obedience to authority, adequate food and material, and high morale. But with weapons now available in the world—nuclear, biological, chemical, and conventional—we are capable of killing everyone three or four times over, and to infer from past tradition that overkill of ten adds to security becomes insane. We lack adequate national security systems and wholly lack such systems worldwide.

Likewise, to our ancestors big families and growth of the survival group was "good." It increased power and security to have plenty of children in nearly all cultures, but now it threatens the whole human species. The reason is the relation of unchecked world population growth to famine, disease, and war. If world population exceeds limits set by technology or ecology, the risk is the decline of civilization through a series of catastrophies. Yet this danger appears all too real in the implications of current world population trends.

World population increases virtually unchecked. Its growth projected only 30 years ahead strains foreseeable resources and projected 150 years ahead reaches theoretically supportable maximums of our present industrial technology. As to growth, it took 2-to-4 million years, since man or his erect relatives had lived on earth, to reach a population of one billion (1850); it took 112 years to reach an estimated 3 billion (1962); but it will take at present growth rates only 30 years to reach 5 billion (2000).

Mankind's history, relating stages of technology to population ceilings, has seen three stages: food-gathering, farming, and industrial. The world population ceiling of man as food-gatherer, reaching through the 600,000 years of the Old Stone Age or Paleolithic period, was about 20 million, based on 2 square miles per person needed in limited areas suitable for hunting. The second stage, beginning about 6000 B.C., brought the agricultural revolution which raised the world population ceiling to one billion. The highest estimate of a population ceiling for the third stage of industrial technology is 50 billion, made by geo-chemist Harrison Brown of the California Institute of Technology. Assuming worldwide industrialization, nuclear and solar power, and all necessary technology now foreseen, Brown concludes the 50 billion people would live in a vast world megalopolis, eat food supplied mainly by algae farms and yeast factories, and use technology employing vast amounts of energy to process mostly air, water, and ordinary rock. Present world population growth, if projected ahead, would bump against the 50-billion ceiling in only 150 years, scarcely more than two lifetimes of 70 years.

Resources and Population

The collision between world resources and population growth, according to evidence cited by Charlton Ogburn, Jr., would come much sooner. Ogburn argues that 5 billion people 30 years from now living at present U.S. consumption standards would overstrain the world's resources. Ogburn concludes "an industrializing world simply cannot afford to have 5 billion people." Brown, however, observes "at the present time we are far from the limit of the number of persons who could be provided for. If we were willing to be crowded together closely enough, to eat foods which bear little resemblance to the foods we eat today, and to be deprived of simple but satisfying luxuries such as fireplaces, gardens, and lawns, a world population of 50 billion persons would not be out of the question." Brown does not, however, minimize the extraordinary changes required in all areas of present culture to achieve such numbers.

The advent of ecology only emphasizes the threat of world population growth. The understanding of ecology—the science of the relationships between living organisms and their living and non-living surroundings—questions the capacity of the environment to support growing numbers and concentrations of people or their increasing production and consumption of material goods or physically-based services created through existing technology. Ecology reveals that, for the first time in history, the extent of man's activities may be limited by the problem of disposing of by-products or effluents, as well as by the depletion of resources needed as inputs. Ecology reveals that pollution of all kinds, traditionally viewed as isolated problems, is inseparable from economic activity. The reason is that all inputs to production (excluding the input of man's collective mind) must ultimately become waste. Long known theoretically, this implication of thermodynamics (entropy) traditionally could be ignored because the summation effects of pollution appeared small. The rising scale of technology increases the extent and spread of summed pollution effects markedly.

A Crisis of Culture

The conclusion seems inescapable that for the world as a whole overpopulation represents a serious survival problem. The clash between population growth, on the one hand, and technology and ecology, on the other, represents a crisis of culture in mankind's history. The symptoms of overpopulation reflect the degree to which present world culture appears out of control despite glowing possibilities for future advance of civilization.

The impending world population crisis is part of a very critical period in mankind's history because it forces his attention on the need to recognize and adapt to the possibility of conscious evolution. As Julian Huxley observes, the new vision of man's destiny, to seek conscious evolution, merely extends the reality of biological evolution which has been going on for three billion years and which has seen life advance in variety and organization from sub-microscopic, pre-amoebic units to vertebrates, to land vertebrates and thence to mankind, Huxley observes the truth that whether mankind likes it—indeed, knows it—or not, he is "the sole agent for the future of the whole evolutionary process on this earth. He is responsible for the future of this planet." To Huxley the present crisis is one in which "quantity is threatening quality...one in which the present is threatening the future." The contrast between the glorious possibilities that are still latent in man, the possibilities of fruitful fulfillment, as against frustration, resemble, for Huxley, the Christian view of salvation as against damnation.

The World Predicament

Recent simulations at MIT of world developments prepared by Forrester and Meadows illustrate the need to ask questions of more significance to mankind's survival than the questions which preoccupy many of us. The project attempts through a set of empirical research and simulation models to identify long term global prospects and evaluate alternative policies for their affects over the next 50 to 200 years. The major model asks the question, What are the interrelations between global population growth, pollution, food production, natural resource depletion, and economic development?

The preliminary conclusions from these modelling studies are at sharp variance with the usual brand of economic theory used by business economists in corporate planning, as follows:

1. There is no possibility of sufficient technological and cultural progress occurring in the next 100 years to sustain as many as fourteen billion people on our globe. Since the doubling time of population is currently 32 years and decreasing, this means that sometime within the next 60 years population growth will undergo a profound deceleration.
2. There is no possibility of bringing the vast majority of those living in the developing countries up to the material standard of living enjoyed by the developed nations.
3. There is a strong probability that the western nations will witness a marked decline in their own material standard of living within the next three or four decades.
4. There is no unique, optimal long-term population level. Rather, there is an entire set of trade-offs between personal freedom, material and social standards of living, and the population level. Given the finite and diminishing stock of resources on this globe, we are inevitably compelled to recognize that more people implies a lower standard of living.
5. There is, in theory, no fundamental human value which could not be better achieved through a substantial lowering of the global population base.
6. There is a very strong probability that the transition to global equilibrium will involve a traumatic decline in population.

Several things can be said about these conclusions. For one thing, they are in general accord with other serious attempts, earlier cited, to trace out global developments. For another thing, all such attempts have assumed that technological progress takes the from of increased productivity as conventionally defined, including conventional definitions of the nature of output and therefore of income and wealth. And in the third place, the conclusions flow from the "existing state of the art" in computer simulation.

In evaluating such conclusions, it is worth keeping in mind that, as Meadows says, "The first version of the main model is very simple and has not been empirically validated." The science fiction writer, Arthur C. Clarke, has often cautioned against categorical negative predictions by scientists, and his caution has enough empirical evidence to support it to be worth mentioning.

The conclusions of the Forrester-Meadows simulations, however, are hardly more significant than their observations about the nature of the interactions that occur in analyzing large and complex systems. Economists have long known that such systems are counterintuitive. "That is," as Forrester puts it, "they give indications that suggest corrective action which will often be ineffective or even adverse in its results . . . choosing an ineffective or detrimental policy for coping with a complex system is not a matter of random choice. The intuitive process will select the wrong solution much more often than not."

It is not so clear, however, that economists have recognized the significance of their own understanding that complex systems are counterintuitive. Although classical price theory fully reflects the crucial operation of information feedback in the behavior of markets seeking equilibrium, economists along with others who advise policymakers often neglect it.

Some examples illustrate the operation of feedback. A road is overcrowded, so we enlarge the road, so more drivers are attracted to the bigger road, so it is even more crowded than the old one. People in cities live in poverty, so we build houses for the poor at low rents, so more poor people move into the city, and so they oversupply existing jobs, so more people in cities are living in poverty. An example economists immediately recognize is the bus company losing money, so raises its fares, which leads to fewer riders, so leads to greater losses for the company.

But how about these examples of Meadows: More people produce more births and more births produce more people. Or, capital investment produces industrial output; greater output, all else equal, results in larger investment, and thus in more capital. Or, output is diverted to consumption and services, so health and education improve, so life expectancy rises, deaths decline, and population grows.

Implications for Policy

Forrester's conclusions from studying the impact of positive feedback in world economic systems are suggestive of new, significant questions. Among the implications for policy that emerge are:

1. Industrialization may be a more fundamentally disturbing force in world ecology than is population. (Medicine and health are included here as a part of industrialization.)

2. Within the next century man may face a four-pronged dilemma—suppression of modern industrial society by a natural resource shortage; decline of world population caused by changes from pollution; population decline from food shortage; or population decline from disease, social stresses, or war.
3. We may now be living in a "golden age" better than what has come before or is to come in the next century or so.
4. Exhortation to population control alone could be self-defeating, by raising per capita food supply and living standards and thus raising population.
5. A society with a high level of industrialization may be nonsustainable.

Looking beyond Forrester and Meadows, one can be briefer. In a brilliant and wise speech recently, Dr. Maynard M. Miller, professor of geology at Michigan State University, points out some more curves besides those of the MIT group. There is the curve of war, which computers predict poorly. There is the "world-is-getting-younger" curve that goes along with population growth. And along with the "world-is-getting-younger" curve there is a curve that might be called "the-world-is-getting-dumber" curve, which rises because there are more heads to fill with knowledge than conventional means to do so.

Issues of Policy

The issue posed by the students of world developments raises a significant question. The question is, what, indeed, is rational? We are victims, it appears, of two harsh and ironic maxims—the French proverb, "Beware lest you get what you want," and Herman Kahn's epigram, "Nothing fails like success." To put the matter plainly, our wealth appears to be killing us.

Is it, then, rational to reject our wealth? The possibility influences men's minds today more strongly than in some time. Thus, we have the British economist, Ezra Mishan, who would consign the automobile to the Devil, from whence Mishan appears to believe it came. Some humanists, in growing numbers, go Mishan one further and would abolish science itself. And finally, a large group of the young, led by such veteran Pentagon marchers as Norman Mailer, disdain more and more even rationality itself, and certainly what Mailer calls "the-logic-of-the-next-step."

Shall we abandon rationality? It would be odd to do so shortly after inventing the computer and shortly after learning once more that man is a part of nature only through new insights derived from knowledge of biology. Shall we abolish science? Again, everyone complains about the same thing—we are engaged in irrationality but we seem so determined to call our behavior rational. Commuters, who rush to the city like lemmings to the sea, feel rational. Minds, schooled to seeking short term gain because in the long run we are all dead, feel rational. In our time we have debased the coinage of that grand word, rational.

Shall we reject our wealth? In order to maintain present standards, we need all the wealth we have to cope with expected growth in world and national population. To reject future wealth is to force a drastic decline in population, a return to a lower level of technology, and to a lower quality of life, if by wealth we mean what men value.

Shall we limit population? Well, of course, but it is not enough. Limiting world population, given present culture, may only lead to increasing it later. Limiting United States population may not, given present culture, reduce appreciably our drain on resources.

What, then, is the significant question for ecology and population? Is the question not far more profound than we have expected? Does the question not go to the nature of our present culture, its values, its perception of wealth, income, productivity, cost, progress, welfare?

Anthropologists use the term culture to mean, generally, the things and devices, including myths, beliefs, and stories, which men use to enhance, protect, or express themselves. The question of environment and population is that of a culture crisis. Anthropologists tell us that the alternatives in a culture crisis are few. When a culture is strained, the population is checked, the culture is fragmented, or some new adaptation of the culture is invented.

The Invention of Culture

In my opinion we are challenged by the environment-population crisis to invent new culture. In principle, and in general, the issue is that of full recognition that our modern scientific revolution centers around the two major concepts of thermodynamics: energy and entropy. The first law of thermodynamics asserts that in any closed energy system, energy is conserved. The second law of thermodynamics asserts that, in any closed energy system, entropy (roughly a measure of disorder) increases until equilibrium is reached. In other words, all systems tend to run down.

Ecological processes offset the disorder arising from entropy by built-in evolutionary tendencies, based on natural selection. In nature, evolutionary movement is from the simple to the complex, from the simple life form to the diverse. Driving these movements is the inclination of living systems to reduce entropy and to foster order by making useful energy available.

In general, our task is to fully recognize the significance of the laws of thermodynamics in our social systems on the globe of Earth. The scientific revolution offers us an escape from the entropy trap depicted by students of world development. One source of escape is to deliver more useful energy to our systems and to substitute energy for matter. This source is in the discovery of the equivalence of mass and energy, and thence to nuclear power.

The Scientific Revolution and Social Life

The other source of escape is to offset the growth of entropy—seen as disorder—through bringing to bear more information in social processes. What is meant is a cultural revolution which systematically applies the spirit and method of classic science—its rules of governance—to the understanding and guidance of the interaction of population, pollution, economic growth, and the quality of life. We need to apply the scientific revolution to social life.

This strategy is not the same as limiting population growth or economic growth. It is several orders of magnitude more complex and significant. It offers a series of positive strategies that add up to the invention of new culture. In my opinion, deeper understanding of the idea involved in the systematic application of the spirit—and I emphasize spirit—as well as the method of science to social processes in the world suggests sub-strategies that are both inspiring and significantly effective.

For one thing, the idea implies an increasing concern for maintaining the world ecosystem in what may be called a "steady state." Already, science empowers us to monitor the world environment by satellite. We are empowered to monitor and understand the world environmental weather.

To establish environmental balance as the concern of economic policy has powerful implications. It is not clear, for example, that our conventional concern for full employment is consistent with environmental balance, if the nature of available jobs remains unchanged. The object is not work for its own sake or as a means to distribute income, but work as a means to achieve environmental balance.

For another thing, the idea implies an increasing interest in redefining wealth. The issue is not to stop the growth of wealth, but to redefine wealth. Our problem is not in the generalized concept of wealth, but in the specific forms of wealth. Our problem is not the empty box of wealth but what we stuff into it in the name of wealth.

In general, we over-value forms of wealth which are entropy-creating and undervalue future forms of wealth which are entropy-offsetting. Thus, there seems little question that, with present patterns of production and consumption, as in the United States, spread over the world, there would result an environmental catastrophe before world population reached five billion people.

Production and Consumption Patterns

The issue, then, is present production and consumption patterns as well as size of population. For example, the present experiment in India of a TV network via satellite for educating Indians about limiting population and improving the quality of life is an immensely valuable form of wealth for mankind, a form of wealth we are tragically neglecting elsewhere in our preoccupation with past forms of wealth. The Indian TV education experiment is substantially an application of the thermodynamic scientific revolution to the increase of wealth for mankind. It markedly increases the evaluation of information and useful energy in our definition of wealth and markedly reduces our use of materials. The Indian TV experiment, indeed, raises the question whether we need all the fantastic proliferation of bricks and mortar that marks our present organizational ideas in education in this country.

At the same time, the perspective of ecological balance offers a deep challenge to conventional ideas of "growth as usual." The perspective is hostile to use of narrow criteria of economic benefit as the only measure of science and technology. Hostility to narrow economic benefit derives from the view that it is not sufficiently rich in rationality. Rebellion against narrow economic benefit energizes inventive efforts to construct social indicators, to link them in social accounting, and to assess social benefits and costs in economic activity not now considered in decision-making. These inventions of culture, if successful, should be at least as important as national income and product accounting.

Assessing Technology

The perspective of ecological balance challenges, as in the SST decision, the modern belief-system, documented by Jacques Ellul, which leads many people to presume that what is technically possible is therefore humanly desirable. Hostility to this belief is energizing the rapid development of a new invention called "technology assessment," aimed at "keeping tab on the potential dangers, as well as the benefits inherent in new technology." Technology assessment is part of a new culture which has abandoned laissez-faire in science and technology.

The perspective of ecological balance requires recognition of the Orphic as well as the Promethean myth; it requires that mankind see himself as part of nature rather than its exploiter. Such a cultural change has highly significant implications to both economic and population policy.

The economic implication is to perceive that "the essential indicator of success is not production and consumption, but the nature, extent, quality and complexity of the total capital stock, including the state of human bodies and individuals in the system," as the President's goals research staff put it. One consequence of such a criterion is that the throughput of materials in the production process will be regarded as something to be minimized, not maximized. Another consequence is recognition of the economic value of human beings as producers of new wealth.

The implication for population policy is to explore provisions of such policy not merely concerned with numbers and geographic distribution of people, but more importantly with viewing "human bodies and individuals" as if they were "part of the capital stock." Both economic and population policy, in other words, would explore the measurable benefits which healthy, well-nourished, genetically well-endowed, educated, skillful and thinking people, free to realize themselves in comprehensive understanding and rational action, could contribute to the growth of income and wealth, the enhancement of the environment, the survival of the species, and the realization of mankind's possibilities.

The Mind of Man

The concept that all systems tend to run down implies that in the production process, all inputs eventuate in waste—except for what has been called "the collective mind of man." The idea is not clear but it is suggestive. Perhaps the best popular explanation is in an essay by Isaac Asimov. It refers to the evolutionary tendency for wealth to flow from ideas, from "the mind of man," which in particular cases can be obscenely erroneous but can also produce ideas of great beauty and worth.

To illustrate, consider once again the doleful implications of Forrester and Meadows and their simulations. If their simulations, however grossly, point in a significant direction, they do so in considerable part only through the use of the computer in new ways. And there is no question that the computer in the future can be used in ever more powerful ways to simulate consequences of given complex systems, including worldwide social systems.

The negative consequences of Forrester and Meadows are derived according to the principle, sharply highlighted by the computer, that analytical output is limited by analytical input. If the MIT simulations have merit, they explore the entropy trap into which our present culture is about to place mankind. If the principle is that of "garbage-in, garbage-out," the garbage is at work on an epic scale. The MIT scholars have offered us, to put the matter in other words, an alternative future. That future follows logically by implication from what the dominant industrial culture now defines as rational. Indeed, many of us business economists, in our long range projections of future markets, are innocently perpetrating some principal canons of the present cultural milieu in visions of more output for more people with more income, world without end. Meanwhile, a quick review of the MIT conclusions, along with those of other students of world development, suggests that they seem to be playing out a funeral dirge for the industrial society which flowed out of the nineteenth century culture that invented it.

The final question for a world facing a growing environmental-population crisis is whether evolution—conscious evolution—is progressive. One answer, all too evident in the sober concerns of population scholars, is No. It is an answer that will come along in due course. It is not the only possible answer, but it is significant. However, mankind does not lack the means to avoid catastrophe any more than it lacks the means to create it. "No" is not the only answer, but it is easier on the mind of the dominant culture.

An Economic Approach to Family Size: A New Perspective on Population Growth

By Donald J. Mullineaux

People are becoming increasingly anxious at the prospect that we humans will someday procreate ourselves right back into our ancestral cave dwellings. This is hardly a new worry. Thomas Malthus, the most pessimistic of a breed Carlyle dubbed the "dismal scientists," averred almost 200 years ago that population growth would inevitably outstrip man's ability to feed and clothe himself. Misery and distress would come to characterize the human condition. Experience has belied the Malthusian prophecy as living standards have risen sharply in most areas of the world. Yet Parson Malthus's theory of population and calamity has shown remarkable resiliency. Like some rubber-legged heavyweights, Malthus has been down but never out. Indeed, in two recent and highly publicized studies[1], the Malthusian outlook has resurfaced, fortified by computer analyses of the world economy and psychosociopolitical theorizing.

Until recently, economists have had relatively little to say about Malthus's views concerning fertility and population *per se*. The Malthusian prophecy was considered faulty because it neglected the saving grace of technology, and nothing needed to be said about family size. Indeed, nothing could be said, since family size was determined mainly by noneconomic factors. Some economists have recently had a change of heart, however. They emphasize that both logic and evidence indicate that economic variables play a role in family decisions about childbearing. One economic approach— sometimes referred to as the "household model"—suggests that neglecting the impact of *prices* on family size can lead to poor forecasts of population growth. In addition, the household model clarifies the relation of education and family size. Finally, the outlook for population growth suggested by this approach allows a much more optimistic view of mankind's future than the bleak Malthusian scenario.

AN ECONOMIC VIEW OF FAMILY SIZE: THE DEMAND AND SUPPLY OF CHILDREN

In recent years, economists have begun to apply their logic and methods in a number of areas once considered beyond the pale of economics. Decisions concerning marriage, childbearing, migration, criminal behavior, church attendance, suicide, and even (with

---

[1]See Donella H. Meadows et al., *The Limits to Growth* (New York: Universe Books, 1972) and Robert L. Heilbroner, *An Inquiry into the Human Prospect* (New York: W. W. Norton and Company, 1974).

Donald J. Mullineaux, "An Economic Approach to Family Size: A New Perspective on Population Growth." *Business Review*, Federal Reserve Bank of Philadelphia, January–February 1976, pp. 3–12. Reprinted with permission.

tongue in swollen cheek) teeth brushing have all been subjected to economic analysis. Sociologists and psychologists have, of course, long studied these kinds of phenomena. The explanations of economists are not intended to displace or denigrate their efforts, but rather to complement psychological or sociological theories and hence provide a fuller elucidation of human behavior.

Many people are offended by the suggestion that children can be treated like any other economic good. Parents in particular are likely to resist attempts to attach a "price" to their children. The reason is that society uses prices to measure value, and most mothers and fathers would not assign a monetary value to their children (although the neighbors' children are often considered "priceless" in quite a different sense than our own). Economists seek to apply their logic to childbearing, however, not to debase the human qualities of children or parents, but to gain insights into behavior which may be useful for problem solving. In other words, economists are trying to abstract from the extremely large number of factors affecting family size and isolate those elements they understand best. This is not to suggest that all behavior is motivated *solely* by economic factors. Economists make no claim to completeness when studying the demand for children (though this is no less the case for automobiles or theater tickets). The point is that where economic factors play *some* role and are ignored, explaining and predicting human behavior and its consequences (such as population growth) will be at best difficult and at worst fallacious.

A popular approach involves treating each household as a miniature firm.[2] A firm purchases materials, equipment, and manpower to produce some product. Similarly, a household purchases goods and services and combines them with its own available time ("manpower") to produce things which give satisfaction to household members. A household for instance employs materials such as bread, wine, steak, vegetables, and the like along with shopping and preparation time to "produce" a meal. Just as the amount

a business manufactures depends on what it has to pay for raw materials and for labor, what a household "produces" depends on the prices of household goods and the value of family members' time. This "household model" also suggests that as the price of a husband's or wife's time increases relative to the prices of other goods, a household will switch to activities requiring less time (just as a firm substitutes machines for labor when wages rise relative to equipment rentals).

The "services" provided by children represent one form of satisfaction produced in many households. Children yield their parents productive services (such as mowing lawns, washing dishes, "doing chores," and the like) as well as nonproductive services. Economists term the latter "psychic income" and it includes the sum of the innumerable joys of watching and helping children grow. Since children yield these services over time, from an economic viewpoint they can be considered akin to "durable goods." Like durables in general, children are costly. Expenditures on food, clothing, health maintenance, education, recreation, and so on can run into many thousands of dollars. In addition, there will be "psychic costs" to child-raising since growing up produces parental heartaches as well as joys.[3]

If children can be thought of as resembling other durable goods in a broad sense, then economists can apply their reasoning to derive suggestions about how people are likely to behave in making decisions about family size. For instance, the demand for "satisfaction" from children should fall when the "price" of children rises. As children become more expensive relative to other means of satisfaction, parents should want to bear and raise fewer children. This presumes of course that the other factors affecting fertility—both economic and noneconomic—are unchanged. Applying economics to childbearing decisions also would suggest that house-

<hr>

[2]Not all economists employ the same framework in studying family size. For an alternative approach to the one outlined in this article, see Harvey Leibenstein, "The Economic Theory of Fertility Decline," *Quarterly Journal of Economics* 89 (1975): 1–31.

[3]Parents presumably compare the benefits of an additional child with the costs involved (such a calculation is, of course, rough at best and perhaps not even consciously undertaken) and adjust their reproductive behavior to add to the size of the family whenever benefits exceed costs. Some may find thinking about behavior this way crass or offensive. It should be remembered, however, that the economic approach is not intended to be the sole explanation of all we do. In addition, whether or not the household model is useful can only be judged in terms of its ability to explain and predict human behavior.

holds should desire more children as family income rises (that is, if children are what economists call "normal" goods). Here is one point where an economic application appears to hit a snag. For the evidence is quite clear that over time and in almost all the various cultures of the world the birth rate *falls* as income increases. In the same vein, wealthier families typically have fewer children than families with lower standards of living. Looking at the relation between family size and income *in isolation*, however, can be misleading. Economists must try to "control" for the effects of other factors which may impinge on childbearing decisions. Recent studies show, for example, that once we take account of the effects of changes in the "quality" and "price" of children, family size on average does increase with income. Thus, income changes cannot explain the long-run decline in birth rates in most developed economies. According to the "household model," declining family size is accounted for mainly by three factors: (1) increases in the average "quality" level of children; (2) the rising "price" of children; and (3) increases in the average education level of parents.

Quantity vs. Quality of Children. The household model approach to family size suggests that children can be viewed much like other durable goods which are desired for the "services" they provide. At first glance, it seems vulgar or offensive to contend that children are wanted for their "services." However, economists define "services" quite broadly. Indeed, *any* kind of "good feeling" that a parent would attribute to having a son or daughter would be considered a "service" from the economist's viewpoint. Friendly greetings on arriving home, long walks in the woods, and games of catch in the backyard are all part of the "service flow" from children.

In many cases, households would like to increase the services provided by durable goods. There are two ways to accomplish this. More units of the good in question can be acquired, or alternatively, a higher quality unit (more BTUs or horsepower) can be purchased. Economists have carried over the quantity-quality distinction to their discussion of the demand for children. In particular, they note that "services" from children can be increased either by adding to the size of the family or by boosting the "quality" of the children parents already have.

By injecting "quality" into their analysis of family size, economists do not mean to suggest that some children are "better" in some moral sense than others. Instead they are simply emphasizing that some parents spend more on raising a family of given size than others. Rather than add further to family size, parents may opt for summer camp and nursery schools for the children they already have. Indeed, households cannot avoid choosing between quantity and quality expenditures in childraising since no family has unlimited resources.

For most durable goods, expenditures on quality seem much more responsive to income gains than does spending on quantity.[4] Several economists have argued that this is likely to be the case for children as well. They note that high-income families typically have only slightly larger or even smaller numbers of children than low-income families, but they spend more on each child. There is some disagreement about why this might be the case. Some have argued that social pressures dictate that children's living standards are inexorably linked to those of their parents. Other economists have contended that producing "quality" children becomes "cheaper" as incomes rise. Whatever the underlying reason, it is clear that ignoring the quality-quantity distinction in relating income and size of family can lead to misleading conclusions since quality can "substitute" for quantity to some extent. Still another factor which must be taken into account, however, is the "price" of children relative to other goods and services.

The Cost of Raising or "Price" of Children. In these inflationary times, everyone recognizes that rearing a family has become an increasingly expensive proposition. But it is difficult to think of any activity that isn't costing more today than yesterday. In fact, childbearing will be discouraged not by inflation *per se*, but by increases in the "price" of children *relative* to the prices of other goods and ser-

---

[4]For example, one well-known study estimates that if total income in the U. S. doubles, total spending on automobiles would rise 200 percent. However, spending on additional numbers of cars would rise by only 31 percent. The difference reflects increased expenditures on quality. See Gregory C. Chow, *The Demand for Automobiles in the United States* (Amsterdam, The Netherlands: North-Holland Publishing Company, 1957).

vices. There is good reason to believe that the relative price of children has been rising sharply over time, at least in the developed countries. The reason is that the "services" that children provide are produced in the home using a resource whose value (relative price) has risen considerably—namely, the parents' (especially the mother's) time.

The dollar cost of the goods and services used in child rearing is only part of the total cost of children. Economists also reckon the "opportunity cost" of the time spent with children as part of the "price" of children. These opportunity costs represent the value parents would attach to *alternative* uses of the time and energy they allot to their children. For instance, to devote her time to her children, a mother foregoes opportunities to earn income in the job market or enjoy leisure activities. Indeed, the "production" of child services requires an extraordinary amount of the parents' time, especially when children are young. In the jargon of economists, producing satisfaction from children is very "time-intensive." Hence, this time or opportunity cost forms an integral part of the "full price" of children.

The value of the opportunities a mother foregoes to raise children can be considered the price of her time, and likewise for the father. For women who spend at least part of their time working in the labor market, their "real wage" (inflation-adjusted earnings) can be taken as a measure of the price of time. In the U. S. as well as in other developed economies, real wages have increased sharply

over time (see Chart 1). Hence, the value of time has been increasing. A rising price of time translates into an increased price of children *relative to other goods and services* because children are *more time-intensive* than other kinds of durable goods. Economic logic dictates that as the relative price of children rises, people will shift to less time-intensive activities to economize on an increasingly scarce resource (time).

Some studies have considered the statistical relationship between family size and the price of parents' time.[5] The relationship between the father's wage and family size is unclear, but several studies have found that a higher value of the mother's time is associated with a lower number of children in the family. These studies typically use a woman's wage or number of years of education as a measure of the value of time. Years of schooling are of course only a "proxy" measure for the value of time. Some researchers employ this measure because wage-rate information is not available for a large proportion of women—mainly those who spend *all* of their time working in the home. The value of the housewife's time must exceed her potential wage in the labor market or she would devote at least some of her time to working outside the home. Studies have shown that the value of the housewife's time will depend on a number of factors,[6] but that education is especially important. Education increases productivity in *work at home* by improving the ability to acquire, evaluate, and use information concerning matters such as consumer products and health maintenance. Since education also has a positive effect on earnings outside the home, it clearly affects the demand for children via its influence on the value of time. But education's impact on family size is not limited to the demand side. It also influences the supply of children by affecting a couple's ability to control the size of their families.

Education and the Supply of Children. Children are unique when viewed in an economic light since they are generally "supplied" by

CHART 1

AS THE VALUE OF TIME HAS INCREASED SHARPLY IN THE POSTWAR PERIOD IN THE U. S. . . .

All Workers
Dollars/hour

Median Annual
Earnings For Women

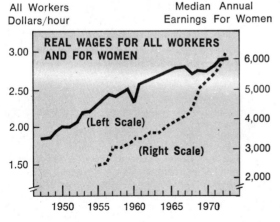

[5]Several studies in the "household model" approach to fertility can be found in T. W. Schultz, ed., *New Economic Approaches to Fertility*, published in the *Journal of Political Economy* 81 (1973): S1–S299.

[6]See Reuben Gronau, "The Effect of Children on the Housewife's Value of Time," in T. W. Schultz, ed., *Economic Approaches to Fertility*, pp. S168–S199.

THE BIRTH RATE HAS DROPPED SIGNIFICANTLY.

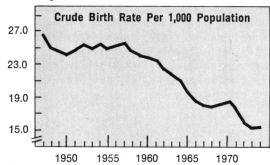

Percentage

Crude Birth Rate Per 1,000 Population

Source: Statistical Abstract of the U. S. & U. S. Department of Commerce, Current Population Reports P-60 Series.

the same individuals who "demand" their "services"—namely, their parents. Having a child is not a perfectly predictable event, however, so that parents cannot expect to be completely successful in matching their "supplies" and "demands" for satisfaction from children. But couples are not completely at the mercy of chance in supplying children. They can exercise some control over the likelihood of having a child.

Trying to increase or reduce the chances of having a child is typically a costly activity. Many couples spend both time and money on family planning. Other kinds of costs may also be involved, such as any expectation of impaired physical health or any conflict with religious beliefs. Couples are willing to bear some of these costs to reduce the chances of having an unplanned child.

Some couples may be more efficient at family planning than others, however. In particular, better-educated couples may be able to reduce the chances of having an unplanned child more efficiently than the less-educated. Researchers have developed evidence which supports this claim. Some have argued that this finding simply reflects the fact that better-educated couples want fewer children (the demand side) and hence have a greater incentive to plan family size more effectively. At least one study has taken the desired number of children into account as a factor in determining family size, and it still remains true that better-educated couples are more effective at family planning.[7]

[7]See Robert T. Michael, "Education and the Derived Demand for Children," in T. W. Schultz, ed., *Economic Approaches to Fertility*, pp. S128–S164.

Within the context of the "household model" approach to family size, then, education clearly plays a leading role in contributing toward an explanation of birth rates. Since it affects both the demand and supply of children, it exerts a clear influence on the "price" of children which has been increasing over time. The notion that the "price" of children is important for predicting family size and population growth is a key one. It differs sharply from past thinking which assigned a role only to income when considering the impact of economic variables on population growth. Once prices are taken into consideration, the outlook for the "human condition" stands at considerable variance with the well-known Malthusian view.

THE LONG-RUN IMPLICATIONS OF THE "HOUSEHOLD MODEL" OF FAMILY SIZE: DOOMSDAY OR PROSPERITY?

Almost all "theories" of population behavior suggest that at some point growth in the number of people on our planet will come to a halt. Many thinkers are at odds, however, about the likely condition of the world once birth rates achieve rough congruence with death rates to produce what demographers call a "population equilibrium." Malthus's own conclusion was straightforward and depressing. Calamity and misery will characterize the human condition in population equilibrium. Recently, the Malthusian outlook appears to be making more and more converts (see Box 1).

The economic approach to fertility outlined in the "household model" yields a different and more optimistic answer about mankind's future. It suggests that population equilibrium is compatible with high living standards and a prosperous human condition. Prosperity prevails over calamity mainly because the "household model" visualizes a different set of factors underlying a decline in birth rates than the Malthusian approach. Malthus and his followers see increases in the relative prices of the *services of natural resources* as the key factor accounting for a leveling off of population growth. Land or energy prices become so high that families can no longer afford to feed or house additional children. According to the "household model" approach, however, an increase in the relative price of *human time* is the driving force which eventually brings worldwide birth rates in line with death rates.

587

POPULATION AND CALAMITY: THE MALTHUSIAN VIEW

Social and natural scientists as well as mathematicians have long been intrigued by the implications of continuously growing numbers of people competing for living space on a finite planet. Thomas Malthus (in essays published in 1798 and 1830) contended that population growth sails along without bound as long as wages remain above the level required for subsistence. While the sum total of people grows and grows, the quantity of land is essentially fixed. Hence, increasing demands for food require that farmers turn to less and less fertile land. These inferior fields yield less and less output per acre (an example of the "law of diminishing returns"). As population doubles and redoubles, the earth is in effect halved until it shrinks so much that food production falls below the level necessary to sustain life. According to Malthus, population growth is eventually held in check by starvation and malnutrition, and hence misery and want characterize the human condition.

Except for incidents isolated in time and space, the Malthusian prediction of calamity has gone unfulfilled. Indeed, during the last 200 years living standards have *risen* sharply rather than fallen. Technological improvement in agricultural production is generally recognized as the providential savior which continuously redeems mankind from a Malthusian hell. Recently, however, debate has resurfaced concerning the outlook for future growth and prosperity, *despite projected advancements in technological wizardry*. In particular, a group of scientists and mathematicians has constructed a computerized "model" of the world economy. They employ a system of mathematical equations to predict future economic activity and population growth. Their conclusion is that continued economic growth is impossible. The earth's natural resources will soon be exhausted, they contend, and increased industrial activity will shortly strangle us in pollution. Furthermore, increasing population will eventually outrun the world's capacity to produce food, and famine will result. Because of the nature of the suggested interaction between depleted resources, pollution, industrial production and population growth, technological innovation cannot prevent or even long forestall the advent of doomsday. These researchers conclude that setting explicit limits on growth in capital (factories, trucks, machines, and the like) and population represents the only means of preventing the eventual realization of the Malthusian forecast.

The conclusions of any mathematical model, however, are only as strong as its weakest equation. One area where the analysis of the neo-Malthusians (as well as Malthus himself) can be challenged concerns the relationship between population growth and economic variables. Malthusians suggest that income is the only relevant economic variable for explaining and predicting fertility and population growth. They fail to consider the impact of *prices*—in particular the "price" of children—on parents reproductive behavior. The household model approach to fertility—which emphasizes the role of the "price" of children (and its relation to the price of time)—yields a different and more optimistic picture of the future.

Procreation is limited in this scenario by the high price (opportunity cost) of children themselves.

Since no amount of technological virtuosity can squeeze more than 24 hours out of a day, time can be considered the ultimate economic resource constraint. Indeed, the *present scarcity* of time relative to other resources is reflected in long-run changes in relative prices. In the U. S., for example, wages adjusted for inflation—a rough measure of the price of time—have moved sharply upwards since the Great Depression (see Chart 2). In fact, total real compensation per hour at work in manufacturing increased between 1929 and 1970 more than *four times* as much as did the rent paid for the services of farmland in the U.S. As time becomes increasingly more expensive, economic logic dictates that households and firms will substitute material goods for human time and engage in less time-intensive activities. If these trends continue on a worldwide basis (see Box 2 on the less-developed economies), the high price of time may become the basic constraint which determines the upper limit of economic growth and population increases.[8] The basic logic is simple. Time is fixed in supply and is becoming more and more expen-

[8]For some discussion about the reasons for the increasing value of time, see T. W. Schultz, "The Increasing Economic Value of Human Time," *American Journal of Agricultural Economics* 54 (1972): 843–50.

sive. Yet consumption takes time. Hence, eventually it is no longer "worth it" to add to the production stream because no time is available to consume the benefits. But the high price of time guarantees—indeed is synonymous with—continued prosperity once growth in production and population ends.

SUMMING UP

The "household model" represents an economic approach to family size, an issue economists in the past have considered outside their analytical domain. While it does not pretend that economics has all the answers, it does suggest that students of population growth may err in their explana-

---

BOX 2

Can Economists Apply Their Fertility Approach to the Less-Developed Countries?

The optimistic outlook for the household model for mankind's future presumes that the relative price of time will continue to rise and that this approach is a useful analytical tool for predicting future population behavior. Some researchers have questioned the validity of this economic approach, particularly as it applies to the less-developed countries (LDCs). In these economies, human time is cheap and women have relatively few opportunities to earn income outside the home. In addition, life expectancy is lower, infant mortality higher, and the availability of family planning techniques (including information about them) is less widespread and hence more costly than in developed economies. The nature of the benefits of children may also differ in LDCs. In particular, more parents may invest in children with a view toward having their offspring support them in old age. This *pension motive* for having children undoubtedly bulks larger in childbearing decisions in less-developed economies where governments have yet to devise public retirement programs (such as Social Security in the U.S.) and where capital markets are not well suited to private pension savings.

None of these differences in the overall economic environment rules out the application of the "household model" to family size decisions in less-developed economies *in principle*. Rather, they require that the mode of analysis be revised to make it more relevant to economies with different characteristics than those of developed economies.* This, of course, does not *guarantee* that this overall approach will successfully explain and predict family size in LDCs. That is for empirical testing to decide, and such tests are just beginning to be undertaken.

At the same time, there is little evidence that the Malthusian approach is best fitted for the study of family size in LDCs. Per capita income is in general not falling in these countries. In addition, there are appreciable gains in living standards which are reflected in improved health conditions and longer life expectancy. Moreover, birth rates are falling in a number of LDCs.

None of this is to suggest that LDCs or even some developed economies do not have a population "problem." In fact, an economic approach to family size clarifies the nature of an overpopulation problem and suggests what may be required by way of a solution. The problem, simply stated, is "too many people" relative to some "desired" population from the point of view of society (as perceived by some agent of society—the government or a planning agency). Such a problem could stem from parents ending up with more children than they want or it may reflect that couples demand more children than is socially desirable. In reality, both factors no doubt play a role. This means, however, that policies designed to reduce the cost of family planning (by devising inexpensive and morally acceptable family planning methods, for example) cannot guarantee a solution to an overpopulation problem. Modern family planning methods only make it easier to control family size. They do not reduce the desired size of the family. To accomplish this, the government must either alter the incentives for childbearing (by changing the "price" or rate of return on children) or directly curtail the freedom of some or all families to choose the number of children they desire. Pills and propaganda are not enough to curb overpopulation, as the economic approach to family size makes clear.

---

*For an analysis in this vein, see Philip A. Neher, "Peasants, Procreation, and Pensions," *American Economic Review* 61 (1971): 380–89.

CHART 2

THE VALUE OF TIME SHOWS A SHARP UPWARD TREND OVER THE LONG RUN IN THE U. S.

Dollars/hour

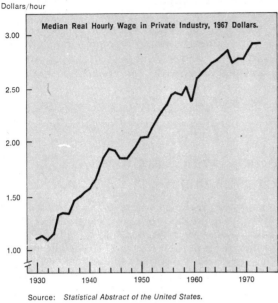

Median Real Hourly Wage in Private Industry, 1967 Dollars.

Source: *Statistical Abstract of the United States.*

economic view also clarifies the nature of the several channels through which changes in the average level of education affect the rate of procreation. Finally, the economic approach foresees a future for mankind which stands at considerable variance with the well-known Malthusian prophecy of gloom and doom. Although some remain skeptical about the "household model" approach, the evidence accumulated thus far seems sufficiently favorable for policymakers to take account of the issues raised in an economic approach when designing population programs. In particular, assessments of the impact of various policies on the "price" of children would seem desirable. Finally, the optimistic conclusions of the "household model" about mankind's destiny should not be taken as a signal for complacency in the face of some obvious population problems in many parts of the world. Economists study only a part of the large puzzle known as human nature. Hence, the contributions of the other social sciences must also be taken into consideration in designing policies. The "household model" approach indeed tells us that doomsday is not the inevitable natural legacy of mankind. But from this we should not conjecture that the only other feasible outcome is prosperity and bliss.

tions and predictions if they neglect the impact of relative price changes on family behavior. In particular, changes in the value of time are likely to exert an influence on birth rates over time and across families. This

SELECTED READINGS

Becker, Gary S. "An Economic Approach to Fertility." in *Demographic and Economic Change in Developed Countries*. National Bureau Conference Series 11. Princeton, N.J.: Princeton University Press, 1960.

DeTray, Dennis N. "Child Quality and the Demand for Children." *Journal of Political Economy* 81, No. 2, supplement (1973): S70–S95.

Gronau, Reuben. "The Effect of Children on the Housewife's Value of Time." *Journal of Political Economy* 81, No. 2, supplement (1973): S168–S199.

Leibowitz, Arleen. "Home Investments in Children." *Journal of Political Economy* 82, No. 2, supplement (1974): S111–S131.

Michael, Robert T. "Education and the Derived Demand for Children." *Journal of Political Economy* 81, No. 2, supplement (1973): S128–S164.

Schultz, Theodore W. "Population Equilibrium: The High Value of Human Time." *Journal of Political Economy* 82, No. 2, supplement (1974): S2–S10.

———. "The Value of Children: An Economic Perspective." *Journal of Political Economy* 81, No. 2, supplement (1973): S2–S13.

Willis, Robert J. "A New Approach to the Economic Theory of Fertility Behavior." *Journal of Political Economy* 81, No. 2, supplement (1973): S14–S64.

Value Systems in Conflict: Economics Versus Ecology

Hazel Henderson

The author calls for an advance in the shared goal of both economists and ecologists, namely a civilized national dialogue concerning the substantive issues. Profits needs redefining. Economic growth requires re-examination. If corporations are to survive the sea changes of the seventies, they will need to restructure themselves along more participatory and democratic lines. The challenge for business economists is to develop new conceptual frameworks, analytical tools and computer models to integrate new variables, such as psychology, physiology, zoology, and anthropology.

I T WOULD be redundant for me to review the various new social manifestations of what has come to be known as "the movement for corporate responsibility". You are all quite familiar with the social and environmental questions now finding their way into corporate proxies, with the annual meeting activists and the many advocates of consumer and environmental protection who attempt to negotiate directly with corporations for the redress of old and newly-perceived grievances.

I am sure that it is equally unnecesary for me to speculate on the reasons for all this new activity. Theories abound. Some cite the speedup of technological change and its disruption of old patterns, combined with a concomitant lag in response time of institutions and political machinery. The corporate responsibility activists believe that the corporation has now become the dominant institution in our society, shaping our culture via advertising, and manipulating political power through lobbying, campaign contributions and its pervasive influence over regulatory agency policies and personnel. These activists, least of all, believe in the existence of a corporate conscience, as their tactics clearly show. Rather they see the cor-

poration as a mindless, amoeba-like system, programmed by its structure and goals to behave in a largely predetermined fashion. In fact, their analysis is remarkably similar to that of Prof. Milton Friedman; that in a private property, free enterprise system, management is still basically the agent of the stockholders and has no right to make decisions of a social nature. In their radically different conclusion, however, the corporate activists believe that only massive public pressure and direct petitioning of the stockholders themselves, can bring about the reformulation of the corporate mandate. At the same time, many others would agree with Prof. Neil Jacoby of the University of California, that "Americans have recently demanded social improvements beyond the capacity of this or any other society to produce." Jacoby maintains that a social problem may be defined as a gap between society's expectation of social conditions and the present social realities.

Of course, there is some truth to all of these contentions, and rather than taking an adversary posture, I would like to share some of my thoughts with you on how we as a society can best mediate our current conflicts, whether they concern the differences in our subjective sets of assumptions and values, or the objective allocations of power and resources in the real world.

Economists and Ecologists

If we view the current conflicts as clashes between differing value systems; for instance, the value assumptions underlying the discipline of economics versus the totally different value systems implicit in the study of ecology, then we may also be able to advance the shared goal of both economists and ecologists: namely a civilized national dialogue concerning the substantive issues. Much of the heat in the current conflicts between us is generated because we fail to explore each others assumptions before we throw the first punch. One set of assumptions underlying economics which ecologists find inconceivable, is the concept that one can construct theoretical models and

---

Hazel Henderson, "Value Systems in Conflict: Economics vs Ecology." *Business Economics,* January 1972, pp. 18–23. Reprinted with permission of the author and the publisher.

simulations of human activities, economic configurations, behaviour of markets or flows of materials and resources, while omitting variables and parameters which ecologists believe are dominant. Conversely, the ecologists begin with the assumption that the only adequate conceptual model on which to hang sub-system simulations, such as those used by economists, is the kind of macro-model of social, technical and natural system interactions on a planetary scale recently attempted by Prof. Jay W. Forrester of the Massachusetts Institute of Technology and described in his new book *World Dynamics*. Or to put it in a nutshell: ecologists see economics as a sub-set of ecology, while economists see ecology as a sub-set of economics! Or to put it another way: economists favor analysis while ecologists prefer synthesis.

Economists, therefore, tend to view ecological questions as a set of irritating but minor variables, which sooner or later, must be accommodated in their models. Naturally, out of this viewpoint grows the conviction that it is not necessary to change the basic model, but merely to incorporate this sudden explosion of new variables, and factor in their effects. Economists have had considerable experience over the years in the handling of new variables. Historically, economics has been forced to embrace ever more variables in its analyses, whether the activities of governments, the vagaries of international trade and currency, the growing power of labor unions, to the recent rise of consumerism and the movements for racial and sexual equality. As each of these formerly minor variables became more dominant, it forced a restructuring and expansion of the theoretical models underlying the economic discipline. I submit that the new ecological variables are so far reaching in their implications that they will require a major restructuring of current economic theories.

Redefining Profit

One of the first concepts that needs redefinition is that of "profit." Economists will have to face the difficult question of whether what we in this country call "profit" and what state-controlled economies call "economic expansion" has not in the past been won at the expense of an equal but unrecorded debit entry in some social or environmental ledger? A graphic telescoping of this issue is visible in Japan's rapid economic expansion and its accompanying environmental chaos. A new definition of profit would reformulate inputs into such indicators as the Gross National Product, and lead to refinement of other measures of well-being, such as social and political indicators. One of the results of such a reformulation of our national economic data might have been a very different set of economic proposals than those put forward by President Nixon to ameliorate our current stagnation, unemployment and inflation. From an ecological viewpoint, our economy is grievously distorted if it must have an adrenalin shot to boost production of automobiles, which have already saturated the nation and produced an incredible backwash of diseconomies, including decaying and abandoned inner cities, 50,000 annual traffic fatalities, an overburdened legal system, some 60% of all our air pollution, and the sacrifice of millions of square miles of arable land to a highway system that is the most costly public works project undertaken by any culture since the building of the Pyramids and the Great Wall of China.

It is also instructive to discover that in spite of the heavy environmental price of two provisions of the President's economic package—the repeal of the 7% excise tax on autos and the acceleration of investment tax credit—to date, the Treasury Department has not released for public discussion the environmental impact statements required under Section 102(2)(c) of the National Environmental Policy Act of 1970. Environmentalists would agree with labor and minority groups that economic stimulation should not trickle down from corporations, but rather "trickle up" from some form of consumer credits to expand purchasing; and that human service programs, which tend to be environmentally benign, should have been extended; such as more day-care centers, health clinics, parks and public improvements, mass-transit facilities, schools and adult education and retraining. Similarly, a national minimum, income program is more needed than ever, since it creates purchasing power for instant spending on unmet needs, such as clothing and food, and also permits the poor greater mobility to seek opportunity in uncrowded areas, thereby relieving the overburdened biosystems of our cities. In addition, we environmentalists have just learned a new lesson, heeded long ago by labor: we must hire our own economists to develop more ecologically-desirable programs to compete with such new retreads of the familiar Eisenhower Administration campaign for prosperity and its slogan "You Auto Buy Now". In fact, we shall generate public pressure to make sure that in future, the President's Council of Economic Advisors includes in its membership an environmental economist as well as a labor economist, a minority bloc economist and a consumer economist.

Economic Growth Re-Examined

Another concept requiring re-examination is that of economic growth itself. Ever since Malthus stated his theories some 150 years ago that food supply would eventually force reduction of population, we have debated this issue. Now, in addition to Malthus' correct indentification of food supply, ecologists bring new inhibiting factors into the consideration of exponential growth. They include depletion of natural resources, pollution, and, in the opinion of many, capital investment itself, which leads to ever faster depletion of resources and increase of pollution. So we must face the implications of continued economic growth in a closed planetary system. Prof. Jay Forrester states flatly in *World Dynamics* that it is not a question of whether growth will cease, but rather whether the coming transition to equilibrium will occur traumatically or with some measure of human intervention, which may head off some of the most tragic outcomes. Indeed, Forrester believes that with all its discontents, we are now living in the planet's "Golden Age" and that we must begin to reduce our more unrealistic expectations.

How will economists respond to all this talk of the "steady state society", zero population growth and a "homeostatic" social system? As one commentator put it "formerly Americans have been urged to hitch their wagon to a star—now they must learn to hitch their star to a wagon." Already some of the euphoria of the fifties over imminent abundance is being reassessed, along with the promise that an ever-bigger pie to share would lead to greater equality. Economists such as Kenneth Boulding, Kenneth Galbraith, Barbara Ward and Ezra Mishan are all wrestling with concepts of economic equilibrium within a closed planetary system. One resulting conceptual tool developed by Mishan which may prove increasingly relevant is that of amenity rights, which he claims should share equal status in law and custom with property rights, with which they often conflict. Another stimulating concept is advanced by ecologist-engineer Prof. Howard T. Odum in his new book, *Environment Power and Society*. Odum suggests that money is no longer an adequate metaphor to describe accurately our various resource allocations and human transactions. The money metaphor needs to be augmented by a system of energy accounting and simulation which could embrace descriptions of how underlying energy/matter exchanges operate and how hidden energy subsidies or outflows obscure or prevent accurate accounting of the real costs, benefits and trade-offs in human activities.

Gloomy Scenarios

But undoubtedly, the most intellectually stimulating set of concepts put forth in support of the equilibrium economy are embodied in Jay Forrester's planetary models and their gloomy scenarios in *World Dynamics*. Some of the shattering implications to current economic assumptions are 1.) There may be no realistic hope that presently under-developed countries will ever reach the standards of living enjoyed by present industrialized nations, 2.) Industrialization may be a more fundamentally disturbing force in world ecology than population, 3.) A society with a high level of industrialization may be non-sustainable and self-extinguishing, 4.) From the perspective of a hundred years hence, the present efforts of under-developed countries may be unwise, because they may now be closer to the ultimate equilibrium with the environment, and in better condition for surviving the forthcoming worldwide pressures than industrialized nations (it is interesting to note that Odum's energy-accounting simulations lead him to the same conclusion). In assessing outcomes of his models, Forrester fears that within the next century man may face formerly externalized costs become internalized and added to the market price of products. This will alter markets and production patterns while it more rationally assigns to the consumer, rather than the taxpayer, the full social and environmental costs of production. For instance, if current promotional rates for electricity are re-structured and include environmental costs, the aluminum industry, which is based on low-cost electricity, would also change. One outcome might be the disappearance of the throwaway aluminum can; another might be wholesale replacement of aluminum in fabricating hundreds of products. Another obvious consequence of restructuring the economy along such lines would be the increasing cost of high-energy and matter input goods, and their gradual replacement by lower energy/matter input goods, and the continued growth of services in the public and private sectors that is already evident. All of this may be initially inflationary while the readjustments and reallocations of resources are occuring, and may cause many American products to face even stiffer competition in world markets. However, this is contested by Prof. James B. Quinn of Amos Tuck Business School writing in *Harvard Business Review* (Sept.-Oct., 1971). He believes that the new environmental costs will eventually be sold as "value added" in products: that new pollution control processes will result in raw materials savings, and that while foreign competition may initially cause some disruption, this problem may be offset by rising ecological wareness in other nations, added exports from a growing domestic pollution control industry, as well as other factors.

The New Ballgame

If this is going to be the new corporate ballgame, will there be any hope at all for profits? I believe there will, and that they can be made in three general areas: 1.) Better energy-conversion ratios. For example, we will no longer be able to afford the thermal inefficiencies of the current generation of light-water nuclear fission reactors or the internal combustion engine, because it is becoming clear that adding pollution-control equipment, such as precipitators and cooling towers or catalytic converters on cars, may on a total energy basis leave us with a trade-off. Only by developing inherently more efficient energy converting systems, such as fuel cells or nuclear fusion can we hope to achieve actual economy and environmental benefit. 2.) Better resource management and rehabilitation. Production loops must be closed by recycling, but probably not in the current mode of recycling of bottles and cans, because it does not constitute a valid negative feedback loop for the container industry and permits them to continue externalizing the severe costs of collection. (Only an energy simulation à la Howard Odum could assess the relative costs and benefits in cleaning and refilling containers versus their destruction and refabrication). 3.) Better and more efficient "market failure research" into those areas where individual consumer choice is inoperative unless it is aggregated, which could provide more flexible and rapid corporate response to social change and indicate where unmet and potentially profitable needs exist in the public sector. This in turn, will require new marketing methodologies which I shall touch on later.

And lastly, it also seems probable that if corporations are to survive the sea changes of the seventies, they will need to restructure themselves along more participatory and democratic lines, so as to increase their own sensitivity to new forces and in accordance with the theories of human motivation of the behavioral scientists such as Maslow, Argyris, Herzberg, McGregor, et al., who have already undermined yet another outworn theoretical model: "homo economicus." A recent survey conducted by *Harvard Business Review* indicates how far corporate democratization has come, particularly in increasing employees' voices in many management decisions, even on selecting candidates for promotion by polling of workers. Also more companies are reaping benefits in productivity and reduced labor strife through various devices for cutting employees in on "a piece of the action" after the style of Louis O. Kelso's Second Income Plan Trusts, which permit corporations to finance new capital equipment with tax-deductible dollars, while apportioning out newly-issued shares representing the expansion to its employees without payroll deductions. Another method of increasing employee identification with the enterprise are the worker's councils at every level within the company, as described by Robert Dahl in his new book *After The Revolution*, as well as other proposals for adding representatives of labor to top management circles and the board of directors. Many variations on this kind of worker participation are well established

in West Germany and due for adoption shortly in Great Britain, Norway, Holland and Sweden.

Negotiating Blocs

In addition, I expect to see other corporate publics, particularly stockholders, consumers, as well as the involuntary consumers of its environmental and other neighborhood effects, organize themselves into coherent negotiating blocs. I expect to see them engage in annual bargaining with corporations, just as labor unions do today and I believe that formalizing such communication channels will civilize and rationalize many of the current ad hoc tactics these forces must now employ in their efforts to change corporate behavior. I also expect to see a restructuring of the board of directors so that it includes representatives of key interest groups, such as consumers, minorities, environmentalists, and others, so that its decision-making can be irrigated beforehand by the same value conflicts it will encounter in the larger society, which will in turn provide valuable market feedforward on social aspirations.

If the ecological view of the future is valid there will be continuing changes in life-styles and consumption patterns. Because external freedoms will become even more circumscribed as population densities increase and resources are depleted, consumers will, and already are, seeking greater psychological freedom and inner space. Leisure activities dependent on high-energy/matter input goods such as hot-rodding and snow-mobiling will give ground to such environmentally-benign activities as hiking, biking, jogging, mountain-climbing, painting, ceramics and handicrafts.

Leisure Life-Styles

One of the most obvious signs of this growing dichotomy in leisure life-styles is the new fight shaping up over interpretation of the Federal Communications Commission's Fairness Doctrine, which has been successfully reinterpreted by environmentalists' litigation so that it now must include controversial products, such as "muscle cars", by giving free air time to environmentalists to extol the virtues of doing without cars or pursuing other forms of recreation. The Fairness Doctrine may now also be invoked to provide equal time to oppose the ads of high-phosphate detergents or heavily-sweetened, nutritionally depleted cereals pushed on children's television programs. It is even possible to speculate that the "back to the land" and the cooperative living, producing and consuming patterns of the commune, and even the new acceptance of non-reproduction oriented sex roles portrayed by the women's movement and gay liberation, are expressions of the innate understanding of the coming population-environment squeeze. As the need to "ephemeralize" our modes of living increases we will probably institutionalize teaching of the joys of meditation and re-training of the senses so as to maximize pleasurable physical sensations of all kinds. Likewise our cities may re-orient themselves away from production, consumption and marketing towards the festival cities of the ancient cultures of pre-Columbian Central America. Similarly, comunications would become the more important side of the coin of human interaction, while the high-energy input transportation side would decrease. This could mean decentralizing of population into smaller, organic-sized communities, managed locally by cable-TV based "electronic town meetings" and all linked into nationhood by mass-media. Likewise, this would lead to decentralizing corporations, both by breaking up their size and some functions as we begin to explore the growing phenomena of "dis-economies of scale." Smaller production units, while somewhat more costly, can be offset by lower transportation and distribution, as well as inventory costs.

Low Consumption Lifestyles

All of this would not necessarily mean a wholesale return to nature or a rejection of technology, because our current population size alone precludes this course. The truly-committed environmentalist is no Luddite. They are merely experimenting with low-consumption lifestyles to see how well they can cope when the crunch comes. Even a cursory reading of their "survival manuals", such as *The Whole Earth Catalog* and *Radical Software* makes this clear. Rather, the environmentalists are seeking an end to the gross, wasteful, "meat-axe" technology which characterizes the receding industrial age. Instead, they seek a second-generation technology, more refined, miniaturized and organic, or what Buckminster Fuller calls "ephemeralization," or doing more with less, and Dr. Carl Madden has called "negentropic industrial activity." Even more exciting is the move toward developing a "counter-technology," particularly using computers and mass-communications, such as TV, not in their centralized and monolithic modes as heretofore, but to rewire the individual citizen back into the central nervous system of the body-politic. Just as information technology can be used to manipulate people's buying habits or intimidate them politically by government surveillance and data-banks; so it can be used for electronic town meetings, instantaneous polling and eventually voting in referenda, as the very hardware of our participatory democracy.

The basic quarrel that environmentalists have with corporations is that their size, power and productive capabilities have insulated them from corrective feedback. They have been allowed to forget the golden rule of marketing: that of accurately assessing real consumer needs and then creating products designed to fill them. Too often corporate marketing men and advertising agencies dream up new products based more on the corporation's capabilities and buttressed by need-oriented market surveys than on real consumer demand, and then sell them with high-powered promotion. We need only look at the proliferation of drugs and toiletries where the packaging and promotion represent more value than the product, and that in some cases, such as marketing of analgesics, it has become necessary to create an imaginary disease like "the Blahs" in order to push the product.

These anomalies occur when the production system has lost adaptive response to negative feedback loops. Meanwhile real unmet needs, many in the public sector, might well become coherently aggregated with a little corporate support of the necessary political activities of citizens groups and other potential consumers working to underpin them with government expenditures. Only these grass-roots coalitions of potential consumers can create enough genuine political steam to capitalize new economic activities. And yet many companies, blind to these new market opportunities, continue to lobby and oppose demands for clean air or mass-transit, while continuing to identify with past vested interests in old, rapidly-saturating markets.

Public Sector Marketing

If corporations can lobby to procure government contracts for military and space products, they can also learn the methodology of the new multi-stage public-sector marketing. First, contact must be established and maintained with citizen, consumer and environmental groups so as to better assess their unmet needs and new expectations, and their design preferences for such public goods as mass-transit systems determined. Then the size and shape of the total market must be measured by extensive polling and interviewing, using additional monitoring of little magazines and underground media to flag new modes of consciousness that will change life styles and expectations. Sophisticated new technology for social choice is now in the experimental stage which has already proved capable of increasing citizens' motivation and participation in articulating public issues, assessing options and formulating community goals and then analyzing and profiling the resulting feedback. This process of collecting "market failure feedback" is described in detail in any forthcoming article in the MBA magazine. Finally, the corporation can use its marketing men to sell these potential groups of consumers on the merits of their product line and join with them in lobbying efforts to pass the legislation or bond issues necessary to create the public-sector markets for these big-ticket items. This was the way the pollution control market developed, and the fledgeling companies in the field put their marketing dollars together to back a trade association program of providing speakers and film strips to inform civic groups of the technology available for the clean-up, and raise enthusiasm for the needed bond issues. The goal of market failure research is to keep producing corporations informed of these social shifts in closer to real time so that new product development can be more rationally based on better information feedforward, and costly response time lags can be reduced. Surely such speeded information flows from consumers to producers and from citizens to governments can only improve the flexibility and competitiveness of our domestic economy.

Organic Technology

In world markets, it is also possible to imagine this kind of organic technological economy as more in tune with the real needs and aspirations of other less-developed nations, as well as our own poorer citizens. If they cannot realistically aspire to our current wasteful consumption patterns, at least such modified life-styles advocated by ecologists provide a more attainable model for emulation. For example, it may be more ecologically and humanly desirable for greater numbers of poor people to own quiet, non-polluting bicycles which don't need costly highways, or individual solar energy heating and cooking devices; than for us to continue flaunting our less attainable, polluting automobiles and power plants. It is widely claimed that the U.S. with 6 percent of the world's population, is already consuming some 40 percent of its non-renewable resources and creating 50 percent of all pollution. We are also told that if everyone enjoyed the living standard of Americans, the planet would have already reached its upper thermodynamic and pollution limits.

In the last analysis, whether you believe or reject this depends on your own particular vantage point within our national sub-system, itself within a labyrinth of sub-systems within the macro-system. And it depends on the inclusiveness of your own mental model of the world system. Does this model include the vantage point of the zoologist, who views the present configuration of life forms, including that late arrival, man, through countless eons of evolutionary selection and adaptation. Does your model include the perspective of the anthropologist, who sees our culture and economic assumptions as but a narrow, fleeting experiment in the vast saga of human interaction? Does it include the view from psychology and physiology which sees the tragic flaws in man's poorly integrated instincts and neo-cortex and his limited range of physical adaptability? These are some of the dimensions of the new variables explosion. Operating managers of our corporations look to you business economists as their oracles. The new challenge that you face is developing new conceptual frameworks, analytical tools and computer models to integrate these variables, while breaking the news gently to management that they must bring their wild expectations more into line with reality. You must help them face the humbling question "Can man evolve and adapt his value system to the requirements of an interdependent world society which must operate in equilibrium on a finite planet?"

If the goal of evolution is survival, then this goal must also be the homeostatic regulation of all sub-systems for the optimal functioning and maintenance of the macro-system. Barbara Ward and Kenneth Boulding call it the space-ship economy. Jay Forrester adds his reminder that the narrow, short-term goals of sub-systems are generally in conflict with the long-term goals of optimizing the macro-system. Biologist Garret Hardin calls it "the Tragedy of the Common." And theologian Rheinhold Neibuhr summed it all up in his concept of that which we call God as, simply, "the ultimate perspective."

Environmental Law
and Occupational Health

By NORMAN J. WOOD

Professor of Economics, University of Georgia.

OVER 80 MILLION American men and women spend a quarter of their lives in their place of work. The deterioration in health which occurs as a result of exposure to hazards in the workplace is not well documented because, until recently, there has been no mandatory national reporting system for occupational illnesses, and the few state reporting systems in existence were incomplete and lacked uniformity. While the incidence of occupational disease is not known, recent estimates indicate at least 390,000 new cases of disabling occupational illness each year.[1] Based on limited analysis of mortality in several industries, there may be as many as 100,000 deaths per year from occupationally caused disease.[2] While disabling job injuries occur five times more frequently, the resulting annual mortality rate is only one-seventh of that for occupational diseases.[3]

Health deterioration at the workplace results from a multitude of hazards and manifests itself in a variety of forms. These range from the overt, classic, occupational diseases such as lead and mercury poisoning, to the insidious, delayed effects of exposure to noise that causes partial or total hearing loss and to dusts that produce fibrosis of the lungs. Even beyond these effects, there is the likelihood that exposure to some occupational hazards will cause, promote, or contribute to the development of cancer, hasten the onset of certain degenerative diseases, or shorten the life span.

Until 1970, the responsibility for the regulation of health and safety in industry was vested in the states. A few states, notably New York, Pennsylvania, and California, had established programs that were given qualified approval by health and safety experts. Many others either had legislation which covered only particular industries or devoted insufficient resources to enforce regulations. A number of

[1] *Executive Office of the President, The President's Report on Occupational Safety and Health* for 1971, 1972 and 1973 (U. S. Government Printing Office, Washington, D. C.).

[2] *Ibid.*

[3] *National Safety Council Accident Facts*, 18 (1972).

states had no law at all until recently. Texas established its first occupational safety statute in 1967. In many states, safety inspectors were chosen for political allegiance rather than professional experience. Occupational health was often misunderstood or ignored completely.

Although health professionals were well aware of the inadequacy of state regulation, the problem was largely ignored by the federal government until recently. The enactment of the Occupational Safety and Health Act in 1970 marked the beginning of federal concern for the harmful effects of the more than 25,000 toxic substances used in the work environment. The Act states that it is the policy of the government "to assure as far as possible every working man and woman in the nation safe and healthful working conditions."

This policy is to be carried out by imposing on each employer two major duties. First, he is to furnish "employment and a place of employment which are free from recognized hazards that are causing or are likely to cause death or serious physical harm to his employees;" and, secondly, to "comply with occupational safety and health standards promulgated under this act."

The standards to be promulgated dealing with toxic materials or harmful physical agents are to be such that each "most adequately assures, to the extent feasible . . . that no employee will suffer material impairment of health or functional capacity even if such employee has regular exposure to the hazard dealt with by such standard for the period of his working life."

The Act applies to all business firms affecting interstate commerce. The only exemptions are employers covered by another federal safety program (e. g. mining companies), state and local government employees, and enterprises operated solely by members of a family.[4] The Act covers over five million establishments employing more than 60 million workers.[5] Since the law became operative in April 1971, compliance officers from the Occupational Safety and Health Administration have made more than 159,000 inspections, issued 106,000 citations alleging over 549,000 violations, and proposed penalties totaling $13.7 million.[6]

In the four years since the Act became law, there has been persistent criticism of the law and its enforcement.[7] Labor union representatives charge that it has been weak and ineffective in protecting employees from exposure to chemical health hazards and job injury. Businessmen assert that the Occupational Safety and Health Administration's (OSHA) standards are vague and difficult to understand, and are too costly for small business firms.[8] A former Assistant Secretary of Labor for OSHA (the title of the agency's head) reacted to these criticisms by telling a congressional committee that "since the criticism of the OSHA program is about equal from all sides, we are probably steering the right course toward accomplishing the objectives

---

[4] While the act defines "employer" in terms excluding the federal government, it also requires, in Sec. 19(a), the head of each federal agency to establish a safety and health program that is consistent with the OSHA program.

[5] *Monthly Labor Review*, at 14 (Vol. 95, No. 3, March 1972).

[6] President's Report, cited in footnote 1.

[7] Steiger, W. A., "OSHA, Four Years Later," LABOR LAW JOURNAL at 723 (Vol. 25, No. 12, December 1974). Congressman Steiger was co-author of the Occupational Safety and Health Act of 1970.

[8] *Wall Street Journal*, August 20, 1974, pp. 1, 33.

of the Act."[9] Another possible conclusion might be that OSHA is doing very little that is right.

The concerns of those affected by the Act indicates the need to examine the effects of the law and its enforcement on industrial health hazards present in the work environment. After reviewing the legislative background and the statutory mandate for government action, this paper will consider three aspects of the government's application of the 1970 Act to industrial health hazards: the establishment of health standards; the impact of state health plans; and the action labor unions are taking to improve occupational health.

Legislative Background

To appreciate the significance of the Occupational Safety and Health Act, it is necessary to go back to 1969, when serious efforts to achieve a federal health law began. At that time, the problem of black lung disease (pneumoconiosis) among coal miners had recently come to public attention, with popular estimates indicating that perhaps 100,000 miners and ex-miners had evidence of the disease. Congress reacted to this health hazard by passage of the Coal Mine Health and Safety Act of 1969, which provides for rigorous federal standards and inspections as well as for federal benefits for victims of black lung disease.[10]

The experience of the coal miners was not lost on employees in other industries. Worker concern for the factory environment was growing. The heat and noise, the dust and other contaminants that often pervaded the factory were being questioned. A 1969 study commissioned by the U. S. Department of Labor focused on the concerns of workers regarding their working conditions.[11] Employees were asked to evaluate 19 labor standards issues with regard to the frequency with which these problems occurred, their severity, and the extent to which they desired protection against these problems. The labor standards which most concerned workers were health and safety hazards, unpleasant physical working conditions, and work-related illness or injury. Inadequate income and fringe benefits ranked well behind these concerns for health and safety.

Congressional hearings on the Occupational Safety and Health Act gave workers and union representatives an opportunity to express their feelings. The major thrust of their testimony was to stress the need for protection against the unseen industrial hazards to health from air contaminants and physical agents. While a number of references were made to the dangers of accidental injury, the great bulk of the anxiety expressed by employees related to the insidious health effects of exposure to dust, fumes, gasses, chemicals, and physical agents.[12]

[9] Testimony of George C. Guenther, Assistant Secretary of Labor for Occupational Safety and Health, in *Hearings on Small Business and the Occupational Safety and Health Act of 1970*, 92d Congress, 2d Sess. (1972).

[10] This law commits the federal government to support disability benefits up to $272 a month for coal miners. *New York Times,* December 31, 1969, at 8, col. 6.

[11] Herrick, N. and R. Quinn, "The Working Conditions Survey as a Source of Social Indicators," *Monthly Labor Review,* at 15-24 (Vol. 95, No. 4, April 1971).

[12] *Hearings on Occupational Safety and Health Act of 1970 before the Subcommittee on Labor of the Senate Committee on Labor and Public Welfare 91st Congress,* and *Hearings on Occupational Safety and Health Act of 1969 before the Subcommittee on Labor of the House Committee on Education and Labor, 91st Congress.*

Much of the testimony at that time was critical of existing state procedures for regulating occupational health. Among the numerous complaints documented were the failure of state laws to provide authority for entry into plants, inadequate funding and staffing, advance notification to employers of inspection, obsolete standards, and failure to furnish reports of inspection to the affected employees.[13] Existing industry programs were characterized as creating employee awareness of safe work habits but were criticized for minimizing administrative and engineering control of workplace hazards. Few industry programs even considered the deleterious effects of toxic substances, partly because of the lengthy studies necessary to establish a correlation between a chemical and its effect on those exposed to it.[14]

While the legislative history of the act cites these failures, it also shows a congressional desire for a multi-faceted approach to the problem of job health and safety. In Senate discussion of the bill, Senator Williams of New Jersey, sponsor of the bill stated:

"Although many employers in all industries have demonstrated an exemplary degree of concern for health and safety in the workplace, their efforts are too often undercut by those who are not so concerned. Moreover, the fact is that many employers—particularly smaller ones—simply cannot make the necessary investment in health and safety, and survive competitively, unless all are compelled to do so. The competitive disadvantage of the more conscientious employer is especially evident where there is a long period

between exposure to a hazard and manifestation of an illness. In such instances, a particular employer has no economic incentive to invest in current precautions, not even in the reductions of workmen's compensation costs, because he will seldom have to pay for the consequences of his own neglect.

"Nor has state regulation proven sufficient to the need. No one has seriously disputed that only a relatively few States have modern laws relating to occupational health and safety and have devoted adequate resources to their administration and enforcement. Moreover, in a State-by-State approach, the efforts of the more vigorous states are inevitably undermined by the short-sightedness of others.

"In sum, the chemical and physical hazards which characterize modern industry are not the problem of a single employer, a single industry, nor a single state jurisdiction. The spread of industry and the mobility of the workforce combine to make the health and safety of the worker truly a national concern."[15]

In the House of Representatives, Congressman William A. Steiger of Wisconsin expressed the intent of the legislation he sponsored, which was combined with the Williams bill to create the Act:

"One of the primary purposes of the bill is to set up a mechanism by which fair and effective occupational safety and health standards can be promulgated so that the many employers and employees throughout the Nation may be guided in their attempts to establish and maintain safe and healthful work environments.

[13] *Ibid.*
[14] *Ibid.*
[15] *Subcommittee on Labor of the Senate Committee on Labor and Public Welfare, 92D*

Congress 1st Sess., Legislative History of the Occupational Health and Safety Act of 1970, at 413.

"The conference reported bill is clearly based on the premise of this House that it is with the cooperation of both employers and employees that the act can most effectively meet the challenge of reducing and perhaps eliminating most of the occupational deaths, tragic injuries, and diseases which take a large annual toll in terms of the human suffering and loss to the economy caused by these tragedies."[16]

The Statutory Mandate

The Act gives the Secretary of Labor broad authority to promulgate and enforce job safety and health standards, a function delegated to OSHA which is located within the Labor Department. The act creating OSHA upgraded HEW's long established Bureau of Occupational Safety and Health to the status of the National Institute for Occupational Safety and Health (NIOSH) and requires this agency to develop criteria and recommended standards for exposures to toxic substances and harmful physical agents, and to carry out various research and educational programs.

The Act defines an occupational safety and health standard as one "which requires conditions, or the adoption or use of one or more practices, means, methods, operations, or processes, reasonably necessary or appropriate to provide safe or healthful employment and places of employment." Because of the scope of this definition, almost any reasonable standard would appear to be permitted.

The Act provides further latitude in its description of the development of standards and the statutory criteria against which they are to be measured: "standards may, but need not be, the product of recommendations by a nationally recognized standards-producing organization, NIOSH, or a statutory advisory committee."[17] Standards are to be based on "research, demonstration, experiments, and such other information as may be appropriate." The statute thus grants to the Secretary of Labor extremely wide-ranging authority to promulgate standards—almost any finding which the Secretary finds persuasive can be the basis for a standard.

The Establishment of Standards

It is estimated that U. S. industry makes use of or generates some 25,000 toxic substances and introduces 500 to 600 new toxic substances annually.[18] OSHA has set human tolerance levels (standards) for only slightly more than 400 of these substances.[19]

The act permits three methods of standard setting. Within two years from the effective date for the act, OSHA could publish as final standards any existing national consensus standards or establish federal standards. On May 29, 1971, OSHA promulgated "Threshold Limit Values" (TLV's)—defined as the concentrations of a given substance to which most workers can be exposed in an average workday without adverse effects—for 400 toxic substances. These TLV's had been previously developed by the American Conference of Government Industrial Hygienists (ACGIH), a private group, and had been adopted as federal stan-

[16] *Ibid.* at 1216.
[17] Sec. 7(b) requires that members of advisory committees represent both employers and employees, and that the committees hold open meetings and make records of their deliberations available to the public.
[18] *General Accounting Office, Report to the Senate Committee on Labor and Public Welfare: Slow Progress Likely in Development of Standards for Toxic Substances and Harmful Physical Agents Found in Workplaces* (1973) at 16.
[19] *President's Report,* cited in footnote 1.

dards in 1969 under the Walsh-Healey Public Contracts Act.[20]

Second, OSHA may set "temporary emergency standards." Such standards are only to be promulgated if employees are exposed to "grave danger" from a hazard, and a temporary emergency standard is necessary to protect against the danger. Such a standard takes effect immediately upon publication in the Federal Register, and lasts no longer than six months.

In the *Florida Peach Growers* case,[21] the Fifth Circuit held that the requirement of "grave danger" means a "serious emergency" and the danger of "incurable, permanent, or fatal" consequences to workers. It was held by the court that the highly toxic nature of pesticides used by the workers in question did not in itself justify issuance of an emergency standard because of the slim evidence that existing safeguards were inadequate or that workers were actually being harmed by the pesticides. This decision led OSHA to become more cautious, and, subsequently, in considering the temporary emergency standard for vinyl chloride, it held a public hearing prior to promulgation of the standard.[22]

The final method by which standards are promulgated is by use of the permanent standard-setting mechanism described in Section 6(b) of the Act. This provides for, but does not require, referral of scientific issues to NIOSH, or the use of an advisory committee, or both. Members of advisory committees represent both employers and employees, must hold open meetings, and make records of their deliberations available to the public. The rulemaking procedure for the promulgation of standards is similar to informal rulemaking but with an oral hearing if requested by any interested person. To comply with the "substantial evidence" requirement set by the Act, OSHA has voluntarily structured hearing procedures more formally—allowing cross-examination, employing a qualified administrative law judge, and keeping a verbatim transcript.[23]

The role of NIOSH in producing criteria documents with standards recommendations is described in Section 20(a)(2) of the Act, and requires NIOSH "to consult with (OSHA) in order to develop specific plans for such research, demonstrations, and experiments—(to enable OSHA to meet its) responsibility for the formulation of safety and health standards under the Act." The procedures followed by NIOSH in developing a criteria document are as follows: (1) a literature search on the toxic substance or physical agent in question; (2) research to fill gaps in the data by the NIOSH staff, or by contract to outside investigators; and (3) a review of the draft of the criteria document by outside consultants, professional societies and other federal agencies prior to its final approval by the Director of NIOSH and the General Counsel of HEW.[24] Step one may typically take from six to twelve months, step two from three to five years, and step three from twelve to fourteen months.[25]

During its first four years of operation, OSHA has adopted the ACGIH

[20] Public Contracts Department of Labor, Safety and Health Standards for Federal Supply Contracts, 34 Fed. Reg. 7946 (1969).

[21] *Florida Peach Growers Ass'n. v. United States Department of Labor*, 489 F. 2d 120 (CA-5, 1974).

[22] See Fed. Reg. 12,342 (1974).

[23] Morey, R. "Mandatory Occupational Safety and Health Standards—Some Legal Problems." *Law and Contemporary Problems*, at 591 (Vol. 38, No. 4, Summer-Autumn, 1974).

[24] GAO Report, cited in footnote 18 at 24-26.

[25] *Ibid.*

consensus standards for 400 toxic substances and has issued health standards for asbestos, pesticides, vinyl chloride, and fourteen cancer-causing chemicals.[26] It is estimated that of the 25,000 toxic substances used in industry, from 1,000 to 2,000 may be highly dangerous to workers' health.[27] To make some headway in the promulgation of standards, NIOSH and OSHA began, in 1974, a 30 month, $3.5 million project to develop standards for handling an additional 400 toxic substances.[28] In keeping with the procedures followed by NIOSH in producing criteria documents (described above), this may take from four and one-half to seven years.

In view of the number of dangerous toxic substances used in industry and considering that there are 100,000 deaths annually from occupationally caused diseases,[29] NIOSH's research and OSHA's issuance of standards is agonizingly slow. Meanwhile, there is no restriction on the right of industry to introduce the hundreds of new toxic substances coming into use each year. Given the vast number of toxic substances already in use and unregulated, it makes little sense to permit industry to introduce new ones without requirements that their occupational safety be established. One writer likens the dilemma of NIOSH and OSHA officials to "men on a handcar pumping their way up a railroad track in pursuit of an express train that has roared through months, if not years, before."[30]

Progress in the formulation of criteria documents by NIOSH depends upon adequate agency funding. Dr. Marcus M. Key, NIOSH's Director until September, 1974, observed that: "NIOSH is not expanding, it is shrinking. It is getting the proverbial meat ax.... Our present laboratory space isn't even adequate for any kind of research. It's substandard.... We have been frozen on hirings for most of our existence, and we are losing key staff right and left because we don't have the grade points to promote them.... I don't think NIOSH is a viable organization at this time (1973)."[31]

NIOSH suffered personnel cuts in fiscal years 1973 and 1974, and its budget for fiscal 1975 was not adequate to remedy this loss.[32]

The Impact of State Plans

In a statutory bow to federalism, Section 18 of the Act provides that a state may reassume responsibility for occupational safety and health by submitting a comprehensive plan for the development and enforcement of its own standards. This plan will be approved by the Secretary of Labor if it meets a series of requirements designed to assure that the state plan is or will be "as effective as" the federal program. Under section 18(c)(2), a state standard also may be developed to replace an existing federal standard covering the same hazard if it is "as least as effective" as the federal standard in protecting safety and health

---

[26] President's Report, cited in footnote 1.

[27] GAO Report cited in footnote 18 at 16.

[28] See statement of John H. Stender, Assistant Secretary of Labor for Occupational Health and Safety, U. S. Department of Labor in LABOR LAW JOURNAL at 77, (Vol. 26, No. 2, February 1975). Secretary Stender states this is to be a two and one-half year project. Ibid.

[29] President's Report, cited in footnote 1 at 111.

[30] Brodeur, P., quoted in Wall Street Journal, August 20, 1974, p. 33, col. 6.

[31] Quoted in Brody, "Many Workers Still Face Health Peril Despite Law," N. Y. Times, March 4, 1974, p. 20, col. 5.

[32] Hearings on Departments of Labor and Health, Education and Welfare Before a Subcommittee of the House Committee on Appropriations 93d Cong., 2d Sess., pt. 3. at 340 (1974) and Labor Law Journal, (Vol. 25, No. 12, December 1974).

and does not "unduly" burden interstate commerce.

Some of the 25 state plans that are either in operation or at least have Labor Department approval are falling short of federal expectations. In Maryland, OSHA found the 40 state inspectors "limited in their knowledge of proper procedure and applicable standards," and found that for serious violations the state proposed an average penalty of $229 compared with $615 under the federal program. In South Carolina, 29 percent of state inspections were conducted in retail establishments, which are less hazardous than factories; by contrast, federal inspectors were spending only three percent of their time inspecting retail firms.[33]

National labor union leaders argue that the states never have done a good job in safety, that state standards are inadequate, that state inspectors are unqualified and too few in number, and that state safety programs are dominated by management.[34] On the other hand, many company managements fear that state-developed standards may bear little similarity to federal standards or those developed by other states.[35] Such a condition would be potentially very disruptive for multistate enterprises.

Because of the opposition of both unions and employers, many major industrial states are now having second thoughts about adopting health and safety plans of their own. Pennsylvania has withdrawn its proposed plan; in New York and New Jersey, the AFL-CIO has been able to block enabling legislation.[36] In Illinois, both labor and business leaders have urged the repeal of the state job health and safety law.[37]

The case for reviving state control is none too persuasive. States are required only to develop plans at least "as effective as" the federal program— and the Secretary of Labor is the final judge. As for surveillance of state programs, the Act says explicitly that the Secretary of Labor "may but shall not be required to exercise his authority." It is easy to imagine his reluctance to enter the thicket of local politics by disapproving, for example, the state selection of safety inspectors. Companies operating in several states are now speaking up for uniform national standards and unions have had too long an experience with the malfeasance and nonfeasance of state programs.

Presumably the justification of the act's "new federalism" is to assure that public tasks are carried out at the level where they can be performed most effectively. Because of the reservations of business and labor with state regulation, there is a strong prima facie case that occupational health and safety can best be regulated by the federal government. The goals of federalism could be accomplished through a different means of state involvement, such as state participation in the development of federal standards, which could then be applied uniformly throughout the country.

Union Involvement

Growing dissatisfaction with enforcement of the Occupational Health Act

[33] *Wall Street Journal*, cited in footnote 30 at 33, Col. 5.

[34] Statement by George Taylor, Industrial Union Department, AFL-CIO, Member National Advisory Committee for Occupational Safety and Health, before a Subcommittee on State Programs in *Official Report of Proceedings* at 56-80 (March 15, 1973).

[35] *Wall Street Journal*, cited in footnote 30.

[36] *Ibid.*

[37] *Wall Street Journal*, December 31, 1974, at 1, col. 5.

has led to increased union involvement in occupational health. There is a strong conviction in a large segment of our labor force that battling complex health problems should be a routine, daily, in-plant duty for organized labor.[38] That view, fueled by rank-and-file concern over job hazards, is spreading through a labor movement that until a few years ago gave little more than lip service to health on the job. At least 35 of the 120 major U. S. unions are taking formal health and safety action.[39]

A prime mover on occupational disease has been the United Rubber Workers. In 1970, this union sought and won a five year employer-paid study of health conditions in all plants of the Big Six rubber manufacturers. The fruits of this research program not only have helped study the problems of vinyl chloride but have begun to turn up other seeming cause-and-effect relationships between rubber-plant chemicals and a number of diseases.[40]

Organized labor is also seeking stricter enforcement of the law. A lawsuit to have approval of all existing state plans rescinded and to prevent states from receiving funds to develop or implement plans has been filed by the AFL-CIO.[41] The suit also seeks to enjoin OSHA from continuing to approve state plans which do not meet the statutory requirements. The suit charges that none of the 25 approved plans meet the requirement that state plans be at least as effective as federal regulations. It alleges that state standards are not as strict as federal standards, and that the states did not give assurance that they would provide sufficient personnel and adequate funds for running their programs.

Proposal

While NIOSH and OSHA may be subject to a multitude of criticisms, the major reason for their failures appears to be the lack of adequate funding. Objective appraisal of both agencies indicates that they would require a budget many times greater than their present one in order to perform the research necessary to issue criteria documents and standards for thousands of dangerous chemicals, and to have the staff of industrial hygienists necessary to enforce such standards. It is not realistic to expect that such funding will be forthcoming.

The scope and variety of beneficial programs competing for limited public revenues makes it unlikely that health legislation, as important as it is, is going to receive the attention that many citizens think it deserves. For example, it will be increasingly necessary to devote large sums of money to achieve such environmental goals as the control of air and water pollution and solid waste disposal. Large public expenditures will also be needed to meet high priority social programs, such as better housing, urban development, the alleviation of poverty and unemployment, and improved mass transportation.

Since it is unlikely that the Occupational Safety and Health Act's approach to employees' health hazards can succeed at present or foreseeable funding levels, some supplementary action is worth considering. One possible approach is suggested by the observation that our national effort to achieve occupational health is inextricably intertwined with state workmen's compensation laws.

---

[38] *Wall Street Journal*, August 19, 1974, at 17, col. 5.
[39] *Ibid.*

[40] *Ibid.*
[41] Docket No. 74-406, U. S. District Court for the District of Columbia.

At present, all state workmen's compensation laws require that medical service be provided for employees suffering occupational diseases. Although full medical treatment is provided in the majority of states, about one-fourth of the states place a limitation on the amount and on the period during which medical and hospital services must be provided. Workmen's compensation laws also provide only partial recompense for loss of wages due to occupational illness. In most jurisdictions, the individual is paid two-thirds of his average weekly wage up to a designated maximum which is typically between $60 and $80 per week. The inadequacy of rehabilitation and benefit payments reflects the fact that many states keep such payments low in order to avoid creating competitive disadvantages for their employers in comparison with other states.

This competitive feature of workmen's compensation could be altered by federal legislation holding all employers responsible for the full costs of occupational diseases.[42] Such a modification in our workmen's compensation laws would provide an incentive for the employer. Achieving a healthful work environment would then become less expensive than the consequences of operating a plant where health hazards abound. If each employer is made responsible for the full costs involved in industrial diseases, he will be stimulated to provide the necessary equipment, education, and training programs, and other precautionary measures designed to prevent occupationally related diseases.

Progress is being made toward this end. The National Commission on State Workmen's Compensation Laws, which was created by the Occupational Safety and Health Act of 1970, submitted a report in 1972 proposing more than eighty improvements in state laws designed to compensate victims of industrial illness or accidents.[43] These recommendations dealt with employee coverage, full medical and rehabilitative services, adequate weekly benefit levels, and elimination of arbitrary limits on the total amount or duration of benefits. The states were to be given an opportunity to improve their laws, and compliance with the essential recommendations of the Commission are to be evaluated during 1975. The Commission asked Congress to take action if the recommendations were not implemented by the end of 1975.

As a result of these recommendations, a number of states have completed comprehensive revision of their workmen's compensation laws since 1972.[44] Eleven have changed their pro-

---

[42] Prior to the enactment of workmen's compensation laws in the United States, employer's liability prevailed. A worker, suffering injury or an occupational disease, might sue in the absence of a suitable settlement. However, the employer had certain defenses which made it difficult for the employee to collect damages. An employer might plead contributory negligence on the part of a worker, or the employer might attempt to prove that the real fault was lodged with a fellow worker—the "doctrine of common employment" or the "fellow-servant doctrine." If these defenses were not available, the employer might plead the "doctrine of assumption of risk" —that the employee was assumed to have had knowledge that he was engaged in a dangerous occupation and, therefore, he had to assume the known risk of injury or disease. For an exposition of employer's liability see Millis, H. and R. Montgomery. *Labor's Risks and Social Insurance* (New York, McGraw-Hill, 1938) at 190-193.

[43] *National Commission on State Workmen's Compensation Laws, The Report of the National Commission on State Workmen's Compensation Laws* 13-27 (1972).

[44] Johnson, F. "Changes in Workmen's Compensation Laws in 1973," *Monthly Labor Review,* at 32 (Vol. 97, No. 1, January 1974) and Johnson, F. "Workmen's Compensation Law Changes in 1974," at 30 (Vol. 98, No. 1, January 1975).

grams from elective to compulsory in nature. Exemptions of small firms based on number of employees have been eliminated or reduced in thirteen states, and several have extended their coverage of agricultural workers. Full coverage of occupational disease is now provided for the first time in six additional states. Finally, most states have liberalized their maximum weekly benefit provisions, and several have reduced the waiting period before benefits become payable.

OSHA is necessary to provide overall standards and an administrative framework for our occupational health program, but without a stronger system of employer incentives to eliminate work related health hazards, OSHA cannot succeed. With greater employer incentive, by the strengthening of our workmen's compensation laws, OSHA has the potential to make a significant contribution to employee health in the work environment.

[The End]

D. Economics of Health Insurance

The Debate Over National Health Insurance

WITH the rapid development of private and public health-insurance programs in the past quarter century, the great majority of Americans now have some protection against the expenses of medical care. Whereas private insurance and various governmental programs together paid for less than one third of all expenditures for personal health care in 1950, such plans defrayed close to two thirds of personal health-care expenditures in 1974.

Even so, gaps in the coverage afforded by private and public plans have attracted increasing attention. Perhaps 25 million people are not covered by any program at all. And many millions of people having some medical coverage lack adequate basic benefits, as well as protection against "catastrophic" costs of serious illness. The rapid spiraling of medical costs has, of course, contributed to the inadequacy of coverage.

Significantly, moreover, the spiral has reflected in part various disincentives under existing financing arrangements to efficient use of medical-care resources and control of costs. Insurance policies, for instance, often pay only for treatment in a hospital, encouraging use of high-cost facilities in numerous instances when lower-cost outpatient treatment would be just as appropriate medically. And with hospitals generally reimbursed for costs and doctors reimbursed for customary charges, neither hospitals nor doctors have much incentive to improve efficiency.

As concern over problems such as these has grown, wide political support has developed for a government initiative to establish a national health-insurance program aimed at extending coverage to a greater part of the population and at increasing health-care efficiency. President Ford's call in January of this year for a moratorium on all new spending programs has temporarily slowed the momentum that had been building for passage of some kind of national health-insurance bill. Nevertheless, enactment of legislation in this session of Congress still seems a distinct possibility. Democratic leaders accord it high priority. And Representative Al Ullman, chairman of the House Ways and Means Committee, has indicated his belief that the House will pass a bill by August and that the Senate will take action later this year or early next year.

If, in fact, legislation is enacted, the costs to taxpayers could be considerable and, what is equally important, the nature of the nation's

---

"The Debate Over National Health Insurance." *Morgan Guaranty Survey,* March 1975, pp. 9–14. Reprinted with permission.

system of financing health care could be significantly transformed. Each of the proposals that has been prominently discussed would add significantly to total national spending on health care (box on page 13). Some would leave pretty much intact the present system of mixed public and private financing, while others would federalize the lion's share of health-care financing.

Senators Russell B. Long and Abraham Ribicoff, who have played a key leadership role in discussions of a national health-insurance initiative, argue that the critical needs are to improve health-care financing for the poor and to provide protection against catastrophic costs of illness. An approach confined to those objectives attracted considerable interest among Congressmen last year—partly no doubt because many legislators believe it would be advisable to begin any new health-insurance program on a limited scale and expand it only as experience is gained.

Significantly, the Administration opposed the approach of the Long-Ribicoff proposal. It argued, in effect, that filling in gaps in coverage was not enough. What the Administration argued for instead was the need for a new approach—for something that would lessen the bias in much existing health insurance toward the use of high-cost hospital facilities and counter other built-in disincentives to efficiency. Specifically, the Administration proposed a comprehensive program that would afford everyone broad basic coverage for outpatient care as well as hospital services.

The Administration's approach

The Administration's bill—as introduced last year—provided, for instance, for unlimited coverage of inpatient and outpatient hospital care, laboratory and X-ray services, treatment by physicians, and prescription drugs. It also provided for selected preventive care, including family planning services, prenatal and maternity care, and additional services for children including check-ups, and eye, ear, and dental care.

This comprehensive package of medical services would have been made available to all age groups and all income groups. Only the extent of beneficiaries' financial contribution would have differed, depending on which segment of a three-part program a particular beneficiary fit into:

1. a plan requiring employers to offer a basic benefit package to full-time employees and their families;
2. an "assisted plan" for low-income and high medical-risk groups which would largely replace Medicaid; or
3. a liberalized Medicare program for the aged.

The first part of the Administration proposal—the employee plan—would be privately financed. Employers would pay 65% of the premium initially and 75% after three years. Employees, who would have an option to enroll or not, would pay the balance. The Administration estimated the average annual premium at $240 for coverage of a single employee and $600 for coverage of an employee and family (entailing premiums for the employee of $60 and $150, respectively, by the time the employer's share rose to 75%). The "assisted plan"—in which part-time employees, the self-employed, and others not eligible under the employee or Medicare plans could enroll if they wished—would be financed partly by premium payments scaled according to income. Beneficiaries of the assisted plan, the Administration estimated, would pay about 20% of the total cost, with the federal government picking up about 60% of the total and state governments the residual 20%. The third plan—for the aged—would be financed by continuation of the Medicare payroll tax, premium payments by covered persons, and federal and state general revenues.

Besides encouraging use of less expensive types of care, the Administration proposal incorporated a number of other provisions aimed at holding down costs. It provided for states, subject to federal guidelines, to set reimbursement rates for providers of health care participating in the program. The Administration intended that states would establish fee ceilings for physicians' services which participating doctors would be obligated to accept as payment in full for

609

patients enrolled in the assisted and Medicare plans. However, doctors could charge patients enrolled in the employee plan more than the state-established fees. For hospital and other institutional services, states would negotiate so-called prospective reimbursement budgets which would set agreed payments per unit of service or per patient day or otherwise establish upper limits on payments. The proposal would have required participating institutions to accept the established rate for a service as full payment under all three parts of the program. Administration officials expect that setting up guidelines for prospective reimbursement of hospitals would involve many complexities, but they believe this method would provide incentives for institutions to increase efficiency that are not present under the prevalent method of reimbursing hospitals for costs after services have been rendered.

Moreover, in order to keep demand for medical services within manageable bounds, the Administration proposal required that all patients share to a limited extent in paying for covered services. Under the employee plan, patients would have been required to pay the first $150 of medical bills (with a maximum of three deductibles per family) and 25% of the costs of covered services above the deductible up to a limit of $1,500 a year for a family. Above that amount all covered services would be provided without further charge to the patient—except for physicians' fees in excess of state-established rates. (Cost-sharing requirements would be reduced for low-income families and the elderly.) As a further cost-control measure, the proposal provided that enrollees in all three plans could elect to receive care from health maintenance organizations (HMOs), which provide comprehensive services to subscribers for a fixed premium paid in advance.* According to several studies, it is not unusual for such groups to deliver care for as much as one fourth to one

third less than the cost of comparable care under fee-for-service practice, with the economies reflecting in large part a significant reduction in hospitalization and surgery.

The Administration proposal assigned to states important responsibilities for overseeing the program — including approval of employee plans, regulation of insurance carriers, and certification of health-care providers as eligible to participate. The federal government's role would be limited essentially to continuing to oversee operation of the Medicare program, setting guidelines for states, and certifying that state laws and regulations meet federal standards.

The Kennedy proposal

Yet another prescription for the nation's health-care ills was offered by Senator Edward M. Kennedy. He shares the Administration's desire to move to a comprehensive medical-care program for the entire population but the particulars of his legislative proposal differed radically from the Administration's. The Senator's plan would provide a standardized health-care package for all beneficiaries with an even broader range of services than the Administration recommended. And such services would be available at no charge to the patient, reflecting the view that everyone should have equal access to health care as a matter of right.

Senator Kennedy's program, as presented to the last Congress, would have been financed by a 3.5% tax on total employer payrolls, a 1% tax on wages and unearned income of employees up to $15,000 a year, a 2.5% tax on earnings of the self-employed up to the same limit, and by contributions from federal general revenues equal to the tax receipts. (The Medicare payroll tax for both employers and employees would be eliminated.) The program would be administered by a special board in the Department of Health, Education and Welfare (HEW). Under the Kennedy proposal (co-sponsored last year with Representative Martha W. Griffiths),

---

* For a discussion of HMOs, see "Changing the System of Health Care," *The Morgan Guaranty Survey*, December 1972.

there would be no role for private insurance companies, even in the processing of claims. HEW would establish a national health budget for each year, which could not exceed the estimated total receipts for that year from taxes and matching general revenues. Funds would be earmarked for particular regions and local areas on a per-capita basis, with predetermined budgets for institutional and professional services in each area. Local administrative offices would directly reimburse hospitals, doctors, and other providers of health care for services rendered. The proposed federalization of health insurance is one of the more controversial aspects of the Kennedy proposal, with supporters stressing the leverage it would give the government in controlling costs and opponents contending that federal intervention in the health-care system to the extent contemplated by this proposal would be both undesirable and administratively unfeasible.

Critics and supporters of the Kennedy proposal differ sharply in estimating the ultimate costs of "free" medical care for the entire population. Far from conceding that the nation's medical-care facilities would be inundated with new demands if the proposed program became effective, Senator Kennedy and his supporters argue that his plan has built-in correctives that would de-emphasize the present bias toward use of high-cost facilities. They maintain that deductibles and coinsurance actually increase over-all costs of medical care by discouraging people who find cost-sharing onerous from seeking early diagnosis and prompt treatment. A rational health-care program, they argue, would remove financial barriers to health care so as to encourage people to seek early attention and thus reduce serious illness. In keeping with that objective, a key feature of the proposed reimbursement system would, in effect, make it more attractive financially for doctors to offer their services via health maintenance organizations than on a fee-for-service basis.

Despite this kind of emphasis on cost savings, many skeptics think the "free-care" feature of the Kennedy plan would flood the delivery system with the demands of people who do not have genuine medical needs and would thus cause the nation's health bill to increase far above its present level. Partly because of the cost controversy, the proposal failed to gain wide support in the last Congress and Senator Kennedy backed away from it temporarily to join Representative Wilbur Mills in sponsoring a compromise measure. The Senator, however, has reintroduced his original proposal this year with some modifications, including an increase in the tax base for employee earnings from $15,000 to 150% of the Social Security tax base (or $21,150 at present). Supporters of the measure apparently are hopeful that the more liberal cast of the new Congress will improve chances of the bill's enactment.

Difficult choices

Obviously very complex issues are involved in the matter of broadening medical-care coverage for the population, and difficult choices clearly lie ahead for the President and Congress in considering what to do and when to do it. The nation has made some serious mistakes in developing the health-care system it now has, and it's to be hoped that something has been learned. One mistake that carries a particularly strong lesson was that of having induced a very rapid expansion in the demand for medical services in connection with the launching of Medicare and Medicaid without having induced a sufficiently accommodative increase in the supply of medical services. That mistake has been rectified somewhat in recent years as various programs have begun to produce significant increases in the number of graduates from the nation's medical, nursing, and other professional schools.

But despite increases in over-all numbers of health manpower and projections of sizable additional increases over the next decade, there are

ESTIMATING THE COST

ESTIMATING the potential costs of various health-insurance proposals involves assumptions that are difficult to make with accuracy. Most importantly, estimates of the increase in demand for health services likely to be generated by any given proposal are bound to involve a particularly spongy set of calculations because no one can judge the precise sensitivity of demand to prices—especially not in the extreme case in which services would be "free."

Nonetheless, the Department of Health, Education and Welfare (HEW) has made an effort to come up with figures indicating what different proposals would do to the nation's total expenditure for personal health care and to the federal budget. HEW estimated that the Long-Ribicoff proposal would add about 4% to total annual spending on personal health care, the Administration proposal somewhat more than 6%, and Senator Kennedy's proposal somewhat more than 12%. With spending already running well in excess of $100 billion annually, all of the proposals would produce significant increases in dollar terms.

Senator Kennedy's proposal, involving as it does almost a total "federalization" of health-care financing, would obviously have a much larger budgetary consequence than other proposals that would keep the present public-private mix of financing essentially intact. The Senator's proposal, by HEW estimates, would balloon federal health spending—and supportive taxes as well—by something in the vicinity of $75 billion. Both the Long-Ribicoff proposal and the Administration proposal, by contrast, would involve federal budget increases in the range of $5 billion to $10 billion. The real question about federalization, of course, is not so much what it does to budget figures per se. It is rather whether it is desirable to have the federal government so dominantly a participant in national health care.

Perhaps the most surprising thing about the HEW analysis is that the estimated increases in total spending for health care under different proposals fall in as narrow a range as they do, particularly considering that patients would have to share in the costs of care under the Administration proposal but would not do so under the Kennedy bill. It is by no means impossible that the true differences in potential cost are much greater.

serious problems associated with the distribution of health-care facilities and personnel. To be sure, the more affluent communities are relatively well supplied with facilities and personnel, and indeed many such areas now have considerable excess hospital capacity. In many other areas, however, particularly inner cities and rural communities, adequate care is simply unavailable at present. In the view of many experts, moreover, an excessively high proportion of doctors has been choosing specialty practice, with the result that there is a "shortage" of physicians in primary or family practice. The nation, in short, is by no means so comfortably supplied with medical resources that it can afford to be incautious in taking actions that would produce another quantum increase in demand. Certainly if Congress takes any action involving potentially larger demand for medical care, it should give very careful attention to supply considerations, both in the aggregate and as to geographic and specialty distribution.

The sheer cost burden involved in expanding the nation's medical-care program is not something that can be undertaken lightly. Total national expenditures on health care, now well in excess of $100 billion annually, have been climbing at a disturbingly rapid pace recently, and the additional cost of a sharp further enlargement in the demand for medical care could be troublesome indeed.

Senator Kennedy's proposal to finance one half of his program by substantial further use of payroll taxes dramatizes this issue. Many people believe that the Social Security drain on payrolls has already pushed payroll taxation close to its practical limits. The additional payroll taxes, it is true, would be offset in some part by reduced private insurance payments. But, as the program evolved over time, the extent of the offset would depend, among other things, on how substantially the demand for medical services was affected, and, in practice, the offset could fall far short of being full. Of course, the Administration's program (involving conventional insurance premiums larger than the total now being paid) could similarly drain away purchasing power.

These costs should obviously be very deliberately weighed. What is to be gained prospectively in terms of health-care improvement from any proposal must be measured, as best it can be, against what will have to be forgone alternatively in terms of people's command over other goods and services. This cost consideration underscores especially the need to devise—either as part of a program that broadens medical-care coverage or independently — inducements for medical resources to be used less indiscriminately and more efficiently than they now are.

Efficiency considerations of another kind weigh heavily, incidentally, against Senator Kennedy's proposal to eliminate entirely private insurance companies from all involvement with a comprehensive health-care program. To shift so dramatically to reliance on federal financing and federal administration of a program would surely entail substantial costs and complications. Achieving order and efficiency has been challenging enough at the federal level in the case of the Medicare program, with its 20 million eligibles. Administering a program in which more than 200 million people were participants would be quite another matter. In fact, a major reason for the partial step proposed in the Long-Ribicoff measure was concern that the federal government does not have the administrative capacity to carry out large new social programs effectively. Implementing the Medicare program, in the view of Senator Ribicoff, a former Secretary of HEW, stretched the government's administrative capacity "close to the limit." The sensible course would seem to be one that involved decentralization utilizing the substantial administrative skills of the private insurance industry.

These are some of the key issues that the new Congress will have to wrestle with when it gets around to a serious look at health care. The dominant needs clearly are for thorough analysis and very deliberate weighing of the pros, the cons, and the risks of all actions that are considered.

Health Care Cost: A Distorted Issue

by Rashi Fein

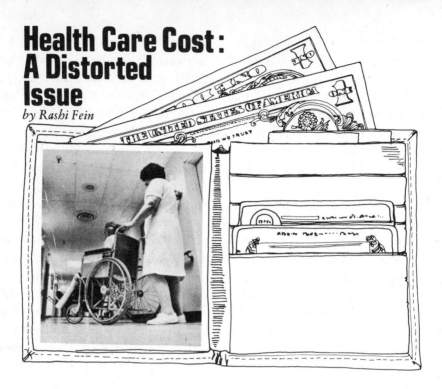

All of us who believe in national health insurance because it is comprehensive, universal, fair and equitable are asked one question: "What will it cost; can we afford it?" Some really wonder, and we owe them an answer. But others are asking not because they really wonder but because they want to muddy the waters and cast doubt. They are not interested in an answer; their problem is they know the answer—and just don't like it.

There is an element of dishonesty in some of the language, questions and issues raised by some who oppose national health insurance. Honest men and women can disagree about a number of issues involving national health insurance. We can and should debate matters relating to financing, to private and public mix of funds, to ways of paying for services. There is a lot, legitimately, to argue about.

Nor do honest men and women all understand the issues of cost perfectly. But some who do understand the issues correctly use scare tactics about cost to confuse the public. They do not believe their own testimony before Congress, but they hope the public will believe it. We ought to recognize that for what it is and turn our attention to the real task before us—explaining the issues to the American people.

What is the story of costs; what can we afford; what is national health insurance all about in dollars and cents? It may be useful to remind ourselves of the situation as it is today and to consider the situation as it will be when national health insurance is enacted.

We are spending over $100 billion a year in the health sector today. In fiscal 1974, the total was $104 billion; and $97 billion of that was for health care and supplies with the remainder for research and construction. That was money spent—dollars transferred from individuals, insurance companies or government to the health sector, to providers of goods and services. There is an ongoing health activity. It employs over 4 million persons, provides over a billion physician visits and about 250 million hospital inpatient days per annum. The health sector is alive and thriving—at least as measured by the dollars flowing into it, 7.7 percent of the gross national product. It is inefficient. It wastes resources. It fails to deliver care to large numbers of people who cannot afford to pay for services or who do not find services available when and where they need them. But it exists; it is financed; it utilizes resources.

We feel the nation should be getting more than we are for the $100 billion. We should, but that is not my point. What is important for the moment is that there is a $100 billion industry out there. We are not talking of creating a new enterprise—a new health industry—when we speak of national health insurance. It is not as if we have nothing today and want to create 350,000 doctors, 1.5 million hospital beds and all the rest and pay for it. We are not an under-

RASHI FEIN is a professor at the Harvard Medical School. This article is excerpted from a paper he presented to a Washington, D.C., conference on Health Security.

Rashi Fein, "Health Care Cost: A Distorted Issue." *The American Federationist*, June 1975, pp. 13–17. Reprinted with permission.

developed country without a health care system engaged in a great debate over whether to invest scarce resources in developing personnel and facilities. We already have a system—a $100 billion enterprise.

All that is important because it lies at the heart of one of the significant differences between national health insurance and other proposed government expenditures and programs. It is at the heart of the discussion about costs and what we can afford.

When government spends money for new desks and chairs, for parks or dams, for the CIA, this represents a change in the way resources are allocated in the economy. In those cases, government pays for things that were not going to be paid for by the private sector. When government builds or pays for a dam, it does not ask whether government should pay for a dam or whether individuals should buy it on their own. It asks, instead, whether we should have a dam at all. And it adds a constraint: if we say "yes," it means we will have to do without something else. To ask "should we have a dam" is to ask a meaningful question—for, if government authorizes a dam, it is a new dam that is created. If government puts new money into new programs that deliver services previously not available or delivered, we are talking about new services: parks, roads, inspection, regulation and so forth. New services require new resources —resources that could have been used for other things in the public or private sector.

If, on the other hand, government talks of assuming the costs of services already being delivered and paid for by the citizenry—as is the case with health services—there are no new total dollars or total resources involved. Every dollar government spends on health relieves us, the public, of dollars that we would have spent on health.

There is, of course, a new and different financing mechanism, a new way of spending old dollars, but that is not the same as new dollars. New parks, roads or bombers represent money for things the people would otherwise not have. But medical care is different: we are already spending $104 billion, and private expenditures account for $63 billion of that total.

So the issue is a non-issue. The question can we, as a people, afford national health insurance really means can we afford to spend what we are already spending —and surely the answer is "yes." The issue is not whether we are spending more than we can. The issues are whether we are getting what we should for our money and whether the present arrangements which make health expenditures depend on a family's income are fair, just and humane.

But, the critics say, what about those people who today cannot afford to purchase medical care. Won't national health insurance cost more than we are now spending when it attempts to provide care to those who today find price a barrier? They ask whether we can really afford a universal national health insurance program that brings health care to the forgotten and the rejected Americans? What does that really mean? Anyone who asks those questions apparently believes that we do not have enough and cannot produce enough medical care services—and that is untrue—and, rather than alter, modify and improve the health care system, prefers to continue rationing health care on the basis of ability to pay—and that is unjust.

In part, of course, the critics say they agree, and that is why they contribute to charity and "support" Medicaid. But, of course, to the extent that charity and Medicaid do purchase health care we are back at square one, talking about dollars that are already being spent. In our view, national health insurance is fiscally a substitute for, not an addition to Medicaid, but it is also different from and better than Medicaid. It is a better way of spending the dollars that are already being spent. No, the reason some of our critics may prefer even Medicaid to national health insurance does not relate to the total dollars going for care. The real reason is some people like the Medicaid system—not because it is efficient, just, humane and decent—but because they feel it is an appropriate system for those whom they consider undeserving. Their chief complaint about it is not that it is a demeaning system in which people are required to trade their dignity for some health care. Their chief complaint is that we are spending too much on it. And when they say, "we are spending too much," they do not mean America cannot afford it. They really mean, "why spend that much on people who aren't making it on their own?"

The fact is that even with Medicaid and other programs, too many Americans still receive inadequate care. National health insurance will permit them to enter the medical care system and will require resources for their care. That is good. That is what we want. That is one of the important reasons we favor the Health Security Act. I am not ashamed of being in favor of decency, humaneness and justice. I am willing to spend dollars, new dollars, to achieve it. In fact, however, I am convinced that we can have a well run system of health care that, by eliminating present waste and inefficiency, can provide care for all the people with fewer resources than are now providing care for only some of the people. For $100 billion we can provide for all 213 million Americans. But even if our critics disagree, even if they argue it will cost more than we are now spending, what would they have us do, continue to deny care to those who need it but cannot pay? Do they really mean we cannot afford it, or do they mean that they prefer not to concern themselves with the problems of the less fortunate?

Unemployment is costing our economy billions upon billions in dollars—aside from the human suffering. Yet we are told the nation cannot provide health care for its people. If we did not have public education, they would tell us we could not afford that either. If we did not have unemployment compensation, they would tell us we could not afford that—or

social security or higher education or workers' compensation. Their economic policies cost the nation tens of billions of dollars in lost wages and products and untold human suffering, yet they ask us whether the nation can afford national health insurance.

Yet another argument is used: if government pays for medical care, it is said, you and I will attempt to get more care than we need. We will flood the hospitals and the doctors' offices, inundate the system and bankrupt the economy. But where is the evidence that we are all so in love with medical care that we will face waiting time, travel costs, absence from work, fear and concern to behave that way? The evidence is not found in prepaid group practices where monetary barriers to care have been eliminated or reduced. It is not found in outpatient departments because they have to mount outreach and follow-up programs to get people to use the services. It is not found in the experience of other nations. Canada can manage to meet its commitments but we, presumably, would be unable to meet ours.

This is the rationale offered for coinsurance and deductibles—for that which is so pleasantly called "cost sharing." Cost sharing is supposed to make you and me behave responsibly, but the real issue is how to induce the system to behave responsibly. You and I do not decide to order unnecessary lab tests; we don't really make the decision that we would like to enter or stay in hospital an extra few days; we are not out there balancing prices and satisfaction and deciding whether we prefer another $10 worth of care or something else. The bulk of those decisions are made for us. High cost sharing is not consistent with the goals and aims of a comprehensive, universal and equitable national health program. Low cost sharing—and that which is low for some is high for others—is not worth the administrative costs. Those who are so concerned about costs might want to join us in eliminating the unnecessary costs involved in administering a system of deductibles and coinsurance. Moving billions of pieces of paper around is expensive—that is waste and, therefore, is something we cannot afford.

At the margin, and for the poor the margin is narrow indeed, price does make a difference. But will the system go bankrupt without price barriers? The U.S. Department of Health, Education and Welfare—a department not known for its support of Health Security—has estimated that the difference in total expenditures—total dollars spent on health, whatever the source of the expenditure—between the Health Security Act and the Administration bill introduced in the last Congress was $6.5 billion on a total estimated expenditure of about $123 billion. We believe that is a substantial overestimation of the costs of the Health Security Act. Among other things, it fails to take account of the very real savings that will come about because of system changes that are part and parcel of the Health Security Act. The HEW estimates assume that the Health Security Act will only finance care and not change the delivery system, and that is not what Health Security is all about. Nevertheless, even HEW admits that the Health Security Act—even without system savings—would add only 10 percent to what the nation will spend if no legislation were enacted and only 5 percent to what the inadequate Administration bill with cost sharing would cost.

Consequently, we are prepared to argue we can afford a Health Security Act and to argue further that with system change the Health Security Act will save, not cost the nation money. There is surely more than 10 percent waste and inefficiency in the present system.

Is the argument really about going bankrupt because of an additional expenditure of some $6 billion? Can anyone say that a trillion dollar economy cannot afford the Health Security Act? The argument is not really about total dollars and total costs but about where the dollars come from and where they will go. That is the real explanation for the cost sharing and also for the mandating proposals that have been offered by the previous Administration. Requiring that patients pay out of pocket or that employers make health insurance available to their employees is not really cheaper—it only looks that way in terms of federal funds. The dollars all stay in the private sector with mandating, and government does not enter the picture. The dollars are not greener nor are they fewer. But they are private; not public. That is the real issue, and that issue is real because the Health Security Act has a social insurance approach—and it is there for a reason. The fact of the matter is that in

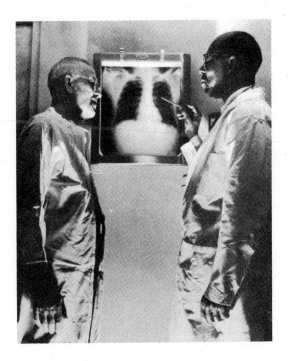

health care private financing, operating with private-insurance principles, has not met the problems of the people. We needed social security. We needed Medicare. We got them because those who fought for those programs understood the basic issues involved. The same issues lie at the heart of the fight for national health insurance.

Keeping things substantially as they are or building upon a weak foundation will not lead to universality or equity. The Administration's bill, after all, would transfer only about 5 percent of total costs from the private to the public sector. This is what they call national health insurance—the Federal Trade Commission ought to look into that kind of mislabeling. Is it not equitable to have low-income employees spend a higher proportion of their income on health care via coinsurance, deductibles and premiums that are fixed amounts and do not vary with income or with payroll. It is not universal to have a multiplicity of plans into which people must be sorted. And in dollar-cost terms all this would increase administrative costs. Whatever they may say about the Health Security Act, at least they must admit that its dollars would go for health care and to the health system—not on paper work and to accountants.

In a March 1975 editorial, the Washington Post suggested Congress should examine the true costs of government programs—not just the costs to government, but the real costs. It said: "The argument over health care provides a classic example of the way the present system works. Health insurance plans before Congress are usually discussed in terms of how much they will cost federal or state governments in tax money. While these figures are of obvious importance, the true cost of any such plan must include the additional expenses the plan will impose on employers and employees. If those additional expenses are paid by the employers, they will be reflected, sooner or later, in prices. If they are paid by the employees, they will be reflected in a loss of buying power. In either case, they are real costs, just as tax increases are real costs.

"In order to get a true picture of the full costs of a health plan or noise reduction regulation or any other federal program, Congress needs an 'economic impact' statement not unlike the environmental impact statements now required of many construction programs. Then it could know how much a particular program or set of regulations really costs."

It surely would be advisable if the Administration prepared economic impact statements such as the Washington Post calls for. We who support the Health Security Act would welcome honest analyses—we have nothing to fear and much to gain from public information and understanding. Social legislation—Medicare, national health insurance—is never harmed by public understanding. It is misinformation that is harmful.

Actually, since the federal Office of Management and Budget (OMB) has not been doing what the Post calls for, proponents of Health Security have done it for them. That is why we know that, in largest measure, the Health Security Act is fiscally responsible. Its economic impact is in terms of equity, not total expenditures. It calls, not for an increase in real costs but, for a shift, a transfer, in expenditures—a shift that is needed and a transfer we can afford. It calls for a social insurance approach.

Thus it follows that the argument that the economy cannot accommodate itself to national health insurance, that it represents an increase in total expenditures and that we have to put national health insurance on the back burner because it is inflationary is false and deceptive. It is an argument without merit, and it does not become any more persuasive when we are told there is no such thing as a free lunch. There isn't, and we know it. But this is a lunch that is already being paid for. In fact, if the Health Security Act were passed and signed into law and if the people who administer it believe in it, the changes in the health care system and in its financing would enable us—for the same money—to have a fine dinner instead of a blue plate lunch.

Recently we were told that the President would veto a national health insurance bill even if spending were delayed a year because enactment of a spending program would encourage an inflationary psychology. If we place the facts before the public and the issues are recognized for what they are—if the public is not misled—no inflationary psychology need result. There are no witches out there, and it is less than honest first to keep frightening us with the imaginary demon of inflation and then to tell us we cannot have national health insurance because some people believe the stories of demons and witches.

Government expenditures on health will go up under the Health Security Act—that is a design feature, not an unfavorable side effect. But private expenditures on health will go down. That is also a design feature. The Health Security Act will be financed out of new revenues which can be obtained in an equitable manner and which all of us will find ourselves better able to pay, in part because we will be saving what we are now already spending on medical care and health insurance and in part because of the growth in tax revenues resulting from the turn around and expansion in the economy. We do not argue that Health Security should come at the expense of other social programs in education, manpower training, income maintenance; we can finance Health Security because we are already financing health care.

Indeed, if people want to talk about inflation, we can respond positively. It is the existing organization and financing of health care that—in the absence of legislation—would continue to contribute to inflationary pressures in the future. The real issue is whether we can continue to afford the waste and inflation inherent in the present system of care and finance. Inflationary pressures, conversely, can be contained and moderated by the kind of responsible intervention that is embodied in the Health Security Act. When it is said that it is automatically inflationary for dollars to be transferred through government back to the private sector for health care, we can respond: "Whose administrative costs are less, the Social Security System which handles Medicare efficiently or the private health insurance sector whose administrative costs are often higher than that of government?"

And so national health insurance is within our means. We are not so poor that we cannot afford one of the hallmarks of a civilized society—the right to health care regardless of income. When all the myths are dispelled, when all the rhetoric and testimony and analyses are over with, we are left with the crux of the matter—the argument about justice for all. Make no mistake about it—the guts of the issue is not about dollars. Those who opposed the Social Security Act, disability insurance or Medicare were not really arguing about money but about how the pie is shared. And the same is the case with national health insurance. The real question is whether resources shall be allocated so that everyone receives his fair share in a system in which the use of medical care is related to medical need, or whether we shall continue, as in the past, to ration care on the basis of income. The answer will be in favor of justice and decency, in favor of national health insurance. A bill will be enacted and will be signed into law.

We must recognize, however, that enactment of a law is only the beginning of a process and not the end of it. The law must be administered. Because we are concerned about cost—about saving money in the health field so that we can devote resources to other social uses, since medical care is not the only unsolved problem on the American agenda—and because we are concerned about equity, all of us will be required to make certain the legislation is administered effectively. Only public vigilance can assure that.

No one will "give" us national health insurance—not the experts or Congress or the Office of Management and Budget. The battle for national health insurance is first a battle for public understanding. Social legislation is not enacted because of the goodwill of special interest groups, but over their opposition. It is not enacted because a few legislators are concerned but because many legislators who would rather sit on the fence find that the pressure of concerned citizens makes fence sitting uncomfortable. We will not convince OMB or the American Medical Association, but we can convince the public.

Thus far, at least on issues of cost, the people have been confused. We have not won the battle of public understanding against those who have sown the seeds of public confusion. I believe it can be won because the facts are on our side. However difficult it is for facts to prevail in a struggle against deception, if enough people work hard enough at it, the public will recognize truth from error. Then, having won the battle of understanding and organization, we will have national health insurance.

MEDICAL CARE

RESOURCE ALLOCATION AND COSTS

One of the major concerns about medical care is the sharp rise in costs. Since 1950 the medical component of the CPI has increased much faster than the overall CPI (Table 37).

Prices of hospital services have increased at a much faster rate than physicians' fees or other medical services. In part this is the result of an increase in the quality of hospital services not fully reflected in the CPI. As indicated in Table 37, when total hospital expenditures per patient day are deflated by a crude price index for hospital inputs, it appears that increases in real resources explain a substantial amount of the rate of increase in expenditures per patient day. During the 5-year period since medicare and medicaid were introduced, 1965 to 1970, the rate of increase of real resources per patient day nearly doubled and accounted for about one-half of the nominal increase in hospital expenses per patient day.

TABLE 37.—*Changes in prices of various medical and hospital services and expenses, 1950–75*

[Percent change; annual rate]

Period	Consumer prices					Hospital expenses and services per patient day [1]		
	All items	All services less medical care services	Medical care services			Expenses [3]	Real expenses [4]	
			All [2]	Semiprivate room	Physicians' fees		Assumption A [5]	Assumption B [6]
Annual average:								
1950 to 1955	2.2	[7]3.8	4.2	6.9	3.4	8.2	3.3	4.3
1955 to 1960	2.0	[7]3.3	4.4	6.3	3.3	6.9	3.3	3.5
1960 to 1965	1.3	1.8	3.1	5.8	2.8	6.7	3.3	4.2
1965 to 1970	4.2	5.4	7.3	13.9	6.6	12.7	6.0	7.4
1970 to 1975	6.7	6.3	7.6	10.2	6.9	12.5	4.8	5.1
Change from preceding year:								
1971	4.3	5.3	7.3	12.2	6.9	13.2	4.5	6.6
1972	3.3	3.8	3.7	6.6	3.1	13.4	6.5	7.8
1973	6.2	4.3	4.4	4.7	3.3	7.6	2.8	1.6
1974	11.0	9.2	10.3	10.7	9.2	11.2	3.7	2.5
1975	9.1	9.1	12.6	17.2	12.3	17.6	6.5	7.3

[1] Beginning 1965, patient days have been adjusted for outpatient visits.
[2] Includes some medical care services not shown separately.
[3] Based on data reported by the American Hospital Association for community hospitals for year ending September 30.
[4] Labor and nonlabor inputs adjusted for price changes.
[5] Deflated by a weighted average of the consumer price index and an index of hospital wages.
[6] Deflated by a weighted average of the consumer price index and adjusted hourly earnings index in the private nonfarm economy.
[7] Change for all services.

Sources: Department of Labor (Bureau of Labor Statistics), American Hospital Association, and Council of Economic Advisers.

"Medical Care—Resource Allocation and Costs." From *Economic Report of the President,* 1976. U. S. Government Printing Office, pp. 124–126.

Resistance by taxpayers to the increasing burden of medicare and medicaid, and pressures to restrain medical costs have led in the past to pressures for a more formal mechanism to control costs. During the period of the Economic Stabilization Program, starting in August 1971 and ending April 1974, the health industry was placed under more stringent price controls than most industries. In addition to price ceilings on individual services, controls were also placed on the increase in total annual hospital expenditures. These controls in effect curtailed the amount as well as the price of the service provided. From 1972 to 1973 increases in hospital resource use per patient day did slow. However, it is not clear whether the slower growth rate represented a gain in efficiency through a more careful use of resources, a curtailment of quality improvements that would have been desirable, or less efficiency through a greater rate of admission of less serious cases. Since the end of controls, real hospital resources have increased at a very rapid rate, partly to "catch up" and perhaps partly in anticipation of a permanent controls program. Hospital expenses per patient day increased at the very high rate of 18 percent from 1974 to 1975.

Some of this expansion in medical resources is probably a desired quality improvement. There is considerable evidence, however, that much is a consequence of the growth of private insurance and public funding, which has led to a system where "third parties" pay for an increasing share of medical services, particularly hospital services. The most common form of health insurance has low or no deductibles and low cost-sharing (coinsurance), especially for hospital care. This type of coverage has been shown to have a substantial effect on the price and quantity of services. For example, families with insurance have a greater number and longer length of stays in hospitals and more visits to physicians. The patients may themselves prefer this extra health care because the extra cost to them is small. In addition, hospitals and doctors, knowing that most of the costs will be paid by third parties who are not in a position to decide on what services should be provided, are also likely to expand the quality, quantity, and price of their services. As a result, patients receive services that they would not value enough to pay for if they were given additional income equal to the cost of the service. In this way too many resources, and probably not the optimal kind, are allocated to medical services. The system encourages the development and use of high-cost techniques and a reliance on institutional rather than home care.

Unlike most other forms of insurance, private health insurance is largely purchased through the employer in a group policy. This practice has been substantially encouraged by the income tax and payroll tax systems, which exempt from taxation the employer's contribution for this form of insurance even though it is really an addition to the worker's income. Up to a point, it is to the mutual benefit of employer and employee to favor wage increases in the form of untaxed fringe benefits rather than in cash. As workers have moved into increasingly higher marginal tax brackets, this incentive has increased. In 1953 employers paid all of the costs for health insurance premiums for 10 percent of employees and none of the costs for 41 percent. By 1970 employers paid all of the costs for 39 percent and none of the costs for only 8 percent. The Government further reduces the cost of insurance by allowing a deduction under the personal income tax of half the cost of premiums paid by the taxpayer up to $150. All medical expenditures, including the other half of the premium cost, that exceed 3 percent of income may also be deducted. Estimated tax losses in fiscal 1977 are $4.2 billion for exclusion of employers' contributions and $2.1 billion for itemized medical deductions, including insurance premiums.

As a result of these tax subsidies, the cost to the consumer of paying for medical care indirectly through insurance is sharply reduced. Indeed, it has been estimated that in 1975 the Federal Government paid 20 to 22 percent of the premium costs of insurance through forgone tax receipts. Even taking into account the insurance companies' administrative costs and the costs of induced additional medical care, a result of the tax subsidy is that families with group coverage, paid for at least in part by the employer, spend less on medical care by buying insurance than they would have done by paying directly. In an unsubsidized market, consumers would have the incentive to pay out of pocket for routine budgetable medical care and to confine their insurance to very large and unpredictable expenditures. Faced with insurance at a substantial discount, they are induced to buy more comprehensive insurance, covering expenditures from the first dollar.

The problems of insurance are exacerbated in the case of medicare and medicaid because the mechanism of higher premiums, which may provide weak incentives to economize in our subsidized private insurance market, hardly works at all in the public system. Although there are medicare deductibles, there is no copayment for the first 60 days of hospital care. Under medicaid there are generally no deductibles and no coinsurance for hospital and physicians' services.

Perhaps the main feature that fosters cost increases is the method by which medicare, medicaid, and most Blue Cross policies reimburse the hospitals. These insurers pay a share of the hospital's costs, based on the percentage of all costs accounted for by their respective beneficiaries. Because hospitals have the assurance that a large percentage of their revenues will be based on cost reimbursement, there is little direct restraint to keep costs down. The Federal Government is now experimenting with prospective reimbursement schemes, whereby hospitals are told in advance how much they will be reimbursed per unit of service provided (e.g., patient admissions, patient days).

E. The Future

SR editors with faculty participants—An exploration of some basic fundamentals.

Recovery and Beyond

An SR-Harvard Business School Colloquium

In any discussion of strategies for prosperity, several basics must be agreed upon if we are to have a clear sense of direction and progress.

To explore these basics, Saturday Review *drew upon the resources of the Harvard Business School, incubator for American business leaders and source of much of the nation's current business operating policies and practices. Five senior professors of business administration, men of national reputation, joined us in a colloquium to review these basics. Each addressed himself to his own area of expertise. The five were George C. Lodge, John Lintner, Jesse W. Markham, Robert Stobaugh, and Ray A. Goldberg.*

The Editors

M*r. Lodge, how do you see the future role of business in our society? Will capitalism as we know it be retained, in strengthened form? Or will we see fairly major changes in the relationship between government and business?*

Professor Lodge: Well, if you'll forgive me, I don't think I'll use the word *capitalism.* Nor will I use *socialism* or *communism,* because I don't think any of these terms mean anything anymore. What I see happening is a widespread systemic disintegration within our country. This disintegration has been going on for about 80 years now. Right now, it's in a very extreme and dangerous phase. Signs of decay are in evidence everywhere: there's the declining motivation in the workplace, the lowering of productivity, increased labor costs, and the

George C. Lodge, John Lintner, Jesse W. Markham, Robert Stobaugh, Ray A. Goldberg, "Recovery and Beyond—An SR-Harvard Business School Colloquium." *Saturday Review,* July 12, 1976, pp. 24, 25, 26, 28, 30, 34. Reprinted with permission.

weakened authority of all our institutions and the people who are supposed to run them.

Another sign of disintegration is our inability to make crucial trade-offs about what the community needs, for example, between clean air, pure water, energy, the economy, jobs. Then there are the many special-interest groups that heavily influence our sorting out of these trade-offs, as in the case of the milk lobby. The upshot is an increasing fragmentation of government in the face of our need for increasing concentration.

Now, let me start off by making some predictions, and then let me explain why I think these predictions make sense. First, it strikes me that sooner or later, in one way or another, we are going to have significantly greater and more comprehensive government planning. The question is not really whether we are going to have more government planning; the question is, Is it going to be effective or ineffective?

Secondly, I predict that there will be more use of the corporate charter and of procedures related to the corporate charter, in order to control corporations —that is, *to harmonize them with the public interest.* Anti-trust laws that simply try to ensure competition and regulation will become less important. I see the corporate charter as being an increasingly important instrument for defining the purposes and functions of giant corporations—the oil companies, for example.

Thirdly, inside the corporation there will be increasing structural reorganization, or else, there will be continued deterioration. And these reorganizations will threaten the old idea of the contract and the old idea of managerial authority based on property rights. I believe more and more employers and employees will think in terms of a consensual, rather than a contractual, process. I would predict that, increasingly, managerial authority will not derive from some mystical body of shareholders operating through some board of directors in a very obscure process. Rather, managerial authority will derive from the managed (the alternate source being, of course, government).

Now then, the issues that all this raises have to do with adaptation and timing— typical issues being the possibility of keeping democracy afloat, centralization versus elitism. These are the kinds of issues that I see.

Now, in order to understand any of these problems, I think one has to take a systemic, overall, holistic approach to the malaise that troubles us. And for that purpose I have found useful the notion of *ideology.* Ideology is a complicated term. The way I define it is this: the bridge by which a society gets from values, essentially non-controversial values such as justice and self-fulfillment and survival, to the real world. It is a framework of ideas for making values explicit and defining them. It is both dynamic and transient. It is not dogmatic. It is that nucleus of ideas by which institutions—business institutions, governments, universities, and so on—are made legitimate. It provides the rationale and justification for these institutions—for their power, their influence, and their work.

Now, what's happening in America— and, as I say, it's been happening for a long time—is that we are operating under an old set of ideas, five in number, which are slipping away. These five ideas used to make our institutions legitimate, but the ideas have been eroded, and a new set of them has been coming in to take their place.

The process has not been a conscious one. It has not been the work of Maoists or some conspiratorial group. Instead, this displacement and replacement of ideas have resulted from pragmatic, experiential activity on the part of corporations and government and universities and all of us.

The five ideas of the traditional dominant ideology are these: individualism, property rights as guarantors of individual rights, the open marketplace as a restraint on property abuses, the notion of the limited state, and specialized scientific analysis as the key to knowledge.

These time-honored ideas are, in important respects, giving way to another set of outlooks, particularly with respect to large corporations. These new ideas haven't been around very long, and we are much less sure of them. But it seems clear that they are inexorably taking the place of the kind of atomism and individualism that is implicit in what might be called the John Wayne conception of society and the individual.

For want of a better term, I have dubbed this new set of societal ideas and ideals "communitarianism." That is to say, we become fulfilled by being part of a group, part of an organization, part of a complex, crowded thing. If this "thing," this societal context, is well designed, it makes full use of our talents and our resources and our capabilities. If it is poorly designed, we are alienated, frustrated, turned off, purposeless, and take to drink and drugs and late-night TV.

So the old idea of equality of opportunity has, as I see it, been replaced by an interesting new one, which you could call equality of result or equality of representation. For instance, the law now says that it isn't enough for a corporation to provide equality of opportunity. It has to have equality of result or representa-

tion: you've got to have so many men telephone operators, so many women vice-presidents. You've got to have minority groups spread up and down the corporate hierarchy, roughly in proportion to their numbers in the community. That's a very new idea, radically different from the old way.

In place of the idea of *contract* I would put *consensus.* Thus, we see a variety of attempts and experiments by business to increase productivity and increase motivation by designing new forms under the heading, "worker participation in management" or "organizational development."

In place of property rights have come the rights of *membership.* Much more important to most individuals in America today than concern over whether they own any property (which increasingly few do) is the question whether they have certain rights as citizens or as members of a large group. That is, as a citizen of the United States, you now have the confident expectation that you will survive. You have a right to survive, you have a right to income, you have a right to health, you have a right to a variety of things that the community has said are yours.

In place of competition to satisfy consumer desires, we see an increasing importance placed on community need, on economies of scale, on efficiency, on beating the Japanese, and on many other things.

The fourth idea among the five "old regime" ideas mentioned a moment ago was Locke's notion that government should be limited, even quiescent. But we are now developing, in a fairly clumsy form, to be sure, an active planning state. We have had this state in varying degrees for the last 50 years or more. One of the difficulties with this whole transition is that nobody recognizes it or makes it explicit.

How we organize state planning depends very much on whether we explicitly acknowledge that the state should

Professor Lintner

have a planning function that it doesn't have now. The question is, Is the change going to happen intelligently, or is it going to happen stupidly and wastefully? And is it going to happen after great institutions have sunk into the mud, or is it going to happen before they do so that we can make these transitions more or less efficiently?

The last of the Lockean Five—scientific specialization—is giving way to *holism*, the conception that a whole cannot be understood without an analysis of its parts. Ecology is perhaps the best example, but there are many others.

We now know that we live in a fragile spaceship, in a fragile biosphere, and that there are limits to growth. We don't quite know what they are, but they're there. We also know that there are scarcities, but that somehow we must manage this, again, holistic, systemic problem.

These, then, are the philosophical basics around which we must build a new prosperity for America.

Any strategy for prosperity must be based upon a clear understanding of our present economic condition. Professor Lintner, could you indicate for us the dimensions of the current recession. How deep is it? How long will it last?

Professor Lintner: There's no question that the American economy is in the midst of its most severe and most protracted recession of the entire post-war period. For example, unemployment did not reach 8 percent in 1958, our sharpest previous post-war recession. Yet it's already quoted at 8.9 percent today—and it's going to be nearly 9.5 percent by mid-year. If all the people who have been discouraged from being part of the labor force are taken into account, unemployment is already in the high 9 percent range. Among younger minority members of the labor force, and in some industries such as the automobile and construction, we have recently had unemployment rates as high as 30 percent—a figure reminiscent of the Thirties.

Real per-capita disposable income, in terms of purchasing power, fell only 0.7 percent in 1958, but it has already declined by over 5 percent through the first quarter of this year. As a result, spending has fallen, and we have had a back-up of inventories. There has been a tremendous (60 percent) reduction—the largest of the post-war period—in housing starts. Plant and equipment outlays have also been falling in real terms. Overall, total output in the quarter just ended was over 7.5 percent below the previous peak level of real GNP. The current decline has been about twice as great as the 1958 decline and has already lasted five quarters while that earlier decline lasted only two quarters.

This recession is also different because it is by far the most *inflationary* of our post-war period. The reasons for this inflation go back to our failure to finance the Vietnam war on a pay-as-you-go, tax-financed basis at the time when we had nearly full employment. This failure led to erratic action on the part of the Federal Reserve, which tried successively to slow down the economy with tight funds for a while but then reversed its field quickly when unemployment started to rise, only to repeat the cycle when business improved and inflation increased again. Since 1965 the inflation rate has been higher at each peak than at the last, and in each trough the inflation rate has also been higher than in the preceding.

Our inflation problem has been complicated by the agricultural situation. Another blow was struck in oil, where, in effect, the oil-producing countries imposed on the American economy a $25 billion excise tax, payable to a foreign government, that is highly deflationary in its longer-run impact on business activity but sharply inflationary in terms of prices.

With inflation rates soaring at 12 to 14 percent rates last year, the Federal Reserve tightened up with still greater determination and converted what would have been a mild slowdown into something far more serious.

By early this year, the risks of a self-reinforcing downward spiral had become so great that a large tax cut was required to turn the economy around. With this $25 billion tax reduction in place, and with easier monetary policy, a solid recovery is now reasonably well assured. The low point in overall production should be reached by summer, and unemployment will begin to decline this fall.

For a variety of reasons, however, I do not believe that we will have a fast snapback from this recession. Consumers have been badly frightened and have felt that administrators were not in control of the economy. The financial position of consumers has deteriorated badly and cannot be restored for some time. These psychological and financial considerations will hold down the pace of the recovery in consumer spending. The financial position of business firms has been seriously weakened, as their debt-to-equity ratios climbed to unprecedented, excessively high levels. The commercial banks also have become over-extended in fulfilling their earlier commitments and lines of credit. Their own investment-to-capital ratios have risen to a level where further expansion has had to be restricted.

Another reason why we may expect a slower recovery than in early periods is that housing is not going to snap back quickly. Many builders are bankrupt, and there is a very heavy overhang of unsold dwellings. Even though money is now flowing into the savings institutions at a record rate, many of these savings institutions themselves have debts to repay, and all must restore their liquidity positions before a large flow of mortgage money can be expected. Housing activity will be showing solid increases by fall, but it will recover more slowly than it has in our previous post-war recessions.

The other principal reason for the general sluggishness of the recovery is that plant and equipment expenditures regularly lag behind changes in final unit sales. The 10 percent investment-tax credit is a powerful stimulus for new investment, but it will not effect rates of spending on capital goods very significantly in the next six months. It will begin to be felt more strongly in about nine months; by the second half of 1976, it will lead to a substantial volume of expenditures that otherwise wouldn't have been made. In the meantime, there is still a heavy stock of excess inventories to be worked off, and business will probably be cautious in restocking for quite a while.

For all these reasons, I think that the recovery will be relatively solid but restrained. Inflation rates have already fallen substantially and—apart from the effects of any bad weather on crops and the chances of further increases in oil—we can expect some further easing in inflation over the next year. The effects of our $25 billion tax cut and of the recent easing in monetary policy will build up over time and lead to a very substantial recovery.

If any further increases in federal spending are of a "self-extinguishing" character—such as increases in unemployment benefits, which are automatically eliminated as recovery proceeds—and if monetary policy prudently, but gradually, moves toward restraint as our resources become more fully utilized, we

Professor Markham

will be in a position where recovery should be substantial *and* sustainable, and without the inflationary overheating that has marred recent expansions.

Mr. Markham, in the face of the recession, what can government, working with business, do about finding immediate and long-range solutions? What, particularly,

is the role and the relative efficiency of the regulatory agencies?

Professor Markham: As a nation, we have, historically, relied very heavily on *market* regulation in those areas where the market seems to function quite well. That is, we leave most business up to market forces to regulate, provided that business itself doesn't capture and control those forces. Government regulation here consists mainly of anti-trust policy.

The second type of situation that introduces government regulation into the picture occurs when this balance of competitive forces is impossible to attain or when these forces are so weak that they will be ineffective. To deal with such situations, we've created a group of rather unique institutions known as public commissions, which are responsible for regulating their respective industries. Nearly everyone agrees that such regulatory commissions have functioned badly and inefficiently, but we are uncertain about what should be put in their place.

A small residual portion of the economy, generally unattractive to private capital, is left to direct government management; for example, TVA and NASA.

I see no evidence that we have developed instruments of public management or public entrepreneurship that hold out any promise of better regulating and governing the large sector of the economy that we historically have left up to the interplay of market forces. Hence, I see no reason for shifting some industrial sectors out of what we call the private sector into either the publicly regulated sector or the public-managed sector. Indeed, there are some

persuasive arguments to support the view that if anything, we perhaps need to shift some industries out of the comprehensively regulated sector.

On that I'm not alone. I really don't see any particular reason for the comprehensive regulation of entry and exit in intrastate trucking or in many other areas. Often, these regulations increase costs, rigidify the industry's structure, and leave uncertain the question of who is really managing the ship.

But let me come back to anti-trust policy itself. I think it's generally agreed that on the whole, anti-trust laws, until recently, have been administered too weakly. There probably is a good bit of informal and formal circumvention of the price system that is never uncovered. By its very nature price fixing is kept secret or is accomplished through informal rules of behavior. But anti-trust policy is clearly being administered much more vigorously now than perhaps it has been at any other time in our history. Anti-trust agencies are presently testing the outer bounds of the meaning of a fairly comprehensive array of anti-trust laws.

The unfortunate part about this whole area of government-business relations is that there is no clearinghouse. Agencies carry out their functions independently. And that is my real concern in this whole government-business relationship. Much has been said about whether or not the market economy has lost its viability and vigor. I think one could make a pretty good case that the complete lack of coordination and the piecemeal interjection of specific regulations to protect certain industries or groups in the economy from the rigors of competition have had a bad effect on the economy. Many regulations have simply grown like Topsy.

The problem, as I see it, is not that the market economy is functioning with less plasticity or with less capacity to adjust, but that government has injected too many rigidities into the economic process. It's the political process by which they get injected that I think ought to be of some concern. We have anti-trust laws, and then Congress passes a fair-trade exemption law, which for all practical purposes lets manufacturers legislate final prices. To protect those who are in industry, we have carried licensing to an extreme.

My point is that in this government-business relationship we need at the federal level the equivalent of the budget clearinghouse just adopted by Congress, and it should become effective next year. It's perfectly apparent to me that many government regulations work in opposition to what we claim to be our national policy. On the whole, they restrain

tremendously the operation of market forces.

So I don't think we'll ever really know what the appropriate role of government is until the conflicting interpositions of government are eliminated from the economy. As matters now stand, it is very difficult to define what the government's purpose is.

In tracing through developments in the economy, I see no persuasive reasons pointing toward a tremendous reshuffling of this division of labor between government and the private sector that I have been talking about. Many voices are calling for such a reshuffling. But I view this matter in very practical terms: who is prepared, for example, to have the government take over the telecommunications system?—which would be, I suppose, a reasonably logical choice. And on pragmatic grounds, it really doesn't make any difference whether the government takes over the railroads—they couldn't be run any worse!

In sum, a return to vigorous prosperity for Americans does not seem to rest upon any major increase in government involvement. Indeed, a strong argument could be made for less.

Mr. Stobaugh, it would seem that America urgently needs to re-evaluate its demand for energy and its attitudes toward energy. Can we ask you to give us your thoughts on the problem?

Professor Stobaugh: Unless some present governmental policies are changed, America is not likely to obtain both a clean environment *and* the amount of energy that it is going to demand. To solve this problem, we should not compromise our environment. But we should remove price controls on domestic production, forget about any scheme for an international floor price for oil, and stock a large inventory of oil to protect our economy in case of a cutoff of imports. Business should take the lead much more than it has in the past.

To be sure, higher energy prices have already caused a certain amount of re-evaluation among consumers. A *decline* in energy consumption has taken place instead of the exponential growth that some people had been predicting. After all, crude oil prices tripled overnight, and this shock to the country's system has been a major problem, but not the only problem. For quite apart from the oil-price crisis, the nation has been facing some tough energy problems for quite a while. In particular, the United States has three key problems that are not solvable by conventional economic analyses. This is unfortunate, because if an economic analysis highlights clearly

625

the best solution for the nation, there is a better chance of gaining wide support for that solution.

One such problem concerns the *extent to which the United States should rely on imported oil as an important energy source*. The U.S. economy can easily handle the balance-of-payments problem, and economists can calculate whether the United States should produce high-cost domestic energy instead of importing lower-cost energy. But the political issues are the overriding ones: how important is it to keep U.S. oil imports low in order to protect our preeminence on the world political scene? How important militarily is it to be relatively self-sufficient in energy?

The second problem not readily solvable by conventional economic models is *energy versus the environment*. This problem causes headaches not only in energy production but also in energy consumption. Take energy production: how much is it worth in terms of energy supply to strip-mine coal? How important is energy supply compared with the "psychic income" that people here in Boston and Cambridge would derive from knowing that reindeer would not have to step over a pipeline in Alaska? How important is energy supply compared with New England's desire not to have drilling off Cape Cod? And on the consumption side, how important is electricity made from high-sulfur coal compared with the sicknesses that the burning of this coal may cause?

The third problem that is inaccessible to economic analysis is the problem of *centralized versus decentralized government*. Because of the mixture of national and local controls, an energy project often requires the approval of governmental organizations at several levels—national, state, county, and city. In one case a company had obtained approvals from 63 governmental bodies but then had a nuclear power plant "out" for six months because it didn't get the sixty-

fourth approval—from the local conservation commission.

In addition to these three areas that don't lend themselves to solution by economic analyses, there is a fourth critical area: the question of whether the nation is going to rely on a government-controlled allocation system in order to determine who gets what energy in what form—or whether we are going to rely on the price mechanism in order to determine allocations. This problem has two sides, the consumer's and the producer's.

First, take the consumer's side and gasoline as an example. The best study of the subject that I've seen comes to the conclusion that the Federal Energy Agency, through its allocations system, caused the long gasoline lines in February 1974. The agency assumed that it knew exactly who needed what, and it told the refineries to produce on that basis without taking into account weather changes or any adjustments in consumption by the consumers. And now Congress is considering whether to maintain price controls, arbitrarily reduce gasoline output by 2 percent, and allocate the available supplies to various states. The result would be more lines at the filling stations.

So the consumers face two alternatives: (1) an allocation system that operates *outside* the price system and that entails an arbitrary allocation for each consumer, perhaps long lines, and a "black market," or (2) a system in which price itself is allowed to allocate the flow of gasoline. Conventional economic theory indicates that consumer satisfaction is maximized if the price system is used rather than the arbitrary allocation system.

For the producer's side, price controls are causing uncertainty; hence people are less willing to spend money on the search for oil. Also, the price controls put a ceiling on the economic incentive to produce. Oil companies are inhibited from injecting high-cost chemicals into "old" oil fields to keep production from falling, because any such oil recovered is subject to price controls. And then there is the familiar problem of natural gas: the controlled prices hold profits so low that producers won't spend money to find enough new gas (and consumers

get natural gas at a lower price than the free market would dictate).

I think it's only fair to say that the energy situation is so complex that we're not going to have—at least not in the near future—a well-coordinated national energy plan. That being so, our immediate actions must be piecemeal.

First, we need tough environmental laws, and business ought to take the

lead in this respect. Business has too often tried to hold back the environmentalist movement; a good example is its opposition to a strip-mining bill. With the enormous rise in oil prices and the concomitant rise in the value of coal, the coal industry could afford to fund environment-rebuilding projects, and the mere existence of tough legislation would remove uncertainty and provide a framework within which to move ahead. Yet the lobbyists fight strip-mining legislation tooth and nail in Congress, and I think that is a strategic mistake.

From other energy industries the uncertainties should be removed so that people can spend money and produce more energy. An essential step in removing uncertainty is the removal of price controls, such as those on oil and natural gas. And if it's politically unacceptable to remove price controls without levying taxes on some of the energy producers, then a combination of removing price controls and imposing taxes would be far better than what we have now. Such tax income could be used for providing reductions in income and sales taxes, among other things.

Both business and government have been less than responsible in the energy picture. Both have taken too much of a short-term view. Business argues for measures that will help it most in the short term. If business wants to drill offshore of New England, the reasoning is, "Let's have the national government control the offshore land and grant us drilling rights." But in regard to the Federal Power Commission's control of natural-gas prices, the reaction is, "Let's get rid of national controls and go to state control."

As for the government, a good example of the problems encountered in solving the energy situation is the hypocrisy in New England. For years New England used low-priced, imported fuel oil, whereas, because of import regulations, the Midwest had to use higher-priced, domestic fuel oil. But when imports were reduced during the oil-supply crisis, New England received a share equal to that of the rest of the country. And now New England politicians do not want a local refinery or drilling off New England; yet they want energy costs as low as those in the rest of the nation, even if getting them will require a subsidy from Washington. I question whether politicians in the rest of the country will allow New England to receive such preferential treatment in the long run, though for a short time they may. But such short-term outlooks by elected officials are a major roadblock in the way of reaching an adequate solution to the long-term problem of bringing energy supply and demand into balance.

Professor Goldberg

Professor Goldberg, what can you tell us about food—both as an industry and as a universal human problem?

Professor Goldberg: Roughly 60 percent of the world's population is involved with food; so it is a basic industry. We'd like to think of the United States as an industrial society. But over 60 percent of the total assets of all U.S. corporations and farms combined is in agribusiness—that is, in the whole food system, from farm supply and farming to food processing and distribution. Some 25 percent of our labor force is employed in agribusiness operations, and roughly 25 percent of our consumer expenditures is for food and clothing made from U.S. farm products.

So agribusiness is a major industry even today in the United States. It's one that's been taken for granted, because we've had excess capacity—excess in the sense that of the approximate 400 million crop acres in this country, roughly 60 million of them have been idled in the last 25 years. We've also built up agricultural surpluses.

In analyzing our food system, we must view it in terms of economic incentives for participants in the system as they respond to consumers' changing nutritional needs. Their responses are more than economic in nature. In the course of the years, what people get paid for producing food and what you and I pay for eating food have always been political as well as economic questions. We've had a bipartisan agricultural or agribusiness policy in this country for many years. And that policy, simply stated, is this: we want to have a minimum price support for our food system to encourage farm production and to encourage the use of modern technology in farming. The assumption is that if we encourage farmers, we will produce enough food at a reasonably low price level.

In the last 25 or 30 years, we've had grain surpluses, and we've supplied roughly 50 percent of all the grain traded in the world. So we are part of a world food system. But we have thought of ourselves as isolated from that system politically, because we have been isolated from it economically.

Traditionally our price support program was, until 1972, higher than the world price, so that we had to pay a countervailing offset for our exporters to be competitive in the world market. Picture, if you will, surpluses being readily available for all the processing people in our country and outside of our country, and for all the people involved in the feed industry and the poultry, livestock, and hog industries. Roughly 80 percent of the grain that we use in our country goes for that livestock and poultry industry. So, our price supports provided price stability not only for the cereal portion of the human food economy but also for the animal section of it, in the form of cheap feed. It also provided price stability for other crops competing for land use.

If you look at the grain price levels, except during the Korean war and the corn blight, with minor exceptions the price level varied very little—maybe 10 or 20 cents a bushel throughout that whole period. Because we were overpricing the rest of the world, we provided price stability not only for the United States but also for the rest of the world, because we were the umbrella beneath which the other nations sold their products. We provided the price incentive for them to produce their products—sort of a *Pax Romana* for grain prices throughout the world.

Most people want our price supports to be geared to some sort of world market, but in fact there's no such thing as a world market. There are 60 or 70 governmental price support programs. How does one fit together a variety of governmental pricing arrangements into an international system? Some firms are doing so on a unilateral basis. Individual sugar users now have five-year contracts with sugar producers on a formula basis. The European Economic Community has a five-year contract with approximately 36 developing countries for a whole variety of commodities.

So some degree of planning is already taking place. And institutions are being created so that the job will get done. The talk is not about a change of ideology, but is rather an explanation that these are our requirements, and this is how we're going to get the job done.

We've paid a big price for not having grain reserves, and one of the persons who paid the biggest price was the livestock and poultry farmer in this country. The members of the livestock industry lost $5 billion of realized losses in 1974 and another 15 billion dollars' worth of inventory losses in one year, because cheap feed was no longer available to them. So I look upon the food system as going back to a reserve system out of necessity.

Judging by the world projections that I see, we'll have surpluses of wheat from now until 1985. We'll have shortages of corn and soybeans because of the feed economy. But if the economy starts getting better—not only our economy but also the worldwide economy, which is also currently in a recession—the surplus in wheat will be used as a feed component to upgrade the diet of the world. I see shortages and surpluses still occurring, but we will develop reserves that tend to moderate that kind of pressure. In addition, our PL 480 Food For Peace Program will be used for those nations that lack the means to pay for food but are trying to organize their food system.

Now, you may ask why food prices are higher, while commodity prices have declined. Part of the reason is an increase in costs—the cost of all labor went up 10 percent in 1974, food-retailing labor more than 20 percent, energy 52 percent, packaging 30 percent, and transportation 10 percent. Profits also rose, reflecting a one-third increase in inventory profits and a catch-up phase after price controls were removed.

What I'm saying, in part, is that our agricultural institutions have left the traditional ideology behind—not 30 or 40 years ago, but back in the revolutionary period of this country when Shays's Rebellion occurred in 1786–87. At that time, the farmers of Massachusetts asked for a paper-money issue so that they could keep their farms, and the State Legislature reacted by exempting certain items from debt process. Today what most companies and most farmers do is to utilize government farm and food programs as part of their own operations.

The immediate problem now is, How do we influence international food policy? First, we don't have those reserve stocks right now. If by chance we have another bad-crop year as we did last year, instead of having to worry about surpluses and building up reserves, we could have another commodity-price-pressure crunch. So we're not out of danger, and I think it's important to recognize for the near term that we are still very much of a weather-vulnerable food economy at the moment.

The attitude of the rest of the world toward food policy is similar to the one with respect to energy policy. Many people like the OPEC approach: they are calling for changes in the coffee agreements and the various types of sugar programs, because they are fearful that once food stocks are built up throughout the rest of the world, they will be under price pressure.

I think that we're going to have to set our agricultural export policy in cooperation with four or five major exporting nations. And we're going to have to figure out some multilateral arrangements for pricing our agricultural commodities versus other commodities. I think that the new social-priority system we've seen emerging domestically is emerging internationally as well.

Finally, high food prices in the United States and in the world have adversely affected the poor, the unemployed, and the elderly. One reaction to this fact has been the development of specific food-aid programs for these consumers, from food stamps to special consumer subsidies. One out of every 10 Americans utilizes food stamps. Such food-help programs will undoubtedly be a continuing part of U.S. and world food policy.

Agribusiness, then, is already an advanced economic philosophy. The resources and means are available to feed the world. A new level of international coordination and an effective coalition of government, business, and finance can move agribusiness to new prosperity. □